BELMONT UNIVERSITY LIBRARY
BELMONT UNIVERSITY
1900 BELMONT BLVD.
NASHVILLE, TN 37212

P9-DCX-526

International Directory of
COMPANY
HISTORIES

International Directory of

COMPANY HISTORIES

VOLUME 17

Editor
Tina Grant

ST. JAMES PRESS
AN IMPRINT OF GALE

Detroit • New York • Toronto • London

STAFF

Tina Grant, *Editor*

Miranda H. Ferrara, *Project Manager*
Laura Standley Berger, Joann Cerrito, David Collins,
Nicolet V. Elert, Margaret Mazurkiewicz, Michael J. Tyrkus, *Contributing Editors*
Peter M. Gareffa, *Managing Editor, St. James Press*

While every effort has been made to ensure the reliability of the information presented in this publication, St. James Press does not guarantee the accuracy of the data contained herein. St. James Press accepts no payment for listing; and inclusion of any organization, agency, institution, publication, service, or individual does not imply endorsement of the editors or publisher.

Errors brought to the attention of the publisher and verified to the satisfaction of the publisher will be corrected in future editions.

The paper used in this publication meets the minimum
requirements of American National Standard for Information Sciences—
Permanence Paper for Printed Library Materials, ANSI Z39.48-1984.

This book is printed on recycled paper that meets Environmental Protection Agency Standards.

This publication is a creative work fully protected by all applicable copyright laws, as well as by misappropriation, trade secret, unfair competition, and other applicable laws. The authors and editors of this work have added value to the underlying factual material herein through one or more of the following: unique and original selection, coordination, expression, arrangement, and classification of the information.

All rights to this publication will be vigorously defended.

Copyright © 1997
St. James Press
835 Penobscot Building
Detroit, MI 48226

All rights reserved including the right of reproduction in whole or in part in any form.

Library of Congress Catalog Number: 89-190943

British Library Cataloguing in Publication Data

International directory of company histories. Vol. 17
I. Tina Grant
338.7409

ISBN 1-55862-351-5

Printed in the United States of America
Published simultaneously in the United Kingdom

St. James Press is an imprint of Gale

Cover photograph: trading floor of the New York Stock Exchange
(courtesy NYSE)

10 9 8 7 6 5 4 3 2 1

187367
BELMONT UNIVERSITY LIBRARY

Ref
HD
2721
.D36
v.17

CONTENTS _____

AAJ—0385

Company Histories

PREFACE

The St. James Press series *The International Directory of Company Histories (IDCH)* is intended for reference use by students, business people, librarians, historians, economists, investors, job candidates, and others who seek to learn more about the historical development of the world's most important companies. To date, *IDCH* has covered over 2,800 companies in seventeen volumes.

Inclusion Criteria

Most companies chosen for inclusion in *IDCH* have achieved a minimum of US$100 million in annual sales and are leading influences in their industries or geographical locations. Companies may be publicly held, private, or non-profit. State-owned companies that are important in their industries and that may operate much like public or private companies also are included. Wholly owned subsidiaries and divisions are profiled if they meet the requirements for inclusion. Entries on companies that have had major changes since they were last profiled may be selected for updating.

The *IDCH* series highlights 10% private and non-profit companies, and features updated entries on approximately 25 companies per volume.

Entry Format

Each entry begins with the company's legal name, the address of its headquarters, its telephone and fax numbers, and, starting with this volume, its URL. A statement of public, private, state, or parent ownership follows. A company with a legal name in both English and the language of its headquarters country is listed by the English name, with the native-language name in parentheses.

The company's founding or earliest incorporation date, the number of employees, and the most recent sales figures available follow. Sales figures are given in local currencies with equivalents in U.S. dollars. For some private companies, sales figures are estimates. The entry lists the exchanges on which a company's stock is traded, as well as the company's principal Standard Industrial Classification codes.

Entries also contain a *Company Perspective* box which provides a short summary of the company's mission, goals, and ideals, a list of *Principal Subsidiaries, Principal Divisions, Principal Operating Units,* and articles for *Further Reading.*

American spelling is used throughout *IDCH,* and the word "billion" is used in its U.S. sense of one thousand million.

Sources

Entries have been compiled from publicly accessible sources both in print and on the Internet such as general and academic periodicals, books, annual reports, and material supplied by the companies themselves.

Cumulative Indexes

IDCH contains two indexes: the **Index to Companies**, which provides an alphabetical index to companies discussed in the text as well as companies profiled, and the **Index to Industries**, which allows researchers to locate companies by their principal industry. Both indexes are cumulative and specific instructions for using them are found immediately preceding each index.

New Series Features

Beginning with Volume 17 *IDCH* features include:

- The company's *URL*
- Citations to on-line research

Suggestions Welcome

Comments and suggestions from users of *IDCH* on any aspect of the product as well as suggestions for companies to be included or updated are cordially invited. Please write:

The Editor
International Directory of Company Histories
St. James Press
835 Penobscot Building
Detroit, Michigan 48226-4094

St. James Press does not endorse any of the companies or products mentioned in this series. Companies appearing in the *International Directory of Company Histories* were selected without reference to their wishes and have in no way endorsed their entries. Companies have been given the opportunity to participate in the compilation of the articles by providing information or reading their entries for factual accuracy, and we are indebted to many of them for their comments and corrections.

ABBREVIATIONS FOR FORMS OF COMPANY INCORPORATION

A.B.	Aktiebolaget (Sweden)
A.G.	Aktiengesellschaft (Germany, Switzerland)
A.S.	Atieselskab (Denmark)
A.S.	Aksjeselskap (Denmark, Norway)
A.Ş.	Anomin Şirket (Turkey)
B.V.	Besloten Vennootschap met beperkte, Aansprakelijkheid (The Netherlands)
Co.	Company (United Kingdom, United States)
Corp.	Corporation (United States)
G.I.E.	Groupement d'Intérêt Economique (France)
GmbH	Gesellschaft mit beschränkter Haftung (Germany)
H.B.	Handelsbolaget (Sweden)
Inc.	Incorporated (United States)
KGaA	Kommanditgesellschaft auf Aktien (Germany)
K.K.	Kabushiki Kaisha (Japan)
LLC	Limited Liability Company (Middle East)
Ltd.	Limited (Canada, Japan, United Kingdom, United States)
N.V.	Naamloze Vennootschap (The Netherlands)
OY	Osakeyhtiöt (Finland)
PLC	Public Limited Company (United Kingdom)
PTY.	Proprietary (Australia, Hong Kong, South Africa)
S.A.	Société Anonyme (Belgium, France, Switzerland)
SpA	Società per Azioni (Italy)

ABBREVIATIONS FOR CURRENCY

DA	Algerian dinar	Dfl	Netherlands florin
A$	Australian dollar	NZ$	New Zealand dollar
Sch	Austrian schilling	N	Nigerian naira
BFr	Belgian franc	NKr	Norwegian krone
Cr	Brazilian cruzado	RO	Omani rial
C$	Canadian dollar	P	Philippine peso
DKr	Danish krone	Esc	Portuguese escudo
E£	Egyptian pound	SRls	Saudi Arabian riyal
Fmk	Finnish markka	S$	Singapore dollar
FFr	French franc	R	South African rand
DM	German mark	W	South Korean won
HK$	Hong Kong dollar	Pta	Spanish peseta
Rs	Indian rupee	SKr	Swedish krona
Rp	Indonesian rupiah	SFr	Swiss franc
IR£	Irish pound	NT$	Taiwanese dollar
L	Italian lira	B	Thai baht
¥	Japanese yen	£	United Kingdom pound
W	Korean won	$	United States dollar
KD	Kuwaiti dinar	B	Venezuelan bolivar
LuxFr	Luxembourgian franc	K	Zambian kwacha
M$	Malaysian ringgit		

International Directory of
COMPANY
HISTORIES

A. T. Cross Company

One Albion Road
Lincoln, Rhode Island 02865
U.S.A.
(401) 333-1200
Fax: (401) 334-2861

Public Company
Incorporated: 1916
Employees: 1,200 (est.)
Sales: $177.1 million (1994)
Stock Exchanges: American
SICs: 3951 Pens & Mechanical Pencils; 5112 Stationery
& Office Supplies; 5199 Nondurable Goods, Not
Elsewhere Classified

The largest and oldest manufacturer of fine writing instruments in the United States, A.T. Cross Company produces and markets a broad line of high-quality pens, pencils, and other gift items throughout the world. For decades a much-coveted status symbol, Cross writing instruments were first made in 1846, when Alonzo Townsend Cross founded the company. Over the ensuing century and a half, the Cross brand developed into one of the strongest names in American business, becoming a fixture in homes and offices everywhere. Although the company suffered a setback during the early 1990s, A.T. Cross remained the leader in its field during the mid-1990s, supported by its pioneering role in the U.S. writing instrument industry and the indisputable quality of its products.

Early History

Two generations of the Cross family directed the fortunes of A.T. Cross during its first six decades of business. The most famous of the Crosses and the man who lent his name to the enterprise was the company's founder, Alonzo Townsend Cross, a 19th-century English inventor who steered his family into pen manufacture in 1846 in the state of Rhode Island—the birthplace and headquarters of A.T. Cross Company. Though the formative efforts of Alonzo Townsend Cross and his descendents gave the company its name and a stable foundation upon which to build, another, similarly named family—the Bosses—exerted greater influence over the history of A.T. Cross's development and controlled the company for a longer period of time. During the 1990s, the third generation of the Boss family, led by Bradford R. Boss and Russell A. Boss, was superintending A.T. Cross's operation, having gained their executive positions atop the A.T. Cross corporate ladder by virtue of Walter Boss's acquisition of the company from the Cross family in 1916. From 1916 forward and from Walter Boss downward, the Boss family built Cross into one of the country's most notable companies, turning the Cross name into one of the most recognizable brands in the history of American business.

Under the Boss reign of command, A.T. Cross developed into a legendary company, ascending to the top of its industry by combining a potent mix of manufacturing quality and efficient marketing. For all intents and purposes, A.T. Cross, while under the stewardship of the Boss family, created the market for high-priced, prestigious pens in America, emerging as the first U.S. manufacturer of fine writing instruments with any appreciable might to compete in an arena dominated by foreign manufacturers. Before A.T. Cross's rise in the fine writing instrument field, the overwhelming majority of pens accorded any prestige were fountain pens manufactured more often than not in Europe; A. T. Cross changed all that with its slender, high-quality ballpoint pens, throwing aside consumer tastes of the past and creating a new trend that consumers wholly embraced.

In the years following the conclusion of World War II, ballpoint pens eclipsed fountain pens as the writing instrument of choice for those seeking the rarified air an elegant writing instrument could impart to its owner. It was a trend sparked by and benefitted from by A.T. Cross, whose silver and gold metal pens and their lifetime warranty of superior performance were the rage for decades. The company was meticulous in its approach to the manufacture of mechanical pens and pencils, dictating exacting standards that A.T. Cross employees adhered to throughout the roughly 150 assembly steps involved in producing Cross writing instruments. Much of this assembly work was done by hand at the company's headquarters in Lincoln, Rhode Island, where skilled employees, each functioning as a quality-control expert, closely monitored the complicated process of making one of the world's most esteemed products. If a Cross writing instrument did not conform to manufacturing tolerances that were as precise as ensuring that engraved grooves were within one ten-thousandth of an inch of perfection, or if a Cross writing instrument demonstrated the slightest hint that its ink ball might clot, the product was summarily discarded. As a result, fewer than two percent of A.T. Cross's writing instruments were returned to the company's headquarters under its much publicized lifetime warranty.

Equally as important as A.T. Cross's emphasis on manufacturing a flawless product was the image associated with the company's writing instruments, which during the 20th century became synonymous with achievement, class, and sophistication. Cross writing instruments became ubiquitous status symbols proudly displayed by those seeking the distinction a superior pen or pencil could engender; a prized gift given to graduates, ascending corporate executives, and anyone else upon whom honor could be bestowed. The emergence of the Cross name as one of the most prestigious brand names in the business world was predicated on the company's renowned attention to the quality of its products and then successfully articulated by effective marketing, but the mysterious forces that elevate a product beyond all others in the minds of consumers also played a part, creating the unique phenomenon of the Cross brand name.

Initial Public Offering in 1971

Underpinned by product quality and global name recognition, A.T. Cross evolved into the preeminent, stalwart force in its industry, dominating competitors and holding a tight grip on the market for fine writing instruments. Perennially, the company controlled 40 percent of the market for fine writing instruments, a market share that gave other writing instrument manufacturers little hope of ever mounting a successful attack on the industry leader. As the decades of Boss leadership progressed, A.T. Cross became increasingly stronger, entrenching itself as a manufacturer and marketer without rival. It was this powerful business force that converted to public ownership in 1971, ending its 125-year existence as a privately held company. In the wake of the company's first public stock offering, A.T. Cross succeeded as it never had before, posting record sales and record profits during the decade that followed its entry into the public spotlight. Between 1971 and 1981, A.T. Cross recorded a remarkable annually compounded growth rate of 19.6 percent in sales and an even more prodigious 21.6 percent in net income, adding considerable momentum to an enterprise that already had loomed as an unparalleled giant in its industry.

During the early 1980s, a national economic recession caused A.T. Cross's annual sales to dip nearly 10 percent and earnings more than 20 percent in 1982, but despite the temporary stain on the company's otherwise exemplary financial record since the 1971 initial public offering, Bradford and Russell Boss were sitting atop the largest and oldest maker of high-priced pens and pencils. Their company was the reigning champion in a $500-million-a-year market, but changes in A.T. Cross's structure and corporate strategy were being orchestrated

by the two brothers that would alter the future course taken by their long-held family business.

1980s Diversification

The corporate strategy implemented during the early 1980s was born during the late 1970s, when the two Boss brothers were cruising Narragansett Bay in a chartered yacht after watching the America's Cup trials. It was the summer of 1977, and the two brothers were discussing A.T. Cross's business. At the time, their company derived 70 percent of its total sales from purchases of Cross products as gifts, which led the two Boss brothers to think about expanding and diversifying into other gift products. As the sensibility of their discussion on Narragansett Bay set in, the two brothers began to reshape their product lines to reflect and tap into the gift merchandising expertise acquired during the more than century-long existence of A.T. Cross, but six years would pass before Bradford and Russell Boss made their decisive move.

After years of contemplating what the appropriate acquisition for A.T. Cross to execute might be, the two brothers finally made their move in 1983. In October 1983, A.T. Cross acquired Mark Cross, Inc., a privately-held company that coincidentally shared the Cross name with its new parent company. A.T. Cross paid $5.5 million for Mark Cross, a store-chain and mail-order retailer of high-priced luggage, handbags, briefcases, other leather goods, and assorted gifts. The bid to acknowledge its gift-business expertise gave A.T. Cross a chain of 17 company-and-licensee-owned retail stores and a mail-order business that added more revenue muscle to an enterprise already posting record financial results.

The acquisition of Mark Cross was followed by the purchase of a similarly-oriented company, Manetti-Farrow, Inc., in 1987. During the years bridging these two acquisitions and the company's evolution into a business focused on the gift-giving market, or at least proclaiming its acknowledgment of itself as a manufacturer and marketer embedded in the gift-giving market, A.T. Cross continued to flourish, becoming what one writing instrument retailer referred to as "a cleverly disguised gift manufacturer." Annual sales marched upward with each passing year, with the company's roughly 50 gold and sterling silver ballpoints, felt tips, desk sets, leather merchandise, and other gift products continuing to attract consumers. Known as a conservative company, Cross was methodically moving forward, yet recording financial growth that belied the staid and steady approach the nearly century-and-a-half-old business was pursuing. A.T. Cross confidently moved forward through the 1980s, reaching $247 million in sales and $36 million in net income by the end of the decade. As the 1990s neared, the road ahead appeared to lead toward continued, tried-and-true success, prompting A.T. Cross's manager of product marketing to note in *Adweek's Marketing Week*, "We do not just catch on to a trend. We may not have the most timely approach, but we'll have the best-researched product."

Changes in the 1990s

The dynamics of the fine writing instrument market were changing, however, as A.T. Cross headed into the 1990s, and the changes underway would catch the venerable giant without a timely response to an emerging trend. Competition had begun to intensify during the mid-1980s, with Germany's Mont Blanc, France's Waterman, and other European pen manufacturers such as Lamy, Aurora, and Ferrari gaining momentum. Pushing these companies forward was the reemergence of the fountain pen as a status symbol and widely desired writing instrument, the same type of pen that A.T. Cross had helped to vanquish from the marketplace three decades earlier. In the hearts and minds of consumers, the fountain pen was back, driving the wholesale sales of the once-obsolete product upward, as people across the country turned back the clock to purchase a product that possessed what one industry observer termed "a beguiling combination of homespun utility, quiet glamour, and fashionable nostalgia."

Wholesale sales of fountain pens doubled between 1986 and 1991, but A.T. Cross, a company that prided itself on its slow and sure strategy, did not flesh out its collection of slender ballpoints with fatter fountain pens until 1990, years after the surge in demand had begun. "Cross had the market locked for so long they took it for granted," remarked one writing instrument retailer to a *Forbes* reporter several years after A.T. Cross introduced its "Signature" line of fountain pens. Financially, the company faltered, as annual sales and earnings fell from their record highs in 1989. By 1993, the $247 million in sales recorded in 1989 had fallen to $165 million, and net income had plunged from $36 million to $8 million, precipitous drops that caused widespread concern among A.T. Cross's executive management.

For a recovery, the fate of the company fell to the hands of Russell Boss, who began to reshape A.T. Cross during the early 1990s. Manufacturing processes were streamlined, parts inventories were reduced, and A.T. Cross employees were encouraged to take early retirement, all in the hope that the company's profitability could be restored. The changes effected saved A.T. Cross roughly $5 million annually, giving it a leaner look for the years ahead. Further changes were soon to follow, including the divestiture of its Mark Cross subsidiary in 1993. Sold 10 years after it was acquired, Mark Cross was purchased by Sara Lee Corporation, a transaction that gave A.T. Cross $7 million, and occurred at the same time the company brought to market in record time the Cross "Townsend" line. Sporting the middle name of A.T. Cross's founder, the Townsend line featured fatter and heavier pens, both in ballpoint and fountain pen models, that were decorated in several shades of lacquer as well as gold and silver metal.

On the heels of these developments, A.T. Cross formed a new products division in 1996 to develop merchandise comple-

mentary to its core business. During his announcement to the press about the formation of the new division, Russell Boss explained his intentions to those in attendance, saying, "In conjunction with leading high-technology companies, we will develop products that combine the functionality and beauty of our distinctive writing instrument products with state-of-the-art technology to meet the needs of this fast-growing market." With this new facet of its business providing an opportunity for growth in the future, A.T. Cross moved forward, past its 150th year of business and toward the late 1990s, still ranking as the dominant leader in its field.

Principal Subsidiaries

ATX Marketing Company; ATX International, Inc.; A.T. Cross Export Co., Ltd. (Virgin Islands); A.T. Cross Limited (Ireland); A.T. Cross Company (France); A.T. Cross Company (Hong Kong); A.T. Cross Company, Spanish Branch (Spain); A.T. Cross (U.K.) Ltd. (England); A.T. Cross Deutschland GmbH (Germany); A.T. Cross (Bermuda) Limited; Cross Co. of Japan, Ltd.; A.T. Cross Distribution (Ireland); ATX Ireland, Limited; A.T. Cross (Europe) Limited (England).

Further Reading

"A.T. Cross Expects Lower Second Quarter Sales and Earnings," *PR Newswire,* July 11, 1996, p. 7.

"High-Class Recession: A.T. Cross Sales and Profits Dip," *Fortune,* March 7, 1983, p. 8.

Leibowitz, David S., "Dream Holdings Redux," *Financial World,* February 18, 1992, p. 87.

——, "Will What Went Down Go Back Up Again?," *Financial World,* February 16, 1993, p. 82.

Levine, Joshua, "Pen Wars," *Forbes,* January 6, 1992, p. 88.

Love, Martin, "Two Bosses, Two Crosses," *Forbes,* December 5, 1983, p. 66.

Michals, Debra, "How Cross Pens Keep the Black Ink Flowing," *Business Week,* August 18, 1986, p. 58.

Oliver, Brian, "The Penpushers," *Marketing,* October 10, 1991, p. 29.

"Pen Maker to Post Drop in Net Income and Sales," *Wall Street Journal,* July 12, 1996, p. 2.

Schuman, Michael, "Thin Is Out, Fat Is In," *Forbes,* May 9, 1994, p. 92.

Toth, Deborah, "A.T. Cross Gets the Lead Out and Expands into Fine-Point Mechanical Pens," *Adweek's Marketing Week,* May 29, 1989, p. 32.

Trachtenhberg, Jeffrey A., "The Not-So-Ugly Americans," *Forbes,* December 1, 1986, p. 212.

—Jeffrey L. Covell

Adelphia Communications Corp.

5 West Third Street
Coudersport, Pennsylvania 16915
U.S.A.
(814) 274-9830
Fax: (814) 274-9112

Public Company
Incorporated: 1986
Employees: 2,564
Sales: $361.5 million (1995)
Stock Exchanges: NASDAQ
SICs: 4841 Cable & Other Pay Television Services

The largest cable operator in western New York and one of the largest in the United States, Adelphia Communications Corp. owns, manages, and operates cable television systems in mid-sized markets and suburban areas where non-cable reception is weak. During the mid-1990s, Adelphia served more than 1.5 million subscribers in a 12-state area stretching from Vermont to Florida, selling its customers video programming distributed through a network of fiber optic and coaxial cables. Recognized as operating one of the most sophisticated and profitable cable systems in the country, the company represented a model for other cable operators to emulate.

Early 1950s Origins

The corporate roots of Adelphia Communications were inseparably linked with the familial roots of the Rigas family, whose experience in the cable television business predated the incorporation of Adelphia Communications by more than three decades. The patriarch of the family, John J. Rigas, first entered the business during its nascence in 1952 when he started his first cable system in Coudersport, Pennsylvania, with his brother Gus Rigas. The name chosen for the company—Adelphia—is the Greek word for "brothers," an apt corporate title for a business that would employ generations of the Rigas family. Then in his early 20s, John Rigas entered an industry in its infancy when he started Adelphia, unwittingly laying the foun-

dation for what would become one of the largest cable television companies in the United States. It would be years, however, before the Rigas family could claim they stood atop a cable empire. Cable television was decades away from enjoying widespread popularity, decades away from the years that would witness the exponential growth in the number of subscribers across the country. Those days arrived during the 1980s, when Rigas, with three decades of experience as a cable television operator, stood well-poised to reap the rewards from an industry fast on the rise. Adelphia Communications would serve as Rigas' vehicle of growth during the cable television industry's rapid expansion, quickly becoming one of the dominant cable systems operators in the nation.

Although Adelphia Communications did not officially exist until 1986, the company entered its inaugural year of business with a considerable head start over other fledgling cable operators. The company served as an umbrella organization for the centralization of the various cable properties owned by Rigas, and, consequently, was supported by more than 30 years of experience from its outset. Adelphia Cablevision, Inc., the cable company started by Rigas in 1952, was the oldest of the of the five cable companies that Rigas reorganized into one company on July 1, 1986. Joining the Pennsylvania-based Adelphia Cablevision were Clear Cablevision, Inc., Indiana Cablevision, Inc., Western Reserve Cablevision, Inc., and International Cablevision, Inc., which combined served 200,000 subscribers. Together, these companies formed the new Adelphia Communications, a Coudersport, Pennsylvania-based cable systems operator beginning business with $30 million in annual sales. In less than a decade, the company's sales volume would increase more than tenfold and its number of subscribers would rise sixfold, as Rigas moved aggressively to expand his cable television holdings. In the years ahead, the five original components of Adelphia Communications would be joined by a host of other established cable systems as Rigas, with his three sons at his side, mounted an aggressive acquisition campaign.

The company achieved prominence early on in western Pennsylvania and in western New York, where Rigas first established a presence in Niagara Falls in 1972. The addition of International Cablevision—one of the five original companies that formed Adelphia Communications—elevated Rigas' company to the number one position in western New York, giving the company 120,000 subscribers to add to its roster of customers. After taking Adelphia Communications public in August 1986, Rigas completed the acquisition of three cable systems before the end of the year, purchasing the Suburban Buffalo System from Comax Telcom Corp., the South Dade System from Americable Associates, Ltd., and New Castle System from Cablentertainment, Inc.

Late 1980s Acquisitions

During the ensuing two years, Rigas spearheaded the acquisition of more than ten cable systems that bolstered Adelphia Communications' presence in western New York and extended its area of service into neighboring states. By the end of 1989, the company owned cable television systems throughout an eight-state region comprising Florida, Massachusetts, Michigan, New Jersey, Ohio, Pennsylvania, Vermont, and Virginia. Adelphia Communications lost money each year during its expansion, but perhaps more important to the long-term health of the company was the manner in which it had expanded.

A strategy had emerged during the first few years of the company's existence, one that dictated the direction of its expansion during the late 1980s and continued to describe its physical growth during the 1990s. Instead of purchasing cable systems merely for the sake of increasing the company's magnitude, Rigas and other Adelphia Communications executives targeted cable systems for acquisition that neighbored existing Adelphia Communications systems, striving to entrench the company's position through acquisition rather than embracing as large a territory of service as possible. The benefits of grouping cable systems together would manifest themselves as Adelphia Communications entered the 1990s, making the company an industry leader and reducing the sting of consecutive money-losing years.

Although the company's profitability had suffered as a result of the ambitious expansion, its revenue-generating capabilities had not. From the $30 million generated in sales during its first year, annual sales shot up to $131 million in 1988, increasing more than fourfold during a three-year span. Further financial growth was expected as the company's physical growth continued unabated, but as before, Rigas made it a practice to set his acquisitive sights on cable systems in proximity to Adelphia Communications systems already in operation. One significant acquisition that conformed to the company's acquisition strategy was the purchase of Jones Intercable in late 1989. Jones Intercable ranked as the third-largest cable system operator in western New York, an area where Adelphia Communications already reigned as the largest cable operator. Further, Jones Intercable, in many cases, operated in towns next to towns that Adelphia Communications already served, making the acquisition a strategic boon to the company's plan to develop an entrenched market position wherever it operated. Noting as much, Michael Rigas (John Rigas's son and Adelphia Communications' vice-president) elaborated on the company's acquisition of Jones Intercable by remarking, "Whenever possible we look for systems that are adjacent to other systems that we own. Generally speaking, we try to cluster our systems together."

Another pivotal transaction completed in 1989 provided Adelphia Communications with a powerful money-making business during the early 1990s. In 1989, the company entered into a partnership with unaffiliated parties to form Olympus Communications L.P., a southeastern Florida cable television joint venture that Adelphia Communications managed for an annual fee. Comprising Adelphia Communications' own South Dade System, which was acquired in late 1986, several neighboring cable systems in West Palm Beach, and several cable systems that were acquired in 1989 from Centel Corporation, Olympus Communications served roughly 250,000 subscribers and epitomized Adelphia Communications strategy to cluster its cable systems together. During the first few years of its operation, Olympus Communications performed admirably, recording double-digit revenue and cash flow growth.

In the wake of the Jones Intercable acquisition and the formation of Olympus Communications, Adelphia Communications was looking to acquire additional cable systems in specific areas, notably in Virginia, West Palm Beach, Florida, Syracuse, New York, and Hilton Head, South Carolina. As the plans for further physical expansion in the 1990s were being formulated, the company was also investing its resources into improving the infrastructure of its various cable systems— something it had been doing since its formation in 1986. In January 1990, the company announced it would start a five-year, $25 million system upgrade to improve picture quality and increase channel capacity for its subscribers. Part of the system upgrade consisted of the installation of 2,000 miles of cable, including a fiber-optic network that would double the number of available stations from 36 to 72, give sharper television images, and lessen the chance of interrupted service.

1990s: National Prominence

Adelphia Communications' continued commitment to improving the quality and technological capabilities of its cable systems stood as one of the hallmarks of its success during the early 1990s, proving to be as instrumental to the company's rise as a national contender as its practice to cluster cable systems together. Another definitive aspect of the company's success was its robust cash flow, which in part was attributable to the economies of scale engendered by the concentration of its cable properties. By 1992, Adelphia Communications had transformed itself through acquisition and internal growth into the tenth-largest television cable systems operator in the country— up from the 25th slot the company occupied in 1986—but in terms of operating cash flow the Coudersport-based firm placed second to no one. Adelphia Communications' operating cash flow margin of 57 percent of operating revenues represented the highest percentage in the U.S. cable industry, far higher than the industry average of 35 percent.

Aside from the company's enviable cash flow performance, there were other characteristics of Adelphia Communications' operations that were indicative of its success in the past and pointed to growth in the future. By 1992, the company had invested nearly $350 million since its formation to achieve what one industry analyst referred to as "among the best channel capacities and addressability in the industry." The company's cable systems were state-of-the-art, capable of providing a quality of service that distanced Adelphia Communications from competitors and kept its customers satisfied. Of the company's 1.2 million subscribers, all had access to at least 30 channels of programming, while 46 percent of the company's subscribers could choose from at least 54 channels; nationally, only 28 percent of cable subscribers had a choice of at least 54 channels.

In terms of cash flow and technological capabilities, Adelphia Communications held a decided lead over other competitors in the cable industry as the company operated during the early 1990s. In terms of the demographics of its markets, Adelphia Communications also could boast superiority over many of the country's cable operators. Since its formation, the company had targeted mid-sized, suburban markets, carving a presence in communities where incomes were high and populations were expanding. The strategy was paying dividends as Adelphia Communications entrenched its position in these lucrative markets, fueling the company's growth. Historically, the primary regions where the company operated had demonstrated household growth rates that eclipsed the national average. By the early 1990s, after years of consistent growth, Adelphia Communications' markets were recording household growth rates nearly 25 percent above the national average, further bolstering hope that the financial growth of the past would continue into the future.

Sales in 1992 amounted to $267 million, up nearly nine times the total collected in 1986. In 1993, sales jumped to $305 million, continuing their solid rise. To sustain this pace of financial growth, Adelphia Communications looked to physical expansion and resumed its acquisition program as it entered the mid-1990s. In 1994, the company agreed to purchase all the cable systems owned by WB Cable Association, Clear Channels Cable TV, and those owned by the Benjamin Terry family. In all, Adelphia Communications gained 62,200 subscribers, a figure that paled in comparison to the nearly 1.5 million subscribers the company served at the time, but the acquisitions strengthened the company's position in key markets. The WB Cable system was situated in West Boca Raton, Florida, where Adelphia Communications served 300,000 subscribers. The Terry family cable systems were located in Henderson, North Carolina and the Clear Channels cable systems were located in the Kittanning, Pennsylvania area. Further additions to the Adelphia Communications system were made in 1995, when the company agreed to buy cable systems from four small operators that included southeastern Florida cable systems owned by Fairbanks Communications, plus others owned by Eastern Telecom and Robinson Cable TV in the Pittsburgh area, and cable systems in New England owned by First Carolina Cable TV. Together, the acquisitions added 108,000 subscribers to Adelphia Communications' network, and each conformed to the company's strategy of clustering its cable system holdings.

As Adelphia Communications prepared for the 21st century, the company was expected to continue adding to its cable system holdings by fleshing out the regions where it already operated through acquisitive means. Supported by its enviable cash flow margins, the economies of scale realized by grouping its markets close together, and its substantial investments in technological upgrades, Adelphia Communications appeared to be solidly positioned for future growth. With a second generation of Rigas family members at the helm, the company prepared for its second decade of existence but had as its support more than 40 years of experience in the cable television market.

Principal Subsidiaries

Adelphia Cablevisions, Inc.; Clear Cablevision, Inc.; Indiana Cablevision, Inc.; Western Reserve Cablevision, Inc.; International Cablevision, Inc.

Further Reading

"Adelphia Agreed to Buy," *Television Digest,* June 19, 1995, p. 7.
"Adelphia Said It Had Agreed to Buy All Cable Systems Owned by WB Cable Assoc., Clear Channels Cable TV and Benjamin Terry Family," *Television Digest,* November 7, 1994, p. 8.
"Adelphia to Install Cable as Part of Upgrade," *Business First of Buffalo,* January 29, 1990, p. 10.
Fazzi, Raymond, "Adelphia Cable to Expand Channel Offerings in Dover Township," *Knight-Ridder/Tribune Business News,* December 27, 1995, p. 12.
Fink, James, "Adelphia Gets Bigger with Purchase of Jones Cable," *Business First of Buffalo,* August 28, 1989, p. 5.
Lindstrom, Annie, "Adelphia Sparks CATV Paging Industry," *Telephony,* January 16, 1995, p. 18.
Mehlman, William, "Adelphia Cash Flow Margin Paces Cable TV Industry," *The Insiders' Chronicle,* August 31, 1992, p. 1.

—Jeffrey L. Covell

Ag-Chem Equipment Company, Inc.

5720 Smetana Drive
Minnetonka, Minnesota 55343-9688
U.S.A.
(612) 933-9006
Fax: (612) 933-7432
Internet: http://www.agchem.com

Public Company
Incorporated: 1963
Employees: 1,393
Sales: $234 million (1995)
Stock Exchanges: NASDAQ
SICs: 3523 Farm Machinery & Equipment; 3559 Special
Industry Machinery Not Elsewhere Classified

Ag-Chem Equipment Company, Inc. is the leader in a specialized market niche of heavy agricultural equipment used in applying liquid and dry fertilizer, crop protection products, and biosolids to fields. The company manufactures and markets high flotation, self-propelled, off-road chassis and product application systems. The main customers for the equipment are professional chemical application businesses rather than the individual farmer.

Ag-Chem, unlike many other agricultural equipment makers, survived the extreme ups and downs of American agriculture in the last half of the 20th century.

From Distributor to Manufacturer: 1960s and 1970s

Ag-Chem Equipment Company, Inc. was established in 1963 as a distributor of specialized spray equipment for agricultural use. The company found itself at a crossroad in 1967, when its major supplier announced that a large agriculture equipment company would begin distributing its line as well. The product line of Hahn, Inc. brought in 95 percent of Ag-Chem sales at the time. Ag-Chem founder A. E. McQuinn responded to the dilemma with a lawsuit against Hahn, and he began transforming his distribution company into a manufacturing business.

Ag-Chem raised $254,000 in capital and produced its first major product, a pull-type field sprayer, in 1968; planning for a new manufacturing facility began that same year. In 1969, Ag-Chem introduced its first self-propelled sprayer, the Ag-Gator, which sold in the $6,500 to $10,000 price range. The product received high marks from customers for its reliability. Ag-Chem also became a publicly-owned company in 1969, with the sale of 100,000 shares of common stock. Sales of Ag-Chem produced products increased by 70 percent over 1968 to $300,000 and rose another 55 percent in 1970.

Ag-Chem completed the transition from distributor to manufacturer in 1971. Company founder, McQuinn was a hands-on manager in those early days of manufacturing, according to a 1973 *Corporate Report Minnesota* article. His concentrated cost-control and marketing efforts brought the new manufacturing business to profitability by its third production year.

The company marked the beginning of its second decade in business with another new product, the Terra-Gator—a forerunner of the high-flotation equipment destined to be a cornerstone for the company. Sales for 1973 reached $3.3 million. Thriving in the strong agricultural market, Ag-Chem made its first acquisition in 1974. AgTec, Inc., a former subsidiary of Stokely-Van Camp, manufactured spray application equipment used in orchards, gardens, groves, and vineyards. A completed plant expansion more than doubled the size of its Jackson, Minnesota, manufacturing facility. Sales for 1974, nearly double the previous year's, climbed to $6.4 million. The lawsuit against Hahn, Inc. was finally settled in 1974 and was ruled in favor of Ag-Chem.

Ag-Chem's growth rate accelerated rapidly in the mid-1970s. Sales for 1976 jumped 51.9 percent $17.1 million, and profits grew by 32.6 percent. The company employed 350 people at its Jackson plant. Jerr Boschee, in a November 1976 article in *Corporate Report Minnesota*, called Ag-Chem's growth phenomenal. But a severe drought in the upper Midwest began to put a damper on sales.

Ag-Chem's agricultural equipment products also did some growing during the mid-1970s. The company began manufacturing application equipment which could treat as much as a

Company Perspectives:

We are a company made up of dedicated employees focused on customer satisfaction, quality, new product development, and long term growth. Our ability to operate profitably enables us to continue to develop new products that meet the ever-changing needs of our customers. We intend to build on our current leadership position through product innovation and reinvestment of profits in our business, while delivering the right products at the right time. We believe in success, and we know we succeed only if our customers do.

1,000 acres in a single day. Ag-Chem was also laying the groundwork for expansion of its business areas. In 1977, the company entered the industrial market with sludge—the by-product of sewage treatment—application equipment. An international marketing effort was put in place and sales were made to customers in Europe and the Mideast in 1976. The first major foreign sale, to the U.S.S.R., came in 1980. Ag-Chem appeared on *Corporate Report Minnesota*'s annual list of the state's top 100 publicly-traded companies for the first time in 1980 and celebrated its 14th consecutive year of sales growth.

Fortune Falls and Rises with the Agricultural Economy in the 1980s

The United States farm economy was severely depressed from 1981 to 1986. With farmers holding off on equipment purchases, the farm equipment industry stumbled. Major U.S. manufacturers were faced with consolidations, takeovers by foreign companies, and the elimination of established product lines. Ag-Chem continued to dominate its markets in 1981 is spite of deteriorating economic conditions. Sales of $31.8 million were only slightly higher than the previous year, but earnings per share actually increased by 49 percent, aided by the implementation of company-wide cost controls and reduction of inventories and short-term debt. The company continued to push forward, acquiring a water tank manufacturer in 1983 and introducing new models in its agricultural equipment line. The industrial division experienced steady growth, supplying equipment to municipalities and the mining industry. But the agricultural depression hit Ag-Chem too: continuous years of growth and profit ended.

Ag-Chem lost money in 1985 and 1986. Its locally traded over-the-counter stock sold for pennies a share. In 1987, the company closed its Salinas, Kansas, plant and consolidated production in Jackson: total company assets were reduced from $21.9 million to $11.6 million. According to the company, its cost cutting programs and the loyalty of employees and suppliers helped Ag-Chem survive the period.

The fortunes of the agricultural equipment industry shifted again in 1988. A drought and subsequent depletion of the grain surplus prompted the United States government to bring farm acreage idled by the Payment-In-Kind program back into production. Demand for equipment rebounded. Ag-Chem's 1988 operating profits increased by 125 percent to $2.8 million, and

revenues rose by 32 percent to $52.4 million. One reporter for the Minneapolis *Star Tribune* wrote in 1989, "That downsizing, plus increased production efficiency, have produced the enormous increases the company is experiencing at the bottom line."

Ag-Chem stock prices rose to $7 per share by February 1989. With sixty-five percent of Ag-Chem stock being held by insiders—Chairman McQuinn alone held 55 percent—investors had to vie for the approximately one million in shares being traded. The newly thriving business was forced to look for outside production assistance to meet consumer demand. Ag-Chem continued to be the leading manufacturer in its specialized niche and planned to stay there by introducing new and more powerful models for the successful Terra-Gator line and by again expanding plant capacity.

New Dimensions in Agriculture: The 1990s

Ag-Chem recorded a company high $6.1 million in net earnings in 1990. Sales and customer support offices had been opened across the United States and in Canada in an effort to expand its business area. Fertilizer dealers made up Ag-Chem's largest customer group. Municipalities and private waste disposal contractors continued to be the primary purchasers in the industrial segment of the business.

In 1991, Ag-Chem purchased Lor-Al, Inc., a Minnesota-based competitor. Lor-Al had initiated a lawsuit for patent and trademark infringement against Ag-Chem in 1988. The acquisition ended the litigation and brought on board Lor-Al's converted truck chassis line of applicators and 60 percent ownership of Soil Teq, Inc., a maker of site-specific application systems. Ag-Chem also paid Lor-Al $4.5 million in damages. Maintaining that it was undervalued, Ag-Chem repurchased some of its own stock in 1991. The Lor-Al settlement combined with nearly flat sales had an impact on net earnings for the year: they fell to $1.25 million.

The new Lor*Al Products, Inc. subsidiary lost money in 1992—during the transition into Ag-Chem's operations—and kept Ag-Chem's earnings from fully rebounding. But the company surpassed the $100 million milestone in terms of sales. Engineering costs shot up in 1992 with the addition of the high-tech farming systems brought in with Soil Teq. New governmental regulations regarding disposal of biosolids—sewage sludge, farm, and organic industrial wastes—were issued in 1992. The company expected sales of subsurface liquid injection equipment and dry sludge spreaders to rise, and said the biosolids reintroduced into the land improved soil fertility and provided other environmental benefits.

Ag-Chem became "a hot though thinly traded stock," according to business writer Lee Egerstrom in the *St. Paul Pioneer Press Dispatch,* by the beginning of 1993. The price went from the $7 dollar to the $20 range in less than six months. The cyclical agricultural equipment business was in an upswing at the time, but Ag-Chem was also benefiting from environmental concerns. To reduce risks more farmers had begun to hire local chemical suppliers to apply their field chemicals, and in turn suppliers who purchased large application equipment were buying Ag-Chem stock.

Ag-Chem's important midwest region was hit by severe flooding in 1993; Minnesota and Iowa markets made up 15 to 20 percent of the company's business. But Ag-Chem was not just waiting for the waters to recede. The company entered a new market that year. Ag-Chem introduced its RoGator line, a mass-produced post-emerge applicator which competed head-to-head with equipment produced by major manufacturers. The high-clearance row-crop applicator, which had been rushed to market, required improvements that cut into the company's yearly profits. Another of its business areas, the small AgTec division which manufactured orchard and row crop sprayers, had its best year on record. Ag-Chem expected the flooding would actually improve sales the next year as farmers worked to replace lost soil nutrients.

In 1994 Ag-Chem announced an alliance with Unisys Corp.'s Electronic Systems Division to develop a navigational system for its site-specific chemical application technology. The SOILECTION variable-blend application system requires an acre-by-acre collection of soil samples. The soil is analyzed and detailed soil maps are created from the data generated. The system helps farmers determine the most effective mixture of fertilizers for specific crop and soil conditions and thereby reducing the amount of chemicals introduced to the environment and maximizing yields. Ag-Chem first used antennas to transmit information to its Terra-Gator applicators; the Unisys system would use satellites. A 1994 article in *Minneapolis/St. Paul CityBusiness* noted that the variable-release technology was "the talk of the farm world," but the expensive systems had not yet taken off in the marketplace.

Ag-Chem sales reached $234 million in 1995; net earnings were up 33 percent to $11.4 million. It was the eighth consecutive year of record sales growth, which averaged out as an annual increase of 25 percent over the time period. International sales grew 97 percent, mainly due to the purchase of its Netherlands distributor. A two-year, $10.7 million expansion of the Jackson plant was concluded with the competition of a new research and development facility and additional manufacturing space. The company spent another $7 million on state-of-the-art manufacturing equipment. The Lor*Al facility where the converted truck chassis and variable release equipment was manufactured was also expanded.

Ag-Chem gained full ownership of the high-tech products and systems maker, Soil Teq, Inc., in 1996. Ag-Chem also announced plans for a new facility dedicated for the training of fertilizer dealers, equipment operators, and farmers in the site-specific agricultural technology. McQuinn said of the project, "We offer the only system which incorporates all the elements necessary to fully practice site-specific farming. Key to the process is the education we provide, along with our data collection, processing, and management functions, which make variable input controls of seed, fertilizer, and ag chemicals a reality." According to its 1995 annual report the company had then spent nearly $3 million on software and hardware development on the system. In 1996, company won five of the technology awards given by the American Society of Agricultural Engineers, including one for a Lockheed Martin navigation system for its site-specific agriculture.

The Future

Ag-Chem's future prosperity was clearly linked to U.S. agriculture. The company was a proven leader in its traditional product line of chemical application equipment. The industrial division had not produced substantial sales, but the company predicted that increased future sales would come as more industries became involved in land treatment. Although the company was committed to the advancement of site-specific agriculture, its market was still being developed. Ag-Chem survived the changing times of the late 20th century agricultural business; it remained to be seen what other changes were on the horizon for the industry and whether or not Ag-Chem was in step with them.

Principal Subsidiaries

Lor*Al Products, Inc. and Soil Teq, Inc.

Further Reading

"Ag-Chem Equipment Co.," *Minneapolis/ St. Paul CityBusiness,* March 18, 1994.

"Ag-Chem Equipment Company Inc.," *Corporate Report Fact Book,* 1996, p. 159.

"Ag-Chem: On Higher Ground," *Star Tribune* (Minneapolis), June 29, 1993.

Boschee, Jerr, "Can the Business Dollar Survive the Drought?" *Corporate Report Minnesota,* November 1976, pp. 32–34, 53–54, 56.

Carideo, Anthony, " 'Drought Plays' a Boon to Ag-Chem," *Star Tribune* (Minneapolis), February 27, 1989.

Egerstrom, Lee, "Ag-Chem Regroups, Considers Expanding," *St. Paul Pioneer Press Dispatch,* February 20, 1989.

——, "Farm Changes Boost Outlook for Ag-Chem," *St. Paul Pioneer Press Dispatch,* March 29, 1993.

Fredrickson, Tom, "Eye in the Sky, Down on the Farm," *Minneapolis/ St. Paul CityBusiness,* July 8, 1994, pp. 1, 29.

Jones, Jim, "Soviets Come to Edina in Hunt for Farm Gear," *Minneapolis Star,* June 3, 1977.

Maler, Kevin, "Ag-Chem Snatches Up Office Space for $4.7 Million," *Minneapolis/ St. Paul CityBusiness,* August 27, 1993.

"A Strong Hand," *Corporate Report Minnesota,* October 1973, p. 25.

—Kathleen Peippo

Alliance Entertainment Corp.

110 East 59th Street
New York, New York 10022
U.S.A.
(212) 935-6662
Fax: (212) 644-6493

Public Company
Incorporated: 1990
Employees: 1,426
Sales: $720.3 million (1995)
Stock Exchanges: New York
SICs: 5099 Durable Goods, Not Elsewhere Classified;
   6719 Holding Companies, Not Elsewhere Classified

The largest full-service distributor of music and music-related products in the United States, Alliance Entertainment Corp. is engaged in the distribution of audio cassettes and compact discs, as well as the exploitation of entertainment properties through acquisition, licensee, and management agreements. Established in 1990, Alliance Entertainment grew quickly under the guiding hand of its founder, Joseph J. Bianco. From its inception through the mid-1990s, the company assumed an aggressive acquisitive stance, purchasing regional music distributors and record labels, both in the United States and abroad. The company distributes its music recordings to small, independent record stores and to large, retail music chains.

Origins

Nearly a decade before he formed Alliance Entertainment, Joseph J. Bianco could be seen cruising through New York City traffic in his $65,000 Lotus Turbo Esprit. On the steering wheel of Bianco's Lotus, "The Wizard" was engraved, a moniker Bianco had earned after leaving a teaching post at Yeshiva University's Cardozo School of Law and throwing himself into the world of high finance. Bianco, in his early 30s at the time, channeled his energies into syndicating venture capital tax shelters in New York, achieving sufficient success to earn the nickname "The Wizard" and to adopt a lifestyle that included the high-priced Lotus, part of the recompense for financing the U.S. distributor of Lotus sports cars.

When federal legislation in 1986 wiped away the profits to be made in setting up tax shelters, Bianco was forced to find a new vocation, and he moved into the business of distributing recorded music. Specifically, Bianco's career change thrust him into a particular segment of the recorded music distribution industry that supplied small independent record stores with music recordings and served as a stopgap source for selections of which the warehouses of large record-store chains had been depleted. Historically, this segment of the recorded music industry was the domain of legions of small regional distributors, but when overnight delivery rates plunged during the mid-1980s the industry began to consolidate. Increasingly, distributors grew larger and larger, swallowing up the smaller regional distributors to form large corporations with national distribution networks. In this rapidly consolidating industry, Bianco embarked on his new venture, intent on creating a national distributor of audio cassettes and compact discs.

1990 Incorporation of Alliance Entertainment

Bianco incorporated Alliance Entertainment in October 1990 and completed his first acquisition the following month when he acquired Jerry Bassin Inc., operator of $60-million-in-sales Bassin Distributors, a Miami, Florida–based distributor of record labels. Established in 1981, Bassin distributed more than 125 lines of recordings through sales offices in New York, Dallas, and Miami, including such labels as Concord Jazz (which Alliance would later acquire), Cheetah, Disney, Syndrome, Select, and Newtown Music. To finance the acquisition of Bassin and the next several acquisitions to follow, Bianco relied on venture capitalists and borrowed money from Cigna, Bankers Trust, and Chase Manhattan Bank, giving his fledgling company the financial backing to begin its march toward becoming a national distributor.

Bianco's next acquisitive move was completed in late 1992 when Alliance purchased Denver, Colorado–based Encore Distributors Inc. With sales offices in Denver, Dallas, Atlanta,

Company Perspectives:

The company is actively engaged in the acquisition and development of proprietary entertainment products in order to enhance its profitability, diversify its operations and capitalize on its leaading position in the distribution of pre-recorded music.

and on the West Coast, Encore Distributors operated as an independent distributor that was also involved in selling merchandise to alternative markets such as lifestyle shops and independent bookstores. Distributing roughly 250 labels and accessories, including Alligator, Fantasy, Higher Octave, Grateful Dead, and Oh Boy, Encore Distributors carried Alliance into new geographic markets and together with Bassin provided Bianco's New York–based Alliance Entertainment with a distribution network whose scope was widening to cover the country. Though Bassin and Encore Distributors were operated as separate entities, industry pundits were beginning to speculate that together the two companies represented the foundation for one national distribution network. Within the next two years, Bianco's strategic moves would create a national distribution network, one that would rank as the largest in the United States.

Following the acquisition of Encore Distributors, Alliance Entertainment picked up the pace of its acquisition program. The company spent $20.2 million in September 1993 to purchase Titus Oaks Distributors, Inc. and in November 1993 merged with Trinity Capital Opportunity Corp. Trinity Capital had been formed two years earlier as a shell company without any assets until a public offering in May 1992 yielded the company its sole asset: cash. When Alliance Entertainment and Trinity Capital merged, Alliance became a publicly-traded company, a conversion from private to public ownership that strengthened Alliance Entertainment's financial stature by reducing debt and making it easier to raise funds for potential acquisitions. Bianco wasted little time in putting Alliance Entertainment's newly-realized purchasing strength to use, completing a series of acquisitions that bolstered the company's distribution network and diversified its interests.

Sales by the end of 1993 amounted to $200.5 million, a total that would more than double by the end of the next year after an acquisition spree orchestrated by Bianco left his company standing alone as the country's largest wholesaler and distributor of music recordings. On the acquisition front, in February 1994 Alliance Entertainment purchased Abbey Road Distributors, a one-stop music wholesaler. Next, the company acquired a clutch of companies that diversified its business domestically and extended Alliance Entertainment's presence overseas. For $3.8 million, Alliance Entertainment picked up Premier Artists Services, Inc., a talent agency that handled the careers of Frank Sinatra, Liza Minnelli, and other acts; Disquemusic, a Brazilian wholesaler of budget and independent labels in Latin America; and Fiebra Latina, a Latin-American distributor.

1994: First Music Label Acquired

Midway through 1994 the company announced its next acquisition, a deal that signaled Alliance Entertainment's move into the music software catalog business where profit margins were higher than in the company's core business area of independent distribution. In late July, Alliance Entertainment submitted a bid to acquire London-based Castle Communications plc, an owner and licenser of pre-recorded audio and video products whose recordings included albums by the Kinks, Motorhead, Black Sabbath, and Uriah Heep. Although a majority of Castle's $51 million in revenues were derived from catalog sales, the company also had some artists under contract, including Ireland's Energy Orchard, Stiff Little Fingers, and the Buzzcocks.

The acquisition of Castle, which was completed in September for $38.5 million, marked the beginning of Alliance Entertainment's strategy to acquire recording labels, a move that added another facet to the company's mainstay distribution business. Another recording label was added before 1994 was through when Alliance Entertainment acquired the Concord Jazz Label, an independent label founded by Carl Jefferson, who established the label after staging the first Concord Jazz Festival in the Northern California town of Concord in 1969. When Alliance Entertainment acquired the label in December 1994, Concord Jazz had more than 500 titles in its catalog, another 130 master recordings yet to be marketed as albums, and a roster of recording artists under contract that included Mel Torme, Rosemary Clooney, Hank Jones, and Pancho Sanchez.

By the end of 1994, Alliance Entertainment was supported by two recording labels—Castle and Concord Jazz—the distribution of music-related merchandise, including T-shirts, baseball caps, videocassettes, and laser discs, and a strong international business, particularly in Brazil. The heart of the company, however, was its distribution business. Alliance Entertainment operated three massive warehouses in California, Florida, and Connecticut through which the company served its two distinct types of customers. One group included the scores of independent record stores scattered across the country that lacked the financial resources to purchase their merchandise in bulk. The other group of Alliance Entertainment's customers looked to the New York–based distributor in times of emergency. When the customers patronizing large record-store chains such as Musicland Stores Corp. and Trans World Music Corp. exhausted the supply of particular recordings, the large chains turned to Alliance Entertainment for the quick delivery of replacements and Alliance Entertainment, in turn, charged a markup of 10 percent of wholesale for its services.

With its distribution business contributing the bulk of its sales and its label and music-related merchandising businesses adding promising avenues of growth, Alliance ended its fourth year of existence on solid footing. When the financial figures for 1994 were announced in early 1995, their magnitude underscored the ambitious achievements of 1994. In 1994, the company eclipsed the $500-million-sales mark, racking up $535.2 million in sales compared to the $200 million generated in 1993. Following a net loss of $895,000 in 1993, which was chiefly due to a one-time charge related to the early prepayment of debt, Alliance Entertainment recorded a heartening $12.8

million in net income in 1994, providing tangible proof that the acquisitions completed during the year had genuinely strengthened the company's position.

The company's fifth year of business was not spent celebrating the financial results achieved in 1994, however. Alliance Entertainment's acquisition spree continued, with the company picking up INDI Holdings Inc., an independent distributor of music, and One Way Records Inc., a distributor of budget label recordings during the year. On the heels of these acquisitions, Alliance Entertainment entered into merger negotiations with Multimedia International Group, but the proposed deal was called off in May 1996 when flagging sales in the music recording industry adversely affected the financial position of Alliance Entertainment.

Despite the suggestion that the company was in a somewhat precarious financial position because of the failed Multimedia International merger, Alliance Entertainment displayed strong signs of financial vitality as it entered 1996, a vitality that instilled the company's management with effusive confidence. During the first six years of its existence, Alliance Entertainment had evolved from a small, regional, and privately-owned music distributor into a large, international, publicly-owned distributor of music with two recording labels added to its business scope. Buoyed by more than 75,000 music master copyrights, sales in 1995 reached $720 million, up exponentially from the $60 million generated by Bassin Distributors, the original component of the company, in 1990.

1996 Acquisition of Red Ant Entertainment

Alliance Entertainment ranked as the largest full-service distributor of music and music-related products in the United States as it charted its course for the late 1990s. Following the failed Multimedia International merger, Alliance Entertainment barely missed a beat and once again resumed its strategy of aggressively seeking acquisitions. Three months after the Multimedia International merger was halted, the company completed an acquisition that not only increased the size of its label business and greatly accelerated the strategy of building both the proprietary content and international components of its business, but also dramatically altered the management of the company.

In August 1996, Alliance Entertainment acquired Red Ant Entertainment, a Los Angeles–based record label whose principal owners included former MCA Music Entertainment Group chairman and chief executive officer Al Teller and the merchant banking firm of Wasserstein Perella. A recently-formed music enterprise when Alliance Entertainment acquired it, Red Ant was in the process of contracting a list of alternative, urban contemporary, and country artists in late 1996, but perhaps its greatest asset was its management. Under the terms of the agreement that ceded ownership of Red Ant to Alliance Enter-

tainment, Teller was to become co-chairman, president, and chief executive officer of Alliance Entertainment.

Upon assuming his three leadership posts at Alliance Entertainment, Teller's assessment was entirely positive and hinted at the course the company would pursue during the late 1990s. In an official announcement marking his arrival at Alliance Entertainment, Teller noted: "Alliance has in place the components upon which to build an important international record company. We intend to accelerate the growth of Alliance's content business through Red Ant, while building an international distribution system that complements Alliance's existing operation. We will also speed up the ongoing consolidation and integration of Alliance's existing distribution operations." Bianco, who became co-chairman of the company he had founded six years earlier, embraced the arrival of Teller, giving his own blueprint of Alliance Entertainment's future: "Al [Teller] is one of the great leaders in the music industry. With his background as chief executive officer of MCA Music and president of CBS Records . . . he is the ideal person to guide Alliance's future. He has the ability and insight to grow Alliance into a major music powerhouse and to guide it into new frontiers of technology." With these two leaders directing the fortunes of Alliance Entertainment, the company embarked on the path toward the robust growth it expected to achieve.

Principal Subsidiaries

Jerry Bassin, Inc.; Encore Distributors, Inc.; Titus Oaks Records, Inc.; Alliance Latin, Inc.

Further Reading

Adilman, Sid, "Alliances Can Take on the World," *Variety,* May 6, 1987, p. 485.

"Alliance Entertainment Acquires Red Ant; Al Teller Becomes Co-Chairman, President and CEO," *PR Newswire,* August 28, 1996, p. 8.

"Alliance Goes for an Encore after '90 Bassin Buy Out," *Billboard,* March 13, 1993, p. 9.

Christman, Ed, "Alliance Breathing Easy after Failed Metromedia Merger," *Billboard,* May 18, 1996, p. 52.

——, "Alliance, Trinity Seal Merger Deal; Wholesaler Back on Acquisition Track," *Billboard,* December 18, 1993, p. 93.

Jeffrey, Don, "Alliance Raises $325 Mil., Partly to Fund Acquisitions," *Billboard,* August 12, 1995, p. 58.

——, "Alliance's '94 Sales Surpass $500 Mil.," *Billboard,* April 8, 1995, p. 89.

——, "Alliance's Sales and Profits Soar," *Billboard,* December 3, 1994, p. 74.

Johnson, Brian D., "Going for the Jugular," *MacLean's,* February 1, 1988, p. 52.

"Metromedia International," *Television Digest,* May 6, 1996, p. 7.

Palmeri, Christopher, " 'That Isn't Napoleon at Austerlitz, but . . . ,' " *Forbes,* December 19, 1994, p. 104.

—Jeffrey L. Covell

AMERIWOOD
INDUSTRIES

Ameriwood Industries International Corp.

171 Monroe Ave. N.W.
Suite 600
Grand Rapids, Michigan 49503
U.S.A.
(616) 336-9400
Fax: (616) 336-9401

Public Company
Incorporated: 1915
Employees: 750
Sales: $100.8 million (1995)
Stock Exchanges: NASDAQ
SICs: 2511 Wood Household Furniture; 2517 Wood TV
& Radio Cabinets; 2679 Converted Paper Products,
Not Elsewhere Classified; 6719 Holding Companies,
Not Elsewhere Classified

Ameriwood Industries International Corp. is one of the leading manufacturers of wood products such as unassembled furniture, stereo speaker cases, and stereo component racks in the United States. The company sells its products to regional discount stores, office and electronics superstores, home improvement chains, warehouse clubs, and catalog showrooms. Ameriwood is also an original equipment manufacturer of various raw wood and laminated particle board products, which it sells to many other manufacturers for use in their own products. Finally, the company produces and markets its own line of stereo speakers through one of its subsidiaries, B.I.C. America. Ameriwood is the corporate successor of Rospatch Corporation, which was a manufacturer of wood products, plastic packaging, printed garment labels, and defense electronics.

Early Years as the Rose Patch and Label Company

Ameriwood's foundations were laid on September 14, 1915, with the incorporation of the Rose Patch and Label Company, a manufacturer of fabric patches and garment labels. The company soon positioned itself as a leader in the industry, and for years it was one of the largest producers of printed garment labels, such as those detailing manufacturer information and care instructions in clothing items. Although business was extremely good, there was little room for growth in its chosen line of business. Therefore, in the 1930s Rose Patch and Label formulated a plan to sell label-making equipment to other companies. This venture was funded by selling shares, shifting the company into the public arena.

Postwar Diversification: Rospatch Corporation

It was not until the 1950s that Rose Patch and Label diversified beyond the business of label production. At that time, the company purchased a plastic packaging company and began creating printed plastic packaging for a variety of retail items, including food and cleaning aids. This shift in focus brought about a company name change in 1968, when in an attempt to accommodate the new business ventures under the corporate umbrella, the Rose Patch and Label Company became Rospatch Corporation.

While the plastic packaging division contributed to Rospatch's yearly sales, the company's principal focus remained the manufacture of garment labels. Throughout the early 1970s, Rospatch searched for another solid acquisition to further boost its profits. In the process it acquired and subsequently divested numerous companies that did not suit its needs, until it bought Jessco Inc. in 1978. A wood and particle-board laminator that sold its product to manufacturers of stereo speaker casings and television cabinets, Jessco boosted Rospatch's yearly sales from approximately $35 million in 1978 to almost $52 million in 1979.

Unfortunately, the success provided by Jessco only hid the fact that Rospatch was beginning to suffer. In mid-1980 Rospatch's President, Richard F. Brush, hired Joseph A. Parini to help begin a restructuring process and be prepared to take over for Brush within a few years. Parini had spent the previous 25 years as an executive in the defense business at Lear Siegler and had just become the head of its aerospace group. Brush died just months after Parini arrived, leaving Parini as Rospatch's new President and Chief Executive Officer.

Company Perspectives:

Ameriwood is developing or manufacturing custom products as far-ranging as cremation caskets, component parts for contract office furniture, point-of-purchase displays, private label furniture for retailers or other items.

A Shift in Focus for the 1980s

Parini immediately began restructuring Rospatch, strengthening management at all levels. He divided the company's existing holdings into two separate operating divisions: the identification products division, which included the printed garment label business and the plastic packaging operation; and the wood products division, which consisted solely of Jessco Inc. He then began laying the foundations for Rospatch to enter into the defense electronics business when he created a third division in 1981, the technical products group, which was to include Rospatch's own research and development division as well as any future defense electronics acquisitions. Recognizing the country's emphasis on modernizing the armed forces, and also taking into account the large amount of defense spending by President Ronald Reagan's administration, Parini saw defense electronics as an excellent opportunity for growth. He began searching for acquisition candidates, screening hundreds of companies before finally settling on three.

In 1982, after selling off the plastic packaging division because it was proving unprofitable, Rospatch made three defense electronics acquisitions in rapid succession. The company purchased Edmac Corp., an $8 million radio receiver and navigational electronic equipment manufacturer; Guidance Technology Inc., a $1.5 million producer of gyroscopes for missiles and military vehicles; and Oaks Development Labs, a $1 million company which dealt in photolithography for the semiconductor industry. Meanwhile, the identification products division was bolstered by its entrance into the business of woven fabric labels, such as those found on neckties, and 1982 sales for the wood products division saw a boost with the acquisition of a ready-to-assemble furniture line, Affordable Furniture.

In order to accommodate heightened manufacturing demands resulting from the addition of the Affordable Furniture product line, Rospatch bought Tiffin Enterprise, Inc., a manufacturing plant in Tiffin, Ohio, in 1984. This plant soon became the site of Rospatch's stereo speaker and original equipment manufacturing (OEM) operations. These operations included the application of wood grain or opaque laminate finishes to particle-board, which was then sold to producers of stereo speaker and component parts and other manufacturers for use in their own products. Use of the Tiffin plant for this purpose enabled the company's manufacturing facility in Dowagiac, Michigan, to focus primarily on the production of retail items such as the new furniture line.

As annual sales in the wood products division increased rapidly, Rospatch continued its push into the defense electronics business with the 1986 addition of the $13.7 million Infrared Industries, Inc., to its technical products group. The purchase strengthened the company's hold in the avionics, antisubmarine warfare instrumentation, and infrared detector businesses, and by 1988 the technical products segment appeared to be Rospatch's most promising opportunity for growth. Rumors of a corporate buyout began to surface, however, signaling problems within Rospatch's empire of three unrelated businesses.

A top contender for purchase of the company was Atlantis Group, Inc., which controlled more than 18 percent of Rospatch's stock by the end of 1988. Nonetheless, Rospatch insisted that it was not putting itself up for sale, and the *Insiders' Chronicle* quoted Parini in November 1988 as saying that he was exploring "various options for the restructuring of Rospatch." Parini first sold the printed and woven label businesses, then, in 1989, he divested the entire technical products division as well.

At that point, Rospatch's largest single shareholder, Atlantis, had increased its stake in the company, which now consisted of only the wood products group, to almost 20 percent. Upon Rospatch's release of the technical products group, Atlantis filed a civil fraud suit against Rospatch in March 1990. The suit alleged that Rospatch had overstated the inventory and assets of the technical products group before it was sold, which led Atlantis to purchase shares of the company under false pretenses. Within months, Parini had left Rospatch, succeeded as chairman by Neil L. Diver and as president and CEO by Joseph J. Miglore.

The 1990s: Ameriwood Is Born

1990 marked the emergence of Rospatch Corp. as a company whose sole focus was the manufacture of wood products. When Diver and Miglore took control, they began creating a three-year strategic plan to increase sales of Rospatch's ready-to-assemble furniture, stereo speakers, and OEM products. They also worked to mount a vigorous defense against Atlantis, which was attempting to gain complete control of Rospatch.

Diver and Miglore managed to realign their company's focus and improve its standing in the wood products industry. In December 1991 a majority vote of Rospatch's shareholders changed the name of the company to Ameriwood Industries International Corp. In September 1991 a U.S. district court judge in Michigan supported a recommendation that the Atlantis suit be dismissed, although appeals by Atlantis were immediately set in motion. By April 1992, Ameriwood and Atlantis had settled their dispute, and Ameriwood repurchased Atlantis's stake in its company.

The next few years were devoted to restructuring the company. Two main operating divisions were created: Ameriwood Furniture and Ameriwood OEM. Ameriwood Furniture became the division responsible for the manufacture of ready-to-assemble furniture for the home and office. Ameriwood OEM served as an original equipment manufacturer of custom stereo speaker and component cabinets, as well as manufacturing wood materials to be used by other manufacturers in their products. Ameriwood also retained its line of stereo speakers, marketed by a subsidiary called B.I.C. America.

The company placed its initial emphasis on the Ameriwood Furniture division, because it offered greater potential for rapid growth than did the Ameriwood OEM or B.I.C. America divisions. Management began plans to broaden Ameriwood's furniture product line, with hopes of gaining the ability to enter more distribution channels and target a greater number of consumers. When Diver and Miglore had taken control of Ameriwood's management in 1991, the company manufactured furniture items that retailed for $100 or less through regional discount stores, and the price of Ameriwood (Rospatch) stock was less than $4 per share. Within two years, Ameriwood was offering furniture products at mid- and upscale price points as well, enabling it to target warehouse clubs and other new distribution channels. Because of this, Ameriwood's stock price had risen to more than $20 per share, and the company began planning to add new machinery to its two manufacturing plants in order to accommodate growing demand.

Among Ameriwood's new mid- and higher-priced offerings were the Members Only and Portfolio furniture lines, which were introduced in 1992. While the company's Affordable brand furniture continued to target the consumers at discount mass-merchant stores, Members Only was channeled into national chains such as warehouse clubs and electronics superstores, and Portfolio entered the home and small office furniture markets. This diversity reduced Ameriwood's dependence on any single distribution channel and allowed the company to reach a broader range of consumers, helping it achieve sales of $87.7 million in 1992.

1993 saw a 34 percent increase in Ameriwood's ready-to-assemble furniture sales, which helped the company break the $100 million mark. This achievement was aided by the introduction of Axial brand furniture for the home office and small business. Ameriwood's increased emphasis on the office furniture market was well planned, as home-based businesses and personal computer use boomed in the early to mid-1990s. Manufacturers including Ameriwood upgraded the quality, style, and ease of assembly of ready-to-assemble furniture at all price levels. For example, Ameriwood instituted a toll-free telephone help line, which not only helped customers who had questions regarding assembly or problems with a product, but also relieved Ameriwood's retailers of such customer service burdens. Such innovations were key to Ameriwood's success in an increasingly competitive environment.

Ameriwood continued to expand and broaden its product offerings in 1994, but was unable to increase its overall sales at the same rate that it had enjoyed during the previous two years. The company's continued focus on the Ameriwood Furniture division had finally taken its toll on the OEM and B.I.C. America operations, both of which suffered decreases in sales. Ameriwood OEM's primary raw material was particle-board, which had increased in price nearly 40 percent in less than two years, due in part to the sudden popularity of ready-to-assemble furniture. Furthermore, electronics superstores had quickly become consumers' preferred retail outlet for electronics, and Ameriwood was just beginning to enter its B.I.C. America stereo speaker line into the superstore channel. Ameriwood

Furniture was the only division to enjoy an increase in sales in 1994, but the higher cost of particle-board affected this segment's profits as well.

1995 was more disappointing: the company experienced a $4.3 million decrease in sales. Joseph Miglore left the company, and Charles Foley was elevated from the position of chief financial officer to president and chief executive officer. Foley and Chairman Neil Diver placed greater emphasis on the Ameriwood OEM and B.I.C. America operations, as Ameriwood sought new channels to market its existing products while also attempting to expand its product line. The furniture division was also expanded, as the company added to its Kids 'N' Kolor children's furniture line, and also began producing an unassembled upholstered furniture line, called Home Suite, which included sofas and futons.

These efforts were rewarded when Ameriwood reported improvements in overall sales for the first half of 1996. Furthermore, the company also experienced an increase in furniture orders by its retailers, which showed a potential for continued future success. Ameriwood's B.I.C. speakers were recognized for their excellent quality in *Consumer Reports'* February 1996 report, giving a boost to speaker sales. During this period Ameriwood OEM was renamed Custom Solutions, as a means of reflecting the expansion of its product line to include such items as cremation caskets and contract furniture. With obvious understanding of its customer base and the importance of altering its emphasis to mirror changing consumer demands, Ameriwood Industries International Corp. entered the late 1990s with great potential for continued growth.

Principal Subsidiaries

Ameriwood Furniture; Ameriwood OEM; B.I.C. America, Inc.; Rospatch Jessco Corp.; Tiffin Enterprise, Inc.; Rospatch Orlando, Inc.; Rospatch Carpinteria, Inc.; Rospatch Exchange, Inc.

Further Reading

"Can He Change the Label?" *Financial World,* February 15, 1983, p. 21.

"Companies Involved in Largest Insider Purchases: Rospatch Corp.," *Insiders' Chronicle,* November 21 & 28, 1988, p. 3.

"Companies Involved in Largest Insider Purchases: Rospatch Corp." *Insiders' Chronicle,* October 28, 1991, p. 3.

Hollow, Michele C., "RTA Furniture Builds on Shoppers' 'Can-Do' Attitude," *Discount Store News,* June 20, 1994, p. 31.

"Particleboard RTA Builds up Finished Look," *Discount Store News,* April 15, 1996, p. 44.

Richman, Tom, "What Business Are You Really In?" *Inc.,* August 1983, p. 77.

"Rospatch Corp.," *Insiders' Chronicle,* August 15, 1988, p. 2.

Zisser, Melinda, "Atlantis Hits Rospatch with Fraud Suit," *South Florida Business Journal,* March 19, 1990, p. 9.

—Laura E. Whiteley

AMPEX

Ampex Corporation

500 Broadway
Redwood City, California 94063-3199
U.S.A.
(415) 367-4111
Fax: (415) 367-4669
Internet: http://www.ampex.com

Public Company
Incorporated: 1944 as the Ampex Electric and
  Manufacturing Company
Employees: 531
Sales: $95.66 million (1995)
Stock Exchanges: American
SICs: 3695 Magnetic and Optical Recording Media; 3663
  Radio and TV Communications Equipment; 3651
  Household Audio and Video Equipment; 3660
  Communications Equipment; 3752 Computer Storage
  Devices; 7819 Services Allied to Motion Pictures

Ampex Corporation is among the world leaders in the fields of magnetic recording, digital image processing, and high-performance digital storage for the visual information age. Ampex introduced video tape recording, and it has applied its resources to other areas of data storage as well. While it continues to supply the radio and television broadcasting industry with professional tape recorders, its electronic data storage systems have applications in any company that handles large volumes of digitized information. The company has been granted thousands of patents in its history and has received numerous awards for technical achievement.

Coming of Age with the Modern Era

Ampex was founded in 1944 by Alexander Mathew Poniatoff, a Russian immigrant to the United States. Poniatoff's early life was full of narrow escapes. As a Russian studying in Germany at the outbreak of World War I, he narrowly escaped home via Belgium, England, and Norway. Later, as a pilot, he ripped his flying boat in two during a takeoff attempt in rough seas. When training to fly fighter aircraft, he narrowly escaped a deadly crash while practicing spins. He retreated with the White forces through Siberia during the Bolshevik Revolution, ending up in Shanghai in 1920.

Poniatoff had a hard time finding passage out of China due to his lack of credentials and linguistic limitations. His knowledge of German, however, did help him obtain a position working for the Shanghai Power Company. Poniatoff's work there brought him into a new field—electrical design. No machinery was manufactured in Shanghai at the time, so Poniatoff was forced to digress from his bent for mechanical engineering, which had been apparent even as a child. The son of a prosperous lumber company owner, Poniatoff had been fascinated by the first visits of locomotives to the rural province of Kazan where he was born.

After seven years in China, Poniatoff at last managed to obtain a passport from the League of Nations, enabling him to sail to San Francisco. He had initially hoped to work the land but was disheartened by the austere conditions farmers in Petaluma, California, faced without the aid of modern machinery. So instead, he decided to travel the country with the aid of a $2,000 bonus he had received as a five-year service award from the Shanghai Power Company. A generous letter of reference then helped Poniatoff land a job with General Electric in Schenectady, New York.

GE assigned Poniatoff to a circuit breaker design group. With the help of a friendly librarian who was also Russian, his grasp of English engineering jargon gradually improved. Poniatoff recalled a most daunting assignment came when he was asked, due to his relative inexperience and unfamiliarity with the concept of the "impossible," to design a new vacuum type of circuit breaker. Though hesitant, he completed the task and, newly confident, once again set forth for San Francisco in 1930.

He was unable to find research opportunities since the Great Depression had made people wary of investing capital. After working briefly for the Pacific Gas and Electric Company, he persuaded the Dalmo Victor company to let him volunteer for three months in developing new appliances. The gambit earned Poniatoff a short-lived position, during which he earned a patent for a temperature control on a permanent wave machine, but he had to return to his

Company Perspectives:

Ampex has excelled at processing and storing visual information for more years than most of today's technology companies have been in existence. As the world increasingly demands that information be created, stored, and transmitted in visual form, Ampex remains at the forefront of innovation.

former job after Dalmo Victor was sued for infringing on an unrelated patent on electric razors. In 1942, he was called back to help Dalmo Victor develop a radar scanner for the U.S. Navy.

Dalmo Victor lacked a steady source for motors and generators for its radar scanners, and Irwin Mosley suggested Poniatoff, whom he had hired, form his own company to produce them. Poniatoff took his advice and on November 1, 1944, founded the Ampex Electric and Manufacturing Company in an abandoned loft in the Dalmo Victor building in San Carlos, California.

Poniatoff wanted to use his initials to name his company, but Aircraft Marine Products, which made electrical connectors, had just registered the name "AMP." Poniatoff added "ex" for "excellent" to form the unique name. He recalled in an address to company engineers that the company's motors and generators performed so much better than the competition that they soon became exclusive suppliers for the Navy.

A Fruitful Postwar Decade

Although a contract to supply motors for furnace manufacturers kept the company busy immediately after the war, Ampex focused its long-term plans on developing a magnetic tape recorder inspired by the Telefunken Magnetophon developed in Germany during the war. (Interestingly, Dr. Heyne, president of Telefunken, had proposed the concept to General Electric, who regarded it as impractical.) Harold Lindsay was hired and given the initial task of developing recording heads for the new machine.

As Ampex desperately lacked capital, Mosley invested in the company, becoming a director and attaining 50 percent control. Bing Crosby Enterprises, the company's first customer, placed a 60 percent deposit on its orders for the new Model 200 tape recorder; eventually it bought 60 units at $4,000 each, reselling the first seven to the American Broadcasting Company. Decca Records placed the next order. A total of 112 units were sold at this price. The first prototype cost Ampex $76,000 to develop; it was manufactured throughout 1948.

Mosley did not feel the company had a future in making tape recorders and the Ayala investment group comprised of Joseph and Henry McMicking, George Long, and Kevin Mallen bought his stake in the company when it again needed capital. When the partnership was dissolved in 1958, Long became president of the company. Ampex began trading stock publicly in 1953, when annual sales were $3.5 million.

The Beginning of the Video Age

Ampex had a goal in mind that would make history: the creation of the first practical television magnetic tape recorder/reproducer, or video tape recorder. However, since its inception in 1951, the project had been continually postponed in favor of more pressing projects.

Charles P. Ginsberg lead the development team, which included Charles Anderson, Alex Maxey, Shelby Henderson, Fred Pfost, and Ray Dolby. Dolby had dropped out of college to join the project and in so doing lost his draft deferment; he was able to return after completing his military service. (This is the same Dolby identified with the noise reduction systems that bear his name.) Unforeseen technical problems arose during the machine's development, such as the "Venetian blind" effect of horizontal line interference and the problem of manufacturing durable video heads in quantity, as well as finding suitable magnetic tape.

Upon its debut, the Ampex VRX-1000 (renamed the Mark IV) recorder was an immediate and sensational success, resulting in dozens of orders, even at $45,000 per unit. By April 1960 the company had sold 603 units. Almost immediately, the tape recorder began recording historic moments. The first broadcast of a taped video program—"Douglas Edwards and the News" on CBS—came on November 30, 1956. While on display at the Moscow Trade Fair, it captured the famous "kitchen debate" between Richard Nixon and Nikita Krushchev. The tape was broadcast across America within two days. The Ampex Video Cruiser introduced the video tape machine itself to the country. The 40-foot-long vehicle carried a crew of ten in addition to the 5,000 vacuum tubes.

In 1957, Ampex agreed to compare notes with RCA, which was working on its own video tape recorder. The deal assured compatibility of tapes between machines and also gave Ampex the technology to record color television signals, a concept which RCA was eager to promote. The VR-2000 recorder was the first practical broadcast quality color video tape recorder. Like the VR-1100, it utilized transistors rather than vacuum tubes.

Thomas E. Davis, sales manager for Crosby Enterprises, the exclusive distributor for Ampex, sought other uses for its recording machines and secured contracts with scientific and military clients. Anything that could be converted into electrical signals was a potential application. Raytheon bought 25 modified Model 300s (called Model 301s) to record flight information while testing its "Loon" missile. Earthquakes and brain waves could also be recorded. A heavy duty recorder (costing $17,250 each) was soon developed for the military and in 1955 a multipurpose recorder was introduced. Ampex also supplied recorders for the nascent automation industry. These machines recorded the steps used by a robot in a manufacturing process.

In 1957, National Cash Register recruited Ampex for help in developing a recorder for its computers. Its primary competitors, IBM and Remington Rand, used their own data tape recorders. Joint ventures with Philco and General Electric soon followed. The storage of digital data would become vital to the company's future development.

The film *Oklahoma,* released in 1955, marked the entry of Ampex into motion picture sound systems. In 1960, this work earned Ampex an Oscar, one of many awards for technical achievement from the film and television industries.

Ampex also began to make sophisticated sound systems for the home. The Model 612, introduced in 1955, was the world's first stereophonic music system; at $700, it sold for more than double the price of a monaural system. The company had traditionally concerned itself with supplying the high end and professional market. However, when prerecorded music on tape became more economical, the company began supplying home tape recorders in earnest. Its United Stereo Tapes (later Ampex Stereo Tapes) subsidiary offered music recordings.

In 1959, the company was restructured into five divisions: The Ampex Data Products Co., the Ampex Military Products Co., the Ampex Professional Products Co., The Ampex Audio Co., and Orr Industries (formerly Orradio Industries, Inc.), an Alabama tape manufacturer which Ampex had recently acquired. It also established Ampex International in Switzerland, which coordinated worldwide marketing and manufacturing in England and Japan. The continuing growth of the company prompted further reorganization.

New Media for the Information Age

In the mid-1960s, Ampex developed a magnetic disc recorder for use in slow-motion replays in televised sporting events. It was considered that tape would not be sufficiently durable for this application. As with tape recording, the disc recording concept found diverse applications in many industries.

Ampex vigorously pursued derivatives of its innovative technologies. In 1962, Ampex introduced a recorder especially designed for closed circuit (CCTV) applications: the VR-1500. At $12,000, it was relatively affordable and could record for five hours on a single tape. In 1963, Ampex introduced EDITEC, which allowed frame-by-frame control in tape editing. In 1970, TeraBit Memory, a high capacity digital storage system utilizing videotape technology, was introduced.

Alexander Poniatoff was named chairman emeritus in 1970. He continued to maintain an interest in the foundations whose research he sponsored in health and preventive medicine. He died on October 24, 1980.

The home videotape recorder, introduced in 1975, changed the entertainment business. Besides recording programs from television, consumers could also peruse video stores for prerecorded movies; eventually a "straight-to-video" market for film producers evolved.

In 1983, Signal Cos. bought Ampex, which failed to produce a profit the next year. In 1985, Allied Corp. merged with Signal. The following year, when revenues were $532 million, Henley Group Inc. bought part of the company. Allied-Signal sold the rest of the company to the New York-based Lanesborough group (later renamed Sherborne Group Inc./NH Holding Inc.) in 1987 for $479 million. In 1992 Ampex was incorporated as a public company.

In the late 1980s, Ampex employed approximately 8,000. In 1989, the company cut its work force by approximately ten percent due to sales growth that was less than expected. Low cost foreign producers by this time had made Ampex the only remaining American videotape equipment manufacturer.

While digital video recording and processing equipment offered unprecedented picture quality and superior flexibility, its high price inhibited buyers. Ampex introduced a sales strategy in 1991 that allowed broadcasters to convert from analog to digital facilities in a gradual, piece-by-piece process.

Terming the U.S. television broadcasting market "mature," Ampex shifted its emphasis away from the analog videotape recording to digital recording and to other applications for digital data storage. It took time for this to prove profitable. In 1995, the company sold its Recording Media division (Ampex Media Holdings Incorporated), which reduced the size of the company considerably but also helped the company retain its profitability. Ampex's "keepered media" technology for extending the capacity and performance of hard disk drives excited investors in 1996 and again stirred rumors of a takeover.

Further Reading

"Allied Nears Ampex Sale for $479 Million, Debt Takeover," *Electronic News,* April 13, 1987, p. 20.

"Ampex Head Says Company Is Back on Track," *Broadcasting,* March 4, 1991, p. 66.

"Ampex is Newest Piece in Diverse Lanesborough Pie," *Broadcasting,* April 13, 1987, p. 38.

"Ampex Lays Off 250 from Recording Media," *Broadcasting,* July 22, 1991, p. 44.

"Ampex Lays Off Personnel, Cuts Inventory," *Broadcasting,* December 11, 1989, pp. 65–66.

"Ampex Proposes Evolutionary Path to All-Digital Production," *Broadcasting,* January 28, 1991, p. 52.

"The Ampex Story," *Monitor,* Redwood, Calif.: Ampex Corporation, 1969.

Bettinger, Jim, "Videorecording," *West,* November 6, 1994, p. 5.

Hostetler, Michele. "Ampex Rewinds the Tape to Profitability," *The Business Journal,* April 10, 1995.

Davey, Tom, "Sale Lets Ampex Wash Some Red Ink Off Its Balance Sheet," *San Francisco Business Times,* May 5, 1995, p. 1.

Deagon, Brian, "E-Systems, Ampex Ready Storage System for '92," *Electronic News,* May 28, 1990, p. 17.

"The Early History of Ampex," Redwood, Calif.: Ampex Corporation, company document.

Euan, Barty, "A Far East Lesson From Ampex," *Electronic Business,* August 1, 1988.

Foisie, Geoffrey, "Ampex Terms U.S. Television Market Mature," *Broadcasting,* June 15, 1992, pp. 22–23.

Ginsburg, Charles P., *The Birth of Video Recording,* Redwood, Calif.: Ampex Corporation, company document.

Levine, Jonathan B., "Little Orphan Ampex Looks for Daddy Warbucks," *Business Week,* April 13, 1987, pp. 39–40.

Lubar, Robert, "Five Little Ampexes and How They Grew," *Fortune,* April 1950.

Marcial, Gene G., "What's Revving Up Disk Drives," *Business Week,* May 20, 1996, p. 100.

Morton, David L., " 'The Rusty Ribbon': John Herbert Orr and the Making of the Magnetic Recording Industry, 1945–1960," *Business History Review,* Winter 1993.

Scully, Sean, "Once-Might Ampex Cuts TV Product Line (To Offer DCT Line of High-End Digital Equipment)," *Broadcasting and Cable,* October 4, 1993, p. 65.

Warner, R. M., Jr., "Ampex and RCA, VHS and Betamax," *IEEE Spectrum,* February 1996, p. 57.

——, "Earl Masterson: A Fresh Slant on Videorecording," *IEEE Spectrum,* February 1996, pp. 51–57.

—Frederick C. Ingram

ANR Pipeline Company

ANR Pipeline Co.

500 Renaissance Center
Detroit, Michigan 48243
U.S.A.
(313) 496-0200
Fax: (313) 496-3299

Wholly Owned Subsidiary of Coastal Corporation
Incorporated: 1945
Employees: 2,039
Sales: $820.7 million (1995)
SICs: 4922 Natural Gas Transmission

ANR Pipeline Company, a subsidiary of the Coastal Corporation, operates one of the largest interstate natural gas pipeline systems in the United States. Through its 12,600 miles of pipeline and 200 billion cubic feet of underground storage, ANR provides transportation, storage and various capacity-related services to a variety of customers in both the United States and Canada.

Company Origins

ANR Pipeline was founded as the Michigan-Wisconsin Pipe Line Company on July 25, 1945, by the large utility holding company American Light and Traction. American Light and Traction was the parent company of the Michigan Consolidated Gas Company, the largest gas company to serve the Detroit region. Until the 1930s, communities like Detroit that were located away from natural gas fields had relied exclusively on gas produced from coal. This manufactured gas produced comparatively little heat per unit burned, and, although gas had been used extensively for lighting and cooking, the cost of gas heating was prohibitive. In the mid-1930s natural methane gas had been used in small areas of Michigan on an experimental basis, and it was found that, with natural gas's higher heat value, gas costs for home heating could be cut by about 50 percent. American Light and Traction entered into an agreement with the largest natural gas supplier at that time, the Panhandle Eastern Pipeline Company, to extend as far as Detroit the Panhandle pipeline which then ran from the abundant Texas gas fields to

Indianapolis. Detroit was converted entirely to natural gas in 1936, and by 1943 Michigan Consolidated's sales of gas for home heating had almost doubled.

While residential gas sales soared, American Light and Traction entered into a long and bitter dispute with Panhandle Eastern over supply to the industrial sector. Industrial gas sales were not subject to government regulation as residential sales were, so that Panhandle Eastern was free to sell gas directly, and at a lower cost, to Detroit industry. Michigan Consolidated insisted that these industrial incursions violated the agreement between the companies, but the utility's bargaining position was severely weakened by its complete dependence on Panhandle Eastern's gas supply. In response to this pressure, American Light and Traction made the critical decision to enter the pipeline business themselves, and Michigan-Wisconsin Pipeline was founded in 1945 to allow American Light and Traction to transport gas directly from the Texas gas fields to the company's utility subsidiaries in Michigan and Wisconsin.

The Michigan-Wisconsin pipeline was met by bitter opposition from Panhandle Eastern as well as from the United Mine Workers and the National Coal Association. Coal interests feared that an abundance of cheap natural gas would mean the end of gas manufactured from coal as well as stiff competition to coal-powered home heating. In spite of these objections, in 1947 the Federal Power Commission finally approved the company's application to build a $52 million, 1,800-mile-long pipeline from Texas to the Detroit–Ann Arbor area and to sections of Wisconsin, Missouri and Iowa. The pipeline's difficulties did not end with the FPC approval as steel shortages and bad weather forced further delays and cost overruns. With the demand for natural gas for home heating and industrial use soaring, however, there was little doubt that the struggle would be worthwhile, and even before the pipeline was completed Michigan-Wisconsin applied to the FPC for authority to double its capacity. On November 1, 1949, the Michigan-Wisconsin Pipeline began operations with 1,500 miles of pipe and three compressor stations. The pipeline ran from Hansford County in Northern Texas through Oklahoma, Kansas, Nebraska, Missouri and Iowa to "Wisconsin Junction," Illinois, where it branched in two with one line to serve Michigan and the other Wisconsin. Although the pipeline would be expanded and ca-

```
+--------------------------------------------------+
|              Company Perspectives:               |
|                                                  |
|  ANR is committed to being the highest value     |
|  provider of natural gas services to our         |
|  customers.                                       |
+--------------------------------------------------+
```

pacity increased many times over the course of the next fifty years, this basic route would remain the core of Michigan-Wisconsin's pipeline system.

Expansion in the 1950s and 1960s

Only two years after the completion of the Michigan-Wisconsin Pipeline, in 1951, the company was furnishing all gas requirements for the Milwaukee Gas Light Co. and the majority of the gas used by Michigan Consolidated in addition to serving 14 smaller utility customers in Wisconsin, Michigan, Iowa and Missouri. Annual sales rose to over $27 million. One of the primary uses for the company's natural gas was to heat homes and offices through the rough Michigan and Wisconsin winters, and gas requirements were therefore highly variable throughout the year. The problem of seasonal demand was ingeniously solved by using gas fields in central Michigan as huge natural storage tanks into which excess gas could be pumped in the summer when demand was low and then exploited during the peak winter months.

As demand for gas grew in the early 1950s, the problem of supply became acute, and gas distributors across the country were forced to place tight restrictions on new sales. Fortunately, discoveries of large natural gas reserves along the Louisiana Gulf Coast were made at this time. American Natural Gas Company, the new name for Michigan-Wisconsin's parent company, moved quickly to exploit this new resource. In 1953 the company formed the American Louisiana Pipeline Company to build a second major pipeline from southern Louisiana to Detroit. Construction on the $130 million pipeline was completed in 1956, and in 1965 the American Louisiana and Michigan-Wisconsin systems were joined.

Through the 1950s and 1960s Michigan-Wisconsin continued to expand its pipeline system both by increasing capacity of existing lines and by extending pipelines into new gas producing areas. Michigan-Wisconsin's major pipeline system from Texas to Michigan and Wisconsin was almost entirely "looped" during the late 1950s. "Looping" involves the laying of a secondary pipeline parallel to the main line, and this process allowed Michigan-Wisconsin to double the gas transportation capabilities of the system without greatly increasing the quantity of compressor fuel needed to transport the gas. Fourteen new compressor stations were built during the same period. New gas gathering lines were constructed in Oklahoma to transport gas from the Laverne, Cederdale and Lovedale fields in the Anadarko Basin area of that state and gas reserves in Kiowa County, Kansas, also began to be exploited by the company. In 1967, Michigan-Wisconsin extended its pipeline system into the Gulf of Mexico with the purchase of an 80 mile offshore line from one of its suppliers. It was also during this period that Michigan-Wisconsin first made purchasing agreements for the

abundant supplies of Canadian natural gas that were made available by the construction of the TransCanada Pipeline. A 1960 contract with the Midwestern Gas Transmission Company promised to deliver 158 million cubic feet a day of Canadian gas to Michigan-Wisconsin through the company's 178 miles of newly constructed trunk lines in northern Wisconsin.

Gas Shortages in the Late 1960s and 1970s

In the late 1960s Michigan-Wisconsin began to search for more direct access to the large Canadian gas reserves, and in 1968 the company formed a joint venture with TransCanada Pipelines to construct a $210 million, 1,000 mile pipeline from the Canadian border in Manitoba to southern Michigan. Called the Great Lakes Gas Transmission Company, this pipeline would remain a crucial link in the Michigan-Wisconsin system into the 1990s both by providing gas to Michigan-Wisconsin's primary markets in Michigan and Wisconsin and by facilitating the sale of transportation services to other natural gas companies. By the late 1960s Michigan-Wisconsin had become the single largest supplier of natural gas to Michigan Consolidated and Wisconsin Gas Company both fellow subsidiaries of the American Natural Gas Company, as well as to 38 non-affiliated gas companies in Michigan, Wisconsin, Indiana, Illinois, Kansas, Missouri, Ohio and Tennessee. In 1970, operating revenues had reached $306 million on sales of 704 billion cubic feet of natural gas.

The 1970s were a period of continued high demand for natural gas. By 1976 the problem of supply had become so severe that Michigan-Wisconsin was forced to institute a sales curtailment that limited the gas supplied to many of its customers. In response to these pressures, Michigan-Wisconsin joined with four other pipelines to build a $350 million pipeline in the offshore Texas gulf. The High Island Offshore System (HIOS) could transport a total of up to two billion cubic feet of gas a day, about 200 million cubic feet of which would be processed through the Michigan-Wisconsin system. As one of the nation's largest interstate pipeline systems, Michigan-Wisconsin was in a position to offer gas transportation and storage services to smaller operations. These services began to contribute significant revenues to the company during the 1970s, climbing from $36 million in 1975 to $118 million in 1982. By 1980, the storage component of these services had become so lucrative that Michigan-Wisconsin's parent, now named the American Natural Resources Company, decided to found a new subsidiary, ANR Storage, to manage the storage needs of non-affiliated companies. Michigan-Wisconsin, however would continue to earn substantial revenues for transporting gas to and from the ANR Storage fields and to offer "bundled" gas services to utilities that included gas supply, transportation and storage commitments.

Deregulation and Restructuring in the 1980s

The natural gas industry underwent substantial restructuring in the early 1980s. Once characterized by a very low-priced product, secure markets and pervasive regulation, the industry now faced wellhead price deregulation and increased competition. To make matters more difficult for pipeline companies, the recession of the early 1980s seriously reduced the demand for natural gas particularly on the part of industry. The gas shortages of the mid-1970s became surpluses in the early 1980s as pipeline volumes dropped 26 percent from 1978 to 1982. Pipeline companies, however, remained saddled with long-term contracts with producers signed during the 1970s that provided high deliverability regardless of market demand. These "take or pay" obligations became the central issue in a lengthy rate dispute with the Federal Energy Regulatory Commission (FERC), which maintained that the advance payments should not be factored into rate increases. Michigan-Wisconsin eventually reached a settlement with the FERC that allowed partial recovery of the "take or pay" payments.

Contrary to initial expectations, government deregulation of the gas industry in the 1980s led to lower rather than higher prices at the wellhead. In spite of poor overall performance in the pipeline industry, Michigan-Wisconsin managed to maintain respectable sales and profits throughout the 1980s. Key to this steady performance in the face of increased competition and lower prices was the company's ability to capture the growing gas transportation market. The relative abundance of gas that had led to lower prices also meant that industrial users were shopping around for their gas supplies and in need of transportation services to deliver this gas to their businesses. By 1985, Michigan-Wisconsin had become the second largest transporter of gas for others in the industry. Led by gains in these services the company's sales rose to $2.4 billion.

Michigan-Wisconsin's parent company, American Natural Resources, undertook a major restructuring and diversification program in the early 1980s in partial response to the changing conditions of the natural gas industry. As part of this reorganization, in 1984, the Michigan-Wisconsin Pipe Line Company's name was changed to the ANR Pipeline Company in order to identify the company more closely with its parent. In addition, ANR's utilities, Michigan Consolidated and Wisconsin Gas, were spun off, removing the company from the marginally profitable gas distribution industry. Under charismatic chairman, Arthur R. Seder, ANR's reorganization plan included the canceling of a proposed $1 billion pipeline joint venture that would have brought Canadian gas from Alberta to markets in the New England states. Ironically the CanAm pipeline was abandoned in favor of an ultimately unsuccessful coal gasification plant, a partial return to the company's coal-based gas of the 1930s.

Acquisition by Coastal Corporation in 1985

In 1985 American Natural Resources was acquired by Coastal Corporation. The takeover began as a hostile bid, but at the eleventh hour the two companies reached an amicable agreement that allowed ANR to retain its top management. Coastal, a diversified energy company with annual revenues of about $6 billion, already owned the Colorado Interstate Gas Company, one of the oldest and largest pipeline companies in the western half of the country. The addition of ANR would make Coastal the second largest natural gas company in the United States.

Under Coastal, ANR Pipeline undertook a number of joint ventures to expand their pipeline system. Stretching from the New York–Canada border to Long Island, the Iroquois Pipeline provided key access to Canadian natural gas for the northeastern states. The Empire State Pipeline, completed in 1993, also ex-

tended ANR's link to Canadian gas for the eastern United States. The creation of a gas hub in Lebanon, Ohio, in the early 1990s provided an interconnection point between ANR's main pipeline system and the major supply and delivery routes of other pipeline companies. In the mid-1990s, ANR announced plans for a joint project with TransCanada Pipelines that would extend the company's pipeline system into Vermont and Maine.

Withdrawal from Natural Gas Merchant Services in the 1990s

The 1980s deregulation of the natural gas industry culminated in 1992 with the Federal Regulatory Commission's megarestructuring ruling, called Order 636. Since the mid-1980s, small gas producers and distributors had complained that interstate pipeline companies offered unfair competition by bundling gas sales with transportation and storage services. These bundled service contracts meant that utilities were often not able to shop around for the lowest priced gas without paying more for transporting that gas. The FERC ruling sought to ensure that the large interstate pipelines provide equal services for all gas suppliers by forbidding the pipelines from offering packages that tied gas sales with gas transportation and storage. After extended negotiations with the FERC over the implementation of this ruling, Coastal decided to take ANR out of the gas supply business altogether and to transfer responsibility for all gas marketing services to a separate subsidiary to be called the Coastal Gas Marketing Company. As of November 1993, ANR Pipeline no longer offered merchant services but concentrated instead on the provision of transportation, storage, gathering and balancing of natural gas for its customers.

The elimination of gas sales had an immediate impact on ANR's revenues which dropped from $1.3 billion in 1993 to only $821 million in 1995. Net income, however, remained relatively steady as almost all of ANR's former gas sales customers chose to retain the storage and transportation services previously included in their "bundled" gas sales services. These services yielded higher and more predictable profit margins than the more volatile gas sales and promised to maintain ANR Pipeline's position as a profitable member of Coastal Corporation's group of companies into the late 1990s.

Further Reading

"ANR: Expanding Out of Natural Gas Puts Pressure on Earnings," *Business Week,* May 23, 1983, p. 138.
"ANR, Paneastern to Share Ohio Gas Line," *Oil and Gas Journal,* March 19, 1990, p. 24.
Bodwin, Amy, "ANR Seeks New Revenue Sources," *Crain's Detroit Business,* January 4, 1993, pp. 1, 20.
"Building on Integrity: ANR Pipeline Company," *Coastal World,* Fall 1990, pp. 10–11.
Clark, Robert, "Not with a Bang," *Financial Planning,* July 1985, pp. 218–20.
Ivey, Mark, and Edid, Maralyn, "The Oil Patch's Slickest Takeover Yet," *Business Week,* April 1, 1985, p. 37.
Norman, James R., "Oscar Wyatt Aims at Sitting Duck," *Business Week,* March 18, 1985, pp. 33–34.
"U.S. Gas Pipelines Respond to FERC Order 636," *Oil and Gas Journal,* May 11, 1992, p. 38.

—Hilary Gopnik

Aprilia SpA

Via G. Galilei 1
30033 Noale (Ve)
Italy
(41) 5829111
Fax: (41) 441054

Private Company
Incorporated: 1979
Employees: 647
Sales: L 558 billion (US $350 million) (1995)
SICs: 3751 Motorcycles, Bicycles & Parts

With revenues quadrupling from 1992 to 1995, Italy's Aprilia SpA is Europe's fastest growing motorcycle maker. In 1995, the company boasted 24 percent of the Italian scooter and moped market, and 34.7 percent of the country's motorcycle business. After establishing European operations in 1993, the firm built up a 16.7 percent share of the continent's scooter/moped market and 13.5 percent of motorcycles by mid-decade. Aprilia also claimed to offer the broadest range of motorbikes in Europe, ranging from 50cc mopeds and scooters to 1200cc street bikes. Aprilia hoped to continue its impressive growth rate through the creation of international operations, joint ventures, and continuing product development. Under the leadership of Ivano Beggio in the mid-1990s, the family-owned firm was expected to go public by the turn of the century.

Postwar Foundation and Developments

Italian motorcycle design was world renowned in the immediate postwar era, but the advent of the Fiat automobile in the late 1950s drew attention and talent from two-wheelers. Aprilia was one of a handful of manufacturers—including Ducati, Piaggio, and Cagiva—who revived the country's motorcycle industry in the 1970s and 1980s. The business was founded in 1955 as a bicycle manufacturer in the medieval town of Noale, just a few miles outside of Venice. When Ivano Beggio joined this, his father's company, in 1968, it had 18 employees and about L 1.5 billion in annual sales. But the son was not interes-

ted in human-powered cycles; he wanted horsepower. He built his first motorbike in 1970 and soon began to collect classic cycles from the 1930s.

Five years later, Beggio convinced his father to begin making motorbikes, starting with the mopeds for which Italians had become famous. Also known as "motorized velocipedes," mopeds originated in the 1950s, when people started adding small engines to bicycles, creating a very light mode of transportation that did not require an operator's license or insurance. Aprilia soon branched out into scooters, small-wheeled motorized vehicles where the rider sits inside the frame instead of straddling it as in most motorbikes. Aprilia and its fellow Italian scooter manufacturers led the world in the production of these low-power vehicles into the mid-1990s.

But Ivano Beggio would not be satisfied with these small-engined (less than 125cc) minibikes. Aprilia began developing full-sized motorcycles in 1981, adding ever more powerful engines and developing broader ranges of styles. To establish a good reputation among the "enthusiasts" to whom it hoped to appeal, the company got into off-road racing, also known as motocross. Aprilia modified these racing cycles for street use, sometimes by simply adding lights, turn signals, and a license bracket. Even Aprilia's mopeds were styled after dirtbikes, featuring knobby tires and high fenders. Dual-purpose models designed for on- and off-road use were also introduced during the 1980s. Aprilia's production volume doubled from 13,000 units per year in 1984 to 28,000 units per year by 1986, and by 1987 it led the 350cc segment of the Italian motorcycle industry.

Much of Aprilia's success has been credited to its potent combination of extraordinarily lean manufacturing and top-notch design. Instead of investing mountains of capital in machines and equipment, Beggio spent his money on design, marketing, and assembly. In fact, more than one-fourth of Aprilia's total staff worked in research and design. Using a strategy it calls "the olonic system," the company outsourced all the parts it needed, then assembled them at Noale. By 1996, it had formed a network of about 250 outside suppliers. Orbital Engine Corporation Ltd.'s Rotax division became Aprilia's primary motor supplier. This manufacturing strategy maintained the company's operating margins at more than ten percent annually, double the industry average. It also allowed Aprilia the flexibility to shift production emphasis quickly from one model or class to another according to demand. From 1989 to 1991, for example, when sales in the 125cc class declined by nearly half in Italy, Aprilia was readily able to increase its production of more popular and less expensive scooters. Thus, although its revenues slid from L 179 billion in 1989 to L 154 billion in 1991, Aprilia remained profitable.

Emphasis on sharp design and attention to detail quickly became two of Aprilia's primary strengths. Kevin Cameron of *Cycle World* praised the company for combining "sensuous design" with "craftsmanship." In 1987, *Cycle World's* Alan Cathcart called Aprilia "perhaps the most exciting motorcycle company to watch in Italy, if not in the world." But, unlike some of its Italian competitors who were criticized for ranking form over function, Aprilia also brought innovations such as liquid-cooled engines and catalytic exhaust systems to the motorcycle world. The company even beat Honda to market with a centrally located rear disc brake in the late 1980s.

Development of Grand Prix Racing Team Paces Growth in the 1980s and 1990s

Although half of Aprilia's annual revenues continued to come from moped sales through the early 1990s, the company, its product line, and its clientele matured, expanded, and grew slightly more mainstream throughout this period. Aprilia branched out into road racing in the mid-1980s, entering its first World Speed Championship in 1984. Like the motocross competitions of the previous years, these races served as proving grounds for the company's forward-looking designs and mechanical innovations. They also became an important factor in the promotion of the Aprilia name, as the company edged closer and closer to the top ranks of the racing world.

The firm nurtured its own team of riders over the course of the decade, eventually securing back-to-back world titles in the 125cc class in 1993 and 1994 and adding victories in the 250cc category in 1994 and 1995. In the latter year, Aprilia was Europe's only cycle maker to enter all three championship classes. The company's winning reputation earned it a devoted following in its home country and bolstered its image abroad. Aprilia's "Replica" line of motorcycles, featuring real grand prix racing engines, parlayed these competitive successes into marketing triumphs. *Cycle World's* Olly Duke called the 250cc version "the hottest road-going race replica" of 1995. By that time, Aprilia had begun to challenge market-leading Japanese imports from Honda and Yamaha.

In 1992, Aprilia signed a joint venture with BMW and Rotax to manufacture "a 650cc endurance bike" assembled by Aprilia, but sold under the BMW nameplate and made according to the German company's specifications. This tripartite effort not only brought Aprilia increased cash flow and boosted its image, but also allowed it to adapt innovations (to quiet engine noise and increase endurance, for example) in the cooperative venture to its own designs.

Motorcycle enthusiast and well-known industrial designer Philippe Starck joined the Aprilia design team in the early 1990s. Together, the two designed the 650cc Moto, a postmodern homage to the everyday street bike of the 1950s and 1960s. Launched in 1995, this model applied Starck's signature style via an expanse of chrome punctuated with a colored gas tank. Chief designer Starck called it "a real motorcycle for the real world." Its down-to-earth price, around US $7,700, signaled the company's continuing evolution from boutique bikes to more mainstream rides. *Business Week* characterized this sleek European alternative to America's hoggy Harley-Davidson as "just about the coolest thing going on Europe's highways." Starck committed to designing a second motorcycle for Aprilia, leading *Cycle World's* Alan Cathcart to speculate that his style would continue to imprint the company's designs through the turn of the century.

Although Aprilia continued to revel in its European origins, it also sought to appeal to Americans' need for power, developing 1000cc and 1200cc models in the mid-1990s. These moves gave Aprilia the broadest range of motorcycles on the European continent.

Although the size and variety of its product line continued to grow into the early 1990s, Aprilia did not abandon its historic small-engine core. In 1993 it launched the 50cc Scarabeo, with a sharp design and top-of-the line mechanics that quickly vaulted it to the summit of the Italian motorscooter heap.

Global Push Highlights Mid-1990s

Having consolidated its domestic position, Aprilia looked to international growth as it entered its fifth decade. The company planned to increase its overseas revenues to 50 percent of total sales by 1999. One of the most fundamental obstacles to international expansion was "the reputation of Italian bikes as exiting, exotic and unreliable." It launched branches in Spain, France, and Germany in 1993, and in the Netherlands three years later. Aprilia planned to establish an American operation by the end of 1996. Mitch Beohm, editor of *Motorcyclist* magazine, corroborated that strategy, telling *Business Week's* John Rossant, "There's a big demand for exotic Italian motorcycles over here [in the United States], and Aprilia has a very good chance of breaking into the market." The company was also in the process of infiltrating the world's fastest growing market for two-wheelers, China.

By 1995, international sales contributed about 43 percent of Aprilia's L 558 billion revenues, and annual production had more than tripled, from 47,200 in 1991 to 167,000 by 1995. The company continued to invest heavily in research and development, nearly doubling the budget from L 7.4 billion in 1994 to L 14 billion in 1995.

Aprilia's rapid growth came during an unusually prosperous period in Italy's economic history. The success of this and other Italian companies has been related to larger trends in the domestic economy, including low inflation, a wage freeze, and low commodity prices. The weak lira helped make Italian products cheaper overseas, thereby benefiting Aprilia's internationalization plan. But at the same time, analysts like *The Wall Street Journal's* Thomas Kamm warned that the country's scandalous collusion between government and industry, a high level of corporate and national debt, and high interest rates threatened to bring a halt to recent industrial success. By increasing its rate of internationalization, Aprilia reduced its exposure to the vacillations of Italian political and economic conditions. CEO Beggio hoped that this ''buffer'' would ensure his company's success in the waning years of the 20th century.

Principal Divisions

Aprilia Spare Parts.

Further Reading

''Aprilia Closes in on Industry Leaders,'' *International Management (Europe),* November 1992, pp. 21–22.
''Aprilia: The Austrian-Italian Connection,'' *Cycle World,* September 1985, pp. 46–48.
Cameron, Kevin, ''Fine Art: Aprilia's AF-1 Is Italy's Newest Masterpiece,'' *Cycle World,* April 1992, pp. 86–91.
Cathcart, Alan, ''Aprilia's Expansion Plans,'' *Cycle World,* October 1987, p. 21.
——, ''Italian Update,'' *Cycle World,* October 1990, p. 18.
——, ''Style Meets Single: Aprilia's Vision for the Year 2000?,'' *Cycle World,* September 1995, p. 50.
Duke, Olly, ''Stroke of Genius,'' *Cycle World,* February 1995, pp. 64–66.
''Inside Aprilia's Race Shop,'' *Cycle,* April 1988, pp. 32–34.
Kamm, Thomas, and Bannon, Lisa, ''Italy's Chaos Depresses Lire But Lifts Exports; Now Firms See Danger,'' *The Wall Street Journal,* February 21, 1995, p. 1.
Rossant, John, ''Aprilia's Leader of the Pack,'' *Business Week,* June 10, 1996, p. 55.

—April Dougal Gasbarre

Avery Dennison Corporation

150 North Orange Grove Boulevard
Pasadena, California 91103
U.S.A.
(818) 304-2000
Fax: (818) 792-7312
Internet site: http://averydennison.com

Public Company
Incorporated: 1977 as Avery International Corp.
Employees: 15,500
Sales: $3.1 billion (1995)
Stock Exchanges: New York Pacific
SICs: 2672 Paper Coated & Laminated, Not Elsewhere
Classified; 2891 Adhesives & Sealants; 3081
Unsupported Plastics Film & Sheet; 3497 Metal Foil
& Leaf; 2679 Converted Paper Products, Not
Elsewhere Classified; 3565 Packaging Machinery;
2759 Commercial Printing, Not Elsewhere Classified

Avery Dennison Corporation was formed in the fall of 1990 by the merger of two *Fortune* 500 companies, Avery International Corporation, based in Pasadena, California, and Dennison Manufacturing Company, headquartered in Framingham, Massachusetts. Best known for its office labels, the merged firm also manufactures consumer packaging labels, self-adhesive stamps, MARKS-A-LOT and HI-LITER markers, automotive films and labels, tapes, specialty chemicals, and stationery.

The two companies had a relationship that dated to 1941, when, following the resolution of a patent dispute involving a dispenser for self-adhesive labels, Dennison became Avery's customer. Avery supplied labels to Dennison that the Massachusetts company sold under the brand name Pres-a-ply, competing with Avery products. By formally joining their two companies Avery and Dennison now share a history dating back almost 150 years.

Dennison Manufacturing Company: 19th Century Origins

Dennison Manufacturing began in 1844 when Aaron Dennison, a Boston jeweler, returned to his family home in Brunswick, Maine, and with his father, Andrew Dennison, and his sisters began making paper boxes. The father and son soon created a machine to facilitate the making of cardboard boxes. At the time most jewel boxes were imported semiannually; the new Dennison business had a ready-made domestic market.

Andrew Dennison presided over the manufacturing of the boxes while Aaron continued working at his jewelry business. As a sideline he purchased materials for the boxes and sold the finished product. In 1849 Aaron Dennison became a full-time manufacturer of the machine-made watch, turning the sales end of the box business over to his younger brother, Eliphalet Whorf (E.W.) Dennison.

Fourteen years later, the family business was a partnership, Dennison and Company, between E.W. Dennison and three nonfamily members. Working out of a small factory in Boston, the company produced jewelry tags, display cards, and shipping tags, while the boxes continued to be made in Maine. The development of the shipping tag represented Dennison's continuing attempt to diversify, to provide a better product than was currently available, and to create new markets. In 1863 Dennison patented the placement of a paper washer on each side of the hole in a shipping tag, thus providing a more durable tag. Dennison and Company sold ten million tags that first year.

By 1878 the company had a large factory in Roxbury, Massachusetts, the box plant in Brunswick, Maine, and stores in New York, Philadelphia, and Chicago. The company incorporated, becoming the Dennison Manufacturing Company, headed by E.W. Dennison. Henry B. Dennison, E.W.'s son, became president in 1886, the year of his father's death. He served until 1892, when a conflict between the production end, which was Henry's responsibility, and the sales management led to his resignation. Henry K. Dyer, based in New York, became president.

Company Perspectives:

The Company's vision is to be the global leader in self-adhesive base materials and self-adhesive office products. An almost unlimited potential for self-adhesive applications and technology allows Avery Dennison to expand its broad industrial and consumer base continually. Self-adhesive products are integral to such diverse industries as data processing, office products, health care, industrial tapes and food. Self-adhesive and other Avery Dennison products can also be found in the transportation, durable goods, apparel and textile and retail markets.

The company returned to family leadership in 1909 when Charles Dennison, another son of E.W.'s, became president. He had previously held positions as vice-president and treasurer. In 1911 Charles Dennison presided over the reincorporation of the company under the same name. When the company originally incorporated in 1878, the managers held all of the stock. Under the terms of E.W. Dennison's will, however, employees participated in profit sharing, receiving stock and the privilege of purchasing additional stock under favorable terms. Over time, people not directly involved in manufacturing acquired on the basis of stock ownership substantial influence on the board and were able to direct policy in ways that Dennison family members found undesirable. The reincorporation plan, spearheaded by Charles Dennison and his nephew Henry Sturgis Dennison, a director of the company, returned control to the managers of production through creation of different categories of stock.

In 1898 under Dyer's direction all of the company's manufacturing operations had been centralized in Framingham, Massachusetts. Under the reincorporation plan, sales operations as well moved to Framingham. By 1911 Dennison Manufacturing's line included tags, gummed labels, paper boxes, greeting cards, sealing wax, and crepe paper. The firm supplied a variety of stationery and paper goods. There were Dennison stores in Boston, New York, Philadelphia, Chicago, St. Louis, and in London, England.

Crepe paper eventually became a major sales item for Dennison Manufacturing Company. In the 1870s the firm began to import tissue paper from England to sell to retail jewelers. Its supplier also provided it with colored paper, which was sold to novelty companies. Crinkling the paper expanded its uses; by 1914 Dennison manufactured its own crepe paper.

The production of crepe paper led to the creation of a line of holiday supplies, including Christmas tags and seals. Eventually the company manufactured items for all of the major holidays including Halloween, St. Valentine's Day, Easter, and St. Patrick's Day. Dennison also had a thriving side business selling pamphlets about parties, crafts, and holidays, highlighting the many uses of Dennison products, particularly crepe paper. The holiday line folded, due to declining profits, in 1967.

Progressive Management in Early 20th Century

In 1917 Henry Sturgis Dennison, grandson of E.W. Dennison, became president of the company; he held the position for 35 years. As a believer in the scientific management theories of Frederick W. Taylor, Dennison initiated many reforms, including reduction in working hours, establishment of health services and personnel departments, creation of an unemployment fund, and nonmanagerial profit sharing.

Although Henry Dennison served as president of Dennison Manufacturing Company until his death in 1952, he made a significant mark on the world outside the family business. Dennison served as a member of the Commercial Economy Board of the National Defense Council during World War I and, following the war, served as a member of President Harding's unemployment conference. He was the author of several books, including *Profit Sharing: Its Principles and Practice,* 1918, written with Arthur W. Burritt and others; *Toward Full Employment,* 1938, written with Lincoln Filene and other industrialists; and *Modern Competition and Business Policy,* 1938, co-authored with John Kenneth Galbraith.

Many businessmen did not support Franklin Roosevelt and the New Deal; Dennison did, chairing the Industrial Advisory Board of the National Recovery Administration (NRA). This body examined all NRA codes while they were being developed. When the Supreme Court declared many of the NRA's codes unconstitutional, Dennison became an adviser to the National Resources Planning Board.

During the Great Depression, Dennison Manufacturing suffered, along with the rest of the nation, recording net losses in both 1931 and 1932. The following year the company recovered, once again showing a profit. Profits, however, did not return to pre-Depression levels, making recapitalization necessary and rendering inoperative the profit sharing plan of 1911.

The war economy of the 1940s helped put Dennison back on its feet, and in 1942 sales passed the level of 1929. By 1951 sales were $37.3 million and net earnings were $2.1 million.

Henry S. Dennison suffered a heart attack in 1937 and turned over the active management of the company to John S. Keir, vice-president. Dennison's death in 1952 ended more than 100 years of Dennison family leadership of the Dennison Manufacturing Company.

Attempts at Diversification in the 1960s and 1970s

During the 1960s Dennison experienced further change when, in 1962, it incorporated in Nevada, in a move to decrease taxes. In 1966 Nelson S. Gifford became a director of the company.

By the 1960s analysts considered Dennison Manufacturing Company as part of the label, or marking, industry. Its major operations focused on paper and tag conversion and the production of imprinting and price-ticketing machines.

In 1964 Dennison became the majority shareholder in Paul Williams Copier Corporation. This step was part of its strategy for producing a copier to challenge Xerox. The plan originated in 1957, when, under license from RCA, Dennison began work on a dry copier that differed in several important technological ways from Xerox machines.

Dennison also produced print-punch machines for generating price tags in a relationship with Cummins, the maker of Data Read Machines. Dennison in the 1960s was a high-tech firm, particularly in the arena of packaging. The company could, through an instantaneous heat process, transfer a graphic design to plastic. The process, therimage, was cheaper than more conventional methods.

Building on this technological base, Dennison continued to invest heavily in research and development. In 1979 Dennison formed a joint partnership with Canada Development Corporation (CDC)—Delphax—to develop high-speed, nonimpact printers. Using proprietary technology, the company sought to create products to compete with laser printers. Xerox subsequently bought CDC's 50 percent interest in Delphax.

Late 1980s Retrenchment

In the 1980s Dennison's other technological ventures took it further afield. The company held the majority interest in Biological Technology Corporation, which was working on diagnostic products, using researchers from Massachusetts Institute of Technology and Harvard University. Potential products included pregnancy test supplies.

Returning to its office products base, Dennison stayed abreast of computer technology, producing floppy discs as well as office furniture. In the 1980s Dennison's stationery division accounted for almost half of sales and profits. The attempt to develop a copier to challenge Xerox, begun in 1957, had not succeeded.

In 1985 Dennison experienced a significant economic downturn, which prompted a five-year restructuring plan. A large source of Dennison's problems came from heavy investments in research and development. In 1985–1986 Dennison, streamlining, sold seven businesses and shut down four others. This process left the company with three key businesses: stationery, systems, and packaging. The stationery division, actually two units, Dennison National and Dennison Carter, remained the major contributor to profit. Systems was divided into retail and industrial units, produced barcode printing machines, and was the world's leading manufacturer of plastic price-tag threads. The ongoing restructuring plan involved the consolidation of Dennison National and Dennison Carter, and the integration of systems was scheduled for completion in 1990.

Because of the company's commitment to this program, the news in the spring of 1990 of a merger between Dennison and Avery caught industry observers by surprise. Both companies, however, had been suffering depressed earnings and sought strength in union.

Avery International Corporation: Founded 1935

R. Stanton Avery founded the company that would eventually become part of Avery Dennison Corporation in 1935 with capital of less than $100 from his future wife, Dorothy Durfee. Avery created Kum-Kleen Products to produce self-adhesive labels using machinery he had developed while working at the Adhere Paper Company.

Based in Los Angeles, Kum-Kleen first marketed its labels to gift shops and antique stores and then expanded to other retail establishments, including furniture, hardware, and drug stores. In 1938, Avery Adhesives, the company's new name, suffered a fire that destroyed all of its equipment except a stock of labels. While rebuilding, Avery implemented changes in the die-cutting machinery; the technology Stan Avery developed remains the standard for the industry.

Before the development of self-adhesives, labels were either pregummed or applied with glue. Initially self-adhesive labels did not have a coating that would facilitate removal of the label from its backing and, therefore, they were difficult to use. Early labels were punched rather than cut. The innovation of Avery Adhesives occurred on two levels: technological, improving and streamlining the manufacturing process; and product definition, creating a market.

World War II and the total economic mobilization it necessitated created problems for Avery Adhesives as well as for other industries. The raw materials needed to produce the adhesive for the labels, natural and synthetic rubber and solvents derived from petroleum, were needed by the military. Avery Adhesives, needing permission from the federal government to continue production and to obtain materials, focused on manufacturing industrial items rather than the labels for consumer goods it had previously produced. Among the products were waterproof labels bearing "S.O.S." in Morse code that were stuck on rescue radios. When the war ended, this focus on labels for industrial and commercial uses persisted. The war economy hastened market acceptance of pressure-sensitive labels.

Postwar Incorporation

In 1946 Avery Adhesives incorporated, becoming the Avery Adhesive Label Corporation. At the time of incorporation, more than 80 percent of the company's output consisted of industrial labels that were sold to manufacturers who placed them on their own products, usually consumer items, using automatic label-dispensing machines. The original retail base of Avery Adhesives persisted, providing ten percent of output. The company sold unprinted labels in dispenser flat-pack boxes to stationery stores and other retail establishments through a distribution network. The final aspect of the new corporation's business consisted of selling pressure-sensitive material to printers and others who used them in other products, such as masking tape. Tape rolls produced by Avery were used in the manufacturing of department store price labels. This aspect of Avery's business, which contributed ten percent to output, was known as converting. These industrial categories were the forerunners of Avery's divisions in the 1960s and 1970s.

In the 1940s Avery perceived itself as the only company in the self-adhesive label industry to offer a full line of products. Competition did exist for transparent mending tape, not part of Avery's line. Minnesota Mining and Manufacturing—3M— was the leader in that field.

A challenge to Avery occurred in the 1950s in the form of a patent suit. Avery had taken out a patent for its method of producing self-adhesive labels. Because other self-adhesive products predated Stan Avery's technological innovations, the label itself could not be patented. In 1950 Avery Adhesive brought suit against Ever Ready Label Corporation, then the leader in the industry, alleging infringement on Avery's basic patent. In 1952 a New Jersey court ruled against Avery, stating that there was "not an invention" and that the patent was only a method, not a unique product.

Meeting the Challenge: The 1960s

The loss of the patent had serious consequences for Avery, ultimately changing the nature of its business, and had a ripple effect on the self-adhesive and label industry. The short-term outcome of the patent decision of 1952 was the creation, in 1954, of a new division, the Avery Paper Company. The division produced and sold self-adhesive base materials, often to competing label companies. Eventually this division dominated manufacturing at Avery, eclipsing label sales.

In the 1960s four different branches made up the loosely defined label industry. There were manufacturers of various rubber stamps for paperwork, metal labelers including engravers and stencilers, adhesive label manufacturers, and producers of specialized marking devices. The total volume of this diverse industry was approximately $150 million with annual growth of three percent. In the adhesive label category the leading manufacturers were Avery Products Corporation (the name was changed in 1964), 3M, the Simon Adhesive Products and Eureka Specialty Printing divisions of Litton Industries, and the Kleen-Stik products division of National Starch and Chemical Corporation.

Avery had four divisions in the marking or identification aspect of the industry. Fasson, the new name of Avery Paper Company, was a supplier of raw materials. A second division used these raw materials to manufacture Avery labels. Another division, Rote, manufactured hand-embossing machines, and Metal-Cal, acquired in 1964, made anodized and etched aluminum foil for nameplates. Another aspect of Avery's business in the 1960s was machines that embossed vinyl tape. Avery's main product continued to be self-adhesive labels used in a range of products, including automobiles and airplanes.

The 1960s represented a period of much growth for Avery and U.S. industry in general. The period witnessed the rise in mergers and the development of the diversified corporation, culminating in the emergence of the conglomerate.

In 1961 Avery became publicly owned; it was listed on the New York Stock Exchange in 1967. That year, the company had 2,500 workers and two major components. Label products included the domestic Avery Label division and four wholly owned foreign subsidiaries. The other component was base materials, predominantly Fasson and Fasson Europe. The major buyers of base materials were industrial firms, including the graphic arts trade. In 1968 Avery's share of the industry's $200 million of sales was $63 million. The late 1960s were good years for Avery, as it developed specific units to target specific markets.

In 1974 Avery made the *Fortune* 500 list for the first time. Avery was last on the list, and its competitor 3M was fiftieth. The 1970s presented Avery with the first major impediment to growth

since World War II. Once again the company faced problems caused by a situation outside its immediate control. The oil crisis of 1975 heavily affected Avery, a company dependent on petrochemicals. Avery faced increased costs, oversupply, and declining demand. The price per share of Avery's stock dropped to $22, from a high of $44 the previous year.

Diversification in the 1980s

By 1980 Avery had reversed its downward slide by diversifying and by controlling costs, prices, and employment levels. The materials units included raw materials, Fasson, and specialty materials, such as Thermark. Thermark produced hot stamping materials for automobiles and appliances. Fasson continued to be the bread-and-butter unit of Avery; its self-adhesives were now being used on disposable diapers. The converting unit had moved into the production of labels for data processing and home and office use. Avery continued to maintain foreign operations, centered in Western Europe and located as well in Canada, Mexico, and Australia.

Seven years later Avery International was the nation's leading producer of self-adhesive materials and labels. The company's revenues were three times greater than ten years previously. In the late 1980s, however, profits flattened. The main reasons were Avery's involvement in the disposable diaper market and its ongoing competition with 3M. Avery first began producing tape for diapers in 1977 and by 1984 was the sole supplier to Kimberly-Clark, manufacturers of Huggies. 3M did the same for Pampers. 3M's tape was one piece while Avery's contained a tiny piece of plastic that could fall off and perhaps be swallowed. Kimberly-Clark turned to 3M. In 1986 Avery developed its own one-piece tape in an attempt to win back Kimberly-Clark's business. Avery also attempted to challenge 3M in two other areas—transparent tape and self-sticking notes. Avery later abandoned this effort.

In a thorough restructuring, beginning in 1987, Avery closed some manufacturing facilities, domestic and overseas, and announced plans to cut the number of employees by eight percent. Avery was, however, succeeding in its attempt to strengthen its share of the diaper tape market.

1990 Merger of Avery and Dennison Caps Decade of Competition

Avery's merger with Dennison was the culmination of 50 years of infrequent negotiations between the two companies. Dennison had made the first overture in 1941, but balked at the $200,000 price demanded by founder Stan Avery. That figure increased considerably in the ensuing five decades. Charles ("Chuck") Miller, who had advanced to Avery's chief executive office in 1977, turned the tables on Dennison, embarking on more than a decade of negotiations. He hoped that Dennison would cap a string of acquisitions in the early 1980s, but the 1987 talks failed once again.

Success came in 1990, when Dennison employees and officers, who controlled more than 20 percent of the company's stock, accepted Avery's $287 million bid. But Miller, who retained the top spots at the merged firm, soon realized that his was a Pyrrhic victory. Dennison lacked proper controls, its overseas operations were losing money, and its domestic businesses were fraught with inefficiencies. To make matters worse, a mild economic recession worsened shortly after the union was completed.

Miller moved quickly to reorganize Dennison while rationalizing it with Avery. He hired a consultancy to evaluate Dennison's subsidiaries and spun off or liquidated about $350 million (sales) unprofitable divisions and product lines by 1995, eliminating about 900 employees in the process. Miller cut another 900 workers outright in the meantime. The adoption of time-based management principles helped the merged companies increase efficiency via inventory reduction and expedited ordering, among other strategies.

Avery Dennison also sharpened its focus on research and development in the early 1990s. By 1996, products developed after the merger contributed one-third of its annual sales. Innovations included America's first self-adhesive postage stamp, PowerCheck on-battery tester (created in cooperation with Duracell Inc.), new Band-Aid adhesives, and Translar recyclable label stock. Perhaps more important, the company instituted a customer-oriented new product development process.

The year in which Avery Dennison became a reality, 1990, was not a good one for the new company. Sales increased only one percent, from $2.4 billion to $2.6 billion, and net income declined from $114.2 million to a scanty $5.9 million. But as CEO Miller's reorganization began to take effect, Avery Dennison's bottom line improved. By 1995, revenues had increased to more than $3 billion, and profits burgeoned to $143.7 million. With its domestic operations back on track, the company could be expected to devote more attention to its neglected overseas businesses in the waning years of the 20th century.

Principal Subsidiaries

A.V. Chemie Ag (Switzerland); AEAC, Inc. (Delaware); Avery (Thailand) Co., Ltd. (Thailand); Avery Automotive Ltd. (United Kingdom); Avery Buroprodukte GmbH (Germany); Avery Chile SA (Chile); Avery China Company Ltd. (China); Avery Coordination Center NV (Belgium); Avery Corp. (Delaware); Avery De Mexico SA de CV (Mexico); Avery Dennison (Hong Kong) Ltd.; Avery Dennison (India) Private Ltd.; Avery Dennison (Ireland) Ltd.; Avery Dennison (Retail) Ltd. (Australia); Avery Dennison Argentina SA; Avery Dennison Australia Ltd.; Avery Dennison CA (Venezuela); Avery Dennison Canada Inc.; Avery Dennison Danmark AS; Avery Dennison Foreign Sales Corp. (Barbados); Avery Dennison France SA; Avery Dennison Holdings Ltd. (Australia); Avery Dennison Mexico SA de CV; Avery Dennison Office Products Co.; Avery Dennison Office Products U.K. Ltd.; Avery Dennison Overseas Corp.; Avery Dennison Singapore (Pte) Ltd.; Avery Dennison U.K. Ltd.; Avery Etiketsystemer AS (Denmark); Avery Etiketten BV (Netherlands); Avery Etiketten NV (Belgium); Avery Etikettier-Logistik GmbH (Germany); Avery Etikettsystem Svenska AB (Sweden); Avery Foreign Sales Corporation BV (Netherlands); Avery Graphic Systems, Inc.; Avery Guidex Ltd. (United Kingdom); Avery Holding AG (Switzerland); Avery Holding BV (Netherlands); Avery Holding Ltd. (United Kingdom); Avery Holding SA (France); Avery International France SA; Avery International Holding GmbH (Germany); Avery International Overseas Finance NV (Netherlands Antilles); Avery Korea Ltd. (South Korea); Avery Label (Northern Ireland) Ltd. (United Kingdom); Avery Maschinen GmbH (Germany); Avery Pacific Corp.; Avery Properties Pty. Ltd. (Australia); Avery Specialty Tape Division NV (Belgium); Avery, Inc.; Cardinal Insurance Ltd. (Bermuda); Dennison do Brasil Industria E Comercio Ltda (Brazil); Dennison International Co.; Dennison International Holding BV (Netherlands); Dennison Ireland Ltd.; Dennison Ltd. (United Kingdom); Dennison Magnetic Media Ltd. (Ireland); Dennison Manufacturing (Trading) Ltd. (United Kingdom); Dennison Manufacturing Co.; Dennison Monarch Systems, Inc.; Dennison Office Products Ltd. (Ireland); DMC Development Corp.; Etikettrykkeriet AS (Denmark); Fasson (Schweiz) AG (Switzerland); Fasson Belgie NV (Belgium); Fasson Canada Inc.; Fasson de Mexico SA; Fasson Deutschland GmbH; Fasson Espana SA; Fasson France Sarl; Fasson Hemel Hempstead Ltd. (United Kingdom); Fasson Ireland Ltd.; Fasson Italia SpA; Fasson Luxembourg SA; Fasson Nederland BV (Netherlands); Fasson Norge AS (Norway); Fasson Osterreich GmbH (Austria); Fasson Portugal Produtos Auto-Adesivos Lda.; Fasson Products (Proprietary) Ltd. (South Africa); Fasson Produtos Adesivos Ltda (Brazil); Fasson Pty. Ltd. (Australia); Fasson Scandinavia AS (Denmark); Fasson Suomi Oy (Finland); Fasson Sverige AB (Sweden); Fasson U.K. Ltd.; Indumarco Comercial Ltda (Brazil); LDNA Corp.; Metallised Films & Papers Ltd. (United Kingdom); Monarch Industries, Inc.; Novexx Modul Vertriebs GmbH (Germany); Presto Sarl (France); Retail Products Ltd. (Ireland); Security Printing Division, Inc.; Soabar Systems (Hong Kong) Ltd.; Soabar Systems Hong Kong BV (Netherlands); Societe Civile Immobiliere Sarrail (France); Tiadeco Participacoes, Ltda (Brazil); Avery-Toppan Company, Ltd. (Japan; 50%); Avery-Petofi Kft (Hungary; 51%).

Principal Operating Units

Materials Group North America; European Operations— Materials; Automotive and Graphic Systems; Chemical Divisions; Office Products; Converted and Fastener Products; European Operations—Converting; Asia Pacific.

Further Reading

Barrett, Amy, "The Loved One," *Financial World,* February 18, 1992, pp. 26–27.

Clark, David L., *Avery International Corporation 50-Year History 1935–1985,* Pasadena, Calif.: Avery International Corporation, 1988.

Darlin, Damon, "Thank You, 3M," *Forbes,* September 25, pp. 86–87.

Dennison Beginnings 1840–1878, Framingham, Mass.: Dennison Manufacturing Company.

Dennison, James T., *Henry S. Dennison,* [n.p.], New York, 1955.

John S. Keir, Portland, Ore.: The Dennison Manufacturing Company, 1960.

Miller, Charles D., "Seeking the Service Grail," *Financial Executive,* July–August 1993, pp. 14–16.

Paley, Norton, "A Sticky Situation," *Sales & Marketing Management,* May 1996, pp. 40–41.

Seventy-Five Years 1844–1919, Framingham, Mass.: Dennison Manufacturing Company.

—Amy Mittelman
—updated by April Dougal Gasbarre

Atmel Corporation

2325 Orchard Parkway
San Jose, California 95131
U.S.A.
(408) 441-0311
Fax: (408) 436-4200

Public Company
Incorporated: 1984
Employees: 3,000
Sales: $634.2 million (1995)
Stock Exchanges: NASDAQ
SICs: 3674 Semiconductors & Related Devices

One of the fastest growing semiconductor companies in the United States, Atmel Corporation designs, develops, and manufactures programmable logic devices, application-specific integrated circuits, and memory and microcontroller devices. During the 1980s and 1990s, the company built its reputation and its business on the design of nonvolatile memory chips, which do not lose their programmed instructions while system power is turned off. In 1989, after five years of existence strictly as a designer, the company entered the manufacturing fray by acquiring a chip-making facility in Colorado Springs. During the first half of the 1990s, as annual sales soared from $60 million to nearly $700 million, Atmel strengthened its manufacturing capabilities, establishing two additional manufacturing plants in Colorado Springs and another in Rousset, France. Catering to a worldwide market, Atmel served customers—mostly large corporations—involved in the computer, communications, consumer goods, industrial, and military industries.

Origins

While he was working for Intel Corp. during the late 1970s and early 1980s, George Perlegos noted the potential for a promising product in the semiconductor market. What interested Perlegos, who was working for Intel as a design engineer, were nonvolatile memory chips and the innumerable applications for the chips in commercial and military markets. During the 1980s, nonvolatile memory chips, once placed in microprocessors, enabled a vast range of products such as toasters, dishwashers, automobiles, portable telephones, and microwaves to "remember" instructions even while power was off. Anticipating the widespread demand for these soon-to-be invaluable chips and the lucrative opportunities open to a small and savvy nonvolatile memory chip designer, Perlegos resolved during the early 1980s to forgo the security of working for Intel and start his own company. In a few short years, the result would be Atmel, one of the fastest growing semiconductor companies in the United States during the 1980s and 1990s.

Before Perlegos found himself facing the career change that would lead to the establishment of Atmel, he acquired the experience that would distinguish him as one of the most successful leaders in the semiconductor industry. Born in Greece, where his father made his living as a grape farmer, Perlegos moved to the United States when he was 12 years old. After earning a master's degree in electrical engineering at Stanford University, Perlegos entered the employment ranks and spent seven years as a subordinate member of the corporate world at Intel. Following the relinquishment of his engineering job at Intel in 1981, Perlegos co-founded a memory chip manufacturer named Seeq Technology. After a short stay at Seeq he laid the groundwork for Atmel, an acronym for Advanced Technology for Memory and Logic.

From its inception in 1984, Perlegos's startup venture excelled at targeting lucrative market niches and quickly designing superior memory chips for those markets. Being small had its advantages, enabling the company to develop chips quickly to meet the demand in specific markets before larger competitors could respond. Perhaps more important to Atmel's early success was the strong engineering talent the company employed. As the years progressed, Atmel consistently delivered memory chips to market that used less battery power than most other memory chips, an enviable trait of Atmel chips that meant batteries lasted longer and chips stayed cooler, improving the performance of portable products.

Before this hallmark of Atmel chips became known to blue-chip consumer corporations throughout the country, the company cleared the most intimidating obstacle facing a startup

Company Perspectives:

Atmel's products provide extra value to the user such as innovative new designs and superior features that improve the performance of each of their products—ultimately enabling the user to gain a competitive advantage. Throughout its increasing growth, Atmel has remained true to its essential belief that the Company's own success depends solely on the success of its customers.

semiconductor designer. Entering the chip business typically required considerable capital, but Perlegos was able to get Atmel off the ground with a $30,000 investment thanks largely to a $5.1 million design contract with General Instrument. Perlegos and the company's handful of other semiconductor specialists designed Atmel's chips and contracted with General Instrument to fabricate the wafers in exchange for an ownership stake in Atmel. The arrangement with General Instrument was followed by a similar agreement with Sanyo Semiconductor, enabling Atmel to get into the business strictly as a designer without the typically massive capital costs incurred from launching a memory chip venture.

Mid-1980s Growth

During the mid-1980s, the qualities that defined Atmel's position in the semiconductor industry and drove its growth emerged. Perlegos and the rest of Atmel's work force succeeded by keeping costs low, identifying lucrative market niches, and supplying those small but lucrative markets with high-performance chips that undercut the power consumption of competing memory chips. The company moved nimbly, made decisions quickly, and responded with superior products that soon attracted a core customer base consisting of large corporations such as Motorola, Nokia, and Ericsson, as well as manufacturers producing military equipment. One of the chief reasons Atmel was able to attract its deep-pocketed clientele was its talent for responding and catering to the needs of its customers, something the management structure of the company encouraged. Though he held sway as president and chief executive officer, Perlegos stood atop a corporate hierarchy that was essentially flat, with no employee more than two positions removed from the top managerial post. Without layers and layers of management, decision making was expedited enormously, giving the entire company the freedom to move in any direction that appeared lucrative.

Atmel's egalitarian management structure created a corporate environment that encouraged initiative, something Perlegos had learned during his stay at Intel where the divisions separating top management from the lowest paid employees were kept to a minimum. Perlegos, in fact, had patterned Atmel's management structure after the managerial system used at Intel, but in one particular area the two companies differed. As Atmel was beginning to gain momentum during the mid-1980s, Intel was on its way toward becoming a leader in nonvolatile memories. Intel, however, decided to concentrate on a technology called flash memory, which worked well in laptop computers but was

not right for appliances. Flash memories allowed customers to erase only large amounts of data, whereas the customers Perlegos had targeted required memory chips that could erase small amounts of data, byte by byte. Accordingly, Atmel focused its design work on a specific type of memory chip called Eeprom, short for electrically erasable programmable read only memory.

Customers like Motorola, Nokia, and Ericsson were drawn to Atmel because of the efficiency of the San Jose-based designer's chips in cellular telephones, which, in turn, allowed cellular customers to change just one telephone number in autodial memory. Eeprom chips paved the way for reprogramming one preset station on a car radio and for reprogramming sundry "smart" appliances that relied on microprocessors to perform various functions, providing Atmel with numerous market niches to penetrate.

Buoyed by this business, Atmel was profitable from its inaugural year to the end of the 1980s. The only mark on its otherwise unblemished record came in the form of a lawsuit filed in 1987 by Intel against Atmel for patent infringement, forcing the company to redesign its chips around the Intel patent. The lawsuit helped Atmel, however, at least according to Perlegos, who explained that the money invested in redesigning its chips gave the company a technological lead over its competitors, further strengthening Atmel's reputation as an elite memory chip designer. Shortly after Intel filed its patent infringement suit, Atmel launched what the business press perceived as a counterattack against Intel by introducing a flash memory chip, thereby entering one of Intel's chief markets. Atmel's flash memory chip stored data faster than Intel's and consumed less battery power, giving Perlegos and his designers a new product line to fuel the company's growth and enhancing the company's reputation as one of the leading memory chip designers in the country.

Manufacturing Begins in 1989

By 1989, Atmel was well on its way toward dominance in the memory chip business, although the company's most prolific growth was yet to be recorded. During its first five years of business, Atmel had recorded a profit every year, and sales had grown exponentially. By the end of 1989, sales for the year would eclipse $60 million, but by the time the year's financial figures were announced, Atmel had completed the first step towards its transformation into a leading manufacturer of memory chips. From 1984 to 1988, the company derived all of its business from designing chips, opting to contract out the manufacture of them. In 1989, however, the company's future course was altered when Perlegos convinced venture capitalists to finance Atmel's entry into the manufacturing side of the semiconductor industry. The company paid $60 million for Honeywell, Inc.'s chip factory in Colorado Springs, Colorado, and then invested more than $30 million in upgrading the facility.

In the years ahead, Colorado Springs would become the chief location of Atmel's manufacturing operations, adding a new geographic base to the San Jose-based company. During the years separating the acquisition of its first manufacturing facility and the establishment of others, Perlegos continued to focus his attention on finding new applications for Atmel's memory and logic chips. By the end of 1990, sales had climbed to $76.9 million, as the company continued to pour a sizable percentage of its revenues into research and development, intent on exploring all the opportunities available in the chip market. With more than a third of its annual sales earmarked for research and development activities, the company was in need of capital to devote to expansion, particularly the capital required to establish or acquire additional manufacturing facilities. To provide for a quick infusion of cash, Perlegos converted to public ownership in 1991, when the company made its initial public offering in March of 5.175 million shares at $13 per share, yielding Atmel more than $65 million to fund its expansion in the coming years.

1990s Expansion

As the company moved forward from the early 1990s into the mid-1990s, considerably more would be spent on expansion than the money gained from the 1991 public offering. In 1993, Atmel acquired Concurrent Logic, a manufacturer of field programmable gate arrays (a user-programmable chip) and announced plans for establishing a second manufacturing facility in Colorado Springs. After considering buying or building a new production plant in New Mexico, Arizona, or Texas, Perlegos decided to remain in Colorado Springs, selecting a 47-acre site for the company's anticipated $200 million expansion. At the end of the year, before any financial gains were realized from the new chip-making facility in Colorado Springs, Atmel's annual sales totaled $222 million, and its net income stood at $30 million. The financial figures represented astounding growth, up substantially from the $77 million in sales generated in 1990 and the $4.2 million posted in net income. Still more robust growth was yet to come, as the ceaseless effort to locate and saturate lucrative niches within the semiconductor market with high-performance chips continued.

In 1994, when the new facility in Colorado Springs began production, Atmel's earnings doubled, reaching $59.5 million, and its sales shot up 69 percent, jumping to $375 million. As for the previous ten years, growth was fueled by developing faster chips that used less power—ideal attributes for chips used in portable electronics. The company's ability to continue designing and manufacturing products that represented the vanguard of chip technology was largely attributable to its steadfast commitment to funding research and development activities. In 1994, the company devoted nearly 50 percent of its revenues to research and development and new capital equipment, compared with the industry average of 35 percent.

After acquiring Seeq Technology in 1994, Atmel ranked as the largest manufacturer of Eeprom chips, having ascended to the top of the market exactly ten years after its founding. Aside from this enviable market position, however, there was much more to support the company's business. In 1995, Atmel produced a dozen product lines, each tailored for and targeted to specific market niches. A third of the company's product lines were still in the developmental stage during the mid-1990s,

providing the means for financial growth during the latter half of the decade.

In 1995 and 1996, Atmel expanded aggressively as the company's rate of financial growth continued unabated. Sales in 1995 rose to $634.2 million, recording another 69 percent gain, and net income soared to $113.7 million, registering a more prolific 91 percent increase. During the year, Atmel moved on the international front by acquiring a French chip maker named European Silicon Structures, which was renamed Atmel-ES2. On the domestic front, the company began building a new chip fabrication plant near its headquarters in San Jose.

In 1996, Atmel increased its presence in France by acquiring Digital Research in Electronic Acoustics and Music S.A. (DREAM), a computer chip company specializing in semiconductors that produced sound in multimedia computers, musical instruments, and karaoke machines. Following the purchase of this French company based in Semur-en-Auxois, Atmel began to formulate plans for the late 1990s and the completion of its second decade of business, intent on maintaining its remarkable rate of financial growth by continuing to penetrate new markets. During late 1996, Perlegos, who continued to serve as the company's president and chief executive officer, was looking to establish another manufacturing plant in Colorado Springs to give Atmel the capability to meet the mounting demand for its widely esteemed chips and further advance the company's transformation into a large-scale manufacturer.

Principal Subsidiaries

Atmel-ES2; Atmel Japan.

Further Reading

"Atmel Adds World's Best 16V8Z," *PR Newswire,* August 26, 1996, p. 8.

Bean, Joanna, "Atmel Corp. Still Plans To Build Colorado Springs Computer-Chip Plant," *Knight-Ridder/Tribune Business News,* July 8, 1996, p. 7.

"CBOE To List Leaps on Atmel Corp.," *PR Newswire,* August 30, 1996, p. 8.

Ferguson, Tim W., "Quiet Wonders of Silicon Valley," *Wall Street Journal,* June 20, 1995, p. B2.

Goldman, James S., "High-Tech Firms Rush to Market: Valley Firms Hit Wall Street with New Stock Offerings," *The Business Journal—San Jose,* March 4, 1991, p. 1.

Hutheesing, Nikhil, "Memories That Linger," *Forbes,* June 5, 1995, p. 42.

Labate, John, "Atmel Corp.," *Fortune,* May 31, 1993, p. 99.

Savitz, Eric J., "Back in the Chips," *Barron's,* September 7, 1992, p. 16.

Schmidt, Joanna, "Two Firms Cleaning Up in Colorado Computer Chip Industry," *Knight-Ridder/Tribune Business News,* October 25, 1993, p. 10.

Welling, Kathryn M., "One Flashy Performance," *Barron's,* July 18, 1994, p. 5.

Zachary, G. Pascal, "Sinking Chips," *Wall Street Journal,* January 11, 1996, p. B1.

—Jeffrey L. Covell

Barilla G. e R. Fratelli S.p.A.

Via Mantova 166
Parma, I-43100
Italy
(521) 2621
Fax: (521) 270621

Private Company
Founded: 1877
Employees: 7,900
Sales: L3.3 trillion (US$2.08 billion) (1995)
SICs: 2098 Macaroni & Spaghetti; 2051 Bread, Cake &
    Related Products; 2052 Cookies & Crackers; 2033
    Canned Fruits & Vegetables; 5149 Groceries &
    Related Products, Not Elsewhere Classified

One of Europe's largest food marketers, Barilla G. e R. Fratelli S.p.A. is a holding company that produces pasta, sauces, and packaged baked goods. The company's namesake branded pasta and sauces lead their respective segments of the Italian market, and its Mulino Bianco brand baked goods hold a 37 percent share of their domestic market segment. Although the company's products are distributed throughout Europe and in the United States, 85 percent of Barilla's sales were still generated in Italy in 1995.

Barilla was owned and operated by family members from 1877 until 1971, when brothers Pietro and Gianni sold it to U.S. conglomerate W.R. Grace & Co. Pietro Barilla repurchased the firm in 1979, and it continued to be privately held into the mid-1990s. By that time, the business was run by Pietro's three sons: Guido, Luca and Paolo.

Company Origins and Development

Barilla was founded in 1877 by another Pietro Barilla as a bakery and pasta shop in Parma, a northern Italian city famed for its pasta and cheese. The company specialized in egg pasta, as opposed to flour and water (glutinous) pasta. In an attempt to increase his income, the patriarch nominally handed over his original shop to his wife and launched a second outlet in 1891. Within just three years, however, he was forced to declare bankruptcy and sell both operations. Barilla made a new start soon thereafter but didn't achieve consistent profitability until 1898, when he added extruded pasta to his small line of hand made noodles and fresh-baked breads.

Production grew exponentially in the late 1800s and early 1900s, fueled by a combination of ever-increasing mechanization and customer-winning quality. Pietro's sons Riccardo and Gualtiero succeeded the founder in 1905. Riccardo oversaw the day-to-day operations of the factory, while Gualtiero focused on sales and promotion. In 1910, they built a new pasta factory nearer railroad and warehouse facilities and installed the region's first continuous bread-baking oven. The Barilla brothers launched the company's first trademark, featuring a "bakery boy" cracking a giant egg into a cart of flour, in 1910. This graphic representation symbolized the simple, yet high-quality ingredients used in Barilla's products.

In these early years Barilla pastas were sold in Parma through company stores and in other cities under exclusive contracts with grocers. Since all the pasta was sold in bulk, these outlets promoted the brand via in-store posters and displays. Barilla's frequent participation in international trade fairs won it awards for quality and wider recognition. By the early 1920s, Barilla pasta was exported (albeit in extremely limited quantities) to France and the United States.

After both Pietro and Gualtiero died in the 1910s, Riccardo's wife Virginia played an important role in the management of the business. Riccardo has been praised for his emphasis on capital investment of profits in plant, process and promotion. During World War I, G. & R. Barilla Company supported its enlisted employees with care packages. The firm was buoyed in the early 1920s by Italy's strong economy, employing 300 in its pasta plant alone by mid-decade. In 1926, Barilla launched a new trademark featuring a "winged chef" carrying a plate of pasta.

Despite the challenges of the Great Depression—including a call for the outlaw of pasta because it was too fattening—Barilla managed to progress on several fronts. Riccardo's son

Pietro, who joined Barilla as head of sales in 1936, was the chief architect of these changes. He exchanged the company's traditional horse drawn carts for bright yellow Fiat autos and launched Barilla's first full-fledged advertising campaigns. His ''Bonaventura'' trading card promotion coordinated newspaper, point-of-sale, radio, and outdoor media and gradually began to broaden the brand's customer base to include much of Northern Italy. However, as Pietro confided to a friend in 1938, he would not be satisfied with part of Italy—he wanted to make Barilla the country's top brand of pasta. Unfortunately, his plan to achieve that goal was interrupted by World War II.

World War II Brings Corporate Crisis

Barilla's mid-century degeneration began when Pietro was drafted into military service in 1939. Wartime rationing and a government-controlled distribution system that funneled much of the company's production to the army eroded the consumer market Barilla had so carefully nurtured in the interwar period. Parma suffered a devastating air raid near the end of the war, and the Barilla plant in particular was sabotaged and fell into disarray. In 1943, the company lost L14 million, and in 1947 Riccardo, who had struggled with poor health throughout the war years, passed away.

Though they were discouraged by the events of the war and the soaring unemployment and inflation left in its wake, Pietro and his brother Gianni resolved to revive their birthright. Led primarily by Pietro, the company shed certain elements of its business and developed a strategy that focused on the consumer pasta market. After the government ended its rationing policy in 1947, Barilla exited its military contracts. During the latter years of the decade, the company sold its bulk retail outlets and divested the breadmaking facilities.

Barilla's postwar plan coalesced in the early 1950s, just as the Italian economy began to gear up for the ''Economic Miracle'' of the 1960s. During this period, the Italian economy was transformed from one of Europe's weakest, most agrarian economies to an industrial and consumer powerhouse. Over the course of the 1950s, Barilla became a shining example of this trend. In 1952, Pietro Barilla traveled to New York to observe packaging, advertising, production and distribution methods used in the world's largest consumer-driven economy. He returned home resolved to build Barilla into Italy's premier pasta brand.

He accomplished this through heavy investments in advertising. Well-known graphic designer Erberto Carboni was charged with creating Barilla's new image, encompassing everything from the corporate logo to delivery vehicles, packaging, and advertising campaigns. His new trademark, a stylized egg lying on its side with the Barilla name in the yolk, would continue to be used (with revisions) throughout the next four decades. Carboni also made the now-famous ''Barilla blue'' background the standard for all packaging. His first tagline, ''It's always Sunday with Barilla,'' won a national advertising prize. Having captured the leading share of the egg segment of the Italian pasta industry in the early 1950s, Barilla's new strategy vaulted it over Buitoni to lead the flour and water sector as well by the end of the decade.

Having established its dominance of the pasta market, Barilla re-diversified in the 1960s. However, instead of making fresh bread, the company capitalized on its existing production and distribution network by adding such nonperishables as breadsticks, cake mixes, sauces and pizza.

National Economic Woes
Trigger Early-1970s Sell-Off

This prosperous period came to a halt in the late 1960s, when rampant inflation compelled governmental price freezes on many staples, including pasta. After nearly 100 years under family control, Gianni Barilla decided that he wanted to sell his share of the business. Unable to buy his sibling's stake, then 61-year-old Pietro Barilla sold the family business to America's W.R. Grace & Co. in 1971 for more than US$70 million.

With pasta prices and profits locked in by federal fiat, Grace turned to new products for growth. Mid-decade the new parent introduced Mulino Bianco (''White Mill'') a premium line of breadsticks, cookies, cakes, biscuits and bread. Grace supported the new brand with a highly successful promotional campaign that encompassed premiums ranging from tableware to toys. Nevertheless, as the Italian economy continued its tailspin in the 1970s, Barilla's new parent grew disenchanted with its foray into food. After owning the struggling pasta maker for eight years, Grace sold it back to Pietro Barilla for US$65 million. Pietro had financial help from Bührle, a Swiss company that continued to own 49 percent of Barilla into the mid-1990s.

Pietro Barilla maintained support of the Mulino Bianco division in the ensuing years. In fact, Barilla relaunched the brand in 1983, increasing the brand's annual sales from US$222 million to US$740 million by 1989. By 1987, Mulino Bianco contributed 50 percent of Barilla's total annual sales and had captured five percent of the European baked goods market. By that time, the brand enjoyed a 26 percent share of Italy's baked goods market.

The return of family management—not to mention the repeal of fixed pasta prices in 1978—revived Barilla's growth. Sales increased from US$288 million in 1979 to almost US$1 billion by 1986. Pietro Barilla also renewed the company's emphasis on marketing after retaking control. In 1984, he hired filmmaker Federico Fellini to direct ''one of Barilla Pasta's most famous campaigns.'' Called ''High Society,'' the ad portrayed pasta not as a mundane dish, but as a sexily simple entree. Advertisements featuring such diverse international celebrities as Paul Newman, Gerard Depardieu, and Cindy Crawford helped make Barilla one of the best-known brands in Italy by the early 1990s.

Challenges in the Mid-1990s

After guiding Barilla for a ''second term'' of 14 years, octogenarian Pietro Barilla died in 1993. His sons Guido, Luca and Paolo took charge as chairman and joint vice-chairmen, respectively. Competition from private labels and cheaper brands combined with the relative inexperience of the new management troika to bruise Barilla's bottom line. By 1996, inexpensive own-label pastas had captured 15 percent of the Italian pasta market and 12 percent of cookies and baked goods.

Barilla's revenues flattened at about US$2 billion, and its profits were halved from $73 million in 1993 to $37.5 million in 1995. The company was forced to close three plants, furlough 1,000 employees, and trim prices by 10 percent.

In 1995, the executive committee asked 66-year-old former Procter & Gamble Co. CEO Edwin L. Artzt to come out of his scant two-month retirement to help Barilla out of its tailspin. Artzt had held the top spot at Procter & Gamble from 1990 to 1995 and had led its battle against no-name brands. His turn-around scheme included several strategies that he had applied at Procter & Gamble, including Everyday Low Prices (EDLP) and an intensified global push. Under his guidance, Barilla cut the prices of products accounting for 70 percent of total sales by an average of 12 percent. He also encouraged more hard-edged advertisements focusing on Barilla's superior quality. The company expected to maintain its traditional high quality by investing US$26 million in a pasta research and development facility.

Another aspect of the strategy was an increased emphasis on global expansion to increase Barilla's proportion of international sales from less than 10 percent in 1994 to 50 percent by 2000. It targeted Asia, Latin America, and especially the United States, which had surpassed Italy as the world's largest pasta consumer in 1990. Although the company only had $10 million in U.S. pasta sales by 1995, it had captured .6 percent of that nation's pasta market after only one year of limited distribution.

Although Barilla faced several formidable competitive challenges in the mid-1990s, the company had faced far greater hazards over the course of its long history. With the benefit of a young, well-educated management team and sound strategies, the company appeared poised to regain consistent, strong profit growth.

Principal Subsidiaries

Barilla Alimentare S.p.A.; Barilla Dolciaria S.p.A.; Barilla Alimentare Dolciaria S.p.A.; Giovanni Voiello Antico Pastificio S.p.A.; Barilla Alimentare Sud S.r.l.; Molino e Pastificio F.lli Quinto e Manfredi S.p.A.; Barilla Alimentare Mediterranea S.p.A.; Forneria Meridionale S.p.A.; Forneria Lucana S.p.A.; Unione Laboratori S.r.l.; Barilla Dolciaria Industriale S.r.l.; Forneria Padana S.r.l.; Pavesi Societa per Azioni; Panifici Italiani S.p.A.; Panem S.r.l.; Barilla Diversi-ficazione S.p.A.; Nuova Forneria Adriatica S.p.A.; Barilla Servizi Finanziari S.p.A.; CO.RI.AL; Barilla France Sarl; Moulin Blanc Sarl (France); Barilla Deutschland GmbH; Misko AE (Greece); Banta EPE (Greece); Barilla International N.V. (Netherlands); Barilla Espana S.A.; Barilla America Inc. (United States); Barilla Luxembourg S.A. Holding (Luxembourg); Italest S.R.l. (63%); Polinvest Societé Anonyme (France) (56.15%); Barilla Suisse S.A.

Principal Affiliates

Panificio S.Antonio Biagio Lecce S.p.A. (30%); Pragma S.r.l. (30%); Pragma 2 S.r.l. (30%); Pragma 3 S.r.l. (30%); Consorzio Politecnico Agroalimentare (33.33%); Filiz Gida Food Industry (Turkey) (35%); Daputa Sp.Zo.o (Poland) (30%).

Further Reading

Bannon, Lisa, "Italians Do Eat Oodles of Noodles, but Trend Is Limp," *Wall Street Journal,* May 10, 1994, pp. A1, A11.

Barone, Amy, and Laurel Wentz, "Artzt Steering Barilla into EDLP Strategy," *Advertising Age,* February 26, 1996, p. 10.

Ganapini, Albino Ivardi, and Giancarlo Gonizzi, eds., *Barilla: A Hundred Years of Advertising and Corporate Communications,* Parma, Italy: Archivio Storico Barilla, 1994.

Giacomotti, Fabiana, "Milan: Y&R Cooks up Pasta Advertisements," *ADWEEK Eastern Edition,* January 16, 1995, p. 39.

Masera, Anna, "Barilla Puts Newman into Santa Claus Suit," *Advertising Age,* November 11, 1991, p. 39.

McCarter, Michelle, "Italian Loss May Mean Gain for Y&R," *Advertising Age,* November 27, 1989, p. 108.

Ono, Umiko, "U.S. Market for Pasta Is Bubbling with Italian Makers' Campaigns," *Wall Street Journal,* April 23, 1996, p. B7.

"Pasta, Present and Future," *Euromoney,* January 1996, pp. 64–66.

Pouschine, Tatiana, "Mangia, Mangia," *Forbes,* November 20, 1987, p. 232.

Sansoni, Silvia, and Zachary Schiller, "Is That Ed Artzt Pushing Pasta?" *Business Week,* April 15, 1996, p. 102.

Taglibue, John, "Family Business (Extended): In Italy, New Generation of Leaders Looks Abroad," *Wall Street Journal,* November 7, 1995, pp. D1, D6.

Tassi, Roberto, and Giorgio Soavi, "The Barilla Collection," *FMR: The Magazine of Franco Maria Ricci,* April 1993, p. 6.

Wellman, David, "Westward Ho!" *Food & Beverage Marketing,* January 1996, p. 33.

—April Dougal Gasbarre

·HOMES·
BEAZER
Beazer Homes USA, Inc.

5775 Peachtree Dunwoody Road, Suite C-550
Atlanta, Georgia 30342
U.S.A.
(404) 250-3420
Fax: (404) 250-3428

Public Company
Founded: 1994
Employees: 1,000
Revenue: $647.8 million (1995)
Stock Exchanges: NYSE
SICs: 1521 Single-Family Housing Construction; 6719
    Holding Companies, Not Elsewhere Classified

Beazer Homes USA, Inc. is the seventh-largest builder of single family homes in the United States. The company concentrates on communities which have higher than average population growth, primarily in the Southeast and Southwest, and targets its projects to first-time home buyers or those making their first move up. In 1996, Beazer Homes operated in nine states, six of which—Arizona, California, Florida, Nevada, North Carolina, and Texas—led the country in housing starts. It also built homes in South Carolina, Georgia, and Tennessee. At the end of the company's 1995 fiscal year (September 30, 1995), total revenue was $647.8 million. During that year Beazer Homes closed the sale of 4.4 million houses, with an average sales price of $148,500.

Early History

In 1968, Brian Beazer became chief executive officer of Beazer PLC, his family's homebuilding company in Bath, England. Over the next 18 years, Beazer built the company into the fourth-largest homebuilder in the United Kingdom, and, with the purchase of the European company French Kier, Beazer became a major civil engineering contractor. Through acquisitions in the United Kingdom and Europe, the company's operations included homebuilding, construction contracting, and real estate.

1985: Coming to America

Beazer PLC entered the U.S. housing market in 1985 with the purchase of Cohn Communities, an Atlanta-based homebuilder. Cohn, a 22-year-old company, had been building homes in the Atlanta area since 1967. The transaction was typical of Beazer: buy a solid local company with management that knows the market and leave the managers in place.

In the United Kingdom, land for housing developments was scarce due to tight regulations and high interest rates. Beazer's strategy was to hold on to the land the company already owned in the United Kingdom and to add to its holdings in the United States. The company began its U.S. expansion in 1987, buying two more established regional homebuilders. The first, Squire Homes had been building homes in the Raleigh, North Carolina, market since 1970, and in Charleston, South Carolina, for two years. Beazer's second purchase, Nashville-based Phillips Builders, was one of the largest homebuilders in Tennessee.

The company organized its homebuilding operations as a wholly owned subsidiary, Beazer Homes, Inc., which performed, in the company's words, under a policy of "decentralized operations with experienced management." Local managers, most from the acquired companies, were responsible for operating decisions regarding design, construction, and marketing. The centralized headquarters dealt with overall strategy, land acquisitions, and financial matters.

However, Brian Beazer was interested in more than the homebuilding segment of the U.S. construction industry, and he soon acquired Gifford-Hill & Co., a Dallas-based cement producer, and Tidewater Construction Co., a heavy construction contractor. Beazer PLC financed all these acquisitions, as well as that of French Kier, by issuing new stock.

With Shearson Lehman Hutton, Inc. as his U.S. investment banker, Beazer went looking for a major producer of construction materials and found Koppers Co., a Pittsburgh conglomerate, whose operations ranged from engineering services to chemical plants to stone quarries. The takeover, however, was not friendly, with opponents fighting the effort on two fronts. The first was in the courts, where one judge initially blocked the

Company Perspectives:

As one of the largest and financially strongest homebuilders in the United States, Beazer Homes is building for growth by remaining focused on its "Formula for Success." This formula—combining decentralized operation with a tight, centrally-controlled conservative financial policy—recognizes the cyclicality of the homebuilding industry and is designed to maintain financial flexibility during market downturns and provide the local control and nimbleness necessary to take advantage of upturns.

deal on antitrust grounds and another delayed action on possible bank-borrowing violations.

At the same time, Koppers' CEO, Charles Pullin, launched a major public relations attack. Beazer PLC, although portrayed as a foreign invader going after a venerable U.S. company, was not the major target. Instead, Pullin focused on Shearson and American Express, which owned 62 percent of Shearson and had put $23 million of its own money into the company Beazer set up to finance the takeover, thus owning a 46 percent interest. As explained in the June 20, 1988 issue of *Business Week,* Shearson had initiated the bid, financed it, and become an equity partner. Koppers' officials and hundreds of other citizens of Pennsylvania cut up their American Express cards. The State's governor and its two senators expressed outrage. Shearson lost an estimated $7 billion worth of business with Pennsylvania, and the mayor of Pittsburgh refused to allow Shearson to underwrite any more municipal bonds for the city.

Yet despite the delays and the actions against Shearson, when Beazer PLC increased its offer from $45 to $61 per share (four times Koppers' book value), the battle was over. Koppers' board accepted the bid in June 1988. For $1.7 billion, Beazer had a major presence in U.S. construction materials. Having financed the takeover completely with bank loans, the company also had a massive debt.

With the acquisition, Beazer became the number two producer of aggregates (crushed stone) and asphalt in the United States. In addition to Koppers and Gifford-Hill, Beazer had building materials operations in northern California and operated more than 100 quarries. As homebuilding continued to slow in the United Kingdom due to tight money policies, the U.S. activities became more important. In 1989, those operations generated more than 50 percent of Beazer's operating profits, and held more than 75 percent of the company's assets. Although homebuilding was a relatively small part of Beazer's operations in the United States, it generated $102.8 million in revenue for 1989 and $106.6 million for 1990.

To cut its debt, Beazer PLC sold off Koppers' chemical division, realizing $650 million after taxes. However, the recession stopped or slowed anticipated road and bridge building and other activities in the construction industry, and Koppers never generated the profit margins Beazer needed to service the debt.

Beazer Homes was also experiencing difficulty. Between 1987 and 1991, housing starts in the United States steadily declined. This was due to a slowing in the number of people forming households, the overbuilding of apartments and other multifamily units, and the recession of 1990–1991.

A variety of things influenced the demand for housing. In the short term, economic factors had the greatest influence on housing construction. These included mortgage rates, the cost of owning a home, the amount of real disposable income people had to spend, and consumer confidence that home ownership was a good investment—that they would make money when they sold their home. Changes in tax legislation, such as the amount of deductibility for home interest payments or capital gains rates, also contributed to the people's home-buying patterns.

1991: The Beazer PLC Acquisition

In 1991, housing starts in the United States fell to a historic low of 1.01 million units. Operating in four states in the southeast, Beazer Homes sold 927 homes that year, at an average price of $105,000. Revenue for the year was $97.6 million. At the beginning of the year, Ian McCarthy was named executive vice-president. McCarthy was a civil engineer and came from Beazer PLC's construction operations in Hong Kong and Thailand. Twenty-two months later he became president of Beazer Homes.

Meanwhile, Beazer PLC was producing annual revenues of about $3.4 billion, but the company's net debt was just over $1.7 billion. On September 11th, Brian Beazer agreed to a refinancing plan which would spin off the company's British and European operations, renamed CHB, and float their stock on the London stock market. Under the plan, Mr. Beazer would retain control of Koppers, Beazer Homes, and the company's other U.S. operations, but lose the business his father started.

Two days after the prospectus detailing CHB's operations was published, Lord Hanson, head of the British conglomerate Hanson PLC, spoke to Brian Beazer about buying the entire Beazer organization and retaining Mr. Beazer as CEO. Shortly thereafter, Beazer's shareholders, one-third of whom lived in the United States, accepted Hanson's agreed takeover offer of £351 million ($612 million).

Christopher Austin noted in *Mergers & Acquisitions,* that the Beazer PLC acquisition was the first takeover in which shareholders in two different countries received a single offer at the same time. For this to happen, the U.S. Securities and Exchange Commission and the U.K. Takeover Panel worked cooperatively to modify merger rules and practices to meet the specific needs of the two companies. *Investment Dealer's Digest* reported the two bodies dealt with five issues in this precedent-setting transaction: disclosure in the preannouncement stage, the form of the public announcement, timing problems with commencement of the offer, delivery of payment for tendered securities, and restrictions on the advisory firms regarding trading Hanson's and Beazer's securities.

As a result of the acquisition, Beazer PLC was restructured and an indirect wholly owned subsidiary of Hanson PLC,

Beazer America, Inc., purchased the U.S. operations, including Beazer Homes, Inc.

1992–1995

During 1992, Beazer Homes entered new markets. Squires Homes expanded from Charlotte to nearby Raleigh, anticipating strong employment growth related to the state government and educational institutions located at the Research Triangle Park. In October, the company bought a condominium development in Clifton, New Jersey. Revenue that year was $127.7 million with closings on 1,182 houses. The average price of a Beazer home was $108,000.

By 1993, single family starts in the United States were nearly 53 percent higher than in 1991. In February, Beazer expanded its operations to the West Coast market with the purchase of Watt Housing Corporation for $116 million. The purchase was financed by borrowing the whole amount from a subsidiary of Hanson PLC.

Watt built homes in developments in California, Arizona, and Nevada under the names Watt Homes, Watt Hancock, and Watt Nevada. To handle its West Coast homebuilding activities, Beazer America established Beazer Homes Holding (BHH), a wholly owned subsidiary. In October, Beazer Homes, Inc., the East Coast homebuilding subsidiary, bought Panitz & Company, a Florida homebuilder, for $3.2 million. Ian McCarthy served as president of both subsidiaries.

In November 1993, the two subsidiaries were combined and incorporated as Beazer Homes USA, in anticipation of going public. Ian McCarthy was named president and CEO, and Brian Beazer became the non-executive chairman of the board. In part because of the acquisitions and expansions, total sales for 1993 increased to $340 million, with 3,163 housing starts and over 2,000 closings. That level of activity earned the company a place on the *Professional Builder* magazine's annual list of major housing builders, where it ranked 17.

In February 1994, Beazer Homes USA went public. A third of the proceeds of the initial public offering went to pay back Beazer America for financing the Watt purchase. Squires Homes continued to grow in the Carolinas, expanding from Charleston, South Carolina, to Columbia, and, in 1995, to Myrtle Beach.

Beazer Homes maintained a conservative financial structure as sales fluctuated in 1995. The company repurchased its outstanding shares previously held by Hanson Industries for $16 a share and issued $50 million of convertible, preferred stock. In April, Beazer Homes moved into Texas, buying Bramalea Homes Texas from a bankrupt Canadian company. Bramalea had projects in the Dallas and Houston markets, two of the top growing cities in the country. The company also closed out the New Jersey development. Although profits for the fiscal year were down due to higher interest rates at the beginning of the year and a weak economy in California, Beazer Homes moved to 13th on *Professional Builder*'s 29th Annual Report of Housing's Giants. Total revenue for the year was $648 million.

1995 and Beyond

Nineteen ninety-six was the best year for homebuilders since 1978, with construction of single-family homes up 15 percent from 1995. In May, Beazer purchased Gulfcoast Homes, Inc., a Florida company building homes in Fort Myers and Naples. In June it bought Trendmaker Homes of Dallas. Markets in which Beazer Homes had developments, including Atlanta, Phoenix, Dallas–Fort Worth, and Houston, were among the busiest, as measured by the number of building permits issued for single-family homes, and the California market began to improve. Revenues for the company's third quarter, which ended June 30, 1996, increased more than 43 percent above the same period in 1995. New orders were up 30 percent for the nine months ending in June.

In looking at the homebuilding industry in the long run, demographics play a bigger role than economics. In a February 7, 1996 news release, *U.S. Housing Markets,* a housing research journal, predicted that an average of 1.25 million new households would be formed annually between 1996 and 2000. Between 1990 and 1995, when about 1.13 million new households were formed each year, it was the 45-to-54 age group—those at the beginning of the Baby Boom generation—who had the greatest household growth. In the second half of the 1990s, the majority of households were expected be formed by 25-to-34-year-olds, Beazer Homes USA's primary target group. While demographic factors appeared to favor Beazer, economic factors could influence whether the households live in rental units, multifamily condominiums, or single family homes. Based on the company's 1996 activities, however, many of those households will be living in homes built by Beazer.

Principal Subsidiaries

Beazer Homes Arizona; Beazer Homes California; Beazer Homes Florida; Beazer Homes Georgia; Beazer Homes Nevada; Beazer Homes Texas; Phillips Builders; Squires Homes.

Further Reading

Austin, Christopher E., ''Drawing a Regulatory Road Map from the Hanson-Beazer Merger,'' *Mergers & Acquisitions,* July/August 1992, p. 48.

''Beazer: A Pittsburgh Exile,'' *The Economist,* September 14, 1991, p. 76.

''Beazer Homes USA (BZH),'' *Barron's,* February 21, 1994, p. 50.

''Beazer USA Changes Name,'' *Wall Street Journal,* February 8, 1985, p. B9.

''British Takeovers: Divide and Lose,'' *The Economist,* September 21, 1991, p. 82.

''Busiest Markets, Single-Family Building,'' *2nd Quarter 1996 Flash Report,* U.S. Housing Markets, http://www.housingusa.com.

Byrne, Harlan S., ''Beazer PLC: Land Scarcity Bodes Well for British-Based Builder,'' *Barron's,* December 25, 1989, p. 29.

Foster, Geoffrey, ''Building Beazer Bigger,'' *Management Today,* October 1986, p. 70.

Hirsch, Albert A., ''Residential Construction from a Long-Run Perspective,'' *Survey of Current Business,* U.S. Department of Commerce, June 1994, p. 30.

''How to Tell Who Your Friends Are,'' *Fortune,* April 25, 1988, p. 11.

Lurz, William H., ''Acquiring Mind: McCarthy Leads Beazer to Top 20,'' *Professional Builder,* August 1994, p. 78.

McCartney, Scott, "Home Building Business Is Losing Its Local Character," *Wall Street Journal,* April 13, 1994, p. B4.

Mencke, Claire, "Homebuilding Stocks: A Tale of Two Tiers," *Investor's Business Daily,* January 15, 1996.

"Mortgage Rates No Deterrent to Eager Home Buyers," *News from U.S. Housing Markets,* July 2, 1996, http://www.housingusa.com.

"New Issue Pipeline: Beazer Homes USA," *Investor's Business Daily,* June 13, 1995.

Popper, Margaret, "Hanson, Beazer Merger Establishes Legal Precedent," *Investment Dealers Digest,* December 16, 1991, p. 16.

"Pulte Surpasses Centex As Nation's Largest Builder, Survey Finds," 1996 Annual Report of Housing Giants, *Professional Builder,* April 1996, http://www.cahners.com/mainmag/pb.htm.

Reina, Peter, et al., "Beazer Builds through Buyouts," *ENR,* April 28, 1988, p. 36.

"Residential Builders Respond to Vigorous New Home Sales Pace," *News from U.S. Housing Markets,* August 1, 1996, http://www.housingusa.com.

Reuters, "Hanson Takes Beazer Homes Public and Sells Property," *New York Times,* February 24, 1994, p. D4.

Schroeder, Michael, and Maremont, Mark, "Why Koppers Fell before Beazer's Bulldozer," *Business Week,* June 20, 1988, p. 82.

"U.S. Homebuilders Match Production to Household Growth," *News from U.S. Housing Markets,* February 7, 1996, http://www.housingusa.com.

Williams, Monci Jo, "Brash New Mogul on Wall Street," *Fortune,* May 23, 1988, p. 91.

—Ellen D. Wernick

Bhs plc

Marylebone House
129-137 Marylebone Road
London NW1 5QD
England
(171) 262-3456
Fax: (171) 262-4740

Wholly Owned Subsidiary of Storehouse plc
Incorporated: 1933
Employees: 14,000
Sales: £749 million (1996)
SICs: 5311 Department Stores; 5621 Women's Clothing
Stores; 5611 Men's & Boys' Clothing Stores; 5712
Furniture Stores

Known for more than 50 years as British Home Stores, Bhs plc ranks among the United Kingdom's largest department store chains. Since its foundation in the late 1920s, this company has haltingly evolved from a variety store focused exclusively on price into a department store with a strong emphasis on apparel. Bhs's 186 outlets (135 company-owned and 51 franchised) carry clothing (mostly womenswear), housewares, and giftware. Many units also feature a restaurant, coffee house, or sandwich shop. The business is a subsidiary of Storehouse plc, a holding company whose operations include maternity and infant goods retailer Mothercare UK Ltd. Led by Keith Edelman, who was also CEO of Storehouse, Bhs enjoyed steadily rising pretax profits in the early 1990s.

Creation and Development

British Home Stores was founded in 1928 by a group of American entrepreneurs. These businessmen modeled their two initial London stores after Woolworth's, which carried no goods that retailed for more than sixpence (ten cents in the United States). So as not to compete directly with its successful predecessor, British Home Stores set its price ceiling a bit higher, at one shilling (double that of Woolworth's). By raising the bar to five shillings in 1929, British Home Stores was able to offer a wider variety of home furnishings, including drapery. Most of the budding chain's locations featured small cafeterias and grocery departments as well. During the interwar period, the company developed several lines of own-label merchandise, including "Twinkle" brand infantswear, "Travair" luggage, and "Request" foods. The chain went public in 1933.

In the postwar era, British Home Stores shifted its strategy from selling strictly on price to focusing more broadly on offering "quality and value for money." The chain adopted the "Prova" brand to designate BHS exclusives in 1960. By the end of that decade, the company employed more than 12,000 and boasted 94 stores nationwide.

British Home Stores continued to distinguish itself from variety stores like Woolworth's over the course of the 1970s by continuously broadening its apparel and housewares lines. The company also formed a joint venture with British supermarket giant J. Sainsbury Ltd. to create a chain of SavaCentre "hypermarkets" (giant supermarkets) during the decade. By the end of the 1970s, BHS had made the transition: it was considered more of a department store, à la Marks & Spencer, than a variety store, like Woolworth's. *The Accountant* characterized British Home Stores as a "strong and efficient" chain in 1980 and compared its earnings growth favorably to market leader Marks & Spencer. In fact, the company's annual revenues had increased from £161.8 million in 1975 to £366.4 million, and its net income before taxes rose from £18.6 million to £41.8 million during that same period.

Gary Warnaby, who examined British Home Stores' history in the early 1990s, asserted, "BHS's advances in trading profit had been due as much to cost containment as to sales growth." Over the course of the 1970s, the chain had only added a net of 30 locations. Indeed, the chain's "back-office" functions—distribution, data processing, etcetera—were highly praised for their efficiency. Some observers, both contemporary and retrospective, noted that despite its apparent strengths, BHS lacked the panache of its department store competitors. Next to Marks & Spencer, British Home Stores was described as "drab" and "dowdy."

Early 1980s Recession Leads to Merger with Habitat/Mothercare

Such criticism came to fruition in the early 1980s, when a global recession bruised the bottom line at many major retailers. In an effort to upgrade its image and increase its sales, British Home Stores consulted with designers at Conran Associates to revamp its merchandise and retail environment. The chain unveiled its first remodeling project late in 1982. The new layout traded in supermarket-style aisles for a curvier, more open floor plan. British Home Stores also continued to add higher-priced goods while working to retain its focus on value.

Perhaps as an outgrowth of its contact with Conran Associates, British Home Stores merged with Sir Terence Conran's Habitat/Mothercare plc in 1986. Widely known as the most important arbiter of postwar Britons' taste in home furnishings, Conran was knighted ''for services to British design and industry'' in 1983. British Home Stores was one of a succession of acquisitions that transformed Conran's chain of Habitat stores from a £67.2 million company into an international retail federation with more than £1 billion in annual sales. Storehouse plc, a holding company, was formed to manage Conran's growing family of companies, which included seven retail outfits and more than six million square feet of selling space. Although all of the chains operated independently, Storehouse CEO Conran hoped that the merger would generate synergies among its primary constituents.

To that end, British Home Stores began to undergo a process of ''Conranization,'' targeting younger customers with updated stores, trendier fashions, and a revitalized corporate image. Sixteen-year BHS veteran Denis Cassidy, who had been appointed CEO of British Home Stores in 1985, became deputy chairman and group managing director of Storehouse in 1986 and advanced to chairman and CEO of BHS in 1987. The parent company chipped in £8.5 million (US 12.6 million) in addition to the chain's existing £50 million modernization program. Before the year was out, British Home Stores had shuttered its 56 food departments and adopted a new logo featuring the ''flying h'': a lowercase swoop of a letter sandwiched between the uppercase ''B'' and ''S.'' (A second round of changes would make the ''s'' lowercase as well.) An increased advertising budget promoted the new ''Bhs.''

These efforts proved to be in vain, however, as the British retail environment went into another tailspin at the end of the decade. *Forbes's* Jeffrey Ferry characterized the Bhs revamp as ''disastrous,'' noting that Storehouse's attempt to appeal to a young, upper-class clientele alienated Bhs's traditional core of mature, budget-conscious customers. In a 1994 interview for Britain's *Marketing* magazine, Bhs executive Helena Packshaw noted, ''Customers knew Bhs had changed in the late '80s but they didn't know what we'd become.'' By mid-1987, even the visionary Conran was ready to decouple Storehouse's disparate interests. Over the span of just a few months, the holding company endured two takeover threats and the October 1987 stock market crash. Top Bhs executive Denis Cassidy resigned in frustration. From 1987 to 1989, group pretax profits dropped from £130 million to £11.3 million, and in 1988, Storehouse's board of directors asked Conran to step aside and accept a titular chairmanship. He resigned in 1990.

Although Bhs and its parent endured a high rate of turnover in the chief executive's offices during the late 1980s and early 1990s, the group benefited from a program of retrenchment. Under the *de facto* direction of Michael Julien from 1988 to 1992, Storehouse decided to restrict its operations to Bhs, which brought in the most revenues, and Mothercare UK, whose focus on maternity and early childhood remained rather unique. Although these two chains were quite different from one another, they were linked in their common target customer: women and their families. In 1989, American David Dworkin, a former executive at Neiman Marcus, Bonwit Teller, and other upscale department store chains, became CEO and chairman of Bhs. Dworkin brought with him U.S.-made clothing and merchandising strategies and furloughed 900 middle managers in an effort to flatten the organization.

When Michael Julien's health compelled him to resign in 1992, Dworkin advanced to the lead roles at the parent company. After less than a year as Storehouse's CEO, Dworkin was hired away by Carter Hawley Hale Stores. In 1993 the board of directors hired an outsider, Keith Edelman, as chief executive officer of both Storehouse and Bhs.

Revenues at Bhs remained flat throughout this period, at around £750 million, but pretax profits more than tripled, from £22.1 million in 1992 to £77.4 million in 1996 (fiscal year ended March 30). Although Edelman has been praised as the architect of Bhs's early 1990s turnaround, it seems clear that the efforts of the previous decade also contributed to the chain's revitalization. Ongoing store renovations kept the selling environments up to date. Rationalization of the chain's suppliers and its distribution scheme cut costs and smoothed inventory replenishment. Company-sponsored clothing design and modeling competitions kept the company's apparel lines fresh and identified new talent. An increased advertising budget featured the chain's first television campaign in years.

After divesting most of its overseas operations in the late 1980s, Bhs undertook a program of international growth through franchising. By early 1996, the chain had established 51 franchised stores in 12 countries, with a particularly heavy concentration in the Middle East. The chain expected to expand this segment of its business to China, Hong Kong, and Moscow in the late 1990s.

With its multidecade transformation from a one-price variety store to a full-fledged department store complete, economic recovery on Britain's horizon, and an apparently dedicated management team in place, Bhs appeared poised for profitable growth in the late 1990s.

Further Reading

''BhS' New Power Supply,'' *Management Today,* January 1986, pp. 11–12.

Born, Pete, ''David Dworkin Leaves Bonwit's for British Post,'' *WWD,* November 9, 1989, p.1.

''British Retailing; Selling by Design,'' *The Economist,* September 20, 1986, p. 82.

Britton, Noelle, and Miles, Louella, ''Chalk and Cheese,'' *Marketing,* July 2, 1987, pp. 26–27.

Collier, Andrew, ''British Home Stores To Cut Staff by 1990,'' *Daily News Record,* May 18, 1990, p. 7.

——, "Dworkin Heading Home To Buy U.S. Apparel," *Daily News Record,* March 2, 1990, pp. 2–3.

"Each Way Bet?," *The Economist,* May 9, 1970, p. 81.

Ferry, Jeffrey, "Broken by the Bottom Line," *Forbes,* November 27, 1989, pp. 180–183.

Great Britain Commission on Industrial Relations, *British Home Stores,* London: H.M.S.O., 1971.

Grofton, Ken, "The Backroom Boys," *Marketing,* September 18, 1986, pp. 31–32.

"High Street Setbacks," *Retail & Distribution Management,* July–August 1986, p. 5.

"Is This the End of a Great Romance? The Problems Facing Storehouse," *Retail & Distribution Management,* July–August 1986, pp. 54–56.

"M&S Up Against New Fashion Rivals," *Retail & Distribution Management,* November–December 1984, pp. 66–68.

Miles, Louella, "The Counter Revolutionaries," *Marketing,* September 25, 1986, pp. 41–43.

Miller, Rachel, "Harvester of a Corporate Culture," *Marketing,* August 24, 1995, p. 20.

Nicholas, Ruth, "Storehouse Set To Build Up BhS," *Marketing,* March 3, 1994, p. 2.

"Super Supermarkets," *The Accountant,* June 26, 1980, pp. 981–984.

Warnaby, Gary, "Storehouse," *International Journal of Retail & Distribution Management,* May–June 1993, pp. 27–34.

"What Lies Behind the Habitat Mothercare-BHS Merger," *Retail & Distribution Management,* January–February 1986, pp. 66–68.

—April Dougal Gasbarre

Big B, Inc.

2600 Morgan Road Southeast
Bessemer, Alabama 35023
U.S.A.
(205) 424-3421
Fax: (205) 425-3525

Public Company
Incorporated: 1981
Employees: 6,300
Sales: $737.1 million (1996)
Stock Exchanges: NASDAQ
SICs: 5912 Drug Stores & Proprietary Stores

Ranking as the tenth largest drug store chain in the United States, Big B, Inc. operates a chain of approximately 400 drug stores in the southeastern United States. During the mid-1990s, Big B operated its drug stores under the names "Big B Drugs" and "Drugs for Less," and operated a smaller chain of stores that sold and rented medical equipment for home use under the name "Big B Home Health Care Centers." Formerly a part of a supermarket chain known as Bruno's, Inc., Big B became a separate corporate entity in 1981 and quickly expanded the number of its retail units, becoming one of the largest and fastest-growing retail prescription providers in the nation. All of the company's stores were located within a 400-mile radius of its distribution center in Birmingham, Alabama, with the greatest concentration of stores existing in Alabama and Georgia. The company also operated more than 50 stores in Florida, Tennessee, and Mississippi.

Origins

Through the entrepreneurial efforts of Joseph S. Bruno, two retail chains were created, both of which flourished in the southeastern United States. The first company founded by Bruno was Bruno's, Inc., a supermarket chain he started in 1932. Twenty years old at the time, Bruno used his family's savings to start the business, investing $600 in the enterprise at the height of the Great Depression. Over the course of the ensuing three-and-a-half decades, the supermarket chain evolved into an unqualified success, proving to be strong enough to shed one aspect of its business as a separate corporate entity. Such was the foundation of Big B, a one-time division of Bruno's, Inc. that was spun off from the supermarket chain to pursue its own development. In roughly a decade, Big B evolved into a formidable retail chain itself, propelled forward by an aggressive expansion program during the 1980s and the first half of the 1990s that elevated the company to the ranks of the largest drug store chains in the United States.

Before Big B gained the stature that described the company during the 1990s, it operated for more than a decade within Bruno's, Inc.'s corporate structure, existing as a division of the supermarket chain from 1968 to 1977. In July 1977, the drug store division of Bruno's, Inc. was organized as a separate business, but remained under the supermarket chain's corporate umbrella as a wholly-owned subsidiary named Big B. Four years later, Big B was spun off to Bruno's, Inc.'s shareholders and emerged as a separate entity. Following the 1981 spin off, Big B spent its inaugural decade entrenching its presence in its home state of Alabama and extending its territory of operations to include neighboring states. Initially, the company operated a chain of retail drug stores under the name "Big B Drugs," which received its merchandise from a distribution center established in Birmingham, Alabama, during the mid-1980s. From this distribution center, which served as the hub of Big B's operations into the late 1990s, the company's stores stocked both brand name and generic prescription drugs, pharmacy-related products, and general merchandise. Gracing the shelves were a broad range of cosmetics, greeting cards, books and magazines, tobacco products, toys, electronics, small electrical appliances, convenience foods, as well as the sundry items found in most drug stores across the country.

The company grew swiftly during the 1980s, by expanding the number of its Big B Drugs stores. Big B Drugs stores averaged 9,000 square feet of retail space and represented the backbone of the company even after the company started another type of retailer in 1988. In response to the rapidly expanding discount drug store market during the 1980s, Big B launched its own deep discount retail concept by debuting

Company Perspectives:

We view our Company as a hard working machine—one which consistently and dependably satisfies the needs of tens of thousands of individuals each day. Keeping pace with the ever changing needs of our customers, the demands of volatile market trends, and the accelerating cycle of new technology often mean reinventing the machine, tuning up the parts, and keeping its mechanisms running as smoothly as possible.

''Drugs for Less'' stores in 1988. Drugs for Less stores were roughly twice as large as their Big B Drugs counterparts, averaging 20,000 square feet of retail space. With these two retail concepts predicating its growth, Big B entered the last year of the decade ready to join the elite company of the country's largest retail drug store chains. An acquisition completed by Big B in 1989, turned desire into reality for company executives at headquarters in Bessemer, Alabama.

Not long after establishing its first Drugs for Less stores, Big B completed a bold move into neighboring Georgia when it acquired 85 stores from Peoples Drugs Stores in February 1989. The stores, which were part of the Reed Drug Co. chain and primarily situated in the Atlanta and Columbus, Georgia markets, cost the company $52.4 million, the price to pay for significantly strengthening Big B's presence in Georgia. The acquisition also brought Big B into the Atlanta market for the first time, setting the stage for a contentious chapter in the company's history seven years later when the battle for supremacy in Atlanta embroiled Big B in a hostile takeover attempt. Before the company would become mired in fending off an unwanted suitor, however, there were years of growth, particularly as the company entered the 1990s and prepared to mount an ambitious expansion program.

Growth in the 1990s

Nine years old as it entered 1990, Big B had accomplished much during its short tenure in the Southeast drug store industry. Further robust growth appeared assured. The company had recently opened its 300th store and construction was underway for a 200,000-square-foot expansion of its existing 220,000 square foot distribution center in Birmingham, Alabama. A third facet to the company's business had also been added when Big B launched a chain of home health stores operating under the banner ''Big B Home Health Care Center.'' Fueled by this growth on all existing fronts and new fronts, sales for the 1989 fiscal year were up a record 54 percent, rising to $418 million, and a record increase—67 percent—in the share of prescription drug sales of the company's total sales was registered. About the only aspect of the company's operations that was less than desirable was its weakened profitability, but even this stain on Big B's balance sheet was a sign of growth. Profits declined by $3.5 million in 1989, but this loss was primarily attributable to the financing costs and other expenses related to the acquisition of the Reed Drug Co. stores and their conversion to the Big B format.

Declining profits, accordingly, were no cause for the company to scale back its plans for the future and reassess its business stance. Instead, Big B executives planned to open 15 new stores in 1990, 12 of which were expected to be Big B Drugs stores and the remaining three slated for establishment as Drugs for Less stores. By this point, Big B operated four Big B Home Health Care Centers in Alabama, 16 Drugs for Less stores in Alabama, Florida, Georgia, Mississippi, and Tennessee, and 277 Big B Drugs stores scattered throughout Alabama and four neighboring states. Nearly half of the company Big B Drugs stores were located in Alabama, where Big B operated 133 stores. The acquisition of the Reed Drug Co. chain, amplified the company's presence in Georgia significantly, increasing its number of stores to 106 by the beginning of summer in 1990. Elsewhere, the number of Big B Drugs stores were less concentrated, with six stores operating in Mississippi and another 13 stores established in Tennessee.

Profits continued their decline in 1991 when Big B lost $1.4 million on sales of $463.6 million, but the following year the company climbed back into the black with strength, posting $6.5 million in profits on sales of $487.8 million. As these encouraging financial figures were being recorded, Big B sold off 2.1 million shares of stock to pay off bank debt and to gain the financial resources to launch an expansion program. The 1992 stock offering, which was expected to bring in roughly $30 million, was an intrinsic part of management's expansion strategy, enabling it to announce with confidence that Big B would open eight to 10 additional drug stores before January 30, 1993 and either open or acquire up to 20 stores by the beginning of 1994. As the company moved forward with its expansion plans it executed them as it had before, never straying beyond a 400 mile radius from its distribution center in Alabama. Though the number of stores would increase in the years to come, it was not the intent of Big B's management to develop any of its retail concepts into national chains. Instead, company executives were looking to saturate markets where the company already had a presence, thereby increasing its market share and enabling it to serve its entire operations from its nearly 500,000 square foot distribution center in Birmingham, Alabama.

Aside from entrenching its position in its five-state service territory, Big B executives were also desirous of increasing the percentage of the company's prescription drug sales. Toward this end, Big B completed two important moves in 1992. During the year, the company started a mail-order prescription drug program and in December acquired a nursing home pharmacy service, which provided medicine for roughly 2,000 beds in Atlanta. On the heels of these two deals, Big B officials announced plans to open 10 to 12 new stores in 1993 and 15 to 20 the following year. By the beginning of summer in 1993, Big B had already exceeded the growth projections for both 1993 and 1994.

Early in 1993, Big B acquired 45 Treasury stores from J.C. Penney Company's Thrift Drug Inc., paying $16.5 million for the Atlanta-based stores. Once integrated into the company's fold, the 45 Treasury stores lifted the number of Big B Drugs stores in the Atlanta area to 109, enough to move the company past Drug Emporium to rank as the second-largest drug store chain in the Atlanta market. By the following year the company ranked not only as a leading contender in the Atlanta market, but also as one of the 17 largest drug store chains in the United States, supported by more than 350 stores.

In 1995—Big B's 1996 fiscal year—the company achieved a record high in sales, generating $737.1 million during the year compared to $668.2 million for previous year. Profits, however, took a precipitous plunge, dropping from $15.1 million to $2.6 million as the company's pharmacy-related gross margins declined. Despite the severe drop in Big B's net income, executives at company headquarters were unruffled. Big B continued to tout itself as "one of the largest and fastest-growing retail prescription providers in the Southeast," according to the company's annual report that announced the drop in profits. During the year, the company filled more than 15 million prescriptions, a total that pointed to the successful efforts of the company during the previous several years to increase the prescription-related segment of its business. As a result, combined pharmacy sales accounted for more than 50 percent of Big B's revenues for the first time, giving the company the sales mix it had been striving to achieve during the first half of the 1990s.

Big B opened 23 stores in 1995, many of them free-standing structures with drive-thru windows and on-site photo labs. By the end of the year, there were 384 stores composing the Big B drug store empire, with 170 stores in Alabama, 161 stores in Georgia, 23 stores in Florida, 23 stores in Tennessee, and seven in Mississippi, all of which were within 400 miles of the company's distribution center in Birmingham, Alabama. The company continued to hold steadfast to its policy of not expanding beyond a 400-mile radius from the Birmingham distribution center even as its charted ambitious expansion plans for the late 1990s. Planning to limit its expansion to markets where the company already had a presence, Big B officials envisioned room for 600 stores within the confines of the geographic boundaries it had established for itself, giving it ample room to continue the pace of expansion it recorded during the first half of the 1990s into the beginning of the 21st century.

Hostile Takeover Attempt

As the company moved toward its goal of establishing a total of 600 stores in the Southeast (operating 389 stores by mid-1996), an unexpected development arose that dominated the company's attention as it planned for the future. In the summer of 1996, Revco D.S., Inc., the second-largest drug store chain in the United States, made a private offer to acquire Big B, an offer Big B officials rebuffed. With a total of 2,200 drug stores, 75 of which were located in the Atlanta metropolitan area, Revco was intent on becoming the largest drug store chain in the Atlanta area, a distinction the acquisition of the 90 Atlanta Big B stores would bestow on the Twinsburg, Ohio-based drug store chain. Two years earlier, Revco had nearly doubled its size by acquiring Cincinnati-based Hook-SupeRx Inc. to become the country's second-largest drug store chain, and as company officials scanned the horizon in 1996, the opportunity to acquire

Big B, which by this point ranked as the 10th-largest drug store chain in the country, was irresistible. Revco did not take "no" as an answer.

Wholly focused on acquiring Big B, Revco announced on September 9, 1996 that it was commencing a cash tender offer for all of the outstanding shares of Big B. The takeover attempt, which D. Dwayne Hoven, Revco's president and chief executive officer, described as "truly a win-win opportunity for Revco and Big B shareholders, employees, and customers," was met with disdain at Big B's headquarters. In response to Revco's unsolicited bid, Big B announced its board of directors had unanimously voted to reject the offer and that a lawsuit had been filed to prevent Revco from contesting the anti-takeover provisions. Big B's anti-takeover provisions, what it called its "poison pill," prompted Revco to file a counterclaim against Big B, alleging that the poison pill created by Big B violated Alabama law. As Big B prepared for 1997, the lawsuits remained unresolved, but the company continued to expand its operations, intent on fending off Revco's offer and pursing its goal of establishing 600 stores in the Southeast on its own.

Principal Operating Units

Big B Drugs; Drugs for Less; Big B Home Health Care Centers.

Further Reading

"Big B Offers Shares to Cut Debt," *Supermarket News,* April 27, 1992, p. 39.

Brookman, Faye, "Big B Getting even Bigger, with Treasury Drug Purchase," *Drug Topics,* May 17, 1993, p. 82.

Elson, Joel, "Big B Increases Sales with Mixed Program," *Supermarket News,* February 16, 1987, p. 38.

Gamboa, Glenn, "Ohio's Revco Launches Hostile Bid for Alabama's Big B Drugstore Chain," *Knight-Ridder/Tribune Business News,* September 10, 1996, p. 9.

Keith, Bill, "Prescription Sales Help to Boost Big B's Fortunes," *Drug Topics,* June 4, 1990, p. 54.

Lee, Georgia, "Big B Stores Angling for Southern Exposure," *WWD,* February 18, 1994, p. S12.

"Revco Announces Offer to Acquire Big B for $15 per Big B Share," *PR Newswire,* September 9, 1996, p. 9.

"Revco Pleased with Expiration of Hart-Scott-Rodino Waiting Period," *PR Newswire,* September 26, 1996, p. 9.

"Revco Seeks to Enjoin Big B Poison Pill," *PR Newswire,* September 30, 1996, p. 9.

Roush, Chris, "Alabama's Big B Rejects Takeover Bid by Ohio's Revco," *Knight-Ridder/Tribune Business News,* September 24, 1996, p. 9.

——, "Hostile Takeover Would Make Revco New Leader Among Atlanta Drugstores," *Knight-Ridder/Tribune Business News,* September 10, 1996, p. 9.

Ukens, Carol, "Big B Chain Seeks Profit in Pharmaceutical Care Capitation," *Drug Topics,* March 4, 1996, p. 47.

—Jeffrey L. Covell

BMC Industries, Inc.

Two Appletree Square
Minneapolis, Minnesota 55425
U.S.A.
(612) 851-6000
Fax: (612) 851-6050

Public Company
Incorporated: 1907 as Buckbee-Mears Company
Employees: 2,000
Sales: $255.4 million (1995)
Stock Exchanges: New York
SICs: 3679 Electronic Components, Not Elsewhere
    Classified; 3851 Ophthalmic Goods

BMC Industries, Inc. is a leading manufacturer in both of its core businesses: precision imaged products and optical products. Operating under the trade name Vision-Ease, BMC has the most extensive product line in the ophthalmic industry, manufacturing polycarbonate, plastic, and glass lenses. In addition, the company is the world's largest fused multi-focal glass lens manufacturer and the second largest supplier of polycarbonate lenses. But, the largest portion of BMC's revenues are derived from aperture masks. BMC is the largest independent manufacturer of the component which directs electron beams in color televisions and computer monitors. BMC pioneered the development of the photochemical machining process used to make the mask.

Roots in the Graphic Arts

Founded in 1907 by cousins Charles E. Buckbee and Norman T. Mears, Buckbee-Mears Company operated one of the Twin Cities' first photoengraving plants. The St. Paul, Minnesota, company quickly added photography to its engraving and creative art departments, and thus became a full-line graphic arts supplier. By 1927, offset printing—a photomechanical process—had been developed and Buckbee-Mears later rendered that service as well.

"It was World War II that brought Norman B. Mears to the forefront in the then-conservative family operation," wrote Dick Caldwell in a 1967 *Minneapolis Star* article. The younger Mears had left his farming operation in South Dakota in 1928 and joined Buckbee-Mears. He then pushed for expansion of the business into photomechanical production. Mears got a big opportunity to experiment with the process when the U. S. Navy needed grids etched on the eyepieces of military equipment. Mears not only led the successful development of a vacuum-etching production line for metal and glass reticles used in fire control (gun sights), radar, and guided missiles, but he created a new industrial division for the company.

A New Focus in the Postwar Years

The industrial skills BMC acquired during the war were transferred to the television industry in peacetime. The Radio Corporation of American (RCA) enlisted Buckbee-Mears to develop an crucial part for color television tubes. In 1963, the company perfected an automated process for the production of the "shadow mask," an extremely thin metal sheet punctured by hundreds of thousands of perfectly positioned holes which directed electron beams toward phosphorous strips that generate the color. The automated chemical etching process had evolved over a 13-year period and several generations of equipment.

Norman B. Mears became company president in 1957 and at one point owned up to 92 percent of the stock. He and Buckbee-Mears were direct beneficiaries of the wave of color television sales they helped set in motion. By 1966 about five million color televisions were sold in the United States; 99 percent of those TV sets contained a Buckbee-Mears mask. The industrial division had doubled it sales from 1965 to 1966, largely due to the shadow masks. The company went public in September 1966.

According to a 1982 *Business Week* article, Buckbee-Mears enjoyed a short-lived high-tech image because of its pioneering work in the television manufacturing field. Growth of the company's other division was steady but less dramatic. When Buckbee-Mears reached its 60th year of business, the graphic arts division primarily served a 13-state area and held a big share of the important Twin Cities' market.

Internal and External Changes in the 1970s

The make-up of the company began to change in the late 1960s and into the mid-1970s. Buckbee-Mears entered the ophthalmic lens business and exited the graphics arts business. Norman B. Mears stepped down from his position as company president. The business environment which had been favorable for Buckbee-Mears also began to change. Color television imports rose from 18 percent of U.S. sales in 1975 to 37 percent in 1976; major domestic television manufacturers, Westinghouse Electric Corp., Motorola Inc., Admiral, and Philco, stopped producing color picture tubes. The loss of business resulted in cutbacks at Buckbee-Mears. Nearly one-third of the workers (75) were laid off at its St. Paul aperture mask plant, and 45 salaried employees also lost their jobs. The company also had aperture mask plants in New York and West Germany.

In December 1976, Everett F. Carter replaced James Bourquin as president. Carter had come to Buckbee-Mears from GTE Sylvania Inc. in 1969, the year Bourquin succeeded Mears as president. The company lost a third of a million dollars in 1976, but became profitable again under Carter; earnings reached $4.3 million in 1979.

Acquisitions Boom of the Early 1980s

Buckbee-Mears Company began the 1980s earning steady profits from its ophthalmic products and the precision metal parts operations of its industrial division. But aperture masks sales stagnated. The company planned to gradually diversify by moving from parts to subassembly to end-product manufacturing. That strategy changed dramatically when the board brought on Ryal Poppa, a high profile manager. Poppa had a number of successful turnarounds associated with his name including Pertec Corp., a Southern California computer equipment maker. His eight-year acquisition drive at Pertec had increased Pertec's annual sales from $28 to $200 million. Poppa, along with a $1 million investment in Buckbee-Mears, stepped into the CEO and chair positions in January 1982. Everett F. Carter retained his position as president, but Norman C. Mears retired from the board. (Carter resigned his position as president as well at the end of 1982.)

As he had with other businesses, Poppa acted quickly and aggressively. A new management team, a new company name, and an ambitious acquisition plan were put in place. Ryal Poppa intended to make the company, renamed BMC Industries, Inc., a major player in the electronic interconnections field. But his first acquisitions were in the optics area. Bolstered by the purchase of Camelot Industries, the optics division contributed about two-thirds of 1982 revenues.

The next year, 1983, was marked by an announcement for a joint venture with Control Data Corporation in the production of semiconductor chip equipment. Four important high-tech businesses were acquired. Total sales reached $155 million with earnings of $4.5 million. With Honeywell's Tampa operations and Advanced Controls of Irvine California included in the electronics division, Poppa was predicting sales to double in 1984. Investors were taking notice of what was happening in St. Paul. St. Paul Pioneer Press Dispatch reporter Dave Beal wrote, "Wall Street loved Ryal Poppa's big adventure; the stock doubled to $27 in just two years."

The Boom Goes Bust

But the adventure came to an end. The environment in which Poppa was trying to diversify BMC was inhospitable: the U.S. electronics industry was struggling under foreign competition and a soft consumer demand. And the new Interconics division, which served the semiconductor and electronic equipment industries, had been funded largely by debt. In December 1984, $30 million in debentures were sold to four companies to pay off some of the heavy debt load.

Return on stockholders equity fell to 2.5 percent in 1984, from over ten percent in the previous three years. Ryal Poppa left BMC early in 1985. The debenture holders sued BMC in order to rescind the notes and call in the debt. Robert J. Carlson, formerly a top executive with United Technologies Corp. and Deere & Co., joined BMC as chief executive in mid-1985. Carlson tried cost cutting measures in an attempt to keep the electronics division Poppa had built in tact. But the recession in the industry and BMC's debt were both too deep. In November 1985 BMC announced that the electronics division would be sold off. Losses in 1985 were nearly $70 million, largely due to business divestment reserves.

BMC's outlook had changed drastically from the aggressive optimism of the Poppa days; 13 high-technology operations—one-third of BMC's assets—were on the sales block, and its $100-million debt was in default. Sales of color television aperture masks and optical lenses both rose in 1986, but profits were drained by the interest on debt and from operating losses in the discontinued businesses. BMC lost another $6.5 million in 1986. Stock prices dropped as low as $3.25 a share, and the company had to ward off a takeover bid.

In 1987, BMC settled the lawsuit by agreeing to pay off the notes, and they began restructuring negotiations on the remaining debt. BMC received $65 million in new loans from institutional investors and used cash from the divestitures to pay off the $100 million debt, as well as, $5 million in interest. The company was back to its pre-Poppa product lines, optical products and precision-etched products, but still held $65 million in long-term debt accumulated from its failed diversification attempt. In terms of production, BMC made a deal with IBM for precision-etched computer parts to be made out of its West German plant. They also entered into a joint venture with an Italian plastic eyeglass lens maker, and made an aperture mask engineering and manufacturing service contract with the Soviet Union. The company also marked 1987 by moving its corporate headquarters from its long-time St. Paul location to a smaller facility in Bloomington, Minnesota.

Growth in the Early 1990s Still Hampered by Debt

Debt hampered capacity expansion in the years following BMC's restructuring, and stock prices generally bounced back and forth between the $5 and $10 per share mark. The company struggled with: production problems in the New York aperture mask plant; slow sales in the St. Paul plant where electronic components and etched glass and large printed circuit boards were made; and a general economic recession. Net earnings for 1990 dropped to $1.8 million, down 66 percent from 1989.

An $18.6 million aperture mask equipment and technology deal with a Chinese company sent BMC earnings upward again in the beginning of 1991. Paul Burke moved up to the position of president; Carlson retained his positions as chairman and CEO. Burke had joined BMC in 1983 as an associate general counsel and at age 29 was appointed general counsel by Carlson. Burke played an instrumental role in the successful divestiture and debt restructuring, and then requested a move to the operations side of the company in 1987. He managed a turnaround at the Florida Vision-Ease Lens plant and became president of the $75-million division two years later. Carlson left BMC in July 1991 and was succeeded by Burke, then 35 years old. Sales for the year reached $203.2 million with record earnings of $8.2 million.

BMC continued to make steady progress toward increasing sales and profits and reducing debt. In 1993 BMC made another deal with a Chinese firm for aperture mask equipment and technology: this time for $26 million. The company was moving away from the manufacturing of the lower-end aperture masks it was licensing, to higher-margin, high-resolution computer monitors and televisions. The precision-etched products division, which made the aperture masks and specialty photo-etched glass and metal parts, provided just under two-thirds of BMC's sales. Eyewear lens sales through the optical products division provided the other third.

BMC debt was down to $32 million toward year-end 1993 and stock price had doubled from the previous year to about $16 per share. A breakthrough deal with a Japanese television manufacturer in 1994 and rising worldwide demand for high-end aperture masks had pushed BMC plants to near capacity. BMC also saw progress in its optical products division in 1994, polycarbonate lens sales jumped 44 percent compared with industry growth of 25 percent. In September of 1994 BMC paid off its debt, giving the company room for capital investment.

Expansion Begins in the Mid-1990s

In 1995 BMC accelerated expansion of its aperture masks production lines, announcing plans for two additional television and one additional computer mask lines. Japanese firms were its only competitors in the high-end market, and they were being hurt by the strong yen which drove up their prices relative to BMC's. The company's other business segment was also doing well with its higher-margin product; in the fast-growing polycarbonate lens market BMC ranked second in sales behind Gentex Optics of Massachusetts. Riccardo A. Davis wrote in July 1995, "BMC has produced 16 consecutive quarters of increased earnings as it has focused on higher margin masks and lenses." In October 1995 BMC stock was split two-for-one.

Buckbee-Mears St. Paul (BMSP), a business area that had been struggling for survival in the early 1990s, increased earnings by 200 percent in 1995 due to increased sales, sales mix changes, and improved production efficiencies. As a world-leader in the field of photo-chemical machining BMSP provided thinner, more detailed pieces, and a greater range of sizes than stamped metal parts. Its products were used in automotive,

electronics, medical, office, consumer, industrial, military and aerospace applications.

The year 1995 also marked a milestone for the company that began as Buckbee-Mears. Norman B. Mears had retired from the board in 1994, leaving the company without Mears's family leadership for the first time. Company-wide profits for 1995 were $24.5 million on total sales of $255.4 million. The precision imaged products group, which included aperture masks and BMSP, brought in 70 percent of BMC's consolidated revenues. The aperture masks alone provided 58 percent total revenue. Optical products brought in 30 percent.

BMC had expanded its polycarbonate lens production capacity in 1993, 1994, and 1995. In 1996, the company announced plans for a $10 million state-of-the-art facility for polycarbonate manufacturing, as well as, centralized distribution, and research and development. (Polycarbonate lens—thinner, lighter, and more impact resistant than plastic or glass lens—were manufactured through a highly automated injection process.) While polycarbonate lenses were the fastest growing segment of the U.S. market, it was actually the smallest segment among BMC's three lens types. BMC held more than 50 percent of the domestic fused multifocal glass lens market and was a major supplier internationally. BMC, like other U.S. manufacturers, began contracting overseas for more labor intensive hard-resin lenses, which held about half of the U.S. market.

Future Hopes

BMC Industries, Inc.'s future hopes were centered on the continued growth in its core businesses. The company planned to continue to shift the mask operation product mix toward high-margin products where there was tight industry-wide supply. Polycarbonate lens sales were expected to grow as the U.S. population aged. Even the much smaller etched products division anticipated growth in response to increased miniaturization in electronics field. But BMC had acquisitions in mind, not only in its core markets, but for development of a third major business area in electronics, metal fabrication or plastics.

Principal Operating Units

Vision-Ease Lens; BMC Mask Operations; Buckbee-Mears St. Paul (BMSP).

Further Reading

"All Ryaled Up at BMC," *Corporate Report Minnesota,* May 1984, pp. 22–23.
Beal, Dave, "BMC May Close Plant in St. Paul to Cut Costs, *St. Paul Pioneer Press Dispatch,* October 2, 1993, pp. 1B, 7B.
——, "Tumult Passed, BMC Now Braves the 90s," *St. Paul Pioneer Press Dispatch,* October 25, 1993, pp. 1E, 6E.
Beran, George, "BMC Chief Advises Patience for Earnings Growth," *St. Paul Pioneer Press Dispatch,* April 29, 1988.
——, "BMC Completes Debt Restructuring," *St. Paul Pioneer Press Dispatch,* July 17, 1987.
"BMC Industries Inc." *Minneapolis/St. Paul CityBusiness,* April 8, 1994.
Caldwell, Dick, "Buckbee-Mears Expanding," *Minneapolis Star,* January 12, 1967, p. 15B.
Carlin, Bing, and Mark Hoonsbeen, "Clear Vision," *Twin Cities Business Monthly,* July 1995.

Carlson, Scott, "BMC Reversal Makes Stock More Attractive," *St. Paul Pioneer Press Dispatch,* February 15, 1988.

Davis, Riccardo A., "BMC's Bright Picture," *St. Paul Pioneer Press Dispatch,* July 19, 1995.

——, "BMC's Vision," *St. Paul Pioneer Press Dispatch,* May 30, 1996.

DeSilver, Drew, "BMC Again Has Its Eye on Acquisitions," *Minneapolis/St. Paul CityBusiness,* June 14–20, 1996.

Feyder, Susan, "BMC Industries Swallows a Strong Dose," *Star Tribune* (Minneapolis), March 31, 1986, p. 1M.

——, "Group Buys into BMC Industries," *Star Tribune* (Minneapolis), January 21, 1987, pp. 1M–2M.

Fifty Years, Minneapolis: Buckbee-Mears Company, 1957.

Fredrickson, Tom, "BMC Breaks Into the Japanese TV Market," *Minneapolis/St. Paul CityBusiness,* February 25, 1994.

Greenwald, John, "TV Imports Hurt Buckbee-Mears," *Minneapolis Star,* March 25, 1977.

Gross, Steve, "Drastic Changes Apparently Working at Buckbee-Mears," *Star Tribune* (Minneapolis), February 13, 1983, pp. 1D, 3D.

Hequet, Marc, "Let's Make a Deal," *Corporate Report Minnesota,* December 1983, pp. 76–78.

McDonnell, Lynda, "A Bet on BMC Is a Bet on Bob Carlson," *St. Paul Pioneer Press Dispatch,* July 27, 1987, pp. 1, 10.

Men, Minds, Microns, Minneapolis: Buckbee-Mears Company, 1967.

"Periscope: BMC Industries, Inc.," *Corporate Report Minnesota,* February 1985, pp. 134–35.

Peterson, Susan E., "BMC Chooses Paul Burke as New Second-In-Command," *Star Tribune* (Minneapolis), May 10, 1991.

——, "BMC Reports Sharp Rise in Earnings; Carlson Retires," *Star Tribune* (Minneapolis), July 16, 1991, pp. 1D–2D.

——, "Young Executive Credited with BMC's Turnaround," *Star Tribune* (Minneapolis), September 9, 1991, pp. 1D, 7D.

"Poppa Tests His Golden Touch," *Business Week,* January 18, 1982, p. 102.

Sarkes Neaville, Lisa, "BMC Industries Building Plant for Lens Molding," *Plastic News,* August 19, 1996.

St. Anthony, Neal, "U.S. Sues BMC, Says it Violated Pension Law," *St. Tribune* (Minneapolis), March 26, 1992.

Strand, Phil, "Checking in Again," *Corporate Report Minnesota,* August 1984, pp. 97–98.

Taylor, Jeff A., "BMC Industries' Paul Burke," *Investor's Business Daily,* March 28, 1996.

Weinberger, Betsy, "After BMC Exec Leaves, Turmoil Follows," *Minneapolis/St. Paul CityBusiness,* May 22, 1992, pp. 1, 30.

——, "Galileo Discovers BMC," *Minneapolis/St. Paul CityBusiness,* February 5, 1993.

Young, Robin, "Profile: Ryal Poppa," *Corporate Report Minnesota,* October 1982, pp. 76–77, 135–36, 138.

—Kathleen Peippo

Bridgeport Machines, Inc.

500 Lindley Street
Bridgeport, Connecticut 06606
U.S.A.
(203) 367-3651
Fax: (203) 335-0151

Public Company
Incorporated: 1939
Employees: 1,024
Sales: $209.2 million (1996)
Stock Exchanges: NASDAQ
SICs: 3541 Machine Tools, Metal Cutting Types

Bridgeport Machines, Inc., is the leading manufacturer of manual milling machines, surface grinders, and computer-controlled metal cutting machine tools in the United States. The company primarily markets standardized, general-purpose machine tools to small and medium-sized machine shops who in turn sell products to the automotive, aerospace, medical equipment, computer, defense, farm implement, construction equipment, and energy industries. In addition to its well-known Bridgeport brand name, the company manufactures and sells surface grinders under the Harig brand name and lathes under the ROMI and EZ-PATH brand names. Bridgeport operates manufacturing facilities in Elgin, Illinois; Leicester, England; and Kempten, Germany; and operates a joint-venture facility in Sicken province, China. It sells its machines through a 150-member sales force and a network of independent distributors throughout the United States and in 60 other countries.

Machines tools are used to cut and shape metal parts for use in a variety of products ranging from automobiles to golf clubs. Although Bridgeport's tools are priced higher than those of its competition, the company enjoys a strong reputation for reliability and attentive service, two factors that have historically mitigated price concerns among buyers. Bridgeport has also benefitted from being a niche player, seeking to retain its top position as a purveyor of metal cutting machines and not to venture into other markets. The company's Series 1 Standard

Mill, a manually operated metal cutting machine, debuted in 1939 and remains one of the best-known machines in the business, with over 330,000 units sold. Since the mid-1980s, Bridgeport has been developing its product line to include high-tech machining centers and computer numerically controlled milling machines. While customers in Europe and Asia seem to prefer the new computerized machines, Bridgeport's U.S. customers primarily purchase manual machines.

Early History

The company's origins date to 1929 when Rudolph F. Bannow, president of Bridgeport Pattern and Model Works, enlisted his customer and friend, Magnus Wahlstrom, to jointly develop an electric hedge clipper. The two worked together on the hedge clipper for over a year when the project was put on the back burner because a company called Atlas Tools asked them to develop a special type of milling attachment. Bannow and Wahlstrom developed the tool, a "portable self-contained ¼ horsepower high-speed milling attachment," which they called the Model C Head upon its introduction in 1932. Despite the drastic decline of the U.S. economy at the time, the tool proved itself to be very versatile in metal shops and soon became a commercial success.

Bannow and Wahlstrom continued to perfect their product and, in 1936, offered a customer a Model C Head that ran on ½ horsepower and incorporated a quill. Again, its versatility in metal shops made it a commercial success. According to company materials, however, "many of their customers had complimented them on their milling head, but expressed their displeasure at having to use an old piece of equipment or make something on which to mount the milling head." The next logical step for Bannow and Wahlstrom was to develop a machine on which the Model C Head could be mounted.

The first drawing of the machine—which was to become a permanent fixture in metal shops throughout the United States—was sketched by Bannow on the back of a paper bag. Actual development took several years, and in August 1939, the company delivered the first machine to Precision Casting Company of Syracuse, New York. Originally marketed as a "Verti-

Company Perspectives:

With over 100,000 different users of our machine tools around the world, perhaps there should be no surprise at some of the end products Bridgeport's machines help to create. Some of the more recognizable items include sporting equipment, airplanes, automobiles, and medical devices.

cal Knee Type milling machine,'' the $995 tool soon became known simply as the ''Bridgeport.''

Bannow and Wahlstrom incorporated their organization that year, under the name Bridgeport Machines Inc. During the 1940s, the company grew steadily, building new products and a name for itself with little competition. Bridgeport Machines profited from the post-World War II manufacturing boom as well. By 1960, the Bridgeport, its original milling machine, had become the standard tool used everywhere from school metal shops and mid-sized companies to large manufacturing facilities.

Textron Purchase and Expansion

In 1968 Textron, Inc., purchased Bridgeport Machines. *Forbes* later declared that the purchase made Bridgeport an ''early victim of conglomeration''; however, Bridgeport soon made improvements to its product offerings with the financial support and direction of its new parent company. The machine tool industry is a cyclical one, and in the late 1960s, the industry was experiencing a slowdown. In an attempt to expand sales by diversifying its product mix, Bridgeport introduced a line of surface, abrasive, and toolroom grinders that became extremely successful. By 1970, Bridgeport had also introduced the Series II milling machine, a larger version of Bridgeport's original machine, and the first numerically controlled Series I milling machine. In the 1970s, Bridgeport purchased the Harig brand of surface grinders. Textron was also responsible for Bridgeport's first foray into the European market when it purchased Adcock & Shipley Ltd., a British manufacturing plant that was converted to build Bridgeport's machines. In 1986 the Adcock & Shipley's name was changed to Bridgeport Machines, Ltd.

Industry Boom

In 1971 demand for machine tools began to skyrocket, fueled by the expanding commercial aerospace and defense industries and a shift among automobile manufacturers to front-wheel drives and four-cylinder engines. Bridgeport's slump was over as it began scrambling to meet new demands. The company successfully filled its orders through 1973, but began to slip as demand outpaced supply. By 1974 the backlog at most manufacturers, including Bridgeport, grew as high as two years. That year, Bridgeport instituted a five-year expansion plan, beginning with the addition of 100,000 square feet of production space in 1975. The company was still unable to make a dent in its two-year backlog, and its primary customers, small and mid-sized shops, were unable to wait that long.

Sensing an opportunity, Asian manufacturers entered the U.S. market in the late 1970s, selling standard machines, CNC lathes, and basic, uncustomized machining centers. Although the influx of Asian machines severely damaged many U.S. machine tool manufacturers, their effect on Bridgeport was less severe. The company continued as it always had, building on its reputation as a manufacturer of reliable, high quality machines. Asian manufacturers did, however, secure a foothold in the computer numerically controlled market. In 1978 Bridgeport responded by introducing a new computer numerically controlled milling machine that reduced programming time by up to 90 percent. Expansion continued through 1979 with the construction of a new 200,000-square-foot plant near the company's headquarters in Bridgeport, Connecticut, the purchase of two Midwest distributors, and the construction of a sales and service center in the Chicago area.

From Boom to Recession

If the 1970s were challenging because of excessive demand for Bridgeport's machines, the 1980s were tumultuous. Just as Bridgeport had expanded to meet increasing demand, a recession hit the United States. Between 1981 and 1982, industry sales dropped by more than 60 percent from $5 billion to less than $2 billion. Although Textron did not release sales figures for its individual subsidiaries, analysts estimated Bridgeport's 1982 sales to have been slightly under $200 million. Textron's Machine Tool and Precision Bearing Group (of which Bridgeport is part) reported an $8 million loss for the year. In 1982 Bridgeport diversified its product line again through an agreement with Romi S.A. of Brazil to import Romi's standard engine lathe. In 1983 the Group posted a $16 million loss, but by 1984, the group was back in the black again, with an $11 million profit.

Also in the early 1980s, Bridgeport filed a claim with the United States International Trade Commission charging more than 20 Korean, Taiwanese, and U.S. machine tool builders with trademark and copyright infringements. Bridgeport pursued the case for over two years. In 1983 the International Trade Commission unanimously rejected Bridgeport's plea, although it did note that it found blatant copying of the company's promotional materials.

The company responded to the recession by diversifying its product line. In 1984 Bridgeport purchased McWilliams Machinery Sales Inc., the exclusive U.S. distributor of Japax electrical discharge machines. The following year, Bridgeport entered into an agreement with a Japanese company, Yasuda Industry Co. Ltd., to market Yasuda's line of horizontal machining centers as part of a long-term strategy to move into the growing market for automated machining centers. 1984 sales were approximately $180 million, comfortably above 1983 figures but well below the company's peak in 1980. The increase was fueled by sales of Bridgeport's new, high-tech machine tools and increased demands in the manufacturing segment of the economy.

Management Buyout

In 1985 Bridgeport's parent company, Textron, acquired a company called Avco Corp. To fund the acquisition, Textron placed Bridgeport and other subsidiaries on the auction block. That year, Bridgeport senior management, led by Bridgeport Division president Joseph Clancy, joined with E. F. Hutton LBO Inc. to purchase a 67 percent stake in the company for $77 million. Clancy and his management team took a risk in their acquisition. According to E. F. Hutton the buyout was highly leveraged, and industry analysts felt the company faced "severe operational and competitive problems," and sales for the following year did not look entirely promising.

To compound the difficulty, Bridgeport's hourly workers unionized a few days after the buyout was finalized. A year later, 220 workers went on strike for increased benefits. Bridgeport's management rolled up their sleeves and joined 128 temporary workers on the shop floor to keep production running. In addition, Clancy and his managers roamed the picket lines to talk informally with the workers. Ultimately, the workers agreed to leave the Teamsters and return to the shop as non-union employees.

Bridgeport continued its investment in automated and computerized machines. In 1987 the company introduced EZ Draft computer-aided-design software and also aligned its EZ-CAM with Apple Computers' macEZ-CAD, to create a team of inexpensive, easy-to-use CAD-CAM milling machines.

The economic recession of the late 1980s hit the company hard, as sales dropped from $185 million in 1989 to $98 million in 1992. Most of its losses were due to the closing of customers' plants; the company responded by downsizing and restructuring its operational and financial organizations. In addition, Bridgeport made an initial public offering of 2.5 million shares of common stock on the NASDAQ exchange in November 1994, raising $12.9 million in the process.

The tide turned again in Bridgeport's favor that year, when the U.S. machinery market entered a boom. "U.S. factories are operating at 84 percent of capacity, their highest rate in more than five years," noted *Business Week*. "After years of underinvestment, there's a pent-up demand for machinery." By the end of 1994, Bridgeport had a backlog of $44 million. By the end of 1995, the backlog had increased to $75 million. Fiscal year 1995 sales rose 39 percent to $148.8 million.

International Expansion

Bridgeport began focusing on international expansion as a means of cushioning itself against the cyclical downturns of the U.S. market. In 1994 the company entered into a joint venture to form P.T. Bridgeport Perkasa Machine Tools to manufacture machine tools in Indonesia for future sale to the burgeoning Association of South-East Asian Nations.

By 1995, 35 percent of Bridgeport's sales were from international markets. That year, the company instituted an international expansion plan with a focus on Asia; business in China alone was expected to grow $10 to $20 million by the year 2000. Bridgeport directly targeted the Chinese market when it entered into a joint-venture/joint manufacturing agreement in 1995 with a long-time strategic partner, Chang Zheng Machine Tool Works. The new company, Chengdu Chang Zheng Bridgeport Machines Ltd., will build two of Bridgeport's "machining centers" for sale to Eastern Europe, North Korea, and China. In June 1995 Bridgeport's British subsidiary purchased a state-of-the-art manufacturing facility in Germany from Deckel Maho AG I.K. for $9.6 million. Production at that facility was used to meet Bridgeport's $44 million backlog in Europe. In the United States, Bridgeport purchased a 19.5 percent share of Engineering Geometry Systems and entered into a strategic alliance agreement with the company to jointly develop and market technology for use in the computer-aided-manufacturing market.

Machine-tool orders continued their record-setting climb in 1996. Fiscal year sales rose 40 percent to $209.2 million, fueled by a 110 percent increase in machining center sales and a 27 percent increase in sales of Bridgeport-Romi lathes.

Bridgeport Machines has proved to be a resilient player in the competitive machine tool market. Having responded well to many industry downturns, the company finds itself in a secure position with a diversified product line and a broadening customer base. Although its joint ventures in China and Malaysia have yet to commence production as of 1996, Bridgeport continues to increase its foreign market presence and is in a strong position for continued, steady growth.

Principal Subsidiaries

Bridgeport Machines, Ltd.; Chengdu Chang Zheng Bridgeport Machines Ltd.; P.T. Bridgeport Perkasa Machine Tools.

Further Reading

Johnson, Stephen S., "The Smell of Grease," *Forbes,* June 3, 1996, p. 74.

Maio, Patrick J., "Stepping up Its Commitment to Int'l Markets," *Investor's Business Daily,* April 3, 1995, p. 4.

Schiller, Zachary, "The Din in Here Is Deafening," *Business Week,* January 9, 1995, p. 65.

—Maura Troester

BROUGHTON

Broughton Foods Co.

210 Seventh Street
Marietta, Ohio 45750
U.S.A.
(614) 373-4121
Fax: (614) 373-2861

Public Company
Incorporated: 1933 as Broughton's Farm Dairy, Inc.
Employees: 375
Sales: $72.3 million (1995)
Stock Exchanges: OTC
SICs: 2026 Fluid Milk; 2024 Ice Cream & Frozen
    Desserts; 5451 Dairy Products Stores; 1382 Oil &
    Gas Exploration Services

Broughton Foods Co. is a regional dairy that distributes its fluid milk, ice cream, and other dairy products throughout the eastern United States. The company has operations in Ohio and West Virginia. Led by members of the Broughton family for its first half century, the public, yet closely held, firm (only nonvoting stock is sold publicly) was guided by Chief Executive Officer Rod M. Collier in the mid-1990s. Members of the founding family continued to play important roles in the day-to-day operation of the company, with Carl L. Broughton acting as chairman of the executive and finance committees, John R. Broughton serving as treasurer and assistant secretary, George W. Broughton in the role of executive vice-president of sales and marketing, and David J. Broughton acting as financial analyst.

Neither a member of a dairy cooperative nor an affiliate of a larger food conglomerate, Broughton Foods is rather unique in the fragmented, competitive dairy industry. Though it is a relatively small player on the national scene, the business has been characterized as "a sizable force in the dairy industry." The company worked diligently in the late 1980s and early 1990s to maintain its independent status in the face of dairy industry consolidation, relying especially on product diversification. By the mid-1990s, its product line included fluid milk, ice cream, frozen yogurt, ice cream novelties, fruit juices, and cottage cheese, among other foods, beverages, and condiments. The company even had three soda fountain-style restaurants serving Broughton's brand ice cream.

Early 20th Century Origins

The history of Broughton Foods Co. can be traced to 1910, when John H. Broughton started selling the yield of his father's Marietta, Ohio, dairy farm. The Broughtons delivered their milk, butter, and vegetables to customers via horse-drawn wagon and sold the farm produce in a family-owned grocery store. They began expanding their dairy business from its headquarters in southeastern Ohio on the Ohio River in earnest in 1919, purchasing a second farm, building their first full-fledged dairy (including an early Universal Milking Machine), and acquiring a dairy delivery truck.

Eldest son Gerald joined the growing business in 1931 following his graduation from Ohio State University with a degree in dairy technology. A second son, Carl, took a more circuitous route to the family farm. After a two-year stint at Ohio State University, he dropped out of that school's business administration program to move to California. When the Great Depression shrunk job opportunities out West, Carl was compelled to return home to the family business, where he, too, would make his career.

In 1933, Broughton patriarch John H. was killed in an accident involving a newly installed ice-making machine. His sons reorganized and incorporated their company as Broughton's Farm Dairy with Carl as president and youngest sibling Robert, who would graduate from Marietta College in 1939, as secretary-treasurer. Broughton's chalked up $30,000 in sales during its first year.

The interwar period brought a period of expansion, especially in the retail end of the business. Gerald Broughton, who continued with the family company, has been credited with launching the ice cream business in 1934. Broughton's opened a restaurant that same year featuring the company's namesake ice cream. Six more store/restaurants located throughout southeastern Ohio and northern West Virginia followed over the course

Company Perspectives:

Broughton Foods Company has been an innovative company guided by traditional wisdom. From its beginnings, the company has grown steadily to become a respected foods producer of premium quality products. The Broughton emphasis has always been on quality. Technology, research and development, the exclusive use of superior quality milk and ingredients, and unparalleled service have given Broughton a reputation for excellence.

of the next seven years. Broughton's promoted itself as the "Brightest Star in the Milky Way" during its early years.

World War II Labor Shortage Brings Contraction

A dearth of employees during World War II (even President Carl Broughton was called to duty from 1943 to 1945) forced the closure of all but one of Broughton's retail stores. The company used a strategy of acquisition to bounce back in the postwar era, acquiring dairies in Ohio, West Virginia, and Kentucky. Having forged a strong position in the business, Broughton began to diversify within the dairy industry via the 1960 creation of the Broughton Foods Division. With primary operations in Parkersburg, West Virginia, this business segment produced portion-controlled dairy and nondairy coffee creamers. These aseptically packaged products were sold to supermarkets, fast food restaurants, and dining facilities in hotels. Relocated to Charleston, West Virginia, by the early 1980s, Broughton's food division had added table cream, nondairy whipped topping, whipping cream, egg nog, dips, and dairy and nondairy sour cream to its roster of products. Meanwhile, the company's dairy division was also growing to produce cottage cheese, yogurt, ice cream, ice milk, and frozen novelties, as well as a full line of fluid milk. By 1975, food products contributed more than 20 percent of Broughton's more than $35 million in annual sales. The company's diversification included a 13-year foray into college and university dining halls. In 1980, it also created Bro-Well, a small oil and gas drilling subsidiary.

Over the decades, Broughton's need for fresh whole milk began to exceed its own dairy's production capacity. As a result, the company cultivated long-standing relationships with many other independent dairy farmers, eventually forging a network of more than 200 exclusive suppliers.

When Carl Broughton retired in 1975, Broughton's board of directors elected Executive Vice-President Samuel R. Cook to succeed him. Cook would serve in that capacity for more than 20 years, when he was succeeded by President Rod M. Collier.

Technological Changes Revolutionize Dairy Business

The perishability of milk and its derivatives has always been a challenge to dairymen. As late as 1919, a lack of refrigeration compelled Broughton to deliver its milk to town twice each day to account for spoilage. The impact of this factor has been mitigated over the course of the 20th century via improvements in processing, storage, and delivery.

Processing advances have concentrated primarily on lengthening shelf life through the elimination of bacteria. The most common method, pasteurization, heats milk to about 160°F (72°C) to destroy microorganisms, thereby extending the shelf life to 14 to 21 days under refrigeration. In the 1970s, many dairies began implementing ultrahigh temperature pasteurization (UHT), which steam-heats milk up to 265°F (130°C) or higher, lengthening shelf life to months instead of weeks. Broughton became the first U.S. dairy to adopt uperization, a European variation on UHT. According to company literature, this technology, which places the product on a spiral flow for more uniform heating, is "100 percent effective against contamination without affecting product taste." By the early 1990s, Broughton was uperizing 3,000 gallons of product per hour. The company applied UHT to the production of half and half, whipping cream, and ice cream and frozen yogurt mixes for food service. The process gave these products a shelf life six to nine times longer than conventional methods, thereby allowing for broader distribution.

Broughton also adopted aseptic packaging processes to lengthen the shelf life of some of its products. Originally developed in Europe after World War II, aseptic packaging unites the product with the packing process in a totally sterile environment. Most familiar to Americans is the aseptic drink box. Broughton applied aseptic packaging principles to its production of table cream, whipping cream, half and half, and related foods, most often portion-controlled for institutional food service. In addition to their longer shelf lives, aseptically packaged products do not require refrigeration until the package's seal is broken. These high-tech processes have helped make the company "one of the nation's leading producers of half and half," with millions of coffee creamers made each month.

Broughton's modes of delivery have also come a long way since the 1920s, when its unrefrigerated Model T truck limited delivery to nearby Marietta. Efficient transportation is a key factor in the perishability equation; every hour that raw milk spends en route from any of Broughton's more than 200 supplier dairies, for example, is an hour subtracted from the processes that extend its shelf life. Over the years, the company accumulated its own fleet of refrigerated tank trucks for transport of raw milk and refrigerated tractor-trailers for delivery of finished product. By the late 1980s and early 1990s, Broughton boasted specialized dual-temperature vehicles that allowed the delivery of frozen and refrigerated products in the same shipment. But as fleet management issues became increasingly complex in the early 1990s, Broughton abandoned its company-owned vehicles in favor of a full-service lease arrangement. This change reduced the company's annual transportation costs by more than $700,000.

High Competition Brings Reduced Returns
in the Early 1990s

Broughton's quest for efficiency was a necessity of doing business in the highly competitive environment of the 1990s. With multibillion dollar giants like Kraft Foods, Dean Foods Co., Borden Inc., and ConAgra Inc. topping the industry,

Broughton executives realized that their work was cut out for them. In 1992, the International Dairy Foods Association forecast that rapid industry consolidation would reduce the number of fluid milk processing plants by 30 percent, to less than 400, by the turn of the 21st century. Although generally regarded as a weakness, Broughton perceived particular strengths in its comparatively small size. In 1990, Executive Vice-President and Director of Marketing George Broughton told *Dairy Foods'* Jeff Reiter, "We hold our own well because we are more flexible than larger competitors, better able to react quickly to changes in the market, and have a better rapport with customers."

In addition to its focus on cost-effectiveness, Broughton concentrated on new product introductions in the late 1980s and early 1990s. In a 1990 profile for *Dairy Foods* magazine, George Broughton called new product development "critical," noting, "Right now, there are a lot of mergers going on in the industry, and we need to either grow or die." Broughton launched nine new product lines in 1989 alone, many of them focused on the growing "healthy" segment of the industry. Consumer demand for foods with reduced fat, calories, sugar, lactose, and cholesterol provided many opportunities for new versions of traditional products. These were distributed by Broughton to private labelers as well as under the company name. To broaden its lines beyond dairy (especially into fruit juices), Broughton also distributed other companies' goods under its trademark.

The company grew and retained its independent status in the early 1990s. But although sales increased 31.7 percent, from $55.9 million in 1990 to $73.5 million in 1994, its net income declined 14.4 percent, from $846,000 to $724,000 during that same period. And as the company cut prices to retain its customer base, it slid into a $380,000 shortfall in 1995. Newly elected Chief Executive Officer Rod Collier blamed fluctuating expenses, overcapacity in particular market segments, and regional competition for the loss, but expressed his belief that "the Foods Division still represents [Broughton's] greatest opportunity for future growth and profits."

Principal Subsidiaries

Bro-Well, Inc.

Principal Divisions

Dairy Division; Ice Cream Store/Restaurant Division; Foods Division.

Further Reading

Doeff, Gail, "A Year of Repositioning," *Dairy Foods,* July 1996, pp. 10–14.

Kimbrell, Wendy, "Broughton Foods Co.," *Dairy Foods,* April 1990, p. 45.

O'Donnell, Claudia Dziuk, "Cutting the Fat," *Dairy Foods,* July 1993, pp. 61–63.

Reiter, Jeff, "Independent Thinkers; Small, Regional Dairy Marketers Use Their Versatility To Compete Effectively," *Dairy Foods,* April 1990, pp. 25–27.

——, "Juices and Drinks with a Twist," *Dairy Foods,* February 1995, pp. 52–56.

——, "Progressive Packaging," *Dairy Foods,* March 1991, pp. 48–54.

"The Story of Broughton Foods Company: 1910–1976," Marietta, Ohio: Broughton Foods Company, [1976].

Valero, Greg, "These Distributors Don't Own Fleets," *U.S. Distribution Journal,* November 15, 1995, p. 22.

—April Dougal Gasbarre

Bucyrus International, Inc.

P. O. Box 500
South Milwaukee, Wisconsin 53172
U.S.A.
(414) 768-4400
Fax: (414) 768-5060

Public Company
Incorporated: 1927
Employees: 1,166
Sales: $231.92 million (1995)
Stock Exchanges: NASDAQ
SICs: 3532 Mining Machinery

Bucyrus International, Inc. is a leading manufacturer of equipment and machines for the global surface mining industry. In 1995 it ranked fifth among U.S. mining machinery manufacturers in total sales. Bucyrus's principal products are electric mining shovels for loading minerals, mining overburden, and rock into trucks or conveyors in copper, coal, and iron mining operations; walking draglines for removing overburden from coal seams in surface coal operations, phosphate and bauxite mining, and land reclamation projects; and rotary blast hole drills for boring large holes in mineral deposits or rock for the placement of the explosives to loosen minerals at mining sites. In addition to supplying its traditional customers in the U.S. coal, copper, iron ore, and phosphate surface mining industry, Bucyrus derived about two-thirds of its shipments from foreign orders for mining projects in the Far East, South America, Australia, and Europe in the mid-1990s.

Digging In: 1880–1921

The birth of the excavating machine industry in the United States was directly tied to the construction of the infrastructure spurred by the nation's rapidly expanding geographical boundaries during the nineteenth century. Dredging rivers, harbors, and canals and laying railroad lines required reliable and efficient digging equipment, and during the 1880s a fledgling U.S. excavating machinery industry rose to meet the need. In 1880 a prosperous Ohio business magnate named Daniel P. Eells saw the opportunity to create a profitable new business sideline for the many railroads to which he had business associations. By purchasing the idle Bucyrus Machine Company of Bucyrus, Ohio, Eells and his associates founded the Bucyrus Foundry and Manufacturing Company, which quickly began producing hand cars, locomotive drive wheels, car wheels and axles, and related components for the expanding railroad industry.

Eells's business took a decisive turn when both the Northern Pacific and Ohio Central Railroads placed orders for steam shovels for their railroad construction operations in 1882. By deploying a sales force and advertising in trade journals, by 1898 Bucyrus's annual output had risen to 24 shovels, and its No. 10 shovel was being hailed by an industry newspaper as "the largest and most powerful steam shovel ever built in this country." Within a year, steam shovels accounted for 80 percent of Bucyrus's business, and Eells and associates decided to transfer the company's assets to a new entity, Bucyrus Steam Shovel and Dredge Co. Because the demand for its standard shovels and dredges was unpredictable, however, Bucyrus increasingly began developing a reputation as a designer/manufacturer of specialized excavating equipment for mining and public works projects.

In 1891, seeking to attract businesses to southeastern Wisconsin, the county of South Milwaukee offered Bucyrus an offer it couldn't refuse: a 15-acre plant site and $50,000 toward construction of a new factory. Bucyrus signed on, but despite the new expanded facilities, by 1895 a national depression and Bucyrus's own troubles with its new Milwaukee labor force had pushed it to the brink of bankruptcy. Eell's son Howard was named the receiver in a court-arranged reorganization that offered Bucyrus's creditors a viable, ongoing business in the form of a new corporation that assumed the assets of the failing company. Realizing that expanded production was the only way to make Bucyrus solvent, Bucyrus increased the output of its new plant threefold between 1897 and 1901. Production innovations such as a new steel foundry, the use of special-alloy steels, and the adoption of new heat-treating techniques began to enhance Bucyrus's reputation as a manufacturer of high-quality steel excavating equipment. Significant technological advances

Company Perspectives:

Bucyrus International ranks as one of the world's leading manufacturers of surface mining equipment. This reputation is the result of over 100 years of providing quality equipment and support to fulfill our customers needs. We continue to solicit feedback from the industry and use this valued input to aid our efforts in providing machinery of optimum design and manufacturing standards. Superior performance is measured by how well we service our customers. Every department is aware that our most important product is customer service. This service takes many forms: concise and complete machine and parts quotations, engineered machine shipments, timely machine erections, and quality produced components. From South Milwaukee to around the world, we are dedicated to ensuring satisfaction. Bucyrus has a commitment to provide the very best surface mining machines that can be manufactured.

enabled Bucyrus to introduce such innovations as the first 180-degree revolving steam shovel; the first back-acting shovel, which could dig below its own level and toward the cab; and, in 1910–11, the first Bucyrus dragline machines, the first Bucyrus tank-tread-style "crawler" shovels and draglines, and the first Bucyrus machines powered by an internal combustion gasoline engine. By the early years of the new decade heavy-duty railroad shovels were accounting for 62 percent of Bucyrus's output, dredges 29 percent, and railroad wrecking cranes and pile drivers nine percent.

In 1904 a recently created federal agency called the Isthmus Canal Commission ordered a 70-ton and two 95-ton Bucyrus shovels for the punishing excavation work that would eventually produce the historic Panama Canal. More orders followed, and between 1904 and 1907 the Bucyrus shovels delivered to the massive undertaking were accounting for a third of all large shovels sold by the firm. Almost all the earth and rock moved during the peak phase of the Canal project was performed by Bucyrus machines. The Panama Canal project not only gave the company priceless public relations opportunities, including a famous photo with President Theodore Roosevelt perched on a Bucyrus machine, it also gave the company invaluable experience in mass-production manufacturing, enabling it to vie with Marion Steam Shovel for dominance in the manufacture of heavy shovels. For the period 1905–07 alone, Bucyrus's corporate profits totaled half a million dollars, and by 1911 its net worth had leaped to $2.3 million.

Bucyrus management quickly capitalized on its Panama Canal success. In 1910, it entered the small revolving steam shovel market by purchasing Vulcan Steam Shovel, acquired a new manufacturing site in Evansville, Indiana, and agreed to purchase the Atlantic Equipment Co. In 1911 the fusion of Bucyrus, Vulcan, and Atlantic produced a new corporation, Bucyrus Company. In the same year W. W. Coleman replaced Howard Eells as company president and led Bucyrus through its brief incarnation as a munitions manufacturer in World War I. In 1915, in a joint venture with three other companies named the

Mississippi Valley Products Co., Bucyrus began work on its first order for high-explosive shell blanks for the British government. The war also precipitated a boom in U.S. nonmilitary construction and mining work, which enhanced sales of Bucyrus's commercial products. Bucyrus created the Wisconsin Gun Company with three other Milwaukee firms to produce artillery barrel and breech mechanisms to meet this demand without interrupting its burgeoning nonmilitary production. By the war's end, Bucyrus annual sales had reached $6.6 million, and by 1922 Bucyrus had definitively surpassed Marion to become the dominant supplier of large mining stripping equipment and medium-sized quarry and mine excavating machines.

Dominance by Diversity

Despite buoyant sales and a growing domestic and overseas market, sales of Bucyrus's small revolving shovels lagged throughout the 1920s. But just as Bucyrus's purchase of Vulcan had enabled it to enter this lucrative new market in 1910, its decision in 1929 to acquire the Erie Steam Shovel Co., then the largest U.S. producer of small excavating machines, catapulted it to the top of the small shovel industry.

While the management of the new Bucyrus-Erie Company was reconciling the two firms' corporate structures and streamlining their overlapping product lines, it expanded again, adding a British manufacturing affiliate in 1930 with the purchase of Ruston & Hornsby, Ltd., the leading British excavating machinery maker, and in 1931 purchasing a controlling interest in Monighan Manufacturing of Chicago, a producer of walking dragline machines. To survive the Depression, management cut back on its work force, closed the Evansville plant, loosened credit arrangements with customers, and minimized product development and plant improvements. Despite the devastation of the Depression, Bucyrus's tight-ship financial system, the assets accumulated through three decades of success, and hold-over back orders from pre-Depression days enabled it to survive the early hardships of the 1930s. In 1932 Coleman announced that Bucyrus was determined to "go after all possible business with courage and the conviction that better times are ahead." Because of its austerity measures, Bucyrus was able to complete the acquisition of the Armstrong Drill Company of Iowa (a manufacturer of churn-type drills) in 1933, and healthy exports combined with a 1935 contract to supply industrial tractor producer International Harvester with tractor parts enabled Bucyrus to post 1937 profits of $2.1 million.

Bucyrus intentionally limited its involvement in munitions production during World War II. As in World War I, the conflict stimulated domestic and military-related sales of its commercial products, and Bucyrus excavators were purchased in dramatically increased numbers for mining domestic coal and minerals, export to U.S. war allies, and use by U.S. armed forces. Between 1940 and 1944, shipments of Bucyrus excavators totaled more than $44 million, and by 1945 three thousand shovels, draglines, and cranes had been sold directly to the military or U.S. allies. Still, nongovernment production stayed above 40 percent, and Bucyrus's only armaments work was for gun carriages and mounts.

Despite Coleman's conviction that the postwar economic boom would play out in two years, by 1947 he admitted that "the demand for Bucyrus-Erie products [was] beyond its capacity to produce." With the outbreak of the Korean War, any fears Bucyrus management had about declining demand were abandoned, and it concentrated on two problems that had bedeviled it in the prewar years: the rising strength of unions and the need to adjust its product lines and plant capacity to meet changing demand. Bucyrus initially took a hard-line stand with national unions, but damaging strikes in the late 1940s softened management's posture, and by the early 1950s the company was more willing to tolerate national union representatives in new labor contract negotiations.

Between 1945 and 1950, demand for smaller excavating machines had grown to $450 million, but Bucyrus represented only 12 percent of the excavating machinery industry's manufacturing capacity in this segment. Bucyrus therefore undertook a plant expansion program that by 1951 had increased its capacity by 25 percent and then followed it with the purchase of the National Erie Corporation, a steel foundry and machine shop less than a mile from Bucyrus's Erie plant. By combining and expanding the two Erie facilities Bucyrus increased its capacity by 50 percent. Bucyrus also expanded its product lines, changing some of the basic designs which had remained the same since the 1930s, and introduced ever bigger, more sophisticated versions of standard models capable of handling larger and larger loads. In 1953 it discontinued dredging equipment production and first began producing rotary blast hole drills, a brand new technology that would remain an integral part of its product line into the 1990s. By 1955, Bucyrus had grown into an industry behemoth employing five thousand people and generating shipments of $72 million a year.

The construction of the St. Lawrence Seaway and the passage of the Federal Highway Act in the 1950s meant intensified demand for Bucyrus shovels and excavators. Bucyrus unveiled a new plant in Richmond, Indiana, in 1955, and the number of foreign markets placing orders had grown to 48. W. W. Coleman's retirement in 1956 fell just before a national recession produced layoffs at Bucyrus plants and the company's first net loss in more than a quarter century. Bucyrus promptly closed the new Richmond plant, slashed inventories, and consolidated and streamlined operations in South Milwaukee, Erie, and Evansville.

By 1963, Bucyrus had bounced back, and for the next decade and a half it would experience breakneck growth and record profits. Bucyrus soon claimed subsidiaries in Brazil, Japan, and Mexico; manufacturing operations on six continents; new plants in Idaho, Pennsylvania, and Racine, Wisconsin; and a backlog so congested it had to reject an offer by NASA to bid on the huge crawler transports for the Apollo moon mission.

The growth in offshore oil drilling offered Bucyrus a valuable new market in marine crane manufacture, and in 1969 Bucyrus unveiled its crowning engineering achievement, the 4250-W coal shovel. Said to be the largest mobile land vehicle ever built, the "Big Muskie" was powered by ten 1,250 horsepower motors and its bucket loaded 325 tons of material in a single pass. By 1971, Bucyrus had soared past the $185 million mark in shipments, and the onset of the energy crisis in 1973 seemed to augur even larger equipment sales to the coal mining industry. In 1973 Bucyrus arranged the third major U.S. equipment sale to the People's Republic of China with a $19 million deal for mining shovels and blast hole drills.

Demand was rapidly outstripping Bucyrus's ability to meet deadlines, and in 1974 management decided to expand its manufacturing facilities 200 percent, by relying on subcontracting and foreign manufacture. With Bucyrus factories virtually on a wartime footing, its workforce was expanded by 80 percent between 1974 and 1975, and in the same two-year period shipments climbed 35 percent to $353 million. The pace continued until by 1979 Bucyrus had broken past the $550 million mark in annual shipments. Bucyrus's production capacity had doubled, sales had grown sevenfold, and profits had skyrocketed 2500 percent since 1962. The boom years of the 1970s seemed to put Bucyrus on solid financial ground as it prepared to celebrate its first centennial.

Disaster: 1980–1996

The celebrations surrounding the anniversary, however, masked a marked dropoff in sales. Confronted with a mature market, Bucyrus began diversifying, buying Western Gear, a California aerospace firm, in 1982, and closing its plants in Idaho and Pennsylvania. With profits still sinking, Bucyrus formed a holding company named Becor Western in 1984 to ward off a hostile takeover. By 1987, however, Becor's consultants reported that "profitability was not likely to improve until 1990, if then" and that Western Gear was an insupportable drain on the corporate purse. Becor's management then made a fateful decision: they decided to sell Western and, in concert with their investment bankers, Goldman, Sachs and Co., execute a leveraged buyout (LBO) of Bucyrus, a move that made the corporation a private company and therefore promised management greater flexibility in steering the company to financial safety. The LBO also promised high cash distributions to shareholders and tax advantages stemming from the service of the debt on the LBO's bonds. It was in the assumption of massive debt—needed to give management the wherewithal to buy Bucyrus out—however, that the inherent risk of the LBO lay.

Shareholders approved the plan, which was completed in February 1988, with Becor broken up into Bucyrus-Erie and a new holding company named B-E Holdings. Damaged by Goldman, Sach's hefty fees, the LBO debt almost immediately began to bury Bucyrus. By the end of 1988, corporate debt had risen to $100 million and equity had plummeted to $16 million. Within a year, B-E Holdings was paying out $21 million annually just to service the interest on its debt. Worse yet, promising new orders only made matters worse. The LBO's financial projections were based on the assumption that Bucyrus would *lose* money in 1990 and 1991. Unanticipated profits only meant that Bucyrus would have to pay even higher levels of debt interest. Bucyrus returned to the financial market to raise more funds in order to avoid paying higher levels of debt interest. Rather than plow the money into much-needed working capital, however, the new influx of cash was applied to debt payment, and Bucyrus was caught in a vicious cycle of acquiring new debt to pay off old.

Following heated negotiations with its creditors, in 1993 Bucyrus proposed a restructuring plan in which it would file for a Chapter 11 bankruptcy but arrange with its creditors beforehand to trade them a combined 87 percent share of Bucyrus stock in return for forgiving $135 million in debt. All Bucyrus's creditors agreed to this so-called prepackaged bankruptcy except Jackson National Bank, which claimed in a lawsuit that false statements about Bucyrus's true financial health had fraudulently seduced it into lending Bucyrus $60 million. Jackson's suit threatened to torpedo Bucyrus's only hope of emerging from bankruptcy intact, and as it headed toward federal court its losses continued to mount. In February 1994, Bucyrus officially filed for bankruptcy, with a ten-month window to secure the judgment before new tax laws went into effect forcing it into further, probably fatal levels of debt. After ten months of deliberation the federal court announced that Bucyrus had been awarded the debt-for-equity bankruptcy it sought and could retain control of its own fate. The worst crisis in its history was over.

Ironically, Bucyrus remained not only a viable but a significant player in the world excavation machinery business before its slide toward bankruptcy began to seem inevitable. The opening of the South African mining machinery market promised greater sources of new sales, and, more importantly, a 1988 contract to provide mining machines to China had been followed by an even larger Chinese order in 1993. And China held the potential of becoming the largest customer for the mining machine industry in the world. If the U.S. market for new mining machinery was exhausted, a large untapped international market seemed capable of offsetting the loss, and between 1994 and 1995 Bucyrus's net sales actually increased almost 20 percent to $232 million.

In July 1995, three senior Bucyrus executives quietly resigned, and a management consulting group shepherded the company during a search for a new CEO. In March 1996, W. R. Hildebrand became president and CEO. He announced the goal of making Bucyrus a customer-driven, employee-empowered enterprise with a modernized accounting system and a new computerized data system. With exports accounting for almost 70 percent of all shipments and new foreign markets offering Bucyrus a chance to grow itself back to health, in May 1996, shareholders officially approved the rebirth of Bucyrus-Erie as Bucyrus International.

Principal Subsidiaries

Bucyrus-Erie Company of Canada Ltd;. Bucyrus Europe Ltd.; Bucyrus (Australia) Proprietary Ltd.; Minserco, Inc. (United States); Boonville Mining Services, Inc. (United States); Bucyrus (Brasil) Ltda.; Bucyrus India Private Ltd.; Bucyrus (Africa) (Proprietary) Ltd.; Bucyrus Chile Ltda.; Bucyrus (Mauritius) Ltd.

Further Reading

Anderson, George B., *One Hundred Booming Years: A History of Bucyrus-Erie Company 1880–1980,* Milwaukee, Wisc.: Bucyrus-Erie Company, 1980.
Gilbert, Nick, "Bleached Carcass," *Financial World,* September 1, 1994, p. 34.
Joshi, Pradnya, "A Surprise at Bucyrus-Erie: Three Execs Resign," *Milwaukee Journal Sentinel,* July 27, 1995, p. 1.
Lank, Avrum D., "Judge Approves Reorganization of Bucyrus-Erie," *Milwaukee Sentinel,* December 2, 1994, p. 1.
——, "The Battle over Bucyrus," *Milwaukee Sentinel,* July 25, 1994, p. 1D.
Savage, Mark, "Bucyrus-Erie Wins Big Chinese Contract," *Milwaukee Journal Sentinel,* August 22, 1995, p. 1.
——, "Bucyrus's Losses Continue, But New Orders Fuel Hope," *Milwaukee Journal Sentinel,* March 7, 1996, p. 1.
——, "Name Change Reflects Business: Bucyrus Taking on International Outlook," *Milwaukee Journal Sentinel,* May 24, 1996, p. 3.
Tessler, Joelle, "China: Wisconsin Companies Move Toward Enormous New Market," *Milwaukee Sentinel,* November 18, 1993, p. 1D.

—Paul S. Bodine

Bundy Corporation

12345 E. Nine Mile Road
Warren, Michigan 48090-2001
U.S.A.
(810) 758-4511
Fax: (810) 758-5167

Wholly Owned Subsidiary of TI Group plc
Incorporated: 1922 as Harry Bundy and Company
Sales: £718 million
Employees: 10,000
SICs: 3714 Motor Vehicle Parts and Accessories; 3585
   Condensers and Condensing Units; 3317 Steel Pipe
   and Tubes; 3498 Fabricated Pipe and Fittings

Bundy Corporation is a subsidiary of the London-based specialized engineering group TI Group plc and a world leader in the design, engineering, and manufacture of small-diameter fluid-carrying systems for the automotive and refrigeration industries (two-thirds and one-third of total Bundy revenues, respectively). Among a wide range of specialized tubing products, Bundy supplies preassembled, integrated brake and fuel tubing bundles for direct, assembly-line installation in car making plants. Bundy's automotive tubing products are also used in transmission lubrication, power steering, cooling, emissions, suspension, and air conditioning systems. Bundy's refrigeration tubing products are used in condensers, evaporators, compressors, and other heating, air conditioning, and industrial applications.

In 1995, the Bundy division of TI Group, which accounted for 42 percent of TI's total sales, operated 73 facilities in 27 countries worldwide. Among Bundy's major automotive customers in the early 1990s were Nissan, Ford, General Motors, Volkswagen, Audi, Volvo, Toyota, BMW, Renault, and Jaguar. In North America alone Bundy supplied products for over eleven million cars and trucks and in 1995 was ranked as the second-largest steel pipe and tube manufacturer in the United States.

Building a Niche: 1922–41

The Bundy Corporation was founded as Harry Bundy and Company in Detroit, Michigan, in 1922 by Harry Warren Bundy, a former mechanic with Detroit Steel Products. Established as a manufacturer of steel tubes used in automobile gas lines, Bundy's first contract was to supply tubing for the Ford Model T, which in 1920 accounted for roughly half the cars on the road worldwide. Bundy's innovation was a tube crafted out of a single strip of steel, which was wound around twice to create a double wall capable of withstanding pressure of six thousand pounds per square inch. At first, Bundy simply sold the straight tubes to Ford whose workers then bent the product to conform to the Model T's chassis. During the initial bending process at Ford, however, the soldered seams of Bundy's tubes broke open, rendering them useless, and Bundy was forced to rethink his design or risk losing the contract.

With the help of his toolmakers, Bundy invented bending machines that could shape the tubes without bursting the seams. This early attempt at "adding value" transformed the auto industry supply business, and by 1923 Bundy had sold 3.5 million feet of tube, and Bundy tubes became the industry standard for automotive steel tubing. Within two years, Bundy moved his operations to the second floor of a manufacturing plant on Bellevue Avenue in Detroit and began selling tubing to the emerging refrigeration industry.

When Harry Bundy's health began to fail in 1926, he sold a three-year option to buy the company, whose assets now totaled $143,000, to Wendell Anderson, a 28-year-old graduate of Yale University. In February 1929, Anderson assumed control of the company (renamed Bundy Tubing Company) and its patents and retained Harry Bundy as the company's advisor. Later that year, Bundy's engineers invented the "Bundyweld" tube, a double-walled steel automotive tube that used brazed copper rather than solder to join the tubes' seams. The result was enhanced torsion and bending qualities, increased resistance to corrosion, and improved fatigue strength. Aided by the rapid development of new automotive applications for its tubing—including hydraulic brakes—Bundy's sales took off.

Company Perspectives:

The company's mission is to maintain a leadership position by providing consistent profitable growth as an integrated manufacturer of fluid carrying systems in global niche markets. The Bundy philosophy is the same throughout our worldwide network: "Commitment to excellence and dedication to providing an assured supply of critical automotive components to meet our customers' requirements."

In 1929 annual sales of Bundy tubing reached 50 million feet and U.S. auto sales continued to climb, reaching 2.8 million cars in 1930 alone. Bundy expanded its production capability for Bundyweld tubing by installing two cracked natural gas hydrogen welding furnaces. In 1931, it initiated commercial production of Bundyweld tubes, selling 35 million feet of product before the year was out. A year after Harry Bundy's death in 1931, the company installed a semicontinuous, automatic hydrogen welding furnace in its Detroit plant, and by 1933 tubing sales had jumped to more than 75 million feet. In 1934 Bundy moved its operations again, to a plant on Hern Avenue in Detroit, where it established its own research and development laboratory.

Despite the worsening Depression, between 1931 and 1934 Bundy sold 200 million feet of Bundyweld tubing and by 1936 was employing over a thousand people. It entered into its first international venture the same year through a license agreement with Armco International Corporation to produce Bundy tubes in France and England, which were soon joined by Bundy affiliates in Italy and Germany. On the eve of World War II, Bundy began manufacturing its second major product, "Electricweld" tubes, a single-walled variant of the Bundyweld tube.

World War II and After: 1941–59

Although new car production in the United States came to a virtual standstill during World War II, Detroit firms manufactured $30 billion of military hardware between 1942 and 1945, representing 20 percent of total U.S. war production. In 1941 Bundy moved into a new 160,000 square foot plant in the Detroit suburb of Warren and converted its entire manufacturing operations to war production. At the end of the war, Bundy closed its Hern Avenue plant, moved its administrative offices to Jefferson Street in Detroit, and divided its operations into two divisions: its Bundyweld tubing operations and its Electricweld, nickel, and monel (an alloy of nickel and other metals) tubing works. The end of the war unleashed four years of pent-up consumer demand, and by 1949 Bundy tubing was being used in such consumer products as umbrellas, toys, steam irons, television antennas, and cribs. By 1950, Bundy had expanded into the manufacture of tubes for the radiant heating equipment industry and announced the sale of its one millionth TV antenna.

In 1947, Anderson's announcement of a new "Cost Savings Sharing Plan" was hailed by the national media as an innovative new trend in U.S. industry, and within a year Bundy had erected a new manufacturing plant in Tamaqua, Pennsylvania. In 1948 Anderson embarked on a round-the-world tour with his son John Anderson II to scout out sites for new international ventures. Visiting Australia, New Zealand, Java, South Africa, and South America, Anderson's expedition ultimately led to the establishment of new Bundy subsidiaries in Australia in 1952, Brazil and Argentina in the 1950s, and Colombia and Mexico in the 1960s. A joint venture with the Usui company of Japan in 1959 inaugurated a Bundy presence in the Far East that by the 1990s would rank as one of its fastest-growing markets.

A year after Bundyweld tubes were first produced in Australia (1954), production in the U.S. auto industry had reached the record-setting level of nine million cars per year. Happily riding the postwar automotive boom, Bundy expanded its Pennsylvania plant in 1956 and enlarged its main Warren, Michigan, plant a year later. When Wendell Anderson Sr. died in October 1959 after three decades as Bundy's president, his 34-year-old son Wendell Jr. assumed the company's reins, and John Anderson II was named executive vice-president of international operations.

Diversification: 1959–88

Shortly after assuming his father's title, Wendell Jr. bought out the Lionel Corporation's share in a marine outboard motor project being developed by Italy's Innocenti Corporation. Explaining the venture to *Business Week* years later, Anderson admitted that "we'd been looking for several years for diversified firms outside our line." In the early 1960s Bundy Marine U.S.A and a new Italian subsidiary, Bundy Marine S.p.A., were thus formed to produce Bundy's outboard engine for the U.S. and European pleasure-boating market.

The unusual move reflected Anderson's growing concern over Bundy's reliance on steel tube manufacturing, which was at the mercy of the feast-or-famine cycles of the world auto industry. That Bundy's earnings had grown 53 percent from 1959 to the mid-1960s made its dependence on a single niche, in Anderson's eyes, no less dangerous. Nevertheless, between 1960 and 1965, Bundy engineers applied the company's Electricweld tubing manufacturing process to the development of automotive push rods (used to operate the valves in internal combustion engines), which culminated in the construction of a push rod manufacturing facility in Kentucky in 1965. By mid-decade, Bundy's sales had broken the $30 million threshold, its share of the automotive steel tubing market had ballooned to 70 percent, and its total workforce numbered 1,600 persons producing 815 million feet of tubing per year. But acquisition feelers from two larger companies convinced Anderson that Bundy had to diversify again to protect itself from takeover. As he told *Forbes* magazine in 1968, "our tubing had penetrated the automobile and refrigeration markets as far as we could expect. In the future we would be dependent on the growth of these industries for our growth. We decided that wasn't sufficient. . . . We decided we wanted to remain independent. At the same time we became quite aware that if we wanted to maintain our growth rate, we would have to move into new products."

In 1967 Bundy therefore moved to definitively establish itself as a multiproduct specialty metals company with the door left open for expansion into plastics and rubber. It dropped "Tubing" from its name in favor of "Bundy Corporation" and acquired National Rolling Mills Company of Pennsylvania, a specialty strip steel producer with sales of $15 million. Following a public stock offering, Bundy's sales rose to more than $60 million in 1968. Throughout the late 1960s and early 1970s, Bundy expanded its position in the international tubing market. It unveiled Bundy New Zealand in 1967, repositioned Bundy of Canada from the international division to divisional status within Bundy Corporation in 1970, merged its Bundy Brazil subsidiary with Bendix Home Appliance do Brazil in 1971, formed Bundy Pacific Tubing (Philippines) Inc. in 1972, acquired 25 percent of Armco-Bundy RoR, A.B., of Sweden in 1973, and reached an agreement with Tubemakers of Australia to spin off Bundy Australia into an independent subsidiary in 1974.

Closer to home, a new headquarters for Bundy Tubing Division was begun in 1969, and a New Business Development Group was founded to pursue such technologies as powder metallurgy (culminating in the creation of the short-lived Metallurgical Products Division in 1970). The passage of the Clean Air Act in 1970 signaled Congress's intent to address the growing problem of auto emissions by forcing U.S. automakers to use more specialized tubing—a niche Bundy was now well positioned to exploit. With evaporative emission control systems now mandated by federal law, sales of Bundy's stainless steel automotive tubing took off, and Bundy expanded plant capacity in Canada; built a new automotive brake tube plant in Coldwater, Michigan; acquired engineered plastic products maker Dixon Industries of Rhode Island; opened a new facility in Mt. Clemens, Michigan; and unveiled a new copper-coating plant in Warren.

In 1974, Anderson announced a new corporate strategy designed to move Bundy from its historical basic tubing "commodity product" niche to the increasingly promising "specialty product" market represented by such high-tech products as its automotive emission control tubing systems. The new strategy led to the sale of National Rolling Mills in May 1974, and in the following year Bundy continued its globalization campaign. It launched Bundy South Africa and Bundy India in mid-decade; secured contracts in Iran and Indonesia in 1978; and formed a joint venture with its Australian and Japanese partners and the Korean Pusan Steel Pipe Company in 1979 to create Pusan Bundy Corporation (Korea). A shaky U.S. economy and the effects of the Arab oil embargo meanwhile led to new federal fuel economy legislation that bolstered sales of fuel-efficient compact cars. Again, Bundy benefited: its North American tubing operations won a substantial portion of the automotive fuel injection tubing business for diesel engines, making Bundy the largest tube supplier for domestic automotive diesel engines by 1980. With sales passing $112 million, Bundy moved into aircraft tubing manufacture in 1978 with the acquisition of Dixon Industries' Titeflex Corporation, built a tubing plant for its refrigeration operations in Arkansas, and established a new tube making facility in Hillsdale, Michigan, in 1979.

The stagflation and continuing energy crisis of the late 1970s, however, battered company profits, and Bundy was forced to close its Tamaqua, Pennsylvania, plant in 1980 and its Penntube (Dixon) plant three years later. But its prowess in bringing new technologies to market continued to augur well for its future: a new "Z-Coat" manufacturing process for Bundyweld and Electricweld automotive tubing, for example, was unveiled in 1980 and during a Japanese tour in 1981 Bundy's Thomas Lauterbach discovered the growing use among Japanese manufacturers of "bundling" technology, in which automotive parts such as fuel systems and brake lines—previously manufactured as separate components—were produced as integrated units for direct installation on the assembly line. Bundy recognized the revolutionary ramifications of the concept, and by 1985 it was selling preassembled tubing bundles manufactured at its Georgia plant.

Strategic acquisitions further bolstered Bundy's long-term prospects. In 1981 it consolidated the newly acquired Bivco Valve Company with its Titeflex subsidiary (which was soon producing hoses for the B-1 bomber, the M-1 tank, and the cruise missile); purchased Bunnell Plastics Inc. of New Jersey, a manufacturer of fluoropolymer-based piping systems and engineered components; and acquired E. I. DuPont de Nemour's product line in 1985 and CHR Industries a year later. New tube bundle manufacturing plants in Georgia, Indiana, and Ohio were unveiled between 1983 and 1986, and in 1983 Bundy consolidated its Dixon, Bunnell, and Titeflex into a new division, Performance Plastics, to complement its Specialty Tubing operations. Internationally, Bundy launched its second Japanese joint venture, DIC-Bundy, in 1984 and in 1986 began supplying tubing to the U.S. plants of Japanese automakers through a joint venture with Bundy-Usui International. Before the year was out it had acquired Bundy Tubing do Brasil and formed Hua Yan Bundy in the untapped megamarket of mainland China.

TI Group: 1988–96

The takeover that Bundy had feared since the 1960s finally arrived in March 1988 when the British specialized engineering firm TI Group plc announced its acquisition of Bundy for $146.5 million. Two years earlier, Sir Christopher Lewinton had been enlisted as TI's new CEO to transform what one journalist called "an aging four-legged metalbasher standing on just one good leg" into a high-tech international engineering dreadnought. Lewinton had immediately begun searching for technology-driven, market-leading acquisition targets, and Bundy fit the bill nicely. TI quickly dispatched Bundy's Performance Plastics Group (except Titeflex) and merged Bundy Corporation and its foreign subsidiaries with TI's smaller engineering firms to form Bundy International, now headquartered in TI's corporate offices in Abingdon, England.

With John W. Potter appointed Bundy's new CEO in 1990, Bundy could focus anew on the changing realities of the auto making business. The auto and auto parts industries had become increasingly global in scope, and radical changes in labor use, technology, governmental regulation, and engineering and manufacturing approaches had revolutionized the industries almost overnight. Automakers were increasingly turning to an ever smaller core of principal suppliers whom they relied on to assume an ever more integral role in the car manufacturing process. Bundy's historically central role in producing critical auto components, its global spread, and its rapid embrace of new technologies left it well prepared to become a major "one-stop, one-source" supplier for the new world auto industry.

By 1992, Bundy's sales (including TI's smaller engineering businesses) had grown to £492.8 million, and, newly energized by TI's aggressive corporate growth strategy, it returned to the globalization plan it had followed in the 1980s. In 1993, it acquired Bundy Venezolana (Venezuela), opened an automotive tubing facility in the Czech Republic, and established a liaison office in Turkey. Its refrigeration segment secured a contract for Goldstar's Italian refrigerator condenser operations, and in the United States Bundy won a major contract to supply all the tubing needs of General Electric's condenser production operations. The introduction of so-called satellite assembly plants in France and Germany enabled Bundy to supply Renault and Volkswagen, respectively, with tubing components as they were needed on the assembly line. Moreover, Bundy engineers were now actually stationed in customers' plants to ensure that Bundy tubing systems met customers' needs. TI's 1991 acquisition of Huron Products of Ohio and its QuickConnects products also dovetailed neatly with Bundy's efforts to improve its tubing line: QuickConnects allowed fuel or coolant lines to be simply and securely snapped together without the limitations of traditional threaded connector fittings. By 1993 TI and Bundy were implementing the QuickConnects technology in its automotive systems plants around the world.

Bundy's affiliation with TI paid off again in 1994 with the acquisition of Technoflow GmbH, a German manufacturer of fuel-carrying hoses and systems, and Arktis, a Hungarian maker of refrigeration condensers. TI's investment in a second Brazilian tubing plant in Brazil and new automotive satellite plants in Europe enabled Bundy to boast a 14 percent growth rate in 1994. The introduction of a new high-performance aluminized, nylon-coated steel tube for the automotive market and a patented "Galfan" anti-corrosion coating further secured Bundy's claim to be the new technology leader of the global tubing industry. In August 1994, Bill Laule, a former executive with Rockwell International, was promoted from the presidency of Bundy North America to CEO of TI's international Bundy division, and Bundy won contracts to supply new BMW and Mercedes plants in the United States. In the Far East, Bundy landed the tubing supply business for Daewoo in Korea and pursued a contract to supply Peugeot and Citroën plants in mainland China.

Bundy's sales increased another ten percent in 1995, spurred by the formation of a joint venture with Tubemakers of Australia to create Bundy Asia Pacific (bought outright by TI a year later), the announcement of an agreement with Volkswagen to supply the brake line components for its new A4 vehicle, and a major contract with Ford to supply the brake, fuel, and transmission line systems for its new rear-drive luxury car project. New satellite tubing plants in Germany, Spain, the United Kingdom, Brazil, and Tennessee extended Bundy's global reach; a major condenser supply contract gave Bundy all of Daewoo's North American refrigeration business; and large refrigeration contracts were signed with customers in Hungary, Slovakia, and Lithuania.

Although Bundy's transformation from a basic producer of steel commodity tubes to a defiantly high-tech supplier of sophisticated tubing "systems," "clusters," and "bundles" rendered its historical link to Harry Bundy's original company almost unrecognizable, in January 1996 TI acknowledged the continuing importance of the Motor City in the world auto industry by transferring the offices of Bundy CEO Bill Laule from Abingdon, England, back to Detroit.

Principal Subsidiaries

Bundy of Canada Ltd.; Bundy Argentina SA; Bundy Brazil; Bundy Colombia; Bundy Mexico SA; Bundy Venezolana CA (Venezuela); Bundy UK Ltd.; Bundy SA (Belgium); Bundy Danmark A/S (Denmark); Bundy SNC (France); Bundy GmbH (Germany); Bundy Kft (Hungary); Bundy SpA (Italy); Bundy SA (Spain); Bundy AB (Sweden); Bundy Tubing Co. (Australia) Pty Ltd.; Foshan Hua Nan Bundy Tubing Co. Ltd. (China); Hua Yan Bundy Tubing Corp. (China); Bundy India Ltd. (India); Bundy Japan Ltd. (Japan); Usui Bundy Tubing Ltd. (Japan); Bundy Tubing (New Zealand) Ltd.; Bundy Systems Ltd. (South Korea).

Further Reading

"A Two-Price Bid to Force a Merger," *Business Week,* February 27, 1978, pp. 35–36.
"British Firm Buys Bundy," *Chicago Tribune,* March 9, 1988.
"Same Players, New Game," *Forbes,* April 15, 1968, p. 70.
"Tube Maker Launches a Boating Venture," *Business Week,* January 21, 1961, pp. 30–32.
Willoughby, N. C. Dylan, "The History of Bundy Tubing Company and Bundy Corporation, 1922–87" (company chronology), Warren, Mich.: Bundy Corporation, June 1996.

—Paul S. Bodine

Burberrys Ltd.

18-22 Haymarket
London, SW1Y 4DQ
England
(71) 839-2434
Fax: (71) 839-6691

Wholly Owned Subsidiary of Great Universal Stores plc
Founded: 1856
Sales: £230.8 million (US$374.1 billion) (1995 est.)
SICs: 2300 Apparel & Other Textile Products; 5651
Family Clothing Stores; 5961 Catalog & Mail-Order
Houses

Burberrys Ltd. is a 140-year-old manufacturer and marketer of men's, women's, and children's apparel, as well as accessories, food and beverages, and fragrances. The Burberry name is virtually synonymous with the tan gabardine raincoat pioneered by the company more than 140 years ago. Writing for *WWD* (*Women's Wear Daily*) in 1989, Andrew Collier described the garment as "a mainstay in outerwear worldwide, [that] symbolizes all that is Britain: sturdy and unassuming, equally at home in fine hotels and muddy lanes."

In the mid-1990s, the company had 18 Burberrys stores in the United Kingdom, 20 in Europe, 23 in the United States, and 162 franchised locations in the Asia-Pacific region. Notwithstanding its varied lines, the company's trench coat—offered in about 100 different styles—accounted for approximately 40 percent of its annual sales, or 8,000 raincoats each week. Ironically, however, private label menswear constituted the largest segment of its sales volume. An icon of classic clothing, Burberrys has utilized licensing and brand extensions to appeal to a younger generation of fashion-conscious customers. The brand's worldwide retail sales, including licensees and other retail distributors, total more than US$1 billion. The company is a subsidiary of Britain's Great Universal Stores plc, the very closely held £2.8 billion mail-order and retail apparel conglomerate.

19th-Century Origins

Founder Thomas Burberry was born in 1835 and apprenticed in the drapery trade, establishing his own drapery business in Basingstoke, Hampshire, in 1856. A sportsman, Burberry was dissatisfied with the then-popular rubberized mackintosh raincoat, which was heavy, restricting, and stifling, and therefore unsuitable for extended outings. Inspired by country folk's loose "smocks," Burberry designed a tightly-woven fabric made from water-repellent linen or cotton yarn. While sturdy and tear-resistant, this "Burberry-proofed" cloth was lightweight and allowed air to circulate, making it considerably more comfortable than the heavy mackintosh. The tailor trademarked his cloth "Gabardine," a Shakespearean term that referred to shelter from inclement weather. Burberry developed five different weights of gabardine: "Airylight," "Double-Weave," "Karoo," "Wait-a-bit," and "Tropical." He even patented "Burberry-proofed" linings made from silk and wool.

Burberry was a shrewd marketer, employing trademarking and advertising to great benefit. Illustrated advertisements touting the clothing "designed by sportsmen for sportsmen" drew customers to Burberry's retail outlet, which was established in London's Haymarket section in 1891. Having used a variety of labels to distinguish its garments from imitations, the company registered the "Equestrian Knight" trademark in 1909, an insignia used continuously through the mid-1990s. Also employed in the corporate logo, this image represents several Burberrys ideals. The armor signifies the protection afforded by the outerwear, the "Chivalry of Knighthood" reflects the company's own standards of integrity, and the Latin adverb "prorsum" ("forward") referred to Burberrys' innovative fabrics and styles.

Although the gabardine name was used under exclusive trademark by Burberrys until 1917, Britain's King Edward, one of the first members of the royal family to don the gabardine coat, has been credited with popularizing the Burberry name by requesting the garment by name. Burberry garments have enjoyed a loyal following among royalty and celebrities around the world ever since. The company's clientele has included Winston Churchill, Gary Cooper, Joan Crawford, Humphrey Bogart, George Bernard Shaw, Al Jolson, Peter Falk, Ronald

Company Perspectives:

Burberrys are recognized internationally as representing the epitome of true British style. With 55 stores worldwide, two Royal Warrants and six Queen's Awards for export, Burberrys has come a long way since its foundation in 1856.

Reagan, George Bush, Norman Schwarzkopf, and Paul Newman. The company also boasts warrants (endorsements of quality) from Her Majesty Queen Elizabeth II and H.R.H. The Prince of Wales. Considered a "rite of passage" by some commoners, a Burberry coat was a prerequisite to a first job interview.

New Products for the New Century

By the turn of the century, Burberrys offered an extensive line of outerwear for both men and women. The company designed hats, jackets, pants and gaiters especially for hunting, fishing, golf, tennis, skiing, archery, and mountaineering. The garments' time- and weather-tested reputation for durability helped make them the gear of choice for adventurers of the late 19th and early 20th century. Balloonists and early aviators wore specially-made Burberry garments that let neither wind nor rain penetrate. Captain Roald Amundsen, Captain R. F. Scott, and Sir Ernest Shackleton wore Burberry clothing and took shelter in Burberry tents on their expeditions to the South Pole in the 1910s.

Burberrys established its first foreign outlet in Paris in 1910 and soon had retail establishments in the United States and South America. It exported its first shipment of raincoats to Japan in 1915. However, it was the First World War that brought widespread acclamation and fame to Burberry. First worn by high-ranking generals during the turn of the century Boer War in South Africa, the Burberry coat was soon adopted as standard issue for all British officers. With the addition of epaulets and other military trappings, the garments came to be known as "Trench Coats," so named for their ubiquity and durability through trench warfare. One Royal Flying Corps veteran wrote a testimonial noting that "During the War, I crashed in the (English) Channel when wearing a Burberry trench coat and had to discard it. It was returned to me a week later, having been in the sea for five days. I have worn it ever since and it is still going strong." The company estimated that 500,000 Burberrys were worn and perhaps more important, brought home, by veterans.

Rainwear became so important to Burberrys that the company soon whittled its lines down to little more than trench coats and tailored menswear for much of the 20th century. The notoriously conservative manufacturer stuck primarily to its well-known raincoats until the 1960s, when a fluke led Burberrys to capitalize on the garments' trademark tan, black, red and white plaid lining. It all started with a window display at the company's Paris store. The shop's manager spiced up her arrangement of trench coats by turning up the hem of one coat to show off its checked lining, then repeated the check on an array of umbrellas. The clamor for the umbrellas was so immediate and compelling that Burberry's made and quickly sold hundreds. This experiment eventually led to the introduction of the cashmere scarf, also a perennial best-seller. By the 1990s, Burberry offered six different umbrella models and scarves in eight color schemes. This turning point in the company's merchandising scheme notwithstanding, rainwear remained Burberrys single largest line into the late 1970s and early 1980s, and menswear continued to dominate.

Exports, Women's and Children's Apparel Emphasized in the 1980s and 1990s

Burberrys export business increased dramatically during the 1980s, fueled primarily by Japanese and American craving for prestigious designer goods. By mid-decade, exports constituted two-thirds of the British company's sales, with over one-fourth of exports headed to Japan and another 15 percent sold in the United States. By 1996, Burberrys had accumulated a record six Queen's Awards for Export Achievement and ranked among Great Britain's leading clothing exporters. Overseas sales continued to grow by double-digit percentages in the early 1990s.

Realizing that "A fine tradition is not in itself sufficient today," Burberrys sought to broaden its appeal to a younger, more fashion-conscious female clientele. Acknowledging that "The first thing people think of when they hear 'Burberrys' is a man's trench coat," U.S. Managing Director Barry Goldsmith asserted in a 1994 *WWD* article that "that's the image we're up against." One result was the Thomas Burberry collection, first introduced in Great Britain in 1988 and extended to the United States two years later. The new merchandise was priced 15 percent to 30 percent less than Burberrys' designer lines, bringing a blouse down to $90 versus the normal $150 to $225, for example. Yet it wasn't just the price tags that set this "bridge line" apart from the brand's more traditional garb. The collection emphasized more casual sportswear, as opposed to career wear. "Updated classics" included youthful plaid mini kilts, jumpers, and snug "jean fit" slacks. U.S. advertising executive David Lipman called the line and its model, Christy Turlington, "modernly relevant, yet classically beautiful." At the upper end of the scale, Burberrys launched a personal tailoring service for the ladies. The company's women's division grew 30 percent from 1994 to early 1996 and was expected not only to overtake menswear, but to constitute over 70 percent of total annual sales by 1999.

Although it continued to manufacture 90 percent of its merchandise in British factories, Burberry's also started licensing its name, plaid, and knight logo to other manufacturers. By the mid-1990s, the Burberrys name added panache to handbags and belts, throw pillows and boxer shorts, cookies and crackers, and fragrances and liquor. Childrenswear, stuffed toys, watches, handbags, golf bags, and even a co-branded VISA credit card sported the Burberry check.

Burberry's efforts at product and geographic diversification appeared to be paying off in the mid-1990s. Sales (including a small sister subsidiary, Scotch House) increased by over one-third, from £200.9 million in fiscal 1994 (ended March 31) to £267.8 million in 1996. Net income before taxes grew twice as fast, from £41.1 million to £70 million, during the same period. Given the company's timeless appeal, reputation for quality, strong licensing program, and its backing by British retail powerhouse Great Universal Stores, Burberrys appeared poised to sustain its record of rapid, profitable growth in the mid-1990s.

Principal Subsidiaries

Burberrys Limited (USA); Burberrys (Products) Ltd.

Further Reading

"Burberrys Goes Casual," *WWD*, December 21, 1993, p. 8.

Burberrys of London: An Elementary History of a Great Tradition, London: Burberrys Ltd., 1987.

"Burberry's Women's Lines Thriving," *WWD*, May 15, 1996, p. 7.

Collier, Andrew, "Burberry Toasts Its History with Museum Exhibit," *WWD*, February 14, 1989, p. 10.

Emert, Carol, "Plaid in Dispute Concerning Sale of Burberrys Items," *Daily News Record*, August 8, 1995, p. 5.

Fallon, James, "Burberrys in U.S. to Get New Line," *Daily News Record*, August 23, 1990, p. 3.

Gray, Robert, "A Green and Pleasant Brand," *Marketing*, July 20, 1995, pp. 22–23.

Pogoda, Dianne M., "Tipping the Sales," *WWD*, May 4, 1994, pp. 8–9.

——, and Friedman, Arthur, "Finally, Some Sunshine for Rainwear," *WWD*, April 16, 1996, pp. 7–8.

Porter, Janet, "Burberrys Weathers Dollar Fall," *Journal of Commerce and Commercial*, February 26, 1987, pp. 1A, 6A.

The Story of the Trenchcoat, London: Burberrys of London, 1993.

Underwood, Elaine, "Check-ing Out," *Brandweek*, December 11, 1995, p. 32.

Woolcock, Keith, "The Great Universal Mystery," *Management Today*, November 1994, pp. 48–52.

—April Dougal Gasbarre

Burger King Corporation

17777 Old Cutler Road
Miami, Florida 33157
U.S.A.
(305) 378-7011
Fax: (305) 378-7262
Internet: http://www.burgerking.com

Wholly Owned Subsidiary of Grand Metropolitan Plc
Incorporated: 1954
Employees: 295,000
Sales: $5.38 billion (1994)
SICs: 5812 Eating Places

Burger King Corporation is the second largest fast-food chain in the United States, trailing only McDonald's. Owned since 1989 by the U.K. food and liquor giant Grand Metropolitan, Burger King franchises more than 7,600 restaurants and owns about 800 for a chainwide total exceeding 8,400, with locations in all 50 states and 56 countries. After nearly a decade and a half of stagnation characterized by several short-term CEOs and a like number of failed advertising campaigns, Burger King seemed to have been revitalized in the mid-1990s with a back-to-basics, value-oriented approach.

Rapid Growth under Company Founders, 1954–67

Miami entrepreneurs James McLamore and David Edgerton founded Burger King Corporation in 1954. Five years later, they were ready to expand their five Florida Burger Kings into a nationwide chain. By the time they sold their company to Pillsbury in 1967, Burger King had become the third largest fast-food chain in the country and was on its way to second place, after industry leader McDonald's.

The story of Burger King's growth is the story of how franchising and advertising developed the fast-food industry. McLamore and Edgerton began in 1954 with a simple concept: to attract the burgeoning numbers of postwar baby boom families with reasonably-priced, broiled burgers served quickly. The idea was not unique: drive-ins offering cheap fast food were springing up all across America in the early 1950s. In fact, 1954 was the same year Ray Kroc made his deal with the McDonald brothers, whose original southern California drive-in started the McDonald's empire.

McLamore and Edgerton tried to give their Burger King restaurants a special edge. Burger King became the first chain to offer dining rooms (albeit uncomfortable plastic ones). In 1957 they expanded their menu with the Whopper, a burger with sauce, cheese, lettuce, pickles, and tomato, for big appetites. But prices were kept low: a hamburger cost 18 cents and the Whopper 37 cents. (McDonald's burgers at the same time, however, cost only 15 cents.) In 1958 they took advantage of an increasingly popular medium, television: the first Burger King television commercial appeared on Miami's VHF station that year.

By 1959 McLamore and Edgerton were ready to expand beyond Florida, and franchising seemed to be the best way to take their concept to a broader market. Franchising was booming in the late 1950s because it allowed companies to expand with minimal investment. Like many other franchisers, McLamore and Edgerton attracted their investors by selling exclusive rights to large territories throughout the country. The buyers of these territorial rights, many of them large businesses themselves, could do what they wanted to in their territory: buy land, build as many stores as they liked, sell part of the territory to other investors, or diversify. McLamore and Edgerton took their initial payments (which varied with the territory) and their cut (as little as one percent of sales) and left their franchisees pretty much on their own.

The system worked well, allowing Burger King to expand rapidly. By 1967, when the partners decided to sell the company they had founded, the chain included 274 stores and was worth $18 million to its buyer, prepared-foods giant Pillsbury.

Difficulties with Franchisees under Pillsbury, 1967–77

The Burger King franchising system also worked well for the franchisees. Under the early Burger King system, some of the company's large investors expanded at a rate rivaling that of

Company Perspectives:

The success and size of Burger King are the result of a tradition of leadership within the fast-food industry in such areas as product development, restaurant operation, decor, service, and advertising.

the parent company. Where this loosely knit franchising system failed, however, was in providing a consistent company image. Because McLamore and Edgerton didn't check on their franchises and used only a small field staff for franchise support, the chain was noted for inconsistency in both food and service from franchise to franchise, a major flaw in a chain that aimed to attract customers by assuring them of what to expect in every Burger King they visited.

It was up to the new owner, Pillsbury, to crack down on franchise owners. But some large franchisees thought they could run their Burger King outlets better than a packaged-goods company. Wealthy Louisianans Billy and Jimmy Trotter bought their first Burger King outlet in 1963. By 1969, they controlled almost two dozen Burger King restaurants and went public under the name Self Service Restaurants Inc. In 1970, when the franchisees in control of the lucrative Chicago market decided to sell out, Billy Trotter flew to Chicago in a snowstorm to buy the territory for $8 million. By the time Pillsbury executives got to town the next day, they found they had been bested by their own franchisee.

The Trotters didn't stop there. By 1971 they owned 351 stores with sales of $32 million. They bought out two steak house chains (taking the name of one of them, Chart House), established their own training and inspection programs, and decided on their own food suppliers. By 1972 they were ready to take over altogether; the Trotters made Pillsbury a $100 million offer for Burger King. When that initiative failed, they suggested that both Pillsbury and Chart House spin off their Burger King holdings into a separate company. When that also failed, they continued to acquire Burger King piecemeal, buying nine stores in Boston and 13 in Houston.

But Pillsbury wasn't about to allow Chart House to gain other valuable territories. They sued the Boston franchisees who had sold to Chart House, citing Pillsbury's contractual right of first refusal to any sale. Eventually Chart House compromised, agreeing to give up its Boston holdings in exchange for the right to keep its Houston properties.

Donald Smith Leads Burger King to Number Two Position, 1977–80

Pillsbury's suit was proof of a new management attitude that involved more central control over powerful franchisees. But it wasn't until Pillsbury brought in a hard-hitting executive from McDonald's that Burger King began to exert real control over its franchisees. Donald Smith was third in line for the top spot at McDonald's when Pillsbury lured him away in 1977 with a promise of full autonomy in the top position at Burger King.

Smith used it to "McDonaldize" the company, a process that was especially felt among the franchise holders.

While Burger King had grown by selling wide territorial rights, McDonald's had taken a different approach from the very beginning, leasing stores to franchisees and demanding a high degree of uniformity in return. When Smith came on board at Burger King in 1977, the company owned only 34% of the land and buildings in which its products were sold. Land ownership is advantageous because land is an appreciating asset and a source of tax deductions, but more importantly it gives the parent company a landlord's power over recalcitrant franchisees.

Smith began by introducing a more demanding franchise contract. Awarded only to individuals, not partnerships or companies, it stipulated that franchisees may not own other restaurants and must live within an hour's drive of their franchise, effectively stopping franchisees from getting too big. He also created ten regional offices to manage franchises.

Smith's new franchise regulations were soon put to the test. Barry W. Florescue, chairman of Horn & Hardart, the creator of New York City's famous Automat restaurants, had recognized that nostalgia alone couldn't keep the original fast-food outlets alive and had decided to turn them into Burger Kings. Smith limited Florescue to building four new stores a year in New York and insisted that he could not expand elsewhere. When Florescue bought eight units in California anyway, Smith sued successfully. Florescue then signed with Arby's, and Smith again effectively asserted Burger King's control in court, based on the franchise contract. His strong response to the upstart franchisee kept Horn & Hardart from becoming too strong a force within Burger King.

Increasing control over franchisees was not the only change Pillsbury instituted at Burger King during the 1970s. Like many other chains, Burger King began to expand abroad early in the decade. Fast food and franchising were unfamiliar outside the United States, making international expansion a challenge. Burger King's international operations never became as profitable as anticipated, but within a decade the company was represented in 30 foreign countries.

At home the company focused on attracting new customers. In 1974 management required franchisees to use the "hospitality system," or multiple lines, to speed up service. In 1975 Burger King reintroduced drive-through windows. While original stands had offered this convenience, it had gradually been eliminated as Burger King restaurants added dining rooms. Drive-throughs proved to be a profitable element, accounting for 60 percent of fast food sales throughout the industry by 1987.

Smith also revamped the corporate structure, replacing eight of ten managers with McDonald's people. To attack Burger King's inconsistency problem, Smith mandated a yearly two-day check of each franchise and frequent unscheduled visits. He also decided that the company should own its outlets whenever possible, and by 1979 had brought the company's share of outlet ownership from 34 percent to 42 percent.

Smith also turned his hand to the food served in his restaurants. He introduced the french fry technique that produced the more popular McDonald's-type fry. In 1978, primarily in response to the appeal that newcomer Wendy's had for adults, he introduced specialty sandwiches—fish, chicken, ham and cheese, and steak—to increase Burger King's dinner trade. Offering the broadest menu in fast food did the trick, boosting traffic 15 percent. A more radical expansion for the Burger King menu came next. After McDonald's proved that breakfast could be a profitable fast-food addition (offering a morning meal spread fixed costs over longer hours of operation) Smith began planning a breakfast menu in 1979. But Burger King had a problem with breakfast: its flame broilers could not be adapted as easily to breakfast entrees as McDonald's grills could. Smith urged development of entrees that could be prepared on existing equipment instead of requiring special grills. He began testing breakfast foods in 1978, but it wasn't until the Croissan'wich in 1983 and French Toast sticks in 1985 that Burger King had winning entries in the increasingly competitive breakfast market.

Troubled Times in the 1980s

Smith left Burger King in June 1980 to try to introduce the same kind of fast-food management techniques at Pizza Hut. (Ironically, when he left Pizza Hut in 1983 he moved into the chief executive position at the franchisee that had given Burger King so much trouble, Chart House.) By following in Smith's general direction, Burger King reached its number-two position within two years of his departure, but frequent changes at the top for the next several years meant inconsistent management for the company. Louis P. Neeb succeeded Smith, to be followed less than two years later by Jerry Ruenheck. Ruenheck resigned to become a Burger King franchise owner in Florida less than two years after that, and his successor, Jay Darling, resigned a little over a year later to take on a Burger King franchise himself. Charles Olcott, a conservative former chief financial officer, took over in 1987.

Burger King did not stand still under its succession of heads, though. The company continued to expand abroad, opening a training center in London to serve its European franchisees and employees in 1985. Besides developing successful breakfast entries, Burger King added salad bars and a "light" menu to meet the demand for foods with a healthier, less fatty image. In 1985 the firm began a $100 million program to remodel most of its restaurants to include more natural materials, such as wood and plants, and less plastic. Burger King also completely computerized its cooking and cash register operations so even the least skilled teenager could do the job. Average sales per restaurant reached the $1 million mark in 1985.

Even some of Burger King's post-Smith successes caused problems, though. The company introduced another successful new entree, Chicken Tenders, in 1986, only to find it that it could not obtain enough chicken to meet demand. Burger King was forced to pull its $30 million introductory ad campaign.

Burger King was still bedeviled by the old complaint that its service and food were inconsistent. The company played out its identity crisis in public, changing ad styles with almost the same frequency that it changed managers. After Smith's departure in 1980, Burger King's old "Have it your way" campaign ("Hold the pickles, hold the lettuce. Special orders don't upset us") was no longer appropriate. That ad campaign emphasized as a selling point what many saw as a drawback at Burger King: longer

waiting times. But under Smith's emphasis on speed and efficiency, special orders did upset store owners. So the company turned to the harder sell "Aren't you hungry for Burger King now?" campaign. The hard sell approach moved the chain into second place, and Burger King took an even more aggressive advertising line. In 1982 Burger King directly attacked its competitors, alleging that Burger King's grilled burgers were better than McDonald's and Wendy's fried burgers. Both competitors sued over the ads, and Wendy's challenged Burger King to a taste test (a challenge that was pointedly ignored). In return for dropping the suits, Burger King agreed to phase out the offending ads gradually, but Burger King came out the winner in its $25 million "Battle of the Burgers": the average volume of its 3,500 stores rose from $750,000 to $840,000 in 1982, sales were up 19 percent, and pretax profits rose 9 percent.

Burger King's subsequent ad campaigns were not as successful. In 1985 the company added just over half an ounce of meat to its Whopper, making the 4.2 ounce sandwich slightly larger than the quarter-pound burgers of its competitors. The meatier Whopper and the $30 million ad campaign using celebrities to promote it failed to bring in new business. All three of the major campaigns that followed ("Herb the Nerd," "This is a Burger King town," and "Fast food for fast times") were costly flops. "We do it like you'd do it" followed in 1988, with little more success.

In 1988, the company faced another kind of threat. Parent Pillsbury, the target of a hostile takeover attempt by the British company Grand Metropolitan PLC, devised a counterplan that included spinning off the troubled Burger King chain to shareholders, but at the cost of new debt that would lower the price of both Pillsbury and the new Burger King shares. Such a plan would have made it highly unlikely that Burger King could ever have overcome its ongoing problems of quality and consistent marketing.

Pillsbury's plan didn't work, and Grand Met bought Pillsbury in January 1989 for $66 a share, or approximately $5.7 billion. Pillsbury became part of Grand Met's worldwide system of food and retailing businesses with well-known brand names. In Burger King, Grand Met got a company with some problems but whose 5,500 restaurants in all 50 states and 30 foreign countries gave it a strong presence.

Turnaround under Grand Met in the 1990s

Grand Met's first move was to place Barry Gibbons, a successful manager of pubs and restaurants in the United Kingdom, into the CEO slot. Soon thereafter, in September 1989, Grand Met acquired several restaurant properties from United Biscuits (Holdings) Plc, including the Wimpey hamburger chain, which included 381 U.K. outlets and 148 in other countries. By the summer of 1990, 200 Wimpeys had been converted to Burger Kings, bolstering the company's foreign operations, a traditional area of weakness. Over the next several years, Burger King was much more aggressive with its international expansion, with restaurants opening for the first time in Hungary and Mexico (1991); Poland (1992); Saudi Arabia (1993); Israel, Oman, the Dominican Republic, El Salvador, Peru, and New Zealand (1994); and Paraguay (1995). By 1996, Burger

King had outlets in 56 countries, a dramatic increase from the 30 of just seven years earlier.

While Gibbons was successful in accelerating the company's international growth, overall his tenure as CEO (which lasted until 1993) brought a mixture of successes and failures. In the new product area, the hamburger chain hit it big with the 1990 introduction of the BK Broiler, a broiled chicken sandwich aimed at fast-food eaters seeking a somewhat more healthful meal; soon after introduction, more than one million were being sold each day. Also successful were promotions aimed at children. In 1990 the Burger King Kids Club program was launched nationwide, and more than one million kids signed up in the first two months. The program continued to grow thereafter; by 1996 membership stood at five million and the number of Kids Club meals sold each month had increased from 6.1 million in 1990 to nearly 12 million. Also hugely successful was the long-term deal with Disney for motion picture tie-ins signed in 1992. Through 1996 (when Disney broke with Burger King to sign a deal with arch-rival McDonald's), the partnership had involved such Disney smashes as *Beauty and the Beast, The Lion King,* and *Toy Story.* In 1996 Burger King signed a new Hollywood deal with DreamWorks SKG.

Gibbons also worked to improve Burger King's profitability, under a mandate from Grand Met. Soon after taking over as CEO, Gibbons cut more than 500 jobs, mainly field staff positions. He also began to divest company-owned stores in areas where the company did not have critical mass, particularly west of the Mississippi. Doing so helped increase profitability, although some observers charged that Gibbons was selling off valuable assets just to improve the company numbers. In any case, during Gibbons's last two years as CEO, profits were about $250 million each year, compared to at most $175 million a year under Pillsbury.

Where Gibbons certainly failed, however, was in addressing Burger King's longstanding problem with image. The advertising program was still in disarray as the firm hired in 1989, D'Arcy Masius Benton & Bowles, created still more short-lived campaigns: "Sometimes you've gotta break the rules" (1989–91), "Your way right away" (1991), and "BK Tee Vee" (1992–93). Neither franchisees nor customers were endeared to any of these. In the face of the improving profitability of the corporation, such marketing blunders led to abysmal chainwide sales increases, such as a 3.6 percent increase for fiscal years 1991 and 1992 combined.

In mid-1993, James Adamson succeeded Gibbons as CEO, a position for which he had been groomed since joining Burger King as COO in 1991. Adamson, who actively sought out the advice of company co-founder James W. McLamore, moved to build on Gibbons's successes as well as rectify the failures. Adamson's most important initiatives addressed key areas: quality, value, and image. He improved the quality of products, such as in 1994 when the size of the BK Broiler, the BK Big Fish, and the hamburger were increased by more than 50 percent. He belatedly added a "value menu" after most other fast feeders had already done so, as well as offering special promotions, such as the 99¢ Whopper. Related to both value and image was the long-awaited successful ad campaign, "Get

your burger's worth," created by Ammirati Puris Lintas, and emphasizing a back-to-basics approach and good value. The focus on the basics also led to a simplification of what had become an unwieldy menu—40 items were eliminated. The new focus was on burgers—with an emphasis on flame broiling—fries, and drinks. By early 1995, Adamson's program was paying off as same-store sales increased 6.6 percent for the fiscal year ending March 31, 1995. Morale among the franchisees had improved dramatically as well.

Adamson resigned suddenly in early 1995 to head Flagstar Cos. of Spartanburg, South Carolina. In July, Robert C. Lowes, who had been chief officer for Grand Met Foods Europe, was named CEO. Later that same year he became chairman of Burger King and gained a position on the Grand Met executive committee, a move that signaled Grand Met's commitment to Burger King and the strength of the company's resurgence. Lowes soon set some lofty goals for Burger King, including $10 billion in systemwide sales by 1997 (from $8.4 billion in 1995) and 10,000 outlets by the year 2000 (there were 8,455 in mid-1996). Burger King seemed well-positioned to reach these goals and to attain new heights of prosperity in the next century.

Principal Subsidiaries

Burger King, Europe/Middle East/Africa (U.K.); Burger King (UK) Limited; Jus-rol Ltd. (U.K.); Fiesta Foods Limited (Netherlands).

Further Reading

Alva, Marilyn, "Can They Save the King?," *Restaurant Business,* May 1, 1994, p. 104.

Collins, Glenn, "Grand Met Names a Chief for Burger King Subsidiary: Turnaround Is Seen at Fast Food Chain," *New York Times,* July 12, 1995, p. C2.

DeGeorge, Gail, "Turning Up the Gas at Burger King: It's Discounting Burgers and Dumping Yet Another Ad Campaign," *Business Week,* November 15, 1993, pp. 62–67.

Emerson, Robert L., *Fast Food: The Endless Shakeout,* New York: Lebhar-Friedman Books, 1979.

——, *The New Economics of Fast Food,* New York: Van Nostrand Reinhold, 1990.

Farrell, Greg, "Burger King: Whopper on the Rebound?," *Brandweek,* February 7, 1994, p. 22.

Gibson, Richard, "Burger King Overhaul Includes Refocus on Whopper: Grand Met Unit Seeks to Cut Costs, Improve Service with Extensive Review," *Wall Street Journal,* December 15, 1993, p. B4.

Howard, Theresa, "BK Looks toward Recovery under New Chief Adamson," *Nation's Restaurant News,* August 2, 1993, p. 5.

Kramer, Louise, "Burger King Gets Back to Basics in Latest Ad Blitz," *Nation's Restaurant News,* April 29, 1996, p. 14.

Luxenberg, Stan, *Roadside Empires: How the Chains Franchised America,* New York: Viking, 1985.

Maremont, Mark, Pete Engardio, and Brian Bremner, "Trying to Get Burger King Out of the Flames: It's a Tall Order, Even for Grand Met Hotshot Gibbons," *Business Week,* January 30, 1989, p. 29.

Pollack, Judann, "Burger King Sizzles in Wake of Arch Deluxe," *Advertising Age,* June 17, 1996, p. 3.

—Ginger G. Rodriguez
—updated by David E. Salamie

Burlington

Burlington Industries, Inc.

3330 West Friendly Avenue
Greensboro, North Carolina 27420
U.S.A.
(910) 379-2000
Fax: (910) 379-4504
Internet: http://www.burlington-ind.com

Public Company
Incorporated: 1923 as Burlington Mills
Employees: 21,000
Sales: $2.2 billion (1995)
Stock Exchanges: New York
SICs: 2231 Broadwoven Fabric Mills, Wool; 2221
    Broadwoven Fabric Mills, Manmade; 2211
    Broadwoven Fabric Mills, Cotton; 2273 Carpets and
    Rugs

Burlington Industries, Inc. is one of the world's leading producers of textiles and related items. Its products include fabrics for home furnishings and apparel, carpeting and rugs, draperies and window shades, and upholstery fabrics. The company operates over 40 plants throughout the United States and Mexico, and functions as a coalition of nine separate businesses joined under the Burlington name.

The Early Years

After returning from military service during World War I, J. Spencer Love went to work in his uncle's spinning mill in Gastonia, North Carolina. There he gained four years of experience before deciding to branch off on his own. He purchased a controlling interest in his uncle's mill, and then convinced the Chamber of Commerce in Burlington, North Carolina, to help him finance the construction of a new plant in that city. Eventually, Love shut down the original mill and moved the equipment to Burlington, forming Burlington Mills on November 6, 1923. The newly-formed company consisted of 200 employees and one building that was situated in the middle of a cornfield.

Textile production was started even before the building's construction had been completed.

Initially, Burlington Mills manufactured several cotton products, including flag cloth, bunting, cotton scrims, curtain and dress fabrics, and a type of diaper cloth called birdseye. Unfortunately for the company, however, many of these products were already becoming obsolete by the time manufacturing had begun. Business faltered for a short time, until out of desperation Love began producing bedspreads out of an experimental fabric called rayon. Consumers responded positively to this shiny new material, and within a few years Burlington became a leader in the manufacture of rayon textile. This success led to the opening of a second mill in 1926, and the achievement of $1 million in sales the following year. A New York sales office was opened in 1929.

During the Depression, Burlington continued to expand even as many competitors closed their doors. The company had a sizable advantage over comparable New England-based firms, due mainly to the lower cost of labor in the southern United States. Using this competitive strength during that period of time, Burlington acquired several mills that had closed as a result of the poor economic times, and subsequently reopened them under the Burlington name.

Diversification Throughout the Mid-1900s

In 1935, the company moved its headquarters from Burlington to Greensboro, North Carolina, in order to have railway access to its operations in New York. In 1937, Burlington consolidated its various operating units and was listed on the New York Stock Exchange. Company revenues had risen to $25 million.

When World War II broke out, the company began producing items for the U.S. government. Its research laboratories also were employed on various government projects, including one that investigated the use of a new fiber, nylon, in making parachute cloth. This initial work provided the foundation upon which the company developed several other uses for nylon-based textiles when the war ended.

Company Perspectives:

We are an organization of people with many special talents and skills, united in our commitment to build a growing, competitive and highly profitable textile company with which our customers prefer to do business, in which our investors prefer to invest and for which we all prefer to work.

Following the war, growth continued rapidly into the 1950s. Plants were often built with one wooden wall that could be taken down, moved, and erected again to expand available floor space. Burlington also acquired several competitors during this time, including Pacific Mills and Klopman Mills. As its diversification strategy began taking the firm beyond its original spinning and weaving businesses, the company changed its name in 1955 to Burlington Industries.

In 1960, Burlington purchased James Lees & Sons, a Philadelphia-based carpet manufacturer. Two years later, Burlington became the first textile firm to exceed $1 billion in sales. To this point, the company's growth had been directed primarily by its founder, J. Spencer Love, who died in 1962. He was succeeded as president by Charles F. Myers. When Myers took over, he changed the company's strategy to more effectively manage increasing labor costs and foreign competition. Under Love, Burlington had provided fabric to other apparel and home furnishings manufacturers. Myers undertook a new approach that directly targeted consumers as the company's customers, and in 1972 Burlington introduced several products under its own name, including towels, blankets, men's socks, women's hosiery, sheets, and draperies.

This activity was accompanied by other changes, including acquisitions of non-textile businesses, development of a consumer advertising campaign, and a major corporate reorganization. One of the acquisitions made during this time, that of the Globe Furniture Company in 1966, furthered the company's goals of getting closer to consumers and of finding new avenues of growth. This became particularly important three years later when a Federal Trade Commission (FTC) decree prohibited Burlington from purchasing any United States textile firms for ten years without prior FTC approval.

Reorganization Into the 1970s

During his tenure, Myers, who became Chairman of Burlington in 1968, engineered a controversial internal restructuring that altered traditional organizational functions, such as marketing and research, and redeployed them into vertically integrated businesses. The company's New York-based executives—along with Ely R. Callaway, who succeeded Myers as Burlington's president in 1968—desired a more centralized operation, while Greensboro-based executives favored Myers' decentralized, divisional structure. In 1973, those who preferred the divisional structure forced Callaway to resign.

Callaway had been charged with running the day-to-day operations of the company, while Myers tended to finances. Callaway had been largely responsible for the company's belated entry into double-knit fabrics, after the popularity of knitwear had seriously begun to reduce the company's sales volume in traditional woven fabrics. Because of this, Callaway's departure was a loss to the company. Fortunately, he was succeeded as president by Horace C. Jones, the former president of the company's Lees Carpets division. Jones ensured that Callaway's work to enter the knitted fabric market was continued. Although faced with rising costs for raw materials that were in short supply, Burlington quickly retooled its worsted fabric production facilities to take advantage of the growing trend toward knit and stretch fabrics. This move resulted in Burlington's recovery.

Also contributing to the company's recovery were U.S. trade agreements in 1971 with four Asian countries that served to reduce import volume. The devaluation of the dollar abroad also helped by giving U.S. goods a price advantage. During this time, the company increased its emphasis on the home furnishings line, which had begun to be marketed under the Burlington House name. In 1973, Burlington ventured into the lighting area with its acquisition of Westwood Industries.

Internally, the struggle for power continued. Following Myers' retirement in 1974, Jones was appointed chairman and CEO, and four executive vice-presidents competed to succeed Jones as president. William A. Klopman, son of Klopman Mills' founder, was chosen for the job. Unfortunately, the recovery that was seen during Jones' presidency was short-lived. By the beginning of 1974, Burlington faced deepening shortages of raw material, fuel, and labor. These setbacks, combined with an inflationary economy, threatened consumer spending for apparel and home furnishings. Demand for double-knit fabrics weakened because the material tended to snag. Luckily, strong sales overseas enabled the company to finally realize a positive return on its ten-year-old investment in its European operations.

In 1976, William A. Klopman was appointed Burlington chairman and CEO. He had joined the company when it had acquired his father's firm in 1956, and had risen through the ranks, to president of the influential yarn and apparel-fabric divisions from 1963 to 1971, and then to president in 1974. Under his leadership, domestic sales finally rebounded in 1977, due largely to gains in the home furnishings and industrial products area. Burlington succeeded in making necessary adaptations in its apparel products to meet changing consumer tastes regarding fashion styles. For example, the company shifted production away from heavyweight woven fabrics into more lightweight textured products, introduced a new washable polyester and wool blend called Burlana, and expanded the manufacture of denim apparel fabrics, which were growing in popularity.

Corporate Restructuring in the 1980s

Burlington entered the 1980s with an eye on its critical foreign operations. It gradually strengthened its financial position overseas by restructuring its French businesses and by selling its German worsted apparel fabric subsidiary. The company's continued emphasis on capital spending, however, met with mixed reviews. Analysts argued that Burlington's object of becoming a low-cost producer supported by technologically superior plants and long manufacturing runs prevented the company from making necessary changes flexibly and quickly enough to keep pace with trends in fashion and consumer demand. Klopman also was criticized for having an impersonal and aggressive management style, for having made incorrect product line decisions, and for creating trade friction between the United States and the Peoples' Republic of China, as he lobbied hard for limits on Chinese imports. Nevertheless, in 1981 Burlington became the first textile firm to surpass $3 billion in sales.

In 1984, Burlington acknowledged the necessity of broadening its product mix and targeting specialized, high-margin niches. The company introduced a lighter-weight crinkled denim fabric to be marketed under designer brand names. Just two years later, however, Burlington decided to place greater emphasis upon its industrial textiles area, and sold the designer bed-linen lines along with the rest of its bedding and bath textiles division, to J.P. Stevens & Company.

Upon Klopman's retirement in 1986, Frank S. Greenberg became Chairman and CEO. Greenberg had joined the company in 1959 when Burlington had purchased Charm Tred Mills, a firm owned by his father. Like his predecessors, Greenberg rose through divisional ranks into the executive suite, beginning as the president of the rug division and later serving as company president. As chairman, Greenberg found himself and the company fighting a takeover attempt by Dominion Textile Inc., Canada's largest textile producer. Many analysts felt that Burlington's prior reluctance to exit the apparel-fabrics business when lower-priced imports began flooding the market had reduced company profits and made Burlington vulnerable to such an attack from outside the firm. Dominion, looking for a way to rejuvenate its own sales in a stagnant Canadian market, viewed Burlington's denim fabric unit as an attractive acquisition.

Burlington was able to thwart the Dominion-Edelman takeover through a leveraged buyout that took the company private. Through an employee stock ownership plan, Burlington's employees became its primary owners. To reduce the significant amount of debt incurred, the company began selling key assets, such as its industrial products segment, while also eliminating 1,200 employee positions and slicing operating expenses to the bare bone. Within one year, Burlington had retired 45 percent of its buyout debt through severe reductions in overhead spending, capitalizing on a favorable market for its divested assets, and strong apparel fabric sales.

The 1990s and Beyond

Operating in the early 1990s as a much leaner organization than in the past, Burlington Industries faced continuing challenges in matching market demand with its manufacturing capabilities and expertise. Burlington's newly streamlined operation and its proven ability to get out from under a massive debt load had given the firm increased flexibility, which enabled the company to explore new trends in textile products. By that point in time, Burlington had positioned itself as the world's largest jacquard weaving manufacturer for upholstery, draperies, mat-

tress coverings, and bedroom linens. Furthermore, its Area Rugs division was the United States' leader, and was experimenting with new patterned color systems as a means of offering customers a broader variety.

One notable change in the early 1990s occurred when Burlington re-entered the public arena with an open stock offering in 1992. With this change, the positive alterations that had taken place when the company operated privately became very evident, as Burlington was immediately able to capitalize on new industry trends. Most importantly, the company was fully able to develop and market new and different products in order to capture consumer interest and set itself apart from the competition. Not only was new product development increased, but so also was Burlington's speed of service to both retailers and customers. It was clear that the company's restructuring efforts after the leveraged buyout in 1987 were finally paying off.

A surge in new housing in the United States during 1994 heightened demand for residential carpeting, even further helping Burlington regain its standing as one of the country's largest and most successful textile businesses. To meet the demand, many of Burlington's plants began running 24 hours a day, seven days a week. Meanwhile, the company continued to invest millions in new product development throughout 1994 and 1995, while virtually extinguishing the remaining debt load left over from the previous years.

At that time, Burlington was searching for attractive acquisition candidates that would diversify its product offerings, while also complementing the items it presently produced. In January 1995, Burlington made the decision to purchase Bacova Guild, Ltd., a company that was the market leader in printed accent rugs and mats. The Bacova Guild joined the Burlington House Area Rugs division, which was already the market leader in dyed bath and area rugs, and together the two operations helped Burlington control those segments of the floor covering market.

Near the end of the century, Burlington was operating over 45 different manufacturing plants throughout the United States and Mexico. As it already enjoyed a standing as the United States' largest apparel fabrics manufacturer, Burlington continued to increase its export volume to further expand its yearly sales. The company entered into a joint venture in 1995 with Mafatlal Industries, Ltd. of India to make and sell denim products in India and other parts of Asia. Burlington decided to sell its struggling knit fabrics division in 1996. Also aiding in Burlington's heightened potential for further growth was the passage of the North American Free Trade Agreement (NAFTA), which helped Mexico and the Caribbean become extremely important sources of apparel items. Burlington had operated out of Mexico for half a century, and an increase in demand and production there was a benefit.

With international markets continually opening up, and with other segments of the world possessing a strong desire for Western-products, Burlington's size and broad scope will be an advantage in its future ability to capture and handle these new markets. The company's emergence from trying times as a stronger and more efficient operation may be indication that Burlington is able to meet the demands of the coming years and promote continued future growth.

Principal Divisions

Burlington Menswear; Burlington Klopman Fabrics; Burlington Denim; Burlington Sportswear; Burlington Madison Yarn Company; Burlington House; Burlington House Area Rugs; Lees Carpets; Bacova Guild, Ltd.

Further Reading

"Burlington Aiming For Joint Venture to Make, Sell Denim in India, Asia," *WWD,* April 4, 1995, p. 16.

"Burlington Industries: A Brief History," Greensboro: Burlington Industries, Inc., 1995.

"Charles F. Myers of Burlington Industries," *Nation's Business,* November 1972.

"Giant Burlington Faces Trying Times for Textiles," *Business Week,* March 2, 1974.

Hage, David, "Sweet Taste of Success: Five Southern Companies Earn Their Just Desserts," *U.S. News & World Report,* March 7, 1994, p. 54.

Lustigman, Alyssa, "Fabric Forecast: Story Time," *Sporting Goods Business,* December 1992, p. 44.

Taub, Stephen, "Burlington's House Is Back in Order," *Financial World,* March 30, 1993, p. 12.

Wright, Annette C., "Strategy and Structure in the Textile Industry: Spencer Love and Burlington Mills, 1923–1962," *Business History Review,* Spring 1995, p. 42.

—Sandy Schusteff
—updated by Laura E. Whiteley

Carr-Gottstein Foods Co.

6411 A Street
Anchorage, Alaska 99518
U.S.A.
(907) 561-1944
Fax: (907) 564-2580

Public Company
Incorporated: 1990
Employees: 3,600
Sales: $601.3 million (1995)
Stock Exchanges: New York
SICs: 5411 Grocery Stores; 5912 Drug Stores &
    Proprietary Stores

The leading food and drug retailer in Alaska, Carr-Gottstein Foods Co. operates a chain of food, drug, and general merchandise stores under the name "Carrs Quality Centers"; a chain of wine of wine and liquor stores operating under the name "Oaken Keg Spirit Shops"; and a chain of stores designed to serve more rural communities known collectively as "Eagle Quality Centers." During the mid-1990s, Carr-Gottstein operated a total of 39 stores: 15 outlets were Carrs Quality Centers stores; 16 outlets were Oaken Keg Spirit Shops; and eight outlets were Eagle Quality Centers. In addition to the retail stores operated by Carr-Gottstein, the company also owned freight operations, which included a 105,000 square foot warehouse and cross-docking facility in Tacoma, Washington, a real estate development company named CGF Properties, Inc., and a warehouse and distribution center in Anchorage, the only facility of its kind in Alaska. The company's Carrs Quality Centers ranged in size from 28,000 square feet to 73,000 square feet. The Eagle Quality Centers stores ranged from 16,300 square feet to 43,900 square feet. The Oaken Keg stores, 14 of which were situated adjacent to Carrs Quality Centers stores, ranged from 900 square feet to 5,300 square feet. Nine of the company's 15 Carrs Quality Centers were located in Anchorage, where nine of the 16 Oaken Keg stores also were located.

In 1986, two companies with decades of experience in Alaska merged together to form what would become the largest Alaska-owned, Alaska-based company in the state, Carr-Gottstein Foods. The elder of the two companies was J.B. Gottstein & Co., a retail grocery and wholesale grocery distributor founded in 1915, but the heart of the company created through the merger was Carrs Quality Centers, an Alaska grocery store company founded 35 years after J.B. Gottstein began business. The founder of Carrs Quality Centers also became the principal personality behind the merged company, a man who served as Carr-Gottstein Foods' chief architect during its first four years of business. His name was Larry J. Carr, a California-raised businessman who spent his adulthood in Alaska, where his professional career was devoted to creating one of the most innovative and successful supermarket chains in the country. Under Carrs' guiding hand, Carrs Quality Centers developed into the leading supermarket chain in Alaska, an enterprise that drew accolades from industry observers in the Lower 48 for its exceptional combination of customer service and innovative marketing strategies. These two attributes represented the chief ingredients of Carrs Quality Centers' success, and in turn, predicated the success of the company's successor, Carr-Gottstein Foods. Though Larry Carr relinquished control over the company in 1990, the legacy of his 40-year tenure at the company was carried on through his disciples as Carr-Gottstein competed during the mid-1990s.

Origins of Carr-Gottstein's Predecessor

Born in Albuquerque, New Mexico in 1929, Carr developed an early interest in food retailing. For as long as he could remember, he later reflected to a reporter from *Alaska Business Monthly,* he had possessed "the desire to own a grocery store," but before store ownership came his way Carr worked as a grocery store employee in his hometown of San Bernardino, California. In California, where his family relocated when he was still a toddler, Carr worked for two grocery stores while attending high school, and during these two short stints was introduced to the important role innovative marketing played in the operation of a grocery store. "Those merchants," Carr later remarked about his high school employers, "were always find-

---

Company Perspectives:

We are focused on delivering value, service and excitement to our customers.

---

ing ways to make shopping more interesting. I knew that if I ever had the opportunity to own a store, change would be a constant challenge.''

Convinced that the key to success lay in marketing innovation, Carr was less convinced about the opportunity to apply his newfound knowledge in California, where the labor pool was saturated by wave after wave of returning World War II veterans during Carr's late teenage years. Returning soldiers, Carr quickly discovered, were given preference for employment over adolescents, so he decided to move elsewhere and settled on Anchorage, Alaska, as his land of opportunity. Carr arrived in Anchorage in 1947 at age 19 and immediately set himself to the task of fulfilling his childhood dream, a dream he was three years away from turning into reality.

After devoting his days and nights to working two jobs during his first several years in Alaska, Carr was able to save enough money to start out on his own and open his own grocery store. In 1950, at the age of 21, Carr and his brother, B.J. Carr, opened their own corner market in Anchorage, a modest business aptly named ''Carr Brothers.'' The trappings of the first Carr Brothers store were quintessentially meager and entirely unlike the expansive, gleaming supermarkets that later bore the Carr name. The first store was a Quonset structure, a prefabricated portable hut bounded by a corrugated metal roof that curved down to form the store's walls. But it was not long before the business began to grow and Carr began to demonstrate his earnest intent to develop a successful and innovative grocery store chain.

After his first year of business, Larry Carr bought out his brother's stake in the business and by the following year was also able to replace the dilapidated Quonset hut with a genuine building. Two years after leaving the spartan surroundings of his portable, metal hut, Carr moved into the mainstream of the business world by completing his first acquisition, a grocery store in Fairbanks that operated under the ''Foodland'' banner. Further acquisitions followed in the decades ahead, with each site meticulously selected in what Carr later remembered as ''a methodical, analytical process.''

Despite the cautious attention given to selecting sites for additional stores, which was guided by careful examination of demographics and based on research conducted by a Harvard professor, there was a sense of urgency in the expansion of the business. During the 1950s, as Carr was developing what eventually would become a retail empire, he was aware of the imminent arrival of supermarket giant Safeway, a California-based chain with deep financial pockets that was eyeing the largely untapped Alaska market as its next territory. As a result, Carr was looking over his shoulder, aware that once a major chain moved into Alaska his chances for securing credit and

seizing the best locations would diminish. Accordingly, Carr set out to capture the prize retail locations in and around Anchorage with a mixture of conservative prudence and pressing urgency pushing him forward.

Thus real estate became crucial to the success of Carr's company. ''We chose to develop our own properties and retain control,'' Carr explained, describing the general theory behind his decision to anchor his grocery stores in shopping malls owned and developed by his company. By obtaining sizeable parcels of real estate when prices were low, Carr created a firm foundation for his chain of Carrs Quality Centers and gained ideal locations for a second retail chain of wine and liquor stores he started, called Oaken Keg Spirit Shops. Both of these chains became the dominant players in their respective markets, with the growth of the Oaken Keg stores driven by the success and popularity of the Carrs Quality Centers supermarkets, which thrived under Carr's business philosophy of providing superior customer service and consistently tinkering with new marketing programs. Since beginning his business, Carr had attended to the particular needs of his Alaskan customers in ways his competitors had not. Carr kept his stores open during the sunny nights of Alaskan summers. He offered customers fresher produce, eggs, and meat than could be typically purchased by shipping perishable foods via chartered plans. He launched the first salad bar service offered by a supermarket on the West Coast and became one of the few retailers to register success early on in selling natural foods and gourmet food selections.

Along the way, as he orchestrated the development of a supermarket chain renowned for its extensive selection of prepared foods, vast produce departments, and general merchandise, Carr earned the esteem of retailers throughout the country. In 1959, he was selected as Retailer of the Year by the National Brand Names Foundation. In 1970, he was awarded first prize for food store advertising by the Women's Day Super Market Institute. Praise was also given to Carr for the working environment he created for his employees, the positive qualities of which cultivated strong employee loyalty.

However, Carr's chain of supermarkets was not the leading retail operation in Anchorage. As expected, Safeway entered Carr's home turf, making its entry into Alaskan markets roughly a decade after Carr opened his first store. For the ensuing 20 years, Safeway reigned as the leading supermarket retailer in Anchorage, its financial resources proving too great for Carr and his collection of stores to outmatch.

1980s: Market Dominance and Gottstein Merger

The tide began to turn, however, in 1980 when Carrs Quality Centers joined Topco Associates, the second-largest food-buying organization in the United States. The affiliation enabled to Carr to discount his prices and compete seriously with major chains such as Safeway. ''We bought better, lowered prices,'' Carr remembered, ''and instantly took command of the market.'' The company's market strength, which was fortified throughout the first half of the 1980s, was made significantly stronger by the 1986 merger with J.B. Gottstein & Co., a retail grocery and wholesale grocery distributor led by Bernard Gottstein. Like Carr, Gottstein had secured prime real estate in Alaska when prices were low, creating a powerful ally for the flourishing enterprise stewarded by Carr. The combined entity was renamed Carr-Gottstein Foods Co., a company that ranked as Alaska's largest food and drug retailer and was supported by the chain of Oaken Keg liquor stores, a real estate subsidiary, a wholesale grocery business, and freight operations.

Under the management of Gottstein and Carr, Carr-Gottstein Foods benefitted from the same business philosophy that had made Carrs Quality Centers one of the remarkable supermarket chains in the nation. "Doing things the way you did them yesterday will eventually make you obsolete," Carr noted several years after the merger. Harkening back to the strategy he had learned during his grocery store apprenticeship in San Bernardino, Carr added, "To be successful over a long period of time, you have to change to fit the needs of tomorrow, not concentrate on what happened yesterday." Despite Carr's focus on the future and his disregard, at least in terms of marketing, for what worked in the past, Carr-Gottstein Foods owed its stature during the late 1980s to the legacy of Carrs Quality Centers' past. Acknowledging the importance of what Carr-Gottstein Foods inherited upon formation, Carr declared, "For the past 30 years, we've probably maintained better demographic information in Anchorage than anybody. We've kept track of neighborhoods and highway patterns. This enabled us, in many cases, to buy sites ahead of growth."

1990 Leveraged Buyout

Major, national chains enjoyed the luxury of vast financial resources, but a locally-owned and locally-operated chain such as Carr-Gottstein benefitted from something perhaps more valuable than overflowing corporate coffers: an intimate, historical knowledge of the markets it served. To retain this advantage over rival, out-of-state supermarket chains, both Carr and Gottstein hoped to pass control of their company to fellow Alaskans as they began to contemplate their withdrawal from overseeing the daily operations of Carr-Gottstein. Out-of-state parties interested in acquiring the chain had made several offers during the late 1980s, but Carr and Gottstein brushed their offers aside. When two senior executives of Carr-Gottstein, John Cairns, the company's general manager, and Mark Williams, Carr-Gottstein's vice-president of operations, tendered an offer buy the company in 1990, Larry Carr and Bernard Gottstein accepted, offering to retain some of the operations composing the Carr-Gottstein enterprise and then lease them back to Cairns and Williams in order to make the price more affordable. In October 1990, when annual sales reached $500 million, the deal was finalized, ceding Cairns and Williams control over Alaska's largest and most profitable supermarket chain.

The financing for the leveraged buyout, the sale price of which was estimated at between $250 million and $300 million, was secured by Leonard Green & Partners, a Los Angeles-based investment banking firm specializing in leveraged buyouts. What specifically Cairns and Williams received for the purchase price gave outside observers a clear picture of the range of businesses developed by both Carr and Gottstein. Included within the new Carr-Gottstein were 13 Carrs Quality Centers, roughly half of which were the anchor tenants in shopping centers developed and owned by the company, and 15 Oaken Keg liquor stores which were situated adjacent to or near each Carrs Quality Center (Alaska law prohibits the sale of alcoholic beverages in grocery stores). Included as well were three modestly-sized stores operating as Eagle Quality Centers, a conventional-store retail format developed for smaller communities. Rounding out the operations that Cairns and Williams found themselves heading in 1990 were Gottstein Co., a wholesale food business, freight operations, and Carr-Gottstein Properties, a real estate development firm.

Once control of the company was passed to new management, Cairns was named president and chief executive officer, and Williams was selected as executive vice-president and chief operating officer. Under their management, the company continued to benefit from innovative marketing programs and an emphasis on customer service, as Cairns and Williams adopted the business strategy used by their predecessors, Carr and Gottstein. "We're always trying something new," Williams declared, echoing the philosophy embraced by Carr. "In this business, you can't stand still and be successful." For Cairns and Williams, "trying something new" during the 1990s generally meant responding to competitive pressures placed on their company by rival retailers. During the early 1990s, wholesale clubs became popular shopping destinations for Anchorage residents, prompting Cairns and Williams to institute a bulk packaging program for meats in late 1991. Several years later, the expansion of several major chains led to what the business press described as the "The Alaska Invasion of 1994," but before Carr-Gottstein found itself facing the stiff competition presented by new Wal-Mart, Kmart, and Fred Meyer retail outlets the company made a move that added new vigor to its growth during the 1990s.

1993 Public Offering

In May 1993, the company announced it was intending to sell 8.8 million shares of stock in an initial public offering (IPO) that would give outside investors a 56.9 percent stake in Carr-Gottstein. Expected to yield $69.2 million, the IPO raised $83.5 million when its was completed in July and Carr-Gottstein began trading on the New York Stock Exchange. With the proceeds from the stock offering, the company reduced some of the debt incurred from the 1990 leveraged buyout and earmarked funds for expansion, taking a fresh look at the opportunities available in Alaska and elsewhere. "With the offering behind us," Williams noted, "we've begun to take a longer view to position this company for the next 10 to 15 years rather than just the next two or three." As Williams looked ahead, he saw his company expanding at a robust pace, a vision that he shared with the public one month after the IPO. In August, Williams announced plans to strengthen Carr-Gottstein's stores base in Alaska by expanding southeast into Juneau and west to the Aleutian Islands, but the most startling news was the announcement that Carr-Gottstein would extend its retail presence beyond Alaska's borders for the first time in its history by expanding into the Pacific Northwest. Slated to begin sometime after 1996, the foray into the Pacific Northwest represented a bold move, but "The Alaska Invasion of 1994" put an end to the optimistic dreams of 1993.

During a nine-month span in 1994, 12 massive stores were opened in Alaska by Fred Meyer, Kmart, Wal-Mart, and Toys "R" Us, creating a fiercely competitive environment for Carr-Gottstein as it plotted its ambitious expansion plans. In total, 1.5

million square feet of new retail space was opened in 1994, quickly eclipsing the 900,000 square feet operated by Carr-Gottstein's. The spate of stores openings during the year began to take its toll on Carr-Gottstein in 1995. Once a stalwart retailer of non-food merchandise in its retail stores, the company watched that segment of its business diminish dramatically in the wake of the 1994 Alaska Invasion. In response, the company heightened its focus on perishable products, specifically prepared foods and bakery products, installed an new bagel program, and in June 1995 began streamlining its financial and wholesale operations with the hope of saving as much as $500,000.

Future Growth

As Carr-Gottstein laid out plans for the late 1990s, its expansion plans were cut back, including its entry into Pacific Northwest markets, which was cancelled in the fall of 1995. Looking ahead, the company planned to bring in more perishable and specialty departments in order to maintain market share in the face of new competition from mass merchandisers, and also to devote resources to the development of a new cigarette and cigar retail chain launched in April 1996, the Great Alaska Tobacco Co. Growth in the future was expected to come from the expansion of the company's Eagle Quality Centers chain rather than from the establishment of additional Carrs Quality Centers, which required a much heavier investment. As the company headed into the late 1990s, a new leader was selected to steward the company's fortunes in the years ahead. In August 1996, Lawrence H. Hayward was named president and chief executive officer of Carr-Gottstein, succeeding Williams, who remained with the company as vice chairman. Hayward's twin

goals of accelerating growth and trimming debt promised to describe Carr-Gottstein's activities as the company moved toward the 21st century.

Principal Subsidiaries

AOL Express; APR Forwarders; J.B. Gottstein; YES Foods; CGF Properties, Inc.

Further Reading

Crispins, Jonna, "Carr's Fights Wholesale Clubs with Bulk Packs," *Supermarket News,* August 10, 1992, p. 40.

D'Innocenzio, Anne, "Carr Gottstein Planning Public Offering," *Supermarket News,* May 31, 1993, p. 7.

Fuerst, Judith, "Larry J. Carr," *Alaska Business Monthly,* January 1988, p. 8.

Scagliotti, Lisa, "Carr Gottstein Foods Co. Looks to Expand to Rural Alaskan Centers," *Knight-Ridder/Tribune Business News,* November 5, 1993, p. 11.

——, "Carr Gottstein to Slow Expansion," *Supermarket News,* May 27, 1996, p. 6.

Snyder, Glenn, "Fighting Back," *Progressive Grocer,* January 1995, p. 14.

Tibbitts, Lisa A., "Prepared in Alaska: Carr Gottstein Is Fending Off New Rivals by Putting an Emphasis on Fresh Foods," *Supermarket News,* June 5, 1995, p. 6A.

Woodring, Jeannie, "Carr-Gottstein Foods Co.: Supermarket Giant Stays on Course," *Alaska Business Monthly,* October 1991, p. 69.

Zweibach, Elliot, "Carr Gottstein's Growing Latitude," *Supermarket News,* August 23, 1993, p. 1.

——, "Carr Gottstein Taps Hayward as President," *Supermarket News,* August 12, 1996, p. 1.

—Jeffrey L. Covell

Champion Enterprises, Inc.

2701 University Drive, Suite 320
Auburn Mills, Michigan 48236
U.S.A.
(810) 340-9090
Fax: (810) 340-935

Public Company
Incorporated: 1953 as Champion Home Builders, Co.
Employees: 5,000
Sales: $798 million (1995)
Stock Exchanges: New York Chicago Pacific
SICs: 2451 Mobile Homes; 3713 Truck & Bus Bodies;
6719 Holding Companies, Not Elsewhere Classified

One of the fastest growing companies in the manufactured housing industry, Champion Enterprises, Inc. manufactures homes that are sold in more than 90 percent of the United States and in western Canada and manufactures a line of mid-size buses, which are sold to municipalities, hotels, hospitals, rental car agencies and other businesses. During the mid-1990s, Champion ranked as the second-largest manufactured home company in the United States, supported by 31 production facilities and a network of 2,000 independent dealers. After reorganizing in 1990, the company began its resolute rise in the manufactured housing industry, more than tripling its sales volume during a five-year span and quickly climbing the industry's rankings. Already recognized as one of the industry's fastest growing companies midway through the 1990s, Champion elevated its stature substantially in 1996 when it merged with the country's third-largest manufactured home company, Dallas, Texas-based Redman Industries, Inc. The merger, once completed, was expected to increase Champion's annual revenue volume to more than $1 billion, add 18 manufacturing facilities, and bolster its independent dealer network by 1,400.

Early History of Mobile Home Industry

Founded in 1953, Champion began business shortly before the mobile home industry in the United States underwent a revolutionary change and blossomed into maturity. With roots stretching back to the 1920s, when mobile homes first began to emerge, the mobile home industry spent the first three decades of its existence struggling in obscurity, desperately trying to spark widespread demand for the products a handful of manufacturers produced. Initially, mobile home manufacturers subsisted on sales to migratory workers such as farm workers and heavy construction workers, whose nomadic life-styles were perfectly suited to the two chief attractions of mobile homes: freedom of movement and affordability. Although migratory workers were not the only purchasers of mobile homes, they did account for the bulk of the industry's sales and, consequently, limited the potential of the industry's future expansion since such workers represented only a trifling percentage of the nation's population. Accordingly, for the first several decades of its existence, the mobile home industry appeared destined to remain a relatively insignificant industry on a national scale, its growth kept in check by serving customers without sufficient purchasing power to launch manufacturers toward exponentially higher sales volumes.

The mobile home industry and manufacturers like Champion were destined for greater prominence and wealth, however. The first signs of the industry's coming growth emerged during the Second World War when the military turned to mobile home manufacturers to provide temporary and transportable housing for defense workers and soldiers. The wartime business gave manufacturers their first upswing in business and, perhaps more important, introduced a sizeable segment of the country's population to "homes on wheels." Once the war ended, business remained strong largely because America, in effect, had a standing army, a new social class of military personnel subject to the frequently itinerant demands of military life. This new facet of the country's social structure created a wealth of prospective customers for mobile home manufacturers, enabling the industry as a whole to generate more than $150 million in sales per year shortly after the conclusion of the Second World War.

Despite the welcomed infusion of business from the Second World War and its after effects, the industry was still several years away from reaching the pivotal moment in its history. That moment, the signal moment in the mobile home industry's development, arrived in 1956 with the introduction of "ten-

Company Perspectives:

"We are not a manufacturer of paper products, spark plugs, or sports apparel. We are not a bureaucracy and we do not focus on management fads. We have no fat. Our passion for quality and success is shared by each of our 5,000 employees at all levels of the company. Champion is a leader in manufactured housing and mid-size bus production. We are aggressive, profitable and growing every day.

wides.'' Until 1956, the size of mobile homes had varied considerably, but always in length and never in width. Every mobile home produced measured eight feet in width to conform to the maximum width permissible by law for vehicles on highways. In 1956, the law changed and manufacturers began producing 10-foot-wide mobile homes, or ''ten-wides,'' forever changing the magnitude and the dynamics of the mobile home industry. The introduction of wider mobile homes was important not only because ten-wides quickly supplanted the production of eight-foot-wide models—representing 85 percent of the industry's total production four years after their introduction—but also because of what the immediate popularity of ten-wides taught mobile home executives. As sales of ten-wides rose sharply after their debut, it rapidly became apparent to manufacturers that mobility was not the primary selling point of mobile homes. Instead, affordability was their distinguishing quality, and manufacturers at last discovered a widespread, national need their mobile homes could fulfill: a dramatically cheaper alternative to traditional housing. As part of this discovery manufacturers realized their business had less to do with the automotive industry and more to do with the construction industry. Though its was just beginning in the mid-1950s, this change in the mindset of manufacturers precipitated the transformation of the mobile home industry into the manufactured home industry and touched off financial growth that would enable the mobile home industry to collect more than $8 billion annually during the 1990s.

Champion Founded in 1953

Champion, incorporated as Champion Home Builders in Michigan three years before the introduction of ten-wides, began business at a propitious time, joining the fray just before the industry was to grow significantly during the late 1950s and 1960s. The company tapped into the prosperous economic conditions promptly and effectively, taking little time to climb the industry's rankings to hold sway as one of the country's elite mobile home manufacturers. Shortly after completing its initial public offering in 1962, Champion was generating more than $30 million in sales annually and drawing praise from the business press for efficient and self-sufficient operations. By the mid-1960s, Champion ranked as one of the five largest manufacturers in the country, who together controlled roughly a third of the $1 billion market for mobile homes.

By the beginning of the 1970s, when annual sales flirted with the $100 million mark, Champion's reputation was solidly established. In its first decade-and-a-half of business, Champion had created an enviable degree of vertical integration that separated its from its rivals. Unlike many of its competitors, Champion manufactured and assembled every component and fixture included in a finished mobile home. From installing plumbing to producing its own roofing materials, Champion carried out everything on its own, manufacturing a wide spectrum of items that ranged from drapes, to furniture, down even to the bedsprings used in the beds. This high level of self-sufficiency enabled the company to achieve exemplary efficiency. Champion could produce one mobile home unit per week with the labor of only two workers, giving it a productivity ratio twice that of nearly all its competitors.

1970s Slump

Strongly positioned by its unique approach toward manufacturing mobile homes, Champion reaped the rewards to be gleaned from its burgeoning industry, registering enough success in its original business to diversify into the production of recreational vehicles and mini motor homes. As a result of its firmly established and extensive mobile operations and its promising subsidiary business, Champion's business was booming during the early 1970s, ranking as strong as any of its competitors, but nothing could protect the company from the disastrous affects of the mid-1970s. Just as the mobile home industry was recording an impressive string of sales gains and building a solid foundation, the bottom dropped out of the business, precipitated by the sudden onset of a national recession. Anemic economic conditions dealt a decisive blow to the industry nationwide, particularly to the handful of publicly-traded companies who stood atop the industry. Companies like Elkhart, Indiana's Skyline Homes, New York's Divco-Wayne Corp., Dallas' Redman Industries, and Champion, who together controlled roughly 30 percent of the national market, all suffered ills from the drastic downturn in business. Industry-wide, sales dropped to $2.5 billion in 1974 after exceeding $4 billion two years earlier, while unit shipments plunged 42 percent. Champion, not immune to the stifling economic climate, recorded a financial loss for the remainder of the decade, lagging behind the recovery of the industry which began in 1976.

For Champion, recovery from the adverse economic conditions during the mid-1970s came not from its mainstay business, but from strong sales generated by products other than mobile homes, specifically its line of recreational vehicles and low-priced mini motor homes. Gradually, however, Champion's mobile home business also began performing well once again, buoyed in part by the escalating prices of new homes, which leaped 61 percent during the mid-1970s. Given a choice between paying an average of $62,500 for new home or $15,000 for a new mobile home, more and more consumers either chose voluntarily or were forced by financial constraints to opt for the more affordable mobile homes. With its mobile home sales invigorated, Champion once again became a consistently profitable enterprise, recording a string of profitable years during the early and mid-1980s.

The recovery effected during the first half of the 1980s was only temporary, however, as the latter half of the decade saw Champion once again struggling to maintain its profitability. The company slipped into the red in 1986 and stayed there for the remainder of the decade. While annual sales totals fluttered between $303 million and $364 million during the late 1980s, the company's net income totals demonstrated more regularity: they consistently slipped downward. The company lost $1.4 million in 1987, $4.9 million in 1988, $7.2 million in 1989, and nearly $14 million 1990, the year Champion began its dramatic recovery.

Animated 1990s Growth

As yearly losses mounted, production facilities were shuttered, stripping the company of some of its manufacturing capability. In 1990, when the company appeared to be on the brink of insolvency, new management was brought in, led by Walter R. Young Jr., Champion's soon-to-be savior. Young, who was named president and chief executive officer, quickly made his presence felt, implementing a corporate restructuring program and shedding Champion's unprofitable operations. A chain of dealers owned by the company was divested, which transferred sales responsibilities to a network of aggressive, incentive-driven independent dealers, and the company exited the retail financial field, thereby limiting its credit operations to financing dealer inventories. In the wake of these changes, Champion climbed out of the red for the first time since 1985, registering a gain of $339,000 on sales of $288 million in 1991.

Profits climbed to more promising levels after the modest gain reported in 1991, as did the company's revenue volume, which for years had been declining as production facilities were dropped from the company's roster of manufacturing operations. The company had closed eight plants since 1986, but after five years of consolidating and decentralizing its operations, Champion found itself in the position to grow its business. After one last necessary divestiture—the company sold its money-losing recreational vehicle division in October 1992 to Firan Motor Coach, Inc. for $621,000—Champion began to expand its business after a lengthy hiatus. Ranking as the fourth-largest manufactured housing company in the country when it began its rise, Champion jumped on the acquisition and expansion track in 1993 when it announced it would pursue prudent acquisitions and invest $6 million to expand four production plants in Colorado, Idaho, and Nebraska, which was expected to increase the company's production capacity 20 percent.

As the company began to actively pursue growth, it did so with the reassurance that its expansion campaign was being launched from a solid financial foundation. After the modest profits recorded in 1991, the company's earnings doubled each year for the next three years, rising to $11.2 million by the end of 1993, by which time annual sales had increased to $341.9 million. On the heels of this encouraging growth, confidence was high at the company's headquarters, a sentiment expressed by Young when he explained to a reporter from *Crain's Detroit Business,* "We're pleased about our past, but more exited about our future." The company's future, or at least its progress for the ensuing several years, was highlighted by strengthening its core modular home business through acquisitions, such as the March 1994 acquisition of Dutch Housing Inc., an $85 million a year modular home manufacturer based in White Pigeon, Michigan. Other acquisitions followed in 1995, when Champion acquired Chandeleur Homes, Inc. and Crest Ridge Homes, Inc. in February, giving the company two businesses that catered to more price-conscious customers. In October, the company acquired Alberta, Canada-based New Horizon Manufactured Homes, Ltd., the addition of which complemented Champion's Moduline International subsidiary and its business of designing highly customized homes.

Once the acquisitions completed in 1995 were brought into the company's fold, Champion's geographic reach extended throughout 90 percent of the United States and into western Canada. By increasing the company's geographic scope and shifting focus toward higher-end products, Young had executed what indisputably was a remarkable comeback for Champion. By the end of 1995, sales reached $798 million, having more than tripled during the previous three years. The company's net income nearly tripled as well in two years, jumping from the $11 million posted in 1993 to $32 million in 1995. Flush with success, Young looked toward a banner year in 1996, mapping out ambitious expansion plans that were aimed at strengthening the company's number two market share of 8.5 percent. In February 1996, the company announced its would open two new plants and significantly expand three of its existing 23 plants. In May, the company's plans became grander with the announcement that it would open five new factories in 1997 and upgrade all of its existing plants. Several months later, however, these expansion plans were dwarfed by an announcement made in August that substantially narrowed the gap separating Champion and the largest manufactured housing company in the country, California-base, Fleetwood Enterprises, which controlled 21 percent of the national market.

On August 14, 1996, Champion announced its merger with the third largest manufactured housing company, Redman Industries, Inc. Based in Dallas, Texas, Redman operated 18 production facilities concentrated in the West, and relied on 1,400 independent dealers. When the merger was completed on October 24, 1996, Young noted the incredible boost the addition of Redman gave Champion on all fronts, declaring, "Today is a momentous day for us. Just five years ago, Champion had sales of less than $250 million annually. With the merger, our 1995 pro forma sales were $1.4 billion, and 1996 sales will be even higher. Our market capitalization has gone from less than $50 million in 1991, to more than $1 billion currently."

After the merger, Champion operated as a manufactured home company with 49 housing production facilities scattered throughout the country and an independent dealer network comprising more than 3,000 retail locations. Strengthened considerably by the absorption of Redman, Champion closed the gap separating it from Fleetwood Enterprises, with each company capable of generating commensurate sales volumes. As Champion prepared for the late 1990s and the beginning of the 21st century, it was intent on galloping past Fleetwood to firmly establish itself as the largest manufactured housing company in the United States.

Principal Subsidiaries

Champion Home Builders Company; Redman Industries, Inc.; Moduline International, Inc.; Dutch Housing, Inc.; Chandeleur Homes, Inc.; Crest Ridge homes, Inc.; Grand Manor, Inc.; Homes of Legend, Inc.; Champion Motor Coach, Inc.

Further Reading

Barkholz, David, "Firm's New Home: Buses," *Crain's Detroit Business,* December 6, 1993, p. 2.

——, "Turnaround Champion," *Crain's Detroit Business,* July 25, 1994, p. 8.

Byrne, Harlan S., "Champion Enterprises: Profits Return on Gains in Factory-built Housing," *Barron's,* April 15, 1991, p. 62.

"Champion Enterprises, Inc. and Redman Industries, Inc. Complete Merger," *PR Newswire,* October 24, 1996, p. 1.

Epstein, Joseph, "Home Cheap Home," *Financial World,* February 26, 1996, p. 48.

Goldenberg, Sherman, "Champion Has 1st Profitable Year Since '85," *RV Business,* June 17, 1991, p. 13.

Halliday, Jean, "Champion Moves HQ to Oakland," *Crain's Detroit Business,* April 6–12, 1992, p. 1.

——, "Champion Poised for More Improvement, Profits in 1993," *Crain's Detroit Business,* May 10, 1993, p. 15.

Pascual, Psyche, "Competitors' Possible merger May Force Changes at Fleetwood Enterprises," *Knight-Ridder/Tribune Business News,* August 21, 1996, p. 8.

Rose, Judy, "Auburn Hills, Mich., Manufactured-Home Builder Balloons in Size," *Knight-Ridder/Tribune Business News,* October 25, 1996, p. 10.

Shellum, Bernie, "Champion Enterprises to Build 5 Factories, Upgrade 27 Plants," *Knight-Ridder/Tribune Business News,* May 8, 1996, p. 5.

—Jeffrey L. Covell

Chart House Enterprises, Inc.

115 South Acacia Avenue
Solana Beach, California 92075-1803
U.S.A.
(619) 755-8281
Fax: (619) 481-0693

Public Company
Incorporated: 1985
Employees: 7,400
Sales: $179.2 million (1995)
Stock Exchanges: NASDAQ
SICs: 5812 Eating Places; 5461 Retail Bakeries; 6794
    Patent Owners & Lessors

Chart House Enterprises, Inc. is a parent company with one primary operating division: Chart House, Inc. In the mid-1990s, the Chart House division, which represented 85 percent of company revenues, consisted of 63 restaurants in 21 states, Puerto Rico and the U.S. Virgin Islands. The majority of Chart House Enterprises' other holdings were sold in 1995. In 1996, Chart House Enterprises, Inc. operated Chart House restaurants and the Solana Beach Baking Company, and held a 25 percent interest in Islands Restaurants.

Origins in the 1960s

The first Chart House restaurant opened as a steak house in Aspen, Colorado, on the Fourth of July, 1961. The upscale chain's rather humble beginning consisted of 14 tables and four bar stools in a converted diner, with charts on the tables, photographs on the walls, and an emphasis on quality dining. Behind the restaurant were the ideas of its two founders—Hawaiian surf legend Joey Cabell and former U.S. Navy frogman Buzzy Bent—and their $5,000 investment. By the first winter, the Chart House was a trendy and crowded dining spot, with nightly customers enjoying teriyaki steaks and artichokes. By 1963, Cabell and Bent opened a second restaurant on Pacific Coast Highway in Newport Beach, California. Additional

coastal locations were opened two years later, on Shelter Island in San Diego, and in nearby Coronado.

The Chart House opening in Coronado was a milestone in the restaurant's history. The opening involved reconstruction of the landmark Coronado Boat House, originally constructed in 1887 as a prototype for the renowned Hotel del Coronado. Until Chart House opted for the neglected site, the building seemed destined to slide into the Glorietta Bay. Chart House impressed the community and local historians by restoring the Victorian construction, which opened for patrons on November 17, 1968. Since that time, Chart House has continued to seek unusual or meaningful sites for its new restaurants, usually in the mountains or near the water.

In this early period, Joey Cabell opened his own Chart House in the islands and then backed out of the business to resume his professional surfing career. Replacing Cabell as Buzzy Bent's partner was Ron Smith, an old diving friend. Smith led the restaurant business through a period of rapid growth and expansion. By 1974, when he followed Bent into retirement, Smith had established Chart House restaurants throughout Southern California, the East Coast, and Hawaii, as a chain known for high quality food, special locations, and good service. Smith selected his own successor, CEO John Creed.

Growth in the 1970s and 1980s

In the mid-1970s, John Creed led Chart House through a period of growth and affluence. The company had plenty of cash and used it to expand and to acquire talented staff. The early 1980s were also successful for Chart House. In 1982, the restaurants earned $18.6 million, an increase over $8.7 million the previous year, with revenues increasing from $354.6 million to $382 million.

In 1983, the Chart House division lured PepsiCo executive Donald Smith to join Chart House Inc. in Lafayette, Louisiana, as chief executive officer. Smith replaced William Hyde, Jr., who became vice-chairman. At this time, Chart House, Inc. operated more than 500 steak, hamburger, barbecue and Mexican restaurants in 32 states, Puerto Rico and the Virgin Islands, and was the largest single franchisee of Pillsbury Co.'s Burger

Company Perspectives:

Chart House Enterprises, Inc. operates 63 Chart House Restaurants. Chart House restaurants are full-service, casual dinner houses with menus featuring fresh fish, steaks, prime rib, seafood, pasta dishes and chicken, and as much salad and bread as the customer desires. The menu is offered in architecturally or historically unique buildings located in a variety of settings, including lake shores, mountains, and seacoasts.

King restaurants, and a franchiser of Luther's Bar-B-Que, a successful "concept" restaurant. With a reputation for empire-building, Smith went to work right away, expanding the Chart House domain. That same year, Chart House, Inc. acquired a 40 percent stake in Godfather's (valued at over $300 million), a national chain of about 800 pizza restaurants.

Almost a decade later, the company continued expanding. Chart House Enterprises obtained the rights to develop and operate Islands restaurants—a 20-unit Southern California gourmet burger chain with a tropical theme. In a forty-year licensing agreement, Chart House promised to develop a minimum of 50 Islands restaurants during the first 12 years, in San Diego, Phoenix, Tucson, Florida, and Hawaii. Chart House paid no upfront fee to Islands but agreed to pay two percent royalties based on restaurant sales. Two new low- and medium-priced restaurants, Mango's and Beaches, were opened experimentally under the licensing agreement. However, the late 1980s and early 1990s held difficult surprises for Chart House.

Difficulties in the Late 1980s and Early 1990s

The national economic recession and the reduction of tourism during the Persian Gulf war brought reduced earnings for Chart House. Between 1987 and 1988, earnings per share had leapt from 44 cents to $1.08, but the next year earnings dropped to 76 cents. In 1991, shares came in at 55 cents, as compared to 80 cents a share the previous year. Revenues, however, continued to grow, creeping up from $133 to $154 million between 1987 and 1990, with an increase in net income from $2.2 million to $6.5 million between those years.

To attend to stock price concerns, a five-year growth plan was stalled, with restaurant openings cut back from a planned seven to an actual two in 1990. Further, through the Islands agreement and lowered prices, Chart House sought to broaden appeal and recoup earnings. By 1994, stock prices had risen. In 1995, no new Chart House restaurants were opened, and three were closed— Idyllwild, California; St. Croix, U.S. Virgin Islands; and Warwick, Rhode Island. However, seven new Islands restaurants were opened in 1995. Revenues increased from $175 million in 1994 to $180 million in 1995, with newly opened Islands restaurants representing a $9 million increase in revenue, offset by decreased customers at Chart House restaurants.

Further change visible in Chart House restaurants in the 1990s was reflected in menu offerings. Since its opening as a

steak house in 1961, the restaurant had retained an emphasis on red meat, with seafood providing variety. In 1994, prime rib was the best single-item seller, but swordfish was quite popular, as the best-selling seafood item, and a new aioli seafood sauce with pineapple-cucumber salsa was frequently requested. Changes were made to the menu in that year, through experiments with several non-seafood items: chicken Marsala, centercut pork chop, baby back ribs, and tomato and basil pasta. Chart House used its Coronado location, an upscale seafood restaurant named Peohe's, for menu tests. By 1995, the typical Chart House restaurant was a full-service, casual dinner house with a menu featuring fresh fish, steaks, prime rib, seafood, pasta and chicken, with bottomless salad and bread bowls. In addition, several Chart Houses featured extensive salad bars with appetizer selections.

1995: A Turning Point

In 1995, Chart House was in trouble. The fiscal year ended with profits down 38 percent to only $2.66 million from $24.29 million the previous year. Sales, however, rose 2.4 percent, to $179.16 million. Management was determined to reorganize company resources, and an executive decision was made to reemphasize Chart House's central division. Through diversification, the company had lost focus, and many premier locations had deteriorated through time and hard use. Chart House initiated sales of all but its flagship division, in order to fully concentrate on restoring its quality and profitability. Paradise Bakery was sold in 1995, and an agreement was made to sell a 75 percent interest in Islands restaurants. To further enhance the new direction and initiate a significant change in leadership, Chart House's CEO John Creed brought in Harry Roberts, a former Starbucks Coffee Company executive and proven marketer, as president and chief operating officer. A five-part strategic plan was employed, consisting of the following components: 1) a four-year revitalization program, allocating substantial cash resources (approximately $700,000 each) to rejuvenation of all 63 Chart House restaurants, including quality controls and menu expansion; 2) a new menu, which debuted in Cincinnati in April 1996; 3) for the first time, a real marketing effort, comprising two percent of annual sales, including the Aloha Club (a frequent diner program which was launched in 1993), in-unit promotions, and local/regional advertising campaigns; 4) a campaign to reduce overhead below eight percent of revenues by the end of 1997; and 5) the strengthening of management, as exemplified by the hiring of Harry Roberts and the promotion of Bill Kuntz to executive vice-president. Restructuring cost the company $4.85 million in fiscal 1995, incurring a $1.51 million loss in the 1995 fourth quarter. The total reimaging campaign required an investment of $44 million.

A goal of the multi-tiered revitalization project was to ensure that Chart House restaurants maintained a high-level profile as classy dining establishments. Harry Roberts told *Nation's Restaurant News* that Chart House viewed its desired competitors as Ruth's Chris, Morton's, and independent steak houses—not the Outbacks of the world. To ensure a sophisticated image, Roberts began to look at replacement of Hawaiian themes and salad bars, preferring a "yacht club" look: wood-fired ovens in the bars and new menu items including tiger shrimp beignets, lobster cakes, grilled artichokes and designer pizzas. Perhaps the most controversial upgrade was the phasing out of Chart House's signature salad bars, a favorite of some longtime patrons. To please these customers, Chart House decided to offer unlimited "just ask" refills on a la carte salads. As part of the revitalization, Joseph Mayhew, Jr. was named director of food service, overseeing new menu item development and service. Mayhew is a graduate of the Culinary Institute of America in Hyde Park, New York.

In addition to food overhauls, alcoholic beverage service became a concern of Chart House in 1995. To attract larger bar checks, the restaurant began to offer premium and super-premium scotches and bourbons and special-label wines. Further, the restaurants updated their specialty drinks, redecorated their bars with new glassware, eye-level beverage displays, and television monitors showing sports and travel videos. To ensure the safety of patrons, Chart House accompanied these alcohol promotions with a message on its menu reminding patrons to appoint a designated driver. The changes in the restaurant's alcohol service were successful in generating a 16 percent increase in alcohol sales (the equivalent of $700,000 in one year).

1996 and Beyond

Such traditional Chart House menu items as steak, prime rib, and fish (all priced over $20), appealed to a customer base that was aging and diminishing rapidly. To market the restaurant to new, younger customers, in 1996, several price-friendly items (under $20) were added to the menus. New items geared to changing palates included such pasta-based selections as prawns and garlic steak on linguine, lobster and monkfish on spinach fettuccine, and a grilled portobello mushroom on fettuccine. The menu expansion was undertaken with the advice of Matteson & Co., a Foster City, California, consulting firm.

In early 1996, Chart House struck a deal to sell its Paradise Bakery division for about $7 million in stock and notes. In April of that year, Chart House sold a 75 percent stake in its ownership of Islands to two affiliated companies formed by Islands Restaurants L.P. These sales were part of the strategy to concentrate on Chart House's main division—Islands units accrued unit volumes of about $1.8 million with average checks of $7 per person, while the typical Chart House customer spent closer to $30 to bring unit volumes to $2.3 million. Several underperforming Chart House locations were shuttered, and a member of the corporate staff was furloughed. In all, these actions comprised an effort to shave $3 million off general and administrative expenses.

Meanwhile, unit renovation was a costly enterprise. The prototype remodeling venture was the Chart House's Malibu location, completed in 1996 at a cost of $1.2 million. The restaurant's former tropical theme was replaced with nautical decor, including raised booths with ocean views, custom hand-blown glass light fixtures, a wood-fired oven, and a new cook line and products. An additional—and somewhat ironic—problem in 1996 was the unexpected success of the Aloha Club frequent diner program. The program offered a free trip for two around the world to anyone who ate their way through every Chart House restaurant. By 1996, a surprising 50 customers complied, and Chart House's travel department was swamped with planning activities from snorkeling in Australia to sight-

seeing in New Zealand. Because of such expense and time for logistical planning, Chart House began rethinking the Aloha Club program.

Having strengthened its basic Chart House division, the company sought to expand once again, opening its first Midwestern Chart House in Cincinnati in April 1996. By May, the Cincinnati location had generated sales 40 percent higher than the chain's average ($2.5 million per location).

In 1996, after more than 20 years in office, John Creed resigned as chief executive officer to pursue personal interests, and Harry Roberts became CEO. Roberts continued the move toward reimaging Chart House, hiring Douglas Zeif—former number two executive of the Cheesecake Factory—as senior vice-president of concept development. Zeif had successfully opened more than 60 restaurants in his career. A new logo and brand identity were designed, symbolizing the break with the past and the new emphasis on revitalization. The new logo, graphically stronger than the old one, displayed a burgee, or swallow-tailed flag used by ships or nautical organizations for signals or identification. Individual burgee flags were developed for each restaurant, with unique symbols for each location borne on menus, clothing, stationery and even china.

The mid- to late-1990s, then, signify a turning point for Chart House. Having built a successful restaurant empire that peaked and then crashed in the late 1980s and early 1990s, the refocusing of the company's resources on its central division offers a strategy for survival. With the new corporate leadership and a different economy, it remains to be seen whether the Chart House of the 1990s will resume its former popularity. For its part, Chart House Enterprises is plunging forward with a strengthened corporate identity, diversified menu, more sophisticated marketing campaign, and newly refurbished restaurants.

Principal Subsidiaries

Chart House, Inc.; Solano Beach Baking Company.

Further Reading

"Acquisitions," *Nation's Restaurant News,* December 19, 1994, pp. 88, 92.

Allen, Robin Lee, "Operators Tap Value Promos to Brew up Sales," *Nation's Restaurant News,* March 20, 1995, p. 64.

Alva, Marilyn, "Have Frequent Diner Plans Become Frequent Headaches?" *Restaurant Business,* July 1, 1996, p. 16.

Carlino, Bill, "Chart House Sells 75% of Islands for $23M," *Nation's Restaurant News,* April 1, 1996, p. 3.

——, "Chart House to Abandon Islands, Focus on Flagship," *Nation's Restaurant News,* January 1, 1996, p. 3.

——, "Reel 'Em in with Broader Menus," *Nation's Restaurant News,* April 4, 1994, pp. 47–52.

Chart House Magazine, May 1996, Solano Beach, Calif.: Chart House Enterprises, Inc.

——, August 1996, Solano Beach, Calif.: Chart House Enterprises, Inc.

"Chart House: Restaurateur Spots Recovery Signs," *Barron's,* January 27, 1992, pp. 42–43.

"Firm Obtains Some Rights for Developing Restaurants," *Wall Street Journal,* November 29, 1991, p. A3C.

"Godfather's to Be Acquired by Chart House," *Wall Street Journal,* September 13, 1983, p. 6.

Guyon, Janet, "Pepsi Is Losing Fast-Food Whiz to Chart House," *Wall Street Journal*, May 13,

Hume, Scott, "Now It's Big Mac; Next, Spoons?" *Advertising Age*, August 22, 1983, pp. 3, 44.

Prewitt, Milford, "Restaurant Stocks Take Beating in 1st Q.," *Nation's Restaurant News*, April 25, 1994, pp. 7, 66.

"Union of Chart House, Godfather's Is Revised; Final Accord Signed," *Wall Street Journal*, October 24, 1983, p. 48.

Zuber, Amy, "Chart House Broadens Menu with Under-$20 Selections," *Nation's Restaurant News*, November 6, 1995, pp. 3, 7.

——, "Starbucks Vet Sets New Course at Chart House," *Nation's Restaurant News*, May 20, 1996, pp. 3, 26.

—Heidi Feldman

Chattem, Inc.

1715 West 38th Street
Chattanooga, Tennessee 37409
U.S.A.
(423) 821-4571
Fax: (423) 821-0395

Public Company
Incorporated: 1879
Employees: 400
Sales: $100.6 million (1995)
Stock Exchanges: NASDAQ
SICs: 2834 Pharmaceutical Preparations; 2844 Toilet
  Preparations; 2869 Industrial Organic Chemicals, Not
  Elsewhere Classified

Chattem, Inc. manufactures and markets a diverse array of brand name pharmaceuticals, toiletries, and cosmetic items. Focusing on smaller product lines that it can market without competing directly against other giant companies in the business, Chattem has had a successful history in helping such products flourish. Over the years, it has manufactured and promoted over-the-counter drugs such as Pamprin, Premsyn PMS, and Norwich Aspirin; analgesics such as Flex-all 454, Icy Hot, and Benzodent; toiletries such as Sun-In Hair Lightener, Ultraswim Shampoo, Bullfrog Sunblock, MUDD Facial Masque, and pHisoderm; and the Corn Silk, Quenchers, and Baby Soft cosmetics lines. Chattem distributes its products across the United States, Canada, Europe, and throughout numerous other international markets.

The Early Years

Chattem's beginnings can be traced to the year 1879, when a small business called the Chattanooga Medicine Company was created to produce and sell Black-Draught, a senna-based laxative. The product had been invented almost half a decade earlier by a doctor who sold it from the back of a covered wagon through a small enterprise called the Dr. A.Q. Simmons Liver Medicine Company. Black-Draught had sold well in the southern United States until the Civil War, but struggled thereafter. It was then that Z.C. Patten purchased all rights to Black-Draught

from Dr. Simmons's son-in-law and founded the Chattanooga Medicine Company to market the product.

With the help of four other Chattanooga businessmen, Patten began an aggressive marketing plan to boost sales of Black-Draught. He used letters of endorsement from satisfied customers to create a stronger trade base in the southern states and, in doing so, posted first year sales of $35,488. This success prompted Patten and his partners to expand their product line; therefore, a menstrual relief product for women called Dr. McElree's Wine of Cardui was introduced in 1880. To maintain the company's building reputation for quality, the new product was delivered to customers with the agreement that they would pay for it only if fully satisfied with its results. Wine of Cardui immediately became successful, as more than 6,500 women reported cures and sent payment to the company for an initial shipment of 7,000 bottles.

With both of its products becoming huge regional successes, the Chattanooga Medicine Company soon implemented a sales force to cover its expanding territories and combat the effects of the slow distribution characteristic of the horse and buggy era. This effort helped the company enter into new areas of the country, where consumers quickly accepted its products. According to the company's historical information, customers were so pleased with the new products that their subsequent communications to the company were massive, and the Chattanooga Medicine Company "quickly became the largest generator of mail in the Chattanooga area and was assigned its own government-paid post office on the premises." Using this resource, the company launched a massive print advertising campaign, which included the distribution of items such as flyers, wall calendars, almanacs, and even songbooks for churchgoers. The prevalence of these items ensured that the company's product names were constantly in the eyes of the public, a tactic that aided in the Chattanooga Medicine Company's rapid growth throughout its early years.

The Early 1900s: A New Era for the Chattanooga Medicine Company

In 1881, an Arkansas crop failure left many of the company's clients unable to pay for the products being shipped to them. Furthermore, two separate fires and a flood in the early

Company Perspectives:

Chattem Consumer Products' mission is the satisfaction of consumer needs in personal and health care areas through the marketing of brand name products which are of excellent quality and proven efficacy. These products are promoted through the national media and are distributed through the mass distribution channels of food, drug and general merchandisers. The objective is to create or maintain a leadership position in each of our domestic markets and to thereby provide superior earnings while also building the value of each brand.

1890s left the company headquarters in near-ruins three different times. Although the company was doing well enough to expand in 1893 to include a branch office in St. Louis, Patten's business partners became uneasy and sold their shares in the company to his nephews, John A. Patten and Zeboim Carter Patten. The two brothers began running the business as partners in 1906, just five years after the Chattanooga Medicine Company had grown to include a second branch office in San Francisco. The company's sales throughout the country were booming, and in the following year Wine of Cardui surpassed the $1 million mark in annual sales.

Unfortunately, John A. Patten died unexpectedly in 1916 at the age of 48, leaving his brother to operate the business alone. Before his death, John A. Patten had not only played a key role in the company's successful use of billboard and print advertising, but had also engineered the company's entrance into the export business on an international scale. His efforts had introduced the company to a great deal of success and affluence, and his death was a huge blow to its continued growth potential. Although his brother did an excellent job in helping the company survive the effects of the Depression, the Chattanooga Medicine Company's growth was stagnant for many years. In 1938, Zeboim Carter Patten passed the modest operation on to his nephew, Lupton Patten, who at age 31 became the youngest president in the company's almost 60-year history.

Lupton Patten immediately began to modernize the company, adding new automated machinery and equipment to the packaging plants and branch offices. He also began using the services of numerous advertising and consulting firms, which resulted in both the creation of the company's own research program and its entrance into the specialty chemicals business. The company began developing specialized chemical products that it could sell to other manufacturers for use in their own consumer products, and this helped generate more annual earnings. The company also got a boost when it was called upon to produce foods and medicines for the U.S. Army during World War II. In addition to the manufacture of its own consumer products, the company actually produced more than 34 million packets of K-rations for U.S. troops. During this time, the company's newly formed research division was continually faced with the need to alter its own products when traditional ingredients became unavailable. The company achieved record earnings during those years nonetheless and was left in excellent financial condition at the conclusion of the war.

Post-World War II Restructuring and Expansion

After the war ended, the company was restructured to include two main operating divisions: the consumer products division and the specialty chemicals division. The consumer products division was responsible for the production and distribution of the company's many food and drug products, and the specialty chemicals division focused mainly on research and development and continued supplying chemical ingredients for other manufacturer's products as well as its own. For example, research and experimentation during the war years led to the creation of a liquid form of Black-Draught, as well as to different aluminum compounds that became important ingredients in other companies' antacids, such as Rolaids.

Then in 1958, in what seemed to be an emerging family and company trend, Lupton Patten also died unexpectedly at the early age of 51. The company's operations were left to his nephew, Alex Guerry, who spent the next decade altering the Chattanooga Medicine Company's financial structure to provide it with greater growth potential. After a decade had passed and the company had continued to prosper in the specialty chemicals realm, he realized that the company's name did not accurately reflect the businesses with which it was involved at that point in time. Therefore, Guerry called for a corporate name change in 1968, and the company became the Chattem Drug and Chemical Company. The following year, Chattem sold its stock in a public offering, which was the first time that the company's stock had been openly available to outsiders.

Guerry then led the company in acquiring several other small businesses, whose products soon supplemented Chattem's own. The first major acquisition was the DePree Company of Michigan, a health and beauty care business that was a successful addition to the consumer products division. That purchase was followed by the addition of the Petrochemicals Company of Texas to Chattem's specialty chemicals division. Meanwhile, Chattem continued to create and market its own successful products. Pamprin, a women's menstrual pain relief medicine, had been introduced in 1962 to take the place of Wine of Cardui, and by 1970 was one of Chattem's leading products.

It was in the mid-1970s that Chattem made a move that became characteristic of its business procedure for many years to come. It began purchasing the rights to small or struggling product lines from other companies, with the intent to help the products flourish by marketing them in small product niches where there would be little competition from the other giant companies in the industry. Within a five-year time period, Chattem acquired Sun-In Hair Lightener, MUDD Facial Masque, and the Corn Silk cosmetics line. The adoption of these products marked Chattem's entrance into the cosmetics and toiletries business, once again rendering the company name an incomplete representation of its business ventures. Therefore, in 1979 the company became Chattem, Inc., a designation that more aptly reflected its rapidly expanding scope of business.

Acquisitions Throughout the 1980s

Chattem's newly acquired products responded positively to the increased advertising and distribution that they received from their new owner, and sales began to rise almost immediately. Therefore, Chattem continued the acquisition trend with the 1980 purchase of Love's Fragrances, a perfume line targeted at teenagers, and the 1983 purchase of Quencher cosmetics. Along with the addition of a liquid form of makeup to the Corn Silk product line, Chattem hoped to round out its cosmetics offerings with the new purchases. Unfortunately, although both products performed adequately for Chattem, neither one possessed the growth potential the company was seeking. As a result, both product lines were sold to outside suitors by 1985. The company also divested its original acquisitions, DePree and Petrochemicals. The consumer products division was still expanding steadily, however, and for the first time ever it began to surpass the specialty chemicals division in annual profits.

The success of Chattem's consumer products division was further bolstered by the 1985 acquisition of Nullo Deodorant tablets and the 1986 acquisitions of Bullfrog waterproof sunblock and Ultraswim chlorine removal shampoo. As with most of its other successful products, these items demanded only small amounts of retail shelf space, due to the fact that they were single products that did not have large line extensions. This helped Chattem convince many stores with limited shelf space to carry its products and made it possible for the company to market the majority of its products nationwide. On the rare occasions when Chattem did extend one of its product lines, it was done to gain a stronger customer base by tailoring the product to the demands of the consumers. For example, in 1988 Chattem added two new variations of its Sun-In Hair Lightener product to store shelves when it unveiled ''Gentle Highlights'' and ''Natural Lemon'' Sun-In. The gentle variety was targeted at younger first-time users, and ''Natural Lemon'' was a means of capturing reluctant clientele.

The year 1989 saw Chattem achieve one of its largest acquisitions with the purchase of Flex-all 454 topical analgesic. At the time of the purchase, Flex-all 454 averaged less than $1 million in annual sales. Chattem immediately launched an extensive $5 million advertising and distribution campaign (the company's largest ever), including television and print advertisements featuring football great Joe Namath. These efforts were incredibly successful, and within a year the product achieved more than $10 million in sales. These new profits were supplemented by the retail sales of another 1989 acquisition, Norwich Aspirin, and together the new products helped Chattem achieve a whopping 27.3 percent return on equity in 1990.

The 1990s and Beyond

After guiding Chattem through some of its most defining years, Alex Guerry died in 1990 and left control of the company to his son, Zan Guerry. Noting the positive results that years of successful product acquisitions had produced, Guerry immediately began negotiating a deal to purchase Icy Hot brand topical analgesic from Procter & Gamble. The transaction was finalized by mid-1991, at which point Chattem had become known as a ''guerrilla marketer,'' defined in a 1991 edition of *The Insiders'*

Chronicle as ''the ability to 'pick a niche and dominate it.' '' The purchase of Icy Hot increased Chattem's share of the market for topical analgesics used to relieve sore muscles to 16 percent.

Meanwhile, Chattem was successfully dominating other product niches as well. Sales of Pamprin had combined with sales of a more recent product, Premsyn PMS, to help Chattem control more than 40 percent of the menstrual symptom relief market. Similarly, the company's Corn Silk cosmetics line was a leader in the oil-absorbent makeup category. When purchased by Chattem, all of these products had been struggling to reach the million dollar mark in sales each year. Years of boosted marketing support, however, had enabled each of them to contribute multimillion dollar sales figures to the company's earnings by the early 1990s.

In 1991 Chattem's specialty chemicals division enjoyed a 45 percent increase in sales, even though the United States' chemical process industries in general experienced decreases. The increase was attributed by some to the fact that Chattem's specialty chemicals division was a leading producer and patent holder of different aluminum compounds that were necessary in the production of many other companies' products. The success of its specialty chemicals division helped Chattem achieve its first $100 million sales year in history and prompted the company to expand itself even further by opening a 1.3 million-share secondary offering of its stock to the public in 1992.

It was not until 1994 that Chattem made another notable acquisition, when it added two new products to its consumer products division: pHisoderm facial cleanser and Benzodent oral analgesic. Chattem's continued emphasis on consumer products expansion then prompted an even more notable 1994 event, as the company decided to put its specialty chemicals division up for sale. The decision was a reflection of the company's desire to focus solely on its consumer products division, which at that point accounted for almost 90 percent of Chattem's yearly income. The specialty chemicals division was purchased by the privately held Elcat Company of New Jersey for $25 million, and the sale was finalized by mid-1995. Elcat then maintained both the division's operations and its name of Chattem Chemicals. Without its specialty chemicals division, Chattem continued its consumer products acquisition process with the purchase of rights to Gold Bond Medicated Powder in early 1996.

After growing from a covered wagon peddler of laxative in the 1800s to a multimillion dollar conglomerate whose products were being distributed worldwide, Chattem entered the late 1990s with the desire and potential to expand further its product offerings and distribution territory. By 1996, Chattem was producing and marketing name-brand products such as Pamprin, Premsyn PMS, Norwich Aspirin, Sun-In, Ultraswim Shampoo and Conditioner, Bullfrog Sunblock, Flex-all 454, Icy Hot, Benzodent, pHisoderm, MUDD Facial Masque, Corn Silk, and Gold Bond Medicated Powder. With a continually increasing list of successful product offerings, and with sales divisions already operating in the United States, Canada, and Europe, Chattem seemed to possess the resources to achieve its goals.

Principal Subsidiaries

Chattem Consumer Products; Chattem International; Chattem (U.K.) Limited; Chattem (Canada) Inc.; HBA Insurance Limited; Signal Investment & Management Co.

Further Reading

Butts, Joan T., "Chattem Nurtures Small Brands to Success," *Soap/Cosmetics/Chemical Specialties,* March 1984, p. 30.

Byrne, Harlan S., "Chattem Inc.: It Scores With Product Lines Bigger Marketers Shun," *Barron's,* August 17, 1992, p. 34.

The Chattem, Inc. History and Background, Chattanooga, Tenn.: Chattem, Inc., 1996.

"Chattem, Inc.," *The Insiders' Chronicle,* September 2, 1985, p. 2.

Mehlman, William, " 'Guerrilla Marketing' Widens Chattem's Product Niches," *The Insiders' Chronicle,* September 30, 1991, p. 1.

"Namath Backs Flex-All," *Advertising Age,* October 30, 1989, p. 60.

Plishner, Emily S., "Profits Continue To Sink, Except for Downstream Operations," *Chemical Week,* March 4, 1992, p. 20.

Schnorbus, Paula, "Grey Matters," *Marketing & Media Decisions,* February 1988, p. 113.

Wood, Andrew, "Fine Chemicals: Chattem Sells Specialties Business," *Chemical Week,* June 7, 1995, p. 18.

—Laura E. Whiteley

The Cheesecake Factory Inc.

26950 Agoura Road
Calabasas Hills, California 91301
U.S.A.
(818) 880-9323
Fax: (818) 880-6501

Public Company
Incorporated: 1978
Employees: 3,100
Sales: $117.2 million (1995)
Stock Exchanges: NASDAQ
SICs: 5812 Eating Places

The Cheesecake Factory Inc. manages a mid-priced, casual dining restaurant chain known for its elegant interiors and its diverse menu. Customers often wait up to two hours for a table in order to select from some 200 items on its 18-page menu, including more than 40 kinds of cheesecake. As of the middle of 1996, the company operated 16 restaurants in seven states and the District of Columbia. Cheesecake Factory leads the industry with its individual restaurants averaging sales of over $8 million a year. Through its bakery subsidiary, Great World Foods, Inc., the company produces cheesecakes and other desserts at a state-of-the-art baking facility in Calabasas Hills, California. These are sold by mail-order and to other restaurants, supermarket chains, and discount stores. Revenues for 1995, from restaurant sales and sales of bakery goods, totaled $117 million.

Early History

Cheesecake first appeared in Greece at least 2000 years ago and was originally made with cottage cheese. By the 1950s, when Evelyn Overton began making cheesecake in her basement in Detroit, cream cheese was the main ingredient. Evelyn's cheesecakes proved so popular with her friends and at bake sales that she and her husband, Oscar, started a bakery business. In 1972, the Overtons moved to the Woodland Hills suburb of Los Angeles and built a wholesale bakery, producing cheesecakes and other desserts for local restaurants.

In 1978, with backing from his parents, David Overton opened a small salad and sandwich shop in Beverly Hills featuring 10 flavors of the Overton's cheesecakes on its one-page menu. "We were completely naive about food service," Overton told Milford Prewitt in a 1995 article in *Nation's Restaurant News*. "We simply wanted to open a restaurant that would showcase our cheesecakes. At that time, most restaurateurs were using every excuse to explain why they could not carry our product, including expenses."

The 1980s

Evelyn's cheesecakes proved popular with California diners, and in 1983, Overton opened a second restaurant, in Marina del Rey. By 1987 the Beverly Hills shop had grown to a 78-seat restaurant and was grossing $3 million a year, even without a bar area, with diners spending an average of $8 for dinner. The Marina del Rey location had a bar and combined indoor and outdoor seating for 270 people. With average checks of $11, that location grossed over $8 million in 1987. In fact, annual sales were increasing by 15 percent a year, and Overton opened a third restaurant, in Redondo Beach, south of Los Angeles. The company spent $2 million renovating the location into a 21,000 square foot, 300-seat restaurant. The new unit was located on the waterfront at King's Harbor, a popular tourist destination.

The chain's one-page menu had expanded, offering items ranging from pizza to meatloaf to omelets to chicken tacos to baby back pork ribs. In the Marina Del Rey kitchen, three prep cooks worked full-time, and separate lines handled broiling, sautéing, frying, and the oyster bar. However, the specialty of the house continued to be cheesecake—fresh banana cream, Southern pecan, Craig's crazy carrot cake, brownie fudge—with 42 varieties baked at the company's facility in Woodland Hills. Despite diets and health consciousness, 70 to 80 percent of Cheesecake Factory customers ordered dessert.

In a 1987 *Restaurant Business* article, Marina del Ray general manager Douglas Zeif told Dolores Long, "Dessert sales boost our check average by about 15 percent. We're just the opposite of most other dinner houses that don't promote desserts because they're anxious to turn the tables. But we want

Company Perspectives:

We draw on a number of key elements—value, large portions, delicious food and beautiful decor. . . . These elements all come together to create an experience that is truly unique to the industry.

everybody eating cheesecake; the profit margin on this item is between 65 and 70 percent for us.''

To encourage such behavior in health-conscious California, work shifts received incentives for the most cheesecake orders, especially for seasonal or special flavors, as well as for daily specials and new menu items. While the company introduced new flavors of cheesecake, strawberry was the favorite, followed by white chocolate raspberry truffle, chocolate mousse cheese, white chocolate macadamia, and chocolate chip.

Although it concentrated on its restaurants, the company also sold a limited number of cheesecake flavors (chocolate chip, lemon twist) at the retail level. Customers included major restaurant chains in Southern California, such grocery store chains as Kroger's and Dominick's Finer Foods in Chicago, and food warehouse companies such as the Price Club in San Diego.

Cheesecake Factory's success directly contrasted with the country's eating habits. According to MRCA Information Services, which monitored in-home and away-from-home eating patterns, the total consumption of cheesecake in the United States fell a huge 27 percent between 1987 and 1988, with the big loser being the ''plain'' cheesecake.

1990 to 1994

Overton began the decade by opening his fourth restaurant, at the Warner Center in Woodland Hills, California. In 1991, the chain took its successful concept across the continent, to Washington, D.C., for its first restaurant outside Southern California. The new location, in the fashionable Chevy Chase section of the District, followed the formula Overton described to Michael Hartnett in a 1993 *Restaurant Business* article: ''Scour large metropolitan areas to find 'trophy sites' offering high visibility, easy access, and close proximity to traffic-builders like shopping centers and tourist attractions.'' Overton built his restaurants to seat between 250 and 750 people and designed them to fit the individual site, incorporating the view if there was one, or, if there wasn't, adding architectural features such as sweeping staircases and dramatic lighting. The average cost for a new location, not counting the land, was $250 to $350 per square foot.

In 1992, Overton and his mother incorporated the company and took it public in September. Cheesecake Factory's stock closed that first day at a price of 18¹¹/₆₄. The company's profits that year were $4.7 million on sales of $51.9 million. Restaurant sales accounted for $42.8 million (82.5 percent of sales) and the wholesale bakery for $9.1 million. Annual sales at the five restaurants averaged $8.6 million, on an average check of $13.57.

Nineteen ninety-three saw the opening of two more restaurants in California (on the water in Newport Beach and in Brentwood) and, in November, the second unit outside California, in the Atlanta suburb of Buckhead. By opening 3 or 4 units a year, Overton hoped to generate 25 percent-a-year sales increases, but this figure was easily surpassed. The three new restaurants contributed to 1993 revenues of $67 million, an increase of 30 percent. In its first 10 days of operations, the 12,000 square foot Atlanta location had sales of $322,000.

Top menu items for the chain were pasta dishes, followed by Cajun Jambalaya and Spicy Cashew Chicken. The company changed the menu twice a year, in June and in December, with new items added from the annual food trips Overton made with his staff to New York and Boston. The list of offerings included pasta, burritos and fajitas, steaks, seafood, ribs, pizza, burgers, omelets, salads, sandwiches, and vegetarian dishes. In addition to cheesecakes, dessert options ranged from hot fudge sundaes to fresh fruit to cakes to apple dumplings.

It is uncertain how much Cheesecake Factory's growth contributed to the comeback of cheesecake eating, but MRCA reported a 4.9 percent increase between 1988 and 1993. More important, in its ''1993 Menu Census,'' *Restaurants & Institutions* magazine found that cheesecake was the most offered dessert on the menus of local fast-food, family-style or white tablecloth restaurants, or local bakery/cafes. Cheesecake was on the menu of 64 percent of the restaurants in the country; apple pie appeared on the menu of 61.5 percent.

The survey also found that cheesecake was the fifth best-selling menu item. It was out-ranked only by french fries, two chicken dishes, and pizza, with pizza beating cheesecake by only one percentage point. Further, the popularity of cheesecake was not limited to restaurant diners. The 1993 Retail Bakery Study conducted by *Bakery Production and Marketing,* reported that 54 percent of retail bakers across the country offered cheesecake, and in-store bakers reported increased sales of prepackaged, frozen cheesecakes. *Bakery* estimated that total sales of cheesecake products in the United States was $430 million, more than $30 million higher than in 1988.

Overton continued to open new restaurants, financing the growth in part from the sale of 1.1 million shares of common stock. By early 1995, the chain numbered 11, with a new unit in Bethesda, Maryland, a Washington suburb, and two restaurants in Florida, in the Miami suburb of Coconut Grove and in Boca Raton. Restaurant sales for 1994 grew by 31 percent to $73 million, and Cheesecake Factory was number 25 in *Restaurant Business*'s top 50 growth chains, ranked by percentage increase in system units. Earnings for the year increased 53 percent, to $7.2 million.

1995 and Beyond

The chain's expansion saw no let up as three more restaurants opened within an 11-week period late in 1995—in Chicago at the John Hancock Center, at the Galleria in Houston, and at the Atrium in Chestnut Hill, a suburb of Boston. Cheesecake Factory's average building costs of about $3.5 million a unit were 2–3 times (or more) those of competitors such as Ruby Tuesday, Applebee's, Landry's Seafood, Chili's, or

Outback or Lone Star steakhouses. The company's new sites were running 14,000 to 24,000 square feet with seating for 400 to 700 compared to chains whose 5,000 to 7,000 square-feet units accommodated about 200 people. Cheesecake Factory filled each seat an average of four times or more a day, and even its smaller units were doing well. The Cocowalk restaurant in Coconut Grove had annual sales of more than $6 million a year—better than $1,000 per square foot. Average sales per square foot were $800 to $900, much higher than comparable casual-restaurant averages of $400 to $500.

The preopening costs for three big restaurants in different areas of the country combined with the expenses of training new staff did have an impact on the company's bottom line in the last quarter of the year—for the first time, the company's net income did not grow. The preopening costs for the Chicago unit were estimated to be near $1 million, for example, but by its third month, that restaurant was generating about $1 million per month in sales. The Chestnut Hill restaurant, although open only a few weeks in December, generated more than a half million dollars in sales in 1995.

In a May 1995 article in *National Restaurant News,* Overton further described what he looked for when selecting sites. "What we like in a site is one that gives us 250,000 people in a five-mile radius, medium-to-high income, and we like opening near apartment dwellers rather than around home owners. Apartment dwellers go out more frequently. People who own homes tend not to go out as much." However, he went on to explain that by the end of the decade, his "trophy sites" would be harder to find, and that the company was therefore already working on a smaller prototype, about 4,500 square feet in size.

One problem the company was experiencing was producing enough bakery goods for its growing number of restaurants, along with its wholesale and mail order business. To correct this, construction began on a new bakery facility, capable of producing 1,000 cheesecakes an hour using vats the size of hot tubs and customized machinery from Italy. The new facility was 45,000 square feet, replacing one only 14,000 square feet. The company's plans for expanding its retail distribution included selling its cheesecakes through Sam's Club and Price/Costco discount stores and additional supermarket chains. It also was working with RJ Nabisco on developing new products.

In July 1995, Overton selected Gerald Deitchle, a former executive at Long John Silver's Restaurants Inc., to be chief financial officer and senior vice-president. Deitchle succeeded William Kling, who retired. In November 1995, Cheesecake Factory appeared on the 1995–96 list of the *Forbes* 200 Best Small Companies in America for the first time, ranking number 79. To qualify for the list, "a company must show a five-year average return on equity of 12.4 percent [Cheesecake's return was 21.1 percent], five-year average earnings growth of eight percent [Cheesecake's was 35 percent], and five-year sales growth of 15 percent [Cheesecake's was over 25 percent, the highest on the list]." The company was ranked sixth of the nine restaurants on the list.

By the end of the year, Cheesecake Factory had moved from Woodland Hills to its new corporate headquarters in Calabasas Hills, California, hiring additional staff, and beginning produc-

tion at the new bakery facility. These costs also contributed to the fourth quarter results. For the year, the company had revenues over $100 million for the first time, reaching $117 million. Although flat in the fourth quarter, net income for the entire year increased to $8.6 million. Restaurant and bakery sales each increased by 37 percent. The workers in the bakery actually produced sales of nearly $1.5 million per month before moving into the new facility. For the restaurants, their unit sales continued to average $8.6 million a year, significantly higher than the $1.3 million considered good by its competitors.

At the end of the year, the company raised its menu prices about 2.7 percent, the first significant price increase in three years. During the summer of 1996, two restaurants opened—in the Old Orchard Center in Skokie, Illinois, and in Baltimore's Harborplace. These brought the total units to 16—and two more were expected to open by the end of the year, at Country Club Plaza in Kansas City and in Old Town in Pasadena, California. The Pasadena unit marked the first new Cheesecake Factory in California since 1993.

In a departure from its traditional distribution strategy, Cheesecake Factory contracted with Host Marriott to set up a dessert outlet at Los Angeles International Airport. If successful, the company expected such licensed outlets could lead to a new component in Cheesecake Factory's brand identity.

Very protective of the Cheesecake Factory name and the concept, David Overton refused to franchise. His plans for the future depended on accelerating the number of restaurant openings and developing new bakery products and customers. Some analysts worried that the expense of building large, opulent restaurants would continue to cut into profits. The company also had to contend with articles such as that in the June 7, 1996 issue of *Time,* which reported "A single slice of the Cheesecake Factory's original plain cheesecake has as much fat (49 grams) as a Pizza Hut Personal Pan Pepperoni Pizza plus two Dairy Queen Banana Splits." Yet customers continued to flock to the restaurants. With no debt, and with those big restaurants generating sales at an impressive pace, the company considered its capital expenditures good investments for the future, and planned to keep opening more.

Principal Subsidiaries

Cheesecake Corporation of America; Great World Foods, Inc.; The Houston Cheesecake Factory Corporation.

Further Reading

Claiborne, Craig, and Pierre Franey, "Naturalizing Cheesecake," *New York Times Magazine,* September 15, 1985, p. 77.

"Deitchle Named New CFO at Cheesecake Factory," *Nation's Restaurant News,* July 24, 1995, p. 12.

Hartnett, Michael, "What a Cakewalk," *Restaurant Business,* November 1, 1993, p. 74.

Krumrei, Doug, "Smile, Say Cheeeeeeese Cake," *Bakery Production and Marketing,* November 24, 1994, p. 18.

Lang, Joan, "Desserts Help Sweeten Profits," *ID: The Voice of Foodservice Distribution,* March 1996, p. 95.

Long, Dolores, "Success Is Sweet for The Cheesecake Factory," *Restaurant Business,* May 1, 1987, p. 128.

Martin, Richard, "Cheesecake Factory Steps Up Growth Pace," *Nation's Restaurant News,* February 14, 1994, p. 3.

"Oh No, Not Again!" *Time,* June 17, 1996, p. 22.

Papiernik, Richard L., "Cheesecake Factory Has Big Design on Hefty Slice of Market," *Nation's Restaurant News,* August 14, 1995, p. 11.

——, "When You're At the Top, Be Sure to Watch for Slippery Slopes," *Nation's Restaurant News,* March 11, 1996, p. 11.

Prewitt, Milford, "Cheesecake Factory," *Nation's Restaurant News,* May 22, 1995, p. 106.

"Restaurant IPOs, Sweet and Sour," *Business Week,* April 15, 1996.

Romeo, Peter, "Top 50 Growth Chains," *Restaurant Business,* July 20, 1995, p. 66.

Schonfeld, Erick, "Say Cheese! This One's Good Enough to Eat," *Fortune,* April 1, 1996, p. 161.

"Slippery at the Top: The Best Small Companies in America," *Forbes,* November 6, 1995.

Taylor, Jeffrey, "Mixing Success with a New Expansion Plan," *Investors Business Daily On-Line,* May 10, 1995.

—Ellen D. Wernick

Chock Full o'Nuts Corp.

370 Lexington Avenue
New York, New York 10017
U.S.A.
(212) 532-0300
Fax: (212) 532-0864

Public Company
Incorporated: 1932
Employees: 1,400
Sales: $328.38 million (1995)
Stock Exchanges: New York
SICs: 2095 Roasted Coffee; 2099 Food Preparations, Not
   Elsewhere Classified

Chock Full o'Nuts Corp. roasts, packages and distributes a variety of regular, decaffeinated, instant, iced, and specialty coffees to retail groceries and foodservice operations. Chock Full sells its coffees under its own brand name, and through its La Touraine Coffee Company and Cain's Coffee Company subsidiaries. The Chock Full o'Nuts All-Method Grind remains the company's flagship brand, supporting Chock Full's more than 20 percent hold of the Northeastern and metropolitan retail coffee markets. Nationally, Chock Full is the fourth largest seller of coffee—and the leading standalone company—holding approximately three percent of the $7 billion domestic market, behind Proctor & Gamble's Folgers, Philip Morris' General Foods (Maxwell House), and Nestle's Nescafe. Through its foodservice operations, Chock Full supplies chain and independent restaurants, hotel, motels, and other lodging establishments, convenience stores, warehouse and club stores, office coffee and vending machine services, and others with Chock Full o'Nuts, Eppens Smith, and other branded coffees, as well as custom manufactured private label coffees. Institutional sales contribute roughly 30 percent of the company's annual sales.

Retail store operations are a fast-growing segment of Chock Full's business. The company operates a chain of eight Chock Full o'Nuts cafes, primarily in Manhattan, featuring gourmet coffees and upscale fast-food items; in addition, the company operates a string of kiosks and carts, also under the Chock Full O'Nuts name. With its Quikava subsidiary, acquired in 1994, Chock Full is rapidly expanding the Quikava chain of drive-through coffee stores, which target suburban commuters with gourmet coffees, bakery, and other foods suited to eating while driving. Quikava stores are located primarily in New England and on Long Island, New York. As of July 1996, there were approximately 25 company-owned or franchised Quikava restaurants, with plans for 40 to open by the end of 1996, and as many as 70 restaurants in operation by the end of 1997.

A Depression Success

William Black, founder and long-time chairman, did not study to be the leader of one of the New York area's most-loved restaurant chains; instead he studied engineering at Columbia University. But after graduating in 1926 and a lengthy job hunt, Black was unable to find engineering work that suited him. Black decided to start his own business, investing $250 in start-up capital into a 6-by-20 basement space located under the stairs of a building on Broadway and 43rd Street, the heart of New York's theater district. The building's landlord was at first reluctant to rent to Black, agreeing to do so only when Black promised not to sell anything that would compete with a drug-store located at street-level in the same building.

Black decided to sell shelled and roasted nuts. Sold both from the store and from a pushcart, these quickly became a hit with the thousands of theatergoers in the district. In its first year, the store, which Black called Chock Full o'Nuts, earned $20,000. Within six years, Black expanded his stores to 18 locations. A shrewd businessman, Black was even shrewder in real estate: many of his stores' locations were to become among the most valuable in Manhattan, with long-term leases, some for as long as 40 years and more, that gave Black not only low rents, but also favorable renewal conditions. Many of the leases Black negotiated included air rights above the Chock Full o'Nuts locations.

But as the country slipped into the Great Depression, nuts quickly became a luxury food, and Chock Full o'Nuts sales dropped steadily. Black was forced to sublease some of his stores, including one to a vendor selling coffee and donuts. Black quickly recognized the potential of this new business. He bought out the vendor, and, between 1931 and 1933, converted all of his nut stores into luncheonettes—forerunners of the modern fast-food restaurant. All of the restaurants featured the same menu, centered around a five-cent nutted cream cheese sandwich and a five-cent cup of coffee, but also including soups, pies, and later donuts and other items. With no table service, food was served quickly. The cream cheese sandwich quickly became a popular item with the Depression-era patron. The restaurants proved popular also because of Black's insistence on cleanliness. Employees never touched the food with their hands, and food was prepared at the counter, not behind a kitchen door. Even the dishes were washed in full view of the customer. Another feature of the Chock Full o'Nuts restaurant was a no-tipping policy that remained in force until the 1970s. Black incorporated the restaurant chain under the Chock Full o'Nuts name in 1932.

Black was among the originators of the franchising concept, allowing him to expand the number of Chock Full o'Nuts locations beyond Manhattan into other parts of the New York metropolitan area, including New Jersey. Black also pioneered employee-friendly policies, including generous benefits, attendance and other bonuses, and food allowances, that set the chain apart from other similar restaurant chains. In the 1950s, the company even bought its own hotel resort in order to offer low-cost vacations to its employees. Black was also an early practitioner of non-discriminatory hiring practices. Indeed, during the 1950s, the company was accused of reverse discrimination not only at the restaurant level, but at the management level as well. For years, the company's management included famed Brooklyn Dodger Jackie Robinson as vice president of personnel. Employees were also encouraged to buy into the company, with discounts on purchases of the company's stock.

The Chock Full o'Nuts restaurants, most of which were located in high-density areas, quickly became a popular New York fixture. By the 1950s, there were 27 restaurants in the chain. In order to service the restaurants, the company built its own bakery in Harrison, New Jersey, and its own commissary in New York. Despite the fact that nuts formed little to no part of the menu, Black kept the Chock Full o'Nuts name.

The Heavenly Coffee of the Fifties

By the 1950s, Chock Full had grown to a $25 million company. Its chain of restaurants sold some 40 million servings per year, including 50,000 cheese sandwiches, 50,000 donuts, and more than 100,000 cups of coffee. By the early 1950s the restaurants' coffee, in fact, had become its largest customer draw. The popularity of its coffee encouraged the company to expand into a new direction. "Many customers like our coffee and wanted to know where they could purchase it for home brewing," Black told the *New York Times*.

In 1953, the company introduced its Chock Full o'Nuts brand of vacuum-packed coffee into New York area stores. In the following year, distribution was expanded into Philadelphia, New England, and upstate New York. Originally, Chock Full had outsourced its coffee roasting, though the company selected and blended its own coffee. But in 1954, the company brought

roasting in-house, opening a Brooklyn-based roasting plant. Within two years, the plant was operating on a 19-hour-per-day, six-day-per-week schedule, prompting the company to invest $500,000 in new equipment to keep up with consumer demand. With consumer demand rising, Black took a calculated risk. He discontinued the company's three traditional coffee blends—for regular, drip, and percolator coffee-making methods and bet instead on a new type of roasting technique that allowed for an all-purpose grind. The coffee's name was changed to Chock Full o'Nuts All-Method Grind.

The new Chock Full grind, packed in the black-and-yellow design found in its restaurants, proved an instant success with retail customers. The company's jingle, sung by Black's second wife, Jean Martin, a popular nightclub singer, became a favorite of a generation. Dubbed the "Heavenly Coffee," the jingle boasted "better coffee Rockefeller's money can't buy." In response to requests from the Rockefeller family, the lyrics were later changed to "a millionaire's." But sales climbed, and Chock Full quickly became the New York area's dominant brand, a position it would hold through much of its later history. Sales expanded beyond the Northeast into eastern and central Pennsylvania, Maryland and Washington, D.C., and to the Midwest, principally Cleveland and Chicago. Meanwhile, the company continued to expand its locations, including the purchase of a prime Wall Street site. Black was also active on the philanthropic front, founding, in 1957, the Parkinson's Disease Foundation, with an initial grant of $100,000. In 1960, Black donated $5 million to fund a new medical research building at Columbia University, then the largest single donation by a living person ever received by the university. In later years, Black's donations sometimes took the form of gifts of company stock, a practice that would come to haunt him in the early 1980s.

The Troubled Years: the Sixties and Beyond

Black took the company public in 1958. Over the next several years the number of restaurant locations rose to 41, and to over 100 by the end of the 1960s. Sales for 1961 climbed to $33.7 million, and by 1965 had risen to $48 million. Yet profits were dropping, bringing Black, who continued to hold tight control over nearly every aspect of the company's operations, into conflict with a growing base of shareholders, many of whom had purchased their stock at an inflated 51 times earnings in 1961. In response to their complaints, Black told *Forbes*, "I agree that people who bought the stock [then] are jackasses. But I didn't ask them to buy it." Black began avoiding stockholders' meetings.

Chock Full's earnings problems stemmed from a series of bad decisions made during the early 1960s. The company rolled out an instant coffee, but its initial packaging in cans, rather than jars, caused it to underwhelm consumers. Next, Chock Full spent $1.5 million building a frozen donut plant, a product that met with little success. In 1963, the company attempted to re-enter the nut market, spending $525,000 to roll out a line of dry-roasted peanuts, almond, cashews, and mixed nuts. This, too, performed poorly. At the same time, the company had embarked on a series of acquisitions, draining the company's bottom line. In 1962, Chock Full purchased Sol Cafe Manufacturing Corp. of Jamaica, Long Island for $900,000. In 1964, the company spent several million dollars more acquiring three coffee companies, Old Judge Coffee Company of St. Louis, Nash's Coffee Company of St. Paul, and Boseul Coffee & Tea Inc. of Philadelphia. These purchases expanded Chock Full's distribution base into 30 states. But the company's earnings fell, from a high of $2.4 million in 1962 to $2.3 million in 1965.

In 1966, Chock Full moved to bring its restaurant operations nationwide, with a Chock Full o'Nuts "Fairs" franchise concept that would help increase the company's restaurant operations to more than 100 units by the end of the decade. Yet Chock Full was already being battered by the surge in fast-food restaurants then sweeping the country. With their old-fashioned and, according to some, "stodgy" restaurant design, Chock Full found it increasingly difficult to compete with the more modern concepts of McDonald's, Burger King, and Kentucky Fried Chicken. Revenues began to fall, dropping to $42 million by 1968. Within the company, Black's insistence on controlling even the most minute details of operations had led to seven presidents in 10 years, including Black himself. Black also became known among advertising agencies as a difficult client; he would write copy for the company's advertisements. Chock Full went through a number of agencies before bringing advertising in-house. By 1970, with revenues of just under $50 million and poor earnings results, Black faced such pressure from shareholders that he vowed never again to attend a stockholders' meeting; a promise he would keep until his death in 1983.

Fomenting a Shareholder Rebellion

A new difficulty awaited the company in 1974, when the company acquired failing Rheingold Breweries from PepsiCo for $1 dollar and assumption of the brewery's $10 million in debt. The acquisition, made more for sentimental reasons—its strength as a regional brewer rested almost entirely in the New York area, and Chock Full would claim it made the acquisition in order to save the brewery's 1,500 jobs—proved costly to the company. During the three years Rheingold operated as a Chock Full subsidiary, it cost the company more than $21 million in pretax losses. In 1977, Rheingold was sold to C. Schmidt & Sons.

Added to the difficulty was the company's struggling restaurant chain. Despite changes in the menu, including adding hamburgers, salads, and breakfast dishes, as well as introducing table service, the restaurants increasingly failed to compete with the new fast-food giants. The attempt to take the chain national had failed, and the chain slowly lost restaurants, dropping to 26 and posting a $1 million loss by the early 1980s. Nonetheless, Black refused to shut down the division, again, in part due to sentimental reasons. As one analyst told *Advertising Age*, "Bill Black refused to close the restaurants for what could be called patriotic reasons. Woody Allen comes to New York to shoot a movie, and when he wants to make sure people know it is in Manhattan, he shoots in a Chock Full O' Nuts."

Rrevenues began a steady decline into the 1980s. Coffee sales slid as more and more consumers turned to colas and other soft drinks, pushing Chock Full's revenues down from $131 million in 1978 to $116 million in 1982. Profits also slid, from $10 million in 1978 to $3.7 million in 1982. By then Black, whose health was failing, had not been seen in the company's headquarters for more than a year. Yet he continued to control the company's operations through memos.

In 1982, the eighty-year-old Black faced down a shareholder rebellion led by well-known New York businessman Jerry Finkelstein. Within two years, Finkelstein had managed to gain control of some 14 percent of the company, and, at the company's annual meeting, sought to oust Black and his management team. The public contest that followed quickly turned bitter. In the end, however, Black prevailed. He died in March of the following year.

Black's place as chairman was taken by Leon Pordy, a cardiologist and Black's personal physician for many years. Under Pordy, the company moved to discontinue its restaurant operations, selling off its leases to Riese Organizations, which ran the Godfather's Pizza and Roy Rogers franchises, among others, for a minimum of $1.8 million per year for 25 years. Riese Organizations began converting the Chock Full of Nuts restaurants, closing the last in the early 1990s.

Perking Up in the Nineties

By the late 1980s, Chock Full seemed ripe for a takeover. In 1986, however, Chock Full moved to enter the institutional foodservice market by acquiring Greenwich Mills Co. and the La Touraine brand for nearly $42 million, and quickly achieved a strong market share. In just five years, the company's retail sales, which had accounted for 85 percent of company revenues, accounted for only 30 percent. In 1991, the company acquired Hillside Coffee Co. of Carmel, California for $24 million, bringing Chock Full into the increasingly popular whole-bean retail market. The rejuvenated Chock Full saw its net earnings jump to $4.4 million on sales of $245 million in 1990. The following year, earnings doubled to $8.8 million.

Sales held steady for the next two years. Then, in 1994, Chock Full decided that it was ready to re-enter the restaurant business. The company sold off its Hillside division to Gourmet Coffees of America, Inc. for $38.5 million in cash. It next completed the acquisition of Quikava, then a small specialty coffee franchise with only four restaurants, for $467,000. While pursuing plans to expand the Quikava chain, Chock Full moved to open a new chain of Chock Full o'Nuts restaurants, cashing in on the sudden surge of gourmet coffee bars, such as Starbucks, that swept the United States in the 1990s. By 1995, Chock Full's sales had jumped to $328 million, for a net income of nearly $5 million. For the future, Chock Full will have to overcome a somewhat "old hat" image; yet the Chock Full o'Nuts name has remained a strong source of goodwill.

Principal Subsidiaries

Chock Realty Corporation; Chock Coffeemaker Acquisition, Inc.; CFN of New York, Inc.; Cain's Coffee Co.; Cain's Holding company; DB Private Brands, Inc.; Quikava, Inc.

Further Reading

"After the Beer at Chock Full o'Nuts," *Business Week*, November 7, 1977, p. 81.

Agovino, Theresa, "Chock CEO Seeks Jolt in New Products," *Crain's New York Business,* July 15, 1991, p. 3.

——, "Chock Full's Brew Tastes a Little Weaker," *Crain's New York Business,* June 20, 1988, p. 15.

Auerbach, George, "Chock Full o' Whatever It Takes," *New York Times,* April 14, 1956, p. 22.

"The Bitter Brew in Chock Full o'Nuts Cup," *Financial World,* August 14, 1974, p. 23.

Bonner, Raymond, "A Heart Doctor Wins a Round in the Spirited Fight Over Chock Full o'Nuts," *New York Times,* December 12, 1982, p. 6.

——, "Battling for Chock Full o'Nuts," *New York Times,* December 1, 1982, p. D1.

Breznick, Alan, "Coffee Firm's Exec Chock Full of Ideas," *Crain's New York Business,* August 24–30, 1992, p. 13.

Hyten, Todd, "Drive-Through Coffee Chain Expands," *Boston Business Journal,* January 26, 1996, p. 9.

Marshall, Christy, "Chock Full of New Marketing Plans," *Advertising Age,* September 19, 1983, p. 4.

Messina, Judith, "Chock Push to Go Upscale Is Facing a Difficult Grind," *Crain's New York Business,* November 14, 1994, p. 12.

Phalon, Richard, "Chock Full o' Woes," *Forbes,* May 24, 1982, p. 37.

Saxon, Wolfgang, "William Black, Founder and Head of Chock Full o' Nuts Corp., Dies," *New York Times,* March 8, 1983, p. A28.

"Yesterday's Hero," *Forbes,* November 15, 1965, p. 45.

Zweig, Jason, "Chock Full o' Potential," *Forbes,* June 22, 1992, p. 52.

—M.L. Cohen

Claire's Stores, Inc.

3 S. W. 129th Avenue
Pembroke Pines, Florida 33027
U.S.A.
(954) 433-3900
Fax: (954) 433-3999

Public Company
Founded: 1961
Sales: $344.8 million (1996)
Employees: 6,650
Stock Exchanges: New York
SICs: 5632 Women's Accessory & Specialty Stores;
    5999 Miscellaneous Retail Stores

A fixture in malls for more than three decades, Claire's Stores, Inc. and its subsidiaries lead the fashion accessory industry with over 1,500 stores in the United States, Canada, England, Japan, Puerto Rico, Scotland, and Wales. The company's perennially popular women's accessories (priced from $2 to $20, with a $4 average) were geared to females aged 13 to 40, a group analysts credited with over $90 million in disposable income each year in the 1990s. Despite an often sluggish economy and a fickle, faddish marketplace ruled by impulse purchases, Claire's Stores' guiding force, Rowland Schaefer, took his company from moderate success to phenomenal sales and profits in the 1990s (from about $190 million in fiscal 1990 to nearly $345 million in fiscal 1996). Through calculated expansion both in the United States and abroad, Claire's Stores became the number one specialty retailer in the world, encompassing the Claire's Accessories, Bow Bangles, Dara Michelle, The Icing, Topkapi, Arcadia, and Art Explosion names.

From Wigs to Accessories, 1961 through the 1970s

What became the Claire's Stores, Inc. of today emerged from two entirely separate companies. Schaefer formed a company named Fashion Tress Industries (FTI) in 1961 to service the increasingly popular wig marketplace in the South. FTI's quality hair pieces were a success with women of the early 1960s, and the company eventually became the world's largest retailer of fashion wigs. Meanwhile, in the Midwest, a small chain of retail outlets named Claire's Boutiques began selling a wide range of accessories from necklaces and earrings to evening bags and pins. Catering to women and teenaged girls, Claire's Boutiques had tapped a rare market niche—when times were tough and people had little to spend, women and young ladies could purchase a few trinkets and accessories to make an old outfit seem brand new. In plush times, these same consumers continued to enhance their wardrobes by purchasing accessories for both old and new outfits.

By the dawn of the 1970s America's fashion trends were changing and women began to turn away from wigs and concentrate on their own tresses instead. As demand for wigs waned, Schaefer looked into diversification and found it in Claire's Boutiques. Based in Chicago with 25 retail outlets, Claire's was still a relatively young enterprise yet with tremendous growth potential. Schaefer bought the midwestern chain and changed his company name from FTI to Claire's Stores, Inc. in 1973. The transition from wigs to accessories proved relatively smooth, and despite some rough times in the early 1980s was a success. Yet few imagined just how successful the Claire's stores would become in the next decade and a half.

Accessorize, Accessorize, Accessorize: The 1980s

By fiscal 1985 (the company's fiscal year ended with the Saturday closest to January 31st) sales for the Claire's chain reached $55.9 million with net income of $6.6 million. The following year, sales climbed to $74.5 million, income to $7.5 million, and stock traded as high as $15 on the New York Stock Exchange. Although sales continued to climb for fiscal 1987 to $87.2 million, net income fell to $5.3 million, an indicator of difficulties to come. Yet from sales alone, Claire's appeared to be on the run, when fiscal 1988 hauled in $103.4 million in sales, and income was back in the black to $6.2 million. Even Claire's Stores' stock held steady at $13, until fiscal 1989 when it plummeted to $2 despite strong sales of $127.3 million and income of $7.1 million.

Company Perspectives:

Our customers know it's hot . . . when they see it at Claire's! Because young fashion trends can change so quickly, Claire's merchandising team continually monitors the television shows, movies and magazines that influence our customers' taste in fashion. Claire's size and international buying presence gives the company a unique ability to adapt to fashion shifts while they're just beginning to take shape.

So what had happened? During fiscal 1989 Claire's ambitious expansion plans took their toll on sales after a burst of openings and the acquisition of the Japanese chain Topkapi (16 stores, bringing total stores to 580). Same-store sales and earnings floundered in red ink during the spring of 1988. Yet Schaefer, aware of the too-aggressive expansion and a temporary loss of control over his ever-growing empire, tightened the reins and initiated a turnaround by the last two quarters of 1988 with Claire's Stores' stock regaining some of its lustre (back to $7) by the end of the fiscal year.

Part of the company's turnaround was the implementation of a $5 million chainwide state-of-the-art computerized cash register and inventory system that linked Claire's stores with headquarters. Daily data capture rose to 99 percent as opposed to 70 percent when performed manually by the Claire's staff. The computer system and the hiring of Claire's Stores' first director of loss prevention further improved the company's numbers by reducing "shrinkage" or theft of the thousands of small items available in each store, with the company keeping this figure to 10 percent or less (1986's figure was as high as 12 percent of sales). Lastly, an increase in Asian imports accelerated gross earnings, and new management selected by Schaefer completely stopped the company's hemorrhaging before any longlasting or irreparable damage was done.

By May of 1989, three months after the end of the previous fiscal year, Claire's posted an incredible sales surge of nearly 79 percent, with same-store increases of 58 percent. Though the company continued expanding, it did so carefully, and by July had 650 outlets in 47 states with some 4,000 employees, nearly two-thirds of whom worked part-time. Claire's finished the year (fiscal 1990) with $190.2 million and a very healthy $19.5 million in net income.

Staying ahead of Competitors and Thriving, 1990–1995

Sales for fiscal 1991 increased 35 percent to $255.2 million, and income was up to $20.5 million partially due to a seven percent rise in same-store sales. The company's stock was up again too—trading at about $14—almost as high as 1985's all-time high of $15. Claire's hoped to add between 125 and 150 new stores by the end of the fiscal year and had even revitalized its ordering system to keep a better tab on trends and delivering merchandise to its stores in far less time. By the spring of 1992 there were a total of 1,006 company-owned stores in 47 states, of these 721 were Claire's, 113 were Topkapi, 32 Dara Mi-

chelle, 32 Arcadia, 20 Art Explosion, and another 90 under the name Art Works or Picture Show. The latter four chains were a departure from Claire's Stores' general trade in women's and girls' accessories. Arcadia and Art Explosion stores were considered "trend" gifts shops stocking calendars, mugs, t-shirts, seasonal and stationery items, unframed posters, and other quick-sale products with a price range from $1 to $75 and an average sale of between $5 and $10. Art Works and Picture Show outlets carried graphic arts, such as framed posters and many other types of matted and framed art work.

The end of the year, however, brought a vast turnaround as fiscal 1992 sales fell to $234.2 million, and Claire's suffered its first loss since 1981. Led by a same-store sales drop of 11 percent, the stunning loss of $8.7 million was blamed on several factors, including too-rapid expansion again (such as ill-fated stores in outlet malls which proved redundant), markdowns on excessive Christmas and Easter inventories (which in turn compounded the problem by tying up space and keeping new merchandise from the shelves and racks), the discontinuation and disposal of the costly graphic arts line of stores (Art Works and Picture Show) for a sizeable hit of nearly $12 million, and lastly, the cost of increased security as Claire's introduced cameras and locked display cases to lower theft rates.

While the company made adjustments to shore up losses and promote sales, Schaefer also looked into diversification. One option was a mail-order sideline with slightly higher-priced items; another was to duplicate the successful $130,000-prototype store that Claire's had opened in the Pembroke Pines Mall near headquarters, filled with black marble, mirrors, plenty of bright neon, mannequins, and several up-scale items like earrings with a price tag of up to $50. Despite its difficulties in the early 1990s, Claire's was still considered a cash cow with some $22 million in cash in fiscal 1992. Additionally, Schaefer, who had long passed the traditional age for retirement (he was 76), sporadically talked about leaving the company or finding a buyer for his 41 percent share of Claire's Stores, Inc. If those on Wall Street were concerned, few showed it for Schaefer was well-liked and respected throughout the industry, and most knew he would never leave his company unstable. Fiscal 1993 brought good news as sales rose to $248 million, and income was back in good form at $14.5 million. By July total stores grew to 1,060 (up from 1,040 the previous year) in 48 states.

Fiscal 1994 proved another successful year for Claire's with $281.7 million in sales and income of 7.9 percent or $23.6 million. Costume jewelry, generally Claire's Stores' biggest selling item, dominated the company's bottom line once again by accounting for $180.3 million or 64 percent of total sales. The same rang true in fiscal 1995 when costume jewelry sales reached $196.1 million of the year's $301.4 million total sales with income at nine percent or $23.9 million. Yet 1995's fiscal figures once again brought a red flag as same-store sales decreased two percent due to what the company deemed as the lack of a discernible "significant" fashion trend.

Near the end of fiscal year 1995, the company bought a $7.4 million new distribution facility in Hoffman Estates, Illinois, a suburb of Chicago. Claire's Stores' other distribution facility, originally leased in 1985 and located in Wood Dale (another Chicago suburb) continued to service the company's merchandising needs (up to five shipments weekly to individual stores with the exception of imported goods like tote bags and costume jewelry) until the new facility was ready in June 1996.

New Acquisitions and What Lies Ahead, 1996 and Beyond

In January 1996, just prior to the end of the company's fiscal year on February 3rd, a three-for-two stock split was declared by the board of directors in the form of a 50 percent stock dividend distribution (9.9 million shares of common stock and 653,807 shares of Class A common stock were given to stockholders of record). Also in January the company moved forward with the first of three major acquisitions, two in the United States and another in the United Kingdom. The first of the U.S. purchases (which counted towards fiscal 1996) involved assets from The Icing, Inc., which had filed for Chapter 7 protection. Assets included 85 property leases in prime locations, retail equipment, fixtures, and furniture. After remodeling, Claire's planned to reopen the stores by May as either "Claire's Accessories" (if no other Claire's store existed in the mall) or as a refurbished "The Icing" if a Claire's store was already in operation.

The second acquisition was a British fashion chain known as Bow Bangles, PLC. Purchased assets included 48 stores throughout England, Scotland, and Wales, as well as related fixtures, furniture, and equipment. Lastly, in April 1996 (fiscal 1997), the company acquired a third chain, Accessory Place, Inc., taking over 31 stores. This brought Claire's Stores' total number of outlets worldwide to over 1,500, with plans to open another 150 locations before fiscal 1997 ended (between 15 and 20 in Canada, 110 to 115 in the United States, and 30 more in Japan). Of the 1,500 stores, 142 were Claire's Accessories stores with each averaging 919 square feet in enclosed and "open-air" malls.

For a start-up cost of about $95,000, using specially-designed display systems, each Claire's Accessories store was ready for business within three months (a relatively short time in the retail industry) and well-stocked in women's (and some unisex) fashion accessories (usually in excess of 6,000 pieces of merchandise) like costume jewelry (bracelets, earrings, hair ornaments, necklaces, pins, etc.), purses, sunglasses, tote bags, some trend gifts, and ear-piercing for a small fee. The other company-owned outlets under the Bow Bangles, Dara Michelle (the more up-scale outlet, with items priced from $5 to $75), The Icing, L'ccessory, and Topkapi names often operated within the same malls as Claire's Accessories stores. This clustering of stores in successfully tested geographical areas kept administrative supervision costs to a minimum and made it easier for refurbishing stores, which the company did on a regular basis.

Although the first quarter of fiscal 1996 found same-store sales lagging, a turnaround began in April and continued. By the third quarter (in October 1995), Schaefer and the company's management were jubilant over record sales and earnings. Stating that the year had proved to be "everything we expected it to be," Schaefer further explained that customer traffic was "excellent," average sales were higher, promotional costs were under budget, and markdowns had been unnecessary. Claire's Stores' finished fiscal 1996 with $344.9 million in sales (an increase of 14 percent over the previous year) and income of $30.9 million, including a rebound in same-store sales to three percent instead of 1995's decrease. Costume jewelry sales remained strong at $244.9 million for about 71 percent of sales, six percent over 1995 and seven percent over 1994.

After three straight years of record sales and earnings, Claire's Stores' prospects appeared strong and steady as the company headed into the 21st century. Though how long Rowland Schaefer remained as president, CEO and chairman was yet to be determined, three other Schaefers—Sylvia (vice-president), Maria (vice-president, fashion merchandising) and Bonnie (vice-president, southeast region real estate) were trusted members of Claire's Stores' top management and well-versed in the elder Schaefer's business savvy and poised to lead the company into the next century.

Principal Subsidiaries

CBI Distributing Corp.; Claire's Accessories U.K. Ltd.; Claire's Boutiques, Inc.; Claire's Canada Corp.; Claire's Nippon Co. Ltd. (50%); Claire's Puerto Rico Corp.

Further Reading

"Claire's Stores, Inc.," *South Florida Business Journal,* July 10, 1989, p. 21.

"Claire's Stores, Inc.," *South Florida Business Journal,* October 28, 1991, p. 18.

"Claire's Stores, Inc.," *South Florida Business Journal,* June 25, 1993, p. 25A.

Coletti, Richard J., "Claire's Renews Its Glitter," *Florida Trend,* February 1993, pp. 26–28.

Collins, Lisa, "Cheap and Cheerful Strategy Fuels Claire's Explosive Growth," *Crain's Chicago Business,* February 18, 1991, p. 16.

Forseter, Murray, "Shedding Light on Claire's Recovery," *Chain Store Age Executive,* July 1989, p. 6.

Marcial, Gene G., "A Costume Jeweler Regains Its Sparkle," *Business Week,* February 13, 1989, p. 88.

"Tempting Takeover Morsels That Could Gain 38%-Plus," *Money,* September 1994, p. 62.

—Taryn Benbow-Pfalzgraf

CLARCOR

Clarcor Inc.

2323 S. 6th Street
Rockford, Illinois 61104
U.S.A.
(815) 962-8867
Fax: (815) 962-0417

Public Company
Incorporated: 1904 as J.L. Clark Manufacturing Co.
Employees: 2,350
Sales: $221 million (1995)
Stock Exchanges: New York
SICs: 3714 Motor Vehicle Parts & Accessories; 2656
   Sanitary Foods Containers; 3542 Machine Tools—
   Metal Forming Types; 3299 Nonmetallic Mineral
   Products, Not Elsewhere Classified

Clarcor Inc. is a leading manufacturer of mobile, industrial, and environmental filtration products and a top producer of specialty packaging products. Despite Clarcor's long history and strong reputation as a maker of top-quality packaging for such consumer goods as battery shells, razor blade containers, and bandage boxes, filtration products account for the largest portion of the company's sales. Clarcor's filtration division, through operating subsidiaries Baldwin Filters, Inc. and Hastings Filters, Inc., both headquartered in Kearney, Nebraska, Airguard Industries, Inc., based in Louisville, Kentucky, and Clark Filter, Inc. in Lancaster, Pennsylvania, contributed 76 percent of the company's 1995 sales and 81 percent of its operating profit for that year. Together, these subsidiaries produce more than 18,000 filtration products, including aftermarket and OEM mobile heavy duty filters, locomotive engine filters, gas turbine filters, and environmental and industrial filtration systems, giving Clarcor the broadest product line in that market.

J.L. Clark, Inc., the operating subsidiary responsible for Clarcor's consumer division, based at the company's original headquarters in Rockford, Illinois, commands a strong position in such niche markets as metal spice packaging, specialty plastic closures, decorative promotional metal packaging, and

others, for such companies as Johnson & Johnson, Gillette, and McCormick & Company, and such brands as Ray-O-Vac batteries, Sucrets, Crayola crayons, and Kodak film containers. Although metalworking has traditionally formed the core of Clarcor's consumer division, since the mid-1980s the company has expanded into plastic packaging, which accounted for nearly 20 percent of consumer sales in 1995. Consumer products formed 24 percent of Clarcor's $290 million in 1995 sales. Given the relatively mature domestic markets for both the company's filtration and consumer products, Clarcor moved to expand its international presence, including joint partnerships and subsidiaries in China, Mexico, Europe, and Australia.

A Turn-of-the-Century Flue Stopper

John Lewis Clark was born in Vermont in 1845, but moved with his family to Rockford, Illinois in 1857. After graduating from high school, Clark joined the Union Navy, serving under Farragut during the Civil War. When that war ended, Clark, then 20 years old, returned to Rockford and obtained an apprenticeship as a tinsmith with a local hardware store. Throughout his apprenticeship, Clark dreamed of opening his own hardware store, which he accomplished in 1874 when he and a friend opened the Robinson & Clark Hardware store in Rockford. This partnership lasted for ten years. The partners eventually sold the store; Clark planned to move west and become a cattle rancher. The day before he intended to leave, however, the new owners begged Clark to buy back the store. Clark did.

The store, especially its tinsmith shop, prospered. In 1889 Clark formed a new partnership and opened a larger store. This partnership, the Clark & McKenney Hardware Co., also lasted ten years, until Clark bought out his partner and brought in his son, Lewis Harold Clark, as a partner. The store was renamed the J.L. Clark Hardware Company in 1899. With the elder Clark's tinsmithing expertise and the younger Clark's Cornell University education, the pair set out to develop a product and move into manufacturing.

One year later, Clark received a patent for an improved flue stopper. These round disks were needed to plug the holes left in walls when oil and coal stoves were dismantled for the summer.

Company Perspectives:

We are a market driven, worldwide provider of quality engineered products and related services to chosen global environmental and consumer products markets, committed to profitable growth through proven innovation, integrity and people orientation.

Clark sold 271 gross of his Gem Flue Stoppers that first year, primarily to local hardware dealers. It cost the store $70 for the dies and punch press needed to start large-scale production of the flue stopper. Originally a flat blank disk, the Gem Flue Stopper was soon available in three styles, with raised and embossed blanks featuring attractive lithographed designs. In 1901, sales of the stoppers grew to 500 gross. Through a small network of hardware sidemen, jobbers, advertisements and direct mailings, sales of the Gem Flue Stopper jumped to nearly 2,400 gross in 1903. The early Gem Flue Stoppers were generally priced higher than competing flue stoppers; the company added a fourth, lower-priced stopper design to the Gem line in 1902.

Clark was not yet satisfied with his relatively inefficient operation. The volume of Gem Flue Stopper sales was not high enough to keep the punch press working full-time. And cutting the blanks for the stoppers left a great deal of scrap metal. To improve efficiency, Clark added a new product line, the Gem Ointment Boxes, cut from the leftover material. In 1903, Clark added two more products, a Crispy Toaster for the stovetop and the Gem Flour Sifter. By the end of that year, the Clarks decided to move fully into manufacturing, and they sold their hardware store.

Renamed the J.L. Clark Manufacturing Company in 1904, the company began operations in a 7,000-square-foot facility in Rockford's Water Power District. With a $25,000 investment, Clark installed a complete line of punch presses, seamers, beading machines, and shear. The company also added a metal lithographing press and baking ovens. Its first lithographing order was for the decoration of fire extinguishers. By then, the company had 13 employees. One of its early major customers was Rockford-based W.T. Rawleigh, then a worldwide distributor of household and pharmaceutical products. As Rawleigh's product line grew, Clark's production expanded into a broad range of containers for products such as cosmetics and spices. In its first year of operation, Clark Manufacturing produced more than 500,000 pieces, including nearly 400,000 Gem Flue Stoppers. By 1905, the number of company employees jumped to 41. Four years later, when Clark added a company-designed-and-produced bodymaker, employment rose to 89.

Production continued to increase and by 1911 the company had outgrown its Water Power District facility, which by then had reached nearly 20,000 square feet. The company purchased a 15-acre tract on the edge of town and designed and built a modern 55,000-square-foot plant, including storage space and corporate offices, which was considered among the most up-to-date in the country. By then, Clark customers included many leading manufacturers, including Milton Bradley and others. Sales of the Gem Flue Stopper continued to rise, topping 500,000. But Clark's other products also contributed to its growth. According to an early newspaper article on the company, Clark's total production volume reached 50 million pieces per year by 1911.

Growth Between the Wars and Beyond

Clark's growth slowed somewhat during World War I (in 1919, the year founder John Clark died, the company posted the first of only two unprofitable years in its history). But with Harold Clark leading the company, Clark regained its momentum in the decade that followed. Photographic lithography processes were added to the production line, and this, coupled with the addition of a rotary printing press in 1925, allowed the company not only to speed up production but also to improve quality, establishing Clark's long-held reputation for excellence. Between 1918 and 1928, sales tripled, from $408,000 to nearly $1.4 million. In 1924, an addition to the plant doubled its production area.

Clark's growth enabled it to survive the Depression of the 1930s. Despite declining sales, down to $800,000 in 1933, in part due to a cutback to a four-day workweek, the number of the company's employees actually grew. The drop in consumer spending during the Depression encouraged companies to turn to quality packaging, which improved the durability of their products and were more attractive to consumers. At this time, 3M, among others, became a long-time Clark customer. This trend helped raise Clark's revenues, to $1.1 million in 1936 and to $1.4 million in 1937. The next year, however, Clark posted its second annual loss. But Clark received a new boost to revenues when the company designed the first metal battery jacket, later to become an industry standard, for Ray-O-Vac. The company also invested heavily in capital improvements, raising the quality and efficiency of production.

The outbreak of World War II stimulated Clark's growth, as production was converted to wartime orders, while the company established three branch plants to continue filling consumer orders. The company added a new major customer, Gillette, in the 1940s, designing and producing the packaging for that company's razor blades. At the same time, Clark began producing Band-Aid boxes, baby powder cans, and tape dispensers for Johnson & Johnson, which soon became the company's largest customer. By 1946, the company was able to add a new addition to its Rockford plant; two years later, the plant expanded again, and in 1950, Clark doubled its lithograph facility. Then, in 1951, Clark completed a 31,000-square-foot expansion of the Rockford plant.

In 1952, long-time employee Ralph Rosecrance replaced Harold Clark, who died the following year, as president of the company. Under Rosecrance, the company made its first acquisition, buying the Liberty Can and Sign Company of Lancaster, Pennsylvania in 1955 for $2 million. The acquisition gave the company increased access to the important East Coast market. Clark's sales, which had reached $10.7 million in 1954, rose to nearly $15 million in 1956.

The Liberty acquisition proved to be the first in a series, as the company moved to expand its product offerings. Significant among these was the 1959 acquisition of G. Felsenthal & Sons of Chicago, which brought Clark into plastics for the first time. The following year, Clark developed a plastic spice can closure to replace the traditional sliding metal closures, which were prone to rust, tended to stick, and were generally difficult to use. A second spice can closure was designed, with lift-tops for a shaker and for spooning, which attracted the attention of McCormick & Company, then the country's largest spice supplier. When Clark was awarded a contract to supply all of McCormick's spice cans, Clark built a 40,000-square-foot plant in California to satisfy the growing demand there. By the mid-1960s, Clark's customers included other major spice companies, including Durkee, French, and A&P. At the same time, Clark added another 41,000 square feet to its Rockford lithographing operations. By 1964, when the company made its initial public offering, sales had reached $23 million, with earnings of $1.2 million.

The newly public company next embarked on a string of acquisitions that not only raised its revenues to $82 million by 1976, but also allowed the company to diversify into a wide range of packaging materials. One of Clark's most important acquisitions was that of Maryland-based Stone Container Corp., which gave Clark a technological and market lead in the manufacture of composite cans. Other acquisitions increased the company's plastic molding capabilities. As then President William Nelson told *Forbes* in 1979, Clark's diversification efforts were made because ''[t]here's always a possibility that metal containers will become too expensive for some uses. Today there's no other firm that can offer such versatility in materials.''

By the end of the 1970s, Clark posted net earnings of $12 million on sales of nearly $105 million. The company's diversification efforts were succeeding, bringing revenues to $124.5 million in 1981, despite the national slide into a recession. But it was in that year that diversification would take on a new meaning for the company.

Becoming a Filtration Giant in the 1980s

Clark had succeeded by pursuing niche markets, avoiding head-on competition with industry giants such as American Can Co., Crown Cork & Seal Co., and Continental Group. In 1981, however, Clark made its largest acquisition to date, that of the J.A. Baldwin Manufacturing Company in Kearney, Nebraska, bringing Clark into a new market altogether. Baldwin was a maker of premium quality heavy-duty filters, with a product line of more than 2,100 filters for oil, fuel, air, coolants, hydraulic, and transmission applications. With a base of 2,500 distributors, Baldwin was a national brand name.

The Baldwin acquisition helped boost revenues to $174 million and net earnings of $16 million by 1984. In addition, filtration was soon to become more important to the company's bottom line. Sales in Clark's packaging division began to slip in the second half of the 1980s as customers turned to other materials or to manufacturing their own packaging. The company began to invest more heavily in its filtration business, acquiring in 1986 Dahl Manufacturing, Inc. of California and

that company's line of marine filters, diesel engine fuel/water separators, and related products. The company further enhanced its nonpackaging business with the acquisition of Michigan Spring Company, adding close-tolerance spring and wire forms to the company's product line and increasing its molded plastics capabilities. Clark began producing its first all-plastic packages, containers for Colgate Palmolive Co.'s Curad bandages.

In 1987, Clark changed its name to Clarcor to emphasize its diversified status. Nelson, by then chairman and CEO, retired and was replaced by Larry Gloyd, former company president. Under Gloyd, the company managed to reverse the slide in its packaging revenues. Yet that market was increasingly seen as too mature for further domestic growth. Accordingly, the company moved to boost its filtration business, acquiring HEFCO of New Jersey, which enabled Clarcor to enter the industrial filtration market. At the same time, the company attempted to move beyond manufacturing and into the services market, with the acquisition of the Furst Group, an executive placement firm, leading to the establishment of a short-lived Services Group. Sales by the end of the 1980s had topped $202 million.

As the 1990s began, Clarcor's filtration business already represented more than half of the company's total revenues. The recession of these years, however, placed pressure on the company's earnings. The company undertook a series of divestitures, exiting all but its filtration and consumer packaging businesses. In 1991, the company entered its first overseas partnership, purchasing a 20 percent stake in GUD Holdings, Ltd., the largest filtration products maker in Australia. The following year, Clarcor expanded its locomotive filter capacity with the acquisition of M&J Diesel Locomotive Filter Co. of Chicago, and made plans to move into other transportation markets, including heavy equipment and boating, as well as nontransportation industries such as generators.

The sale of Clarcor's precision products subsidiaries enabled the company, in 1993, to purchase with cash Airguard Industries, Inc., a Louisville, Kentucky-based maker of commercial environmental control systems, allowing the company to take advantage of business generated by the passage of the Clean Air Act. The company also purchased Eurofilter Airfilters Ltd. of England, giving the company access to the European market and expanding its product line to include gas turbine filters. At the same time, Clarcor entered a joint venture agreement with Filtros Continental in Mexico City, forming Filtros Baldwin de Mexico. The following year, Clarcor acquired Filtros Continental, the second-largest filter maker in Mexico, changing its name to Fibamex.

These acquisitions helped fuel a growth in revenues, with a 20 percent rise both in 1993 and 1994. The 1995 purchase of Hastings Manufacturing Company of Michigan, which added filtration products for the automotive and light truck markets, helped boost Clarcor's sales that year to $290 million and net earnings to $22 million. By 1996, Clarcor was present in nearly every filtration market, with a dominant position in many of the market segments. A joint venture with Weifang Power Machine Fittings Ltd. in China, closed at the end of 1995, continued Clarcor's international expansion. Overseas sales, which accounted for 13 percent of the company's revenues in 1995, were expected to rise to 25 percent or more by the year 2000.

Principal Subsidiaries

Airguard Industries, Inc.; Baldwin Filters, Inc.; Baldwin Filters N.V. (Belgium); Baldwin Filters Limited (England); Baldwin Filters (Aust.) Pty. Limited (Australia); Filtros Baldwin de Mexico (Fibamex) (Mexico); Baldwin-Weifang Filters Ltd. (China); Clark Filter, Inc.; Hastings Filters, Inc.; J.L. Clark, Inc.

Further Reading

Berman, Phyllis, "Virtue Well Rewarded," *Forbes,* August 20, 1979, p. 120.

Clarcor Inc., *From Hardware Store to ... Clarcor: 1904–1989,* Rockford, Ill.: Clarcor Inc., 1989.

Liebowitz, David S., "Playing with the Big Boys," *Financial World,* June 8, 1993, p. 88.

Murphy, H. Lee, "Acquisitions Fueling Expansion at Clarcor," *Crain's Chicago Business,* April 18, 1994, p. 28.

——, "Clarcor Repackage Tied to Expansion," *Crain's Chicago Business,* April 18, 1988, p. 40.

——, "Clarcor Set To Add Overseas Plant To Support Global Push at Home," *Crain's Chicago Business,* April 10, 1995, p. 49.

—M.L. Cohen

Conair Corp.

1 Cummings Point Road
Stamford, Connecticut 06904
U.S.A.
(203) 351-9000
Fax: (203) 351-9180

Private Company
Incorporated: 1959 as Continental Hair Products, Inc.
Employees: 3,200
Sales: $524 million (1994)
SICs: 2844 Perfumes, Cosmetics & Other Toilet
    Preparations; 3631 Household Cooking Equipment;
    3634 Electric Housewares & Fans; 3661 Telephone &
    Telegraph Apparatus; 5064 Electric Appliances,
    Television & Radio Sets; 5122 Drugs, Drug
    Proprietaries & Druggists' Sundries

Lee Rizzuto started a hair care business in a Brooklyn basement in 1959 and developed it into a leading manufacturer and marketer of personal care and beauty aid products and consumer electronic and kitchen appliances. Conair Corp., a leading manufacturer and distributor of nationally branded personal and health care small appliances, markets various liquid hair care products both to the consumer and the beauty professional.

Continental Hair Products, 1959–1975

Continental Hair Products, Inc., established and incorporated in 1959, was founded by Julian Rizzuto and his son Leandro (Lee). Julian had invented the "machineless permanent wave," a chemical process that replaced electric hair curlers for a time. He ran a beauty parlor on Manhattan's East 42nd Street with his wife, but this business collapsed in the late 1950s. This left him with only an improved, fast-drying hair roller he had invented. Continental Hair was launched in a Brooklyn basement to produce these premium-quality, premium-priced hair curlers for sale to the beauty salon business.

The start-up capital was $100, raised from the $5,000 sale of Lee's Cadillac, with the rest of the money going to pay off family debt. The business was an instant success, requiring the Rizzutos to expand their assembly capacity nine times in four years. Within a few years the firm was selling curlers and Japanese-made hair clips at the rate of ten million per month.

Continental Hair suffered a setback when a fire in 1965 destroyed its underinsured Brooklyn quarters. Julian Rizzuto died two years later. The company began recording remarkable and uninterrupted progress during 1968–1969, however, when it developed and introduced hot combs, curling irons, and the first of a line of pistol-grip hair styler-dryers, which helped to popularize blow-dried hair styles. Initially made exclusively for the professional beauty care market, the hair dryers were immediately embraced as superior to the conventional bonnet-type, salon-type dryers. Continental Hair also began selling retail lines of electric hair appliances in late 1971, when it introduced the "Conair Pro-Style" dryer. Sales grew from $1.1 million in 1968 to $12.6 million in 1973. Net income rose from $52,000 to $910,000 in the same period.

Continental Hair was also designing and marketing a wide variety of electric appliances by 1974, including other hand-held dryers under the Conair name, and hot combs, curling irons, shampoos, conditioners, and other hair care accessories. It was manufacturing the Vidal Sassoon line of hand-held dryers, brushes, and cutlery, as well as producing a number of private-label products. In 1973 it acquired Ethical Personal Care Products, Ltd., which became a subsidiary selling a line of hair dryers to mass-merchandise chains under the brand name "Superstars." Also in 1973, the company entered the liquid end of the business by acquiring Jheri Redding Products, Inc., whose product line, including shampoos, conditioners, and other hair care products, had a strong and wide following among hair stylists and beauticians throughout the United States.

Continental Hair's first venture into manufacturing as well as marketing its products occurred in 1972, when it purchased a one-third interest in a Hong Kong company. In 1973, 85 percent of the hair dryers sold by Continental Hair were produced by this firm, but the company remained substantially dependent on independent Japanese suppliers who could not sufficiently meet its demands for stepped-up production. Continental Hair, therefore, built a combination warehouse/manufacturing facility in Arizona in 1974 and moved its headquarters in 1975 from Brooklyn to a newly purchased assembly plant in Edison, New Jersey. Also in 1975, the company added personal care products to its line. The principal items were two shower massage units manufactured in Edison and marketed under the trade name "Waterfingers."

Public Company, 1972–1985

Continental Hair made its first public offering of stock in 1972 to raise funds for working capital and expansion, but the majority of the shares remained in management hands. Net sales reached $24.7 million in 1975, and net income was $1.9 million. The company's name became Conair Corp. in 1976, when net sales reached $36.4 million and net income $2.2 million. The following year sales increased to $53 million and net income rose to $3.5 million.

In 1977 Conair's principal product line remained its electrical hair care products, headed by eight basic models of pistol-grip hair dryers plus variations of these models. It commanded the nation's largest overall share of this market. The Conair appliance line also included five models of curling irons, an airstyling hot comb, and an infrared standing model lamp sold exclusively to the professional market and used for hair drying, permanents, and coloring. In the shower massage market, Waterfingers was second only to Teledyne's Water-Pik. These and other Conair hair care and personal care products were being sold in thousands of stores. The company also was conducting hundreds of "seminars" a year to demonstrate its products to professional customers.

The company's growth, which had been averaging an annual 32 percent on equity, came to a screeching halt in 1978, when it lost $2.1 million on sharply reduced sales of $40 million. A 1977 strike at the Edison plant had set the target dates on some Conair products behind by six months to a year—a virtual lifetime in the hotly competitive market for personal care appliances. Because of the delay, the company's new "Pro Baby" yellow, curved, freestanding hair dryers were released hastily, untested; they proved to be costly flops. Waterfingers sales also dropped sharply. In addition, a new IBM database system proved so complex that it took a year and a half to become operational.

Conair was able to unload its huge unsold Pro Baby inventory by using its component parts for the Pistol Power 1200, which by mid-1979 had become the hottest compact dryer on the market. To make itself less dependent on hair dryers (which were accounting for 80 percent of Conair's sales), the company introduced an affordable espresso/cappuccino coffeemaker and two new lines of liquid hair products for retail distribution: Royal Persian Henna shampoos, conditioners, and sprays; and "nucleic" hair care products, so called because they contained nucleic acids, which are thought to benefit hair. Sal DiMascio, an experienced corporate controller, was hired as chief financial officer to impose more sophisticated financial controls and procedures. The manufacturing of appliances was shifted from Edison to Hong Kong and Taiwan.

The most lasting consequence of the Pro Baby debacle was Conair's decision to shift its emphasis from hard goods to toiletries, specifically to the Jheri Redding line of liquid hair care products. Originally geared to the professional market, this line was renamed "Milk 'n Honee" for 1981 retail distribution. Bottles that sold for $3.50 to hairdressers were doubled in size and sold for $1.99, yet Conair still made money, partly because of economies of scale, partly because the salons had been selling these products to their customers for an exorbitant profit. By 1982 some 70 percent of company sales (85 percent by 1983) were being made directly by Conair through its own sales force and representatives, instead of 70 percent by distributors.

Conair's sales rose to $50.8 million in 1979, $64.7 million in 1980, and $87 million in 1981, and net income was $1.25 million, $2 million, and $3.1 million, respectively. In late 1982 the company held 30 percent of market share in hair dryers, almost twice that of its nearest competitor. This business accounted for 40 percent of its 1981 sales. Other personal care appliance lines, including curling irons and brushers, hairsetters, lighted makeup mirrors, and muscle relaxers, accounted for 45 percent. "Milk 'n Honee" products accounted for about 10 percent of company sales in its first year of distribution. The company's short-term debt of $10.6 million was liquidated completely in 1981, and long-term debt as a percentage of total capitalization was a modest 16 percent in late 1982.

Conair entered consumer electronics in 1983, when it began selling a line of telephones under the Conair Phone brand name. The new consumer electronics division's other products included telephone answering devices and cordless telephones.

1985 Leveraged Buyout

In June 1985 Conair arranged what was called the first leveraged buyout to be financed through the public sale of debt securities (in this case junk bonds), rather than a privately arranged bank loan. The financing called for Rizzuto to sell $190 million of debt securities through a new company that he wholly owned, Conair Acquisitions Corp., which then merged into Conair Corp. Proceeds of the debt sale were used to buy $169 million of common stock from Conair shareholders.

The buyout was a windfall for Rizzuto, who had owned 40 percent of Conair's stock and emerged with $25 million in cash as well as complete ownership of the new, private Conair and a ten-year employment contract as chairman and president at $750,000 per year, not counting bonuses. Conair's shareholders also were well rewarded, receiving the highest price level in the company's history for their stock. An investor putting $8,750 into Conair's initial public offering of stock in 1972 would receive almost $300,000 before taxes. The new Conair's debt consisted of $80 million in zero coupon financing, with no cash payments required before 1990, and $110 million in interest-bearing debentures, due near the turn of the century.

Private Company, 1985–1995

Conair moved its headquarters to Stamford, Connecticut, and entered the kitchen appliance field, a market five times the size of personal care, in 1986. Launching a line called Conair Cuisine for delivery in 1987, the company introduced a downsized food processor, a countertop can opener, a five-speed hand mixer, and a two-slice toaster. The Conair Cuisine line, in late 1988, also included an automatic drip coffeemaker, microwave oven, shake and beverage maker, and three battery-powered gadgets. An Ultra line of more deluxe items also had been added, including an electric juicer, cordless can opener, programmable coffeemaker with automatic shutoff, and microwave oven that also baked, broiled, and toasted.

Conair's net sales rose from $235.4 million in 1986 to $256 million in 1987 and $282.2 million in 1988. Net income increased from $628,000 in 1986 to $6.3 million in 1987 and $118.4 million in 1988. The latter figure reflected the sale of the hair care products division, a wholly owned subsidiary named Zotos International, Inc., to Japan's Shoseido Co. for more than $329 million. Conair had bought Zotos in 1983 for $71 million. In 1988 Conair had manufacturing facilities in Taiwan and Hong Kong and warehouses in Phoenix and East Windsor, New Jersey. The following year it also began to produce toiletry products in Rantoul, Illinois, and appliances in Costa Rica. Conair's long-term debt fell from $272.5 million at the end of 1987 to $145.6 million at the end of 1988 as the company used proceeds of the Zotos sale to pay off zero coupon notes.

Rizzuto had sought to buy Cuisinart Inc., manufacturers of the first food processor for home use in the United States, in 1986. After the company filed for bankruptcy in 1989, following a botched leveraged buyout, Conair paid about $17.7 million for the trademarks, patents, and assets of the $40- to $50-million-a-year company. It was not responsible for Cuisinart's debts, which eventually were settled for less than 50 cents on the dollar. In 1995 the Cuisinart product line included food processors, stainless steel cookware, accessories, and other kitchen appliances, such as pasta makers, hand mixers, chopper/grinders, toasters, blenders, and coffeemakers.

At the National Houseware Manufacturers Association's show in January 1990, Conair introduced, in the personal care segment of its business, three high-fashion hairstyling products for the home, two compact products for easy storage and travel, and a facial sauna. In the kitchen appliance segment, it introduced products with the Cuisinart label on them in two new categories: espresso makers and microwave ovens. Another new Cuisinart product was a juice extractor/juicer. Contrary to speculation, the Cuisinart cookware line was retained. Conair also announced plans to enter a joint venture in Japan to market the Cuisinart line.

Conair's reputation for quality was underlined by *Discount Store News* surveys in 1989, 1990, and 1991 that found the company, in the opinion of both shoppers and store managers, to be tops in the field of personal care appliances. Twenty-three percent of discount shoppers rated Conair a preferred brand in 1991, compared with 14 percent for the runner-ups, Norelco, Clairol, and Vidal Sassoon. In 1994 Conair was still tops in this field among discount shoppers.

In 1995 Conair acquired Babyliss, S.A., a manufacturer and marketer of personal care appliances, principally in Western Europe, for about $38 million. During the early 1990s it signed long-term licensing and distribution agreements giving it exclusive rights to market telephones under the Southwestern Bell name and personal care products in Western Europe and Mexico under the Revlon name and in the Asia Pacific region under the Vidal Sassoon name.

Conair's net sales rose from $361.8 million in 1992 to $442.6 million in 1993 and $524.4 million in 1994. Net income rose from $1.2 million to $12 million and $20.5 million in these years, respectively. Of 1994 sales, personal care appliances accounted for 43 percent, consumer electronics for 29 percent, toiletries and professional salon products for 17 percent, and Cuisinart products for 11 percent. More than five percent of sales was international. The company's long-term debt was $100.4 million at the end of 1994.

At the end of 1994 Conair owned manufacturing facilities in Rantoul, Illinois, and Cartago, Costa Rica, and it was leasing a manufacturing facility in Highland Park, Illinois, where it started production of toiletry and household maintenance products in 1993. It also owned an assembly plant in Wandre, Belgium, that manufactured about 30 percent of Babyliss's products. The company owned warehouse and/or distribution facilities in East Windsor, New Jersey; Rantoul; Phoenix; Wandre; and Valenciennes, France. It leased such facilities in Toronto; Breda, Netherlands; and Dusseldorf, Germany. The corporate executive offices in Stamford were owned. Continental Conair Ltd. had leased offices in Hong Kong, and Babyliss had leased offices in Montrouge, France.

Principal Subsidiaries

Babyliss S.A. (France); Conair Consumer Products, Inc. (Canada); Conair Costa Rica, S.A. (Costa Rica); Conair UK, Ltd. (UK); Continental Conair Ltd. (Hong Kong); Continental Products, S.A. (France; 50%); Cristal Gesellschaft fur Beteiligungen und Finanzierugen, S.A. (Switzerland); Cuisinart-Sanyei Co., Ltd. (Japan; 50%); HERC Consumer Products, LLC (50%); Rusk, Inc. (50%).

Further Reading

Eckardt, Dorothy, "Conair Corporation," *Wall Street Transcript,* November 8, 1982, p. 67726.
Ellis, Beth R., "Conair's Commodity Savvy," *HFD,* November 16, 1987, pp. 141–143.
Gissen, Jay, "Update Conair: 'Class to the Mass,' " *Forbes,* February 1, 1982, p. 104.
Griffin, Marie, "Conair Adds Novelty to Items in Kitchen Electrics Assortment," *HFD,* November 7, 1988, pp. 77, 80.
Mayer, Ted, "Conair Corporation," *Wall Street Transcript,* April 11, 1977, pp. 46715–46716.
Monaghan, Jean, "Electrical Hair Items Spur CONH's Growth," *Investment Dealers' Digest,* September 9, 1975, pp. 16–17.
Smith, Geoffrey, "You Don't Learn Anything from Success," *Forbes,* September 3, 1979, pp. 98, 100, 102, 104.
Trachtenberg, Jeffrey A., "Make My Day," *Forbes,* July 29, 1985, p. 74.

—Robert Halasz

CoreStates Financial Corp

Broad and Chestnut Streets
P.O. Box 7618
Philadelphia, Pennsylvania 19101-7618
U.S.A.
(215) 973-3100
Fax: (215) 786-6545

Public Company
Founded: 1803 as The Philadelphia Bank
Employees: 19,000
Total Assets: $45.2 billion (1996)
Stock Exchanges: New York
SICs: 6712 Bank Holding Companies; 6021 National
  Commercial Banks; 6022 State Commercial Banks;
  6282 Investment Advice

CoreStates Financial Corp is a major, Philadelphia-based regional bank holding company whose basic banking services are concentrated in Pennsylvania, New Jersey, and Delaware. However, beyond these "core states," the holding company also operates a national lending operation (Congress Financial) and is a leader in processing electronic transactions for other banks.

The core of CoreStates is what started out in 1803 as The Philadelphia Bank (later Philadelphia National Bank), though today's CoreStates can claim roots that go back even further in American financial history. Well before there was a Constitution, the Continental Congress in 1781 granted the first commercial banking charter to The Bank of North America, which more than two centuries and a number of mergers later became part of the CoreStates family in 1990. Two other forerunners, barely younger than The Philadelphia Bank, were the 1804-founded Trenton Banking Company in New Jersey, and the Farmers Bank of Lancaster, which opened in that Pennsylvania city in 1810. Another venerable forerunner was The Pennsylvania Company for Insurances on Lives and Granting Annuities, which received an insurance charter in 1812 but in time became a major Philadelphia bank. And a more recent major CoreStates acquisition—Meridian Bancorp, which was merged in the

spring of 1996—traces its ancestry to the 1828-founded Bank of Penn Township.

A New Country and a New Banking Community

The Philadelphia Bank began as the pet project of John Welsh. A self-made man who had become a prominent shipowner, Welsh nonetheless was still an outsider in the city's mercantile establishment. Much of that establishment cherished both business and emotional ties to Britain (a good many continued to keep their books in pounds and pence) and tended to be staunch Federalists. Welsh and his friends in the new entrepreneur class were more inclined toward Jeffersonian ideals and argued that the existing Philadelphia banks were uninterested in serving small merchants or meeting the needs of the entire community. However, Welsh was shrewd enough to bring in as first president George Clymer, a signer of both the Declaration of Independence and Constitution and a well-connected member of the Federalist establishment. The new bank was organized in August 1803 at Welsh's countinghouse with a capitalization of $1 million. It opened for business on September 19, 1803.

Clymer served as president until his death in 1813. For his part, John Welsh never held an executive post at the bank, but his influence was great. He remained a director all his life. When he died at 84 in 1854, a memorial resolution declared "to him is justly due the appellation 'the Father of the Bank.' " The same resolution remarked that the "triumph" to which Welsh led the bank "was achieved over the powerful, bitter and uncompromising opposition against which it had to contend in its earliest history and for many succeeding years."

When Welsh and Clymer opened their bank, there were already three well-established banks in the city. Robert Morris, who helped finance the Continental Congress and government during the Revolution and officially became its Superintendent of Finance in 1781, was instrumental in founding the Bank of North America (as noted, a future CoreStates partner) with the primary purpose of lending to the hard-strapped Continental Congress. The Congress granted a charter on December 31, 1781, and the bank began business a week later. Although Cornwallis had surrendered in October 1781, it took three more

---

Company Perspectives:

Stated below are our CoreValues. . . . We value people. We will treat all people with respect and courtesy and create an environment that supports the attainment of their personal and professional aspirations. We value performance. *Exceptional contributions by individuals and by teams are critical to CoreStates successful performance. Such contributions at all levels of the organization will be appreciated and recognized.* We value diversity. *We will actively promote an atmosphere of mutual respect for each other's differences, recognizing that our diversity creates a breadth of perspectives which strengthens our organization.* We value teamwork. *Teamwork is critical to our success. Trust and mutual respect for each other's responsibilities, functions, skills and experience are essential ingredients of teamwork.* We value communication. *Open, candid communication flowing in all directions will be the norm. We emphasize that listening is a crucial component of the communication process.* We value integrity. *We will strive to be recognized as an organization of the highest ethical standards and unquestioned integrity.*

---

years of semi-hostilities, with the concurrent military and financial strain, before peace was secured.

Because the Continental Congress's powers were so uncertain, a state charter was obtained in April 1782—not without considerable opposition in the Legislature. It was revoked in 1785, but the bank managed to stay in operation; it also threatened to move to more hospitable Delaware. After a new legislature was elected, a Pennsylvania charter was granted again in 1786, and the bank prospered while helping finance both government and business.

Once the Federal government was established under the Constitution, Treasury Secretary Alexander Hamilton pushed hard for a federally chartered Bank of the United States, patterned in many ways after the century-old Bank of England. Congress approved a 20-year charter and the bank was established in 1791 in Philadelphia, then the national capital as well as the preeminent financial center of the young nation.

Some rival merchants tried to form a Bank of Pennsylvania as an alternative to the Bank of North America in 1784 but settled for the right to receive stock in the older bank at the original issue price of $400 a share. (The North America directors had wanted to sell new stock in their successful enterprise for $500.) But in 1793 a new Bank of Pennsylvania was organized and over the next decade the three banks found they were all able to thrive nicely.

However, the trio was in no mood to welcome additional competition. For some time they refused to accept bank notes issued by The Philadelphia Bank and lobbied hard against a legislative charter which the newcomer was finally able to obtain in 1805.

The Philadelphia Bank also suffered from internal problems—not the least of which was its first cashier's absconding

to Georgia in 1805. However, the bank was able to survive with the support of prominent customers like E. I. DuPont. Once it gained strength, its directors, following the example of its rivals, paid generous dividends and established branches in outlying parts of the state. When the depression of 1819 hit, the bank found its latest dividend had been paid partially out of capital. John Read, a lawyer and long-time director who took over as president in 1819, introduced belt-tightening and managed to sell the money-losing branches. He was able to resume dividends by 1820 and, as the country expanded during the decade, began to develop correspondence relationships with banks in the South and West.

In the mid-1830s, the Second Bank of the United States—which had received a 20-year Congressional charter in 1816 but was denied renewal in a bitter battle with the Andrew Jackson Administration—tried to linger on locally and managed to get the Philadelphia banks to lend it $5 million, $1 million of which was subscribed by The Philadelphia Bank. Despite that, the Second Bank of the United States failed in February 1841, putting severe strain on the other banks of the city, all of whom suspended specie payment (exchanging their bank notes for gold or silver). Three large banks in the city collapsed, moving The Philadelphia Bank to the lead position. However, as prosperity returned in the mid-1840s, the bank stuck to conservative growth policies, allowing old rival Bank of Pennsylvania, which had almost collapsed in 1842, to surge back to top spot in the city.

In size, The Philadelphia Bank was also outpaced by the Farmers' and Mechanics' Bank. But its careful management was able to resume dividends in 1844 and uninterrupted payments have now been kept up for more than a century and a half. In 1852, the Philadelphia bankers formed a Board of Presidents. They aimed to establish a clearinghouse to facilitate transactions and make the true financial condition of each bank more visible. The effort was blocked by vigorous opposition from the Bank of Pennsylvania. When that bank finally failed in 1857, the others founded the Philadelphia Clearing House Association in 1858. And the next year The Philadelphia Bank moved into a fine new building (acquired at half price) that had been erected for the defunct Bank of Pennsylvania.

The Civil War Years

Once the Civil War started, Treasury Secretary Salmon P. Chase found Philadelphia financier Jay Cooke an able seller of public debt by going directly to the public instead of conservative bankers and a few wealthy families. Chase also got Cooke (whose later manipulations were to make him a leader in infamy) to use his publicity talents to promote passage in early 1863 of the National Bank Act, which established the federally printed greenbacks and authorized national banks. Cooke promptly organized the First National Bank of Philadelphia (another future CoreStates entity) which was awarded national charter Number One. The city's established banks had to wait until August 1864 for the Pennsylvania legislature to authorize them to give up their state charters. Shortly thereafter, all the city's banks switched—and The Philadelphia Bank became the Philadelphia National Bank.

Both competition and growth continued during the rest of the century. In 1893, Fourth Street National, founded only a decade earlier, took the lead among Philadelphia banks. Meantime, Philadelphia National, also growing fast, passed old leader Farmers' and Mechanics'. By 1900, Fourth Street and Philadelphia National were both more than twice as big as any of their rivals.

Into the Twentieth Century

Under Levi Rue, who had started as a stenographer in 1878 and was named cashier in 1894 and president in 1907, Philadelphia National actively pursued accounts in the Midwest, entered foreign banking, and participated in underwriting syndicates (chiefly with New York-based giants J.P. Morgan and Kuehn, Loeb). Correspondence banking was also beefed up aggressively. By 1914, Philadelphia National had edged out Fourth Street as the city's biggest bank.

In 1900, Philadelphia National merged with City National—a small transaction, but notable as the bank's first acquisition. Then, in 1918, it bought Farmers' and Mechanics,' the onetime leader that had long been declining in strength, but which brought in important lines of business as fiscal agent for the city and state.

The late 1920s totally reordered the Philadelphia banking scene. In 1926, Fourth Street National, which had been losing ground since 1914 and was now No. 4, merged with No. 3 Franklin National. While Philadelphia National was still first in size, president Levi Rue (about to retire) considered the new "Franklin Fourth Street" a strong challenger and countered by negotiating a merger with No. 2 bank Girard National to form Philadelphia-Girard National. Then in 1928 the two newly merged organizations entered into a merger with each other, so that what in 1926 had been the four largest Philadelphia banks were now one under the Philadelphia National Bank name.

The Post-World War II Era

The bank sailed safely through the Depression (president Joseph Wayne had sharply cut back on brokers' loans in 1929) and World War II. After the war, under the leadership of president Frederic Potts, management moved back toward John Welsh's original goal of serving small merchants. A bank brochure conceded that, after 100 years of emphasizing wholesale banking, "the bank had long since lost touch with the small borrower and the small depositor." In fact, only a few personal accounts were handled for very substantial customers.

In 1951, Philadelphia National absorbed Ninth Bank & Trust, which helped it "inaugurate an all-inclusive program of personal banking service, including neighborhood branches, complete trust services, small loans and special checking accounts." Of course, "commercial loans continue[d] to represent the back bone of the bank's business." In 1953, the bank was able to make its first cross-county move (since the original branching days of 1809–1820), acquiring the First National of Conshohocken, and a number of other suburban acquisitions followed.

The Pennsylvania Company's Rise to Prominence

By 1955, Philadelphia National had grown to a billion-dollar bank. But that same year it lost top place in Philadelphia through a merger of major rivals. The key player was another

company which could point to John Welsh as one of its founders. Welsh was a leader of a merchant group that saw the need for a locally based insurance company and started soliciting subscriptions in 1809. The legislature rebuffed their initial effort but, with the approach of the War of 1812 adding to the urgency, a charter was granted in March 1812 for The Pennsylvania Company for Insurances on Lives and Granting Annuities. One seemingly minor clause in the charter authorized the insurance company to invest in any chartered or incorporated bank, a provision that was to assume vital importance a couple of decades later.

Capitalizing on these incidental investment powers, the company in 1829 and 1836 obtained charter amendments that broadened its powers to invest in government, municipal, and corporate securities and engage in trust activities. Trust operations soon became far more important than insurance activities. In 1853 the company was authorized to act as executor or administrator. Insurance activities played a progressively lesser role and in 1872 were discontinued altogether, leaving the Pennsylvania Company strictly a bank and trust company.

After considerable growth over the years, the Pennsylvania Company in 1929 merged the Robert Morris-founded Bank of North America, and the name of the nation's first bank disappeared. Several more banks were acquired in the early 1930s and still others soon after World War II. Also in 1947 directors, realizing that the old "Insurances on Lives" title was, as a company history put it, "a befuddling name for a bank," changed to the still lengthy but more descriptive The Pennsylvania Company for Banking and Trust. Then in 1955 the bank merged Jay Cooke's old First National Bank of Philadelphia and as the new leader on the Philadelphia banking scene adopted the name of The First Pennsylvania Banking and Trust Company.

Philadelphia National tried to regain the lead in 1960 by merging the Girard Trust Corn Exchange Bank (no relation to the 1926-merged Girard National), but in 1963 the Supreme Court upheld the government's anti-trust objections. Disappointed Philadelphia National soon snapped back with an aggressive branch building program. It also moved briskly into a number of new fields.

In 1965 it opened its CompuCenter in Carlisle, Pennsylvania, designed to provide data processing services for correspondent banks. The next year it became one of the charter members issuing the BankAmericard (later renamed VISA) credit card. And in 1967 it took advantage of more liberal regulatory attitudes to buy New York City-based Congress Factors. This unit later became known as Congress Financial. Factoring (buying a supplier's receivables) would represent only one-sixth of business in the 1990s; the rest would be mostly asset-based lending. The Congress Financial of the 1990s would account for about one-tenth of CoreStates profits.

Forming a Holding Company in the 1960s

In 1969 Philadelphia National joined the move of most major banks to form a one-bank holding company, which provided more flexibility and diversification opportunities. It named the holding company PNB Corporation. Actually, Philadelphia National had been emphasizing its initials as a stream-lined identifier since the mid-fifties and "PNB" blazed from the new headquarters building it opened in 1956. But officially, the bank and its branches retained the full name, and indeed carried it into the 1990s. And only in 1996 was it able to complete its "one bank, one name, one mission" aim, with a "CoreStates Bank" shingle at every branch.

Bank watchers found a downside to the PNB acronym in a state where the two major cities shared the same first letter. The potential for confusion had escalated when the fast-growing Peoples First National Bank & Trust became Pittsburgh National Bank in 1959. A head-on collision of initials was avoided when Pittsburgh National at first named its 1969-formed holding company Pittsburgh National Corp. Clarity was further served when in 1973 PNB Corp. renamed itself Philadelphia National Corp. However, informal use of the handy abbreviation PNB—and even PNC—continued. Meanwhile, in 1983—the year in which Philadelphia National was to adopt the CoreStates name for the parent corporation—Pittsburgh National followed the "initials" trend and became PNC Financial Corp. PNC went on to acquire a far more wide-spread group of banks and as of mid-1996 was easily the largest Pennsylvania-based banking company (ranked 13th nationally), some 60 percent bigger than runner-up CoreStates, whose $43.7 billion assets ranked it 21st in the United States at that time.

Expansion in the 1980s

Even so, Philadelphia National and its successor continued substantial growth. Once Pennsylvania authorized statewide banking in 1982, the bank quickly arranged to move into the central part of the state through a merger with National Central Financial, whose chief unit was Lancaster-based Hamilton Bank. The merger (which technically used the National Central charter) was completed in 1983 and the combined organization adopted the name CoreStates. Meantime, in 1982, Philadelphia Bank (Delaware) had been formed, primarily to take over credit card activities which had suffered under Pennsylvania's rigid limits on permissible charges. Banking expansion into New Jersey, made possible by new laws in both states, came in 1986 with the acquisition of Trenton-based New Jersey National Bank.

Back in Philadelphia, CoreStates in 1990 acquired the venerable First Pennsylvania, whose nearly two-century history had so often paralleled Philadelphia National's. Chairman and CEO Terrence Larsen bluntly conceded CoreStates was concerned by the prospect that "one of the strongest local institutions" would be purchased by an out-of-area competitor. He noted that of the eight large independent banks based in Philadelphia in the late 1970s, all but CoreStates had since been acquired, mostly by outsiders. First Penn also provided welcome strength in consumer banking and middle-market businesses.

In 1995, CoreStates considered a first inter-regional merger with Bank of Boston, but to the overwhelming relief of Wall Street analysts who saw a poor fit and considerable weaknesses, the talks were soon ended. On the other hand, there was strong acclaim for the merger with Meridian Bancorp, based in Reading, Pennsylvania, which was completed in April 1996, and brought with it $15 billion in assets and strengthened operations

in the CoreStates area. While most CoreStates competitors in the Philadelphia market (including Pittsburgh-based PNC and Mellon) operated over a fairly wide area, CoreStates retail banking had not ventured beyond eastern and central Pennsylvania, central and southern New Jersey and northern Delaware by the mid-1990s.

However, in other endeavors, the CoreStates reach was far broader. Philadelphia National had started a foreign department in 1910, opened two Edge Act banks (which helped finance foreign trade) in the 1960s and by 1996 had some two dozen overseas branches and representative offices scattered from London and Hamburg to Tokyo and Sydney. It also had investments in a number of foreign financial institutions and "longstanding" business relationships with nearly 1,200 institutions. International business brought in about one-tenth of CoreStates profits.

In the United States, CoreStates leveraged an early interest in electronic banking technology to become one of the foremost "third-party" service providers. Philadelphia National first offered a 24-hour automated teller machine (ATM) in 1972 and in 1979 launched Money Access Service (MAC). Initially it provided an ATM network covering 13 banks, with PNB handling the processing. In 1992 CoreStates and three partners (a fourth joined later) formed Electronic Payment Services (EPS) as a broad-based, fast-growing processor of ATM, credit and debit card transactions. In 1996, EPS was working with MasterCard on a rechargeable "smart card" that could be used instead of cash for small purchases.

Also in the mid-1990s CoreStates' wholly owned subsidiary QuestPoint operated units that handled check processing for other banks (J.P. Morgan became the first major customer), provided cash management services to some 70 major banks, and took care of the highly complex requirements of corporate credit card servicing. As more banks, including very large ones, outsourced all these specialized processing tasks (often to non-bank operators), CoreStates felt it had a niche business that would provide a dependable and increasing flow of fee income.

In May 1996, CoreStates named Rosemarie B. Greco to the post of company president, "making her the highest-ranking woman in commercial banking," according to *American Banker* magazine. Greco asserted that her role at the bank would first focus on making the merger with Meridian work. While aware that in an era of mega mergers, diversification, and technological advances the banking scene was in flux as the 20th century came to a close, CoreStates remained a major, soundly based regional bank, an important player in a number of related financial areas, and a leader in technological services.

Principal Subsidiaries

CoreStates Bank, N.A.; Congress Financial Corporation; CoreStates Bank International; Philadelphia International Investment Corporation; QuestPoint; CoreStates Investment Advisers, Inc.; Electronic Payment Services, Inc. (20%).

Further Reading

Chase, Brett, "CoreStates' Incoming President to Be Top Woman Exec in Banking," *American Banker,* May 28, 1996, p. 8.

"CoreStates Trims at Top," *The Star-Ledger* (Newark, NJ), October 17, 1996, p. 42.

Elstein, Aaron, "CoreStates Transaction Shows Short-Selling's Role in Buybacks," *American Banker,* December 2, 1996, p. 29.

Larsen, Terrence A., *CoreStates Financial Corp: Drawing Strength from History, Community and Diversity,* New York: Newcomen Society, 1993.

Perkins, Edwin J., *American Public Finance and Financial Services 1700–1815,* Columbus: Ohio State University Press, 1994.

Since 1803: A Look at Executive Leadership, Philadelphia: Philadelphia National Corp brochure, 1976.

The Bank, 1781–1976, Philadelphia: First Pennsylvania Bank, 1976.

—Henry R. Hecht

COURTAULDS

Courtaulds plc

18 Hanover Square
London, W1A 2BB
England
(44) 171 612-1000
Fax: (44) 171 612-1500

Public Company
Incorporated: 1913 as Courtaulds Ltd.
Employees: 18,100
Sales: £2.2 billion (US$3.3 billion) (1995)
Stock Exchanges: Geneva London
SICs: 2851 Paints & Allied Products; 2820 Plastics
Materials & Synthetics; 3086 Plastics Foam Products;
2891 Adhesives & Sealants; 2869 Industrial Organic
Chemicals, Not Elsewhere Classified

Courtaulds plc is the world's second-largest producer of acrylic fibers and a major global producer of rayon. With a history going back to 1816, the firm split into two independent companies, Courtaulds plc and Courtaulds Textiles plc, on January 1, 1990. As an independent company, Courtaulds plc comprises five divisions: coatings, chemicals, fibers and films, performance materials, and packaging.

18th-Century Origins

The Courtauld family migrated to England from France at the end of the 17th century and became successful gold- and silversmiths in London. Its first link with textiles was forged in 1775 when George Courtauld was apprenticed to a silk throwster—''throwing'' is the equivalent in silk manufacture of spinning in cotton or wool—in Spitalfields. In 1816, George Courtauld's eldest son, Samuel, set up independently, and the family textile firm was first established, in Essex. Vigorous, impatient, and autocratic, Samuel Courtauld moved from silk throwing to the mechanized manufacture of a textile fabric popular in Victorian Britain: silk mourning crêpe. By the 1870s, when it employed about 3,000 workers, Samuel Courtauld &

Company had become one of the biggest firms in the British silk industry. It had become so profitable that the partners were then earning an average of more than 30 percent on their capital, and Samuel Courtauld himself was drawing an income of about £46,000 a year from his investment in the business.

Fashions began to change, however. Crêpe prices fell, and after Samuel Courtauld's death in 1881 the firm's leadership faltered. Losses were suffered in the 1890s. The partnership was turned into a private limited liability company, and new managers were brought in to modernize the business. H. G. Tetley was made a director in 1895, as was T. P.—later Sir Paul—Latham, in 1898. These two men, outsiders to the family business, virtually controlled the company for the next quarter-century and in the process created the multinational Courtaulds Ltd. in 1913 as the world's largest producer of the first manmade fiber, rayon. Under the new management some modernization and diversification was achieved, but by the turn of the century a plateau had been reached. As Tetley told his fellow directors in April 1904, Samuel Courtauld & Company (Courtaulds) needed ''a new source of profit to replace crêpe profits—which are leaving us.'' It was the adoption of his proposed remedy for this problem that put the firm on a wholly new course.

Turn-of-the-Century Foray into Rayon

Three independent lines of inquiry—none of which involved Courtaulds—led to the discovery of rayon, which is technically a regenerated cellulosic fiber. One line of inquiry was pursued in France by Count Hilaire de Chardonnet, who set up the first factory to make artificial silk in 1892. Another, by a different process, led to a factory in Germany in 1899. The third, in Britain, was potentially the simplest and cheapest route. This ''viscose'' process—consisting basically of treating wood pulp with caustic soda and other chemicals and spinning the resultant substance into fibers—was developed and patented by three inventors working in a pilot plant near London. Most of the various national patent rights had been sold off when Tetley visited the plant early in 1904. He reported back enthusiastically. After successful flotation as a public company in July 1904, Samuel Courtauld & Company Ltd. bought the British rights to the patents for approximately £25,000.

A factory was built on the outskirts of Coventry. Production commenced in July 1905, but the factory was still operating at a loss in 1907. By 1913, however, it was turning out over three million pounds of rayon per annum, and Courtaulds had emerged as easily the largest and strongest of all the firms that had bought the viscose rights. It had been able to buy out the holders of the U.S. rights in 1909, set up a wholly owned subsidiary in the United States, and float Courtaulds Ltd. as a new £2 million company on the basis of a ten-for-one bonus issue.

It soon became evident that the process that Tetley had bought was unreliable. A small group of chemists and engineers at Coventry, operating largely by hit-or-miss methods, made the technical breakthrough in making the process reliable and capable of producing a fiber of consistent quality. Technical cooperation with the purchasers of the French rights and a favorable legal judgment in a patent action helped. An important reason for the company's success lay in the fact that of all the purchasers of the viscose patent rights, only Courtaulds was a textile manufacturing firm. Those directing the efforts of the chemists and engineers knew what technical qualities were needed to make a yarn useful and salable; the textile machinery and the dye house at the Essex mills were available for experimentation; and the whole range of commercial contacts made by the company in its textile business, skillfully exploited by Latham, were used for the marketing of the new product. The real architect of the achievement was Tetley. Not only did he drive the company forward in Britain but his purchase of the U.S. rights led to the foundation of the American Viscose Corporation (AVC). Starting production in 1911 and operating inside a tariff barrier, by 1915 AVC reached an output that surpassed that of its parent, and it was soon contributing massively to profits. The combined profitability of the U.K. and U.S. sides of the business allowed not only the payment to Courtauld's shareholders of substantial dividends but also the making of further bonus issues in 1919 and 1920, thus bringing the ordinary share capital to £12 million.

Return to Family Leadership in the 1920s

Tetley had become chairman of Courtaulds in 1917. On his death in 1921 the leadership of Courtaulds passed into the hands of Samuel Courtauld, great-nephew of the Samuel who had founded the family business. Under the leadership of the second Samuel Courtauld, the company became a highly respected multinational concern, and its great financial strength was not matched by any comparable enterprise in technical innovation. Samuel Courtauld became known to a wider public as a patron of the arts. His collection of Impressionist paintings became the basis of the Courtauld Institute of Art, which he set up and endowed in 1931. As the leadership of Courtaulds changed, so also did the circumstances in which the firm operated. The end of World War I approximately coincided with the expiration of the basic patents. New firms moved into the rayon industry all over the world. New rayons, notably that made by the cellulose acetate process, were developed. Filament yarn, seen as a substitute—though rather a poor one—for silk, was joined by staple fiber, used as a substitute for cotton or even wool. The result was a gigantic boom in the output of rayon. From 1920 to 1941, world output rose from 32 million pounds to over 2.8

billion pounds. Moreover, as competition grew fiercer and as costs were cut, rayon prices fell sharply, much more than those of silk, cotton, or wool. Cheap woven or knitted fabrics and hosiery in rayon or rayon blends made cheaper stockings, underwear, furnishing fabrics, and dress materials.

Courtaulds participated in the boom in sundry ways. New plants were built—in the Midlands, North Wales, and Lancashire—for yarn production and processing. To the existing textile mills in Essex were added others in Lancashire and Yorkshire to demonstrate the uses of staple fiber. Across the Atlantic, AVC built more yarn mills, and a subsidiary was established in Canada. In Europe a French company—La Soie Artificielle de Calais, renamed Les Filés de Calais in 1934—began production in 1927, and a joint enterprise, Glanzstoff-Courtaulds, started in Germany. Processing mills were set up in India, Denmark, and Spain, and a major investment was made in the biggest of the Italian rayon companies, Soria Viscosa. By 1928 Courtaulds' total issued capital had risen to £32 million, and nearly half of the company's gross income came in the form of dividends from AVC, about whose profits and performance Courtaulds remained secretive.

Great Depression

The 1929 stock market crash and the Depression of the 1930s did not afflict Courtaulds in Britain with anything like the hardships felt in older industries or by some other firms. Profits, however, were lower than in the heyday of the 1920s; the dividends from AVC came tumbling down, and in 1938 there were none. Overseas difficulties increased. The financial results of the French, German, and Canadian yarn factories were poor, and the yarn-processing mills were all sold. The value of many investments had to be written down drastically. AVC's performance was particularly worrying. The quality of its output was questioned, and a thoroughgoing inquiry into its technical and managerial shortcomings was instituted. In 1937 AVC's British boss was replaced by an American, and a substantial modernization program was launched. At home, output rose dramatically, especially in staple fiber. High-tenacity yarn, used in tire manufacture, was successfully developed. In 1935 a new venture, British Cellophane, was started for the manufacture of transparent film. However, the relative backwardness of the company in research was brought home to Samuel Courtauld by du Pont's development of nylon in the United States in 1938. Although Courtaulds' laboratories proved their practical value in a variety of ways, the money spent on basic research remained very small. The need for directed research work was just dawning when war came again.

World War II Increases Hardships

World War II brought to Courtaulds, as to other firms, various domestic problems, including shortages of raw materials and of labor, wartime controls, higher taxation, and damage from air raids. Such troubles, however, were minor compared with one event: the forced sale in 1941 of AVC. Dictated by the U.S. government, it reduced Courtaulds to about half its former size. In 1942 a tribunal awarded Courtaulds some £27 million in compensation.

These substantial cash reserves helped to shape the course of postwar recovery. This proceeded, from 1947 to 1962, under the chairmanship of J. C. (later Sir John) Hanbury-Williams, who succeeded Samuel Courtauld. The first tasks—the requisite renewals and replacements postponed by war—were joined to efforts to implement those greater changes that belatedly had been deemed necessary just before the war. New appointments were made to the board; expenditure on directed research was increased substantially; modernization programs were begun; but financial policy continued to be conservative. New rayon plants were built, mainly for staple fiber and industrial yarns. Research on the acrylic fiber Courtelle was pushed ahead. Just before the war Courtaulds had secured an interest in nylon by entering into an agreement with Imperial Chemical Industries (ICI), which had obtained the British rights to this du Pont invention. A jointly owned company, British Nylon Spinners (BNS), was set up and output grew rapidly from the 1950s. Overseas, a yarn plant was built in Australia, and the U.S. market was reentered by the establishment of a large rayon staple fiber plant in Alabama. Fears of a world shortage of the wood pulp used in rayon manufacture led to the formation of the South African Industrial Cellulose Corporation (SAICCOR) to produce pulp from eucalyptus trees.

Diversification via Acquisition in the 1950s and 1960s

For a time these recovery and expansion measures seemed to be working, and profits rose during the decade 1944 to 1954. Soon after, they started to slip and, as the full impact of nylon and other new synthetic fibers began to be felt, the whole future of rayon was in question. New policies were contrived, owing much to Frank (later Lord) Kearton, who joined the board in 1952. Expansion and diversification were the main themes. Between 1957 and 1963 British Celanese—the main producer of acetate fibers—and five other rayon companies were bought; Courtaulds' existing interest in packaging, through British Cellophane, led to the acquisition of firms making various sorts of containers. Its chemical interests, reinforced by the acquisition of British Celanese, pointed the way to a move into paints, especially with the purchase of Pinchin, Johnson Ltd. in 1960.

The process was interrupted by a takeover bid from ICI, launched in December 1961. This resulted in a three-month wonder, at that date the biggest takeover battle in Britain, causing much public debate. In March 1962 ICI conceded defeat, having secured only about 38 percent of Courtaulds' equity. In 1964 Courtaulds' share in BNS was exchanged for ICI's holdings in Courtaulds' equity. Meanwhile, the bid battle had caused some upheaval on the Courtaulds board. Kearton, who had played a major part in opposing the bid, took over the chairmanship in 1962. The last two members of the Courtauld family to sit on the board retired in 1965 and 1966. Under Kearton's aegis the company then embarked on a massive series of acquisitions in the cotton and hosiery industries. This was dictated primarily by the fear that the Lancashire cotton industry, weak and decaying in the face of inexpensive imported Asian textiles, would disappear and with it Courtaulds' biggest market for staple fiber. The hosiery industry, expanding on a growing enthusiasm for knitted fabrics, was seen as a profitable outlet for acetate and nylon yarns. It was hoped that the creation

of a vertically integrated fibers-textiles group would solve the company's excessive reliance on rayon. By 1968 Courtaulds controlled about 30 percent of U.K. cotton-type spinning capacity as well as 35 percent of warp-knitting production and smaller but significant shares in weaving and finishing.

In the short term the policy paid off. Profits rose to a high in 1975. Despite much reorganization carried out by Kearton—who left Courtaulds in 1975—and his immediate successor from 1975 to 1979, A. W. (later Sir Arthur) Knight, Courtaulds was not in good shape to cope with the recession of the late 1970s and especially with the crisis affecting the European manmade fiber and textile industries. Profits fell sharply in 1976 and, after some recovery, dropped in 1981 to the lowest point since World War II.

1980s-Era Reorganization

Sir Arthur Knight's successor as chairman in 1979 was C. A. (later Sir Christopher) Hogg, who began a gradual and total reorganization of the company. In the course of the ensuing decade, much of the edifice created by Kearton's move into spinning, weaving, and the mass production of textiles was dismantled. Despite investment in new machinery, yarns and fabrics had made losses or very small profits in the face of cheaper imports and falling markets overseas. Substantial closures of spinning and weaving mills followed. Restructuring overseas included the sale of the South African pulp interests. Employee numbers fell: the 1975 work force of well over 100,000 in the United Kingdom alone had contracted by 1988 to 46,000 in the United Kingdom and 22,000 overseas. In contrast, the other part of Kearton's diversification, into paints, chemicals, and packaging, fared much better and provided the basis for Hogg's achievements in expanding these and related aspects of the company's activities on a worldwide basis. The final logic of the textile-chemical mix created by the original success with the 1904 purchase of the viscose patents came with the demerger of 1990.

Courtaulds plc emerged from the breakup as a specialty materials industrial manufacturing company producing paints and coatings—accounting for 33 percent of profits in 1990—manmade fibers and films—30 percent—acetates and other chemicals—23 percent—packaging materials, and sundry specialized products. It operated in 37 countries. Courtaulds Textiles plc, with 28,000 employees and annual sales of £983.8, was primarily a U.K.-based operation with nearly 80 percent of its work force in that country. Its chief activities were the making of apparel and furnishing fabrics, the manufacture of garments under various brand names, and a much-reduced spinning section.

1990s Bring New Leadership, New Fibers

In 1991 30-year Courtaulds veteran Sipko Huismans advanced to the company's chief executive office, succeeding Christopher Hogg, who assumed the title of chairman. Huismans has been credited with reinvigorating Courtaulds plc by concentrating on new product development, consolidation via joint ventures and acquisitions, and geographic expansion. Asserting in a 1990 *Chief Executive* article that ''Ironically, the demerger made the mature fibers businesses an even larger proportion of the new Courtaulds,'' Huismans focused new product development on fibers that would demand higher margins. The most celebrated of these was Tencel lyocell, a cellulosic (wood pulp) fiber that boasted strength, softness, washability, and dyeability. The company started mass production of this ''luxury fiber'' in 1992 at a U.S. plant, and marketed it primarily in Japan. Brisk sales prompted rapid increases in manufacturing capacity; Courtaulds had added a second U.S. factory by 1996 and expected to bring a U.K. plant into operation in 1997. Huismans forecast annual Tencel capacity of 150,000 metric tons by 2002.

However, Huismans didn't remain with the company to see whether that prediction would become a reality. The 54-year-old executive retired in July 1996, noting in a *Daily News Record* piece that ''The main objectives I set myself—putting Tencel on the road to becoming a world-class fiber, developing a major presence in the Asia-Pacific region and rationalizing our fibers and coatings businesses in Europe and the U.S.A.—have all been set well on their way.'' Some observers disputed his analysis, however, citing Tencel's continued unprofitability in the face of high materials, capital investment, and marketing costs. It remained to be seen whether his replacement, Gordon Campbell—himself a 28-year Courtaulds veteran—would see the fiber through to profitability.

Further Reading

Coleman, D. C., *Courtaulds: An Economic and Social History,* 3 vols., Oxford: Oxford University Press, 1969–1980.

Fallon, James, ''Courtaulds Fiber Net Down 26.6% in Year,'' *Daily News Record,* May 23, 1996, pp. 2–3.

——, ''Courtaulds Fibers Profits Down 9.7% for the Year,'' *Daily News Record,* May 25, 1995, pp. 2–3.

——, ''Name Campbell Courtaulds CEO, Effective July 16,'' *Daily News Record,* December 5, 1995, pp. 2–3.

——, ''UK M-MF Producers Realign Operations,'' *Daily News Record,* June 25, 1991, p. 9.

Huismans, Sipko, ''The Parent Trap,'' *Chief Executive,* April 1995, pp. 46–49.

Jackson, Debbie, ''Courtaulds: Making Money from Mature Businesses,'' *Chemical Week,* November 17, 1993, pp. 34–35.

Knight, Arthur, *Private Enterprise and Public Intervention: The Courtaulds Experience,* London, Allen & Unwin, 1974.

Rotman, David, and Wood, Andrew, ''Trendy Fibers Lifted by Growing Fashion Markets,'' *Chemical Week,* January 27, 1993, p. 57.

Singleton, John, *Lancashire on the Scrap Heap,* Oxford: Oxford University Press, 1991.

—D. C. Coleman
—updated by April Dougal Gasbarre

Cumberland Farms, Inc.

777 Dedham Street
Canton, Massachusetts 02021
U.S.A.
(617) 828-4900
Fax: (617) 828-9012

Private Company
Incorporated: 1957 as Cumberland Farms Dairy, Inc.
Employees: 3,800
Sales: $1.32 billion (1995)
SICs: 2051 Bread & Other Bakery Products, Except
Cookies & Crackers; 5172 Petroleum & Petroleum
Products Wholesalers, Except Bulk Stations &
Terminals; 5411 Grocery Stores; 5541 Gasoline
Service Stations

Founded in 1938 as a one-cow dairy farm, Cumberland Farms, Inc. grew to become a billion-dollar-a-year corporation. In the early 1990s it ranked third among the nation's convenience store chains and was also a leader in both the retail and wholesale distribution of petroleum products. A closely held private company since its inception, it was still fully owned in the 1990s by members of the founding Haseotes family.

From Dairying to Convenience Stores

Vasilios and Aphrodite Haseotes were Greek immigrants who bought a Cumberland, Rhode Island, farm in 1938, reportedly for $84. Eventually the company they formed grew to become the largest dairy farm operation in Massachusetts, with herds of more than 3,000 cows, heifers, and calves. In 1956 the company opened a jug-milk store in Bellingham, Massachusetts.

Few convenience food stores, offering dawn-to-midnight service every day of the week, existed in the 1950s, and most of them were limited to the South. By 1967, however, there were some 8,000, with more than $1 billion per year in sales. The typical convenience food store concentrated on selling milk,

soft drinks, dairy products, snack items, tobacco, and, where legal, beer, also providing a parking lot with space for up to 15 automobiles. Their profit margins averaged 2.3 percent, compared with only 1.3 percent for the higher-volume supermarkets. With some 400 stores, Cumberland Farms Dairy, Inc. was among the industry leaders. Most of the stores were in rural and suburban areas, where land was cheaper and crime rates lower than in the cities.

In its early years as a convenience store chain, Cumberland Farms relied heavily on sales of gallon and half-gallon jugs of milk to draw in customers. These were often loss leaders, compensated for by prices on other grocery items higher than those charged by supermarkets. In 1962, when Cumberland Farms had 32 stores in four New Jersey counties, it was described as the greatest threat to the status quo in New Jersey's milk industry, which relied on state-mandated price floors. Cumberland Farms wanted to lower the price of milk by four cents a quart and contended that the reduced price would save consumers $34 million annually. To focus attention on its campaign to eliminate milk price controls in the state, it announced that it was issuing refund coupons good for 18 cents on each gallon and nine cents on each half gallon.

Cumberland Farms tried, but failed, to overturn New Jersey's milk-support law in court. It also brought suits against various New England milk-pricing boards on behalf of what it called the public's right to buy low-priced milk. In Massachusetts, however, the attorney general's office ordered Cumberland Farms in October 1973 to return at least $17,500 to customers to compensate for the alleged sale of short measured half-gallon milk containers.

Expanding into Gasoline Sales in the 1970s

In 1970 Cumberland Farms added, for the first time, a gas station to one of its stores. When major gasoline dealers abandoned their service stations in the wake of the 1973–1974 Arab oil embargo, Cumberland Farms was quick to snap up choice locations in the Northeast and Florida, although the company itself had been badly hurt by the cutoff of gasoline supplies. In 1975 Cumberland Farms opened its thousandth store. The following year it also opened a 550,000-square-foot bakery and warehouse in Westborough, Massachusetts.

Cumberland Farms, in 1985, purchased 550 Gulf and Chevron service stations and related assets in ten Northeastern states for $250 million. The transaction included 25 marketing terminals and contracts to supply gasoline to about 1,700 Gulf dealers and 2,000 stations supplied by jobbers, making Cumberland Farms the largest independent seller of gasoline in the United States and also a supplier of heating oil and aviation fuel. By this time Cumberland Farms had about 1,200 stores, of which about half were selling gas.

Cumberland Farms had tried since the 1970s to build petroleum refineries in Rhode Island and Massachusetts to protect itself from any future foreign oil embargo but had been stopped by local opponents. In 1986 it purchased a mothballed oil refinery in Come-by-Chance, Newfoundland, for $1 Canadian. The purchaser of record was Newfoundland Processing Ltd., a wholly owned subsidiary of Newfoundland Energy, Ltd., a Bermuda holding company. Demetrios B. (Jim) Haseotes, chairman and chief executive officer of Cumberland Farms, was the sole owner of Newfoundland Energy and also of Cumberland Crude Processing, Inc., which supplied crude oil to the refinery and sold its refined petroleum products, receiving funds from Cumberland Farms. Newfoundland Processing and Cumberland Crude Processing were subsequently deemed unable to repay Cumberland Farms for $47 million in cash advances. The sale of the refinery in 1994 raised about $22.1 million in funds repaid to Cumberland Farms.

Legal Challenges in the 1980s

Cumberland Farms received unwelcome publicity when the U.S. Environmental Protection Agency charged it, in 1985, with selling gasoline adulterated with alcohol beyond legal limits at 24 of its service stations. The company also was in trouble with environmentalists on a number of fronts. For example, it had for years drained a swamp in Plymouth County, Massachusetts for corn planting, despite state and federal efforts to stop the action. In 1987 the U.S. Supreme Court rejected its appeal of a federal court order to pay a $540,000 fine or restore 600 acres of the swamp to its original wetlands state. Cumberland Farms won a round in 1992, however, when a federal appeals court upheld a ruling clearing the company of responsibility for the pollution of water wells serving 40,000 people in Dedham and Westwood, Massachusetts.

Cumberland Farms withdrew from agriculture in 1986, selling 5,000 acres of Cape Cod land, along with a cranberry processing plant and freezer facilities, for $30 million. At about the same time it closed down its 400-acre dairy farm in Bridgewater, Massachusetts, pocketing $2.7 million from the federal government to slaughter the herd under a program designed to cut the nation's chronic oversupply of milk. The company next proposed to establish a $150 million waste-to-energy incinerator on 400 acres of its Bridgewater farm. The site, however, was found to contain hazardous waste substances in water and soil samples.

A full-fledged scandal struck Cumberland Farms in 1990, when two former company officials said the company had a longstanding policy of coercing confessions of theft from employees, often without corroborating evidence. Some 275 former company cashiers, several of whom filed lawsuits, said they had been falsely accused of stealing, intimidated by company officials into signing false confessions, and forced to pay the company money as restitution. The story made headlines in many newspapers and *Newsweek* and was also featured on the television program "60 Minutes."

Growing Sales and Debt

Bad publicity did not seem to be hurting the company's bottom line, however. Annual sales for its 1,150 stores was estimated as high as $3 billion in 1990. The company, while closing more than 300 of its less profitable stores, refurbished other ones. Fast foods, including sandwiches heated in microwave ovens, had been added to the 3,000 to 3,500 items sold in its stores, which included goods from the company's own bakery. Some stores also rented videotapes. To cut labor costs and increase reporting efficiency, Cumberland Farms introduced a personal computer sales and ordering system in its outlets, uploading the data nightly to the mainframe at corporate headquarters in Canton, Massachusetts. A more advanced system was introduced in 1995, supporting back-office functions, point-of-sale transactions, and scanning.

The fuel business, however, was proving more contentious. In 1991 Cumberland Farms decided to cut off supplies to gasoline jobbers in favor of the company's own service stations. As a result breach-of-contract suits were filed in several states, and about 100 distributors simply dropped the Gulf brand. In early 1992 Cumberland Farms agreed to sell one-third of its fuel marketing business, including day-to-day control, to Catamount Petroleum Corp. for more than $125 million. A limited partnership, Gulf Oil L.P., was to be formed, with Cumberland Farms holding the majority interest, while Catamount marketed the gasoline and other light petroleum products as the minority partner.

The creation of this limited partnership was delayed because, on May 1, 1992, Cumberland Farms, which had been buffeted by the recession of the early 1990s, unexpectedly filed for Chapter 11 bankruptcy protection. It placed responsibility for the action on the Industrial Bank of Japan Trust Co., which replied that the company had defaulted on a $175 million loan that the bank had renegotiated several times since 1988 and owed $65 million to a banking syndicate it led.

Cumberland Farms reportedly had a long history of slow payments to creditors. In addition, the company's "revolving-door" management was reported to have "given creditors the jitters," according to a 1992 *Boston Globe* story. Francis Alger became the first nonfamily executive to serve as president of Cumberland Farms, in 1986. Peter G. Pantazelos, brother-in-law of Jim Haseotes, succeeded Haseotes as chairman and chief executive officer of the company in March 1989 but resigned just six months after assuming the job. He was succeeded as chief executive by Richard A. Jensen, not a family member. Lily Haseotes Bentas, sister of Jim Haseotes, was appointed chairman and president of the company at the same time. According to a court document, Bentas, George Haseotes, and

Byron Haseotes owned three-quarters of the company's stock in 1992.

In October 1993, a federal judge approved a reorganization plan that proposed paying Cumberland Farms' creditors in full. The plan allowed the company to stretch payments over ten years to secured creditors owed more than $300 million, including International Bank of Japan and Chevron Corp. Unsecured creditors, who held about $35 million in debt, were to be paid over five years, without interest. An outsider-controlled board was established to oversee plans to close stores and reduce staff as well as to pay the creditors. Company lawyers said Cumberland Farms had earned $13 million on revenue of $1.2 billion in 1992.

Reemergence from Bankruptcy in the 1990s

Cumberland Farms emerged from 18 months of bankruptcy in December 1993 under this reorganization plan. The Gulf Oil L.P. joint venture went into effect in 1994, selling primarily to the convenience stores and service stations owned by Cumberland. A fiscal 1995 disclosure filing to the Securities and Exchange Commission, however, listed $11.9 million in payments of debt at less than face value and forgiveness of debt. The outsider-directed company also charged breach of fiduciary duties and violations of the reorganization plan in connection with acquisitions by an affiliate of Jim Haseotes of certain of the company's certificates. Following a court order unfavorable to Haseotes, the company purchased the certificates from this affiliate. The company also instituted legal proceedings to seek, in its words, "an accounting and possible disgorgement of funds received by Mr. Haseotes in connection with the sale of the refinery and an accounting of funds distributed to Mr. Haseotes to pay certain tax liabilities."

At the end of fiscal 1995, Cumberland Farms consisted of three divisions. The Cumberland Farms division included the convenience store, retail gasoline, and manufacturing operations. The Gulf Oil division marketed refined petroleum products on a wholesale basis to lessee dealers as well as to company-operated locations. The VSH Realty division acquired and constructed real property for lease to the other divisions of the company and others for use as retail and wholesale sales locations.

In late 1993 Cumberland Farms had about 900 convenience stores and about 2,000 Gulf gasoline stations operating in New England, the mid-Atlantic states, and Florida. Its revenues rose from $1.1 billion in fiscal 1993 (the fiscal year ending September 30, 1993) to $1.19 billion in fiscal 1994 and $1.32 billion in fiscal 1995. Net income was $7.7 million in fiscal 1993, followed by a loss of $1.7 million in fiscal 1994 and a net profit of $34.8 million in fiscal 1995. The long-term debt was $236.7 million at the end of fiscal 1995.

These figures did not include Gulf Oil L.P., whose assets included a 5.5-billion-barrel gasoline storage system made up of 14 terminals in the eastern United States, including a massive "tank farm" on Neville Island, Pennsylvania. Gulf Oil's revenues were in excess of those of Cumberland Farms itself. It had sales of $1.34 billion in fiscal 1994 and $1.82 billion in fiscal 1995. Net income came to $15.1 million and $20.7 million, respectively.

Principal Operating Units

Cumberland Farms; Gulf Oil; VSH Realty.

Further Reading

Biddle, Frederic M., "Cumberland Farms Seeks Bankruptcy Protection," *Boston Globe,* May 2, 1992, pp. 1, 13.

Cotter, Wes, "New Venture Tries To Boost Gulf Name in Pittsburgh Area," *Pittsburgh Business Times,* January 31, 1994, pp. 1–2.

"Cumberland Farms Dairy Facility Auctions Off Its Heavy Machinery," *Boston Globe,* April 26, 1987, p. 39.

Dumanoski, Dianne, "High Court Upholds Order on Restoration of Wetlands," *Boston Globe,* February 23, 1987, pp. 17, 22.

Gorov, Linda, "Cumberland Buying 520 Chevron Units," *Boston Globe,* November 9, 1985, p. 8.

Hammer, Joshua, "Fear in the Back Room," *Newsweek,* September 24, 1990, p. 64.

McKibben, Gordon, "Making Money, Not Friends, Far from the Farm," *Boston Globe,* January 20, 1987, pp. 39, 43.

Marder, Dianna, "Security Pair Describes Cumberland Policy," *Boston Globe,* August 16, 1990, pp. 55–56.

Pastore, Richard, "Cumberland Looks to PCs To Compete in Crowded Field," *Computerworld,* August 27, 1990, pp. 33, 40.

Russell, Gerard F., "Cumberland Farms Rises Out of Ch. 11," *Boston Globe,* October 23, 1993, p. 29.

Sullivan, Joseph, "Politicians Make Milk an Issue," *New York Times,* August 5, 1973, p. 65.

—Robert Halasz

The Daiei, Inc.

4-1-1, Minatojima Nakamachi
Chuo-ku, Kobe 650
Japan
(81) 78 302-5001
Fax: (81) 78 302-5572
Internet: http://isr.co.jp/daiei/index.html

Public Company
Incorporated: 1957
Employees: 16,612
Sales: ¥3.2 trillion (1995) (US $30 billion)
Stock Exchanges: Tokyo Osaka NASDAQ Brussels
    American
SICs: 5300 General Merchandise Stores; 5331 Variety
    Stores; 5411 Grocery Stores; 5140 Groceries &
    Related Products; 5130 Apparel, Piece Goods, &
    Notions; 5090 Miscellaneous Durable Goods

The Daiei, Inc. is Japan's largest retailer, ranking sixth among the world's leading retailers. Daiei founder, Chairman and CEO Isao Nakauchi, once boasted that his company sells "everything except ladies and opium." Indeed, the group includes more than 7,700 outlets in more than 50 retail categories, from supermarkets to department stores to warehouse clubs and convenience stores. The company even has more than 400 "superstores," each featuring a massive supermarket on the ground floor and a department store on the upper floors. Not limited to retailing, Daiei also owns and operates the Fukuoka Dome and Fukuoka Daiei Hawks, a major league baseball team, as well as Western-style fast food restaurants, a financial services network, and real estate.

1950s Origins

Nakauchi founded Daiei in his hometown of Osaka in 1957; the company's name is a complicated play on words that means both prosperity of Osaka and big prosperity. A pharmacist's son, Nakauchi had made a small fortune in the years after World War II by participating in a venture that sold penicillin at above the legal price. His brother and some associates were arrested for their roles in the scheme, but the experience taught Nakauchi that risk taking and making money were inseparable. His first Daiei store was a pharmacy called Housewives' Store Daiei. He gave its parent company the name Daiei Pharmaceutical Company. Japan's post-Korean War depression was then reaching its lowest point, and Osaka shoppers appreciated Daiei's discount pricing policy. Its initial success soon inspired him to open more stores in the Osaka area.

The poor economic conditions also proved fortuitous for Daiei at the wholesale level. Manufacturers were grateful for the fact that Nakauchi always paid cash for their goods. He also bought whatever surpluses overextended manufacturers may have accumulated and passed on the savings to consumers. Thus Daiei quickly ceased to be merely a drug store chain; as Nakauchi would recall years later, "We soon moved from drugs into candies and other foods and from cosmetics and toiletries into hard goods." In 1970 the company dropped the focus on specialized retailing and shortened its name to its current form.

Achieves National Dominance in 1970s

Daiei expanded to become a nationwide chain. By the time it celebrated its fifteenth anniversary in 1972, the company was operating 75 superstores and had become Japan's largest supermarket operator and second largest retailer. It had achieved such rapid and overwhelming success by breaking many of Japanese retailing's time-honored rules. In a nation where small shops often banded together in cartels to keep prices artificially high, Daiei was a high-volume, low-price retailer. "Even our barbers and laundries have self-protective cartels," Nakauchi once complained. Nakauchi, an unlikely but open admirer of Mao Tse-tung's strategic wisdom, cast Daiei in such a mold to draw on the strength of "the masses," offering quality goods at the lowest possible prices. In 1970, when outraged consumers realized that Japanese television sets were being sold for less in the United States than at home, Daiei leapt into the breach, signing a marketing deal with Crown Radio and selling Crown sets under their own name for less than half the going rate. Daiei was a pioneer in introducing the concept of house brands to

Company Perspectives:

In order to create stores adapted to the lifestyles and the needs of our customers, Daiei has adopted a system of companies that hold distinct functions. With this structure as a foundation, Daiei is striving to create sales areas and product lines adapted to each locality as well as to strengthen product development and purchasing capabilities. We have continued to put together a low-cost mass-merchandising system through increased attention to improved productivity and to more efficient store operations. Daiei has also worked tirelessly to recover from the effects of the Great Hanshin Earthquake. Daiei's basic policy is "For our Customers—Good Products at Lower Prices for a More Bountiful Society." With this as our motto, we will continue to implement sound measures to realize our goal of Everyday Low Prices.

Japanese consumers, who were used to paying higher prices for recognized brand names. The following year, Daiei acquired Crown and added more electronics goods and household appliances to the Daiei name. Nakauchi kept his overhead low by opening stores in the suburbs, rather than the densely populated, high-rent urban areas favored by Japanese department stores. For his iconoclasm in a consensus-oriented society, he was reviled by ex-friends, threatened by irate competitors, and ostracized by the business establishment, but this treatment did not deter him from his vision of revolutionizing Japanese retailing, an arduous process he once compared to Mao's travails.

In the 1970s the company began to internationalize, diversifying its range of goods and services even further. In 1972 it created Daiei U.S.A. as a wholly owned subsidiary and opened a branch in a Honolulu shopping center. Taking advantage of the liberalization of Japanese laws regarding the presence of foreign retailers, Daiei entered into joint ventures to open branches of U.S. department store Joseph Magnin and Swift & Company's Dipper Dan Ice Cream Shoppe chain in Japan.

In 1974 Daiei surpassed the sales of department store giant Mitsukoshi to become Japan's largest retailer. Once again, Nakauchi's ambitions were scarcely satisfied. In the spring of that year, Daiei began selling J.C. Penney merchandise as part of an arrangement with the U.S. retailer to test its popularity in Japan. The venture proved successful, and several months later, Daiei and J.C. Penney entered into a joint venture to open stores in Japan under the Penney name, beginning in 1976. Under the agreement, Daiei and Penney each owned 47.5 percent, with the remaining five percent going to trading company C. Itoh.

In 1978 Daiei continued to capitalize on the popularity of Western goods in Japan when it became the sole Japanese agent for British department store Marks & Spencer. Daiei chose Marks & Spencer merchandise because of its reputation for price competitiveness, especially in food and clothing. For its part, Marks & Spencer, which already had a substantial presence in Hong Kong, saw Japan as its largest remaining potential export market.

Diversification into Fast Food Intensifies in the 1980s

In 1979 Daiei joined with Wendy's International to open Wendy's fast food restaurants and Victoria Station steak houses in Japan. Wendy's Japanese rollout did not progress as quickly as hoped because of the inflexibility of the American parent organization. Portions and stores, for example, were too big for Japanese tastes. And although the chain expanded too fast early on, it had fewer than 30 restaurants by 1988 and the operation had yet to earn a profit.

Other cross-cultural ventures undertaken during the decade were more successful. In 1980 Daiei made its first serious incursion into the U.S. market when it acquired in its entirety Holiday Mart, a three-store discount chain in Honolulu, Hawaii. It also opened its first U.S. purchasing office. Not least of all, it joined with Au Printemps to open branches of that venerable French department store in Japan; the first Au Printemps Japon opened in Kobe in 1981, followed by stores in Sapporo in 1982 and in Tokyo the year after that.

Daiei's supermarket operations continued to flourish. At the outset of the 1980s, Daiei controlled one-fifth of the entire Japanese food retail market. In 1981 it reorganized that side of its business somewhat when it merged its Sanko affiliate with food store chain Maruetsu. Daiei and Maruetsu each owned 50 percent of the new company, which immediately became the nation's ninth largest retailer, boasting 140 branches. Also in 1981, Daiei acquired a 10.5 percent stake in Takashimaya, another department store chain, making it that company's principal shareholder.

In 1984 Daiei's sales reached ¥1.4 trillion, and its chain of superstores had grown to 160. Daiei continued to expand at a breakneck pace, opening a branch in Tokyo's expensive Ginza district during this same period. Nakauchi financed this continuous augmentation with heavy borrowing, and the cost of financing this debt forced the company to post a ¥11.9 billion loss in 1984, despite its massive sales. The next year, it lost ¥8.8 billion, spurring speculation among some analysts that Daiei's sixty-something year-old founder and CEO had lost his Midas touch.

Nakauchi insisted all along that these deficits were part of his plan and that continued expansion would pay off in the long run. Daiei had cleverly spread its borrowing among four different banks—contrary to the usual Japanese corporate practice of borrowing from one bank, which then allowed that bank to become the company's principal stockholder. This wise move enabled Daiei to preserve its independence; indeed, Nakauchi has always been Daiei's principal shareholder. In 1986 the company returned to profitability, earning ¥1.1 billion, and by 1987 it was healthy enough to acquire bankrupt sewing machine manufacturer Riccar at the request of the Ministry of International Trade and Industry. In that same year, it announced a five-year plan to install an electronic information network to link all of its branches, offices, and affiliates, starting with an ¥11 billion point-of-sale (POS) system for its superstores. POS systems give retailers quick and accurate information on sales and inventories, information that can be used to improve inventory control.

Retail Powerhouse Rolls on in the 1990s

Although some Japanese retailers began to follow Isao Nakauchi's price-slashing lead in the 1990s, none could keep up with his pace. He created Japan's first wholesale membership club in 1992. (Like Sam Walton's groundbreaking stores, the new chain operated under the name Kuo's, an alternate pronunciation of Nakauchi's given name.) In 1992 he brought "everyday low pricing" to the country, even abbreviating the concept as "EDLP" in Roman letters for advertisements. Daiei's Big-A Co. box stores hoped to mimic ALDI's international success with limited lines of nonperishable staples in bare-bones stores. But even this was not enough for Nakauchi; in 1995, he announced his goal to slash consumer goods prices in half by 2010. This strategy continued to enjoy success: in the mid-1990s, Daiei accounted for 13 percent of Japan's grocery sales.

Nakauchi formed a Chinese joint venture and opened his first supermarket there in 1995. He also continued to invest in his Hawaiian operations, acquiring a supermarket in 1994 and expanding his shopping center there two years later. In 1993, the company opened the first phase of its Fukuoka Dome in Japan, home of the Fukuoka Daiei Hawks baseball team. By 1998 this twin-domed retail and entertainment complex was expected to have a 1,000-room hotel, amusement rides, and shopping.

Daiei's revenues increased to more than ¥3 trillion in fiscal 1995 (ended February 28), but its net income slid dramatically, from ¥10 billion in 1992 to ¥5.4 billion in 1994. Nature conspired to inflict a ¥50.7 billion loss on the group in 1995, when a January earthquake demolished eight superstores in the Kobe area. Daiei experienced a partial rebound in fiscal 1996, when it recorded a ¥5 billion profit.

The Daiei's erratic fiscal performance again raised the question of its future leadership. Although septuagenarian founder and CEO Isao Nakauchi appeared unmotivated to relinquish control of the company, he had prepared for that eventuality by grooming son Jun Nakauchi as executive vice-president and chief operating officer.

Principal Operating Units

Beijing Liaison Office (China); Seoul Liaison Office (Korea); Shanghai Liaison Office (China); Taipei Liaison Office (Taiwan, R.O.C.); Hong Kong Liaison Office; Bangkok Liaison Office (Thailand); Hi-Daiei Trading Co., Ltd. (Philippines); Jakarta Liaison Office (Indonesia); Sydney Liaison Office (Australia); D International, Inc. (United States); Los Angeles Liaison Office (United States); New York Liaison Office (United States); Amsterdam Liaison Office (Netherlands); Milano Liaison Office (Italy); Printemps Ginza S.A., Paris Office (France); London Liaison Office (United Kingdom); Kaheka Office (United States).

Further Reading

Bulman, Robin, "Price-Cutting Effort by Store Group in Japan May Help US Exporters," *Journal of Commerce and Commercial,* April 18, 1994, p. 3A.

Butterfield, Fox, "Japan's Retailing Colossus," *The New York Times,* November 3, 1974.

"Daiei's Discount Empire Prospers," *World Business Weekly,* January 12, 1981.

Holden, Ted, "A Retail Rebel Has the Establishment Quaking," *Business Week,* April 1, 1991, pp. 39–40.

"Japan: Mao in the Supermarket," *Time,* June 28, 1971.

Markowitz, Arthur, "Daiei Opens Kuo's, Japan's First Club," *Discount Store News,* October 5, 1992, pp. 1–2.

Merrefield, David, "Big-A Powers Growth at Daiei," *Supermarket News,* October 5, 1992, pp. 11–15.

——, "Japan's Pricing Pioneer," *Supermarket News,* October 5, 1992, pp. 11–15.

O'Brien, Tim, "Japan's Fukuoka Dome Set To Open in March," *Amusement Business,* September 28, 1992, pp. 1–2.

"The Perils of Popularity," *The Economist,* August 24, 1996, p. 53.

"Retailers Get Ready To Move into the U.S.," *Business Week,* August 4, 1980.

Sherrid, Pamela, "What Barriers?" *Forbes,* October 10, 1983, p. 180.

Simmons, Tim, "Big Business," *Supermarket News,* October 5, 1992, p. 2.

Smith, Lee, and Griffiths, Philip Jones, "Japan's Autocratic Managers," *Fortune,* January 7, 1985, pp. 56–65.

Zwiebach, Elliot, "Daiei Net Tumbles in Quake Wake," *Supermarket News,* May 22, 1995, p. 23.

—Douglas Sun
—updated by April Dougal Gasbarre

Dawn Food Products, Inc.

2021 Micor Drive
Jackson, Michigan 49203
U.S.A.
(517) 789-4400
Fax: (517) 789-4465

Private Company
Incorporated: 1920
Employees: 1,200
Sales: $350 million
SICs: 2045 Blended & Prepared Flour; 2099 Food
Preparations

Dawn Food Products, Inc. is the largest, oldest, most experienced and renowned bakery mix producer in the United States. The company makes a large assortment of mixes, icings, fillings, and frozen products that are marketed, sold, and distributed to both major retail supermarket chains and small, owner-operated grocery stores who run their own in-house bakeries. The Dawn Food Products line includes such items as Hand-Cut Donut Mixes, Blueberry and Cherry Cake Donut Mixes, Apple Cake Donut Mixes, Sour Cream Old-Fashioned Donut Mixes, Holland Creme Filling, French Donut Mix, RTU Donut Icings, RTU Donut Glazes, Carrot Cake Mix, Sponge Cake Mix, Cream Cheese Icing, Caramel Glossy Icing, and a host of other products such as pie glazes, pie fillings, danish fillings, brownie mixes, muffin mixes, bagel mixes, bread mixes, and frozen kosher fruit sticks. Through expansion of its distribution and sales network overseas, the company has established a presence in Costa Rica, the Dominican Republic, England, Jamaica, Japan, Malaysia, and Mexico.

Early History

During the period immediately before America's entry into World War I, Eugene Worden and Grover Lutz, both from Union City, Michigan, decided to open a bakery of their own. The two men, with extensive training and experience as bakers, were determined to establish a new business that made a whole range of fresh-baked goods such as donuts, breads, pies, and cakes. Knowing their reputations as bakers, the local townspeople encouraged Worden and Lutz in the pursuit of their dream. With a small loan from the local bank and savings they had accumulated for many years, the baking entrepreneurs opened their own store located at 112 East Michigan Street in the small town of Jackson, close to Union City. Named the Century Bakery, the new bakery was an immediate success, and both Worden's and Lutz's reputations as bakers spread throughout the local vicinity.

During the First World War, there was no interruption in the production of pastry and breads by the Century Bakery. In fact, the bakery's product line was growing at a fast rate, and the two owners could hardly keep their ovens hot enough for the increased demand. The bakery's most popular and largest selling item, however, was a light, fluffy donut that, according to legend, made people's mouths water. Soon the company's donuts products were in greater demand than any other item, including bread. By the time the war ended on November 11, 1918, Century Bakery had become widely known as the preeminent bakery in the region. Most important, numerous bakers in neighboring communities began to ask Worden and Lutz for the mixes to their products. The greatest demand was for the bakery's donut mixes.

In a change of direction that was to have far-reaching consequences for their bakery, Worden and Lutz decided to begin selling prepared pastry mixes to other bakeries in the vicinity. As the demand for prepared mixes grew, the owners finally recognized that their company was making more money by selling its mixes than it was by selling its bakery products through the store on East Michigan Avenue. After some intense deliberation, Worden and Lutz decided to close the bakery and its retail operation and open a company devoted exclusively to producing, marketing, and selling pastry mixes. Named Dawn Food Products, for the time of day that donuts are made, the country's first industrial mix company was formed and incorporated in 1920.

Since the location on East Michigan Avenue was well suited for a small bakery, but hardly adequate for the manufacture of mixes on a large scale, the owners moved the entire operation to

Company Perspectives:

Dawn's bigger now, with international expansion and a product line that practically grows daily! To meet increasing customer demands, we utilize the latest equipment and procedures in all our facilities. Our product development team works hard to anticipate market trends and formulate new mixes, icings, fillings and frozen products for today's customers. But some things about Dawn remain the same—products that, most importantly, taste delicious. Fresh, high quality ingredients. Demanding, quality control testing of every batch. Personal "Dawn family" supervision of every aspect of the business from our door to yours. And you have our promise that Dawn will continue to help grow your business in every way we can . . . because our success depends on your success. That's what our Dawn "Circle of Excellence" is all about: Great People—Making Excellent Products—Taking Good Care of Our Customers.

330 Otsego, a location within Jackson that allowed for extensive expansion. As the company grew during the decade of the 1920s, its product line became more and more varied. Dawn Food Products began to sell prepared mixes not only for a wide variety of donuts, but also for bread and other kinds of pastries. By the end of the decade, the company was supplying mixes to bakeries throughout western and central Michigan.

The Great Depression and World War II

When the stock market crashed during the autumn of 1929, Dawn Food Products was affected like most other companies in America. Numerous employees who had been hired during the previous years were laid off, and the wages of those who remained were frozen. Production dropped precipitously, especially in pastry mixes, since most people during the early 1930s did not have the money to spend on items such as desserts. Demand for bread mixes remained, however, at a constant level and actually helped keep the company solvent during the harshest years of economic upheaval. The one thing people did need was bread.

In 1936, a young man named Marlin Jones joined the company. Although the Great Depression would not end until the beginning of World War II, the worst years for Dawn Food Products were over, and the country once again began to resume its normal course of activities. These activities included, of course, the increased consumption of pastries, and the demand for Dawn's mixes began to increase slowly. As the company's financial situation became more stable, it started to hire more employees, with the ultimate intention of returning to the pre-Depression level. One of the new workers was Marlin Jones. Ambitious and industrious, Jones was quickly noticed by management and given greater responsibilities in marketing and sales.

When America formally declared war on Germany and Japan in December of 1941, the entire agricultural industry, from small farms to large cooperatives, was organized by the federal government to ensure the flow of food to the country's soldiers serving both at home and overseas. Commodities such as flour and corn grew scarce, as the nation converted its industrial base and agricultural produce to a wartime footing. Jones, now a part of Dawn's management team, was assigned the task of supplying a constant flow of necessary grain for the production of bread and various other mixes. Traveling from one state to another across the broad expanse of the American landscape, he made arrangements with both the federal government and farmers to commit large tracts of grain fields to Dawn Food Products for specific kinds and quantities of food production. By the time World War II ended in 1945, numerous soldiers had tasted the wares that came from Dawn's packaged mixes.

Postwar Transition and Growth

In spite of the developments during the war years, and the benefits the company garnered through its association with the federal government, Dawn Food Products, Inc. remained a relatively small and highly localized operation. After the original owners passed away, their families were not inclined to assume leadership of the company. Sensing an opportunity that comes once in a lifetime, Marlin Jones decided to purchase control of the company in 1955. The transition in ownership did not signify any changes in the company's basic product, namely, pastry mixes, but in terms of long-term strategy and operational matters, Jones was ready to implement a comprehensive development program. The new owner's first step was to expand the product line to include icings and fillings for pastries, as well as increasing the number of different types of donuts mixes available to bakeries and other retail food establishments. One of the most important developments during this time was the formation of Dawn Equipment Company. Created in 1957, just two years after he took control of the firm, Dawn Equipment Company began to manufacture bakery equipment for large volume users. One of the first pieces of equipment sold was a bakery fryer that produced donuts.

From the time Jones took control of the company, he was committed to expanding its presence from a local operation to a nationwide organization. Consequently, a new marketing strategy was initiated and directed to bakeries and supermarket chains across the country. As the company continued to grow, Jones decided to build a new plant in Jackson's Micor Industrial Park. Completed in 1967, the new building featured an office area, a total of three floors devoted just to production, and a mixing tower that rose five floors high. The building and its facilities was, at the time, a reflection of state-of-the art technology in the mixing industry.

During the 1950s and 1960s, Marlin Jones's sons began their association with Dawn Food Products. During summer vacations and other holidays during their college schooling, Ronald, Steven, and Miles began to work at various odd jobs around the company's production and distribution facilities in Jackson. Starting at the bottom of the ladder, the brothers first unloaded boxcars of sugar and flour for use in production. Later, at the suggestion of their father, the three young men worked in the plant and learned the intricacies of mixing different concoctions for pastry, bread, and a wide variety of other products. As they grew older, with each successive summer holiday they learned more and more about the company and were given greater responsibilities. Before long, the three young men just out of college were ready to assume the leadership roles within the company for which their father had prepared them.

Continued Growth and Expansion in the 1980s

Many changes were to take place at Dawn Food Products during the 1980s. Marlin Jones died during the early part of the decade, but his cultivation of family ownership, control, and hands-on management continued through his three sons. Readily prepared to run the company, Ronald became the president of the firm. Steven served as executive vice-president and Miles was appointed vice-president of operations. Marlin Jones, during the time of his tenure from 1955 to 1983, had increased the company's annual sales from less than $1 million to more than $27 million. Without changing the direction and purpose of Dawn Food Products, the three sons developed the company's marketing techniques and production facilities with uninterrupted resolve.

A typical week at Dawn's mixing plant during the late 1980s involved the use of more than one million pounds of flour, 300,000 pounds of sugar, 20 different varieties of shortening products, and, something that an industry analyst would not expect of an American firm, spices and herbs from as far away as East India and other exotic locations around the world. The new generation of management renewed its commitment to quality control and guaranteed that the same mixes would bake the same way all of the time. To ensure this type of quality control for all of its products, Miles made certain that a sample of the baking mix was extracted for testing from each batch. As the reputation of the company grew, annual sales increased and more expansion was undertaken. Soon the company's product mixes were sought after by companies in other countries, and management arranged licensing agreements with firms in Canada and Japan to use its tested formulas to produce mixes for pastries and breads.

The 1990s and Beyond

During the late 1980s and early 1990s, the trend toward in-store bakeries became more and more pronounced within large supermarket chains across the United States. In-store bakeries that were in full operation—baking breads, preparing birthday cakes, and making donuts—were beginning to reap large profits for their retailers. As a result, Dawn Food Products decided to capitalize on this movement by providing a planning and operational package for supermarkets to employ. Dawn emphasized the importance of product consistency to its customers, stressing that the single most important factor in keeping customers happy was that all mixes, fillings, icings, toppings, and frozen products exhibit the same taste from one day to the next. When large supermarket chains began to contract with Dawn to help set up their own in-store bakeries, the company was ready with

more than 3,500 manufactured products of its own to provide to retailers.

Relying heavily on consumer research and sophisticated marketing techniques, Dawn helped in-house bakeries customize their products to the needs of its clientele. One such program, called the "Select Cake Program," used socioeconomic data gathered from customers to tailor its cake assortments to the preferences of the neighborhood within which the supermarket was located. By the mid-1990s, cakes accounted for approximately 30 percent of in-house bakery sales volume, and there was no indication that the trend would diminish. Equally important as the demographic research for its Select Cake Program, management at Dawn started to give greater weight to children as one of the preeminent and fast growing consumer segments. Through its marketing and research department, Dawn discovered that children influence decisions on what to buy in the in-store bakeries, and the company began to develop promotions and products that were sure to appeal to these young customers. Another development at the company was its emphasis on "better for you" bakery products. Once again, Dawn's marketing and research development department had discovered that people were willing to pay a bit more for natural ingredients in the food that they eat. If they could believe the manufacturer's list of ingredients on the package, and the product tasted good, consumers were more than ready to take these items home to their families.

Although some management changes occurred at the top in the 1990s (for example, Peter Staelens was brought in as chief financial officer), the three Jones brothers continued to retain their ownership, control, and management of Dawn Food Products. The family business had no intention of slowing down and, by the mid-1990s, Dawn had established distributorships in each of the contiguous states as well as numerous offices worldwide, including Canada, Japan, Costa Rica, the Dominican Republic, England, Jamaica, Malaysia, and Mexico.

Further Reading

Dawn: The Family Album, Jackson, Mich.: Dawn Food Products, Inc., 1994.

Dowdell, Stephen, "The Right Stuff," *Supermarket News,* March 11, 1996, p. 36.

Krumrei, Doug, "Let the Good Times Roll," *Bakery Production and Marketing,* June 24, 1995, p. 62.

Malovany, Dan, "Don't Change That Dial," *Bakery Production and Marketing,* May 24, 1995, p. 68.

——, "How New Products Drive Automation," *Bakery Production and Marketing,* June 24, 1995, p. 18.

"Voice of America," *Bakery Production and Marketing,* January 24, 1995, p. 62.

—Thomas Derdak

DeKalb Genetics Corporation

3100 Sycamore Road
DeKalb, Illinois 60115
U.S.A.
(815) 758-3461
Fax: (815) 758-6953

Public Company
Incorporated: 1917 as the DeKalb County Agricultural
    Association
Employees: 1,797
Sales: $430 million (1995)
Stock Exchanges: NASDAQ
SICs: 0115 Corn; 0116 Soybeans; 0119 Cash Grains, Not
    Elsewhere Classified; 8731 Commercial Physical
    Research

DeKalb Genetics Corporation is one of the largest and most successful international research, production, and marketing firms in the agribusiness industry. The company's focus is on seed products, including hybrid corn, sorghum, sunflower, varietal soybeans, and alfalfa. DeKalb is also one of the world's leaders in the research and production of hybrid swine breeding stock. Devoting 14 percent of every dollar to research, the midwestern company has created an impressive portfolio of biotechnological patents, such as the first fertile transformed corn patent, the first patent for insect-resistant corn, and a host of transgenic corn production and breeding technique patents. With 34 research facilities in the United States and 16 overseas, the company has garnered a large portion of the agribusiness market in Canada, Argentina, Mexico, France, Germany, South Africa, and Thailand. Selling 2.5 million units of corn, 4.5 million units of soybean, and 350,000 units of sorghum in 1995 alone, company sales reached an all-time high of $430 million.

Early History

DeKalb Genetics Corporation had its start in the farming land of the Midwest. During the late 1890s and early 1900s,

farmers in DeKalb County, Illinois, began to develop an awareness of the many agricultural problems that confronted them. Although their farms were prosperous, they recognized the need for improved soil fertility, balanced rotation of crops, a pure seed law, more farmer control over the pricing and marketing of farm produce, and the improvement of crop varieties. These needs led the farmers to organize the Farmers' Institute, the purpose of which was to invite university professors to talk about different aspects of better farming in counties throughout the state.

As the popularity of and interest in groups such as the Farmers' Institute began to grow, the farmers realized that they needed bankers and newspapermen to help in expanding the information that was being provided about farming. In January of 1912, farmers, bankers, and the county board of supervisors from DeKalb met and pledged $10,000 to sustain an annual budget for a new organization that would attack the problems of soil fertility and legume seed. The group traveled to the University of Illinois and hired W.G. Eckhardt to act as the organization's first farm advisor. One of the first farm groups in the United States supported by farmer contributions, the new organization was called the DeKalb County Soil Improvement Association.

As the organization and its membership grew over the next few years, Eckhardt began to make numerous trips to and from Idaho to buy good seed. Illinois had no seed law and, as a result, nearby states used counties such as DeKalb as dumping grounds for inferior seed. Securing a reliable seed was an important and far-reaching project, therefore, and considerable amounts of money were used during the purchases in Idaho. Since the DeKalb County Soil Improvement Association was formed primarily for educational purposes and not for business transactions, the membership decided to create the DeKalb County Agricultural Association to take care of the seed business and also to conduct the business affairs of the DeKalb County Soil Improvement Association.

On June 2, 1917, the DeKalb County Agricultural Association was incorporated, and its first business transaction was to purchase legume seed and limestone, which was spread over farmland before legumes could be grown, and to handle seed

Company Perspectives:

At the heart of our company are dedicated, knowledgeable, well-trained professionals who are working to improve the productivity of agriculture. They are a diverse group of people including plant breeders, geneticists, technicians, accountants, agronomists, salespersons, statisticians, writers and secretaries. They are willing to go the extra mile because they believe in the importance of what they are doing and the mission of DEKALB: to provide our customers with quality products and services that will increase their productivity and profitability.

corn. In those days, seed corn was openly pollinated and consequently varied in quality significantly from one year to the next. Most farmers in the Midwest tried to select their own seed during good years and then turned to commercial sources during the poor years, especially when early freezes had damaged the quality of the crop. One of Eckhardt's priorities was to develop a seed corn that was of extremely high quality and increased yield and could be sold to farmers in the area.

Eckhardt hired a man named Charlie Gunn as the Association's corn breeder, and Gunn went to work immediately. The corn that the Association had been handling at the time was Webb's Western Plowman, a relatively good variety of corn. Gunn wanted to produce an earlier strain, and he accomplished this feat by selecting ripe ears from green stalks. Called Gunn's Western Plowman, the selection was grown throughout northern Illinois. Yet Gunn wanted to improve both its earliness and its yield, so he blended various types of seed to produce a better yielding strain of corn.

During the early 1920s, Tom Roberts, a graduate from Iowa State College, replaced Eckhardt as farm advisor to the Association. Like his predecessor, Roberts continued to work closely with Gunn on the improvement of corn. Production of a utility type of corn, which was resistant to disease, involved ear-to-row testing techniques and many other methods, but progress was slow and cumbersome. When the two men heard of a new hybrid idea in corn, they believed that this new method might be the way to improve the corn then being grown.

Experimentation During the 1930s and 1940s

It was not until 1932 that the first cross-breeding of corn was tested by the Association. The results were so successful, however, that a large field of the variety was planted in 1933. That fall, the new type of corn had yielded 21 bushels more per acre than open-pollinated Western Plowman. In the spring of 1934, Tom Roberts decided to grow the new type of hybrid seed corn in anticipation of selling it to local farmers on the open market. Production was estimated at 300 bushels, but, unfortunately, the dust storms of the 1930s began to take their toll. Temperatures rose suddenly, rain was nonexistent, and the seed crop began to suffer. Artificial irrigation was used, yet only 350 bushels of seed graded out 325 bushels of kernels. The seed was sold to nearby farmers, and preparations were made for the next plant-

ing season of 1935. With a different hybrid combination, and more irrigation, the planting was a huge success. The Association began selling the hybrid corn seed as DeKalb 601 to farmers across the nation, and the results were overwhelming. A higher quality and increased yield revolutionized farm productivity. Most important, however, the hybrid corn seed increased farm income and helped pay off farm mortgages, thus saving an untold number of family farms at the height of America's Great Depression.

In searching for an appropriate logo that would incorporate the activity of the Association, Tom Roberts recalled from his earliest memories that, during the early 1900s, dairy cattle were called "mortgage lifters," since it was the cattle that provided enough income for farmers to retain their property during hard economic times. During the 1920s, the raising and selling of hogs for commercial purposes helped farmers pay off their mortgages. When the Association developed hybrid corn, Roberts was certain that a 20 percent increase in a farmer's yield from DeKalb hybrid corn would provide more income to pay for mortgages than dairy cattle or hogs. In a burst of inspiration, he said, "Let's put wings on an ear of corn to represent the lifting of the mortgages," and a soon-to-be famous logo was created.

As a natural extension of its activities in the United States, near the end of the 1930s and during the early 1940s, the Association began to export its hybrid corn seed to Canada. The fields and soil of Alberta and Saskatchewan were perfect for developing an even higher quality and increased yield hybrid corn. During the Second World War, the DeKalb County Agricultural Association worked in concert with the U.S. government to provide a constant flow of agricultural products for the Allied war effort. Increasing the yield of its hybrid corn allowed the United States to help Britain and other Allied nations to weather the war years, during which starvation was just around the corner for many people.

Postwar Developments and Expansion

After the Second World War, the American Midwest became the "breadbasket to the world," and DeKalb was at the forefront of increasing production and developing higher quality seed during these years. In the decade of the 1950s, the company established an entomology department, which began to study the effects insects have on a wide variety of crops, but especially corn and sorghum. The company also established numerous test plots throughout the Midwest to gather hybrid and variety crop data. At approximately the same time, DeKalb initiated a major research program that placed crops across the United States and tested the potential for top performing hybrids and varieties by sampling weather and soil conditions as well as insect and disease situations. In 1956, DeKalb was the first company to produce a high-quality, high-yield hybrid sorghum.

The company's investment in research and development continued during the 1960s. Dekalb created a pathology department to study the diseases and the changes in those diseases in both new and existing hybrids. A germplasm resources department was also created to collect germplasm from around the world and evaluate it for disease and insect reactions. In addition, a biotechnology research laboratory was formed to begin experimenting with the possibility of making genetic improvements in corn and other seed, which could not be achieved by using the traditional techniques of plant breeding. All of these developments enabled DeKalb to reach the pinnacle of success by the late 1960s and early 1970s. A new hybrid alfalfa was created in 1967, and hybrid sunflowers were developed in 1972. By 1974, the company had captured 23 percent of the corn seed market, second only to Pioneer Hi-Bred International.

Transition During the 1970s and 1980s

Unfortunately, the company's success was not to last. Tom Roberts, still influential at DeKalb even though his son Tom Roberts, Jr. was now chairman, convinced the Board of Directors to make the momentous decision to diversify into energy businesses at the height of the diversification craze in corporate America. DeKalb Energy, a producer of oil and gas, and Pride Petroleum Services, an oil and gas well support services firm, were created as part of the new diversification strategy. Management's concern with these new operations, however, took time and energy away from the company's concentration on the seed market. As a result, management began to miss opportunities, and the changing seed market passed them by. By 1982, DeKalb's market share had dropped from 23 percent to nine percent, and Pioneer Hi-Bred International scooped up much of DeKalb's former business.

Having seen enough of DeKalb's fall from grace in the agribusiness industry, Tom Roberts, Jr. sold all of the company's energy holdings and started a comprehensive plan to refocus on the seed market. His first move was in 1982, when he arranged a joint venture in genetics research with the seed division of Pfizer drug company. The decision had the immediate effect of halting DeKalb's precipitous market share decline, but over the next few years the joint venture was unable to develop many new products that would attract farmers back to the company. To compensate for the lack of new product development, Tom Roberts, Jr. decided to initiate a strategic expansion and marketing program that he thought would help regain DeKalb's lost market share. Production facilities and distribution offices were set up in Iowa, Ohio, Texas, Oklahoma, Nebraska, and Georgia. Corn research facilities were established in such faraway locations as Argentina, Brazil, France, Thailand, Italy, and Germany. Licensees were contracted in countries such as Hungary, India, Portugal, Turkey, Egypt, Bolivia, Indonesia, and Zimbabwe, just to name a few. Yet by 1991, the company's share of the seed market remained at nine percent and Tom Roberts, Jr. decided that it was time for him to leave the company.

The 1990s and Beyond

After Roberts's departure, DeKalb Genetics Corporation, directed by President and Chairman Bruce Bickner, slowly reestablished itself in the seed market and regained some of its former market share. Most of the gains came from a concerted attempt by management to devote large sums of money to research and development. Part of this strategy included arranging major joint ventures with larger, more established firms in the field of agricultural biotechnology. In February of 1996, DeKalb and Monsanto Company reached such an agreement. Monsanto agreed to invest $160 million in a significant minority share of DeKalb and pay the company $19.5 million annually over a period of a ten-year collaboration to develop new products in corn seed, sorghum, wheat, oilseeds, soybeans, and other produce.

By the mid-1990s, DeKalb Genetics Corporation, still the second leading agribusiness firm in the United States, was beginning to regain its former place in the hearts and minds of farmers across the Midwest. The company had also made significant inroads to capture a larger share of the international seed market through its growing presence in many foreign countries. Research and development, especially in the field of agricultural biotechnology, became the focus of the company's efforts and would soon lead DeKalb back to the preeminent position it once held in the seed product industry.

Principal Subsidiaries

DEKALB Argentina, S.A.; DEKALB Canada, Inc.; DEKALB Centroamericana, S.A.; DEKALB Italia, S.p.A.

Further Reading

Berss, Marcia, "Gone to Seed," *Forbes*, December 19, 1994, pp. 166–168.

DeKalb County Agricultural Association: A History, DeKalb, Ill.: DCAA, 1955.

"DeKalb Genetics Corporation," *The Wall Street Journal*, October 16, 1995, p. B6(E).

"DeKalb Genetics Sells Unit," *The Wall Street Journal*, May 1, 1995, p. A2(E).

"DeKalb Genetics Stock Drops 12.6%," *The New York Times*, July 9, 1993, p. D3(L).

"MGI Pharma Sells Patent Rights," *The Wall Street Journal*, January 4, 1996, p. B3(E).

"Monsanto and DeKalb Genetics in Joint Venture," *The New York Times*, February 2, 1996, p. D4(L).

Smith, Rod, "DeKalb Reports New Products," *Feedstuffs*, March 7, 1994, p. 6.

——, "DeKalb Sees Stronger Year for Corn, Swine Breeding Stock," *Feedstuffs*, January 15, 1996, p. 6.

Wyatt, Edward, "Corporate America Is Courting Agricultural Bio-Tech," *The New York Times*, March 3, 1996, p. F11(L).

—Thomas Derdak

Deposit Guaranty Corporation

2100 East Capitol Street
P. O. Box 1200
Jackson, Mississippi 39215-1200
U.S.A.
(601) 354-8564
Fax: (601) 354-8192
Internet: http://www.dgb.com

Public Company
Incorporated: 1968
Total Assets: $6.03 billion (1995)
Employees: 2,613
Stock Exchanges: NASDAQ
SICs: 6712 Bank Holding Companies; 6021 National
    Commercial Banks

Deposit Guaranty Corporation (DGC) is a bank holding company formed in 1968 to provide its predecessor and principal subsidiary, Deposit Guaranty National Bank, with greater flexibility within the banking industry and a means to expand into new banking services. In 1996, DGC—the 115th-largest bank holding company in the United States—consisted of four banking operations: Deposit Guaranty National Bank, the second-largest bank in Mississippi; Commercial National Bank (of Shreveport, Louisiana), the fifth-largest bank in Louisiana; Deposit Guaranty National Bank of Louisiana; and Merchants National Bank of Fort Smith, Arkansas. Through its subsidiaries, DGC offered banking, trust, mortgage, insurance, and investment services to individual, commercial, industrial, and agricultural customers primarily in Mississippi, Louisiana, and Arkansas. Real estate mortgage loans comprised nearly half of DGC banks' outstanding loans in 1995, followed by commercial, financial, and agricultural loans (28 percent); consumer loans (24 percent), and real estate construction loans (three percent). In 1996, DGC's core institution, Deposit Guaranty National Bank, maintained 146 branches in 18 of Mississippi's 20 largest markets, and Commercial National Bank operated 24 branches in the Shreveport area.

"Grow with Us": 1925–65

The forerunner of Deposit Guaranty Corporation was the brainchild of 14 prominent Jackson, Mississippi, businessmen who in 1925 decided to break into the city's traditionally tight banking community by establishing a new thrift as a vehicle for investing in bank stock. The name Deposit Guaranty Bank and Trust Co. was chosen because, its originator argued, "any name long enough to learn is good enough to be remembered always." The state collector of internal revenue, a Spanish-American War veteran named Major George L. Donald, was enlisted as the bank's first president, and in mid-1925 1,000 shares of stock and the following newspaper ad were offered to Jackson's banking public: "On June 15th this bank, headed by executives of many years experience in business and banking, will formally open with ample capital and surplus to carry out a policy of positive safety and to take care of its patrons, large and small, at all times. . . . Our service will be general banking, including checking accounts, savings accounts, trust department, real estate loans, and renting safe deposit boxes." The announcement struck a chord, for by the end of its first year in business, Deposit Guaranty was claiming deposits of $739,000 and assets of almost $900,000.

By 1929 and the onset of the Great Depression, Deposit Guaranty had paid off its startup debts, opened a full-time trust department, and issued its first stock dividend. Moreover, more than two months after the stock market crash, Deposit Guaranty's assets were still climbing toward the $2 million mark and, more urgently, the bank had managed to stave off a run on its deposits by panicked customers. But stockholder worries forced Deposit Guaranty to cancel its annual meeting in 1930, and as the nation's financial climate worsened management reluctantly imposed salary cuts (ten percent for employees making more than $100 a month and a full 15 percent for the bank's officers).

At the gloomy 1933 shareholders' meeting Major Donald entreated his employees to trust in "counsel, courage, and common sense" to see them through to the inevitable economic turnaround. Deposit Guaranty itself meanwhile seemed almost impervious to the forces claiming hundreds of other U.S. banks, including Mississippi's largest thrift, Merchants Bank: Deposit

Company Perspectives:

Deposit Guaranty continues to be very much a network of community banks providing friendly, personal service for our customers who value face-to-face relationships and want to use traditional channels to access financial services. We will continue to stress this approach and are focusing on sales and service skills throughout our system of community banks. We also recognize that a growing number of our customers are not only more comfortable with technology but are, in fact, demanding it to make their lives easier. For them, good customer service means offering technology to handle their banking. The challenge for all financial institutions is to operate in both worlds simultaneously, providing a balanced mix of both ''high-tech'' and ''high-touch'' services. We are committed to meeting this challenge.

Guaranty had close to 4,800 depositors by 1933 and deposits of almost half a million dollars. A $250,000 stake Deposit Guaranty had purchased in 1929 in the Canal Bank and Trust Co. of New Orleans finally brought the Depression unambiguously to the bank's doorstep. The failing economy had forced Canal Bank into receivership, immediately freezing more than half of Deposit Guaranty's cash reserves. With the help of Mississippi's bank commissioner, Deposit Guaranty's executives convinced some of Canal Bank's Mississippi bank correspondents to unfreeze their holdings in the doomed New Orleans bank, enabling Deposit Guaranty to purchase the remainder of the frozen assets and free itself from the debacle.

As Franklin Roosevelt's New Deal legislation was beginning to pull the economy out of the worst phase of the Depression, Deposit Guaranty applied for membership in the new federal Temporary Deposit Insurance Fund and agreed to comply with all the requirements of the Banking Act of 1933. It then picked up where it had left off before the Canal Bank crisis: doubling its assets to $7.3 million in 1934 and opening a new personal loan department to offer ''Banking Credit for Everybody'' in the form of $50 to $500 loans. In 1937 the 17-story headquarters of the now defunct Merchants Bank was purchased for Deposit Guaranty's new offices, and by the onset of World War II Deposit Guaranty had become the largest bank in Mississippi with more than 10,500 customers and assets of $15 million.

When Major Donald died in early 1941, William M. Mounger, an associate officer and director of the bank, was named Deposit Guaranty's second president. With America now in the war, the bank guaranteed the jobs of employees leaving for military service, and as assets spiraled past $50 million in 1944 Deposit Guaranty began preparations for financing the local construction projects expected to accompany the postwar boom in consumer demand.

In Jackson and the nation at large that boom lasted longer than anyone had anticipated, and by 1948 Deposit Guaranty had made its first acquisition, purchasing the Bank of Clinton, Mississippi, amending the bank's charter to allow the new

addition to become a full-fledged branch of Deposit Guaranty. As it approached its 25th anniversary year, Deposit Guaranty instituted an employee profit-sharing program and opened its second branch office in Jackson. That branch's profitability and a 1953 merger with the Commercial Bank and Trust of Jackson helped Deposit Guaranty become Mississippi's first $100 million bank by the end of the year, and the traditional claim of New Orleans and Memphis to dominance of the deep South's banking community suddenly seemed less certain. Following William Mounger's death in 1957, W. P. McMullan became Deposit Guaranty's new chairman of the board and CEO, and the bank celebrated its new leadership, $170 million in assets, and the opening of its expanded downtown headquarters by inviting Miss America of 1959, Mississippi native Mary Ann Mobley, to preside over the ribbon-cutting ceremony of the ''new'' Deposit Guaranty.

Although in 1959 the widespread reliance on computers to process large volumes of business data was still several years away, Deposit Guaranty's management authorized the establishment of an electronic data processing department, anticipating the day when all banking transactions would be routinely processed by automated technology. Deposit Guaranty's record growth continued into the new decade. A $23 million increase in assets in 1961 was surpassed by a $38 million leap in 1964, and throughout the early 1960s Deposit Guaranty extended its reach into untapped Jackson-area markets with a series of new branch openings.

Statewide: 1965–87

In September 1965, Deposit Guaranty's board of directors voted to change the bank's charter from that of a state bank to a national bank, shifting the bank's regulatory framework from the state of Mississippi to the federal Comptroller of Currency. Among other benefits, the new federal charter enabled the renamed Deposit Guaranty National Bank to establish branch offices and involve itself in such lucrative fields as real estate and government securities. Deposit Guaranty launched an expansion drive that within six months included the acquisition of Greenville Bank and Trust Co. of Greenville, Mississippi; Mechanics State Bank of McComb; and Lawrence County Bank of Monticello. Energized by these new sources of income, Deposit Guaranty's assets rose from $338 million at the end of 1966 to $395 million a year later. Management's early decision to embrace computer technology was vindicated in late 1967 when its new automated Operations Center began processing the bank's financial transactions. An intense promotional blitz led to the successful launch of Deposit Guaranty's first credit card product, the Bank Americard, in mid-1968, and the acquisition of City Bank and Trust Co. of Natchez (1967) and Rightway Travel Agency (1968) signaled Deposit Guaranty's intention to continue expanding in new directions.

In October 1968, the bank's board voted to establish a bank holding company, to be named Deposit Guaranty Corporation, that would exchange its stock for Deposit Guaranty's on a share-by-share basis. Reconstituted as a bank holding company and its subsidiary, Deposit Guaranty would now be able to operate with greater flexibility in the banking industry while venturing into new services and activities. In 1969, Russ M. Johnson, who began his career with Deposit Guaranty as a teller in 1933, was named chairman and CEO, inheriting an enviably prosperous institution; by the end of the decade Deposit Guaranty had expanded to 14 locations, and in the 1960s alone assets had grown from $169 million to almost $500 million, making it the richest bank in Mississippi.

Since its inception, Deposit Guaranty had identified itself closely with Mississippi's economy, loaning businesses and consumers the capital that helped transform the largely agricultural Mississippi economy of the 1920s into one of the fastest-growing manufacturing regions of the New South. Acknowledging the energy of the state's business climate in the early 1970s, in 1973 Deposit Guaranty established the first industrial development department of any Mississippi bank. While continuing its expansion strategy through such acquisitions as Bridges Loan and Investment Co. (1972) and Leflore Bank and Trust Co. (1973), Deposit Guaranty also demonstrated its readiness to exploit new banking products coming to market. It introduced its "Mini-Bank" automatic teller machines (ATMs) in 1972—Mississippi's first 24-hour ATMs—and beefed up its data processing operations center by merging it with a recently acquired computer company to form Bankers Data Processing Center, which marketed its services to other Mississippi banks in addition to handling Deposit Guaranty's data processing work. In 1972 Deposit Guaranty formed DGC Services Company to provide management services to the bank and the holding company as well as the larger bank market. And in the same year a full-time bank officer was brought aboard to oversee Deposit Guaranty's international department, which quickly began establishing correspondent relationships with several overseas banks.

Despite the recession of the early 1970s, Deposit Guaranty's assets vaulted past the $800 million mark in 1973 and by its fiftieth anniversary year in 1975 were closing in on $1 billion. J. H. Hines replaced the retiring Russ Johnson as chairman of the board and CEO in 1974 and soon began implementing a new corporate and management structure to reflect the new realities of the U.S. banking industry. When Deposit Guaranty moved into its newly completed 22-story headquarters three months before the anniversary celebrations began, it had been decentralized into eight major divisions—administration, corporate, investment, marketing, operations/finance, retail banking, state banking, and trust—each empowered to manage its affairs without continual oversight from above.

Less than ten years into its second half century, Deposit Guaranty's total assets had passed $2.5 billion, and its mid-1970s reorganization had given way to periodic restructurings that sought to maintain continually streamlined operations in a banking environment that seemed to be changing almost month to month. In 1985, Deposit Guaranty, now under the dual leadership of President Howard L. McMillan Jr. and chairman of the board and CEO E. B. Robinson Jr., assumed sponsorship of Mississippi's only PGA-sanctioned golf tournament, and the rechristened Deposit Guaranty Golf Classic was soon generating $15 million annually for Jackson's economy. A new business banking department was formed in 1983 to provide business and personal financial services to companies with over $1 million in annual sales, and new products unveiled in mid-decade included home equity loans, a "phone-a-loan" rapid loan approval service, and a new personal credit line program.

Then in 1986 Deposit Guaranty's dogged efforts to convince the Mississippi legislature to revise the state's restrictive banking laws finally paid off when the state announced that, beginning in 1987, Mississippi banks would be permitted to merge with other banks anywhere in the state. One year later the state's thrifts would be permitted to acquire banks in the bordering states of Arkansas, Louisiana, Tennessee, and Alabama, and on July 1, 1990, the entire south-central and southeastern portion of the United States—from Missouri to Florida—would be opened to Mississippi's banking industry. Deposit Guaranty immediately moved to capitalize on the new banking climate, merging with banks in DeSoto County, Mississippi, near Memphis, as well as Tupelo and Starkville and breaking ground on a new branch in the vital Gulf Coast region. By the end of 1987 Deposit Guaranty could claim 111 locations in thirty-eight Mississippi communities.

Regionwide: 1988–96

Deposit Guaranty entered the new era of interstate banking with assets of more than $3.2 billion and only some lingering—and soon-to-be-eliminated—bad loans to Latin America from the 1970s blemishing its balance sheet. After a 1987 U.S. Supreme Court decision vindicated its claim that the principle of "competitive equality" allowed it to challenge Mississippi's banking laws by establishing a branch on the Gulf Coast, the bank moved to exploit the opportunities offered by the increasingly deregulated U.S. banking industry. New product lines were developed to capitalize on the youth, mature (50 years old and up), upscale, and small business markets; branch automation and integrated banking software systems were implemented to, in the words of one Deposit Guaranty vice-president, "turn a hog into a more sleek animal"; a "Shop 'N' Bank" agreement was reached with a major Mississippi grocery chain to operate full-service Deposit Guaranty branches in selected food stores; and mergers with banks in the Mississippi towns of Meridian, Corinth, and Southaven were given shareholders' stamps of approval. By the end of 1988, Deposit Guaranty's intrastate strategy of opening branches in every major market in the state was virtually complete. As the U.S. Congress moved to bail out and reform the troubled savings and loan industry through the Financial Institutions Reform Recovery and Enforcement Act of 1989, Deposit Guaranty closed the decade with 131 branches in 41 communities and more than $3.5 billion in total assets.

When interstate banking finally arrived in Mississippi in July 1990, Deposit Guaranty had already lined up its first acquisition in the promising "ArkLaTex" region to the west, and the $1 billion Commercial National Bank (CNB) of Shreveport, Louisiana, was added to Deposit Guaranty's stable. As assets climbed toward $5 billion in 1991–92 Deposit Guaranty unveiled a full-service investment services subsidiary named Deposit Guaranty Investments, Inc. and initiated plans to acquire the First Columbus Financial Corporation of Columbus, Mississippi. The $200 million First Columbus deal was closed in 1994, and Deposit Guaranty soon purchased $300 million in assets by acquiring banks in West Monroe and Hammond, Louisiana.

Amidst rumors that Deposit Guaranty was being targeted for acquisition, management, keen to be "the acquirer rather than the acquiree,'' stayed on the acquisitions offensive in 1995 and 1996, adding a Clarksdale, Mississippi, bank; Merchants National Bank of Fort Smith, Arkansas; and the Louisiana banks Tuscaloosa Bancshares Inc., Bank of Gonzales, and Jefferson Guaranty Bancorp (later merged as Deposit Guaranty National Bank of Louisiana). With the aftermath of the savings and loan crisis fueling a wave of consolidation in the U.S. banking industry in the mid-1990s, regional players like Deposit Guaranty looked to new technology and efficiency measures to protect market share and increase their customer base. In 1995 alone, for example, Deposit Guaranty introduced touch-tone phone-based and on-line PC-based banking services, an Internet web site, and a business-to-business electronic data interchange service for its business customers. By mid-decade Deposit Guaranty's long road from an $880,000 community thrift to a $6-billion mega-regional made it one of the two largest banks in the Mississippi, with the state's most extensive retail banking network, its biggest trust and international banking departments, and its largest brokerage and residential mortgage operations.

Principal Subsidiaries

Deposit Guaranty National Bank; Merchants National Bank; Deposit Guaranty National Bank of Louisiana; Commercial National Bank.

Further Reading

Brinson, Carroll, *The First Fifty: The Story of Deposit Guaranty National Bank,* Jackson, Miss.: Deposit Guaranty Corporation, 1976.

Cline, Kenneth, ''Mississippi Bank Mining Its Reserves for Profits as Loan Demand Lags,'' *American Banker,* September 28, 1995, pp. 4–5.

——, ''Mississippi's Deposit Guaranty Plans Louisiana Purchase.'' *American Banker,* August 29, 1996, p. 4.

——, ''Pleasant Problem in Mississippi: Swollen Reserves,'' *American Banker,* June 11, 1993. p. 1.

Pesek, William, Jr., ''Deposit Guaranty Plucks Customer Data Right from Mainframe,'' *American Banker,* April 26, 1993, pp. 8A–9A.

Prestridge, Sam, ''DGNB Unveils Subsidiary,'' *Mississippi Business Journal,* September 16, 1991, pp. 1+.

Zack, Jeffrey, ''New ABA Chief Still Minding the Store at Deposit Guaranty,'' *American Banker,* November 21, 1994, pp. 1A, 6A–7A.

—Paul S. Bodine

DONNKENNY, INC.

Donnkenny, Inc.

1411 Broadway
New York, New York 10018
U.S.A.
(212) 730-7770
Fax: (212) 228-6036

Public Company
Incorporated: 1934 as Nadler Sportswear
Employees: 1,595
Sales: $210.3 million (fiscal 1995)
Stock Exchanges: NASDAQ
SICs: 2331 Women's, Misses & Juniors' Blouses &
    Shirts; 2335 Women's, Misses & Juniors' Dresses;
    2339 Women's, Misses & Juniors' Outerwear, Not
    Elsewhere Classified; 2341 Women's, Misses',
    Children's & Infants' Underwear & Nightwear; 2369
    Girls', Children's & Infants' Outerwear, Not
    Elsewhere Classified; 5621 Women's Clothing Stores;
    5641 Children's & Infants' Wear Stores; 6719
    Holding Companies, Not Elsewhere Classified

Donnkenny, Inc., a holding company, designs, manufactures, imports, and markets a broad line of moderately priced women's sportswear and sleepwear through its several subsidiaries and divisions. In addition, men's, women's, and children's sportswear and intimate apparel featuring various cartoon character images were being manufactured, imported, and marketed by the company.

Steady Growth to 1978

Based in New York City's garment district, Donnkenny was a successor company to Nadler Sportswear, founded in 1934 by Murray Nadler and his brother Leon. This enterprise originally manufactured blouses only. After Murray returned from army service in World War II the firm began production of other sportswear items. In about 1957 it moved its manufacturing operations from New Jersey to Virginia. In that year it had net income of $115,338 on net sales of $3.3 million.

At the end of 1961 Donnkenny acquired the entire stock of six corporations, which became wholly owned subsidiaries. The consolidated company went public the next year, but 77 percent of the shares were held by Murray Nadler, president and chairman; Leon Nadler, secretary; and Glenn O. Thornhill, treasurer. Donnkenny was leasing three Virginia manufacturing plants and in 1961 had net income of $334,199 on net sales of $6.8 million.

In 1965 Donnkenny was producing a complete line of moderately priced misses' and young women's sportswear apparel, including blouses, pants, skirts, and jackets, with particular emphasis on casual wear. More than 80 percent of its sales were in the retail price range of $3.98 to $6.98. Styling and manufacturing emphasized coordination of separate items in the firm's line, so that they could be worn in a variety of combinations as part of an ensemble. All of Donnkenny's goods were manufactured by nonunion labor in the company's five leased Virginia plants. They were marketed through more than 4,000 retail outlets, including department stores, specialty shops, and women's apparel outlets throughout the country under the registered name "Donnkenny."

Donnkenny acquired Dunwoodie Manufacturing Co., a producer of ladies' blouses and tailored shirts, in late 1965. It enjoyed rapid growth in the mid-1960s, climbing from $11.6 million in net sales in 1964 to $22.8 million in 1966. Net income rose from $427,000 to $728,000 in this period. The company added permanent press, sold under the "Donnypress" label, to its line of cottons, woolens, corduroys, and synthetic fabrics. A sixth Virginia plant was opened in 1966. Designs were being turned out four times a year by the company's own staff to conform to the selling seasons. Sales were supported by a national advertising program, including ads in many of the leading fashion publications.

Interviewed by the *New York Times* in 1971, Murray Nadler said it had become more difficult to anticipate consumer needs in the sportswear business in the past five years because of the growth in new lines and patterns. By the end of that year Donnkenny was operating two more Virginia factories and was turning out an average of 9,000 dozen garments a week, which were mainly selling at retail from $7 to $15 under the labels Donnkenny, Xtrovert, R.B.K., Kenny Classics, Melray, Durbin, and Dunwoodie. The company had recently inaugurated a junior division in sizes below eight for shorter girls and was importing knitted sweaters and skirts from the Far East. Forty-five percent of its 1970 sales were through department stores, 26 percent from major chains and discount houses, and 24 percent through specialty and women's apparel shops.

Donnkenny passed the million-dollar mark in net income in 1970 and the $30-million mark in net sales the following year. Its growth continued unabated through the next several years, and it had 18 wholly owned subsidiaries by 1974. Revenues increased every year between 1973 and 1977, and record profits were reported for every year except 1974. Net sales totaled $82.2 million and net income amounted to $3.8 million in 1977.

Troubled Private Firm, 1978–1985

Financially speaking, Donnkenny was a very conservative company, paying for expansion from its own earnings rather than taking out loans or mortgages. That all changed in November 1978, when it was acquired by the investment house Oppenheimer & Co. for $27.5 million in a leveraged buyout that privatized the company. Of this sum, only $3.5 million was equity, with the rest senior and subordinated debt. Minority shareholders were bought out; insiders, principally the Nadler (46 percent) and Thornhill (12 percent) families, received shares in a closed-end investment company holding a portfolio of tax-exempt municipal securities. Murray Nadler, Thornhill, and three other company officers kept their jobs, receiving substantial raises in salary, deferred compensation, and profit-sharing incentives.

The deal soured for Oppenheimer, which in August 1981 dismissed not only the management but the office staff, right down to the switchboard operator. In a lawsuit the investment banking firm charged that it had overpaid for Donnkenny because the management had cooked the books and diverted profits, accusing the firm's accountants and a Thornhill-controlled company of "racketeering activity," "breaches of fiduciary duty," and a conspiracy "to systematically defraud and loot" the company. Among the charges were that, during the negotiations to buy out Donnkenny, Nadler and Thornhill secretly began arranging to contract out work from the company's two dozen manufacturing subsidiaries to the Thornhill-controlled company and other plants owned by Thornhill. In addition, the investors' representatives on Donnkenny's board of directors allegedly were given doctored figures to conceal siphoned off profits.

The Donnkenny investment group, which included Security Pacific Bank, installed Al Paris as president. Control of Donnkenny passed to Odyssey Partners, a spin-off headed by several of Oppenheimer's founders. It was announced in April 1982 that the company's parent, Donnkenny Holding Co., and Donnkenny, Inc. itself had been recapitalized under favorable terms of bank and institutional debt and that the Paris Group, which included other Donnkenny managers, had acquired majority ownership of the holding company. In 1985 this group transferred its holdings back to Odyssey, restoring it to full ownership of the firm.

Frazzled Donnkenny ended 1985 with the biggest loss in its history—$12.5 million. At this time the firm had ten plants in the South and about $85 million in annual sales, according to its management. Richard Rubin, a ten-year sales veteran who was vice-president in 1985, got the job of turning the company around. It returned to profitability in 1986, and Rubin was rewarded with the titles of chairman and chief executive officer as well as president.

Thornhill won vindication in 1985, when a Virginia jury awarded him $1.28 million in damages against Donnkenny for breach of his employment contract and "willful, malicious, wanton and oppressive conduct." This verdict appeared to end Donnkenny's $8 million suit against Thornhill, which was transferred to Virginia from New York because the jury decided he was improperly fired despite the company's allegations of misconduct.

Prosperity in the 1990s

In 1989 Donnkenny was acquired by Merrill Lynch Interfunding Inc., and Donnkenny management was involved in another leveraged buyout that added $58.7 million to the company's debt. Its managers included Rubin, who took a 28 percent share; Merrill Lynch Interfunding took 66 percent. In 1991 Donnkenny announced plans to go public, selling about 40 percent of the shares. Merrill Lynch Interfunding planned to keep another 40 percent and Rubin kept 17 percent. The estimated proceeds of $27 million were to be used to reduce debt. Donnkenny reported sales of $108 million in fiscal 1991 and earnings of $2.7 million.

Donnkenny did not go public until June 1993. By the end of the year its stock had risen about 50 percent over the initial offering price, and it had worked off 54 percent of the debt it had assumed in the 1989 buyout. The company's core business was still women's sportswear and sleepwear, with more than 90 percent of its garments produced at ten Virginia plants. Its fastest selling line, however, was Mickey & Co., consisting of Disney-licensed clothing for men and children as well as women. Lewis Frimel sleepwear and intimate apparel, also featuring cartoon characters, were produced under the Warner Brothers/Looney Tunes label.

The Donnkenny of the mid-1990s was aggressively expansion- and acquisition-minded, with the stated intention of tripling its sales to $456 million by 1998. In 1994 it signed a licensing agreement to produce a better-priced sportswear and knitwear line under the label of the noted designer Arnold Scaasi, with distribution confined to department and specialty stores. These stores were also to carry a new line of natural fiber, moderately priced coordinated women's sportswear and related separates under the J.G. Hook label.

Armed with a new $85 million bank loan, Donnkenny made two important acquisitions in 1995, purchasing Beldoch Industries Corp. for about $15 million and the sportswear division of Oak Hill Sportswear Corp. for about $14.6 million. Beldoch held the license for all Pierre Cardin women's wear in the United States and was manufacturing sweaters bearing the Cardin name. It also marketed other knitwear for women. Oak Hill's sportswear unit marketed women's sportswear, knitwear, sweaters, and shirts under the Victoria Jones and Casey & Max names. Donnkenny planned to open almost 1,200 Mickey & Co. concept shops in J.C. Penney stores by August 1996.

As part of Donnkenny's diversification strategy, Rubin emphasized in a 1995 *WWD* interview that he was focusing on "middle America," or, in his words, "women who can't afford to spend more than $100 for an outfit." He said the company's licensed cartoon endeavor accounted for 60 percent of business and was expected to grow at a rate of 25 percent. In 1994 Donnkenny signed a license to market apparel featuring the Felix the Cat cartoon character, and in 1995 it introduced Sleepy Heads, a nylon pajama pouch cut to look like the profile of a cartoon character, for the Lewis Frimel/Flirts and Mickey & Co. lines.

Net sales rose from $126.5 million in fiscal 1992 (the year ended December 5, 1992) to $210.3 million in fiscal 1995 (the year ended December 1, 1995). Net income rose from $4.5 million in fiscal 1991 to $9.8 million in fiscal 1994, and then fell to $5.8 million in fiscal 1995.

Donnkenny in 1995

Donnkenny Classics, the company's core products, primarily for women over 35, included year-round pull-on stretch gabardine pants and skirts and coordinated gabardine jackets and blouses, plus tops, blouses, pants, skirts, and jackets in styles varying from season to season. The D.K. Gold division produced private-label related sportswear. The Beldoch subsidiary manufactured and imported women's knitted sweaters sold under the brand names Beldoch Popper and Knitmakers. In addition, it had the right to manufacture, import, and sell women's sportswear in the United States with the Pierre Cardin trademark and was manufacturing sweaters under this trademark. Beldoch also intended to manufacture knitwear under the Alberoy name in the fall of 1996.

The Lewis Frimel/Flirts product line (acquired in 1977) consisted of women's and girls' sleepwear and sportswear and, since fall 1993, panties and boxer shorts. Licensed images on this product line included characters in the Garfield and Peanuts comic strips, Looney Tunes characters, and classic Muppet characters. The Mickey & Co. line included boxer shorts, T-shirts, sweatshirts, sweaters, toppers, leggings, jackets, underpants, underpants sets, and sportswear imprinted with various Disney characters. In 1996 Donnkenny was licensed rights, which it sublicensed, to sell this product line in China. Donnkenny also was designing and/or manufacturing custom products for private labels such as Polo/Ralph Lauren, Tultex, and Cross Creek.

In fiscal 1995 about 51 percent of the products Donnkenny sold were manufactured in the United States, of which a majority were manufactured at the company's Virginia facilities or West Hempstead, New York. The remainder of its products were produced abroad and imported, principally from China, India, Guatemala, Turkey, and Bangladesh. Donnkenny was shipping orders to about 27,000 stores in the United States. In fiscal 1995 specialty retailers accounted for about 36 percent of net sales, department stores for about 23 percent, chain stores for about 23 percent, mass merchants for about eight percent, catalogue customers for about five percent, and other customers for about five percent. J.C. Penney accounted for 15.5 percent of net sales.

At the end of fiscal 1995 Donnkenny was operating nine Virginia, two Mississippi, and two New York facilities. It also had a small administrative facility in Hong Kong. The principal showroom was in New York City; the others were in Atlanta, Charlotte, Chicago, Dallas, Denver, Elmont, New York, Los Angeles, Minneapolis, and Seattle. Corporate headquarters were in New York City. The company planned to operate a Charleston, South Carolina, facility by the mid-1990s. Donnkenny also operated 14 outlet stores to market out-of-season and irregular merchandise. These were situated primarily in Virginia, with additional locations in Alabama, Florida, North Carolina, Pennsylvania, and Tennessee.

Principal Subsidiaries

Beldoch Industries Corp.; Christianburg Garment Co.; Donnkenny Apparel Inc.; MegaKnits, Inc.

Principal Divisions

D.K. Gold; Lewis Frimel/Flirts; Oak Hill Sportswear.

Further Reading

Brody, Michael, "Cloak and Suit: The Strange Case of Donnkenny," *Barron's*, April 5, 1982, pp. 13, 22, 24.
Dann, Arthur, "Donnkenny, Inc.," *Wall Street Transcript*, November 8, 1971, pp. 26–35.
D'Innocenzio, Anne, "New 'toons for Donnkenny," *WWD*, May 3, 1995, p. 10.
"Donnkenny Cuts a Stylish Growth Pattern by Hitting Right Market," *Barron's*, September 20, 1965, p. 25.
"Enlarged Line Enables Donnkenny To Sew Up Stylish Profits Gains," *Barron's*, March 20, 1967, pp. 30–31.
Koshetz, Herbert, "Donnkenny Projects Increases This Year," *New York Times*, April 11, 1971, Sec. 3, p. 14.
"Ladies Sportswear Maker Donnkenny Is Fashioning a New Earnings Rise," *Barron's*, December 6, 1971, p. 29.
Seckler, Valerie, "Donnkenny To Buy Beldoch, Oak Hill Unit," *WWD*, May 16, 1995, p. 11.
Tell, Lawrence J., "Donnkenny Donnybrook," *Barron's*, October 21, 1985, p. 75.

—Robert Halasz

Dreyer's Grand Ice Cream, Inc.

5929 College Avenue
Oakland, California 94618
U.S.A.
(510) 652-8187
Fax: (510) 601-4905

Public Company
Incorporated: 1928
Employees: 2,500
Sales: $678.8 million (1995)
Stock Exchanges: NASDAQ
SICs: 2024 Ice Cream & Frozen Desserts

Dreyer's Grand Ice Cream, Inc. is one of the leading ice cream manufacturers and distributors in the United States. The company sells its premium ice cream products under the Dreyer's Grand name throughout the western United States, Japan, and other markets in the Far East; the same product line is also available in the United States east of the Rocky Mountains under the Edy's Grand name. Dreyer's and Edy's products are sold through grocery stores, convenience stores, ice cream parlors, restaurants, and other food service outlets. The company utilizes nationwide direct-store distribution in conjunction with regional manufacturing to facilitate sales throughout the country. The company also distributes products manufactured by such other companies as Ben & Jerry's, Healthy Choice, Dove, and Nestlé.

Early History

Dreyer's Grand Ice Cream, Inc. was founded in 1928 by William Dreyer and Joseph Edy when the two men opened an ice cream and candy shop on Grand Avenue in Oakland, California. With their goal being to make and sell the best tasting ice cream possible, Dreyer (an ice cream maker) and Edy (a candy maker) focused on creative innovations to fuel their small venture. For example, the two men used Edy's knowledge and expertise in candy-making to create the original Rocky Road ice cream. The chocolate, marshmallow and nut flavor was created in late 1930 and was named Rocky Road as a means of describ-

ing the ice cream's texture as well as the troubled economic times of the Great Depression. Dreyer and Edy are also credited with originating the Toasted Almond and Candy Mint flavors.

Within a short time after its introduction, Dreyer's Grand ice cream gained a faithful following in the San Francisco Bay area. Prior to Dreyer's and Edy's exotic flavor creations, ice cream was available mainly in such basic flavors as vanilla, chocolate, and strawberry. The addition of traditional sundae-topping items such as nuts and candy into the ice cream itself was a novel approach to ice cream production. Such innovations were enthusiastically accepted by consumers, however, and Dreyer and Edy continued to experiment with different flavor combinations. At that time, Dreyer's Grand ice cream was delivered to and sold in ice cream shops and soda fountains throughout the San Francisco area.

It was not until the 1960s that Dreyer's Grand began to be packaged in containers for sale in supermarkets and other retail outlets. During the era surrounding World War II, the average home refrigerator had extremely limited freezer space in the form of small ice cube compartments, and therefore could not accommodate large containers of ice cream or other frozen foods. By the 1960s, however, most families had larger freezers that were suitable for food storage, and the popularity of quart and half-gallon size containers of ice cream increased dramatically. Dreyer's began distributing its ice cream to supermarkets and retail outlets around San Francisco and the surrounding areas.

Expansion in the 1980s

In the 1970s, the company's business expanded beyond the San Francisco area to other Northern California markets, and distribution throughout all of Northern California and Los Angeles was in place by 1976. In 1977, the $6 million company was sold by Kenneth Cook, a longtime Dreyer's employee, to T. Gary Rogers and William F. Cronk. Prior to the purchase, Rogers and Cronk had attended the University of California at Berkeley together in the 1960s. After graduating, Rogers joined the army and later went on to Harvard Business School, while Cronk became a stockbroker. The two men joined forces again in the 1970s to start a restaurant, and when the venture failed, they decided to purchase Dreyer's. Rogers became chairman of

---

Company Perspectives:

Our mission is to make Dreyer's Grand Ice Cream, Inc. the leading premium ice cream company in the United States.

---

the board and chief executive officer of Dreyer's, while his partner, Cronk, was named as the company's president. Together, the two began formulating a plan to introduce the company's product nationwide and to make Dreyer's the leading premium ice cream in the country, filling the gap between Haagen Dazs (super premium) and Sealtest (generic), both of which were already found on the national level.

Under the leadership of Rogers and Cronk, Dreyer's had introduced its products into the states of Washington, Oregon, and Arizona by 1979, using the company's unique direct-store distribution system. Direct-store delivery was a strong advantage in Dreyer's quick expansion throughout the West, in that it allowed the company to tailor each delivery to the tastes of consumers in any particular area. Dreyer's was therefore able to ensure that it could meet the demands of its customers, making retail outlets more willing to stock Dreyer's products. Direct-store delivery also enabled Dreyer's to avoid the costs of building numerous manufacturing facilities to coincide with existing distribution companies throughout its market areas.

With a strong hold on the market in the western United States, Dreyer's became a public company in 1981, selling shares of its stock to fund further expansion and distribution around the United States. Because another premium ice cream company by the name of Breyers already existed in much of the eastern portion of the country, Dreyer's agreed to market its product east of the Rocky Mountains under the Edy's Grand name. Edy's Grand Ice Cream was introduced in Chicago and Kansas City in 1981, offering 23 different flavors to its retail customers. In 1983, as Edy's Grand Ice Cream began to be marketed in St. Louis, Milwaukee, and parts of Ohio, Dreyer's Grand Ice Cream, Inc. was named to *Forbes* magazine's prestigious list of "Up & Coming" companies. At that point, Dreyer's had experienced a 959 percent increase in sales since Rogers and Cronk bought the company, and its market value was estimated to be $192.2 million.

In December 1985, Dreyer's made a strategic move to accommodate its growing distribution needs in the eastern United States when it acquired Berliner Foods Corp., a distributor in Maryland, for $8.4 million. Prior to the purchase, Berliner had distributed 55 manufactured gourmet ice creams and ice cream novelty items, the most notable of which was Haagen Dazs, throughout the states surrounding Maryland. Dreyer's used Berliner as a means of distributing its Edy's Grand product line around the mid-Atlantic region to test the eastern market, and eventually used its success in that area as a springboard to enter the New England region and the remainder of the East Coast. Meanwhile, in December 1986, Dreyer's acquired Midwest Distributing Co., Inc. for $5.2 million and used it to enter the Minnesota, Wisconsin, and Michigan markets.

Dreyer's then expanded its product line in 1987 with the introduction of Dreyer's and Edy's Grand Light, the first premium light ice cream in the United States. The ice cream contained half the fat content and a third fewer calories than regular Dreyer's or Edy's Grand Ice Cream. Grand Light was quickly accepted by the many consumers who were becoming more and more health-conscious, and by the end of 1988 sales of the product had doubled from the previous year. In 1987 the company also established the Dreyer's Grand Ice Cream Charitable Foundation, an organization committed to supporting community, youth and K–12 public education programs. The Foundation soon spread its reach throughout the country, localizing itself mainly in the many communities where Dreyer's held operating facilities.

In 1989, the company once again led the market with the national introduction of frozen yogurt in quart and half-gallon containers. Available in almost every popular flavor, the frozen yogurt was the best-selling packaged yogurt in the United States within three years, and its success soon ushered in six flavors of Dreyer's completely fat-free frozen yogurt. Nineteen eighty-nine also marked the beginning of an extremely important partnership between Dreyer's Grand Ice Cream, Inc. and Ben & Jerry's Homemade, Inc. For $3.1 million, Dreyer's purchased the rights to distribute the Ben & Jerry's super premium products in selected areas of the nation, along with its own premium line of products. Because Ben & Jerry's butterfat level classified it as a super premium, and because it was packaged in pints only, it was the perfect complement to the Dreyer's and Edy's product line, without competing with it. Distributing the two products together also helped bolster the sales of each, as the availability of one item was often a selling point with retailers for stocking the other.

The 1990s and Beyond

In early 1990, drawing from the quick success of their distribution partnership with Ben & Jerry's Homemade, Inc., Dreyer's acquired Barkulis Bros., Inc., the Chicago-area distributor of Mars Inc.'s DoveBars, for $9 million. Dreyer's also sealed a distribution deal with NutraSweet in April of the same year, after NutraSweet's Simplesse fat substitute was approved by the FDA for use in frozen desserts and the introduction of Simple Pleasures fat-free frozen dessert began. Dreyer's received the rights to distribute Simple Pleasures throughout the country, and began delivering it to stores that summer alongside its own Dreyer's and Edy's Grand products, the DoveBar products, and Ben & Jerry's products.

With sales in its U.S. markets booming, Dreyer's expanded into the international market by entering a joint venture with the Japanese trading firm Nissho Iwai Corp., to market and sell the Dreyer's line of products in Japan. Because politically powerful dairy farmers had kept Japan's dairy prices at an extraordinarily high level for many years, Dreyer's sales potential in Japan looked very promising. Trade pressure from the United States had forced Japan to lift restrictions on the import of dairy products, making it possible for Dreyer's to ship its products to Japan directly from its manufacturing sites in California. Dreyer's hoped that its price advantage would help it gain ten percent or more of the Japanese market and even further increase its almost $300 million in annual sales.

Nineteen ninety also saw the introduction of Dreyer's American Dream, a 99 percent fat and cholesterol-free dessert made with the same ingredients as ice cream, but which did not contain a fat substitute. The product marked Dreyer's increasing commitment to serving the health-conscious consumer, and, within a year it became the leading premium nonfat brand in almost all of its markets. Dreyer's continued its product line expansion in 1992 with the unveiling of Dreyer's and Edy's No Sugar Added, which appealed to consumers who wished to limit their sugar consumption for health or dietary reasons. The success of these products, combined with Dreyer's successful expansion throughout the country during the 1980s, had solidly placed Dreyer's line of products as the second-leading premium brand in the United States in 1992, with competitor Breyers at the head of the premium market.

Continuing its emphasis on product development, Dreyer's began manufacturing frozen dessert novelty items in 1993. The company introduced Dreyer's and Edy's Ice Cream Bars and Tropical Fruit Bars, and set its sights on capturing an even greater number of consumers based on the variety and convenience provided by the new items. Dreyer's also created a soft-serve variety of its ice cream and frozen yogurt, dubbed Dreyer's Premium Soft, to be sold in restaurants, ice cream shops, and other outlets in the food service industry. In order to meet the demand for its increasing number and variety of products, Dreyer's utilized over fifty distribution centers around the country, which were served by five different manufacturing facilities located in Union City and Commerce, California; Denver, Colorado; Houston, Texas; and Fort Wayne, Indiana. The company's efficiency in manufacturing and distribution was recognized by *Industry Week* magazine when it named the Fort Wayne facility as one of the country's ten best manufacturing plants in 1993.

By the end of 1993, Dreyer's annual sales had increased to over $470 million, and it was poised to take the lead in the race with Breyers to become the country's leading premium brand. Dreyer's continued its nationwide expansion with successful entrances into the Florida and Texas markets, using its direct-store distribution system as its strongest strategic asset. By early 1994, Dreyer's products were being sold in every major grocery chain in the state of Florida, and the company had entered into an agreement with Sunbelt Distributors, Inc. of Texas to begin distribution of the Dreyer's line of products on a long-term basis. Within one year, Dreyer's had earned almost ten percent of the ice cream market in Houston. Furthermore, Dreyer's added Lactose Reduced Ice Cream to its product line, and began offering prepackaged Ice Cream Cones and Yogurt Bars as novelty item selections.

Taking into account the broad array of products it had on the market, and also its continued expansion around the country, Dreyer's began to focus more on advertising its product line in the mid-1990s. Using the slogan "Evidently it's not your normal ice cream," Dreyer's introduced a fantastically popular series of television commercials that humorously depicted the outrageous things people would do for a taste of Dreyer's or Edy's Grand products. In one television spot, grandpa jumps up and does the splits upon learning that Dreyer's is for dessert; in another, grandma lifts a car in a supermarket parking lot in order to retrieve a container of the product which has rolled underneath.

Possibly the most popular version, however, was that in which a previously-bored baby stands up and begins break-dancing when his mother announces, "Mommy's gonna put you in your high chair and fix you some Dreyer's Cookies 'N Cream.''

Having grown from a small neighborhood ice cream maker into one of the largest ice cream companies in the United States, Dreyer's Grand Ice Cream, Inc. entered the late 1990s in a position of dominance in the premium ice cream industry. The company began an aggressive marketing plan, which included quadrupling its advertising budget. These measures helped T. Gary Rogers' and William F. Cronk's company surpass its rival Breyers in market share in early 1995. In celebration of the success, the company chartered three DC-10 airplanes to fly all of its employees to a party in Oakland, California, near the site of the original Dreyer's Ice Cream Parlor. It also increased the scope of the Dreyer's Grand Ice Cream Charitable Foundation with the addition of a new foundation effort called the Grand Expectations Program. The purpose of the new program was to support creative projects around the country which affect a significant number of children and promote excellence in their actions.

Throughout the years, Dreyer's commitment to innovation and serving consumers' needs aided it in the development of numerous products focusing on both health and convenience. Furthermore, its direct-store distribution system had proven to be so effective that the company's portfolio of partner brands had grown to include Ben & Jerry's, ConAgra's Healthy Choice, Mocha Mix, Nestlé Ice Cream novelties, and Lemon Chill, among others. In 1995, its partner brands accounted for 34 percent of Dreyer's total revenues. With sales steadily climbing in the geographic areas already served by their distribution system, and with several other national and international market areas still open, Dreyer's possessed seemingly-unlimited potential for continued growth and success.

Principal Subsidiaries

Edy's Grand Ice Cream; Edy's of Illinois, Inc.; Dreyer's International, Inc.; Grand Soft Capital Co.; Grand Soft Equipment Co.; Systems International, Inc.; Portofino Co.; M-K-D Distributors, Inc.

Further Reading

Autry, Ret, "Dreyer's Grand Ice Cream," *Fortune,* August 27, 1990, p. 81.

Brown, Paul B., and Kichen, Steve, "The Class of 1983: Breaking the Barriers," *Forbes,* November 7, 1983, p. 168.

"Dreyer's Grand Ice Cream, Inc.," *San Francisco Business Times,* September 20, 1991, p. 22.

"Dreyer's Grand Ice Cream Licks Both Fat and Cholesterol," *Distribution Journal,* July 15, 1990, p. 64.

Dunn, Laurence, "Just Desserts," *California Business,* June 1991, p. 60.

Lubove, Seth, "The Berserk-ley Boys," *Forbes,* August 14, 1995, p. 42.

Martin, Sam, "Gourmet Ice Cream, Soy-Bean-Based Imitations Create Excitement," *Quick Frozen Foods International,* July 1985, p. 29.

Royall, Roderick, "Ice Cream Wars," *Baltimore Business Journal,* April 28, 1986, p. 1.

Schlax, Julie, "Cone-ichiwa," *Forbes,* July 9, 1990, p. 107.

—Laura E. Whiteley

Duplex Products Inc.

1947 Bethany Road
Sycamore, Illinois 60178
U.S.A.
(815) 895-2101
Fax: (815) 895-7028

Wholly Owned Subsidiary of Reynolds and Reynolds
Company
Incorporated: 1958
Sales: $275 million (1996)
Employees: 1,852
Stock Exchanges: American
SICs: 2758 Commercial Printing; 2761 Manifold Business
Forms; 2678 Stationery, Tablets & Related Products

Duplex Products Inc. is one of America's leading manufacturers and suppliers of business information products, services, and technologies. The company offers a comprehensive array of paper-based and electronic-based business information products, including custom and stock business forms, custom and stock pressure sensitive labels, integrated form/label combinations, electronic printing and mailing services, forms management services, and a wide variety of services related to check fraud prevention, electronic forms, and information flow services. Duplex Products Inc. has manufacturing plants located in ten states across the United States, and numerous direct sales offices throughout America and Puerto Rico. Yet during the early 1990s the company experienced the harsh reality of shrinking markets and intense competition. In the spring of 1996, with declining sales and a recent reorganization program less than successful, the company was purchased by Reynolds and Reynolds Company, one of the largest manufacturers and distributors of business information products in the country.

Early History

Founded in 1947 by a group of businessmen interested in taking advantage of the growing market for business forms within both the local and federal governments, Duplex began to design and manufacture simple business forms such as carbon copies, invoices, and a wide variety of other information materials. At first, the firm specialized in designing stock business forms and labels, but within a few years branched out into the design and production of custom business forms for regular government clients. At this time, most of the company's designs were for either hand-written forms or for forms inserted into manual typewriters. Although the firm grew slowly, it gradually carved a niche for itself as one of the pre-eminent business forms manufacturers and suppliers in the Midwestern United States.

As the company's reputation grew during the 1950s, management began to broaden the scope of its products and services in order to keep pace with the needs of clients and the changing nature of information management. Although carbon-based business information forms remained the company's primary product, management began to expand its products and services to include customized labels, continuous and multi-part custom business forms, and a consulting arm to advise clients how to improve the processing of information while lowering costs at the same time. These added products and services brought more and more new clients to the firm, from industries as diverse as retail, industrial, and financial, and sales began to increase dramatically.

During the 1960s and 1970s, the company continued to expand its product line. Forms for management services, printing services, and various other documentation were designed and manufactured by the company. As sales and services began to increase, Duplex began a comprehensive training program for its marketing employees on new selling techniques. This program soon became one of the most important within the company since it served as the impetus for establishing sales offices throughout the United States. During the late 1970s, the company began to open business service centers for its expanding list of clients, including warehousing, customer inventory management and reporting, and various on-site business form productions. By 1978, sales had surpassed the $200 million milestone and, even though one major company maintained a stranglehold on the business forms industry, Duplex was quickly becoming one of the premier manufacturers in the marketplace.

Company Perspectives:

Duplex takes pride in its team of business specialists with a total market orientation. We offer the most extensive printing and distribution services in the industry; engineering and research professionals who understand your business requirements; responsive sales consultants dedicated to finding creative solutions for your concerns; and a performance-based reporting system to measure our success.

Expansion and Growth during the 1980s

During the late 1970s and early 1980s, the business forms industry experienced a downturn following the fortunes of the American economy. However, when the economy began to recover in 1982, Duplex took advantage of the opportunities and increased its market share and profitability. By 1984, the company reported sales of $242 million, an increase of nearly 17 percent over the previous year, and its momentum did not appear to diminish in the least. Management decided to sell its wholesale office-supply division during this time, but reaped the rewards of a higher consumer demand for its products, increased productivity, and lower than average raw materials costs. During the same year, the company upgraded much of its equipment and manufacturing facilities within the United States. A catalogue sales facility was built in Mechanicsburg, Pennsylvania, and the company's existing forms plant in Orlando, Florida, was completely replaced with a newer, modernized facility. Major renovations were undertaken at the company's West York, Pennsylvania plant, along with numerous others along the East Coast. In addition, demand for the company's Form/Serv systems was also growing. Designed to computerize the ability of a customer to reorder forms, control inventory, identify obsolete forms and provide various other business forms analyses, the program was one of the most successful ever designed and manufactured by Duplex. By 1985, Duplex was operating 15 business forms manufacturing facilities in the United States, and was planning to open another plant in Salt Lake City, Utah.

Projections for future growth gave management even greater confidence in the company's future. The United States Department of Commerce issued a report for the year 1984 which reported a total of $5.7 billion in business form shipments. This amount was expected to increase by an average of 5 percent through the late 1980s. Most of the increased demand for business form products and services was the result of phenomenal and unexpected technological advances in office automation and data processing, closely connected to the expanding use of word processors and microcomputers by businesses of various sizes. The Department of Commerce further estimated that over three million microcomputers were being employed by companies and organizations throughout the United States, and the percentage of installations of such equipment was expected to grow by approximately 20 percent from 1985 to 1990. Thus Duplex management was anticipating an increase of between 10 and 20 percent in shipments of its business forms materials. The predictions by the Department of Commerce proved true. By the end of fiscal 1985, Duplex Products reported sales of $326.5 million, the best year for sales revenues in the company's history.

Industry Changes during the late 1980s and early 1990s

Although management was confident that the company could sustain its rate of growth and continue to increase its sales volume, the market for traditional business forms in the United States gradually began to decline during the late 1980s. Operating in a highly competitive and extremely mature market, Duplex felt the initial effects of vast industry changes. Large corporations and organizations moved away from paper-based information systems for two reasons: the expanding use of personal computers to store information and the technological advances in document publishing software packages that enable firms to design and print a wide variety of business forms on their own. By the early 1990s, approximately 20 percent of the $8 billion business forms industry was controlled by one large competitor, and the remaining market was shared by some 600 other companies. Duplex had grown so quickly and so large that it was ranked as the sixth largest among these companies. Yet this was somewhat of a dubious achievement since the excess of supply over demand was crowding firms out of the market. In an industry where pricing structure, paper quality, on-time delivery, and customer service were the most important competitive factors, over-capacity was giving rise to pricing pressures that most companies, including Duplex, could not overcome.

By the early 1990s, Duplex Products was producing a wide variety of business forms and offering a comprehensive array of services from ten facilities located in Illinois, Pennsylvania, Indiana, Florida, Ohio, California, Utah, Maryland, and Georgia. One of the most promising developments during this time was the establishment of a envelope manufacturing operation, Puerto Rico Envelopes, Inc., situated in Bayamon, Puerto Rico. With a lower wage scale than the company's continental U.S. operations, management intended to drastically reduce its overall operating budget. These developments appeared somewhat to counteract the industry trends of increasing competitiveness in an overcrowded market. Unfortunately, however, after a lengthy period of time which saw a decline in paper prices, suddenly bond paper prices dramatically shot up. The company's selling prices were adjusted to reflect this increase, but pressure on profit margins remained intense, and the marketplace became all the more competitive. By the end of fiscal 1993, Duplex Products reported a drop in sales volume to $258 million.

Restructuring during the mid 1990s

In 1993, Benjamin L. McSwiney was hired as president and chief executive officer of the company, and given the authority by its board of directors to do whatever was needed to reverse declining sales and shrinking profits. McSwiney, who had extensive management experience and had served as president of WhiteStar Graphics and general manager of Williamhouse Regency, immediately implemented a comprehensive and far-reaching restructuring program designed to revitalize the company's prospects. To reduce operating expenses, he closed six of the company's facilities, and abruptly terminated nearly 30 percent of its entire workforce. The company sold its envelope manufacturing plant in Puerto Rico and its catalog operation at approximately the same time. To emphasize his no-nonsense approach in turning Duplex Products around, he replaced eight of the firm's nine senior management executives and issued a memorandum stipulating the a large percentage of the company's products were to be outsourced from that time forward.

At the same time, McSwiney launched a major corporate initiative that was designed to add a broad range of new products, services, and technologies to its existing line of traditional business forms and products. The new president saw high potential growth in areas such as pressure sensitive labels, short-run preprinted cut sheets, electronic printing and mailing services, demand printing, and forms automation. Implementing services that assisted customers in reducing their cost and handling of information, including the integration of electronic and paper documents, and the development and enhancement of new business processes, were regarded as forerunners of a more prosperous future. McSwiney was convinced that the increase in information generated by the expanding age of computer processing would increase opportunities in the field of paperless communications, and enable companies like Duplex gradually to replace the declining segments of the traditional paper-based business forms market with high technology products and services for the electronic information highway.

Unfortunately, sales continued to spiral downward. Above normal price discounting within the business forms industry, large increases in bond paper prices, and growing selling expenses placed Duplex in a vulnerable economic position. Unable to satisfy the growing demands of the company's board of directors for an immediate turnaround, and unable fully to implement his strategy for reinvigorating Duplex Products, McSwiney was forced to resign in June of 1995. At a special meeting of the board, Andrew A. Campbell, vice president of finance and chief financial officer, was appointed the new president and CEO of the company. Prior to joining Duplex, Campbell had served as the vice president and chief financial officer of General Electric's Motor Group. More comfortable with the conservative Campbell, the board of directors gave him the directive to turn the company around as soon as possible.

Campbell continued, albeit at a slower pace, the electronic-based solutions, the emphasis on customer service, and the development of cost-effective business information forms that McSwiney had initially designed and implemented. New products and services were also introduced, including personal computer-based requisitioning software, a highly sophisticated check fraud prevention program, and an information process analysis service. Campbell also poured significant amounts of money into the company's electronic printing and mailing centers located in Chicago, Illinois, and Baltimore, Maryland, and the recently acquired facilities in Sacramento, California. The resignation of McSwiney and the efforts of Campbell, however, did not provide the solution to Duplex's problems. In the spring of 1996, unable to prevent the loss of the company's market share, the decline of its sales volume, and the growing perception that Duplex Products was not positioned well enough to recover from its tribulations, the board of directors decided to accept an acquisition offer from Reynolds & Reynolds, one of the largest business forms manufacturers in the industry. As of the summer of 1996, details concerning the acquisition were still pending, but it was agreed upon by industry analysts and representatives from both companies that the purchase of Duplex Products by Reynolds & Reynolds was a done deal.

The future of Duplex Products, Inc. is uncertain. Reynolds & Reynolds, the company's new owner, might decide to partition its operations, and sell off those that are less profitable, while reorganizing the high technology services to provide maximum profitability. Or the new management might decide to pump significant amounts of capital into its operations in order to revive the company's deteriorating market share. Whatever happens in the future, Duplex Products is certain to undergo many changes.

Further Reading

"Catching Up," *Barron's,* May 13, 1985, p. 57.

Cohen, David, R., "Office Equipment and Supplies Industry," *Value Line Investment Survey,* October 28, 1994, pp. 11–16.

"Duplex Products, Inc.," *Barron's,* December 17, 1990, p. 61.

"Duplex Products Purchase Completed for $90 Million," *Wall Street Journal,* May 21, 1996, p. C4(W).

Murphy, H. Lee, "Duplex Products Forms Plan to Reverse 5 Years of Decline," *Crain's Chicago Business,* March 20, 1995, p. 34.

"Outsourcing Forms Trims Buying Tab," *Purchasing,* February 16, 1995, p. 77.

—Thomas Derdak

Duriron Company Inc.

P.O. Box 8820
Dayton, Ohio 45401-8820
U.S.A.
(513) 476-6150
Fax: (513) 476-6231

Public Company
Incorporated: 1912 as Duriron Casting Company
Sales: $532 million
Employees: 3,900
Stock Exchanges: New York
SICs: 3492 Fluid Power Valves & Hose Fittings; 2822
 Synthetic Rubber; 3569 General Industrial Machinery,
 Not Elsewhere Classified

Duriron Company Inc. is one of the world's leading manufacturing firms in specialized process fluid handling systems. The company offers a variety of products, including automatic control valves, valves and actuators, pumps, sealing systems, filtration equipment, pipes and fittings. Duriron's product line is used in the intricate process systems of the chemical, petrochemical, refining, food and beverage, pharmaceutical, pulp and paper, and aerospace industries. Since the beginning of the 1980s, Duriron has significantly expanded its presence around the world. The company has service centers, manufacturing operations, and licensees in 170 cities and 29 countries, including England, Ireland, Holland, Belgium, France, Italy, Switzerland, Germany, Brazil, Japan, China, Korea, Australia, Singapore, South Africa, India, and Saudi Arabia.

Early History

During a trip through Europe before the outbreak of World War I, a young DuPont Chemical Company engineer and acid plant supervisor, John R. Pitman, was impressed by the development of an iron-like material called "tantiron." Tantiron had been developed for use in the production of materials and equipment that normally employed highly corrosive acids. Chemicals were infrequently used in the manufacture of heavy equipment during the early years of the 20th century, and therefore there was no need for materials that could withstand intense corrosive attack. However, the exception to this was the production of explosives. The corrosive acid mixtures that were employed to make gunpowder actually destroyed the processing equipment which was used in its production. Ordinarily, each manufacturer regarded it as an inevitable burden that the pipes, valves, and fittings used in the production of gunpowder required replacement on a regular basis due to the effects of corrosion. The development of "tantiron," therefore, constituted a revolutionary event in the world of manufacturing.

When Pitman returned to the United States, he contacted William E. Hall, a lawyer and financier in New York City. Hall recognized the potential of "tantiron" for the American manufacturing industry and suggested that the two men work with Peirce D. Schenck, an eccentric but brilliant engineer living in Dayton, Ohio, to develop their own unique alloy. Intrigued by the challenge of creating a new corrosion-resistant material, Schenck set up a makeshift foundry on the porch of his home and began conducting experiments that lasted from one week to the next. After months of research and experimentation, the Yale engineer finally succeeded in producing a high silicon content iron alloy. The most durable iron material ever made, Schenck, Hall, and Pitman named it "duriron."

Schenck, Hall, and Pitman met in New York to incorporate the Duriron Casting Company on May 16, 1912. Capitalized at $50,000, the company opened its first sales office at 90 West Street in New York, with Schenck as president, Pitman as vice-president and general sales manager, and Hall serving as legal adviser. Schenck returned to Dayton and arranged an exclusive licensing agreement with Dayton Malleable Iron to pour metal and furnish castings made from duriron. By the end of 1914, the Duriron Casting Company was selling its products at a brisk rate, and management decided to open both an office building and a foundry. At this time, the company primarily acted as a castings supplier for the equipment of various other companies' designs but had also developed a small product line of its own, including kettles, tanks, troughs, towers, and concentrator tubes.

America's entry into World War I changed the fortunes of the company forever. Demand for Duriron's products skyrock-

Company Perspectives:

The Duriron Vision: Duriron will be a global growth company recognized by our stakeholders for providing superior total value and as the preferred total quality supplier of specialized products for the process industries.

eted since it was the sole domestic source of the corrosion-resistant, high-silicon iron alloy which was essential to the control of chemical acids for the production of munitions. A new foundry was built during 1918 to meet the increasing demand of the U.S. government and the Allied war effort for the company's products. When Schenck enlisted in the U.S. Army and was assigned to overseas duty in Europe, production began to decline so dramatically that the federal government considered nationalizing Duriron Casting Company to assure the uninterrupted flow of products for the manufacture of munitions. Alarmed by the prospect of a government takeover, Hall and Pitman arranged for Schenck to return and manage the company's production facilities. Government officials agreed to refrain from nationalizing the company and deferred all Duriron employees from military service during the war since the company was considered an ''essential industry'' to the U.S. military effort. By the end of the war, the company employed over 1000 men and women and produced more than 40,000 tons of Duriron.

Unfortunately, the immediate postwar period was not as lucrative for the company. Business plummeted largely because munitions were no longer in demand, and the nation's economy had stagnated. Yet by the mid-1920s, Duriron was on the rebound and began to invest large amounts of capital in research and development. During this time, the company developed Alcumite, an aluminum and bronze alloy with magnesium and iron added for strength and corrosive resistance. By the end of the decade, the company was producing high-quality stainless steel, one of the most important materials used during the 20th Century.

The Great Depression and War Years

The Great Depression swept over millions of Americans like an economic plague after the Wall Street stock market crash of 1929, but Duriron Company was not as severely affected as other U.S. businesses. Although stunned by the death of Peirce Schenck, the man most responsible for the company's initial success and subsequent development, Duriron's research laboratory continued its experimentation with various materials and products. One of the most important developments during this time was an austenitic stainless steel named Durimet 20. A high-quality, special-purpose material with substantial resistance to corrosion, the product became the basis for an entire range of alloys that quickly set Duriron apart from the rest of the industry as a leader in process equipment. By 1939, over 20 additional corrosion-resistant metals had been formulated for the manufacture of steel, magnesium, copper, aluminum, synthetic rubber, plastics, petroleum, alcohol, vitamins, paper, textiles, and pharmaceuticals.

The hectic pace of research and development conducted by Duriron during the 1930s was interrupted by the advent of World War II. As in the First World War, Duriron was classified as an essential industry for the production of munitions, and its employees were exempted from conscription. Although the company reported $5.3 million in sales during 1942, most from the production of processing equipment for making munitions, the most important work going on in the research lab involved the atomic bomb. Duriron was instrumental in making products that could successfully process and concentrate uranium and plutonium, the two essential ingredients for the atomic bomb.

Technical Developments during the 1950s

By the end of the war in 1945, Duriron had strategically placed itself to take advantage of the explosive demands that occurred within the petrochemicals industry. Manmade fibers like nylon and plastic were replacing wool and metals. A foundry modernization program, designed to incorporate these new developments in materials and products, was implemented and concluded with efficiency. By the mid-1950s, the company had sales outlets in 34 cities, and representatives in 10 countries overseas. In 1953, Duriron sales surpassed $10 million for the first time in the company's history.

The research and development laboratory was working at what seemed like a frenetic pace during this decade. Duriron introduced a plastic sleeve plug valve, noteworthy because it was the first successful application of Teflon in processing equipment for the severe chemical services. The company also developed a back pull-out process pump, the first of its kind in the world. In 1954, research led to the introduction of the first cathodic protection anodes, which were designed to protect buried metal structures from corrosion through the process of electrical transfer. In 1957, the first line of epoxy pumps was designed and produced by Duriron and, in the same year, a revolutionary one-piece epoxy resin sink designed for chemical waste disposal was also introduced. By the end of the 1950s, Duriron was one of the leaders in the field of applying plastics to processing equipment.

Growth and Expansion during the 1960s, 1970s, and 1980s

Although a new facility was built in 1961 to house the burgeoning Corrosion-Resistant Plastics Division, three years later another expansion of the plant was necessary. New valve production facilities, testing labs, engineering offices, and foundry shops at the company's main headquarters in Dayton were also built during this time. By the end of 1962, at the company's 50th anniversary celebration, management could report that sales had climbed to $15.7 million. The decade of the 1960s also marked the first time that management turned its attention to the international marketplace. Duriron of Canada, Inc., was organized as a sales subsidiary in 1964, and a European sales office was opened in Brussels, Belgium, in 1968. By 1970, Duriron had opened its first overseas production facility in Liege, Belgium.

The 1960s were also marked by significant technical developments in the company's research laboratory. The MARK II Stand Chemical Service Process Pump become the model of choice in the petrochemical processing equipment industry, while another first for the company involved the development of a fully Teflon lined valve which resisted chemical corrosion. Two additional developments late in the decade included DC-8 and Durcomet 100, both rapidly becoming widely used within the industry due to their unparalleled resistance to corrosion and wear.

Duriron continued its development of new products during the 1970s. Specially designed sealed pumps, in-line pumps, and a revolutionary fiber reinforced plastic pump were introduced during the early years of the decade. DurcoShell, a proprietary ceramic shell molding technique designed in the company's research laboratory, was introduced to the market with great fanfare. The process, which significantly reduces carbon content, one of the major causes of casting failure because of corrosion, removed doubt from anyone within the industry that Duriron was the technological leader in foundry processing equipment. In 1973, Duriron reported total sales of $52 million; by 1976, company sales had passed the $100 million mark. In 1978, Duriron was selected by *Fortune* magazine as one of the largest and most successful manufacturing companies in the United States.

By 1980, sales had surpassed $140 million, but the energy crisis, the development of offshore chemical capacity, and the generally harsh conditions of the process industries necessitated a change both in the company's market strategy and its operational management. As a result, management decided to implement a thorough plant and equipment modernization, along with an aggressive acquisitions policy. In 1980 alone, over $7 million was spent in updating machine tools and process techniques. In 1981, a new materials and hydraulic lab was built, and a new valve facility. Plant expansion occurred once again at Duriron headquarters in Dayton, Ohio, as well as other manufacturing facilities across the United States. In 1982, the company constructed a new manufacturing plant in Tarragona, Spain, and in 1985, one of the major foreign acquisitions of the decade was made in Belgium. A manufacturer of engineered plastics, N.V. Janssen M&L, the company was one of the leading firms in western Europe. The most important domestic acquisition during this time involved Valtek Incorporated, a recognized leader in designing and manufacturing high-quality automatic control valves, actuators, and various related component parts. At the end of the 1980s, Duriron Company Inc. stood as the world's leading supplier of chemical process equipment.

The 1990s and Beyond

During the early and mid-1990s, the company initiated a comprehensive reorganization of its operations that resulted in

the following four business groups: the Industrial Products Group, including manual valves and valve actuation equipment, filtration systems, metering pumps and foundry products; the Flow Control Group, including automatic control valve products of its Valtek subsidiary; the Rotating Equipment Group, consisting of chemical process pumps; and the Fluid Sealing Group, including whole new lines of mechanical sealing products. This last group was created with the acquisition of Durametallic Corporation, the company's largest acquisition in its history. In addition to the Durametallic acquisition, Duriron has purchased Sereg Valves, Kammer, and Mecair, three European firms which increased international sales to almost 40 percent of its total sales volume. Forays into China and Saudi Arabia also promised to increase revenues over the long term.

Duriron has been fortunate throughout its long history to have been extremely well managed. This is especially true during the 1990s when the marketplace demands sophisticated expansion policies and cost-cutting operational strategies. Duriron has created a pre-eminent leadership position for itself in the chemical process equipment industry that it is not likely to relinquish in the near future.

Principal Subsidiaries

Durco Pumps; Valtek International, Inc.; Durco Valve; Kammer Valves, A.G.; Automax; Sereg Valves, S.A.; Durco Filtration Systems; Atomac; Mecair, S.p.A.; Engineered Plastic Productions.

Principal Divisions

Durco Foundry Division.

Further Reading

"Duriron Agrees to Buy Durametallic for $150 Million," *New York Times*, September 12, 1995, p. D4(L).

"Duriron Company," *Wall Street Journal*, January 5, 1996, p. B5(E).

"Duriron Selected as Supplier," *Wall Street Journal*, June 7, 1995, p. A6(W).

"Duriron Will Acquire Durametallic for Stock Valued at $150 Million," *Wall Street Journal*, September 12, 1995, p. C16(E).

"Empowerment Pumps Duriron Productivity Up," *Tooling & Production*, October 1994, p. 13.

A *Legacy of Quality, 1912–1987: The Duriron Company*, Dayton, Ohio: Duriron Company, 1987.

—Thomas Derdak

E! Entertainment Television Inc.

5670 Wilshire Boulevard
Los Angeles, California 90036
U.S.A.
(213) 954-2400
Fax: (213) 954-2793

Private Company
Incorporated: 1989
Employees: 330
Sales: $120 million (1996 estimate)
SICs: 4841 Cable Television Services

E! Entertainment Television Inc. is one of the fastest growing cable companies in the United States. The company's circulation jumped to 31.2 million subscribers in just a little more than five years, a phenomenal increase in the cable television industry, especially considering the fact that cable TV is already saturated. With an aggressive and youth-oriented programming strategy, E! Entertainment has become widely known for its irreverent talk shows, such as ''Talk Soup,'' ''The Gossip Show,'' and ''The Howard Stern Show,'' with a host whose format and jokes are controversial but who is able to boost the ratings of his parent company. In the mid-1990s, E! Entertainment made a major move into the international arena, snatching up such clients as Sky Channel in the United Kingdom, StarTV in Asia, and Orbit in the Middle East.

Early History

The brashness of E! Entertainment Television is reflected in the overwhelming and uninhibited confidence of its creator, Lee Masters. Masters had worked for a number of years as the general manager of MTV, cable television's most successful music channel. While at MTV, Masters cleverly guided its programming and music to appeal to the 14-year-old to 20-something crowd, a major accomplishment in itself. Masters was a major influence behind the controversial ''Beavis and Butthead'' cartoon serial as well as programs such as ''The Week in Rock'' and ''Remote Control.'' While at MTV, Mas-

ters developed the ingenious idea of allowing celebrities more control over the interview process, which translated into more unusual and less predictable entertainment.

In 1989, Masters was lured away from his position at MTV to take control of the Movietime cable channel. Movietime was owned by a consortium of cable television companies, including Time Warner HBO, Continental Cablevision, Comcast Corporation, Cox Cable, and Tele-Communications, Inc. The programming at Movietime, however, was dreadful. Movietime was placed at the higher limits of the cable television dial and played previews of movies over and over again. With only 15,000 subscribers, which some cable television wags described as insomniacs, Movietime was not an exciting channel for viewing. Masters was hired with the understanding that he would have complete authority and control to implement a total reorganization of the cable channel.

Innovative Programming in the Early 1990s

Using the knowledge about cable television, demographics, and celebrity publicity and exposure he gained while working at MTV, Masters began his turnaround of Movietime. The new chief executive officer's first decision was to rename the cable television network E! Entertainment Television Inc. Masters's second move was to change the programming completely. Since Americans are generally in awe of film, radio, and television celebrities, Masters decided to develop programs that would provide those celebrities with significant exposure, but in a way they could control. Thus the audience would get to see celebrities, and celebrities would maintain a certain amount of control over their exposure to the public.

This strategy of ''controlled publicity'' first took the form of talk shows and entertainment news that was filled with ''star-studded'' celebrities. Without much money to work with, Masters approached the controversial and provocative radio show host and celebrity Howard Stern and convinced Stern to allow E! Entertainment to install robotic video cameras that taped the radio show and all of Stern's antics while on and off the air. Stern agreed to Masters's proposal, and E! Entertainment got excellent programming material of one and one-half hours per day at the bargain basement rate of $33,000 per episode, plus a cool $1 million in compensation to Stern. Within a few months of its introduction on E! Entertainment, the "Howard Stern Show" was the cable television's hottest and highest rated program.

One of Masters's most successful ideas evolved into the hit show "Talk Soup." Airing six times a day, the show excerpted highlights of mainstream daytime network talk shows, such as those hosted by Jerry Springer, Geraldo Rivera, Richard Bey, Montel Williams, and Oprah Winfrey, and juxtaposed this material with out-of-the-ordinary, quirky skits produced by the show's host and comedian, John Henson. The genius of the show, which reflected the entrepreneurial spirit and creativity of Masters, was that production costs were next to nothing. The network talk shows agreed to give E! Entertainment clips free of charge, in exchange for promoting the next day's programming. With this free material, the cost of a 30-minute production of "Talk Soup" was approximately $10,000, which was $20,000 to $30,000 less than the costs to produce one of the talk show segments featured on "Talk Soup." Moreover, advertisers like Nike and Visa paid approximately $1,000 for a typical 30-second advertising slot on the show. Revenues from advertising, from the time the show went on the air, climbed to nearly $30,000, which left a hefty profit of approximately $20,000 per show. From the beginning of its run, "Talk Soup" aired 260 times per year, resulting in a pretax income of more than $5 million annually.

Perhaps the most successful and most lucrative of all of Masters's cable productions was the creation of "E! News Daily." The show's format was ostensibly that of a newscast, but the news was strictly Hollywood. Masters would send out a total of eight camera and sound crews to record premieres, award shows, and movie productions, and to arrange on-the-spot, impromptu interviews of cinema celebrities on a daily basis. The cost for a 30-minute production of "E! News Daily" ran about $15,000 per show, most of which was recovered through advertising slots during the first time the show was aired. Since the show aired three times per day, commercial revenues began to mount by the end of each month. In addition, Masters reached an agreement with the parent company of NBC, General Electric. In exchange for free videotape from crews working at NBC, Masters would give the mainstream network footage from "E! News Daily" for it to run during the late evening and early morning hours when viewership was at its lowest. According to Masters, everybody won since costs were kept low and yet television entertainment continued.

One of the genuine masters of recycled material, Masters then promoted and sold "E! News Daily" to foreign television outlets and to major international airlines, which used selected footage of the program to show to passengers during lengthy intercontinental flights. One would think this idea would be the limit of Masters's creative entrepreneurism. But it was not. By building a library of tapes that his roving Hollywood crews compiled during the production of "E! News Daily," Masters had amassed a library of more than 200,000 segments, which ranged from long interviews with celebrities to short, quirky out-takes from movies. At no additional expense, Masters arranged for in-house editors and voiceovers to produce 30-minute specials on celebrities such as Robin Williams and

Whoopi Goldberg and behind-the-scenes perspectives on the making of a movie. Again, Masters sold these special segments to foreign outlets and major international airlines, but at a relatively low cost. The goodwill he created from selling inexpensive programs to his customers translated into an agreement with his operators to carry E! at a lower channel number, closer to where the mainstream networks are located. Knowing that millions of people around the world who subscribe to cable TV are in the habit of channel surfing, especially during primetime commercials, Masters arranged to run E! Entertainment's commercials at times different from the times chosen by the mainstream broadcasting networks, thereby increasing the chance that people who channel surf will stay tuned to his programs.

When the O.J. Simpson trial was first aired on television, with gavel-to-gavel coverage by CNN and Court TV, E! Entertainment began to notice a significant decline in its viewership. As a result, Masters decided to cover the trial as intensely as the other cable television networks. Of course, E! Entertainment's coverage was not quite the same. For example, one of its reporters began to read faxes on the air from people who commented on the trial, and also began to compare the fashions, hairstyles, and jewelry of the lawyers. Although this unorthodox approach to reporting the trial was controversial and soundly criticized by other members of the media, nonetheless, E! Entertainment's coverage brought back its viewership.

Growth and Expansion in the Mid-1990s

As revenues began to increase and viewership began to climb, E! Entertainment was able to surprise some of the analysts within the cable television industry. One of the most unexpected moves came when Masters decided to purchase the off-network rights to "Melrose Place," the megahit with the 20- and 30-something crowd produced by Fox. Masters agreed to pay the price of $200,000 per episode, for more than 100 installments of the primetime soap opera, to build a loyal following and, at the same time, increase his viewership. In addition, Masters reached an agreement with Brandon Tartikoff, head of New World Entertainment, that allowed for the use of E!'s production facilities as an experimental laboratory, so to speak, for innovative shows. In return, E! Entertainment received new shows that were on the cutting edge of hip-hop programming.

By the mid-1990s, Masters was taking a hard but cautious look at the syndication market. E! Entertainment had received numerous unsolicited queries from syndicators and finally decided to take the plunge by signing a major deal with Columbia TriStar Television Distribution for "E! News Daily." Yet when Warner Brothers decided to produce "Extra—The Entertainment Magazine," Masters thought it wise to step back from the deal and wait to judge the competition. Masters did not hesitate, however, to enter into an agreement with NBC whereby E! Entertainment would give the mainstream network entertainment news for its various affiliates across the United States. Still, Masters remained wary of making new deals since widespread agreements to syndicate E! Entertainment programs would actually take viewers away from his own cable network.

What catapulted E! Entertainment to the top of the cable television industry was its low production costs. The cable TV industry measures costs in terms of household, and E! Entertainment's costs in the mid-1990s were well below any of its competitors, hovering at approximately $221, in comparison with the Comedy Channel and Turner's TNT network where costs per household were reported at $333 and $567, respectively. Masters knew that the only way to keep costs down was to develop inexpensive programming, since both domestic and overseas cable operators were searching for low-cost programs to increase viewership. Acquisition of the ''Melrose Place'' programs was part of this strategy, as well as a new 30-minute show that reduced and condensed full-length movies to the best parts. The show, called ''Cut to the Chase,'' was scheduled to lead into reruns of ''Melrose Place.''

Additional cost-cutting agreements became part of Masters's specialty. He negotiated a contract with Westwood One Radio Network so that a daily newsfeed from E! Entertainment would be shown on Westwood's 6,000 international affiliates. In return, Westwood agreed to promote programs on E! Entertainment through its syndicated shows, such as ''Casey Kasem's Top 40,'' ''In Concert,'' and ''Country Countdown USA.'' Masters also acquired more than 500 episodes of ''Late Night with David Letterman'' and numerous episodes of ''The Smothers Brothers Comedy Hour.'' ''The Letterman Show,'' shown seven nights a week in primetime, heightened E! Entertainment's profile in cable television and brought along a legion of diehard Letterman fans.

One of the most important developments for E! Entertainment came in 1995, when the company made a commitment to expanding its international coverage. Masters signed a pact with the Australian commercial cable system, Optus Vision, to show five of its programming series on the airwaves of three start-up channels. In Europe, Masters signed an international distribution agreement with Reservoir Productions, located in Paris, to license ''E! Newsfeed'' and ''E! News Week in Review.'' Another international distribution deal was arranged with Channel 4 in the United Kingdom to show episodes of ''F.Y.E!: For Your Entertainment.''

In the mid-1990s, E! Entertainment was on course to increase its viewership to more than 40 million by the year 2000 and, as revenues continued to climb, there was a very good likelihood that the company would achieve its goal. Ten years before, demographic studies indicated that viewers between the ages of 12 and 34 mentioned the three mainstream channels of ABC, NBC, and CBS as their primarily watched networks. By the mid-1990s, however, those statistics changed: the same age group mentioned only one or two of the mainstream channels, along with either cable television's Disney channel, MTV, or E! Entertainment.

Further Reading

Burgi, Michael, ''Cable's Menu Expands with Original Fare,'' *MEDIAWEEK,* April 11, 1994, p. 24.

——, ''Living on a No-Juice Diet,'' *MEDIAWEEK,* October 30, 1995, p. 12.

——, ''Looking for a Home on E!asy Street,'' *MEDIAWEEK,* May 23, 1994, p. 28.

Darlin, Damon, ''E!,'' *Forbes,* November 6, 1995, p. 118.

''E!, Cassaro, Take Entrepreneurial Approach,'' *Broadcasting & Cable,* May 22, 1995, p. 73.

''E! Entertainment Television,'' *MEDIAWEEK,* November 8, 1993, p. 43.

Flint, Joe, ''After Five-Year Fight, E! Strikes Black Ink,'' *Variety,* February 6, 1995, p. 25.

Jessel, Harry A., ''Turner, E! Make Deals with Telcos,'' *Broadcasting & Cable,* December 4, 1995, p. 62.

Johnson, Debra, ''E! Entertainment Television,'' *Broadcasting & Cable,* September 18, 1995, p. 42.

McClellan, Steve, ''E! To Supply NBC News Channel,'' *Broadcasting & Cable,* January 9, 1995, p. 22.

Miller, Stuart, ''Cable Gets a Broadcast Blast,'' *Variety,* May 10, 1993, p. 73.

Petrozzello, Donna, ''Westwood, E! Interface,'' *Broadcasting & Cable,* May 23, 1994, p. 100.

''Stern, E! Strike a Deal,'' *Broadcasting & Cable,* June 6, 1994, p. 24.

''Warner Brothers, MCA/Universal and E! Entertainment Television,'' *MEDIAWEEK,* November 29, 1993, p. 8.

''Worldvision Enterprises,'' *MEDIAWEEK,* January 30, 1995, p. 6.

—Thomas Derdak

EBSCO Industries, Inc.

P.O. Box 1943
Birmingham, Alabama 35201-1943
U.S.A.
(205) 991-6600
Fax: (205) 991-1479
Internet: http://www.ebsco.com

Private Company
Founded: 1944 as Military Service Company
Employees: 4,000
Sales: $865.2 million (1995)
SICs: 7389 Business Services, Not Elsewhere Classified

EBSCO Industries, Inc. is a diverse and international conglomerate that built itself on magazine subscription services. Still the company's mainstay, EBSCO Subscription Services is the world's largest subscription management agency, serving clients through 30 regional offices on six continents. The parent company operates many media related companies, including EBSCO Graphics and EBSCO Media, two commercial printing companies, EBSCO Publishing, a distributor and publisher of electronic reference sources and databases for libraries and organizations, and EBSCO Curriculum Materials, a publisher of educational materials for elementary, secondary, and vocational schools. The company also manufactures such diverse products as fishing lures, carpeting, and pool tables, among others. Ranked second on the *Birmingham Business Journal*'s list of 100 privately-held local companies, EBSCO's diverse offerings prompted the *Journal* to create a new category called "service sector" to try to encompass all that EBSCO offered. The company's broad base of operations stabilizes and strengthens its subscription services; Dun and Bradstreet gave EBSCO the highest financial strength rating in the serials information industry in 1996.

Selling Started It All

When Elton B. Stephens graduated from the University of Alabama School of Law in 1936, he figured he could earn ten times the salary of a lawyer by selling magazines. Selling was not new to Stephens. Growing up in a poor family of eight children in rural Clio, Alabama, Stephens told *Forbes* he spent his youth selling "everything I could get my hands on." He had paid for college selling magazines door-to-door and selling socks and shirts in a dry goods shop. Though he was an enthusiastic salesman, Stephens told *Forbes* he hated selling magazines door-to-door. "You'd get the door slammed in your face. You'd get cussed at by husbands. You had to bounce back." Nevertheless, he went on selling and eventually hired others to sell for him. By 1937 Stephens purchased a Keystone Readers' Service franchise, which served subscribers for publishers of magazines.

During World War II, Stephens realized the great potential for success in selling to military bases, and by 1944 he and his wife, Alys Robinson Stephens, had invested $5,000 into their own partnership, the Military Service Company, which sold magazines, personalized binders, and racks. When Keystone fired Stephens for spending too much time with his own company, Stephens offered the publishers who had supplied Keystone better terms and took their business. And Stephens' treatment of Keystone became typical of his management style. If a supplier impeded the progress of a division, EBSCO would start its own venture or acquire another to replace it.

Stephens' desire to make his business as effective as possible and his youthful drive to "sell anything he could get his hands on," set the stage for EBSCO's growth. In an interview with *Forbes,* Stephens estimated that he launched between 60 to 80 companies over his 60 years in business, noting that 30 percent of them had failed. He recalled telling someone once "that I'd like to have five companies. That way, if one or two of them don't make it, I'll still have something to hang my hat on." By the 1990s, EBSCO was active in 28 industries.

Stephens started his company with the idea that he would work on an all-cash basis, and for 20 years he managed his company without a long-term loan. With cash on hand, Stephens formed Metal Fabricators and Finishers to manufacture display stands, Vulcan Binder and Cover to manufacturing binders, and Vulcan Enterprises to provide community related messages for binder covers; he purchased Hartsfield Printing

Company Perspectives:

EBSCO's goal is to deliver useful products and services with results that enable improvement and growth. The main lesson learned from our past is to put the customer first. While EBSCO has many customers, it is very important that each be respected and served as if they were the first and only. Customers teach and sponsor the ingenuity EBSCO needs to develop better products and services. While EBSCO takes pride in its selling, satisfied customers serve as the company's most effective ambassadors. EBSCO employees work for EBSCO customers.

Company to supply personalized stationary to the military; and he acquired Hanson-Bennett Magazine Agency of Chicago and National Magazine Company of San Francisco. But by 1964, Stephens had learned that loans help business grow and took on EBSCO's first long-term debt. Remembering a lost opportunity because of his reluctance to take on debt, Stephens told *Forbes* "Had I done that, I would probably be worth another three or four million dollars. But I'm not."

Nevertheless, since the 1960s, EBSCO—so-called after the initials of its founder's name along with the abbreviation for "company"—continued to grow, as did Stephens' fortune. In 1971, Stephens turned over EBSCO's presidential duties to his son, J. T. Stephens. Under the leadership of J. T. Stephens, EBSCO flourished. One year after taking the presidential position, J. T. Stephens saw EBSCO's sales volume double with the purchase of Franklin Square Agency, Ziff-Davis' international subscription service. And like his father, J. T. Stephens seems to be comfortable selling just about anything.

While the company remained focused on maintaining the prominence and leadership of its magazine subscription division, it broadened its base of operations to include unrelated industries such as National Billiard, Fine Craft Carpets, and PRADCO, the country's largest manufacturer of fishing lures. Elton B. Stephens remained as chairman of EBSCO, overseeing the company's charitable contributions and profit sharing investment trust. And in 1981, he started his second career as a banker, launching Alabama Bancorp.

Information Leaders

To maintain its leadership in the magazine subscription services industry, EBSCO is sensitive in its role as an information handler. EBSCO researches the needs of each of the different types of libraries it services: academic/research, law, biomedical, school, public, and special/corporate. Staff members organize seminars and forums to create a mutually beneficial working relationship with customers, seek electronic connections between EBSCO and automated library systems, and develop special reports that aid libraries in analyzing their journal collections. EBSCO employees also help develop library communication standards and support the library profession through membership and active participation in many library associations including the American Library Association, Medical Li-

brary Association, Special Libraries Association, National Information Standards Organization, Serial Industry Systems Advisory Committee, and the International Committee on Electronic Data Interchange for Serials. EBSCO strives to make subscription management as easy and efficient as possible. To that end it developed the world's first online data communications network for serial management. Developed in the late 1970s to connect all EBSCO Subscription Services regional offices with the central computer in Birmingham, in the 1990s EBSCONET acts as a link between EBSCO and customers worldwide. Customers can place orders and claims, order missing issues, search EBSCO's title database, send e-mail to EBSCO or other EBSCONET users, review their list of subscriptions ordered through EBSCO, access the Internet, and search for and order individual articles through the CASIAS (Current Awareness Service/Individual Article Service) option.

EBSCO's understanding of the importance of accessing information quickly and easily has helped it become one of America's leading producers of CD-ROM reference products. In the 1980s, EBSCO Publishing emerged from the combination of *Popular Magazine Review,* a publisher with abstracting and indexing capabilities which EBSCO renamed Magazine Article Summaries in 1987, and Horizon Information Systems, a producer of CD-ROM search and retrieval software. The first product of EBSCO publishing was *The Serial Directory: An International Reference Book.* The archives of Magazine Articles Summaries was converted to electronic format and published on CD-ROM in 1989.

EBSCO Publishing was the first to provide abstracts and keyword searching to full text or general magazines in electronic format. And in 1993, Carol Tenopir and Péter Jacsó noted in a study for *Online* that given a choice between indexes with or without abstracts they thought most users would choose those with abstracts "every time." The leading CD-ROM indexes for the layperson in 1993 were H.W. Wilson Company's Readers' Guide Abstracts, UMI's Periodical Abstracts Ondisc (and its subfile, Resource-One), and EBSCO's Magazine Article Summaries. Tenopir and Jascó attempted to differentiate between these competitors based on the quality of their abstracts. The authors looked at the consistency of style and readability in the abstracts, the extent to which the ANSI standard (The American National Standards Institute's standards for abstracts developed in 1979) was observed, and the informativeness of the abstracts. Readers' Guide Abstracts best met the test for informativeness and were two-and-a-half times longer than the others. The Magazine Article Summaries abstracts were very brief, but described the information in the article. The authors noted that EBSCO did not claim to offer full abstracts but rather summaries of articles.

Such a test may not indicate the desires of those who use indexes, however, and that is the market EBSCO desires most to please. Tenopir and Jascó wrote that some instructors and librarians preferred "an index with shorter, less informative abstracts because they didn't want students to rely on abstracts without having to go to the original article." Indeed, EBSCO's customers are the center of product development. Joseph Tragert, EBSCO Publishing's manager of product development, remarked in *Information Today* that "our objectives for 1996 are a direct result of focus groups, surveys, communication with industry professionals, and feedback from our customers and our sales team regarding the needs of libraries.'' In describing the product development cycle at EBSCO Melissa Kummerer noted in *CD-ROM Professional* that ''we can never consider a product to be finished. We can always make it better: by adding features, adding editorial content, or reducing memory requirements. We believe that quality is not a static term.'' In 1996 EBSCO planned to increase the number of titles abstracted and indexed to over 3,800 and full-text titles covered to over 1,500.

In keeping with EBSCO's interest in developing new products, it began offering an online search and retrieval system called EBSCOhost in 1996. EBSCOhost featured the same searching capabilities made popular by CD-ROM but could be accessed on the Internet. Jascó hailed the emergence of EBSCO online because, he said, ''for many magazines, EBSCO is the only abstracting/indexing and/or full-text source.''

EBSCO's growth has strengthened the company and its surrounding community. Elton B. Stephens founded the Alabama ''%'' Club, whose member companies donates two, five, or ten percent of their pre-tax income to foundations or other charitable projects. EBSCO is a member at the five percent level. In addition, EBSCO funded the nation's largest endowment for a chair of library science at the University of Alabama. Of the company's success, Elton B. Stephens told *Forbes,* ''I never dreamed that we would accomplish anything like what we have.''

Principal Subsidiaries

EBSCO CASIAS, Inc.; Valley Joist, Inc.; EBSCO Investment Services, Inc.; EBSCO International, Inc.; EBSCO Worldwide, Inc.

Principal Divisions

Military Service Company; Vulcan Service-Periodical Sales; EBSCO Subscription Services; EBSCO Advertising Specialties; EBSCO Curriculum Materials; EBSCO Telemarketing Service; EBSCO Reception Room Subscription Services; EBSCO Furniture Pavilion; Publisher Promotion and Fulfillment; Directional Advertising Services; EBSCO Publishing; EBSCO Interiors; NSC International; National Billiard Company; Vulcan Binder and Cover; Vulcan Industries; EBSCO Media; EBSCO Graphics; EBSCO Carpet Mills; Four Seasons Garment Company; H. Wilson Company; Plastics Research and Development Corp. (PRADCO).

Further Reading

Beiser, Karl, ''From Print to Electronic Form: The Sum Greater Than the Parts,'' *Database,* October 1993, pp. 97–99.

Bell, Suzanne S., ''The Serials Directory/EBSCO CD-ROM,'' *Information Today,* October 1993, pp. 24–25, 27.

''EBSCO Offers New Search and Retrieval System for Libraries,'' *Information Today,* September 1995, p. 43.

Jacsó, Péter, ''CD-ROM Publishers Come Online,'' *Information Today,* September 1995, pp. 32–33.

Kummerer, Melissa, ''Perpetual Product Development: EBSCO's CD-ROM Development Strategy,'' *CD-ROM Professional,* November 1993, pp. 104–108.

McMenamin, Brigid, ''The Afterlife of a Salesman,'' *Forbes,* May 24, 1993, pp. 206–208.

Milazzo, Don, ''EBSCO Is a Category Killer,'' *Birmingham Business Journal,* November 6, 1995, p. 1.

''News from EBSCO Publishing,'' *Information Today,* March 1996, p. 4.

''OCLC and EBSCO to Offer Full-Text Images of Articles from 1,000 General Reference Journals,'' *Information Today,* April 1995, p. 18.

''Online Data Communications Network Provides Speedy Customer Service,'' *Data Management,* December 1985, pp. 46–48.

Pollard, Jonathan, and Anne Marie Downing, ''Ziff Boosts Computer Library Availability with Major Distribution Agreements,'' *Business Wire,* November 2, 1988.

Rifkind, Eugene, ''EBSCO Primary Search,'' *Information Today,* January 1995, pp. 20–21.

Rosen, Linda, ''EBSCO Magazine Article Summaries Full Text Elite CD-ROM,'' *Information Today,* June 1993, pp. 26–27.

''Subscription Service Credits Its Swiftness to On-line Net,'' *Computerworld,* March 19, 1984, p. 38, 40.

Tenopir, Carol, and Péter Jacsó, ''Quality of Abstracts,'' *Online,* May 1993, pp. 44–55.

Tenopir, Carol, and Timothy Ray Smith, ''General Periodical Indexes on CD-ROM,'' *CD-ROM Professional,* July 1990, pp. 70–81.

—Sara Pendergast

Ellett Brothers
As big as all outdoors.

Ellett Brothers, Inc.

267 Columbia Avenue
Chapin, South Carolina 29036
U.S.A.
(803) 345-3751
Fax: (803) 345-1820

Public Company
Incorporated: 1933 as Ellett Brothers
Employees: 354
Sales: $150.4 million (1995)
Stock Exchanges: NASDAQ
SICs: 5091 Sporting & Recreational Goods

A leading national distributor of outdoor sporting goods, Ellett Brothers, Inc. specializes in marketing and supplying hunting and shooting sports equipment. All of Ellett Brothers' merchandise, which also included marine accessories, camping equipment, and general outdoor sporting accessories, was sold by the company's telemarketing sales force and through numerous product catalogs. During the mid 1990s, Ellett Brothers marketed and distributed more than 60,000 different items and targeted a clientele consisting primarily of small, independent retailers located in all 50 states and in 16 foreign countries.

Although Ellett Brothers underwent numerous changes during its first six decades of business, two characteristics remained constant throughout its history: the Ellett Brothers name and the location of the business. Founded in 1933, Ellett Brothers was established in Chapin, South Carolina, where the company operated as a regional sporting goods distributor. Initially, the company distributed fishing equipment exclusively, deriving all of its business from fulfilling the requests of independent sporting goods dealers located in its home state, North Carolina, and Georgia. For the first quarter century of its existence, Ellett Brothers operated as such, serving a three-state territory with fishing equipment during the economically depressed 1930s and throughout the 1940s. The company's second quarter century of business was decidedly more dynamic, encompassing sweeping

changes that shaped the Chapin-based company into the Ellett Brothers of the 1990s.

1950s: A Product Line for the Future

The first significant change occurred in 1957, when Ellett Brothers began distributing hunting and shooting sports products and outdoor accessories throughout an expanded geographical area. The foray into hunting and shooting products and outdoor accessories marked the introduction of what quickly would become the company's core business, a product line that has defined Ellett Brothers since the 1960s. Not long after this signal move, the company abandoned its original business by discontinuing the distribution of fishing equipment. From the 1960s forward, Ellett Brothers' sales force focused their efforts on selling firearms and outdoor accessories to a largely rural clientele comprised mainly of independent, "mom-and-pop" retailers.

Like other sporting goods wholesalers, Ellett Brothers relied on a sales force that traveled throughout the company's area of service to solicit business. For distributors like Ellett Brothers, the art of convincing retailers to buy merchandise was done face to face, an all-important task undertaken by a field sales force that travelled a circuit, visiting prospective retailers and signing them on as customers. For 40 years, Ellett Brothers approached this integral aspect of the wholesaling business much like its competition, but in the early 1970s the company adopted a different approach that distinguished it from other sporting goods distributors and spurred sales growth significantly. During the early 1970s, Ellett Brothers' management directed a group of its salespeople to market the company's products over the telephone, marking the beginning of telemarketing at the Chapin headquarters.

For a brief period the company was supported by a two-pronged marketing program: some salespeople traveled in the field soliciting business from independent retailers in person, while others solicited business over the telephone. It was not long until the latter approach proved to be dramatically more effective than the former, leading the company to eliminate all field sales personnel and rest its fortunes exclusively on its

Company Perspectives:

Our strategy is to expand our use of the business unit concept by focusing on newly identified markets, similar to the archery group started in 1994. In addition, we will continue to pursue strategic acquisitions whose product lines are compatible with Ellett's existing products, are additive to margins, and create new channels of distribution. We will apply a business unit approach to acquisitions, where it is appropriate. We will also continue to identify distribution opportunities, targeting specific markets where we can effectively implement our teleservicing and business unit approaches.

telemarketing program. Business soared as a result, lifting sales and profits substantially. By the late 1970s, Ellett Brothers ranked as a leading national distributor of outdoor sporting goods products thanks largely to the effectiveness of its less-than-decade-old telemarketing program. Ahead were years of continued robust financial growth, as the company honed its telemarketing talents and matured into a highly-efficient and focused telemarketer and distributor of sporting goods. But the years ahead also brought their own anguish.

1980s Misstep

Ellett Brothers entered the 1980s with its primary focus on the sale and distribution of hunting and shooting sports equipment. But the late 1980s saw a number of changes resulting from a transfer of ownership of the company. In 1985, a subsidiary of a privately-owned, Rocky Mount, North Carolina-based investment firm named Tuscarora acquired Ellett Brothers. Tuscarora soon implemented two major changes, only one of which proved successful. Under Tuscarora, Ellett Brothers introduced a marine accessories product line in late 1988. The company's marine accessories business proved to be a natural, complementary addition to its core outdoor sporting goods business, contributing $2.6 million in sales for 1989 and giving the Chapin-based company a promising new facet to its business that augured growth for the 1990s.

Meanwhile, however, the company was acting on less prudent decisions and straying far afield. Instead of celebrating the encouraging results registered by the newly-formed marine accessories venture and the arrival of the company's 60th anniversary year, Ellett Brothers ventured into unexplored territory. In 1989, executive management launched a veterinary pharmaceutical business that represented a dramatic departure from the company's traditional business. The diversification into the veterinary pharmaceutical business proved to be Ellett Brothers' undoing, drawing attention away from the company's traditional business and tainting its enviable historical record of profitability. By the summer of 1990, with profits sagging, Ellett Brothers' board of directors had begun to take action, quickly realizing that the foray into veterinary pharmaceuticals was causing the company to flounder. Executive management was removed as a result, devolving control over the company to middle-management and Tuscarora representatives from the

summer of 1990 to the spring of 1991. During this precarious period in the company's history, those in charge attempted to restore profitability by concentrating on strengthening Ellett Brothers' primary outdoor sporting goods business and by limiting the losses from unprofitable operations. Meanwhile, the search was on for a new executive management team.

1990s Recovery

The veterinary pharmaceutical business was sold by the beginning of the summer of 1991 and by the end of the summer a new executive management team was in place. Led by Joseph F. Murray, a veteran of the sporting goods distribution business who joined the company in June 1991, Ellett Brothers' new management team followed up on the work started by middle-management and Tuscarora representatives and restored profitability by the end of 1991. The following year, Ellett Brothers surged resolutely forward, casting aside any ill effects from the misadventure into veterinary pharmaceuticals by posting record sales and net income levels. Once again pointed in a positive, profitable direction, the company rallied forward during the ensuing two years. During 1993 and 1994, developments that affected Ellett Brothers' business were outside the company's control but provided a welcomed boost to business, completing its recovery from the problems of the early 1990s.

As Ellett Brothers entered 1993 and its 60th anniversary year, the company's marine accessory business was performing admirably. By the end of 1992, revenue generated by the sale marine products eclipsed $7 million, up substantially from the $2.6 million posted in 1989. More significant growth was recorded during 1993, however, when the company's mainstay business was buoyed, ironically, by recessionary economic conditions. Flagging firearm sales during the early 1990s forced manufacturers to slash their prices by 1993, a response to the anemic economic climate that benefitted distributors like Ellett Brothers. Lower prices meant firearm distributors attracted more customers, pushing sales upward.

Ellett Brothers by this point was deriving the bulk of its business from hunting and shooting sports equipment, with camping and boating equipment rounding out the company's roster of merchandise. The company went public in June 1993, making its initial public offering at $9 a share, and went on to record a banner year, as Ellett Brothers telemarketers were kept busy taking orders for the company's 44,600 different items. Half of Ellett Brothers 240 employees were employed as salespeople in 1993, all of whom were stationed at the company's headquarters in Chapin, the sole location of Ellett Brothers' operations.

Ellett Brothers' salespeople were making 4,000 telephone calls a day by this point and serving 17,600 sporting goods retailers across the nation, most of whom were small, independent retailers located in rural areas. By dealing with small, "mom-and-pop" stores, Ellett Brothers was able to realize higher profit margins than it would have by supplying more competitive sporting goods chains with merchandise. The smaller retailers, in turn, were attracted by Ellett Brothers' quick shipping service—90 percent of the company's orders were shipped via two-day Federal Express service—and its wide selection of products, enabling small stores to keep tight control over inventory.

By the end of 1993, sales had eclipsed the $100 million mark for the first time, reaching $118.6 million. Further sales growth was achieved in 1994 when Ellett Brothers posted record firearm sales for the year. Again, as in 1993, external developments outside the company's control were responsible for spurring sales growth. In 1994, a host of regulatory issues such as the Brady Bill and the Crime Bill sparked widespread consumer demand for firearms, lifting buying levels to unprecedented heights. Firearm aficionados were afraid federal legislation would either ban firearm sales in the United States or at least make the purchase of firearms a more difficult process, so they snatched up guns in a rush. Hunting and shooting sports equipment sales at Ellett Brothers soared 40 percent during the year as a result, driving total sales up to $160.1 million.

Though the financial gains achieved in 1993 and 1994 were credited to recessionary economic conditions and the threat of pervasive gun control, much of the company's success was owed to the marketing efforts of Ellett Brothers' sales force in Chapin. In addition to the company's telemarketing program, its never-ending series of product catalogs also played an important role in generating business. For years catalog advertising had been a key component of the company's marketing strategy, an advertising approach that placed the Ellett Brothers' name and its wide selection of merchandise at retailers' fingertips. Designed to be used at retail sales counter as a reference source and sales guide, the company's annual catalogs were produced for each major product group, with the photographs and names of Ellett Brothers' sales personnel included in each volume. Aside from the annual catalogs, Ellett Brothers' also frequently published promotional "mini-catalogs" that concentrated on a limited assortment of merchandise and advertised seasonal specials.

Coming off of two banner years, Ellett Brothers entered 1995 as a flourishing enterprise. Its mainstay hunting and shooting sports equipment business had registered a record sales year and its marine accessories business, one of the newer facets of Ellett Brothers' operations, was growing steadily. Sales derived from boating equipment and supplies had increased 50 percent in 1993, creating a burgeoning force within the company's operations that required additional space to grow. In late 1994, Ellett Brothers purchased a 106,000-square-foot facility near Chapin and in early 1995 began to move its marine accessories business into this new facility. By the end of 1995, marine accessories sales had reached $18.4 million, posting a 20 percent increase from 1994's total and substantially outpacing the average industry growth rate of 8.9 percent, as reported by the National Marine Distributors Association. The company's other product lines, however, did not perform as well, making 1995 a year of disappointment for those anticipating growth at company headquarters.

Camping, archery, and outdoor accessories sales increased a modest two percent in 1995, but hunting and shooting sports products sales declined 20 percent, leading to a six percent slip in total sales for the year. Despite the slip in sales, Ellett Brothers assumed a decidedly aggressive acquisitive stance during the year, purchasing three companies that established a presence outside of Chapin for the first time in the company's history. In May 1995, the company acquired Houston, Missouri-based Evans Sports, Inc., a manufacturer of outdoor sporting accessories and wooden nostalgia boxes. Next, Ellett Brothers acquired Denver, Colorado-based Safesport Manufacturing Company, an importer and marketer of camping and backpacking accessories, sporting cutlery, outdoor safety products, and other outdoor leisure products. Completed in August 1995, the purchase of Safesport was followed in September with the acquisition of Taylorsville, North Carolina-based Vintage Editions, Inc., a specialty manufacturer of nostalgia products such as wooden boxes, storage chests, serving trays, dart board cases, and compact disc racks.

The acquisitions completed in 1995 were indicative of Ellett Brothers' new growth strategy to broaden its product lines and increase its channels of distribution. Late in 1995, the company formed a wholly-owned subsidiary, Leisure Sports Marketing Corp., to serve as the owner and operator of Ellett Brothers' three new subsidiary operations and entered 1996 looking for further potential acquisitions. The essence of this acquisition program was described by the company's president and chief executive officer Joseph Murray, who explained after the acquisition of Safesport that "[Ellett Brothers'] acquisition strategy has been to acquire companies whose products will benefit from Ellett's marketing expertise, while expanding our product sources and channels of distribution." With this strategy leading the company forward, Ellett Brothers moved toward the late 1990s intent on building sales growth and increasing its gross margins.

Principal Subsidiaries

Evans Sports. Inc.; Vintage Editions, Inc.; Leisure Sports Marketing Corp.; Safesport Manufacturing Company.

Principal Divisions

Hunting and Shooting Sports; Camping, Archery, and Outdoor Accessories; Marine Accessories.

Further Reading

"Ellett," *Boating Industry,* June 1991, p. 17.
"Ellett Brothers Inc.," *Boating Industry,* June 1993, p. 10.
Ellett Brothers, Inc. Annual Report, Chapin, SC: Ellett Brothers, Inc., 1995.
Henschen, Doug, "Ellett Bros. Netting Second Year of Dramatic Growth," *Boating Industry,* October 1994, p. 16.
James, Frank, "Ellett Brothers: As Big as All Outdoors," *Shooting Industry,* December 1993, p. 114.
Michels, Anthony J., "Ellett Brothers," *Fortune,* October 4, 1993, p. 123.
Tosto, Paul, "Sporting Equipment Supplier Ellett Brothers Reports Lower Earnings," *Knight-Ridder/Tribune Business News,* February 27, 1996, p. 22.

—Jeffrey L. Covell

Envirodyne Industries, Inc.

701 Harger Road
Oak Brook, Illinois 60521
U.S.A.
(708) 575-2400
Fax: (708) 571-0959

Public Company
Incorporated: 1969
Employees: 4900
Sales: $650.21 million (1995)
Stock Exchanges: NASDAQ
SICs: 3081 Unsupported Plastics Film & Sheet

Envirodyne Industries, Inc. is the holding company for three plastics specialty companies: Viskase Corporation; Sandusky Plastics, Inc.; and Clear Shield National, Inc. Viskase is the worldwide leading producer of cellulosic (plastic) casings for the preparation and packaging of processed meat products, especially hot dogs, and a leading manufacturer of heat-shrinkable plastic bags and a variety of specialty plastic films for the packaging and preserving of fresh meat, cheese, and poultry products. Viskase brand names include NOJAX cellulosic casings, Filmco shrink films, and PERFLEX shrinkable bags. Viskase also provides graphic arts services for its clients, providing custom artwork for its bags and films. Headquartered in Chicago, Viskase operates nine manufacturing facilities in the United States, and facilities in France, Puerto Rico, Brazil, Canada, Mexico, England, and Wales. Viskase's annual sales make up approximately 80 percent of Envirodyne's total revenues.

Sandusky Plastics, based in Sandusky, Ohio, manufactures thermoformed and injection-molded plastic containers for dairy and delicatessen products, as well as horticultural trays and inserts. The majority of Sandusky sales go to dairy product manufacturers in the form of cottage cheese and yogurt containers and the like. Sandusky also provides custom graphics and printing of its customers' container purchases. The third Envirodyne subsidiary, Clear Shield National, is a leading U.S.

maker of plastic cutlery, custom dining kits, drinking straws, and related plastic products. Clear Shield, based in Wheeling, Illinois, sells primarily to institutional customers such as hospitals and schools, and to major fast-food restaurant chains such as Burger King, McDonald's, KFC, Taco Bell, Pizza Hut, and others. Clear Shield also sells its plastic cutlery and other products under the Clear Shield and Carnival brand names to the retail consumer market.

Envirodyne, which emerged from Chapter 11 bankruptcy in December 1993, had revenues totaling $650 million in 1995, for an operating income of $38 million but a net loss of more than $20 million. Until 1995, the company was headed by Donald P. Kelly—of Beatrice Cos. leveraged buyout fame—who served as chairman, chief executive officer, and president. Succeeding Kelly was F. Edward Gustafson. Principal shareholders in the company include Malcom I. and Avram Glazer, through Houston-based Zapata Corp., which controlled 40 percent of Envirodyne stock in mid-1996. Envirodyne has come under increasing threat of a hostile takeover by Zapata.

Founded as an Engineering Consultant in 1969

Envirodyne took the long way into plastics manufacturing. The original focus of the company was, in fact, geared toward high technology industries, in keeping with company founder Ronald K. Linde's background. Linde held master's and doctorate degrees in material science from the California Institute of Technology. By 1969, at the age of 29, Linde was the director of physical sciences at the Stanford Research Institute (SRI) in Menlo Park, California. There, Linde worked in such areas as explosion dynamics and the effect of extreme heat and pressure on various materials. But in 1969, with $1,800 in savings, Linde set out to form his own company.

"I ran what was like a subsidiary of a company [at SRI]," Linde told the *Chicago Tribune,* "I had my own financial statements to worry about and had to know how to generate business. . . . I looked at starting my own business as a chance to get into the real world."

Linde seemed to take a backwards movement into his own business. "Unlike most who go into business, I didn't start with a bright new idea or an invention,'' he told the *Chicago Tribune.* Instead, Linde determined to start up a technology-based company, although he had not yet decided upon a particular technology, telling *Engineering News Record (ENR)* only that: ''I wanted to go into areas that were fragmented.'' Linde's first step was to establish Envirodyne as a broad-based consulting firm. From that vantage, Linde hoped to identify emerging areas of technology.

Linde's search for fragmented, low-competition technologies led him to focus the company on the fields of environment and energy. He next set out to acquire companies specializing in these areas. Envirodyne's initial acquisitions primarily involved small engineering consulting firms involved in projects that included designing wastewater treatment plants, slaughterhouses, and even bakeries. In order to finance these acquisitions, Linde initially attempted to take Envirodyne public in 1970. But the times and the market were not ripe for public offerings from small companies. Linde was forced to take a different route to becoming a public company.

Linde began searching for an already established public company to merge into Envirodyne. He found Pony Meadows Mining Company, an inactive mining concern in Nevada, which traded in the over-the-counter market. That company possessed, apart from two undeveloped silver mine claims, some $160,000 in cash and, more importantly, authorization to capitalize six million shares of common stock. At the time, only about one million of those shares had been issued, trading at prices ranging from $1.33 to $4.70 per share. Linde was able to convince Pony Meadows management and stockholders to merge into Envirodyne.

With these new assets, Linde set about building Envirodyne's consulting capacity. Over the next several years, Envirodyne acquired six engineering consulting firms covering a range of fields. These purchases were accomplished in large part through stock swaps. Acquisitions took up much of Linde's time during this period. ''For every one of the . . . companies we acquired, we looked at 50,'' Linde told *ENR,* ''and we at least started negotiations with 100.'' Linde's activity paid off, at least in the stock market, raising Envirodyne's stock to a high of $16 per share by 1972.

Linde envisaged forming Envirodyne into a manufacturing-engineering conglomerate based on the synergistic model popular through the 1960s. By 1975, Linde was ready to expand the company into manufacturing. Over the next two years, Envirodyne would increase the number of its acquisitions to 18, bringing in a variety of small industrial manufacturers. The majority of these companies were active in production for environmental or energy uses, including manufacturers of air purification equipment and pipe insulation. Another company acquired during this period was Pulsar Instruments, Inc., which manufactured electronic instruments such as noise-level meters. Envirodyne also worked on developing technology, chiefly in sonics technology, using sound waves as a power source.

Linde also began raising capital by selling stock in the company. Avoiding investment banking firms and acting instead as the company's salesman, Linde managed to generate some $4.5 million in stock sales. Yet Linde would tell *Business*

Week that the company's early manufacturing efforts were ''toe-in-the-water things.'' Envirodyne soon sought a faster entry into high technology and, in 1977, Linde prepared a new acquisition that would take the company on a headlong dive into manufacturing. Company revenues reached $24 million in 1976. Net earnings that year, however, were slightly more than $250,000.

The Wisconsin Steel Debacle of 1980

Linde soon brought his deal-making experience to bear on a much larger target: the failing Wisconsin Steel division of International Harvester (IH; later Navistar) in Chicago. Wisconsin Steel, with some $200 million in revenues, was roughly 10 times Envirodyne's size. Yet Linde discovered that IH was anxious to sell off its Wisconsin Steel division, which had lost more than $30 million over the previous five years. IH was said to want to sell the concern, rather than invest in capital improvements later estimated to require some $100 million. The purchase price for Wisconsin Steel was set at $65 million.

In acquiring Wisconsin Steel, Linde orchestrated his most impressive deal, and one that involved virtually no money—and little risk—from Envirodyne itself. Wisconsin Steel, Linde discovered, had about $40 million in iron ore, steel, and coal inventories. Linde was able to convince Chase Manhattan Bank to make a commodity loan of $50 million against Wisconsin Steel's inventory. Linde managed to secure the loan in part by arranging a deal with Engelhard Minerals Corp., a metals broker, that had that company agreeing to purchase the Wisconsin Steel inventories from Chase in the event Envirodyne defaulted on the loan. In return, Engelhard was given 10 percent of Wisconsin Steel's pretax profits for seven years. Engelhard also agreed to act as an agent for Envirodyne's steel output.

From the Chase loan, IH would receive $15 million cash; the remaining $50 million of the purchase price would be paid off over the next 10 years through 8.5 percent notes. In addition, IH was given the rights to convert $10 million of those notes to Envirodyne stock at a fixed price of $10 per share, which at the time traded at about $3 per share. Finally, IH agreed to purchase about 30 percent of Wisconsin Steel production for the next several years. Envirodyne would use the remaining $35 million of the Chase loan to make capital improvements. Now a $250 million company, Envirodyne moved its headquarters to Chicago. Linde proudly forecasted $1 billion in revenues by the mid 1980s.

The deal catapulted Envirodyne into the manufacturing big time. But from the outset, the Wisconsin Steel acquisition seemed doomed to failure. For one thing, the U.S. steel industry was undergoing its own depression as it faced increasing competition from overseas. Linde was able to turn this to the company's advantage, applying almost immediately after the acquisition for a $90 million load guarantee from the Economic Development Administration (EDA), which sought to stimulate domestic steel production. Despite being among the first to apply for the EDA loan guarantee, however, Envirodyne struggled to meet EDA loan conditions.

Yet the EDA loan was sorely needed: chief among Wisconsin Steel's problems was its aging equipment. Breakdowns and production bottlenecks had reduced its output to less than 75 percent of production capacity. Much of its equipment, such as the essential blast furnaces, were described as being years beyond their operating life. New environmental control laws enacted by the federal and Illinois governments also required Envirodyne to pour more than $20 million into immediate pollution control improvements, depriving Wisconsin Steel of much-needed capital improvements. Breakdowns were costing the company as much as $22 million per year; unable to meet shipments, the company saw many of its customers turning elsewhere for their steel needs.

Even with all these problems, Envirodyne almost managed to turn Wisconsin Steel around. Despite continued losses totaling close to $20 million in 1978 alone, sales rose 22 percent in 1978, and productivity was heightened, with man-hours per ton dropping from 14 to 10. The company was also gaining new customers, adding some 200—for a 50 percent rise—in two years, and increasing its share of the high-alloy steel market to 4.4 percent from 3.8 percent. And in November 1979, the EDA finally granted Envirodyne the loan guarantee it needed.

It was too late, however. By then, Wisconsin Steel's blast furnaces were described as "literally falling apart." Both IH and Chase provided emergency loans to Envirodyne. But just as the EDA loan was approved, new disaster struck in the form of a strike by IH workers. The strike ended IH purchases, which by then accounted for about 40 percent of Wisconsin Steel's output. Envirodyne's lenders, arranged under the EDA guarantee, balked at providing capital. Then in March 1980, IH foreclosed on its notes, and told Chase that it would no longer secure the bank's emergency loans. In response, Chase bounced paychecks to Wisconsin Steel workers. Envirodyne, protected from the Wisconsin Steel failure, was nonetheless out of the steel business. The following year its revenues dropped to $4.5 million. Its stock, too, had dropped, to the neighborhood of 12 cents per share.

Reengineered for the Eighties

"It was like starting over again after Wisconsin Steel," Linde would tell the *Chicago Tribune,* "but we've come back stronger." Indeed, Linde took Envirodyne in a new direction in 1982, with the purchase of Clear Shield Inc. That purchase, which boosted Envirodyne's revenues to $35 million in 1983, was accomplished in part by selling 1.5 million common shares to Clear Shield's parent, Artra Group Inc. Artra would gain an additional 2.5 million shares four years later for a discounted price of $3.25 per share as a "finder's fee" for helping arranged Envirodyne's next, and most successful, acquisition. This was the plastics and film division of Union Carbide—then reeling under its Bhopal, India disaster—renamed Viskase after Envirodyne's $215 million cash and notes purchase in February 1986. Viskase's revenues had been $275 million in 1985.

By then, Linde finally seemed to have found the industry he had always been looking for: in December 1986, Envirodyne paid $34 million to acquire Filmco Industries (later merged into Viskase), expanding Envirodyne's reach into the food-packaging materials market. These acquisitions—and a fire at a chief Viskase competitor's plant—helped boost Envirodyne's revenues more than 525 percent, to $316 million. Net income

boomed to $16.3 million. The following year, sales reached $475.7 million, gaining Envirodyne a position on the Fortune 500 (at number 493).

Linde had just enough time to complete the last of Envirodyne's major plastics acquisitions, making a 1988 purchase of Sandusky Plastics for $22.6 million in cash and retirement of about $3.5 million in debt. But Envirodyne faced new troubles: its performance had made it a ripe takeover target. Meanwhile, Artra, with nearly a 30 percent share of Envirodyne, was posting losses and looking to sell its Envirodyne stock. By 1989, a potential buyer loomed: Donald P. Kelly, former chairman of the Beatrice Cos., working together with Salomon Bros. Inc. as Emerald Corp., offered $38 per share, worth more than $800 million. In exchange for its Envirodyne stock, Artra received $75 million in cash and an additional $50 million in notes. Artra was also given a 27.5 percent share in Emerald Corp. The new owners took the company private and proceeded to run Envirodyne into bankruptcy.

Bankrupt and Revitalized in the 1990s

Emerald financed the leveraged buyout through bank debt and subordinated debt, leading Envirodyne into 1990—and the worldwide recession—with more than $800 million in long-term debt. By 1991, the company was struggling to repay its senior debt, about $275 million. Revenues had reached $544 million in 1990, but the company's losses were mounting, rising from $15 million in 1990 to $31 million in 1991. The rising price of oil—a necessary component in the company's plastic products—prior to the outbreak of the Gulf War added severely to the company's losses. At the same time, traces of highly toxic benzene were found in one of Viskase's products, forcing the company to shut down production and chasing away many of the subsidiary customers. Added to the company's financial problems was a pending $33 million tax bill.

Despite these problems, Kelly continued collecting nearly $1.2 million per year between them in management fees, another $1.7 million per year for Envirodyne's use of his corporate jet. Kelly and two partners also paid themselves $800,000 each in annual salaries. In addition, Salomon Bros. collected more than $33 million in various fees between 1989 and 1991. Envirodyne attempted to pay down some of its debt by entering into a $171.5 million sale-leaseback arrangement with GE Capital Corp., involving four Envirodyne subsidiary plants. But unable to pay its debt, Envirodyne filed for Chapter 11 protection in January 1993.

Reorganized and Public in the Mid 1990s

The company remained in bankruptcy for less than a year, however. In November 1993, the company surprised its creditors with an aggressive reorganization plan, which, among other elements, allowed Kelly to remain at the head of the company and to continue, through his DP Kelly partnership, to collect management fees worth more than $4 million over two years. Kelly would also come out of the reorganization with about the same percentage of Envirodyne stock he had held before the bankruptcy. Envirodyne managed to convince a majority of bondholders to accept the reorganization, and the company emerged from bankruptcy on December 31 of the same year.

Five days later, the company once again went public. Kelly retired from the company in 1995.

Once out of bankruptcy, Envirodyne continued to face a difficult climb back to profitability. The baseball strike of 1994 cut into hot dog sales—and, correspondingly, Viskase revenues—leading Envirodyne to a net loss of $3.6 million on $599 million in revenues. And in 1996, Viskase, which continued to contribute the largest share of Envirodyne revenues, faced new competition with the re-entry of Viscofan, of Spain, into the U.S. market. That company had been banned from the United States after being charged with stealing Envirodyne trade secrets in the mid 1980s. Envirodyne's losses continued into 1995, reaching $21.5 million on revenues of $650 million. By mid 1996, the company faced a new takeover threat, led by Zapata Corp., a natural gas company founded by former president George Bush. Zapata had gathered some 31 percent of Envirodyne by 1995; in July 1996, Zapata upped its stake to 40 percent, prompting Envirodyne to institute a shareholder's rights plan to thwart Zapata's possible takeover.

Principal Subsidiaries

Clear Shield National, Inc.; Sandusky Plastics, Inc.; Viskase Corporation.

Further Reading

"Acquisition-Hungry Envirodyne Leaps into Steel," *Business Week,* September 12, 1977, p. 96.

Bukro, Casey, "After Bankruptcy Battle, a Repackaged Envirodyne Again Eyes Growth," *Chicago Tribune,* February 28, 1994, Bus. Sec. p. 5.

Cleaver, Joanne, "Envirodyne's Wrapping Up Plastic-Covering Market," *Crain's Chicago Business,* June 1, 1987.

"Consultant Expands Via Steel Mill Purchase," *Engineering News Record,* November 30, 1978, p. 30.

"Envirodyne's Digestion Difficulty," *Business Week,* August 6, 1979, p. 34.

Keefe, Lisa M., "Kelly's Envirodyne LBO Bleeding," *Crain's Chicago Business,* September 9, 1991, p. 1.

Lashinsky, Adam, "While Envirodyne Sinks, Kelly Gets His Fees," *Crain's Chicago Business,* January 25, 1993, p. 3.

McAfee, Andrew, "Savvy Acquisition Set to Boost Envirodyne," *Crain's Chicago Business,* May 26, 1986, p. 4.

Sherrod, Pamela, "Envirodyne Moves Past Steel Failure," *Chicago Tribune,* June 28, 1987, Bus. Sec. p. 1.

Snyder, David, "Learning the Hard Way about When to Hang It Up," *Crain's Chicago Business,* March 7, 1994, p. 13.

—M. L. Cohen

ERLY Industries Inc.

10990 Wilshire Boulevard #1800
Los Angeles, California 90024
U.S.A.
(213) 879-1480
Fax: (310) 473-8890

Public Company
Incorporated: 1964 as Early California Foods, Inc.
Employees: 1,500
Sales: $487 million (1996)
Stock Exchanges: NASDAQ
SICs: 2044 Rice Milling; 2084 Wines, Brandy & Brandy
   Spirits; 8748 Business Consulting Services, Not
   Elsewhere Classified

Owner of one of the largest rice companies in the world, ERLY Industries Inc. operates as an international agribusiness company through three principal subsidiaries: American Rice, Inc., Chemonics International—Consulting, and Chemonics Industries—Fire-Trol. In 1995 ERLY Industries derived $373 million of its $459 million in sales from its American Rice subsidiary, one of the world's largest processors and marketers of branded rice products. American Rice's geographic reach extends far and wide, with its branded rice products market leaders in the United States, Canada, Haiti, Puerto Rico, Mexico, Saudi Arabia, and Asia. The brand labels marketed by American Rice included "Comet," "Adolphus," "Blue Ribbon," "Abu Bint," "Green Peacock," and "AA." ERLY's two other major subsidiaries, Chemonics International—Consulting, an international agribusiness consulting firm, and Chemonics Industries—Fire-Trol, which produce forest fire-retardant chemicals for the U.S. and Canadian Forest Services, contributed $64 million and $23 million in sales in 1995, respectively.

Origins

For the first two decades of its existence ERLY operated as a vegetable processor, relying on its "Early California Foods" label to sustain and propel its growth. Incorporated in 1964 as Early California Foods, Inc., the company was formed by Gerald

D. Murphy through the merger of B. E. Glick & Sons and Pacific Olive Company. Early California Foods, Inc., existed for four years until the company began to diversify through a long series of acquisitions. The acquisition spree, touched off in 1966, engendered a new name in 1968: Early California Industries, Inc.

Pacific Cherry & Fruit Corporation was acquired in 1966, followed by the addition of White House Foods, Inc., and its wholly owned subsidiary, Lady's Choice Foods, in 1967. Next, the company acquired two pickle processing and packaging companies, Eastern Pickle Products, Inc., and International Pickle Briners, in early 1968. Later in the year, when the name change to Early Industries, Inc., was effected, the company acquired Arizona Agrochemical Corporation, a producer of agricultural chemicals, fertilizers, insecticides, and fire retardants.

1970 Acquisition of Comet Rice

In 1969 four new companies were purchased: Fairfax Food Corp.; Festival Foods of Los Angeles; Clarke Publishing Company, publisher of a weekly shopping newspaper in Portland, Oregon; and Coronet Foods Corporation. In April 1970 Early California Industries acquired Houston, Texas-based Comet Rice Mills, Inc., for $4 million, thereby laying the foundation for the company's future as one of the world's leading processors and marketers of rice. Over the next 20 years, "Comet" brand rice grew into a widely recognized label, becoming one of the leading brands of rice in the United States, Canada, the Caribbean, Mexico, and South America.

During the 1970s, Early Industries acquired businesses involved in newspaper publishing and wine production (Sierra Wine Corporation), as well as the Maxwell, California-based United Rice Growers.

1985: The "New" ERLY Emerges

The company's founder, Gerald D. Murphy, remained on as chairman and chief executive officer, and in 1985 Murphy began making changes that launched ERLY's global expansion. To a reporter from *California Business,* Murphy said, "Never before has the case for global expansion been so compelling. Change necessitates adaptation and innovation."

In 1985 the vegetable processing division was sold, marking the exit of the brand name Early California Foods. The following year the company adopted the name ERLY Industries Inc. Two years later, Murphy began gradually to distance his company from the wine business. At the same time the company began displaying its first interest in the troubled TreeSweet Company, a fruit juice producer mired in Chapter 11 bankruptcy protection.

1988 Acquisition of American Rice

In 1988 ERLY acquired 48 percent of Texas-based American Rice, Inc., an agricultural co-operative. Once American Rice was merged with ERLY's Comet Rice processing and marketing subsidiary, the basis was established for one of the largest rice companies in the world.

Elsewhere within ERLY's operations, preparations were being made to enter the juice business in earnest. In September 1988, Murphy completed the acquisition of the citrus division of Kraft, Inc., located in Florida. ERLY also obtained several packing plants in the Midwest, which strengthened the capabilities of the ERLY-owned TreeSweet once the juice maker emerged from bankruptcy in 1989.

By the end of the 1980s, the pieces were in place for the construction of the new ERLY, and the company began showing encouraging financial gains. In 1990 annual sales climbed to $431 million from $313 million the year before, and a $2 million loss in net income in 1989 was transformed into an impressive $14 million profit in 1990. Business was moving forward on all fronts. The company's juice business, was demonstrating profitability, its rice interests showed great promise, and the company's two smaller divisions, a manufacturer of fire-retardant chemicals for crops and an agricultural consulting group that assisted governmental agencies in developing countries, were poised to garner a high percentage of profits by virtue of their low overhead costs.

Confidence was high at the company's executive offices, prompting Murphy to declare that it was ERLY's objective "to be a global company of over a billion dollars of annual sales" by fiscal 1993, an objective that would require the company to more than double in size within two years. Instead, however, ERLY stumbled, as political developments outside the company's control sent profits tumbling.

Effects of the Gulf War

During the late 1980s the Middle East, and Iraq in particular, became a primary market for ERLY. The single biggest buyer of Comet rice in the Middle East was the Iraqi Grain Board, the official buyer for Saddam Hussein's regime. When the Gulf War broke out in 1991 and touched off a U.S. embargo of Iraq, the company lost a $130 million market, causing earnings to fall sharply. ERLY lost $12.5 million in 1992 and another $8.6 million in 1993, while sales shrank from $218 million in 1991 to $214 million in 1992 and down to $169 million in 1993, the year Murphy had hoped sales would eclipse $1 billion.

To make matters worse, the company was delisted from the NASDAQ exchange from July 2, 1993 to August 15, 1994 for capital insufficiency, adding further pain to the damage inflicted by the Gulf War and requiring an immediate response from Murphy and the rest of ERLY's executive management. To effect a recovery, Murphy restructured operations and trimmed debt. Payroll was reduced, several divisions were consolidated, and some operations were divested, including ERLY's juice division in 1993. That same year, the company increased its ownership stake in American Rice to 81 percent and began to substantially reduce its reliance on rice markets in the Middle East. The changes sparked growth throughout ERLY's operations during 1994. By the end of the year, sales had climbed to $284 million, and, perhaps more encouraging, net income had soared to $17.6 million, up from a $8.6 million loss the year before.

ERLY entered 1995 once again on strong footing, with record earnings achieved by each of the company's three principal subsidiaries. American Rice, two years after depending on business in the United States and in the Middle East to provide nearly 80 percent of its total sales, derived less than 50 percent of its total volume from these two massive markets in 1995. Ambitious worldwide expansion had compensated for the reduction, and as the rice processor and marketer headed toward the late 1990s, it was selling rice in 44 countries, with no single foreign country accounting for more than 14 percent of total sales. By year's end, global expansion had pushed sales up 31 percent to a record $373 million.

Chemonics International—Consulting, meanwhile, completed its first year as an independent entity in 1995, after having completed consulting contracts in 92 countries since its formation by ERLY in 1975. As the ERLY subsidiary prepared for the late 1990s, it was widening its scope as an agribusiness consultant and casting itself as an organization able to help developing countries clear the hurdles toward privatization. In 1995 the consulting subsidiary was involved in 46 contracts that were regional or worldwide in geographic scope, including work in Egypt, the Philippines, Central and South America, Nepal, Indonesia, and Russia. Collecting more than half of its sales from countries in the Near East and Eastern Europe, Chemonics International—Consulting registered record sales in 1995 of $64 million, a 64 percent increase from the previous year's total.

The smallest of ERLY's subsidiaries recorded the greatest gain in sales. Chemonics Industries—Fire-Trol controlled 45 percent of the U.S. market for forest fire retardant chemicals and 80 percent of the Canadian market, supported by a Fire-Trol product line with more than 42 registered patents. Sales increased an impressive 173 percent for the subsidiary in 1995, reaching a record $23 million and rounding out the company's financial gains.

Principal Subsidiaries

American Rice, Inc. (81%); Chemonics International—Consulting; Chemonics Industries—Fire-Trol.

Further Reading

Berger, Robin, "ERLY Industries Denies Allegations Reported in *New York Times* Story," *Los Angeles Business Journal,* October 18, 1993, p. 8.
"A Rice Trader May Start to Steam," *Business Week,* September 26, 1994, p. 112.
Walsh, James, "ERLY Industries: A Tale of Strategic Positioning," *California Business,* July–August 1991, p. 12.
Wells, Shan, "Market," *California Business,* June–July 1993, p. 43.

—Jeffrey L. Covell

Expeditors International of Washington Inc.

19119 16th Avenue South
Seattle, Washington 98188
U.S.A.
(206) 246-3711
Fax: (206) 246-3197

Public Company
Incorporated: 1979
Employees: 2,500
Sales: $584.6 million (1995)
Stock Exchanges: NASDAQ
SICs: 4731 Freight Transportation Arrangement

A fast-growing shipping services company, Expeditors International of Washington Inc. provides international freight-forwarding and customs-clearance services to large, globally-oriented corporations through a vast network of sales offices scattered across six continents. Expeditors robust pace of financial growth began during the early 1980s when the company started providing both freight-forwarding and customs-brokerage services, a novel concept at the time for companies involved in coordinating international cargo transportation. Propped up by its ability to orchestrate the transportation of cargo and clear such cargo through customs, Expeditors recorded animated growth during the 1980s and the first half of the 1990s as customers increasingly sought the aid of full-service shippers.

Origins of a Unique Shipping Services Company

Expeditors' history was shaped not by the company's founders but through the vision of Peter J. Rose. Rose, a Canadian-born son of a National Express employee who spent his life in the shipping business, and four of his colleagues, Kevin Walsh, Glenn Alger, Robert Chiarito, and James Wang, each of whom shared experience in the business of shipping freight, changed the business focus of Expeditors. But from the group, Rose emerged as the prominent, guiding personality. More than a decade after the incorporation of Expeditors, one industry observer noted that the company mirrored the person-

ality of the person chiefly responsible for its enviable record of financial growth, Peter Rose.

Rose was born in Montreal, Quebec, and, as the story went, entered the vocation that would occupy his professional career at the age of five when he donned his father's cap and delivered packages door-to-door. As a young adult, Rose attended Sir George Williams University, then after shelving dreams of becoming a professional hockey player, embarked on his career when he went to work for Canadian Pacific. Rose's entry into the transportation field would define his working life in the decades to follow, but his greatest success would be achieved in the United States where Rose accumulated the experience that eventually predicated Expeditors' existence. Rose arrived in the United States in 1965 and immediately began working as the Inward Traffic Manager for Compass Agencies, a steamship agent. From there, Rose went on to work for other companies involved in the transportation business, serving short stints at Harper and Circle Airfreight. Rose finished his long-served apprenticeship in the freight-forward business by the late 1970s, and from the 1980s Rose orchestrated the growth of a unique shipping services company.

After joining Circle Airfreight in 1975, Rose returned to Harper, where he and several other Harper executives discussed the possibilities of creating a superior and unique type of shipping service for the corporate world. The business approach discussed by these Harper executives was simple yet novel. They resolved to fuse the functions of a freight-forwarding company and a custom-house broker at a time when other shipping services companies either shipped cargo or facilitated the clearance of cargo through customs, but rarely offered both services. By offering both services, Rose and his other Harper executives could offer the full gamut of services sought by international, blue-chip corporations. ''We wanted to take big freight,'' Rose later explained in a hypothetical example, ''and be able to move it from the door in Hong Kong to the door in Minneapolis,'' which the company did, but without its own transportation equipment. Instead, the handful of Harper executives planned to move cargo via other companies' transportation equipment, ensuring that the cargo moved through customs speedily and reached its ultimate destination.

Company Perspectives:

The company's mission is to set the standard for excellence in global logistics through the total commitment to quality in people and services, with superior financial results.

Once the plans for this door-to-door, customs-clearance, and freight-forwarding company were finalized by Rose and his associates, during a late-night drinking session on the island of Lantau, the course was set for a new force in the shipping services industry. That night, on the island near Hong Kong, the talks transformed into action. In 1981, the group joined Expeditors, a company with an office in Seattle that had been founded two years earlier. Rose was immediately named Executive Vice President of Expeditors, and before the year was through sales offices were established in San Francisco, Chicago, Hong Kong, Taipei, and Singapore.

Despite its far-ranging sales offices, the company was a contrastingly modest enterprise during the early days following the arrival of Rose and the other Harper executives. As Rose would later reflect, Expeditors was a modestly-sized enterprise during the early 1980s, "almost that proverbial phone booth and a note pad," he later remembered. Though the company grew quickly and swiftly became the leading U.S.-based airfreight importer from the Far East, it did not lose the lean and focused quality to its operations that described Expeditors during the early years of the decade. Operating without ownership of any transportation equipment or any of the attendant responsibilities of owning capital equipment, Expeditors focused on service, service that attracted the business of the nation's largest corporations who appreciated the benefits a genuine full-service shipper could provide. The business strategy formulated by Rose and his colleagues worked, and worked unexpectedly well, prompting Rose, more than a decade after he joined Expeditors, to confide, "I wouldn't have believed we could've done this . . . we created this monster; it has to be fed."

Robust Growth Begins in Early 1980s

Rose fed the "monster" by entering the export market in 1982 and the ocean freight market in 1985. Sandwiched in between these two diversifying moves was Expeditors' initial public offering in 1984, which was completed in September and yielded the company the financial resources to expand its operations on a worldwide basis. Though the trappings at Expeditors' headquarters near Seattle-Tacoma International Airport (Sea-Tac) remained unassuming throughout its explosive rise in the shipping industry, the company's network of international sales offices grew increasingly formidable. In the wake of the 1984 conversion to public ownership, Expeditors grew vigorously, adding sales offices in the Far East, where the company first had distinguished itself, and by branching out into other overseas markets. The company entered the expansive European market in 1986, with an office in London, and continued to flesh out its network of foreign offices as the decade progressed.

As Expeditors recorded exponential financial growth during the latter half of the 1980s, the company began to attract the attention of industry observers and the mainstream business press. *Inc.* magazine ranked Expeditors as one of the 100 fastest growing companies in the United States in 1987 and other testaments to the company's prolific growth were soon to follow. By 1988, sales had been increasing at a rate of more than 50 percent during the previous five years, fueled by the business garnered from clients such as Apple Computer, IBM, Nike, and Motorola who helped Expeditors generate nearly $150 million that year. By the end of the following year, when the company's number of sales offices had increased to 22, annual sales neared $200 million, a volume derived from 42 countries.

Growth in the 1990s

Entering the 1990s, Expeditors' global reach was extensive, extending across the world and enabling the company to meet the variegated shipping needs of large, international companies. Though much had been achieved during the 1980s, the company's growth during the 1990s would overshadow the accomplishments of Expeditors' inaugural decade of business as a freight-forwarder and customs-house broker. As if anticipating the rapid growth to come during the 1990s, the company expanded its headquarters near Sea-Tac during the early months of 1990, increasing the square footage at its executive offices from 13,000 to 26,000, then set about expanding its network of sales offices as well. In 1991, the company opened an office in Kuwait and placed representatives in offices in Istanbul, Cairo, Athens, and Dubai. Expeditors also opened an office in Antwerp, Belgium, two offices in Portugal, and four offices in Germany. On the domestic front, the company expanded as well, establishing new offices in Louisville, Kentucky, and Phoenix, Arizona. The spate of new office additions enabled Expeditors to generate a record $254 million in revenue in 1991 and an unprecedented $10.2 million in earnings, the bulk of which was earmarked for financing further expansion, as were the profits from earlier years.

Focused on growth and service, Expeditors grew rapidly during the early 1990s, winning customers from its competitors with its capacity as a dual shipping service provider and earning praise from the business press. The company was selected as one of *Forbes'* 200 best small companies in the United States in 1990 and again in 1992. Not lost on the industry pundits who lauded Expeditors' innovative business strategy and its financial vitality was the company's performance during the economically recessive early 1990s, a time when the Sea-Tac-based shipper was growing by leaps and bounds. As many businesses reeled from the stifling affects of waning consumer confidence and bleak economic forecasts, Expeditors surged ahead and opened 14 new sales offices in 1992, helping the company post $333.2 million in sales and $11.3 million in earnings.

Financial growth continued unabated in 1993, when Expeditors generated $361.4 million in sales and more than $10 million in earnings, although the company's physical pace of growth slowed in comparison to 1992. After establishing 14 new sales offices in 1992—most of which were located in Europe and Asia—the company opened only four new offices in 1993, but its coveted ability to coordinate cargo movement and consolidate shipments to win low rates pushed revenues upward, nonetheless. As 1994 began, Expeditors moved resolutely forward with its expansion program, opening two new sales offices each in Sweden, Spain, and South Africa early in the year. An office in New Delhi was opened in March, with an office in Bombay slated to open by the end of the year.

In addition to the company's expansion of its sales office network, Expeditors was also diversifying the value-added services it provided to its customers by signing long-term contracts for customs brokerage and by making its foray into distribution. The company's first customer in the distribution business was Koss Corp., for whom Expeditors agreed to distribute imported headphones throughout the United States. Expeditors' customs-brokerage operations, meanwhile, received a substantial boost in business when the company signed a contract with retailer Montgomery Ward in early 1994. Under the terms of the contract, Expeditors was expected to clear imported merchandise through customs for Montgomery Ward's 360 retail stores, with the bulk of the activity to take place in the Los Angeles area. Growing and diversifying on all fronts, Expeditors entered the mid-1990s with sanguine hopes, an optimism that prevailed not only at the company's headquarters but outside the company as well. Noting Expeditors' strategic expansion and its evolution as a freight forwarder and customs broker, one industry analyst remarked to a reporter for the *Puget Sound Business Journal*, "It's becoming a global company. They're diversifying well geographically and I think they're doing a good job of diversifying away from import air freight. I think they're in a good position to benefit from worldwide economic recovery."

Future Growth

Twelve new sales office were opened in 1994, with another six slated to open in 1995, as Expeditors continued to broaden its presence overseas. China was considered as one of the important markets for the company as it prepared for the late 1990s and looked to sustain its consistent, record-setting pace of financial growth, with markets in South America and India offering strong opportunities for future growth as well. Annual sales, which in 1995 totaled $584.6 million, had been increasing 25 percent to 30 percent annually during the 1990s, setting the stage for commensurate growth during the latter half of the decade.

As the company headed toward the late 1990s, with 25 percent to 30 percent annual increases in sales projected through the year 2000, Rose was confident that Expeditors' future would be as profitable as its past, prompting him to promise that he and the company's more than 2,400 employees would "continue on

in our boringly consistent manner." Whether or not the company's financial growth would continue to be "boringly consistent" in the future remained to seen, but considering Expeditors' record of physical expansion during its first decade-and-a-half of business, progress appeared to be inevitable as Rose and other executives set their sights on new and potentially lucrative markets. With sales operations on six continents and more than 100 offices worldwide during the mid-1990s, the company still had room to grow as it embarked on its future course, intent on securing its position as one of America's leading shipping services companies.

Principal Subsidiaries

E.I. Freight Canada, Ltd.; E.I. Freight (H.K.) Ltd. (Hong Kong); E.I. Freight SDN. BHD. (Malaysia); E.I. Freight (USA) Inc.; Expeditors International Philippines Inc. (60%); Expeditors International (U.K.) Ltd. (England); Expeditors Overseas Mgt. (H.K.) Ltd. (Hong Kong); Expeditors Private Ltd. (Singapore); Expeditors International Pty. Ltd. (Australia) (50%); Expeditors International Sverige AB (Sweden); Pac Bridge International Ltd. (Hong Kong); Pac Bridge Shipping, Ltd.

Further Reading

Armbruster, William, "Expeditors' Next Stop: India and the Middle East," *Journal of Commerce and Commercial*, September 14, 1994, p. 3B.

Fagerstrom, Scott, "Expeditors International to Relocate from SeaTac Airport to Seattle," *Knight-Ridder/Tribune Business News*, May 9, 1996, p. 50.

"Freight Forwarder's Unique Idea Brings Growth, Honors," *Puget Sound Business Journal*, May 14, 1990, p. S15.

Knee, Richard, "Expeditors Contracts with Hanjin, OOCL," *American Shipper*, October 1991, p. 74.

Levere, Jane L., "Movers and Shippers," *Journal of Commerce and Commercial*, February 27, 1995, p. S17.

Robertshaw, Nicky, "Expeditors, Memphis Newcomer," *Memphis Business Journal*, June 3, 1996, p. 16.

Smith, Sarah, "Expeditors International of Washington Inc.," *Fortune*, June 6, 1988, p. 152.

Wilhelm, Steve, "Airborne, Expeditors Ride Outsourcing Boom," *Puget Sound Business Journal*, August 19, 1994, p. 1.

——, "Expeditors International Hits Fast-Forward Mode," *Puget Sound Business Journal*, March 11, 1994, p. 3.

——, "Globe-Trotting Peter Rose Mirrors Reality of Expeditors International," *Puget Sound Business Journal*, September 11, 1992, p. 1.

——, "Personal Service Packs a Payoff for Expeditors," *Puget Sound Business Journal*, January 22, 1990, p. 10.

—Jeffrey L. Covell

EXPRESS ℞SCRIPTS.

Express Scripts Incorporated

14000 Riverport Drive
Maryland Heights, Missouri 63043
U.S.A.
(314) 770-1666
Fax: (314) 567-3082
Internet: http://www.express-scripts.com

Public Company
Incorporated: 1986
Employees: 1,127
Sales: $544.46 million (1995)
Stock Exchanges: NASDAQ
SICs: 5961 Catalog & Mail-Order Houses; 7374 Data
    Processing & Preparation

Express Scripts Incorporated (ESI) is the leading independent pharmacy benefits manager (PBM) in the United States. Headquartered outside of St. Louis, with a second and larger service facility in Tempe, Arizona, ESI provides the full range of PBM services from claims and mail-order processing to benefit design consultation, formulary management, drug utilization review, and data analysis. ESI also provides vision care services and infusion therapy services. The company's subsidiary, Practice Patterns Science (PPS), launched in 1995, provides data analysis services by developing, marketing, and supporting proprietary software technology.

With the rising dominance of managed health care and increasing pressure to contain health care costs, ESI has grown rapidly in the 1990s. The company's net revenues reached $544 million in 1995, for a net income of over $18 million, sustaining annual growth rates of up to 50 percent. ESI's pharmacy networks cover more than 46,000 pharmacies in the United States. ESI fills pharmacy orders for more than nine million customers, through such managed care providers as FHP, Inc., NYLife Care Health Plans, Inc., Coventry Corporation, and the 1,700-hospital alliance APS Healthcare, as well as unions, self-insured employers, and insurance companies. Approximately 55 percent of ESI customers are members of HMOs; roughly 22

percent of the company's 1995 net revenues were generated through managed care providers NYLife (formerly Sanus) and FHP. In 1996, ESI expanded into Canada, servicing agreements with the Canadian divisions of Manufacturer's Life, Prudential, and Aetna, among others, with the acquisition of a Canadian PBM, Eclipse Claims Services. ESI has also formed an alliance with CIBA Vision Ophthalmics U.S. to market disease management programs using technology developed by ESI's PPS subsidiary.

ESI's position as the sole independent among the country's top PBMs has proved a strong selling point with its customers. The five other largest PBMs are closely affiliated with pharmaceutical companies: Medco Containment is owned by Merck & Company; PCS Health Systems was purchased by Eli Lilly in 1994; Diversified Pharmaceutical Services is owned by Smith-Kline Beecham; Value Health Inc. has entered a joint venture with Pfizer Inc.; and Caremark has developed exclusive agreements with several pharmaceutical companies. ESI's independence is likely to continue, as more than 90 percent of the company's stock is owned by its former parent, NYLife Healthcare Management, a subsidiary of New York Life Insurance Company, making the company an unlikely takeover target.

Founded in the 1980s

Express Scripts was born out of the boom in health management organizations of the late 1970s and early 1980s. In 1983, two employees of McDonnell Douglas, then one of Missouri's largest employers, left that company to start up their own HMO, called Sanus Corp. Health Systems. Backed by major investors McDonnell Douglas and General American Life Insurance Co., the private Sanus grew quickly, expanding into the Dallas, Fort Worth, Houston, and Washington, D.C., markets, as well as in St. Louis, signing up 90,000 members and reaching revenues of $30 million by 1985. One year later, Sanus's membership had swelled to 200,000, and revenues topped $100 million. As Sanus grew, it expanded its range of services as well. Considered innovative at the time, Sanus operated not only a HMO but also a preferred-provider plan, or PPO, and a standard health insurance plan. The expansion of Sanus's services led the company to establish GenCare Health Systems as an umbrella

---

Company Perspectives:

Express Scripts has been providing integrated mail and network pharmacy benefit management services since 1986. Since our inception, our mission has been to provide superior services while managing the pharmacy benefit, not maximizing mail order or certain manufacturer products. In addition, we strive to: ensure quality and cost-effective pharmacy services through partnerships with our clients; apply proven managed care principles; provide high-quality customer service.

---

operation for the Sanus plans. By then, Barrett A. Toan had joined the company to serve as executive director.

Toan, who held a bachelor's degree from Kenyon College and a master's degree from the University of Pennsylvania's Wharton School of Finance and Commerce, came to the private sector after years in public service. Early in his career, after a period of working as a high school teacher, Toan served as the assistant director with the office of state planning and development in Pennsylvania, and later as a budget analyst and deputy director for the Illinois Bureau of Budget. In the late 1970s, he was appointed commissioner of the division of social services for the state of Arkansas under Governor Bill Clinton, then in his first term as governor. In 1981, Toan moved to Missouri, where he was named director of that state's department of social service.

As director of social service, Toan was placed in charge of Missouri's Medicaid system, which had seen a 40 percent rise in costs in the year before alone. Toan convinced the state legislative to enact major changes in Medicaid, especially in that system's pricing structure. Where previously doctors and hospitals had been allowed to bill Medicaid for services after they were performed, which led to the charging of inflated fees, Toan argued for set fees to be negotiated in advance of treatment. These price caps forced providers to control their own costs, a trend that would lead to the rise of the HMO as the dominant form of health care provision by the mid-1990s.

Toan left public service in 1985, joining GenCare as its executive director, and GenCare, with additional investments from New York Life, expanded into the New York, New Jersey, and Maryland markets. Despite the greater efficiency of managed care over traditional health insurance plans, GenCare found itself paying high prices for its members' prescriptions. Hiring a claims examiner to process prescriptions, however, would not have provided the company greater efficiency. Instead, Toan negotiated with St. Louis–based Medicare-Glaser to process and fill GenCare and Sanus members' prescriptions. Data on prescription orders were then provided to GenCare, eliminating the need for GenCare to enter the data on its own. Medicare-Glaser was, at the time, one of the 25 largest pharmacy chains in the United States, operating nearly 90 pharmacies and full-line drug stores, as well as optical and home health centers, principally in Missouri, but also in Illinois and Connecticut.

Toan quickly recognized that this arrangement had applications beyond the GenCare-Sanus network. In late 1986, GenCare and Medicare-Glaser formed ESI as a joint venture providing mail-order prescription drug and claims processing. Under the agreement, Sanus members in Missouri and Illinois continued to receive their prescription benefit through the Medicare-Glaser pharmacy chain. The remainder of Sanus's 200,000 member network became ESI's initial customers; however, the company quickly began marketing its services to health care providers across the country. Early ESI clients included the cities of Baltimore, Memphis, and San Antonio. Toan became head of ESI, while continuing to lead GenCare.

By 1987, New York Life had begun to increase its investment in Sanus Health Systems, investing more than $50 million in the company, and increasing its investment to as much as $75 million in the following year. New York Life was also an early investor in ESI. In 1988, Medicare-Glaser began to stumble as Walgreen's moved to expand aggressively in the former company's core St. Louis market. By early 1989, with losses mounting, Medicare-Glaser announced it was merging with SupeRx of Arizona, Georgia and Alabama Corp., moving its headquarters to Arizona. At the time of the merger, Medicare-Glaser agreed to sell its 50 percent interest in ESI to Sanus, giving New York Life, which had already gained controlling interest in Sanus, full ownership of both GenCare and ESI. Medicare-Glaser subsequently filed for bankruptcy and closed or sold off all of its stores.

New York Life quickly sold GenCare back to General American, retaining the Sanus HMO and ESI. Toan, however, continued to serve as the head of both GenCare and ESI, both of which were based in St. Louis. Toan remained with GenCare through 1991, when he took the company public. Toan left GenCare in 1992 to turn his full attention to ESI.

Explosive Growth in the 1990s

ESI revenues rose rapidly as it entered the 1990s, from $27.4 million to nearly $72 million by the end of 1991. Membership in ESI prescription plans had also increased, to more than 1.5 million. Part of the company's growth could be attributed to the evolving role of PBMs in general, from mail-order prescription drug discounters and claims processors to playing an active role in patient pharmaceutical management. By 1991 less than 80 percent of ESI revenues were achieved through its mail-order sales. PBMs also began to play a more prominent role in health care management: as managed care slowly became the dominant form of health insurance, patient prescriptions became one of the most expensive insurance benefits. PBMs offered not only discounted drugs but also the ability to offer increased data analysis of the care process, working with providers to define cost-effective treatment, offer patient drug education services, and alert providers to potential inappropriate drug treatment stratagems. ESI's services also expanded to provide eye wear and home infusion therapy programs.

Toan took ESI public in 1992, joining a wave of health care-related firms filing initial public offerings in the early 1990s. ESI's IPO, which raised more than $28 million, was made in part to enable New York Life Insurance to maintain control over the company. ESI offered two classes of stock. The class A stock, which accounted for most of the shares being sold, gave shareholders one vote per share. The class B stock, of which New York Life, through its NYLife Healthcare Management subsidiary, controlled nearly 97 percent, gave shareholders 10 votes per share. In addition, only the class A stock would be traded on the NASDAQ index. Toan was named CEO of ESI, which by then had more than 220 employees and 1,150 clients. Sanus members, however, continued to account for nearly 55 percent of all ESI sales.

ESI stock rose rapidly, from its IPO of $13 per share to a high of $35.25 per share early in 1993. However, investors grew nervous after the inauguration of President Clinton and his attempted health care reforms. ESI stock slipped to $28 per share and then to $21.50. However, ESI continued to grow, expanding its pharmacy network to 28,000; membership reached two million customers in 1992. The following year, ESI signed on FHP International Corp. and Maxicare Health Care, both based in California, which together held three percent of the national HMO market. ESI also added such corporate clients as Lockheed Corp., Service Merchandise Co., and Ingersoll-Rand Co. These new clients doubled ESI's customer base, boosting its share of the pharmacy mail-order market to 2.5 percent—behind leader Medco's 50 percent. In 1993, ESI more than doubled its revenues, to $264.9 million for net income of over $8 million. In response to the increase in its West Coast business, ESI opened a second mail-order service facility in Tempe, Arizona.

ESI was also helped by another trend that swept through the PBM industry. In 1993, Merck & Co. paid $6.6 billion for Medco. This acquisition was quickly followed by SmithKline Beecham's $2.3 billion purchase of Diversified Pharmaceutical Services. Then PCS was purchased by Eli Lilly & Co. for $4 billion. Caremark, a division of J.C. Penney with roughly 15 percent of the PBM market, instituted alliances with Pfizer, Bristol-Myers, Rhone-Poulenc, and Lilly in 1994. The last of the large PBMs, Value Health, announced its joint venture with Pfizer in 1995. Distrust of these new relationships—and suspicion that the drug companies would exert too much influence on the PBMs to include their parent companies' drugs in their formularies, that is, the list of drugs approved for their customers' use—proved beneficial to ESI. The company's independent status helped lure FHP as a client—one executive at FHP told the *New York Times*: "Large employers and health plans don't want to get in bed with Lilly or Merck." In 1994, Coventry Corp., a national HMO based in Nashville, also chose Express Scripts as their PBM.

By 1994, ESI had expanded its pharmacy network to 34,000 stores. Its revenues reached $384.5 million, producing a net income of $12.7 million. The company expanded its services by adding workers' compensation prescription services, and also reinsurance. The company's growth also fueled its stock price, which reached $50.50 per share in April 1994. In that year, the

company also began to emphasize computer technology, introducing its RxWorkbench software used for analyzing patient prescription data. By the end of 1994, ESI membership had grown to 5.7 million.

The following year, ESI reached an agreement with San Diego–based American Healthcare Systems Purchasing Partners L.P. to provide for that group's network of 800 hospitals and 100 nursing homes. The company also made a deeper investment in information technology by launching its Practice Patterns Science (PPS) subsidiary. PPS offered clients the ability to combine medical and pharmaceutical data in order to identify treatment and spending patterns, allowing for improved patient outcomes at lower cost.

ESI's purchase of Canadian PBM Eclipse Claims Services allowed it to move into that market in 1995. Canadian customers included divisions of Aetna, Prudential, and Manufacturers Life insurance companies. The company also instituted an agreement with CIBA Vision Ophthalmics U.S. to form a managed eye care alliance, marketing disease management programs using technology developed by PPS. By the end of 1995, ESI's revenues had increased nearly 42 percent over the previous year, to $544 million, for net earnings of over $18 million. The company's pharmacy network increased to 45,000 stores, while its membership swelled to more than eight million people.

That number jumped past nine million early in 1996 when APS Healthcare—newly formed in a merger among American Healthcare Systems, Premier Health Alliance, and SunHealth Alliance—signed ESI to provide pharmacy benefits. Despite the gains of ESI and the PBM industry in general in the first half of the 1990s, a majority of large employers still had not switched to the greater discounts offered by PBMs—a situation that only spelled future growth potential for ESI.

Principal Subsidiaries

Practice Patterns Science, Inc.; ESI Canada Inc.

Principal Divisions

Infusion Therapy (IVTx); Managed Vision Care (MVC).

Further Reading

Chesler, Caren, "Leader's Success," *Investor's Business Daily,* December 20, 1993, p. 1.

Jacobson, Gianna, "Independence Creates Niche in Health Care," *New York Times,* July 15, 1995, Sec. 1, p. 40.

Lau, Gloria, "Concentrating Drug Purchases to Reduce Costs," *Investor's Business Daily,* April 20, 1994, p. A6.

Steyer, Robert, "Rx for Growth: Express Scripts Pays off Quickly for Investors," *St. Louis Post-Dispatch,* March 1, 1993, Sec. Business. p. 12.

—M. L. Cohen

E-Z Serve Corporation

2550 North Loop West, Suite 600
Houston, Texas 77092
U.S.A.
(713) 684-4300
Fax: (713) 684-4367

Public Company
Incorporated: 1986 as E-Z Serve Inc.
Employees: 5,156
Sales: $748 million (1995)
Stock Exchanges: American
SICs: 5541 Gasoline Service Stations; 5411 Grocery
Stores; 6719 Holding Companies, Not Elsewhere
Classified

As the seventh largest convenience store operator in the United States, E-Z Serve Corporation owns and operates 737 stores and 13 franchised stores in 15 states, with the majority of the company's stores located in the southeastern United States. During the mid-1990s, E-Z Serve operated its convenience stores, mini-marts, and gas marts under the names "E-Z Serve," "Jr. Food Stores," "Majik Market," "Taylor Food Mart," and "Time Saver." At 681 of the company's convenience stores and at 204 noncompany-operated retail outlets, E-Z Serve also retailed gasoline under its proprietary "E-Z Serve" brand name and a number of major brands, such as CITGO, Texaco, Conoco, and Chevron. For much of its history, E-Z Serve was primarily concerned with marketing gasoline, but in 1991, when new management developed a new business strategy for the company, its business focus was dramatically altered. From 1991 onward, the company's chief aim was to develop into a major convenience store operator and to derive the majority of its profits from the retail merchandising of traditional grocery and nongrocery lines typically found in convenience stores, rather than continuing to generate the bulk of its revenues and profits from the more volatile and less profitable business of marketing gasoline. Through a series of acquisitions completed during the early and mid-1990s, E-Z Serve

transformed itself into one of the largest convenience store operators in the nation.

Origins

E-Z Serve achieved its greatest prominence as an operator of convenience stores, quickly becoming the seventh largest independent convenience store company in the country. For the first 20 years of the company's history, however, it was involved in a distinctly different business. The two periods encompassed two eras in the company's history: one spent as a privately owned petroleum marketing company and the other spent as a publicly traded operator of convenience stores. The first chapter in E-Z Serve's history began in 1971 when the company was organized in Houston, Texas, just as the Texas oil boom period of the 1970s was about to usher in a decade of prolific growth for all those associated in the production and marketing of petroleum products.

Initially, E-Z Serve operated a motor fuels wholesale business and a motor fuels supply and trading business, making a name for itself by marketing gasoline to service stations and convenience stores located in a large territory surrounding its corporate headquarters in Houston. E-Z Serve, which operated as E-Z Serve Inc. for the first 15 years of its existence, grew steadily during its first decade and a half of existence, eventually extending its service territory to include 20 states and roughly 800 retail locations by the mid-1980s, the bulk of which were situated in rural areas. It was at this juncture in the company's history that the first signs of the changes to come became apparent.

Ironically, the developments that precipitated E-Z Serve's exit from petroleum marketing as its primary business arose from its prowess as a marketer of petroleum. During its first decade and a half of business, E-Z Serve had developed renowned marketing expertise, a skill that made the company an attractive entity to independent oil and gas exploration companies looking to diversify their operations to include the marketing side of the petroleum business. One such company was Harken Energy Corporation, a publicly held, Dallas-based exploration and production company that acquired E-Z Serve on

Company Perspectives:

We at E-Z Serve are totally committed to becoming the most customer-driven company in our markets.

the last day of 1986. At the time of the acquisition, E-Z Serve had offices in Abilene and Houston and supplied roughly 900 service stations and convenience stores in 24 Sunbelt states and Hawaii. The deal, which cost Harken $36.3 million, was executed through E-Z Serve Holding Co., a subsidiary formed by Harken to complete the transaction.

Under the corporate umbrella of Harken, E-Z Serve continued to conduct the same type of marketing work as it had before the acquisition, but under the stewardship of new management. Led by this new leadership, in 1988 and 1989 E-Z Serve acquired 49 convenience stores—the foundation upon which the company's future chain of convenience stores would be built. In September 1988, E-Z Serve paid $10 million for control of Allen's Convenience Stores, Inc. and in March 1989 acquired 17 retail gasoline outlets, including six convenience stores, and supply agreements at 25 branded locations from Harris Oil Company.

1991: New Plan for the Future

Following these acquisitions, E-Z Serve entered a decade of dramatic transformation, one that would chart the brisk rise of the company as a convenience store operator and mark the beginning of the second chapter of its corporate history. This second phase of development was touched off by E-Z Serve's return to operating as an independent company. In 1991, following a rights offering, E-Z Serve was cut free from Harken, once again gained new management, and began to develop a new business plan. As discussions were held about the future course of the company, a new business strategy was adopted that steered E-Z Serve in a different direction and set the stage for the development of one of the country's largest convenience store operators. E-Z Serve's executives resolved to increase per store profitability and corporate growth through the acquisition of convenience stores, opting to forgo the years of marketing gasoline as the exclusive engine driving the company's growth. Instead, E-Z Serve officials decided to concentrate their efforts on merchandise sales in company-owned retail units. Though E-Z Serve would continue to market gasoline as the 1990s progressed, the primary focus of the company during the decade would be to increase the profits derived from convenience store merchandise, thereby avoiding the cyclical nature of gasoline sales and the various economic and political influences that made marketing gasoline a decidedly capricious business and moving the company into a business that, as a rule, yielded higher profit margins.

As the new cadre of E-Z Serve's management plotted its course, there was much to be done to transform the company into a major player in the convenience store industry. First and foremost, the company needed to acquire additional store units. When E-Z Serve was formulating its plans to become a prominent convenience store operator, the company owned 54 retail

units located primarily in southern Texas. Considering that the company operated 750 stores in 15 states four years later, the quantity of E-Z Serve's convenience store holdings in 1991 represented only a fraction of the size the company would soon become. To make the leap from 54 stores to 750 stores in four years, much of the growth had to come through the acquisition of existing stores. The company did this, beginning in 1992.

Acquisitions in the 1990s

In 1992, E-Z Serve completed two acquisitions, purchasing Taylor Petroleum, Inc. and TOC Retail Inc. from Tenacqco Bridge Partnership and renaming the properties E-Z Serve Convenience Stores, Inc. (EZCON). The acquisitions raised the number of company-operated convenience stores to a total of 523 and dramatically increased E-Z Serve's presence in metropolitan markets. In the space of a few short months, E-Z Serve had fashioned a substantial foundation to support its bid toward becoming a convenience store powerhouse. Further prodigious growth was in the offing as the company assimilated its 1992 acquisitions into its network of retail units, but it would be another three years before any deals were completed that rivaled the magnitude of 1992's achievements.

E-Z Serve's next pivotal acquisition was completed in early 1995, when the company purchased Time Saver Stores, Inc., a chain of 116 convenience stores located primarily in the New Orleans, Louisiana area. Six months later, in July, the company completed another significant acquisition when it purchased Sunshine Jr. Stores, Inc., a chain of 205 convenience stores situated primarily in the Florida Panhandle. Together, the two acquisitions nearly doubled the size of E-Z Serve, adding 321 store units to its fold for a total of 750 and giving it a major presence in key market areas along the Gulf Coast from New Orleans to Tallahassee, Florida. Separately, the two acquisitions strengthened E-Z Serve's geographic stance in their own particular way. The addition of the Sunshine Jr. chain, which was based in Panama City, Florida, gave E-Z Serve 120 stores in the Florida Panhandle, with the remainder—all full-sized food stores—located in Alabama, Mississippi, Georgia, and Louisiana. The acquisition of the Time Saver chain, meanwhile, positioned E-Z Serve as the dominant convenience store operator in the New Orleans market. There were 148 Time Saver retail units located in and around New Orleans, the absorption of which immediately ranked E-Z Serve as the market leader, by far eclipsing the store count of any of the company's competitors.

The financial totals recorded by E-Z Serve in 1995 reflected the positive strides the company had achieved toward becoming a leading convenience store operator. Sales, which had amounted to $563.1 million in 1994, rose by 33 percent in 1995, reaching $748 million. Equally as encouraging to company executives in Houston as the robust jump in total sales was the increase in E-Z Serve's general merchandise sales. For the year, merchandise sales swelled by 47 percent, increasing from $181.1 million in 1994 to $266.7 million in 1995.

Once the store units gained through the acquisitions completed in 1995 had been added to the company's network, E-Z Serve stood positioned as a convenience store operator with outlets spread across a broad geographic base. Although the company was supported by operations in 20 states, the majority of its stores were located in Texas, Louisiana, Georgia, and Florida, where 505 of the company's stores were situated. Of the company's total of 750 stores, 13 of which were franchised, nearly 260 were operated under the E-Z Serve banner. Majik Market represented the second most widely used name for the company's stores, with 150 units bearing the Majik Market name. Taylor Food Mart was used as the name for 66 stores, Jr. Food Store as the name for 200 locations, and Time Saver as the name for 46 stores. Merchandise sales collected from all of the company's units accounted for 36 percent of E-Z Serve's total annual revenues, and gasoline sales accounted for 51 percent of the company's revenue total.

Plans for the Mid-1990s and Beyond

In the wake of the great strides achieved in 1995, E-Z Serve assimilated the retail units it acquired during the year into its network. By early 1996, most of the Sunshine Jr. stores had been converted to E-Z Serve stores. Aside from the acquisitions completed in 1995, the company also made a number of significant changes within its stores that were expected to attract more customers and lift the percentage of merchandises sales in relation to total sales. Cappucino and breakfast rolls were added to the merchandise lines in many of the company's stores and Blimpie was signed on as a provider of fast foods to the company's stores, bolstering the list of branded food items offered by E-Z Serve. In addition, Baskin-Robbins ice cream was introduced at E-Z Serve stores during 1995, and the number of stores outfitted with automated teller machines (ATMs) increased to more than 200, adding the opportunity to conduct rudimentary banking services as a customer draw.

With further acquisitions in the offing as E-Z Serve charted its course for the late 1990s, the company's continued expansion appeared inevitable. Aside from increasing the number of retail units composing its chain, E-Z Serve's management was also determined to flesh out the merchandise lines at its stores. For 1996, a new pastry merchandising program was slated to begin and the number of fast food facilities at company stores was expected to increase. In 1995, E-Z Serve opened eight branded fast food facilities, including national brands such as Subway, Baskin-Robbins, Hot Stuff Pizza, and Blimpie. In 1996, the company planned to increase its branded food lines by adding ten fast food facilities. Other plans for 1996 called for the expansion of its ATM program by installing an additional 277 ATMs in its chain of stores and the expenditure of $10 million to remodel some of the company's retail outlets. With this work under way, E-Z Serve headed into the late 1990s, its frenetic yet successful years of growth during the first half of the 1990s providing a valuable blueprint for the company's expansion during the second half of the 1990s and the beginning of the 21st century.

Principal Subsidiaries

E-Z Serve Convenience Stores, Inc.; E-Z Serve Petroleum Marketing Company.

Further Reading

Murphy, Marvin, "Producers Finding Know-How Crucial in Successful Switch to Marketing," *The Oil Daily,* January 12, 1987, p. 4.
Steffy, Loren, "Analysts Question Harken's Timing on Refinery Acquisition," *Dallas Business Journal,* October 12, 1990, p. 18.
Williams, Scott, "Harken Subsidiary Sells Parent's Stock to N.Y. Brokerage," *Dallas Business Journal,* October 11, 1991, p. 10.

—Jeffrey L. Covell

Fanuc Ltd.

3580, Shibokusa Aza-Komanba
Oshino-mura
Minamitsuru-gun
Yamanashi 401-05
Japan
(0555) 84-5555
Fax: (0555) 84-5512

Public Company
Incorporated: 1972 as Fujitsu Fanuc Ltd.
Employees: 2,166
Sales: US$1.01 billion (1993)
Stock Exchanges: Tokyo
SICs: 3625 Relays & Industrial Controls

Headquartered at the base of Japan's Mount Fuji, Fanuc Ltd. is the world's leading manufacturer of numerical control (NC) equipment for machine tools, devices that put the automation into automated factories. NC devices are the forerunners of industrial robots. Fanuc, whose name is an acronym for Fuji Automatic Numerical Control, has been a world leader in robotics since the 1970s.

Founded as a Subsidiary of Fujitsu

Fanuc was founded as a wholly owned subsidiary of Fujitsu in 1955, after that electronics giant decided to enter the factory automation business. Its first employees were a team of 500 engineers, and Fujitsu chose from among them a young executive engineer named Seiuemon Inaba to head the subsidiary. It was a move that would prove beneficial for both the company and the man. Inaba, who received a doctorate in engineering from Tokyo Institute of Technology after joining Fujitsu in 1946, has since remained at the top of Fanuc's chain of command. His name has become virtually synonymous with that of the company.

At first, Fujitsu Fanuc devoted itself solely to research and development. U.S. companies led the way in automation tech-nology at that time; in fact, no Japanese company produced NC machine tools until the mid-1960s. Once the Japanese NC industry entered the field of play, however, Fujitsu Fanuc dominated the game. By 1971, it controlled 80 percent of the domestic market for NC equipment. In 1972 Fujitsu spun-off its highly successful subsidiary, retaining a substantial minority interest. The remaining shares were put on the open market. In 1975 Seiuemon Inaba became president of the new company.

Fujitsu Fanuc, as it continued to call itself until 1982, began its life as an independent company with numerous marketplace advantages. As a major Japanese NC manufacturer, it was well suited to spearhead the Japanese NC industry's entry into the export market. In 1975 it licensed U.S. manufacturer Pratt & Whitney to market its NC drilling machines in North America. In the same year it entered into a licensing agreement with German engineering firm Siemens, which was also a minority shareholder in the company, giving Siemens the exclusive right to market Fujitsu Fanuc products in Europe. In 1985 the European Economic Community would find that the deal violated its rules regarding monopolies and fined the companies $840,000. In 1978 Fujitsu Fanuc took its manufacturing operations abroad, building a plant in South Korea. By 1982, it had captured half of the world NC market.

Captured Leading Position in Robotics in the 1980s

Its position as an NC manufacturer notwithstanding, it is the company's commitment to the related field of robotics that has brought it the most attention and acclaim. Fujitsu Fanuc started selling robots in 1975, but they accounted for only a tiny percentage of sales at first, Kawasaki and Hitachi being the leading Japanese robotics companies at the time. Inaba sought to change that situation in the 1980s. In January 1981 Fujitsu Fanuc opened a showcase plant in Yamanashi Prefecture, in which robots and NC machine tools made parts for other robots. The factory, which would otherwise require 500 human workers, was run by a staff of 100 people, whose duties consisted of maintaining the robots and assembling the parts into finished products.

This vision of robots manufacturing other robots caught the fancy of the press and, evidently, other robotics companies. A string of joint ventures followed the opening of the new plant. In 1982 Fujitsu Fanuc granted Taiwan's Tatung Co. sole import rights for its robots. In 1983 it also joined with the 600 Group, a British machine tool manufacturer, to form 600 Fanuc Robotics, which would sell Fanuc robots in the United Kingdom.

Fanuc's most important move in 1982 was to enter into a joint venture with General Motors (GM), called GMFanuc Robotics, to produce and market robots in the United States. The new company was 50 percent owned by each partner and was based in Detroit, with GM providing most of the management and Fanuc the products. This was not the first alliance between Japanese and U.S. robotics concerns; Japanese companies on the whole lacked the advanced technology necessary to create sophisticated robots, while the U.S. plants lacked Japanese manufacturing skill. By linking up with its largest single potential customer in the United States, Fanuc all but assured itself of a lucrative share of the U.S. market. In its early years, GMFanuc Robotics chiefly made automobile assembly robots and sold them to GM. Although both companies denied it at the time, few industry observers doubted that GM gave preferential treatment to GMFanuc robots when considering bids from suppliers. GMFanuc sales described a steep upward curve, and within six years it became the world's largest supplier of robots.

Inaba's goal of increasing Fanuc's robot sales was not simply a business matter, but a reflection of his personal interest in robots. Known in Japan as the Emperor of Robots, Inaba said in 1981 that it was his dream to develop within four years a robot that would help assemble Fanuc's robot-made robot parts into finished robots. By the middle of the decade, Fanuc had indeed developed assembly robots, which were used to put together parts for motors at its motor factory.

Fanuc's success in robotics has brought Inaba to the attention of the U.S. financial press. There is his passion for the color yellow, for instance, because, as he put it, "In the Orient, yellow is the emperor's color." Fanuc factories, offices, and assembly lines are all painted in such a shade. The workers' jumpsuits are also yellow, head to toe. Inaba is known for his demanding and authoritarian management style—at meetings, his subordinates are not allowed to speak unless spoken to; for his company's commitment to a futuristic industry like robotics; and for the profoundly scenic location of its headquarters.

In the mid-1980s, sales of automation equipment dropped substantially. Manufacturers who pumped large amounts of capital into automation equipment suddenly found themselves with weak cash flows and were unwilling to invest further. GM cut back on its commitment to robotics, GMFanuc sales fell, and Fanuc was further hurt by the relative strength of the yen against the dollar, making its products more expensive in the United States. Fanuc, nevertheless, managed to maintain a healthy profit margin despite these difficulties, and it kept expanding its activities.

In 1987, it tightened its grip on the U.S. market by entering into a joint venture with another pillar of U.S. industry, General Electric (GE). The two companies formed GE Fanuc Automation to manufacture computerized numerical control (CNC) devices. The deal marked something of a defeat for GE, which had failed in its attempt to become a factory automation power-house. GE stopped making its own CNC equipment and turned its Charlottesville, Virginia, plant over to the new company, which equipped it to produce Fanuc CNC devices.

In 1988 Fanuc once again joined forces with General Motors, this time to form GMFanuc Robotics Europa, to market robots in Europe. In 1989 it took advantage of relaxed East-West tensions to increase its presence in the Soviet Union. It joined with Mitsui, a huge Japanese trading company and with Stanko Service, a Soviet machine-tool service organization, to form Stanko Fanuc Service, which would maintain and repair Fanuc products there.

Fanuc's success has always been derived from the circumstances that its products are the most reliable and yet the least expensive on the market, allowing it to better its competition in good times and to maintain its advantage in lean times. In a cutting-edge field like automation, a huge commitment to research and development is required, and fully one-third of Fanuc's nearly 1,800 employees are engaged in such activity, the highest ratio of any Japanese manufacturer. As with every other facet of the company's operations, Fanuc's R&D bears the personal stamp of Seiuemon Inaba. He once gave his Product Development Laboratory a clock that ran ten times faster than normal, as a gentle reminder of the importance of staying ahead of the competition. Inaba has made the German engineering slogan *Weniger Teile,* which means "fewer parts," Fanuc's slogan; machines with fewer parts are cheaper to produce and easier for automatons to assemble.

Difficult Years in the 1990s

Inaba has garnered publicity for the extensive benefits he provided his employees. At the Yamanashi Prefecture plant, located in a rural setting at the base of Mount Fuji, Inaba included a medical center, a gymnasium, a 25-meter heated swimming pool, a culture center, employee living quarters, and a pub. In the late 1980s and early 1990s, these attractive benefits helped Fanuc counter a labor shortage affecting many Japanese firms.

In the early 1990s, however, Fanuc faced more than just a difficult labor market. Revenues and earnings declined as the entire machine tool industry in Japan suffered from slackened demand compared to heyday of the 1970s and 1980s. In the midst of this downturn, Fanuc gained an increased presence in foreign markets when it purchased GM's half-interest in GMFanuc and renamed it Fanuc Robotics Corporation, which became a wholly owned subsidiary of Fanuc Ltd. Fanuc Robotics, in turn, held two subsidiaries—Fanuc Robotics North America, based in Auburn Hills, Michigan, and serving the North American and Latin American markets; and Fanuc Robotics Europe GmbH (formerly GMFanuc Robotics Europa), based in Luxembourg, which served the European market.

To maintain Fanuc's dominant position in automation technology in the face of the industry slump, Inaba determined to further bolster Fanuc's R&D. In 1994 the Fanuc Berkeley Laboratory was established in Union City, California. Inaba also sought to reduce costs by purchasing more raw materials outside of Japan, taking advantage of the strength of the yen.

Longer term, Inaba committed Fanuc to a strategic emphasis on robots.

Unlike other Japanese robotics firms, Fanuc did not shift production to the United States during this period. Demand for robots was growing dramatically in North America in the early 1990s thanks to a rebounding automobile industry. Fanuc could continue to profitably manufacture in Japan based on two factors. First, Fanuc's production process was cheaper than competitors because of its highly automated "lights out" plant, which was capable of producing one thousand robots a month. Second, Fanuc could take advantage of its world leadership in production of CNCs—a key component in robots—to keep its production costs down.

These strategies seemed to be paying off as Fanuc's revenues and earnings rebounded in 1994 and 1995. A master businessman as well as a master engineer, Seiuemon Inaba has guided his company along a steep ascent and through some challenging conditions as well.

Principal Subsidiaries

Fanuc Robotics North America, Inc. (U.S.); Fanuc U.S.A. Corp.; GE Fanuc Automation Corporation (U.S.); Beijing-Fanuc Mechatronics Co., Ltd. (China); Fanuc Europe GmbH (Germany); Fanuc Germany GmbH; Fanuc France S.A.; Fanuc Iberia, S.A. (Spain); Fanuc Italia S.p.A. (Italy); Fanuc Sweden AB; Fanuc India Limited; Fanuc Korea Corporation; Fanuc-Machinex Ltd. (Bulgaria); Fanuc Oceania Pty. Limited (Australia); Fanuc South Africa (Proprietary) Limited; Fanuc Southeast Asia Pte. Ltd. (Singapore); Fanuc Singapore Pte. Ltd.; Fanuc Hong Kong Limited; Fanuc Thai Limited; Fanuc Taiwan Limited; Fanuc U.K. Limited; P.T. Fanuc Indonesia.

Further Reading

Bylinsky, Gene, "Japan's Robot King Wins Again," *Fortune,* May 25, 1987.

"Fanuc Edges Closer to a Robot-Run Plant," *Business Week,* November 24, 1980.

"Fanuc Throws One-Third of Its Entire Labor Force into the Most Powerful R&D Setup of the Industry," *Business Japan,* April 1989.

"GM to Sell Its 50% Stake in GMFanuc, a Robotics Firm, to Japanese Partner," *Wall Street Journal,* June 4, 1992, p. B3(W), p. B4(E).

Nakamura, Minoru, "Trouble in the Robot Kingdom," *Tokyo Business Today,* June 1994, pp. 44–45.

Wiegner, Kathleen K., "The Dawn of Battle," *Forbes,* October 26, 1981.

Winter, Drew, "Eastward Ho: Japanese Robot Builders Shift Production to U.S.," *Ward's Auto World,* July 1995, p. 81.

—Douglas Sun
—updated by David E. Salamie

Fay's Inc.

7245 Henry Clay Boulevard
Liverpool, New York 13088-3571
U.S.A.
(315) 451-8000
Fax: (315) 457-1266

Wholly Owned Subsidiary of Thrift Drug
Incorporated: 1966 as Fay's Drug Co., Inc.
Employees: 9,000
Sales: $973.8 million (1996)
SICs: 5912 Drug Stores & Proprietary Stores; 5921
Liquor Stores; 5961 Catalog & Mail-Order Houses

Fay's Inc. was the nation's 12th largest drug-store chain at the end of 1995 and the largest operator of super drug stores in the Northeast. After the sale of an office-supply division in mid 1996, it consisted of 273 discount drug stores, almost all in New York and Pennsylvania, and one liquor store. More than half of Fay's drug stores were situated in four upstate New York metropolitan areas: Albany, Buffalo, Rochester, and Syracuse. They were located in suburban shopping centers with adjacent paved and lighted parking facilities and ranged in size from 12,000 to 16,000 square feet. A mail-order pharmacy-services division marketed mail-order prescription services to prescription-benefit programs.

Fay's announced in August 1996 that it had agreed to be acquired by the J. C. Penney Co. for $285 million in stock. The merger agreement was completed in October of that year and Fay's became a subsidiary of Thrift Drug, making that subsidiary of Penney's the eighth largest drug store chain with over $3 billion in sales.

The Early Years: 1958–76

Fay's originated in 1958, when Henry Panasci and his son, Henry A. Panasci, Jr., both graduates of the University of Buffalo pharmacy school, opened a drug store in Syracuse. Fay's Drug Co. was incorporated in 1966 to acquire the six existing retail outlets and their distribution center in Liverpool, a suburb of Syracuse that also served as company headquarters. By 1969, when the company first offered stock to the public, there were (either in operation or planned for opening prior to June 1970) 11 Fay's Drugs stores in central New York. These were discount drug and general-merchandise stores ranging in size from 8,000 to 35,000 square feet. For the fiscal year 1967, the company had $8.4 million in revenues and net income of $245,309. For 1968 and 1969 revenues were $11.3 million and $13.6 million, respectively, and net income $158,330 and $358,072, respectively.

In 1969 Fay's Drug launched an ambitious expansion program that, by late 1972, had increased the number of stores in operation to 27. All of them were in New York except one in Pennsylvania and were located around the periphery of fast-growing communities, in suburban shopping centers and mini-malls adjacent to supermarkets. A typical store had about 15,000 square feet of space and included a prescription department, health and beauty aids, and a full line of sundries, including toys, automotive products, hardware, housewares, small appliances, sporting goods, stationery, tobacco products, and seasonal items. These self-service outlets were open seven days a week, from about 9 a.m. to 10 p.m., except for the Pennsylvania store, which was closed on Sundays.

Fay's Drug's growth was attributed to a strong senior management team assembled by the junior Panasci and to the company's training and incentive programs for the middle managers who were recruited from pharmacy schools to actually run the stores. A computerized system of financial and management controls included sales, budgets, and inventory control for each store. In fiscal 1972 (ended January 31, 1972), company revenues reached $30.5 million and net income $595,113. Dividends began to be paid out in 1975.

By early 1976 Fay's Drug operated 40 stores of 11,000 to 80,000 square feet. It was filling more than two million prescriptions a year. Prescription departments accounted for about 10 to 11 percent of sales, and Fay's Drug's private-label line to almost five percent. Cash flow had increased to the point where the company was financing about 80 percent of its capital requirements. Its long-term debt was about $2.5 million.

Southern Expansion and Hasty Retreat

Fay's Drug expanded southward during 1978 and 1979 by acquiring the seven Berkeley Drugs stores in Charleston, South Carolina, and the 14 Craft's Drug Stores in Greenville and Spartansburg, South Carolina. Panasci said he was attracted to these two chains because they did 40 percent of their trade in prescribed medicines, compared to Fay's Drug's 19 percent. The company was using this segment as the core of its ever-expanding general-merchandise wares. Another inducement was the chance to move into an area growing in population, unlike stagnant-to-declining New York. Nine more southern stores were opened in 1979. The southern strategy proved a failure, however, because the acquired stores had less than half the selling space of the existing ones, and the lack of a company distribution center in the area mandated reliance on high-priced jobbers. Fay's sold its 31-store southern division to Rite Aid Corp. in 1981 for $10 million.

Fay's Drug also expanded by acquisition in the North in 1979 when it bought 20-unit Key Drug Co. of Rochester, New York, a chain with annual sales of over $29 million, for $10 million in cash. After the disposal of the southern units the company was a more compact operation of 81 stores, all within 150 miles of its Liverpool headquarters and warehouse. Hard goods and miscellaneous general merchandise were accounting for 40 percent of Fay's Drug sales in 1980. Health and beauty aids and stationery, candy, and magazines each accounted for 15 percent. Tobacco products brought in another ten percent and pharmacy the remaining 20 percent. A computerized pharmacy system was installed in early 1982 to facilitate such services as the tracking of prescription usage and the detection of possible drug interaction. It also allowed acceleration of collections from third-party payers.

Revenues in fiscal 1980 (ending January 31, 1980) came to $194 million and net income to $3 million. During the next year sales increased to $243.1 million, but net income fell below $1 million, leading to the sale of the southern division. The company rebounded in fiscal 1982, earning $3.1 million on sales of $238.2 million. By early 1983 Fay's Drug had 92 outlets, including 24, 13, and 12 in the Rochester, Syracuse, and Buffalo metropolitan areas, respectively. Sixty-five percent of its products were coming from the company's warehouse. That year the company's common stock split two for one, and it moved up to the New York Stock Exchange from its previous listing on the American Stock Exchange.

New Acquisitions: 1984–94

In early 1985 Panasci received an award from the *Wall Street Transcript,* and a securities analyst cited Fay's Drug for being "one of the best in an area of the country that's not particularly known for growth." The company had opened 17 new stores in 1984 and had bought Wheels Discount Auto Supply, a deep-discount New York chain. It had also opened Paper Cutter, a chain in New York and Pennsylvania selling discounted stationery, greeting cards, books, and office and party supplies. During fiscal 1985 the company earned a record $8.7 million on sales of $366.7 million.

Fay's Drug entered the Springfield, Massachusetts, and Hartford, Connecticut, metropolitan areas in 1985 by acquiring eight Genovese drug stores. Forty percent of Fay's drug stores were less than three years old at the end of the year. By the end of 1986 there were 13 Fay's outlets in Massachusetts and Connecticut, but in 1988 nine were sold to Melville Corp. and the others were closed.

Fay's Drug Co. changed its name to Fay's Inc. in 1989 to reflect its diversification into Wheels and Paper Cutter. Later that year there were 190 Fay's Drug stores in New York and Pennsylvania, 26 Wheels stores in upstate New York, and 25 Paper Cutter stores in New York, New Jersey, and Pennsylvania. Panasci's son David was president of the Paper Cutter division. Company revenues were $527 million in fiscal 1989, and net income was $10 million.

In 1991 Fay's purchased the capital stock of Rome, New York-based, 48-store Carls Drug Co., Inc., a company founded in 1939 by Panasci's uncle Carl A. Panasci, from Victory Markets Inc. for $35.5 million. In 1993 it agreed to sell ten drugstore locations in southeastern Pennsylvania to the CVS division of Melville Corp. The company bought the assets of 26 National Auto Supply Stores and four Whitlock Auto Supply Stores from WSR Corp. in 1994, adding them to the Wheels Discount chain. Also in 1994, Fay's completed the purchase of the capital stock of Peterson Drug Co. of Western New York, Inc. That year David H. Panasci was named president and chief operating officer of Fay's, moving him in line to succeed his father, who remained chairman and chief executive officer.

Three-Stage Sellout: 1995–96

Fay's found itself the object of takeover rumors in late 1995, a year in which it lost money for the first time. To fend off unwelcome suitors, the company, which was about 31 percent owned by management and directors, adopted a poison-pill defense in August 1995 to counter what it called "abusive takeover tactics, including attempts to acquire control of the company at an inadequate price." During fiscal 1995 (ending January 28, 1995) the company had passed $1 billion in sales and had earned a record $12.6 million, but in fiscal 1996 (ending January 27, 1996) its sales fell to $973.8 million, and it lost $9.6 million. Fay's problems arose from some underperforming and undersized drug stores and the sharp decline of gross margins due to a higher percentage of sales made through third-party prescription plans. The figures were somewhat misleading because the company took a $4.1 million loss from discontinued operations and a $12.5 million after-tax restructuring.

To restore his business to financial health and raise capital for future operations, Panasci decided to concentrate on drugstore operations and jettison the peripheral businesses. Accordingly, Fay's sold Wheels Discount to Western Auto Supply Co., a wholly owned subsidiary of Sears, Roebuck and Co., in November 1995 for $39 million in cash. It was renamed Parts America. Fay's sold Paper Cutter to Party Stores Holdings Inc. for $14 million in June 1996.

Stripped of its peripheral businesses, Fay's became a more attractive takeover target. According to the terms of its August

1996 agreement with J.C. Penney, its stockholders were to receive $12.75 in tax-free Penney stock for each share of Fay's stock, whereas on June 9, 1996, the day Fay's announced it was engaged in talks to sell the chain to J.C. Penney, its stock closed at $8.625. Among the beneficiaries would be Henry Panasci, who held 2.8 million of the company's 20.9 million shares of common stock, and David Panasci, who held 334,000 shares.

At the end of fiscal 1996 there were 218 Fay's Drug Stores, of which 192 were located in upstate New York, 23 in Pennsylvania, two in Vermont and one in New Hampshire. The company was also responsible for the operation of 55 other drug stores—45 of which were operated under the trade name "Fay's Cornerdrug"—acquired from independent owners, and a liquor store. Of the 55 total, 49 were in upstate New York, five in Pennsylvania, and one in Vermont. All stores were being leased. Most ranged in size from 12,000 to 16,000 square feet and were located in suburban shopping centers with adjacent paved and lighted parking facilities.

In addition to PostScript, its mail-order pharmacy-services division, Fay's introduced Optima Pharmacy Services, a pharmacy-benefits management group, in 1994. Optima Pharmacy Services provided administrative and management services to managed-care organizations and other plans and programs paying for prescription drug benefits. It was intended to lower the cost of providing prescription benefits by designing plans, monitoring drug usage, and promoting the use of generic drugs in appropriate situations.

In fiscal 1995 prescription and proprietary drugs accounted for 52 percent of Fay's sales. Health and beauty aids accounted for ten percent, tobacco for six percent, consumer hard goods for six percent, and miscellaneous merchandise for the remaining 26 percent. The company's long-term debt was $75.4 million in October 1995.

Further Reading

"Fay's Drug Chain off and Running on Comeback Trail," *Drug Topics,* December 15, 1986, pp. 116–118, 120.
"Fay's Drug Writes Own Prescription for Success," *Investment Dealers' Digest,* October 10, 1972, pp. 22–23.
"Fay's Focuses on Core Growth," *Central New York Business Journal,* December 11, 1995, p. 6.
"Fay's Knocks on the Major League Door," *Discount Merchandiser,* April 1980, pp. 57–58.
"Fay's Moves to the Big Board," *Discount Merchandiser,* March 1983, p. 18.
"Fay's to Sell Paper Cutter Unit," *Wall Street Journal,* June 10, 1996, p. B10.
"J. C. Penney to Buy Fay's Drugstore Chain," *New York Times,* August 7, 1996, p. D4.
Marcial, Gene, "Fay's Drugs: Fit to Be Swallowed?" *Business Week,* January 8, 1996, p. 48.
Rosenbaum, Michael, "Neat Formula: Fay's Drug Thrives on Low Prices and House Brands," *Barron's,* August 30, 1982, p. 40.
"TWST Names—Retail/Drug Chains," *Wall Street Transcript,* February 4, 1985, p. 76799.

—Robert Halasz

Fleming Companies, Inc.

Fleming Companies, Inc.

6301 Waterford Boulevard
P.O. Box 26647
Oklahoma City, Oklahoma 73126-0647
U.S.A.
(405) 840-7200
Fax: (405): 841-8003
Internet: http://www.fleming.com

Public Company
Incorporated: 1915 as the Lux Mercantile Company
Employees: 42,400
Sales: $17.5 billion (1995)
Stock Exchanges: New York Pacific Midwest
SICs: 5141 Groceries, General Line; 5199 Nondurable
Good, Not Elsewhere Classified

Fleming Companies, Inc. is the largest food wholesaler in the United States. The company stocks the shelves of more than 3,500 supermarkets and other retail food stores in 42 states and the District of Columbia, as well as in several foreign countries. Fleming has shown exceptional innovation in meeting the changing needs of the independent grocer over the years. The company's taste for the most up-to-date technology and its knack for making healthy acquisitions has catapulted it to the forefront of the wholesale foods industry. Today the company not only supplies its customers with food products but also assists with new store planning and financing, marketing, accounting, and operations management. In the 1990s, Fleming has sought to expand its presence on the retail end of the food industry and has increased its retail revenue to more than 21 percent of total revenue.

Founding and Early Development

In 1915, O. A. Fleming, E. C. Wilson, and Samuel Lux founded the Lux Mercantile Company in Topeka, Kansas, to sell produce to local merchants. The company's name was changed to Fleming-Wilson three years later. In 1921, Ned Fleming, the son of the company's cofounder, joined the firm. He was promoted to general manager a year later and held that position until he was elected president in 1945.

Throughout the 1920s, the Fleming-Wilson Company operated locally in Kansas. In 1927, it joined the Independent Grocers Alliance (I.G.A.), a voluntary grocery store chain and one of the largest independent chains today. In such voluntary chains, affiliated stores agree to buy most or all of their merchandise from one distributor and receive collective buying power in exchange, enabling them to compete with larger corporate supermarket chains. Voluntary chains have historically made up the largest share of the wholesaler's business, and they contributed significantly to Fleming-Wilson's growth.

The Depression took a particularly heavy toll on the lower Midwest and the Southwest. Though many industries in the region were virtually paralyzed, Fleming-Wilson managed to survive. In 1935, it acquired the Hutchinson Wholesale Grocery Company, another Kansas-based distributor, the start of a period of growth that has continued virtually unbroken to the present day.

In February 1941 the company changed its name to Fleming Company, Inc. That same year it branched out of Kansas when it acquired the Carol-Braugh-Robinson Company of Oklahoma City. By the end of World War II the fate of the independent grocer was uncertain, and Ned Fleming was faced with new challenges. Americans were moving out of the cities and into the suburbs. As shoppers drove their new automobiles to the new supermarkets, independent "mom and pop" corner stores fell by the wayside, and supermarket chains grew at a frantic pace. It was the voluntary chain concept that rescued the independent grocer. Voluntary chains expanded tremendously after the war, and as a result so, too, did Fleming. The company reported steadily increasing earnings throughout the late 1940s and the 1950s.

In 1956, Fleming Company bought Ray's Printing of Topeka, renamed General Printing and Paper. Fleming itself was General Printing and Paper's biggest customer, consistently accounting for more than half the company's sales.

Acquisitions and Diversifications in the 1960s and 1970s

The 1960s were a decade of exceptional growth, as Fleming expanded nationwide through the acquisition of other regional wholesalers. Throughout the early 1960s, the company acquired several companies and facilities in the Midwest and Southwest, including the Schumacher Company of Houston, Texas, in 1960.

In 1964, Ned Fleming became chairman of the board of directors and Richard D. Harrison became the company's president. Under this new leadership, Fleming began an even more ambitious campaign of expansion and acquisition. In 1965, Fleming purchased Thriftway Foods, which operated in the East with headquarters in King of Prussia, Pennsylvania. Three years later, Fleming tapped West Coast markets when it bought Kockos Brothers, Inc. in California. However, at the end of the decade profits slowed for the first time in many years.

Fleming began to diversify again in the 1970s. The company bought a semi-trailer manufacturing unit in 1970, and in 1972 it created the Fleming Foods Company, which ran the food distributing operations as a semi-autonomous unit. Later that year Fleming bought the Quality Oil Company, of Topeka, Kansas. Quality Oil operated about 50 retail gas stations in the Midwest and proved to be a wise investment. A year after the acquisition, the subsidiary was contributing more than ten percent of Fleming's pretax profits. Fleming also branched into health foods distribution when it bought Kahan and Lessin in 1972. At that time, K&L delivered to about 1,200 health food stores and 1,000 supermarkets. Fleming's venture into health foods proved to be less profitable than petroleum: K&L lost money in 1973 and showed only a slight profit in 1974.

In 1974, Fleming bought Benson Wholesale Company and the Dixieland Food Stores retail chain, both headquartered in Geneva, Alabama. In 1975, the company pushed into the New Jersey and New York markets by purchasing Royal Food Distributors. Finally, in 1979 Fleming acquired Blue Ridge Grocery Company of Waynesboro, Virginia, capping off a decade of acquisition and growth.

Renewed Focus on Wholesaling in the 1980s

In 1981, Fleming Companies reincorporated in Oklahoma, and its corporate headquarters moved to Oklahoma City. In March 1981, Richard D. Harrison was elected chairman of the Fleming Companies board of directors, and E. Dean Werries, who had previously headed the Fleming Foods division, replaced him as president, while Harrison remained CEO.

This new leadership steered Fleming in a slightly different direction. Harrison and Werries stressed wholesale food distribution over diversification. Throughout the 1980s, Fleming made more and larger acquisitions of food wholesalers as part of its growth strategy. In 1981, it bought McLain Grocery in Ohio. In 1982, it bought the Waples-Platter Company for $91 million, which included the White Swan Foodservice division in Texas. A month later, in January 1983, it purchased the bankrupt American-Strevell Inc. for $14 million. Fleming also purchased Giant Wholesale of Johnson City, Tennessee, that year. In 1984, Fleming acquired United Grocers, a cooperative

wholesaler in California. It further strengthened its hold on the northern California region by purchasing a huge distribution center in Milpitas, California, from the Alpha-Beta Company a year later. In 1985, Associated Grocers of Arizona, Inc. was purchased for $47 million. In 1986, Fleming purchased the Frankford-Quaker Grocery Company in Philadelphia and the Hawaiian distribution warehouse of Foodland Super Markets. In 1987, it acquired the Godfrey Company of Wisconsin, and in July 1988 Fleming became the largest wholesaler in the country when it acquired the nation's fourth-largest wholesaler, Malone & Hyde Inc.

Fleming's incredible spree of acquisitions was not completely free of complications. In particular, the acquisition of Associated Grocers of Arizona posed some new problems for Fleming. Because the wholesaler had previously operated as a cooperative, owned by those supermarkets it serviced, Fleming had difficulty implementing its own corporate style of management. Associated Grocers customers were not at first supportive of the changes that were necessary to transform the company into a profitable unit for Fleming. Despite such minor setbacks, Fleming continued to look for possible mergers to strengthen the company. Cooperative distributors who lacked the capital to reinvest in new facilities and found it increasingly difficult to compete with the streamlined corporate wholesaler were likely candidates.

At the same time Fleming concentrated on acquiring food wholesalers, it divested some of its other units. In 1982, it sold Quality Oil, and in 1983 it sold General Printing and Paper. In 1984, it sold its health foods specialty distributor, Kahan and Lessin. K&L's performance had been inconsistent ever since its acquisition in 1972. In addition, in 1982 the Justice Department charged the subsidiary, along with three other health food distributors, with fixing prices. The company was fined $75,000; Fleming reported a $862,000 expense as a result of the litigation. Also divested were M&H Drugs, the retail drug subsidiary of Malone & Hyde, and White Swan; both were sold in 1988.

Wholesale food distributors traditionally operate on profit margins of less than one percent. Increased productivity of even fractions of a penny on each dollar of volume can make a noticeable difference in earnings. For this reason, Fleming was quick to implement technological developments to increase productivity. In its newest warehouses, a computer breaks down orders by product, allowing a worker to fill several orders at once. The worker puts the total number of cases of one product ordered on a conveyor belt. A laser scanner sends each unit to the proper shipping bay to be loaded for delivery. This system increased productivity an average of 11 percent in those warehouses where it was employed. In warehouses in which it was impossible to mechanize without significantly disrupting operations, Fleming established standards of productivity as an alternative way to increase its profit margins. The procedure improvement program (PIP) measured each worker's productivity by computer. Before doing a specific task, a worker inserted a card into a computer, which calculated the standard amount of time for the task and evaluated the worker's performance. A worker who consistently fell below standard faced dismissal. Such work standards programs were, naturally, not always popular. In early 1986, workers went on strike at Fleming's warehouse in Oaks, Pennsylvania, in opposition to the work standards program and an increase in the standard number of cases moved per hour, from 125 to 150. The strike was settled when the Teamsters agreed to the new standard, and the company lengthened the five-step disciplinary review procedure to six steps.

Rapidly Changing Fortunes in the 1990s

Fleming went through a number of significant shifts in the 1990s, starting in 1990 with the loss of a major client when Albertson's became a self-distributing chain. This led to a $400 million loss in volume for Fleming and the closure of the company's Fremont, California, distribution center. Fleming quickly moved the following year to more than recover the lost revenue with a $80 million purchase of the warehousing and transportation assets of the Lubbock, Texas–based Furr's Inc. The deal garnered Fleming about $650 million in wholesale volume from the Furr's stores operating in Texas, New Mexico, and Oklahoma. Soon, however, Fleming relinquished the top spot in U.S. food distribution to Supervalu Inc.—based in Eden Prairie, Minnesota—when Supervalu, in 1992, acquired Wetterau Inc. of St. Louis in a $1.1 billion deal.

Fleming also lagged behind Supervalu in profitability, in part because Supervalu had a larger retail operation (retail marketing typically provides higher margins than wholesaling). In early 1992, Fleming derived only seven percent of its revenues from retail, compared to 20 percent for Supervalu. Over the next several years, however, Fleming would dramatically increase its retail base.

In mid-1992 Fleming spent $50 million to acquire a ten-store chain in Omaha, Nebraska—Baker's Supermarket. This was the company's first retail purchase in several years. The following year, Fleming signed a long-term (six-year) deal with Kmart to supply Super Kmart Centers with food products in those areas in which Fleming operates.

Early in 1994, Fleming began a major reengineering effort under the guidance of new company president and CEO, Robert E. Stauth. As originally envisioned, the program focused on downsizing and streamlining operations, including a nine percent (2,000-employee) workforce reduction, the closure of five regional sales offices, and a reduction in operating costs of $65 million per year. This effort had only begun to be implemented when officials at Scrivner Inc., then the number three U.S. food wholesaler, approached Fleming about a possible sale. On June 1, the two Oklahoma City–based companies announced that Fleming would pay Scrivner's owner, the German firm Franz Haniel & Cie, GmbH, $1.085 billion for all of Scrivner's stock.

The Scrivner acquisition catapulted Fleming back to the number one position with revenues of $19 billion, surpassing the $16 billion of Supervalu. The deal also brought Fleming an increased national presence by adding seven specific markets to the company's domain: Iowa, the Carolinas, western Pennsylvania, New York, Illinois, and Minnesota. Perhaps most important, however, was Scrivner's large retail operation, which increased Fleming's retail revenue to 15 percent of total revenue, derived from a combined total of 315 corporate retail stores. Fleming quickly bolstered its retail sector further when it ac-

quired controlling interest in CMI in August 1994. CMI operated 24 stores primarily in Missouri, but with operations in Arkansas and Kansas as well. These stores garnered $225 million in annual revenue, bringing Fleming close to the $3 billion level in retail.

Following the acquisition of Scrivner, the company reengineering program was expanded into a consolidation effort as well. With 21 Scrivner distribution centers added to 31 existing ones, Fleming closed eight redundant centers for a final total of 44. Back on the reengineering side, Fleming announced early in 1995 a new approach to selling, called the Flexible Marketing Plan, whereby retail customers would be charged Fleming's net acquisition cost of goods plus the costs of storage, handling, delivery, and other services used by the customer. Another reengineering effort involved an aggressive approach to gaining new customers through a newly created New Sales Development organization.

In 1996 Fleming enhanced its retail operation again with the acquisition of ABCO Markets, a 71-supermarket chain in Arizona. This increased the company's retail sector to 21 percent of total revenues. Fleming was thus closing in on a goal it had recently set to increase retail to 25 percent of total revenue by the year 2000.

Fleming then suffered a potentially severe blow when the company was found guilty of fraud, breach of contract, and deceptive practices in a case brought by David's Supermarkets based in Grandview, Texas, a customer which accused Fleming of inflating manufacturer's prices and overcharging David's. It was estimated that damages could exceed $200 million, but Fleming received at least a temporary reprieve when the judge in the case ordered a new trial after Fleming discovered that the judge had had past financial dealings with David's and should have excused himself. Nevertheless, the judgment had an immediate impact as Fleming's stock moved down sharply, and the company reduced its dividend for the first quarter of 1996 by 93 percent. On the heels of the David's suit came a class action suit filed against Fleming charging violations of securities laws for not disclosing the existence of the David's suit; although filed in August 1993, Fleming did not disclose the suit until about the time of the jury's verdict. The company's potential difficulties were compounded by the high debt load taken on in order to purchase Scrivner's and earnings that were lagging because of the major reengineering efforts.

The late 1990s will be a critical time for Fleming Companies. The outcome of the various lawsuits and the success or failure of its reengineering efforts will go a long way toward determining whether Fleming can maintain its top position in food wholesaling.

Principal Subsidiaries

Baker's Supermarkets, Inc.; Certified Bakers; Fleming Co. of Nebraska, Inc.; Fleming Finance Corp.; Fleming Foods of Alabama, Inc.; Fleming Foods of Missouri, Inc.; Fleming Foods of Ohio, Inc.; Fleming Foods of Pennsylvania, Inc.; Fleming Foods of Tennessee, Inc.; Fleming Foods of Texas, Inc.; Fleming Foods West; General Merchandise Distributors, Inc.; Fleming Company; Clearwater Mill, Inc.; Consumers Markets Inc.;

Crestwood Bakery; Hub City Foods; Sentry Drugs, Inc.; Sentry Market, Inc.; Store Equipment, Inc.; Malone & Hyde, Inc.; Megamarkets, Inc.; Hyde Insurance Agency, Inc.; M & H Financial Corp.; Piggly Wiggly Corp.; Royal Food Distributors, Inc.

Further Reading

Bennett, Stephen, "Aiming for $1 Billion," *Progressive Grocer,* January 1995, p. 103.

"Fleming Sees Its Future," *U.S. Distribution Journal,* March 15, 1994, p. 31.

"Fleming's 'Strategic' Buy," *U.S. Distribution Journal,* July 15, 1994, p. 9.

Friend, Janin, "Fleming Sifts Options after $200 Million Legal Defeat," *Supermarket News,* March 25, 1996, p. 1.

Garry, Michael, "Linchpin of the New Fleming," *Progressive Grocer,* January 1995, p. 57.

Jones, Kathryn, "A Move along the Food Chain: A Large Wholesaler Expands into Retail," *New York Times,* July 2, 1994, p. 17(N), p. 33(L).

Margulis, Ronald A., "The Trials of Staying No. 1," *U.S. Distribution Journal,* September 15, 1990, p. 26.

Mathews, Ryan, "Bloodied but Unbowed," *Progressive Grocer,* May 1996, p. 48.

—updated by David E. Salamie

Foamex

Foamex International Inc.

1000 Columbia Avenue
Linwood, Pennsylvania 19061
U.S.A.
(610) 859-3000; (800) 776-FOAM
Internet: http://www.foamex.com

Public Company
Incorporated: 1993
Employees: 5,600
Sales: $1.3 billion (1995)
Stock Exchanges: NASDAQ
SICs: 2821 Plastics Materials & Resins; 6719 Holding
    Companies, Not Elsewhere Classified

Foamex International Inc. (FMXI) is North America's largest manufacturer and marketer of flexible polyurethane foam and foam products, through its subsidiary, Foamex L.P. Its foams are used in four markets: carpet cushions and other carpet products (it controls approximately 36 percent of the carpet cushion market); cushioning foams for furniture, bedding, packaging, and health care; automotive foams for protective material in headliners and doors, seat upholstery, floor mats, sound absorbers, and interior trims, with about a 60 percent market share; and technical foams for products ranging from batteries to baby diapers. In November 1995, the company decided to focus completely on its core foam products through its Continuous Improvement Process program. As a result, FMXI put on the market its subsidiary, JPS Automotive L.P., which makes carpets and other textiles for the automobile industry, and its subsidiary, Perfect Fit Industries, a manufacturer of mattress pads, pillows, and draperies. It sold Perfect Fit in 1996. Foamex International is ultimately controlled by Marshall Cogan through his holding company, Trace International Holdings, Inc. The company conducts its operations in 43 locations in the United States, Mexico, and Canada. Revenues in 1995 were $1.3 billion.

Early History

In 1983, "21" International Holdings, owned by financiers Marshall Cogan and Stephen Swid, bought Scott Paper's foam division, its first investment in the polyurethane foam industry.

Foam sales in 1984 came to $82 million. In 1986, Cogan and Swid split up. Swid bought the music publishing division of CBS Inc., and Cogan, who kept most of the conglomerate's assets, bought Foamex Products, a former division of Firestone Tire & Rubber. Two years later he added three regional foam producers: Miller Companies' Millfoam, Sheller-Globe's Tupelo, and Reeves Brothers' Curon. By 1989, Cogan had built foam sales to $422 million. In 1990 he acquired a U.S. foam business owned by Recticel S.A., the largest European foam producer. To consolidate his growing foam activities, Cogan created a holding company, Foamex L.P.

1991–1994: A Growing Company

With the passage of the Clean Air Act at the beginning of the decade, foam manufacturers had to reduce emissions during their production process. In 1992, Foamex L.P., in partnership with Recticel S.A. of Belgium and equipment supplier Beamach Group Ltd., began working on a new technology to eliminate chlorofluorocarbons and volatile organic blowing agents from the production of flexible foam.

Meanwhile, Cogan kept buying companies for Foamex L.P. In 1993, the company made three big acquisitions: Great Western Foam Co., a major foam producer on the West Coast; General Felt Industries, a leading manufacturer of carpet cushions; and Perfect Fit Industries, a North Carolina company that made and distributed decorative bedding, pillows, mattress pads, and drapes. In September 1993, Cogan created Foamex International Inc. in order to acquire a 99 percent interest in Foamex L.P. and, in December, completed an initial public offering. Foamex International acquired a direct 95 percent limited partnership interest in Foamex L.P., and FMXI, Inc., a wholly owned subsidiary of the company, acquired a four percent managing general partnership interest.

In March 1994, the company bought TEFSA (Transformación De Espumas Y Fiéltros S.A. de C.V.), a leading Mexican foam manufacturer, for $4.5 million. In June, it bought JPS Automotive, a leading supplier of automotive textiles, including molded floor carpet systems, headliner fabric, airbag fabric, and other interior and trunk trim components. The total JPS Auto cost was approximately $264 million.

Company Perspectives:

Our mission is to be the premier supplier of foam and related products in markets in which we compete; to maintain our dominant market position in North America, and by the year 2000 to be the premier global company supplying products that add comfort and value; to maintain good employee relations; and to develop, produce and market innovative products that provide comfort and value to our customers.

Foamex International appeared to be well positioned with the vertical integration of its new subsidiaries. The purchase of Perfect Fit increased the company's access to products using cushioning foams, one of the largest product categories in the polyurethane industry. Scott Star, Perfect Fit's director of merchandising, explained the benefits in a March 1994 interview with *HFN*. "As a subsidiary of Foamex International, Perfect Fit produces the raw materials that are used in its products, possesses unsurpassed processing capabilities and quality standards, and is armed with a vast distribution network. . . . These strengths . . . will allow Perfect Fit to deliver innovative, feature-rich products at highly competitive prices." With money and equipment from its new parent, the Perfect Fit Home Comfort Products division opened three new manufacturing plants.

General Felt Industries was the leader in the $800 million carpet cushion industry, making all types of padding to go under carpets: rubber, natural felt, synthetic felt, recycled textile fiber cushion, and both prime and recycled polyurethane cushion. In 1994, Foamex engineers developed a prime polyurethane carpet cushion that absorbed shocks better because of its unique hexagonal design containing five times as many air pockets as other prime cushions. In a departure from normal practice within the industry, Foamex gave the new cushion a brand name, Comfort-Wear, and launched a print and television advertising campaign aimed at consumers. According to the ads, ComfortWear offered a more luxurious feel than standard padding and was 40 percent more durable. Its ability to extend the life of a carpet allowed Foamex to offer a five-year warranty on any no-mat/no-crush carpeting installed on it. By combining the ads with promotional displays at major floor covering retailers, people buying carpet asked for ComfortWear by name, a first for carpet padding.

The acquisitions helped 1994 sales grow to $1.08 billion, up from $696 million in 1993. In late 1994, however, prices for raw materials such as TDI and polyol began to climb. By the fourth quarter of 1995, Foamex was paying about 70 cents a pound for polyol, 25 percent more than the year before, and about $1 for a pound of TDI, a 30 percent hike. These were the highest prices in 13 years. Although the company could pass on about half the added costs to its own customers, it was having to absorb the remainder, approximately $25 million. At the same time, carpet sales weakened, causing a drop in the volume of carpet cushion needed by retailers. Although net sales for 1995 were higher than in 1994, most of that was due to the increase in automotive textiles sales resulting from a full year of operations for JPS Automotive. Gross profit, on the other hand, decreased 13.4 percent.

The company was also confronted with various legal problems. Bulk foam purchased from Foamex L.P. and Trace Holdings was used to make a polyurethane foam covering for certain silicone gel implants. As a result, Foamex L.P. and Trace Holdings, along with other defendants, were parties in suits filed on behalf of more than 4,000 recipients of breast implants. Foamex L.P. was also one of several defendants accused of violating Tennessee hazardous waste regulations at its plant in Morristown.

1995 and Beyond: New Focus, New Products

As chemical prices began to rise, Foamex International's support of new technologies began to pay off. The Foamex/Recticel/Beamach research partnership came up with a new, proprietary production method called variable pressure foaming (VPF). Foamex installed its first VPF line in Mississippi in 1994. The new process was important in two ways. First, it exceeded the federal emission standards for eliminating chlorofluorocarbons and volatile organic blowing agents. Second, it made it possible to create foam with new types of molecular structures that gave them unique mass and hardness characteristics no one else in North America could duplicate.

Under conventional production methods, TDI and polyol were combined with water and poured onto an open conveyor mold. In VPF, production took place in a closed chamber, which eliminated chlorofluorocarbons from production, making the manufacturing of flexible foam environmentally friendly.

The closed chamber also provided direct control of air pressure, temperature, and humidity, any of which can be regulated to change the density of the foam. As the foam rose, its density was determined by the pressure in the chamber. The higher the chamber pressure, the higher the density of the foam; the lower the pressure, the lower the density. As a result, the process could produce low-density, ultrasoft foams not previously available. In addition, the foams coming out of the chamber were free of defects. "We're creating whole new polymers," Vincent Bonaddio, Foamex's manager of research applications development, told *Plastics World* a May 1996 article.

By 1996, the company had developed three new categories of foams with VPF: Ultrafirm, Ultrasoft, and Breathable. New markets opened by VPF included replacement products for the polyester fiberfill used in upholstered furniture and bed pillows, alternatives for polystyrene and polyethylene packaging materials, and a new, breathable polymer for medical and consumer applications. Action Furniture by Lane was one of the first customers for the new products, using a VPF product with very low compression in certain recliners. Berkline and King Hickory soon followed, using VPF on upholstered furniture products. The new product was popular because it did not mat or lose shape as quickly as fiberfill.

Foamex engineers also used VPF in their efforts to design a more energy-absorbent polymer for the automobile industry. In August 1995 new federal safety regulations began requiring car makers to provide better head protection inside cars and light trucks and greater side impact protection over the next five years. "We had the technology set to go when the regulations came out," a Foamex manager told *U.S. Auto Scene*. Foamex's energy-absorbent foams were already being used by Ford and Chrysler in dashboards and door panels. And scientists at Lawrence Livermore Laboratory, a federal energy and military research facility, were conducting computer modeling of the VPF process to help find the most efficient polymers as quickly as possible. Industry observers saw the regulations adding $40 million per year to the foam market, and the company saw opportunities for introducing energy-absorbing forms into side support pillars, headliners, and sun visors.

A second patented technology was developed by Foamex and JPS Automotive. Surface Modified Technology (SMT) gave Foamex the ability to produce foams with very economical and unique surface cuts. "For the first time, we can create multiple patterns, spaces and depth-of-cut in a single process throughout the entire top surface of a piece of foam," Bonaddio explained in an article in the August 1, 1994 issue of *HFN*. The 1997 all-purpose vans from General Motors featured an SMT foam-backed carpet with a cut for the oil pan, allowing a nearly flat floor. The carpet also reduced overall vehicle weight by two to six pounds per vehicle and cut noise by up to four decibels, twice that of conventionally backed carpet systems. Outside the automotive area, Perfect Fit used SMT in its PowerPuff and PowerPuff Plus bed support pillows as well as in its tri-zone and single-zone foam mattress cushions. GTI's ComfortWear pad was also an SMT product.

The third area in which Foamex introduced innovations was composites technology. This involved fusing foam with other materials, usually fabric or carpeting. Most of the new composites products were developed for the automotive industry, such as cabin filters and package shelves. One of the most important products was CustomFit, a composite process that made it possible to attach foam to fabric by heat, using a flame. This eliminated the costly cut-and-sew process and was first used in manufacturing headliners, the cushioning between the car roof and occupants' heads. CustomFit headliners were made from layers of polyurethane, fabric, and encapsulated fiber mat and weighed less and were easier to handle and install than traditional fiberglass headliners. The first cars using the new headliners included the Chrysler minivan, the Jeep Grand Cherokee, and the Ford Taurus and Sable.

As all this was going on, Cogan and John Rallis, president and chief operating officer of Foamex International, brought in a new leader for Foamex L.P. In July 1995 they selected Salvatore ("Sam") Bonanno, a 30-year international manufacturing veteran of Chrysler, to be Foamex's executive vice-president of manufacturing and president of Foamex L.P.

Bonanno joined a company heavily in debt from its acquisitions. Chemical prices kept increasing, competition intensified, and manufacturing facilities were not fully utilized. The company had grown quickly, particularly since 1993, but was not able to maintain its profit margin. Management undertook an examination of the company's operations, and in October 1995, the Board of Directors agreed to focus the company on its core operations and reduce its total debt of $723 million to around $400 million.

The board approved a plan to consider selling JPS Automotive and Perfect Fit Industries. It also initiated a three-part plan to try to improve the profitability of the company's foam products segment through restructuring. First, the company introduced its Continuous Improvement Plan (CIP). As described in the 1995 annual report, the CIP "requires Foamex employees to rethink each step of the manufacturing, distribution and marketing process, eliminating unnecessary procedures and constantly seeking ways to improve the quality of our products and level of our service." To implement the plan, the company created an office of quality and productivity responsible for employee training and CIP oversight. At the same time, the company began closing underused facilities, including the consolidation of 13 foam production, fabrication, or branch locations, and increased efforts to control costs. From these activities the company hoped to save $30 million in 1996 and more than $50 million per year after that.

By the second quarter of 1996, the company was reporting record net sales of $616.3 million and savings of $11 million. Chemical prices had stabilized, and there was greater demand for carpet cushions and automotive foam. In August, Foamex completed the sale of Perfect Fit Industries for $50 million to PFI Acquisition Corp., an investor group led by Perfect Fit's senior management. The sale of JPS Automotive, however, was still pending.

Part of the company's long-term strategy was to expand its markets outside North America. In June the company announced a strategic alliance with Recticel S.A. to design, manufacture, and market products for the auto industry in Europe and North America. Both companies would provide auto suppliers on both continents with their products. These products included roll goods, energy absorbing foams, foams for headliners, and SMT acoustical foam components for automobile carpets.

In August Foamex International announced another international initiative, the creation of a new division, Foamex Asia. Stephen Scibelli was named president of the division and charged with expanding the company's presence in China, Indonesia, Malaysia, the Philippines, Singapore, and Thailand.

With its cost reduction plan, restructuring, and international expansion, Foamex appeared to be on the road to financial health, according to various analysts. The major risks were the cyclical nature of its markets and the potential for increases in the price of raw materials.

Principal Subsidiaries

Foamex, L.P. (99%); General Felt Industries, Inc.; Great Western Foam Products Corp.; JPS Automotive L.P.

Principal Divisions

Foamex Canada Inc.; Foamex Latin America Inc.; Foamex Asia Inc.

Further Reading

Button, Graham, "Marshall Makes Out," *Forbes,* November 23, 1992, p. 104.
"Foamex International Completes Sale of Perfect Fit Industries," New York: Foamex International, Inc., August 1, 1996 (Press Release).

"Foamex International Plans To Expand Presence into Asia-Pacific Rim," New York: Foamex International, Inc., August 12, 1996 (Press Release).

"Foamex International Inc. Reports Record Results for Second Quarter 1996," New York: Foamex International, Inc., July 24, 1996 (Press Release).

Frinton, Sandra, "A Perfect Fit Bid: Managers Plan To Make Offer," *HFN: The Weekly Newspaper for the Home Furnishing Network,* December 18, 1995, p. 19.

Keenan, Tim, "Strategic Foam: Foamex, JPS Alliance Is Paying Dividends," *Ward's Auto World,* June 1995, p. 45.

Khermouch, Gerry, "Carpet Pads Crave Brand Image," *Brandweek,* February 28, 1994, p. 4.

Maio, Patrick J., "Getting a Cushion from Cost-Cutting," *Investor's Business Daily,* August 26, 1996.

"New Head Impact Rules Spur Research," *Automotive & Transportation Interiors,* April 1996, p. 28.

"New Surface Process from Foamex Debuts," *HFD—The Weekly Home Furnishings Newspaper,* August 1, 1994, p. 38.

"Recticel S.A. and Foamex International Enter into Strategic Alliance," New York: Foamex International Inc., June 19, 1996 (Press Release).

Sorge, Margorie, and Norman Martin, "Quiet, Please," *Automotive Industries,* September 1995, p. 67.

Slutsker, Gary, "The Sour Smell of Success," *Forbes,* January 26, 1987, p. 54.

Smock, Doug, "Foamex Develops New Flexible Urethane Polymers," *Plastics World,* May 1996, p. 12.

Wattman, Karla, "Perfect Fit Readies Foam Entries," *HFD—The Weekly Home Furnishings Newspaper,* March 28, 1994, p. 43.

Weber, Joseph, "Chemicals: The Cauldron Is Brimming with Profits," *Business Week,* January 9, 1995.

Werner, Johannes, "Auto Interior Suppliers Look at Regulations," *U.S. Auto Scene,* May 13, 1996.

Woods, Wilton, "Cushy Carpet Cushion," *Fortune,* June 27, 1994, p. 131.

Zweig, Jason, "The New Marshall Plan," *Forbes,* October 15, 1990, p. 216.

—Ellen D. Wernick

Forever Living Products International Inc.

P.O. Box 29041
Phoenix, Arizona 85038
U.S.A.
(602) 968-3999
Internet: http://www.foreverlivingproducts.com/

Private Company
Incorporated: 1978
Employees: 1,536
Sales: $1.1 billion (1995)
SICs: 2844 Toilet Preparations; 5999 Miscellaneous
Retail Stores, Not Elsewhere Classified

With more than $1 billion in annual sales, Forever Living Products International Inc. is Arizona's largest privately held company and one of the world's largest direct marketers. The nearly 20-year-old firm has millions of representatives in North and South America, Europe, Africa, Asia, and Australia. Forever Living's product line includes aloe vera-based drinks, lotions, supplements, cosmetics, and detergents. The company owns 5,000 acres of aloe plantations and facilities capable of processing 6,000 gallons of raw aloe each day. Forever Living also owns and operates more than a dozen resorts and attractions, including Dallas's Southfork Ranch.

Late 1970s Origins

The company was founded in 1978 by Rex Maughan. Raised on a farm in Idaho, Maughan worked his way through Arizona State University, earning a degree in business administration with a concentration in accounting in 1962. Upon graduation, Maughan served as a Mormon missionary in Western Samoa. Back home, he started as an accountant in a Phoenix firm and then entered the real estate industry in 1964. Three years later, he took a top management position with real estate developer Del E. Webb Corporation. After ten years there, however, Maughan realized that he was not likely to rise to that company's presidency, so he started to look into creating his own enterprise.

Before deciding on a product or service, he focused on devising a marketing plan. Maughan quickly homed in on multilevel marketing, researching well-known direct sales firms like Avon, Amway, Tupperware, and Shaklee. Also known as MLM or network marketing, multilevel marketing is a method of direct selling whereby each distributor/salesman brought into the company brings in several new distributor/salesmen who become part of his "downline." The original distributor makes profits not only on his own sales, but also earns commissions on downline sales. A key advantage of this strategy is that it relies on word-of-mouth networking for growth, thereby eliminating the need for an advertising budget.

Although the direct sales industry in general and MLM in particular have been blighted by illegal pyramid schemes, several standards guide the operation of lawful organizations. A company must offer a legitimate product or service that is fairly priced to distributors; offer commissions on sales, as opposed to downline sponsorships; provide sales and recruitment training; and not exaggerate earnings potential. The Federal Trade Commission legalized multilevel marketers who adhered to these guidelines in 1979.

Maughan first got involved with multilevel marketing as a distributor selling gasoline additives in his free time, but soon observed that "most [network marketing companies] seemed to be top-heavy—designed to benefit the guys who founded them. So I started developing my own plan for a company." He and an associate who had some experience in the field drew up a business plan and started recruiting their own downlines in 1978.

Only after they settled on a marketing scheme did the two partners seek a product. Maughan was convinced that they needed to offer something expendable to encourage repeat sales. In a 1995 interview with *Success* magazine's Duncan Maxwell Anderson, the Forever Living founder reflected, "Water purifiers and burglar alarms were very popular, then, but I didn't want anything that wasn't consumable. I was interested in health products and thought other people might be, too. But I didn't want a me-too item like diet products, soaps, or vitamins." Maughan found what he thought was an ideal candidate—aloe vera.

Commonly known as the "first aid plant" or the "burn plant," aloe vera is a succulent whose juicy middle has been used cosmetically and medically for centuries. The Bible notes that aloe was used to anoint Jesus' body before it was entombed, and other sources claim that the substance was used by Cleopatra and Alexander the Great. Maughan stumbled upon a group of doctors in Dallas who had developed a method of stabilizing and storing the highly perishable aloe gel, which they used in a sunburn lotion. The Dallas group, Aloe Vera of America, had been trying to sell its product in health food stores with little success. Maughan and his partner believed that the products would benefit from the direct selling method, which relies heavily on demonstrations, testimonials, and word-of-mouth sales.

Maughan, who continued to hold his day job with Del Webb, rented an office in Phoenix and warehoused product in his garage. From an initial investment of $10,000 in 1978, he and his partner recruited about 40 people who sold $700,000 worth of aloe-based products under the Forever Living name that first year. Within just two years, annual sales had increased to more than $30 million. Feeling confident that he had achieved "financial freedom," a 43-year-old Maughan quit Del Webb to concentrate on Forever Living Products (FLP) full time in 1980.

Growth Accelerates in the 1980s

In 1981, Forever Living Products purchased Aloe Vera of America's patents, its cosmetic production plant, and its field processing operations. From 1980 to 1981, the company's sales more than doubled to more than $71 million, ranking FLP among America's fastest growing firms. This rapid expansion drew the attention of "dozens" of brokers seeking to take the company public or merge it with another firm. But Maughan was not ready to cash out. In the mid-1980s, he reflected, "I was not interested then, nor now. I'm still in it to help other people." Of course, every person Maughan "helps" brings him increased profits, too. As Forbes's Christopher Palmeri noted in his August 1995 article on Forever Living Products and its founder, "More money works its way to the top than stays at the bottom. The big money is not in selling the stuff, but in recruiting people to sell the stuff." In 1983, Maughan solidified his position at the top by buying out his partner's half interest.

Forever Living Products exceeded $100 million in revenues and 500 employees by 1985, when the company had more than 1,000 acres of aloe growing in Texas's Lower Rio Grande Valley. By this time, the company also owned processing plants and research labs in Dallas, a fleet of trucks, and an official headquarters in Tempe.

Capitalizing on his experience as head of recreational properties at Del Webb, Maughan formed a resort division in 1981. By the mid-1990s, Forever Living owned 18 resorts in Nevada, Missouri, Kentucky, Texas, California, Wyoming, Arkansas, Colorado, Indiana, Arizona, and Georgia. Properties included Southfork Ranch, made famous in the "Dallas" television series. Maughan bought the ranch from its cash-strapped owner at auction in 1992 and refurbished it to feature a convention center, "Dallas" museum, and rodeo. Cut-rate trips to the resorts are used as rewards for productive Forever Living representatives and are also open to the public.

Maughan refined Forever Living's MLM plan over the years. By the mid-1990s, sales people were ranked from beginner-level "Distributor" to high-flying "Double Diamond Manager." The company supported these representatives with training materials ranging from booklets and videotapes to "ForeverVision," a bimonthly satellite broadcast featuring product information and motivational programs. In addition to downline bonuses, distributors had the potential to earn vacations to Forever Resorts, autos, electronics, and other incentives.

Product and Geographic Diversification Drives Continued Growth in the 1990s

Although aloe is most commonly used topically, Forever Living's key product has been its aloe vera beverage. The substance has long been used as a purgative agent, to which Maughan may have been referring when he asserted, "Aloe vera helps our bodies perform like they are supposed to." By the mid-1990s, the company had developed three flavors of aloe "juice": cranberry, apple, and natural. Although Forever Living promotes the natural flavor as "exotic," Christopher Palmeri characterized the taste as more near that of "turpentine" in his 1995 piece. The nutritional benefits of aloe consumption remain debatable. Some doctors note that aloe products are at worst ineffective, while others, like Mount Sinai School of Medicine's Dr. Victor Herbert, have asserted, "There is no reason for humans to drink it." Aloe drinks generated about 50 percent of Forever Living's annual sales into the mid-1990s.

The company also made dozens of skin care products from aloe, including lotions, creams, soaps, hair care products, deodorant, aftershave, lip balm, and a burn treatment. Other aloe-based goods included toothpaste, colognes and perfumes, and laundry detergent.

FLP launched its line of Forever Bee Products in 1983. At the core of this group of nutritional supplements is "Royal Jelly," a food created by honeybees especially for the queen bee. Some scientists attribute the queen bee's growth, reproductive ability, and comparative longevity to her consumption of royal jelly. The company offered royal jelly in 250 mg tablets, bee pollen (the worker bees' food source) in 500 mg tablets, bee propolis (from the walls of the hive) in 500 mg tablets, and pure honey. Forever Living made absolutely no claims that humans who consumed these products would obtain the same health benefits apparently enjoyed by the bees, making assurances only about the source, potency, quality, and purity.

Although the founder has asserted that, initially, he was not interested in selling vitamins and diet products, nutritional supplements would become an important segment of the Forever Living line. The company combined aloe with vitamins, ginseng, minerals, fish oils, garlic, and other substances to make an array of nutritional supplements. Forever Living's promotions were peppered with pseudo-scientific terms like "flavonoid extract" and "bioflavonoids," but the most the company would guarantee was that its products would "make people feel better and more beautiful."

Forever Living took even greater pains to avoid making specific health claims in the wake of a 1992 lawsuit. That year, the Texas state attorney general brought suit against the company, charging that a Spanish language infomercial made unfounded claims that consumption of aloe could control diabetes.

Having fleshed out its product lines, Forever Living began to diversify geographically in 1983. The company focused first on the Far East, where natural remedies enjoy a strong heritage and high esteem. By 1995, FLP had distributors in 40 countries.

Although Rex Maughan calls his company "the best-kept secret in Arizona," Forever Living's fame grew in line with its sales in the late 1980s and early 1990s. Revenues mounted from $100 million in 1985 to more than $200 million in 1990 and surpassed $1 billion in 1995. Although some observers warned that multilevel marketing could reach a saturation point, where virtually everyone was a distributor, there seemed no limit to Forever Living's growth.

Further Reading

Anderson, Duncan Maxwell, "Invisible Giant," *Success,* September 1995, pp. 20–22.
——, "The Secret War: Regulators Are on the March Against MLM," *Success,* July–August 1993, p. 12.
Huston, Jenni, "No. 2 Private Company Is 'Best-Kept Secret' in State," *The Business Journal—Serving Phoenix & The Valley of the Sun,* November 12, 1993, p. 23.
Marth, Del, "A Sales Plan Gels," *Nation's Business,* January 1986, pp. 89–90.
Palmeri, Christopher, "The Aloe Juice Man," *Forbes,* August 14, 1995, pp. 98–99.
Schultz, Leslie, "A Good Garage Is Hard to Find," *Inc.,* April 1983, pp. 91–97.

—April Dougal Gasbarre

Fossil, Inc.

2280 North Greenville Avenue
Richardson, Texas 75082
U.S.A.
(214) 234-2525
Fax: (214) 348-1366

Public Company
Incorporated: 1984 as Overseas Products International
Employees: 555
Sales: $181.1 million (1995)
Stock Exchanges: NASDAQ
SICs: 3873 Watches, Clocks, Watchcases & Parts; 3171
   Women's Handbags & Purses; 2389 Apparel &
   Accessories, Not Elsewhere Classified

Owner of one of the most popular brand names in the United States, Fossil, Inc., designs, markets, and distributes fashion watches, leather goods, sunglasses, and other merchandise for retail sale on an international basis. Fossil grew quickly during the 1980s, propelled by the retrospective designs of its watches, which were inspired by magazine advertisements from the 1930s, 1940s, and 1950s. After recording phenomenal success with the sale of its watches in the United States, the company entered international markets and diversified its product line to include leather goods and sunglasses during the 1990s. In addition to marketing merchandise under the Fossil brand name, the company also marketed a line of less expensive fashion watches under the Relic label.

Fossil's 1984 Beginning

Founded in 1984, Fossil represented the second entrepreneurial effort launched by Tom Kartsotis, a Texas A&M dropout living in Dallas. When he was in his early twenties, Kartsotis and a partner operated a ticket brokerage business in Dallas, where the two entrepreneurs enjoyed moderate success by hawking tickets to Dallas Cowboy football games and other events. But "I didn't want to be a 30-year-old ticket scalper," Kartsotis confided to *Forbes* a decade after founding the business that would launch him toward fame and wealth. The inspiration that led Kartsotis into his second business venture came from a suggestion by his older brother, Kosta Kartsotis, a merchandising executive at Sanger Harris, a large, Dallas-based department store chain. Kosta told Tom about the large profits that could be made from importing retail goods made in the Far East, particularly the money that could be made in importing moderately-priced fashion watches. At the time of Kosta Kartsotis' suggestion, Swiss-based Swatch watches were the rage of the day, enjoying international popularity as trendy fashionable timepieces. Tom Kartsotis was intrigued enough by his brother's comments to withdraw his savings and sell his half of the ticket brokerage business, which gave the young entrepreneur $200,000 to start his new business.

Tom Kartsotis flew to Hong Kong without any concrete plans about his business future except to investigate the possibilities of starting an import/export business. During his travels around Hong Kong, Kartsotis explored various import/export possibilities, including dealing in stuffed animals and toys, but finally settled on the suggestion made by his brother. Kartsotis hired a Hong Kong manufacturer to produce 1,500 watches and brought the products back to the United States where he sold the watches to Dallas department stores and boutiques. These sales marked the fledgling moments of his new company, Overseas Products International.

Shortly after embarking on his new enterprise, the 24-year-old Kartsotis hired a friend, Lynne Stafford, as Overseas Products' designer and created the "retro" design style that predicated the company's existence and fueled its growth throughout the 1980s and into the 1990s. With Kartsotis at the helm, the company grew exponentially during the 1980s by attracting consumers with designs reminiscent of an era only their parents or grandparents had live through. Targeting middle- and upper-income consumers in their teens, twenties, and thirties, Kartsotis and Stafford designed watches that imitated the styles of the 1930s, 1940s, and 1950s. For inspiration, Kartsotis and Stafford (who were later married) pored over old issues of *Look, Life,* and *Time* magazines, taking careful note of the fashion styles illustrated in advertisements and devising a design concept that was embraced by a new generation of consumers.

Company Perspectives:

The company's primary objective is to create value by building the FOSSIL brand name.

Before consumers could flock to their local stores and snatch up Fossil watches, Kartsotis needed to broaden and deepen his distribution network. The watch designs touched a nostalgic chord in the hearts of the company's early customers, but the company itself was little more than a startup venture just emerging on the retail scene, unable to attract legions of consumers. With financing from Asian manufacturers and after several years of peddling his products to an increasingly greater number of retailers, however, Kartsotis' company stood on the brink of explosive growth. By 1987, Fossil, Inc., as the company was now called, was collecting $2 million in sales a year after having established a solid reputation among Texas retailers. Kosta Kartsotis joined the company in 1988, midway through the most prolific period of growth in Fossil's short history. Kosta Kartsotis' job was to help the company sells its watches to department stores—the area of his expertise—and ensure that as many retailers as possible stocked Fossil watches.

Explosive Late 1980s Growth

By the end of the decade, there was ample evidence that the efforts toward increasing Fossil's distribution network were successful. In 1989, the company generated $20 million in sales, having increased its revenue volume tenfold in two years, and made one important change in its marketing approach that spurred further growth in the years ahead. In 1989, the company began packaging its watches in elaborately decorated tin containers and wooden boxes, which strengthened the nostalgic appeal of Fossil merchandise. To further excite consumer demand, a marketing campaign was launched featuring Fossil watches on the wrists of models engaged in adventurous activities in exotic settings, an approach that evoked comparisons to the popular mystique surrounding the "Indiana Jones" films.

The leap from $2 million to $20 million in sales between 1987 and 1989 bred irrepressible optimism for the 1990s, as the company quickly evolved from an entrepreneurial whim to a fast-rising company attracting considerable attention from the retail business press. As with any company able to register robust financial growth, an equal, if not greater pace of expansion was expected in the future, something Kartsotis hoped to achieve during the 1990s by penetrating international markets, expanding domestically, and diversifying into other product lines.

Early 1990s

During the first few months of the 1990s, Fossil was deriving nearly all its business from selling watches in the United States. Roughly three percent of the company's sales came from international markets when the decade began, but this would soon change. So too would its reliance on the sale of watches as the sole source of revenue. In 1990, the company introduced a line of leather goods and it introduced a new brand of watches. The line of leather goods expanded as the years passed, growing to include handbags, wallets, and belts, among other items, while the new watch brand, Relic, was marketed as a lower-priced alternative to Fossil watches and sold to retail chains such as Sears and J.C. Penney. Concurrent with the introduction of these two new lines, Fossil began to develop its international business more diligently, moving into Europe first, where it established a subsidiary in Traunstein, Germany. Although the push overseas had begun, it would be several years before the company possessed adequate financial resources to expand internationally with vigor.

Enviable sales growth continued as Fossil entered the 1990s, with sales climbing from $20 million in 1989 to $32.5 million in 1990. A greater increase was recorded the following year, when sales leaped to $57.1 million, as the strength of the Fossil brand name increased and drove sales upward. Heightening the awareness of the Fossil name was one of the chief objectives of the company during the 1990s, and toward this goal Kartsotis achieved much by allying the Fossil name with one of the most well-known retailers in the country. In 1991, Macy's opened a 300-square-foot Fossil Watch "Super Shop" in one of the most ideal locations for a small, but fast-growing company to attract attention. Located on the main floor of Macy's flagship store in New York City, the Fossil shop represented a marketing boon for the Texas-based company, its debut a precursor to the retail outlets Fossil would open on its own during the mid-1990s.

Sales in 1992 jumped to $73.8 million, more than 90 percent of which was generated by the sale of Fossil and Relic watches. The company's foray into the design and marketing of leather goods accounted for less than five percent of total sales by this point, but this complementary side business would become more important to Fossil's bottom line in the near future. Although tremendous financial growth had been achieved during the first two years of the decade, Fossil had not yet expanded overseas in earnest nor pursued the strategic objectives that would describe the company's progress during the mid-1990s. International expansion, building brand name recognition, and strategic diversification became the mantra of Fossil's management during this period, but before these three objectives were fully embraced the company made a move that provided the financial resources to execute its plan for the future.

1993 Initial Public Offering

In June 1993, Fossil completed its initial public offering of stock, selling 20 percent of the company to investors, with Tom Kartsotis retaining 40.5 percent control over the company and his brother Kosta retaining 18.8 percent ownership. The proceeds from the conversion to public-ownership yielded Fossil $19 million, half of which was earmarked for reducing the company's debt, while the remainder was set aside as working capital.

The year of Fossil's initial public offering of stock proved to be a busy one for the nine-year-old company. By this point, Fossil was producing more than four million watches a year, the actual manufacture of which took place overseas and was conducted by contracted manufacturers. Retailing between $45 and $110 dollars, Fossil watches were sold at more than 2,000 locations, including the department store units of companies such as Carter Hawley Hales Stores, Dayton Hudson Corporation, Dillard Department Stores, Federated Department Stores, May Department Stores Company, and R.H. Macy, as well as specialty stores. Relic watches, on the other hand, were targeted for a different market, appearing in retail units operated by Ames Department Stores, J. C. Penney Co., Service Merchandise Co., and Target Stores. For these retailers and the growing numbers of Fossil customers, the company provided an ever-changing selection of Fossil merchandise, striving to ride the crest of the fashion wave. Fossil's 500-watch product line was revamped five times a year, giving consumers a vast selection of designs to choose from and refreshing the innovative yet retrospective design styles that fueled the company's financial growth.

It was this strong domestic business that the company sought to extend overseas during its inaugural year as a publicly-traded company. In 1993, Fossil operated several subsidiaries in Europe, led by Fossil Europe GmbH, the company's primary European operation located in Germany. Other subsidiary companies on the Continent included Fossil France SARL and Fossil Italia SRL, which served as Fossil's marketing and distribution entities in these countries. Fossil B.V. was formed in 1993 as a holding company for these three European subsidiaries, with Texas-based Fossil, Inc. controlling 70 percent of its newly formed European holding company.

The restructuring of Fossil's European operations was indicative of the company's intent to bolster its foreign sales, increase brand name recognition, and diversify product lines. In 1994, the company achieved strides in each direction through three noteworthy developments. Early in the year, Fossil announced plans to add a line of men's leather goods to its merchandise mix, scheduling the shipment of leather key fobs, money clips, and wallets to arrive in time for Father's Day. Next, in April, Fossil moved into what one company official described as "another substantial international market" by signing an agreement with rival Seiko Corporation. Under the terms of the five-year deal, Fossil gave Seiko the rights to distribute Fossil products in Japan through Fostim, a wholly owned subsidiary controlled by Seiko, thus allowing the Texas-based company entrance into the Japanese market. On the heels of this agreement with Seiko, Fossil announced its intention to open 150 concept shops within departments stores and also laid out future plans to increase the number of its outlets to 500 shops by 1996.

By the end of 1994, sales had reached $161.1 million, up dramatically from the $105.1 million generated in 1993. Despite the continued surge in sales, the company's anticipated rate of expansion was falling short of expectations. Domestic sales of Fossil watches were flagging as the company moved past its 10th anniversary year and into 1995, prompting Kartsotis and the rest of Fossil management to intensify their efforts toward increasing the market presence of the company on a worldwide basis and to continue diversifying. In the summer of 1995, Fossil introduced a line of sunglasses, lessening its reliance on watch sales to fuel growth, and in October increased its stake in Fossil B.V., the holding company

for the Fossil subsidiaries in Europe. By paying $1.7 million, Fossil increased its ownership in Fossil B.V. to 88 percent, giving the company more control in a region that was expected to compensate for fluctuating watch sales in the United States.

In 1995, the extensive line of Fossil fashion watches were sold in department stores and in other upscale retail settings in more than 50 countries, giving the company a broad geographic foundation to support its business. International sales, particularly those derived from European markets, were accounting for much of the company's sales growth by the end of 1995 as sales growth in the United States began to ebb. By early 1996, the company was operating 20 retail outlets compared to four units the year before and was counting on overseas markets to provide financial growth for the late 1990s. Toward this end, the company acquired 81 percent of the Seiko-owned Fostim in April 1996, paying $700,000 in cash to gain greater control over the distribution of Fossil products in Japan. Under Seiko's control, Fostim had placed Fossil products in more than 180 retail location in Japan. After the acquisition Fostim was renamed Fossil Japan and figured to be one of the primary areas of focus for Fossil as the company charted its plans for the late 1990s. Although prolific sales growth had characterized the company's existence during its first decade of business, the next decade was expected to bring more prosaic growth. Nevertheless, Fossil management was optimistic about the future of the company and the ability of the Fossil brand name and its distinctive image to attract consumers around the globe.

Principal Subsidiaries

Arrow Merchandising, Inc.; Fossil East Limited (Hong Kong); Fossil Intermediate, Inc.; Fossil New York, Inc.; Fossil Overseas, Ltd. (British Virgin Islands); Fossil Stores I, Inc.; Fossil Stores II, Inc.; Fossil Trust; Amazing Time, Ltd. (Hong Kong; 60%); Fossil Europe B.V. (Netherlands; 70%); Fossil Europe GmbH (Germany); Fossil Italia, S.r.L. (Italy; 60%); Pulse Time Center Company, Ltd. (Hong Kong; 60%); Trylink International, Ltd. (Hong Kong; 51%).

Further Reading

Barrett, William P., "Selling Nostalgia and Whimsy," *Forbes,* November 8, 1983, p. 224.
Bowen, Bill, "Fossil Digs Up Big Sales in Foreign Markets," *Dallas Business Journal,* October 8, 1993, p. B5.
"Fossil Acquires Controlling Stake in Fossil Japan from Seiko," *Daily News Record,* April 19, 1996, p. 5.
Fossil, Inc. Annual Report, Richardson, Tex.: Fossil, Inc., 1995.
Hart, Elena, "Macy's N.Y. Flagship Unfurls Fossil Shop," *Daily News Record,* November 15, 1991, p. 3.
Meadus, Amanda, "Fossil Falters but Watches Tick On," *WWD,* December 11, 1995, p. 8.
Vargo, Julie, "Fossil's New Fuel," *Daily News Record,* February 11, 1994, p. S12.
Welch, David, "Despite Stock Slide, Fossil Still Has Some True Believers," *Dallas Business Journal,* December 1, 1995, p. 7.
Wood, Sean, "Watchmaker Plans IPO to Fund Acquisitions, Expansion," *Dallas Business Journal,* February 7, 1992, p. 3.

—Jeffrey L. Covell

FSI International, Inc.

322 Lake Hazeltine Drive
Chaska, Minnesota 55318
U.S.A.
(612) 448-5440
Fax: (612) 448-2825

Public Company
Incorporated: 1973
Employees: 1,125
Sales: $190.4 (1995)
Stock Exchanges: NASDAQ
SICs: 3559 Special Industry Machinery, Not Elsewhere
Classified

FSI International, Inc., a leading producer of automated equipment used in the manufacture of integrated circuits, has served a worldwide market since its founding in 1973. The Minnesota-based company concentrates on three distinct technologies: silicon wafer cleaning systems; self-contained, robotics photolithography systems; and chemical delivery, blending, and generation systems. The company staged a dramatic comeback after faltering within a year of its first public stock offering in 1989.

FSI's Origin

The history of FSI may be traced to the 1966 formation of Fluoroware, Inc., a custom fabricator for the electronics industry founded by Victor Wallestad. When Wallestad established Fluoroware, he recruited Joel Elftmann for his start-up team. Elftmann, a technical school graduate, had worked as mold maker at Booker & Wallestad and had also worked a second shift as a die maker for another company, while making custom molds in his shop at home in his spare time. Elftmann would later figure prominently in the founding of FSI.

Fluoroware's core product was a Teflon carrier which held silicon wafers in position during the manufacturing process. Such large manufacturers as Delco, Texas Instruments, and Fairchild Semiconductors were among its early customers. When Fluoroware was contracted by a division of Collins Radio to build a drying mechanism for silicon wafers, Elftmann, as supervisor of design and tool making, lead his production team in the invention of the first centrifugal "spin dryer" for semiconductor manufacturing. The success of the spin dryer lead to development of the first automated silicon wafer rising and drying system using a spray technology.

The spray technology provided an alternative to the immersion cleaning method used to remove impurities from silicon wafers during the manufacturing of computer chips. The rinser/dryer equipment required technology more advanced than what was necessary for Fluoroware's core business area. So in 1973, Vic Wallestad founded a company to develop the product. FSI International, Inc. was begun on $60,000, with Wallestad owning 75 percent and Elftmann owning 25 percent of the new business.

The Years of Private Ownership

FSI established itself as an international supplier of semiconductor manufacturing equipment from the beginning of its existence; exports brought in at least a quarter of total sales. In 1975, Elftmann used his experience gained through establishing a European sales and distribution organization for Fluoroware to co-found, with Fluoroware, Metron Semiconductors Europa, an independent organization which sold wafer processing equipment and provided technical support to customers. A similar arrangement was made with Fluoroware in 1985 via the founding of Metron Semiconductors Asia which served Korea, Taiwan, Singapore, China, and Hong Kong.

An innovator, FSI was among the first semiconductor equipment suppliers to establish its own computer chip processing laboratory. Opened in 1978, the lab helped FSI to more accurately identify customer production needs in relationship to its equipment. The company also lead in the commercialization of chemical management and distribution technology as an alternative to bottled chemicals. A joint venture with Texas Instruments, initiated in 1985, resulted in the creation of the first vapor-phase cleaning system, which greatly reduced water and chemical consumption.

Company Perspectives:

FSI International, Inc. is a successful supplier, preferred by the semiconductor industry in strategic technology segments, proactively providing high value solutions with consistent performance; high reliability; on-time delivery; competitive cost; total support.

As micro chips became smaller and more complex, FSI technology became an increasingly crucial part of the semiconductor manufacturing process in which layers of conducting and insulating materials are applied and etched away from silicon wafers in order to form the electronic circuits. The chemical cleaning process must be performed repeatedly during manufacturing: impurities of even a fraction of a micron can render a chip useless. FSI's ''wet-process'' equipment, which measured, timed, and released a liquid chemical spray, sold for $40,000 per unit or up to $600,000 per system; in 1987 FSI held just over 20 percent the $125 million market segment. That same year, FSI introduced the first gas-cleaning system, the ''Excalibur,'' which sold for $250,000 to $500,000.

In 1988 FSI was a leading supplier—among about forty competitors—of cleaning machines for the computer chip industry, with total sales of about $45 million. ''Excalibur'' gas-cleaning system was named one of the nation's 100 best new technology-oriented products by *Research & Development* magazine. International sales had risen to 45 percent, and the company employed 350 people. The company's main concerns seemed to be the volatility of the industry—there had been four serious downturns since FSI started business in 1973—and reliance on one customer for a significant proportion of its business. IBM, including both domestic and overseas operations, accounted for 31 percent of FSI's sales. FSI's first decade and a half of business had been marked by solid leadership and financial stability. The company posted net profit in all but two years.

Troubled Times Mark Transition to Public Company

FSI went public in January 1989 with an initial public offering of 1.45 million shares of common stock priced at $7.50. A reporter for the *St. Paul Pioneer Press Dispatch* wrote in April 1989, ''FSI had been flirting with the idea of going public for years, getting as far as an initial draft of a prospectus in 1985.'' But a computer chip industry downturn forced FSI to scrap the public offering and make cut backs. When the switch from a private to public company finally was accomplished, the day-to-day leadership changed too. In August 1989 the board moved Richard Jackson, a professional manager with FSI since 1982, into the CEO position. Elftmann retained his position as chairman of the board but turned his attention to foreign distribution and industry concerns.

Annual revenues for the fiscal year ending in August 1989 were $61.6 million, and net income was $3.2 million, but FSI would not record another profitable year until 1993. Problems in the three years from 1990 to 1992 added up to $8 million in loses for the newly public company. Trouble was already on the horizon at the end of 1989, the beginning of FSIs 1990 fiscal year. First quarter operating income had fallen sharply compared to the previous year: from $908,000 to $391,000. One piece of bad news followed another, and it was colored by the aftereffects of the national economic recession of the late-1980s, as well as a changing international business environment.

The dismantling of the former Soviet Union and resulting economic chaos caused FSI's Eastern European sales to drop from $7 million to $1 million by 1990. FSI lost another $6 million in sales when a German company failed to renew its licensing agreement for photolithography technology, a process of circuit pattern imprinting. Although FSI promptly signed on with Texas Instruments (TI) for similar technology, TI's own difficulties resulted in suspension of development support in June 1991. Two FSI expansions, one in California and the other in Japan, failed and cost another $1 million. To make matters worse, the company had to pull newly upgraded cleaning equipment from some customers' plants and re-engineer others. In a rush to get the equipment up and running FSI skipped on-site testing; this proved to be another costly error.

Faced with the loss of market share, customer good will, and bleak prospects for the future, Elftmann resumed day-to-day management of FSI in May 1991. Projected sales were down nearly $20 million from 1989. The August order backlog fell to about $5 million. In November 1991, employees were asked to take Thanksgiving week off without pay, while the senior management team met. Elftmann later recalled in a 1994 *Minneapolis Star Tribune* article, ''We started with a blank sheet of paper, examined our strengths and weaknesses and proceeded to tear the organizational chart apart.''

The process resulted in a plan that included: the elimination of some long-term managers in order to strengthen FSI technical and managerial expertise; the phase out of a number of products—including the spin dryer that launched the company—while refocusing on three core businesses; and a financial commitment to engineering, research and development in order to elevate the level technology.

It was no easy task to implement the plan. FSI had been dropped as a customer by both its banks, and Elftmann had to personally guarantee $1.5 million in credit in order to finance the turnaround. Elftmann held 18 percent of the company's stock and used that and his personal assets as security. The company pushed forward and opened a new development facility in Dallas; former TI employees with industry know-how came on board. Elftmann reached out to its customers, such as Motorola and TI, for guidance on improving on product quality. Steve Wilson, a senior Motorola engineer was quoted in *Corporate Report Minnesota* in 1995 as noting, ''One of the things that really distinguished FSI is that they asked for our help.''

The Early 1990s Turnaround

FSI's hard work began to pay off. Sales for fiscal year 1993 reached $77 million, and net profit was $3.2 million. Sales jumped to $94 million in 1994, and net profit more than doubled. FSI's comeback was bolstered by a strong semiconductor industry: chip sales rose to $102 billion in 1994, a hike of $25 billion from the previous year. FSI had moved itself into position to capitalize on the gains.

Further evidence of the company's turnaround came from customer and industry endorsement. TI named FSI vendor of the year in 1994. In 1993 and 1994, surveys conducted by a California-based consulting group, VSLI Research, showed that semiconductor equipment customers ranked FSI among the best process equipment suppliers. FSI received its International Standards Organization (ISO) certification in recognition of its quality assurance processes in 1994. And *Semiconductor International* magazine selected three FSI products for its 1994 Editor's Choice Best Product Award.

FSI's success continued in 1995. Each of its three divisions was gaining world-wide market share: surface conditional area held 7 percent of a $1.2 billion market; microlithographic technology held 9.5 percent of a $1.1 billion market; and chemical management held 35 percent of a $150 million market. The Chemical Management division was enhanced by the acquisition of Applied Chemical Solutions. The Surface Conditioning division made headway in Japan through its joint venture m*FSI Ltd, which had been established in 1991. The company's backlog of business reached a record $115 million at the end of the fiscal year.

FSI was in a growth period. Two stock offerings made in 1995 raised more than $100 million, which was targeted for capital expenditures and acquisitions. FSI's stock rose to a high of $51.75 in June of 1995; the stock was split two-for-one that same month. Sensitive to the fortunes of the large semiconductor manufacturers, FSI stock prices dropped to around $12 per share in the beginning of 1996.

But FSI appeared to be taking a stance of optimism in 1996. New products, new markets, and new technologies were driving the chip manufacturers to expand their facilities. And counted among its customers were Intel, Motorola, TI, AMD, DEC, Fuijitsu, AT&T, and IBM. To meet demand and keep up with state-of-the-art production facilities, FSI continued its move to upgrade its operations and technologies. Expansions of facilities in Texas and Minnesota were announced. The engineering, research and development budget was set at $39 million. FSI licensed IBM's Cryogenic Aerosol Cleaning Technology, and

acquired Semiconductor Systems, Inc., which it consolidated as part of the microlithography division.

On to the 21st Century

Based on the rapid growth of products utilizing semiconductors—such as cellular phones and pagers—industry analysts were predicting that the annual world-wide semiconductor market could reach $300 billion by the year 2000. FSI is positioning itself to capture significant additional market share in each of its business areas by the turn of the century. The company expected a continued commitment to successful strategies, such as the licensing of new technology, support of internal research and development, and the pursuit of joint ventures with or acquisitions of companies with complementary technologies.

Principal Subsidiaries

Applied Chemical Solutions Inc.; Semiconductor Systems, Inc.

Further Reading

Abelson, Alan, "Up & Down on Wall Street," *Barron's,* December 1989.

Beal, Dave, "Chip Cleaner Stays Ahead of the Game," *St. Paul Pioneer Press Dispatch,* April 3, 1989, pp. 1, 8.

Carideo, Anthony, "When Chips Are Down, This Firm Cleans Them," *Star Tribune* (Minneapolis), December 25, 1989, pp. 1D, 5D.

"FSI International Has Record Sales, Profits," *St. Paul Pioneer Press Dispatch,* March 28, 1989.

"FSI International, Inc.," *Corporate Report Fact Book 1996,* p. 251.

"FSI Moving Assembly of Polaris 200 Clusters to Texas Lab Early Next Year," *Star Tribune* (Minneapolis), May 24, 1996, p. 3D.

Gross, Steve, "FSI Cleaning Up in Removal of Computer Chip Impurities," *Star Tribune* (Minneapolis), September 29, 1988, pp. 1D, 4D.

Schafer, Lee, "Re-Engineering FSI," *Corporate Report Minnesota,* June 1995, pp. 36–38.

"Victor Wallestad, Founder of Fluoroware," *Star Tribune* (Minneapolis), November 17, 1993, p. 7B.

Youngblood, Dick, "FSI Co-Founder Owns Up to Woes, Looks to Future," *Star Tribune* (Minneapolis), February 21, 1994, p. 2D.

——, "FSI Stock's Soaring, but Elftmann Still Finds Things to Worry About," *Star Tribune* (Minneapolis), May 31, 1995, p. 2D.

—Kathleen Peippo

Fuqua Enterprises, Inc.

One Atlantic Center, Suite 5000
1201 W. Peachtree Street, N.W.
Atlanta, Georgia 30309
U.S.A.
(404) 815-2000
Fax: (404) 815-4529

Public Company
Incorporated: 1900 as Seagrave Corporation
Employees: 710
Sales: $117.13 million (1995)
Stock Exchanges: New York
SICs: 3111 Leather Tanning and Finishing; 2599
Furniture and Fixtures, Not Elsewhere Classified;
5047 Wholesale Trade—Medical, Dental, and
Hospital Equipment and Supplies

Fuqua Enterprises, Inc., through its principal subsidiaries, is a leading supplier of processed leather to manufacturers of finished leather goods and a growing manufacturer of medical products for the institutional and home health care markets. In 1995 the company changed its name from Vista Resources, Inc., to Fuqua Enterprises, reflecting the growing involvement of the Fuqua family, headed by 77-year-old John B. Fuqua and his son, 44-year-old J. Rex Fuqua. Not to be confused with the similarly-named Fuqua Industries, Inc. (see *International Directory of Company Histories,* Vol. I), Fuqua Enterprises sold off its insurance subsidiary in 1995 and decided to get into the growing medical products market by acquiring two companies in that industry in 1995 and 1996. The company also retained its leather tanning businesses, the Irving Tanning Company, which was acquired in 1962, and Kroy Tanning Company, acquired in 1965.

Vista Resources, Inc.

As the company began its second century of operations in 1980, it changed its name from the Seagrave Corporation to Vista Resources, Inc. Seagrave and its subsidiaries manufac-

tured a wide range of products, including paint, industrial coatings and chemicals, glass products, and metal windows and related products for large buildings, among others. They were also involved in leather tanning, the sale of architectural products, and the marketing of solid waste disposal systems.

Along with changing its name, Vista decided that its future was in the leather tanning business. It sold off all of the assets or capital stock of its other operating businesses effective September 30, 1980, for approximately $20.3 million and the assumption of certain liabilities. The businesses that were sold generated approximately $86.4 million in annual sales in 1979. Vista retained its leather business and $6.5 million in cash.

The late 1970s were an era of escalating inflationary and deflationary pressures. Interest rates were soaring and federal monetary policies were generally unfavorable to business. The sale of more than $20 million in assets, primarily for cash and in excess of their net worth, significantly helped Vista increase its liquidity and book value while reducing its fixed debt. In light of the prevailing economic conditions, the company made a strategic decision to focus on building the per share value of its stock and having cash resources sufficient to ride out money shortages and credit crunches.

In 1981, its first full year of operations as Vista Resources, the company's leather operations show improved sales volume, produced a better quality of leather products, and upgraded its equipment. Vista terminated a joint venture with its Spanish partners and took over ownership of the Wilton, Maine facilities, which would be used exclusively for the production of lambskins by its subsidiary, Kroy Tanning. Financial results showed a significant improvement in earnings per share, to $2.28, on sales of $45.8 million. At this time Vista's stock was traded on the NASDAQ exchange.

For most of the 1980s, Vista's sales volume fluctuated between a low of $42.3 million in 1982 and highs of $60 million in 1984 and 1986. The company paid its last cash dividend in 1988. Economic conditions in general were not favorable for Vista's leather operations. Lower offshore labor costs attracted much of the domestic market for shoes and other finished leather goods, and U.S. leather production declined during the 1980s. Personal consumption of finished leather goods was adversely affected by a recession. The only benefit to Vista was that its raw material costs, primarily leather hides and lambskins, also declined. Lower raw material costs, combined with more efficient production, enabled Vista to improve its profit margins.

According to *Barron's,* Vista in 1989 was a cash-rich company, holding cash or cash equivalents equal to 73 percent of the value of its stock. In April 1989 John B. Fuqua, aged 70, acquired 35 percent of Vista Resources from Vista's long-time president and CEO, Arnold A. Saltzman. J.B. Fuqua, as he was known, became chairman of the board and brought in his associate Robert S. Prather, Jr., as president and CEO. He moved the company's headquarters to Atlanta from New York City and had Vista's stock listed on the New York Stock Exchange.

Sensing a takeover, Wall Street pushed Vista's stock price up from about $9 to $18. Investors were already familiar with the Fuqua name. As chief executive officer (CEO) of Atlanta-based Fuqua Industries, Inc., J.B. Fuqua transformed the small brick manufacturer in 1965 into a $2 billion conglomerate in the 1980s that sold lawn mowers, sporting goods, and photo finishing. In 1989 he sold his seven percent stake in Fuqua Industries to Intermark and retired as CEO.

Under new management in 1989, Vista's leather sales improved to more than $70 million. The company declared a 400 percent stock dividend in August of 1989 in lieu of a cash dividend. Adjusted for the split, its stock traded in the $15.25 to $7.375 range in 1989. The next year was even better. Leather sales reached a historical high of $71.9 million, two percent higher than 1989. Financially, 1990 was a year for the company to "clean up its balance sheet," according to the annual report. Vista "wrote off goodwill and provided for certain foreseeable contingent and real liabilities," according to Chairman Fuqua. The company recorded $2.026 million in corporate expenses and took a $1.515 million loss from discontinued operations and from the settlement of litigation as well as a $1.715 million loss from continuing operations. The loss from discontinued operations represented $.41 per share.

The year 1991 began with the installation of new management. Fuqua's associate Robert Prather left under friendly terms as president and CEO. Fuqua brought in Samuel P. Norwood III, to take over as president and CEO. Norwood had worked with J.B. Fuqua for approximately 20 years in corporate development at Fuqua Industries. As Chairman Fuqua noted in the company's annual report, "As has been my practice in other companies over the past 30 years, a portion of [management's] personal compensation is determined by the earnings for which each one is responsible, and is also tied to the increase in the value of the stock you and I own." He also noted that leather was not a high-growth industry, hence the compelling need to diversify through acquisitions. In fact, leather sales declined ten percent in 1991, due to lower selling prices and to a lower quantity of leather produced. Modernization of the company's tanneries, located in Maine, produced a positive effect on profits for the second half of 1991 and allowed the company to reduce its inventories.

Still flush with cash, Vista announced in September 1991 that it had reached an agreement to purchase the stock of the

Atlanta-based American Southern Insurance Co. from InterRedec, Inc., which was based in Savannah, Georgia. The sale price of $30 million included $20 million cash at closing, a five-year note of $8 million, and $2 million payable in five years based on meeting specific earnings targets in 1992, 1993, and 1994. As reported in the *Journal of Commerce,* closing of the deal was subject to regulatory approval and "the absence of any governmental action precluding the transaction." What the *Journal of Commerce* did not point out, but the *New York Times* did, was that American Southern's parent, InterRedec, was the holding company for the American investments of Saudi Arabian Ghaith Pharaon. Pharaon was a central figure in the unfolding Bank of Credit and Commerce scandal, and the U.S. government had frozen his American assets in September of 1991. However, InterRedec was allowed to withdraw funds to finance its operations, but it had to put up as collateral its large estate at its headquarters in Richmond Hill, Georgia. The government's action to freeze its assets was simply designed to keep Mr. Pharaon from taking any cash out of the country.

In October, the sale of American Southern to Vista was approved by Georgia's insurance commissioner. The insurance company had annual revenues of about $40 million. It specialized in six distinct types of insurance, but its primary niche was insuring fleet vehicles owned by state and local governments. The company was licensed in 15 states and conducted business on a "non-admitted" basis in two other states. At the time of the sale it had 39 employees, low overhead, and an experienced claims management staff. It also had a high-quality investment portfolio, with only short-term liabilities and no debt.

With the acquisition of American Southern, Vista was divided into two groups, the Leather Group and the Insurance Group. After sales for the Leather Group increased in 1992 by 30 percent as a result of increased domestic market share and growing export sales, the company posted sales of more than $100 million in 1993 for the first time in its history. American Southern contributed about $40 million.

In 1993 J.B. Fuqua paid $1 million to buy back the Fuqua Industries name from the company that subsequently renamed itself Actava Group, Inc. After J.B. left Fuqua Industries in 1989, the company had fallen on hard times. It was eventually merged into Metromedia International in 1995. In a 1991 article in *Business Atlanta,* Vista's new president, Samuel Norwood III, noted that "keeping the Vista name is not important." Few investment analysts had followed the company during the 1980s, so it was not a well-known name on Wall Street. In fact, Norwood didn't rule out the possibility of merging Vista with another, more well-known company as a way of enhancing its value when he came on board in 1991.

In 1994 sales rose to $126.5 million. During the year John J. Huntz, Jr., 43, was named to the new post of senior vice-president for corporate development. He was formerly managing partner of Noble Ventures International, a venture investment firm. At the end of the year Vista and its subsidiaries employed 672 people. The company owned active tanneries in Hartland and East Wilton, Maine, which it was in the process of modernizing, and a discontinued tannery in Ellsworth, Maine, plus corporate offices and insurance operations in Atlanta, Georgia.

In mid-1995 Vista announced that it was planning to change its name. It originally planned to change its name to Fuqua Industries, Inc., but instead changed it to Fuqua Enterprises, Inc. The name change reflected the growing investment and commitment of the Fuqua family to the enterprise. J.B. Fuqua brought in Lawrence Klamon, 58, a member of the prestigious Atlanta law firm Alston & Bird, to replace Samuel Norwood as president and CEO. Klamon was an officer of the former Fuqua Industries, Inc., for 24 years, rising from general counsel to serve as its president and CEO from 1989 to 1991. J. Rex Fuqua, son of J.B. Fuqua, became vice chairman whose duties included guiding strategic planning. John J. Huntz, Jr., was promoted to executive vice-president and chief operating officer. As the name change and new management were announced, J.B. Fuqua, then 77, was quoted in the *Wall Street Journal* as saying, "We're trying to see if you can go back and do a thing over again." Together, J.B. Fuqua and his son owned nearly 40 percent of the company's common stock.

Fuqua Enterprises, Inc.

Immediately following its change in name and management, Fuqua Enterprises announced in October 1995 that it was selling off its insurance unit, American Southern Insurance Co., to Atlantic American Corp. The sale price of $34 million was $4 million more than Vista paid for it in 1991. Although American Southern was a solid and profitable company, Fuqua Enterprises did not wish to remain in the insurance business. Keeping American Southern was "not consistent with our strategic direction," according to the company's 1995 annual report. The company expected to use the proceeds from the sale to expand further into growth industries in general and the medical equipment market in particular.

In November Fuqua Enterprises entered the medical equipment field with the purchase of privately-held Basic American Medical Products for $16 million. In addition to using cash for the acquisition, the company issued an additional 600,000 shares to Basic's primary shareholder. Basic was an Atlanta-based maker of healthcare equipment, primarily for institutional markets. Its products included patient beds, furniture, wheelchairs, and other patient aids for hospitals, extended care facilities, and home care. The acquisition of Basic also brought in SSC Medical Products, which Basic acquired subsequent to its agreement with Fuqua Enterprises. SSC was based in Tupelo, Mississippi, and produced home care beds. In the company's annual report, J.B. Fuqua noted that the medical equipment industry was a growing one.

In addition to getting into medical equipment, Fuqua Enterprises maintained its commitment to its leather tanning business, which continued to be profitable. In January 1996 the company decided to discontinue the operation of Kroy Tanning Co. and its tannery in East Wilton, Maine, which had been historically unprofitable. Kroy produced sheepskin and deerskin leathers which were sold mainly to garment manufacturers. All of the company's leather operations would be concentrated in its subsidiary, the Irving Tanning Company, and its 444,000-square-foot facility in Hartland, Maine. Over the past five years, Irving had undergone a $14 million capital improvement program.

Fuqua's leather business was now an international business that involved selling to Nike in Indonesia, Doc Martens in Thailand, and Reebok in China. Fuqua was also working on completing a joint venture in China that would use low-cost hides for products in Asia. In March 1996 Fuqua agreed to acquire a 70 percent interest in this joint venture for about $1.5 million. Under the joint venture, Fuqua would provide machinery and raw materials to a Chinese tannery. The joint venture provided Fuqua with a market for the lower-grade hides that it bought when it purchased truckloads of hides of varying grade levels. By exporting the lower-grade hides to China, Fuqua would be able to devote more of its tanning facilities to processing the higher grade leathers that were primarily used by its customers. Although Fuqua's leather operations were not dependent upon a single customer or a few customers, one individual customer in 1995 accounted for sales of $23.662 million, and another for $15.938 million. While the company had no foreign leather operations, sales to customers in foreign countries accounted for 27 percent of 1995 leather sales, down from 30 percent in 1994.

In March 1996 Fuqua Enterprises furthered its strategy to become a major provider of medical products by acquiring the Lumex medical products division of Lumex, Inc., for $40.75 million in cash. The division's major market was home health care, to which it sold specialty seating and healthcare beds, including wheelchairs, hospital beds, and reclining chairs for dialysis. It had sales in 1995 of about $63 million. It also sold to institutional markets, such as acute care and extended care facilities and dialysis clinics. The Lumex brand name had been in existence for over 35 years, and Fuqua acquired rights to use the name. Lumex was based in Bay Shore, Long Island, New York.

Soon after the acquisition Fuqua appointed a new president of Lumex and new head of marketing. It also eliminated about 60 redundant jobs at the Long Island facility and announced the closing of Lumex's Pennsylvania manufacturing plant, with operations to be transferred to Basic American's Mississippi and Wisconsin facilities. These moves were expected to lower production costs and improve capacity utilization of the company's facilities. The company's medical products were manufactured in Fond du Lac, Wisconsin, Toccoa, Georgia, and Tupelo, Mississippi. It also maintained a 50,000-square-foot medical products showroom in Atlanta.

With the acquisition of Lumex, Fuqua Enterprises was positioned to compete in two of the fastest growing medical markets, extended care and home health care. Together, Lumex and Basic American were projected to provide Fuqua with sales of $100 million in medical equipment alone.

Fuqua Enterprises expected to have a significant increase in net income and earnings per share in 1996, due to the addition of revenue from Basic American for a full year and from Lumex for approximately nine months. The outlook for the firm's leather operations was good, with strong retail demand and steady or falling raw materials prices. The joint venture in China was moving forward faster than expected. The company would also have use of the proceeds from the sale of American Southern. Results from the first half of 1996 supported the company's high expectations. Income from continuing operations for the first six months of 1996 was $3.4 million, or $.76 per share, on revenues of $78.7 million, compared with $2.0 million and $.52 per share on revenues of $58.1 million the previous year.

Principal Subsidiaries

Basic American Medical Products, Inc.; Irving Tanning Company; Lumex Medical Products, Inc.

Further Reading

Anason, Dean, "Fuqua Sends Signal to Wall Street with Health-Care Buyout," *Atlanta Business Chronicle,* October 13, 1995, p. 3A.

"Atlantic American's Acquisition of American Southern Insurance Co. from Fuqua Enterprises Inc.," *Wall Street Journal,* October 18, 1995, p. A6 (West).

Brooks, Rick, "A Reincarnated Fuqua Enterprises Soon Could Gain Some Visibility," *Wall Street Journal,* February 28, 1996.

"Fuqua Enterprises, Inc.," *PR Newswire,* July 26, 1996.

"Fuqua Enterprises, Inc., to Acquire Basic American Medical Products Inc.," *New York Times,* October 10, 1995, p. D4.

"Fuqua Enterprises Selling Insurance Unit," *New York Times,* October 18, 1995, p. C4.

"Fuqua Enterprises to Buy Lumex Medical Unit," *New York Times,* March 15, 1996, p. D3.

"Georgia Approves Sale of Saudi Company," *New York Times,* October 3, 1991, p. D9.

"Lumex Unit to Be Bought in $40.8 Million Accord," *Wall Street Journal,* March 15, 1996, p. B4.

Marcial, Gene C., "Fuqua's New Guise—and Old Gusto," *Business Week,* May 13, 1996, p. 110.

McKenna, Jon, "Vista Resources Keeps Searching," *Atlanta Business Chronicle,* March 12, 1993, p. 3.

Palmer, Jay, "Wealth of Possibilities: A Screen Turns Up a Trove of Cash-Rich Companies," *Barron's,* April 10, 1989, p. 20.

Smith, Faye McDonald, "Fuqua Infuses Life in Vista Resources," *Business Atlanta,* November 1991, p. 64.

Tedeschi, Mark, "Irving Scores with Customers as a Heavyweight," *Footwear News,* August 30, 1993, p. 17.

"Vista Resources Inc.," *Atlanta Business Chronicle,* June 25, 1993, p. 49B.

"Vista Resources Inc.," *Atlanta Business Chronicle,* March 19, 1990, p. 28A.

"Vista Resources Inc. Expects to Post Drop in 4th-Quarter Profits," *Wall Street Journal,* February 10, 1993, p. B5.

"Vista Resources Plans To Change Its Name, Look for Acquisitions," *Wall Street Journal,* July 21, 1995, p. B5A.

"Vista to Buy Stock Of American Southern," *Journal of Commerce,* September 20, 1991, p. 8A.

"Who's News: Vista Resources, Inc.," *Wall Street Journal,* March 3, 1994, p. B11.

—David Bianco

Gantos, Inc.

3260 Patterson Southeast
Grand Rapids, Michigan 49512
U.S.A.
(616) 949-7000
Fax: (616) 949-5884

Public Company
Incorporated: 1932
Employees: 2,106
Sales: $192.8 million (1995)
Stock Exchanges: NASDAQ
SICs: 5621 Women's Clothing Stores

Gantos, Inc. is a nationwide retailer of women's clothing and accessories. The company's 113 stores are located in upscale malls in 23 states. Gantos's primary customers are women aged 30–50 who are shopping for moderate to higher priced, career-oriented clothing. Over the 65 years since the company's founding, Gantos stores have built a reputation for providing a range of quality merchandise and a high level of customer service.

Company Origins

Gantos was founded in Grand Rapids, Michigan in 1932 by Theodore (Ted) and Haseebie Gantos. The Gantoses were Lebanese immigrants who had met and married in Grand Rapids. Ted sold linens door to door in summer resort areas in western Michigan but dreamed of opening his own store. He flirted with his dream briefly in 1929 when he opened a linen store in downtown Grand Rapids, but the Great Depression soon put an end to this fledgling enterprise, which closed after only a few months in business. Three years later the Gantoses were ready to try again. After a few months in a rented store front on Ottawa Avenue in Grand Rapids, the Gantoses moved their small linens business to a tiny eight foot by twenty foot shop on Monroe Avenue, Grand Rapids' main shopping thoroughfare. By this time an agreement with a hosiery manufacturer allowed Gantos to add hosiery to his stock of fine linens and baby clothes, thus entering the women's wear market that would become the center of Gantos's trade.

For the new store's first five years of operation Ted continued to travel throughout western Michigan, selling his stock of fine linens and tablecloths door to door to help finance the Grand Rapids business. This left Haseebie in charge of all of the day-to-day operations at Monroe Avenue, including selling, window dressing, accounting, and ordering new stock. Her virtual one-woman operation prospered and, at her suggestion, ladies' sportswear, lingerie, and blouses were added to their original linen and hosiery inventory. By 1937 annual sales for the store had attained the $10,000 mark and Ted felt secure enough to quit the road and concentrate his energies on the Monroe Avenue venture. By this time, the tiny store had been expanded twice and could boast 500 square feet of floor space. With Ted in charge of the store on a full-time basis, Haseebie, by now the mother of two young sons, could scale back her commitment, although she continued to contribute both her advice and hard work to the concern for the remainder of her life.

Growth in the 1940s and 1950s

The war years were prosperous for the Gantos women's wear store. Although sales help was difficult to find because of war production jobs and rationing meant that obtaining merchandise often required hours of frustrating travel and calls, Gantos's persistence paid off and he was often able to provide women with the precious stockings that other retailers had run out of. By the end the war, annual sales had multiplied to $100,000.

By the mid-1940s the Gantos family had grown to include four sons: Douglas, Richard (Dick), David, and Daniel. With the business thriving, Ted Gantos began to formulate what he called his four-D plan in which he envisioned opening a branch store for each of his sons to manage. Although none of the boys were old enough to take over a store in 1949, Gantos proceeded with his expansion plan and opened a new branch on Division Avenue in the Burton Heights district of Grand Rapids. Two years later, in 1951, Gantos opened a third outlet on Coit Avenue in the Creston area on Grand Rapids' northeast side.

Company Perspectives:

Gantos' mission is to increase shareholder value by operating a highly profitable, nationwide, retail specialty organization offering a full range of moderate-to-better priced women's apparel and accessories for the fashion conscious consumer. Our mission will be accomplished by providing, with recognized excellence and dedication, customer service and quality merchandise at price levels which represent real value to our customers. We will continue to treat each and every customer as though she were a guest in our home.

The two branch stores were virtually carbon copies of the original downtown location, carrying the same wide range of ladies hosiery, lingerie, accessories, sportswear, and blouses. The Creston store would add semiformal dresses, suits, and coats to this product mix.

The three Gantos stores were bringing in annual sales of $300,000 when Ted's eldest son, Douglas, came home from fighting in Korea in 1955 to join the management of the small chain. Douglas urged his father to modernize Gantos's inventory system. He also insisted that the neighborhood locations of the current Gantos stores were in decline and that shopping centers and malls were going to become the dominant force in the retail world. Father and son fought bitterly over the direction the business should take, according to a company history written in the 1980s. "We were at it every other day," Douglas said in an interview. "We would be at each other's throats." In the end, economics proved Douglas's point as Ted realized that his neighborhood stores were losing sales to the suburban malls. In 1958, with great reluctance, Ted Gantos closed the original Gantos store on Monroe Avenue in downtown Grand Rapids. Two new small suburban stores were opened in its place, one in Grandville, to be managed by Douglas's younger brother David, and the other in the Towne and Country Shopping Center on the outskirts of Grand Rapids.

Regional Expansion in the 1960s and 1970s

Douglas Gantos's campaign to expand into suburban malls was won decisively in 1963 with the opening of a Gantos branch in the Breton Village Shopping Center in the suburbs of Grand Rapids. This new store was designed to have a more upscale look than the traditional Gantos outlets and included the distinctive arch motifs and split levels that were to become characteristic of Gantos store layouts. The merchandise to be carried was also upgraded. The more staid housecoats and lingerie were dropped from the inventory and a broader line of business-oriented suits and formal dresses were introduced. The new look was a hit as sales from Breton Village surpassed those from the four other Gantos outlets in the first year. Following the success of the Breton Village venture, Ted Gantos turned the day-to-day management of the company over to Douglas, who became general manager of all of Gantos's operations. In 1964 a new Gantos outlet following the Breton Village model was opened in Rogers Plaza, Grand Rapids' first shopping mall,

and within a year total annual sales for Gantos's stores had reached $1 million.

After opening a still more successful outlet at Eastbrook Mall in Grand Rapids, Douglas Gantos felt that the now established Gantos image of elegantly designed stores and mid-priced, fashionable, yet not extreme, women's fashions would sell in other cities. Beginning in 1969 the Gantos brothers, now including Douglas, David, and Daniel, began to expand the Gantos concept to other towns in Michigan. This expansion was opportunistic rather than planned as the brothers took advantage of the many new malls opening during the early 1970s. By 1973, there were Gantos stores in Lansing, Kalamazoo, Jackson, Ann Arbor, and Saginaw, Michigan as well as two stores in towns in Indiana. During this same period Gantos developed the concept of the "Bargain Boutique," whereby marginally profitable Gantos branches were turned into clearance outlets for slow-selling merchandise from the successful stores. This allowed Gantos management to clear unwanted inventory without resorting to image damaging, and margin lowering, clearance sales at their more upscale locations. These bargain outlets would remain a feature of Gantos's marketing into the 1990s.

During the mid-1970s the somewhat haphazard expansion of the Gantos chain brought the company into difficulties as corporate structure lagged behind expansion. Communication and organizational snags became common and the three Gantos brothers decided that the family company would have to develop a more sophisticated managing strategy if the enterprise were to continue to grow. Richard (Dick) Gantos, the fourth link in the 4-D chain, who had become a professor of mathematics at the University of Wisconsin, agreed to return to the family business following founder Ted Gantos's death in 1972. Richard was put in charge of the reorganization plan, which included computerization of inventory and accounting, a systematized training program for staff and management, and a division into regional operating units. With this new corporate structure in place, Gantos was ready for further expansion. By 1980 Gantos had opened eight new stores in Detroit and five in the Chicago area to make a total of 30 Gantos branches, with annual sales totaling almost $40 million.

National Expansion in the 1980s

By the mid-1980s the Gantos brothers, still under the leadership of eldest brother Douglas, had opened 20 more stores in the Midwest. Sales were booming and operating margins, notoriously low in the retail clothing industry, rose to more than seven percent. In 1986, the stores brought in revenues of more than $3 million on sales of $77 million. In the wake of five very successful years, in 1986 the Gantos brothers decided to take the company public to raise cash for additional expansion. An IPO of 1.4 million shares netted $11.6 million in a short period of time, and analysts were predicting that the financially strong Gantos firm was set for further impressive growth.

It was around the nature of this expansion that the 55-year-old family firm began to break apart. Douglas Gantos, who had remained president of the company, wanted to take advantage of their current success to expand quickly and across a wide geographic region. Brothers Richard and David felt that a more steady and cautious approach was called for to avoid the cash crunch that would come with over-expansion. Just as in his battle with his father about expansion some 30 years earlier, the domineering Douglas eventually won out. All three of his brothers sold their stock in the company to Douglas in the late 1980s and the eldest sibling was left in sole charge of Gantos, Inc.

Douglas Gantos's rapid expansion program was an initial success. After a second stock offering raised an additional $20 million in 1989, Gantos was able to double the number of stores in only two years. By 1990, 140 Gantos stores were scattered across the country from New Hampshire to California. In 1989 revenues had mounted to $240 million and earnings reached $7 million, a respectable three percent net return. Gantos stock, which was being touted by analysts as a success story in the making, climbed from $14 to $32 per share. Inevitably, however, the high debt to capital ratio incurred from the new store openings could not be fully counterbalanced by sales gains, particularly since clothing stores are rarely profitable in their first year of operation. By the close of 1990 it became clear that Gantos was in serious trouble. The company had incurred a net loss of $13 million and was unable to generate enough cash flow to meet the interest expense on its mounting debt.

Bankruptcy and Beyond in the 1990s

Pressed by falling sales, growing debt, and plummeting stock Douglas Gantos was forced to retrench and put a halt to further expansion. In an effort to restore stockholder confidence, for the first time in the company's history an outsider was hired as Gantos president in the spring of 1992. The new president, Michele Fortune, set out to close unprofitable units and cut costs across the board, but her reorganization plan reportedly met with resistance from Douglas Gantos. "When there's founder involvement like with Doug, the store image is wrapped up in who he is," Fortune remarked in a 1994 article in *Forbes.* "When it came down to it, he just wouldn't close [money-losing] stores." Disagreements about management policies eventually became irreconcilable and Fortune left Gantos in 1993 after barely a year on the job.

With Fortune's departure, Douglas once again took over management of the troubled firm. Despite sales gains in 1991 and 1992, however, Gantos was unable to emerge from accumulated debt. To compound the company's problems, the merchandise decisions made for the summer season of 1993 proved disastrous and Gantos stores were forced to take large markdowns on fashions that would not sell. By the fall of that year it became clear that the company was headed for a record loss and, with vendors refusing to extend credit, there was no option but to file for protection under Chapter 11 of the Bankruptcy Code.

Under the reorganization plan required by the bankruptcy filing, Gantos closed 50 underperforming stores and reworked the company's merchandising policy. In the spring of 1995, Gantos's reorganization was approved by creditors and stockholders and the company was able to emerge from bankruptcy protection. With the reduced number of stores, sales dropped in 1994 and 1995 but the company was able to return to profitability, with net income rising to $3.7 million in 1995.

In 1996, Douglas Gantos stepped down as CEO of Gantos, Inc., although he retained his position as chairman. Appointed in his place was Arlene H. Stern, a former executive vice-president with the Women's Specialty Retailing Group. From the perspective of the mid-1990s it remained to be seen whether Stern could restore the struggling Gantos clothing stores to a top position in the retail industry.

Further Reading

Bancroft, Thomas, "Dog with Bone," *Forbes,* May 25, 1992, pp. 144–145.
Book, Esther Wachs, "Hands-On Mismanagement," *Forbes,* November 7, 1994, p. 12.
"Gantos Draws on Merchandising Savvy," *Chain Store Age Executive,* February 1987.
Gantos: The History of a Family Business 1932–1982, Grand Rapids, Mich.: Gantos, Inc., 1982.
"Gantos To Emerge from Bankruptcy; Creditors and Shareholders Happy," *Detroit Free Press,* March 8, 1995, p. E1.

—Hilary Gopnik

Genesco Inc.

P.O. Box 731
Nashville, Tennessee 37202-0731
U.S.A.
(615) 367-7000
Fax: (615) 367-8278

Public Company
Incorporated: 1925 as Jarman Shoe Company
Employees: 3,750
Sales: $434.6 million (1996)
Stock Exchanges: NYSE
SICs: 3143 Men's Footwear Except Athletic; 3144
Women's Footwear Except Athletic; 5661 Shoe Stores

Genesco Inc. is a major producer, wholesaler, and retailer of brand name shoes and boots for men and women. The company also owns Volunteer Leather Company, a leather tanning and finishing business. Among the shoe brands Genesco owns or produces under license are Johnston & Murphy dress shoes for men, J. Murphy men's casual and dress casual shoes, Domani European-style dress shoes for men, and Dockers and Nautica casual footwear. The company also manufactures and sells Laredo, Code West, and Larry Mahan western boots. More than 5,000 retailers, including leading department stores, discount, and specialty stores, offer Genesco footwear. The company itself operates 463 retail shoe outlets, including Johnson & Murphy, Jarman, Journeys, Factory To You, Boot Factory and J&M Factory stores. In the fiscal year ending January 30, 1996, the company had sales of $434.6 million.

Early History

James Franklin Jarman began manufacturing $5 shoes in Nashville, Tennessee, in 1924 and incorporated the following year as Jarman Shoe Company. His son, Walton Maxey Jarman, soon joined the company, dropping out of MIT to do so. Maxey, as he was known, first worked a year at the Nashville plant as a laborer earning $10 a week, then began selling the company's product.

Maxey didn't want to be an electrical engineer, but he did want to build something. In 1933, at age 29, he got his chance. The senior Jarman made Maxey company president and moved up to chairman. Maxey changed the company name to General Shoe Corporation, and, despite the troubled economy of the Depression, started moving the company into shoe retail. He took this step since many shoe stores simply were not interested in more shoe brands, and he saw stores owned by General Shoe as the best way to distribute the company's footwear.

Maxey established four retail chains, bought a tanning plant in Michigan, and, to keep everything in-house, began producing shoe boxes. Through a subsidiary, he provided the manufacturing plants with cement, chemicals and finishes. Maxey became chairman in 1938 upon his father's death, and in 1939 he took the company public, offering 150,000 shares at $15.25 a share.

Opening brand name shoe stores in key cities helped make the Jarman and other General Shoe brands popular. Once that occurred, big independent retailers wanted to have them in stock. The company-owned stores also served as laboratories, providing immediate signals as to what the factories should make. By 1941, General Shoe had sales of $24 million, selling its shoes through its own 43 retail stores and 10,000 other outlets. In 1946, the company made a second stock offering, at $40 per share, with the proceeds going into its general fund.

Growth through Acquisitions from 1950 to 1956

Maxey Jarman was a devout Southern Baptist and an avid reader. He was reserved by nature, and the results of company psychological tests (which he took under an assumed name) indicated he was too shy to succeed in management. Yet he loved his business, had a great curiosity, and worked hard to overcome his shyness. He also had an entrepreneurial flair.

Aided by the postwar economic boom, General Shoe started the decade by manufacturing and selling $84 million worth of shoes and making a net profit of $4 million. Maxey continued to buy other shoe companies, including Massachusetts' W.L. Douglas Shoe Co., which made men's shoes, and Nisley Shoe Co., with 45 retail stores in the Midwest. Most of the company's brands were moderately priced, in the $10.95 to $18.95 range.

Company Perspectives:

Genesco's mission is to become the most customer-focused company in the footwear industry, with consistent performance in the top quartile as measured by market share, sales growth, return on assets employed and operating income.

With the 1951 purchase of the Johnston & Murphy Shoe Company, Maxey took his company into the high-price ($27.50–$39.50) end of the shoe market. J&M was 101 years old at that time, and its customers had included Teddy Roosevelt and Henry Ford. Part of J&M's marketing strategy, in fact, was to send a pair of shoes to the White House when a new President took office. Within 18 years of becoming head of the company, Maxey had built it up from a single plant in Nashville to the fourth largest shoe company in the United States, with 23 plants, over 200 stores, and 10,000 employees.

But he didn't stop there. Over the next four years he bought 15 more shoe manufacturers and retailers, becoming the country's second largest shoe company. In 1955, the Justice Department brought an anti-trust suit against General Shoe, charging that the effect of the purchases since 1950 "may be substantially to lessen competition or to tend to create a monopoly." Although the company claimed it made only five percent of the shoes manufactured in the United States, it settled with the government out of court in February 1956. General Shoe agreed not to buy any shoe companies for eight months. Then, for the next five years, the company could not make any mergers or acquisitions in the shoe industry without government approval. The decree also required General Shoe to buy 20 percent of its shoes from other manufacturers and enjoined it from requiring independent shoe retailers to buy a specific portion of the company's products.

1956 through 1969: Diversifying into Apparel

The success of General Shoe provided Maxey a model for expansion outside the shoe industry. His company was involved in both manufacturing and retail, and General Shoe offered shoes for every taste, from $1.99 to $200. The consent decree may have been the impetus for Maxey to apply that model to the apparel industry.

Five months after the settlement, General Shoe announced it had bought a 65 percent controlling interest in the Hoving Corporation, which controlled seven Bonwit Teller stores and jeweler Tiffany & Co. According to a July 28, 1956 article in *Business Week*, General Shoe paid over $10 million in cash for the shares. The move built on General Shoe's 1953 purchase of Whitehouse & Hardy, a chain of men's shoe and clothing stores.

In 1957, Maxey's son, Franklin, joined the company as a trainee. In June that year, the company continued its move into clothing retail with the purchase of 100 percent of Henri Bendel Inc., a high-fashion women's specialty shop based in New York. That move seemed to make particular sense since General

Shoe already owned Frank Bros. and I. Miller, which operated Bendel's shoe department.

Early in 1959, Maxey gave a clear indication of his plans when he changed the company's name again, to Genesco, dropping all reference to shoes. Shortly thereafter, Genesco moved into the apparel manufacturing business with the purchases of girdle maker Formfit Co. and Kingsboro Mills, Inc., a lingerie manufacturer. In 1960, the company bought L. Greif & Bro. Inc., which made men's clothing. The title page of Genesco's annual report that year proudly announced the company was "First in apparel and footwear." The company had sales of $321 million (not counting $40 million of sales to its own retail stores), with shoes accounting for about half the volume.

As the company grew, Maxey gave each division's management a great deal of autonomy, while insisting the divisions maintain their distinctive personalities. A 1962 *Time* magazine article quoted a Wall Street analyst: "Genesco gives a lot of leeway to the divisions, and Maxey runs around ready to throw the book at them if they don't perform."

By the end of 1962, Genesco operated 80 factories in 17 states, manufacturing 51 brands of shoes, making girdles and lingerie for women and suits for men, and selling its products through its 1,500 retail outlets. And Maxey kept buying. While most acquisitions were shoe or apparel companies, in 1963 the company went slightly afield with the purchase of the S.H. Kress & Co. chain of variety stores. Frank Jarman was then company treasurer, and Kress was his first acquisition. As Frank told *Business Week* in a March 10, 1973 article, "I decided that we should buy a company as large as we were. Our net worth at that time was $103 million, and Kress's was $104 million."

In 1968 Maxey achieved his dream. Genesco became the world's first apparel company to reach $1 billion in sales.

1969 to 1977 Turmoil at the Top

Maxey retired in 1969, leaving a company with 85 divisions, 198 manufacturing plants and 1,630 retail stores. Frank was named president. Four months later he was promoted to chairman. Maxey assumed the new position of chairman of the combined finance and executive committees. In 1970 Maxey ran unsuccessfully for governor of Tennessee. In May 1971, with Genesco's earnings falling, Maxey stepped back in to take control.

The next several years were hard ones for Genesco. A steep increase in hide prices in early 1972 hurt the shoe manufacturing side of the business. Even more critically, the company was having problems with many of its apparel and other retail divisions. Kress was not profitable, due largely to its many downtown outlets and the decisions by former variety store competitors such as Kresge and Woolworth to move heavily into discounting. Roos-Atkins, a staid, West Coast chain selling quality clothing had been turned into a promotional chain, competing with discounters, and the move bombed. Additionally stockholders were suing the company. Although sales for 1972 increased six percent (to $1.4 billion), net income was down 45 percent, to $8.9 million. The shoe division, with its 16 shoe companies, was one of the few bright spots.

Early in March 1973, Frank took back control and became chief executive as well as chairman. He rebuilt Genesco's management structure with fairly tight controls over the 85 operating divisions and settled stockholder lawsuits. He also laid off more than 10,000 employees, including some 900 managers, and closed down or sold off losing operations including 177 Kress stores, 10 apparel plants, and I. Miller women's shoe stores. In Europe, Frank sold off San Remo, a manufacturer of men's suits, and five smaller subsidiaries. The $60 million reserve fund needed for the closures caused a $52.9 million deficit that year.

As Frank explained in a May 18, 1974 article in *Business Week,* ''All our businesses have to do with wants, not needs. In managing them, you must somehow give the operating company managers enough authority to react to fashion changes, but at the same time keep tight controls on finances and inventories.'' Fiscal year 1974 saw earnings from continuing operations increase 18 percent over 1973, to $17.1 million.

However, Frank took over just before the beginning of a long and increasingly steep recession which had a severe impact on apparel sales and manufacturing. With about 60 percent of Genesco's sales coming from apparel—from 22 separate manufacturing companies and the rest from retail chains—1974 saw another deficit for the company, of $14.3 million. Analysts agreed, however, that the loss would have been much larger if Frank had not taken the belt-tightening steps he did.

In addition to the financial problems, Frank was also confronted with the inevitable and on-going clash between the money side and the creative side of the business. A ''numbers freak'' who always had a calculator close at hand, Frank selected people with management or people skills for top positions in the company. Despite introducing Laredo, a line of traditional western-style boots, the fact that few of the executives had merchandising experience drew complaints from the operating divisions.

Management discontent combined with shareholders who were angry that they hadn't received a dividend since 1973 and creditors who were worried about $70 million in debt, added up to a bleak outlook for Frank. In January 1977, despite a profit of $16 million for 1976, the board ousted Frank as president and chief executive. Although Frank remained chairman, the fifty-three years of Jarman family control were ended.

1977 through the 1980s—Turnaround Attempts

John Hanigan, retired chairman of Brunswick Corp., became CEO, with a four-year contract. Hanigan arranged a new $130 million line of credit and began negotiations to sell various parts of the company. ''I found an organization that over the years had focused on gross sales. I had to change that focus,'' Hanigan told *Business Week* in April 1978. After his first year, the company reported a net profit of 84¢ a share, compared to a loss of $11.12 for 1977. Hanigan sold or closed almost 50 of the 80 companies the Jarmans had bought—60 percent of the non-shoe retail business. On the retail side, he sold the Bonwit Teller, Plymouth Shops and Whitehouse & Hardy chains, the Henri Bendel store in New York City, Baron's menswear units in New York and Atlanta and Burkhardt/Davidson's in Cleve-

land. He closed Kress and the Roos-Atkins stores. He also took Genesco completely out of the business of making women's and children's clothing and, except for some profitable men's suit makers, out of men's apparel manufacturing as well. ''This is going to be run again as a shoe company,'' Hanigan told *Business Week* in 1980. ''It took a while to get that accepted by everyone around here, but we're all singing from the same hymn book now.''

Hanigan shifted the company's footwear focus from manufacturing to retail, largely in recognition of the impact of shoe imports. He built 100 new shoe stores in 1979, bringing the total to 960, and directed the stores to sell any brand that was in demand, not just Genesco brands. By the end of 1979, shoes accounted for nearly half Genesco's sales of $849 million, up from only one-third in 1970. However, the emphasis on retail rather than manufacturing resulted in the closing of six of the company's 18 shoe plants over a two-year period.

In April 1980, Richard W. Hanselman was selected as president and heir apparent to Chairman Hanigan. Hanselman headed the $1.5 billion Samsonite Corp. under Beatrice Foods Co., and a plaque in his office reminded visitors that he had trebled sales at Samsonite to $296 million and increased net profits sevenfold to $43 million.

Hanselman agreed with Hanigan that shoe retailing was the company's future and—as an experienced marketer—stressed brand loyalty. He concentrated his efforts on improving the market share of the company's mid-priced brands—Jarman, Flagg and Hardy—and thinning out the number of retail store names, but corporate debt thwarted his plans.

In January 1986 Hanselman resigned as the company announced it had lost almost $34 million for the fiscal year and its banks were refusing to extend its credit lines. William Wire II, the company's chief financial officer who had been with Genesco since 1962, was promoted to president and chairman.

Wire's first priority was to raise money. He sold off company divisions which did not relate directly to the businesses of footwear and men's clothing, including BBC and Camp Hosiery and the box making company. In 1987 he sold the company's Canadian operations for $63 million. He also moved several shoe plants abroad and downsized some of Genesco's retailing and men's suits businesses. In addition, he dismantled the company's centralized operations. According to a May 11, 1987 article in *Barron's,* what Wire wanted to do was simple: ''I keep saying to everyone here that we will never, ever be the low-cost producer of shoes. So we've got to be something else: fast and flexible, with the right product. And the best way to do that is to have small units that can move very quickly.''

Wire's approach began to pay off. He reduced debt significantly and, after a year of assuming control, reported net earning of $20.4 million, and a book value at $2.45 a share, up from 77¢ in 1986. The Johnston & Murphy division set sales records, the Mitre Sports soccer footwear unit moved successfully into softball and baseball shoes, and Greif Cos. turned an operating loss of $2.4 million into an operating profit of $2.5 million for its men's suits. The company introduced the Code West brand of boots for the fashion segment of that market, and the plant making those and Laredo boots worked overtime shifts. With an exchange in 1988 of about 5.5 million common shares of stock for most of the company's preferred shares, he eliminated over $28 million in dividend and redemption arrearages. That move cleared the way for the company to pay dividends on its common stock.

Early 1990s

The beginning of the new decade brought additional downsizing to the company. In January 1991, Wire closed Genesco's footwear components plant in Reynosa, Mexico, and in February, sold parts of The Charm Step/Easy Street division and liquidated the remaining assets.

By 1992 he felt confident enough about the financial picture to introduce new lines of men's casual shoes. Genesco got the exclusive license to market Levi Strauss's Dockers in the United States and the exclusive worldwide license for the more expensive Nautica brand of canvas footwear. In April, Wire selected E. Douglas Grindstaff, a 30-year marketing veteran from Proctor & Gamble, to become Genesco's president.

Grindstaff had headed P&G's Canadian activities, more than doubling sales there in five years. His first steps were to fill gaps in the company's product line with a younger, less expensive line of Johnston & Murphy shoes called J. Murphy, and an expensive Italian soft-soled loafer called Domani. He also poured money into advertising Genesco's western boot brands and added new colors and styles to the Code West line, taking advantage of the western-look fad. The boot lines were so popular that stores easily sold out of stock. To meet the demand, Grindstaff switched production lines, replacing low-margin shoes with more boots.

Grindstaff also started buying companies with well-known brands, taking the company into new footwear markets. In May, he acquired British soccer shoe maker Mitre Sport U.K. from Grampian Holdings plc for about $29 million. A few months later he expanded Genesco's children's shoe division with the $8 million purchase of Toddler U Inc. and its popular Toddler U brand, the second largest name in the children's market. At the end of the fiscal year, earnings were up to $9.7 million on sales of $540 million, a 14 percent sales increase. A large part of the increase was due to boot sales, which increased 50 percent.

In January 1993, Grindstaff was named CEO, Wire became chairman, and the Johnston & Murphy unit continued its marketing tradition by sending President Clinton a pair of handmade blue suede loafers. However, a new resident in the White House was not the only change occurring. The recession was ending, styles in men's footwear were more casual, and men were buying almost twice as many shoes as they had ten years before.

Grindstaff indicated the company would focus on developing strategies for its 14 brands of shoes, hoping to double sales over the next five years. Unfortunately, Grindstaff misjudged the western boom. After an unexpected $38 million writedown, sales for the year ended January 31, 1994, were $573 million, but the company had a loss of $51.8 million.

Grindstaff initiated a company-wide reorganization aimed at improving the company's bottom line within 12 months. He began closing several footwear and men's clothing manufacturing plants, eliminating approximately 1,200 jobs (20 percent of the company's work force), and shutting down 58 retail stores. In the middle of the downsizing, however, the company's subsidiary, GCO Apparel Corporation, bought the men's tailored clothing manufacturing assets of LaMar Manufacturing Company.

Despite Grindstaff's measures, the picture did not improve. For the six months ended July 31, 1994, the company had a net loss of $3.2 million on sales of $271.6 million. The company traced the weak results to the tremendous fall off in the sales of women's western boots, a sharp drop in sales for the University Brands division, the departure of Toddler University founder and president Jeff Silverman, and continuing problems in the retail division. In a May issue of *Fortune,* Nancy Rotenier also pointed to problems resulting from trying to take the Mitre soccer brand into clothing and pricing the Levi's Docker shoes too high. In October, Grindstaff resigned, and David M. Chamberlain, a Genesco director since 1989, was named interim president, CEO and chairman.

In November, the company's board approved a plan to concentrate on men's and women's footwear. As part of the 1995 restructuring, Genesco sold its children's shoe business (University Brands) and the Mitre Sports soccer business. Getting out of the men's apparel business altogether, it liquidated the Greif companies and sold GCO Apparel Corporation. By the end of 1995, net sales from ongoing operations in both the retail and wholesale operations were up. The Volunteer Leather Company was a major supplier to the U.S. military for its boots and other footwear.

1996 and Beyond

Genesco was once again solely a manufacturer and retailer of footwear and appeared to be stabilizing. Net sales from ongoing operations for the first half of its fiscal year increased 17 percent to $203.2 million and net earnings were $3 million, at 11¢ per share, compared to a net loss of $164,000 in the first half of 1995. Demand for boots and western wear continued to be soft, but new lines introduced during 1996, including the high-end Larry Mahan western boot and a work boot with western influences, appeared to be popular. The company also planned to introduce a boys' line of Nautica footwear. Chamberlain announced he would stay as chairman and CEO through the year and that Neale Attenborough, president of the Laredo Boot Company, and Ben Harris, president of Genesco's retail operations, had been named executive vice-presidents for operations.

Since its near bankruptcy in the late 1960s the company has made numerous turnaround attempts by refocusing on its core footwear business. Perhaps this latest effort, which succeeded in eliminating all non-footwear operations, will prove successful.

Principal Subsidiaries

Volunteer Leather Company.

Further Reading

Carruth, Eleanore, ''Genesco Comes to Judgment,'' *Fortune,* July 1975, p. 108.

"The Choices Narrow for Troubled Genesco," *Business Week,* September 19, 1977, p. 41.

"Curbs on Shoes and Shubert," *Business Week,* February 25, 1956, p. 32.

"Does Genesco Face a Takeover Bid?" *Business Week,* April 11, 1977, p. 29.

"End of a Family Fight," *Time,* January 17, 1977, p. 49.

"Frank Jarman's Radical Surgery on Genesco," *Business Week,* May 18, 1974, p. 88.

Gellers, Stan, and Nannery, Matt, "Hear Greif Cos. Getting Takeover Bids; Genesco Put Clothing Unit on Block Last Week," *Daily News Record,* November 14, 1994, p. 4.

"General Shoe, Expanding out of Shoes, Buys Henri Bendel Specialty Shop," *Business Week,* June 15, 1957, p. 54.

"General Shoe Takes Another Stride into the Retail Apparel Field," *Business Week,* July 28, 1956, p. 64.

"Genesco: An Apparel Empire Returns to Its Retailing Base—Shoes," *Business Week,* June 23, 1980, p. 90.

"Genesco Form 10-K," Washington, D.C.: Securities and Exchange Commission, January 31, 1996.

"Genesco Reports Second Quarter Earnings," Nashville: Genesco Corporate Relations, August 21, 1996.

Henriques, Diana, "Firmer Footing: Genesco Treads the Path to Recovery," *Barron's,* May 11, 1987, p. 16.

Henry, David, "Round-Trip to Nowhere," *Forbes,* July 28, 1986, p. 43.

"How Far Can a Producer Retail?" *Business Week,* January 21, 1961, p. 77.

"The Impatient Shoemaker," *Time,* November 23, 1962, p. 76.

Kern, Beth Sexer, "Grindstaff Leaves Helm at Genesco," *Footwear News,* October 17, 1994, p. 1.

Koselka, Rita, " 'Worst Case' Wire's Smart Hire," *Forbes,* April 26, 1993, p. 100.

Marcial, Gene C. "Inside Wall Street: Is a Go-Go Sixties Stock about to Do an Encore?" *Business Week,* August 22, 1988, p. 85.

"New Shoes," *Time,* August 13, 1951, p. 92.

"Profitable Oedipus," *Time,* July 5, 1976, p. 74.

"Putting Genesco Back on Track," *Business Week,* April 3, 1978, p. 70.

"The Recession Balks Genesco's Turnaround," *Business Week,* July 7, 1975, p. 66.

Rieger, Nancy, "Genesco's Growth Path Strewn with Brands," *Footwear News,* August 9, 1993, p. 23.

Rotenier, Nancy, "Footloose," *Forbes,* May 9, 1994, p. 14.

Rooney, Ellen, "Genesco Outlines 5-Year Growth Plan," *Footwear News,* January 25, 1993, p. 8.

——, "Grindstaff Is Named to Genesco CEO Post," *Footwear News,* January 18, 1993, p. 2.

Santry, David G., "Inside Wall Street: Genesco Hits a Snag En Route to Recovery," *Business Week,* December 4, 1978, p. 89.

Seckler, Valerie, "Genesco to Put All Its Eggs in Shoe Basket," *Footwear News,* November 7, 1994, p. 1.

Sender, Isabelle, "Blueprints for Success," *Footwear News,* February 12, 1996, p. 18.

——, "Mitre, U.B. Fair Game for Bargain Hunters," *Footwear News,* November 14, 1994, p. 1.

Sherrid, Pamela, "Trudging toward Recovery," *Forbes,* November 9, 1981, p. 176.

Sohng, Laurie, "T.U. Adjusts to Life with Genesco," *Footwear News,* February 15, 1993, p. 72.

"Where Genesco Goes from Here," *Business Week,* March 10, 1973, p. 104.

—Ellen D. Wernick

Gold Kist Inc.

244 Perimeter Centerparkway, N.E.
Atlanta, Georgia 30346
U.S.A.
(404) 393-5000
Fax: (404) 393-5061
Internet: http://www.goldkist.com

Cooperative Company
Incorporated: 1933 as Georgia Cotton Producers
    Association
Employees: 15,700
Sales: $1.7 billion
Stock Exchanges: NASDAQ
SICs: 2015 Poultry Slaughtering & Processing; 5261
    Retail Nurseries & Garden Stores

With operations in 17 states, more than 15,500 employees, and nearly 30,000 active members, Gold Kist Inc. is America's second largest poultry processor and ranks second only to Coca-Cola Co. among the state of Georgia's largest businesses. Its broilers are sold throughout the country under the Gold Kist Farms brand. This diversified farm cooperative is the nation's third largest feed manufacturer and a high-ranking pork producer. Gold Kist's more than 90 retail outlets sell farm supplies throughout the southern United States. In a partnership with Archer Daniels Midland Co. and Alimenta (USA), Inc., the co-op owns a one-third stake in America's leading peanut procurement, processing, and marketing company in the United States, Golden Peanut Company. Other operations include: a joint venture pecan processor, a hybridizing operation, a metal fabricator, a farm financing firm, an aquaculture division, pet food production, and fertilizer plants.

Depression Era Origins

The first 35 of Gold Kist's more than 60 years in business were dominated by David William Brooks, a man who has been lauded as one of agriculture's "senior corporate giants." The Georgia native was born in 1901, the youngest son of a well-to-do farmer-merchant. D.W. was the only one of his siblings to follow his father into agriculture, earning a degree in agricultural economics and science from the University of Georgia at the age of 19. Brooks later reflected in a company-published biography, "Realizing I was a few years ahead of the game, thought maybe I needed a little maturity." Taking a teaching position at the school, he pursued a master's degree in agricultural economics.

But witnessing the extreme poverty of many of Georgia's small farmers (*annual* per capita income averaged less than $75), Brooks was inspired to organize the Georgia Cotton Growers Cooperative Association (GCGCA) in 1921. With roots in the Grange and Populist movements of the late 19th and early 20th centuries, American agricultural cooperatives numbered in the thousands by 1930. These organizations brought efficiency of scale, increased buying clout, and innovative methods to small farmers across the country. But up to this time, they had been concentrated in the northern states and limited to production of perishables like dairy products. Some co-ops sought to raise commodity prices by limiting supply, even resorting to destroying their own crops at times. Brooks hoped to use the cooperative structure to help local farmers increase their productivity and market their produce more profitably by eliminating the middleman at several levels of trade. By doing elementary processing and marketing themselves, for example, co-op members could demand higher prices for their goods and retain more of the proceeds.

Over the protestations of his father and the president of the College of Agriculture, Brooks resigned his teaching position in 1925 to supervise field operations for the struggling group. Despite his efforts, the GCGCA failed in 1933. That same year, Brooks and a core of true believers founded a new cooperative, the Georgia Cotton Producers Association. With a $10,000 loan from the American Cotton Cooperative Association, Brooks bought warehouses and fertilizer plants at pennies on the dollar from sellers motivated by Depression era devaluation. Brooks even executed what would now be called LBOs (leveraged buyouts), borrowing funds to buy whole companies and liquidating assets his co-op did not need to pay off the debt. Apply-

---

Company Perspectives:

Since its founding in 1933 as a cotton marketing cooperative, Gold Kist has been dedicated to helping farmers in the South profitably meet the rapidly changing demands of agriculture and helping them feed and clothe people from Alabama to Asia. Through innovative research, rapid adaptation of new technology, extensive employee training, substantial investments in modern facilities and equipment and aggressive marketing, Gold Kist is successfully fulfilling its corporate mission to improve the economic well-being of its members.

---

ing what he had learned in college, Brooks helped member-farmers increase their yields with improved varieties, high-quality fertilizers and insecticides, and better seed and livestock feed.

By the end of its first year, the Georgia Cotton Producers Association had grown from 13 members to about 7,000 and had achieved a net profit on its operations. That first year, the co-op established a long-held precedent of paying out half its profits in dividends (or credits toward the next growing season's supplies) and reinvesting the remainder. Having expanded far beyond the borders of its home state to become a regional influence by the end of the 1930s, the cooperative dropped "Georgia" from its name.

Diversification of Products and Services in the 1940s and 1950s

Notwithstanding the co-op's early success, Brooks soon perceived that the group would not last long if its members concentrated their efforts exclusively on cotton production. By the early 1940s, a number of factors had combined to shift cotton production from the small farms of the Southeast to large-scale operations in the Southwest. As a result, Brooks began to engineer a shift from cotton to poultry. As he had with cotton, the leader emphasized high yields as well as cooperative processing and marketing. Although co-op members continued to produce and process cotton through the mid-1990s, this singularly southern crop declined as a proportion of the group's sales in the intervening years.

During World War II, the Cotton Producers Association harnessed its nitrogen-producing fertilizer plants to produce ammunition for the allied effort. A 1951 diversification into pecan processing brought more than a new product to the Cotton Producers Association, it also instituted a new name for the cooperative. Over the course of the next two decades, the CPA slowly assumed the Gold Kist moniker, making it official in 1971. By 1950, the cooperative's membership had grown to 108,000 and its net worth burgeoned to $2.7 million.

CPA/Gold Kist diversified into property and casualty insurance during this period as well. During the Depression, many despairing farmers had burned their own homes and barns to collect insurance payouts. By the early 1940s, several insurers

began to cancel farmers' policies across the board and pull out of the market. In desperation, farmers, many of whose loans were secured in part by their insurance policies, turned to their cooperative for help. The CPA organized Cotton Farmers Mutual Insurance Association in 1941, establishing strict standards so as not to get "burned." The co-op added life insurance in 1955. (It appeared to have terminated both of these businesses by the mid-1990s.)

Gold Kist started to expand internationally in the immediate postwar era, establishing sales offices first in Europe, then in Asia and the Middle East in the 1950s. By 1980, the cooperative ranked among America's fifty largest exporters.

Brooks's Retirement Signals End of an Era

By the time D.W. Brooks entered semiretirement in 1968, Gold Kist Inc. was the South's largest farm cooperative, with more than $270 million in annual revenues and a net worth of $53 million. Brooks relinquished the day-to-day details of the operation in favor of a slightly less taxing chairmanship. He held this transitional post until 1977, at which time he became chairman-emeritus and head of the policy committee. Brooks had garnered many honors over his lifetime of service to farmers, including "1966 Man of the Year in Agriculture" from *Progressive Farmer* and induction into the University of Georgia's Agricultural Hall of Fame. He was even nominated for the Nobel Peace Prize for his efforts to end hunger around the world. Brooks was also known as an "advisor to presidents," having officially consulted with every president from Harry Truman to Jimmy Carter (with the notable exception of Richard Nixon). Brooks continued to serve the company in an advisory capacity, working three days each week into the mid-1990s.

After its more than three decades under one leader, Gold Kist endured a tragically high rate of turnover in its top executive office during the 1970s. C. Wesley Paris succeeded Brooks as general manager. He had spent his entire career with the cooperative, having started out as an office boy in 1934. Paris held Gold Kist's top post until his death in 1972, at which time the corporate governance was changed to a three-man executive committee consisting of the chairman, the chief executive officer, and the president. Paris was succeeded by G.A. Burson, who was at the helm of the company when it crossed the $1 billion sales mark in 1977. Burson served as president until his death in 1978, when he was succeeded by Donald W. Sands.

Agricultural Crisis Bruises Bottom Line in 1980s

Up until the 1980s, Gold Kist's growth had been interrupted by only one annual net loss, when drought and other factors caused a $4 million shortfall in 1971. Although the cooperative's sales neared $2 billion, a number of factors—double-digit interest rates, inflation, the energy crisis, a severe drought, and America's grain embargo on the USSR—converged to bring a $1.6 million loss in fiscal 1979–1980. It was a traumatic beginning to a decade that saw the number of agricultural cooperatives nationwide decline by about 12 percent through a combination of failure and merger.

This difficult era's interest rates, which soared as high as 20 percent, influenced a dramatic change at Gold Kist. In September 1986, the cooperative made a public stock offering of 27 percent of its Golden Poultry subsidiary, which itself constituted one-sixth of the entire Gold Kist organization. The initial public offering went against some of the most strongly held beliefs of conservatives in the cooperative movement. In a 1987 article for *Forbes* magazine, David Henry noted that some observers accused Gold Kist of "behaving more like big business than like the farmer's answer to big business." But when faced with the choice between incurring more debt or selling equity to raise capital to pay for expensive poultry processing plants, the company chose the latter. Gold Kist President Donald Sands told *Forbes's* David Henry, "Until that time, I think you would have almost had a lynching of anyone who wanted to go public with anything." That fiscal year's net profit of $22.3 million, however, seemed to validate the executive decision.

The 1990s and Beyond

Poultry continued to be Gold Kist's primary product into the 1990s, constituting about 74 percent of net sales volume in fiscal 1995. Chicken became an increasingly important part of the American diet during this period, with per capita annual consumption surpassing pork in 1985 and beef in 1995. By the latter year, Gold Kist was processing an astonishing 14 million broilers each week. The co-op's poultry exports also expanded rapidly during the early 1990s, from $46.3 million in 1990 to more than $70 million in 1995. In line with founder D.W. Brooks's focus on continuous innovation, the company automated its inventorying, delivery, and invoicing through the use of computerized barcode scanners and implemented highly efficient and forward-looking processing techniques. The cooperative's marketing methods also grew significantly more sophisticated. In conjunction with a change in the poultry brand name to Gold Kist Farms, the company launched its most ambitious poultry marketing program in 1996. The campaign included television, radio, print, and point-of-sale advertising to support the brand rollout.

But in acknowledgment of the vagaries of commodities markets, Gold Kist did not put all of its eggs in the poultry basket. Guided by an executive committee consisting of Chairman and CEO Gaylord O. Coan (who succeeded the retiring Harold O. Chitwood in 1996) and President and Chief Operating Officer John Bekkers, the company diversified into pork, pet food, and catfish farming in the early 1990s. Gold Kist executives and members alike hoped that these efforts would help even out the co-op's profitability, which continued to be erratic during this period. After declining to barely $1 billion in 1988, Gold Kist's sales grew to $1.7 billion in 1995, and net income fluctuated from a high of $46.4 million in 1989 to a $20.6 million loss in 1992. Net income stood at a rather dismal $11.8 million in 1995.

Principal Subsidiaries

Golden Poultry Company; Carolina Golden Products Company; Golden Peanut Company; Young Pecan Company; AgraTrade Financing, Inc.; Luker Inc.; Agvestments, Inc.; AgraTech Seeds Inc.

Principal Divisions

Poultry Group; Agriservices Division; Cotton Division; Fertilizer and Chemical Division; Pet Food and Animal Products Division; Aquaculture Research Center.

Further Reading

Alster, Norm, " 'Getting the Middleman's Share': A New Wave of Midwest Farmers' Co-Ops Is Challenging the Processors," *Forbes,* July 4, 1994, pp. 108–109.

Bennett, Stephen, "Plumping Up Sales," *Progressive Grocer,* December 1993, p. 79.

Demetrakakes, Pan, "Harvesting Heat," *Food Processing,* January 1995, pp. 55–57.

Dwyer, Steve, "The Co-Operative Evolution," *Prepared Foods,* July 1996, pp. 27–28.

"Gold Kist Taps Coan as Chairman, CEO," *Nation's Restaurant News,* November 27, 1995, p. 36.

Henry, David, "Capitalist in the Henhouse," *Forbes,* January 26, 1987, p. 37.

Lightsey, Ed, "D.W. Brooks: Georgia's Senior Corporate Executive," *Georgia Trend,* September 1995, pp. 74–76.

Looker, Dan, " 'Farmers Have To Ask Themselves If They Want To Be Just Farmers or If They Want To Be Farmer Businesspeople,' " *Successful Farming,* September 1995, p. 15.

Martin, Harold H., *A Good Man, A Great Dream: D.W. Brooks of Gold Kist,* Atlanta, Ga.: Gold Kist Inc., 1982.

Rice, Judy, "Just-In-Time Invoicing," *Food Processing,* May 1996, p. 133.

Salerno, Lynn M., and Esposito, Allison I., "The Big Business of Farm Cooperatives," *Harvard Business Review,* pp. 122–131.

Soslow, Robin, "Patience in the Pacific," *Business Atlanta,* April 1991, pp. 40–45.

Welytok, Daniel S., "Doing Business as a Cooperative in the Face of Increased Challenges from IRS," *Journal of Taxation,* January 1996, pp. 37–43.

—April Dougal Gasbarre

Groupe André

28, Avenue de Flandre
75949 Paris Cedex 19
France
1 44 72 38 43
Fax: 1 40 36 44 49

Public Company
Incorporated: 1903 as Chaussure André de Paris
Employees: 11,000+
Sales: FFr 10.37 billion ($2.1 billion) (1995)
Stock Exchanges: Paris
SICs: 5661 Shoe Stores; 5621 Women's Clothing Stores;
    6719 Holding Companies, Not Elsewhere Classified

Headquartered in Paris, Groupe André oversees one of the largest groups of shoe and clothing retailers in Europe, offering products in markets ranging from discount family wear to high fashion styles. In recent years the company has also ventured into the home furnishings market. With outlets primarily in France, the company's shoe stores include La Halle aux Chaussures (France's top shoe retailer), and the Chaussland, André, Orcade, Minelli, and François Pinet chains. The company's apparel chains include La Halle aux Vêtements, Vetland, Megal 1, Spot, Kookaï, Caroll, Creeks, and Liberto. Finally, Groupe André includes among its holdings Adolphe Lafont, retailer of menswear, and Didier Lamarthe, a retailer of women's fine leather handbags. While the company reported net losses of FFr28.9 million ($5.8 million) for the year ended August 31, 1995, which it largely attributed to costs associated with restructuring, consolidated sales rose 5.2 percent for the year.

An Early History of Rapid Growth

The company traces its beginnings to May 1896 when Albert Lévy, originally from the Alsace region, opened a small shoe factory on the Rue de Rome in Nancy, 170 miles east of Paris. Four years later, Jérôme Levy (the two men shared the same name but were not related) joined him in the business. Albert functioned as the manufacturer and merchant, while Jérôme, who previous worked as a notary in Toul in northeast France, served as administrator and financial officer. In 1903, the small company's first stores were opened in Paris and in the provinces under the name Mathieu. However, a year later, two new stores in Paris bore the name Chaussure André de Paris, and the company was known as such until it became Groupe André in 1992.

Quickly outgrowing the Rue de Rome factory, Albert and Jérôme built an larger factory on the Rue de L'Abbe Gidel in Nancy in 1910. An existing factory on the city's Quai Claude Le Lorrain was purchased in 1914. By the outbreak of World War I, André boasted 57 stores, more than half of which were in Paris' most popular neighborhoods. Each shop, about the size of a modest boutique, employed one or two managers and several salesclerks. The inventory was limited: 250 designs, all in the same price range. Nonetheless, the company was already selling 500,000 pairs of shoes each year.

When the war ended, Albert and Jérôme decided to move the company's headquarters to Paris. A six-story building facing the Rue de Soissons offered the spacious office and storage space that the burgeoning company needed. Management offices were set up on the first floor with the inventory filling the lower and upper floors. By 1922, the basement was taken over by the company's own tannery where, until 1963, thousands of skins were sorted annually. Within a decade, however, shoes were being stacked in every available space; hallways and stairways became impossible to navigate because of the encroaching inventory. To alleviate the overcrowding, the company opened a central warehouse in Pantin, a suburb northeast of Paris. From there, André's products were distributed to 132 shops in France, Algeria, and Tunisia. Unfortunately, Jérôme was only able to enjoy the beginnings of the company's success; he died in 1926.

Economic and Political Forces
Challenge Company's Creativity

The worldwide economic crisis of the 1930s and increased foreign competition forced André to revamp its production and sales operations. Assembly lines were instituted at the Gridel factory, a leather sole tannery was opened in Longjumeau, and a heel factory was opened in Châtillon-sur-Seine. By streamlining the manufacturing process, André was able to step up mass production and reduce prices. In addition to increasing sales (from 3,200,000 pairs in 1931 to 6,300,000 in 1935), holding the line on prices was a positive public relations move. The company's advertising tag line, "André le chausseur sachant chausser," André, the shoemaker who understands feet," was reflective of the public's perception of the firm as a friendly, caring one.

André's successes were dampened by the death of Albert Lévy's in 1935. Two members of the second generation were now in charge: Albert's son Georges stepped in to replace him as president and Jérôme's son Roger was second in command. By the end of the decade, the company's 132 stores were selling 5,200,000 pairs of shoes each year and had become a force to be reckoned with in the French shoe industry.

German occupation during the Second World War was psychologically and physically devastating to the French. In spite of the upheaval, many companies such as Group André hung on tenaciously. A flurry of activity marked André's postwar years. New locations were opened at a rate of three or four per year. In 1947, an aggressive 31-year-old named Jean-Louis Descours joined the company as its real estate, financial, and administrative director. Descours was intrigued by American business practices and quickly embarked on a series of visits to the United States, bringing new ideas back to André. By 1960, the company employed 5,500 workers, the three factories in Nancy were producing 3,900,000 pairs of shoes annually, and 161 André stores in France and Algeria were selling 7,750,00 pairs to the tune of 150 million francs. The year also marked the death of Georges Levy. Descours succeeded him as president and began an overhaul of the company in earnest.

A New Era Dawns Under Descours' Leadership

Foremost in Descours' plans were the modernization of the manufacturing process, contracting production to countries with lower labor costs, expanding the product line, and exporting products to new markets. Descours had been especially influenced by the success of discount retailing in the United States and in Belgium. In spite of the fact that half of André's board of directors opposed the changes, Descours forged ahead with his plans. While French shoppers had already been introduced to discount shopping through so-called hypermarkets, the André low-cost centers offered the new concept of self-service. The company's first discount store, La Halle aux Chaussures (HAC), opened in a dilapidated warehouse in rural Dombasle. Consumers responded so favorably that HAC stores soon appeared in suburban towns and shopping malls. Today 80 percent of the discount shoes, featuring leather uppers with synthetic soles, are manufactured in Europe. Of that, 15 percent are made in Groupe André factories. The remaining 20 percent are produced in the Far East.

As part of Descours' plan for modernizing the manufacturing process, Groupe André built new factories in Nancy, Rupt-sur-Moselle, Champigneules, and Dombasles in the late 1960s and early 1970s. Not only did the new facilities streamline production, the working conditions were much improved as the company management staff became more aware of employee needs. In 1962, the installation of a computer system revolutionized the company's inventory control and computer programs were quickly set up to execute accounting procedures, employee compensation plans, and financial reports.

Restructuring and expansion took a toll on the company's profit margins in the 1970s. Fortunately, a steady rise in sales allowed the company to return to its traditional profit pace by 1978. Acquisitions further added to the company's growth. Jallate, a leading manufacturer of work shoes and boots was acquired in 1981. Minelli, with a reputation for high-fashion women's shoes, was purchased in 1984. The Raoul, Dressoir, and Pinet network of designer shoe stores was acquired in 1985. In late 1989, André celebrated the opening of its 500th store and the annual sale of 18 million pairs of shoes.

Expanding into Clothing Markets and Making Plans for the Future

The 1980s also signalled André's move into the clothing market with the establishment of La Halle aux Vêtements, a chain of low-priced garment stores opened in suburban locations. When asked in a 1993 interview why the company chose to diversify into clothing sales, Descours said that they wanted to avoid saturation in the shoe industry. Once La Halle aux Vêtements was established, Groupe André further strengthened its position in the clothing marketing with the acquisition of Caroll, purveyor of women's fashions, in 1988; Creeks-Liberto and Didier Lamarthe in 1989; Kookaï, which specializes in young women's clothing, in 1990 and the discount family apparel chain, Spot, in 1991. By the mid-1990s, André was also venturing into the home furnishings market with La Halle a la Maison.

In the mid-1990s, Groupe André's staff of slightly more than 11,000 was relatively young; the average employee age was 32 years. Not only did the company's fashion products demand a youthful focus, the management welcomed the ideas that younger employees generated. The company offered flexible work schedules and made a practice of promoting from within. By the end of the decade, Groupe André plans to create 6,000 additional positions to keep pace with the company's growth.

By 1992, international operations accounted for 20 percent of the company's revenue. Continuing this trend, expansion into Eastern Europe was a project just beginning to take shape. In France, Groupe André faced increased competition as consumers became more enamored of discount shopping and demanded higher quality. Several of the company's divisions, notably Caroll and Creeks, suffered financial loses early in the decade, prompting a restructuring designed to decrease overhead and revamp the stores' collections.

Speculation about Descours' personal plans occasionally swirled around the business world. Known to be a shrewd businessman with a strong grip on the company's operations, his holding company, Groupe Jean-Louis Descours, owned a 20 percent interest in Groupe André in 1995. Industry analysts predicted that Descours, approaching 80 years old, would engineer a sale of the larger company rather than give up his post. Descours, on the other hand, insisted that he would be replaced from within Groupe André and that no one would notice his departure.

Principal Subsidiaries

Adolph Lafont (93%); André Facon; Caroll International; Compaignie des Halles aux Textiles; Compagnie Internationale de la Chaussure; Compagnie Internationale du Textile; Creeks (75%); Esprit (80%); Kookaï (79%); Kookoo (71%); Vetland.

Further Reading

"Groupe Andre," *Footwear News*, January 22, 1996, p. 20.

Groupe André: L'Histoire, Paris: Groupe André, 1990.

Weisman, Katherine, "Descours: The Man Behind Groupe André," *Footwear News*, July 26, 1993, p. 2.

——, "La Halle aux Chaussures Strikes Bargain with French Shoppers," *Footwear News*, February 20, 1995, p. 76.

—Mary McNulty

Hamilton Beach/Proctor-Silex Inc.

4421 Waterfront Drive
Glen Allen, Virginia 23060
U.S.A.
(804) 273-9777
Internet: http://www.hambeach.com

Wholly Owned Subsidiary of Nacco Industries Inc.
Incorporated: Founded 1901 as Wear-Ever Aluminum
Employees: 4,113
Sales: $377.5 million (1994)
SICs: 3634 Electric Housewares & Fans; 3631
   Household Cooking Equipment

Hamilton Beach/Proctor-Silex Inc. is a leading manufacturer of more than 27 different household appliances, from coffeemakers to blenders, toasters to irons. A combination of two revered names in household appliance manufacturing, the company has taken a number of steps in the late 1980s and 1990s that have made it a leader in every field it enters, with double-digit market share in nearly every product group. Although, traditionally, Proctor-Silex had been known as a maker of heating appliances and Hamilton Beach had been known for its motorized appliances, the management of the joined company opted to spread product mix across the two brands, positioning Proctor-Silex as the entry brand and Hamilton Beach as the premium brand. This strategy, along with other innovative management and development techniques, has made Hamilton Beach/Proctor-Silex a strong player in the stable of its parent company, Nacco Industries, of Mayfield Heights, Ohio.

From Old Companies, New Ideas

Although Hamilton Beach/Proctor-Silex Inc. (HB/PS) is now a fully modernized and diversified appliance manufacturer, it traces its origins to some of the innovators in the field of household convenience. The Hamilton Beach Manufacturing Company began when two young employees of the Arnold Electric Company of Racine, Wisconsin, Chester Beach and L. H. Hamilton, teamed up to invent a motor that could run off either AC or DC electricity. At a time when different regions of the United States

used different types of power, the "universal motor" allowed the company to begin offering the first commercial drink mixer to a national market beginning in 1911. Their timing was right, for malted milks were the latest health drink in drugstores across the nation and the mixers sold well. Soon the entrepreneurs adapted their motor for sewing machines, mixers, can openers, electric knives, and other motorized appliances. For decades thereafter Hamilton Beach operated as a successful, though undynamic, maker of quality home appliances.

The Proctor-Silex brand also traces its beginnings to a young inventor, in this case a 14-year-old Jackson, Michigan boy named Joe Myers. Myers tinkered with his mother's single-setting iron, inventing an adjustable temperature control that he tried to sell to several appliance companies without success. Finally, Myers convinced a Cleveland, Ohio company to back him in displaying the first adjustable temperature iron at the United States sesquicentennial celebration in 1926. The iron attracted the attention of automatic toaster inventors Proctor & Schwartz, who purchased Myers's Liberty Gauge Company and began marketing both the toaster and the iron in 1929. Thirty years later, in 1960, Proctor & Schwartz acquired the coffeemaker manufacturer Silex to form the Proctor-Silex company. The new company soon branched out into the manufacture of can openers, popcorn poppers, and toaster ovens.

Like Hamilton Beach, Proctor-Silex enjoyed a steady though unspectacular success through most of its history. The company went through a number of management changes over the years: it was acquired by SCM in 1966, then sold to Wesray and Management in 1983. A year later, Wesray merged Proctor-Silex with Wear-Ever, an aluminum cookware company founded in 1901 as part of the United States Aluminum Co. After enjoying two years as a publicly owned company, in 1988 Wear-Ever/Proctor-Silex was purchased outright by NACCO Industries for $104.6 million in cash. NACCO dumped Wear-Ever less than a year later, on January 31, 1989, for $39.7 million and renamed the company Proctor-Silex Inc. On October 11, 1990, NACCO merged Proctor-Silex Inc. with its newest acquisition, Hamilton Beach Inc., to form Hamilton Beach/Proctor-Silex Inc. Thus out of two old companies, a new company was formed.

Company Perspectives:

It is our policy to provide quality products and services that meet or exceed both consumer and customer expectations. We will use sound practices to ensure products and services of excellent quality and value. We are committed to continuous quality improvement in all aspects of our business.

Teaching an Old Dog New Tricks

Managers at HB/PS were faced with a number of problems in making their company a success. Not least among these problems was the inherently cyclical nature of the small appliance business. When the economy was booming, appliance makers could count on their goods flying off the shelves. But when the economy was bad—as it had been in the early 1980s—appliance makers truly suffered, for their profit margins were never substantial to begin with. Both Hamilton Beach and Proctor-Silex had suffered through the recession of the early 1980s, plagued by high manufacturing costs and declining product quality. Moreover, increased competition from European appliance makers like Krups and Braun forced the companies into the lower end of the market, where profit margins were especially slim.

When George Nebel became president of HB/PS early in 1991, he sought to turn the difficulties of the appliance business into virtues. *HFD* reporter Linda Purpura noted that most executives see "low-margin business as inflexible and risky ventures that require keen management, savvy, strong brand strength, and highly efficient manufacturing to avoid losses." But with the backing of the NACCO board, Nebel took steps to turn his new company into an efficient and, above all, profitable enterprise. Nebel closed two factories, slashed personnel and advertising, and sought to increase the efficiency of existing operations. By 1992 the latter step was clearly taking effect, as factories were running at 70 to 80 percent capacity and plant managers were encouraged to reach 90 percent capacity by 1993. These steps returned the company to profitability by the end of 1991. Earnings for that year were $2.8 million on sales of $392 million. But Nebel was not yet satisfied. "As a public company, HB/PS must show an acceptable level of profitability to its shareholders, which we define as 5 percent after tax profit," he told Purpura.

Nebel next set out to reposition the Hamilton Beach and Proctor-Silex brands in an incredibly competitive market. HB/PS sought to maintain its historic strength in offering lower-priced appliances. "But equally important to HB/PS," noted Purpura, "is leveraging the popularity of its lower-priced goods to win placement for its higher-priced, and better-featured merchandise." Achieving such a goal required that HB/PS broaden its line of products, improve product quality, get these products into stores, and convince consumers to buy them. Achieving the profitability that Nebel desired meant that HB/PS needed to learn to succeed at each of these different tasks. Remarkably, they did.

New product development became an important project for HB/PS. Parent company NACCO invested more than $15 million in product development, engineering, and molding equipment. "We recognize that technology changes," Nebel told Purpura. "We can't be the low-cost producer with the last generation of technology." The addition of computer-aided design (CAD) equipment cut development time to less than six months and allowed HB/PS to stay abreast of current styling trends. By 1993 HB/PS had introduced new lines or expanded old lines in its best-selling ranges of coffeemakers, toasters, blenders, and irons. The logic behind the new product development was to create a Hamilton Beach or Proctor-Silex brand product for each price point in a product range. With this expanded line, customers who had purchased the inexpensive Proctor-Silex coffeemaker when they first started a household could now move up to the full-featured Hamilton Beach Aroma Elite coffeemaker as their earning power increased.

The mere existence of an expanded product line was attractive to retailers, who in displaying the entire range of HB/PS products could offer their customers a range of value without having to purchase from a variety of manufacturers. But HB/PS did not rest on new products alone. They also instituted an aggressive marketing plan to get their products into every available market. "Our mission has been to become the vendor of choice in the small appliance industry," Judy McBee, executive vice-president of marketing, told *HFN*'s Michelle Nellett Abdeddaim. HB/PS marketers and salespeople worked to educate existing retailers about how best to display and market HB/PS products and sought to open new channels of distribution. In 1994, *HFN* reported that the company "restructured its sales staff to service department stores and specialty shops with a sales force trained specifically for these distribution channels." Such stores were expected to be the premier distribution channel for the new Hamilton Beach Professional Line of products, as well as carriers of other Hamilton Beach and Proctor-Silex products.

Finally, HB/PS sought to improve upon its brand recognition with an expanded and innovative advertising campaign. Print advertising in home magazines served as one channel to let consumers know about the new face of HB/PS products. In addition, the company initiated an innovative new idea in television marketing: an infomercial that promotes an entire range of products rather than just a single item. The "Hamilton Beach Showcase" infomercial, which featured television personality Sarah Purcell and Piero Biondi, host of the radio program "Chef Piero's Food and Wine Show," began airing in 1993 and featured the Steam Grill, the Food Steamer/Rice Cooker, and the Super Shooter cookie press. "The Hamilton Beach Showcase really illustrates the numerous benefits of the three products—benefits like ease, speed and convenience," Ian Sole, vice-president of marketing, told *HFD*.

Market share information for the years 1992 and 1993 showed that HB/PS's tactics paid off, for the company held double-digit market share in nearly every category in which it placed a product. HB/PS led all manufacturers in the toaster market with a 39 percent market share, held second place in the blender and electric knives markets, with 26 and 20 percent, respectively, and claimed 15 percent of the portable mixer market and 10 percent of the electric can opener market, all according to *Appliance Manufacturer* magazine. In the overall core electric housewares market, HB/PS held a 26.4 percent market share, just behind Black & Decker's 28.6 percent and ahead of competitors Sunbeam, Mr. Coffee, Toastmaster, Braun, Rival, Oster, and a host of other smaller manufacturers, according to *Appliance* magazine.

Innovations and Future Prospects

Nebel left HB/PS early in 1995 to head consumer electronics manufacturer Gemini Industries, and he was replaced in 1996 by former S. C. Johnson & Son Inc. executive Richard Posey. NACCO Chairman and Chief Executive Officer Alfred M. Ranking, Jr. told the Richmond *Times-Dispatch* that Posey "brings to the company the leadership experience and strategic vision vital to the company's continuing growth and reputation." Mike Morecroft, vice-president of engineering, added, "The main thing he brings is consumerism. . . . How do we give the consumer what he wants?"

Posey inherited from Nebel a product development and testing staff that was eager to produce the most consumer-friendly products it could build. Engineers, market researchers, and industrial designers teamed to develop products that combined the latest features with a high degree of usability. Referring to product development as a painstaking and detailed process, Morecroft told *Times-Dispatch* reporter Chip Jones, "Sometimes my mind is blown by the millions of dollars in computer power [it takes to make] a $9 coffee maker." Once the basic product was designed, marketers tested colors and features with focus groups to come up with a product line that would appeal to the greatest number of consumers. In the product testing lab at corporate headquarters in Glen Allen, Virginia, technicians put the products through a diabolical series of tests designed to tease out any faults a consumer might find in years of usage. "We do abusive things to our products," Chris Zachwieja, manager of product safety and reliability, told Jones.

An example of the output of such a process was the cow line of Proctor-Silex products that was introduced in 1994. Four products—a coffeemaker, a toaster, an electric can opener, and a slow cooker—all bore the distinctive image of a healthy black-and-white spotted cow. "You don't have to be a cow lover to appreciate the line's classic good looks," marketer Sole told *HFD*. Such research also led to careful choices of colors to match contemporary home decor and to extensive focus-group testing of the features offered on irons.

HB/PS entered the digital age shortly after Posey's arrival with the debut of its site on the World Wide Web, an informa-tion network available to many computer users. The site invited browsers to imagine themselves in a home environment in which they can choose just the items they need to suit their lifestyles—and in which they can quickly consult an expert willing to offer advice and information about Hamilton Beach and Proctor-Silex products. Included in the multilayered web site were a Virtual Kitchen, Products on Parade (a richly photographed catalog), and At Home Suites (depicting designer suites of specialty appliances). The web site allowed the company to create a world in which the consumer is surrounded by its products, a marketer's dream world. Left to be seen, however, was whether such a site was also a consumer's dream world. To their credit, the site's designers left visitors with a way out, in the form of links to other sites on the World Wide Web. The site was given the Top Shopping Site award by the All-Internet Shopping Directory in 1996.

HB/PS prepared to enter the 21st century in strong shape. With 1994 sales of $377.5 million, a slowly expanding mid-decade economy, and aggressive plans for further product development and placement, the company stood poised to challenge for the leading market share in every market it entered. With Posey's consumer focus and a skilled and efficient manufacturing base, this combination of two venerable appliance makers intended to extend its longstanding record of success.

Further Reading

Abdeddaim, Michelle Nellett, "Ham Beach Awaits CEO," *HFN*, February 27, 1995, pp. 36, 69.

"Consumers Speak, Ham Beach Listens," *HFD*, January 11, 1993, pp. 150, 159.

"Ham Beach Pushes Restyled Blenders," *HFD*, February 1, 1993, p. 48.

"Ham Beach Sales Staff To Target Dept. Stores," *HFD*, December 5, 1994, p. 51.

Jones, Chip, "CEO Offers Fresh Perspective," *Times-Dispatch* (Richmond, Virginia), March 26, 1996, p. C1.

——, "The Making of a Better Coffee Pot," *Times-Dispatch* (Richmond, Virginia), May 20, 1996, p. D18.

Martin, Terry, "Role Model: Plant Honored for Cleaning Up Its Act," *Winston-Salem Journal*, September 4, 1995, p. B1.

"1992 Core Electric Housewares Market Share," *Appliance*, September 1993.

"Proctor-Silex Sees Line as Cash Cow," *HFD*, May 9, 1994, p. 55.

Purpura, Linda, "Effecting Efficiency," *HFD*, February 1, 1993, pp. 48–49.

"Scovill Hits the Comeback Trail," *Financial World*, January 25–February 7, 1984, pp. 24, 28.

—Tom Pendergast

Harper Group Inc.

260 Townsend Street
San Francisco, California 94107-0933
U.S.A.
(415) 978-0600
Fax: (415) 978-0699

Public Company
Incorporated: 1898 as F.F.G. Harper Co.
Employees: 3,150
Sales: $346.6 million (1995)
Stock Exchanges: NASDAQ
SICs: 4731 Freight Transportation Arrangement

Harper Group Inc. is an international provider of freight forwarding, customs brokerage, and logistics management services. Harper's primary operating subsidiary, Circle International, Inc., operates essentially as a travel agent for goods—managing the door-to-door delivery process including booking ground transport, air cargo and ocean cargo services, consolidating cargo from various shippers, clearing customs, warehousing, and tracking products as they travel to their destination. Indeed, Circle International is the second largest customs broker in the United States and the top air freight and logistics provider to Latin America; among its major corporate customers are Levi Strauss, Polaroid, and Ford, as well as the 1996 Atlanta Olympic Committee. The company has offices and agents in 356 locations in 96 countries. Following a period of financial challenge in the early 1990s, Harper came under new management in 1996 and looked forward to continued strengthening of its position as an industry leader.

19th Century Origins

Harper Group traces its history to San Francisco in 1889, when the F.F.G. Harper Co. was established to serve as a customs broker for San Francisco's burgeoning trade industry. At that time, the goods flowing through San Francisco's ports were primarily food items and art objects brought in via clipper ships from such places as Shanghai, Hong Kong, and Japan.

From a one-room office, F.F.G. Harper Co. processed entries using a wooden abacus; entry fees were paid in gold, which messenger boys carried in sacks from the bank to the U.S. customs house.

In 1906 an earthquake devastated San Francisco and destroyed Harper Co.'s original office. Undaunted, the small organization moved to a new office at 510 Battery Street. Also during this time, a 12-year-old named Ray C. Robinson joined the staff as a messenger boy, hauling gold from bank to customs house. As the company grew steadily (and was considered one of the leading customs brokers on the West Coast by 1921), the young messenger boy, Robinson, gradually assumed greater duties at the company. By 1940 he had taken over the role of company president from F.F.G. Harper, who had retired.

The Growth of Harper, Robinson & Co. in the 1940s

Around this time, Harper passed away, and Robinson bought the customs brokerage from the founder's heirs for $15,000. Robinson changed the company's name to Harper, Robinson & Co. and oversaw operations, with a reduced staff of three, during the war years. When the war ended, Robinson's two sons, John H. and Ray C., Jr., returned home and joined the company, where they began developing the strategy that would carry the company into the 20th century. At this time, Harper, Robinson & Company's work force numbered 12.

According to company documents, the Robinson family determined that flexibility would be essential to the success of the company. In order to "satisfy the logistics and transportation needs of individual companies in very different industries," according to John H. Robinson, "we decided that if it had tires, wings or floated, we wouldn't own it." The organization, therefore, positioned itself as a "freight forwarder," purchasing cargo space on airplanes, ships, and trucks, and then selling that space to its customers. As part of their vision for growth, Harper Robinson & Co. applied for the IATA freight forwarding license in 1949 and became one of four San Francisco companies to win the honors.

Company Perspectives:

We will provide integrated door-to-door transportation and logistic solutions on a time-definite basis. We will be an essential part of our client's supply chain from sourcing to delivery of product to the ultimate customer.

Postwar Expansion

In the early 1950s, Harper Robinson & Co. entered an era of tremendous national and international expansion. Internationally, the customs broker and freight forwarding company grew its business through establishing alliances with freight forwarders native to specific countries. At home, the company continued to open local offices and by 1969 had 40 offices across the United States. To accommodate such expansion, the company created four new subsidiaries to handle the various processes involved in buying space with carriers, consolidating shipments, and moving them internationally. Harper Robinson & Co. maintained its customs brokerage business and also took on the duties of ocean forwarding; Circle Air Freight was created to handle air freight forwarding transactions; Western Navigation handled ocean cargo consolidation; and Harper Shipping Co. and Pacific Intermodal Corp. handled affairs such as Spanish documentation, marine insurance, and international banking.

This growth strategy had reportedly been set into motion in 1951, when John H. Robinson flew on Pan American Airlines' inaugural flight from California to Japan. During his stay in Japan, the young Robinson made contacts with several Japanese businessmen who would become instrumental in the company growth, among them Shoshi Idemitsu (who later became chairman of the board of Idemitsu Oil Company) and a man who would become chairman of Nippon Express. These Japanese companies would purchase American goods which Harper, Robinson & Co. would then transport from the Midwest to Japan via San Francisco. "Through my Japanese contacts we eventually built our business representing Japanese companies purchasing American goods," said Robinson. In fact, the company built its first satellite office in Los Angeles the following year. Robinson's flight to Japan proved lucrative in several ways; in the mid-1950s, when Pan Am began air cargo service to Japan, Harper Robinson & Co. was appointed its first freight forwarding agent in San Francisco, and in 1956 the company became an official freight forwarded handling shipments of oil refinery to Japan.

Early Computerization and Expansion Efforts

When the elder Robinson retired in 1963, his son John took the helm as president and CEO and began a series of computerization efforts which would prove fundamental in the company's market leadership position of the 1990s. "Robinson watched his accounting team pull on the long arm of an old IBM computer," company documents noted, adding "As the machine groaned, it dawned on him how important information systems would be to the forwarder of tomorrow." Under John Robinson's direction, Harper, Robinson & Co. began establish-

ing an extensive information technology system that evolved as the company grew and eventually placed the firm among the few freight forwarders that offered "100 percent true information control of in transit cargo."

If the 1950s was a decade for expansion into Asia, the 1960s was the time for expansion into Europe. Harper, Robinson & Co. set the groundwork for this expansion "by riding the tails of Fortune 500 expansion," according to company literature. As these growing American companies expanded their markets into Europe, Harper, Robinson & Co. grew through providing customs brokerage, ocean forwarding, air freight forwarding, ocean cargo consolidation, marine insurance, and international banking.

Formation of the Harper Group

In 1970, the Harper Group was created to serve as a parent company uniting the financial operations and statements for Circle Airfreight Corp., Harper, Robinson & Co., Robinson Shipping Co., Western Navigation Corp., and Pacific Intermodal Corp. Also that year, Harper opened its first international office in Japan. The company's Circle subsidiary had grown to become the third largest international freight forwarder. "Going overseas was unbelievably tough," said Marty Collins who joined in 1970 as Harper's new controller. "Every country was different. You had to cross cultures, and were operating in a different environment while managing it long distance. To support this expansion we discovered how important it was to have—in place—an integrated communications network," he observed. Harper's office in Japan was successful, and soon it had expanded its network of offices to Hong Kong, Singapore, Taiwan, the Philippines, and Korea. In 1972 the company acquired a freight forwarding subsidiary, J.R. Michaels, and inaugurated an internal computer system, HARPRCON, that proved instrumental in supporting its overseas expansion. In 1974, Harper opened offices in Sao Paolo, Brazil; Johannesburg, South Africa; and Beirut, Lebanon. As it expanded across international borders, the company significantly strengthened its foothold in the ocean, air, and intermodal transport industries.

Going Public in the 1970s

In 1977, Harper Group made an initial public offering on the NASDAQ exchange. Annual revenues that year were $63 million; net profit was $43 million. Harper had grown to be one of the world's largest buyer of airfreight space and the sole international freight forwarding company with strong groups in ocean, air, and intermodal transport.

Shortly after Harper went public, deregulation hit the transportation industry and completely altered the company's business environment. "It changed from a fixed environment to an entrepreneurial environment," said a Harper official, adding "We had to negotiate for everything—truck, ocean, air." By the 1980s deregulation was having its effect on Harper's business in another way: tough competition.

1980s: Boom Years

Harper retained its competitive edge by standardizing and streamlining its information processing systems. It was one of the first companies to use personal computers and electronic mail systems. Harper also responded by opening branch offices around the globe, and by 1988 had opened offices in Egypt, Scotland, Spain, Germany, Portugal, Peru, Colombia, Malaysia, the United Kingdom, France, India, Mexico, Panama, Colombia, Haiti, Trinidad, and Puerto Rico. From 1986 to 1991, the company experienced compound annual growth of 22 percent.

Some of this growth was realized through the opening of branch offices, but much also was obtained through a lengthy series of acquisitions that began around 1985 and ended in 1992. Harper's purchased over 40 companies during that time, including Bowater Freight Services group in the United Kingdom (subsequently renamed Baxter Gruenhut Management Ltd.), Challenge Freight Services in New Zealand, Darrell J. Sekin Transport Co. in Texas, and a 70 percent stake in S.W. Air Freight, an airfreight forwarder based in Paris.

Dubbed an industry pioneer by some and a "bit kooky" by others, John Robinson's unusual management style gained attention in the transportation industry. Credited with training some of the top managers in the field and with building Harper from "one San Francisco office into an international powerhouse," Robinson realized early on that the future of freight forwarding rested not solely in the movement of goods around the world, but in *information* about the goods as they moved from the supplier to the customer. What truly set Robinson apart form his peers, however, was his practice of using positive imagery as "a means of overcoming obstacles and effectively reaching goals." Robinson became interested in the technique in 1971 in an effort to understand his son's learning difficulties and slowly began incorporating the practices into his business. Robinson also invested heavily in education, building a company training center in 1984 in the wine region of California, and sending senior management to attend graduate programs at Northwestern University and the University of California at Berkeley.

Analysts generally gave Robinson credit for his pioneering vision. However, in 1992, when Harper was forced to take a $48.3 million writedown, some accused him of overly optimistic accounting practices. "Mr. Robinson was out to reestablish Harper as the largest and most successful of the forwarders before retiring," one reporter noted, adding "it was simply a case of damn the torpedoes, full speed ahead and pickup the pieces once the war is over." Others called such accusations ludicrous. Nonetheless, the company completed a financial reorganization in 1993, and liquidated its real estate holdings, primarily warehouses, valued at $80 million total. In addition, Peter Gilbert, Harper's president, assumed Robinson's duties of chief executive officer, while Robinson remained chairman of the board.

Having essentially learned the business under Robinson's tutelage, Gilbert was well suited to fill some of Robinson's duties. A native of Barcelona, Spain, Gilbert moved to the United States in 1965 to play in the U.S. professional soccer league. He began working at Harper as a messenger at age 22 and rose from messenger to truck driver to mailroom clerk before he transferred to the company's ocean freight forwarding department, where he eventually worked his way up to the position of manager. In 1981, he was appointed senior vice-president, but left the company three years later to purchase and run Darrell J. Sekin Transport Co., a bankrupt trucking firm in Texas. Gilbert returned that company to profitability, and in 1991, when Harper bought Sekin for $21 million, Gilbert took on a senior management position with the firm.

Reorganization in the early 1990s

Gilbert was given a mandate to consolidate the company's sprawling network of offices and subsidiaries. In 1992, the company reduced its U.S. work force to improve efficiency and began offering "value added" services such as transport management, purchase-ordering, freight insurance, and temporary warehousing. The company continued to focus on trimming operating costs and improving profitability. In 1994, the company underwent a major reorganization plan, divesting its 20 percent stake in Intercargo, a cargo insurance underwriter, and consolidated Circle Airfreight Corp. and Harper Robinson & Co. into Circle International, its primary operating subsidiary. In the process, Harper integrated the marketing efforts of the two companies so that sales people were better able to sell all company offerings, from air freight space to overall logistics management.

During this time a trend emerged among international traders to contract out logistics management responsibilities, and Harper began marketing itself as a provider of such integrated services. To realize its goals, the company began recruiting from outside in an effort to bring the industry's "best and brightest" to Harper. In March 1996, Steven D. Leonard, a former airline executive, was named president and chief operating officer of Circle International. In June 1996 James A. McKinney, former Navy fighter pilot and president of Fed Ex Logistics Services, was appointed president of Harper Group. Commenting on the addition of McKinney, Chairperson Gilbert explained that the company sought "new dimensions in logistics knowledge, best practices, and user-driven technology development to help fuel our growth as a full service global logistics provider and trace facilitator." Given the trend toward outsourcing warehouse, distribution, trade finance, and customs brokerage services, Harper Group seemed assured of doing increased and brisk business in that industry into the next century.

Principal Subsidiaries

Circle International, Inc.; Circle Freight International; Con-Carriers; Max Gruenhut International; Sekin Transport International; United Intermodal Lines.

Further Reading

Armbruster, William, "Harper Group Guarantees On-Time Delivery to UK," *Journal of Commerce and Commercial,* September 14, 1993, p. B3.
Burstiner, Marcy, "For Sale: $80M in Worldwide Properties," *San Francisco Business Times,* September 1, 1995, p. 1.
——, "Freight Financing Arm Helps Harper Deliver the Goods," *San Francisco Business Times,* May 20, 1994, p. 4.
——, "Growth by Acquisition," *San Francisco Business Times,* April 14, 1995, p. 1.
Johns, Brian, "Harper Group Chief Says Firm Will Build on Recent Gains," *Journal of Commerce and Commercial,* May 13, 1994, p. B2.

Knee, Richard, "Harper Completes a Sale and a Purchase," *American Shipper,* October 1991, p. 71.

——, "Harper Group Changes Strategy," *American Shipper,* February 1993, p. 55.

Manolatos, Spyros, "The Power of Positive Imagery," *Forbes,* April 16, 1990, p. 105.

Nelson, Eric, "John Robinson's Visionary Style Propels Harper Group's Growth," *San Francisco Business Times,* February 1, 1991, p. 12.

——, "Peter Gibert Named Heir at Harper Group," *San Francisco Business Times,* June 14, 1991, p. 1.

Perser, John H., "Contract Logistics Providers Optimistic on Growth, but See Shakeout to Come," *Chicago Tribune,* August 15, 1993, Bus. Sec.

Tangeman, Nanci A., "The International Logistics of Freight Forwarding: Performance Measurement at the Harper Group," *National Productivity Review,* Winter 1993, p. 107.

Wastler, Allen R., "Harper's Numerous Acquisitions Give Company a Financial Headache," *Journal of Commerce and Commercial,* November 9, 1992, p. B2.

—Maura Troester

Communications

Harte-Hanks Communications, Inc.

P.0. Box 269
San Antonio, Texas 78291-0269
U.S.A.
(210) 829-9000
Fax: (210) 829-9403

Public Company
Incorporated: 1928 as Harte-Hanks Newspapers
Employees: 4,957
Sales: $532.85 million (1995)
Stock Exchanges: New York
SICs: 2711 Newspapers; 7331 Direct Mail Advertising
    Services; 833 Television Broadcasting Stations

Harte-Hanks Communications, Inc. is a diversified communications company. Its six newspapers *(Abilene Reporter-News, Corpus Christi Caller-Times, San Angelo Standard-Times,* and *Times Record News* in Texas, and *Anderson Independent-Mail* in South Carolina) make up 25 percent of its sales. Nearly 40 percent of sales come from the company's Direct Marketing division, which offers full-service marketing programs from market research to advertising design and delivery. More than one-third of company revenues are generated by the company's 570 zoned editions of its four free advertising shoppers, also known as pennysavers, which together reach nearly seven million households each week in the Dallas/Ft. Worth, Southern and Northern California, and Miami/Ft. Lauderdale markets.

In 1996 Harte-Hanks expanded its shoppers' potential reach by launching World Wide Web sites featuring searchable databases of shopper ads. The company is also the long-time owner of KENS-TV in San Antonio, a CBS affiliate. Together, Harte-Hanks divisions produced nearly $533 million in revenues in 1995 for net income over $10 million. Principal shareholders include Houston H. and Ed Harte, sons of company founder Houston Harte, with more than 31 percent combined, and Andrew Shelton, son-in-law of company founder Bernard Hanks, with 15 percent; Houston H. Harte serves as chairman of the board. President and CEO Larry Franklin and other officers hold an additional ten percent of the company's stock.

Partnership Between Rivals in the 1920s

Houston Harte, owner of the *San Angelo Standard,* and Bernard Hanks, owner of the *Abilene Reporter,* met for the first time at a publishers' meeting in Dallas in the early 1920s. Their papers, located only 90 miles apart, had for years competed fiercely in the primarily rural areas where their territories overlapped. That rivalry, which continued throughout their partnership, did not prevent the two from taking a liking to each other. When Harte heard about an opportunity to purchase a weekly in Lubbock, Texas, he joined with Hanks and another investor to purchase it. The partnership might have ended with the sale of that paper six years later; however, a new purchase by Harte and Hanks, of the *Corpus Christi Times,* sealed their relationship.

By then, both men had several decades of newspaper experience. Born in 1883 in Knob Noster, Missouri, Harte worked as a reporter for the *Los Angeles Examiner* while studying at the University of Southern California. In 1913, while finishing a journalism degree at the University of Missouri, Harte bought his first newspaper, the *Knob Noster Gem.* Three years later, Harte took over the *Central Missouri Republican,* based in Boonville. The U.S. entry into World War I briefly interrupted Harte's newspaper career; by 1920, however, Harte had returned to civilian life, selling his Missouri paper and moving to Texas, where he began publishing the *San Angelo Standard,* a paper founded in 1884. Harte worked to expand the paper's circulation, slowly widening its reach into 40 West Texas counties. In 1922 Harte purchased two more papers. Soon after that, he and Hanks formed their partnership.

Hanks, born in 1884, began his newspaper career as a horseback carrier for the *Abilene Reporter* when he was 12 years old. When Hanks's father moved to another town, Hanks moved in with *Reporter* publisher George Anderson. In 1907 Anderson incorporated his newspaper and allowed Hanks to purchase shares in the new company. In 1923 the company separated into two parts: Anderson took over the printing operation, while Hanks became the newspaper's publisher and owner.

After selling the Lubbock weekly, Harte and Hanks decided to remain partners. Harte had heard that the owner of a Corpus Christi paper, the *Times,* was having financial problems. Hanks and Harte took out an option to buy the paper, and went down to Corpus Christi to inspect it. As reported in a company publication, Harte recalled: "The *Times* was printed on an old flatbed press on a vacant lot in back of its building. . . . It was under a tarpaulin. It was quite a feat to print the paper out in the open in the South Texas rain." The partners nevertheless bought the paper.

The *Corpus Christi Times* was then the number two paper in town; a dismal first year brought Harte-Hanks Newspapers only $2,800. Instead of fighting a newspaper war, the young partnership took a different approach: they formed a new partnership, called Texas Newspapers, Inc., with two other investors, and bought out the rival paper. Texas Newspapers would go on to buy several more Texas papers over the next three years, but moving into the Depression the partnership proved unprofitable and was disbanded. Harte-Hanks took control of the *Corpus Christi Times* and a second paper, the *Paris News,* in Paris, Texas. By then, Harte-Hanks had also added the *Big Spring Herald* to their newspaper chain. Nevertheless, the Harte-Hanks partnership remained a more-or-less informal arrangement, with no written contract. Harte tended to handle the operational and editorial end, while Hanks focused on the partnership's finances. Newspapers were primarily bought on credit, with the former publisher holding the note, and often a share in the newspaper as well. Harte-Hanks generally retained a newspaper's former management. Purchases usually involved buying a town's second paper, which often would suffer from poor circulation and operations.

Harte-Hanks added several more newspapers, all based in Texas, during the 1930s and 1940s. In 1945 the partners took on their first corporate employee, Bruce Meador, who would later become trustee of Hanks's estate. Bernard Hanks died in 1948. By then, the second generation—Houston H. and Ed Harte, and Andrew Shelton—were already learning the newspaper trade. The company continued adding newspapers to its fold. One acquisition, of the *Greenville Daily Banner,* sparked a bitter newspaper war that led Harte-Hanks to purchase and then consolidate the rival *Greenville Herald.* The owners of that paper took Harte-Hanks to court, charging them with unfair competition, but Harte-Hanks was acquitted of this charge.

New Media in the 1960s

During the 1960s, Harte-Hanks acquired a number of newspapers, including its largest to date, the *San Antonio Express* and *News.* By the end of the decade, Harte-Hanks controlled a 13-paper empire. In 1962 the company moved beyond newspapers for the first time with the purchase of KENS-TV, a CBS affiliate based in San Antonio. Prior to the Harte-Hanks acquisition, that station had been under-staffed and under-budgeted and was consistently ranked last in its market. Under Harte-Hanks, however, the station's fortunes improved, and it quickly captured its market's top rating, a position it would hold until the 1990s. The company moved its corporate headquarters from Abilene to San Antonio in 1968.

As the company moved into the 1970s, however, the family faced the future with uncertainty. Harte's health was failing, and the chain—made up of 27 family-owned corporations—offered no clear line of succession. New technology was also entering the newspaper industry, and the company worried about its ability to keep pace. Meador, who by then was running the company, approached outside consultants. They proposed three options for the company: do nothing, which might lead the company to break up; sell out; or go public. Over Harte's objections, the family chose the last option. Their first step, in 1971, was to consolidate the 27 corporations into a single entity, called Harte-Hanks Newspapers, Inc. Their next step was to find the person to lead the company into its initial public offering.

At about the same time, Robert G. Marbut, a graduate of the Harvard Business School and a former corporate director with Copley Newspapers, was making plans to start his own publishing company. Marbut approached Harte-Hanks for financial backing for his venture; instead, the Harte family proposed that Marbut lead their company instead. Harte-Hanks went public on March 13, 1972. Houston Harte died six days later.

Marbut set about transforming the company, instituting a modern control system, a budgetary process, market research, and, as a first for the company, a system of long-range planning. Marbut also took Harte-Hanks outside of Texas, beginning in 1971, by buying the *Hamilton* (Ohio) *Journal-News.* Other new markets included Ypsilanti, Michigan; Anderson, South Carolina; and Yakima, Washington. Funds raised in the IPO allowed the company to step up its expansion: by the end of 1972, the chain had more than doubled, to 27 newspapers. Importantly, Marbut began to transform the character of the newspapers themselves, adding lifestyle and other service features to the newspapers to boost their circulation, and turning at least some of the papers into what *Forbes* described as "aggressive marketing vehicles tailored for advertisers."

While adding new papers, Marbut also began shedding others. Harte-Hanks focused its chain on smaller markets where its newspapers could hold monopoly positions. The average circulation of these papers was 10,000 to 30,000. Larger papers—such as the *San Antonio Express-News,* bought by Rupert Murdoch for $19 million in 1973—were sold, with the exception of the Corpus Christi paper, which had a circulation of about 85,000. By 1974, the company's revenues had reached $79 million, with profits of $6.5 million, compared to income of around $1.5 million at the time of the company's IPO.

The number of available small-market papers was shrinking, however. To continue expanding company revenues, Marbut took Harte-Hanks deeper into other communications areas. In 1975 Harte-Hanks bought a second television station, WTLV in Jacksonville, Florida, an NBC affiliate. Two more stations were added by the end of the decade in Greensboro, North Carolina, and Springfield, Missouri. The company also moved into radio with the 1978 purchase of Southern Broadcasting's AM and FM station holdings. By then, Harte-Hanks had also began to build its advertising shopper empire. While newspapers remained the company's chief revenue source, its growing diversity prompted a name change, to Harte-Hanks Communications. Revenues jumped to $243 million in 1979. Income topped $19 million.

By 1980, the company's holdings included 29 daily newspapers, 68 weekly newspapers, four VHF television stations, 11 radio stations, four cable television systems, and three trade publications. Its fastest-growing division was its Consumer Distribution Marketing (CDM) unit, which consisted of its advertising shoppers, three market research firms, and three direct mail distributors. Also included in CDM were electronic publishing and video entertainment software businesses. Moving into the recession of the early 1980s, Harte-Hanks's emphasis fell more heavily on CDM. As one analyst told the *New York Times,* "Harte-Hanks is much less newspaper-oriented than the other newspaper companies. It's more interested in information transfer. It's much more financially oriented." Marbut confirmed this, telling the *New York Times,* "Our job is not just to produce newspapers. Our job is to meet people's needs for information."

By 1983, CDM represented 28 percent of the company's revenues. Holdings had expanded to include 23 direct mail systems, seven research companies, a cable television shopping channel, seven delivery systems and a trucking service, and nine shoppers. Harte-Hanks revenues neared $445 million, with earnings over $33 million, placing it on the Fortune 500 list. But the emphasis on CDM, as well as Harte-Hanks's plans to invest aggressively in cable television, had begun to make investors nervous: by 1984, the company's stock was trading below $20 per share, despite being valued as high as $30 per share. The company was becoming a potential target for a hostile takeover. To prevent this, Marbut, along with Houston and Ed Harte, Andrew Shelton, and other corporate directors, took the company private in a leveraged buyout.

Private for the 1980s, Public in the 1990s

The LBO, executed in 1984, saddled the company with $1 billion in debt, just as the Texas economy, crippled by the oil crash of the 1980s, was going sour. The company began streamlining its operations, quickly shedding 56 of its 113 units, including three of its four television stations, its cable television systems, and all of its radio stations. Sales of these units, of which all but three were profitable, brought $200 million to pay down debt. The company also traded seven of its Texas, Washington, Ohio, and Michigan papers for 19 papers in Dallas and Boston. By 1988, revenues had grown to $450 million, with operating income of $70 million. The company had reduced its debt to just $375 million in zero coupon debentures, bringing its interest payments down from $81 million paid in 1986 to $20 million.

By 1990, the company had reinvented itself. The company's restructuring had turned its focus to three key areas—the shoppers, by then zoned into 465 separate editions, reaching 5.8

million households, which made Harte-Hanks the largest distributor of advertising shoppers; direct marketing; and the company's nine newspapers. KENS-TV also continued to contribute a small share to the company's revenues. Marbut retired in 1991, turning the company over to Larry Franklin, his long-time chief operating officer and executive vice-president. By 1992, the company enjoyed revenues of $423 million and had reduced total long-term debt to less than $220 million. Yet, with stock divided among the Harte and Shelton families, the company once again faced a problem of succession. In 1993, the company went public for the second time.

Revenues grew to $463 million in 1993. But problems with Harte-Hanks's 14-paper Boston chain drove the company to a $52 million net loss that year. The company sold off the Boston papers in 1995. In the meantime, the company acquired Select Marketing, a high-tech industry marketer, and Steinert & Associates, another marketing group. With revenues topping $532 million in 1995, the company continued to shore up its marketing and high-technology industry capacities; its efforts included purchasing a minority interest in the SiteSpecific Internet ad-placement firm.

Principal Subsidiaries

Harte Hanks Community Newspapers.

Principal Divisions

Caller Times Publishing Co.; Data Technologies Division; Harte-Hanks Direct Marketing Co.; Independent Publishing Co.; Potpourri Shopper Group Inc.; Reporter Publishing Co.

Further Reading

Barrett, William P., "I'm Real Happy about the Way It's Turning Out," *Forbes,* April 18, 1988, p. 44.

"The Education of Bob Marbut," *Forbes,* December 15, 1976, p. 53.

Jones, Alex S., "A Media Industry Innovator," *New York Times,* April 30, 1984, p. D1.

Kleinfeld, N. R., "Rise of an Information Empire," *New York Times,* October 30, 1980, p. D1.

O'Donnell, Thomas, "Forget Glamour, He Will Deliver the Mail," *Forbes,* April 11, 1983, p. 166.

Phelps, Christi, "Harte-Hanks Charts Post-Divestiture Path," *San Antonio Business Journal,* March 2, 1987, p. 1.

Valentine, Tammy, "Harte-Hanks: The First 50 Years," *Harte-Hanks Commemorative Series,* San Antonio: Harte-Hanks Communications, Inc.

Williams, Norma Joe, and Dick Tarpley, "Harte-Hanks: The Founders," *Harte-Hanks Commemorative Series,* San Antonio: Harte-Hanks Communications, Inc.

—M. L. Cohen

Healthtex®

Healthtex, Inc.

2303 West Meadowview Road
P.O. Box 21488
Greensboro, North Carolina 27420-1488
U.S.A.
(910) 316-1000
Fax: (910) 316-1022

Division of VF Corporation
Incorporated: 1921 as the Standard Romper Co.
Employees: 1,400
Sales: $80 million (1995 est.)
SICs: 2321 Men's/Boys' Shirts; 2325 Men's/Boys'
Trousers & Slacks; 2361 Girls'/Children's Dresses &
Blouses; 2369 Girls'/Children's Outerwear, Not
Elsewhere Classified

Healthtex, Inc., a division of the VF Corporation, is one of the leading manufacturers of children's playwear in the United States. In business since 1921, the company has undergone a number of changes in ownership and management style over the years but has maintained a reputation for producing durable, versatile clothing for children from birth to adolescence.

Company Origins

Healthtex was founded in 1921 by Louis Russek as the Standard Romper Company. Russek had worked previously as a salesman in the children's garment industry, and company tradition holds that it was his personal charisma and skill as a salesman that created and maintained Standard Romper's success for almost half a century. Russek ran his small manufacturing concern from a warehouse in Manhattan, producing flannel pajamas, creepers and rompers for infants and toddlers. He sold his products, marketed under the brand name "Stantogs," directly to small apparel stores in the Northeast.

By the 1930s Standard Romper had expanded their market with a line of sturdy, practical play clothes for children up to age seven and had leased showrooms in Chicago and San Francisco to establish a national presence for the growing firm. The Health-tex brand name was introduced in 1937 in order to emphasize the "healthy" cotton and wool textiles that the company used in their clothing. Health-tex quickly became the dominant brand name for Standard Romper although the label "Health-tex Stantogs" continued to be used through the 1970s. Standard Romper had begun advertising their children's apparel line in trade publications in the 1930s, but in the 1940s the company extended this campaign directly to consumers through advertisements in such journals as *Good Housekeeping* and *McCall's*. The promotion of the Health-tex brand name directly to the public would prove to be crucial to the long term success of the apparel company.

Growth in the 1950s and 1960s

Standard Romper and the Health-tex brand continued to expand through the 1950s and 1960s. By 1960 Health-tex had become the country's best known brand of young children's clothing. Louis Russek, who was responsible for leading the company throughout this period, maintained a policy of avoiding selling to large discount stores which he felt would cheapen the Health-tex brand. Instead, Health-tex clothes were marketed to smaller children's specialty stores and middle market department stores. By 1967 sales had reached $34 million and the company was operating five manufacturing facilities in Rhode Island, Maine, Alabama and Virginia in addition to the company offices in New York City and showrooms in Dallas, Los Angeles and Chicago.

In 1966, Health-tex launched what would prove to be one of the most successful advertising campaigns ever for a children's branded clothing line. Called "The Handy Answers to Hard Questions Asked by Children in the Health-tex Years," the campaign featured colorful print ads which provided concise answers to some of the questions commonly asked by preschool age children. The ads, put together by the AC&R agency, were illustrated with sweet cartoon-like drawings of children dressed in Health-tex clothes and included a postscript which highlighted the versatility and durability of the Health-tex line. Every time a new ad in the series appeared, Standard Romper was deluged with requests for reprints from parents and

---

Company Perspectives:

As Healthtex introduces new products and continues to build its brand, it is quite clear that the company will continue working towards one mission: To be the most responsive kidswear company in understanding and meeting the needs of the consumers and retailers with durable branded everyday playwear while aggressively understanding and attacking competitors for share in our marketplace.

---

teachers who were impressed with the clear but cute answers. This ad campaign, which continued through the early 1980s, was largely responsible for making the orange Health-tex logo one of the most recognizable children's clothing labels in the United States.

The 1970s: The Chesebrough-Pond's Years

In 1971 Standard Romper officially changed its name to Health-tex, Inc. in acknowledgement of the well established public recognition of the brand name. By this time the Health-tex brand had become so popular that the company was having trouble meeting the demand for its products. The apparel maker was forced to limit the number of retail outlets which could be offered Health-tex goods and to institute a tight allocation program to ensure that each regular customer received a fair share of Health-tex clothing to sell. In the late 1960s the growing Standard Romper went public in order to finance further expansion of manufacturing facilities, and by 1972 annual sales had soared to $64 million.

By the early 1970s, the success of Health-tex began to attract the attention of other corporations in search of profitable acquisitions, and in 1973 Chesebrough-Pond's, Inc. reached an agreement to acquire the apparel company for a stock swap worth $229 million. Formed in 1955 by the merger of Chesebrough Manufacturing Co. and Pond's Extract Co., Chesebrough-Pond's had traditionally been a health and beauty aids company with a number of long standing successful brands like Vaseline, Q-tips and Pond's. In the late 1960s, under the leadership of CEO Ralph Ward, the company had begun a program of acquisitions which would eventually extend its product range to include such diverse goods as spaghetti sauce, shoes and hospital supplies. Ward sought out Health-tex as a prime acquisition candidate because of the company's high level of brand recognition combined with its great potential for further growth.

Chesebrough-Pond's first move on acquiring Health-tex was to build new manufacturing facilities to increase production of the sought after children's clothing line. Four new plants were added within the first year of the company's new ownership, and by 1975 production had been increased by 50 percent, allowing the tight allocation program on Health-tex clothes to be relaxed. While new supplies meant that Health-tex sales and earnings rose dramatically, increased costs associated with the start up of new facilities saw profit margins fall. By the mid-1970s the company had run into serious problems with distribution and inventory controls on the rapidly expanding

production line. Bottlenecks developed at manufacturing plants, and retailers ended up with long waits for promised merchandise. Although sales climbed to over $150 million in 1978, Health-tex earnings declined for the first time in decades, dropping a dramatic 24 percent over the previous year. Chesebrough-Pond's brought in a new management team led by Chesebrough Vice-President Robert Breakstone to help straighten out the struggling company.

Breakstone had no previous experience in the children's apparel industry, but CEO Ward felt that what was needed to improve profits was organization rather than innovation. Breakstone, who had a background in data processing, immediately brought in a team of systems engineers to restructure the company's inventory control systems and by the end of the decade production and distribution problems had largely been overcome. In addition to the reorganization of management controls, under Breakstone Health-tex introduced a successful line of clothing for children age 7–14 as well as a line of activewear including swimsuits and windbreakers. During the late 1970s and early 1980s department and specialty stores began to look to more fashion-oriented children's clothing in order to differentiate their merchandise from the mass-produced inexpensive clothes being offered by competitive discounters. Health-tex responded by revamping their design process to include a high level of vertical integration between their knit textile production facilities, which manufactured two-thirds of the fabric used in Health-tex clothing, and their New York based fashion designers. This allowed the company to produce a line of original print and solid coordinates that could be combined in a wide variety of ways. The ability to mix and match Health-tex clothing encouraged brand loyalty on the part of consumers and became a major selling point for the company.

Breakstone's reorganization and line extensions of the late 1970s proved successful, and by 1983 Health-tex sales had surpassed $300 million with operating profits near $40 million, a more than 30 percent rise in two years. Sales in the new lines for older children and in fashion-oriented clothing were particularly strong. By this time, Health-tex's share of the once fragmented children's apparel market had grown to an impressive 35 percent, putting the company well ahead of their closest competitor, the William Carter Company. In 1984, Chesebrough-Pond's purchased the Imperial Reading Corporation a maker of children's apparel under the Britannia brand name. This acquisition was incorporated into the company's Health-tex division and helped increase sales still further. In addition to strong growth in the American market, in 1983 Health-tex won approval from the Canadian Foreign Investment Review Board to open a Canadian subsidiary which would operate Health-tex retail outlets, selling the company's merchandise directly to consumers.

Decline in the 1980s

In spite of the success of their Health-tex subsidiary, parent company Chesebrough-Pond's ran into difficulties in the mid-1980s. Rising debt and management turnover led to fears of a hostile takeover, and in 1985 CEO Ward made the controversial decision to purchase the ailing Stauffer Chemical Company for $1.25 billion in order to fend off a possible takeover. This purchase increased ChesebroughPond's debt to a daunting

73 percent of capital, forcing the sale of other assets. A group of investors led by Health-tex president Robert Breakstone had already made an offer to acquire the children's apparel division from Chesebrough, and in June 1985, a deal was reached between Chesebrough and Breakstone's management group. Health-tex, which by this time had grown to employ 9,000 workers in 16 plants, was taken private by Breakstone and his fellow investors by means of a leveraged buyout financed largely by heavy borrowing.

Although Breakstone was confident that the burdensome debt caused by the buyout could be repaid from the company's operating profits, it quickly became clear that Health-tex would be forced to sell assets and close plants. Even before the buyout, profits had declined by ten percent from the peak reached in 1983 because of a failure to keep pace with quickly changing fashions. Now, with no capital to invest in innovative product design, Health-tex's market share dropped still further. By 1988, the struggling firm had closed all but five of its manufacturing plants and had laid off over half of its workers. Sales fell by more than 50 percent to an estimated $150 million. Unable to make interest payments on its leveraged buyout loan, the Health-tex management group undertook a major reorganization in order to appease worried lenders and avoid bankruptcy. CEO Robert Breakstone resigned and a turnaround specialist, Gilbert C. Osmos, was appointed to replace him. Osmos's first move was to reduce the number of styles in the Health-tex line and concentrate instead on "fashion basics." The company also began to look for distribution to the large discount retail outlets like Kids 'R' Us that had traditionally been avoided by the image-conscious Health-tex. Most significantly, Osmos retained an agency to look for a buyer for the financially troubled firm.

Revival in the 1990s under VF Corp.

In 1991 Osmos successfully reached an agreement with the VF Corporation to purchase substantially all of the operating assets of Health-tex, Inc. for an estimated $29 million, a fraction of the price paid to Chesebrough-Pond's by Breakstone's group only six years earlier. VF Corp. was a Fortune 500 apparel conglomerate whose stable of brands included Lee, Wrangler, Girbaud, Jantzen and Vanity Fair. The new parent moved immediately to replace and reorganize the management of Health-tex, consolidating all management functions into new headquarters in Greensboro, North Carolina. The new management team then undertook a major campaign to revitalize the somewhat tarnished Health-tex brand image. Finding that consumers sometimes mistook Health-tex for a health care firm, VF removed the hyphen from the division name to de-emphasize the "health" component of the brand name. The new Healthtex was also given a new, brighter, logo and a $3 million ad campaign to reintroduce the brand to consumers was launched. In addition to the renewal of the brand, Healthtex management moved to revamp the Healthtex product line after mothers in focus groups complained that the quality and design of Healthtex clothing did not match their expectations for the brand. A new design team using a Computer Aided Design system was put in place to add "cute" to Healthtex basics, and all stages of the manufacturing process were reviewed to determine the source of quality slips. The "mix-and-matchability" of Healthtex clothes, which had been a feature of the line since the late 1970s, was now emphasized at the retail level with displays highlighting possible clothing combinations.

The new, improved Healthtex was an almost immediate success. By 1993 sales were up by almost 80 percent since the acquisition, and the division was able to report "solidly profitable" results for the first time in years. Market share for Healthtex, which had dropped to a dismal 3.5 percent during the nadir of the late 1980s, was also once more steadily gaining ground. Although the 75-year-old brand could no longer boast of the leading position in the children's branded apparel market, Healthtex clothes were among the top sellers in the industry. By the mid-1990s, under the leadership of division president, Gary Simmons, Healthtex seemed poised to enter another period of prosperity and growth.

Further Reading

Barnes, Peter W., "Chesebrough Agrees to Sell Health-tex Inc.," *Wall Street Journal,* June 20, 1985, p. 14.

Blyskal, Jeff, "Filling up the Table," *Forbes,* December 6, 1982, pp. 100–01.

"Chesebrough: Finding Strong Brands to Revitalize Mature Markets," *Business Week,* November 10, 1980, pp. 73–77.

"Chesebrough-Pond's to Buy Health-Tex for $229.5 Million," *Wall Street Journal,* February 27, 1973, p. 10.

Forman, Ellen, "Health-tex to Reduce Its Styles, Return Focus to Fashion Basics," *Daily News Record,* July 11, 1988, p. 5.

"Healthtex 'Solidly Profitable' in 1993," *Children's Business,* March 1994, p. 116.

Rohde, Ellen, "Turning around a Troubled Company," *Working Woman,* November 1993, pp. 34–36.

Rudnitsky, Howard, and Gissen, Jay, "Chesebrough-Pond's: The Unsung Miracle," *Forbes,* September 28, 1981, pp. 105–09.

"Standard Romper Ads Are Delight to Moms, Teachers," *Advertising Age,* September 12, 1966, p. 74.

Trachtenberg, Jeffrey, "Clothing Union to Make Offer for Health-tex," *Wall Street Journal,* June 13, 1989, p. 12.

Understanding Families: Healthtex since 1921, Greensboro, N.C.: Healthtex, Inc., 1996.

"VF Corp. Completes Purchase of Health-tex Inc.," *Wall Street Journal,* March 12, 1991, p. 12.

—Hilary Gopnik

Herbalife International, Inc.

9800 South La Cienega
Inglewood, California 90301
U.S.A.
(310) 410-9600
Fax: (310) 216-7454

Public Company
Incorporated: 1979
Employees: 862
Sales: $489 million (1995)
Stock Exchanges: NASDAQ
SICs: 5963 Direct Selling Establishments; 5499
    Miscellaneous Food Stores

Herbalife International, Inc. markets and distributes a broad spectrum of 62 herb- and botanicals-based weight management and dieting products, personal care products, and food and dietary items through a worldwide network of 750,000 independent distributors in 32 countries. Herbalife products, sold under a variety of brand names, include the Thermojetics Weight-Management Program, the Health & Fitness Bulk & Muscle Program, the Dermojetics herbal and botanical skin-care products, the Cell-U-Loss cellulite-attacking supplement, and Nature's Raw Guyana, a stimulant supplement, as well as perfumes for men and women under the Vitessence brand name. A company that has thrived in spite of wide criticism, it has come under attack for false marketing claims and for the potentially dangerous ingredients of some of its products—Thermojetics products, for example, may contain the Chinese herb ma huang, which contains ephedrine, suspected to cause hypertension and other health complications when used in large doses—Herbalife has most consistently been faulted for its unconventional distribution methods.

"Herbalife uses 'network marketing' as a way to describe its marketing and sales programs as opposed to multi-level marketing," according to the company's 1995 annual report, "because multi-level marketing has had a negative connotation in certain countries in which Herbalife does business." Nevertheless,

Herbalife's distribution network closely resembles the typical multi-level marketing approach—sometimes referred to as a pyramid scheme—and has been accused of crossing the line into the illegal endless-chain marketing. Multi-level marketing remains legal in most states in the United States, with the condition that the company's sales force of distributors actually receive earnings by selling products to people not related to the company. In an illegal endless-chain scheme, earnings are achieved primarily through recruiting new salespeople into the pyramid.

In the Herbalife network marketing plan, potential distributors buy into the network by purchasing Herbalife products, generally at a 25 percent discount off the retail price, which they may then in turn sell to others. Once they place orders above a certain amount—ranging from $2,000 to $4,000—a distributor may become supervisor, at which point they receive a 50 percent discount on Herbalife products. Distributors also become supervisors by recruiting new distributors into the network. They then receive a percentage of each recruit's sales—usually about eight percent. As supervisors rise higher in the pyramid, their earnings have the potential of rising dramatically, depending on the number of supervisors below them.

Herbalife distributors are supported by a range of company career and training programs. Among these are the company's annual distributor convention, called the Herbalife Extravaganza, which features five-day intensive training; HBN, a private satellite broadcasting network that provides training in recruitment and retention techniques, as well as marketing support and training; bonus vacation programs for top-selling distributors; and the company's own magazine, featuring testimonials of success stories by Herbalife distributors and customers. Top distributors may earn $250,000 per year and more; nonetheless, the average annual earnings among all Herbalife distributors has been estimated at $1,500. As independent contractors, distributors receive no salary or benefits from the company.

At the top of the Herbalife pyramid sits 40-year-old company founder and CEO Mark Hughes, who owns more than 50 percent of the company. In 1995, Hughes received an estimated $10 million in pay and bonuses. The company's retail sales in that year reached $932.64 million. Because distributors receive

Company Perspectives:

Our mission is to take Herbalife's philosophy of good nutrition, herbal-based products and our unique business opportunity to every corner of the world.

discounts of up to 50 percent and more on the products they sell, the company's net sales were $489 million in 1995, for net earnings of $19.7 million.

American Success Story Begins in 1980

Master salesman Mark Hughes began Herbalife in a Beverly Hills warehouse in 1980, selling the new company's dieting aids from his car. Hughes, whose parents were divorced soon after his birth in 1956, was raised in Lynwood, California, outside of Hollywood. By ninth grade, Hughes had dropped out of high school. He became involved in drug use and by the age of 16 was sent to the Cedu School, a private residential home for emotionally disturbed and troubled teenagers. It was there that Hughes developed a knack for salesmanship, rehabilitating himself by selling door-to-door raffle tickets in support of the school. By the end of his tenure, Hughes had joined the school's staff.

Another turning point for Hughes came at the age of 18, when his mother died due to an overdose of diet pills. As Hughes would tell it, according to *INC.* magazine: "My mom was always going out and trying some kind of funny fad diet as I was growing up. Eventually, she went to a doctor to get some help, and he prescribed . . . a form of speed, or amphetamine. . . . After several years of using it, she ended up having to eat sleeping pills for her to sleep at night. And after several years of doing that, her body basically began to deteriorate." The death of his mother stimulated Hughes's interest in herbs and botanicals, the use of which had become popular during the 1960s. Hughes set out to develop a dieting program based on herbal and botanical products that would enable people to lose weight safely.

Before founding Herbalife, Hughes the salesman received another kind of training when, in 1976, he began selling the Slender Now diet plan from multi-level marketer Seyforth Laboratories. Hughes quickly rose to become one of the pyramid's top earners. When that operation collapsed, Hughes joined another multi-level marketer, selling Golden Youth diet products and exercise equipment. By 1979, however, Hughes, then 23 years old, decided to form his own company.

Together with Richard Marconi, former manufacturer of the Slender Now products, Hughes developed the first Herbalife line of diet aids. Marconi, who claimed to hold a Ph.D. in nutrition, would later admit that his doctorate was a mail-order certificate from a correspondence school; nevertheless, Marconi would remain an officer at D&F Industries, Inc., which would continue to manufacture much of the Herbalife line throughout the company's history. Also joining Hughes in the new venture was Lawrence Thompson, formerly of Golden Youth, and earlier, Bestline Products, which in 1973 was fined $1.5 million for

violating California's pyramid scheme laws. At both Bestline and Golden Youth, Thompson worked with Larry Stephen Huff—later to become a Herbalife distributor—who was involved in what *Forbes* labeled the "father of all pyramid schemes," Holiday Magic, Inc., a multi-level marketer charged by the Securities and Exchange Commission (SEC) in 1973 with defrauding its distributors of $250 million.

The Herbalife plan involved limiting meals to one per day, and supplementing the diet with protein powders and a regimen of as many as 20 pills per day. According to the company, Herbalife was an instant success, selling $23,000 in its first month, and $2 million by the end of its first year. Hughes, described by *INC.* as "a honey-tongued spellbinder" and "a tanned and blow-dried California swashbuckler," and by *Forbes* as a "firebrand preacher," brought multi-level marketing to a new height, by taking the Herbalife message to television. Booking two- to three-hour slots on cable television, including the USA Cable Network, Herbalife was an early purveyor of the so-called "infomercial." The Herbalife television programs, led by Hughes himself, were, as described by *Forbes,* "full of inspiring testimonials from common people and resemble[d] old-style revival meetings in their fervor." At the same time, Herbalife published its own magazine, *Herbalife Journal,* equally filled with testimonials, for which the company reportedly paid $200 each, from distributor success stories to weightloss victories of Herbalife customers. Within a short time, the Herbalife slogan "Lose Weight Now—Ask Me How" began appearing on buttons and bumper stickers everywhere.

Legal Challenges in the Mid-1980s

Herbalife grew rapidly. By 1985, the company appeared on *INC.* magazine's list of fastest growing private companies. (That magazine labeled Herbalife's five-year growth "from $386,000 to $423 million, an increase of more than 100,000 percent, [as] by far the highest growth rate in the history of *INC.* 500 listings.") In that year, the company claimed over 700,000 distributors in the United States, Canada, United Kingdom and Australia, bringing annual (gross) revenues of nearly $500 million. Yet, as early as January 1981, the Food and Drug Administration (FDA) began receiving complaints of nausea, diarrhea, headaches and constipation, which were attributed to the use of Herbalife products. Herbalife distributors reportedly were instructed to assure customers that these side-effects were the result of the body purging itself of toxins. By 1982, when the company published that year's edition of the *Herbalife Official Career Book*—a guide given to distributors that contained a full product list and descriptions of the uses and benefits for each product, as well as advice on building their Herbalife sales—the FDA took action against the company.

Among the complaints leveled against the company were a number of the claims Herbalife made for its products in the *Career Book.* The Herbal-Aloe drink, for example, was said to help treat kidney, stomach and bowel "ulcerations"; and Herbalife Formula #2 was said to be a treatment for 75 conditions ranging from age spots to bursitis to cancer, herpes, and impotence. In the summer of 1982, the FDA sent Herbalife a "Notice of Adverse Findings" requiring the company to remove the mandrake and poke root ingredients—both considered unsafe for food use—of Slim and Trim Formula #2, while finding questionable the existence of "food-grade" linseed oil also in the product. In response, Herbalife removed the mandrake and poke root, and promised to modify the product claims found in the 1982 *Career Book.*

Herbalife was well into its surging growth—and Hughes was riding high himself, purchasing for $7 million the former Bel-Air mansion of singer Kenny Rogers, and marrying Angela Mack, a former Swedish beauty queen—when the FDA released a "Talk Paper" on its complaints against Herbalife to the press and public in August 1984. The company's troubles increased several months later when Canada's Department of Justice filed 24 criminal charges for false medical claims and misleading advertising practices against Herbalife. In December of that year, Hughes went on the attack, filing a suit against both the FDA and the U.S. Secretary of Health and Human Services, accusing them of "grossly exceeding their authority by issuing false and defamatory statements and by engaging in a corrupt trial-by-publicity campaign against the company." In a press release, Hughes said: "[We're] not about to stand around and let this agency or anyone else issue blatant lies about us or our products, or to lie down and roll over while they take pot shots at us. In the five years we've been in business, literally billions of portions of Herbalife products have been consumed by millions of people. And we have never been sued or subjected to any formal proceedings by the FDA." In the same press release, Hughes also suggested that the FDA "attack" on Herbalife was inspired by legislation pending in Congress that sought to regulate the rapidly expanding dietary supplement market.

Although Hughes would withdraw the lawsuit the following year, Herbalife began to suffer from the negative publicity surrounding not only its products, but also its marketing tactics. After a still-strong first quarter, the company ended 1985 with only $250 million in retail sales. In March 1985, Herbalife itself was charged in a civil suit brought against it by the California attorney general, the California Department of Health and the FDA. That suit, which included Hughes as a defendant, charged Herbalife with making false product claims, misleading consumers, and with operating an illegal endless-chain scheme. At the same time, both the U.S. Senate and U.S. Congress began investigations into the company, during which time the investigating subcommittees pursued allegations that Herbalife products had been responsible for as many as five deaths. While the civil suit was based in California, the Washington investigations brought the negative publicity surrounding the company nationwide.

With sales stalling, the company cut its work force—which had reached approximately 2,000 people—laying off 270 in April 1985, and nearly 600 more the following month. Herbalife distributors were also hard hit, leaving many with unsalable inventories of Herbalife products and many others seeing their income drop to nothing overnight. Sales dropped even more precipitously the following year. Despite repeated vows to fight the charges against his company, Hughes reached an out-of-court settlement with the California attorney general's office. Under terms of the settlement, Herbalife paid $850,000 in civil penalties, investigation costs and attorneys' fees. Herbalife also agreed to discontinue two of its products, Tang Quei Plus and

K-8 at FDA insistence that, while the products posed no safety risks, the claims made for them by the company would require them to be considered as drugs under the Food, Drug and Cosmetic Act. In addition, the company agreed to make further changes to its *Career Book,* including dropping claims for its Cell-U-Loss product as a natural eliminator of cellulite. By the end of 1986, Herbalife posted a $3 million loss.

Going Overseas and Back Again in the 1990s

Herbalife's domestic sales were at a standstill, so Hughes took the company overseas to expand its international markets. In order to finance the expansion, the company went public in December 1986, merging with a public Utah-based shell company, which allowed the company to go public much faster than if it had been required to file an initial public offering. Hughes became chairman of the new company, now called Herbalife International, taking 14.8 million of 16.8 million shares of outstanding common stock. The remaining two million shares went to newly named director and executive vice-president, Lawrence Thompson.

By 1988, Herbalife had moved into Japan, Spain, New Zealand, and Israel, and soon added Mexico as well. The company's aggressive expansion forced it to take a loss of nearly $7 million that year, but international sales built quickly, raising worldwide sales to $191 million in 1991. Meanwhile, domestic sales continued their slide, reaching a low of $42 million that year. At the same time, critics of the company pointed to an emerging pattern: that in many of the countries Herbalife entered, sales would surge initially, then plunge, often in the face of government scrutiny.

Nonetheless, Herbalife continued to grow strongly through the first half of the 1990s. Retail sales doubled to $405 million in 1992 and jumped again to nearly $700 million in 1993. While 80 percent of sales still came from international markets, Herbalife's U.S. sales began to climb, reaching $85 million. Buoyed by this growth, Herbalife filed for a secondary offering of five million shares in 1993.

However, the company came under attack again. A Herbalife program introduced in 1992 called Wealth Building—in which newly recruited distributors could achieve supervisor status, with an immediate discount of 50 percent, if they made a first purchase of $500—was seen as skirting the edge of an illegal endless-chain scheme. The company's newly introduced Thermojetics Program of products were also criticized by the FDA and others for containing the Chinese herb ma huang, which contains ephedrine. In response to a Canadian threat to ban Thermojetics, the company agreed to reformulate the product. Despite this publicity, sales of Thermojetics were credited with raising Herbalife's retail sales still higher, to $884 million in 1994 and to $923 million in 1995, for net earnings of $46 million and $19.7 million, respectively.

Herbalife's legion of distributors also grew, once again to more than 750,000 worldwide. Many of these distributors dreamed, no doubt, of the Herbalife path to untold wealth—much like Herbalife's founder and majority shareholder, Mark Hughes.

Further Reading

Barrett, Amy, "A Wonder Offer from Herbalife," *Business Week,* September 13, 1993, p. 34.

Cole, Benjamin Mark, "Herbalife Plans Share Offering of $101 Million," *Los Angeles Business Journal,* August 23, 1993, p. 1.

Day, Kathleen, "Herbalife Lays off 573, Blames Slowing Sales," *Los Angeles Times,* May 29, 1985, p. D1.

Evans, Heidi, "Agencies Sue Herbalife, Alleging False Claims," *Los Angeles Times,* March 7, 1985, p. D1.

Hartman, Curtis, "Unbridled Growth," *INC.,* December 1985, p. 100.

Linden, Dana Wechsler, and Stern, William, "Betcherlife Herbalife," *Forbes,* March 15, 1993, p. 46.

Paris, Ellen, "Herbalife, Anyone?" *Forbes,* February 25, 1985, p. 46.

"Self-Healing," *Forbes,* November 17, 1986, p. 14.

Shiver, Jube, Jr., "Herbalife Says All Queries into Tactics Now Resolved," *Los Angeles Times,* October 17, 1996, p. D4.

Svetich, Kim, "Herbalife Seeking to Rebuild Its Domestic Market," *California Business,* February 1990, p. 18.

Yoshihashi, Pauline, "The Questions on Herbalife," *New York Times,* April 5, 1985, p. D1.

—M. L. Cohen

Hickory Farms, Inc.

1505 Holland Road
Maumee, Ohio 43537
U.S.A.
(419) 893-7611
Fax: (419) 893-0164
Internet: http://www.hickoryfarms.com

Private Company
Incorporated: 1960 as Hickory Farms of Ohio, Inc.
Employees: 2,300
Sales: $160 million (1995 est.)
SICs: 5499 Miscellaneous Food Stores; 5147 Meats and
Meat Products; 5143 Dairy Products; 7331 Direct
Mail Advertising Services

Once the nation's largest specialty food retailer, Hickory Farms Inc. has been called "Middle America's gourmet." While the company's chain of mall stores and kiosks specializes in summer sausage, cheeses, candies, fruit baskets, nuts, and specialty meats and seafood, an increasing emphasis on mail order marketing characterized the early 1990s. Founded in Toledo, Ohio in the late 1950s, Hickory Farms went public in 1970 and was acquired by General Host Corp. in 1980. After two decades of unabated growth, Hickory Farms suffered two consecutive annual losses under its new parent. The chain was then spun off to a management-led investment group in 1987, and it remained privately-held into the mid-1990s.

Post World War II Origins

The roots of Hickory Farms stretch back to the late 1940s, when Richard Ransom and his cousin Earl Ransom started a produce business in Sandusky, Ohio, known as Dick's Markets. Seeking a business to even out their highly seasonal work, the cousins casted around for new opportunities. Convinced that there was demand for old fashioned wheels of Swiss and cheddar cheeses like those they remembered from their youth, they tested their idea in a small booth at a 1950 home show in Toledo. That first booth was so successful that the partners

began licensing two-person crews to set up kiosks at local and regional fairs around the country. They soon added a four-pound, two-foot-long smoked summer sausage dubbed the "beef stick" to their product line, and renamed their business "Hickory Farms" after the hickory-smoked sausage. By 1959, Hickory Farms was selling 1.5 million pounds of beef stick via over 250 temporary booths as well as mail order. By 1964, the company claimed to have booked more booth space at fairs and exhibitions than any other business in the world.

The Ransoms established their first retail outlet in Toledo in 1959. The company fostered a country store image with storefronts modeled after a red barn and friendly staffers wearing red and white checked shirts and denim skirts. Heavy sampling of sausages, cheeses, and jams was the order of every day. Richard Ransom, who quickly emerged as the company leader, put a great deal of stock in this marketing method, saying, "We think we have the finest products on the market and the best way to get people to agree with us is to give them a sample." Ransom positioned sample displays in the doorways of his store to attract customers, then offered free coffee to keep them in the store for an extended period of browsing, tasting, and, it was hoped, buying.

Hickory Farms opened its first franchised store outside Toledo in 1960, the same year the company was incorporated. The stores quickly evolved into "seasonal monsters." In Hickory Farms' case, 40 percent of its sales were made during the fourth-quarter gift-giving holiday season, when its annual balance sheet traditionally went from the red to the black.

Chairman and chief executive officer Ransom earned a reputation as a strict manager with rigid standards and "Prussian discipline," known for his "obsessive" control of—and support for—franchisees. He insisted on tight controls because, as he told *Marketing Magazine's* Steve Blickstein in a June 1972 interview, "the public can get along without our product very well." Ransom charged a low initial franchise fee, then collected five to six percent of each outlet's weekly gross sales. He insisted on standardization, asserting in the *Marketing Magazine* interview that "A successful franchise is nothing more than the continuation of a good idea. It's a repetition of success that eliminates excuses for failure." Ransom was especially sold on the power of promotion,

230

Company Perspectives:

With a gift from Hickory Farms, you never have to worry about the correct size, color or fit because everyone loves great-tasting food! You can send a gift from Hickory Farms with complete confidence knowing your friends, family and co-workers will savor, share, and enjoy it . . . and appreciate your thoughtfulness. Hickory Farms: It's the gift everyone loves to get!

---

requiring each franchise to invest at least five percent of its gross sales on advertising, asserting that when "advertising goes down, sales go down. It's that simple." He gauged each store's success according to weekly sales reports.

Ransom's rigidity notwithstanding, Hickory Farms franchises were so highly sought-after that the CEO stopped "selling" them in 1965, when he said he started "granting" them. The chain achieved rapid growth by encouraging its franchisees to own more than one store. Hickory Farms had 57 retail outlets by 1965, and opened its 100th store just three years later. The parent company's revenues exceeded $3 million by the late 1960s.

Highly Successful 1970s Give Way to Dismal 1980s

Hickory Farms' 1971 initial public offering launched a decade of rapid growth, when annual revenues multiplied tenfold. By 1975, franchising had enabled the chain to grow to over 300 units in 43 states and Canada. Although the franchise strategy had encouraged growth without significant capital expenditures by the parent company, Ransom sought to retain more profits in the corporate coffers by acquiring franchises and establishing company-owned stores. By late 1977, the parent company owned 60 outlets.

Ransom, who moved from president to chairman and chief executive officer in 1975, revived the booth idea that year, using small kiosks in malls to penetrate markets too small for a full-sized store and to supplement permanent store sales during the holiday season. Hickory Farms enjoyed an average annual growth rate of 20 percent during the decade. By 1980, the chain had over 500 stores, 80 of them company-owned. Chain-wide revenues grew from about $100 million in 1976 to over $164 million in 1979.

This phenomenal growth attracted a suitor at the dawn of the new decade. After an initial purchase of 15 percent of the chain's equity, General Host Corp. acquired all of Hickory Farms from its founder and shareholders for a total of $40 million. The specialty foods chain became the most profitable subsidiary in General Host's $750 million family, which included L'il General convenience stores, Hot Sam's pretzel shops, and Van de Kamp's Frozen Foods, among other holdings. Hoping to use Hickory Farms as the core of a successful food retailing group, the new parent acquired the new subsidiary's largest single franchisee, Hickory Farms Sales, for $11 million. The 113-store addition brought the number of company-owned stores even with franchised units, at about 200 locations each.

But General Host's hopes that the steady growth and high profitability enjoyed by Hickory Farms would be repeated throughout the conglomerate were not realized. Instead, Hickory Farms began to resemble its erratically profitable parent. Although it was "America's best-known brand of specialty foods" and owned more individual stores than ever, the chain suffered back-to-back losses totaling $3.5 million in 1985 and 1986. Retail analysts blamed mismanagement, declining mall traffic, and increasing competition from upstart specialty foods sellers like HoneyBaked Ham, for the chain's decline.

No matter what the causes, by 1986 General Host had decided to refocus on it subsidiary Frank's Nursery and Crafts, the 157-store chain of gardening superstores it had acquired in 1983. Divesting its other interests, including Hickory Farms, took more than a year of fits and starts. Two deals—one with a management group and one with Nutrition World, Inc., a Chicago operator of specialty food stores—fell apart due to the acquirer's inability to secure financing. Finally, in 1987, a group of managers and investors led by Robert DiRomualdo—who had succeeded Richard Ransom as president and CEO mid-decade—were able to garner the $51 million financing necessary to acquire their company. They paid $38 million for Hickory Farms, and used the remaining $13 million to get the company on its feet.

DiRomualdo was credited not only with returning Hickory Farms to profitability, but also with re-engineering it for new market realities. But after four years at the helm, he surprised the company's employees and officers alike when he resigned abruptly and without comment in 1988. Hickory Farms brought in an outsider, Thomas Frank, to guide the company into the 1990s. The 47-year-old boasted two decades of experience with Kentucky Fried Chicken and Procter & Gamble.

The 1990s and Beyond

The Hickory Farms of the early 1990s was a much smaller operation than that of the early 1980s, with less than 200 full-sized stores total—less than half its peak number of outlets. As many longtime franchisees neared retirement age, the parent organization sought to boost the number of company-owned stores through acquisition. Hickory Farms purchased its largest remaining franchisee, Hickory Farms Northwest, in 1991, adding 14 stores in Washington and Oregon. Other smaller store purchases brought the total number of company-owned stores to over 100 and reduced franchised locations to 55 by 1992. CEO Frank also scaled back Hickory Farms' packaging operations, closing plants in California, New York, and Oregon and consolidating that work at the Toledo headquarters.

Frank set out to revitalize Hickory Farms' mall stores and simultaneously cultivate more vital marketing outlets. The new CEO established a National Training Center in Toledo to reemphasize the service component that had always been so important to Hickory Farms stores. But recognizing the ascendance of catalog shopping in the harried 1990s, Frank also resurrected a mail order operation that had been phased out in the early 1970s. The company diversified from its traditional country-style beef stick and cheeses through acquisition of several catalog operations in the early years of the new decade. In 1991, it bought Blue Diamond Growers' Almond Plaza catalog business, which sold almonds and other nuts. The acquisition of Catalogue Marketing, Inc. a California-based division of Geo. A. Hormel & Co. followed in 1992. This purchase added Mission Orchards, a cataloger featuring premium fruit gifts; California Cuisine, a mail order gourmet food seller; and mail order meat gifts from Austin Street Market. In 1994, Hickory Farms acquired ConAgra Inc.'s ConAgra Consumer Direct, which included a mail order catalog business selling steaks and snacks. Renamed Catalog Marketing of Illinois, the ConAgra purchase also complemented Hickory Farms' growing premium/incentive business, which sold gift packages used by employers to reward their employees. A site on the World Wide Web promoted these relatively new operations electronically. By the mid-1990s, Hickory Farms' product line had burgeoned to include fresh fruits, sun dried tomato pesto, brie, steaks, seafood, and petit fours. By 1995, the chain's estimated sales had nearly recovered to the high of $164 million recorded in 1979, with about 15 percent of the total coming from mail order marketing.

Principal Divisions

Catalog Marketing of Illinois; Hickory Farms Inc. Catalogue Marketing Division.

Further Reading

Baessler, Jack, "Frankly Stated," *The Toledo Blade,* November 15, 1992, pp. 1C, 3C.

Blickstein, Steve, "Supersalesman Dick Ransom: Fattening the Averages at Hickory Farms," *The Marketing Magazine,* June 12, 1972, pp. 27–30.

Curtis, Carol E., "Middle America's Gourmet," *Forbes,* March 14, 1983, pp. 90–91.

"Fresh Profits Advance Seems in Store for Hickory Farms," *Barron's,* November 21, 1977, pp. 41–43.

"General Host Officially Acquires Hickory Farms," *The Toledo Blade,* August 1, 1980.

"General Host to Keep Hickory Farms," *The Toledo Blade,* April 9, 1987.

"Hickory Farms Elects President," *The Toledo Blade,* February 26, 1975.

"Hickory Farms Enters Premium/Incentive Market," *Toledo Business Journal,* September 1990, p. 6.

"Hickory Farms Founder Plans Sale of Firm," *The Toledo Blade,* June 21, 1980.

"Hickory Farms, HoneyBaked Increase Area Presence," *Toledo Business Journal,* July 1992, p. 11.

"Hickory Farms Opening New Home," *The Toledo Blade,* November 11, 1964, p. B1.

Judy, Bernard, "Hickory Farms Doing Nearly $2 Million Business Annually in 'Beef Sticks,'" *The Toledo Blade,* May 31, 1959.

McLaughlin, Mary-Beth, "Hickory Farms Buys Catalog Company, Expands Mail-Order," *The Toledo Blade,* July 8, 1991, pp. 20–21.

——, "Hickory Farms Plans Expansion 'In The Heartland'," *The Toledo Blade,* February 11, 1990, p. E6.

Powell, Mary Alice, "Shopping in a Store That Smells Good," *The Toledo Blade,* May 5, 1968.

Terhaar, Joyce, "Hickory Farms Buys Co-Op's Mail Order Unit," *Sacramento Bee,* July 9, 1991, p. 1E.

Towle, Michael D., "DiRomualdo Quits As Hickory Farms CEO," *The Toledo Blade,* September 27, 1988, pp. 22–23.

——, "Hickory Farms' Buy-Out Deal Works Because of Innovative Banking Idea," *The Toledo Blade,* May 23, 1988.

——, "Hickory Farms: How Dick Ransom Built It, General Host Broke It, and Robert DiRomualdo Is Fixing It," *Toledo Magazine,* October 2, 1988.

"Why Hickory Farms Goes To the Fair," *Business Week,* September 4, 1965, pp. 70–72.

—April Dougal Gasbarre

HMI Industries, Inc.

3631 Perkins Avenue
Cleveland, Ohio 44114
U.S.A.
(216) 432-1990
Fax: (216) 432-0013

Public Company
Incorporated: 1968
Employees: 1,187
Sales: $137.6 million
Stock Exchanges: NASDAQ
SICs: 3635 Household Vacuum Cleaners; 3317 Steel
Pipe & Tubes; 3544 Special Dies, Tools, Jigs &
Fixtures; 3559 Special Industry Machinery, Not
Elsewhere Classified

Known until early 1995 as Health-Mor Inc., HMI Industries has diversified from its core in high-end vacuum cleaners to develop a product line that includes items ranging from automotive components to health care equipment. Offered in nearly 50 countries worldwide, the company's "home cleaning systems" are sold primarily through an 8,000-member direct sales force. Although HMI's Filter Queen, Majestic Triple Crown, and Princess vacuums comprise far less than five percent of the United States sweeper market, their $1,000-plus price tags help compensate for their meager market share. Under the direction of Canadian Kirk W. Foley, HMI surpassed the $100 million sales mark in 1993. The CEO, who himself owned an estimated 50 percent of HMI's equity, predicted that the company would top $300 million in sales by 1998. He expected to achieve that goal by continually introducing new products and increasing international sales.

Creation and Early Development

The business was created in 1928 as Sanitation Systems, Inc., a Chicago-based distributor for Cleveland's Scott & Fetzer. The founders included Martin Callahan, his son Frank, and their associate Ray Owen. Within just two years, these energetic salesmen had sold enough of Scott & Fetzer's home cleaning systems to make their venture the largest organization of its type in greater Chicago.

Buoyed by their "sweeping" success, the three men contracted with one of America's most experienced vacuum manufacturers, Cleveland's P.A. Geier Company, to make an upright vacuum for them to sell. In 1930 the company name was changed to Health-Mor Sanitation Systems, Inc. to reflect its new product. The distributorship forged a strong relationship with its new supplier in the early 1930s, and by 1936 Health-Mor was one of P.A. Geier's largest clients.

At the end of the decade, Health-Mor acquired the patent on a vacuum cleaner that utilized centrifugal force to generate suction and trap dirt simultaneously. A team of P.A. Geier engineers, including Max Fairaizl, Ted Fistek, and Gene Martinec, refined the concept into the Health-Mor Model 200, later renamed the Filter Queen 200. By incorporating proprietary technology, this appliance distinguished Health-Mor from many of its competitors.

A generational change in administration at P.A. Geier in the early 1940s combined with the manufacturing imperatives of World War II to bring a temporary halt not only to vacuum cleaner production, but also to appliance research and development. The business continued to struggle in the immediate postwar era, and its new leadership was reluctant to invest its meager resources in research and development. As a result, P.A. Geier engineers Gene Martinec, Max Fairaizl, Ted Fistek and their secretary Annette Clark left that company to form an independent firm called Team (later Jem) Development in 1947. Within a year, the group had created three prototypical Model 350 Filter Queen vacuums. Health-Mor paid the design company a 35-cent royalty on each appliance, and P.A. Geier manufactured the machines.

This tripartite arrangement crumbled in the early 1950s, when P.A. Geier suffered a bankruptcy, hostile takeover, and name change to Royal Appliance Mfg. Co. When the new owners broke their contract with Health-Mor, the latter company elected to undertake its own manufacturing operation. While maintaining its corporate headquarters in Chicago, the company launched its first self-produced vacuum cleaner in 1952.

Company Perspectives:

Our relationship with our customers worldwide adds value to the organization each and every day. We measure our growth through our customers, and our success by their continued satisfaction. And that translates directly to the bottom line. As we incorporate this annuity value into our plans, our products and our programs, we truly make our customers our most valuable asset.

Health-Mor's strong emphasis on engineering and design won it several vacuum industry firsts over the ensuing years, including the first painted and chrome models with automatic cord reels. Led by co-founder Frank Callahan, the company incorporated in 1968 and made its initial public offering the following year. Although Health-Mor's direct sales scheme and high prices (about 20 times the average retail vacuum) consigned it to a niche position in the overall vacuum market, the company's multipurpose home cleaning systems won it a loyal core clientele. With a coterie of attachments, the Filter Queen could function as an air filter and freshener, paint sprayer, hair dryer, sander, polisher, and upholstery and carpet cleaner. By the end of the decade, Health-Mor's 161 employees generated about $9 million in annual sales and the company's net income stood at $1.3 million.

Although sources conflict with regard to corporate leadership, a company history notes that President John Licht tested retail sales in the early 1970s. Finding that the new outlet cannibalized existing direct sales, Health-Mor developed an alternate model, the Princess, especially for the retail market. Over the course of the decade, company sales tripled to $30.1 million in 1979. Net income growth nearly matched that performance, burgeoning to $3.3 million.

1980s Era Decline Reversed by New Management

Health-Mor's lackluster performance under John Licht in the early to mid-1980s has been, justifiably, criticized. Sales slid from more than $30 million in the late 1970s to less than $25 million in 1986, and net income dropped to a low of $100,000 in 1987. That year, Health-Mor was reborn under the leadership of Canadian Kirk W. Foley.

Having gone into early retirement at the age of 44, Foley acquired vacuum parts maker Tube Fab Ltd. An associate who had invested in Health-Mor affiliate Filter Queen-Canada convinced Foley that Health-Mor was a worthwhile, but mismanaged, investment. Foley and his colleague teamed up to acquire 40 percent of Health-Mor via Filter Queen-Canada, thereby winning board seats and eventually negotiating the merger of the two companies with Foley's own Tube Fab Ltd.

Starting in 1988, the new CEO launched a threefold turnaround program that began with the consolidation of manufacturing and administration at Cleveland and included product and geographic diversification. Product diversification, both within the core vacuum cleaner industry and via peripheral markets, was achieved through a combination of internal research and development and corporate acquisition. The merger with Filter Queen-Canada, for example, added central vacuum systems to Health-Mor's product line. These whole-house systems, which account for about 15 percent of all Canadian vacuum purchases, cost about $1,000 and are best installed during a home's construction. Health-Mor's tube fabrication subsidiary developed several consumer-oriented products, including a luggage caddy, flagpole, and firewood caddy. The 1993 acquisition of Canada's Household Rental Systems gave Health-Mor an edge over typical carpet shampooer rental companies by offering delivery and pickup of rental units.

Health-Mor broadened its manufacturing capacity largely through acquisition in the late 1980s and early 1990s. The company purchased three tube makers—Precision Tube Formers, Inc., Ultrametl Mfg. Co., and Advanced Metal Technologies Inc.—in 1990 alone, thereby adding to its varied line of products for the aerospace, military, communication, and appliance industries. That year also saw Health-Mor's largest-ever acquisition, that of Youngstown, Ohio's Bliss Manufacturing Co. The $15 million purchase gave the company a position in the production of metal stampings for the automotive industry. In 1994, Health-Mor's Manufactured Products Division, encompassing the tube and automotive operations, surpassed its Consumer Goods Division in terms of sales.

Foley transformed Health-Mor from what he characterized as "a member of the Flat Earth Society" into a company striving for and thriving on global expansion. From its base in the United States and Canada, Health-Mor carefully sought new geographic markets for its core home cleaning products in the late 1980s and early 1990s. The company targeted Japan, for example, because of the market's relative affluence and its cultural obsession with cleanliness. Although Health-Mor's vacuums sold under the Princess brand for about $2,500 in Japan, sales there climbed to about $7 million by 1991. Health-Mor made a timely push into another affluent market, Kuwait, in the aftermath of the Persian Gulf War. In 1991 the company acquired Holland Electro B.V., a European manufacturer of vacuum cleaners and vacuum cleaner motors, via a stock swap valued at about $900,000.

The turnaround at Health-Mor under Foley was a success on several fronts. Vacuum production, for example, increased from 25,000 in 1988 to 180,000 in 1993 and 250,000 in 1994. This unprecedented growth prompted the 1995 purchase of a new plant that had the potential to double the company's production capacity. The combination of geographic and product expansion fueled a tripling of sales, from $39.3 million in 1989 to 133.6 million in 1994. Profits mounted even faster during this period, from $1.4 million to $7.2 million. Industry observers ratified HMI's achievements. The company was ranked among *Forbes* magazine's Best Small Companies of 1994 and had earned four consecutive spots on Northeast Ohio's Weatherhead 100 by 1995.

Growth in the Late 1990s and Beyond

Having made its inaugural diversification in the late 1980s, HMI brought out a parade of divergent products in the mid-1990s. The Comfort Lounger, for example, was a portable, adjustable bed powered by a vacuum cleaner motor. The Activa AdvantaJet needleless insulin injection system (a relative bargain at $700) offered an alternative to traditional insulin delivery systems. The AdvantaJet, which used air pressure to inject insulin, was competing with about six other similar medical devices for the nation's 13 million diabetics. In 1995 Health-Mor created a new subsidiary, Personal Care Corp., to manage this product line. Health-Mor simplified its corporate moniker to HMI Industries, Inc. that same year in recognition of its varied product line.

With its program of geographic expansion firmly in place, the company forecast double-digit growth in Europe, Asia, the Middle East, and Central and South America. By 1995, international sales contributed more than 40 percent of HMI's annual revenues.

HMI suffered a slight setback in 1995, when its net earnings slid 13 percent to $5.6 million. Foley attributed this "uninspiring performance" to several factors, including a labor dispute at Bliss (which was resolved with a six-year contract) and the Mexican economic downturn.

Principal Subsidiaries

Tube Form, Inc.; Tube-Fab Ltd.; Bliss Manufacturing Company; Health-Mor B.V. (Netherlands); HMI Inc. (Canada); Health-Mor Acceptance Corp.; HMI Acceptance Corp. (Canada); Health-Mor Acceptance Pty. Ltd.; Health-Mor Mexicana S.A. de C.V. (Mexico); HMI Personal Care Products; Home Impression Inc.; Experimental Distributing Inc.

Further Reading

Cleaver, Joanne, "Health-Mor Eyes Markets for Built-Ins," *Crain's Chicago Business,* June 27, 1988, p. 19.

"A Look Back," *The Health-Mor World,* company publication.

Phillips, Stephen, "HMI Industries Is Looking To Move," *Cleveland Plain Dealer,* March 11, 1995, p. 1C.

Prizinsky, David, "Health-Mor Looks East," *Crain's Cleveland Business,* March 16, 1992, pp. 1, 29.

Sabath, Donald, "Health-Mor CEO Sees Growth, New Products," *Cleveland Plain Dealer,* June 14, 1994, p. 1E.

——, "HMI Expects Air Cleaner To Fuel '96 Sales, Profits," *Cleveland Plain Dealer,* January 25, 1996, p. 2C.

——, "HMI Industries Says Labor Woes Held Down Earnings," *Cleveland Plain Dealer,* December 7, 1995.

Silverstein, Evan, "Non-Needle Technology Offers Diabetics Freedom From Pain," *Cincinnati Business Courier,* December 13, 1993, p. 32.

Solov, Diane, "Health-Mor Cleans Up with Pricey Vacuums," *Cleveland Plain Dealer,* July 4, 1992, pp. 1E, 9E.

——, "Health-Mor Meeting Is Bit Unusual," *Cleveland Plain Dealer,* January 22, 1993, p. 1F.

—April Dougal Gasbarre

Howard Johnson International, Inc.

339 Jefferson Road
Box 278
Parsippany, New Jersey 07054-0278
U.S.A.
(201) 428-9700
Fax: (201) 428-6057

Wholly Owned Subsidiary of Hospitality Franchise Systems Inc.
Incorporated: 1961 as Howard Johnson Co.
SICs: 6794 Patent Owners and Lessors; 7011 Hotels and Motels

Howard Johnson International, Inc. is the 15th largest lodging chain in the United States, with 523 properties and 57,200 rooms at the end of 1995. Most of these hotels and motels also feature swimming pools, restaurants, and gift shops, catering to the leisure-travel market and, to a lesser extent, the business traveler. The company is a subsidiary of Hospitality Franchise Systems Inc. (HFS), which runs Howard Johnson as a franchise operation. Interestingly, Howard Johnson was once the largest restaurant chain in the world, but such fast-food outlets as McDonald's came to replace "HoJo" in America's affections, and a 1985 sale of the company essentially divided it into separate lodging and dining operations. By 1994 there were only about 100 Howard Johnson restaurants left.

Inception and Growth Before World War II

A World War I veteran with only a grammar-school education, Howard Dearing Johnson started out as a salesman for his father, a Boston cigar jobber. As smokers increasingly turned to cigarettes, however, the business fell into debt and, after his father died, Johnson closed it. Looking for a better enterprise, he bought a store selling candy, newspapers, and patent medicines in Wollaston, a Boston suburb, in 1925 for $500 he borrowed, picking up also its debts of at least $28,000. Johnson revived the store's moribund soda fountain and, seeking a quality product that would bear his name, introduced chocolate ice cream with a "secret" formula—a butterfat content almost twice the standard. It proved a hit, so he added other flavors and opened a beachfront stand where he sold $60,000 worth of ice-cream cones in a single summer. By 1928 his gross sales of ice cream had risen to $240,000.

When Johnson opened his first restaurant, in neighboring Quincy in 1929, he made fried clams and broiled swordfish the specialties and also included homemade baked beans, brown bread, and pastries. But he was frustrated in his desire to expand by lack of capital before 1935, when he persuaded an acquaintance to open a restaurant in Orleans, on Cape Cod, and sell his ice cream under a franchise. By the following summer there were four Howard Johnson franchised restaurants—called "Howard Johnson's"—and 13 small Johnson-owned roadside stands being converted into restaurants. By the end of the year 39 more franchised restaurants had been opened.

Howard Johnson's phenomenal growth was based on the application of two relatively new and untried concepts. Its founder, unable to obtain loans from bankers, was a pioneer in the franchising field. Licensees, rather than the chain, bore the start-up costs, which included an initiation fee paid to the company, which then made more money by selling food and other supplies to the licensees. And Howard Johnson foresaw that the growing popularity of the automobile would send millions of hungry Americans out on the road.

By the end of 1939 there were 107 Howard Johnsons along the eastern seaboard as far south as Florida, mostly along highways. Gross receipts came to $10.5 million, and profit to $207,000. The following year the company won a contract to locate 24 restaurants on the newly completed Pennsylvania Turnpike, holding a monopoly on the heavily traveled route until 1979. Generally situated along major highways and drafted by Johnson's staff of 27 architects, Howard Johnson's were easily distinguished by porcelain roof tiles of a special orange color, scientifically determined as the best shade for attracting a motorist's attention. A New England-style blue cupola was mounted on the roof. "Site engineers" determined the locations, and supervisors hired and trained cooks, waitresses, and counter clerks. Quality control from headquarters assured that the 28 flavors of ice cream, fried clams from the company's own clam bed off Ipswich, Massachusetts, pies baked on the premises according to company recipes, and other items would meet the standards of the Howard D. Johnson Co. The company lured the family trade with children's portions.

The Booming Fifties

With America's entry into World War II gasoline rationing took such a toll on the Howard Johnson chain that the number of restaurants fell in little more than a year from about 200 (75 of them company-operated) to about 75. By the summer of 1944 only 12 remained in business. The company took up part of the slack by turning some of the restaurants into jam factories and by operating cafeterias for workers in war plants. Once the war had ended, Howard Johnson adopted a policy of smaller units in place of big, showy "roadside cathedrals." By the summer of 1947, construction was under way on the first of 200 new branches to stretch across the Southeast and Midwest. Still owned exclusively by its founder, the Howard D. Johnson Co. was providing its restaurants with some 700 items, including the saltwater taffy always found on the counters. Gross sales totaled $115 million in 1951 (25 percent from ice cream), and net income came to $656,000.

By 1954 there were about 400 Howard Johnson restaurants in 32 states, of which about 10 percent were highly profitable company-owned units on turnpike locations. That year Howard Johnson entered the motel business. In 1959 the company founder, who had accumulated three homes, a 60-foot-long yacht, an art collection, and four wives, turned the reins over to his son, 26-year-old Howard Brennan Johnson, who succeeded him as president of the company. The junior Howard Johnson, a graduate of Andover, Yale, and Harvard Business School, quipped, "My father felt that I should start at the top and work my way down." Years later, in a more serious vein, he told a *New York Times* reporter, "I knew from the age of five I wanted to join the company. It was all we talked about at home. I saw my father working so hard. He was the kind of person you almost couldn't let down." He established executive offices in New York City's Rockefeller Center, although corporate headquarters remained in Wollaston. The senior Johnson remained chairman and treasurer of the company until 1964. He died in 1972.

Going Public in the Sixties

When Howard Johnson Co. went public in 1961, it consisted of 605 Howard Johnson restaurants (265 operated by the company and 340 by licensees), ten Red Coach Grill company-owned restaurants (a chain started in 1938 and specializing in steak and lobster), and 88 Howard Johnson's Motor Lodges, all of them franchised, in 33 states and the Bahamas. There were 17 manufacturing and processing plants in 11 states. Net sales came to $95 million in 1960 (compared to $31.8 million in 1951), and net income to $2.3 million. Both annual sales and earnings per share increased every year between 1959 and 1966. Between 1961 and 1967 the company's founder, his son, and his daughter sold nearly two million shares of stock for a sum estimated in the neighborhood of $1 billion.

In 1963, when the firm's profit margin rose to an all-time high for the fourth straight year, the number of company-owned Howard Johnsons exceeded the franchised units for the first time. "It's simple," Howard B. Johnson explained to a *Forbes* reporter in 1962. "Last year our own 279 stores [i.e., restaurants] had sales of nearly $79 million, on which we got both the wholesale and the retail profit. Naturally, we'd like more of these double-barreled profits." The number of motels reached 130 in 1964, each with a Howard Johnson restaurant on the site or adjacent to it. Popular Howard Johnson staples were now being frozen and distributed through supermarkets in the Northeast. In the mid-1960s Howard Johnson became a coast-to-coast chain for the first time by opening California outlets. Ground Round, a limited-menu, pub-style suburban chain with banjo-strumming entertainment, was initiated in 1969.

Challenges of the Seventies

Marked by occasional gasoline shortages and frequent gas price hikes, the 1970s were a difficult decade for companies catering to motor traffic, but especially for Howard Johnson, which depended on highway operations for 85 percent of its business. Yet except for 1974, the first full year of the energy crisis, Howard Johnson continued every year to post record sales and earnings per share. It reacted to the challenge by instituting around-the-clock service in more than 80 percent of the company-owned restaurants, installed cocktail lounges in place of soda fountains in about 100 of these locations, increased seating capacity, and stepped up special menu promotions. New HoJos, the company's leader pronounced, would be concentrated in population centers rather than along highways. By the end of 1975 the HoJo empire had grown to 929 Howard Johnson restaurants (649 company-operated), 32 Red Coach Grill restaurants, 63 Ground Round restaurants, and 536 motor lodges (125 company-operated) in 42 states, the District of Columbia, Puerto Rico, the Bahamas, the British West Indies, and Canada.

Nevertheless, in the competitive struggle for the traveler's dollar, Howard Johnson was falling behind fast-food franchisers like McDonald's and Burger King and growing lodging chains like Holiday Inns, Ramada Inns, and Marriott. The classic orange-roof Howard Johnsons especially were perceived as past their prime. Customers complained of agonizingly slow service and overpriced, bland, predominantly frozen food that gave rise to the gag, "Howard Johnson's ice cream comes in 28 flavors and its food in one." HoJo outlets accounted for 78 percent of the restaurant group's sales volume in 1977 but only 57 percent of pretax profit. By contrast, the company's motels, although also cited as increasingly behind the times, accounted for only 16 percent of the company sales in 1978 but more than 43 percent of its earnings.

Criticized for choosing to stand pat and hoard company cash, Howard Johnson told a *Forbes* reporter in 1978, "My expansion plans got stalled in the 1974 oil embargo. I overreacted. I stopped all expansion, and once you stop, you know how hard it is to get the monster going again." Others, however, blamed management's tight-fisted concentration on the balance sheet for the company's lack of dynamism. One of its former executives said, "HoJo always seemed to have ideas to upgrade the restaurants and hotels. But they never wanted to spend the money." By the late 1970s the Howard Johnson Co. had a balance sheet more inspiring than its future. It held $90 million in cash and marketable securities and carried no long-term debt aside from $143 million in capital-lease obligations for its company-owned units.

Under British Rule: 1980–1985

Although Howard Johnson had professed no interest in selling his namesake company, in September 1979 he accepted, as too lucrative to pass up, an acquisition bid of $28 a share, or $630 million in all, from Imperial Group Ltd. of Great Britain, a tobacco, food, beer, and packaging conglomerate. For its money Imperial received 1,040 restaurants (75 percent company-owned) and 520 motor lodges (75 percent franchised). Howard Johnson, who had collected $35.2 million for his shares, resigned as chairman, president, and chief executive officer of the company at the end of 1981. He was succeeded by G. Michael Hostage, a manager who had worked his way through business school washing dishes and digging sewers before spending 15 years with the Marriott Corp.

Hostage inherited a declining balance sheet. In 1979 the company had earned $34 million before taxes on sales of $588 million, but earnings dropped to only $14.7 million in 1980 and never fully recovered during the four succeeding years. Sales grew only 22 percent during this period. Hostage vowed to integrate adjacent HoJo restaurants and motels—often under different ownership—by unifying their staffs and offering food-and-lodging package deals and to cut costs by allowing restaurant managers to buy food from a variety of sources rather than exclusively from the company. Some new entrees and a low-cholesterol breakfast were added. The successful Ground Round chain was expanded, growing to 210 units in 1985.

In order to lure business travelers to its motels, which trailed the industry average in occupancy rate and had fallen to sixth place among lodging chains, Howard Johnson initiated corporate discounts and a new reservations system and raised the advertising budget. It gave licensees the choice of accepting low-interest loans to refurbish their properties by mid 1987 or losing their franchises. A new mid-priced Plaza-Hotel chain for the business traveler was opened in 1983, with 90 or more planned over five years at an average cost of $20 million each. These units would include amenities business people expected but were not receiving from the traditionally family-oriented HoJos: restaurants and lounges, banquet and meeting rooms, and executive floors.

Divided Between Marriott and Prime

In September 1985, however, Imperial threw in the towel, selling the Howard Johnson Co. to Marriott Corp. for $314 million. Marriott kept the 418 company-owned restaurants but immediately sold the franchise system and the company-owned lodging units to Prime Motor Inns Inc. for $97 million. Prime also assumed Howard Johnson's $138 million in debt. For its money Prime received the Howard Johnson trade name and trademark, 125 hotels and motor lodges operated by Howard Johnson, 375 franchised lodges, and 199 franchised restaurants. Imperial kept the Ground Round chain because Marriott was not interested in buying it.

Neither did Marriott have an interest in prolonging the life of a restaurant chain whose name was also held by a lodging

operation in competition with its own. The corporation intended to convert these units to Big Boy and Saga restaurants which would in turn be sold. By the end of 1987 only 90 Marriott-owned Howard Johnson restaurants remained, and by mid 1991 only 50. Similarly, Prime wanted to wash its hands of the independently owned units once the franchise agreements expired.

Claiming that their interests were being set aside, about 150 Howard Johnson restaurant franchisees retained former U.S. attorney general Griffin Bell and began threatening a class-action suit against Marriott and Prime. After eight months of negotiations, the parties reached an agreement in May 1986 by which Prime granted to Franchise Associates, Inc., a company established by the franchisees, a perpetual exclusive license to the Howard Johnson name in connection with the operation of Howard Johnson restaurants in the United States, Panama, and the Bahama Islands, and granted Franchise Associates the exclusive right to use the Howard Johnson name or license it to others for Howard Johnson Signature Food Products in these locations. From Marriott the operators won the free use of HoJo recipes.

Franchise Associates bought 17 of Marriott's HoJos in 1991. It even built a prototype restaurant with a toned-down version of the orange roof and required all new franchisees to hew to the design. Oat bran muffins, salads, and garden pizzas were among the health-conscious fare added to the familiar standbys in a new menu introduced in 1990. A stockholders' company of 65 franchisees, Franchise Associates owned and operated about 85 of the 110 franchised HoJo restaurants in 1991.

Prime was described by a securities analyst as the fastest-growing company in the lodging industry with the highest profit margins. In 1988 it announced a joint venture to build 20 Howard Johnson suite hotels a year for the next five years at an annual construction cost of about $100 million. A Prime subsidiary was to supply the financing, while AAA Development Corp. would build the hotels. Suite hotels were a fast-growing segment of the lodging industry largely favored by business travelers, and Howard Johnson was planning to charge $55 to $90 a night. The following year Howard Johnson initiated a $25-million marketing plan centered on the idea of advertising the chain as ''home of the road warrior''—the industry name for frequent travelers. Figures showed that 22 percent of U.S. business travelers were responsible for 56 percent of hotel stays.

New Ownership in the Nineties

In order to reduce its $280 million in bank debt, Prime, which had become the nation's second-largest hotel franchiser, sold its Howard Johnson and Ramada systems to Blackstone Capital Partners L.P.—an affiliate of Blackstone Group—in 1990 for $170 million. A downturn in the lodging and real-estate industries and problems in the high-yield, high-risk junk-bond market had dried up financing sources for hotels and caused Prime's stock to lose 75 percent of its value in seven months. Blackstone Group, an investment-banking firm, added the Days Inn chain and renamed the operation Hospitality Franchise Systems Inc. The company went public in 1992, but Blackstone retained 65 percent of the shares.

Hospitality Franchise Systems changed its name to HFS Inc. in 1995 and the name of its Howard Johnson Franchise Systems subsidiary to Howard Johnson International, Inc. in 1996. In February 1996 HFS announced that it would require its Howard Johnson franchisees to upgrade their properties, including establishing a rating system designating properties as either full-service hotels or limited-service units and posting a new sign with a bright blue background. It was also considering discontinuing the distinctive orange roofs that still topped about 30 percent of the lodges. While conceding that the orange roof is "an American icon—as American as apple pie and Chevrolet," HoJo President Eric Pfeffer declared, "As we change with the times, we've got to show the newness." Pfeffer, who discontinued the franchises of 37 Howard Johnson properties in 1995 for quality shortfalls, said the company would be expanded worldwide.

At the end of 1995. there were 523 properties with 57,200 rooms in the Howard Johnson lodging system, throughout North America and also in Europe, the Middle East, and Central and South America. They were midpriced, averaged 110 rooms each, and most had a swimming pool, gift shop, and restaurant. HFS received monthly marketing and reservation fees from its Howard Johnson franchisees, based on a specified percentage of gross room sales.

Further Reading

Casper, Carol, "Howard Johnson's," *Restaurant Business,* January 20, 1991, pp. 78, 80.

Ettorre, Barbara, "Dry Spell for Howard Johnson," *New York Times,* August 6, 1979, pp. D1, D3.

Hooper, Laurence, "Blackstone Is Planning Public Offering of Shares in Motel-Franchising Business," *Wall Street Journal,* August 31, 1992, p. C9.

Howard, Theresa, "Howard Johnson," *Nation's Restaurant News,* February 1996, pp. 85, 88.

"The Howard Johnson Restaurants," *Fortune,* September 1940, pp. 82 +.

"Howard Johnson's New Flavor," *Business Week,* October 19, 1963, pp. 109–110, 112.

Kleinfield, N.R., "Can HoJo's Regain Its Luster?" *New York Times,* April 21, 1985, Sec. 3, p. 4.

Kulkosky, Edward, "Howard Johnson's New Formula," *Financial World,* October 1, 1978, pp. 13–15, 17.

McLaughlin, Mark, "A Whole Lot of Shakin' Going On Under Orange Roofs of HoJo Franchisers," *New England Business,* October 6, 1986, pp. 41–42.

Preer, Robert, "For Venerable HoJo's Restaurants, a Second Serving," *Boston Globe,* September 5, 1993, South Weekly, pp. 1, 4.

"Prime Motor Inns, Marriott to Acquire Howard Johnson's Motels, Restaurants," *Wall Street Journal,* September 21, 1985, p. 5.

"Putting the HJ Seal on Motels," *Business Week,* October 23, 1954, pp. 126, 130, 132.

Salmans, Sandra, "Remodeling Howard Johnson," *New York Times,* November 12, 1982, pp. D1, D15.

"Tinting Supermarkets with Orange and Blue," *Business Week,* July 2, 1966, pp. 42–43, 46.

"To Be and What to Be—That Is the Question," *Forbes,* May 1, 1978, p. 25.

Weber, Joseph, "Got My Hojo Workin'," *Business Week,* March 4, 1996, p. 46.

—Robert Halasz

HUNT-WESSON, INC.
Hunt-Wesson, Inc.

1645 W. Valencia Drive
Fullerton, California 92633-3899
U.S.A.
(714) 680-1000
Fax: (714) 449-5100

Wholly Owned Subsidiary of ConAgra, Inc.
Incorporated: 1890 as Hunt Brothers Fruit Packing
  Company
Employees: 8,000
Sales: $2.3 billion (1995)
SICs: 2033 Canned Fruits & Vegetables; 2032 Canned
  Specialties

Hunt-Wesson is one of the nation's largest and most successful food companies. It markets and manufactures a wide range of brand name grocery and foodservice products through its independent operating companies: La Choy / Rosarita Foods Co., Orville Redenbacher / Swiss Miss Foods Co., Hunt Foods Co., and Wesson / Peter Pan Foods Co. Hunt-Wesson operates over 20 manufacturing plants, 14 distribution and customer service centers, and 45 grocery retail and foodservice sales offices in 24 states and Canada. Hunt-Wesson itself is an independent operating company and wholly owned subsidiary of ConAgra, Inc., a $24 billion diversified international food company.

19th-Century Origins

In 1890 brothers Joseph and William Hunt incorporated their company as the Hunt Brothers Fruit Packing Company in Santa Rosa, California. At a time when food products were delivered to market by horse-drawn carriage, they established a reputation for quality and freshness. As their business grew, they relocated to a larger headquarters in Hayward, California.

Nearly 45 years later in Fullerton, California, a young entrepreneur named Norton Simon bought an inactive orange juice canning plant and in 1934 started Val Vita Food Products. Starting with annual sales of only $45,000, he built the business into a

$9 million company in less than a decade, becoming something of a star in the California canning business in the process.

In 1943 the Hunt Brothers Packing Company merged with Norton Simon's Val Vita Food Products to form a new company, Hunt Foods. The company was located in Fullerton and headed by Simon. Over the course of the next decade, Simon diversified and expanded the company by establishing a can-making plant and a glass plant and introducing new products. He achieved national distribution and launched innovative advertising and marketing programs. By the mid-1950s, Hunt Foods was nationally known. In 1956 it was renamed Hunt Foods and Industries to reflect the company's diversification.

Hunt-Wesson in the 1960s

In 1960 Hunt Foods merged with the Wesson Oil and Snowdrift Company, another leader in the food industry. By 1964, sales of the combined companies exceeded $400 million, and the company was renamed Hunt-Wesson Foods. In 1968 Hunt-Wesson Foods, Canada Dry Corporation, and McCall Corporation consolidated to form Norton Simon, Inc., a $1 billion corporation. While Norton Simon's headquarters were relocated to New York City, Hunt-Wesson's headquarters remained in Fullerton.

During the 1970s Hunt-Wesson continued to grow. It expanded its line of tomato and oil products. It introduced new products, including Manwich Sloppy Joe Sauce, Big John's Beans 'n Fixins, Snack Pack, and flavored tomato sauces. Acquisitions also played a significant role in Hunt-Wesson's growth. In 1976 it acquired the Orville Redenbacher Gourmet Popping Corn company. Hunt-Wesson sales topped $1 billion for the first time in 1979.

Starting in 1983, a series of important changes began for Hunt-Wesson. Norton Simon, Inc., was purchased by Chicago-based Esmark, Inc. Then in 1984, Esmark was acquired by Beatrice Companies, Inc., another Chicago-based company. The following year, Beatrice became a private company under the direction of the investment firm of Kohlberg, Kravis, and Roberts (KKR). It was renamed BCI Holding Company.

Company Perspectives:

Across the board—ranging from the multinational strength of its parent company through to the strong franchise of its individual brands—Hunt-Wesson is an innovative and ever-growing company committed to maintaining its leadership position in the food industry. To assure that leadership position, the company continues to identify ways to be the highest quality, most cost effective producer utilizing the latest in manufacturing technologies and systems. To keep focused, Hunt-Wesson continually benchmarks its products and business practices versus the best of its competition. Over the years, the introduction of new and improved products has driven the company's success. In addition, with the support of ConAgra, the company continues to pursue and integrate acquisitions which make good business sense for the future.

During this period of changing ownership, Hunt-Wesson continued to grow. It took on responsibility for other food businesses, including Peter Pan Peanut Butter, Swiss Miss, La Choy, and Rosarita. It developed a strong sales and distribution network, and sales topped $2 billion annually.

Acquisition by ConAgra in 1990

In 1990 the BCI Holding Company was acquired by ConAgra, Inc., a diversified food products conglomerate based in Omaha. ConAgra paid $1.36 billion to KKR for the three remaining Beatrice Divisions: Hunt-Wesson, Swift-Eckrich, and Beatrice Cheese. While the acquisition added $4.3 billion in sales, ConAgra also assumed $1 billion of BCI's debt and had to borrow heavily to finance the acquisition.

ConAgra had high expectations for Hunt-Wesson. ConAgra president Phil Fletcher was quoted in *Prepared Foods* as saying, "We see Hunt-Wesson as a very strong franchise. It has great potential." ConAgra required Hunt-Wesson to be more aggressive. In 1990 and 1991 Hunt-Wesson introduced 41 new grocery products and 33 new foodservice products. The most notable were Wesson Pure Olive Oil, the first major American brand of olive oil marketed nationwide, Wesson Canola Oil, and Wesson Lite No-Stick Cooking Spray. Two new sizes of plastic containers were introduced for Hunt's Ketchup, giving it the most extensive line of ketchup available in plastic containers.

Under ConAgra, Hunt-Wesson's businesses were organized into independent operating companies (IOCs) in 1991. The IOC philosophy was integral to the way ConAgra was organized and did business. Hunt-Wesson itself operated as an IOC with ConAgra as its parent company. At each of Hunt-Wesson's IOCs, brand management teams were made responsible for achieving the goals of the IOC business across all business areas, including marketing, manufacturing, technology / research and development, marketing services, and sales and business administration.

Hunt-Wesson was organized into four major IOCs and three smaller companies. The four major IOCs were La Choy /

Rosarita Foods Co., Orville Redenbacher / Swiss Miss Foods Co., Hunt Foods Co., and Wesson/Peter Pan Foods Co. The three smaller companies were ConAgra Grocery Products Companies International, Hunt-Wesson Foodservice Sales Company, and Hunt-Wesson Grocery Products Sales Company.

Through its four major IOCS, Hunt-Wesson marketed and manufactured a wide range of shelf-stable grocery products. La Choy / Rosarita Foods was focused on ethnic foods. It included five major product lines: 1) La Choy Products, including bi-pack dinners, noodle entrees, chow mein noodles, fried rice, and fortune cookies; 2) Chun King Products, which included vegetables, dinners, sauces, and chow mein noodles; 3) Rosarita Products, a line of Mexican food that included refried beans, salsas and sauces, and taco and tostado shells; 4) Gebhardt Products, a line of spicy foods that included chili products, canned beans, and spices and mixes; and 5) Healthy Choice Soups, a non-ethnic line of low-fat canned soups.

The brand soon spread to virtually every grocery product category, and Hunt-Wesson was given the Healthy Choice line of low-fat soups, which were produced by the La Choy / Rosarita Foods IOC. Hunt-Wesson expanded the line by introducing new products, including Chicken Corn Chowder and Clam Chowder in 1995. Corporate standards for the Healthy Choice brand included less than 30 percent of calories from total fat, less than 10 percent of calories from saturated fat, and reductions in sodium and cholesterol where appropriate.

Another major IOC was the Orville Redenbacher / Swiss Miss Foods Co., which was focused on snacks and desserts. Its five major product lines were as follows: 1) Orville Redenbacher Popping Corns, including jarred and microwaveable products; 2) Swiss Miss Products, including hot cocoa packages and cannisters, apple cider mix, and premier cocoa mixes; 3) Orville Redenbacher Pop and Top Oil; 4) Swiss Miss Snack Pack Pudding Products; and 5) Snack Pack Pudding and Gelatin Products.

The IOC with the oldest heritage was Hunt Foods Co., with more than 100 years of history in tomato products. Its line of tomato products included canned whole, stewed, and diced tomatoes, tomato paste and sauce, ketchup, tomato juice, barbecue sauce, spaghetti sauce, Manwich Sloppy Joe Sauce, and Healthy Choice Pasta Sauce. In 1995 Van Camp's was acquired by Hunt Foods, adding such product lines as Van Camp's Pork 'N Beans, Wolf Brand Chili, and Beanee Weenee. Hunt's tomato products were traditionally Hunt-Wesson's biggest business.

Hunt-Wesson's fourth major IOC, Wesson / Peter Pan Foods Co., combined two brand leaders in the oil and peanut butter businesses. Operating in large and mature categories, the company has grown through product innovations and the introduction of new varieties. Its major product lines included Wesson Cooking Oils, Wesson No-Stick Cooking Spray, Peter Pan Creamy and Crunchy Peanut Butter, and Smart Choice Reduced Fat Peanut Butter Spread.

Continued Growth through New Product Development

Hunt-Wesson's growth has been driven by the introduction of new and improved products. A good example is the way Hunt-Wesson created an entire grocery products category from a single variety of popcorn. When Hunt-Wesson acquired Orville Redenbacher's Gourmet Popping Corn business in 1976, there was only one variety offered in a glass jar. In 1980 the company began exploring the possibility of a microwave product. By 1983 it introduced the first shelf stable microwave popcorn—Orville Redenbacher's Microwave Popping Corn. Hunt-Wesson was surprised when this product became an overnight success, eventually creating a completely new grocery products category: microwave snack foods.

Hunt-Wesson continued to expand the product category with new and improved products. In 1985 two new salt-free varieties of popcorn were offered. In 1987 the company was the first to offer flavored popcorns. Then, in 1989, with consumers looking for more healthful food options, Hunt-Wesson capitalized on the trend and offered the first "Light" popcorn, which was followed by "Smart Pop," an extra light version. Four years later Reddenbudder's Movie Theater popcorn gave consumers more popcorn choices. Movie Theater Butter became the best-selling item in this category. Hunt-Wesson soon thereafter introduced a "Light" version of Redenbudder's Movie Theater popcorn, and in 1995 flavored White and Golden Cheddar varieties of Redenbudder's was offered to the public. Popcorn cakes were also introduced in 1995.

An aggressive leader in grocery food products, Hunt-Wesson continued to seek ways to grow and expand its business in the mid-1990s. In 1995 it made three major acquisitions: Chun King, Van Camp beans and chilis, and Knott's Berry Farm jams. The Van Camp acquisition also included Wolf Brand chili products, and the Knott's Berry purchase also included jellies, preserves, salad dressings, syrups, and gift packs.

In 1995 Hunt-Wesson also named a new president, Dave Gustin, who was well-suited to provide aggressive leadership. He replaced former Hunt-Wesson president Al Crosson, who was promoted to president and chief operating officer of ConAgra Grocery Products Companies. Gustin was a veteran of the coffee wars between General Foods and Procter & Gamble in the 1970s. Then he was involved in the cereal wars against Kellogg in the early 1980s, followed by a stint at Frito-Lay where he was involved in the snack wars. As he told *Brandweek,* "Those war experiences taught me the incredible value of brands, because in each of those 'let the best man win' setups, it's almost always the case that the best brand wins."

The development of new products also remained a key component of Hunt-Wesson's plans for growth. With a new product development cycle of three to five years, Gustin explained, "I've also learned to constantly focus on where consumers are going, not where they are." One area that the company was focused on for the coming decade was "healthy, phenomenally good-tasting snacks." Gustin noted for *Brandweek* that Hunt-Wesson's pudding business had been growing 15 percent a year and was one of the company's fastest-growing businesses.

Gustin also planned to move the company from less emphasis on ingredients to more emphasis on finished, ready-to-eat products. "Everything that takes time is our enemy," Gustin said. "Our competition isn't other branded stuff in the super-

market—it's the restaurant business." With consumers more concerned about convenience and health, Hunt-Wesson's competition was seen to be coming from ready-to-eat foods from other sources. One new ready-to-eat product line that was in the works involved new recipes for Rosarita's slow-simmered beans line.

A third area of growth for Hunt-Wesson was ethnic cuisine. With its Rosarita line of Mexican grocery products, the company was positioned to expand the line to take advantage of what Gustin termed "a vastly under-developed" ethnic cuisine. Hunt-Wesson's La Choy and Chun King products gave it a very strong presence in the Chinese food business, with growth coming from the introduction of innovative new products. Another aspect of ethnic cuisines that Hunt-Wesson was looking at for growth involved combining healthy ingredients and product offerings with new and existing ethnic grocery products. In early 1996 Hunt-Wesson announced a new, branded concept for on-site foodservices to be called Terri-Yaki. It would use the company's La Choy products and could be a servery fixture or one element of a food court.

Snacking continued to be a major trend, and Hunt-Wesson planned to take advantage of the desire for healthy snacks by narrowing the gap between "the regular stuff and the good-for-you stuff," as Gustin described it for *Brandweek.* The company planned to introduce new varieties of popcorn-based snacks as one aspect of this phase of future growth.

Hunt-Wesson, along with ConAgra's other Grocery Products Companies, was expanding its grocery sales force. Hunt-Wesson in particular was reengineering its entire sales system by moving from a geographic system to one focused on specific accounts. According to Hunt-Wesson's president, Dave Gustin, in *Brandweek,* "Concentration in the grocery trade means only 25 accounts make up 50 percent of our volume." Also helping the company provide better customer service was a Grocery Products Service Center that was established in 1995 to support the services of the Hunt-Wesson companies and ConAgra Frozen Foods.

Principal Subsidiaries

La Choy / Rosarita Foods Co.; Orville Redenbacher / Swiss Miss Foods Co.; Hunt Foods Co.; Wesson / Peter Pan Foods Co.; ConAgra Grocery Products Companies International; Hunt-Wesson Foodservice Sales Company; Hunt-Wesson Grocery Products Sales Company.

Further Reading

Fusaro, Dave, "Wealthy Choices: ConAgra Blitzes the Competition," *Prepared Foods,* September 1994, p. 34.
King, Paul, "Branding Out of Control: Who's Driving This Train, Anyway?," *Nation's Restaurant News,* March 4, 1996, p. 18.
Meyer, Ann, "Healthy Choice Transforms the Freezer," *Prepared Foods New Product Annual 1991,* p. 34.
Spethmann, Betsy, "Real Gustin at Hunt-Wesson," *Brandweek,* March 18, 1996, p. 37.

—David Bianco

Hyde Athletic Industries, Inc.

Centennial Industrial Park
Centennial Drive, P.O. Box 6046
Peabody, Massachusetts 01961
U.S.A.
(508) 532-9000
Fax: (508) 532-6105

Public Company
Incorporated: 1912 as A.R. Hyde and Sons
Employees: 362
Sales: $102.56 million (1995)
Stock Exchanges: NASDAQ
SICs: 3149 Footwear Except Rubber, Not Elsewhere
    Classified; 3021 Rubber & Plastics Footwear; 3949
    Sporting & Athletic Goods

Peabody, Massachusetts-based Hyde Athletic Industries, Inc. produces the top-rated Saucony line of quality athletic footwear, as well as footwear for coaches and sports officials under Hyde's Spot-Bilt brand. Hyde's Brookfield division markets roller skates, in-line and hockey skates, and other recreational and enthusiast sports products, including protective wrist, elbow, and knee pads, primarily for children and young adults. Brookfield products are marketed under the Brookfield, Hyde, and Spot-Bilt brands, as well as under brand names such as Barbie, Playskool, Spalding, Mickey and Minnie, and Nerf, licensed from Mattel, Inc., Hasbro, Inc., Spalding, Inc., Walt Disney Co., and Franklin Sports, Inc. Hyde's acquisition of Quintana Roo adds that branded line of road, triathlon, and mountain bicycles, and wet suits. Hyde also operates a chain of six factory outlet stores selling the company's discontinued and factory-second merchandise, as well as sports-oriented third party merchandise. Most Saucony products are assembled at the company's Bangor, Maine factory, from parts manufactured in China, Taiwan, and Thailand. Products in Hyde's other branded line are manufactured and assembled entirely in the Far East.

Hyde, still controlled by its founding family, generated $102.5 million, for a net income of $1.6 million, in 1995. The

Saucony brand, which includes running, cross training, walking, and hiking shoes, contributes more than one-third of Hyde's annual revenues. Saucony ranks fifth in sales among leading producers of athletic footwear, with a market share of seven percent. International sales of both Saucony and Brookfield products account for approximately 25 percent of total annual revenues.

Early History

Cobbler Abraham Hyde emigrated to the United States from Russia in 1890. Hyde established a reputation as a shoemaker and, in 1910, opened his own store. His first products were carpet slippers, so called because they were crafted from carpet remnants. Two years later, Hyde was successful enough to purchase a wood frame house in Cambridge, Massachusetts. In that year, Hyde established A.R. Hyde and Sons. Joined by son Maxwell C. Hyde, the small company's product line grew to include women's and children's shoes. By the 1930s, however, ice skates, ladies' figure skates, and roller skate boots figured strongly in the company's sales. When Maxwell Hyde took over operations, Hyde added more products to its athletic line, including baseball and bowling shoes.

At the outbreak of the Second World War, Hyde ceased production of civilian shoes, turning instead to manufacturing boots for the U.S. Army. For its wartime efforts, Hyde was the only shoe company to be awarded the Army-Navy E Award for excellence in manufacturing. The company returned to civilian production in 1946, now concentrated on athletic footwear. In 1952, Hyde made its first acquisition, purchasing the Athletic Shoe Company and adding that company's Spot-Bilt line of team sports shoes. With the acquisition completed, Hyde changed its name to Hyde Athletic Industries, Inc.

Hyde renewed its government contract work in the early 1960s, when NASA awarded the company the contract to supply footwear for the first astronauts. When the first astronaut walked in space, he wore boots made by Hyde. Yet Hyde remained a small company. By 1967, its annual revenues had grown to only $5.5 million. Earnings in that year were a slight $196,000.

Company Perspectives:

We believe that our most valuable resources are: one, our customers, to whom we are committed to providing the very best in world quality service and support; two, our employees, whose individuality we respect and whom we offer an environment where creativity, risk taking and effort are encouraged and rewarded; and three, our shareholders, to whom we commit to a philosophy of long-term strategic planning that yields superior return on investment.

Passed by the Fitness Boom of the 1970s

The next phase in Hyde's development was again fueled by an acquisition. In October 1968, the purchase of Saucony Manufacturing Company added that company's branded line of athletic footwear. A second acquisition, of K&B Shoe Co., Inc., was merged with Saucony to form Hyde's new Saucony Shoe Manufacturing Co., Inc. division. The company's expanded product line helped raise revenues to nearly $9 million in 1969, for net earnings of $4.5 million. One year later, the company's revenues topped $10 million for the first time. The company's production facilities had by then grown from its single Cambridge location to a factory in Bangor, Maine, three plants in Pennsylvania, and three additional plants in New Hampshire, California, and Chicago.

By the 1970s, the company's product line had expanded to include footwear for ice skating and roller skating, bowling, soccer, football, track, tennis, jogging, and other sports. The company also manufactured a line of figure skating and ice hockey outfits. Products were sold under the Hyde, Spot-Bilt, and Saucony trademarks. The 1970 purchase of 60 percent of Mitchel & King Skates Ltd. of England, later boosted to 70 percent, brought Hyde into production of ice skating blades as well, under the MK trademark. By 1976, Hyde's revenues grew to $15 million. In 1977, Maxwell Hyde retired, turning over the company to son-in-law Leonard R. Fisher.

By then, the United States was undergoing a fitness craze, with running and jogging, popularized by personalities such as Jim Fixx, providing a boom to athletic shoemakers. Early industry leaders, such as Adidas and Puma, would soon give way to new giants Nike and, later, Reebok. Endorsements by professional athletes were providing a new boost, and brand loyalty, to sports shoe sales. By the late 1970s, most manufacturers had shifted production overseas, primarily to the Far East, a trend that had already begun in the late 1960s. Hyde, however, continued to manufacture solely in the United States. It also refused to buy professional endorsements.

Nonetheless, Hyde's Saucony line helped fuel the company's sales, raising revenues to $21 million in 1977. In that year, a leading consumer magazine gave Saucony running shoes its top rating. Saucony became a favorite shoe among the small but growing population of professional runners. Yet Hyde's refusal to seek endorsements limited its acceptance by the broader public. Hyde sales grew only slowly, reaching $23 million in 1978 and $26 million in 1979. Despite the rise in sales, however, net earnings were slipping. In 1978, Hyde posted a net profit of only $320,000. The following year, the company posted a loss of $69,000. The pressures of maintaining its domestic manufacturing facilities were crippling the company. Hyde was also saddled with high interest payments, which had reached $2 million per year. At last, Hyde was forced to undergo a drastic restructuring.

The company sold its interest in Mitchel & King in 1979. Hyde then began to shift production overseas, closing all of its domestic plants except its Saucony facility in Bangor, Maine. The restructuring caused losses to deepen to $471,000 in 1980. But Hyde was back in the black the following year, earning a net just over $400,000 on $26 million in sales. By 1982, when Hyde completed its plant closings, sales jumped to nearly $37 million, bringing net earnings of almost $5 million.

Building a Professional Reputation in the 1980s

The company was poised to expand. But a family dispute erupted after Fisher, with his wife Phyllis, acquired a controlling interest in the company's stock. After a lengthy court battle, the Fishers agreed to a settlement in which Hyde posted a second public offering, reducing the Fishers' share to 41 percent. Rumors that the company might be sold placed a hold on Hyde's expansion, just as the boom in running shoes was building. Fisher, joined by his son, John H. Fisher, helped rebuild confidence in the company, when, as reported by the *Boston Globe,* he stated that the settlement "will put to rest the endless speculation about the company's future . . . This company is not for sale."

Nevertheless, sales of the Saucony line, which by then enjoyed a strong reputation among serious and professional runners, helped to raise total revenues to $44.5 million, for net earnings of nearly $3 million in 1983. The company also turned to professional endorsements and sponsorships, hiring O.J. Simpson as its vice-president of promotions. The company added several new products, including basketball and tennis shoes, as well as a line of performance running shirts and shorts, rain suits, and warmup suits under the Saucony Magic brand name. Sales continued strongly into the next year, building to $47 million. With an eye on further expansion, Hyde began construction on a new $5 million headquarters facility, which also housed a warehouse, pilot plant, and research and development laboratories, and moved the company from its Cambridge home to nearby Peabody, Massachusetts the following year. By the end of 1985, the company's revenues rose to $54 million.

The company also made a new acquisition that year, purchasing the Brookfield Athletic Shoe Company, also of Massachusetts. Brookfield helped extend Hyde into the children's and young adults' market. The Brookfield acquisition also brought Hyde the venerable PF Flyer brand. The canvas PF Flyers, which with Keds had been the most popular kids' sneaker in the postwar years, had faded significantly with the advent of leather-topped shoes in the 1970s. But Hyde hoped to capitalize on the surging demand for canvas sneakers in the mid-1980s (Keds sales had more than tripled between 1985 and 1988) in the 20- to 35-year-old adult market. The company's revenues rose to nearly $68 million in 1987, with net earnings of $2.2 million.

Consumer Reports *to the Rescue*

Yet Hyde faltered badly in 1988. Revenues plunged to $55 million, forcing a net loss of $1.75 million. By the end of that year, Hyde had agreed to be acquired by Silvershoe Partners, a New York-based investment partnership. Terms of the deal would have provided $8.50 per share, for a total of $23 million, while retaining the Fisher family in management. Little more than a week later, Hyde received an offer from a European-based investment group for $9.50 per share. But Hyde's agreement with Silvershoe precluded the company from entertaining the new offer.

By August of 1989, however, the merger acquisition with Silvershoe still had not been completed. When Silvershoe proved unable to arrange financing for the merger, the acquisition agreement was ended. Hyde's sales barely grew to $57 million, with a net loss of $650,000, for the year. As explained in that year's somewhat bitter annual report, the uncertainty surrounding the Silvershoe deal had cut deeply into Hyde's ability to compete in the booming athletic shoe market. Over the next two years, the company rebuilt its profit, although slowed by the looming recession, posting net earnings of $611,000 in 1990 and more than $1 million in 1991. Sales were relatively flat, however, hovering around $57 million. In a market dominated by Nike and Reebok, Hyde struggled to maintain a three percent share.

But the following year marked a turning point for Hyde. In a review of running shoes, *Consumer Reports* awarded Saucony's Jazz 3000 shoe its top rating, as well as its "best buy rating." The magazine, with a subscriber base of five million and an estimated readership of 15 million, had long been acknowledged as a powerful force in consumer spending. Hyde, led by John Fisher since his father's death in 1990, saw a surge in orders. The number of outlets carrying the Saucony brand rose by 25 percent in one year, including the 170-store Oshman's Sporting Goods chain. By the end of 1992, Hyde's sales, led by its Saucony line, had risen to $81 million, for net earnings of nearly $3.5 million.

Hyde responded by retooling its Bangor facility, thereby tripling its production capacity. The company also increased its advertising budget to $5 million from $2 million. But many analysts doubted Hyde's financial ability to capitalize in the long term on the *Consumer Reports* article. Nevertheless, sales continued to gain strongly in 1993, helped in part by a new *Consumer Reports* article recommending the Saucony walking shoes, posting a 28 percent increase in sales, to nearly $104 million, and a 46 percent earnings increase, to $4.6 million. Hyde's market share also grew, to seven percent of the athletic shoe market. At the same time, Hyde posted a new stock offering, creating nonvoting Class B shares. With the money raised, about $19.5 million, Hyde increased its stake in its foreign joint venture distribution partnership. The creation of the new class of stock was also seen as a means of thwarting a possible hostile takeover: potential buyers would be forced not only to control all of the company's Class A shares, but also to achieve a required percentage of Class B shares.

Yet by the end of 1993, Hyde's growth spurt was already slowing. The market for athletic shoes was being pummeled by the surge in outdoor shoe sales, led by Timberland's hiking boots. Among young adults, the athletic shoe was increasingly being replaced by Doc Martens. In response, Hyde introduced its own line of outdoor footwear. But added to Hyde's difficulties were well-publicized false advertising charges from the Federal Trade Commission (FTC) against Hyde and competitor New Balance, Inc. Both companies were accused of falsely labeling their products as "Made in USA" when most of the components for the shoes were manufactured overseas. Hyde, which had never disguised the fact that its domestic plant assembled its shoes from foreign-made components, settled with the FTC, agreeing to relabel their products. New Balance, however, chose to fight the FTC's complaint, prompting a renewed discussion, given the growing global economy, of the meaning of the "Made in USA" claim. The controversy did not help Hyde sales, which rose only slightly, to $107 million in 1994.

The following year, Hyde's sales slumped, with a poor fourth quarter showing dropping sales to $103 million. In its annual report, the company attributed this performance to a failed "cosmetic attractiveness of our footwear models. Fashion has become almost synonymous with success in all athletic footwear categories in today's retail environment." Nonetheless, most analysts agreed that the Saucony line's core customer, the professional and serious athlete, would likely remain loyal to the brand. Reinforcing this image, Hyde acquired Quintana Roo, Inc. of California in 1995, adding that company's line of professional and triathlon racing bicycles and triathlon wetsuits and swimwear.

Principal Subsidiaries

Spot-Bilt, Inc.; Brookfield Athletic Company, Inc.; Hyde International Services Ltd. (Hong Kong); Hyde Securities Corp.; Saucony, Inc.; Saucony Sports BV (Netherlands; 76%); Saucony Deutschland Vertriebs GmbH (Germany); Saucony Canada Inc. (Canada; 85%); Saucony Sp Pty Limited (Australia; 50%).

Further Reading

Barry, David G., "Hyde Running Strong after Stock Offering," *Boston Business Journal,* June 18, 1993.

French, Destree, "Hyde Back in the Running," *Boston Globe,* June 12, 1984, p. 42.

Neale, Stacy, "Hyde's Run Looks To Be Slowing," *Boston Business Journal,* November 12, 1993.

——, "Hyde Stock Falls after Poor Quarter," *Boston Business Journal,* March 4, 1994, p. 6.

Shapiro, Eben, "Getting a Running Shoe in the Door," *New York Times,* August 13, 1992, p. D1.

—M.L. Cohen

Hyster Company

P.O. Box 847
1901 E. Voorhees Street
Danville, Illinois 61832
U.S.A.
(217) 443-7293
Fax: (217) 443-7494

Wholly Owned Subsidiary of NACCO Industries Inc.
Incorporated: 1929 as the Willamette Ersted Company
Employees: 250
Sales: $700 million (1996 est.)
SICs: 3537 Industrial Trucks & Tractors; 5013 Motor
Vehicles Supplies & New Parts

The Hyster Company is one of the leading forces in the North American lift truck industry. Founded in 1929 by E. G. Swigert as an equipment supplier to Oregon's lumber industry, Hyster has been among the top three lift truck manufacturers in North America since the 1950s. A strong international presence has been an important part of Hyster's corporate plan since the 1950s, and manufacturing plants in England, Scotland, the Netherlands, Brazil, and Australia have been integral to the company's entry into the international market.

Company Origins

Hyster Company was founded as the Willamette Ersted Company in 1929 by Ernest G. Swigert. The company began business as a manufacturer of winches and lifting machines for the Pacific Northwest logging industry. Ernest's father, Charles Frederick Swigert, was the founder of ESCO Corp., a large steel works, and ESCO remained a major shareholder of Hyster through the 1980s. Hyster Company headquarters were located in Portland, Oregon, near the logging and timber country that the company served. The name Hyster was adopted as an evocation of the command ''hoist her,'' shouted by the loggers when a fallen tree was secured and ready to be lifted. ''Hyster,'' a slang corruption of the phrase, quickly became associated with the lifting machinery, and in 1934 the Willamette Ersted company adopted the term as a name for their product line. In

1944 the company name was officially changed to the Hyster Company.

One of the Hyster Company's most important early customers was the huge Caterpillar Tractor Company, which had an exclusive contract with Hyster to supply winches for its logging tractors. In 1936 Hyster opened a warehouse and distribution center in Caterpillar's hometown, Peoria, Illinois, and in 1940 the company began full-scale manufacturing there. The Peoria plant established a foothold in the Midwest that would become Hyster's center for manufacturing in the ensuing decades. In the same year, the company extended its production beyond the logging industry by beginning production of industrial lift trucks for other exterior applications. Among Hyster's important products during the 1930s and 1940s were the massive Karry Kranes, lift trucks designed for loading and unloading the huge cargo ships that were the center of the import-export trade at that time. The Karry Kranes were used in every seaport in the United States by the late 1930s and assumed a crucial role internationally during World War II when Allied forces relied on the versatile lift trucks to unload ships even at bomb-damaged ports. Almost 1,000 Karry Kranes were used during the war years, setting an important precedent for the international expansion that Hyster was to undertake in the late 1940s and 1950s.

International Growth and Diversification in the 1950s and 1960s

When the war ended, Hyster was in a position to capitalize on its new export business and, in order to meet growing demand for its lift trucks both at home and abroad, the company opened a new manufacturing plant in Danville, Illinois, that was to become the heart of Hyster's manufacturing operations for the next 50 years. By 1953 Hyster's sales had reached almost $26 million. The company was ranked third in sales of lift trucks in North America behind Eaton Manufacturing's Yale division and the industry-leading Clark Equipment Company. In 1956 day-to-day operations of the growing firm were taken over by Vice-President Philip S. Hill, who had worked for the company since 1933, beginning as a machinist. Hill would go on to become president of Hyster in 1960 and CEO in 1966 upon Ernest Swigert's retirement. Under Hill's leadership, the

Company Perspectives:

Hyster Company is the dominant force in the North American lift truck industry today. Our intent is to capitalize on that position. To do so, we need to act with a sense of urgency, exercising judgement and flexibility, to take advantage of business opportunities. In pursuit of this endeavor, we owe this to our stakeholders: Employees ... To be a fair, progressive employer that provides opportunity for employment security, career advancement, and competitive, performance-related compensation and employee benefits in a satisfying, empowering work environment. Customers ... To offer products that can and will fulfil their materials handling requirements while returning the best value on their investment. Community ... To be a responsible corporate citizen that strives to provide long-term stable employment in a safe working environment that conforms to area environmental standards, while supporting community growth and services. Internal Suppliers ... To be a company that achieves its marketing plans, providing accurate forecasts of product needs with minimal changes. External Suppliers ... To be the industry leader, financially strong, creating long-term business relationships with excellent credibility, integrity, and quality expectations. Dealers ... To be the company that provides the best materials handling distribution opportunity while offering dealers complete, quality products and support. Senior Management ... To be an organization providing a cohesive, professional management team which meets or exceeds divisional objectives while containing operating costs within AOP guidelines.

company entered the indoor or warehousing end of the forklift business, producing smaller and more manoeuvrable trucks for indoor applications. Hyster also diversified into road construction equipment including road bed compactors and levelling equipment for a variety of industries. "We feel we are diversified because we service so many industries and professions, including the grave diggers," Hill said in a 1970 interview with *Investor's Reader.*

Beginning in the mid 1950s, Hyster began to make a serious push into the international market. Over the course of the following decade the company opened manufacturing plants and distribution warehouses in Scotland, Australia, the Netherlands, the Philippines, Brazil, South Africa, and Canada. By 1964 $27 million of Hyster's $63 million total annual sales were provided by the company's international operations.

From 1960 to 1970 Hyster sales more than quadrupled, rising from about $50 million to over $220 million. This growth could be accounted for in part by a rise in international sales, which made up 35 percent of Hyster's business by the early 1970s. The domestic lift truck industry also prospered during the 1960s, averaging a growth rate of about 11 percent through the decade. By 1970, lift trucks were providing over 85 percent of Hyster sales. Of this segment over 60 percent of Hyster lift trucks were sold for indoor warehouse use, an impressive accomplishment since the introduction of the line in the mid 1950s. Hyster also continued to serve the cargo ship industry

that had launched the company's international business during the war years, landing a $2 million contract for "floating" lift trucks for the States Steamship Company. New manufacturing plants in Illinois and Alabama helped the company meet the rising production demanded by soaring sales.

Although Hyster's sales growth during the 1970s could not match the pace set in the 1960s, sales nonetheless more than tripled over the course of the decade, reaching $683 million by 1979. Even more significantly, a program to cut costs and improve plant efficiency resulted in increases in return on shareholder equity and higher profit margins. The growth rate in earnings per share far outstripped sales growth, rising from $2.36 in 1970 to $10.42 in 1979. As part of the company's modernization campaign, new manufacturing plants with state-of-the-art facilities were opened in Kentucky and Indiana and extensions were made to the Danville, Illinois, operations. Lift trucks now accounted for over 90 percent of Hyster sales, and the company decided to extend its competitive position in this segment by introducing a line of electric powered trucks that were particularly popular in the European market. In 1978 Hyster, at the peak of a period of growth and seeking to expand its material handling capabilities, acquired Fabtek Inc., a major manufacturer of personnel lifts based in California. By the end of the decade Hyster had outstripped its closest competitor, Eaton's Yale division, to take the number two spot in lift truck sales behind industry leader Clark Equipment.

Japanese Competition in the 1980s

The prosperity that fueled the lift truck industry in the 1960s and 1970s came to an abrupt halt in the early 1980s. The recession of the early 1980s hit hard for many industrial companies like Hyster, but the forklift industry received a double blow as large Japanese auto companies began to make serious inroads into the American lift truck market. Toyota, Mitsubishi, Nissan, and Komatsu, among other Japanese firms, had introduced low-cost, high-efficiency forklifts to Australia in the mid 1970s, and Hyster had seen its once-dominant 30 percent market share cut in half. Similar inroads were made in Europe during the late 1970s, but overall market growth in these areas dampened the effect of the increased competition from Japan. By the end of the 1970s, however, Japanese firms had begun to enter the low end of the U.S. market, targeting smaller customers like lumber yards and food warehouses that didn't need, or couldn't afford, the expensive options included in most domestic lift trucks. By 1982, Japanese companies had gained control of about 20 percent of the American market, and domestic materials handling companies were scrambling to prevent further erosion. The combined effect of the recession and Japanese competition caused Hyster sales to drop to $422 million, and in 1982 the company incurred its first unprofitable year, posting a $22 million net loss.

Hyster responded to these new threats by implementing an across-the-board restructuring program. Manufacturing plants in California and Belgium were closed and facilities in the Netherlands and Australia were heavily downsized. Overall, about 2,000 Hyster employees were laid off, and the remaining employees saw salaries cut back or frozen. Key to Hyster's recovery plan was the development of a low-end line of its own that would compete directly against Japanese imports. The XL Challenger line of gas-powered lift trucks was designed to meet these goals. The $18,000 to $22,000 price tag of the XL trucks was aimed at those customers who couldn't afford the $300,000 top-of-the-line Hyster models and whose needs could be met by the reduced lift capacity of the less expensive models. Introduced in 1981, by the following year the XL Challenger series had improved Hyster's market share in the low-capacity product category by six percent, and Challenger sales represented ten percent of new factory orders.

An important and somewhat controversial part of Hyster's recovery plan was the lobbying of various levels of government both to complain about unfair subsidies to Japanese companies and to demand aid for struggling Hyster plants. As outlined in a 1983 article in *Forbes,* in September 1982 Hyster Chairman William Kilkenny and President William Fronk addressed letters to five states and four nations in which the company built trucks, detailing Hyster's battle with foreign competition and offering to maintain precious jobs only in those areas that would offer monetary incentives for the company to stay. In a recession-plagued economy, governments felt they had no choice but to respond and retain scarce jobs at all costs. By February 1983, U.S. municipalities and states had contributed about $28 million in direct grants and subsidized loans to keep Hyster plants operating in their communities, and the United Kingdom offered a reported $20 million to save 1,500 jobs in Irvine, Scotland.

Most importantly, the new inexpensive line of Hyster lift trucks was to be exclusively produced in a new, highly automated and heavily subsidized manufacturing plant in Craigavon, Northern Ireland. Half of the $42 million construction and equipment costs at this plant were supplied by the United Kingdom, and a $50 million interest-free loan from the EEC helped defray operating costs. In addition, in 1982, Hyster built a new $8.2 million plant in Blanchardstown, Ireland, using funds provided by Ireland's Industrial Development Authority, which also contributed $16 million toward operating costs. This plant was to produce warehouse automation systems that Hyster then thought would be the direction of the future for materials handling companies. As it turned out, the automated systems were more expensive to produce and more difficult to sell than Hyster had anticipated. In June 1987, as reported in *Forbes,* the Blanchardstown plant was closed, much to the distress of the IDA, which would not recover its investment, and the Irish workers who, irate at the loss of their jobs, occupied the plant in a stormy protest.

Recovery in the 1980s and 1990s

Hyster's campaign to combat Japanese competition and retain market share was, by and large, a success. In 1987 the company won an anti-dumping case it filed against Japanese corporations with the International Trade Commission, resulting in the imposition of 50 percent import duties on Japanese lift trucks. Although the duties temporarily halted Japanese inroads on the American market, Japanese firms quickly set up their own U.S. assembly plants, and held onto their 50 percent market share. Almost all of the Japanese incursion on market share, however, was at the expense of Hyster's competitors, Clark Equipment, Caterpillar Inc., and Yale Materials Handling. Clark, which had dominated the American lift truck industry for years, was the big loser, as it failed to come up with a credible alternative to the Japanese products and saw its market share drop to less than 20 percent. Hyster was the only lift truck manufacturer that managed to remain profitable throughout the 1980s, retaining its 17 percent market share. Although net income never reached the 1979 high of $63 million, sales had rebounded to $776 million and profits to a respectable $22 million by the close of the decade.

In 1984 Hyster was taken private in a leveraged buy-out by longtime shareholder ESCO Corp., and in the late 1980s ESCO decided to cash in on its investment by selling the company to the highest bidder. NACCO Industries Inc., a former coal-mining company, was in the process of diversifying and had already purchased Hyster competitor Yale Materials Handling Corp. In May 1989 NACCO acquired Hyster for $620 million and an agreement to assume some $80 million of the company's debt. Hyster operations were joined with those of Yale, and the Hyster-Yale Materials Handling division of NACCO became the number one producer of lift trucks in North America. The management of the two companies was split by NACCO in a 1995 restructuring, and Hyster was then run as an independent operating unit of the NACCO Materials Handling Group.

The American lift truck industry which had struggled so bitterly through the 1980s began to rebound in the mid 1990s. A strengthening economy caused industries that had been delaying investment in new equipment to undertake new purchasing programs. As a joint company, Hyster-Yale Materials Handling posted record sales of $1.2 billion in 1994, although plant ramp-ups and heavy investments in strategic customer service and product development programs kept profits down to $15 million. As the Hyster Company entered the late 1990s, operating once again as an independent unit, the lift truck industry seemed to be regaining the vitality that had lifted Hyster sales through the almost 70 years of its corporate history.

Further Reading

Cieply, Michael, "Do-It-Yourself Industrial Policymaking," *Forbes,* July 18, 1983, pp. 30–31.

Doran, H. V., "Hyster's Efforts Bearing Rich Fruit," *Investment Dealers' Digest,* August 16, 1965, pp. 30–31.

"Hyster: A Top-of-the-Line Producer Tries to Beat Japan at Its Own Game," *Business Week,* February 8, 1982, pp. 99, 101.

"Hyster Lifts the Stakes," *Sales and Marketing Management,* November 15, 1982, pp. 53–56.

Kevin, K., et al., "How U.S. Forklift Makers Dropped the Goods," *Business Week,* June 15, 1992, pp. 106–107.

"Materials Handling: Big Lift at Hyster," *Investor's Reader,* February 5, 1964, pp. 7–8.

"Materials Handling: Oregon-Based Hyster Is Specialist in Load Lifting Equipment," *Investor's Reader,* November 4, 1970, pp. 15–16.

Rutgers, Carolyn G., "Old Principle Gives Hyster a New Profit Outlook," *Investment Dealers' Digest,* March 2, 1964, p. 30.

"Spotlight on Hyster Company," *Journal of Commerce,* October 3, 1973, pp. 3, 22.

Troxell, Thomas N., Jr., "Results at Hyster Get Lift from Efforts to Pare Costs," *Barron's,* January 16, 1978, pp. 30–31.

"When I Was a Boy," *Forbes,* October 1, 1969, p. 68.

Wiegner, Kathleen K., "Lessons from Ireland," *Forbes,* September 7, 1987, pp. 37–38.

—Hilary Gopnik

IHOP Corporation

525 N. Brand Boulevard
Glendale, California 91203-1903
U.S.A.
(818) 240-6055
Fax: (818) 240-0270

Public Company
Incorporated: 1958
Employees: 2,500
Sales: $164.32 million (1995)
Stock Exchanges: NASDAQ
SICs: 6794 Patent Owners & Lessors; 5812 Eating Places

IHOP Corporation develops, operates, and franchises the International House of Pancakes restaurant concept in the United States, Canada, and Japan. Through a focus on franchising and a long-term program of unit renovations and menu diversification, IHOP transformed itself from a struggling chain of pancake houses into a three-meal-occasion family dining empire. In fact, IHOP is among those companies responsible for the prevalence of affordable full-service family dining. In 1996 the IHOP system included over 700 International House of Pancakes restaurants in 36 states, Canada, and Japan.

Founding in the 1950s

The first International House of Pancakes restaurant opened in 1958 in Toluca Lake, California, under the direction of founder Al Lapin, Jr. After winning consumers over with its affordable pancake breakfasts and numerous flavored syrups, the business quickly expanded into a small chain of restaurants. Weekend patrons were often confronted with lines that stretched all the way out the establishments' doors. A year later, in 1959, the IHOP chain became an operating division of International Industries, a public company that held more than 20 different businesses and was strongly rooted in the franchising concept. Along with the newly acquired IHOP chain, International Industries franchised many other restaurant and food service concepts, including Copper Penney coffee shops, Love's Wood Pit Barbecue, and the Orange Julius chain.

While IHOP grew steadily throughout the 1960s, International Industries continued to expand its portfolio by obtaining additional businesses each year. By the early 1970s, International Industries was overflowing with businesses, but IHOP was one of only two that were producing a profit. The other, the Orange Julius chain, was sold to keep the company afloat, and IHOP's profits were used to support the rest of International Industries' holdings. IHOP soon began to suffer as well, unable to support International Industries' unprofitable ventures. By 1975, International Industries folded, releasing its unprofitable divisions and leaving IHOP on its own. Its chief financial officer, Richard K. Herzer, saw promise in the previously successful IHOP division, and began working with its creditors to keep the IHOP concept alive.

Herzer had come to IHOP in 1967 as a controller for International Industries. He was appointed chief financial officer in 1974, just before the company folded. In 1976 he rearranged a payment schedule with the banks, and the International House of Pancakes, Inc., became the principal operating subsidiary of a new parent, the IHOP Corporation. The restaurant chain was suffering, however, having had none of its profits reinvested toward improvements and developments in years.

In 1979 a majority of IHOP Corporation's stock was purchased by Wienerwald Holding, a Swiss company that controlled other restaurant chains in the United States, including the 225-unit Lum's chain. With the purchase, Wienerwald inherited IHOP's debt obligations, momentarily lifting the burden from Herzer and allowing him to focus instead on restructuring and improving the IHOP chain. Herzer was appointed president of IHOP by Wienerwald's chairman, Swiss entrepreneur Friederich Jahn. Herzer held to the belief that franchising the IHOP units would prove to be the best business strategy. He reasoned that an equity-involved franchisee would deliver superior restaurant operations to those of a salaried manager who had no individual stake in the company. IHOP implemented a process by which the corporation developed and operated each restaurant unit before eventually franchising it.

Company Perspectives:

Numbers are not our business. Our business continues to be people and the excitement of interacting with our guests and co-workers. Our success comes from hard work and a dedication to always being responsive to the needs of our guests. Success is not a birthright. It must be earned each day. To be successful, we focus on our restaurant operations.

In 1981 IHOP became a private company when Jahn repurchased 52 percent of its stock. Unfortunately, while many thought that Jahn had used the profits from Wienerwald to enact the purchase, he had actually borrowed $8 million to complete the $12 million transaction. Wienerwald declared bankruptcy in August 1982, leaving IHOP to SVIDO, a Swiss holding company which had no restaurant management background and left IHOP's management in place to run the chain.

Restructuring in the 1980s

Herzer was named IHOP's chief executive and chairman in 1983 and began the long process of restructuring IHOP in order to position the restaurant chain as a dominant presence in the family restaurant business. First, the company assessed the financial well-being of each of its restaurant units, ultimately closing the unprofitable ones and beginning a refurbishing program for the rest. Slowly but steadily, the company began remodeling the 88-seat, A-frame units, making way for larger and more contemporary units with twice the seating capacity and a muted decor that was deemed more pleasant for family dining. The number of two-seat stations in each of the new units was also increased, in order to accommodate more people (typical weekday patrons were individuals or couples on their way to work) and decrease waiting time by freeing up larger tables for those who actually needed them. Unit renovations often also included the implementation of a double-galley kitchen, which consisted of two identical smaller-scale kitchens, one of which could be closed down during slow periods in order to avoid excessive operation expenses.

While the unit renovations were taking place, Herzer also began a long-term program to broaden the menu selections by adding more non-breakfast items, holding to his belief that success in all three meal segments would be the key to expanding the IHOP chain. Knowing that the company's earlier attempts to enter the lunch and dinner segment had been ineffective, the IHOP management engaged in an extensive market research program in order to formulate a successful approach. Herzer insisted that the new lunch and dinner items be designed to use each IHOP unit's existing kitchen equipment, so as to avoid the necessity of spending additional money on items such as ovens, which no unit possessed. Using advertising slogans such as "Man does not live by pancakes alone" and "Good things cooking at breakfast, lunch, and dinner," IHOP introduced 26 new lunch and dinner items to its menu between 1983 and 1987, phasing in each item gradually after testing it in the Los Angeles market first. To ensure the success of the new

lunch and dinner program, an extensive training program for all employees was created.

IHOP also began offering special breakfast promotions and deals at its restaurants, believing that customers captured during the breakfast hours would be more likely to return at lunch and dinner as well. Promotions such as the Rooty-Tooty Fresh 'n Fruity Breakfast special, the T.S.B.S. (Truly Special Breakfast Special), and the Passport Breakfast Combo offered restaurant patrons heaping portions of fresh-cooked food in a full service atmosphere, at prices that were very competitive with those of fast food chains. For example, in 1985 the Rooty-Tooty Fresh 'n Fruity special was offered in various markets for either $1.99 or $2.49, including two eggs, two sausage links, two bacon strips, two fruit pancakes, and coffee. Similar dinner specials were soon introduced at most locations, at prices that placed IHOP solidly into the budget and fast-food pricing arena. The lunch and dinner menu was also crafted to accommodate the eating habits of IHOP's more nutritionally aware customers by offering vegetarian plates, chicken, and seafood.

Shortly after the commencement of unit renovations and the introduction of lunch and dinner items, IHOP began experiencing a steady increase in sales. Most newly renovated IHOP restaurants doubled their annual sales, and soon many of them were breaking the $1 million mark each year, up from $300,000 a year before the changes. Many franchisees attributed this sudden success in the lunch and dinner market to the attractive prices offered at IHOP. One of IHOP's largest franchise groups, FMS Inc. in Florida, noted to *Nation's Restaurant News* that dinner at IHOP was "appealing to Florida's senior citizens as well as blue-collar workers and single parent families, all people on budgets who like to eat out frequently." While enjoying its financial success, IHOP continued the expansions and revisions, gradually restructuring the company into a solid, profitable entity.

Leveraged Buyout in 1987

Meanwhile, SVIDO had begun searching for a buyer for the IHOP Corporation. After approximately four years of unsuccessful attempts to sell the company to an outside suitor, Herzer and other members of IHOP's management began planning a leveraged buyout, enlisting the services of several different institutional investors. In May 1987, this investment team, led by Herzer, purchased IHOP from SVIDO for an estimated $50 million. IHOP went public again in July 1991 after four years as a successfully self-owned corporation. It sold over eight million shares of its stock in a public offering at $10 per share. This shift back into the public arena paid off for IHOP, and as its month-to-month revenue continued to increase, the value of its stock doubled in less than a year.

In early 1992 IHOP introduced "America's regular guy" Cliff Bemis as its television spokesman. Past spokesmen for IHOP had included MacLean Stevenson of the television show *M.A.S.H.* and Jack Snow of the Los Angeles Rams. Bemis began appearing regularly in nationwide television commercial spots, known only as "Cliff" and using the new promotional tag "Nobody does breakfast like IHOP does breakfast." This new slogan was designed to emphasize IHOP's historical strength in breakfast, once again supporting Herzer's notion that clientele captured during the breakfast hours would be likely customers at other meal times as well. Accompanying Bemis's emergence as the IHOP spokesman was the reappearance of meal specials from the past, such as the Rooty-Tooty Fresh 'n Fruity Combo. These efforts were very successful: by 1994 the IHOP corporate logo had achieved an 80 percent consumer recognition level, which was the second highest rating among sit-down restaurants in the country.

In August 1992, IHOP made another strategic move in its effort to dominate the family-dining market when it acquired 23 units in the Pacific Northwest from JB's Restaurants, Inc. Prior to the acquisition, this geographic area had been almost completely controlled by Denny's, Inc., another large full-service chain whose primary focus is family dining. IHOP's management saw the 23 JB's units as a prime opportunity to penetrate the Pacific Northwest market, and quickly began converting the restaurants to the IHOP concept.

In 1993 IHOP introduced the first major addition to its menu since the 1980s, unveiling Country Griddle Cakes in September 1993, pairing itself with Nabisco, whose Cream of Wheat product was a primary ingredient in the pancakes. The partnership between the two companies came on IHOP's 35th anniversary and on Nabisco's 100th, and provided each with an excellent advertising opportunity. The new pancake was supported by television spots featuring Cliff, who promoted the new IHOP product as well as Nabisco's Cream of Wheat. Furthermore, almost 20 million coupons offering a free stack of Country Griddle Cakes with the purchase of an IHOP entree were distributed on Nabisco Cream of Wheat boxes across the country.

The introduction of Country Griddle Cakes came at an excellent time for IHOP, and the new pancakes and their advertising campaign were a quick success. The 1990s saw a more nutritionally aware clientele, and pancakes have a good overall nutritional profile. This was especially true for Country Griddle Cakes, which contain nonfat yogurt, Cream of Wheat cereal, and skim milk. A *Restaurants & Institutions* survey revealed that the top trends for the food service industry to follow were home-style value meals, combo breakfasts, anything in a skillet, and pancakes. It seemed that IHOP's strategic priorities were right on the money, and the company entered the mid-1990s in a position to strengthen its standing in the family dining market.

"Overnight" Phenomenon, 1990s

After years of slowly restructuring the company and reinvesting its profits in further improvements, IHOP and its stock were continuing to soar. Suddenly, financial analysts were taking note, hailing the corporation as an overnight phenomenon with the potential of a gold mine. *Forbes* magazine ranked IHOP 102 out of 200 among the best small companies in the United States, one of only three food service companies to be included. Analysts were predicting huge rises in the stock's value, some as high as 60 percent. Although IHOP had just

brought attention to itself by entering the public arena in 1991, it had actually been enjoying increases in its revenues every month since the early 1980s. Roger Lipton, of the New York firm of Ladenburg Thalmann & Co., Inc., expressed as much to *Nation's Restaurant News,* stating, "This company is not a 90-day phenomenon. They've always had a good value image and customers are comfortable with them. People are returning to IHOP."

By 1995, IHOP was opening more than 50 new restaurants each year in the United States, Canada, and Japan, and was planning to open almost 90 new units in 1996. Almost 90 percent of IHOP's units were franchised, with its largest concentrations of restaurants in California, Florida, Texas, and Japan. Systemwide sales continued to increase, leading IHOP into the late-1990s in a position of dominance in the family-dining market.

Principal Subsidiaries

International House of Pancakes, Inc.; IHOP Realty Corp.; Copper Penney Corp.; III Industries of Canada Ltd.; Blue Roof Advertising, Inc.; IHOP Properties, Inc.; IHOP Restaurants, Inc.

Further Reading

Alva, Marilyn, "IHOP Franchise Group Breaks Breakfast Mold," *Nation's Restaurant News,* March 9, 1987, p. 3.

"Basic Breakfast Puts the Bounce in IHOP," *Restaurants & Institutions,* June 15, 1994, p. 85.

Bruno, Karen, "IHOP Develops Eight Lunch, Dinner Items," *Nation's Restaurant News,* January 19, 1987, p. 3.

Carlino, Bill, "IHOP Hopes Everyone Will Remember Cliff's Name," *Nation's Restaurant News,* January 6, 1992, p. 12.

———, "IHOP Serves Up 'Hot' Griddle Cakes Systemwide," *Nation's Restaurant News,* September 13, 1993, p. 7.

———, "Richard K. 'Kim' Herzer: Keeping the Bounce in IHOP," *Nation's Restaurant News,* September 19, 1994, p. 170.

———, "Spruced-Up IHOP Shows Soaring 3rd-Q Profits," *Nation's Restaurant News,* November 16, 1992, p. 14.

"Family Dining Chains Scramble," *Restaurants & Institutions,* July 15, 1993, p. 90.

Hughes, L. A., "Chains Hungry for Expansion," *Miami Review,* August 23, 1985, p. 1.

Liddle, Alan, "IHOP to Acquire 23 JB's Units in Northwest," *Nation's Restaurant News,* August 3, 1992, p. 7.

Long, Dolores, "IHOP Plays off Morning Strength," *Restaurant Business,* April 10, 1986, p. 252.

———, "Kim Herzer, Chairman, IHOP," *Restaurant Business,* August 10, 1986, p. 62.

Martin, Richard, "IHOP, Free of Parent, Plots Growth," *Nation's Restaurant News,* May 25, 1987, p. 1.

———, "IHOP Rolls Bargain Breakfast, Readies 2nd Repositioning Drive," *Nation's Restaurant News,* January 21, 1985, p. 2.

"Stacked Stock," *Forbes,* July 6, 1992, p. 128.

—Laura E. Whiteley

Information Access

COMPANY

Information Access Company

362 Lakeside Drive
Foster City, California 94404
U.S.A.
(415) 378-5000
Fax: (415) 378-5199
Internet: http://www.iacnet.com

Wholly Owned Subsidiary of Thomson Corp.
Incorporated: 1977 as Information Access Corporation
Employees: 950
Sales: $110 million (1995)
SICs: 2741 Miscellaneous Publishing; 7373 Computer
    Integrated Systems Design; 7375 Information
    Retrieval Services

Information Access Company (IAC) is among the world-wide leaders in providing periodical indexes and the articles accompanying them in electronic form. IAC is also considered a pioneer in the various means of delivery of this information—on microfilm, optical disc, and the Internet—and has developed the software and provided the hardware needed to access its databases. The company's innovations have helped change the way millions of library users conduct research.

The 1970s: Start-Up Years

IAC had its origins in a consulting business which advised libraries on how to automate their card catalogs. Based in Los Altos, within the high-technology region known as "Silicon Valley," the start-up was a partnership between Brett Butler, Lyle Priest, and Harold (Buster) Spiwak. Butler held both MBA and Master of Library Science (MLS) degrees and knew the library business well. Spiwak was an entrepreneur with a background in sales. Priest was a computer hardware and software innovator. The three men had already established another company, an enterprise called Information Design, which was engaged in putting library card catalogs on microfilm. They had run this company for several years before selling it.

In 1976, Butler, Priest, and Spiwak got back together to do some consulting work and soon decided to found another company, one that would develop its own index product. They thus took on a fourth partner, Dick Kollin, who had an MLS degree and considerable experience developing periodical indexes in the publishing industry. The new company was incorporated in Los Altos on June 2, 1977 as Information Access Corporation. Buster Spiwak was named chairman of the board, with his wife Phyllis Spiwak serving as secretary and treasurer, while Butler became president and Priest and Kollin each became vice-presidents.

IAC's first product, largely Kollin's idea, was Magazine Index, an index of about 400 popular magazines similar in scope to the *Reader's Guide to Periodical Literature*. Magazine Index, however, was created as a computerized database and was delivered not in printed volumes but as computer-output microfilm. Users read the product through automated microfilm readers, which Priest had pioneered back at Information Design. IAC was the first company to use microfilm as a means of providing public libraries with periodical indices; since the microfilm was computer-output, it was easy to keep the index continuously cumulative, giving it a substantial advantage over printed indexes.

The first indexers, all of whom had MLS degrees, were hired in August 1977. They initially used IBM optical scan typewriters but in late 1978 were given personal computers, Apple IIs, to perform their work. As the computers were not networked at that time, the indexers had to bring their completed work on floppy disk to another computer for transmission.

Magazine Index was introduced by IAC at the California Library Association's fall conference in 1977, and the first deliveries were made to libraries in spring of the following year. IAC also made Magazine Index available as an online database for use by professional searchers and corporate librarians through the commercial database vendor Dialog Information Services. Although other computerized databases were available on Dialog, Magazine Index was the first general interest database among the other highly specialized ones. Dialog, which was located in nearby Palo Alto, was not the only online vendor in the United States, but it was the leading one. The head

Company Perspectives:

People who work or study in public and academic libraries, corporations, governments, hospitals, schools, and homes rely upon Information Access Company for useful, current information in databases that are easy to access and simple to use.

of Dialog at the time, Roger Summit, was a personal acquaintance of Butler's, and thus agreed to lend IAC about $250,000 in exchange for an exclusive online distribution contract.

Over the next three years, IAC introduced a new database product each year, and its indexing staff grew accordingly. In 1979 it came out with National Newspaper Index, an index featuring citations from five of the nation's leading newspapers. In 1980 IAC introduced an index to 700 law journals known as Legal Resource Index in its online form and Current Law Index in its print form. Then in 1981 the company introduced an index to trade journals called Trade & Industry Index in its online form and Business Index in its microfilm form.

IAC soon outgrew its small Los Altos office and moved to larger quarters in nearby Menlo Park in spring 1980. Boasting a work force of 40, IAC was growing and its products were successful. However, the company was not yet profitable, as its expenses were high. The company had not received any additional large investments since the loan from Dialog, and revenues from the dwindling consulting business had ceased in 1979. However, it had always been the intention of the founders to one day sell the company.

Growth under Ziff-Davis

On June 6, 1980 IAC was acquired by Ziff-Davis Publishing Co. IAC's name was modified to Information Access Company, and it became a division of Ziff. Although they no longer owned the company, the four founders each stayed on for awhile. In fact, Butler continued to run the company until the following year, when Ziff appointed one of its own executives, Larry Parkis, as acting president. Butler then remained with IAC in a less formal role until 1984. Kollin continued to run the indexing operations of IAC until 1982, when he left to take a position as senior vice-president at another indexing company. Spiwak stayed on in a consulting role until 1985, by which time he had turned 60 and retired. Priest remained a consultant to the systems department of IAC into the late 1990s.

Following the acquisition by Ziff, dedicated marketing, sales, and customer service departments were created at IAC. Ziff's experience in marketing and a dedicated sales force led to a boom in sales for IAC within a year. Another consequence of the sale to Ziff was that the exclusive online distribution contract with Dialog was terminated. Thus, in addition to having its index databases on Dialog, IAC added other online vendor distributors. Over the years these came to include Lexis/Nexis, Dow Jones News/Retrieval, Data-Star, and M.A.I.D.

In February 1982 Ziff sent a permanent president to IAC; Morris Goldstein assumed the duties which Butler and Parkis had been sharing. Although an outsider, Goldstein soon developed a good working relationship with the managers and staff of IAC. Although a division of Ziff, IAC retained a very separate identity, and, similarly, Goldstein became strongly identified with IAC as he oversaw the growth of company revenues and work force. In fact, IAC's rapid growth in the 1980s necessitated a move to larger facilities in the San Francisco suburb of Belmont in 1984, and then to an even larger headquarters in nearby Foster City in 1988.

The acquisition by Ziff not only helped IAC achieve profitability but also provided capital for acquisitions. Harfax Database Publishing, Area Business Data Bank, Management Contents, and Wards Business Directories were all acquired in the 1980s and were then merged into IAC's operations. Moreover, in 1985 Management Contents Co., acquired by Ziff in 1980, was merged into IAC. This company produced two periodical index products, which also included abstracts: Management Contents, which focused on the field of business management, and Computer Database. In 1986 production of both databases was integrated into the IAC indexing systems, when the company switched from the Apple II to a newer indexing system based on the Wang minicomputer. Management Contents and Computer Database would continue as distinct database products among IAC's offerings, production of Management Contents was later outsourced to an offshore vendor. Computer Database was temporarily transferred to a different division of Ziff in the early 1990s to coordinate its marketing as part of suite of other computer-related resources called Computer Library.

In 1985 IAC acquired Wards, which published a directory of companies uniquely strong in private company data. IAC thus started sharing company data between periodical indexers and the company researchers. IAC continued to publish the print directory under the *Wards* title for a few years by itself and later, starting in 1989, jointly with reference book publisher Gale Research Inc. IAC also integrated the company directory with data from its Trade & Industry database to create the new Company Intelligence database.

Database Delivery Innovations of the 1980s

In addition to new database products, IAC also developed new ways for users to access its databases and greater content for those databases. In the early 1980s IAC developed and sold a software package—Search Helper—to help searchers of Dialog develop their search strategies off-line and thereby save connect-time charges.

IAC also became a pioneer in providing full-text access to the articles it indexed. For microfilm, in 1983 IAC developed a product called Magazine Collections, which aimed at supplementing a library's collection of periodicals by offering the text of over 250 publications on microfilm. The index citations from then on included Magazine Collections cartridge and frame numbers, so that the user could quickly find the article on a separate dedicated microfilm Collections reader. Business Collections, offering the microfilmed texts of business and trade journals to correspond with Business Index, was subsequently added.

In online databases, IAC also begin introducing full text in 1983, when it began indexing and providing text from the PR Newswire in its new Newswire ASAP database. IAC was the first database indexing company to provide the full text of articles on Dialog. Subsequently, IAC began adding full text to selected journals in its other online databases. Including the full text involved negotiating royalty payments to the publishers, distinct from the microfilm rights, which initially were set as a 50–50 split. At that time few publishers could or would provide the electronic files of their publications, so IAC had to have all the articles retyped. For this manual task, IAC contracted out the work overseas. Within a few years the manual keying was partially replaced by scanning an optical character recognition.

In January 1985 IAC introduced a revolutionary new database delivery mechanism called InfoTrac, a turn-key computer hardware/software system for use by library patrons. Until then, databases searchable by computer were available only on expensive online services used by librarians. InfoTrac offered greater speed in searching than by microfilm. Specifically, it allowed a user to browse the thesaurus of subject headings, instantly jump to cross-references, and print out the citations, yet it required little or no user training. For InfoTrac, IAC developed its own unique search software and interface, and over the years all versions of IAC's microfilm indexes and most of its online indexes were made available on InfoTrac.

When InfoTrac was introduced, CD-ROM technology was still in its infancy, and reliable premastering studios and duplicating services for high volumes were nonexistent. Thus, for storing the data, IAC chose an earlier form of optical media, the 12-inch videodisc or laser disc. The videodiscs, like IAC's CD-ROMs of the 1990s, were updated on a monthly subscription basis. As with the microfilm readers, IAC owned all the equipment, leasing it to libraries and providing repair or replacement services. In 1987 IAC introduced a CD-ROM version of the InfoTrac system. Over the next two years IAC replaced the videodisc hardware with the CD-ROM systems for all of its subscribers.

At the same time, IAC began making its databases available to larger libraries in yet another format by directly leasing its databases on computer magnetic tape for the libraries to load onto their own computer systems and online public access catalogs (OPACs). By 1990 IAC was actively marketing such tape lease databases in a program named InfoTrac 2000. Rather than market to the libraries themselves, IAC marketed InfoTrac 2000 to companies that supplied OPAC software.

The availability of IAC's databases on OPACs, in combination with the new ability to dial into a library's catalog remotely, enabled people with computers and modems to access IAC's databases from home for the first time. IAC also began serving the home market when, starting in 1989, it made its databases available through the consumer online service CompuServe. On CompuServe IAC offered full-text databases from the onset. IAC also developed two new databases in the late 1980s: Health Index, introduced in July 1988, and Academic Index, introduced in April 1988. In 1991 IAC began adding abstracts to most of the citations in most of its databases.

Challenges of the 1990s

Throughout most of the 1980s, IAC grew with little direct competition. This began to change, however, in the late 1980s and early 1990s. Traditional print index publishers, such as H. W. Wilson, the publisher of the *Reader's Guide to Periodical Literature,* began releasing versions of their indexes on CD-ROM and online formats, and even Dialog began marketing its databases on CD-ROM. At the same time new electronic publishers, such as EBSCO, emerged.

In order to offset the effects of increased competition, IAC decided to step up its marketing efforts in the corporate market. Toward that end, IAC made its biggest acquisition, purchasing its leading competitor in online business databases, Predicasts Inc. of Cleveland, Ohio, in September 1991. Predicasts' sales were estimated at $60–80 million, slightly higher than those of IAC, which the trade journal *Online* estimated at between $40 and $50 million.

IAC continued production of all of the former Predicasts online, CD-ROM, and print products: PROMT, F&S index, MARS (Marketing & Advertising Research Services), A/DM&T (Aerospace/Defense Markets & Technology), Newsletter Database, New Product Announcements, Forecasts, and U.S. Time Series. Under IAC, Infomat's International Business, produced in the United Kingdom, was renamed Globalbase, and a few print products were discontinued.

Then, in an effort to place equal emphasis on the library and corporate markets, IAC created two market-oriented divisions in early 1994: Corporate Division and Library Division. Plans were also laid for a consumer division to be called the At-Home Division. Each division, headed by a general manager, had its own sales, marketing, product development, and product management staffs.

In another move aimed at strengthening its position in the corporate market, in March 1994, IAC acquired SandPoint Corp., a developer of intelligent agent software, known as Hoover, for Lotus Notes. IAC hoped to combine this technology with its database content to provide a current awareness service. Towards that end, IAC introduced an entirely new database in July 1995 called Industry Express. SandPoint's operations were merged into the Corporate division of IAC in late 1995. However, as Hoover proved less successful than hoped for, IAC sold SandPoint to Individual Inc. in October 1996.

The emergence of the Internet as a viable means of long distance commercial data communications allowed IAC to expand its methods of delivering its databases, as well as to become a competitor of the database vendors and OPAC companies with which it had traditionally worked. In late 1993 IAC began utilizing a central computer facility shared with other Ziff companies, called Ziff Information Services (ZIS), to offer libraries 24-hour access to its databases through a telnet connection over the Internet. The service was called InfoTrac Central 2000.

IAC Under Thomson

In January 1994 Goldstein resigned from IAC to accept a position as head of ImagiNation Network. IAC's executive vice-president and general manager, Robert Howells, was named company president. Then, in June of that year, Ziff's owners announced that they were putting all of its holdings up for sale. In December 1994 IAC was acquired by The Thomson Corporation for $465 million. Thomson, a multinational company based in Toronto, owned hundreds of periodical, print, and electronic publishing companies, in addition to a travel service. Just prior to the sale, Ziff's Computer Library operations were segmented, with Computer Database reverting back to IAC. IAC also gained another Computer Library operation, Data Sources of Cherry Hill, New Jersey, which produced computer company and product directory. IAC also retained the computer center, ZIS, in Medford, Massachusetts, renamed the Information Access Center, or IACenter. Howells remained president of IAC under Thomson and assumed the additional position of chief operating officer, while Goldstein rejoined IAC as the company's first chief executive officer.

Formerly a division of Ziff, IAC became a wholly-owned subsidiary of Thomson. The company thus assumed even greater independence in its operations and market strategies. Furthermore, new opportunities opened up for strategic partnerships with other Thomson companies. In fall 1996 Goldstein left IAC to take a newly created position in Thomson with the aim of fostering the sharing of resources among affiliated Thomson companies. Another result of becoming a part of a multinational conglomerate was a new emphasis on international markets. In February 1996 IAC created an International Division, and the activities of its existing U.K. office were expanded. IAC planned to introduce its first foreign language product, a Spanish magazine index and full-text database, in 1997.

Meanwhile, the growth of the Internet's World Wide Web meant a growing market for IAC's nascent At-Home Division. IAC's first Web-based service, called Cognito!, was aimed at the high school student/home market. It included Magazine Index, with text, and the indexed articles of two encyclopedias. In addition to reference books, the At-Home Division marketed other databases that were not periodical indexes. In 1994 IAC had established a partnership with Access Dynamics Inc., called the Automotive Information Center (AIC), which contained a searchable database of new car specifications; in 1996 IAC relocated the headquarters of the At-Home Division to AIC's offices in Westborough, Massachusetts.

In 1996 IAC's Library and Corporate Divisions also introduced web-based services. InfoTrac Searchbank, with the option of a web browser interface, replaced the InfoTrac Central 2000 service used by libraries and OPAC vendors. InSite, with flat-fee subscriptions for a single user, shared workstation, or site-licenses, was introduced as a web-based service for the corporate market.

The proliferation of the Internet and the concept of the information superhighway in the mid-1990s meant that IAC's products and services, originally aimed exclusively at libraries, were of potential interest to a much broader spectrum of society. Greater opportunities and greater competition thus lay ahead for IAC.

Principal Divisions

IACenter Division; Library Division; Corporate Division; At-Home Division.

Principal Operating Units

Computer Library; Automotive Information Center.

Further Reading

Carney, Richard, "Information Access Company's InfoTrac," *Information Technology and Libraries,* June 1985, pp. 149–153.
Davis, Lisa, "Information Access Spreads the Word," *San Francisco Business Times,* January 9, 1989, pp. 1+.
Flanagan, Patrick, "Talking CD-ROM with Sean Devine of Information Access Company," *CD-ROM World,* October 1993, pp. 26–27.
"IAC Announces New Licensing Program," *Information Today,* November 1990, p. 56.
Lane, Patricia, "Predicasts, On the Move," *Information Today,* September, 1992, p. 1.
——, "Ziff Communications Acquires Predicasts," *Information Today,* October 1991, pp. 1, 7.
Levison, Andrew, "Ziff-Davis: Sale of Publishing Giant Impacts Online Industry," *Online,* September–October 1994, pp. 31–38.
"Magazine Index—A New Database Aimed at the Markets of the Reader's Guide and the *New York Times* Information Bank—Due Online in January," *Online,* January 1978, pp. 7–8.
Pemberton, Jeffrey K., "Database Interviews Morris Goldstein, President of Information Access Company," *Database,* October 1989, pp. 29+.
——, "Online Interviews Delores Meglio of Information Access Company," *Online,* July 1987, pp. 17–24.
"Predicasts Sold to Ziff Communications Company," *Online,* November 1991, p.8.
Quint, Barbara, "Information Access Co.," *Database Searcher,* January 1992, pp. 16–17.
"Ziff-Davis Electronic Information Acquires SandPoint," *PR Newswire,* March 1, 1994.
"Ziff Family Sells Information Access Company to The Thomson Corporation for $465 Million," *PR Newswire,* October 31, 1994.

—Heather Behn Hedden

Interbrew S.A.

Vaartstraat 94
3000 Leuven
Belgium
+32 (16) 24-71-11
Fax: +32 (16) 24-74-07

Private Company
Incorporated: 1988
Employees: 13,237
Sales: BEF 81.4 billion (1995)
SICs: 2082 Malt Beverages; 2086 Bottled and Canned
Soft Drinks; 5181 Beer & Ale; 5149 Groceries and
Related Products, Not Elsewhere Classified; 6719
Holding Companies, Not Elsewhere Classified

With operations on every continent on the globe, Belgium's Interbrew S.A. ranks fourth among the world's brewing companies and first in its home country. The company emerged as a top European brewer in the late 1980s, when two Belgian brewing families merged their closely-held, centuries-old interests to form Interbrew. Under the direction of a succession of chief executive officers, the firm advanced from the middle ranks of the global beer hierarchy to the upper echelon via the US$2.7 billion acquisition of Canada's John Labatt Ltd. in 1995. Interbrew continued to be privately held into the mid-1990s.

Interbrew's strategy for growth has contrasted sharply with that of the beer industry's "Big Three." Anheuser-Busch, Heineken NV, and Miller Brewing Co. all focus on pushing their flagship brands throughout the world, while Interbrew has grown by acquiring leading national and regional brands, then investing in production and promotion to increase those beers' sales. By 1995, the company's stable of brands included Hungary's Borsodi Világos, Mexico's Dos Equis, America's Rolling Rock, and Canada's Labatt Blue. Interbrew cashed in on this cadre of specialty beers by exporting select brews, including its own Stella Artois, from one region to another.

Origins and Development

Interbrew was formed through the 1987 union of the Artois Brewery, owned by the de Spoelberch clan, with the Van Damme family's Piedboeuf Brewery. Artois traced its history to the late 14th century, when the Den Horen brewery was established in Louvain, Belgium. This business was acquired and renamed by master brewer Sébastien Artois in 1717. It is not clear when the de Spoelberchs assumed ownership of the company, which retained the Artois moniker throughout the remainder of the 20th century. The Piedboeuf family brewery, on the other hand, was established in 1853 and acquired by Albert Van Damme in 1920.

Both companies undertook programs of European expansion through acquisition in the late 1960s, and even joined forces in 1971 to effect the joint purchase of a third Belgian brewery. The multi-brand strategy developed over the course of three decades, as both companies bought competitors in the Netherlands, France, Italy, and Belgium, yet retained these new affiliates' disparate brewing heritages and brands. This policy fostered the development of two families of truly distinctive beers. Stella Artois enjoyed a legacy that extended back to 1366, Leffe Blond was brewed in a tradition that could be traced to a mid-13th century Belgian monastery, and Hoegaarden was a white beer with more than five hundred years of history behind it.

When Artois and Piedboeuf merged in 1987, the joint owners hired José Dedeurwaerder to rationalize operations. A citizen of both Belgium and the United States, the new CEO shed inefficient plants, won concessions from organized labor, and invested heavily in the newest brewing technology. His efforts nearly tripled overall productivity, from 2.5 hectoliters (66 gallons) per man-hour in 1990 to 6.5 hectoliters (429 gallons) in 1995. In spite of these apparent successes, Dedeurwaerder abruptly resigned in early 1993. He was succeeded by Hans Meerloo.

Interbrew continued to pursue its strategy of growth through acquisition in the early 1990s. The company achieved full ownership of Belgium's Belle-Vue brewery and Hungary's Borsodi Világos brand beer in 1991. These acquisitions provide insight in to Interbrew's multibrand strategy. The firm groomed Belle-Vue for export to the French market, targeting this cherry-flavored wheat beer at women. A reinvigorated advertising campaign helped sell eight percent more Borsodi Világos in its first year under new management. Interbrew continued to penetrate Eastern Europe with the 1994 acquisitions of Rumania's Bergenbier and Croatia's Ozujsko. Although some analysts viewed Interbrew's burgeoning cadre of international beers as a liability, others noted that the company's ''connoisseur'' brands accounted for over one-fourth of its net income and only 13 percent of sales. While vital to Interbrew's overall strategy, all the company's late 1980s and early 1990s acquisitions paled in comparison to the events to come.

Interbrew Emerges as a Global Brewing Powerhouse in the 1990s

By the early 1990s, Interbrew was Europe's fourth-largest brewer, with $2 million in sales and distribution throughout 80 countries. While impressive, the company's owners and executives realized that its status as a middling brewer on the global stage threatened its profitability and competitiveness. Furthermore, the company's core European market was showing signs of decline. Specifically, per capita beer consumption on the continent slid six percent in the early 1990s as the result of health concerns and more stringent drunk driving legislation. Interbrew's erratic fiscal results reflected this troublesome trend, as annual sales vacillated from a high of BEF 59.1 million in 1991–1992 to a low of BEF 48.7 million in 1993–1994. As a result, Interbrew started seeking a way to penetrate the all-important North American beer market. This was no easy task: Anheuser-Busch and Miller commanded a combined total of two-thirds of the U.S. market, leaving the rest of the industry's competitors to fight over the dregs.

But Interbrew got a couple of very important breaks in the mid-1990s. First was a market trend that saw craft beers and imports chalking up double-digit sales increases as consumers sought out unique tastes. But even more importantly for Interbrew, an overall consolidation of the global beer industry saw Canada's John Labatt Ltd. put into play in 1995. Gerald Schwartz's Onex Corp. soon launched an uninvited attempt to take over Toronto's John Labatt Ltd. for US $2.3 billion. Labatt CEO George Taylor put out a summons for a ''white knight'' that was answered with a personal response from Interbrew CEO Hans Meerloo. By mid-year, Interbrew was able to bring a successful US $2.7 billion offer for Labatt.

Although some industry observers thought the price, at 14 times cash flow, was steep, Interbrew CEO Meerloo perceived several valuable factors in the deal. Chief among these was Labatt's extensive North American distribution system, which could be used to peddle the parent company's trendy European brands throughout the United States and Canada. Labatt's patented process for making ''ice beer'' held out the potential for increased brand differentiation, global licensing revenues, and cost reductions. Not to mention the fact that Labatt's flagship brand ranked second among Canada's beer labels, with a 45 percent share. Significantly, Labatt was also Canada's most profitable brewer. Finally, the new subsidiary's multi-brand strategy (''50 beers exported to 40 countries'') meshed well with Interbrew's own program. The acquisition brought with it a 22 percent stake in Mexico's Dos Equis brand, which boasted a 45 percent share of that country's market, as well as Amer-

ica's Rolling Rock brand. The merger nearly doubled Interbrew's annual revenues and advanced it from fifteenth among the world's brewers to fourth.

Interbrew maximized the purchase of Labatt by spinning off what it considered extraneous activities that were significantly less profitable than the core brewery operation. These included Labatt Communications Inc., which encompassed a Francophile sports network, the Discovery Channel, and BCL Entertainment (involved in concert promotion). The company also sold its 20 percent share of Canada Malting Co. to ConAgra Inc. and expected to divest the Toronto Argonauts football team, the Toronto Blue Jays Major League Baseball club, and its 42 percent stake in the Toronto SkyDome. Company spokesman Gerard Fauchey told Maclean's Andrew Willis that ''It's very simple. We're brewers, not managers of hockey or baseball teams or television stations.'' These sales of these assets was expected to net US $1 billion and helped reduce the US $1.6 billion debt accumulated in the friendly takeover.

It seemed that CEO Meerloo's two-year term in office had been highly successful. Not only did he elevate Interbrew to the upper echelon of the brewing industry, but he was also credited with more than doubling the corporation's net margins via an early 1990s reorganization. The BEF 20 billion program cut costs and reinvigorated marketing across-the-board, thereby doubling profits from BEF 1.3 million in fiscal 1992 to BEF 2.7 million in fiscal 1994 despite a 17 percent reduction in annual revenues over the same period.

Notwithstanding these achievements, the Van Dammes and the de Spoelberchs were apparently unhappy with the Labatt pricetag. Represented by board members Viscount Philippe de Spoelberch and Alexandre Van Damme, the families apparently blamed Meerloo, who resigned in the fall of 1995. A 1995 Forbes article asserted that ''Interbrew is now without a clear leader. Johnny Thijs in Europe and Hugo Powell in Canada are chief operating officers who report to Chairman Paul De Keersmaeker . . . a crony of the owners.'' Some analysts have cited dissension among the de Spoelberch and Van Damme factions for the high turnover in the chief executive office.

Following the Labatt acquisition, Interbrew was reorganized into two primary divisions. One focused on Europe, Asia, and Africa, while the other concentrated on the Americas. Interbrew began importing its Stella Artois to the People's Republic of China via joint ventures formed in 1994 and 1996. The company hoped to establish a strong foothold in what was expected to be the world's fastest-growing consumer market of the 21st century. The continuing decline of European beer consumption and subsequent price wars not only encouraged Interbrew's expansion outside the Continent, but also fueled the divestment of some European interests. In 1995, for example, Interbrew sold its Italian affiliate to Heineken NV. The company also revealed its plan to divest its limited mineral water and soft drink interests and use the proceeds to reduce debt.

Dominated by Labatt, the Americas division focused on rationalizing the newest operations into Interbrew's global beer family. In his first annual report, division COO Hugo Powell emphasized globalization, cost-cutting, fortification of brands, and capital investment as keys to this business's future.

Interbrew shifted the end of its fiscal year from September 30 to December 31 in 1995, and therefore counted 15 months in its 1995. This new accounting made it difficult to compare that year's performance to either the previous year's or future years' results. Nevertheless, the company claimed BEF 81.4 million in 1995 sales, an 84 percent increase over fiscal 1994. Profits of BEF 3.5 million bested the preceding year's mark by 29 percent.

Principal Subsidiaries

Interbrew Belgium; Interbrew Netherlands; Interbrew France; Labatt Brewing U.K.; Labatt Retail U.K.; Birra Moretti SpA (Italy).

Principal Divisions

Interbrew Americas; Interbrew Europe-Asia-Africa.

Further Reading

"Belgians Take Off out West," *Beverage World,* June 1992, p. 10.

Clarke, Hilary, "Belgium's Strong Drinks," *International Management,* June 1992, pp. 62–64.

Khermuch, Gerry, "Labatt Shuffles U.S. as Interbrew Charges In," *Brandweek,* June 12, 1995, p. 3.

Munk, Nina, "Make Mine Hoegaarden," *Forbes,* December 18, 1995, pp. 124–126.

Parker-Pope, Tara, "Beer Consumption in Europe Wanes in Wake of a Widespread Recession," *Wall Street Journal,* February 21, 1995, p. A13.

Symonds, William C., and Linda Bernier, "A Belgian Brewer's Plans Come to a Head," *Business Week,* June 19, 1995, p. 56.

Willis, Andrew, "The Winning Brew," *Maclean's,* June 19, 1995, pp. 44–45.

——, "A Bidding Battle: Labatt's Sale of Hot TV and Sports Assets Draws a Crowd," *Maclean's,* June 26, 1995, pp. 24–25.

—April Dougal Gasbarre

Items International Airwalk Inc.

P.O. Box 951
Altoona, Pennsylvania 16603-0951
U.S.A.
(814) 943-6164
Fax: (814) 943-3921
Internet: http://www.airwalk.com

Private Company
Incorporated: 1976 as Items International Inc.
Employees: 110
Sales: $200 million (1995)
SICs: 5139 Footwear

Items International Airwalk Inc. designs and markets, through its Carlsbad, California–based subsidiary Airwalk, a popular line of casual, active casual, and specialty sports shoes targeted almost exclusively at people under the age of 25. Airwalk's line of snowboarding boots is the top seller in its category; the company also designs and markets a branded line of snowboards, bindings, and other accessories for that rapidly growing segment. Together with Vans, Airwalk remains the unofficial shoe of the skateboarding set, with a line of shoes specially designed to stand up to the rigors of that activity. Airwalk has also entered the relatively new biking category, marketing specialized shoes for the growing segment of professional and amateur mountain biking athletes.

The company has seen its greatest growth, however, in its branded line of casual and active casual shoes, which feature such styles as sandals, clogs, and oxfords, and active styles, including its popular One, Blammo, and Jim shoes. Airwalk also markets a list of lifestyle accessories, including t-shirts, sweatshirts, hats, and other garments, and sponsors such activities as the alternative rock festival Lollapalooza, and a number of professional skateboarding, snowboarding, and mountain biking athletes. In 1996, Airwalk expected to double its sales from the $200 million the company recorded in 1995. A growing percentage of its sales come from Europe and other parts of the world eager to emulate the Californian youth culture. Euro-pean sales already represent approximately 25 percent of sales of Airwalk, and are expected to grow to $100 million by 1997. Since the mid-1990s, Airwalk has undergone extraordinary growth, in large part through word of mouth. In the mid-1990s, the company stepped up its advertising spending, and by 1996 its advertising budget grew to $40 million, making that the fifth largest in the athletic shoe industry.

Airwalk is the sole subsidiary of Items International. Corporate and administrative functions are centered in the company's home base of Altoona, Pennsylvania. Design and marketing activities for Airwalk are performed at the company's Carlsbad headquarters, where the company can remain close to its source of inspiration, the casual California lifestyle. The company does not manufacture its own shoes but, instead, outsources production to factories in Asia. Items International continues to be led by founder and CEO George Yohn. The Airwalk line operates under the leadership of 34-year-old Lee Smith.

Unbranded in the 1970s

By the time Items International added Airwalk to its name, the company's founder, George Yohn, already had some 30 years in the shoe industry. Yohn was raised in Altoona, Pennsylvania, where he started his first company, Blair Co. Blair manufactured unbranded shoes in classic styles for such major department store and footwear chains as J.C. Penney, Kinney, and Sears. That company eventually grew to $12 million in sales, but by the mid-1970s, the rising costs of manufacturing footwear in the United States began to cripple the company's profits.

More and more footwear manufacturers began to outsource their production to plants in Asia, where wages were far lower and environmental regulations far less restrictive than in the United States. Yohn joined this trend in 1977, starting up a separate company, Items International, to produce similar unbranded and private label classic shoes for the U.S. market. Items International's higher profits soon convinced Yohn to shut down Blair Co. and focus on the new company.

Joining Yohn at Items International was president Bill Mann, a former art student with a background as a buyer for athletic gear and women's shoes for Payless Shoe Corp. and Shoe Corporation of America. Items International continued Blair Co.'s business of producing classic shoe styles for its clients' private label lines. However, Yohn and Mann sought greater growth for the company. At first, Items International attempted to enter more upscale dress shoe styles; the company opened offices in La Costa, California, in part to be closer to its Asian manufacturers, but this market failed to flourish for the company. As Mann told *Children's Business,* "I was going to be the first one to have the Orient make shoes that had the appearance of an Italian line of dress shoes. And then it dawned on me. You can't live in Southern California and be in the dress shoe business. Why? Because I can't compete with the Paris look. However, they can't compete with me . . . because I live in Southern California."

Persistence in the 1980s

The athletic craze had been building throughout the 1970s, originating in California and spreading nationwide in the next decade. Such companies as Adidas, Puma, Nike, and Pony were proving that there was a market for a new type of athletic shoe that went beyond the canvas styles of the past to offer performance features designed for serious athletes. As the footwear market began to segment, into categories such as basketball, jogging, running, and walking shoes, Yohn and Mann decided to build their own line of branded shoes, which offered the lure of double the profit margins of the company's private label business.

Then in 1983, Mann spotted an ad for a new type of exercise program that was rapidly gaining in popularity across the country. Aerobics had quickly become a staple of exercise regimes, especially among women, and a number of different styles of aerobics were emerging. One of the early programs was called Jazzercise, which, with its dance-like movements, appealed especially to women. Mann approached Jazzercise Inc. with the idea of licensing the name for a line of footwear specifically designed for aerobics. Jazzercise officials, who had already been interested in licensing footwear, agreed.

Mann sent one of Items International's designers to join a Jazzercise class and create a shoe specifically designed for aerobics, and especially the nearly half million women participating worldwide in Jazzercise programs. "I merely listened," Mann told *Footwear News,* "and put together what the women wanted." The result was a lightweight shoe with technical features such as a lower heel, a flexible sole, and foam padding for absorbing the shock of the high-impact aerobic movements. However, Mann had trouble locating a factory to build the new shoe, and it would take 16 months to bring the Jazzercise line to market.

By then it was too late, as step aerobics began to capture the market from Jazzercise. Led by Reebok, step classes became ubiquitous at gyms across the country and all over the world. As Jazzercise faded, so did Items International's hope for its aerobic shoes. The company continued in its attempt to develop a branded product, trying jogging shoes and tennis shoes, but the company made little headway in these categories, which were already dominated by such companies as New Balance, Reebok, and others.

Then Mann discovered a sport that had remained relatively untapped by the footwear industry: skateboarding. When Mann's wife originally suggested the idea, however, Mann was not enthusiastic. It was only after talking to his then 11-year-old son that Mann began to consider the idea. As Mann told *Children's Business*: "When he said, 'Dad, I'm bored with wearing white leather Reeboks,' it turned the light bulb on. I realized millions of kids probably felt the same way." Seeing that a skateboarder did not want to wear the same shoes "his mom wore to her aerobics class," as he told *Footwear News,* Mann began to study his son and his friends and other skateboarders. "I would scout the skate parks and see how they were wearing their shoes out," Mann continued in *Children's Business,* "While everyone else wears shoes on the bottom, these kids were wearing them all over—the uppers, the sides, the backs, and the toes. I realized that a more durable product was needed—one that gripped the boards and helped the kids do their tricks better."

Mann took another clue from a popular skateboarder's trick, called airwalking, and took the name for the new subsidiary launched by Items International in 1986 to pursue its new market. While developing the technical aspects of the new type of shoe, Mann also went to work on its styling. "My wife and son both recognized that kids were dressing differently and had different attitudes about things," Mann told *Children's Business.* "They like to look unique and not be bored. So I came up with more colorful, fresher looks that befit this new generation's attitude." By then, too, another shoe manufacturer, Vans, had begun to make waves in the youth market, when their checkerboard style sneaker achieved massive popularity after Sean Penn was featured wearing a pair in the movie *Fast Times at Ridgemont High.* Airwalk took the styling of its shoes even further, producing shoes in many different colors and patterns, and introducing different types of fabrics—among its popular shoes were ones made of tennis ball fabrics; the company would also produce shoes made of the material used to make basketballs.

Mann at first believed that the Airwalk styles, sold primarily in surf and skate specialty shops, would remain limited to California. However, he told *Children's Business,* "I quickly realized that kids were dressing the same all over the world. They all wanted to emulate the same California lifestyle and attitude." Within a year and a half after launching the company, Airwalks were selling by the millions worldwide. The subsidiary moved its headquarters from its 3,000 square-foot space in La Costa to a 48,000 square-foot facility in Carlsbad. By the end of 1987, Airwalks were available in over 100 styles, selling for relatively low prices, between $20 and $30, "low enough," Mann told *Footwear News,* "for kids to buy multiple pairs." In addition, Mann saw the company's growth linked to the growth of skateboarding itself, adding: "There are more kids that are skaters than football and basketball players combined. We feel that with this sport, we have a chance to be one of the major shoe companies."

Airwalk quickly broadened its line beyond its original 14-year-old target to include children's and adult sizes. Skateboarding, meanwhile, had also begun to influence clothing fashions in general among the youth market. Airwalk responded by adding a line of accessories, from caps, socks, t-shirts, and sweatshirts, to watches, stickers, and bags. The company also moved to extend its brand name into older categories, by bringing out a leather performance shoe. Toward the end of the decade, the company attempted to enter the apparel market; however, Airwalk found little success there. By 1990, Airwalk's sales had topped $20 million.

Success in the 1990s

Before achieving its runaway success of the mid-1990s, however, Airwalk weathered the collapse of its core skateboarding market. The sudden proliferation of skateboard parks across the country soon sparked a backlash against the sport. Many of the skateboard parks were closed, and Airwalk saw its sales slump to $8 million in 1991. Mann was replaced as president in 1992 by Lee Smith. (Mann joined rival Vans, Inc. as vice-president of foreign sourcing in 1994.) Before leaving Airwalk, however, Mann had already brought the company into two new categories—the newly emerging snowboarding and mountain biking markets—helping to redefine the company's image from the skateboard leader to an action sports company. Revenues rose again to $20 million in 1992, with sales overseas—where mountain biking and snowboarding saw its fastest growth—providing the largest boost. Under Smith, the company moved to extend its brand even further.

Taking a cue from Nike, which had successfully moved its shoes off the basketball court and onto feet all over the world, Airwalk began to promote its brand name—and the accompanying image of the California lifestyle—beyond the skateboarder set to the mainstream teenage market. While jettisoning its failed apparel line, Airwalk began to produce its first casual and active casual shoes. Yet finding outlets for these new fashions proved difficult. With a limited advertising budget, the company instead relied on its sales force to convince stores to stock its shoes. As Smith told the *San Diego Union-Tribune,* "We sought to get established as a fashion company rather than those kooky skateboard guys."

Meanwhile, sales of snowboarding boots were helping to firm up sales. Snowboarding was becoming increasingly popular—and accepted—by the skiing industry. By 1994, Airwalk had taken the lead in sales of snowboarding boots, just as snowboarding was becoming the country's fastest growing sport. Sales for that year reached $60 million. The company by then had managed to place its products into more than 1,200 outlets; that number would more than double over the following year as Airwalk launched its line of casual and active casual shoes, sparking the company's biggest growth. Separating the company into three divisions—action sport and leather and active casual—the company pushed to promote the Airwalk as a lifestyle brand. Under pressure from retailers the company also began marketing accessories to complement sales of its shoes. Teenagers all over the world responded, boosting company sales to $200 million by 1995.

Airwalk stepped up its advertising budget, in part to counter attempts by Nike—then facing a drop in demand for basketball shoes as the athletic market as a whole began to slip—and others moved to enter the action sports arena. Spending $30 million in 1995, the company pledged another $40 million for 1996, as sales were expected to double in that year. Yet the company's real challenge lies in maintaining sales while preserving its image as the hip, alternative lifestyle brand. As Smith told *Mediaweek,* "It's like walking a razor. You can't be too mainstream and you can't be too core. You have to keep yourself exciting."

Principal Subsidiaries

Airwalk Footwear.

Further Reading

Biederman, Danny, "California Kicks," *Children's Business,* July 1990, p. 42.
Brown, Christie, "For Cool Old Dudes Only," *Forbes,* August 12, 1996, p. 81.
Gallagher, Leigh, "Lee Smith: President, Airwalk Footwear," *Sporting Goods Business,* July 1996, p. 48.
Low, Kathleen, "Bill Mann Hopes to Ship a Million Jazzercise," *Footwear News,* June 25, 1984, p. 21.
Miller, Cyndee, "Shoe for Hipsters Targets Mainstream Teens," *Marketing News,* August 12, 1996, p. 2.
Rottman, Meg, "Skateboard Line Demand Overwhelms Airwalk," *Footwear News,* October 5, 1987, p. 2.

—M. L. Cohen

Jack Henry and Associates, Inc.

663 Highway 60
PO Box 807
Monett, Missouri 65708
U.S.A.
(417) 235-6652
Fax: (417)235-8406

Public Company
Incorporated: 1977
Employees: 350
Sales: $46.12 million (1995)
Stock Exchanges: NASDAQ
SICs: 7373 Computer Integrated Systems Design

Jack Henry and Associates, Inc. (JHA) is a leading supplier of in-house integrated computer systems for community banks in the United States. While most of JHA's customers are banks and other financial institutions with assets of less than $2 billion, upgrades to the IBM computers that run JHA's core software have expanded the company's potential market to include banks with assets of up to $10 billion. The company's main products are the CIF 20/20 and the Silverlake System, both of which run on IBM midrange computers. These turnkey systems, which are virtually complete and require little modification, support the core operations of banks and other financial institutions. While banks may access JHA software through service bureaus and facilities management operations, JHA's marketing strategy is designed to convince banks that it is feasible and more efficient to operate their computer systems themselves. JHA often bundles its software with IBM hardware, and the company is known for its high level of customer service, including maintenance and support.

Starting Up in the 1970s

Through acquisitions and strategic alliances, JHA has improved its position in the banking software industry since it was founded in 1976. That year, John W. "Jack" Henry, Jerry D. Hall, and a third person founded the company as a partnership to develop, market, maintain, and support integrated data processing systems for in-house automation of standard banking and accounting applications in commercial banks and other financial institutions. The company targeted community banks and marketed a bank automation system that used IBM's System/36 midrange computer. The firm was first incorporated in Missouri in 1977 but remained a private company until 1985. Its headquarters were established in Monett, Missouri, a small city located in the southwest corner of the state.

JHA reincorporated in Delaware on November 12, 1985, making an initial public offering on November 20 of that year. Approximately 1.1 million shares were offered at $6.75 per share, with the company realizing $6.21 per share. Of the shares, 725,000 were sold by the company and 375,000 by selling stockholders. Henry and Hall owned about 60 percent of the outstanding common stock of the company following the public offering. By this time revenues had grown to approximately $12.5 million, up from $5.5 million the year before. The company's main sources of revenue were software licensing and installation, maintenance and support, and hardware, with hardware sales accounting for most of 1985's new revenue. JHA had 46 employees, plus 22 employees in its unconsolidated affiliates, at the end of 1985.

Growth and Challenges in the 1980s

In 1986 JHA attempted to expand into financial services, acquiring FinSer Capital Corporation, a securities brokerage operation based in San Antonio. The new acquisition became a wholly owned subsidiary of JHA, but after three unprofitable years, JHA divested it in May 1989, transferring ownership to FinSer's chairman and CEO, Fred L. Baker, following a 40 percent drop in gross revenues that was attributed to generally poor performance in the industry at that time.

On March 31, 1988, JHA entered into a product development and marketing agreement with Unisys, a Detroit-based supplier of mainframe computers and related equipment. The next day IBM terminated its agreement with JHA. Under the original agreement between JHA and Unisys, JHA software would have been installed on more than 300 of the Unisys A

Company Perspectives:

Our mission, briefly, is to protect and to increase the value of our stockholders' investment by providing quality products and services to our customers. To accomplish this, we intend to: concentrate on what we know and do best—information systems and services for banks and financial institutions; provide outstanding commitment and service to our customers, so that the perceived value of our products and services is always consistent with their real value; maintain a work environment that is personally and financially rewarding to our employees.

Series computers, which were comparable to IBM System/36 midrange computers. However, the deal with Unisys soured, and JHA filed suit for breach of contract against Unisys a year later, in July 1989. Claiming that Unisys failed to pay approximately $1.7 million due on May 30, JHA sought $13.5 million, an amount that would have been due under the remaining portion of the contract. At the same time it filed the lawsuit, JHA announced that it had reestablished a remarketing agreement with IBM.

Henceforth the company would devote practically all of its efforts to two software systems that ran on IBM hardware: the CIF 20/20, which was designed for community banks with assets of less than $200 million and ran on the IBM System/36 midrange computer; and the Silverlake System, which ran on IBM's AS/400 system, a higher-grade midrange computer than the System/36, and was designed for mid-sized institutions with $100 million to $2 billion in assets. A new generation of AS/400 computers that was introduced in the early 1990s allowed the Silverlake System to service institutions with assets of up to $10 billion. The software systems were often sold bundled with IBM System/36 or IBM AS/400 systems through the remarketing agreement with IBM.

In June 1990 JHA announced a promising merger with Peerless Systems, Inc., a bank software company based in Richardson, Texas, with about 250 customers. The merger would have resulted in a banking software vendor with revenues projected at $20 million and about 850 customers, but in July JHA unexpectedly called it off. After four weeks of negotiations, it appeared that it would have taken too long to reach an agreement. One possible problem affecting negotiations may have been JHA's continuing lawsuit against Unisys.

New Leadership in the 1990s

In August, Colin McAllister quit as CEO at JHA, after serving for two years. Under McAllister, JHA had become embroiled in its lawsuit with Unisys, attempted to diversify into financial services by acquiring FinSer, and failed to consummate a promising merger with Peerless. President Jerry D. Hall immediately assumed the duties of CEO.

In 1990 JHA paid its first dividend, $.28 per share, a practice it has continued to follow. The declaration may have been

motivated in part as a move to bolster the stock price, which was trading in the $1.5–$3.5 range that year. The company reported negative income on revenues of $15 million.

The next year, fiscal 1991, saw the beginning of five consecutive years of profitability, with revenues increasing from $20.737 million in 1991 to $46,124 in 1995. Net income grew from $2.181 million in 1991 to $7.978 million in 1995. The stock price began to recover in 1991, trading in the $1.5 to $6.125 range. The number of employees increased by about 20 percent to 110, a trend that would continue for the next several years.

In January 1992 JHA acquired the banking software contracts of Bankers Own Software Systems (BOSS), the first of four acquisitions of bank software system businesses that it would consummate over the next few years. In December it acquired the business operations of Fremont Software, Inc., of Fremont, Indiana. Like JHA, Fremont marketed banking software and was an authorized remarketer of IBM computer equipment to small and medium-sized banks. These acquisitions served to expand JHA's customer base.

The end of 1992 also saw a favorable out-of-court settlement with Unisys, which agreed to pay $4 million to JHA. JHA was to receive $3,464,000 in cash, with the remaining $536,000 to be paid by eliminating charges against Unisys. JHA announced the settlement income would be added to working capital and that the company was pleased to reach a settlement, noting that a continuing legal battle could have significantly drained its resources.

Finally, in 1992 Michael E. Henry, the son of founder Jack Henry, was named to the board of directors and became vice-president of research and development. He had been with the firm since 1979. Michael R. Wallace also joined the board and was named vice-president of installation services. These two promotions marked the beginning of an orderly management change to a younger generation of executives that would be completed in 1994, when Michael E. Henry became chairman and chief executive officer and Michael R. Wallace, by then president, assumed the additional role of chief operating officer.

JHA continued to seek ways to expand its business in 1993. In January it announced the formation of a marketing alliance with BankVision Software, Ltd., of Durango, Colorado. By August JHA purchased BankVision for $2 million in stock and future payments based on earnings. BankVision added about 35 domestic customers, but its primary focus was to provide software and services for the international banking community.

By the end of 1993 JHA reported that it had software installed at more than 910 banks and financial institutions worldwide. Revenues had reached $32.6 million, net income was up to $6.259 million, and the stock was trading in the $10.25 to $17 range (adjusted). For the first time the number of stockholders had dramatically increased to nearly 2,000, and the company employed some 154 workers.

By 1994 the company had more than 3,000 stockholders, but the stock price was down in the $6.5 to $11.25 range due to flat earnings. JHA bolstered its stock price by increasing the quarterly dividend and reporting an increase in earnings by the end of the calendar year. Revenues were more heavily weighted toward the two most profitable segments, software and service, a trend JHA officials expected to continue.

In mid-1994 JHA acquired CommLink Corp., described in the company's annual report as "a rapidly growing electronic transactions company that handles automated teller machine (ATM) switching and point-of-sale (POS) technology for both financial and nonfinancial institutions." JHA paid $2.5 million, plus potential payments based on specific performance targets. CommLink, based in Houston, Texas, would operate as a subsidiary of JHA and be run by Thomas D. McCarlet, its founder, president, and CEO. CommLink had a customer base of approximately 100 customers for its ATM products and services. JHA regarded this as an important complementary service that could be marketed to its existing bank customers, to banks not served by JHA, and also to nonfinancial institutions such as gas stations and casinos that might someday have their own ATM cards.

The CommLink acquisition was followed in September 1995 by the acquisition of Central Interchange (CI), a small ATM provider located in Kansas City, Missouri, for common shares valued at $250,000. CommLink and CI together provided ATM networking products and services to more than 150 customers.

Always looking for new services to market to its established customer base, JHA formed a new division to develop, market, and support its own line of check imaging systems in October of 1994. After JHA developed software that would allow banks to electronically scan and store digitized images of checks that had cleared, the first test site became operable during fiscal 1995, with general release of imaging software expected to occur by December 31, 1996. This was regarded by JHA as a promising future source of revenue and profitability. Recent advances in check imaging technology had made it affordable for community banks. By offering its own imaging product, JHA became the first company to offer such an integrated product to its customers. Banks could access the check images immediately for their customers, and having check imaging capability gave smaller community banks a competitive edge over larger regional banks, many of which did not yet offer check imaging.

In 1995 JHA made several significant deals that further expanded its customer base and added new services that it could market. The first was a "technical services alliance" with Integrated Systems Solutions Corp. (ISSC), a subsidiary of IBM. The deal stemmed from the longstanding relationship between JHA and IBM. JHA had more than 1,000 installations of software on IBM's AS/400 computer line. Under the agreement, ISSC could use JHA's Silverlake System in service bureau arrangements, whereby several banks operated out of a single data center, or in facilities management contracts, where IBM installed and maintained a computer system on-site at the bank's location. Now IBM was able to offer banks with assets in the $500 million to $10 billion range an outsourcing option based on the AS/400, using JHA's Silverlake software. This represented a new market for JHA software in terms of the size of the banks it could service. The first contract realized from the arrangement with ISSC resulted in a $617,000 contribution to net income in the first quarter of fiscal 1996 for JHA, and JHA expected two or three such contracts per year, not all of them of the same magnitude.

In June 1995 JHA purchased two banking software businesses, significantly increasing its customer base. The first involved the SECTOR business unit of Nationar, located in Danbury, Connecticut, with a customer base of 34 customers concentrated in the northeast. Like JHA, SECTOR marketed software to banks. It was a cash transaction in the neighborhood of $883,000, with two possible future payments dependent on customers renewing their contracts with JHA.

The second, and perhaps the most important acquisition in the history of the company, involved Broadway & Seymour's community banking business, which JHA acquired for approximately $12 million. The transaction price included fees for certain distribution and marketing rights and fees for management services to be provided by B&S during the 12 months following the sale. Of the $12 million, JHA paid $6 million in cash and $6 million in installments through April 1, 1996.

As a result of the acquisition, JHA gained about 340 bank customers in 35 states of the Liberty banking system, thus increasing its customer base by one-third. The new subsidiary was called Liberty Software, Inc., with headquarters in Charlotte, North Carolina, and had approximately 150 employees. The subsidiary also provided revenue from service bureau contracts, disaster recovery, and a forms and supplies business.

In early 1995 JHA announced the restructuring of its unprofitable BankVision subsidiary, which was involved in developing and marketing international banking software. The unit was relocated from Durango, Colorado, to JHA's corporate headquarters in Monett, Missouri, in June. The division's president, Raymond L. Walters, was relieved of his duties as a result of the restructuring. JHA officials expected BankVision to negatively impact earnings for the current quarter and possibly the next. The BankVision unit was expected to break even or even become profitable during fiscal year 1996 beginning July 1, 1995.

William M. Caraway, senior vice-president of JHA, was named BankVision's president. He kept his sales and marketing duties for JHA. According to the company's annual report, the reorganization "eliminated significant overhead and minimized the loss potential for the BankVision operation." The reorganization gave JHA better control over its international operations and allowed the company to better focus its international marketing efforts. The company planned to expand BankVision more conservatively, and its major focus would be developing the Latin American market. However, at the end of fiscal 1996, JHA discontinued BankVision, taking a $1.68 million loss.

The Mid-1990s and Beyond

As a result of these acquisitions and reorganizations, 1995 was the best year financially in the history of the company. Revenues increased 20 percent to $46.1 million, and all major revenue categories showed significant gains. As demand for bank software took off, JHA reported a $16.4 million order backlog at the end of fiscal 1995, a 56 percent increase from the previous year's levels. Forty percent of the increase in order backlog was attributed to the company's core business, while the balance came from the newly formed Liberty Software subsidiary that was acquired in 1995 from Broadway & Seymour.

American Banker, which tracks JHA and other bank technology stocks, reported that JHA led all bank technology stocks with a 154 percent gain. According to *American Banker,* bank technology stocks gained an average of 35 percent during 1995, which was comparable to the one-third gains posted in 1995 by the Dow Jones industrial average and Standard & Poor's index of 500 stocks. During the year JHA stock traded in the $8.75 to $25.50 range.

According to *American Banker,* analyst Kevin J. Dyches of George K. Baum & Co. attributed JHA's stock gain to its June acquisition of the community banking software business of Broadway & Seymour Inc. The acquisition resulted in a 33 percent increase in JHA's customer base, and Dyches was quoted as saying, "At that time their market value was about $150 million, and they bought a company that was one-third their size for $12 million." The acquisition turned an immediate profit for JHA in the subsequent quarter.

In March 1995 JHA announced plans to develop a home banking software system that would become available through the Internet and online service Compuserve. JHA would develop the new product for Block Financial, owner of Compuserve and a wholly owned subsidiary of H&R Block, Inc., and offer it to its banking clients. The software package would allow a bank's customers to check account balances, pay bills, and get stock quotes using their personal computers. They would also have access to nonfinancial services as well as tax software from H&R Block through Block Financial's web site. A final agreement was reached with Block Financial in May 1996.

By March 1996 JHA's customer base had risen to 1,240 financial institutions. Financially, the company was in excellent condition. Its balance sheet remained debt-free, and the company was able to finance its acquisitions using its sizeable cash reserves and excess cash flow. JHA was poised for exceptional earnings growth from its acquisitions and core business. From 1993 to 1996, it increased its market share from eight to 12 percent of the nation's banks. According to a Sovereign Equity Management Corporation research analysis, JHA enjoyed several strategic advantages over its competitors. Its flexible software was among the most popular in the industry. It was the leading banking industry reseller of IBM hardware, which had the dominant share of the bank hardware market. Its superior service reputation was based on regular software upgrades, frequent regional and national user meetings, and timely re-

sponses to customer calls. And its low-cost operations had led to bigger net margins.

Principal Subsidiaries

Jack Henry International, Ltd.; CommLink Corp.; Liberty Software, Inc.

Further Reading

Barthel, Matt, "Unisys Paying $4 Million to Settle Dispute with Bank Software Firm," *American Banker,* January 5, 1993, p. 3.

"Block Unit, Jack Henry In Home Banking Pact," *American Banker,* March 19, 1996, p. 18.

Dyches, Kevin J., "Jack Henry & Associates, Inc.," *George K. Baum & Co. Equity Research,* March 28, 1996.

"Jack Henry Announces Management Shift," *American Banker,* November 21, 1994, p. 14.

"Jack Henry Plans Joint Marketing with BankVision," *American Banker,* January 14, 1993, p. 3.

"Jack Henry Purchases Software Firm," *American Banker,* February 1, 1993, p. 17A.

"Jack Henry, Small-Bank Software Firm, Posts Record Profit," *American Banker,* January 19, 1994, p. 23.

Layne, Richard, "Another Blow for Jack Henry; Chief Executive Officer Quits," *American Banker,* August 8, 1990, p. 3.

——, "Jack Henry Calls Off Talks On Merger with Peerless," *American Banker,* July 5, 1990, p. 3.

——, "Likely Merger Would Create Big Vendor to Small Banks," *American Banker,* June 8, 1990, p. 3.

Marjanovic, Steven, "Broadway & Seymour Spinning Off Core Software Business to Jack Henry," *American Banker,* June 22, 1995, p. 16.

Tracey, Brian, "Hogan and Jack Henry Gained in 2Q as Demand for Software Took Off," *American Banker,* July 31, 1995, p. 14.

——, "IBM Unit Gets Access to Jack Henry Package for Outsourcing Deals," *American Banker,* January 23, 1995, p. 10.

——, "Software Firm Jack Henry to Develop Own Check Imaging Unit," *American Banker,* October 24, 1994, p. 14.

——, "Systems Developer Jack Henry Posts Earnings Gain," *American Banker,* January 25, 1995, p. 13.

Tyson, David O., "Jack Henry Claims Breach of Contract in $13.5 Million Suit Against Unisys," *American Banker,* July 20, 1989, p. 2.

——, "Jack Henry Posts Loss for Quarter," *American Banker,* June 7, 1989, p. 11.

—David Bianco

HARLAND

John H. Harland Company

P.O. Box 105250
Atlanta, Georgia 30348
U.S.A.
(770) 981-9460

Public Company
Founded: 1923
Employees: 7,000
Sales: $561.6 million (1995)
Stock Exchanges: New York
SICs: 2759 Commercial Printing, Not Elsewhere
    Classified; 2752 Commercial Printing Lithographic;
    3577 Computer Peripheral Equipment, Not Elsewhere
    Classified

John H. Harland Company, an S&P 500 company, provides the financial industry with marketing and strategic planning services, checks and forms, and loan automation and compliance software. Harland is the world's second-largest check printer and the major collector of demographic consumer information for financial institutions. The company operates primarily in the United States and Puerto Rico, and has a joint venture, Galas Harland, with Mexico's largest check printer. Harland's subsidiary Scantron provides education technology and produces optical mark reading and optical character recognition forms and equipment. These are used in grading standardized tests, surveying hotel customers, inventorying warehouse contents, and selecting meals in hospitals. In 1995 Harland had sales of $561.6 million, 90 percent of which was to the financial services market. Its primary customers are banks, credit unions, brokerage firms, and personal financial software companies.

Early History

John Harland, a school dropout, came to the United States from Ireland at the turn of the century. After working in Providence and New York, he moved to Atlanta in 1906 and began his career as an office boy. He was promoted to cashier, and eventually to company treasurer. In 1922 he married Wilhelmina Drum-

mond, who had repaired ambulances in France during World War I and delivered hospital beds to Belgrade after the Armistice. It was Wilhelmina who convinced Harland to start his own company in 1923.

The new John H. Harland Company consisted of a printing plant, which produced stationary and business forms on a second-hand lithography press, and an office supply store. During the first year, Harland employed ten men and women and recorded sales of $113,000.

Business was good, and in 1926, the company moved to a new building. But the stock market crash and the business failures that followed nearly killed the young company. In his history of the company, Chairman Robert Woodson related that in 1931 profits were only $1,400. Things got worse: in 1932, the company made a profit of 31 cents.

In 1993 John Harland and his employees took advantage of an opportunity that eventually set the company on a new course. The banks in the Atlanta Clearing House had decided to issue emergency certificates, or scrip, to be used in case people panicked and tried to withdraw their money. The Clearing House awarded the contract for three million certificates to the John H. Harland Company—if they could deliver the certificates in one week.

Employees worked day and night, as armed guards (hired by the government) protected the plant and armored trucks lined up at the loading dock. The company met the deadline. Although the emergency certificates were never used, the banks were impressed. They soon asked Harland to add check printing to its office supplies and form printing businesses.

By the late 1940's, factions within the company were debating which segment of the business to concentrate on. One group wanted to stay with office supplies. A second thought the company should put more effort in the check printing business. The third segment wanted to concentrate on jobs that paid the most, preparing insurance policies and large contracts. According to Woodson, the check-printing group won out by convincing the others that with enough $2 and $3 dollar check orders, the company would have sales in the thousands.

Company Perspectives:

For over 70 years, John H. Harland Company has built its reputation on providing premier products and services to the financial services marketplace. Our services are designed to increase the profitability of financial institutions, while serving the changing needs of their customers. We have built valuable relationships with the nation's leading banks, credit unions, brokerage firms and financial software companies. These relationships, based on mutual trust and experience, provide a franchise and foundation for introducing additional value-added products and services.

1950's and 1960's—Concentrating on Checks

With the decision made, the company expanded during the early 1950's, opening check printing plants in Orlando, Nashville, Greensboro, and New Orleans. During this period, the banking industry (and much of the rest of the corporate world) became interested in automation. The American Bankers Association (ABA) set out to automate the reading and processing of checks, using a process called Magnetic Ink Character Recognition (MICR).

Harland was one of a few printing companies selected by the ABA to work on developing MICR. To implement the automation, a new typestyle, called E-13B, was designed. (These are the strange characters now common across the bottom of all checks.) However, once the MICR process was ready, check printers had to decide whether they wanted to meet the very stringent standards required to print MICR-encoded documents. Most of the companies that did not move into that technology disappeared. John H. Harland Company decided to go with MICR printing, and by the mid-1960's, the company had sales of more than $10 million and 750 employees running ten plants. In 1964 Robert Woodson joined the company, as comptroller. He had been an accountant with the firm of Haskins and Sells, and performed the annual audit of the Harland Company.

Much of the company's success appeared to come from its responsiveness to consumer demands, as in its introduction of scenic checks, which included designs and photography. Soon people were paying their bills with checks portraying their pets, flowers, views of mountains, and sea shells. As Chairman Woodson wrote, "Scenic checks transformed a dull transaction into an entertaining event, and checks became mini-billboards which people could distribute about town."

The company offered customers even more self-expression through its ability to print customized checks. Woodson described checks depicting Hollywood starlets and the Spruce Goose designed for the estate of Howard Hughes; a farmer's prize cow; and a man kissing his second wife, on checks with which to pay alimony to his first wife.

In 1969 Harland named William Robinson president and CEO. Robinson took the company public that year.

1970's and 1980's—Bank Deregulation

Harland died in 1976, but the company continued to move into new markets. By 1979, John H. Harland employed over 3,000 people in 32 plants, and had sales of $94 million. However, the check-printing business was about to go wild.

In 1980 Congress deregulated the financial industry. Suddenly everyone—large banks, small banks, credit unions—was offering checking accounts and wanted checks. At the San Diego plant, check orders jumped from 3,000 to 15,000 overnight. In keeping with the company's ability to recognize early shifts in market demand, Harland was the first company to provide checks to brokerage houses, and eventually became the check supplier for the majority of U.S. brokerage firms.

Checks were a high-profit item for banks and other financial institutions, who marked up the price by 20–30 percent. By 1988, consumers were turning to mail-order check printers whose checks were much less expensive. When appropriate, according to the company's annual report, Harland provided these high-margin checks through direct mail and specialized retail outlets.

Another new distribution channel was providing checks in conjunction with personal financial software programs. With personal computers becoming more affordable, small businesses and individuals liked the idea of printing out checks from the computer. Harland pioneered the strategy of marketing checks through financial software companies such as Peachtree Software, Solomon, and RealWorld.

Harland was also exploring other printing options, and in 1988 bought Scantron Corporation as a wholly owned subsidiary. This California company produced scannable answer forms for schools and other educational institutions and manufactured an electronic scanner that read and graded the tests. Scantron's strategy was to sell a school system the test forms and, if it couldn't afford to buy a scanner, to lend it for free, for as long as the customer kept ordering Scantron's forms.

In 1989 the check printing business was growing at about three percent, and Harland was printing 23 percent of the checks in the country, second only to Deluxe Corporation, which had 50 percent of the check printing business. That year, for the 40th year in a row, Harland increased its sales, to $344.7 million. For the 36th year in a row it had profit and dividend growth, which was the longest record of any company on either the New York or American stock exchanges.

1990's—Diversification

The 1990's saw increased competition in the check printing business as banks consolidated, becoming regional and even national institutions, and electronic money transfers became more prevalent. Harland, along with Deluxe Corporation and Clarke American, Inc., dominated an industry that had far fewer participants than ten years before.

The process of printing checks had changed as well, with companies switching from letterpress to less labor-intensive offset printing. Printers upgraded their plants and invested in computer technology. Harland spent millions upgrading or building new plants, training employees, and creating computerized networks that connected their customers to their facilities. In 1990 the company experienced its best productivity gains in four years, according to *graphic arts monthly.*

At the same time, banks were competing for customers' deposits and looking for ways to keep existing checking accounts or to attract new ones. In March 1990 Harland's sales representatives began selling the company's new Viewpoints line of checks. For no additional charge, customers could choose from 21 political messages, such as "Farmers Feed America," "Save Our Earth," "World Freedom," "Black Pride," or "Just Say No." In October, with American military units stationed in Saudi Arabia as part Operation Desert Shield, the company introduced checks with an American flag theme and the message, "Love the USA." The company also offered a line of checks endorsed by John Denver's environmental group, the Windstar Foundation, which received a portion of the order price.

In late 1990 the company announced plans to purchase Courier Dispatch Group, Inc.; however, the following spring, Courier's board took the air and ground courier private in a management buy-out to avoid the takeover by Harland.

In 1991 Bill Robinson retired and Robert Woodson was named president and CEO. Woodson continued strengthening the company's core check printing business. In 1992 Harland acquired Interchecks, Inc., of Seattle, the fifth-largest check printer in the country, with sales of $70 million. The move gave Harland a larger presence on the West Coast and brought with it a piece of BankAmerica Corporation's business. In 1993 the company bought Rocky Mountain Bank Note Co. Harland also produced new check designs, including those with the logos of major league football and baseball teams. At the end of that year, the printing of checks and forms accounted for 80 percent of the company's revenues.

Woodson also moved Harland into the financial software and services arena. In order to differentiate itself from other check printers and to provide more services to its retail banking customers, Harland built alliances with a variety of companies. Through its alliance with and investment in Bottomline Technologies, which produced hardware and software for encoding checks with magnetic ink, the company offered banks the Smarter Starter, a desktop printing system which made it possible for a bank branch to provide new customers personalized checks the minute they opened an account. Working with Telecheck Services, Inc., Harland offered check cashing services, account screening, debt referral and recovery, and lost and stolen check services to its financial customers. Through Cardpro Services Inc., a maker of magnetic stripe cards, Harland could provide automated teller machine (ATM) cards.

In January 1994 Harland switched from developing alliances to buying companies. Harland's strategy was to sell the software systems and services offered by these companies to Harland's customers as individual products or packaged with Harland's check printing services.

The first acquisition was Marketing Profiles Inc., a Florida company with 1993 revenues of approximately $13 million. Bankers used MPI's database software system and consulting

services to track customer data and build a marketing customer information file (MCIF). The system collected customer, product, and account-level information from a bank's pertinent data centers, and the results could be used to market the bank's products. In March Harland bought FormAtion Technologies, a Denver company. With FormAtion's loan origination software, a bank branch could instantly produce loan forms that complied with federal, state, and local regulations. Harland's subsidiary Scantron purchased Omaha-based Financial Products Corporation. The new subsidiary, Scantron-FPC, provided installation, maintenance, and repair services for computers, peripherals, networks, and operating systems. Harland also formed The Check Store to sell checks directly to customers.

That same year, the company introduced its Smart Document Series™, to help reduce the counterfeiting of checks on photocopies and laser printers. Banks could choose from eight security features, such as a microprint signature line whose words "authorized signature" appeared as a broken line if copied; ink that dissolved on contact with organic solvents; the appearance of the word "void" across the bottom of a photocopied document; and a three-dimensional holostripe which was almost impossible to reproduce. As William Borkland, a Harland executive, told *American Banker,* "We specialize in serving small to mid-sized banks so we wanted to create a product offering with pricing and feature flexibility."

Following the signing of the North American Free Trade Agreement (NAFTA), Harland moved into the international market. The company formed a joint venture, Galas Harland, with the Mexico City printing company, Miguel Galas S.A., to print personal and commercial checks for the Mexican market. Within a year Harland was providing checks and specialty printing for markets in Central and South America and throughout the Caribbean.

In 1995 the company signed a five-year exclusive contract with Intuit, Inc., becoming its sole provider of checks and forms. Intuit was the country's largest provider of personal financial software, with seven million people using its Quicken software. To meet this demand, Harland purchased dataPRINT of Seattle, which produced computer-compatible forms and was a major supplier to Intuit. Continuing to expand its educational technology division, the company bought Quality Computers & Applications. The new company, Scantron QCA, developed and distributed educational hardware and software such as theLINQ, the first filtered access system to the Internet.

Harland also developed and began testing a self-service interactive kiosk, using its SuperLink™ technology. Customers could simply go up to the stand-alone unit, touch the screen, and be able to get information about an account, apply for a loan, and order checks. The same technology also allowed customers to order checks through automatic teller machines (ATMs) and banks' automated telephone systems or Voice Response Units. The company began making its products available on banks' Internet sites and was the sole supplier of checking products to First Security Network Bank, the first all-Internet bank.

Continuing to enhance its core check business, Harland introduced new check designs, including drawings from the Monopoly® board game, Mighty Mouse®, and comic strip characters, and designed customized check packages for customers, such as the Charles Schwab & Co.'s ''e.Schwab Online Investing''™ account. Customers could also order checks to support such causes as the National Association for Sickle Cell Disease and the Humane Society of the United States.

In October 1995 Robert J. Amman was selected as the new president and CEO of Harland. Amman was president of Western Union and vice chairman of its parent company, First Financial Mortgage Corp. Woodson continued to serve as chairman.

Total sales for 1995 were $561.6 million, an increase of 7.7 percent from 1994. However, net income decreased, largely due to rising paper prices and the cost of the acquisitions. In January 1996, for the first time in 41 years, the company announced that it would not raise quarterly dividends.

In 1996 the company announced that it would begin an extensive review of its business. After first-quarter earnings fell 34 percent, Amman announced he would close some plants and lay off employees. The *Atlanta Journal Constitution* reported in April that Amman was considering selling Scantron, since it did not fit with the company's focus on the financial market. In June the company merged Formation Technologies, its compliance software subsidiary, into its Financial Markets segment. With that move, all the company's various financial service functions became a single operation under the Harland name.

The same month, Harland purchased OKRA Marketing Corporation, a Tampa-based database marketing service, for $25 million. OKRA's mainframe system was designed for large financial institutions and complimented the PC-based system of MPI which served mid-sized institutions. With the acquisition, Harland had the top two companies in that market.

Principal Subsidiaries

Scantron Corporation; Scantron FPC; Scantron QCA; The Check Store, Inc.; Galas Harland, S.A. (50%).

Further Reading

Allen, Pat, ''Mail Order Firms Make a Play for Check Print Orders,'' *Savings Institutions*, October 1988, p. 115.

Associated Press, ''Bank Check Maker Shutting Down, 53 Layoffs Announced,'' *San Diego Daily Transcript*, May 21, 1996.

Associated Press, ''Mexico Printing Venture,'' *New York Times*, March 17, 1994, p. D6.

''Courier Dispatch Group Inc.,'' *Wall Street Journal*, May 8, 1991, p. C21.

Cross, Lisa, ''The New Face of Financial Printing,'' *graphic arts monthly*, July 1991, p. 42.

Epper, Karen, ''Harland Reinventing Itself as a Supplier of Branch Systems,'' *American Banker*, March 30, 1994, p. 14.

Ezell, Hank, ''Harland Plans to Buy Seattle Rival,'' *Atlanta Constitution*, January 10, 1992, p. G3.

''Harland Offering Checks Aimed at Reducing Fraud,'' *American Banker's Management Strategies*, March 28, 1994, p. 16A.

Higginbotham, Mickey, ''Harland to Slice 2,500 Jobs,'' *Atlanta Journal Constitution*, April 23, 1996, p. B9.

——, ''Harland Considers Sale of Testing, Grading Unit,'' *Atlanta Journal Constitution*, April 27, 1996, p. H3.

Husted, Bill, ''Harland Co. Plans to Buy Control of Courier Service,'' *Atlanta Constitution*, October 5, 1990, p. B1.

Lyman, Ralph, ''Give 'Em the Razor, Sell 'Em the Blades,'' *graphic arts monthly*, January 1989, p. 74.

''New Checks Offered with a Flag Theme,'' *American Banker*, October 11, 1990, p. 6.

Poole, Shelia M., ''Harland Breaks String of Dividend Boosts,'' *Atlanta Constitution*, January 30, 1996, p. D1.

Sands, David R., ''Checks to Include Political Messages,'' *Washington Times*, March 29, 1990, p. C1.

Shultz, Matt, ''Shake-up Costs Formation Separate Status at Harland,'' *American Banker*, June 6, 1996, p. 10.

Slovak, Julianne, ''Companies to Watch,'' *Fortune*, March 27, 1989, p. 104.

Sullivan, Deidre, ''Harland Offers Features to Fight Counterfeiting,'' *American Banker*, February 7, 1994, p. 14.

Tracey, Brian, ''Check Printing Firm Buys Florida Data-Base Marketer,'' *American Banker*, January 12, 1994, p. 15.

——, ''Harland Signs Pact with Intuit to Supply Checks for Quicken,'' *American Banker*, September 11, 1995, p. 38.

——, ''Ex-Western Union Chief Named CEO at Harland,'' *American Banker*, November 13, 1995, p. 18.

Woodson, Robert R., *John H. Harland Company: A Proud Past, A Promising Future*, New York: The Newcomen Society of the United States, 1992.

—Ellen D. Wernick

WILEY

John Wiley & Sons, Inc.

605 Third Avenue
New York, New York 10158
U.S.A.
(212) 850-6000
Fax: (212) 850-6088

Public Company
Incorporated: 1962
Employees: 1,680
Sales: $331.0 million (1995)
Stock Exchanges: NASDAQ
SICs: 2731 Book Publishing; 2711 Newspapers; 2721
  Periodicals

A leading publisher of textbooks and professional books in science and technology and business, John Wiley & Sons, Inc. operates worldwide through its headquarters in New York City and through foreign subsidiaries in Europe, Asia, Canada, and Australia. Founded in 1807, John Wiley & Sons began as a publisher of American fiction writers, then moved into the science and technology segment of the publishing market after the American Civil War. From the late 19th century on through the 20th century, the company continued to publish academic, professional, and scientific titles, achieving encouraging success as one of the oldest independent companies in all of American industry. Led by a succession of Wiley family members, John Wiley & Sons entered the 1990s with Bradford Wiley II, the great-great-great-great-great-grandson of the company's founder, in control. In 1995, the company derived roughly 40 percent of its total sales from outside the United States.

In the early 1980s, Bradford Wiley uttered the obvious when he told a reporter from *Publishers Weekly,* "I guess you can say that we Wileys are survivors." In reference to a family whose business dated from the time of the presidency of Thomas Jefferson, this comment by Bradford Wiley was an understatement. Chairman of John Wiley & Sons at the time, Bradford Wiley was the great-great-great-great grandson of the company's founder, who established a business during the dawn of

the 19th century that would employ generation after generation of Wiley family members. Over the course of nearly two centuries the Wiley name was closely linked to the publishing business, a span of time that nearly encompassed the existence of the United States and charted the family tree of one of the oldest business dynasties in American industry. From the founder of the company to Bradford Wiley, to Bradford Wiley II, who directed the fortunes of the family business during the 1990s, a long line of Wileys orchestrated the growth and perpetuation of their publishing empire, creating one of the most venerable enterprises in the history of the country that John Wiley & Sons helped put on the publishing map.

Early History

The founder of John Wiley & Sons was not John Wiley, but his father Charles Wiley, the first of numerous Wileys to earn his money in the publishing business. Charles Wiley began all that would follow in 1807, when he opened a small printing shop alongside One Reade Street in New York City. Framed by a paperhanging shop on one side and a soapmaking shop on the other, Charles Wiley's business was a modest one, a trait of John Wiley & Sons that would continue to characterize the company for more than a century. Early on, however, the small shop on One Reade Street played an integral role in the emergence of the American literary movement.

During its first years in a young country, Charles Wiley's small printing shop served as a bastion for America's struggling yet superlative writers. Among the roster of notable writers whose words went to print at One Reade Street were Herman Melville, Edgar Allan Poe, Nathaniel Hawthorne, and James Fenimore Cooper. Each was an associate of Charles Wiley, who helped establish Cooper as perhaps America's first major novelist by publishing *The Spy* in 1821. All of these famous authors outlived the instrumental Charles Wiley, however, who died in 1826, leaving the business he had founded to his son, John Wiley.

When he took control of the Wiley publishing business in 1826, John Wiley was only 18 years old, but his youth did not prevent the second generation of the Wiley publishing family from taking the company in new directions. John Wiley contin-

Company Perspectives:

Our goal is to satisfy customer needs for information and education, while generating financial results that yield attractive returns for all members of the Wiley partnership: shareholders, authors, and employees.

ued where his father had left off by bringing the words of American writers to the public, but he also embraced the English literary scene by shifting the company's geographic stance overseas, making the Wiley business the first American publisher to offer royalties to foreign authors. To a list that already included Melville, Hawthorne, Poe, and Cooper, John Wiley added such distinguished English literary figures as Charles Dickens, Samuel Taylor Coleridge, John Ruskin, Thomas Carlyle, and Elizabeth Barrett Browning. During his tenure, John Wiley also launched *Literary World,* a book trade weekly that was in publication from 1847 to 1853, representing a precursor to the influential *Publishers Weekly,* which held sway in the publishing world during the 1990s. Other business avenues were pursued as well, including John Wiley's foray into selling nonbook items. The sale of pencils, school slates, violins, and stereoscopic equipment and pictures was added to the Wiley business, lending a hint of diversification to the operations at One Reade Street more than a century before such strategic moves would become a prevalent aspect of corporate existence.

The association the Wiley business had with the 19th century's greatest writers gave the company a unique and pivotal role in the development of the American publishing community. For the future of the company itself, though, the next Wiley to assume command of the company would direct the publisher toward the path it would pursue until the end of the 20th century. The years of disseminating the country's greatest literary works were over for the company. Ahead was the entry into a segment of the publishing market that would describe John Wiley & Sons during the 1990s.

Post-Civil War Shift in Business Focus

Taking over during the years following the American Civil War was William Wiley, son of John Wiley and a former soldier for the Union Army. Aside from being the son of John Wiley and thereby accounting for the corporate title the Wiley business adopted, William Wiley's influence on John Wiley & Sons was definitive. Trained as an engineer, the grandson of the company's founder instilled his passion for engineering and the sciences in the company he led, transforming John Wiley & Sons into a different type of publisher. Under William Wiley's stewardship, the company began publishing textbooks and professional books, a strategy that would fuel its growth for the remainder of the 19th century and carry John Wiley & Sons into the 20th century.

By 1914, when annual sales exceeded $300,000, four decades of operating as a publisher focused on science and technology books had propelled the company forward. Between 1875 and the beginning of World War I, John Wiley & Sons' sales

volume tripled, as did its payroll, which by the mid-1910s numbered 18 workers. Instead of publishing the novels of Melville and Dickens, the company was making its money in another field, earning its largest profits from publishing books on mechanical and electrical engineering. Such would be the future of the company, as it focused its efforts on the less glamorous, yet nevertheless profitable, science and professional side of publishing.

During World War II, John Wiley & Sons' business received a boost after several of the company's texts were adopted for use in training Armed Forces personnel, one of the lucrative markets opened up to the company as a scientifically and technologically oriented publisher. Another lucrative market for John Wiley & Sons expanded dramatically after the conclusion of World War II, when college enrollment swelled across the country, as veterans returned home and economic prosperity spread from coast to coast. Sales of textbooks climbed steadily as college enrollment rose in the United States, while in Asia and in Europe, where countries struggled to rebuild themselves in the postwar era, the demand for textbooks increased as well. John Wiley & Sons answered the call by exporting titles to Europe and Asia, substantially increasing the company's international business.

Post-World War II Growth

It was during this postwar upswing in business that Bradford Wiley, the great-great-great-grandson of John Wiley, rose to the top of John Wiley & Sons' executive ranks, becoming president of the company in 1956. The company's first overseas subsidiary was established four years later in London, touching off a period of international expansion that over a two-decade period would see John Wiley & Sons foreign subsidiaries established in Canada, Australia, Latin America, India, and Singapore. On the domestic front, John Wiley & Sons sidestepped the prevailing trend toward consolidations and takeovers that produced numerous conglomerate corporations during the 1960s. Despite eschewing the corporate maneuvers of the day, John Wiley & Sons did go public early in the 1960s, making its initial public offering of stock in 1962. It also executed several acquisitions during the decade, most notable of which was its purchase of Interscience, which substantially strengthened John Wiley & Sons' list of scientific titles and for the first time steered the company into the area of encyclopedia and journal publishing.

After serving as president for 15 years, Bradford Wiley ascended to the top of John Wiley & Sons' executive ranks in 1971, the year he was named chairman of the company, and then during the ensuing decade watched over the family business as it evolved into a thoroughly modern corporation. After establishing a medical division in 1973, which a decade later would publish an average of 60 medical titles a year, Bradford Wiley took steps toward repositioning the company to compete in the future. Titles were grouped into product lines, and in 1978 John Wiley & Sons' business activities were restructured into four major groups, comprising the company's professional, educational, international, and medicine business areas.

By the beginning of the 1980s, as it had done for decades, John Wiley & Sons ranked as a leading publisher of textbooks and professional books in science and technology, with offices situated around the globe. In its 175th year of business, the company generated record high totals in sales and earnings, collecting $137 million in sales and earning slightly more than $10 million, fueling confidence that the years after 1982 would continue to bring robust growth. The company by this point in its lengthy history was publishing more than 1,000 titles, 50 percent more than a decade earlier, and with the groundwork laid for John Wiley & Sons' expansion into electronic publishing, expectations ran high, with company officials projecting $300 million in annual sales by 1987. The company's 175th year of business, however, marked the beginning of bad times. Quickly, confidence was replaced by consternation.

Faltering Steps During the 1980s

Amid the celebrations heralding the company's 175th year of business and its record financial highs, John Wiley & Sons acquired Wilson Learning Group, a company founded in 1965 by Larry Wilson, co-author of *The One Minute Sales Person*. A creator of training programs for businesses, Wilson Learning Group added a new facet to John Wiley & Sons' operations, giving the publishing company a new enterprise to help offset flagging book sales. Starting in the late 1970s, college enrollment in the United States began to ebb, causing the sales of college textbooks to drop as well. The sale of such books accounted for one-third of John Wiley & Sons' total annual sales, and as the growth of college textbooks fell from double-digit percentage figures, the Wiley publishing firm began to feel the pinch. By 1984, the growth rate of college textbook sales had dropped to 4.8 percent, significantly weakening one of John Wiley & Sons' chief markets. If help was expected from the 1982 acquisition of Wilson Learning Group, it did not materialize. The subsidiary had been given considerable autonomy, but that proved to be its undoing, as Wilson Learning Group recorded robust growth—expanding at a 30 percent clip—but posted paltry profits.

In 1986, Wilson Learning Group registered a $754,000 loss, prompting one John Wiley & Sons official to remark that the subsidiary was "growing in an undisciplined manner." Two years later, the subsidiary lost a deleterious $2.2 million, which, coupled with John Wiley & Sons' difficulties in the college textbook market, left the publisher hobbled. In 1988, John Wiley & Sons earned $4.7 million on $241 million in sales, totals that when compared with the record year of 1982 pointed to serious problems. In 1982, the company earned more than twice as much as it did six years later on slightly more than half the sales volume, a phenomenon that no one at John Wiley & Sons wanted to perpetuate.

Ruth McMullin, who was recruited from General Electric, was hired in 1987 as chief operating officer to lead John Wiley & Sons toward recovery. When McMullin was talking with a *Forbes* reporter two years after joining the publishing firm, she reflected on her assessment of the company at the time. "It was clear this company became complacent about its uninterrupted record of success," McMullin noted, "and complacency led to an inattention to being tough and disciplined." To bring back these qualities, McMullin reorganized John Wiley & Sons' businesses into three divisions—educational, professional and trade, and training—and sold much of the company's floundering medical division, as well as closing the company's West Coast distribution center. Further changes were in the offing, as John Wiley & Sons entered the 1990s and steadily moved toward complete recovery.

Recovery in the 1990s

A new management team took over during the 1990s, led by Bradford Wiley II, the son of Bradford Wiley and the great-great-great-great-great-grandson of Charles Wiley. In 1990, John Wiley & Sons launched a sweeping strategic program aimed at restoring the company's profitability. The program called for the divestiture of poorly performing businesses, the strengthening of core businesses, and entry into new niches of the publishing market; its success restored the image of one of the country's oldest companies.

In 1991, the failing Wilson Learning Group subsidiary was sold, yielding John Wiley & Sons $30 million, and a medical book series was divested. A year that saw the company's college textbook sales record an encouraging gain also brought a new entity into John Wiley & Sons' fold. The law publications division of Professional Education Systems, Inc. was acquired, giving the company entry into a new publishing niche and marking the beginning of a concerted attempt to build John Wiley & Sons into a publisher of legal-oriented titles. Further gains were recorded in this area in 1992, when the company acquired Chancery Law Publishing Ltd. in the United Kingdom and the paralegal publishing line belonging to the James Publishing Group in the United States. By 1993, John Wiley & Sons' college division was recording double-digit leaps in revenues, concurrent with international expansion in Europe and Asia.

In a few short years during the early 1990s, John Wiley & Sons regained the luster lost during the mid- and late 1980s. By 1995, after recording 14 consecutive quarters of earnings increases, the company was generating $331 million in sales and posting $18.3 million in net income, achieving performance levels company executives had projected to reach nearly a decade earlier. Despite the less-than-spectacular performance demonstrated during the 1980s, John Wiley & Sons was firmly positioned for strong growth during the 1990s, its nearly 200-year-old presence in the publishing business and its resolute recovery during the 1990s sparking confidence for the future. As the company moved past its 190th year of existence and toward its third century of business, John Wiley & Sons was expected to continue its reign as one of the oldest companies in the United States and as one of the preeminent publishers in American business history.

Principal Subsidiaries

Wiley Europe, Ltd.; John Wiley & Sons (Asia) Pte. Ltd.; John Wiley & Sons Canada, Ltd.; Jacaranda Wiley, Ltd.

Further Reading

Anthony, Carolyn T., "John Wiley at 175," *Publishers Weekly*, September 24, 1982, pp. 42–46.
Poole, Claire, "Stubborn Patriarch," *Forbes*, February 6, 1989, p. 99.
"Wiley's Long March," *Forbes*, November 22, 1982, p. 155.

—Jeffrey L. Covell

Kent Electronics Corporation

7433 Harwin Drive
Houston, Texas 77036-2015
U.S.A.
Phone: (713) 780-7770
Fax: (713) 978-5892
Internet: http://www.kentelec.com

Public Company
Incorporated: 1973
Employees: 1,191
Sales: $372 million (1996)
Stock Exchanges: New York
SICs: 3679 Electronic Components, Not Elsewhere
     Classified

Kent Electronics Corporation is a distributor and contract manufacturer of specialized electronic components. Since it became a public company in 1986, it has grown steadily through selected acquisitions and internally to become the largest publicly traded specialty electronics distributor of interconnection and passive component products in the United States in 1996. In October 1996 the company realigned into four business units. The company's core distribution business, conducted by the Kent Components business unit, distributed electronic connectors, wire and cable, capacitors, resistors, and other passive and electromechanical products to original equipment manufacturers (OEMs) and industrial users in the United States. Another unit, Kent Datacomm, was focused on distributing interconnect wiring products for local area networks (LANs), wide area networks (WANs), and internal communication systems. The company's contract manufacturing unit, K*TEC Electronics, worked closely with OEM customers to provide fully integrated electronic manufacturing services, including assembly and testing of printed circuit boards, electronic interconnect assemblies, specially fabricated battery power packs, plastic injection molding, and system integration. The fourth business unit, Futronix Systems, was a specialty wire and cable redistribution operation consisting primarily of the recently acquired Futronix Corporation and Wire and Cable Specialties Corporation.

Founded in 1973

Kent Electronics was established in 1973 by Morrie Abramson and James Corporron. The two men, then in their mid-30s, purchased the radio and television parts business from their employer, Sterling Electronics Corporation, located in Houston. They used their own money, persuaded other Houston investors to participate, and borrowed from a venture capital firm, to whom they also sold a partial equity stake.

As the retail prices of radios and televisions fell, demand for radio and television parts slackened in the late 1970s. Kent phased out its radio and television parts business in 1978 and began selling industrial parts, mainly to the oil and gas industry in Texas. By April of 1982, Kent was generating 80 percent of its $8.6 million in sales from selling its broad line of electronics products to the oil service industry. That was the month that oil prices began to slide from a peak price of $35 per barrel. That was also when the phones stopped ringing at Kent. As Abramson told *Forbes* magazine, "When they started ringing again, the calls were cancellations. We were one of the first dominoes to fall."

After meeting with his top executives in a marathon session, Abramson and his team decided that the way to keep Kent in business was to reduce the company's product line. Instead of selling a broad range of electronics products to a single industry, Kent would sell a more focused product line of electronics connectors, such as wire and cable, sockets and receptacles, and other connectors, to a broader base of customers. It was this strategy, which significantly reduced the company's risk, that guided Kent throughout its steady growth phase in the late 1980s and 1990s, after it became a publicly traded company in 1986.

The company shrank its product line from more than 100 products to 20. As it did so, Kent's sales force became more knowledgeable about its offerings and was able to provide a higher level of customer service. As stated in its 1989 annual report, "The company as it is today was conceived in adversity

Company Perspectives:

The company's objective is to continually strive to be the best specialty electronics distribution and custom contract manufacturing company—as measured by our service to customers, returns for shareholders, and rewarding work experience for associates—and to consistently maintain these qualities as we grow and expand.

in the middle of an economically depressed market. We learned a lot from that experience. We learned that being the best in a niche in the market is better than being everything to everyone in a very large market. We learned that developing long-term relationships with a broad base of customers doesn't happen overnight. But it happens when you give the customer the same high level of service and products over and over again, no matter how large or small the order.''

Seeking to distribute electronic connectors, Abramson contacted AMP Inc., the leading manufacturer of electronic connection devices, which was located in Harrisburg, Pennsylvania. In late 1982 Kent became the AMP distributor for Texas. As Kent picked up other suppliers, AMP continued to be one of its major suppliers. In fiscal 1996, purchases from AMP represented approximately 22 percent of the company's total purchases.

Contract Manufacturing in the 1980s

In 1983 the company expanded into contract manufacturing and established K*TEC Electronics in Houston as a wholly owned subsidiary. K*TEC was set up to manufacture passive electronic components, including interconnect assemblies and custom fabricated portable and standby battery power sources. By adding contract manufacturing capabilities, K*TEC allowed the company to diversify within its vertically integrated product niche.

One of K*TEC's first customers was Compaq Computer Corporation, which *Forbes* described as ''then an obscure computer manufacturer operating out of a small office on the second floor of a suburban Houston bank building.'' K*TEC manufactured cable assemblies to Compaq's specifications for a prototype computer. By 1990, K*TEC was Compaq's primary supplier of cable assemblies and battery packs. Compaq accounted for approximately 30 percent of K*TEC's sales in fiscal 1990, and in fiscal 1996 sales to Compaq, by then a leading computer manufacturer, accounted for 12.2 percent of Kent Electronics' net sales.

K*TEC reflected the company's desire to provide customer solutions, not just parts. K*TEC's engineers became closely involved with its OEM customers in prototype development. As the company was wont to point out in its annual reports, K*TEC's products and services usually accounted for only one or two percent of the sale price of its customers' products; but the components that K*TEC provided were essential ones. Therefore, K*TEC's customers sought the involvement of

K*TEC's engineers early on in the development of prototypes for next generation products.

To facilitate prototype development, K*TEC enhanced its computer systems by adding Computer Aided Design (CAD) capability. This allowed K*TEC's engineers to be online with the OEM's engineers when developing and changing component designs. In December 1987 K*TEC opened a second manufacturing facility in Dallas, bringing it closer to a large number of OEMs in diversified industries.

K*TEC continued to capture a larger share of the available OEM market throughout the 1980s and 1990s. It benefitted from several market trends, such as the miniaturization of end products that required K*TEC's advanced technological manufacturing skills. K*TEC was also positioned to take advantage of increased outsourcing by OEMs.

K*TEC also expanded its manufacture of custom fabricated portable and standby battery power sources as it became standard practice to integrate such power sources in a wide range of electronic equipment. The company's 1988 annual report described how power sources manufactured by K*TEC were used miles in space and thousands of feet below ground, as well as in medical facilities across the United States. As demand increased, a separate division, K*Power, was set up in 1989 to market and manufacture the K*Power line of power sources.

The manufacturing capability that K*TEC brought to Kent Electronics allowed the company to provide customer solutions based not only on the specialty products that it distributed, but also to custom manufacture parts according to customer specifications. As Kent Electronics created new subsidiaries, such as Kent Datacomm, to provide additional solutions to new and existing markets, K*TEC's manufacturing capabilities could be called on to provide custom fabricated parts as needed by the new subsidiary's OEM customers.

By 1990 K*TEC had manufacturing facilities located in Houston, Dallas, and Santa Clara, California, in the heart of Silicon Valley. From these three locations, K*TEC was able to make just-in-time (JIT) deliveries to its customers. Its customers included manufacturers of computers and peripherals, electronic products for the telecommunications and medical industries, and other capital equipment and industrial applications. Major customers included Abbott Laboratories, Apollo Computer, Compaq Computer, Control Data, Fisher Controls, and Texas Instruments. It received the prestigious ''Texas Instruments' Supplier Excellence Award'' in 1988.

Parts for Voice and Data Communication Networks

Kent Datacomm was formed as a wholly owned subsidiary in 1987 to offer a broad range of equipment, products, and services to the end-user in the growing voice and data communications aftermarket. With demand for LAN interconnection expected to increase dramatically, Kent Datacomm was positioned to serve architects, consulting engineers, electrical contractors, and computer professionals who installed or serviced voice and data communications networks.

In January 1988, Kent Datacomm launched an aggressive marketing campaign that included distributing a catalog to voice and data communication end-users to increase the new company's visibility. Datacomm's large dedicated inventory represented the major vendor lines, including Alpha, AMP, Belden, IBM, and Panduit. It was able to provide customers with immediate off-the-shelf delivery of many voice and data communication products as well as products for the IBM Token-Ring, Ethernet, and other LAN systems. Quality custom fabricated products could be supplied through K*TEC's manufacturing operations.

As part of Datacomm's marketing program, inside and field sales representatives in Houston, Dallas, and Austin accounted for a growing number of sales to aftermarket customers for large and small projects in a wide range of industries, including manufacturing, airline, government, food, medical, media, financial, and aerospace. By targeting a broad range of industries, management hoped to build Kent Datacomm into a recession-proof business. It sought a competitive advantage by offering a unique range of services, equipment, and products, including both manufacturing and LAN system design capabilities.

Kent Datacomm was quickly established in southern California in 1989 to take advantage of the still-emerging industry of linking computers together. It continued to expand its product lines to stay abreast of LAN industry advances. For example, it broadened its inventory of fiber optic connectors and cables, which were in greater demand as customers installed faster computer equipment. A further geographic expansion took place in January 1990, as Kent Datacomm entered the Midwest market with a center in Chicago.

Purchases of connectors and cables for voice and data communication networks tended to be complex, since several different manufacturers of computers and peripherals may be included in a network. The individuals who made purchases from Kent Datacomm were primarily system integrators, who typically had to network a variety of computers and peripherals. The company demonstrated its ability to add value through its distribution methods when it received the prestigious "Spirit of Communications Award" from AT&T in 1991, an award that was given to only one AT&T distributor that year.

Throughout the early 1990s Kent Datacomm benefitted from the explosive growth in networking. In 1993 it strengthened its position as a single source for the networking needs of its customers by expanding its offerings to include intelligent products such as hubs, routers, bridges, and modems. Kent Electronics integrated Kent Datacomm operations into several existing components facilities, including those in St. Paul, Phoenix, and Boston. These locations represented new markets for Datacomm's LAN products. Existing Datacomm facilities were expanded and automated to provide additional distribution capacity and improved productivity.

Into the Silicon Valley in the Early 1990s

Kent launched its strategy to become a multiregional distributor and manufacturer of electronics connectors by purchasing Electro-Sonic Components, located in southern California, in September 1987 for $204,000 in cash and a promissory note for $400,000. Electro-Sonic was a specialty distributor of electronic parts. The acquisition provided Kent with access to many new customers in a wide range of diversified industries. Located in the center of a market that accounted for roughly one-third of all U.S. electronic component sales, Electro-Sonic formed the base for Kent's expansion into a new geographic market.

In 1989 Kent formed a new subsidiary, Kent Electronics Corporation-West, which entered into an option agreement to purchase all of the assets of Pyramid Electronics Supply, Inc., in exchange for common stock and the assumption of certain liabilities. Pyramid was headquartered in Santa Clara, California, and employed about 135 people at industrial distribution facilities in Redmond, Washington, and Santa Clara, Fullerton, and San Diego, California. It also had a custom contract manufacturing facility in Santa Clara. Pyramid projected revenues of $20 million for fiscal year 1990 (which coincided with Kent's fiscal year). Kent had reported net sales of approximately $36.5 million for its fiscal year 1989, so the acquisition of Pyramid would substantially increase Kent's net sales.

Kent completed its acquisition of Pyramid on January 16, 1990, for 166,667 shares (with a market value of $8 per share) and the assumption of certain liabilities. As was the company's practice when making an acquisition, it proceeded to integrate the operations of the acquired company with its own.

Becoming a National Distributor

Kent moved to become a national distributor and manufacturer in its specialty electronics field when it negotiated an option agreement on April 4, 1991, to acquire Shelley-Ragon, Inc., an electronics distributor located in St. Paul, Minnesota. Under the agreement, the two companies would work cooperatively for up to one year before deciding whether Kent would exercise its option to purchase. Shelley-Ragon had 14 sales offices and distribution centers and two manufacturing facilities in eleven states. In its last fiscal year, Shelley-Ragon reported sales of about $47 million. It employed about 250 people. The acquisition would substantially increase Kent's sales, complement its product line, and expand the company's customer base and geographic presence.

Kent completed its acquisition of Shelley-Ragon in fiscal year 1992 (ending March 28, 1992). During the same year it made a public offering of 1.625 million shares, with proceeds of approximately $23.3 million to the company. Kent's geographic expansion since 1986 had been dramatic, but it was also the result of a disciplined, orderly expansion plan. In 1986 the company served six states representing about ten percent of the U.S. electronics market. Its facilities were located in three Texas cities. With the acquisition of Shelley-Ragon, it was positioned in proximity to approximately 80 percent of the domestic electronics market. The acquisition added distribution facilities in several key markets, including Minneapolis/St. Paul, Denver, Boston, and New York. Kent now had approximately twenty sales offices and distribution centers in twelve states, and five manufacturing plants located in four states. Kent was truly a national organization.

Throughout the first half of the 1990s Kent continued to gain market share by offering a wide variety of materials management services and solutions to an expanding customer base. During fiscal year 1993 it successfully integrated Shelley-

Ragon's operations, increasing its geographic presence and adding product lines. Net sales jumped to $154.7 million from $94.7 million the previous year. The company's product line included connectors, capacitors, resistors, wire and cable, and other electromechanical and passive components. Its suppliers included AMP, AVX/Kyocera, Belden, 3M, Molex, Philips Components, and the Vishay companies.

In 1993 Kent received national authorizations for key lines, including AMP, AVX/Kyocera, Philips Components, and the Vishay companies. This opened up a host of new markets for the company. It also became one of only four AMP Nationally Authorized Distributors. Kent's entire sales force received training at the AMP Institute in Harrisburg, Pennsylvania.

Noting a trend toward comprehensive materials management services and solutions, Kent entered into a non-exclusive strategic marketing partnership with Anthem Electronics that allowed each company to draw upon the other's franchised product strengths. The two companies had complementary product lines and similar geographic coverage. Advantages to customers included offering more effective local JIT delivery systems, in-house stores at customer locations, and third-party manufacturing. These were the types of materials management services and solutions that helped customers reduce their overall acquisition costs.

Following the acquisition of Shelley-Ragon, Kent created the Kent Electronics Custom Services Division (KECS). With five locations across the US, KECS provided value-added services to customers needing cable and battery assembles. Shelley-Ragon had provided these types of custom services for 20 years.

Kent reported net sales of $372 million for the fiscal year ending March 30, 1996. That marked 11 consecutive years of growth since the company made its initial public offering in 1986. During that time Kent kept strict control over its costs, and its gross margins typically exceeded industry averages. Just as net sales increased year over year for eleven straight years, net earnings also increased each year. The company reported net earnings of nearly $28 million for fiscal 1996, compared with net earnings of just $410,000 for fiscal year 1986.

Kent began expanding its physical facilities in Texas in March 1995, when it purchased a 66-acre parcel of land with an option to buy an additional 30 acres in Sugar Land, Texas, located near Houston. By January of 1996 the company had completed building some 210,000 square feet of its new facility for manufacturing and warehouse operations and approximately 40,000 square feet for offices. A second phase of building was expected to add an additional 210,000 square feet by the end of 1996. By mid-1996 a new 215,000-square-foot distribution facility, also located at the Sugar Land location, was in the design phase.

Just prior to reorganizing into four business units as described above, Kent entered into an agreement to acquire two specialty wire and distribution companies, Futronix Corporation of Houston, Texas, and Wire and Cable Specialties Corporation of Atlanta, Georgia. The two companies had combined sales of more than $35 million during the first six months of 1996. In October 1996 Kent announced that its fourth new business unit, Futronix Systems, would be headed by Terrence M. Hunt, the founder of Futronix Corporation. This new business unit was expected to serve more than 1,000 electrical distributors through thirteen distribution centers and sales offices located across the United States.

Principal Subsidiaries

Kent Components, Kent Datacomm, K*TEC Electronics, Futronix Systems.

Further Reading

Auguston, Karen, "Streamlined Handling Triples Warehouse Productivity," *Modern Materials Handling,* March 1995.
Bower, Robert, "Automatic Replenishment: How EDI Sparked More and Better Business for Kent Electronics," *Automatic I.D. News,* August 1996.
Poole, Claire, "Quick-Change Artist," *Forbes,* December 10, 1990.
Sperry, Paul, "Trendscape: The Knowledge Substitute," *Investor's Business Daily,* May 28, 1996.

—David Bianco

Knape & Vogt Manufacturing Company

2700 Oak Industrial Dr. N.E.
Grand Rapids, Michigan 49505
U.S.A.
(616) 459-3311
Fax: (616) 459-3290

Public Company
Incorporated: 1898
Employees: 1,400
Sales: $183 million (1995)
Stock Exchanges: NASDAQ
SICs: 2541 Wood Partitions & Fixtures; 2542 Partitions
and Fixtures, Except Wood; 3429 Hardware, Not
Elsewhere Classified; 3496 Miscellaneous Fabricated
Wire Products

Knape & Vogt Manufacturing Company is one of the United States' leading suppliers of large adjustable steel shelving units, such as those used for the display of merchandise in stores, and has also long been a leading producer of drawer slides used by makers of cabinetry and office furniture. It is a producer of many storage and hardware products, which it distributes to other manufacturers for use in their own products, or to retail outlets for sale to the general consumer. Numerous acquisitions and mergers throughout the years have helped Knape & Vogt improve its own product offerings, while also adding retail items such as storage and organizational systems, home workshop components, and ready-to-assemble furniture to its product lists.

The Early Years

The company's beginnings can be traced to the late 1800s, when German brothers-in-law John Knape and Englebert Vogt arrived in Grand Rapids, Michigan, and began working on Knape's idea for a chainless bicycle. Knape saw great potential in his design, but another inventor's creation of the chain-drive coaster brake rendered Knape's idea unnecessary. Therefore, he

and Vogt founded the Knape & Vogt Manufacturing Company in 1898, and began producing specialty machinery and tool and die products in order to make a living.

John Knape passed away in 1914, and the business was continued by his three sons and Vogt. The company soon expanded its scope and began producing specialty hardware for local furniture manufacturers in addition to its machinery products. It was at this time that Knape & Vogt entered into the business of producing drawer slides, which became one of its most important products throughout the rest of the century. By the 1920s, the company was also supplying hardware to makers of store display fixtures and showcases around the United States. This broadening of production focus led to the creation of Knape & Vogt's own adjustable shelving hardware, and Joseph J. Knape's 1934 invention of the company's patented adjustable standards and brackets.

By the time the United States entered into World War II, Knape & Vogt was supplying its products to other manufacturers around the country and was also continuing to develop new products. The war effort, however, caused the company to temporarily abandon the production of its regular product lines and instead begin completing contract work for the military. Knape & Vogt's plant in Grand Rapids contributed to the production of glider wings, shell casings, and bandolier clips throughout the war. As was also the case with many other manufacturing companies, the increased production demands of the war left Knape & Vogt in good financial condition at the conclusion of the war in 1945.

Post-World War II Diversification

Interestingly, as wartime led to an increase in Knape & Vogt's production, so did peacetime. The late 1940s saw the beginning of the "baby boom," as thousands of soldiers returned home to start families. As these families started seeking ways to expand and improve the their homes without spending large amounts of money, the "do-it-yourself" concept began to gain popularity. Knape & Vogt decided to take advantage of this shift by expanding its product line to target the retail market as well as the other manufacturers to which it already supplied

---

Company Perspectives:

The corporate philosophy emphasizes providing a stable investment return for shareholders, a secure work environment and quality of life for employees and being a conscientious corporate citizen. We are a leader in the hardware and home center market with storage, workshop and specialty hardware products and a major source for metal drawer slides and related hardware for original equipment manufacturers. We pride ourselves on being a builder of quality products sold at competitive prices.

---

hardware. Therefore, in the 1950s the company developed different shelving and storage systems to sell to consumers for their homes.

The success of its entrance into the retail market led Knape & Vogt to go public in 1961; at the same time, the remaining members of the Vogt family divested their shares of the company. Two years later, John Knape's grandson, Raymond Knape, left a promising law career to join Knape & Vogt under his cousin, Donald, who was at that time president of the company. Raymond Knape believed that the company's future growth potential was dependent upon its acquisitions of other companies with complementary product lines. He helped engineer the company's first major acquisition in 1967, when Knape & Vogt purchased Modar, a furniture components manufacturer. The purchase strengthened Knape & Vogt's standing in the retail arena, as Modar began supplying laminated wood-fiber shelving and ready-to-assemble furniture to Knape & Vogt's retail offerings.

Under Donald and Raymond Knape, the company proceeded to manufacture and distribute its products throughout the 1970s, while also beginning to emphasize new product development. It began redesigning and improving its hardware items, such as drawer slides and shelving brackets, and also continued the development of new retail items such as Modar's ready-to-assemble furniture and storage items. Whereas much of Knape & Vogt's hardware items had previously been used in raw store shelving displays and fixtures, the improvements and new developments led to its use in high-quality kitchen cabinetry and wood office furniture. By the mid-1980s, the company had created and begun to market its 8000 line of precision ball-bearing drawer slides, a product line which was soon in high demand among Knape & Vogt's customers.

Acquisitions and Expansion in the 1980s

In 1985 Donald Knape died, leaving Raymond Knape to take over as president and assume control of the company. Raymond Knape immediately began evaluating the company and its future potential, and came to a number of conclusions. He realized that the company was relying on mature product lines with little or no opportunity for future growth. Revenue gains were coming mainly from yearly price increases, and unit sales for many products were actually decreasing. Knape also recognized that since the company's 1967 purchase of Modar,

the only other additions to Knape & Vogt's product offerings had been small improvements or changes to certain hardware items. Therefore, Knape decided that the next few years would have to be devoted to increased research and development efforts, and a search on his part for new acquisitions that could offer Knape & Vogt the opportunity to grow.

Knape & Vogt began investing heavily in product development in the late 1980s, spending approximately $8 million per year on the creation of new items. The company's research and development philosophy, which had previously been to find out what could be created using existing equipment, soon became market-driven as the development teams instead asked themselves what items needed to be created in order for Knape & Vogt to expand and succeed. Meanwhile, Raymond Knape had been negotiating with potential acquisition candidates, which resulted in the 1987 purchase of Roll-It of Canada, Knape & Vogt's largest competitor in the market of store shelving and display fixtures. Another acquisition took place in early 1988, as Knape purchased Feeny Manufacturing of Indiana, a leading supplier of wire storage parts to cabinet manufacturers.

1988 also saw major changes take place in Knape & Vogt's manufacturing plant in Grand Rapids. First came the purchase and implementation of a $2 million computerized manufacturing resource planning system, which was used to help run production as the plant continued to handle more material each year. Also new was the introduction of an employee suggestion system, which Raymond Knape instituted under the belief that the workers on the production floor knew more about the actual job than did those in management. Within a year, changes generated by the suggestion program helped Knape & Vogt realize over $360,000 in yearly cost savings, five percent of which went to the employees themselves. Finally, a profit-sharing program was implemented, which also helped boost the employees' interest and involvement in their company.

By 1989, Knape & Vogt's sales had reached $114 million, with the company's line of adjustable shelving for store displays making up almost 45 percent of that figure. Another third of the income was derived from sales of Knape & Vogt's drawer slides, a segment of the business that had grown considerably in 1989 due to the addition of heavy-duty and epoxy-coated European drawer slides to its product line. Most important, however, was the fact that the company's recent emphasis on product development was beginning to pay off, with sales of new items bringing in three times as much money as five years earlier.

The 1990s and Beyond

Introduced in early 1990, a newly-developed shelving system called Variations was backed by high expectations on the part of the company's management. Considered at the time to be revolutionary, Variations was a ready-to-assemble wood and glass storage unit that was attractive enough to be found in the living room of consumers' homes. Variations won awards as one of the outstanding new products of the year but failed to capture consumer interest and did not perform as well as had been predicted. Another decorative shelving unit, Shelf Anchor, had received considerably less attention when also introduced in 1990, and soon greatly exceeded Knape & Vogt's expectations and generated an abundance of sales. Shelf Anchor, which used a patented bracketless-mount design, quickly became a bestseller in the retail arena.

Unfortunately, the failure of Variations was one of the factors leading to a 40 percent decrease in earnings during the following year. Retail outlets began submitting smaller orders for Knape & Vogt merchandise, as a slump in the do-it-yourself market affected the entire industry. Luckily, the 1993 acquisition of the Hirsh Company of Illinois for almost $30 million gave Knape & Vogt the boost it needed. Hirsh, also a producer of freestanding steel shelving, as well as home workshop items and closet storage systems, helped Knape & Vogt double its shelving offerings. Through the purchase, the company also gained Hirsh's top three customers: Kmart's Builder's Square, Dayton Hudson's Target, and Wal-Mart.

The sudden expansion in product offerings that came with the acquisition of Hirsh prompted Knape & Vogt to restructure its organization of items into four separate product lines under the Knape & Vogt brand name. Shelf Help Shelving Systems came to include the company's steel shelving and store display items; Space Solutions Storage Systems encompassed all of the company's different home storage and ready-to-assemble offerings; Iron Horse Work Systems was made up of home workshop items; and finally, Knape & Vogt Drawer Slides rounded out the company's offerings. Leading this reorganization effort was Allan E. Perry, who in 1994 became the first non-family member in company history to be named president and chief operating officer.

In 1995 the Space Solutions line was bolstered by the addition of a ready-to-assemble wood closet storage system, with marketing of the item being based on its attractive appearance and ease of assembly by consumers. Modar's manufacturing facility in Michigan immediately began playing a large role in the production of the new Space Solutions items, which helped both Modar and its parent company generate profits. Although raw material costs were steadily on the rise and negatively affected the company's earning potential, Knape & Vogt managed to add some retail customers to its distribution list, enabling the company to increase its 1995 sales to $183 million.

In 1996, Raymond Knape continued to pass on more of his responsibilities on to Allan Perry, in an attempt to prepare him to take over as chief executive officer when Knape retired on his 65th birthday in December of that year. After almost 34 years with the company, Raymond Knape had helped Knape & Vogt expand and diversify through his emphasis on product development and his negotiation and acquisition skills. In 1996, the ready-to-assemble market was thriving due to the popularity of both home-based business operations and personal computer use. With operation and manufacturing sites spread across the United States and Canada to handle heightened demand for its products, Knape & Vogt entered the end of the century poised to strengthen its presence in the hardware, home center and drawer slide markets.

Principal Divisions

Knape & Vogt Canada; Modar; The Hirsh Company; Roll-It; Feeny Manufacturing Company.

Further Reading

"Knape & Vogt Manufacturing Co.," *The Insiders' Chronicle,* March 5, 1990, p. 3.
Palmer, Jay, "On the Shelf No More?: The Outlook Improves for Knape & Vogt," *Barron's,* January 13, 1992, p. 16.
Whisenhunt, Eric, "Wall Eyed: Knape & Vogt Doesn't Let Dust Settle on its Shelves," *Michigan Business,* October 1989, p. 32.

—Laura E. Whiteley

Kruger Inc.

3285 Bedford Ch.
Montreal, Quebec H3S 1G5
Canada
(514) 737-1131
Fax: (514) 737-1001

Private Company
Incorporated: 1921 as Kruger Paper Company Ltd.
Employees: 6,000
Sales: $800 million (1995 est.)
SICs: 2621 Paper Mills; 2631 Paperboard Mills; 2653
Corrugated & Solid Fiber Boxes; 6710 Holding
Offices

A leading manufacturer of recycled newsprint and other paper products, Kruger Inc. is the largest, privately owned forest products company in Canada. During the mid-1990s, Kruger produced 1.8 million metric tons of paper products per year. The company's two largest paper mills were located in Bromptonville and Trois-Rivieres, Quebec. Aside from these two major mills, the company operated several other mills in Canada and a recycling center in Albany, New York for collecting wastepaper.

Early 20th Century Origins

The first stirrings of what eventually became the largest, privately owned forest products company in Canada began in New York at the turn of the 20th century. It was there and then that the patriarch of the Kruger family, Joseph Kruger, worked as a paper merchant, plying his trade in a business that would make the Kruger name synonymous with the production of paper products for the next century. Along with the inseparable link connecting the Kruger family name with paper production came enormous wealth and widespread prominence for Joseph Kruger's descendants, but the family did not begin its rise until Joseph Kruger decided to settle elsewhere. New York proved to be only a way station along the family's path to greatness. It was in Montreal that the Krugers rose to distinction in the paper products industry, establishing a business legacy there that was renowned for its privacy and astute management, and one that began in 1904 when Joseph Kruger moved from New York and settled in Montreal.

In 1921, Joseph Kruger formally established the predecessor to Kruger Inc., a wholesale fine papers business known as Kruger Paper Company Ltd. Though Joseph Kruger founded the family business, the credit for developing the business into one of Canada's largest companies fell to his two sons, Gene and Bernard. The duties of stewarding the fortunes of the family business were passed to these two second generation representatives of the Kruger family at an early age, for six years after he officially established Kruger Paper Joseph Kruger died, never knowing that the small business he had created would develop into one of Canada's preeminent enterprises.

At the time of Joseph Kruger's death, Kruger Paper employed a total of five employees. Four workers were assigned to the company's warehouse to distribute the fine paper sold to wholesale customers, and the remaining member of the company's payroll wore two hats, serving as Kruger Paper's secretary and bookkeeper. At the age of 25, Gene Kruger took control of the enterprise. He had spent the previous five years working at Kruger Paper with his father; his brother Bernard, 15 years old at the time of his father's death, remained in school. A year later, in 1928, Bernard joined his brother at Kruger Paper, marking the beginning of a fraternal partnership that would span a half century.

The transformation of Kruger Paper from the small, wholesale fine papers business left by Joseph Kruger into one of the largest newsprint producers in North America began quickly under the guidance of the two Kruger brothers, albeit in a direction far removed from newsprint production. In 1929, the Krugers diversified into the aluminum business, founding Aluminum Rolling Mills and Dominion Foils Ltd. Both were based in Quebec, with Dominion Foils registering the greatest success of the two. A manufacturer of foil for the packaging industry, Dominion Foils was one of the first companies to master the production process involved in combining foil and soft paper for holding cigarettes in their packaging, spurring the two Kruger brothers forward in their involvement in the aluminum business. In the decade leading up to World War II and after the war, the Krugers continued to invest in aluminum production properties by acquiring or building plants throughout Canada and in Holland.

Within a few short years of their father's death, Gene and Bernard Kruger had distanced themselves from the business that Joseph Kruger had created. Joseph Kruger had established a business that never pretended to be more than a small-scale, entrepreneurial venture capable of supporting a family. The Kruger brothers, on the other hand, quickly embarked on a course that, in retrospect, pointed to the development of a business empire. Although the two Kruger brothers kept both their personal and business dealings close to the chest, preferring to remain out of the public spotlight, later publicity about the power dynamics between the two brothers cast the elder bother, Gene, as the orchestrator of all that followed the death of Joseph Kruger.

For nearly all of their years spent together directing their family-owned business, Gene and Bernard maintained a low social profile and avoided political involvement. During the decades that spanned the development of their family fortune, however, a few employees and friends shed light on what was occurring within the Kruger inner circle. To a reporter from *MacLean's,* a former employee noted that Gene Kruger was always on the phone ''yelling and screaming.'' The same employee described Bernard as the epitome of affability, remarking that, in contrast, Bernard was a gentle and gracious person who mixed easily with his employees. The divergent personalities of the brothers defined their dealings with each other: Gene was in charge and Bernard generally responded dutifully to his brother's bidding. Bernard admitted as much, confiding to a *Maclean's* reporter that ''if there was a disagreement, we would do things Gene's way.'' Consequently, Gene Kruger received much of the credit for the success recorded by Kruger Paper and later by Kruger Inc., earning a reputation within the Canadian forest products industry that perhaps was justly deserved. One industry consultant later remarked, ''Gene Kruger was always one of the brightest and most innovative men in the business.'' Despite the uneven power relationship between the two brothers and the accolades heaped upon Gene Kruger, there was no power struggle between the two brothers. In one of his few comments to the press, Bernard Kruger described his feelings for his brother to a *Canadian Business* reporter, explaining, ''It was the greatest relationship in the world; we trusted each other implicitly.''

Post-World War II Expansion

The Kruger brothers worked well together, and the growing magnitude of their business interests reflected as much. While the pair built up their holdings in the aluminum business before and after the war, they did not neglect the development of the paper business. Increasingly, the brothers became involved in paper production and related ventures, executing their boldest moves following the conclusion of World War II. In 1950, they completed their first major acquisition when they purchased the Richmond Pulp and Paper Company in Bromptonville, Quebec. The acquisition gave the Kruger business a paper production plant that would serve as the company's flagship paper facility for the remainder of the century, touching off decades of

energetic physical growth, as the two brothers narrowed their sights on the paper business. It was during this period that Gene Kruger's strategy for growth was most discernible. As the company grew exponentially from the 1950s forward, it did so by purchasing old pulp and paper mills and then revamping those facilities into modern production facilities. This approach predicated the company's expansion strategy for the decades ahead, remaining a key tenet of Kruger Inc.'s development even after the departure of Gene and Bernard Kruger.

During the 1950s, the Kruger brothers went on an acquisition spree, quickly adding to the breadth of their paper business. Among the companies acquired during the decade were Matane Pulp & Paper Company in Matane, Quebec, Sherbrooke Paper Products Ltd. in LaSalle, Quebec, which produced corrugated boxes, and Montreal-based Turcot Paperboard Mills Ltd. By 1961, the Krugers owned ten pulp and paper companies and ranked as a leading paper producer in their home province of Quebec; their nonpaper business interests, meanwhile, were gone. As the brothers increased their stake in paper production, they concurrently began shedding businesses that did not add to their stature as a paper producer. By the beginning of the 1960s, all of the nonpaper operations had been divested (the last business was sold in 1961), leaving the Krugers entirely dependent on yet strongly supported by the growing roster of pulp and paper facilities composing their growing empire.

Expansion continued under the aggressive and ambitious tutelage of Gene Kruger throughout the 1960s and 1970s, both within Canada and abroad. In 1955, the Krugers acquired 50 percent interest in, and then later purchased the balance of, Papeles Venezolanos C.A., a Venezuela paper mill company. Although this property was organized as a company separate from Kruger, Inc., the move to foreign shores established a precedent. In the late 1960s, the Krugers purchased Italy-based Velcarta S.p.A., a one-machine mill that produced wrapping tissue. On the domestic front, a second box production plant was erected in Rexdale, Ontario in 1964, and a second paper mill was added in 1973 through the purchase of Three Rivers Pulp and Paper Company. The paper mill, located in Trois-Rivieres, Quebec, represented a significant addition to the company's operations, ranking as important as the purchase of the Bromptonville plant 23 years earlier.

By the time the Trois-Rivieres plant was acquired, Kruger Inc. had completed a sweeping modernization program. Many of the company's facilities were thoroughly revamped to meet the mounting need for paper products, particularly for newsprint, which ranked as Kruger Inc.'s single most important product. The investment in the Bromptonville plant represented a telling example of the company's commitment to establishing itself as a large-scale paper producer. It also provided a glimpse into Gene Kruger's strategy to purchase old plants and enhance their technological capabilities and capacities. When the Krugers purchased the Bromptonville newspaper mill in 1950, the plant contained one machine that could produce roughly 9,000 metric tons of newsprint per year. By 1973, after years of investment, the plant housed three machines capable of producing 168,000 metric tons of newsprint per year.

After the modernization program was completed, Kruger Inc., to a certain extent, was beginning anew; a gradual change in the company's leadership added to the sense that a new chapter in the company's history was beginning. In 1968, Gene Kruger's son Joseph Kruger II was appointed to Kruger Inc.'s board of directors, marking the arrival of the third generation of the Kruger family to the company's upper ranks of control. By the mid-1970s, Gene was giving his son more and more responsibilities and, according to Bernard, Joseph began to wield this new-found power freely, occasionally stepping on his uncle's toes as he did so. Before long, Bernard began to feel uneasy about the situation at Kruger Inc. In his mind, his position was being eroded by his nephew. Bernard Kruger no longer knew where he stood and saw no resolution to the new power dynamics reshaping Kruger Inc.'s executive ranks without creating considerable friction among family members. In 1979, Bernard Kruger left the company of which he had been an integral part for 51 years, opting to retire rather than engaging in a power struggle at the company's headquarters.

Family Feud Erupts in the 1980s

Bernard's departure did not ease the troubles that began brewing in the late 1970s. The uneasiness remained, particularly in Bernard's mind, as he began to wonder exactly how much he owned of the family's various ventures and what his own children could expect as an inheritance. Inquiries into these matters caused Gene to take umbrage, and quickly the dispute turned into a battle waged in the courts and in Kruger Inc.'s boardroom. In 1982, a legal fight over the central issue of Bernard's family's rights as minority shareholders was brought to the courts. Bernard charged that his brother and representatives had attempted to bilk his family out of its fair share of Kruger Inc. and other offshore ventures. Further, Bernard contended that Gene's family, who owned 61 percent of Kruger Inc.'s shares, was not paying out sufficient dividends, that he had stopped receiving his $40,000-per-year pension, that his secretary had been fired, and that his company credit cards had been cancelled. As the owner of 32.5 percent of Kruger Inc.'s 11 million shares, Bernard's family asked the courts for compensation for years of low dividend payments, a demand that Gene and his son found specious. Although Gene's side of the family kept their comments to the press to a minimum, flatly stating that Kruger Inc.'s dividend policy was "moderately reasonable," the family feud was the stuff of headlines. The bitter battle brought the lives of a family that had shunned the scrutiny of the public eye for decades into the open.

Amid the turmoil, however, Kruger Inc. continued to perform admirably. Despite board meetings that Bernard's son David, a Kruger Inc. board member, compared with "the way Lee Iacocca described Ford meetings under Henry Ford," the company reigned as a dominant force in the Canadian forest products industry. The dispute between Gene and Bernard was eventually settled during the late 1980s in a secret, out-of-court deal in which Joseph agreed to buy Bernard's 32 percent share in the company for $99 million, but Kruger Inc. never missed a step throughout the decade. While tempers were at their hottest during the early and mid-1980s, the company had secured a major contract with Gannett Supply to provide newsprint for the publisher's new newspaper, *USA Today*. The deal was significant not only for the volume of business it represented but also because *USA Today* required the most demanding quality specifications in the newsprint business, which meant that Kruger Inc. could count itself among the most sophisticated newsprint producers on the continent. The newspaper's four-color pages were the first in the industry, and Kruger Inc. was one of the first newsprint suppliers to qualify as a supplier. By the late 1980s, when newspaper publishers were rapidly moving toward color printing, there was a dearth of qualified newsprint mills capable of meeting the expected demand. There were, in fact, only eight newsprint mills in North America that qualified as suppliers for *USA Today* and Kruger Inc. operated two of them.

Kruger Inc.'s strong technological lead over many of its North American competitors during the late 1980s served the company well as it entered the 1990s. Newsprint production would continue to be the company's mainstay business in the decade ahead, but, with Joseph Kruger at the helm as chairman, Kruger Inc. also made an aggressive effort to strengthen its position in the recycling business, specifically in its capacity to produce recycled newsprint. Toward this end, the company purchased Manistique Papers Inc. in February 1991 for roughly $68 million. Located in Michigan, the mill obtained through the purchase accelerated Kruger Inc.'s foray into recycled newsprint production and strengthened the company's presence south of the border, where the bulk of its newsprint shipments were delivered. Next, the company acknowledged its need to develop further its operations in the United States by forming a U.S. subsidiary in 1992. The subsidiary operation, located in Albany, New York, was established to generate baled wastepaper for use by the company's linerboard and newsprint mills in Quebec. Concurrent with this move, the company also opened a $55 million deinking facility at its mill in Bromptonville.

By the mid-1990s, Kruger Inc.'s strength was considerable. The company's largest market share continued to be in newsprint production, which was generated by ten machines capable of producing approximately 980,000 tons of newsprint per year. All totaled, the company's facilities were capable of producing 1.8 million metric tons of paper products per year, making Kruger Inc. the largest, privately owned paper products company in Canada. Supported by this mammoth production capacity, Kruger Inc. stood well-positioned for future growth in the late 1990s and continued vitality as it prepared for its second century of business.

Further Reading

Beirne, Anne, "Kruger vs. Kruger; Gene and Bernard Kruger Spent More Than 50 Years Building Kruger Inc. into a Giant Paper Company," *Canadian Business,* January 1986, p. 61.

Glowacki, Jeremy J., "Kruger Inc.: Newsprint Market Dominance," *Pulp & Paper,* February 1996, p. 34.

Ingman, Lars C., "Kruger Inc. . . . One of the Quality Leaders," *Pulp & Paper,* August 1989, p. 135.

"Kruger Feud Erupts with C$40-Million Lawsuit," *Pulp & Paper,* June 1993, p. 29.

Patrick, Ken L. "Kruger Boosts Newsprint Production with New Machines at Trois-Rivieres," *Pulp & Paper,* August 1991, p. 100.

Wallace, Bruce, "A Family Dynasty on Trial," *Maclean's,* June 2, 1986, p. 42.

—Jeffrey L. Covell

Lend Lease Corporation Limited

Level 46
Australia Square Tower
Sydney NSW 2000
Australia
(61) 2 236-6111
Fax: (61) 2 252-2192

Public Company
Incorporated: 1958
Employees: 4,000
Operating Revenues: A$2.05 billion (1996)
Stock Exchanges: Australia New Zealand
SICs: 1542 Nonresidential Building Construction; 6311
   Life Insurance; 6331 Fire/Marine/Casualty Insurance;
   6552 Subdividers & Developers, Not Elsewhere
   Classified; 6282 Investment Advice; 6726 Investment
   Offices, Not Elsewhere Classified

Lend Lease Corporation Limited is one of Australia's top 20 public companies and a leading real estate development corporation, with branches and subsidiaries throughout the world. Fiscal 1995 marked the company's 20th consecutive year of profit growth, as it earned A$260 million (after tax) on revenues of A$1.5 billion. From its inception the company has been an integrated property service, engaged in property development, management and investment, as well as construction of residential, commercial and industrial facilities; in more recent years, Lend Lease added funds management to its roster of services.

Post World War II Foundations

In the late 1940s, Australia was basically a nation of sheep farmers. The country, with a population of 8.3 million, was undeveloped and maintained a colonial dependence upon Europe and other nations for many of the basic necessities of life, in exchange for wool. World War II showed the danger of such an existence, and the nation was very much in favor of developing its own natural resources and skills.

Australia's dry climate made a source for a plentiful supply of water necessary to the development of the nation. The solution lay in a project called the Snowy Mountains Scheme, which entailed the taming of a snow-fed alpine river by the interruption of its seaward course. The river would then be sent through 130 kilometers of tunnels through a mountain range and a system of holding reservoirs to join rivers on the other side, 900 meters below. This design, however, was beyond the resources of this relatively small nation. What became known as the Snowy Mountains Hydro-Electric Authority (SMHA) was the trigger that implemented Australia's most ambitious immigration program. A government mission traveled worldwide, recruiting tradesmen, engineers, and laborers.

In Amsterdam the call was answered by Bredero's Bouwbedrijf of Utrecht (Bredero's) and The Royal Dutch Harbour Company. Bredero's sent a 30-year-old engineer, Gerard J. Dusseldorp, to Australia on a fact-finding tour for the Dutch construction firm. What he discovered was a country ripe for development and about to enter a period of great growth and prosperity. His report convinced the two firms to embark on a joint venture. They formed a company called Civil & Civic Contractors and put Dusseldorp in charge. Its first assignment was to supply and erect 200 prefabricated houses for the Snowy Mountain project. The 35 workers for the job were recruited in Holland by Dusseldorp and brought to Australia under the liberalized immigration laws.

Civil & Civic completed its first assignment within 15 months, but out of the SMHA came further jobs for the fledgling company. Bridges, houses, flats, and hospital extensions were added to the projects the company was to complete in the area of Cooma and Canberra. As a result, a locally engaged work force was soon growing around the nucleus of the original 35 Dutch workers.

At all times, however, G.J. Dusseldorp, who was by then Civil & Civic's managing director, was looking for a way to expand the company's operations. He focused on Sydney, Australia's largest city, which was about to experience the largest building boom in its history.

Evolution of a Full-Service Contractor in 1950s

Dusseldorp, as a developer, was constantly seeking a better way to do things, not only to boost company profits, but also to set standards of excellence within the industry. For him, the traditional system of tendering (or subcontracting) was, in his words, "a gushing stream of waste." When other firms were unreliable, the contractor had to shoulder the burden of their mistakes. He wanted to establish a system that was to remain the foundation of the company's philosophy—undivided responsibility for any project from start to finish.

Civil & Civic had a chance to try out the new system when a small project in Sydney in 1953 was presented to the company. Dusseldorp was determined to prove that there was a better way to handle a construction project. An oil refinery needed a gatehouse to be added to a new plant currently under construction. Civil & Civic designed and built it within six weeks. It was the firm's first design and construction project.

In 1954 Dusseldorp's chance had come to put Civil & Civic on the map by building Sydney's first concrete skyscraper. He was determined, however, to become the sole entrepreneur, thus ensuring complete control over the project. He wanted to take over the option, the council-approved plans, and the services of the architect and engineer. All that Dusseldorp now lacked was the money.

He approached Bredero's in Holland for a £100,000 loan which he was refused, but the president of the Reconstruction Bank of Holland was present at Dusseldorp's presentation. He was impressed with Dusseldorp's style, determination, and confidence, and backed the loan.

When building work began Dusseldorp was faced with yet another problem besetting the construction industry—industrial action by the workers' unions. He therefore proposed to the unions an agreement which among other things would include a productivity bonus. Although viewed at first with skepticism, it proved a great success as building workers began to feel like valued employees.

Caltex House was finished months ahead of the original schedule and established Civil & Civic as a leading contractor. Now the company could sell itself as a new composite building service which operated in conjunction with leading architects and engineers. Such a service was designed to eliminate delays and reduce costs.

Creation of Lend Lease in Late 1950s

Yet Dusseldorp was not satisfied. He was still searching for a better package to present to prospective buyers or leasers. During the building boom of the early 1960s there was a great need for new construction of all kinds. Many companies, as a result of their own success, were being forced to build larger premises. The buying of larger premises inevitably meant tying up capital that was needed for business operations. Dusseldorp concluded that what most businesses were looking for were premises which they could lease.

He also saw a need for cooperative projects which would bring together people with a common interest, such as doctors who needed professional consulting rooms. Such professionals would not be able to finance such projects independently. Dusseldorp had the solution.

He decided to float a finance and investment company and go to the Australian public for funds to finance Civil & Civic projects on completion, thus gaining entrepreneurial control over their projects. In April 1958, Lend Lease Corporation Limited was established and floated on the stock exchange with Civil & Civic holding 40 percent of the shares.

This original share issue was floated to finance the construction of a seven-story building containing professional consulting rooms. The deal was that North Shore Medical Centre Pty, Ltd., which owned the land, had the right to occupy or nominate the occupant of specified areas in the building. Lend Lease was to take up the whole of the issued capital of the company on completion of the building and would then sell the professional suites on term contracts over varying periods, while retaining part of the space in the building as an investment—in other words, lending and leasing.

It was not long before Lend Lease began to acquire its own sites, plan the development, and construct buildings in cooperation with Civil & Civic. They were set to provide and complete development of large-scale projects of real estate.

Both Civil & Civic and Lend Lease were out to gain prestige and publicity. They began to tender for projects that would put them in the public eye. Buildings such as the Academy of Science in Canberra would win them the Sulman prize for architecture. It was not until February 1959, however, that Lend Lease became a household name. It was at that time that the company contracted to build stage one of the Sydney Opera House.

Civil & Civic and Lend Lease were not ordinary construction outfits. The management of both organizations had an interest in urban planning and renewal. Plans for new building sites would always include open areas with fountains and plazas so that beauty as well as commerce might be enjoyed.

As the organization grew, it also had to change. Between 1959 and 1962 Lend Lease acquired its original sponsor, Civil & Civic, as well as six companies whose manufactured products were useful to their construction business. These companies supplied Lend Lease with elevators, windows, and building materials. The company also bought a ski resort and a motel chain. It was set to change from the role of financier of other people's projects to that of developing and managing real capital assets for long-term property investors.

In June 1960 a subsidiary company was formed to take control of Lend Lease's joint operations with Civil & Civic. The parent company formulated policy and provided specialist advisory skills. It also developed new projects and raised the money to carry these projects out. The subsidiary, Lend Lease Development Pty. Ltd., selected and purchased the sites, dealt with the authorities, and managed the design and construction of the site, as well as the sale or lease of projects.

Lend Lease was now involved in a multitude of projects from commercial buildings to suburban housing to recreational sites. The group was expanded to include 14 operating companies. Their presence was virtually ubiquitous in Australia, especially in the cities of Sydney, Canberra, Melbourne, Launceston, Brisbane, and Perth.

In May 1968 one of Lend Lease's largest projects, Australia Square, was officially opened by the Duke of Edinburgh. It won the Sulman Award for Architectural Merit, and the Civic Design Award of the New South Wales chapter of the Royal Australian Institute of Architects for a work of outstanding design.

By 1971 property values in Australia were peaking. Dusseldorp could see that the bottom was soon going to drop out of office development market and it was decided that Lend Lease would end its work in this field. It would instead turn its attention towards shopping centers. The shift in activities was not unusual for this corporation. The key to its success was its ability to keep its finger always on the pulse of change.

Lend Lease continued to retain a long-term interest in properties developed without long-term capital investment, and to be free of fluctuations in the property market through public subscription and independent property trusts. Lend Lease was the first developer to go public and to form in 1971 General Property Trust, a publicly owned real estate trust to hold its properties.

International Growth in 1970s

On June 30, 1971, G.J. Dusseldorp's contract with Bredero's, which made him available as principal executive of the group, expired. Dusseldorp agreed to be retained until June 30, 1975, with a renewable clause thereafter. The new agreement allowed Dusseldorp to have interests outside Australia. Dusseldorp wanted to try his style of business in the United States. Through its subsidiary, U.S. Lend Lease, established in 1972, formed International Income Property (IIP).

Despite the multitude of activities in which Dusseldorp and his team were involved, he was nonetheless paving the way towards his own retirement by grooming his executives for future management. His contributions to the success of Lend Lease were considerable. Although he surrounded himself with a team of some of the best people in the business, there is no doubt that the inspiration for the projects, as well as the new ways of handling development and finance, all sprang from the mind of Dusseldorp. His aversion to borrowing kept the firm's debts below 50 percent of its total capital, a low figure compared to those of rival developers. Year after year, despite an adverse financial climate and lows in the property market, Lend Lease was to produce profits for its shareholders. The firm did not retain its own publicity department, but worked quietly and expertly at all its projects, so much so that it prompted the *Financial Times* to comment, "Unlike many prominent Australian companies, it [Lend Lease] attracts little publicity and even less adverse comment from analysts."

In 1971 Bredero's sold its shareholding in Lend Lease, and J. DeVries, a founding director of Lend Lease, retired from the board. W.M. Leavey, managing director of Lend Lease, replaced him. S.G. Hornery became managing director of Civil & Civic, with R.G. Robinson as chairman.

In 1978 Dusseldorp commented in the annual report, "In the conditions which have prevailed, to have obtained one million

dollars worth of business every working day represented an extraordinary effort by everyone in the group." It was also the year in which employees became the largest shareholding block, holding 26 percent of the shares.

Lend Lease's success—during one of the greatest slumps in the property market—lay in its concentration on earnings and cash flow rather than ownership of assets. It acted as a service corporation. It also stuck to a policy of refusing to undertake construction unless an end-buyer was in place.

New Chairman Leads Group Into the 1990s

In 1988 Dusseldorp retired as chairman and was succeeded by S.G. Hornery. Dusseldorp left a corporation in which 30 percent of all projects were planned, designed, built, fitted, financed, managed, and refurbished for their economic life. It was a company with novel staff ownership schemes, well-tended links with investors, and numerous corporate sponsorships. Dusseldorp cultivated good relations with employees, shareholders, and local communities alike.

Hornery also made a mark on the firm bringing in insurance and related financial services to the group by acquiring MLC. Lend Lease was able to provide, through MLC, savings, mortgage investment, and superannuation as well as life and general insurance products which would cover its clients from cradle to grave. The financial services division proved a shrewd diversification for the early 1990s, contributing nearly half of Lend Lease's after-tax profit by 1991. The conglomerate's 1993 acquisition of a minority stake in Australia's oldest bank, Westpac Banking Corp. was interpreted by some analysts as a step toward its goal of becoming that country's largest financial services company. Lend Lease would, however, begin phasing out their stake in Westpac by 1996.

During the 1990s, Hornery's objective for the group of companies will be steady and continuous growth through extending MLC's offshore investments and developing global property investment capability. The company's property investment funds focused on emerging markets, especially in Asia. By 1995, it had funds targeting Thailand, Indonesia, and other Asian nations. International expansion of Lend Lease's construction interests continued as well. The corporation acquired U.S.-based Yarmouth Group, Inc., in 1993 and purchased a minority stake in Hoyts Theaters cinema chain with locations in the United States, Australia, and New Zealand, in 1994. In addition to his company's new business interests, Chairman Hornery also remained committed to continuing the company policy of enhancing the urban environment and playing a leading role in changing Australia's cities for the better.

While Lend Lease's sales declined from A$1.7 billion in fiscal 1990 to A$1.5 billion in 1995, the company continued to add to its 20-year record of increasing after-tax profit, which grew from A$160.5 million to A$260 million during the first five years of the decade. The company reported revenues of A$2.05 billion in 1996 as well as another increase in profits despite a declining Australian property market. As it approached the 21st century, Lend Lease was intent on succeeding in an increasingly competitive industry and on becoming a truly global concern.

Principal Subsidiaries

Civil & Civic Pty. Ltd.; Lend Lease Property Management Pty. Ltd.; Lend Lease Corporate Services Ltd.; Lend Lease Development Pty. Ltd.; Lend Lease Interiors Pty. Ltd.; Lend Lease Property Funds Management Ltd.; Lend Lease Property Investment Services Ltd.; Lend Lease Residential Pty. Ltd.; Lend Lease Management (NSW) Pty. Ltd.; The Lend Lease Design Group Ltd.; Civil & Civic (NZ) Ltd. (New Zealand); Lend Lease Asia Holdings Pte. Ltd. (Singapore); Lend Lease Asia Pty. Ltd.; Lend Lease International Holdings Ltd. (United Kingdom); Lend Lease Corporation Ltd.; Lend Lease (New Zealand) Ltd. (New Zealand); Lend Lease Advisor Services Ltd.; MLC Client Services Ltd.; MLC Investments Ltd.; Lend Lease Corporate Services Ltd.; Lend Lease Corporate Services Asia Pte. Ltd. (Singapore); Lend Lease Custodian Pty. Ltd.; Lend Lease Finance International Ltd.; Lend Lease Capital Services Asia Pte. Ltd. (Singapore); Lend Lease Capital Services Ltd.; Lend Lease Project Finance Pty. Ltd.; Lend Lease Securities & Investments Pty. Ltd.; Lend Lease Asia Water Pty. Ltd.; Lend Lease Finance Ltd.; Lend Lease Learning Pty. Ltd.; MLC Computer Pty. Ltd.; Serenia Pty. Ltd.; Staff Shares Pty. Ltd.; The MLC Ltd.; City Centre Development Ltd.; Lend Lease Estates Pty. Ltd.; Limosa Pty. Ltd.; Limosa Unit Trust.

Further Reading

Harris, Mike, "Oz's Hoyts Breaking Chains: Firm Selling Cinema Franchises to Frisco Bank, Aussie Investor," *Variety,* September 12, 1994, p. 29.

"Lend Lease's Morschel Resigns as Top Officer, *Wall Street Journal,* March 8, 1995, p. 4B.

Murdoch, Blake, "Hoyts Confirms Theaters Sale," *Hollywood-Reporter,* September 13, 1994.

Murphy, Mary, *Challenges of Change: The Lend Lease Story,* Sydney: The Pot Still Press, 1984.

Rudnitsky, Howard, "A Hand from the Grave," *Forbes,* May 11, 1981, pp. 83–84.

Witcher, S. Karene., "Australian Sells Westpac Stake to Lend Lease, *Wall Street Journal,* May 12, 1993, p. B3B.

—Anastasia N. Hackett
—updated by April Dougal Gasbarre

Life Technologies, Inc.

8717 Grovemont Circle
Gaithersburg, Maryland 20877
U.S.A.
(301) 840-8000
Fax: (301) 670-1394

Public Company
Incorporated: 1983
Employees: 1,380
Sales: $272 million (1995)
Stock Exchanges: NASDAQ
SICs: 2835 Diagnostic Substances; 2836 Biological
    Products, Except Diagnostic Substances; 8731
    Commercial Physical Research

Life Technologies, Inc. develops, manufactures, and markets products chiefly used in life science research and biomedical manufacturing, using genetically engineered cells. In 1995 its more than 3,000 products were being sold to more than 20,000 customers, including hospitals, research and clinical laboratories, and pharmaceutical and biotechnology companies. One of its biggest clients was the National Institutes of Health, which maintained dozens of laboratories on its campus in nearby Bethesda, Maryland. Life Technologies was 53.8 percent owned in 1995 by Dexter Corp., a manufacturer of specialty materials for the aerospace, automobile, food packaging, and medical industries.

Founded in 1983 Merger

Life Technologies was founded in 1983 by the merger of Bethesda Research Laboratories, Inc. and GIBCO Corp., a subsidiary of Dexter Corp. GIBCO was an amalgam of some 40 businesses acquired over a 15-year period by North American Mogul Products Co., a firm incorporated in 1915 that changed its name to Mogul Corp. in 1968 and was acquired by Dexter in 1977. GIBCO had sales of $77.3 million and net income of $4.5 million in 1982.

Bethesda Research, by contrast, was a struggling private company that, according to its chairman, Frederick Adler, was within a week to ten days from filing for bankruptcy in 1982. Adler, described in a *Barron's* news story as a "flamboyant venture capitalist and turnaround artist," laid off about half of the company's 500 employees and lopped off marginal research and unprofitable product lines. According to Adler, Bethesda Research was on the verge of launching an initial public offering of its own when it merged with GIBCO. It became profitable during the last quarter of 1983.

Dexter took a 64 percent stake in newly formed Life Technologies. The first chairman was Adler and the first president was M. James Barrett, a microbiologist who Adler had lured to Bethesda Research from SmithKline. The firm originally had headquarters at GIBCO's old offices in Chagrin Falls, Ohio. Net sales came to $91.4 million and net income to $3.7 million in 1983.

In 1985 Life Technologies was producing and selling more than 3,000 products used in scientific and medical research, human health diagnostics and treatment, biotechnology, and industrial applications. Among its units, the Invenex Laboratories division, located in Orlando Florida, was specializing in the production and sale of small-volume parenteral solutions such as nutritional supplements, electrolytes, antihistamines, antibiotics, diluents, anticholinergics, and generic diuretics. This division was sold to LyphoMed Inc. in 1985 for $39.5 million in cash and notes.

In 1986, the year it went public with an offering of about seven percent of its outstanding common stock, Life Technologies believed itself to be the leading supplier of sera and other cell-growth media. It was also a leading supplier of enzymes and other biological products necessary for recombinant-DNA procedures. In December of that year the company completed the sale of its Sensititre product line to Radiometer A/S, a Danish instrumentation company. By then the company had moved its headquarters to Gaithersburg, Maryland. In 1987 the company signed a technology transfer and licensing agreement with Toray Industries of Tokyo. This agreement conferred on Toray exclusive marketing rights in Japan, Korea, and Taiwan for products based on Life Technologies' nonisotopic DNA technology for detecting hepatitis B and human papillomavirus (HPV), with the company receiving a sum of $2 million over three years.

Life Technologies had net sales of $75 million in 1984, $84.4 million in 1985, $98.3 million in 1986, and $121 million in 1987. Its net income, $4.2 million in 1984, advanced to $17.1 million in 1985, fell to $3.7 million in 1986, and rose to $11.1 million in 1987. The company announced plans in November 1987 for a $4.8 million expansion and upgrade of its cell biology operations in Grand Island, New York, to increase its production of cell biology products. Revenues increased to $130 million in 1988, and profits rose to $12 million.

Successes and Setbacks

Life Technologies beat out two other firms to win, in January 1989, approval from the U.S. Food and Drug Administration to market a test for HPV, a sexually transmitted infection linked to cervical cancer. The test was designed to be used in conbination with the Pap smear that most doctors recommended annually for female patients. This Life Technologies product was seen as providing the company with between $4 million and $5 million in revenue in 1989, and a company officer suggested this sum could reach $50 million per year within five years.

During 1989 Life Technologies introduced more than 100 products and was granted 15 patents. In July it purchased products and technology for separating different elements of blood serum from New Zealand's Waitaki International Biosciences Co. for $3 million. Life Technologies' revenues came to $134 million in 1989 ($4 million more than during the previous year), and net income rose to $13.2 million.

Life Technologies was the only profitable biotechnology company in the Washington, DC area during 1990. That year it opened a 51,000-square-foot manufacturing plant in Frederick, Maryland and a 7,500-square-foot training center in Beltsville, Maryland to offer classes to its customers on how to use the most recent research techniques and the company's newest supplies. The company decided to drop its HPV test, however, and seek a buyer for the molecular diagnostics division, which was responsible for the test's development. The company's vice-president for finance told a *Washington Post* reporter it had been decided "that the business wouldn't develop as quickly as we had hoped." A research analyst estimated that the molecular diagnostics division was losing $4 million per year. It was sold in December 1990 for $3.6 million.

Life Technologies had record revenues of $151.6 million per year in 1990 and record net income of $15.4 million. Despite an economic slowdown in the United States during the year, the company benefited from a weak dollar to make half its sales overseas. It also purchased Tekmunc A/S, a Danish distributor, for $1.5 million. In February 1991, after abandoning a two-year search for a suitable acquisition, the board of Life Technologies declared the company's first dividend, a special payment of $3.50 per share that was followed thereafter by an annual one of 20 cents per share (raised to 24 cents in 1996). With a total payout of $50 million to $52 million, or about a third of

company assets, the special dividend left Life Technologies with about $5 million in cash and no debt.

During 1991 Life Technologies earned $170.9 million but, for the first time since 1986, its net income fell, to $12.1 million. It attributed this setback to the cost of making fetal bovine serum, which was used to grow cell cultures in biology research and was its most important product. The company took a charge of $1.2 million from the elimination of 40 jobs, which was equal to about five percent of its U.S. work force. It increased investment in research and development, however, to nearly $13 million and was operating in 17 countries during the year.

During 1992 Life Technologies raised its sales to $197.6 million and its profit to $15.5 million. Its production of fetal bovine serum continued to account for about 20 percent of sales. The company invested $13.9 million in research and development during the year and introduced more than 400 new cell culture and molecular biology products. Its total number of products remained about 2,000. Life Technologies acquired certain assets of Telios Pharmaceuticals, Inc. for $1.3 million in October 1992.

Life Technologies had net income of $16.6 million on revenues of $205.6 million in 1993, both records in spite of a slowdown in sales to pharmaceutical and other health care companies during the second half of the year. The company blamed uncertainties about health care reform and the possibility of price controls on drugs for the sales slowdown and also cited adverse currency exchange rates on foreign sales. During the year Adler, no longer board chairman but still a director and investor, was named to the annual list of the Top 100 "Molecular Millionaires" published by *Genetic Engineering News*. This widely read publication in the biotechnology industry valued Adler's stock holdings in Life Technologies at $13.3 million.

Expansion in the 1990s

The revenues of Life Technologies rose to $235.3 million in 1994, and its net income increased to $18.2 million. These figures increased to $272.3 million and $22.3 million, respectively, in 1995, both records. During 1995 Life Technologies took full control of a joint venture laboratory it maintained with Protogene Laboratories Inc. for the manufacture of custom-made DNA. Previously, Protogene had owned 75 percent of the venture. Life Technologies also established wholly owned subsidiaries in Italy and Spain during 1995 and bought a majority stake in a joint venture that it had operated in Japan with Tokyo-based Oriental Yeast Co. In February 1996 it purchased Custom Primers, a manufacturer of custom oligonucleotides sold to researchers in gene sequencing and other clinical studies.

In 1996 Life Technologies was building a new $40 million red brick headquarters complex in Gaithersburg to house its administrative offices, training center, and much of its research and development facilities. Plans called for the complex to be completed around the end of 1997. The company had been leasing space in five spread-out buildings in a Gaithersburg office park a few miles from Interstate 270, Maryland's "technology corridor." Life Technologies was also planning to spend $60 million over five years to upgrade and expand its facilities around the world, including major research manufacturing centers in Scotland and New Zealand as well as Grand Island, New York.

Among Life Technologies' customers in 1996 was the nation's second largest biotech company, Genentech Inc., which was using its medium to grow the genetically altered cells composing the protein used in TPA, a drug that breaks up blood clots. Japan, Europe, and Southeast Asia were areas of major overseas business. "Boringly successful," as the company's chief financial officer called it, Life Technologies ranked third among 26 public biotechnology companies surveyed for profitability, with an average five-year return on equity of 14.9 percent during the first half of the 1990s.

In November 1995 Adler held 410,934 shares of the 15.2 million shares of Life Technologies common stock. All officers and directors of the companies held a combined 834,983 shares. The company's long-term debt was only $1.4 million in March 1996. J. Stark Thompson had been the company's president and chief executive officer since 1988.

In addition to its 30,000-square-foot leased Gaithersburg quarters, Life Technologies owned or leased, in 1995, properties in Grand Island, New York; Frederick, Maryland; Burlington, Ontario; Paisley, Scotland; Auckland, Christchurch, and Nelson, New Zealand; Roskilde, Denmark; Eggenstein, Germany; Ghent, Belgium; Cergy Pontoise, France; Basel, Switzerland; and the New Territories of Hong Kong. The Frederick, Grand Island, Auckland, and Paisley properties were in excess of 25,000 square feet. Production facilities were operating at about 85 percent of capacity during the year.

Cell culture products were being marketed under the GIBCO name and molecular biology products were marketed under the Bethesda Research Laboratories name in 1995. The former accounted for 58 percent of Life Technologies' 1995 sales and the latter for the remaining 42 percent. Fetal bovine serum comprised 16 percent of sales. Most of Life Technologies' products were being sold by its own sales force, but agents and distributors were also used. North America accounted for 56 percent of net sales in 1995, Europe for 36 percent, and the Pacific area for the remaining eight percent.

Principal Subsidiaries

Canadian Life Technologies, Inc. (Canada); Laboratory Services Ltd. (New Zealand); Life Technologies A.S. (Denmark); Life Technologies Asia Pacific Inc.; Life Technologies Foreign Sales Corp. (U.S. Virgin Islands); Life Technologies GIBCO BRL Co., Ltd. (Taiwan; 51%); Life Technologies Holdings Unlimited (Scotland); Life Technologies Investment Holdings, Inc.; Life Technologies Italia S.r.l. (Italy); Life Technologies Ltd. (New Zealand); Life Technologies Oriental K.K. (Japan; 51%); Life Technologies (Pacific) Ltd. (Hong Kong); Life Technologies Pty. Ltd. (Australia); Life Technologies S.A. (Spain); Life Technologies Sweden AB (Sweden); Serum Technologies Holdings, Inc.

Further Reading

Day, Kathleen, "Building a Future in Biotech," *Washington Post,* June 3, 1996, Bus. Sec., pp. 25–26.

Gibson, W. David, "216 Years Old and Sexy," *Barron's,* June 13, 1983, pp. 14, 18–19, 22.

Gladwell, Malcolm, "Life Technologies Faces Hurdles in Marketing Diagnostic Test," *Washington Post,* January 9, 1989, Bus. Sec., p. 6.

"Life Technologies Sells Invenex Laboratories," *Wall Street Journal,* June 19, 1985, p. 21B.

Potts, Mark, "Life Technologies To Start Division for Medical Tests," *Washington Post,* June 4, 1990, Bus. Sec., pp. 5–6.

Webb, Margaret K., "Life Technologies Expands Amid Biotechnology Slump," *Washington Post,* October 29, 1990, Bus. Sec., p. 5.

—Robert Halasz

Luby's Cafeteria's, Inc.

2211 Northeast Loop 410
P.O. Box 33069
San Antonio, Texas 78265-3069
U.S.A.
(210) 654-9000
Fax: (210) 599-8407

Public Company
Incorporated: 1959
Employees: 11,000
Sales: $419 million (1995)
Stock Exchanges: New York
SICs: 5812 Eating Places

Luby's Cafeterias, Inc. is the largest chain of cafeterias in America. From one small cafeteria in 1947 located in downtown San Antonio, Luby's has steadily expanded, first in Texas and then in other southern states, to become the most profitable cafeteria chain in the United States with over 200 cafeterias. In 1996, the company operated 147 units in Texas; 12 in Arizona; ten in Tennessee; nine in Oklahoma; five in Florida; four each in Arkansas, Kansas, and New Mexico; three in Missouri; two in Louisiana; and one in Mississippi. Unlike many restaurant chains, Luby's does not franchise its units, but it does compensate each unit manager with a generous portion of the profits from the unit the manager runs.

With its motto of "Good food from good people," the Luby's cafeterias offer freshly-prepared, family-style food at reasonable prices served in attractive settings. The cafeterias cater primarily to shoppers and to store and office personnel at lunchtime, and to families for the dinner meal. The cafeterias do not serve breakfast. The individual units are generally 10,000 to 11,000 square feet in area, can typically accommodate up to 300 people and are located in shopping and business developments as well as in residential areas. Luby's cafeterias are part of the social fabric and a tradition in many parts of the southern United States, "In San Antonio, they say you have to beat the Baptists out of church on Sunday to get a seat at Luby's," *Forbes*

magazine writer William P. Barrett observed in an article in the November 12, 1990 issue.

Coupled with this down-home style is a stellar financial record. Luby's leads its publicly-held competitors in growth benchmarks in sales, earnings, earnings-per-share, return on average equity and average sales-per-unit. Since 1965, Luby's has paid consecutive quarterly dividends and has increased the dividend every year. With the exception of a brief time in the late 1970s, the company has shown no long-term debt on its balance sheet. Luby's growth has been financed from internal cash flow, periodic stock offerings and, on occasion, from short-term lines of credit from banks. *Forbes* magazine wrote that Luby's executives and individual unit managers "do try to stick to what they know, and so far have done that brilliantly." Comparing Luby's to its cafeteria-field competitors such as Morrison's, Furr's/Bishop's and Piccadilly, *Forbes* noted that "none cuts a better hog" in terms of return on equity.

Luby's Origins

Luby's roots run through America's political, social, and economic history, beginning with the first unit and extending through every successive decade of the 20th century. Although Luby's was incorporated in 1959, the company's history was planted in 1909 when clothes merchant Harry Luby made a business trip from his home in Springfield, Missouri, to Chicago, Illinois. Luby was captivated by a new type of restaurant where patrons picked the food items they wanted from a counter and carried their own trays to dining tables.

Luby immediately saw that the Chicago restaurant was employing the then-emerging concepts of mass production and assembly lines in the restaurant business. Two years later, Luby opened a similar operation in Springfield, Missouri. From a 12-foot counter he built himself, Luby dished out freshly-prepared food at reasonable prices. One year later in 1912, Luby opened a second cafeteria in Springfield. From Missouri to Oklahoma to Texas, Luby opened one cafeteria after another over the next ten years. In stepping stone fashion, Luby would sell outright or retain a partial interest in a unit before moving southward to establish his next eatery. In 1927, the 39-year-old

Company Perspectives:

Recipe for Success. Take liberal quantities of: Luby's Fresh Foods and Variety. *Add large portions of:* Luby's Organization and Entrepreneurship. *Fold in:* Luby's Ability to Choose and Train Good People. *Season with:* Luby's Convenience and Service. *Top with:* Luby's Dedication to Public Service

Harry Luby had made enough money to retire in San Antonio where he oversaw his investments in seven cafeterias in Texas and one in Kansas.

Amiable and generous, Harry Luby had operated his restaurants on some very simple concepts: good food at reasonable prices for the customers and a generous portion of profits for the managers. "Share the work, share the risks, share the profits" was a guiding principle for Luby. Thus, as an investor in eight cafeterias, Luby gave 40 percent of profits to the unit managers, an unusually large percentage at the time as well as in the years that followed.

A New Generation of Leadership

Harry's son Robert M. Luby grew up in the restaurant business, playing after school in cafeteria basements as a young child and working in cafeterias cleaning grease traps as a teenager. After graduating from college, Bob Luby and his cousin Earl Luby set their entrepreneurial sights on San Francisco where they opened a cafeteria which failed to produce the Texas-sized profits his father's restaurants generated. Bob returned to Texas undeterred in his goal to establish and run a successful cafeteria. That goal was reached with a cafeteria in Dallas on Live Oak Street. Luby next enlisted his aunt, uncle, and brother-in-law George H. Wenglein to invest in, establish, and operate a cafeteria in El Paso, Texas.

While Bob Luby's cafeterias prospered during the 1930s, business was bleak for others. Homeless, hungry people often visited Luby's for sustenance. During the Depression, the cafeterias associated with Harry and Bob Luby served needy people from the food left over at closing time.

World War II and its wake profoundly altered America, sparking social changes and robust economic growth. Forced to sell his Dallas cafeteria when he enlisted in the Army Air Corps, Luby's thoughts returned to the cafeteria business even while serving as an intelligence officer. The contacts he made while serving his country constituted the foundation of a management team for the cafeteria chain to come.

Postwar Expansion

In 1946, Bob Luby hung up his military uniform and began plans with his cousin, Charles R. Johnston, to establish a cafeteria for the postwar era. In the decade following the war, household incomes would rise, families would move from cities to suburbs, and lifestyles calling for convenient products and services would reshape the fabric of American life. Amid such awesome change, Americans also would seek the threads of the past.

In 1947, Luby and Johnston recognized the promise of these postwar stirrings and opened a cafeteria with capacity to seat 180 people. Located in downtown San Antonio, the restaurant was an immediate success thanks to returning servicemen in the area and to the post-war housing shortage which had forced many people to live in downtown hotels. Nearby movie theaters provided brisk business in the evening. The cafeteria was managed by Norwood W. Jones, a fellow officer of Luby's while stationed at Santa Ana Army Air Base.

Luby and Johnston's next restaurant was located in the growing and affluent San Antonio suburb of Alamo Heights. Brother-in-law Wenglein was persuaded to co-manage the cafeteria with John Lee, a prewar Luby's associate. The Alamo Heights cafeteria served as a model for future Luby's units.

From the front seat of a sporty Studebaker serving as their office, the two entrepreneurs traveled the Lone Star State in search of new locations. Luby and Johnston were careful to open new cafeterias only when they had managers to operate the units according to the standards Harry Luby had pioneered.

By 1958, Luby and Johnston had opened 11 cafeterias, each of which had a different configuration of investors. In order to build and operate new Luby's cafeterias, the investors formed a new corporation—Cafeterias, Inc.—on February 4, 1959. The pre-existing cafeterias were not affected by the new structure because those units provided the cash to help the investors finance the new corporation.

The new corporation launched its first cafeteria in March 1960 in a strip shopping center in Corpus Christi and two others followed within 60 days. Although in the black, the three units were not generating the profits normally associated with Luby's cafeterias. Downtown locations proved to be a problem while an experiment to serve breakfast was a mild failure.

Luby's hit pay dirt with its fourth cafeteria located in a far north San Antonio suburb in a retail development called North Star Mall. Bob Luby recalled, "Some people thought we had lost our minds because it was so far out that the city buses didn't serve the mall adequately. We actually had to subsidize the bus service in order to get our employees to work." But the fast-growing affluent suburbs surrounding the mall would fill the fourth corporate Luby's restaurant with patrons and provide profits to build more cafeterias.

With Bob Luby as president and Charles Johnston as executive vice-president, Luby's entered the Houston market in 1965 with an upscale cafeteria which offered an expanded menu and more expensive food items. Operating under the Romano name, the cafeteria quickly became a huge money-maker. The modern structure with its rich decor served as a model for revamping efforts at existing Luby's and proved a market existed for cafeterias with a very modern style and design.

Luby's growth in the Houston market was propelled, in part, by the nation's space program, initiated in the early 1960s, with its mission control headquarters in the area. In subsequent years, the oil industry and its attendant financiers in the banking and financial services industries would fuel the economy further.

Consolidating Operations and Going Public in the 1970s

The corporation forged a link with the original Luby's cafeterias in 1969 when it agreed to manage those units for the next 15 years, bringing the number of corporate-managed units to 26, of which 17 were company-owned. Luby and Johnston passed their executive management reins to George Wenglein and to Norwood Jones, respectively, in 1971. Luby, who remained chairman of the board, recalled the reason for stepping aside at age 61: "I had run the company with Charles since the beginning. . . . Before we started selling stock to the public, I wanted to be darn sure the company could operate without me as president. So Charles and I stepped down earlier than we had to."

In January 1972, the company's stock was offered to the public in the over-the-counter market. The company continued to expand into new markets such as Dallas and to strengthen its internal operations creating the new corporate position of area manager to oversee existing units and to launch new ones in a specific market.

The Yom Kippur War in October 1973 ushered in an era in which the Texas economy would be inexorably tied to Middle Eastern oil and the volatile political situation in that part of the world. The war created gasoline shortages in the United States but no shortages of customers at Luby's which offered a reasonably-priced, convenient suburban alternative to consumers whose pocketbooks were pinched by higher gas prices and whose auto travel was circumscribed by scarce fuel.

High oil prices soon began to work to Luby's advantage as energy exploration and development in Texas, Oklahoma, and Louisiana injected billions of dollars into the region's economy. With more cafeterias opening to meet the demand, Luby's created a formal training program to ensure that each new cafeteria would have adequate managerial staffers who were service-oriented to their customers, sensitive to their employees, and cost-conscious to the bottom line.

Establishing a School of Management

The Luby's Story, a history of the company published in 1988, explained that trainees were schooled in the theory and practice of running a cafeteria. The boot-camp style training taught the recruits "the intricacies of butchering a side of beef, baking a lemon meringue pie, and mopping the floor," as well as how to clean the restaurant equipment and replenish the cafeteria serving line.

Trainees also learned to show respect to all Luby's employees. "In the kitchen, the young recruit is taught to show deference to his instructors—the fry cook, the baker, the butcher, and the salad maker. Clearly the young college graduate is the disciple and the veteran cook his master," the corporate history stated.

The deference and respect has resulted in a stable workforce at the individual Luby's cafeterias. Luby's has recorded one of the lowest turnovers of support staff in the restaurant industry. That low turnover has translated into experienced and consistent service for the customers and minimal training costs for the individual units. After graduation, the prospective managers

spend seven to ten years of additional training in individual cafeterias moving from assistant manager to associate manager to manager, and from manager of a small unit to manager of larger and larger units.

Luby's cafeteria managers are given a high degree of autonomy. This has enabled them to cater to customer tastes in their local markets with specialized menu offerings. The majority of the food ingredients have been purchased locally by the individual cafeteria management team. This permitted managers to take advantage of price bargains in the local wholesale markets and to quickly respond to local product shortages.

A few items such as fried haddock are carried by every cafeteria in the Luby's network. Ingredients for these signature items have been centrally sourced by the company. The management team of the individual cafeterias received their compensation based on the financial performance of each cafeteria. The management team consisted of a Manager, an Associate Manager and two to three Assistant Managers. Each team received 40 percent of the unit's operating profits. After the salaries of the assistant managers are deducted, the remainder in profits was divided in a 65/35 percent split between the manager and associate manager, respectively.

The opportunity for autonomy and for attractive financial compensation has given Luby's managers a strong incentive to operate profitably for the long-term. Approximately 85 percent of the company's unit managers have been with Luby's for ten years or more.

Growth in the 1980s

The year 1980 saw corporate revenues surpass the $100 million mark, and the company adopted a new name, Luby's Cafeterias, Inc. On February 22, 1982, Luby's entered the financial big league when its stock began trading on the New York Stock Exchange under the LUB symbol and since May 16, 1985, Luby's stock has been included in the Standard and Poor's 500 Composite Stock Price Index.

The 1980s represented a period of expansion outside Texas which was suffering from slumping oil prices. Luby's Texas cafeterias weathered the economic downturn by avoiding waste and cutting labor costs. While others in the restaurant industry expended millions of dollars on advertising and borrowed heavily, Luby's relied on word-of-mouth recommendations to build its customer base and internally-generated profits to build new cafeterias.

In a much publicized incident, random and bizarre violence hit a Luby's restaurant in Killeen, Texas, on October 16, 1991. A lone gunman entered the restaurant filled with patrons and employees, shot and killed 23 people, wounded 25 more, and then turned the gun upon himself. When the killing ended, Luby's had acquired the unwanted distinction of being the site of the worst mass shooting in the history of America. The killer took his motive for the murders with him to the grave.

When word of the massacre reached company headquarters in San Antonio, Luby's chairman and several senior executives immediately flew to Killeen to provide aid and comfort to the victims' families, the survivors, and to the community. In fact,

Luby's management was praised for its sensible and sensitive handling of the crisis surrounding the shooting. When the Killeen Luby's reopened on March 12, 1992, hundreds of people, including some of the survivors, came to the cafeteria to eat freshly-prepared jalapeno corn bread, pan-grilled catfish, and Jefferson Davis pie.

The 1990s and Beyond

The 1990s brought a more vibrant economy to the markets Luby's served and some new directions in its operations. In 1991, the company began developing a new marketing program using television and radio advertising in order to build repeat business and to position itself for youthful customers. "Luby's TV ads cut the mustard, go heavy on the wry" was the double entendre headline over an article appearing in the December 5, 1994 issue of *Nation's Restaurant News*. The article noted Luby's ads used humor to convey the message that its restaurants catered to patrons of every age. Unlike the ads for other chains, Luby's did not merely feature glittery shots of the food and the cafeteria.

During fiscal year ended August 31, 1994, Luby's conducted its first cooperative promotion, joining forces with Southwest Airlines, Sea World of Texas and Karena Hotels of Texas to target families with children. Favorable results from the advertising and promotional campaigns led Luby's to earmark two percent of sales for marketing efforts in fiscal 1996.

At its January 1996 annual meeting, Luby's unveiled joint venture plans with Waterstreet Inc. for five to seven seafood restaurants over the next five years. Waterstreet's five restaurant in three cities serve moderately priced, Gulf-of-Mexico-style seafood.

With a possible hint of a major new direction for the company as it moves toward the twenty-first century, Luby's Chairman Ralph "Pete" Erben told shareholders, "We will actively explore other potential concepts for diversification and enhancement of shareholder values." He said the company expected the joint venture to furnish Luby's with "restaurant concepts that provide growth and profitability into the future."

Luby's successful strategy has been recognized by the press. "Why They're Lining Up at Luby's" was the headline for an article by *The New York Times* in the August 18, 1985 issue describing the company's recipe for success. *Kiplinger's Personal Finance Magazine* included Luby's in its list of "39 Stocks for Your Portfolio" which appeared in the August 1994 issue. An October 19, 1990 article in *The Wall Street Journal* examined how the company maintained its profitability during an economic recession. *Forbes* magazine named Luby's among

the top 200 Best Small Companies for eight of the ten years the publication has conducted the survey.

Restaurant management publications have also awarded Luby's with top honors. *Restaurant Business* profiled Luby's in a May 1989 article entitled "Slow and Steady Wins." In 1996, for the sixth time in seven annual surveys conducted nationally by *Restaurant & Institutions* magazine, consumers voted Luby's as their favorite in the cafeteria/buffet category.

With firm roots in the local communities it served, Luby's cafeterias have been closely involved in local community events and philanthropic endeavors. When Hurricane Carla crashed into the Texas Gulf Coast in September 1961, the Corpus Christi Luby's served as an outpost for the National Guard and scores of emergency workers. Using gas-fired stoves, Luby's dispensed food and hot drink to police, guardsmen, and neighbors. "We didn't charge a thing, but we made a lot of friends," cafeteria manager Bill Lowe recalled. When the cafeteria reopened for normal business, Lowe remembered, "We were swamped with customers."

In addition to such ad hoc measures, unit managers have been given a budget to spend on public service in their areas. The company's largest civic program is the Community Drug Education System. Initiated in 1987, the program has received a Presidential Citation for educating students, parents and teachers in 11 states about the dangers of substance abuse. By the end of fiscal 1996, Luby's had spent over $1.3 million on the program.

Further Reading

Allen, Robin Lee, "Luby's Eyes Updated Image with Two New Campaigns," *Nation's Restaurant News,* June 6, 1994, p. 12.
Barnhill, Steve, *The Luby's Story,* San Antonio: The Watercress Press, 1988.
Barrett, William P., "The Best Little Hash House in Texas," *Forbes,* November 12, 1990, pp. 220–221.
Barrier, Michael, "First in Line at the Cafeteria," *Nation's Business,* February 1991, pp. 29–31.
Dorfman, John R., "Luby's Cafeterias' Steadiness Seems Suited to
Withstand a Forced Diet for the Economy," *Wall Street Journal,* October 19, 1991, p. C2.
Krajewski, Steve, "Luby's: Dining Humor," *Adweek,* August 22, 1994, p. 4.
McDowell, Bill, "The People's Choice," *Restaurants & Institutions,* February 1, 1996, pp. 43–65.
Reinhold, Robert, "Why They're Lining Up at Luby's," *The New York Times,* August 18, 1985, p. F11.
Ruggless, Ron, *Luby's TV Ads Cut the Mustard, Go Heavy on the Wry,*" *Nation's Restaurant News,* December 5, 1994, p. 12.

—Lynn W. Adkins

Luxottica SpA

Agordo
Belluno 32021
Via Valcozzena, 10
Italy
(39) 437 626 41
Fax: (39) 437 638 40
Internet: http:www.luxottica.it
http:www.lenscrafters.com

Public Company
Founded: 1958
Employees: 3,350
Sales: L812.7 billion (1995) (US$1.2 billion)
Stock Exchanges: New York
SICs: 3851 Ophthalmic Goods

The world's largest manufacturers and distributors of eyeglass frames, Luxottica SpA is the lifework of Italy's Leonardo Del Vecchio. Del Vecchio, who with his family continued to own over two-thirds of the company's equity in the mid-1990s, has been praised as "the quintessential entrepreneur." Luxottica's success had made this "King of Spectacles" Italy's highest paid citizen. Over the course of the company's history, he has transformed the firm into a vertically integrated enterprise that extends from drawing board to the craftsman's bench to the retail counter. The 1995 acquisition of the LensCrafters chain made Luxottica the world's largest retailer of optical goods. By the mid-1990s, it was churning out over 16 million pairs of glasses each year. All of Luxottica's frames are manufactured in Northern Italy, then sold through wholly-owned distributors in the United States, Canada, Italy, France, Spain, Portugal, Sweden, Germany, the United Kingdom, Brazil, Switzerland, and Mexico. The company also holds controlling interests in distributors in Belgium, Greece, the Netherlands, Finland, and Japan.

One overriding theme has distinguished Luxottica's history: eliminate the middleman. In the 1950s and 1960s, Del Vecchio honed his own skills, meticulously learning every facet of the ophthalmic frame manufacturing process. In the 1970s, he worked to automate the process with machinery of his own design, then linked every stage of production, from design to inventory, via computers. In the 1980s, Del Vecchio began acquiring Luxottica's formerly independent international distributors. The 1990s have seen what may be the culmination of Luxottica's drive for vertical integration, the acquisition of retail outlets. Each of these steps has resulted in increased efficiency, paving the company's route to profitable, rapid growth.

Post-World War II Creation and Development

Born in 1935 in Milan, Luxottica founder Leonardo Del Vecchio has been called "Italy's version of Horatio Alger." His father, a street merchant who hawked vegetables, died five months before Leonardo was born, leaving the family so destitute that the youngster spent seven years of his childhood in an orphanage. As a youth, Del Vecchio apprenticed as a designer in a tool and die factory specializing in small metal components. After studying drawing and engraving at the Brera Academy of Art, the young designer struck out on his own in 1958, manufacturing molded plastic eyeglass components in Milan. With financial backing from two key customers, he moved his 14-man shop in 1961 to Agordo, a picturesque mountain town in a region of Northern Italy known for its hand-crafted jewelry.

Although he had no formal training in economics, the young entrepreneur soon realized that he could retain more profits through vertical integration. Del Vecchio renamed the business Luxottica and set out to expand its capacity to include the full range of eyeglass components. Over the course of the decade, he added metalworking capabilities, plastic milling, and other processes to his company. In a 1991 interview, Del Vecchio told *Financial World's* Stephen Kindel that "by mastering all the technologies, we [became] very competitive on price, without having to compromise our quality." This process culminated in the 1969 launch of Luxottica's first complete set of optical frames.

Luxottica had a brush with oblivion in 1971, when the company's two outside investors called in their 190 million loans to Del Vecchio. But Del Vecchio's fortunes quickly reversed when

Company Perspectives:

Unlike most competitors, Luxottica's success to date has been based on total vertical integration, whereby the Company directly controls the design, production and distribution of its frames and sunglasses. Luxottica's success is based on four key factors: 1) Broad and diversified product line; 2) Efficient manufacturing facilities; 3) Strong worldwide factory direct distribution network; 4) Excellent customer service.

the entrepreneur brought in a new partner, Scarrone, then bought out this former competitor within the year.

Drive for Integrated Production Marks 1970s

Del Vecchio continued to systematically integrate his eyeglass business, focusing on technological advances throughout the 1970s. Noting that it was not materials, but retooling to accommodate fashion changes, that drove cost increases, Del Vecchio began to tackle that side of his business. Having taken courses in advanced machine design in 1969, he began to devise automated molding and milling equipment. He also adopted techniques from allied industries, borrowing specialized electroplating procedures from local jewelers, for example. Ample funding for research and development in plastics compounding, metallurgy, and basic chemistry ensured the quality of future products.

Perhaps most importantly, Del Vecchio guided Luxottica's implementation of computerization. By the end of the decade, the company had integrated all facets of its process, from design to manufacturing and inventory control. This early application of computer technology not only gave Luxottica a significant cost advantage over its competitors, but also helped make small production runs more efficient. This factor would become increasingly important as the influence of ever-changing fashion trends impacted the eyewear industry.

Geographic Consolidation through Acquisition in 1980s

Luxottica concentrated on consolidating its international distribution network in the 1980s. International sales have always been vital to Luxottica's success. In fact, the very first sets of the company's frames were not sold in Italy, as one might expect, but in the United States. In 1970, the company assigned exclusive rights to distribute its eyewear in the United States to Avant Garde. The Luxottica line was not offered in Italy until 1975. After taking control of Avant Garde in the early 1980s, Luxottica increased its U.S. market share from less than two percent to over seven percent, enough to lead this highly fragmented industry.

Under the direction of Leonardo Del Vecchio's son and expected successor, Claudio, revenues from the American division—which constituted more than half of the Italian firm's total sales—increased from $28 million in 1982 to $143 million by 1990. Over the course of the decade, Luxottica acquired 9 of its 12 international distributors and took significant equity positions in the remainder with an eye toward full ownership. The company applied its own finely-honed standards to its new affiliates, winning opticians' and retailers' loyalty by offering computerized ordering, inventory services, and just-in-time delivery. And in the early 1990s, Luxottica found itself in the unusual position of increasing brand awareness and penetration in Europe, where it only had about five percent of the market.

Fueled by acquisitions and continual economizing, Luxottica's revenues increased from L16 billion in 1979 to L194 billion in 1985. But in spite of this spectacular financial and geographic expansion, Leonardo Del Vecchio remained ''Signor Nessuno'' (Mr. Nobody) among Italy's leading businessmen.

Designer Lines Spark Late 1980s Growth Spurts

Three principal trends converged in the late 1980s to jump start Luxottica's sales and earnings growth. Prescription eyeglasses evolved from a fashion liability into an important accessory, to the point that even those who did not need to correct their vision might wear frames with non-corrective lenses just to complete a particular ''look.'' Luxottica capitalized on this trend by amassing a collection of designer labels in the late 1980s and early 1990s. To its own Luxottica and Sferoflex ophthalmic frames and Sfersol sunglasses, the company added Giorgio Armani, Genny, Byblos, Giugiaro, Valentino, and Yves Saint Laurent. Del Vecchio correctly reasoned that people who might not be able to afford a Giorgio Armani suit might opt instead for the designer's eyewear.

As the share of company sales generated by designer glasses increased from nil to over 38 percent, Luxottica's revenues and earnings mounted. Sales increased from L194 billion in 1985 to over L460 billion in 1991, by which time net income exceeded L60 billion. By the early 1990s, designer eyewear drove the company's gross margins to an astonishing 70 percent.

Luxottica went public on the New York Stock Exchange with a January 1990 floatation of 23 percent of the company's equity in the form of American Depositary Receipts (ADRs). Luxottica was the first Italian company ever to bypass the Milan Stock Exchange to list on the New York Stock Exchange. Company executives treated financial analysts to their stylish sunglasses to help promote the initial public offering. Luxottica Chairman Roberto Chemello told Lisa Bannon of *WWD* that ''We want to show the financial world our image is international, not just Italian, which is in line with the international nature of our business.'' Del Vecchio elaborated in a 1991 interview with *Forbes'* Katherine Weisman: ''If we listed [on the Milan Exchange], we would have been a piccolissima cosa [teeny thing]. On the NYSE, c'e rispetto [there's respect] for everybody, piccolo e grande.'' The founder treated himself to the US$80 million proceeds of the initial public offering. Debt-free Luxottica did not need the money, and he had certainly earned the reward. By 1994, the shares had quadrupled in value.

Acquisitions Bring Integration Full-Circle in Early 1990s

In 1995, Del Vecchio and Luxottica took its largest single step toward vertical integration with the hostile US$1.4 billion takeover of United States Shoe Corp. This initially surprising development was precipitated by heightened competition in the frame industry and reduced reimbursements from third-party payers like insurers and health maintenance organizations. Luxottica had traditionally sold to individual opticians, and had over 28,000 clients in the United States by the early 1990s. But at that time, the company increasingly found itself squeezed between shrinking insurance allowances for frames and its competitors' price cuts to match those limits. Del Vecchio knew he couldn't rely on the designer market alone for continued profitable growth, but he also didn't want to start chasing the industry's lowest common denominator. He found an oblique solution to the dilemma in U.S. Shoe Corp.

Luxottica was not interested in the target's shoe manufacturing business or its retail apparel subsidiaries. Instead, Del Vecchio was eager to capitalize on its chain of nearly 700 LensCrafters optical stores and that operation's $767 million annual sales. Established in 1983, LensCrafters was one of the first businesses to combine vision professionals, eyeglass frames, and prescription lens processing in one easily-accessed mall location. The company's "about an hour" turnaround time completed the convenient package. Anticipating the immense potential of this new concept, U.S. Shoe acquired the budding three-store chain barely a year after it was founded. The financial backing of this billion-dollar conglomerate helped LensCrafters become America's largest retail eyewear chain by 1988. It achieved global sales leadership in 1992.

As part of the 1995 transaction with Luxottica, U.S. Shoe sold its footwear group to Nine West Group Inc. for $600 million prior to its own acquisition. But Luxottica was unable to find a buyer for U.S. Shoe's 1,300 money-losing apparel retailers, which included the Casual Corner, Petite Sophisticate, August Max, Casual & Co., and Capezio chains. As a result, the parent transferred this division to La Leonarda Finanziaria Srl, a separate Del Vecchio interest. The addition of LensCrafters more than doubled Luxottica's annual revenues from L812.7 billion in 1994 to L1,848.9 billion in 1995.

The Mid-1990s and Beyond

Luxottica faced the end of the 20th century with an array of growth strategies in its arsenal. The company hoped to further increase sales of designer eyewear, which had already topped 50 percent of annual revenues, by placing stronger emphasis on these more expensive lines in LensCrafter stores. Luxottica planned to continue its diversifications into sunglasses and

sports eyewear, as witnessed by the 1995 acquisition of Italian sunglass manufacturer Persol SpA. By that time, sunglasses constituted more than one-third of annual sales. And in a radical shift from its traditional trade-only promotions, Luxottica planned to boost its consumer advertising with an image-oriented campaign.

Principal Subsidiaries

La Meccanoptica Leonardo SpA; Brico Srl; Persol SpA; Avant Garde Optics Inc. (United States); Luxottica Fashion Brillen Vertriebs GmbH (Germany); Luxottica Portugal SA; Mirari Japan Ltd. (50%); Luxottica France S.a.r.l.; Luxottica Iberica SA (Spain); Luxottica U.K. Ltd.; Luxottica Canada Inc.; Luxottica Belgium N.V. (50%); Luxottica Hellas AE (Greece) (51%); Luxottica do Brasil Ltda. (51%); Luxottica Sweden AB; Luxottica (Switzerland) A.G.; Luxottica Nederland B.V. (51%); Oy Luxottica Finland AB; Luxottica Vertriebsgesellschaft m.b.H. (Austria) (75%); Luxottica México SA de C.V.

Further Reading

Babej, Marc E., "Italy," *Forbes,* July 18, 1994, p. 199.
Bannon, Lisa, "Luxottica Planning a Listing on NYSE," *WWD,* November 28, 1989, p. 11.
Costin, Glynnis, "Luxottica's Designing Eyes," *WWD,* September 14, 1990, pp. 6–7.
D'Angelo, Luca, "Luxottica Group—A Transition from a Workshop to a Global Firm," Master's thesis, Massachusetts Institute of Technology, 1994.
Goldoni, Luca, *A Far-Sighted Man,* Verona, Italy: Luxottica SpA, 1991.
Hessen, Wendy, "Customers Eye Luxottica's Big Move," *WWD,* May 1, 1995, pp. 20–21.
Kindel, Stephen, "Frame Up," *Financial World,* January 22, 1991, pp. 58–59.
Lowengard, Mary, "Gimmicks of the Year," *Institutional Investor,* April 1991, pp. 92–94.
Morais, Richard C., "Luxottica's Golden Spectacles," *Forbes,* May 20, 1996, pp. 98–99.
Saporito, Bill, "Cutting out the Middleman," *Fortune,* April 6, 1992, p. 96.
Seckler, Valerie, "Luxottica Aims to Find Buyer Fast for U.S. Shoe's Apparel," *WWD,* April 18, 1995, p. 2.
——, "Luxottica Sells Women's Group of U.S. Shoe," *WWD,* June 26, 1995, p. 2.
"Silver Europe," *Financial World,* July 19, 1994, pp. 46–49.
Weisman, Katherine, "Piccolisima Cosa No More," *Forbes,* April 29, 1991, pp. 70–71.

—April Dougal Gasbarre

Mac Frugal's Bargains - Closeouts Inc.

2430 E. Del Amo Boulevard
Dominguez, California 90220-6306
U.S.A.
(310) 537-9220
Fax: (310) 632-4477

Public Company
Incorporated: 1953 as Freight Outlet
Employees: 8,200
Sales: $704.9 million (1996)
Stock Exchanges: New York
SICs: 5710 Furniture & Homefurnishings Stores; 5331
   Variety Stores

When many manufacturers need to unload products—discontinued items, production overruns, canceled orders, inventory liquidations, etc.—they turn to Mac Frugal's Bargains - Closeouts Inc. to take that stock off their hands quickly, usually quietly, and always cheaply. Mac Frugal's is California's—and one of the country's—largest closeout retailers. Each of the company's 311 retail stores carry an ever-changing assortment of more than 30,000 items and offer products at 40 to 70 percent below retail price; these prices are generally 25 percent more than Mac Frugal's pays for them. Unlike discounters such as Kmart and Wal Mart, Mac Frugal stores carry no continuing lines: stores are stocked with whatever bargains Mac Frugal buyers are able to find. This "treasure hunt" experience has built a loyal following among the company's chiefly middle-class customers, many of whom return several times a month to browse the shelves. Mac Frugal stock is geared toward impulse buying, offering items ranging from books and corkscrews for under a dollar, to vacuum cleaners for $80, to decorator bath sets, health and beauty aids, and outdoor and other furniture. Many of these items feature prominent and national brand names.

The company operates 157 stores under the Pic 'N' Save name in its core California market; the other stores, known as Mac Frugal's, operate in Texas, Arizona, Nevada, Florida, Colorado, Utah, Louisiana, and ten other states, including Illinois, Oklahoma, Kentucky, Indiana, and Tennessee. The company reaps additional savings by leasing and subleasing spaces from failed supermarkets and other stores. Mac Frugal stores are generally located in or near working-class and middle-class neighborhoods, and usually avoid low-income areas; average store size is 20,000 square feet. The company also operates a warehouse and distribution center in Los Angeles; a second distribution center in New Orleans was destroyed by fire in March 1996. Mac Frugal's produced nearly $705 million in revenue in 1995. In the mid-1990s, Mac Frugal's has made aggressive expansion moves, opening 35 stores in 1995 alone.

Started with World War II Surplus

Long before he opened his first store William Zimmerman had been active in sales. Raised on New York City's Lower East Side, Zimmerman's sales career began as early as age nine, just as the country verged on the Depression. Zimmerman would make the 20-minute walk to Chinatown, where he bought stalks of sugarcane. Returning to his neighborhood, Zimmerman cut the stalks into slices, which he sold for two to three cents a piece, netting 50 to 75 cents profit on each stalk. As he moved into his teens, Zimmerman switched to clothing, buying used clothing door-to-door in the morning and selling his purchases from a small store in the afternoon.

Even the Second World War could not interfere with Zimmerman's sales career. Stationed in the Philippines, Zimmerman began selling costume jewelry—mailed to him from New York—to Filipinos. After the war, Zimmerman moved to Los Angeles. Working as a welder at night, Zimmerman made the rounds of manufacturers by day. As Zimmerman told *Forbes,* "Buying and selling was what I knew. So I ran around to see what manufacturers had left over." These leftovers ranged from shirts, which Zimmerman hawked on the street, in bars, and other places, to plastic household wares, sold directly to grocery stores. Zimmerman soon began selling from the back of a truck; by 1950, he opened his first retail store in Culver City, California, moving his family into an apartment in the back of the store. Called Freight Outlet, the store featured war surplus and other items. Zimmerman's wife tended the store while he searched for merchandise.

By the mid-1950s, Zimmerman was able to open a second store. Arthur Frankel, a cousin who had been working as a lathe operator in New Jersey while working weekends peddling war surplus hardware at flea markets, flew out to Los Angeles to join Zimmerman's business. Zimmerman took charge of locating and buying merchandise, usually paying on the spot in cash; Frankel picked up Zimmerman's purchases, storing them in a warehouse or stocking the stores.

The pair slowly expanded the Freight Outlet chain, primarily in the Los Angeles area, then moving into other areas in California. In the 1960s, Zimmerman changed the name of his stores to Pic 'N' Save, in part to distance the chain's image from its army surplus origins as the company moved to sales of new merchandise exclusively. By then, Zimmerman had already begun to build a reputation among manufacturers as the place to unload their overruns, discontinued merchandise, and commercial failures. Sales by the end of the decade topped $10 million.

Public in the 1970s

Lewis Merrifield, who had worked as a law clerk for Supreme Court Justice William O. Douglas, joined the company as corporate counsel in 1971, and led the company into its initial public offering the following year. The IPO, involving 250,000 shares priced at $14.50 per share, quickly sold out. Zimmerman was named chairman; Frankel became the company's president and chief executive officer. The company continued to expand, although slowly, generally adding only about five stores each year. By the mid-1970s, the company's chain of Pic 'N' Save outlet reached 47 stores in California (29 in the Los Angeles area), with its first out-of-state store in Arizona. Between 1972 and 1976, sales more than tripled, to $43.6 million. Earnings grew from less than $1 million in 1972 to nearly $5 million in 1976, a jump attributable to Zimmerman's desire to keep cash on hand for swift purchasing power instead of investing in more rapid expansion.

By 1976, the company employed more than 1,000 people, and operated its own 35-truck fleet, with warehouse space in four Los Angeles facilities. Almost all of its stores were leased, and about 40 percent were subleased. The company owned only one store outright, as well as its 10-acre corporate headquarters site. More Pic 'N' Saves were added through the end of the decade, but the company continued on its slow expansion course. By 1981 the company achieved $133 million in revenues at its 78 stores, providing net earnings of over $8 million. Zimmerman's 31 percent share of the company was already valued at over $100 million.

The company was also valued by thousands of manufacturers across the country. Where Zimmerman once made the rounds of manufacturers, many were now coming to Pic 'N' Save's team of buyers. As Frankel told *Forbes*, "the fun part of the business is never knowing what merchandise is going to walk through the door next." The company not only took unwanted merchandise off manufacturer's hands—one example was Richardson-Vick's aborted attempt to market a mint-flavored, green-tinted Cepacol to compete with Procter & Gamble's popular Scope—but also showed a willingness to do so on the manufacturer's terms, which often included agreements not to advertise the product, or to resell to direct competitors in the

manufacturer's ordinary distribution channels. These arrangements allowed manufacturers to discontinue failed and overstocked items quietly, without damaging the image of their brand names. For its part, Pic 'N' Save rarely spent more than one percent of revenues on advertising, depending instead on strong word-of-mouth and the loyalty of its customers. Operations expanded into Nevada, Texas, New Mexico, and Utah, raising the number of stores in the chain to 87, with sales of $227 million by 1983. Net earnings were also on the rise, reaching nearly $36.5 million in 1983, up from $27 million in 1982. A two-for-one stock split in 1983 followed on a three-for-one split in 1981. In 1984, the company opened its first store in Colorado, although Pic 'N' Save continued to resist a more aggressive national expansion.

The company's rising fortunes soon attracted the interest of outside investors. The Zimmerman family appeared ready to sell. But when a New York-based investment fund offered $23 per share ($3 per share over the current value) to acquire the company, an offer worth about $720 million, Frankel rejected it. Instead, the company agreed to buy back Zimmerman's five million shares of stock, giving Pic 'N' Save control of more than 22 percent of its stock. Zimmerman remained on as chairman; however, he retired from the company the following year. Merrifield was named chairman, while Frankel remained as president and CEO. Not long after Zimmerman left Pic 'N' Save, he joined in a leveraged buyout of the similarly named Pay 'N' Save, a Seattle-based discount retailer with more than $1 billion per year in sales. Zimmerman, who had taken a number of Pic 'N' Save buyers with him, attempted to duplicate the Pic formula at Pay 'N' Save, with disastrous results. By 1988, Pay 'N' Save was bought up by Pacific Enterprises' Thrifty Corp.

While Pay 'N' Save floundered, Merrifield took Pic 'N' Save on an expansion surge: between 1984 and 1988 the company nearly doubled the number of its stores. Sales at the 136-store chain reached $362 million in 1987, with a net income of over $47 million. When Frankel retired in 1988, Merrifield took over as president and CEO, while remaining chairman of the company.

Slumping in the Nineties

Merrifield abandoned the company's former slow growth strategy, propelling Pic 'N' Save into new markets in the South and Southeast. To supply the new stores, the company began construction on a new warehouse-distribution center in New Orleans. With a projected cost of $50 million, and at 1.4 million square feet, it was to be one of the largest warehouse facilities in the country. But the expansion of the chain was placing pressure on the company to find enough merchandise to stock the stores. New competition came from the larger, Midwest-based Consolidated chain of closeout stores, which was also expanding aggressively. And the push to expand into New York and other East Coast Markets slashed at the company's bottom line. While sales rose to $475 million in 1989, profits dropped to $30.9 million.

This set the stage for a hostile takeover attempt and a bitter proxy battle, led by David Batchelder, former Boone Pickens/ Mesa Petroleum corporate raider partner. Batchelder won that fight, forcing a restructuring that gave him two of eight seats on Pic 'N' Save's board. Shortly afterwards, Merrifield was replaced by Len Williams, whose 30-year retailing experience included serving as president of Caldor and CEO of Lion-Nathan's retail operations. Taking over as chairman was Peter Willmott, formerly chairman of Carson Pirie Scott. The company saw its income shrink, primarily because of $19 million spent fighting the takeover, and was forced to place part of its expansion drive on hold, slowing to a more modest 10 new stores per year, while fixing up many of its aging existing stores. At the same time, the company delayed opening its New Orleans facility. A bloated administration was also hampering profits.

The company faced a new challenge in 1991. Its expansion into the southeast brought the company into conflict with National Merchandise Corp., which had been licensing the nearly identical Pic N' Save name in the 1950s and had registered it in 1968, a move that Pic 'N' Save had neglected. The company first tried out a new name in that market, opening stores under "The Wow! Stores" name. But a court fight with National Merchandise led to a more drastic name change. Under a settlement, Pic 'N' Save was allowed to keep its name for its California stores. All other stores, as well as the corporation itself, were to be given a new name. Instead of hiring outside consultants and market research experts, the company held a contest among its store employees. The winning name was Mac Frugal's. The corporation formally changed its name to Mac Frugal's Bargains - Closeouts Inc. in 1992.

The name change and a variety of cost-cutting measures, coupled with merchandising successes—such as selling 90,000 pairs of LA Gear sneakers, normally priced at $65, for $19; and 50,000 pairs of Lady Gitano jeans for $10.99 rather than the going retail price of $18—helped sparked a turnaround. Net income for the year ending February of 1992 doubled over the previous year, to $34 million on sales of $542 million. But the turnaround proved short-lived. Difficulties in finding big name merchandise the following year turned away many customers, ballooning the company's inventory. The New Orleans center was opened by the end of 1991, but was operating at barely 40 percent of capacity. With the company's East Coast expansion on hold, the New Orleans facility dragged on the company's earnings; in late 1992, Mac Frugal's disposed of the facility in a sale-leaseback arrangement, forcing the company to take a $36.6 million writedown. Income for that year slipped to $11 million; sales, too, were off, dropping to $540 million.

The company responded by once again stepping up expansion of the chain; instead of pushing into new markets, however, the company at first concentrated on its core areas. Between 1993 and 1995, the company opened more than 100 new stores, including an aggressive 1995 push into the Midwest market, adding 17 stores in that region in 1995 alone. Sales rose to $682 million in 1994, with a net income of $38.8 million. But by 1995, the company faced a changing retail environment. The line between discount retailers, such as Kmart, and closeout retailers was becoming blurred, and Mac Frugal's found it difficult to maintain its traditional 40 to 70 percent pricing edge. As president and CEO Phil Carter, taking over for the retiring Williams in 1995, told *HFN*: "It's not that our pricing has gone up. It's because competitors are coming down and down over time, and the gap that we used to have . . . is in some areas now only 5 to 15 percent off. That's not enough." By 1995, revenues had topped $700 million; yet income slumped to $14.5 million, thanks to a $21 million after-tax charge related to inventory liquidation.

Mac Frugal's moved to cut expenses, including cutting salaried staff, and restructuring benefits. The company also worked on improving its merchandise mix, adding more consumer electronics and other items, while shrinking its apparel goods. The launch of a chain of seasonal stores featuring holiday related goods added to fourth-quarter sales. With its streamlined administration, revitalized merchandise mix, and continued expansion plans, Mac Frugal's appeared certain to regain its reputation as one of the country's most profitable retail chains.

Further Reading

Barrett, William P., "Pic 'N' Run," *Forbes,* October 12, 1992, p. 48.

Erlick, June Carolyn, "Rock Bottom: Mac Frugal's Aims for Lower Prices," *HFN: The Weekly Newspaper for the Home Furnishing Network,* October 2, 1995, p. 1.

Gilbert, Les, "Pic 'N' Save: Powerhouse of Close-outs," *HFD: The Weekly Home Furnishings Newspaper,* September 24, 1984, p. 112.

Groves, Martha, "Pic 'N' Save Goes Shopping," *Los Angeles Times,* September 11, 1989, Bus. Sec. p. 4.

Halverson, Richard, "Pic 'N' Save Head Sees Promise in Retail Turmoil," *Discount Store News,* January 7, 1991, p. 1.

Merwin, John, "Lemons to Lemonade," *Forbes,* August 30, 1982, p. 60.

Sorcher, Jamie, "Bargain Power, Mac Frugal's," *HFN: The Weekly Newspaper for the Home Furnishing Network,* August 14, 1995, p. 11.

—M.L. Cohen

Marsh Supermarkets, Inc.

9800 Crosspoint Boulevard
Indianapolis, Indiana 46256-3350
U.S.A.
(317) 594-2705
Fax: (317) 594-2705

Public Company
Incorporated: 1933 as Marsh Food Stores, Inc.
Employees: 12,400
Sales: $1.39 billion (FY ended March 30, 1996)
Stock Exchanges: NASDAQ
SICs: 5411 Grocery Stores; 5912 Drug Stores &
    Proprietary Stores

Marsh Supermarkets, Inc. is one of the top 50 supermarket chains in the United States, despite limiting its operations almost entirely to Indiana and western Ohio. Many of the 78 Marsh Supermarkets feature a superstore concept, which, with an average 60,000 to 80,000 square feet, house various departments emphasizing fresh, perishable, and takeout foods, as well as video rental, pharmacy, and other services. The company also operates the 12-store chain of Lo Bill Foods, a smaller concept store focused on low prices and located primarily in urban markets. Marsh's chain of Village Pantry convenience stores has grown to 181 stores, 70 percent of which sell gasoline, making Village Pantry the largest distributor of gasoline in Indiana. Marsh's Convenience Store Distributing Company (CSDC) supplies Village Pantry and more than 1,300 unrelated stores in a nine-state area. The company's Crystal Food Service is Indiana's largest catering and food service operation. The company also operates eight stores in New Delhi, India. Marsh is led by chairman, president, and CEO Don Marsh, son of company founder Ermal Marsh. In the fiscal year ended March 30, 1996, Marsh recorded sales of nearly $1.4 billion.

A Depression-Era Success

The first attempt by a member of the Marsh family to enter the grocery business came in 1922, when Wilmer Marsh left farming to buy a small grocery and general goods store in North Salem, Indiana, population 75. All seven of Marsh's children helped in running the store, but it was Ermal Marsh, the second youngest at 12-years-old, who took the most interest in the store's operations, taking charge of the books and ordering merchandise. The store did well enough; but in 1925, during a holdup by a member of the Al Capone gang, Wilmer Marsh was shot in the head. Although he suffered only a flesh wound, Wilmer Marsh sold the store and returned to farming.

Two years later, however, Wilmer Marsh bought a new store in New Pittsburg, Indiana, population 50. That store was successful enough for Marsh to open a second store in Ridgeville, Indiana in 1929. Ermal Marsh, then completing his first year of college at Ball State, left school to manage the new store. Grocery stores of the era were small, about 2,400 square feet, and sold a variety of dry goods in addition to foods, which the grocer would gather from the shelves for the customers. For the new store, Ermal Marsh joined the Independent Grocers Association (IGA), which advocated new selling techniques, such as advertising and allowing the customer to choose their purchases for themselves. Three weeks after the Ridgeville store opened, the stock markets crashed, and the Depression era began. Despite the bleak economy, the new store proved successful and was operated by brother Estel, when Ermal Marsh returned to college.

In order to finance his education, Ermal Marsh opened his own store in Muncie, Indiana, in 1930, borrowing $2,900 from an older brother. The first day's sales totaled $7 dollars. Yet the store, an IGA affiliate, proved successful enough for the newly graduated Ermal Marsh to open a second store two years later. The following year, Marsh closed that store and moved its stock to a new store located in Muncie's commercial district. He also incorporated his business as Marsh Food Stores, Inc., listing himself as secretary and treasurer, and his older brother as president.

Marsh sought financing to expand his company, but banks were reluctant to lend in the early Depression years, especially to the low-margin grocery business. By 1935, however, Marsh had arranged sufficient financing to open a third Muncie grocery. The next year, Marsh closed his second store and reopened it in a new, larger location. The new stores, both IGA affiliates, featured meat counters, fresh produce, and a sound system providing background music and in-store announce-

Company Perspectives:

Marsh Supermarkets, Inc. strives to attain and maintain a position of leadership and market dominance in Indiana and other outlying territories. It is the company's intention to accomplish this through aggressive marketing of new products, accompanied by service innovation with the support of a first class sales organization, support staff and community involvement. As the company progresses, it will improve profits through efficient management. Above all, providing excellence to the customers we serve, remains our first priority.

ments. By the end of the decade, Marsh sought to expand again. He sold one store and opened another, larger store. Then, together with several other store owners, Marsh formed the Carload Buyers Association to purchase dry goods at wholesale for distribution to its member stores. The association next teamed up with another wholesaler, changing its name to Mundy Sales, Inc.

The U.S. entry into the Second World War barely slowed Marsh's growth. By 1943, Ermal Marsh had added three more stores to his operations. The following year, he opened his first store outside of Muncie, in the Jay County seat town of Portland. Two more stores were added that same year, in Dunkirk and Marion, and in 1946, Marsh opened a new store in Muncie, closing his original store. However, Marsh's biggest advancement would occur the following year.

Post–World War II Growth

Marsh opened two new groceries in 1947 and planned to open a third, somewhat larger store that year, complete with a parking lot. Unable to get permission to break the curbstones for entrances, Marsh decided to use the parking space to expand the size of the store. The new store, at 6,430 square feet, became Marsh's—and Muncie's—first supermarket. Called Marsh Foodliner, the store proved profitable in its first week. Encouraged by the store's success, Marsh determined to convert his operation entirely to supermarkets. The company began to expand its corporate staff; by then, too, Marsh operated its own fleet of trucks to service its stores. Over the next three years the company opened four more stores—including a second Foodliner in Muncie, helping to prove the viability of the supermarket concept. Store size was reaching 9,000 square feet in size. The company started up its own bakery in 1949, and then added a new sideline business, making ice cream in the basement of one of the stores. Sold in gallon containers, Marsh Ice Cream proved immediately popular with customers—selling five million gallons by 1957 and eventually making Marsh the country's largest distributor of gallon ice cream—beginning a long line of Marsh private label products.

By 1951, Marsh was outgrowing its facilities. In that year, the company purchased an abandoned milk condensery in Yorktown, Indiana, and began construction there on the Marsh Food Center—housing production, distribution and warehouse facilities, and corporate headquarters. In order to finance the construction,

Marsh went public, issuing 40,000 shares of non-voting stock. The following year, Marsh restructured the company's various operations as a single entity under the name Marsh Foodliners, Inc. The supermarket chain had grown to sixteen stores, all in Indiana. That changed in 1956, when Marsh opened its first two stores in western Ohio. Until this time, Marsh supermarkets were found only in mid-sized towns and cities. In 1957, the company opened its first store in a large urban market, Indianapolis. Sales for that year reached $34 million.

Marsh stepped up its expansion in the final years of the 1950s when it acquired the eight-store Food-Lane Stores, Inc. chain based in South Carolina and Georgia. Marsh followed that acquisition with the purchase of Bellman Markets, a five-store supermarket chain with an average store size of 13,000 square feet, based in Toledo, Ohio. Ermal Marsh's five-year plan called for even faster growth, but he did not get to see completion of his plan. Ermal Marsh died in 1959 when the plane he was piloting crashed.

Settling in—the 1960s and 1970s

Marsh's brother Estel, then serving as executive vice-president, took over as head of the company, now renamed Marsh Supermarkets, Inc., and continued the pattern of growth set by Ermal Marsh. By 1960, the chain had expanded to sixty-two stores, reaching annual sales of $80 million. The company maintained its rapid expansion, adding thirty-four stores between 1960 and 1963. By 1966, Marsh had topped $100 million in sales. By then, the supermarket concept had captured the grocery market, ending the era of the small grocer. The demise of the small stores opened a new market for the increasingly mobile American public. Convenience stores had begun to appear in various parts of the country, but Indiana's restrictive laws regarding sales of beer and gasoline—the most profitable aspects of the convenience store business—left that state largely free of competitors.

Marsh opened its first Village Pantry convenience store in Muncie in 1966. That division, led by then executive vice-president Don Marsh, oldest son of Ermal Marsh, grew quickly, adding nine more Village Pantries in two years. The company also experimented with another type of store concept, called Family Market, which offered a no-frills concept. When Estel Marsh was appointed chairman in 1968, Don Marsh was named president of the company. Following the lead of other supermarket chains, Marsh moved into the drug store business, opening its first Marsh Drug Store in 1969. Under Don Marsh's leadership, the company exited the food production business, contracting with outside companies to supply its private label products, in order to concentrate on its growing retail empire. Marsh closed out the 1960s with revenues of $122 million.

Marsh continued to expand its operations at the start of the 1970s, but a slowdown in the economy, rising building costs, and increasing price competition with other supermarket chains cut deeply into the company's profits. With a 49 percent drop in net income in 1971, the company closed its Family Market operation, then sold its truck fleet in a sale-leaseback arrangement. The company stepped up the growth of its Village Pantry chain, bringing the total to 30 stores by 1973. In that year, the company acquired 15 convenience stores from Nite Owl Food Marts, Inc., and, with the addition of more Village Pantries, the convenience store division reached 62 stores by 1974. However, by then the Arab oil embargo and the resulting surge in inflation began to restrict Marsh's growth.

Nevertheless, Marsh made international news in 1974 when its Troy, Ohio, supermarket became the first in the world to offer Universal Product Code scanning. The new system would greatly enhance the company's ability to track its customers' purchases; linked to inventory, scanning also helped streamline its ordering and delivery processes. Before long, UPC scanning became ubiquitous in the supermarket industry and soon spread to nearly every retail industry.

Through the second half of the 1970s, Marsh, by then topping $200 million in annual sales, continued adding to its chains, although its growth was slowed somewhat by the economic problems of the day. To aid in its expansion, the company adopted a "last-in, first-out" accounting method. During this time, Marsh also began moving away from leasing its Village Pantry locations to owning them outright. The advantages of owning also led the company into acting as its own building contractor for the construction of new Village Pantries. Meanwhile, Marsh unveiled a new supermarket concept in the mid-1970s when it opened its first integrated supermarket-drug store site. The new prototype stores, called "Combos," were former Marsh supermarkets that had been expanded to an average 25,000 square feet. Two years later their success led the company to developing an all-new store concept, this time built from the ground up, with selling area and warehouse space growing to more than 35,000 square feet.

Estel Marsh retired in 1978 and was replaced by Don Marsh as CEO and chairman. By the end of the 1970s, the company had grown to include, in addition to its supermarket chain—which had launched a new, expanded prototype called Marsh Xtras—109 Village Pantries, fifteen Marsh Drug Stores, and three new ventures: the first of a chain of restaurants called Foxfires; a seven-store chain of Tote 'N' Save markets, a return to the no-frills shopping concept, and the first store of another division, called Farmer's Market, specializing in produce sales. None of these new ventures would survive the coming decade, however.

Price Wars in the 1980s and Beyond

Marsh had successively competed in its Indiana market with other, national supermarket chains, but a new type of grocer soon threatened the company. The 1983 entry of Cub Foods and its warehouse concept stores into Indiana sparked a vicious price war that would last more than two years, driving down the profits of the larger chains and forcing at least 35 independent grocers to close. Yet Marsh, which saw its net income drop to $1.6 million on sales nearing $600 million in 1984, managed to come out of the fray intact. Better, the company actually saw an increase in its market share, capturing many of the customers of the failed supermarkets. Marsh responded to the store wars by increasing its operating efficiency and cutting out luxury expenditures, such as the company's fleet of jets. Marsh also began heightening its customer service, adding bulk food items, increasing its range of fresh foods, such as cheese, and including other services such as in-store banking and video rental. By

1985, despite a meager four percent revenue growth, to $628 million, over the previous year, Marsh was able to post a net profit of $4.7 million.

Not all of the Marsh empire came out unscathed. The company sold off its drug store division to the Peoples drug store chain. Marsh also unloaded its restaurant division, and shut down both its Tote 'N' Save and Farmer's Market divisions. The company instead returned its focus to its supermarkets and Village Pantries, raising the number of Marsh supermarkets to 76 and the number of Village Pantries to nearly 170 by the end of the decade. The company also picked up CSDC to serve its Village Pantry stores and other convenience stores in the Midwest. By 1990, sales had topped $1 billion.

The 1990s brought a new growth spurt to the company, which moved its headquarters to Indianapolis in 1991. The launching of a new superstore concept—with stores of 60,000 to 80,000 square feet—sparked several years of intensive capital investment. The company also rolled out its Lo Bill store concept, offering lower prices and more limited selection—and offering the company the ability to convert its older, smaller Marsh supermarkets to the new concept. The company added another new division, Crystal Food Services, bringing the company into the catering and food service area.

In the mid-1990s, the company faced the emergence of a new competitor in its core Indiana market. Michigan-based Meijer, a chain of "hypermarkets" with warehouse-style stores averaging 200,000 square feet, entered Indiana in 1993—with a reputation for allowing new stores to take losses until they had beaten competitors. Marsh responded by adding warehouse-style departments to its superstores, launching more superstores and expanding the fresh foods departments of existing stores, while appealing to six-decades of Marsh family service to its Indiana and Ohio customers. The strategy appeared to be working: despite the entry of 14 direct competitors, Marsh's revenues rose to $1.4 billion, and net income increased to $9 million.

Principal Divisions

Marsh Supermarkets; Village Pantry; Lo Bill Foods; Convenience Store Distributing Company; Crystal Food Services.

Further Reading

Higgins, Will, "Marsh Benefits from Price War Industry Fallout," *Indianapolis Business Journal,* June 24, 1985, p. 9.

Johnson, J. Douglas, "CEO of the Year: Don Marsh," *Indiana Business,* December 1993, p. 8.

Kukolla, Steve, "Marsh Takes on Meijer, Disputes Meager Predictions by Analysts," *Indianapolis Business Journal,* June 27, 1994, p. 3.

Lasting Values: The First Half-Century of Marsh Supermarkets, Inc., Yorktown: Marsh Supermarkets, Inc., 1984.

Marsh, Don E., *Marsh Supermarkets, Inc.: Sixty-Four Years of Continuous Smiles,* New York: The Newcomen Society of the United States, 1996.

Sherman, John, "Don Marsh Talks Shop," *Indiana Business,* March 1986, p. 46.

"Marsh Knows Supermarketing," *Progressive Grocer,* December 1992, p. M6.

—M. L. Cohen

Masland Corporation

50 Spring Road
Carlisle, Pennsylvania 17013
U.S.A.
(717) 249-1866
Fax: (717) 386-1833

Wholly Owned Subsidiary of Lear Corporation
Incorporated: 1991
Employees: 3,100
Sales: $496.6 million (1995)
Stock Exchanges: NASDAQ
SICs: 2273 Carpets & Rugs; 2396 Automotive &
Apparel Trimmings; 6719 Holding Companies, Not
Elsewhere Classified

A leading North American designer and manufacturer of car-interior components, Masland Corporation operates ten manufacturing facilities in the United States, Canada, and Mexico. Founded as a yarn dye business in 1866, Masland entered the automotive industry in 1922 when it first sold woven carpet to Ford Motor Company. From that year forward, the company derived much of its business from supplying car manufacturers with floor materials and then diversified into the design and manufacture of other car-interior components. In 1996, Masland was purchased by Lear Corporation, a $5-billion-a-year company involved in the production of a full range of car-interior components.

Though Masland's business was fully entrenched in the automotive industry during the 1990s, the company's historical roots stretch back decades before the first ''horseless carriages'' began motoring about the nation's cities, towns, and countryside. More than a half century would pass after Masland's establishment before it would enter the business and industry that would predicate the company's existence for much of the 20th century, a span of time that represented one era in Masland's evolution from a 19th century textile business into a 20th century automotive parts business. The transformation did not occur overnight; instead a series of milestone moments in the company's history steered Masland toward the business

areas that would ultimately describe the company at the end of the 20th century. Often, these definitive junctures in the course of the company's development were separated by decades. The result was a corporate history that befitted a more-than-a-century-old company, a story that charted the growth of a business born not long after the American Civil War and its transformation into a leading manufacturer in the automotive industry poised for the 21st century.

19th Century Origins

The long, winding road that led to the Carlisle, Pennsylvania home of Masland during the 1990s originated more than a century earlier in Philadelphia. There, in 1866, one year after Union and Confederate soldiers ended their four-year, epic struggle against one another, a young Charles H. Masland, fresh out of military uniform, founded a business that would outlive his great-great-grandchildren and capture headlines during the 1990s. In Philadelphia, Masland opened a yarn dye house, hoping to share in the explosive growth of the city's textile industry. It was a prudent and financially rewarding decision, one that enabled his fledgling enterprise to take root in Philadelphia and enjoy sufficient prosperity to finance the acquisition of a carpet mill near Philadelphia 20 years later, in 1886.

The move into carpet manufacturing would prove to be one of the most significant developments in the company's history, guiding the Masland venture into the business area that would fuel its growth during the 20th century. Nearly all of the financial and physical growth that resulted from the acquisition of the carpet mill, however, occurred after the company's headquarters were moved from Philadelphia to Carlisle in 1919, three short years before the most pivotal moment in the company's history would occur. Although C.H. Masland & Sons, as the company was known at the time, had already moved past its 50th year of business when it relocated to Carlisle, in many respects the history of the Masland business was just beginning.

Entry into the Automotive Sector in 1922

By the time of the move to Carlisle, Masland had been involved in carpet manufacture for more than four decades, relying on the production of flooring material to grow into a

---

Company Perspectives:

Masland's business strategy is to retain market share in core business with primary customers; to increase market share through further market penetration; to expand into complementary product areas; and to expand geographically.

---

modestly sized firm with more than half a century of business experience. By all accounts the company was a success, but in 1922 Masland made a move that would forever change the magnitude and scope of its business. That year, Frank Masland, a descendant of Charles H. Masland and one of the reasons the company operated under the name "C.H. Masland & Sons," sold his first shipment of woven carpet to Ford Motor Company. The C.H. Masland & Sons carpet was first used in Ford's Model T, but Masland-manufactured carpeting would find its way into countless Ford automobiles, as well as the sundry models manufactured by other car manufacturers, becoming one of the most widely used types of automobile floor material during the ensuing decades.

Frank Masland's first step into the automobile industry in 1922 steered C.H. Masland & Sons toward a business area that would serve as the foundation for the company in the future and it introduced the company to its most important customer. Seventy years later, Ford ranked as Masland's largest customer by far, accounting for more than 60 percent of the sales collected by the Carlisle-based manufacturer. Once Ford began purchasing Masland-made woven carpet, other car manufacturers quickly followed suit. General Motors was the next manufacturer to look to C.H. Masland & Sons for floor material and then, as Masland's presence in the automobile industry matured, a full range of domestic and foreign car manufacturers turned to Masland for automobile floor carpeting.

During the decades following the first foray into the automobile industry, Masland refined its products and deepened its involvement in the automotive sector, building a reputation that was strengthened with each innovation the company brought to market. Among the highlights of the company's rise during the 20th century was its development of molded auto-carpet pieces in 1955. The molded, multipiece floor systems did away with the old "cut-and-sew" technique and C.H. Masland & Sons' limited role as a manufacturer and marketer of rolls of carpet. From the 1950s forward, the company's design contributions to car floor systems picked up pace, placing a greater emphasis on the expertise C.H. Masland & Sons' employees were rapidly developing. During the 1960s, the first one-piece molded floor systems went into production, engendering the introduction in 1968 of a carpet system that covered both the frontseat and the backseat areas inside automobiles. The 1970s, in turn, brought their own innovations, including the creation of floor systems that possessed noise- and vibration-abatement features. By the 1980s, the company's legacy of offering a consistent supply of new and improved floor systems had earned the respect of the world's largest car manufacturers, who demonstrated their faith in C.H. Masland & Sons by awarding product design and engi-

neering responsibilities to the Carlisle-based company during the middle years of the decade.

1986 Acquisition by Burlington Industries

By this point, as Masland entered its 120th year of business, the company was collecting nearly $200 million per year in sales and nearly $7 million per year in earnings, displaying sufficient financial health to attract an eager suitor in 1986. The company intent on acquiring C.H. Masland & Sons was Burlington Industries, Inc., a $2.8 billion-in-sales company that offered $68 a share, or roughly $109 million, for the Carlisle-based carpet and rug manufacturer. Less than a week after the offer, Masland's board of directors met to discuss the deal and unanimously voted to reject the offer, calling the $68-a-share cash tender offer "inadequate." Beryl C. Gardner, Masland's president and chief executive officer at the time, reiterated the rejection of the Burlington bid, telling business reporters, "In our view, Masland is positioned to continue achieving meaningful growth in its earnings and revenues," financial objectives he and the rest of Masland's executives clearly wished to pursue as an independent company. Burlington, however, was not to be denied. Rebuffed and perhaps angered by Masland's quick decision, Frank S. Greenberg, Burlington's president and chief operating officer, responded to the refusal by saying, "We regret that the Masland board has seen fit to reject our offer without even meeting with us or discussing it with us."

Burlington's executives vowed to continue their pursuit of Masland after it had brushed their first offer aside, intent on bringing the carpet and rug manufacturer into their fold despite the objections of the Masland board of directors. The chase did not take long, ending just a few weeks after Masland's board of directors unanimously voted against the acquisition. In June 1986, Masland agreed to Burlington's $73-a-share bid, ending 120 years of independence for the carpet and rug manufacturer. Gardner, who had staunchly opposed the merger, tried to put a positive spin on the outcome, but his words betrayed a half-hearted acceptance of the deal. "Change is sometimes hard," Gardner said, "but it is often necessary and positive."

Masland's acquisition by Burlington marked the beginning of a new era in the company's history, and, for a time, it appeared that the effect of Burlington's control of the company would be to completely wipe away a more-than-a-century-old business. In early 1988, Burlington put Masland Automotive, the automotive products division of C.H. Masland & Sons, up for sale. Masland Automotive, the source for $200 million of C.H. Masland & Sons' total annual sales volume, represented the heart of the company, ranking as one of the country's major suppliers of molded floor carpets, trunk liners, and interior trim parts to car and truck manufacturers in North America. Not long after the announcement that Masland's automotive products division was slated for divestiture, Burlington announced it was putting Masland's residential carpet division, Masland Floorcovering, on the block. As it turned out, however, only Masland Floorcovering, a manufacturer of high-fashion, high-quality carpet and area rugs for designer, residential, and commercial markets, was actually sold, stripping the company of $70 million in annual sales and leaving it wholly focused on the design and manufacture of car-interior systems.

Meanwhile, as these events were unfolding, Burlington was struggling to contend with problems of its own. A 1987 leveraged buyout of the company had financially weighed it down, causing the massive company to take staggering steps as it entered the 1990s. In addition to the financial problems associated with the 1987 leveraged buyout, Burlington's condition was made more precarious by a series of financial losses stemming from its anemic textile business and high interest costs. In trouble, Burlington struggled to effect a turnaround, and it cut loose its ties to Masland in 1991 as part of its recovery program.

Slightly more than five years after its affiliation with Burlington had begun, the relationship was over, ending formally in August 1991, when a group of investors and Masland's management purchased the business of C.H. Masland & Sons from Burlington and created Masland Corporation and its chief operating subsidiary, Masland Industries. Once again on its own, Masland moved forward with its focus entirely on the design, manufacture, and supply of automotive components.

As the company pushed ahead with its new-found freedom, it was coming off of two decades devoted to making Masland products for a range of car interior parts. The company's entry into the automotive sector in 1922 had begun with the manufacture of carpet, and for several decades Masland confined itself to producing only flooring materials. Beginning in the 1970s, however, the company began to make other products for other car-interior components. The departure of the residential carpet and area rug division in 1988 had intensified the company's concentration on car interiors, giving Masland one objective to purse in the future. In 1992, the company bolstered its car-interior component business by acquiring K.W. Muth Company, a manufacturer of automotive dash insulators, vinyl floor systems, and various other acoustic products.

On the heels of this acquisition, Masland converted to public ownership, making its initial public offering of stock in 1993. By the end of the year, sales totaled $353.5 million and net income amounted to $13 million. The next year sales rose solidly to $429.8 million, but on the financial front the most dramatic gain was the remarkable 61 percent leap in net income, which soared to $21 million.

1996 Acquisition by Lear Corporation

During the mid-1990s, the big news for Masland was the arrival of another company intent on acquiring the Carlisle-based designer and manufacturer. This time, ten years after Burlington had offered its first bid for Masland, Lear Corporation made an offer for Masland midway through the company's 130th anniversary year of business. Lear, a $4.7 billion-in-sales supplier of car seats and car parts, was involved in an ambitious

expansion program that was focused on enabling the company to furnish car manufacturers with complete interior systems, or, as Lear's chairman phrased it, to offer "one-stop shopping for interiors." For Lear, the addition of Masland represented an important piece to the total package it was striving to assemble. Masland controlled 40 percent of the floor systems market in North America in 1996 and operated facilities devoted to the production of interior trim and luggage compartments and acoustical systems.

The union of Lear and Masland was announced in May 1996, then completed for $384 million two months later in July, leaving Lear in pursuit of only one more piece to complete its total package: an instrument panel manufacturer. With Lear expecting to supply its first complete interior system by the beginning of the 21st century, Masland headed into the late 1990s operating as the Masland Division and striving to help its parent company reach its objective.

Principal Subsidiaries

Masland Industries, Inc.; Masland of Wisconsin; K.W. Muth Company, Inc.; Consorcio Industrial Mexicano de Autopartes (Mexico; 99%).

Further Reading

"Burlington Bids $109 Million for C.H. Masland," *Daily News Record,* May 22, 1986, p. 8.
"Burlington Has 92% of Masland," *Daily News Record,* July 10, 1986, p. 7.
"Burlington Puts Masland Carpet Unit Up for Sale," *Daily News Record,* February 16, 1988, p. 16.
"Burlington Puts Masland's Auto Unit Up for Sale," *Daily News Record,* January 12, 1988, p. 16.
Dochat, Tom, "Carlisle, Pa.-Based Masland Corp. Fielded Auto Supply Offer Before Lear Deal," *Knight-Ridder/Tribune Business News,* June 6, 1996, p. 6.
——, "Lear Corp. Interest in Purchasing Masland Corp. Began with a Call," *Knight-Ridder/Tribune Business News,* June 11, 1996, p. 6.
"Lear Corporation Completes Acquisition of Masland Corporation," *PR Newswire,* July 1, 1996, p. 70.
"Masland Agrees to $73 a Share Bid by Burlington," *Daily News Record,* June 17, 1986, p. 2.
"Masland Cancels Stock Split, Cites Takeover Bid," *Daily News Record,* June 9, 1986, p. 3.
"Masland Corp.," *HFN,* November 6, 1995, p. 10.
"Masland Says No; Burlington Continues Bid," *Daily News Record,* May 30, 1986, p. 11.
Rutberg, Sidney, "Burlington Continues To Pay for '87 Buyout," *Daily News Record,* August 2, 1991, p. 10.
Sorge, Marjorie, "Interior Powerhouse Lear Buys Masland," *Automotive Industries,* June 1996, p. 94.

—Jeffrey L. Covell

Matria Healthcare, Inc.

1850 Parkway Place
Marietta, Georgia 30067
U.S.A.
(770) 423-4500
Fax: (770) 423-4640

Public Company
Incorporated: 1995 as Matria Healthcare, Inc.
Employees: 1,431
Sales: $87.5 million (1995)
Stock Exchanges: NASDAQ
SICs: 8082 Home Health Care Services; 3845
    Electromedical Equipment

As the leading provider of high-risk, home health care obstetrical services in the United States, Matria Healthcare, Inc. offers services and provides products that assist physicians in the management of high-risk pregnancies, as well as providing home health care services for the management of other obstetrical and gynecological conditions. Matria, which was formed in 1995 through the merger of Healthdyne, Inc. and Tokos Medical Corporation, produced the only home uterine activity monitors approved to be marketed for earlier detection of preterm labor.

Origin of Eldest Predecessor

Although Matria did not officially exist until late 1995, the company's corporate roots date to 1971, when one of its predecessor organizations first emerged on the business scene. That company, the elder of the two entities that merged to form Matria, was Healthdyne, Inc., a business created out of the deep despair of its founder, Parker (Pete) H. Petit. Petit's life changed forever in 1970 when his six-month-old son Brett died from sudden infant death syndrome. As would be expected, the loss of his infant son shattered Petit, 30 years old at the time. But the young Georgia Tech-educated aerospace engineer did not sit home lamenting Brett's arbitrary death. Instead, Petit did what he could to keep other parents from suffering from the same

tragedy. As he later explained to a reporter from *Forbes* magazine, "Everybody deals with grief in different ways." Petit's catharsis occurred with the formation of Healthdyne and the development of a device that trimmed the number of deaths resulting from sudden infant death syndrome.

Following his son's death, Petit worked furiously to develop a monitoring device that would sound an alarm if the heartbeat or breathing of a sleeping child stopped. Within weeks, Petit's efforts paid off and a marketable monitoring device had been discovered, prompting him to solicit financial help from friends and business acquaintances to bring his creation to market. Toward this goal, Petit once again was successful, obtaining enough money ($60,000) to allow him to quit his job at Lockheed in Atlanta in 1971 and establish Healthdyne, the company that for the ensuing decade would derive its sales from Petit's invention.

A year after his son's death, Petit found himself in a new line of work and sitting atop a fledgling enterprise that had a product to market but little else. Initially, the infant monitors were marketed through a network of independent medical products distributors, enabling the company to develop a customer base that soon provided the means for survival. Healthdyne operated as such, marketing its infant monitors through distributors, throughout its inaugural decade of business, developing, during that time, into a flourishing concern. By 1981, the company had exceeded Petit's highest expectations, evolving from the all-consuming need of a father to recover from the loss of his son into a thriving enterprise that had carved a new niche in the medical equipment industry and helped curb the number of deaths resulting from sudden infant death syndrome. Ahead were years of rapid growth and tumultuous change, as the success achieved during the 1970s spawned a decade of diversification that widened Healthdyne's business scope and then sent the company reeling from the frenetic pace of expansion.

1980s Diversification by Healthdyne

At the time of Healthdyne's tenth anniversary in 1981, it stood as an unqualified success, with annual sales eclipsing the $10 million mark for the first time and the infant monitor

Company Perspectives:

We will carry on our tradition of innovation and working relationships in all areas of our business: clinical services, information systems, diagnostic products and managed care programs. All of which can now be provided with greater efficiency as the result of our merger. Many factors will influence our business, most especially, the way our health-care delivery system is transformed and financed. However, the consequences and costs of poor birth outcomes have become a higher priority on the national agenda. And Matria will be on the forefront with the most experience, capabilities, qualifications and outcome data.

business expanding at a 70 percent annual rate. Despite the vibrancy of Healthdyne's business and its industry, Petit decided early in the decade that to continue Healthdyne's steady pace of financial growth he needed to diversify the company's business interests. To reduce the company's reliance on infant monitor sales and enter new business lines, Petit first needed the money to fund Healthdyne's diversification. Accordingly, in late 1981 he sold 26 percent of Healthdyne to the public and raised $11 million to mount an ambitious acquisition program. Additional public offerings of Healthdyne stock in 1982 and 1983 yielded $74 million, bolstering the company's ability to acquire a collection of companies and immediately diversify its business mix. This the company did in an aggressive fashion, acquiring more than 20 medical-related companies during the early 1980s that transformed Healthdyne in a matter of months into a diversified health care company.

The spate of acquisitions brought Healthdyne into a number of different business fields and expanded its product line dramatically to include medical equipment such as surgical instruments, incubators, and oxygen concentrators, which turned room air into pure oxygen for people suffering from respiratory problems. Along with the acquired businesses came an enormous boost for the company's revenue volume, with the financial figures recorded during the early 1980s providing tangible evidence that the push was on at Healthdyne headquarters in Marietta, Georgia. Sales, which exceeded $10 million in 1981 after a decade of growth, tripled the following year, and rose even more the next year, soaring to $133 million in 1983. Company executives were exuberant, with Petit leading the way. In two short years, Healthdyne had transformed itself from small player in its industry to a diversified, rising force evidently on its way toward greatness. Petit noted as much in the company's 1983 annual report containing the financial figures charting Healthdyne's exponential sales gain from $30 million to $133 million. "It's always been our goal," Petit wrote, "to become a major health care company." Quickly, however, that lofty aspiration would fade from the minds of Petit and other executives. Ahead were the most difficult years in Healthdyne's history.

Healthdyne's Mid-1980s Tailspin

In the best of times, the efficient assimilation of more than 20 acquisitions completed during a two-year period would be a

difficult task for any company, but Healthdyne quickly found itself in the unfortunate position of having to orchestrate the organization of its new businesses at the worst of times. First, changes in Medicaid's reimbursement policies significantly weakened the company's formerly stalwart position. In October 1983, when the state- and federally-funded health care program altered its reimbursement policies, hospitals responded by drastically slashing their medical product budgets, thereby directly affecting companies like Healthdyne that relied on the business derived from health care institutions. To make matters worse, the Health Care Financing Administration made budget cuts of its own, sharply reducing the amount it would reimburse for Healthdyne's oxygen concentrators. Perhaps the most damaging development, however, was yet to come, and for this the company could not point fingers at federal or state officials. In its attempt to build around its mainstay infant monitor business, the company, as one industry pundit charged, was distracted from the development of its second-generation infant monitor and put the new product on the market with a serious design flaw. Sales of the infant monitor plunged, dropping by 80 percent. The company's stock responded in kind, dropping in value as investors grew wary of tying their investments to a company suffering from the effects of rapid, ill-timed expansion.

Financial figures again told the tale of Healthdyne's fortunes, as they had during the company's rise during the early 1980s. Between 1984 and 1988, Healthdyne recorded $66 million in losses, with each new year adding to the woes of a company whose financial health had taken a turn for the worse. In response to the company's floundering status, Petit divested all of the hospital supply businesses, shedding most of what had been gained during the early 1980s, and refocused the company's energies on the fast-growing home health care industry. Further, Petit invested $35 million in a line of fetal monitors and a nationwide service operation for women with high-risk pregnancies. With these moves, the stage was set for the company's recovery, giving it the product lines that would record the greatest growth during the 1990s. There was, however, still one more hurdle Petit had to clear before Healthdyne could embark on the path toward full recovery.

Although the company was on the mend, the very fact that it had once struggled and then showed signs of recovery made Healthdyne an attractive acquisition for corporate suitors. During the late 1980s, companies were on the lookout for weakened but resurging prey, and Healthdyne fit the description perfectly. In 1988, Englewood, New Jersey-based Continental Health Affiliates aped the prevailing trend of the day and attempted a hostile takeover of Healthdyne. Petit was adamant in his refusal to give up Healthdyne's independence, and after persuading the company's board to fight off Continental Affiliates' unsolicited offer, he succeeded, leaving Healthdyne on its own to pursue its course.

As Healthdyne exited the 1980s, the path ahead looked promising. Considering the sweeping changes the company underwent during the decade, Healthdyne entered the 1990s as a company much different from what it had been as it entered the 1980s. As a result of Medicaid's change in reimbursement rules for hospitals, Petit had shed a division that sold equipment to hospitals in 1986, one of a series of divestments made during the years of staggering financial losses. Another was made in late 1989 when the company's health care services group, which was primarily involved in rentals of medical equipment and supplies through a dealer network, was sold. Consequently, after a decade that saw Healthdyne's operations expand and contract like an accordion, the company was reshaped for the 1990s, its primary focus on certain areas of the rapidly expanding market for home health care products, including infusion services and high-technology home health systems and equipment.

Healthdyne in the Early 1990s

Of the businesses composing Healthdyne as it entered the 1990s, the most instrumental operating company was Home Nutritional Services, one of the vestiges of Petit's acquisition spree during the early 1980s that survived to see the 1990s. The primary contributor to Healthdyne's sales and earnings growth, Home Nutritional Services ranked as the third largest provider of home infusion therapies, a business that was experiencing rapid growth as hospital costs soared by offering services such as sterile nutritional solutions, antibiotic therapies, and chemotherapy, along with a range of other infusion programs. Although not as strong a contributor to the company's financial growth as Home Nutritional Services, Healthdyne's manufacturing arm, Healthdyne Technologies, was recording a faster rate of earnings growth than was Home Nutritional Services. Healthdyne Technologies produced equipment for monitoring and treating sleep and respiratory disorders and focused its efforts on four segments of the market for home care products: respiratory disorders, sleep disorders, sudden infant death syndrome, and high-risk pregnancies. Aside from the oxygen concentrators and infant monitors Healthdyne Technologies manufactured (which brought in close to $40 million a year), the manufacturing division's work was also highlighted by the introduction in 1990 of a device that pumped air through face masks for sufferers of sleep apnea, a chronic closing of the throat that afflicted roughly two million generally overweight adult males. Rounding out the company's operations was perhaps the most promising aspect of its business: Healthdyne's Perinatal Services division, a business formed in 1987 that provided home monitoring of women with high-risk pregnancies.

Healthdyne's Perinatal Services division represented the future of the company, and like the company as a whole, was recording encouraging financial growth as the 1990s began. Healthdyne's financial health was invigorated in December 1989 when the company raised more than $60 million by selling to the public a one-third interest in Home Nutritional Services. Buoyed by the infusion of this cash, which was used to reduce bank debt and strengthen working capital, Healthdyne once again took on the luster lost during the mid-1980s. After recording losses of $21.3 million, $5.5 million, and $5.4 million in 1986, 1987, and 1988, respectively, Healthdyne posted a promising $7.1 million gain in 1989. Revenues, meanwhile, had also surged ahead, increasing from $48.3 million in 1987 to $103.4 million by the end of 1989. Further financial growth was expected in the years ahead, particularly from the company's Perinatal Services division, which was expected to record a strong sales gain from the introduction of what the company called "System 37," a device for home monitoring of uterine activity. The only hitch in the company's plan to realize what was expected to be an 80 percent increase in Perinatal Services' sales total was approval by the Food and Drug Administration

(FDA) to put System 37 on the market. While awaiting the nod from federal officials, Healthdyne was beaten to the punch by a rival home health care services company that took its name from the Greek word for "childbirth," Tokos Medical Corporation, Healthdyne's future partner.

Tokos Medical During the 1990s

The nation's leading provider of home health care services to women at risk of premature labor, Santa Ana, California-based Tokos Medical Corporation pioneered the market of home obstetrical care in 1983 and, as the 1990s began, stood as the only company in the country to boast a uterine monitor approved for home use by the FDA. Healthdyne failed in January 1991 to get FDA approval for its own uterine monitor version, making Tokos Medical the industry leader and Healthdyne a distant second, with the two companies controlling 60 percent and 30 percent of the perinatal services market in the United States, respectively. Tokos Medical's uterine monitor, which was worn like a belt, could detect premature labor long before its wearer could and early enough to allow medical intervention to delay delivery, alerting medical personnel through readings transmitted via modem. The device was used on an outpatient basis, thereby eliminating the need for costly hospital observation. The financial merits of the device to health care insurance companies were easily discernible. As one investment analyst noted in *Barron's* magazine, "The company [Tokos Medical] is providing a service at $100 a day to which the alternative, if they don't provide that service, is $1,000 a day."

Much the same could be said of the financial benefits realized from using Healthdyne's services, which held the company in good stead as health care costs soared during the early 1990s and insurance companies increasingly sought cheaper alternatives to lengthy hospital stays. During the years leading up to its merger with Tokos Medical, Healthdyne once again took on the accordion-like behavior that characterized its movements during the 1980s by gradually stripping itself of business interests to leave only its core Perinatal Services holdings. In 1993, Healthdyne sold 19 percent of its Healthdyne Technologies subsidiary in an initial public offering, which produced a pretax gain of $9.5 million. Two years later Healthdyne completely spun off its manufacturing arm. Home Nutritional Services, meanwhile, was sold to W.R. Grace Co., leaving Healthdyne as strictly a services and software company by the mid-1990s. Against the backdrop of Healthdyne's waning stature, Tokos Medical struggled financially, recording a $5.8 million loss in 1994 on revenues of $100.7 million. "Both companies," Petit confided as Healthdyne and Tokos Medical were contemplating their union, "have struggled the last three years."

1995: Matria Is Created

In October 1995, the merger between Healthdyne and Tokos Medical was announced, paving the way for the creation of a $160 million maternity-management company. Expected to create a more efficient company, the merger was applauded by industry pundits who perceived the corporate marriage of the two industry leaders as a prudent strategic move. "These are, by far, the two major players in the field," one analyst noted, "it's sort of like Coke and Pepsi merging."

The merger was completed on March 8, 1996, creating Matria Healthcare, Inc., a leading provider of specialized obstetrical home health care services. Retaining the headquarter offices that were formerly occupied by Healthdyne in Marietta, Georgia, Matria took its two top executive positions from Healthdyne and Tokos Medical, with Petit named as chairman and Robert F. Byrnes, Tokos Medical's chairman and chief executive officer, selected as Matria's president and chief executive officer. As the company headed toward the late 1990s, the integration of Tokos Medical and Healthdyne was expected to save Matria roughly $30 million, providing a much-needed lift for a new company charting its plans for the future.

Further Reading

Allgood, Lyn, "Is Healthdyne Rebounding?," *Atlanta Business Chronicle,* May 20, 1985, p. 1A.

Byrne, Harlan S., "Healthdyne Inc.: It Stands To Prosper in Home Infusion," *Barron's,* September 10, 1990, p. 54.

Greene, Jay, "Four Executives Laid Off from Tokos Medical, Healthdyne To Share $8.5 Million," *Knight-Ridder/Tribune Business News,* February 14, 1996, p. 21.

Marcial, Gene G., "Bringing Home Hospital Care," *Business Week,* May 7, 1990, p. 136.

Miller, Andy, "Marietta-Based Healthdyne To Merge with Its Rival Santa Ana-Based Tokos," *Knight-Ridder/Tribune Business News,* October 3, 1995, p. 1.

Neumier, Shelley, "Tokos Medical," *Fortune,* March 23, 1992, p. 109.

Palmeri, Christopher, "Born Again," *Forbes,* December 23, 1991, p. 64.

——, "Emmett's Guardian Angel," *Forbes,* December 23, 1991, p. 66.

Zipser, Andy, "Taken with Tokos," *Barron's,* April 1, 1991, p. 34.

—Jeffrey L. Covell

Maxco Inc.

1118 Centennial Way
P.O. Box 80737
Lansing, Michigan 48908-0737
U.S.A.
(517) 321-3130

Public Company
Incorporated: 1946
Employees: 500
Sales: $80 million
Stock Exchanges: NASDAQ
SICs: 6719 Holding Companies; 5039 Construction
Materials, Not Elsewhere Classified; 5013 Motor
Vehicle Supplies & New Parts; 3089 Plastics
Products, Not Elsewhere Classified

Maxco Inc., is a mini-conglomerate of four active subsidiaries and two divisions that has invested in three primary industry segments: distribution, manufactured products, and real estate development. The distribution segment consists of a division of Maxco, Ersco Corporation, and Wisconsin Wire and Steel. The manufactured products segment consists of Wright Plastic Products and Pacer Tool and Mold, serving the automotive component industry, and Pak-Sak Industries and Akemi, serving the industrial products industry. The real estate segment consists of a division of Maxco, Maxco Development Company, and two partnerships, Riverview Associates One Limited Partnership and CJF Partnership. Maxco is also owns 19.7 percent of the outstanding common stock of Medar, a leading supplier of microprocessor-based process monitoring and control systems for use in resistance welding and optical disc inspection.

Max Coon to Maxco: Company Origins

Working as a partner in a local accounting firm in Lansing, Michigan, in the late 1960s, Max A. Coon became interested in owning his own company. To start, Coon purchased a third share and later a 50 percent share of his client Lloyd Barnhart's local underground construction company, Barnhart Construction Com-

pany, and offered stock according to the law at the time, which allowed companies to sell stock to ten people per year without being registered. Coon considers the true beginning of Maxco to be July 1, 1969, when he used debt to purchase his first additional companies: Triquet Paper Company, Triplex Engineering Company, and Ollie's, Inc. After two years of juggling his work at the accounting firm and his work at Maxco, Coon decided to pour all his energies into his own venture.

Maxco became a highly leveraged company, using debt and stock to acquire companies with strong potential. During Maxco's first decade, the company purchased the mainstays of its financial base. In 1972 Ersco Corporation, a fabricator of reinforcing steel and distributor of concrete construction products and accessories for road and commercial building construction, became a division of Maxco. In the mid 1990s, net sales of the construction supplies group, which consisted of Ersco and Wisconsin Wire and Steel, were approximately 50 percent of consolidated net sales. The purchase of Pak-Sak Industries in 1973, Auto Body Supply Company in 1973, Akemi Plastics in 1977, and Medar in 1978 gave stability to Maxco into the 1990s. Pak-Sak Industries and Akemi made up the industrial products group of Maxco and accounted for approximately 28 percent of consolidated net sales in the mid-1990s. Coon commented in an interview that he consciously stayed away from low-margin industries like food and liquor, seasonal, and recreational industries. ''From my experience as an accountant,'' he noted, ''I knew these industries were hard to manage.''

Medar, Inc. Acquisition

Medar and Auto Body Supply Company (now FinishMaster) have been the shining stars of Maxco's holdings. Purchased January 1, 1978, Medar has grown into a leading supplier of resistance welding controls for on-line inspection of storage media such as Audio Compact Discs (Audio CDS) and Compact Disc Read-Only Memory (CD-ROMs). Maxco owned 100 percent of Medar until 1983 when it took the company public. Since 1983, Maxco has held a variable amount of stock in Medar. Maxco has been instrumental in helping Medar with its bottom line. In 1992, for example, Maxco received shares of Medar in exchange for the retirement and cancellation of outstanding promissory notes and accrued interest. The move gave

Company Perspectives:

It is the mission of Maxco, Inc., through the ownership of operating subsidiaries and investments, to excel in the creation of economic value for its shareholders. Maxco will promote the creation of economic value within its investments and subsidiaries by establishing a culture for its people that promotes entrepreneurial growth. Maxco will support this growth by providing the highest level of corporate resources to its subsidiaries. We believe our people are our most valuable resource; we will pursue a continuous quest for quality in everything we do; our conduct will reflect the highest standards of integrity; we are committed to the health and well being of the environment and communities within which we live and work. To the extent that we act according to these values, we believe we will excel in the creation of value for our shareholders.

Medar more flexibility. According to Medar president Charles Drake in *Business Wire,* the exchange served "a number of purposes for Medar, all of which go hand in hand with a high-tech company experiencing significant growth. The debt retirement eliminates the need to fund the continuing interest obligation and the principal repayment, permitting the company to redeploy these financial resources to fund the growth ahead, while also serving to increase earnings per share."

Maxco's support and the good management of Medar have paid off. Though Medar acquired debt due to the cutback of automated factory equipment purchase in the auto industry in the late 1980s, its acquisition of Automatic Inspection Devices Inc., a manufacturer of systems to inspect the quality of compact discs, began paying off in 1991. The sales of the CD-inspection machines jumped from 17 to 31 percent of Medar's sales from 1990 to 1991 and brought the company back into the black. The company expected demand for its welding controls to continue to be a significant part of its business, however. Medar president Charles Drake noted in *Crains Detroit Business* that the auto industry will require new welding machines each time automakers try to increase market share by introducing new models. A 1994 public offering of Medar's stock led Maxco to report what it called a "significant gain" in its first quarter. Maxco realized $3.1 million in pre-tax gains from the offering. In 1996 Maxco continued to be the largest single shareholder of Medar.

FinishMaster Acquisition

FinishMaster, Maxco's first cash purchase, was the brightest star of Maxco's holdings. When FinishMaster was acquired in 1973 as Auto Body Supply Company it operated out of one location and had revenues of less than $700,000. James White had founded the company in 1968; five years later he sold the company to Maxco to finance growth. Maxco acted as a silent partner, allowing White to grow the company according to his own plan. "From the outset, my idea was to start a paint business and follow the lines of automotive parts divisions, like NAPA has," he commented in the *Grand Rapids Business Journal.* He began to acquire new stores in 1975, and by 1996, FinishMaster had grown to include 56 outlets in 12 states. "It's

not a case that we want to be the biggest in the world. We just want to be the best in our line of business," White told the *Grand Rapids Business Journal.* Maxco took FinishMaster public in 1995, and FinishMaster realized a 23 percent increase in sales and a 61 percent increase in net income.

Coon credited FinishMaster's success to its excellent record of building on existing business, purchasing power, strong management organization, and emphasis on service and training. *Ernst and Young, Inc. Magazine* and Merrill Lynch named James White the Entrepreneur of the Year for the state of Michigan in 1995. In 1996, while James White served on the company's executive board, his son Ronald served as president and CEO.

Unlike Medar and FinishMaster, not all of Maxco's holdings have proved brilliant investments. During Maxco's second decade, the company experienced operating losses due to such troubled projects as the Zilwaukee Bridge, whose delays and cost overruns cost Maxco nearly $5 million. Despite rough times, Coon nurtured his close ties to Maxco's lenders. "I never lied to my bankers; they're my friends," Coon said. "I let them know of problems beforehand. I never surprised them with trouble." And in 1996, Coon was able to demonstrate his financial savvy.

In 1996 Lacy Diversified Industries Ltd. purchased a controlling interest in FinishMaster for $63 million. With the proceeds of the sale, Maxco was able to eliminate its debt for the first time in its history. Coon said that the move made Maxco more conservative. "I see us becoming more of an investment company than a mini-conglomerate," he said. Given the stability of its executive team, some members of which have been with the company for more than ten years, and Maxco's record of profitability, the company seemed well prepared to embark on its new course.

Principal Subsidiaries

Ersco Corporation; Maxco Development Company; Wisconsin Wire and Steel; Wright Plastic Products, Inc.; Pak-Sak Industries, Inc.; Akemi, Inc.; Medar, Inc. (19.7%); CJF Partnership (25%); Riverview Associates One Limited Partnership (2%).

Further Reading

Child, Charles, "Enjoying the Payoff," *Crains Detroit Business,* November 18, 1991, sec. 1, p. 2.

Coon, Max, "Maxco's FinishMaster, Inc., Announces Acquisition, Expands Midwest Operations," *PR Newswire,* February 3, 1993.

——, "Maxco Increases Equity Position in Medar through Debt Exchange," *PR Newswire,* June 29, 1992.

Drake, Charles J., "Medar Reports Debt to Equity Exchange," *Business Wire,* June 26, 1992.

Galasso, Joseph, Jr., "Decade Ends on Flat Note for Most Public Companies," *Michigan Business,* October 1990.

Howes, Daniel, "1994 Michigan Corporate Report Card: Serving the Shareholders," *Detroit News,* December 11, 1994, sec. D, p. 1.

Luymes, Robin, "FinishMaster Is Showing Growth," *Grand Rapids Business Journal,* July 2, 1990, sec. 1, p. 5.

Schneider, A. J., "Buying Binge Lifts LDI," *Indianapolis Business Journal,* June 10, 1996, p. 1.

VanderVeen, Don, "Flourishing Company Forges New Frontier," *Grand Rapids Business Journal,* September 11, 1995, p. A11.

—Sara Pendergast

The Men's Wearhouse

The Men's Wearhouse, Inc.

40590 Encyclopedia Circle
Fremont, California 94538
U.S.A.
(510) 657-9821
Fax: (510) 657-0872

Public Company
Founded: 1973
Employees: 4,100
Sales: $406.3 million (1995)
Stock Exchanges: NASDAQ
SICs: 5611 Men's and Boy's Clothing Stores

The Men's Wearhouse, Inc. is one of the most successful men's specialty store chains in the United States, dominating the men's tailored clothing field. It has accomplished this by offering men a comfortable environment in which to buy high quality suits, dress slacks, sport jackets, and sweaters at 20 to 30 percent below department store prices. In June 1996, the company operated 299 stores in 29 states, and was opening about 50 new stores a year. To attract men, who notoriously dislike shopping, the stores were located in upscale strip shopping centers that were convenient to customers' homes and workplaces and eliminated the need to hike through large malls. A well-trained, friendly staff provided exceptional customer service, with tailors in every store and free pressing for the life of a garment. The combination of these factors plus aggressive radio and television advertising led to consistently increasing sales and earnings in a highly fragmented industry. Net sales for 1995 totaled $406.3 million, an increase of 28.1 percent over the previous year. Net earnings increased 36.3 percent in the same period. CEO George Zimmer and his family own 42 percent of the stock.

Early Years

In 1972 George Zimmer had been out of college for two years and was just back from a year in Hong Kong, where he had set up a factory for his father's raincoat manufacturing business. He became a manufacturer's representative for his father's company,

living in Dallas and driving throughout Texas, Louisiana, and Oklahoma to sell boys' raincoats to stores.

When the buyer at Foley's in Houston, his biggest account, complained about racks of unsold raincoats, Zimmer talked his father into taking back $10,000 worth of merchandise. When Foley's dropped the raincoat line anyway, Zimmer got angry. In a 1993 *Forbes* article he explained, "As Tom Peters says, you have to be a monomaniac to build a business. The fuel for my monomania came from that situation with Foley's."

Taking $7,000, Zimmer rented a small store in a strip shopping center on the west side of Houston and stocked up with name-brand suits. He opened The Men's Wearhouse in August 1973, selling the suits well below the prices charged at Foley's and other department stores. With him at the opening were his father and Harry Levy, a good friend from college.

It took his father's firm more than six months to find a replacement for him. So from Monday through Thursday Zimmer was on the road, selling raincoats. On Friday and Saturday he would be in Houston, on the sales floor of The Men's Wearhouse. In those days, blue laws kept stores closed on Sundays. Harry Levy, who eventually became senior vice-president of planning, covered the store during the week.

Once he was able to devote his full time to The Men's Wearhouse, Zimmer quickly opened two more stores and incorporated the company. He promoted his three stores with small advertisements in the Saturday sports section of local newspapers. In the first year he had sales of $1 million and lost $20,000. At a friend's suggestion, he switched to TV, filming inexpensive ads and buying unsold commercial space at a discount. Executive Vice-President Richard Goldman, who joined the company in 1974 after selling Zimmer advertising space, told *MR Magazine,* "Mary Hartman Mary Hartman becomes the #1 rated TV show in Houston at 10:30 p.m.; commercials cost $700 each, except for ours, which we bought before the series started at $18.25 per spot." By 1981 there were 12 Men's Wearhouses, and by the end of 1985, the chain had grown to 25.

During those early years, Zimmer, Levy, and Goldman established the conceptual basis of their business, which has not

Company Perspectives:

The mission of The Men's Wearhouse is to maximize sales, provide value to its customers and deliver top quality customer service, while still having fun and maintaining the company's values. The Company's commitment to operate a growing, profitable and socially responsible compay is a commitment of which its shareholders can be proud. The Company seeks to adhere to its culture, not only as a means for achieving economic success, but because adherence is a worthwhile goal in and of itself.

changed. Goldman explained to *MR Magazine,* "Our strategy is to be like the old time men's clothing store around the corner, except that we add price as a key ingredient. We realize that men hate to shop, so we actually try to make it fun!"

The company targeted the moderate-income professional and semi-professional male worker. It kept its stores relatively small, between 4,000 and 4,500 square feet, because, as Zimmer told the *Daily News Record* in 1996, "Men don't really like taking their pants off in places larger than 5,000 square feet." The stores were clustered in a mid-sized city to take advantage of advertising and distribution savings and to make them convenient to get to. This was important because a customer had to go to the store twice (once to buy and get measured and again to pick up and try on the suit after alteration). The company expanded the merchandise mix, adding other tailored clothing—sport coats, dress shirts, and dress slacks—to its suits and offered accessories such as ties and belts.

The company emphasized integrity and service. Employees, trained in customer service skills, were also treated as family, with everyone on a first-name basis, and most were hired full time. Zimmer began donating a percentage of pre-tax profits to charities, establishing a reputation for the company as being socially responsible. Vendors were also treated well, and the company never canceled an order. One of The Men's Wearhouse's biggest customers told Jeffrey Arlen of *Discount Store News,* "They do what they say they are going to do. They are very focused and honorable."

Some of the company's competitors disagreed. In the mid-1980's The Men's Wearhouse moved into California. Following its successful Texas formula, the company would open a store, advertise heavily with Zimmer doing his own television ads, and then open several more stores in the area. In 1989 Nordstrom Department Store sued The Men's Wearhouse for false advertising, disputing the company's claim that Men's Wearhouse suits were identical to those sold by Nordstrom. In 1990 C&R Clothiers also sued, complaining about false claims regarding pricing. Both suits were settled when The Men's Wearhouse agreed to stop running the ads.

1990–94: Explosive Growth

The first half of the 1990s saw tremendous growth for the company. It opened 17 new stores in 1990 and 19 the following

year. In April 1992 Zimmer took the company public, selling 2.25 million shares at $8.67 per share and raising $12.7 million. That year new store openings jumped to 31, including the first Men's Wearhouse outlet center, in Houston. At over 7,000 square feet, this was much larger than the regular Men's Wearhouse stores. The outlet had limited services and carried greater quantities of merchandise.

In the fall of 1992, the company introduced Made by America (MBA), a sportswear catalog. The catalog contained only quality, U.S.-made sportswear. In keeping with its ecologically and socially responsible culture, the company avoided mass mailings by distributing the catalogs through its retail stores. When that proved unsuccessful, the company mailed catalogs to customers who had previously bought clothing through the mail. Although cleverly written (and with a percentage of sales going to reduce the national deficit), the catalog did not generate sufficient sales and was discontinued in 1993.

1993 was a rough year for most discount stores, with the *Discount Stores News* Stock Index of 86 stocks falling 5.9 percent. Except for its MBA catalog, however, The Men's Wearhouse had a great year. The company's second public offering raised $10.4 million, with 1.3 million shares selling at $12 per share. This allowed Zimmer to pay off debts while opening 40 stores during the year, including two more outlet stores. The company ended the year with net sales of $240.4 million and earnings of $8.7 million. Between 1991 and 1993, The Men's Wearhouse doubled its net earnings on a net sales increase of 80 percent.

In May 1994 the company completed its third public offering of one million shares at $29 per share, which generated net proceeds of $14.5 million. This provided the financing to open more stores and to acquire the licenses for tailored clothing produced for French designer Pierre Balmain and Italian designer Vito Rufolo. The company began manufacturing as well as selling the new lines, using its direct-sourcing capabilities in the United States and overseas. In addition to its private labels, the company offered brand name suits including Pierre Cardin, Geoffry Beane, Calvin Klein, and Oscar De la Renta.

The company purchased the Coach House in Pittsburgh, which gave the company a major presence in western Pennsylvania. In June The Men's Wearhouse hired Michael Batlin from Macy's West to expand its shoe business. The company had started selling shoes three years earlier, offering Rockport, Florsheim, and Bostonian; it began offering its own private-label brand in early 1994.

The company also decided to offer Big and Tall sizes. To provide the space for these expansions, it increased the floor space of its new stores an additional 500 square feet to 5,000 square feet. Company growth was aimed at the Southeast, and by the middle of the year, there were ten stores in Florida, five in North Carolina, 11 in Georgia, and about a dozen in neighboring states. At the end of 1994, there were 230 stores, more than double the number existing when the company went public in 1992. Net sales for the year increased 32 percent, to $317.1 million.

1995 and Beyond

1995 saw the opening of a 35,500 square foot office, training, and redistribution facility in California. Staff training had always been an important part of The Men's Wearhouse strategy, and all employees went through a three-day Suits University program, conducted at the company's executive headquarters. Richard Goldman explained the company's thinking in a 1995 interview with *Discount Store News.* "We want our people to feel they are being treated fairly, and it all starts at Suits U. First of all it's an all-expenses-paid trip to Northern California, which can mean a lot to a new employee. Once we get them at Suits U. we don't teach people how to use the cash register; that they can learn in the store. What we do is inculcate them with the corporate culture." Sessions included selling techniques, product information, in-store training meetings, and social events. Employees were trained in helping customers select an entire wardrobe, not just a suit or a pair of slacks.

During the year the company executed a revolving loan agreement of $100 million to be used primarily to pay for the company's planned growth and, in July, filed a secondary offering of two million shares. In September The Men's Wearhouse acquired the North American rights for exclusive use of the Botany, Botany 500, and Botany Couture labels. These had been owned by the McGregor division of Samsonite Corporation, which sold the tuxedos, sport coats, and suits through its 500 Fashion Group. Botany 500 became a prominent label in the industry in the 1930's. When Botany went bankrupt in 1972, its labels were bought by Joseph H. Cohen (JHC) of Philadelphia. JHC became a division of Rapid-American, which, after numerous acquisitions and name changes, was the predecessor of Samsonite Corp.

Although the company had planned to expand its Big and Tall inventory into more stores, it found the line selling better than expected in the first 50 stores, which, paradoxically, limited its expansion. "We weren't able to roll it out to as many stores as we wanted to. We had to go back and fill in at the stores where it was selling well," Richard Goldman told *Daily News Record* in a January 1996 interview.

1995 also saw the company move into new markets, including Cincinnati, Milwaukee, and Chicago, which was one of the top five markets for men's tailored clothing. The company's biggest competitor in Chicago, Today's Man, was facing financial difficulties, and within a year had closed all its stores in that market. In the meantime, sales in the new Men's Wearhouse stores were higher than expected.

Industry consolidation and weak sales were taking their toll on department and menswear specialty stores. Traditionally, most suits were sold in department stores or small mom-and-pop operations with one or two stores. In the first half of the 1990s, according to Kernkraut and Abramowitz at Bear Sterns, approximately 4,000, or 23 percent, of the men's clothing boutiques closed, and department stores cut back their men's suit departments. 1995 was a particularly bad year for the industry. Brooks Brothers, a subsidiary of Mark & Spencer, lost $4 million during the first half of the year; the 114-store Britches of Georgetown was put up for sale; Hartmarx sold its

Kuppenheimer stores division; and several regional chains declared bankruptcy.

A major factor in the decreasing sales of tailored clothing was the move toward more casual business dress. The Men's Wearhouse responded to this trend by slightly increasing its stores' selection of sport coats and slacks, replacing about 60 suits with an equal number of sport coats. At the same time, the company increased the training employees received, stressing all aspects of a customer's business attire needs.

In late 1995 the company produced a video entitled "How to Dress Casually and Still Mean Business," in which a sales associate led the viewer on a guided tour of what is needed for a complete office wardrobe. The video was distributed to each Men's Wearhouse store. While managers could show it in the store (it was only seven minutes long), the company had a larger objective: staging free "how-to" fashion shows at local businesses. Managers mailed free copies of the video to human resource directors or other company contacts, with an accompanying letter offering to conduct a live fashion show for male employees, either on-site or at the store.

The company used a similar approach in an 1996 advertisement about business casual wear on *Houston Chronicle* Interactive, the *Houston Chronicle*'s web site. That piece discussed textures and colors of jackets and sport coats, with tips such as "the belt should match your shoes," and "business casual socks are printed socks you can wear with a suit."

George Zimmer received some free advertising on the World Wide Web courtesy of Steve Kubby, publisher of *Alpine World,* an on-line magazine. In a letter to readers, Kubby wrote, "Several months ago we approached The Men's Wearhouse about supporting a tree-free alternative to magazines printed on paper made from trees. . . . I learned that under George's leadership, The Men's Wearhouse was actively involved in recycling, in using hemp paper, and in supporting environmental causes. So they agreed to 'advertise' with us—only they didn't want an ad!" Kubby also wrote that Zimmer actively participated, with money and time, in making the Oakland zoo "one that is endorsed by animal rights activists around the world."

During 1996 the company opened its first store in the Washington, D.C., market, marking its initial entry into the Northeast. It planned to open several more in the Washington-Baltimore area and to enter the Boston-Providence market before the end of the year. First quarter net earnings were 53 percent higher than in 1995, and comparable store sales rose 7.6 percent, compared to a 4.3 percent increase for the same period the previous year. As analysts at Robertson, Stephens & Company noted in their recommendation of April 30, 1996, "The Men's Wearhouse has never depended on strong industry growth but solely on the company's superior fundamentals and growth prospects."

Further Reading

Arlen, Jeffrey, "The Men's Wearhouse: Tailoring an Off-Price Mix," *Discount Store News,* February 20, 1995, p. A16.
Evenson, Laura, "Nordstrom, Men's Wearhouse Settle," *San Francisco Chronicle,* May 12, 1989, p. C2.

Gellers, Stan, and Jean Palmieri, "Men's Wearhouse Acquires License for Three Botany Clothing Labels," *Daily News Record,* September 21, 1995, p. 1.

Giroux, Stephanie, "The Men's Wearhouse," PaineWebber, November 15, 1995.

Grossman, Karen Alberg, "Something More," *MR Magazine,* p. 12.

Houston Chronicle Interactive, "The Men's Wearhouse—How to Dress: Business Casual," Houston Chronicle Marketplace, http://www.chron.com, July 1996.

Karr, Arnold, "Jockeying for Position," *MR Magazine,* June 1995, p. 56.

Kernkraut, Steven, and Pamela Abramowitz, "Recommendation and Follow-Up—Men's Wearhouse, Inc.," New York: Bear, Stearns & Co. Inc., November 13, 1995.

Kloppenburg, Janet, and Carolyn Capaccio, "The Men's Wearhouse, Inc.," San Francisco: Robertson, Stephens & Company, April 30, 1996.

Kubby, Steve, "The Men's Wearhouse: An Unsolicited Testimonial by the Publisher," Alpine World Publishing, http://www.alpworld-.com, July 1996.

Mammarella, James, "Dim the House Lights and Educate the Client," *Daily News Record,* January 15, 1996, p. 60.

McAllister, Robert, "Men's Wearhouse Putting Shoes on Expansion Track," *Footwear News,* July 25, 1994, p. 6.

"Men's Wearhouse Launches MBA Catalog," *Catalog Age,* January 1993, p. 44.

"Men's Wearhouse Net Jumps 38% in 4th Quarter," *Daily News Record,* March 7, 1996, p. 2.

"Men's Wearhouse Obtains $100 Credit Agreement," *Daily News Record,* March 15, 1995, p. 10.

"Men's Wearhouse Files Secondary Stock Offering," *Daily News Record,* July 28, 1995, p. 10.

Motamedi, Beatrice, "Men's Wearhouse Agrees to Pull Ads," *San Francisco Chronicle,* July 19, 1990, p. C1.

Narum, Beverly, "Clothing Chain Opening First Outlet Center," *Houston Post,* September 3, 1992, p. B4.

Nordby, Neil, " '93 Discount Stocks on Sale Rack," *Discount Store News,* January 17, 1994, p. 1.

Palmeri, Christopher, "MBA as d-u-d," *Forbes,* January 17, 1994, p. 20.

Palmeri, Jean, "The Man Who Would Be King of Clothing," *Daily News Record,* January 22, 1996, p. 16.

——, "Good Causes Are Always in Stock at Men's Wearhouse," *Daily News Record,* June 13, 1994, p. 8.

——, Jean, "Men's Wearhouse to Build up Its Big & Tall Biz," *Daily News Record,* October 4, 1994, p. 2.

Poole, Claire, "Don't Get Mad, Get Rich," *Forbes,* May 24, 1993, p. 58.

Power, Gavin, "Building a Retail Empire," *San Francisco Chronicle,* November 26, 1993.

Ruth, Alice A., Elizabeth Beach Mills, and Sharon A. Singer, "The Men's Wearhouse, Inc.," San Francisco: Montgomery Securities, June 1, 1995.

Tuller, David, "Men's Wearhouse Ads False, Nordstrom Says," *San Francisco Chronicle,* March 25, 1989, p. B1.

—Ellen D. Wernick

MGM Grand Inc.

3799 Las Vegas Boulevard South
Las Vegas, Nevada 89109
U.S.A.
(702) 891-3333
Fax: (702) 891-1114

Public Company
Incorporated: 1986 as MGM Grand Inc.
Employees: 7,120
Sales: $721.8 million (1995)
Stock Exchanges: New York
SICs: 7011 Hotels & Motels

A leading hotel and casino operator, MGM Grand Inc. operates an entertainment, hotel, and gaming company in Las Vegas. During the mid-1990s, MGM Grand owned and operated the MGM Grand Hotel, Casino & Theme Park in Las Vegas, which ranked as the largest hotel and the largest casino in the world when it opened its doors in late 1993. In addition to the company's $1.1 billion entertainment complex in Las Vegas, it also operated a MGM Grand hotel and casino in Darwin, Australia and held a 50 percent stake in Las Vegas-based New York-New York, a 2,035-room hotel and casino slated to open in the winter of 1996/1997.

Origins

The formation of MGM Grand Inc. in 1986 marked the rebirth of sorts of the hotel and casino operations that at one time were part of entertainment giant Metro-Goldwyn-Mayer. The hotel and casino operations became a separate entity in 1980 when Kirk Kerkorian orchestrated the breakup of Metro-Goldwyn-Mayer into two distinct companies: Metro-Goldwyn-Mayer Film Co. and MGM Grand Hotels Inc. Kerkorian, a self-made millionaire who first made his fortune trading war surplus airplanes during the 1950s, was in his early 60s when he divided Metro-Goldwyn-Mayer in two, having earned vast wealth and a renowned reputation as a savvy financier during his three decades in the business spotlight. In the years following the 1980

split of Metro-Goldwyn-Mayer, Kerkorian would continue to command considerable attention in the financial community, his clout left undiminished by the breakup of one of the film industry's oldest and largest conglomerates. Kerkorian, after the 1980 division of Metro-Goldwyn-Mayer, owned 47 percent of Metro-Goldwyn-Mayer Film Co. (later MGM/UA Entertainment) and more than 50 percent of MGM Grand Hotel Inc. With sizable stakes in each of these companies, Kerkorian continued to hold sway in the entertainment industry during the 1980s. Of particular interest, however, was his stewardship over the hotel and casino operations that half a decade later became MGM Grand Inc.

The first year of MGM Grand Hotel Inc.'s existence as a separate corporate entity also marked the year a fire swept through the company's Las Vegas hotel and casino. Aside from the property damage caused by the fire, the November 1980 blaze mired the company in legal difficulties that portended its possible collapse. A proposed $200 million facility in Atlantic City, New Jersey was aborted as a result of the fire, but the most damaging aftereffect of the fire was the $1 billion in lawsuits the company faced nearly a year after the fire had been extinguished. This massive sum crippled Kerkorian's ambitious plans for expansion. Investors were wary of funneling their cash into an enterprise awaiting the drop of a gavel that could summarily wipe away their investments. For years, the specter of the November 1980 fire hobbled MGM Grand Hotel Inc.'s financial capability to expand, giving the company little chance to execute what Kerkorian had in mind.

Despite the unfortunate effect of the 1980 fire on the fortunes of MGM Grand Hotel Inc., Kerkorian increased his ownership stake in the company in 1984, purchasing enough shares to give him nearly an 80 percent interest in the company. A year after Kerkorian upped his ante in MGM Grands Hotel Inc., the company entered into negotiations with Bally Manufacturing, operator of Bally's Park Place, one of the most profitable casinos in Atlantic City. By December 1985, an agreement was reached between the two companies for the sale of MGM Grand Hotel Inc.'s two hotels and casinos in Las Vegas and Reno to Bally Manufacturing for $440 million. Under the terms of the purchase, which was completed in early January 1986, Bally

Company Perspectives:

*We consistently provide the premier entertainment experi-
ence while maximizing value and opportunity for our guests,
Cast Members, business partners and shareholders.*

Manufacturing assumed ownership of the two properties, renaming them "Bally Grand," and Kerkorian, the majority
shareholder of MGM Grand Hotel Inc., was granted the exclusive rights to the MGM Grand name and logo, to be used in
whatever future hotel and casino operations he chose to undertake. Kerkorian did not wait long to put the exclusive rights to
the MGM name and logo to use. Shortly after the Las Vegas and
Reno properties were sold to Bally Manufacturing, Kerkorian
embarked on the development of a new but similarly named
enterprise: MGM Grand Inc.

1986: The "New" MGM Grand Is Formed

MGM Grand Inc. was incorporated on January 28, 1986, a
company with a highly marketable name but with little else to
attract the attention of investors or customers. A year after its
formation, MGM Grand moved in a direction different from
that of its predecessor organization by launching an airline
service that offered luxury flights between New York and Los
Angeles. The following year, in 1988, the company moved into
a more familiar arena when it purchased the Desert Inn Hotel
and Casino in Las Vegas, 48 acres of adjacent undeveloped
property, and the Sands Hotel and Casino from Summa Corporation, Hughes Properties, Inc., and Howard Hughes Properties,
Ltd. for $167 million. With this foundation in the hotel and
casino business, Kerkorian embarked on a path that would
establish MGM Grand as a high-profile giant in the Las Vegas
hotel and casino business and lead to the creation of a new breed
of entertainment facilities in the country's gambling mecca.

In 1989, the first signs of Kerkorian's bold and ambitious
plans became evident when MGM Grand announced its intentions to build a movie theme park and new hotel in Las Vegas.
At the time, the project was to include a massive 4,000-room
hotel and an expansive casino—the financial backbone of the
complex—but the unique component of the company's project
was the theme park. Hollywood-style studio theme parks were
on their way to becoming the rage of the day in certain areas of
the country, as entertainment companies concentrated their efforts on attracting families. Prior to MGM Grand's announcement that it planned to build a theme park in Las Vegas, Walt
Disney Co. and MCA Inc. had each committed more than $1
billion to similar attractions in central Florida, pledging themselves to large-scale, family-oriented complexes. Although
MGM Grand embraced the theme park concept perhaps more
fully than others, the company was not alone in its attempt to
attract families through the establishment of theme parks. Other
Las Vegas hotel and casino operators followed suit, creating a
movement that the *Los Angeles Times* would later refer to as the
"Disney-fication of Las Vegas." For Kerkorian and the MGM
Grand management team that carried out his orders, bringing

the proposed project to fruition would take years, as the idea of
the complex crystallized and construction began.

As the company entered the 1990s, the Las Vegas project
began to take shape, evolving from an idea on paper into reality.
In January 1990, when the project was being heralded by company officials as "the largest hotel complex in the world," MGM
Grand acquired the Marina Hotel & Casino, the proposed site for
the hotel and casino that was expected to be completed in 1992.
The following month the company acquired the 113-acre Tropi-
cana Hotel Golf Course in Las Vegas as the site for its theme
park, which together with the adjoining hotel and casino represented a $700 million project. In May 1991, while the company's
business was being generated by its operation of MGM Grand Air
and the Desert Inn and the MGM Marina Hotel, MGM Grand
further refined the details of its Las Vegas project. The complex
by this point was expected to cost $910 million and consist of a
5,011-room hotel and a 35-acre theme park based on the Wizard
of Oz books and movie, with construction expected to break
ground by the end of the summer of 1991.

1993 Grand Opening

In July 1992, MGM Grand moved its headquarters from
Beverly Hills to Las Vegas to position management closer to the
construction of what by this point was being referred to as the
MGM Grand Hotel and Theme Park. The official name of the
complex would eventually become the MGM Grand Hotel,
Casino & Theme Park, a $1.1 billion project situated on a
112-acre site deep in the heart of the Las Vegas strip. The
complex opened in December 1993, amid the fanfare one would
expect for the completion of what stood as the premier hotel-
casino-theme-park in Las Vegas. The 33-acre theme park,
which was operated by MGM Grand Adventures, included eight
separate themed areas based on the Wizard of Oz, seven amusement rides, five theaters, three arcades, and a host of restaurants
and retail shops. The casino, featuring standard table games
such as blackjack, craps, poker, and baccarat, measured 171,500
square feet and was not only the largest casino in Las Vegas but
the largest in the world. The hotel was not to be outdone by the
stature of the casino. With more than 5,000 rooms, the hotel also
ranked as the largest in the world, featuring 751 luxury suites,
52 of which were two stories in height and included internal
elevators, formal dining rooms, and dual master bathrooms,
each with their own hot tub.

The MGM Grand Hotel, Casino & Theme Park represented
a project of unprecedented scale. Aside from the sheer size of
the complex, the sprawling Las Vegas structure was adorned
with trappings to attract every type of customer. The entrance to
the complex was dominated by a seven-story lion. Inside, a 75-
foot-tall reproduction of the Wizard of Oz's Emerald City created an eye-catching, fantasy land. Nearby, the theme park, with
its lights, rides, arcades, restaurants, and shops, served as a
welcome diversion for those not drawn to the ranks of gaming
tables inside the casino.

During its first year of operation, the MGM Grand Hotel,
Casino & Theme Park generated $742 million in revenues and
posted a heartening $75 million in earnings, drawing more than
60,000 visitors per day. While the Las Vegas property was
working its way toward recording its inaugural financial figures,

Kerkorian led MGM Grand in other directions and into other projects. In August 1994, the company announced plans to build two multimillion dollar resort-casinos in the People's Republic of China, a first for the country. Expected to be established on Hainan Island in the South China Sea, the resort-casinos were anticipated to become popular vacation havens for all of Asia. A month after the announcement of the proposed projects in China, MGM Grand formed a joint venture with Primadonna Resorts Inc. to build and manage a resort in Las Vegas to be called New York-New York. The $300 million project, which was slated to begin construction in late 1994 on an 18-acre site across the street from the MGM Grand Hotel, Casino & Theme Park, was designed with many of the same components as its much larger, future neighbor. New York-New York, as plans were being formulated during late 1994, was to include 1,500 rooms, a casino, a theme park, and a recreation of the New York city skyline.

Profitability Declines in the Mid-1990s

In early 1995, MGM Grand followed up on its announcements to expand by moving in the reverse direction. In January the company sold its MGM Grand Air subsidiary, which had been providing scheduled and charted air service between Los Angeles and New York, to a cargo airliner named American International Airways. On the heels of this divestiture, the luster of the MGM Grand Hotel, Casino & Theme Park began to fade. The most pressing problem with the complex was the $110 million theme park operated by MGM Grand Adventures. The theme park was "sometimes eerily empty," as one *Wall Street Journal* reporter noted during a visit, and its attendance figures had not been bolstered significantly by a reduction in its 1994 admission price of $25 to $15 by 1995. Regarding the floundering state of its MGM Grand Adventures subsidiary, MGM Grand's management was remarkably candid, quickly realizing its errors. The company's chief operating officer, Alex Yemenidijian, confided to a *Wall Street Journal* reporter, "We did not understand the theme-park business. . . . For us to succeed in that segment, we need to joint venture with the pros, those who have made the mistakes there are to make and learned what there is to learn."

While the company talked with major entertainment companies during the first half of 1995 about revamping its theme park, deeper problems with the Las Vegas complex had to be addressed. Once the rush and excitement created by the opening of the MGM Grand Hotel, Casino & Theme Park had ended, the complex's business began to wane. Midway through 1995, the company was projecting $725 in sales from the Las Vegas hotel-casino-theme park operation, down slightly from the first year's total, and earnings were expected to suffer a more precipitous drop, falling to $24 million from the $75 million earned the previous year. The drop in earnings pointed to MGM Grand's most glaring weakness: profitability. Other large-scale Las Vegas hotel and casino operators were enjoying net margins that ranged between 9.7 percent and nearly 13 percent, but MGM Grand was recording a paltry 3.3 percent during 1995. The company's anemic profitability prompted Kerkorian to take action, which he did in the summer of 1995.

After MGM Grand's president and chief executive officer Robert Maxey resigned in mid-1995, Kerkorian replaced him

with 52-year-old J. Terrence Lanni, president of Caesars World from April 1981 to February 1995. The task facing Lanni, who was named chairman and chief executive officer, and Yemenidijian, who had been promoted to president, was to increase MGM Grand's profitability. Lanni welcomed this challenge, telling a *Forbes* reporter, "It's not very exciting to go somewhere that has great margins already." To increase the company's profitability, Lanni endeavored to attract higher-stake gamblers, hoping to bring in customers who would lay down their money in the casino rather than merely tour through the complex and exit without spending substantial sums of money. Aside from accomplishing this objective, Lanni had other ideas in mind as MGM Grand moved past 1995 and into its tenth year of business. Lanni announced plans to establish a sound stage in front of several restaurants within the complex and to erect a recreation of Hollywood Boulevard, as well as to create a "Sidewalk of the Stars" to commemorate high-rollers at the company's casino.

Expansion Plans for the Mid-1990s and Beyond

As MGM Grand entered 1996, Lanni was searching for an experienced joint venture partner to manage the company's struggling theme park. Despite the problems with the theme park and the poor profitability of the MGM Grand Hotel, Casino & Theme Park as a whole, however, the company's tenth year of business was highlighted by several announcements that set the stage for expansion during the late 1990s. In early July 1996, the company announced it had entered into an agreement with Forest City Ratner Companies to develop 30 acres of land on the Atlantic City, New Jersey boardwalk. Several weeks later, the company received a Statement of Compliance from the New Jersey Casino Control Commission that completed the first step in the licensing process toward MGM Grand's plans to establish its Atlantic City resort. Describing the company's plans for its Atlantic City project, Yemenidijian declared, "We intend to invest in excess of $700 million to develop a majestic destination resort that will be the pride of Atlantic City, and we will complete it as quickly as the entitlement process will allow us."

As the Atlantic City project was getting under way in July, the company also announced it had reached an agreement to act as the exclusive project developer and manager for Tsogo Sun Gaming & Entertainment, which planned to apply for a minimum of 15 casino gaming licenses in the Republic of South Africa. The execution of the company's two new development projects in Atlantic City and South Africa highlighted its expansion plans as MGM Grand moved toward the late 1990s, with New York-New York, the 2,035-room hotel and casino jointly developed with Primadonna Resorts, scheduled to open in Las Vegas during the winter of 1996/1997.

Principal Subsidiaries

MGM Grand Hotel Inc.; MGM Grand Hotel Finance Corp.

Further Reading

"Atlantic City Reshuffle," *Fortune,* December 23, 1985, p. 8.
Block, Alex Ben, "Kerkorian's Master Plan," *Forbes,* May 20, 1985, p. 166.

Faust, Fred, "MGM Grand Opens Casino/Theme Park in Las Vegas," *Knight-Ridder/Tribune Business News,* December 20, 1993, p. 12.

"Freshly Picked," *Barron's,* September 2, 1991, p. 12.

Lubove, Seth, "The Wrong Kind of Carriage Trade," *Forbes,* October 23, 1995, p. 42.

"MGM Grand, Inc.," *The Insiders' Chronicle,* June 22, 1992, p. 3.

"MGM Grand, Inc.," *PR Newswire,* July 24, 1996, p. 7.

"MGM Grand, Inc.," *PR Newswire,* July 31, 1996, p. 7.

Post, Theresa J., "MGM Grand Unveils Plan To Build $910 Million Complex in Las Vegas," *Travel Weekly,* May 23, 1991, p. 1.

Waddell, Ray, "MGM Grand Has Plans To Build a Themer/Hotel Complex in Las Vegas," *Amusement Business,* September 30, 1989, p. 1.

Zeilenziger, Michael, "MGM Grand Announces Plans for Casinos in China," *Knight-Ridder/Tribune Business News,* August 10, 1994, p. 8.

—Jeffrey L. Covell

Michaels Stores, Inc.

8000 Bent Branch Drive
Irving, Texas 75063
U.S.A.
(972) 409-1300
Fax: (972) 580-1345

Public Company
Incorporated: 1962 as Dupey Enterprises, Inc.
Employees: 19,330
Sales: $1.29 billion (1995)
Stock Exchanges: NASDAQ
SICs: 5719 Miscellaneous Home Furnishings Stores

The largest specialty retailer of arts, crafts, and home decor in the United States, Michaels Stores, Inc. is based in Irving, Texas. During the mid-1990s, the company operated 450 Michaels stores in 45 states, Puerto Rico, and Canada. Through its wholly owned subsidiary, Aaron Brothers Inc., Michaels also operated 68 Aaron Brothers stores, which were located in California, Arizona, and Nevada. Averaging 16,000 square feet of selling space, Michaels stores stocked more than 35,000 items, drawing their greatest percentage of sales from silk and dried flowers and plants. Although the company was headquartered in Texas, its greatest concentration of stores was in California, where 81 stores were located.

The First Ten Years

Two decades before the 450th Michaels arts and crafts store opened in 1996 the first store was established, its creation the work of a young, enterprising businessman that retail analysts would later hail as a "merchandising genius." His name was Michael Dupey, and he got his start in 1973 when he converted one of a group of Ben Franklin stores operated by his father into an arts and craft store that operated under the name Michaels. Located in Dallas, the first store became part of the Dupey family business, a company headed by Michael Dupey's father, Jim Dupey, and aptly named Dupey Enterprises, Inc. Founded in 1962 and the predecessor to Michaels Stores, Inc., Dupey

Enterprises controlled the first store and transformed the retail concept into a chain, adding additional stores as the 1970s progressed.

Dupey Enterprises controlled the Michaels retail concept for ten years. With Michael Dupey leading the way, the Dupey family business expanded the number of Michaels stores, assembling a small chain of stores comprising 11 units—nearly all of which were located in Texas—by the time its era of ownership was over. Although the Michaels retail concept enjoyed an encouraging start, the period of Dupey ownership would stand as the least prolific decade in the retailer's first 30 years of existence. Michael Dupey created the concept, but the work of transforming Michaels into a national chain and building it into the largest retailer of its kind in the United States fell to the new owners who took control of the company in 1983. The year marked the beginning of the Wyly era in Michaels's history, a period during which Michaels arts and crafts stores proliferated throughout the United States and into Canada and Puerto Rico.

1983 Acquisition by the Wylys

In 1983, Dupey Enterprises sold Michaels to Peoples Restaurants, Inc., a company controlled by renowned Dallas entrepreneurs Sam Wyly and his older brother Charles J. Wyly, Jr. Among his numerous accomplishments in the business world, Sam Wyly had founded University Computing Company, a computer software and services company, in 1963. He had co-founded Earth Resources Company, an oil refiner and miner of gold and silver, and, along with his brother, had acquired a 20-unit restaurant chain named Bonanza Steakhouse in 1967. Under the stewardship of the Wyly brothers, Bonanza Steakhouse ballooned into a sprawling 600-restaurant chain during the ensuing two decades, recording an impressive rate of expansion that the Wylys would match with their new acquisition, Michaels.

As part of the deal that brought Michaels into the Peoples Restaurants fold, Michael Dupey successfully negotiated for ownership of two Dallas Michaels stores and was granted the exclusive, royalty-free rights to open licensed Michaels stores in Dallas and area counties. Other than this proviso, Peoples

Company Perspectives:

Michaels mission is to operate the most exciting arts and crafts stores in the world, excelling at satisfying the creative and fun needs of our customers while contributing to the growth and well-being of our associates.

Restaurants assumed full control over the 11-unit Michaels chain, but the company did not hold onto the retailer for long. In 1984, one year after acquiring the retailer, Peoples Restaurants spun off Michaels to Peoples Restaurants shareholders in a rights offering at $2.50 per share, making the arts and crafts retailer a separate, publicly traded corporate entity. On May 6, 1984, the company began trading its stock on the NASDAQ exchange, with the Wylys ranking as the largest shareholders in Michaels Stores, Inc.

Concurrent with the company's initial public offering, Sam Wyly was named chairman of Michaels and a seat on the company's board of directors was taken by his brother Charles, who was named vice-chairman in 1985. Under the leadership of the Wylys, Michaels expanded aggressively, casting aside the prosaic growth that characterized the first decade of its existence to emerge quickly as a strong, regional competitor in the arts and crafts retail industry. During their first five years of directing the company, the Wylys (with Sam in charge) devoted more than $100 million dollars toward the acquisition of small arts and crafts chains and toward opening new stores, embarking on this course shortly after taking the retailer public.

1980s Acquisitions

In July 1984, two months after the company's initial public offering, Michaels acquired Montiel Corporation, operator of a 13-unit chain with stores scattered across Colorado, Arizona, and New Mexico. Having already doubled the size of their company in eight weeks, the Wylys pressed forward, opening additional Michaels stores while they searched for further acquisitions. In 1985, six more retailers were purchased, and in 1987 the company acquired Moskatel's, Inc., a 28-store chain in California, where the greatest concentration of Michaels stores would be located in the future.

By the time these acquisitions were completed, Michaels already represented a promising chain on the verge of breaking into the ranks of national arts and crafts retailers. The company's vast selection of merchandise, which included silk and dried flowers, oil paints, picture frames, model airplanes and ships, greeting cards, and party favors, attracted a specific and loyal clientele. Nearly all (90 percent) of Michaels's customers were female, and 25 percent patronized a Michaels store at least once a week. Largely due to the popularity of the Michaels retail concept and the ambitious expansion orchestrated by the Wylys, Michaels's sales and earnings rose strongly during the mid-1980s, reaching $167 million and $4.9 million, respectively, in 1987.

In 1988, Michaels acquired a division of Wal-Mart Stores, Inc. named Helen's Arts & Crafts. The sale by Wal-Mart repre-sented the massive retailer's exit from the business of selling arts and crafts supplies, but Michaels was fast on the rise and the addition of another arts and crafts retailer represented yet one more step toward national prominence. By this point in the company's history, Michaels had recorded incredible growth. The 11 stores acquired by the Wyly-controlled Peoples Restaurants in 1983 had grown into a chain comprising more than 100 stores. Much had been achieved, but as the company exited the late 1980s and prepared for the 1990s, a regrettable event interrupted Michaels's otherwise steady rise toward becoming the preeminent arts and crafts chain in the United States.

By the late 1980s, Michaels's success had attracted considerable attention from both those involved in the arts and crafts industry and the business community in general. One of those drawn to the company was famed investor Richard Bass, who with his firm, Arcadia Partners, attempted a leveraged buyout of Michaels. The particulars of the deal were negotiated during much of 1989 before the proposed $225 million transaction was terminated in January 1990. At Michaels's headquarters in Irving, Texas, executives were dismayed, particularly Sam Wyly. After the pain resulting from the foundered deal had ebbed somewhat, Wyly told a reporter from the *Dallas Business Journal,* "We wasted almost a year on that deal that failed. It was a major distraction and we will never do that again."

Because of the failed leveraged buyout, Michaels was forced to take a $5 million pretax charge on its balance sheet, which trimmed earnings from $5.2 million to a paltry $13,000, even as annual revenues rose 20 percent to $290 million. The lesson learned from the failed deal was a hard one, but in the wake of Michaels's "major distraction" the company effected sweeping changes that made its operations stronger than ever before. The changes first became apparent in August 1990 when Michaels's president, B.B. Tulley, was replaced by a Michaels director, Donald G. Thomson. Michael Dupey, who at the time was operating his 24-unit MJDesigns chain, was brought in as a special consultant, marking the return of the "merchandising genius," and purchasing was dramatically streamlined. Quickly, the company was moving forward on all fronts with positive momentum. The Michaels chain comprised 140 stores by the end of 1990, with sales reaching $362 million and debt down from $34 million to $9 million after one year.

Animated Growth During the 1990s

By early 1991, the Michaels empire was flourishing once again, prompting one retail analyst to remark, "They [Michaels] are marketing better and buying better. The management restructuring seems to be helping them; they are running a tighter operation." Merchandising and advertising functions had been centralized, profitability was made a primary focus, and regional and district manager positions had been created. At this point, confidence ran high enough to lead Sam Wyly to project that the company would eclipse the $1 billion-in-sales plateau in the next five years, an objective that, remarkably, Michaels achieved.

With a goal of reaching $1 billion sales in the next five years, Michaels's strategy was clear as it prepared for 1992 and the remainder of the 1990s: aggressive expansion throughout the United States. Midway through its plan to open 35 stores in 1992, the Michaels chain consisted of 157 stores, each selling more than 30,000 different arts and craft items and each averaging more than $3 million in sales annually, roughly twice the arts supply industry average. During the previous five years, store sales had more than doubled and profits had quadrupled, a rate of financial growth that ranked the company as one of the hottest retail stories during the early 1990s. The popularity of Michaels stores was credited to the retailer's vast product selection, with silk and dried flowers representing its largest product category in terms of sales generated. Product selection told only half the tale of the company's success, however, because much was owed to the service provided by Michaels's store employees. Amid the display booths and product departments that filled the selling space in a Michaels store, employees taught in-store art classes, providing instruction for various arts and crafts projects, including how to create T-shirt designs and how to make festive centerpieces. With service, product mix, and rapid expansion propelling the company forward, it was only a matter of time and money before Michaels stores dotted the nation's landscape.

The stores opened in 1993 extended Michaels's presence from its base in the Southeast and Southwest to Ohio, Virginia, Oklahoma, Washington, and Iowa, and carried the company beyond U.S. borders for the first time, as two Michaels stores made their debut in Toronto, Canada. The strategy was to cover as much territory as possible with Michaels stores before competitors had the time to catch up. In 1994, any hope of catching the Irving-based retailer was lost as Michaels completed an unprecedented year of physical growth by increasing its store count more than 70 percent.

In terms of acquisitions, 1994 got off to a start in March when Michaels acquired Oregon Craft & Floral Supply, staking a presence in the Oregon arts and crafts retail market. The company then purchased H&H Craft & Floral, which fleshed out its presence in southern California. Next, in April 1994, Michaels acquired Seattle, Washington-based Treasure House Stores, Inc., moving the company into Washington where it had little market presence. These three acquisitions added 25 stores to the expanding Michaels chain, but the company's next acquisition quickly overshadowed the gains made during the spring months of 1994. In July, Michaels acquired Leewards Creative Crafts Inc., a 101-unit chain of arts and crafts stores that gave Michaels solid footing in the Midwestern and Northeastern markets, areas where the company had achieved scant market penetration.

In addition to the stores gained through acquisitions during 1994, Michaels opened 32 new stores on its own, helping drive sales up to $995 million. At the beginning of 1995, there were 380 stores composing the Michaels chain, with stores scattered throughout 41 states and in Canada. For 1995, 55 stores were expected to be added to the chain, including units in Alaska and Puerto Rico, as efforts were under way to round out the company's presence throughout North America, particularly in the Northeast. The company's stores by this point averaged 16,000 square feet and were located in highly visible strip shopping centers near shopping malls. Of the merchandise gracing the company's store shelves—general crafts, home decor items, picture frames, art and hobby supplies, party supplies, wearable art, and seasonal and holiday goods—silk and dried flowers and

plants still accounted for the bulk of Michaels's sales, generating a fifth of its annual revenue volume.

As store expansion continued in 1995, Michaels added another retail concept to its widely popular Michaels format. In March 1995, the company acquired Aaron Brothers Holdings, Inc., operator of a 71-unit chain of specialty framing and art supply stores. Located primarily in California, where the greatest number of Michaels stores were located, the Aaron Brothers stores offered professional custom framing services, sold photograph frames, and stocked a full line of ready-made frames, as well as a broad selection of art supplies.

Buoyed by the addition of Aaron Brothers and the more than $50 million in sales the retailer generated the year before its acquisition, Michaels entered 1996 as the country's largest arts and crafts retailer. The $1 billion-in-sales mark had been reached in 1995 when the company recorded $1.29 billion in sales. The company anticipated opening between 50 and 55 new Michaels stores in 1996, but was beginning to scale back its expansion plans to achieve greater operational efficiencies. Between 1991 and 1995, the company's expansion of store units had increased at a compounded annual rate of 33 percent; for the future the store growth rate was targeted at 15 percent. As the company charted its course for the late 1990s and the beginning of the 21st century, Michaels officials saw the potential for 900 stores in the United States and in Canada, an estimation that set the stage for another decade of robust growth for the 23-year-old company.

Principal Subsidiaries

Aaron Brothers, Inc.

Further Reading

Bond, Helen, "Management Shake-Up at Michaels Earns Kudos from Stock Analysts," *Dallas Business Journal,* April 5, 1991, p. 2.

Coleman, Lisa, "Glue-On Eyeballs, Anyone?," *Forbes,* August 17, 1992, p. 58.

"Corporate Snapshot: Michaels Stores, Inc.," *Dallas/Fort Worth Business Journal,* September 14–20, 1987, p. 13.

Hall, Jesse, "Michaels Shops for New Metroplex Digs," *Dallas Business Journal,* February 10, 1995, p. 1.

"Jack Bush Joins Michaels Stores," *Discount Store News,* July 22, 1991, p. 2.

Lisanti, Tony, "The SPARC Awards Are Where Good Guys Finish First," *Discount Store News,* September 18, 1995, p. 15.

Lundegard, Karen M., "Texas Crafts-Supply Retailers Bringing Feud to Maryland," *Baltimore Business Journal,* September 29, 1995, p. 2.

Smith, Sarah, "Michaels Stores Inc.," *Fortune,* June 6, 1988, p. 152.

"Taking Stock: Michaels Stores Inc.," *Dallas Business Journal,* August 6, 1990, p. 13.

"13D Highlights: Michaels Stores, Inc.," *The Insiders' Chronicle,* April 30, 1990, p. 42.

Wilensky, Dawn, "Michaels Crafts Future with Superior Mix, Service," *Discount Store News,* January 16, 1995, p. 19.

Wilson, Marianne, "Michaels Artfully Crafts High Performance," *Chain Store Age Executive with Shopping Center Age,* November 1995, p. 39.

—Jeffrey L. Covell

Midland Bank plc

27–32 Poultry
London EC2P 2BX
United Kingdom
(0171) 260-8000
Fax: (0171) 260-7065

Wholly Owned Subsidiary of HSBC Holdings plc
Incorporated: 1836
Employees: 50,728
Total Assets: £93.63 billion (1995)
Stock Exchanges: London
SICs: 6081 Branches & Agencies of Foreign Banks;
    6282 Investment Advice

Midland Bank plc is one of the leading deposit banks in the United Kingdom. Following its heyday in the first half of the 20th century, when it was the largest bank in the world, Midland flirted with disaster in the 1980s due to an ill-conceived international expansion and then recovered some of its luster after its acquisition by HSBC Holdings plc.

Rapid Growth in the 19th Century through Acquisitions

The Birmingham & Midland Bank was founded in 1836 as a joint-stock company. The leading figure among its founders was Charles Geach, a 28-year-old Bank of England clerk stationed in Birmingham who quit his job to become the new institution's general manager, which he remained until his death in 1854. Midland's starting capital was a very modest £28,000, but the bank quickly proved to be a successful enterprise. It prospered until 1851, when it acquired Bates & Robins, a Stourbridge private bank. In 1862 it added Baker & Crane, another private bank. These two acquisitions marked the beginning of a long series of amalgamations that would turn Midland into a banking powerhouse by the early years of the next century.

Despite its early success, Midland remained a relatively small institution for the next 20 years, its operations limited to Birmingham and the immediate area. But the bank expanded in the 1880s, beginning with the acquisition of Union Bank of Birmingham in 1883. Amalgamation with Coventry Union Banking Company and Leamington Priors & Warwickshire Banking Company followed in 1889, as well as Derby Commercial Bank, Leeds & County Bank, and Exchange & Discount Bank, Leeds in 1890.

Edward Holden became Midland's general manager in 1891, and it was under his guidance that the bank experienced its greatest rise in stature. Perhaps the most momentous decision of his career as the head of Midland was also one of its earliest: in 1891, Midland acquired Central Bank of London. In one leap, the bank transformed itself from a provincial institution with a presence limited to the industrial Midlands to one with nationwide ambitions and a strong presence in the financial capital of the world. Midland moved its headquarters to London that year and renamed itself London & Midland Bank (it would drop the first half of the name in 1923, giving it its current form).

A further wave of acquisitions in the 1890s established Midland's presence throughout England, from the Scottish border in the North to the Channel Islands in the South. By 1898, it had 250 branches in England and Wales and £32 million in deposits. Holden's expansion policy was nothing if not aggressive; a contemporary cartoon portrayed him as a hunter bagging hares labeled with the names of Midland acquisitions. He would make an unsolicited takeover offer for a bank and, if it refused, open a Midland branch to compete with it as soon as possible.

Continued Expansion in the Early 20th Century

Midland's expansion continued into the early years of the 20th century. The acquisition of North & South Wales Bank in 1908 was one of its more important acquisitions, giving Midland stronger Welsh connections. In 1914 it took over Metropolitan Bank, a substantial institution in its own right with deposits of almost £12 million. In that same year, Midland expanded its presence into Northern Ireland with the purchase of a large interest in the Belfast Banking Company. And in 1918, the bank made its largest acquisition to date when it bought out the London Joint-Stock Bank, with more than £60 million worth of deposits.

Midland also took an increased interest in foreign loans and underwriting during this time. After assuming the title of managing director in 1898 and delegating much of his authority to senior executives, Holden traveled to North America and became convinced that his bank ought to do more overseas business. His straightforward manner won him friends in the American banking community, and he once considered opening Midland branches in New York and Chicago. At Holden's instigation, Midland opened a foreign exchange department in 1905 and was the first British deposit bank to do so. His London colleagues criticized the move as unconventional, but it proved so successful that all of Midland's major competitors eventually followed suit. The bank's traveler's check business and its installation of branch offices on Cunard ocean liners in 1920 both stemmed from this interest in foreign business.

Sir Edward Holden (he had been made a baronet in 1909) died in 1919. He had started out as a bank clerk and worked in the banking business all of his life; it was a sign of the stature that Midland Bank had achieved during Holden's reign that his successor as chairman was a Cambridge graduate who had served as first lord of the admiralty, home secretary, and chancellor of the exchequer in the liberal government of Prime Minister Henry Asquith. The Rt. Hon. Reginald McKenna left politics in 1917 to become Holden's heir apparent, but remained an outspoken authority on economic matters all of his life and was a noted ally of John Maynard Keynes.

Under McKenna, Midland stopped its practice of expansion through acquisition, but only because treasury regulations in the 1920s made mergers virtually impossible. The purchase of North of Scotland Bank in 1924 would be Midland's last acquisition for more than 40 years. Despite these difficulties and the political and economic instability of the interwar years, Midland still prospered and expanded through its branch network. By 1939, it had more than 2,100 branch offices. By 1934, it had become the largest deposit bank in the world, with more than £457 million in assets.

Reginald McKenna died in 1943. During the 1940s and most of the 1950s, Midland was comparatively dormant, at first because of the disruption and destruction caused by World War II, and after the war had ended, because of tight credit restrictions. Expansion of its branch network stopped.

Falling Behind Competitors: 1950s–1970s

The government eased credit restrictions in 1958 and expansion resumed, but Midland found that it had fallen behind its major competitors—Barclays, Lloyds, National Provincial, and Westminster formed the Big Five deposit banks along with Midland—in developing its foreign operations, an area in which it had once blazed the trail. To rectify this situation, Midland combined with the Commercial Bank of Australia, Canada's Standard Bank, and the Toronto-Dominion Bank in 1963 to form Midland and International Bank. The new institution was designed to engage in both merchant and development banking activities, and it also marked the first time that a British bank participated in an international banking joint venture.

In 1967 Midland scored another first when it purchased a 33 percent interest in the merchant bank Samuel Montagu. This marked the first merger in Britain between a merchant bank and a deposit bank and was taken as a sign that the Bank of England was willing to blur the traditional lines between financial companies. Midland wanted to diversify its activities and also sought Montagu's expertise in international markets, and Montagu felt that it would gain business among Midland customers.

During the late 1960s, as Midland shed its image as a banker's bank and a correspondent bank, it cofounded Bank Européene de Credità Moyen Terme and several other consortium banks, with Deutsche Bank, Amsterdam-Rotterdam Bank, and Société General de Banque, but later divested itself of these consortium banks.

In 1974 Midland increased its stake in Samuel Montagu to 100 percent. It also acquired another merchant bank, the Drayton Corporation, and merged it with Montagu. This stronger commitment to merchant banking did not work entirely to Midland's advantage, however; Montagu's financial performance had been solid, but Drayton came with many questionable real estate investments, causing Midland's position in merchant banking to slip somewhat after the acquisition. In 1982 it sold a 40 percent stake in Montagu to Aetna Life and Casualty, only to buy it back in 1985.

International Ventures in the 1980s

Despite its international ventures, Midland still lagged behind its rivals in establishing an overseas presence in the late 1970s. The problem was that Midland had done all of its foreign business through correspondent banks, consortiums, and joint ventures and had little direct representation abroad. Midland promptly tried to make up for lost time, but with mixed results. In 1979 it acquired 67 percent of Banque de la Construction et les Travaux Public, a French mortgage and real estate bank. That year it also made a bid for the American financial company Walter E. Heller, but called it off after discovering that Heller held an unusually high number of problem loans in its portfolio. In 1980 Midland purchased 60 percent of Trinkaus und Burkhardt, West Germany's largest privately owned bank, from Citicorp. And in 1982 it acquired a 69 percent interest in Handelsfinanz Bank of Geneva from Italy's Banca Commerciale Italiana. These acquisitions gave Midland a substantial expertise in foreign markets.

But the centerpiece of this strategy was an unqualified disaster. In 1981, Midland acquired a 57 percent stake in Crocker National Bank, the fourth largest bank in California and twelfth largest in the United States, for $820 million. It was the largest foreign takeover, ever, of an American bank. Midland, of course, sought to establish a large direct presence in one of the most prosperous regions in the country through the deal, and Crocker felt that the increase in capital would allow it to expand. Midland, already the third largest deposit bank in Britain, became the tenth largest banking organization in the world when the deal was consummated.

But the honeymoon did not last long. Crocker's financial performance began to falter almost from the moment Midland took it over, and it collapsed in 1983 when it posted a loss of

$62 million for the fourth quarter. Plagued by bad real estate loans and a substantial share of Latin American debt, it went on to lose $324 million for its parent company in 1984, causing *The Economist* to exclaim in one headline, "What a big hole Crocker is making in Midland's pocket." Nevertheless, Midland stuck by its beleaguered subsidiary, even buying out the rest of Crocker's stock in 1985 after it hit its rock-bottom price of $16.25 per share, down from $90 in 1983. Before long, however, Midland decided that it had had enough. In 1986 it sold Crocker National to one of its California rivals, Wells Fargo & Company, for $1.1 billion, roughly the same amount of money that Midland had sunk into Crocker.

But the Crocker debacle did not end there. Five years of nursing a major acquisition had stunted Midland's capital base while its competitors increased theirs. So when Sir Kit McMahon, an Australian-born former deputy-governor of the Bank of England, became chairman and CEO in 1987, his first priority was to bolster Midland's capital by means of a rights issue and by selling assets. Profitable regional subsidiaries in Scotland, Ireland, and Northern Ireland were divested in 1987. In the same year, Midland Montagu was established, combining the group's treasury, global corporate, international, and investment banking businesses. Midland Montagu was the result of the merger of Samuel Montagu & Company; Greenwell Montagu Gilt-Edged, the leading British government bond primary dealer; and Midland's international corporate banking operations. Overall, the bank aimed to concentrate on its core domestic banking business, deemphasizing international operations.

Optimism about Midland began to surface again in the securities markets, and its depressed stock looked like a bargain. In 1987 several parties purchased substantial interests in the bank. Hanson Trust acquired 6.5 percent, tabloid publisher Robert Maxwell acquired 2.5 percent, and Prudential Insurance Company bought two percent. In 1988 the Kuwaiti Investment Office disclosed that it owned a 5.1 percent stake in Midland. All of this led to speculation in the financial press that Midland might itself become a takeover target. Midland reacted in late 1987 by agreeing to let the Hongkong and Shanghai Banking Corporation acquire a friendly 14.9 percent of its stock. Hongkong agreed to hold the stake for a standstill period of three years while the two banks consolidated and rationalized their international businesses, with Hongkong to concentrate on Asia and Midland on Europe.

Acquisition by HSBC

Midland's 1987 results illustrated that the bank was recovering from, but still seriously affected by, its disastrous international forays. Operating profits before provisions increased 18 percent over the previous year to £511 million, but because the bank was forced to take a huge provision for bad debt (primarily to guard against defaults on shaky Third World loans undertaken earlier in the decade), it posted an overall operating loss of £505 million. On the positive side, the asset sales, rights issue, and outside purchases of Midland stock had improved the bank's capital strength.

The three-year agreement between Midland and Hongkong was an important component of Midland's newfound domestic focus. For example, in 1988 Midland Bank Canada was transferred to Hongkong Bank of Canada. Although the agreement was not renewed in 1990, Hongkong retained its large stake in Midland. The two companies entered into merger talks in 1990, but the talks broke off late in the year because of what were termed "financial difficulties."

In 1991 Midland was still struggling to recover when McMahon resigned in March; he was replaced as chief executive by Brian Pearse, who had been finance director at Barclays. The same week as McMahon's departure, the bank announced that its dividend would be reduced from 18p to 9p, the first time in history Midland had cut its dividend.

Meanwhile, Hongkong reorganized itself in 1991, creating a new holding company, HSBC Holdings plc, and making Hongkong a subsidiary of HSBC Holdings. HSBC stock was set up on both the London and Hong Kong markets, showing the importance Hongkong placed on Europe (and London) for its future. This emphasis was borne out the following year when the long-anticipated merger of Hongkong and Midland finally occurred.

In March 1992 HSBC Holdings made a friendly takeover offer for Midland, amounting to 378p for each share of Midland stock. The next month Lloyds contemplated entering into the bidding with a hostile takeover offer of 400p per share. For Midland, a merger with HSBC would keep its domestic operation fairly intact; HSBC planned to earn back its investment from synergies that would develop between the two largely complementary operations. By contrast, merging with Lloyds would mean the end of the Midland name and huge reductions in branches and employees; Lloyds planned to cut costs dramatically to make the takeover pay off. The sharp differences between these choices quickly became moot when HSBC upped its offer in June to 480p per share, leading Lloyds to decide not to pursue Midland anymore, concluding that the price had grown too high. HSBC ended up paying £3.9 billion (US $7.2 billion) to acquire Midland. About the same time this deal was being concluded, Midland continued its focus on banking by divesting its travel agency subsidiary, Thomas Cook Group Ltd., through a £200 million (US $363.9 million) sale to the LTU Group, a German travel operator.

Over the next few years, HSBC worked to revamp Midland and bring the bank under HSBC control. Management was almost immediately shaken up, as Midland's two management boards were reduced to one, an entire layer of management was eliminated, and HSBC executives were brought in to take over key slots. In July 1992 two senior Midland executives—Gene Lockhart, head of domestic banking, and George Loudon, head of international banking—resigned, and Keith Whitson, who had headed up HSBC's Marine Midland (no relation to Midland Bank) subsidiary based in New York, was brought in as deputy chief executive reporting to Pearse. Whitson soon moved into the top spot, replacing Pearse, who took "early retirement." HSBC placed its own people in the other key positions as well. Another change was the merger of Midland's corporate and institutional banking operations.

Overall, a few years after its completion, the merger was viewed positively by most analysts. Thanks to its improved capital base, Midland's market share was improving because the bank could seek out younger, riskier customers who bring in more profits. Companywide, profits recovered and grew steadily: £844 million before tax in 1993, £905 million in 1994, and £998 million in 1995.

Midland Bank, although no longer an independent firm, faced a much brighter future in the mid-1990s than it did just a few years earlier. Backed by the deep pockets and international strength of HSBC Holdings, Midland was well positioned to regain some of its past glory.

Principal Subsidiaries

Forward Trust Limited; Griffin Factors Limited; HSBC Limited; Midland Bank Trust Company Limited; Midland Life Limited; Swan National Leasing Limited; Midland Bank SA (France); Trinkaus & Burkhardt KGaA (Germany; 71%); Midland Bank International Finance Corporation Limited (Jersey); Guyerzeller Bank AG (Switzerland).

Further Reading

"After the Dust of Battle," *Banker,* August 1992, p. 36.

Ashby, John Frederick, *The Story of the Banks,* London: Hutchinson & Company, 1934.

Bennett, Neil, "Decline of a Heavyweight," *Accountancy,* September 1992, p. 30.

Bose, Mihir, "Breathing Fire into the Griffin," *Director,* October 1994, pp. 60–64.

Green, Edwin, *Banking, An Illustrated History,* New York: Rizzoli, 1989.

Green, Edwin, and Holmes, A. R., *Midland: 150 Years of Banking Business,* London: BT Batsford, 1986.

"Keith Whitson—Putting the HSBC Stamp on Midland," *Banking World,* May 1994, pp. 22–24.

"Merger Progress: Hongkong/Midland," *Economist,* December 26, 1992, p. 104.

"The Middle Game: Midland's Merger," *Economist,* May 16, 1992, p. 109.

Mitchell, Alan, "Midland Listens Harder," *Marketing,* July 2, 1992, p. 2.

Taylor, Michael, "Wedding of the Century," *Far Eastern Economic Review,* April 23, 1992, p. 64.

—updated by David E. Salamie

Milliken & Co.

920 Milliken Road
Spartanburg, South Carolina 29308
U.S.A.
(864) 503-2020
Fax: 864) 503-2100
Internet: http://www.milliken.com

Private Company
Incorporated: 1890 as Deering-Milliken & Co.
Employees: 15,000
Sales: $2.00 billion (est. 1995)
SICs: 2211 Broadwoven Fabric Mills-Cotton; 2221
Broadwoven Fabric Mills-Manmade; 2281 Yarn
Spinning Mills

Milliken & Co. is one of the largest privately owned companies of any kind in the United States, although the precise rank of this closely held firm is difficult to ascertain; Milliken has never released sales statistics. For decades Milliken & Co. has been the clear industry leader in technology and research and, to many observers, in quality and services as well. Chairman Roger Milliken, grandson of company founder Seth Milliken, has been recognized as a giant of the textile industry since his ascension to the company's chairmanship in 1947. The two characteristics that have defined Roger Milliken's reign are his commitment to research and technological innovation and his commitment to secrecy regarding company matters. The former is best illustrated by the patents held by Milliken & Co. on inventions ranging from computerized dyeing equipment to color-enhancing chemicals; the latter is reflected by the fact that most of the company's shareholders, largely Milliken family members and friends, do not have access to financial information.

Milliken & Co. controls about 30 percent of the U.S. stretch-fabric market, about 40 percent of the market for acetate and acetate blends used in linings for coats and outerwear, and around 25 percent of the market for automotive fabrics. By the mid-1990s the diversified company manufactured carpeting and rugs, chemicals, automotive, industrial, and apparel fabrics. In 1995, Milliken boasted more than 55 plants in ten countries worldwide.

19th Century Origins

Milliken & Co. first appeared as Deering-Milliken & Co., a general store and selling agent for textile mills, in 1865. Deering-Milliken was a Portland, Maine-based partnership formed by Seth Milliken and William Deering. The company moved its base of operations from Maine to New York a few years later. Soon after that, Deering left the company for Chicago, where he formed the Deering Harvesting Machinery Company (now Navistar). Seth Milliken continued to operate under the Deering-Milliken name as a selling agent for woolen mills in New England. In the 1860s, he was selling for 16 different mills. Deering-Milliken made its first southern contact in 1884, when it began its long-standing and successful connection with Pacolet Manufacturing Company, headed by Captain John Montgomery of Spartanburg, South Carolina.

From his vantage point as part owner, sales agent, and factor (purchasing and procurement aide) for textile mills in both New England and the South, Milliken was able to determine when a mill was struggling financially, and much of Deering-Milliken's early growth sprang from the acquisition of these concerns. In 1890 Deering-Milliken & Co. was incorporated. Under Seth Milliken, the company eventually acquired interests in at least 42 mills, helping develop the textile industry in the southern United States by financing local manufacturing firms. Seth Milliken died in 1920 and was succeeded by his son Gerrish Milliken, who had joined the company in 1916. During Gerrish Milliken's tenure as head of Deering-Milliken, the company's primary role was that of sales agent and factor for southern mills.

The company's lasting tendencies toward free-flowing cash investment and technological farsightedness were already evident during the Gerrish Milliken era. For example, by keeping debt low and capital liquid during the Great Depression, Deering-Milliken was able to acquire controlling interest in several mills that faced bankruptcy while heavily indebted to Deering-Milliken. In addition, Gerrish Milliken recognized early on the potential importance of man-made fibers. He acquired the gigantic Judson mill in Greenville, South Carolina, and tested rayon, a new fiber, there.

WWII Spurs Research and Development

The onset of World War II created great demand for new, more durable textiles. Deering-Milliken was among a handful of companies that led the industry in the development of synthetics for military use. Mills that sold their goods through Deering-Milliken were commissioned by the War Production Board to produce a variety of fabrics and yarns to meet government specifications. In 1944 Deering-Milliken was designated to build a mill that would process a new man-made fiber for military tire cord. The DeFore mill, built on the Seneca River near Clemson, South Carolina, was the first windowless textile mill equipped with complete air-clearing and -cooling systems; it set the plant standard for years to come. Throughout the war years, demand also continued to grow for the company's New England-produced worsteds and woolens, and more southern mills were purchased.

Gerrish Milliken died in 1947, and his son Roger Milliken took charge of the company. Gerrish Milliken Jr. and Minot Milliken, two other grandsons of Seth Milliken, were also given official positions in the company. Roger Milliken began to shift the company's emphasis away from commission selling toward its own manufacturing. Eight new mills were built between 1940 and 1953. The first mill Roger Milliken built was the Gerrish Milliken Mill, in Pendleton, South Carolina. In addition to weaving Orlon and nylon, this plant, along with two others, doubled as a cattle farm.

By the mid-1950s, Deering-Milliken & Co. was the third largest textile chain in the United States. About 19,000 workers were employed by the company, ranging geographically from New England through the South.

In 1956 the company became entangled in one of the ugliest and most drawn-out affairs in the history of labor relations, a case that continues to be studied by experts in labor law. On September 6, 1956, workers in Darlington, South Carolina, ignoring Roger Milliken's threats of a plant shutdown, voted to bring in the Textile Workers Union of America to represent them. The textile industry historically had been hostile to organized labor—15 percent to 20 percent of the industry had union representation by the mid-1970s—and Roger Milliken had been among the most vocal of union opponents. Milliken made good his threat, and the Darlington plant was closed. In 1962 the National Labor Relations Board ruled that the closing constituted an unfair labor practice, but this decision was reversed by a federal appeals court. The case was ultimately decided by the Supreme Court, which ruled that a plant could not be closed to discourage union activity at other company locations. It was not until 1980, after 24 years of litigation and negotiation over a formula for calculating back pay, that the case was finally settled. The company agreed to pay a total of $5 million to the 427 workers still alive and the survivors of the 16 workers who had died since 1956.

Originally, the mills controlled by Deering-Milliken were separate corporations, some of which had outside shareholders. By the end of the 1950s, Roger Milliken had succeeded in buying out all of them, integrating them into a single corporate entity.

The year 1958 marked the opening of Deering-Milliken's gigantic research facility in Spartanburg, located on a 600-acre complex that became the company's headquarters. From this facility, the most sophisticated in the textile industry, flowed a steady stream of new fabrics and processing techniques. It was here that "durable press" and "soil release," important advancements in polyester treatment, were developed through irradiation.

New Products, Policies Highlight 1960s and 1970s

Under Roger Milliken's leadership, Deering-Milliken continued in its role as industry groundbreaker into the 1960s. In the early 1960s Milliken began to question the conventional thinking of most textile executives regarding inventories. Traditionally, manufacturing and marketing were treated as separate functions, often resulting in excessive inventories. Milliken commissioned a study that indicated an inverse relationship between inventory size and profits. This led Milliken to keep tighter control of inventory by adjusting the rate of production. Deering-Milliken began its European operations in 1965, opening mills and offices in England, France, and Belgium.

In 1967 Deering-Milliken eliminated 600 mid-level management jobs in a consolidation to cut overhead. Deering-Milliken was among the trail-blazing companies in the 1960s, however, in producing double-knit fabrics. Toward the end of the decade, the company unveiled one of its most important inventions, Visa. Visa is a fabric finish that resists stains and is used on a wide variety of products, including clothing and tablecloths. The original irradiation process for making Visa has been replaced by a chemical process. The development of Visa strongly reaffirmed the company's position as a leader in developing patented fabric finishes. It also produced huge profits.

For decades, Roger Milliken has been an active force in conservative politics. Milliken demonstrated the depth of his right-wing convictions in 1967, when, after viewing a television documentary on UNICEF aid to communist-governed countries sponsored by Xerox, he quickly had all Xerox copiers removed from company offices. Company executives routinely receive subscriptions to conservative publications. By the late 1980s, however, the company began using Xerox machinery again, and Xerox was its major copier supplier in 1991.

In 1978 the name Deering was finally removed from the company, more than a century after company founder Deering's departure. The year also marked the 25th anniversary of a Milliken & Co. tradition known as the breakfast show. Each year, retail store buyers and other industry professionals are invited to a Broadway-style musical revue featuring big-name performers and staged at a major New York venue. The breakfast show has a run of 13 performances, nine actually at breakfast and four at cocktail hour, and is seen by more than 30,000 people annually. The show was essentially a glamorous advertisement for Milliken products and has featured Phyllis Diller, Cyd Charisse, Ray Bolger, and Bert Parks, among others.

1980s Bring Rising Tide of Imports

The first half of the 1980s was difficult for the textile industry. One reason was the doubling of textile imports between 1980 and 1985. During that period, Milliken & Co.

closed seven plants, reducing its total to 55 in North Carolina, South Carolina, and Georgia, and a quarter of its work force was laid off. These circumstances led Roger Milliken to depart from his general policy of avoiding the press. He began speaking out in favor of protectionist policies, recommending limiting the growth rate of imports to the growth rate of the U.S. market. By 1991 58 percent of the fabric and apparel sold at retail in the United States was imported. Milliken & Co. was also hurt during this period by Milliken's refusal to adjust to the trend among U.S. consumers toward wearing natural fibers. He believed that because synthetics required less labor, a shift in emphasis was not practical.

In 1984 Roger Milliken survived a helicopter crash. Some who knew him believe that this event brought about a new willingness to deal with the public. He began assuming leadership roles in a number of industry organizations, most notably the Crafted with Pride in U.S.A. Council. Milliken's increased public involvement resulted in his being named Textile Leader of the Year in 1986, the first such honor awarded by *Textile World,* an industrial magazine.

Despite Milliken's objections to textile imports, between 1985 and 1989 Milliken & Co. purchased 1,500 modern Japanese looms, and in 1989 the company bought 500 more from Belgium, because U.S. weaving machinery manufacturers no longer existed. These looms are able to detect defects, stop themselves, and then start up again on their own. In 1987, the company fought fire with fire, establishing a subsidiary in Japan. This operation imported commercial (mostly modular) carpet until 1991, when Milliken brought its first Japanese manufacturing plant on line.

During the late 1980s Milliken & Co. began to show signs of moving toward diversification. The company opened a second chemical plant in 1988 in Blacksburg, South Carolina. The plant makes Millad, a clarifying agent for polypropylene products. The company's first chemical plant had been opened in Inman, South Carolina, in 1963. It made chemical products used in the textile manufacturing process, as well as chemical additives for paint, crayons, markers, plastics, and other products.

TQM Brings Awards, Accolades in Late 1980s and Early 1990s

Roger Milliken named 17-year company veteran Dr. Thomas Malone president in 1984. In response to the competitive challenges of the 1980s, the duo borrowed ideas from several management philosophies to create what soon came to be known as the "Milliken Quality Process." In the early 1980s, for example, they embraced the principles of Total Quality Management (TQM) espoused by Philip Crosby. Known as Pursuit of Excellence (POE), this program flattened the organization via the creation of relatively autonomous teams of "associates," not employees. By 1984, the company had increased its quality and simultaneously reduced its costs.

Having implemented this internal strategy, the company turned outward in a quest for customer satisfaction in the late 1980s. For this stage of Milliken's transformation, the company looked to management guru Tom Peters. In fact, the textile manufacturer implemented his theories so successfully that Pe-

ters dedicated his book, *Thriving on Chaos,* to Roger Milliken. The company "cherry-picked" dozens of other modern management concepts to create its own strategy. In 1989, the U.S. Department of Commerce recognized Milliken's achievements by awarding it the Malcolm Baldrige National Quality Award. (Ironically, that year's other winner was Xerox, the company that Roger Milliken had shunned more than 20 years earlier because of his rigid political beliefs.)

Instead of resting on its laurels, Milliken established a new set of quality, customer satisfaction, and innovation goals. Its ongoing quest has earned it an astounding array of awards, including the European Quality award (1993), *Textile World's* "Best of the Best" (1993), and the Warren Featherbone Foundation Award for American Manufacturing Excellence (1996), to name just a few. The company even succeeded in turning a crisis, a devastating fire that destroyed the La Grange, Georgia plant in January 1995, into yet another citation. Milliken not only rebuilt the mill in less than six months, it also managed to keep most of the factory's 700 associates employed during the interim by transferring them to the company's British plant. These heroic efforts earned the 1995 Model Mill award.

There is but one visible chink in the Milliken & Co. armor. A struggle over future control of the company developed during the late 1980s as Roger Milliken entered his mid-70s. The family of Joan Milliken Stroud, Roger Milliken's late sister, owns about 15 percent of the company and has indicated that it resents its lack of input on company decisions. The Stroud family had sued Milliken and his board of directors at least three times by 1989 in attempts to win shareholders' information and input. When the Strouds threatened to sell their stock, Milliken countered by making new rules that require approval by 75 percent of the voting power before the company can be sold and hand-picking a new, self-perpetuating board dominated by outside directors and managers. Roger Milliken, Gerrish Milliken Jr., and Minot Milliken control about 50 percent of the company common stock. It has been suggested that they have stymied the Stroud family's attempts to sell their stock because it is their wish to keep the company private. Nevertheless, in December 1990 the *Daily News Record* reported that the Stroud family had sold "a small amount of Milliken stock" to Erwin Maddrey and Bettis Rainsford, executives of Delta Woodside Industries Inc. The two investors hinted at the possibility of purchasing the remainder of the Stroud faction's stock.

Among textile industry insiders Milliken & Co. has for generations been associated with quality products and services—quality usually achieved through foresight and innovation. Roger Milliken has been, arguably, among the most important individuals in the textile industry during the 20th century. The success of Milliken & Co. in the future will depend largely on the company's ability to continue with its steady technological and organizational advancement in the absence of the management leadership the Millikens have provided for so long. This will be the case whether the company becomes publicly owned or remains firmly in Milliken family hands.

Further Reading

Andrews, Mildred Gwin, *The Men and the Mills,* Macon, Georgia: Mercer University Press, 1987.

Caulkin, Simon, "The Road to Peerless Wigan," *Management Today,* March 1994, pp. 28–32.

Christiansen, Laurence A. Jr., "There's Been Nothing Like It!," *Textile World,* September 1995, p. 13.

Clune, Ray, "Delta Execs Not Now Buying Milliken Stock," *Daily News Record,* December 27, 1990, p. 9.

Furukawa, Tsukasa, "Milliken Unit To Build Carpet Plant in Japan," *Daily News Record,* October 5, 1990, p. 3.

"How Roger Milliken Runs Textiles' Premier Performer," *Business Week,* January 19, 1981.

Isaacs, McAllister III, "Define Excellence: Milliken & Co.," *Textile World,* June 1996, pp. 64–66.

Kalogeridis, Carla, "Milliken in Motion: A Pursuit of Excellence," *Textile World,* December 1990, pp. 42–46.

Konrad, Walecia, "How Milliken's Tightly Knit Empire Could Unravel," *Business Week,* May 28, 1990, p. 27.

Lappen, Alyssa A., "Can Roger Milliken Emulate William Randolph Hearst?," *Forbes,* May 29, 1989.

"Mind Your Ts and Qs," *Management Today,* March 1994, p. 3.

Ostroff, Jim, "AAMA Convention Urged To Steer New Course of Business or Sink," *Daily News Record,* April 30, 1996, pp. 6–7.

"Textile World's 1994 Leader of the Year: Dr. Thomas J. Malone," *Textile World,* October 1994, pp. 34–41.

—Robert R. Jacobson
updated by April Dougal Gasbarre

Moore Medical Corp.

389 John Downey Drive
P.O. Box 1500
New Britain, Connecticut 06050
U.S.A.
(860) 826-3600
Fax: (860) 223-2382

Public Company
Incorporated: 1969 as Optel Corp.
Employees: 450
Sales: $289 million (1995)
Stock Exchanges: American
SICs: 5122 Drugs, Proprietaries & Sundries; 5047
    Medical & Hospital Equipment

A leading distributor of health-care products, Moore Medical Corp. sells approximately 13,000 pharmaceutical, medical, and surgical products through direct mail, telemarketing, and a small field sales force. During the mid-1990s, Moore Medical fulfilled orders at four regional distribution centers located in New Britain, Connecticut, Jacksonville, Florida, Lemont, Illinois, and Visalia, California. Through these facilities and through two telemarketing centers in Connecticut and California, where the majority of the company's orders were processed, Moore Medical catered to a nationwide customer base, serving approximately 90,000 customers. The bulk of the company's business was derived from sales to either professional health-care practitioners or wholesale customers who purchased Moore Medical products for resale. Although Moore Medical was founded as a wholesaler of brand name pharmaceuticals, the company was moving in a different direction during the 1990s. Higher-profit-margin generic pharmaceuticals and medical and surgical supplies were the company's chief areas of focus as it completed its first half century of business and embarked on its second. As a result of the new strategy adopted during the early 1990s, Moore Medical's sales were declining during the first half of the decade, but its profits were on the rise. In 1995, the company recorded $2.3 million in net income on $289 million in sales compared to $645,000 in net income on $306 million in sales in 1990.

Late 1940s Origins

Established in 1947, Moore Medical began as a mail-order distribution business housed in the back room of a local drugstore. Originally, the company's product line comprised brand name pharmaceuticals that were sold to independent drug stores throughout the country, a customer base that the fledgling drug wholesaler targeted through unconventional means. Typically, companies of Moore Medical's ilk during the late 1940s marketed their product lines through catalogs—a medium Moore Medical would later use—but early on the company placed advertisements in trade journals and printed sales information on post cards, which were then mailed to prospective drug store customers.

With its foundation in the wholesale drug distribution business established, the company slowly began to broaden the scope of its business, making its first noteworthy move more than a decade after its formation. Cosmetics were added to company's product line in 1960, when H. L. Moore Drug Exchange, as the company was then known, employed roughly a dozen employees. Entry into the generic pharmaceutical business had also been completed, giving the company two facets to its business as the 1960s progressed.

By the end of the decade, Moore Medical was supported by a promising generic drug trade and its more than 20-year-old brand name wholesale business, enterprises that began to draw the attention of interested buyers from the national business community. Such interest touched off a period in Moore Medical's history that saw the company's control pass from one new owner to another. Holbrook, Massachusetts-based Parkway Distributors acquired Moore Medical in 1969 and superintended the company's development for the next six years, until Levitt Industries acquired Parkway Distributors in 1975. Three years later, Levitt Industries merged with Optel Corp., a company based in New York that was founded in 1969 as a liquid crystal display (LCD) designer and manufacturer. It was at this point that the name Moore disappeared from the corpo-

---

Company Perspectives:

The mission of Moore Medical Corp. is to market competitively priced health-care products with delivery and service standards that meet or exceed customer expectations. Our goal of increasing share in the markets we serve will be achieved through a team of motivated employees that work in an environment that encourages the realization of their full potential. Through excellence in marketing and service, we will achieve growth in value to the benefit of customers, employees and shareholders.

---

rate ranks of U.S. businesses, but its departure was only temporary. In October 1985, Optel changed its name to Moore Medical Corp., ushering in an era in the health care distributor's history that witnessed the New Britain company reposition itself for growth during the 1990s and the 21st century.

During the years of fluttering from one parent company to another, Moore Medical had started to merchandise medical and surgical products, one of the most important product lines during the company's existence in the 1990s. Other developments that took place in the wake of the name change from Optel to Moore Medical also played a part in the company's operation during the 1990s. In July 1986, Moore Medical moved to 389 Downey Drive, the address of company headquarters during the 1990s, and two years later acquired West-Ward Pharmaceutical Corporation. The acquisition of West-Ward Pharmaceutical, completed in January 1988, gave Moore Medical a generic drug manufacturing division, something new for the New Britain company.

Years had past since Moore Medical had relied on post cards and advertisements in trade journals to generate business. The company, like numerous other drug wholesalers, began to distribute catalogs delineating its product lines, thereby adopting the approach use by its competitors, but in one other respect Moore Medical was unlike many of its competitors. Typically, drug distributors were manufacturers as well, but for years Moore Medical did not possess any pharmaceutical production capabilities. The acquisition of West-Ward Pharmaceutical Corp. gave the company manufacturing capabilities, but Moore Medical did not hold on to the generic drug manufacturer for long. Its divestiture marked the beginning of a new strategy for Moore Medical during the 1990s, signaling the start of a period in the company's history that moved the drug distributor and marketer toward products with higher profit yields.

New Strategy Adopted during the 1990s

West-Ward Pharmaceutical was sold in 1991, a year that saw Moore Medical change its market approach and adopt a new strategy to carry the company through the 1990s. For years Moore Medical's management had focused its efforts on increasing the company's market share, a strategy that at times meant sacrificing profitability. Concurrent with the sale of West-Ward Pharmaceutical, this strategy was abandoned, as management revised its pricing policies and began to shape the

company into a distributor whose hallmark qualities were low prices and quality service. Specifically, the company became less aggressive about competing in the brand name pharmaceutical market, where Moore Medical had first fought for business during the late 1940s. Despite its link to Moore Medical's first days as an enterprise, the brand name pharmaceutical business offered low profit margins to competitors during the early 1990s, something the company's management was intent on avoiding in the new decade ahead.

For the 1990s, management instead concentrated its efforts on higher-profit-margin generic drugs and the expansion of its medical and surgical supply business. The new approach meant lost sales, but increased profits, a function of Moore Medical's strategy for the 1990s that was borne out in the financial figures posted by the company during the first half of the decade. Between 1990 and 1995, annual sales dipped from $306 million to $289 million, recording a six percent slip. The company's net income during the first five years of the 1990s, on the other hand, increased exponentially, rising from $645,000 to $2.3 million in 1995, a 260 percent leap.

In retrospect, the financial totals recorded between 1990 and 1995 pointed to the validity of the new strategy embraced in 1991. The intervening years, however, told the tale of Moore Medical's progress with its new plan before industry analysts could point to the five-year financial figures. With its hopes on expanding its medical and surgical supply business and its generic pharmaceutical business, Moore Medical's management moved forward in 1991 endeavoring to improve the company's marketing and distribution systems. A new distribution facility in Visalia, California, opened in March 1992, replacing the company's outmoded warehouse in Hayward, California, which was half the size of the new Visalia building. Further additions to the company's distribution center network were in the offing as Moore Medical restructured itself for the coming years, tailoring its operations and marketing approach to reflect the changing focus of its business.

In 1993, Moore Medical divided its customer base into three groups: independent pharmacies, pharmacy chains and specialty retailers, and health-care professionals working in non-hospital settings. By this point the company sold more than 12,000 products to 66,000 customers and derived its revenue from the sale of generic pharmaceuticals, medical and surgical supplies, and brand name pharmaceuticals. To generate business, Moore Medical marketed its products through a small field sales force, catalogs, and telemarketing. Although two years earlier the company had decided to put less effort into developing its brand name pharmaceutical products, Moore Medical had by no means abandoned the business. Brand name pharmaceuticals continued to contribute substantially to the company's bottom line, but the future rested on the growth of the prescription generic drugs sold under the ''Moore'' label and the over-the-counter prescription generic drugs packaged by manufacturers under the ''Valumed'' trademark.

The expansion of Moore Medical's medical and surgical supplies business also figured heavily into the company's future. With a product line that included disposable products, diagnostic tests, instruments, and rehabilitation equipment, and everything from hospital gowns and bandages to stethoscopes and latex gloves, Moore Medical's medical and surgical supplies business was a much-used source for professional health-care practitioners across the country. The company had been involved in this field for roughly 20 years by the 1990s, but during much of that time the sale of medical and surgical supplies represented a small percentage of Moore Medical's total sales. In 1990, for instance, medical and surgical supplies sales contributed only slightly more than 10 percent of Moore Medical's revenue volume for the year, a percentage that the company's management hoped to increase in the years ahead. Toward this goal the company achieved considerable success, as more resources were funnelled into the medical and surgical supplies segment of Moore Medical's operations. In 1995, the sale of medical and surgical supplies ranked as one of Moore Medical's most important businesses, accounting for more than one-fifth of total revenue volume for the year.

By the mid-1990s, the changes initiated in 1991 had delivered their desired effect, but further changes were still to come as Moore Medical sought to position itself for the future ahead. A new, 60,000-square-foot distribution center was opened in Jacksonville, Florida, in March 1995, an addition that improved the company's service in the Southeast. Later in the year, management reorganized Moore Medical's operations into eight business units, each concentrated on a particular market type. Five of the new business units created during the latter half of 1995 were structured to serve markets that addressed professional practitioners administering health care. The remaining three units were charged with marketing products that were purchased for resale.

By this point, nearly 50 years into its corporate existence, Moore Medical ranked as a leading, national distributor of medical and pharmaceutical supplies, its high industry standing owing to an effective combination of competitive pricing and helpful service. During the mid-1990s, Moore Medical was focused on the markets that were expected to yield the highest profits and selling and distributing health-care products to more than 20 targeted customer groups. By 1995, the company was selling 13,000 products to roughly 90,000 customers and marketing its pharmaceutical and medical/surgical supplies through the conventional industry methods. The company continued to rely on a small field sales force, two telemarketing centers in Connecticut and California, and catalogs, but as the late 1990s neared Moore Medical adopted a new marketing approach.

In 1996, after one year of development, Moore Medical began shipping CD-ROM and diskette versions of its 350-page, full-color catalogs. Shipments of the CD-ROM and diskette versions of Moore Medical's catalogs began in July, with both formats featuring an on-line ordering system that confirmed inventory and pricing 24 hours a day.

It was a move that firmly positioned Moore Medical as a company responsive to the needs of its customers. Mark Karp, the president and chief executive officer of Moore Medical at the time, noted as much, describing the technological changes that had affected the company's clientele. "The PC," Karp said in July 1996, "is a central part of virtually every clinic, pharmacy, office, EMS organization or institution these days. . . . as more and more organizations move toward a paperless environment, Moore Medical wants to be 100 percent responsive to the health care market's need for simplification." With this focus on service and the company's intent on distributing high-profit-margin products characterizing its stance during the mid-1990s, Moore Medical charted its course past its 50th year of business and into the late 1990s.

Further Reading

Arnott, Nancy, "Moore Medical Corporation: Dispensing Service," *Sales & Marketing Management,* October 1994, p. 81.

Burck, Charles G., "Optel's (Mis)adventures in Liquid Crystals," *Fortune,* October 1973, p. 193.

"Moore Arranges Lease for $6.5 Million Medical Project," *Denver Business,* December–January 1990/1991, p. 20.

"Moore Medical Announces Second Quarter Results," *PR Newswire,* July 17, 1996, p. 71.

Moore Medical Corp. Annual Report, New Britain, Conn.: Moore Medical Corp., 1995.

"Moore Medical Introduces Electronic Catalog with On-Line Electronic Commerce System," *PR Newswire,* July 29, 1996, p. 72.

Salmon, Kenneth S., "Moore Medical Corp.," *CL King & Associates,* April 14, 1993, p. 1.

Schneider, Stephen I., "Moore Medical Corp.," *Stifel, Nicolaus & Company, Incorporated,* May 4, 1995, p. 1.

Spangle, Peter, "Origins of Moore Medical Corp.," *The Manifest,* November 1987, p. 1.

—Jeffrey L. Covell

Mothercare UK Ltd.

Cherry Tree Road
Watford, Hertfordshire WD2 5SH
England
(44) 1 923 33577
Fax: (44) 1 923 816733

Wholly Owned Subsidiary of Storehouse PLC
Incorporated: 1972
Employees: 2,300
Sales: £306.2 million (1995 est.)
SICs: 5641 Retailer of Maternity Wear & Children's
Apparel

With more than 370 stores throughout Great Britain, Europe, and the Middle East and Asia, Mothercare UK Ltd. is Britain's largest retailer of clothing and accessories for mothers and their young children. Along with BHS (formerly British Home Stores), Mothercare is the second major component of the Storehouse PLC retail group. An independent operation until late 1981, this unique retailer's profits peaked in 1980 and only began to approach a full recovery in the mid-1990s.

Creation and Development

Mothercare founder Selim Zilkha was born and educated in the United States and served in the U.S. armed forces during World War II. Descended from an affluent banking family, Zilkha began to seek alternate business interests in Britain during the late 1950s. After touring France's Prenatal shops, he sought to import the concept of a one-stop maternity and infant store to Great Britain. Moving quickly, Zilkha assembled a group of investors to acquire the 10-store Lewis and Burrows nursery furniture chain. Zilkha converted a section of one of these stores to a "mother-to-be-and-baby department" and hired several buyers to choose merchandise. The experiment, which lost £180,000 over a two-year period, was later characterized as "a complete fiasco."

Zilkha sold the chain in 1960 but did not give up on the concept. Before the year was out, he acquired the 50-store W. J.

Harris chain, which sold very traditional baby carriages and nursery furniture. He shuttered half the stores, changed the chain's name to Mothercare, and revamped its merchandise to offer "everything for the mother-to-be and her baby under five." This one-stop concept included modestly priced maternity apparel, infant and children's wear, furniture, strollers, and even baby food. Zilkha also hired Prenatal's M. Mazard as an adviser but was still unable to mirror the French chain's success.

In 1963, the frustrated banker-turned-retailer invited an acquaintance, Barney Goodman, to join him in the business. The move proved a catalyst for success. The partners split the corporate responsibilities with special concentration on personnel, merchandising and distribution. Their "systems-based" management scheme included the adoption of a computerized ordering and distribution system as early as 1964. This highly efficient centralized purchasing program helped give Mothercare more purchasing power than the independent boutiques that constituted most of its competition. These controls in turn allowed the budding chain to offer its goods at lower prices while maintaining high profit margins.

After going public in 1972, Mothercare enjoyed several years of growth and prosperity. Barty Phillips, author of *Conran and the Habitat Story,* characterized the company as "one of the very few British firms who have had the courage to go into Europe and the determination to make it work." International expansion started in 1968, when Mothercare launched its first location in Denmark. Over the course of the next nine years, it established operations in Switzerland, Norway, Germany, Austria, Holland, and Belgium. Mothercare acquired an American maternity apparel chain in 1976 and converted it to the British format the following year. The chain expanded from 139 stores to 417 by 1981, and pre-tax profits multiplied from £3 million in 1972 to £22.3 million in the fiscal year ended March 1980.

Merger with Habitat

The magic began to wear off in the early 1980s, however: pre-tax profits slid nearly 19 percent to £18.1 million in fiscal 1981. Several factors induced the decline. Although the American operation had expanded to nearly 200 stores by the early 1980s, it had yet to achieve consistent profitability. At the same time, Mothercare allowed its image to erode. Instead of going upmarket, the chain tried to compete on price with bargain outlets like Woolworth's, Boots and Littlewoods. Stores and merchandise were characterized as "dull" and "clinical." Gary Warnaby, writing for the *International Journal of Retail & Distribution Management* in 1993, also noted that "Selim Zilkha seemed to have lost interest in the company."

Whatever the causes, in 1981 Zilkha and Goodman sold their 423-store Mothercare chain to Habitat PLC, a 52-unit home furnishings chain founded by Terence Conran. The leveraged buy out cost tiny Habitat £50 million (US$239 million). Barney Goodman, who had moved to the United States to launch operations there, returned to Great Britain to help smooth the transition.

Although Habitat was only one-third the size of Mothercare, it had cultivated a much more upscale image. Both chains had originated in the early 1960s. Habitat's moderately-priced, own-design furniture was a British decorating phenomenon—Conran was even knighted "for services to British design and industry." The charismatic designer hoped to imbue Mothercare with Habitat's cachet while maintaining its much-heralded back-office strengths. Habitat, in turn, would use Mothercare's established operations in 10 countries as jumping-off points for its own internationalization. Over the ensuing 18 months, Conran undertook a gradual, subtle revamp of the Mothercare stores and merchandise that culminated in a mid-1983 relaunch featuring a new catalog and gala fashion show. Habitat/Mothercare's first year together appeared a success; profits of £19 million seemed to bode well for the coming decade.

Mothercare was the first in a series of acquisitions that expanded Habitat from a strictly British chain with about £67.2 million in annual revenues to an international retail empire with over £1 billion by 1986. Habitat/Mothercare PLC capped its growth spurt with the 1986 acquisition of British Home Stores, a troubled 130-unit department store chain. Conran hoped that he could do for British Home Stores what he had done for Mothercare: infuse the "dowdy" chain with Habitat's marketing and design savvy.

A new holding company, Storehouse PLC, was formed with Conran as chairman and CEO. Mothercare was one of seven chains in the group, which boasted more than six million square feet of selling space. Over the next three years, Storehouse attempted to reposition British Home Stores, but a serious retail downturn in the late 1980s thwarted the turnaround. By mid-1987, the conglomeration appeared to have failed so miserably that even Conran flirted with breaking up the retail group. The October 1987 stock market crash and two takeover attempts brought an end to Conran's career at Storehouse in 1988. Group pre-tax profits plunged from about £130 million in 1987 to £11.3 million in 1989.

Mothercare struggled unsuccessfully to regain its former glory during this turbulent period. A 1988 attempt to adopt barcode scanning backfired and resulted in what *Marketing* magazine's Suzanne Bidlake called "a stock replenishment and customer service fiasco." Competitors took advantage of the corporate confusion: by 1992, Britain's Adams chain had grown to within 14 stores of Mothercare's 254 domestic units, and department stores like Woolworth's, C&A, and Marks &

Spencer expanded their maternity and children's offerings as well as their market shares. While the Storehouse subsidiary maintained dominant stakes in the British maternity wear and nursery equipment markets, it fell to third in infants' and children's wear by the end of 1992.

At the end of the 1980s, Storehouse executives decided to limit their efforts to Mothercare UK and British Home Stores (subsequently renamed BHS). Having spun off most of its smaller chains (including Habitat), Storehouse sold Mothercare Stores, Inc., the U.S. arm of its maternity chain, to American investment company Bain Capital Inc. in 1991. The £7.5 million (US$13.5 million) loss on the transaction contributed significantly to Mothercare's £3.9 million pre-tax loss on the fiscal year ended March 28, 1992.

Turnaround Gains Momentum in the Early 1990s

Backed by an economic upswing, Mothercare's turnaround proceeded gradually under the direction of a succession of CEOs over the ensuing years. Derek Lovelock replaced exiting chief Peter James in 1990. Lovelock emphasized international growth (excluding the United States) via franchising. In 1992, he hired marketing specialist Patricia Manning away from competitor Woolworth's in an effort to boost Mothercare's market share. Marketing strategies in the early 1990s included cross-brand promotions and point-of-sale displays.

Lovelock led the subsidiary until mid-year, when American Ann Iverson was hired away from Bonwit Teller. Iverson stepped up the pace of the reorganization, leading the first full-scale revamp of Mothercare's store concept in nearly 20 years. The new store layout featured a park-like setting complete with lampposts and talking trees. Many locations were enlarged, and the variety of products was scaled back. In 1993, Iverson told *WWD*'s James Fallon that "In trying to offer everything, we offered too much." By the end of 1995, 127 of Mothercare's stores had been converted to the new format. A new advertising campaign featuring television, print, and outdoor media helped promote the changes.

Iverson's cost-cutting efforts, which included a reduction of middle management, began to bear fruit in the mid-1990s. In a press release summarizing the first six months of fiscal 1995 (ended October 14, 1995), Storehouse chairman Ian Hay Davidson called Mothercare's performance "particularly pleasing." Same store sales had increased two percent year-over-year, and pre-tax profits nearly doubled. The company expected to achieve a net of £17 million on the year, nearing its 1980 record of £22 million. In an apparent show of confidence, Storehouse announced its plan to acquire Boots Company PLC's Children's World for £62.5 million (US$95.8 million).

Although the chain had, in the words of Verdict Research's Hilary Monk, "lost a lot of credibility" over the course of its decade-long decline, a Mothercare executive asserted that "No one has such a strong brand name in kids as we do." It remained to be seen whether that trademark would regain its market dominance in the mid-1990s.

Further Reading

Bidlake, Suzanne, "City Jitters Persist in Wake of Storehouse Loss," *Marketing*, June 8, 1989, p. 13.

——, "Mothercare in Global Push," *Marketing,* February 8, 1990, p. 1

——, "Rebirth for Mothercare?" *Marketing,* March 5, 1992, p. 2.

Fallon, James, "Bain Capital Acquires Mothercare for $11M," *WWD,* March 20, 1991, p. 12.

——, "The Nurturing of Mothercare: A Fun Conception," *WWD,* February 16, 1993, p. 12.

Ferry, Jeffrey, "Broken by the Bottom Line," *Forbes,* November 1989, p. 180.

"Homing in on Mums," *Marketing,* March 15, 1990, p. 13.

Lebow, Joan, "Conran's Sibling Targets Moms and Kids," *Crain's New York Business,* November 17, 1986, p. 6.

Phillips, Barty, *Conran and the Habitat Story,* London: Weidenfeld and Nicolson, 1984, pp. 108–116.

Robins, Gary, "Downsizing Trims Cost at Mothercare," *Stores,* October 1991, p. 28.

Robinson, Jeffrey, "A Touch of Class; It's Paid Off for Habitat-Mothercare," *Barron's,* December 3, 1984, pp. 68–69.

Smith, Geoffrey N., "Another Try," *Forbes,* August 11, 1986, p. 112.

" 'Storehouse PLC' Born of UK Retailers' Merger," *Daily News Record,* January 8, 1986, p. 17.

Warnaby, Gary, "Storehouse," *International Journal of Retail & Distribution Management,* May–June 1993, pp. 27–34.

Whelan, Sean, "Battered Storehouse Tightens Up Its Act," *Marketing,* December 8, 1988, pp. 13–16.

—April Dougal Gasbarre

Movie Star Inc.

136 Madison Avenue
New York, New York 10016
U.S.A.
(212) 679-7260
Fax: (212) 684-3295

Public Company
Incorporated: 1935 as Industrial Undergarment Corp.
Sales: $102 million (1995)
Employees: 2,300
Stock Exchanges: American
SICs: 2339 Women's, Misses' & Juniors' Outerwear, Not Elsewhere Classified; 2341 Women's, Misses', Children's and Infants' Underwear & Nightwear; 2384 Robes & Dressing Gowns; 5621 Women's Clothing Stores

The company incorporated in 1935 as Industrial Undergarment Corp. went through two name changes and two mergers before adopting the name of one of its merged partners, Movie Star Inc. Movie Star, in the 1990s, specialized in the design, manufacture, marketing, and sale of an extensive line of ladies' sleepwear, robes, leisurewear, loungewear, panties, and daywear. It also operated a chain of 25 retail outlet stores in Mississippi and Georgia. When the company hit a rough patch in the mid-1990s and lost a substantial amount of money, it restructured its operations and discontinued its men's work- and leisure-shirt product line.

Stardust Inc., 1968–1981

Incorporated in 1935, Industrial Undergarment Corp. was one of many small firms in New York City's garment district. Its change of name to Stardust Inc. in 1946 presumably reflected a conversion to women's intimate apparel. By 1968, when the company went public, it was designing, manufacturing, and selling a diversified line of popularly priced women's daywear and nightwear lingerie. Stardust's subsidiaries at that time, all

wholly owned, were Hazlehurst Manufacturing, Starcrest, Helen of Troy, Orocovis Manufacturing, and Orocovis Embroidery. It operated facilities in New York, Georgia, California, Miami, and Puerto Rico with a total of 255,000 square feet of space, of which 63,000 square feet were leased. Lewis Ratner was president of the company, which employed 1,100 people.

Stardust had sales of $14.4 million in the fiscal year ended June 29, 1968, $14.9 million in the fiscal year ended June 28, 1969, and $15 million in the fiscal year ended June 27, 1970. Net income was $734,771, $637,712 and $740,546, respectively. Long-term debt was $9.3 million in the latter year. Sales and profits continued at this general level through fiscal 1974, although dividends ceased after 1972. In 1975 Stardust's sales plunged to $11.9 million, and it suffered the first of five losing years through 1980. By that year the company had disposed of its California, Miami, and Puerto Rican facilities and had closed one of its three Georgia factories.

In 1981 Stardust merged with Sanmark Industries, Inc., a private New York company with two Pennsylvania factories and nearly the same markets and manufacturing methods as Stardust. The exchange of 15 shares of Stardust stock for one share of Sanmark stock left Sanmark stockholders with 79 percent of the consolidated company. The David family held about two-thirds of the stock, and Abraham David, previously head of Sanmark, became chairman and president of the resulting Sanmark-Stardust, Inc.

Sanmark-Stardust, 1981–1992

Sanmark-Stardust was in appreciably better financial shape than Stardust. In fiscal 1980, just prior to the merger, Sanmark had $13.6 million in sales, compared to $11.3 million for Stardust, and net income of $910,000, compared to Stardust's net loss of $656,000. Under a program of aggressive expansion, the sales volume of the consolidated company grew from $27.1 million in fiscal 1981 to $60.6 million in fiscal 1987. Net income, $919,000 in 1981, rose as high as $2.8 million in 1986. The company declared stock dividends in 1981, 1983, and 1985.

Sanmark-Stardust opened the Anne Leslie division in 1983 for the manufacture of robes and leisurewear and added a manufacturing plant in Lebanon, Virginia, the following year. In 1985 it acquired Claxton Manufacturing Co. of Claxton, Georgia, a panties maker, for about $7 million, and in 1987 it bought the major assets of Fountain Manufacturing Corp., a manufacturer of children's jeans and other clothing for infants and toddlers, for $1.2 million. Sanmark-Stardust also bought Mark Trouser, Inc., in 1987, a privately held manufacturer whose products were being sold in better-priced department stores and specialty shops. Mark Trouser's main brands were Cuteslumber, a line of infants' and toddlers' overalls, shortalls, jumpers, tops, slacks, and jeans; Pure Gold 13 boys' fashion jeans and casual wear; and Mark of Fifth Avenue boys' dress slacks.

In November 1987 Sanmark-Stardust bought a 64.5-percent interest in Movie Star, Inc. for $8 a share and began an $8-a-share tender offer for the remaining shares. The selling shareholders of Movie Star, which like Sanmark-Stardust was an intimate-apparel company, were primarily the family of the company's founder—the late Milton Herman, including Irwin Goldberger, the chairman and Herman's son-in-law, and Goldberger's two sons—and other members of management. Two months later, when the offer expired, Sanmark-Stardust reported that it had purchased about 97 percent of Movie Star's outstanding shares, at a total cost of $6.7 million.

This acquisition further broadened Sanmark-Stardust's scope. Movie Star, incorporated in 1946, was producing, in addition to women's sleepwear, daywear, and loungewear under the brand names Movie Star, Cinema Etoile, and Cine Star, a line of men's work and leisure shirts in its Irwin B. Schwabe division. By 1986 it had facilities in New York, six southern states, and Puerto Rico, plus 26 factory outlet stores. Its sales grew to $77 million in fiscal 1985, when its net income was $774,000, but it lost $2 million in fiscal 1986.

The newly consolidated company now had 20 factories manufacturing most of its products. It lost $1.8 million on sales of $96.2 million in fiscal 1988 but earned $4.8 million on sales of $126.6 million in fiscal 1989 and declared a five-for-three stock split. During the next three fiscal years, net sales ranged between $117.7 million and $124.7 million, while net income ranged between $289,000 and $1.2 million. No dividends were declared after 1988.

Sanmark-Stardust's rapid expansion had brought its long-term debt up to $28 million, and, in the soft economy of the early 1990s, it found it had no choice but to retrench. Six factories, including both remaining Georgia plants, were closed between 1990 and 1992, and additional downsizing measures followed.

Movie Star, 1993–1995

Sanmark-Stardust changed its name to Movie Star at the start of 1993. At the end of fiscal year 1993 (ending June 30, 1993) Movie Star sold its children's ready-to-wear division to the manager of that division and others. Fiscal 1993 was a good year for Movie Star, with net income of $2.3 million on net sales of $120.3 million. Nearly $1 million of the profit came, how-

ever, from the sale of plant facilities. To combat certain unfavorable trends in retailing, which the company cited as "inventory tightening, chain consolidation, and pricing pressure," Movie Star consolidated its eight divisions into four and streamlined its manufacturing. The consolidated divisions were Cinema Etoile for better-price sleepwear, loungewear, and daywear; the Sanmark Group for similar innerwear categories at moderate prices and aimed at the mass market; Movie Star outlet stores; and Irwin B. Schwabe, the division for men's work and leisure shirts.

In fiscal 1994 Movie Star's net sales dropped to $103.1 million, and the company sustained a loss of $4.2 million. This figure chiefly reflected a $3.8-million charge taken for inventory markdown. During the calendar year the company restructured its Sanmark division, focusing entirely on larger, higher-margin private-label customers representing national and regional chains. This division formerly also had sold its products to mass merchants and lower-margin smaller accounts. The change in operations reduced inventory by more than $7 million. In fiscal 1995 the company closed the Taiwan office it had established in 1985 for a new international division and transferred the responsibility for monitoring the quality and progress of manufacturing of finished products purchased in the Far East to independent agents in the countries of manufacture.

Despite these economy measures, in fiscal 1995 Movie Star's sales not only dropped to $102 million, its loss widened to $5 million. In September 1995 the company announced that it would discontinue the Schwabe division because of inadequate return on capital and would take a special charge to reflect the writedown of assets tied to the men's-shirt business. Accordingly, it closed three shirt manufacturing plants in northern Mississippi and liquidated Schwabe's other assets. This division had sales of $20 million in fiscal 1995, about half to one customer.

During fiscal 1996 Movie Star took other steps to restructure its operations. It consolidated its facilities, outsourced product from foreign manufacturers, and wrote down inventories. A new chief executive officer, Barbara Khouri, appointed in August 1995, concentrated on cutting costs and emphasizing Movie Star's original and higher-margin products. She resigned eight months later, saying she had finished the task she set out to do, and was succeeded by Mark M. David, who had held the job before her.

Movie Star felt confident enough in its future, however, to open a new apparel division, SunWorks, in 1995. SunWorks was to focus on novelty apparel items with designs that when, exposed to sunlight, would appear in vivid colors. The first offerings in this line were to be T-shirts, followed by sweatshirts and baseball caps. By mid 1996 SunWorks T-shirts were selling nationally in over 700 stores. Movie Star also formed a partnership with GSR, Inc. to market the patent-pending process under the company name of SunMax and, with GSR, granted a license to Guilford Mills of North Carolina, the world's largest warp knitter, to print fabrics with the SunMax technology.

Movie Star continued in the red during the first half of fiscal 1996 (the second half of calendar 1995). It lost $2.3 million on sales of $57.6 million over this six-month period and, in April 1996, had to negotiate a deal to avoid default on its debentures. Long-term debt was $22.5 million in September 1995. Total assets were $57.2 million at the end of fiscal 1995.

Movie Star's Operations in 1995

In 1995 Movie Star was selling an extensive line of women's intimate apparel, including sleepwear, robes, leisurewear, loungewear, panties, and daywear to discount, specialty, national and regional chains, mass merchandise and department stores, and direct-mail catalog marketers throughout the United States at prices ranging from $2 to $70. It also operated 25 retail outlets. National chains and mass merchandisers accounted for some 45 percent of sales, with Sears, Roebuck and Co. alone accounting for 22 percent, of which more than half were men's work and leisure shirts. Sales of the company's own manufactured goods accounted for 30 percent of the sales volume of the retail outlet stores, operating under the name Movie Star Factory Outlets, at discounted prices. These sales accounted for less than 10 percent of the company's total revenues.

At the end of fiscal 1995 Movie Star owned manufacturing facilities in Petersburg, Pennsylvania; Lebanon and Honaker, Virginia; and two plants in Mississippi. It also owned a warehouse and distribution center on the Petersburg and Lebanon sites and vacant properties in Hazlehurst, Georgia, and Evansville, Indiana. It was leasing a manufacturing plant in Puerto Rico, five warehouses in Mississippi, its headquarters in New York City, and its 25 retail stores in Mississippi and Georgia. By the end of the fiscal year Movie Star had closed nine manufacturing plants in five years in an effort to lower its costs.

About four percent of its raw materials and 14 percent of its finished goods were imported, and about seven percent of its finished goods were assembled in the Caribbean and Central America during the fiscal year.

Mark M. David, chairman and chief executive officer of Movie Star, was also the chief stockholder in 1995, with almost 21 percent of the shares. Mrs. Abraham David held nearly 12 percent, and an employee plan held more than 10 percent.

Principal Subsidiaries

Cuteslumber Inc.; P.J. San Sebastian, Inc.

Principal Operating Units

Cinema Etoile; Movie Star Factory; Sanmark; SunWorks.

Further Reading

Gladfelter, Elizabeth, "Movie Star Draws on Power of Sun to Launch New Color Change Apparel Division," *WWD*, July 17, 1996, p. 27.
Monget, Karyn, "Khouri Quits as Movie Star CEO," *WWD*, April 19, 1996, p. 5.
"Movie Star Ends Men's Shirts," *WWD*, September 11, 1995, p. 8.
"Movie Star's Losses Down in Period; Yearly Profits Up," *WWD*, September 30, 1993, p. 6.
"Sanmark Buys Kids' Firm," *WWD*, June 25, 1987, p. 8.
"Sanmark-Stardust Now Holds 97% of Movie Star's Shares," *Daily News Record*, January 29, 1988, p. 5.

—Robert Halasz

Neutrogena®

Neutrogena Corporation

5760 West 96th Street
Los Angeles, California 90045
U.S.A.
(310) 642-1150
Fax: (310) 337-5537

Wholly Owned Subsidiary of Johnson & Johnson
Incorporated: 1962
Employees: 670
Sales: $281.70 million (1993)
SICs: 2844 Toilet Preparations; 2841 Soap & Other
   Detergents

An independent company until its 1994 acquisition by Johnson & Johnson, Neutrogena Corporation manufactures and markets a line of premium-priced skin and hair care products that are distributed in more than 70 countries. The company is especially known for its innovative niche marketing and its leading product, the clear, clean-smelling glycerine soap bar that established its role as a pioneer in the skin care arena.

Company Foundations, 1930–60

Headquartered in Los Angeles, California, the company was founded by Emanuel Stolaroff in 1930. In its early years, the company name was Natone, and its function was to supply specialty cosmetics to beauty salons related to the Hollywood film industry. Expansion began in the 1940s, when Natone spread its manufacturing and distribution of cosmetics to the larger retail market.

A 1954 business trip to Europe inspired Stolaroff to follow a new product direction that would chart the future course of Natone's operations. Belgian cosmetic chemist Dr. Edmond Fromont had developed a new soap which rinsed quickly and easily, leaving no soap residue. In fact, eleven minutes after washing with Fromont's soap—just one minute longer than with pure water—a person's skin pH would return to normal. This unique soap was called "Neutrogena." Believing that Fromont's

soap would be well received by the U.S. market, Stolaroff made arrangements to import and distribute it in the United States. Early marketing plans emphasized the soap's transparency and targeted department stores and drug stores as sales venues.

Instrumental in the design of the first marketing strategies for the Neutrogena soap was Lloyd Cotsen. A former archaeologist with a history degree from Princeton, Cotsen married Stolaroff's daughter, Joanne Stolaroff, in 1953, and then went to Harvard for his M.B.A. Beginning in 1957, he became an integral and personally invested player in the family business (he retained ownership of approximately half of Neutrogena's stock until the company's 1994 acquisition). In fact, Cotsen's strategies made the soap such an important aspect of Natone's business that in 1962 the company name was officially changed to Neutrogena Corporation. In 1967 Cotsen became president of the company. Neutrogena's sales in that year were approximately $3 million, with the major product being the glycerine soap.

Niche Marketing Strategy, 1960s

Soon after his presidency began, Cotsen created the niche marketing strategy that would shape the success of Neutrogena for almost three decades. According to *Business Week,* Cotsen's motto has always been: "I'm not that smart, and I don't like competition." Priced midway between soaps like Ivory and Clinique, and positioned between elite skin-care products and mundane toiletries, Neutrogena was safe from competitive price wars waged by bigger companies for most of the company's history. Cotsen kept credibility high and marketing costs low (12 percent of sales in 1981, as compared to 20 percent at Clinique) by promoting Neutrogena soap through the cultivation of relationships with two institutions: dermatologists and luxury hotels. Free samples left in dermatologists' offices and repeated visits each year led to Neutrogena's unrivaled success in the soap market. As of 1981, a dedicated force, comprising 16 out of 66 salespersons, was assigned the sole responsibility of visiting 5,000 dermatologists each year, developing personal relationships with advocates in the profession. Similarly, one-ounce bars of Neutrogena were distributed to luxury hotels and resorts, where—Cotsen theorized—businessmen's wives would be likely to see them. Cotsen insisted that the mini-bars of Neutro-

While continuing the Neutrogena past formula for success, the company will head in new strategic directions using the vast resources of Johnson & Johnson to help further distinguish itself as a world class organization. Neutrogena's vision is: 1) to become the worldwide leader of consumer products recommended by medical professionals and recognized by consumers as providing real improvements in the health and beauty of skin and hair; and 2) to be widely available and command a premium price due to the originality, quality, and credibility of Neutrogena's product formulations and positioning.

gena retain the company name and logo, promoting name recognition along with the soap's unmistakable look and smell.

Similarly, Cotsen targeted book-review readers rather than comics-readers as his primary market, and shunned supermarket sales for years. Drugstores comprised the primary sales venue, sideskirting the problem of competition with mass-produced brands and stressing the high quality of the product. In 1966 Neutrogena was one of eleven companies named in a lawsuit by two wholesale drug companies, H. L. Moore Drug Exchange and Hyman Boxer, alleging that the refusal of Neutrogena and other companies to sell to the plaintiffs led to the elimination of price competition.

During the 1970s, the company began to explore marketing and research efforts to expand its skin care product line. Promotions for Neutrogena's new acne cleansing soap in teen publications offered a free trial-size bar. The ads proclaimed, "If you have acne, we need your help," and Neutrogena asked teens to send a quarter (to cover handling) and to give the company honest answers about the success of the soap. Over 57,000 teenagers sent in their quarters, constituting the highest response in the company's history, and a newly penetrated market. In 1973 the company went public, with a market value of $11 million. By 1980, Neutrogena entered hair care with a new product, and acne preparations soon followed.

Tragedy and controversy linked to the family business befell Neutrogena's president, Lloyd Cotsen. In 1979, while Cotsen was in New York on a business trip, his wife, son, and a young house guest were murdered in the family's Beverly Hills home. An investigation by Beverly Hills police pointed to the guilt of the Belgian businessman who had originally sold the Neutrogena rights to Emanuel Stolaroff. Stolaroff and the Belgian rival were involved in litigation, and the police contended that Lloyd Cotsen was the intended target of the murderer. The Belgian committed suicide shortly before his scheduled interview by detectives, leaving the crime unsolved. Cotsen remarried in 1981, to Jacqueline Brandwynne, a New York consultant. In 1992 Brandwynne sued Cotsen for divorce and $1.5 million, claiming that he had convinced her to quit her $150,000 a year job in New York on the condition that she would be paid in an equivalent number of Neutrogena shares each year. In return, she helped to formulate Neutrogena's success strategies. According to Brandwynne, the

Neutrogena shares never materialized during the ten years of her marriage to Lloyd Cotsen.

Dramatic Growth, 1970 and 1980s

Between 1973 and 1980, sales leaped by 339 percent to $29 million, and earnings grew 190 percent to $2 million. Between 1975 and 1980, return on equity averaged 21 percent, and the company distinguished itself by remaining debt-free. Neutrogena was featured in *Forbes*'s 1979 "Up & Comers" class (the first year the magazine published such a list).

However, when the 1980s began, it appeared that Neutrogena might have drifted too far from the job it always had done best—niche marketing of its trademark soap. The company introduced new soap categories that may have confused consumers—"normal to oily" and "normal to dry"—resulting in a ten percent decrease in sales in 1981. The company heeded the warning and returned to its previous packaging and promotional strategies: changing the soap categories back to their original "dry skin formula" and "acne cleansing formula;" reviving 12- to 18-month advance planning of promotions and presentations to lock Neutrogena into retailers' schedules; returning to the practice of underselling merchandise to avoid overstock on shelves; and bolstering the dermatology sales force (now serviced by 19 salespersons) by increasing the number of samples left in doctors' offices. Back-to-basics marketing paid off for the company: profits rose 15 percent in 1982, reaching the $3 million mark, with total sales of $39 million (a 19 percent increase over fiscal year 1981), including a 28 percent leap in formerly flagging soap sales. In 1982 Lloyd Cotsen was named CEO.

Neutrogena's subsequent performance in the 1980s was brilliant. Between 1981 and 1986, the company's annual profit growth averaged 22.5 percent, with an exceedingly high 32 percent average annual return on equity. Between 1983 and 1988, Neutrogena stock demonstrated a phenomenal burst from $3 to $44. The trademark soap represented over a third of the company's $75 million annual revenues in 1985.

Aging baby boomers seemed to provide the ticket to the future for Neutrogena's marketing teams in the 1980s. Skin dries with age, and by 1989 the skin care market would burgeon to $1.5 billion. Research efforts in the 1980s thus were directed to the development of creams, lotions, moisturizers, and a liver-spot cream. Sideline efforts included the loan of a Neutrogena chemist (on moonlighting hours) to Gus Blythe, founder and CEO of the SecondWind company. The Neutrogena chemist helped Blythe create a cleaning and deodorizing formula for shoes that is not harmful to shoes or skin.

Other efforts, specifically the launching of an expensive skin-care line called "Origine Suisse System," proved unprofitable in early stages. Similarly, Neutrogena's shampoo, introduced in 1980, received a sluggish reception at first. The company demonstrated its characteristic "if it's broken let's fix it" marketing ingenuity, promoting the shampoo as a product to be used once every two weeks to remove the residue left by other shampoos. Shampoo sales grew 80 to 100 percent annually after this directional change, representing more than one-third of total sales in 1987.

When the stock market crashed in October 1987, Neutrogena was one of the last stocks to fall, and one of the quickest to recover. By April 1988, the stock was running at 31 times projected earnings of $1.05 a share for the previous fiscal year, and 1988 sales hit $179 million, with earnings as high as $23 million. With a 1989 market value of $570 million, Neutrogena had found a permanent place in *Forbes*'s "200 Best Small Companies." With a 33 percent average annual increase in net income since 1981, the only significant concern of investors was whether Neutrogena could grow fast enough to support multiple increases more typically associated with higher technology outfits than soap companies. Some speculators, fearing slowed growth, rid themselves of the company's stock. However, long-term holders had reasons to retain Neutrogena: in 1989, *Forbes* pointed out that a $10,000 investment in Neutrogena in 1979 would now be worth $286,000.

In October 1989, however, *Financial World* asked whether Neutrogena had already saturated its upscale markets, highlighting the difficulty of identifying more buyers without lowering prices or altering image. Having penetrated 85 percent of drugstore markets, and with control over 50 percent of the specialty soap market, Neutrogena was finally beginning to lose its middle-area niche. A sure marker of this change was the imitation of Neutrogena's products by large-scale competitors including Johnson & Johnson and Revlon. When quarterly earnings growth slid from an unsustainable 70 percent to 47 percent and then to 32 percent in the first three fiscal quarters of 1988 (and when stock dropped 5½ points after the third quarter announcement), Cotsen turned his attention to the broadening of Neutrogena's markets.

One way to achieve mass marketing would have been supermarket distribution, but Cotsen chose to forestall the placement of $2.25 Neutrogena bars next to 40-cent Ivory bars, instead electing to bolster proven areas. Advertising expenditures were increased from 15 percent of sales in 1981 to approximately 22 percent—twice the industry average—in 1988. Part of this increase was channeled into experimentation with television advertising. Another solution might have been a small acquisition, easy enough for the company to achieve with $15 million in the bank and no debt. Again, Cotsen instead chose to focus on the development of Neutrogena's own products. During the 1988 fiscal year, the company increased its introduction of new products, bringing out four instead of the more typical two, while simultaneously decreasing R&D expenses.

1989 was a difficult year amid company growing pains. Earnings of $26.7 million on sales of $203.2 million compared with earnings of $23 million on sales of $178.9 million from the previous year. A new product introduced in early 1990 was a shampoo and conditioner for hair with color and/or permanent treatment. At the close of fiscal year 1990, Neutrogena was forced to announce that fourth quarter earnings, at $3.2 million, would be 41 percent lower than the $5.4 million earnings of the previous year's final quarter, due to softness in sales of several products in September. Sales of a tinted moisturizer and a sun block were suspended due to quality concerns. However, the company maintained that the setback was more than offset by increased international sales.

In 1987 the company's foreign subsidiaries had lost $514,000. Cotsen returned to the roots of the company's unique soap in an effort to speed foreign expansion. The Belgian company from whom Cotsen's father-in-law had purchased the Neutrogena trademark also sold the name to firms all over the world. Cotsen began negotiations to purchase the trademark from these companies in Venezuela, Australia, New Zealand, and Scandinavia. French marketing executive Christian Bardin had been hired by Neutrogena in 1982 in order to boost international sales. Bardin devised a global strategy that worked. In fact, by 1992 over 20 percent of revenues ($231 million) were generated abroad, with international sales growing by 49 percent and international sales finally contributing to the company's $21 million in earnings. Bardin's strategy was to tailor promotions to the cultural preferences of each country. Bardin achieved considerable success in Latin American markets, where sales jumped from $0 to $2 million between 1990 and 1992. In Japan, however, blunders (including an uninformed distributor, inadequate research, and failure to introduce new products over time) led the company to fail. A surprise success was achieved in the Middle East, where ads—aimed at women whose skin is hidden under veils—revealed considerably less skin than those aimed at Western markets.

A major executive transition occurred in 1991. After 24 years as president of Neutrogena, Lloyd Cotsen stepped up to become chairman (a position that had remained vacant since founder Emanuel Stolaroff died in 1984). Moving into the slot of president and CEO was Allan H. Kurtzman, former president of Max Factor & Co.

Acne product sales were flat in 1992, but Neutrogena introduced a new product—Antiseptic Cleaning Pads for Acne-Prone Skin—in hopes that anticipated growth in the number of teenagers would spur the market. An additional market for the product was women in their 20s and 30s, who are known to suffer from acne more than their male contemporaries. In 1993 the company made a delayed entrance into the skincare market with a new Active Cleansing range (comprising facial wash, cleansing lotion, and toner). The launching of this new product gave Neutrogena a complete skincare range for the first time in the company's history.

Acquisition by Johnson & Johnson, 1994

Competitors continued to emulate Neutrogena, and in 1993 Wal-Mart stores released a premium private label brand to compete against Neutrogena's glycerine soap at a lower price. Consolidation and acquisition of small, family-owned companies like Neutrogena became a prominent phenomenon, with larger companies seeking strategic opportunities. In 1994, after a prolonged period of speculation regarding a potential buyout, Neutrogena was acquired by Johnson & Johnson, the world's largest health products company, with a $4.5 billion corner on the consumer products market, and a major competitor. Johnson & Johnson paid a premium of $924.1 million, and $35.25 cash for each Neutrogena share (a 63 percent premium over the market price). The acquisition united Neutrogena's skin care products with Johnson & Johnson's Baby Shampoo and Baby Oil, as well as Tylenol, Band-Aids, and Retin-A (an acne treatment). In addition, Johnson & Johnson's product research resources would now aid Neutrogena in its development of more sophisticated products, to compete with Oil of Olay and Avon. Finally, Johnson & Johnson's international expertise would help Neutrogena boost international sales, which still had not taken off at noticeable levels. Neutrogena is considered an autonomous member of the international network of Johnson & Johnson companies.

At the time of the company's sale, Lloyd Cotsen owned 9.87 million of the 25.7 million outstanding company shares. The *Los Angeles Times* estimated that he would personally receive $347.9 million before taxes from the transaction.

In 1996 Neutrogena's skin and hair care products were distributed in more than 70 countries around the world. Facial care products included the trademark Neutrogena cleansing bars, as well as several types of cleansers, toners, deep pore treatments, moisturizers, lotions, and acne treatments. Body care products included shower and bath gel, oil spray, body mist, lotion, emulsion, hand cream, and a variety of sun blocks and sunless tanning lotion and spray. Hair care products included shampoos and conditioners, hair spray, and antipruritic liquid to relieve itchy scalp. The company's acquisition by Johnson & Johnson will certainly begin a new chapter in its history, potentially bolstering international and research efforts. How Neutrogena will adapt its long-respected marketing techniques, family management style, and niche product development to its new role as a subsidiary of the largest health products company in the world remains to be seen.

Principal Subsidiaries

Neutrogena (Mexico); Neutrogena (England); Neutrogena (France); Neutrogena (Germany).

Further Reading

Barman, Sharon, "The Business of Beauty," *Working Woman,* April 1993, p. 82.

Benoit, Ellen, "The Family That Buys Families," *Financial World,* June 30, 1987, pp. 24–28.

Bradley, Sam, "Adbank's Brand Watch," *Brandweek,* September 5, 1994, p. 37.

Brower, Alison, "ADBANK's Brand Watch," *Brandweek,* February 28, 1994, p. 27.

——, "ADBANK's Brand Watch," *Brandweek,* May 3, 1993, p. 37.

Carson, Teresa, "In Personal Care, Small Can Be Beautiful," *Business Week,* No. 2950, Industrial/Technology Edition, June 9, 1986, pp. 96–97.

Cole, Jeff, "Neutrogena Corrects Earlier Statement, Discloses Talks with Potential Buyer," *Wall Street Journal,* August 11, 1994, p. A7(W), A6(E).

Davis, Donald A., "The Changing Face of the Cosmetic Industry," *Drug & Cosmetic Industry,* July 1992, pp. 8–16.

Dent, Harry S., Jr., "Branding Strategies," *Small Business Reports,* September 1990, pp. 62–66.

Eaton, Leslie, "Blind Faith," *Barron's,* May 17, 1993, pp. 41–42.

Freeman, Laurie, "In Zany Shampoo Arena, P&G Rebuffs Helene Curtis," *Advertising Age,* September 29, 1993, pp. 13–16.

Fuller, Doris A., "Neutrogena Sticks with Its Niche; Soap Maker's Sales, Profits Double in 5 Years," *Los Angeles Times,* June 11, 1985, p. 1.

Harris, Roy J., Jr., and Elyse Tanouye, "Johnson & Johnson to Buy Neutrogena in Bid to Boost Consumer-Products Unit," *Wall Street Journal,* August 23, 1994, pp. A3(W), A3(E).

Harris, William, "If I Have the Doctor," *Forbes,* March 30, 1981, pp. 63–64.

Heins, John, "Neutrogena Defends Its Turf," *Forbes,* June 26, 1989, pp. 80–88.

Holzinger, Albert G., "The Sweet Smell of, Well . . . ," *Nation's Business,* August 1988, p. 56.

Hoppe, Karen, "Neutrogena," *Drug & Cosmetic Industry,* February 1993, pp. 46–48.

"J&J Buys 98.6% of Neutrogena," *Wall Street Journal,* September 27, 1994, p. C22(W), C7(E).

Jaffe, Thomas, "Where Are They Now?", *Forbes,* September 12, 1994, p. 290.

"Johnson & Johnson to Buy Neutrogena for Over $900 Mil.," *Corporate Growth Report* (Weekly), September 5, 1994, p. 7424.

Lipman, Joanne, "Neutrogena Decision (Carlson & Partners and Atlas Citron Haligman & Bedecarre Win Accounts)," *Wall Street Journal,* January 7, 1992, p. B3(W), B6(E).

——, "Decision Expected (Neutrogena's Ad Account)," *Wall Street Journal,* January 6, 1992, p. B4(W), B4(E).

Lubman, Sarah, "Neutrogena's Chief Is Sued by His Wife (Jacqueline Brandwynne Cotsen; Lloyd E. Cotsen; Breach of Contract Lawsuit)," *Wall Street Journal,* February 28, 1992, p. B7B(W), B8A(E).

Meeks, Fleming, Steven Ramos, and Christopher Palmeri, "The 200 Best Small Companies in America: How to Tell an Eagle from an Icarus," *Forbes,* November 13, 1989, pp. 213–76.

"Neutrogena Corp. (Who's News)," *Wall Street Journal,* November 3, 1992, p. B12(W), B11(E).

"Neutrogena Corp. (Who's News)," *Wall Street Journal,* July 26, 1991, p. B4(W), B2(E).

"Neutrogena Estimates Results (Neutrogena Corp.)," *Wall Street Journal,* February 16, 1989, p. A2(W).

"Neutrogena Net Fell 41% in Its 4th Period as U.S. Sales Decline," *Wall Street Journal,* December 11, 1990, p. C9(W), C25(E).

"Neutrogena Sees the Way More Clearly," *S&MM,* January 17, 1983, pp. 22–23.

Olmos, David R., "Johnson & Johnson to Soak up Neutrogena; Health Products Company Will Pay a Premium Price to Expand Its Line of Skin and Hair Care Products," *Los Angeles Times,* August 23, 1994, p. D1

Ozanian, Michael K., Ellen Benoit, Suzanne Loeffelholz, and Tani Maher, "Today's Best Bets—Stocks," *Financial World,* October 4, 1988, pp. 58–63.

"Personal-Care Firm's Profit Will Drop in 4th Quarter (Neutrogena Corp.)," *Wall Street Journal,* October 12, 1990, p. C12(W), B4(E).

Ranzal, Edward, "2 Drug Wholesalers Accuse Producers," *New York Times,* November 16, 1966, p. 65.

Riddle, Judith Springer, "Wal-Mart Looks to Clean Up," *Adweek* (Eastern Ed.), September 6, 1993, p. 10.

——, "Wal-Mart Soap Opera Hits Sour Note for Brands," *Brandweek,* September 6, 1993, pp. 1, 6.

Rosendahl, Iris, "Hand and Body Lotions Targeting Special Niches; Integrate Hand, Body Lotions for Best Results," *Drug Topics,* September 21, 1992, pp. 105–107.

——, "Medicated Shampoos Fill a Consumer Need," *Drug Topics,* February 22, 1993, p. 60.

——, "New Products Add Life to Acne Sales; Build Acne Remedy by Staying Informed, *Drug Topics,* August 17, 1992, pp. 91–93.

——, "What's Moving for the Christmas Season, *Drug Topics,* August 20, 1990, pp. 75–76.

Salwen, Kevin G., "Neutrogena Investors Aren't Losing Any Sleep Over the Skin-Care Concern's High P-E Ratio (Heard on the Street)," *Wall Street Journal,* April 7, 1988, 51(W), 57(E).

Savona, Dave, "The Art of Exporting," *International Business,* September 1992, pp. 66–70.

"Skin Care Market Shows New Signs of Vitality," *Drug & Cosmetic Industry,* August 1992, pp. 28–29.

"Skin Care Products Concern Expects 50% Earnings Drop (Neutrogena Corp.)," *Wall Street Journal,* April 18, 1990, p. A4(W).

Sloan, Pat, "Beauty Business' New Complexion," *Advertising Age,* August 29, 1994, p. 4.

——, "Beauty Marketers Look for a Good Fit," *Advertising Age,* August 1, 1994, p. 8.

——, "Neutrogena, Lehn May Vie for Buyers," *Advertising Age,* August 15, 1994, p. 8.

Tyrer, Kathy, "Crystal Cruises into Ad Review," *Adweek* (Western Advertising News), August 15, 1994, p. 3.

Tyler, W. D., "Is TV Strongest Tool? Jell-O Ads Point Up Advantages of Print," *Advertising Age,* December 8, 1975, pp. 40–42.

Walters, Donna K. H., " 'Soap Salesman': Neutrogena CEO Takes a Modest View of His Success (Lloyd E. Cotsen)," *Los Angeles Times,* August 23, 1994, p. D3.

Wyatt, Edward A., "Charting the Market," *Barron's,* August 29, 1994, p. MW103.

—Heidi Feldman

New Valley Corporation

100 Southeast Second Street
Miami, Florida 33131
U.S.A.
(305) 579-8000
Fax: (305) 579-8006

Public Company
Incorporated: 1851 as New York & Mississippi Valley
    Printing Telegraph Company
Employees: 294
Sales: $67.7 million (1995)
Stock Exchanges: New York
SICs: 7389 Business Services, Not Elsewhere Classified;
    4822 Telegraph & Other Communications

The inheritor of the businesses once owned by Western Union Corporation, New Valley Corporation is the owner of an investment banking and brokerage business and a commercial real estate management business. Although New Valley traces its origins back to 1851, when the predecessor to Western Union Telegraph Company was established, the company was not formed until 1991. The two businesses that constituted New Valley during the mid-1990s—Ladenburg, Thalmann & Co. Inc. and the New Valley Realty Division—were brought into the company's fold in 1995 and 1996, respectively.

The corporate name New Valley first surfaced in 1991 as a shroud to protect one of the most familiar brands in the history of American business. Western Union was floundering after a century of dominance, its preeminence in the telecommunications industry only a memory. To mitigate any further damage to the brand name's image, the company's shareholders voted on April 18, 1991, to adopt the New Valley name, thereby lessening the sting of witnessing the business press chart the fall of their once-great enterprise. New Valley Corporation was a new company in name, but one with a lengthy history.

19th Century Genesis of Western Union

Western Union rode the crest of the telecommunication industry's technological wave from its first days as a corporate entity. Incorporated as the New York & Mississippi Valley Printing Telegraph Company in 1851, the company was founded seven years after Samuel F. B. Morse tapped the first electro-magnetic telegraph message between two cities, a historic correspondence traveling between Washington and Baltimore. From 1851 forward, the telegram business represented Western Union's foundation, propelling the company forward and creating one of the most recognizable names in American business.

In 1856 New York & Mississippi Valley Printing Telegraph Company was renamed Western Union Telegraph Company. Five years later Western Union constructed the first trans-continental telegraph line, laying the groundwork for coast-to-coast communication, then introduced the commercial telegraph machine three years later.

20th Century Domination and Missteps

By the 1930s, after decades of growth fueled by the pervasive use of telegrams, Western Union reigned as a powerful force in the telecommunications industry, holding sway, according to one industry observer, as "a fat, happy monopoly." The Western Union name was familiar to generations of Americans who associated it with the dramatic announcements of life, including messages that told of birth, death, and homecomings, all handed to the recipient by a Western Union messenger. The company represented the fastest and trustiest messenger service in the country.

While carving its leading position in the telegram industry, Western Union missed the boat on the next huge technological development to dramatically alter long-distance communication. When Alexander Graham Bell tried to sell the patent for the telephone to Western Union for $100,000, the company refused the offer, opting to stick with its telegraph business. Later, Western Union executives did make some investments in telephone technology, acquiring several patents—including one filed by

Thomas Edison—after realizing that the telephone was a good idea. Despite their belated attraction to the telephone business, company leaders decided that however promising the new invention was it was not the business for Western Union, so all the patents were sold to a new, rising power called AT&T.

In retrospect, the decision to forgo the telephone business during its early years was a regrettable move, but Western Union was a thriving enterprise that needed little else other than its rapidly expanding telegraph business to drive its growth during the late 19th century and the first half of the 20th century. After the 1930s, Western Union began to diversify gradually, establishing a private line communication service in the 1940s and creating a telex business following the conclusion of World War II. The introduction of telex messages by Western Union in 1958 marked the birth of what would serve as the company's second chief source of revenue.

However, the pervasive use of telegrams began to diminish and other forms of communications surged ahead. By the mid-1960s, the telegraph, which represented a substantial portion of Western Union's business, was well on its way out, usurped by the telephone. In response, Western Union executives changed the company's direction by refocusing on the telex as a major business and by continuing to explore other business areas. As the company's telex business expanded during the 1970s, several innovative developments offered hope that Western Union could restore its former luster, including the introduction of Mailgram service in 1970 and the operation of the first domestic satellite communications system, Westar, which was launched in 1974. As it turned out, however, Western Union was on the decline.

1980s: The Fall of Western Union

The company's telex business achieved encouraging success for a while, but when it became cheaper to send data over telephone lines the telex business began to suffer and Western Union found itself in dire straits. The company lost $59 million in 1983, and the following year, when annual sales eclipsed $1 billion, another $58.4 million was recorded as a deficit. Clearly, something needed to be done to arrest the slide.

In 1984 Western Union stopped paying dividends on its stock, and its banks cut off its lines of credit; over the next few years Western Union inched closer and closer to bankruptcy. It was during this period in the company's history that the next telling name change occurred, a move orchestrated by a turn-around artist named Bennett S. LeBow. LeBow entered the picture in 1987, when Western Union Telegraph Company became Western Union Corporation and LeBow was named the 136-year-old company's chairman. Together with Robert J. Amman, who was tapped as the company's chief executive officer, LeBow initiated sweeping changes throughout the Western Union organization, hoping to reposition the company as a technologically modern corporation able to compete in the world of sophisticated telecommunications.

When LeBow and Amman took charge, Western Union was a $940 million company deriving 75 percent of its revenue from its telex, money-transfer, and telegram services. In the future, the two leaders hoped to transform Western Union into a high-

technology electronic messaging and consumer services company and collect the bulk of its sales from the telex business, its financial services subsidiary, and a newly formed travel services unit.

1990s: Bankruptcy and Birth of New Valley

As Western Union entered the 1990s, its telex business was shrinking 20 percent annually. The restructuring program implemented upon LeBow's arrival in 1987 had saddled the company with enormous debt, and its telegram and telex businesses had been damaged by new technology. The specter of bankruptcy, which had hovered over the company for nearly a decade, seemed inevitable as Western Union prepared for its 140th anniversary year. It was the fear of imminent bankruptcy and the attendant negative publicity bankruptcy would generate that led the company and its shareholders to effect a name change during Western Union's celebratory 1991 fiscal year, a move intended to keep its severe financial problems from further damaging the reputation of its subsidiary businesses. One of Western Union's original businesses, its money-transfer subsidiary Western Union Financial Services Inc., was demonstrating encouraging profitability as the 1990s began, but there was concern that if the Western Union name were dragged through bankruptcy court the subsidiary would suffer as result. Accordingly, on April 18, 1991, Western Union Corporation shareholders voted to change the name of their company to New Valley Corporation, hoping to shield the Western Union name from the public eye.

Western Union Financial Services Inc., as an independent subsidiary, would be able to conduct business as usual if its new parent company plunged into bankruptcy. New Valley assumed the debt accrued by its predecessor, and by the early 1990s, the debt had ballooned to $800 million, weighing the company down enormously as it tried to muster a recovery.

For the mid-1990s and the future, New Valley was working to reshape Western Union Financial Services Inc. to become a financial services provider to middle- and low-income consumers, making their company a "bank" for the estimated 15 million households in the United States without a traditional banking relationship. However, in 1993 New Valley slipped into bankruptcy, and in 1994 the company sold Western Union Financial Services Inc., all the Western Union money-transfer trademarks and tradenames associated with the Western Union name, and various other businesses, for $1.19 billion.

On January 18, 1995, New Valley emerged from bankruptcy and tried to reposition itself for the future. In May 1995 the company acquired Ladenburg, Thalmann & Co. Inc., a full-service broker-dealer involved in investment banking and securities and over-the-counter trading. Next, in 1996, New Valley acquired four commercial office buildings and eight shopping centers, giving the company a second facet to its business for the late 1990s and the years ahead. Thoroughly revamped for the 21st century, New Valley, the inheritor of a more than 150-year-old business icon, was transformed into the parent company of an investment banking and brokerage business and the owner of a business engaged in the ownership and management of commercial real estate.

Principal Subsidiaries

Ladenburg, Thalmann & Co. Inc.

Principal Divisions

New Valley Realty Division.

Further Reading

Andrews, Greg, "Vulture Snaps up Anacomp Securities," *Indianapolis Business Journal*, June 19, 1995, p. 1A.

"At a Loss for Words," *Financial World*, November 28, 1984, p. 23.

Eng, Paul M., "Western Union's New Name Is Forgettable, by Design," *Business Week*, May 6, 1991, p. 120E.

Frank, Robert, "LeBow's New Valley Gets FTC Approval to Buy a 15% Stake in RJR Nabisco," *Wall Street Journal*, August 30, 1995, p. A2.

Ginsberg, Stanley, "This Time, Maybe?," *Forbes*, March 3, 1980, p. 82.

Hammonds, Keith H., "Vultures in the Valley?," *Business Week*, November 7, 1994, p. 42.

Hindlin, Eric, "Western Union, IBM to Link E-Mail Services, Allowing Message Exchange," *PC Week*, March 31, 1987, p. 14.

Keller, John J., "Bob Amman Tries to Reinvent the Onion," *Business Week*, June 13, 1988, p. 33.

Kretchmar, Laurie, "Gary L. Breitbart," *Fortune*, June 3, 1991, p. 212.

Light, Larry, "The Vulture Investors Circling New Valley," *Business Week*, April 11, 1994, p. 4.

Mintz, Steven, "Western Union Bets on the Money," *Sales & Marketing Management*, August 15, 1983, p. 37.

Sutor, Ruthanne, "Lost Horizons: Missed Opportunities Have Nearly Wrecked Venerable Western Union," *Financial World*, April 18, 1989, p. 60.

"Tough Tidings: The Messenger Bearer's Woes," *Time*, March 18, 1985, p. 45.

Woolley, Suzanne, "Western Union Banks on the 'Unbanked,' " *Business Week*, April 5, 1993, p. 71.

—Jeffrey L. Covell

NIPPON STEEL

Nippon Steel Corporation

6-3, Otemachi 2-chome
Chiyoda-ku, Tokyo 100-71
Japan
(81) 3 3242-4111
Fax: (81) 3 3275-5607
Internet: http://www.nsc.co.jp/

Public Company
Incorporated: 1971
Employees: 27,583
Sales: ¥2.95 trillion (US $27.78 billion)
Stock Exchanges: Tokyo Osaka Nagoya
SICs: 3310 Blast Furnace & Basic Steel Products; 1791
Structural Steel Erection; 2999 Petroleum & Coal
Products, Not Elsewhere Classified; 3325 Steel
Foundries, Not Elsewhere Classified; 3577 Computer
Peripheral Equipment, Not Elsewhere Classified

As the spearhead of Japan's economic transformation after World War II, Nippon Steel Corporation rose from virtual annihilation to a position of world leadership in the space of 25 years. With Japanese shipbuilders, automakers, and other heavy steel consumers achieving prominence in world markets, Nippon Steel enjoyed annual sales gains of 25 percent and more during the late 1950s and the 1960s and, by 1975, was the world's largest steelmaker. In the waning years of the 20th century, however, neither Japan's domestic economy nor those of the other developed nations have need of the enormous steel supply they once did. As a result, Nippon faced problems of static demand and fresh competition from countries such as South Korea, busily forging their own "economic miracles."

Like other of the world's steelmakers, Nippon drastically reduced capacity after the oil crisis of 1973–1974 and followed the example of other Japanese industrial powers in diversifying from basic commodity products toward specialty steels and wholly unrelated activities. Nippon Steel continued to rank as the world's top steelmaker in 1996. After a succession of retrench-

ments in the 1980s and 1990s, the company cut billions of dollars in costs, but was also expected to downsize itself out of the global industry's top spot by 1998. Although steel production continued to constitute more than two-thirds of Nippon's sales in the mid-1990s, the company had also diversified into industrial engineering, chemicals, nonferrous metals, and ceramics.

Late 19th Century Origins

The history of Nippon Steel closely parallels, and in some cases is identical with, the history of Japanese steel as a whole. In the centuries of isolation before the opening of trade with the West in the 1850s, Japan had manufactured what little steel it needed by an ancient method of smelting adequate to the demands of a pre-industrial economy. Prodded by the need to defend itself against the incursions of Western steamships, the Japanese government lifted its ban on the production of large ships in 1853, and a number of dockyards soon sprang up around the country, all of them in need of unprecedented amounts of steel. In 1857, Japan's first blast furnace was installed near the Kamaishi iron mines, an accomplishment that still left the Japanese 400 to 500 years behind the West in metallurgy. The Kamaishi furnaces were successful, however, and the Japanese government nationalized them in 1873 to hasten the development of this basic constituent of an industrial economy.

In its race to catch up with the Western powers, Japan faced a number of formidable obstacles. Not only was the country without engineering expertise, it also lacked all but trace amounts of coking coal and iron ore, the key ingredients of iron and steel. Its mineral poverty would later play a critical role in Japan's foreign policy, but in the early years of its steel industry the first need was for technical guidance. Most of this was supplied by Germans, in particular Curt Netto, professor of engineering at Tokyo University from 1877 to 1885, and Adolf Ledebur, another professor of engineering who was instrumental in coordinating the work of German design firms on behalf of Japan's early steel mills. Under the tutelage of these and other German experts, Japan soon developed its own circle of metallurgists and engineers, including, most notably, Kageyoshi Noro and Michitaro Oshima. When the Japanese government renewed its commitment to steel with the opening

Company Perspectives:

Nippon Steel continues to build on its proud technical heritage and its ability to supply a diversity of materials, equipment, and services while boasting of the world's cleanest and most environmentally advanced production facilities.

of a vast new plant at Yawata in 1896, its construction was entrusted to a German firm and Michitaro Oshima was named managing director of the newly created Imperial Japanese Government Steel Works at Yawata. The Yawata works became the nucleus of today's Nippon Steel.

The Yawata works did not get under way until 1901, when its target for the year's production was 60,000 tons of steel. In comparison, U.S. steel capacity in 1901 was ten million tons. Yawata's primary customers were shipbuilders and weapons makers. The state of Japan's armed forces prompted the government to take a direct role in the development of its steel industry and pour its resources into the nascent steel works at Yawata. Even so, production at Yawata was poor at first, with many technical failures during the early years. By 1904 most of these difficulties had been overcome, and Yawata was running a smooth, if modest, operation.

Quest for Raw Materials Dominates Early 20th Century

Having borrowed the technology it needed from the Germans and the English, Japan faced a second and more intractable problem—its lack of raw materials. The dominant steelmaking nations, chiefly the United States, England, Germany, and France, had achieved their positions with the help of native supplies of iron ore and coking coal. Japan had practically none and, with the primitive modes of transport then available, believed that it would never become an industrial power without taking steps to secure convenient and stable supplies of these basic ingredients. Its poor supply of raw materials played at least a contributing role in the growth of Japan's territorial claims in the first half of this century. Both of its closest neighbors, Korea and China, were rich in iron ore and coal, and as early as 1910 Japan had formally annexed Korea and was jockeying for position in northern China. In the following decades Japan would take what it needed from these two countries while also shifting a significant amount of its steel production to these countries.

Japan's steel industry remained incapable of supplying the country's urgent need for steel for years. In 1913, production at Yawata reached 200,000 tons of crude steel, which was 85 percent of all the steel made in Japan but less than 30 percent of that needed by the nation's growing shipbuilding and munitions industries. World War I provided an important stimulus for all segments of the Japanese economy. Shipping, railroads, electrical industries, and Japan's now-numerous manufacturers all required far more steel than the Imperial Works could supply, and even the gradual appearance of privately owned steel companies could not close the gap. The country remained precariously dependent on foreign sources of pig iron, scrap iron, coal, and iron ore as well as finished steel products.

Great Depression Spurs Six-Company Merger

The Great Depression added a fresh impetus to Japan's aggressive foreign policy. Military leaders were inspired by a rising tide of ultraconservative political sympathy to demand a more rapid pace in Japan's continental expansion. In such a climate, the country's relatively backward steel industry became all the less tolerable, and in 1934 the Japanese government took a major step toward finally gaining self-sufficiency in steel. The Imperial Works at Yawata was merged with six leading private steelmakers—Wanishi, Kamaishi, Fuji, Kyushu, Toyo, and Mitsubishi—to form Japan Iron & Steel Company, Ltd., which was about 80 percent owned by the government. At the time of its formation, Japan Iron & Steel's crude steel capacity was estimated at 2.12 million tons, about 56 percent of the total for Japan. Under its first president, Reisaku Nakai, Japan Iron & Steel immediately began an ambitious and highly successful expansion of its facilities. Two plants were completely overhauled and given much larger blast furnaces, and a new mill was added in northern Korea near plentiful sources of iron and coal. With Korea and Manchuria now supplying more than 50 percent of Japan's coal and much of its iron ore, an increasing proportion of iron and steel production was moved to the mainland. This trend in turn seemed to confirm the military's insistence on further imperialist expansion. At Japan Iron & Steel, production was geared ever more closely to the needs of the military.

In a remarkably short time, Japan Iron & Steel and the rest of the industry caught up to the level of domestic steel consumption. By the beginning of World War II in 1939, Japan had become the world's fifth-leading steelmaker, with production reaching 5.8 million tons, and the industry was able to supply most of the needs of Japanese manufacturers, with the striking exception of armor plating. Yet even in its newfound strength, the Japanese industry was quite small by the standards of the United States, which in that year produced 28 million tons. Japan was not in a position, because of shortages of steel and a dozen other crucial resources, to wage a world war, and yet it was precisely this lack of materials that made war seem inevitable to the Japanese. Wartime steel production hit a peak of 12 million tons, but in that same year the United States alone launched 19 million tons of merchant shipping. At Japan Iron & Steel, only three of its many blast furnaces remained operable at the end of the war.

Postwar Reconstruction Brings Rapid Growth

A nation in ruins, postwar Japan was in need of vast amounts of steel. With the close cooperation and financial support of the United States, Japan Iron & Steel was rebuilt from the ground up according to the latest and most efficient designs. The new Japanese plants were larger, more completely integrated, and technologically more advanced than any others in the world—a complete overhaul that would not be possible for the older steel industries of Britain and the United States. Once given this technological edge, Japan Iron & Steel used its favorable labor rates to produce the world's best steel at the lowest possible prices for the next 30 years, until South Korea employed the same tactics to displace Japan in the 1980s.

Japan Iron & Steel met the same fate that most of the *zaibatsu*, combines of banks and industries, had suffered at the hands of the Allied occupation forces. In 1950 it was broken into four privately owned companies to promote American-style competition in the steel business. Of the four firms, the largest by far was Yawata Iron & Steel Co., Ltd., made up mostly of the plants of the old Imperial Works. Two others were much smaller specialty companies, but the fourth became Japan's second largest steelmaker, Fuji Iron & Steel Co., Ltd. Fuji and Yawata spent the next 20 years engaged in intense competition without ever forgetting their common origins, until in 1971 they again merged to form today's Nippon Steel.

The Korean War gave Japan its first inkling of the role it would play in the post-World War II economy, as the Western powers looked to Japan for basic industrial goods and supported its growth into a bulwark against Asian communism. In response, the steel industry in Japan embarked upon its First Modernization Program in 1956. In the first of these united efforts some ¥128 billion was invested, in the second ¥625 billion, and a third program initiated in 1961 used more than ¥1 trillion. The most important results of these enormous expenditures fall into three categories. First, beginning in the early 1950s, Japan led the world in its adoption of the basic oxygen furnace technology, arguably the most important steelmaking innovation of the postwar era. Second, in 1957 Yawata Iron & Steel was one of the first steel companies to install the LD converter, which consumes far less scrap iron during the steel-making process than the formerly universal open-hearth method. Third, the Japanese pioneered continuous casting, the integration of steel production with the milling and shaping process, which until this time had been kept inefficiently separate. All three of these improvements eventually were adopted around the world, but the Japanese were the first to use them and were similarly advanced in their introduction of computer controls in the early 1960s.

In 1959, Yawata Iron & Steel's annual sales reached US $340 million, making it the largest industrial company in Japan. Fuji sales stood at US $250 million, or third largest. The bulk of the two companies' revenue was generated by domestic sales, as the Japanese economy still absorbed nearly all the steel the country could make. The trend in postwar Japanese consumption was away from military and railroad contracts and toward the burgeoning automobile, shipbuilding, and construction markets, which together were expanding the Japanese economy at the rate of about ten percent per year. In the next ten years Japan enjoyed the decade of its most spectacular growth and began the heavy exporting of goods that has made it the wonder of the economic world. Growth in the Japanese steel industry in the 1960s averaged 25 percent per year, and the country's paucity of raw materials no longer seemed the problem it once had. In the meantime, the more mature U.S. economy used a decreasing amount of steel, and the U.S. steel industry fell irretrievably behind the Japanese.

The end of the 1960s saw another leap in worldwide demand for shipping tonnage, mainly to ferry oil, and the Japanese steel industry agreed to spend the unprecedented sum of ¥3 trillion on yet another round of capital improvements. The two chief descendants of the old Japan Iron & Steel, Yawata and Fuji, announced in 1969 that they were to re-merge and form a new steel giant called Nippon Steel. Many other former *zaibatsu* holdings had similarly gravitated back together. The new Nippon Steel had combined revenue of about $2.3 billion, making it Japan's largest business of any kind and second only to U.S. Steel Corporation among world steelmakers. Top management was carefully divided between Shigeo Nagano from Fuji and Yoshihiro Inayama from Yawata, but for a number of years there was factional bitterness between the newly merged partners.

Global Energy Crisis of 1970s

At its height in the early 1970s, Nippon Steel's 80,000 employees directed a network of furnaces and mills capable of producing 47 million tons of crude steel per year, or four times the wartime capacity of Japan as a nation. It was hoped that combining the two great steelmakers would eliminate duplication of effort, increase scale efficiencies, and help pump up the steel industry's thin bottom line. The 1973–1974 oil crisis and the changing nature of the world economy rendered these hopes vain, however. The oil crisis brought to an abrupt halt the booming market for Japanese shipping, approximately quadrupled the cost of Nippon Steel's power and fuel, encouraged the construction of lighter automobiles containing less steel, and in general dragged the world's heavy industries into a long slump. The effects on Nippon's performance were immediate. Fiscal year 1975 showed a paltry profit of $50 million on declining sales of $7 billion, and by 1977 production was down to 32 million tons and nine of the company's 25 furnaces had been shut down.

Nippon's fortunes were also affected by Japan's changing place in the world economy. By 1975, when Nippon passed U.S. Steel as the world's largest steelmaker, Japan was no longer a young industrial nation requiring vast amounts of steel to build its infrastructure and heavy export goods. Similarly, the developed Western nations upon whom Nippon depended for export sales were all well into the postindustrial age; their need for steel was essentially static and increasingly weighted toward various specialty products. The oil shock only accelerated a trend toward reduced steel usage and Third World competition.

The combined impact of these events on Nippon Steel and the world steel industry was devastating. Worldwide, steel employment dropped 43 percent between 1974 and 1987. At Nippon Steel it was halved in the same period, and overall capacity was cut back from 47 million tons to about 27 million in the mid-1980s. The recession of the early 1980s was especially hard on Japanese steel, which as a whole reported losses in 1983 for the first time in many years. Four years later Nippon and the other leading Japanese steelmakers all showed a year-end loss, the first time that had happened since World War II. The next few years offered a mild recovery, with national production reaching 108 million tons, still less than the peak year of 1980 and not significantly greater than what it had been 20 years earlier. Nippon managed a return to the two percent to three percent profit margin it has traditionally shown.

Adjusting to New Realities in the 1980s

Nippon's response to the erosion of its markets has been typical of large Japanese combines. While cutting expenses to the bone and shedding excess labor (generally by attrition and in the form of employee "loans" to other companies), Nippon also moved swiftly into an array of new fields. To its core steelmaking, the company added nonferrous metals, a wide variety of heavy construction projects, and a catch-all grouping of new materials development. Nippon used this latter category to range far afield, launching an amusement park called Space World, a silicon wafer plant, and a U.S. venture to manufacture notebook computers.

Notwithstanding these diversifications, steelmaking continued to constitute more than two-thirds of Nippon's business. In the late 1980s and early 1990s, the company adopted new production methods and developed innovative products. In response to competition from minimills, which used electric furnaces to process ferrous scrap, the company accumulated shares in more than a dozen of its upstart competitors. Internally, the integrated giant adopted its own scrap-melting process to increase productivity and licensed the Romelt process to reduce costs and pollution. Nippon also increased its presence in the U.S. steel market through a number of substantial joint ventures with Inland Steel Industries, in which it, not coincidentally, owned a 13 percent stake. Nippon Steel stepped up the pace of international investment, often through joint venture, in the early 1990s, focusing especially on emerging economies like Thailand, India, Brazil, and China.

Contrary to most analysts' predictions, however, Japanese steel production actually increased in the late 1980s and early 1990s, as the country's auto and construction markets flourished. Nippon Steel's mid-decade reorganization, which had cut US $3 billion in costs by 1987, helped it recover from a US $84 million loss in 1987 to record a US $700 million profit in 1991. Thanks to its preemptive reorganization, Nippon Steel maintained its profitability until 1992, when Japan's "bubble economy" burst. At the same time, the rising yen made Japanese exports less competitive on world markets.

Led by 35-year company veteran Takashi Imai, who advanced to president in 1993, the company undertook a second major restructuring. By 1997, Nippon Steel expected a combination of reengineering, employee reductions, and operational rationalizations to cut US $3 billion in expenses. As it had in the past, the company honored its lifetime employment clause by permanently "loaning" workers to affiliated companies, retraining them for new jobs, or via early retirement buyouts. In total, the steelmaker expected to reduce its employment by one-third, from 30,000 to 20,000. Nippon Steel also implemented an automated computer shipping network and reduced overhead by negotiating reduced raw materials and energy prices. As a result of its downsizing, the company achieved its first annual profit in three years in fiscal 1996 (ended March 31). Nippon Steel was the only of Japan's "big five" steelmakers to do so. But the company's downsizing had another, perhaps unexpected, effect. In 1995, *New Steel's* Bryan Berry noted that Korea's Pohang Iron and Steel Co. (Posco) would likely surpass Nippon as the world's largest steelmaker in 1998.

Principal Subsidiaries

NS Tek, Inc. (U.S.A.); NS Kote, Inc. (U.S.A.); NS Pipe Technology, Inc. (U.S.A.); NS Sales, Inc. (U.S.A.); Nippon Steel Metal Products Co., Ltd. (95.4%); Nittetsu Steel Drum Co., Ltd. (57.8%); Nippon Steel Welding Products & Engineering Co., Ltd. (68.2%); Nippon Steel Bolten Co., Ltd.; Nippon Tubular Products Co., Ltd.; Fuji Tekko Center Co., Ltd. (51%); Nittetsu Corrosion Prevention Co., Ltd. (54.2%); Nittai Corporation (60%); Chukyo Seisen Co., Ltd. (80%); Nippon Steel Chemical Co., Ltd. (57.1%); Nittetsu Cement Co., Ltd. (55%); Chemirite, Ltd. (U.S.A.; 77.9%); Kankyo Engineering Co., Ltd. (55%); Nittetsu Electrical Engineering & Construction Co., Ltd.; Nittetsu Plant Designing Corporation; Electro-Plasma, Inc. (U.S.A.; 76%); Nittetsu Transportation Co., Ltd. (86.4%); Nittetsu Transport Service Co., Ltd.; Nittetsu Ryutsu Center Co., Ltd. (60%); Nippon Steel Shipping Co., Ltd. (76%); Nippon Steel Information & Communication Systems Inc.; Nippon Steel Life Planning Co., Ltd.; Tetsubiru Co., Ltd. (91.7%); Sakai Tekko Building Co., Ltd. (75%); Yuwa Sangyo Co., Ltd; Nittetsu Finance Co., Ltd.; Nippon Steel U.S.A., Inc. (U.S.A.); NS Invest, Inc. (U.S.A.); NS Invest II, Inc. (U.S.A.); NS Finance, Inc. (U.S.A.); NS Finance III Inc. (U.S.A.).

Further Reading

Berglund, Abraham, "The Iron and Steel Industry of Japan and Japanese Continental Policies," *Journal of Political Economy,* October 1922.

Berry, Bryan, "The Top Two: Nippon Steel and Posco Trade Places," *New Steel,* December 1995, pp. 20–29.

"Dumping Charges Miff Nippon Boss," *American Metal Market,* August 30, 1993, p. 2.

Eisenstodt, Gale, "If at First You Don't Succeed," *Forbes,* January 20, 1992, p. 68.

Furukawa, Tsukasa, "Financial Woes Plague Japanese Steelmakers," *American Metal Market,* December 1, 1993, p. 8.

——, "High Tensile Strength Steel Bows," *American Metal Market,* December 22, 1993, p. 8.

——, "Imai To Focus on Management," *American Metal Market,* April 29, 1993, p. 2.

——, "In Japan It's Godzilla vs. Mini-Godzilla," *American Metal Market,* December 6, 1994, p. 10A.

——, "Japanese Steel Restructures Under the Weight of the Yen," *American Metal Market,* October 4, 1994, p. 12A.

——, "Nippon Steel Launches Computerized Shipping," *American Metal Market,* April 16, 1993, p. 4.

——, "Nippon Steel Unveils Three-Year Restructuring," *American Metal Market,* March 31, 1994, p. 12.

——, "Nippon To Enter Scrap Recycling Arena, Boss Says," *American Metal Market,* July 22, 1993, p. 7.

History of Steel in Japan, Tokyo: Nippon Steel Corporation, 1972.

"Lights Out, Workaholics," *Time,* November 30, 1992, p. 22.

"Nippon Steel: How a Lifetime Employer Displaces 10,000," *New Steel,* January 1995, p. 8.

Scheier, Robert L., "Sun Sets on Nippon Steel's U.S. Notebook Subsidiary," *PC Week,* September 7, 1992, pp. 121–122.

Weisman, Jonathan, "Firms See Door Closing on Japanese Vault," *The Business Journal,* September 7, 1992, pp. 1–2.

—Jonathan Martin
—updated by April Dougal Gasbarre

Nokia Corporation

Etelesplanadi 12
P.O. Box 226
Helsinki 358018071
Finland
(358) 1 18071
Fax: (358) 1 656388
Internet: http://www.nokia.com/

Public Company
Incorporated: 1865
Employees: 34,000
Sales: FIM 36.81 billion (US $8.4 billion)
Stock Exchanges: Helsinki Stockholm London Paris
   Frankfurt New York
SICs: 3630 Household Appliances

With a stock market value that equals more than one-third of Finland's gross domestic product, Nokia Corporation is that country's largest company. The firm's tens of thousands of employees make it one of Scandinavia's largest employers. Over the course of its more than 130 years in business, the company has evolved from a concentration in pulp, paper, and other basic industries to a focus on electronics, especially telecommunications. In the mid-1990s, the company had three business groups. The most important of these was Nokia Mobile Phones. With about 20 percent of the global cellular phone market, this division ranked as the continent's largest and the world's second largest producer of mobile phones. Nokia Telecommunications was a highly profitable supplier of digital phone exchanges and other cellular network equipment, ranking second among manufacturers adhering to the GSM (Global System for Mobile Communication) digital standard. The General Communications Products group was created through the mid-1995 combination of the company's Consumer Electronics division with its Cables and Machinery group.

19th Century Origins

Originally a manufacturer of pulp and paper, Nokia was founded in 1865 in a small town of the same name in central Finland. Nokia was a pioneer in the industry and introduced many new production methods to a country with only one major natural resource, its vast forests. As the industry became increasingly energy-intensive, the company even constructed its own power plants. But for many years, Nokia remained an important yet static firm in a relatively forgotten corner of northern Europe.

The first major changes in Nokia occurred several years after World War II. Despite its proximity to the Soviet Union, Finland has always remained economically connected with Scandinavian and other Western countries, and as Finnish trade expanded Nokia became a leading exporter.

During the early 1960s Nokia began to diversify in an attempt to transform the company into a regional conglomerate with interests beyond Finnish borders. Unable to initiate strong internal growth, Nokia turned its attention to acquisitions. The government, however, hoping to rationalize two underperforming basic industries, favored Nokia's expansion within the country and encouraged its eventual merger with Finnish Rubber Works and Finnish Cable Works. When the amalgamation was completed in 1966, Nokia was involved in several new industries, including integrated cable operations, electronics, tires, and rubber footwear, and had made its first public share offering.

In 1967 Nokia set up a division to develop design and manufacturing capabilities in data processing, industrial automation, and communications systems. The division was later expanded and made into several divisions, which then concentrated on developing information systems, including personal computers and workstations, digital communications systems, and mobile phones. Nokia also gained a strong position in modems and automatic banking systems in Scandinavia.

Oil Crisis in the 1970s Triggers Corporate Change

Nokia continued to operate in a stable but parochial manner until 1973, when it was affected in a unique way by the oil crisis. Years of political accommodation between Finland and the Soviet Union ensured Finnish neutrality in exchange for lucrative trade agreements with the Soviets—mainly Finnish lumber products and machinery in exchange for Soviet oil. By agreement, this trade was kept strictly in balance. But when world oil prices began to rise, the market price for Soviet oil rose with it. Balanced trade began to mean greatly reduced purchasing power for Finnish companies such as Nokia.

Although the effects were not catastrophic, the oil crisis did force Nokia to reassess its reliance on Soviet trade (about 12 percent of sales) as well as its international growth strategies. Several contingency plans were drawn up, but the greatest changes came after the company appointed a new CEO, Kari Kairamo, in 1975.

Kairamo noted the obvious: Nokia was too big for Finland. The company had to expand abroad. He studied the expansion of other Scandinavian companies (particularly Sweden's Electrolux) and, following their example, formulated a strategy of first consolidating the company's business in Finland, Sweden, Norway, and Denmark, and then moving gradually into the rest of Europe. After the company had improved its product line, established a reputation for quality, and adjusted its production capacity, it would enter the world market.

Meanwhile, Nokia's traditional, lower-technology heavy industries were looking increasingly burdensome. It was feared that trying to become a leader in electronics while maintaining these basic industries would create an unmanageably unfocused company. Kairamo thought briefly about selling off the company's weaker divisions, but decided to retain and modernize them.

He reasoned that, although the modernization of these low-growth industries would be very expensive, it would guarantee Nokia's position in several stable markets, including paper, chemical, and machinery productions, and electrical generation. For the scheme to be practical, each division's modernization would have to be gradual and individually financed. This would prevent the bleeding of funds away from the all-important effort in electronics while preventing the heavy industries from becoming any less profitable.

With each division financing its own modernization, there was little or no drain on capital from other divisions, and Nokia could still sell any group that did not succeed under the new plan. In the end, the plan prompted the machinery division to begin development in robotics and automation, the cables division to begin work on fiber optics, and the forestry division to move into high-grade tissues.

Electronics Come to the Fore in the 1980s

Nokia's most important focus was development of the electronics sector. Over the course of the decade, the firm acquired nearly 20 companies, focusing especially on three segments of the electronics industry: consumer, workstations, and mobile communications. Electronics grew from ten percent of annual sales to 60 percent of revenues from 1980 to 1988. In late 1984 Nokia acquired Salora, the largest color television manufacturer in Scandinavia, and Luxor, the Swedish state-owned electronics and computer firm. Nokia combined Salora and Luxor into a single division and concentrated on stylish consumer electronic product, since style is a crucial factor in Scandinavian markets. The Salora-Luxor division was also very successful in satellite and digital television technology. Nokia purchased the consumer electronics operations of Standard Elektrik Lorenz A.G. from Alcatel in 1987, further bolstering the company's position in the television market to the third largest manufacturer in Europe. In early 1988 Nokia acquired the data systems division of the Swedish Ericsson Group, making Nokia the largest Scandinavian information technology business.

Although a market leader in Scandinavia, Nokia still lacked a degree of competitiveness in the European market, which was dominated by much larger Japanese and German companies. Kairamo decided, therefore, to follow the example of many Japanese companies during the 1960s (and Korean manufacturers a decade later) and negotiate to become an original equipment manufacturer, or OEM, to manufacture products for competitors as a subcontractor.

Nokia manufactured items for Hitachi in France, Ericsson in Sweden, Northern Telecom in Canada, and Granada and IBM in Britain. In doing so it was able to increase its production capacity stability. There were, however, several risks involved, those inherent in any OEM arrangement. Nokia's sales margins were naturally reduced, but of greater concern, production capacity was built up without a commensurate expansion in the sales network. With little brand identification, Nokia feared it might have a difficult time selling under its own name and become trapped as an OEM.

In 1986 Nokia reorganized its management structure to simplify reporting efforts and improve control by central management. The company's 11 divisions were grouped into four industry segments: electronics; cables and machinery; paper, power, and chemicals; and rubber and flooring. In addition, Nokia won a concession from the Finnish government to allow greater foreign participation in ownership. This substantially reduced Nokia's dependence on the comparatively expensive Finnish lending market. Although there was growth throughout the company, Nokia's greatest success was Mobira.

Having dabbled in telecommunications in the 1960s, Nokia cut its teeth in the industry by selling switching systems under license from a French company, Alcatel. The Finnish firm got in on the cellular industry's ground floor in the late 1970s, when it helped design the world's first international cellular system. Named the Nordic Mobile Telephone (NMT) network, the system linked Sweden, Denmark, Norway, and Finland. A year after the network came on line in 1981, Nokia gained 100 percent control of Mobira, the Finnish mobile phone company that would later become its key business interest. Mobira's regional sales were vastly improved, but Nokia was still limited to OEM production on the international market; Nokia and Tandy Corporation, of the United States, built a factory in Masan, South Korea to manufacture mobile telephones. These were sold under the Tandy name in that company's 6,000 Radio Shack stores throughout the United States.

In 1986, eager to test its ability to compete openly, Nokia chose the mobile telephone to be the first product marketed internationally under the Nokia name; it became Nokia's "make or break" product. Unfortunately, Asian competitors began to drive prices down just as Nokia entered the market. Other Nokia products gaining recognition were Salora televisions and Luxor satellite dishes, which suffered briefly when subscription programming introduced broadcast scrambling.

The company's expansion, achieved almost exclusively by acquisition, had been expensive. Few Finnish investors other than institutions had the patience to see Nokia through its long-term plans. Indeed, more than half of the new shares issued by Nokia in 1987 went to foreign investors. Nokia moved boldly into Western markets; it gained a listing on the London exchange in 1987 and was subsequently listed on the New York exchange.

Crises of Leadership, Profitability in the Late 1980s

Nokia's rapid growth was not without a price. In 1988, as revenues soared, the company's profits, under pressure from severe price competition in the consumer electronics markets, dropped. Chairman Kari Kairamo committed suicide in December of that year; not surprisingly, friends said it was brought on by stress. Simo S. Vuorileto took over the company's reins and began streamlining operations in the spring of 1988. Nokia was divided into six business groups: consumer electronics, data, mobile phones, telecommunications, cables and machinery, and basic industries. Vuorileto continued Kairamo's focus on high-tech divisions, divesting Nokia's flooring, paper, rubber, and ventilation systems businesses and entering into joint ventures with companies like Tandy Corporation and Matra of France (two separate agreements to produce mobile phones for the U.S. and French markets).

In spite of these efforts, Nokia's pretax profits continued to decline in 1989 and 1990, culminating in a loss of US $102 million in 1991. Industry observers blamed cutthroat European competition, the breakdown of the Finnish banking system, and the collapse of the Soviet Union. But, notwithstanding these difficulties, Nokia remained committed to its high-tech orientation. Late in 1991, the company strengthened that dedication by promoting Jorma Ollila from president of Nokia-Mobira Inc. (renamed Nokia Mobile Phones Ltd. the following year) to group president.

Forbes's Fleming Meeks has credited Ollila with transforming Nokia from "a moneylosing hodgepodge of companies into one of telecommunications' most profitable companies." Unable to find a buyer for Nokia's consumer electronics business, which had lost nearly US $1 billion from 1988 to 1993, Ollila cut that segment's work force by 45 percent, shuttered plants, and centralized operations.

The new leader achieved success in the cellular phone segment by bringing innovative products to market quickly with a particular focus on ever-smaller and easier-to-use phones featuring sleek Finnish design. Nokia gained a leg up in cellphone research and development with the 1991 acquisition of the United Kingdom's Technophone Ltd. for US $57 million.

Ollila's tenure brought Nokia success and with it global recognition. The company's sales more than doubled, from FIM 15.5 billion in 1991 to FIM 36.8 billion in 1995, and its bottom line rebounded from a net loss of FIM 723 million in 1992 to a FIM 2.2 billion profit in 1995. Securities investors have not missed the turnaround: Nokia's market capitalization multiplied ten times from 1991 to 1994. There is no reason to believe that this leader will not guide his company to even greater profitability in the waning years of the 20th century.

Principal Subsidiaries

Nokia Cellular Systems Oy; Nokia Data Systems Oy; Nokia Cable Machinery Oy (61%); Nokia Kaapeli Oy; Nokia Matkapuhelimet Oy; Nokia Renkaat Oy (80%); Nokian Paperi Oy; Salora Myynti Oy; Shkliikkeiden Oy (65.6%); Telenokia Oy; British Tissues Ltd (UK); Graetz Strahlungsmesstechnik GmbH (West Germany; 99.7%); Horda AB (Sweden; 91.1%); Ibervisao-Audiovisao Iberica S.A. (Portugal; 99.7%); Kabmatik AB (Sweden; 61%); Luxor AB (Sweden; 90%); Maillefer S.A. (Switzerland; 61%); Monette Kabel-ud Elektrowerk GmbH (West Germany); Nokia A/S (Norway); Nokia Audio Electronics GmbH (West Germany; 99.7%); Nokia Consumer Electronics GmbH (West Germany; 99.7%); Nokia Consumer Electronics Ltd (UK; 99.7%); Nokia Consumer Electronics Italia S.r.l. (Italy; 99.7%); Nokia Data AB (Sweden); Nokia Data A/S (Denmark); Nokia Data A/S (Norway); Nokia Data BV (Netherlands); Nokia Data GmbH (West Germany); Nokia Data Ltd (UK); Nokia Data S.A. (France); Nokia Data S.A. (Spain); Nokia Data Systems AB (Sweden); Noki Graetz Holzwerke GmbH (West Germany; 99.7%); Nokia Kunststofftechnik GmbH (West Germany; 99.7%); Nokia Ltd (Ireland); Nokia Mobira AB (Sweden); Nokia-Mobira A/S (Denmark); Nokia Mobira A/S (Norway); Nokia-Mobira Inc. (USA); Nokia-Mobira UK Ltd; Nokia Interhaltungselektronik (West Germany; 99.7%); Novelectric AG (Switzerland; 99.7%); Oceanic S.A. (France; 99.9%); Salora AB (Sweden); Sodipan-Nokia S.A. (France); Trkkablo A.O. (Turkey; 51%).

Further Reading

Berkman, Barbara N., "Brainstorming in the Sauna," *Electronic Business,* November 18, 1991, pp. 71–74.
——, "Sagging Profits Spark Identity Crisis at Nokia," *Electronic Business,* March 4, 1991, pp. 57–59.
Furchgott, Roy, "Nokia Signals Desire for Higher Profile," *ADWEEK Eastern Edition,* June 12, 1995, p. 2.
Heard, Joyce, and Keller, John J., "Nokia Skates into High Tech's Big Leagues," *Business Week,* April 4, 1988, pp. 102–103.
La Rossa, James Jr., "Nokia Knocks on U.S. Door," *HFD—The Weekly Home Furnishings Newspaper,* February 10, 1992, pp. 66–67.
Lineback, J. Robert, "Nokia's Mobile Phone Unit Is Ringing Bells," *Electronic Business Buyer,* June 1994, pp. 60–62.
Meeks, Fleming, "Watch Out, Motorola," *Forbes,* September 12, 1994, pp. 192–194.
"Not Finnished Yet," *The Economist,* February 9, 1991, p. 73.
Salameh, Asad, "Nokia Repositions for a Major Cellular Marketing Initiative," *Telecommunications,* June 1992, p. 43.
Silberg, Lurie, "A Brand Apart," *HFD—The Weekly Home Furnishings Newspaper,* September 5, 1994, pp. 54–55.
Williams, Elaine, "100-Year-Old Nokia Experiences Fast-Growth Pains," *Electronic Business,* June 26, 1989, pp. 111–114.

—updated by April D. Gasbarre

Oglebay Norton Company

1100 Superior Avenue
Cleveland, Ohio 44114-2598
U.S.A.
(216) 861-3300
Fax: (216) 861-2863

Public Company
Incorporated: 1924
Employees: 1,579
Sales: $193.6 million (1995)
Stock Exchanges: NASDAQ
SICs: 4432 Freight Transportation on the Great Lakes;
    1011 Iron Ores; 1221 Bituminous Coal & Lignite—
    Surface; 3297 Nonclay Refractories

With a cargo capacity of about 400,000 tons and a dozen ships, Oglebay Norton Company owns the largest U.S.-flagged fleet of bulk carriers on the Great Lakes. Great Lakes transportation and iron ore mining have been the primary foci of the business throughout its more than 140-year history, but the company expanded into coal, industrial sands, and other minerals during the 20th century. Oglebay Norton and its predecessor companies played a vital role in the development of Cleveland's steel industry, and the business's rich heritage is peppered with highlights that affected the Great Lakes shipping industry overall.

19th Century Antecedents

Oglebay Norton's history can be traced to the 1851 creation of Hewitt & Tuttle, an iron ore brokerage. The principals, Henry Blakeslee Tuttle and Isaac Hewitt, were also investors in the 1853 launch of Cleveland Iron Mining Company (later Cleveland-Cliffs Inc.), one of the first businesses organized to develop the iron ore reserves discovered in the Marquette Range of Michigan's upper peninsula in the 1840s. They launched their independent business to buy the high-quality iron ore mined by Cleveland Iron Mining, transport it via the Great Lakes to Cleveland and Pittsburgh, and then sell it to proces-

sors. In fact, Tuttle and Hewitt managed the very first shipment of iron ore from Lake Superior to Cleveland, Ohio, in 1852.

In the early days, this was no small feat. Labor and transportation costs were prohibitive because, until the Sault Ste. Marie shipping canal linking Lake Superior and Lake Huron was completed in 1855, the ore had to be portaged around the 19-foot Saint Marys Falls—not to mention the river's many rapids—by hand and mule team and then brought to Ohio via rail. Tuttle and Hewitt made Great Lakes shipping history again in July 1855, when their ship *Columbia* became the first to carry iron ore through the Saint Marys Canal's Soo Locks and proceed on to Lake Huron. By the late 1860s, Tuttle had resigned from Cleveland Iron Mining, acquired full control of the Lake Superior Iron Co., renamed it after himself, and brought his two sons, Horace and Frederick, into the business.

Rapid technological change and ever-increasing demand fueled dramatic expansion of the iron ore industry and H.B. Tuttle and Company. By the time the founder died in 1878, he owned a growing fleet of vessels dedicated to iron ore shipping, as well as a 3,000-acre iron ore mine in the Menominee range. Shipbuilders progressed from wooden sailing vessels in the mid-1800s to steel steamships by the 1880s, and cargo capacities increased from a few barrels to several tons. Consequently, shipping costs declined from $3 per ton in 1855 to 60 cents per ton by the turn of the century.

But with such rapid growth came intense competition. In addition, the burgeoning capital requirements of mining and shipping made them increasingly risky businesses. In the waning decades of the 19th century, many of the industry's leaders began to forge strategic alliances to survive and compete effectively. The Tuttles formed transient partnerships with several companies and independent operators during the 1870s. Then, in 1884, they merged with the Benwood Iron Works. Benwood was also in its second generation of management. Banker and industrialist Crispin Oglebay had invested in this West Virginia company in the early 1860s. Having inherited this "coal country" iron processor, son Early W. Oglebay sought to integrate vertically via the purchase of iron ore mines in the Gogebic Range on the southwestern shores of Lake Superior. The union of the two families' businesses as Tuttle, Oglebay and Company

---

Company Perspectives:

Oglebay Norton is a company whose future growth will flow from marine transportation services and a more diversified approach to basic metals and mineral-related industries. Our approach to business will be customer driven as we respond aggressively to the constantly changing needs of our customers. We are committed to narrowing the focus of Oglebay Norton business operations, while at the same time intensifying the diversification of our customer base. Recognizing the employees of Oglebay Norton to be our greatest strength, we are committed to an aggressive policy of investing in the ability of our employees to plan and implement our future growth strategies. We are equally committed to a style of management which empowers our employees to participate in the management of the company, holds them accountable for their actions and rewards them for their continued contributions to the company's growth and profitability. We will continue to a take a more aggressive approach to corporate financial growth, thus increasing the market value of our common stock to the benefit of our investors and employees.

---

created a vertically integrated system that spanned from extraction of ore to processing at several iron works. The business's network of mines included America's largest underground mine, the Montreal in Wisconsin. This single source generated 30 million tons of ore from 1886 to 1962.

Formation and Development of Oglebay, Norton & Co.

Tuttle, Oglebay and Company was a short-lived entity. When Horace Tuttle died in a railroad accident in 1889, Earl Oglebay bought out the surviving Tuttles and dropped their name from the corporate moniker. One year later, Earl Oglebay joined forces with well-connected Cleveland banker David Z. Norton to form Oglebay, Norton & Co. Norton, who by this time was president of the $4 million (capital) Citizens Saving and Trust Company, brought with him a lucrative contract to organize, transport, and broker rich iron ore mined by John D. Rockefeller's Lake Superior Consolidated Mines Company in the recently discovered Mesabi Range. (Incidentally, Rockefeller had worked for Hewitt & Tuttle as a teenager in the 1850s.) Oglebay, Norton received its first two-ton shipment of Minnesota's "red gold" in November 1892. They would continue to manage sales and shipping for Rockefeller's mining interests until 1901, when the oil magnate sold Lake Superior Consolidated Mines to the U.S. Steel Corporation.

For almost a decade, cash flow from this business enabled Oglebay, Norton to adopt the technological improvements made in the shipping industry at the turn of the 20th century, including mechanical unloaders, self-unloading ships, and vessels equipped with cranes. The iron and steel trade grew in tandem during the early 20th century, fueled by industrial demand for steel in all its forms that was used to fill consumer demand for everything from autos and appliances to homes and high-rise buildings.

Although Oglebay, Norton and its predecessors had operated their own shipping vessels since the mid-19th century, the company did not create a true fleet until 1920. At that time, it acquired the late Captain W.C. Richardson's 11 Great Lakes freighters and organized them as The Columbia Steamship Company, named for Henry Tuttle's very first "brig."

When Earl Oglebay and David Norton both died in the mid-1920s, a second generation of corporate management led by Crispin Oglebay and Robert C. Norton advanced to the fore. Earl's nephew Crispin Oglebay, who held the presidency until 1949, has been credited with leading the company into a period of expansion. Following its 1924 incorporation, Oglebay, Norton diversified into the sale of steelmaking fluxes for the manufacture of alloys, ceramics, and chemicals. Over the course of the decade, the firm expanded into mining and selling coal, marketing fluorspar and ferro-alloys, and manufacturing ceramic insulators known as "hot tops" in the steel industry. During the 1930s, it began to manage docks at Toledo, Lorain, and Fairport along the south shore of Lake Erie and acquired coal mines in Ohio and West Virginia. In 1949, the company installed Ohio's first continuous coal mining machine.

The Postwar Era Brings Industrywide Change

Four forces converged on the iron ore industry and Oglebay, Norton to bring about fundamental changes in the business in the late 1940s and early 1950s. World War II's military requirements had driven ravenous demand for high-quality iron ore. Given the high costs (and unpredictable payoff) of domestic underground exploration, iron and steel producers began to seek alternative sources of high-grade ore through overseas exploration and research into converting low-grade ores like taconite and jasper into more useful materials. Oglebay, Norton had started to investigate the development of America's abundant sources of low-grade minerals with the 1939 creation of the Reserve Mining Co. This effort reached its summit with the creation of a large taconite mine in Eveleth, Minnesota, in the early 1960s.

Operations at this mine, which was cooperatively owned yet managed by Oglebay, Norton, focused on iron ore pelletization. This two-step process originated in Europe during the early 20th century. In the first phase, machines pulverized the taconite and sifted the ore from the other elements. The second step formed the ore into pellets that could be used in blast furnaces. By the 1970s, this processed taconite would be the most important product of Minnesota and Michigan mines.

By the mid-1950s, Oglebay, Norton & Co. had developed an unusual and complicated corporate structure. Over the course of the early 20th century, the firm had taken substantial, but not full, positions in a variety of companies, and then managed those businesses for a fee. The arrangement made for intricate intercompany accounting and sometimes internecine competition. Harrie S. Taylor, who succeeded Crispin Oglebay as president in 1949, and Executive Vice-President E.W. Sloan, Jr. began to press for a reorganization in the 1950s. After commissioning a highly critical assessment of the corporate structure,

Oglebay, Norton & Co.'s relatively small group of shareholders voted overwhelmingly to merge its ten affiliates into a single corporate entity in 1957. The move united Columbia Transportation Co., Montreal Mining Co., Ferro Engineering Co., Saginaw Dock & Terminal Co., Richwood Sewell Coal Co., North Shore Land Co., Standard Box Co., Fairport Machine Shop, Inc., Pringle Barge Line Co., and Oglebay, Norton & Co. as Oglebay Norton Company.

During this challenging period of corporate restructuring, Oglebay Norton and the U.S. steel market were inundated with high-grade, yet inexpensive, foreign ore. Imports increased from eight percent of domestic consumption in 1953 to 36 percent by 1963. The combination of high costs, competition, war-driven overcapacity, and exhaustion of higher-grade domestic ore sources forced hundreds of American mines out of business in the postwar era.

Diversification in the 1960s and 1970s

Like many of its colleagues in the iron and steel industries, Oglebay Norton undertook a diversification program in the hopes of reducing its dependence on the cyclical, competitive steel industry. Oglebay Norton acquired three companies and created six others from 1961 through 1976, thereby expanding into industrial sands, foundry, and metal stamping. By the early 1980s, revenues from nonsteel goods and services surpassed steel-related sales. The diversification program helped compensate for downtrends in steel: overall sales increased from $52.5 million in 1960 to $83.6 million in 1975, and profits surged apace, from $2.4 million to $8.7 million.

But this modest diversification was not the most newsworthy of the company's activities in the 1970s. In November 1975 Oglebay Norton's fleet lost its flagship in what has been called "the most famous shipwreck in Great Lakes history." During a terrible storm that year, the freighter *Edmund Fitzgerald* split in two and sank in Lake Superior. The catastrophe, in which all 29 hands were lost, was later immortalized in a popular song by Gordon Lightfoot.

Difficulties Persist in the 1980s

The U.S. iron mining and shipping industries continued to be battered throughout the 1980s, as increasing imports and two severe recessions shuttered one-third of America's iron ore mines. After operating at 75 percent of capacity in 1982 and just over half capacity in 1983, Oglebay Norton and its partners closed the Eveleth Mines for two months that fall to reduce ore inventories. It was the first shutdown in the mines' history.

Oglebay Norton's revenues and net income climaxed in 1981, and the company suffered back-to-back operating losses in 1986 and 1987. The deficits forced the firm to cut its dividend for the first time since becoming a unified company in 1957. Other issues cropped up as the 1980s wore into the recessionary early 1990s. In 1986, LTV Steel Co.'s Chapter 11 bankruptcy erased $50 million in iron ore contracts from Oglebay Norton's books. A 1990 strike at the Eveleth Mines only complicated the situation.

Not surprisingly, these financial woes prompted a rash of shareholder uprisings. In 1987, Hong Kong's Industrial Equity (Pacific) Ltd. acquired a 24 percent stake in the company. There was never any real takeover threat: four board members held a cumulative 50 percent share, and U.S. maritime law limits foreign ownership of U.S.-flagged shipping companies to 25 percent. Oglebay Norton adopted anti-takeover measures nevertheless, including staggered director's terms and a requirement for a 75 percent supermajority to approve a merger. By the end of the year, Oglebay Norton had repurchased the Asian investment company's shares for about $20 million.

Having diffused the previous year's investors, Oglebay Norton executives faced a new challenge in 1988, this time from Brent D. Baird's First Carolina Investors Inc. Having increased its stake in the company to more than eight percent by that fall, this large, Buffalo-based family trust began clamoring for representation on the board. Baird had a reputation for investing in depressed stock that were likely to gain in the long term, and he had earned directorships of other companies in which his fund had a substantial stake. He won a place on Oglebay Norton's board in January 1990 after agreeing not to make a takeover attempt or increase his stake to more than 11 percent. Analysts pointed out that many members of the board of directors had held their seats since the 1950s and 1960s, and that Baird brought a fresh perspective to this administrative body.

Investor John D. Weil was not quite as welcome at Oglebay Norton. Having increased his stake in the company from about five percent in 1990 to more than nine percent in 1992, the Missourian requested a seat on the board of directors. Unable to negotiate a directorship, Weil threatened to launch a proxy fight in 1992. By this time, board members owned just over one fourth of the stock, so although they had a great deal of influence, they did not have a voting majority. Weil was nominated and elected to the board shortly thereafter.

A New Generation of Leadership for the 1990s

R. Thomas Green Jr., a 54-year-old, 25-year veteran of Oglebay Norton, advanced to chairman, president, and chief executive officer in 1992, replacing septuagenarian Chairman Courtney Burton, who had served in that capacity since 1957, and 65-year-old Renold D. Thompson, who had worked at the company since 1952. A steady rate of turnover reduced the average age of the top six corporate officers from the mid-70s to the low-50s.

Upon advancing to the presidency, CEO Green surveyed management in preparation of a five-year strategic plan designed to shed noncore interests, increase efficiency, and boost profitability. From 1992 to 1994, the company reduced expenses by cutting its work force by about 29 percent, from 1,995 to 1,417. Beginning in 1992, the company shed its coal mining and foundry interests and halved its dividend to generate funds for four key businesses: marine transportation, iron ore, refractories and minerals, and industrial sands.

After suffering an extraordinary loss of more than $56.6 million to establish a reserve for employee health and retirement benefits in 1992, the company appeared to have returned to a pattern of growing profitability by the mid-1990s. Revenues increased from $148.8 million in 1991 to $193.6 million in 1995, and net income tripled from $5.1 million to $15.4 million during the same period.

Principal Subsidiaries

Canadian Ferro Hot Metal Specialties Ltd. (Canada); Laxare, Inc.; Oglebay Norton Industrial Sands, Inc.; Oglebay Norton Refractories & Minerals, Inc.; Oglebay Norton Taconite Co.; On Coast Petroleum Co.; ONCO Eveleth Co.; ONCO WVA, Inc.; Saginaw Mining Co.

Principal Divisions

Marine Transportation; Iron Ore; Refractories & Minerals; Industrial Sands.

Further Reading

"Fresh Start for Oglebay Norton," *Business Week,* February 1958, pp. 162, 164.

Gerdel, Thomas W., "Green Named Oglebay Executive VP," *Plain Dealer,* September 1, 1990, p. 2D.

——, "Hong Kong Firm Boosts Stake in Oglebay Norton," *Plain Dealer,* July 18, 1987, p. 3B.

——, "Investor Takes Oglebay Seat," *Plain Dealer,* January 19, 1990, p. 12B.

——, "New Top Officer Signals End of Era at Oglebay," *Plain Dealer,* February 27, 1992, p. 1F.

——, "St. Louis Investor Boosts His Stake in Oglebay Norton," *Plain Dealer,* August 7, 1990, pp. 1E, 4E.

Gleisser, Marcus, "Investor Increases Family's Holdings," *Plain Dealer,* May 3, 1991, p. 1E.

Hillstrom, Kevin, *Encyclopedia of American Industries,* Detroit: Gale Research, Inc., 1991, pp. 338–344.

"The Iron Mining Giants Go Prospecting," *Business Week,* April 26, 1982, p. 120.

Karle, Delinda, "Group Ups Stake in Oglebay Norton, Seeks Board Seat," *Plain Dealer,* September 26, 1989, p. 1C.

Leibowitz, David S., "Something for Nothing," *Financial World,* May 31, 1988, p. 127.

Orth, Samuel P., *A History of Cleveland, Ohio,* Chicago: S.J. Clarke Publishing Co., 1910.

Rose, William Ganson, *Cleveland: The Making of a City,* Kent, Ohio: Kent State University Press, 1950.

Scolieri, Peter, "Oglebay, Baird in 'Standstill' Pact," *American Metal Market,* January 24, 1990, p. 2.

——, "Oglebay To Fund Core Business," *American Metal Market,* November 23, 1992, p. 3.

Strozier, Geraldine M., "4 Ore Firms Demanding Competitor Protection," *Plain Dealer,* July 12, 1983, p. 1D.

Taylor, Harrie S., *"Oglebay, Norton" 100 Years on the Great Lakes,* New York: The Newcomen Society, 1954.

Van Tassel, David D., and Grabowski, John J., eds., *The Encyclopedia of Cleveland History,* Bloomington: Indiana University Press, 1987.

Vernyi, Bruce, "Iron Mine Closings Continue; Soft Steel Demand Forcing Inventory Cuts," *American Metal Market,* July 21, 1983, p. 1.

—April Dougal Gasbarre

OLD AMERICA
CRAFTS ★ FRAMES ★ FLORAL ★ DECOR

Old America Stores, Inc.

811 North Collins Freeway
Highway 75 North
Howe, Texas 75459
U.S.A.
(903) 532-3000
Fax: (903) 532-6708

Public Company
Incorporated: 1980
Employees: 1,800
Sales: $134.6 million (1995)
Stock Exchanges: NASDAQ
SICs: 5949 Sewing, Needlework & Piece Goods; 5999
Miscellaneous Retail Stores, Not Elsewhere
Classified; 6719 Holding Companies, Not Elsewhere
Classified

One of a handful of retailers who redefined the arts and crafts industry during the 1980s and 1990s, Old America Stores, Inc., through its wholly owned subsidiaries, Old America Store, Inc. and Old America Wholesale, Inc., operates a chain of stores that feature a vast selection of craft, framing, floral, and home decorating products. With 95 stores scattered throughout 25 states, Old America ranked as one of the leading multiregional arts and crafts chains in the United States, drawing the majority of its business from its chief areas of operation in the Southwest, Midwest, and Southeast. The company's stores, which ranged in size from 12,000 to 40,000 square feet, were primarily located in small and medium-sized towns and stocked roughly 28,000 products. Although described as an arts and crafts retailer, Old America did not derive the bulk of its sales from the retail sale of traditional arts and crafts items. Instead, the company focused its efforts on selling silk and dried flowers, picture frames, and prints, the fastest growing and most profitable segment in the arts and crafts industry during the 1990s. The company's flower, picture frame, and print sales, which accounted for 53 percent of its total sales in 1995, were enhanced by free framing services, including while-you-wait service for

ready-made frames, and free floral arrangement services, provided the framing and floral materials were purchased at the company's stores. Based in Howe, Texas (55 miles north of Dallas) Old America relied on a 96,000-square-foot distribution center adjacent to its executive offices to serve as the primary waystation for its merchandise.

Arts and Crafts Industry during the 1980s

The most successful retailers during the 1980s were those who aped the prevailing trend of merchandising on a mammoth scale. Big was better for retailers of all types during the decade, as the benefits of volume purchasing and a broad merchandising mix manifested themselves in the proliferation of massive retail units and the decided rise in the number of national and multiregional chains. Small retail establishments, once pitted against much larger stores that offered greater product selection at substantially lower prices, watched their business decline in the face of the sprawling national giants who usurped their markets and drew away their customers. The era of individually operated, ''mom-and-pop'' stores was coming to an end. The race was on to see who could secure the greatest number of markets first, a chess game that more often than not resulted in national and multiregional chains reigning victorious at the expense of small, privately owned retailers. One company that could count itself among the winners during the 1980s was Old America, a retailer that began its corporate life as a small, unassuming company and then expanded vigorously, wholly embracing the strategy of operating as a large volume purchaser with a broad merchandise selection.

Like the U.S. retail industry as a whole, the arts and crafts retail industry became the domain of large-scale operators during the 1980s. In an industry that, historically, had been highly fragmented, or primarily composed of small specialty shops and variety stores, competition was intense, but generally limited to small areas, with one small store doing its best to secure a hold on its local market and fend off a small number of independently operated rivals. Though the arts and crafts market amounted to a considerable sum on a national basis, there were essentially no arts and crafts retailers who could boast that they controlled an appreciable portion of the industry's national

Company Perspectives:

Our formula for growth is simple: Satisfy our customers. Old America's 1,800 associates are committed to this goal, and our team is better trained and prepared than ever before to make it happen.

market. This characteristic of the industry began to change during the 1980s when a few specialty retailers recognized the growth that could be achieved by greatly expanding the square footage of an arts and crafts store, stocking that store with a vast array of products, and transforming this retail prototype into a regional or national chain. These retailers were the "winners" in the arts and crafts industry during the 1980s and the companies that ranked as the dominant forces during the 1990s. Old America's development during the 1980s and the description of its operations during the 1990s exemplified what it took to be an industry leader in the arts and crafts industry.

The Birth of Old America

The course of Old America's development during the 1980s neatly framed the arts and crafts industry's decade of change, beginning with the establishment of the first Old America store in 1980. Although the company's pace of expansion would be at its greatest during the 1990s, when the number of retail units more than doubled during the first half of the decade, Old America by no means remained idle during the 1980s. Instead, the company spent its formative years establishing itself as one of the new breed of retailers that were altering the composition of the arts and crafts industry. By the end of the decade, the company had developed into a multiregional chain, quickly adding to the solitary store opened in 1980. With the exception of an acquisition completed in 1988 that gave Old America two stores, all of the company's stores established during the 1980s were funded principally by equity capital, borrowings, and internally generated reserves of cash. Eschewing the acquisition of existing retail establishments, Old America erected its own stores, developing into a chain with a strong presence in the Southeast, Midwest, and Southwest.

By establishing a network of stores (more than 40 were opened during the 1980s), Old America was able to realize the cost efficiencies achieved by purchasing its merchandise in large amounts. This, in turn, allowed the company to price its merchandise significantly lower than the small, independent competitors who constituted the bulk of the company's competition. From the beginning of its expansion program, Old America stuck to its strategy of establishing stores in small and medium-sized towns, thereby ensuring that much of its competition consisted of small, locally owned and operated retail outlets. The company's penchant for small and medium-sized towns also kept the price of establishing new stores to a minimum, positioning it where real estate and labor prices were substantially lower than in cities.

The location of Old America stores was a distinctive characteristic of the company's operations; so too were the products

that filled the shelves of its retail units. Inside a typical Old America store, roughly 28,000 products were stocked, the breadth of which distinguished the company's stores from the small, independent outlets against which it competed and the composition of which differentiated Old America from the national and multiregional arts and craft chains. By stocking a far greater number of products than its direct rivals, Old America held an obvious advantage over the smaller stores situated in the company's market areas. Given a choice of frequenting a store with a limited supply of arts and crafts items or a store that stocked a vast array of merchandise, customers generally opted for the latter and flocked to the superior merchandise selection housed in Old America stores. The fact that the company's retail units offered their broad range of merchandise at prices significantly lower than the prices charged at the less well-stocked stores of its competition further strengthened the company's customer-drawing power, giving Old America a basic formula for success in the small and medium-sized towns where the company operated the majority of its outlets.

Other arts and crafts retailers could claim a variety of merchandise as bountiful as Old America's, particularly the national and multiregional chains that, along with Old America, were changing the dynamics of the arts and crafts industry during the 1980s. Operators such as Michaels Stores, Inc. (Old America's chief competitor), M. J. Designs, Inc., Hobby Lobby Stores Inc., and Amber's Stores, Inc. stocked a full array of merchandise as well, but Old America distinguished itself from its larger-sized competitors by the makeup of its merchandise mix. As the company developed into a steadily growing chain during the 1980s, the unique composition of Old America's merchandise stood as the hallmark of its success, predicating the company's business during the 1990s.

Although the company carried a broad selection of decorative accent products and craft supplies for do-it-yourself home decorators and craft hobbyists, it did not derive the majority of its business from the sale of traditional arts and crafts items. Instead, Old America concentrated on selling picture frames and flowers, which typically yielded much higher profit margins than could be realized from the sale of traditional arts and crafts products. The merchandise strategy to focus primarily on the sale of flowers and frames proved to be a boon to Old America's business, positioning the company in the fastest growing segment of the arts and crafts industry. There was more to the company's strategy, however, than merely stocking store shelves with a preponderance of silk and dried flowers and picture frames. Unlike most of its competitors, Old America offered free floral arrangement and framing services to customers who purchased materials at company-operated stores, adding an extra enticement to lure customers through the doors of Old America's stores. The free services increased the volume of sales of high-profit-margin merchandise and led to impulse purchases of other merchandise, rounding out the company's business strategy with an innovative flair and giving the company a winning formula to carry it into the 1990s.

Rapid Growth during the 1990s

As Old America entered the 1990s, it embarked on the greatest period of growth in its history. The company opened more stores during the first half of the 1990s than it had during the first ten years of its existence, recording a pace of growth that extended the company's presence throughout half of the United States. As the company's expansion program moved forward during the 1990s, it did so in the same fashion as it had in the past: new stores were primarily situated in strip shopping malls near major thoroughfares and small and medium-sized town were selected over larger population centers. In 1991, five new stores were established, giving the company a total of 52 stores by the end of the year. As a national economic recession intensified during the early 1990s, making the going particularly rough for retailers throughout the country, Old America moved aggressively forward, its expansion unchecked by a stifling economic environment. Ten new stores were opened in 1992, 12 more were established in 1993, when the company completed its initial public offering of stock, and a record-setting 17 stores were opened in 1994, lifting the number of Old America stores to 91 after the four-year spree of new store openings.

At this point in the company's history, as the pace of expansion slowed, Old America's management initiated meaningful changes that were expected to strengthen the company's position during the late 1990s. While the company was busily establishing 17 new stores in 1994, it also took time to conduct a review of its merchandise policies. Following the review, company officials resolved to trim the inventory and selling space devoted to furniture products and to certain craft categories. Management also formulated a more aggressive policy concerning product markdowns to invigorate inventory turnover and speed the introduction of new products. On the heels of these changes, the company launched a store renovation program in late 1994 aimed at increasing store productivity, quickening inventory turnover, and improving the financial performance of the company as a whole.

By late 1995, the store renovation program was completed in 87 stores, each of which contained a wide center aisle the company called a "power aisle." The addition of the wide aisles was expected to accelerate the company's ability to turn over its fastest selling merchandise and provide a highly visible location for the fastest selling items of each season. Concurrent with the creation of power aisles, the company committed itself to offering a greater selection of merchandise associated with the three longest seasons in the crafts industry—spring, fall, and Christmas—and, to a more limited extent, with the Easter and Halloween seasons.

Future Expansion

By the end of 1995, after establishing three new stores during the year, Old America operated 94 stores, 48 of which had been opened during the previous five years. The company's area of operation by this point covered a 25-state area, with the greatest number of outlets located in Florida, where the company operated 14 outlets, and in Arizona and Louisiana, where there were 11 stores in each state. Another store was added to the company's network of outlets in Louisiana in August 1996, when a store opened in Hammond that represented the prototype for future Old America stores. With decor, floral, and framing merchandise occupying 75 percent of the store's 20,000-square-foot floor plan, the Hammond store exemplified Old America's stature as a home decor store with some arts and crafts merchandise, rather than as a genuine arts and crafts retailer.

As the Hammond store was recording a highly successful grand opening, the company was pursuing the objectives it had laid out for 1996, which included opening as many as 16 stores during the year. Given the company's exemplary record of expansion throughout its history (only six stores were closed during Old America's first decade and a half of business), the addition of further units in 1996 and during the late 1990s promised to add to the company's strength. With plans to accelerate expansion during the late 1990s, Old America appeared destined to remain among the ranks of the country's premier arts and crafts retailers.

Principal Subsidiaries

Old America Store, Inc.; Old America Wholesale, Inc.

Further Reading

Murchinson, Robin S., "Old America Stores, Inc.," *Southwest Capital Corporation,* August 29, 1996, p. 1.

—Jeffrey L. Covell

OM Group, Inc.

3800 Terminal Tower
Cleveland, Ohio 44113-2203
U.S.A.
(216) 781-0083
Fax: (216) 781-0902

Public Company
Incorporated: 1991
Employees: 324
Sales: $360.96 million (1995)
Stock Exchanges: NASDAQ
SICs: 2899 Chemical Preparations, Not Elsewhere
Classified; 5162 Plastics Materials & Basic Shapes;
2819 Industrial Inorganic Chemicals, Not Elsewhere
Classified; 2869 Industrial Organic Chemicals, Not
Elsewhere Classified

Created through the 1991 merger of America's Mooney Chemicals, Inc., Finland's Kokkola Chemicals Oy, and France's Vasset, S.A., OM Group, Inc. is one of the world's largest producers of specialty chemicals made from cobalt and nickel powders and inorganic salts. These seemingly obscure metals are used in hundreds of applications, including (but not limited to) glassware, PVC plastics, industrial and household paint, tires, rechargeable batteries, and ceramics. When formed, OM Group was 96 percent owned by Outokumpu Metals & Resources Oy (former parent of Kokkola and Vasset) and four percent owned by James P. Mooney. OM Group went public in 1993 with an initial stock offering valued at about $129 million. The union's success is illustrated by OM's subsequent growth: sales increased 79 percent from $201.2 million in 1992 to $361 million in 1995 and net income more than doubled from $12 million to $25.9 million during that same period.

Although OM Group operates in what has been called an "arcane niche" of the specialty chemicals market, it boasts leading positions in several of its industry segments. The Finnish operation, for example, is the largest nickel inorganic salt plant in the world, with the capacity to process 6,000 metric tons per year. And although it was the smallest of the three merged businesses, Mooney Chemical ranked as America's leading producer of metal carboxylates for the rubber and paint markets. According to company figures, OM Group has built up 22 percent stakes in both the cobalt carboxylates and cobalt salts markets, 15 percent of the cobalt powders industry, and 13 percent of nickel salts.

Postwar Foundation and Development

Predecessor Mooney Chemical Co. was founded in 1946 in Cleveland, Ohio by namesake James B. Mooney and a partner, Carl A. Reusser. The firm manufactured carboxylates (metal soaps) from a variety of metals, with an emphasis on cobalt. Isolated by Swedish chemist Georg Brandt in 1730 or 1742, cobalt ore was long used by potters and glassmakers to give their wares a rich blue color. The metal's name is German in origin; copper miners who discovered this vexing substance mixed in with their target material cursed it as "Kobold," the "devil's imp." Later research showed that cobalt (like lead) was useful as a drier in paint, printing inks, and petroleum. Cobalt, nickel, lead, and other metal "soaps" were sold by Mooney Chemical under the "Organ-o-Metal Chemicals" brand. Leading paint companies headquartered in Cleveland became Mooney Chemical's most important customers.

The African country of Zaire (specifically its Shaba province) became the world's leading cobalt producer in the 1920s and continued to occupy that position throughout the 20th century, producing about one-third of the world's output in the late 1980s. The vast majority of cobalt ore is found in the presence of copper and nickel ores. The cobalt is separated from the other ores during the smelting process, when it is concentrated in the slag layer. A variety of processes can then be used to extract the cobalt from the slag.

By forging strong ties with copper and nickel miners in Zaire and Zambia, James B. Mooney was able to obtain cobalt-laden slag direct from the source. The personal contacts and high level of vertical integration developed during Mooney Chemicals' early years would become key contributors to the company's success in the decades to come. Strong business relationships helped Mooney maintain its supply of cobalt despite the countries' political and economic vacillations. In 1994, James P. Mooney asserted, "When [cobalt] supplies are limited, we're at the head of the line." Vertical integration helped Mooney Chemicals maintain some of the highest levels of productivity in the cobalt specialty-chemicals industry. In the mid-1990s, for example, OM Group's sales per employee were more than double the industry average, at $850,000 compared with less than $300,000.

Cobalt markets were largely limited to paint and petroleum manufacturers in the 1940s and 1950s, but intractable strikes at Canadian nickel mines helped boost awareness and use of cobalt as a nickel substitute in the late 1960s. Although cobalt was more expensive than nickel, it was harder and more heat resistant. "Superalloys" (combinations of metals that had properties well-suited for particular applications) developed in the 1960s and 1970s further expanded the markets for cobalt to include aerospace, magnets, catalysts, and electronics.

Family Succession Portends Corporate Reorganization

Seventh of the founder's 14 children, James P. Mooney emerged as the one with the interest and intelligence needed to run the family business. Having been immersed in the cobalt trade from childhood (he dined with African mining executives as a teenager, for example), the younger Mooney joined the company in 1971 at the age of 23. Just four years later, he advanced from a sales position to join three of his brothers at the company's top executive offices. That is when the patriarch, who had been diagnosed with Lou Gehrig's disease, retired and moved to Florida.

Because of a corporate aversion to debt, acquisitions were infrequent. Nevertheless, Mooney expanded its product line through the purchases of a Mobil Oil Co. subsidiary in Pennsylvania, Chicago's Lauder Chemical, and Cleveland's Harshaw Chemical in the 1960s, 1970s, and 1980s. By 1984, the niche company's 40 employees generated about $2 million in annual sales.

After about 45 years of family ownership, many in the Mooney clan were ready to divest their stakes in the business. Unwilling to relinquish his birthright, President James Mooney sought out a sympathetic acquirer. He found it in Finnish mining powerhouse Outokumpu Oy, which was then looking for a way to spin off its peripheral cobalt operations. In 1991, Mooney Chemicals, Inc. was acquired for about $50 million and merged with Outokumpu's Kokkola Chemicals Oy (in Finland) and Vasset, S.A. (in France). Renamed Outokumpu Metals Group, the reformed company operated as a subsidiary of the Finnish giant until 1993, when the parent company spun off its 96 percent share to the public as OM Group. James Mooney continued to own about four percent of the "new" firm and serve as its chief executive officer.

The merger dramatically expanded Mooney's geographic reach as well as its product line. OM Group emerged as the self-proclaimed "world's first company to manufacture a complete line of cobalt and nickel powders and inorganic salts." New products targeted customers in the steel, magnet, and battery industries. Foreign sales increased from ten percent of annual revenues pre-merger to just over 50 percent by the end of 1993.

The Mid-1990s and Beyond

OM Group looked forward to reaping the benefits of increased capacity, a strategic partnership, and acquisitions in the mid- to late 1990s. In 1994, the company invested $19.7 million in a physical plant, increasing its capacity to produce specialty chemicals vital to the manufacture of rechargeable nickel-hydride and lithium-ion batteries for the growing array of portable electronic cellular phones, laptop computers, and cordless tools. The mid-1995 creation of D&O Inc., a Japan-based joint venture between OM and Dainippon Ink & Chemicals Inc., was a key component of this strategy. OM hoped that its cooperative enterprise would capture 15 percent of the $470 million Japanese market for cobalt-nickel inorganic compounds by the turn of the century.

OM Group also boosted its capacity to manufacture polyvinyl chloride (PVC) heat-stabilizers. These specialty chemicals composed of barium and calcium zinc were an environmentally correct additive used to help PVC plastics retain their color and strength during manufacturing. These highly specialized substances ended up in such mundane household items as shower curtains, garden hoses, and toys.

In the fall of 1995, OM entered the chemical recycling industry through the acquisition of Hecla Mining Co.'s Apex mining division in Utah. Born of the 1976 Resource Conservation & Recovery Act, companies like Apex recycle used electroplating solutions and chemical and petroleum catalysts and extract the valuable cobalt, nickel, and other metals. These materials can then be reused in (and resold to) the oil refining and electroplating industries.

Although OM's array of products had increased to more than 350 items for more than a dozen industries by the mid-1990s, more than two-thirds of those chemicals were still derived from the company's core metal, cobalt. An estimated one-fifth of OM's revenues continued to be derived from paint ingredients and another fifth was generated by petroleum refining catalysts. The remaining 60 percent of sales were distributed among the plastics, ceramics, rubber, glass, and adhesives industries.

After nearly a quarter-century with the company, James Mooney set up an orderly plan of succession with the promotion of North American operations head Eugene Bak to the dual offices of president and chief operating officer in 1995. Despite all of the changes endured by the company and the industry, this realigned management team faced many of the same challenges and enjoyed several enduring corporate strengths nurtured throughout OM's history. Potential pitfalls included high capital expenses; ongoing turbulence in the cobalt market due in part to upheaval in supplier countries like Zaire; and currency fluctuations, especially against the Finnish markka. OM Group faced these hazards armed with high levels of vertical integration and productivity, a conservative balance sheet, and a zeal for innovation.

Principal Subsidiaries

Kokkola Chemicals Oy (Finland); Vasset S.A. (France); OMG Americas, Inc.; OMG Asia Pacific Co., Ltd. (Taiwan); OMG Europe, GmbH (Germany).

Further Reading

Chapman, Peter, "Metal Chemical Recycling Grows," *Chemical Marketing Reporter,* December 25, 1995, pp. 7, 22.

Chynoweth, Emma, "Mooney Merges with Outokumpu," *Chemical Week,* October 2, 1991, p. 14.

Coeyman, Marjorie, "OMG's Chemistry Turns Cobalt to Gold," *Chemical Week,* January 19, 1994, pp. 60–61.

Cohn, Lynne M., "Eugene Bak Appointed OM Group President, Chief Operating Officer," *American Metal Market,* July 25, 1994, p. 5.

——, "Life-Long Interests Focused on Metals," *American Metal Market,* May 12, 1994, p. 6.

Croghan, Lore, "OM Group: Watch the Earnings," *Financial World,* May 9, 1995, p. 24.

Ember, Lois R., "Many Forces Shaping Strategic Minerals Policy," *Chemical & Engineering News,* May 11, 1981, pp. 20–25.

Fine, Daniel I., "The Growing Anxiety Over Cobalt Supplies," *Business Week,* April 16, 1979, pp. 51, 54.

Furukawa, Tsukasa, "Dainippon, OM Group Form Alliance," *American Metal Market,* June 8, 1995, p. 5.

"Metal Chemical Recycling Grows," *Chemical Marketing Reporter,* December 25, 1995, pp. 7, 22.

Mooney, Barbara, "Overcoming Cobalt Blues," *Crain's Cleveland Business,* January 24, 1994, p. 2.

"Outokumpu Prepares To Sell Cleveland-Based OM Group," *American Metal Market,* April 7, 1993, p. 5.

Plishner, Emily S., "OM Group To Go Public," *Chemical Week,* April 14, 1993, p. 13.

Sherman, Joseph V., "No Cobalt Blues," *Barron's,* May 11, 1970, pp. 11, 17.

Yerak, Becky, "Expansion, New Products Help OM Meet Goals," *Plain Dealer,* May 16, 1995, p. 12C.

——, "Mooney Chemicals Merges," *Plain Dealer,* October 3, 1991, p. 2E.

—April Dougal Gasbarre

Orchard Supply Hardware Stores Corporation

6450 Via Del Oro
San Jose, California 95119
U.S.A.
(408) 281-3500
Fax: (408) 629-7174

Public Company
Incorporated: 1986 as Orchard Supply Hardware Stores
Corporation
Employees: 4,980
Sales: $532.4 million (1996)
Stock Exchanges: New York
SICs: 5251 Hardware Stores; 5261 Retail Nurseries &
Garden Stores; 5211 Lumber & Other Building
Materials; 6719 Holding Companies, Not Elsewhere
Classified

A leading home improvement retailer in California, Orchard Supply Stores Corporation operates a chain of hardware stores through its operating subsidiary, Orchard Supply Hardware Corporation. During the mid-1990s, the Orchard Supply chain comprised 60 stores, all located in California. Designed to attract customers seeking to complete the small tasks associated with repairing and maintaining a home, the company's stores occupied a niche in the highly competitive California home improvement market that positioned Orchard Supply as an alternative to the warehouse retail concept most prevalent during the 1990s. Featuring garden and nursery products and houseware merchandise, Orchard Supply stores attracted equal numbers of male and female customers, a rarity in the home improvement industry. In 1993, the company entered the southern California market, and as it laid plans for expansion during the late 1990s, many of the new stores established were expected to be situated in southern California.

Early History

A world of difference separated the Orchard Supply of the 1990s from its origins. The modern version of the company was a sprawling, ever-expanding 60-unit retail chain with 45,000-square-foot stores stocking more than 45,000 products, a retailer engaged in one of the most fiercely competitive industries in U.S. business. Its origins were entirely dissimilar. The company was established in 1931 as a supply cooperative for farmers residing in the Santa Clara area, its formation occurring as the cooperative movement in the United States was in full swing. The company remained a farmer's cooperative for the next two decades, then began selling general hardware merchandise during the 1950s, a retail category that would predicate the company's business for the next half century and beyond.

Throughout much of its history, Orchard Supply operated as a modestly sized enterprise, a hardware store indistinguishable from the thousands of other hardware stores scattered throughout the country. For decades, the company confined its operating territory to the northern California area, restricting itself to its home territory and operating as the quintessential "mom-and-pop" business. In comparison with the frenetic growth that would characterize the company during the 1990s, Orchard Supply pursued a serene and staid approach to business during its formative decades.

Ownership Changes During the 1980s

By the late 1970s, after shedding the cooperative vestiges of its past and moving into the retail sale of general hardware goods, Orchard Supply comprised seven stores, all located in the upper reaches of California. The company was supported by these seven stores when W.R. Grace & Co. purchased Orchard Supply from its original owners in 1979. During the next seven years, the size of the retail chain more than doubled, as expansion picked up pace under the aegis of an owner with deeper financial pockets. Orchard Supply was a 19-store company by July 1986, when Santa Monica-based Wickes Companies, Inc. acquired the retailer from W.R. Grace & Co. The transaction was completed six months before the arrival of the individual that would lead Orchard Supply toward accelerated growth and prominence in the home improvement industry. Under the guiding hand of Maynard Jenkins, Orchard Supply wrested free from its sleepy origins, ending a half century of measured growth to embark on a future that would position the company as an industry leader a decade later.

Company Perspectives:

Since 1931, Orchard Supply Hardware has maintained its strategy of providing a broad merchandise selection, outstanding service, convenient, well organized stores and fair everyday pricing, encouraging its customers to perceive Orchard as the primary destination for their "fix-it" needs. Orchard strives to offer the same quality, service and convenience of a "mom and pop" operation and a greater depth of products in its core product categories than other large warehouse facilities and home center chains.

Born in Orange, California during the early years of World War II, Jenkins grew up in nearby Huntington Beach and attended Orange Coast College. Jenkins's roots in southern California would stand as a symbolic indication of what the future would hold for Orchard Supply, but before Jenkins and Orchard Supply were introduced to each other, the southern California native spent his early professional career as a J.C. Penney management trainee. Jenkins later jumped ship to a competitor, spending time working for Sears, Roebuck & Co. before settling down at the Gemco division of Lucky Stores. Jenkins spent 15 years at Gemco learning the retail trade and then was hired as president and chief operating officer of a 107-unit chain of drug stores operated by Seattle-based Pay 'N Save Stores in 1985. After a year at the dominant Pacific Northwest retail chain, Jenkins switched employers once again, joining Orchard Supply shortly after Wickes Companies acquired the 19-unit hardware retailer from W.R. Grace & Co.

By the time Jenkins joined Orchard Supply, the chain had added two stores, increasing to a 21-store company. This was the starting point of the Jenkins era, a tenure that ten years after his arrival would witness the expansion of the Orchard Supply chain to 60 stores. Before this expansion occurred, Orchard Supply underwent several more ownership changes, as the company was tossed from parent company to parent company, led to private ownership and then toward public ownership.

Late 1980s: Maynard Jenkins Spurs Growth

Exactly two years after Jenkins's arrival Wickes Companies was purchased by Blackstone Capital Partners and Wasserstein Perella Partners, a transaction that also gave Orchard Supply new owners. As far as Orchard Supply was concerned, the relationship lasted less than a year. In June 1989, Jenkins and other Orchard Supply management sought to restore the retailer's independence, enlisting the help of a limited partnership organized by the Los Angeles-based investment firm of Freeman, Spogli & Co. The result was a $134 million leveraged buyout that returned Orchard Supply to private ownership.

Coming off of $255 million in sales in 1988, Orchard Supply generated $280 million in sales during the year of the leveraged buyout. The financial increase was not an anomaly during the first years of Jenkins's influence over the fortunes of Orchard Supply. Between 1987 and the beginning of the 1990s—the first three years of the Jenkins era—Orchard Supply had added

ten stores and had posted consecutive record sales and earnings levels. By the beginning of the 1990s, Jenkins was sitting atop a 33-unit chain as president and chief executive officer, ready to lead the company toward expansion.

Although Orchard Supply was a nearly 60-year-old business as it entered the 1990s, longevity gave no retail competitor an edge during the decade ahead. In addition to the sweeping changes that had revolutionized the home improvement retail industry and dramatically altered the formula for success, the industry had become one of the most hotly contested businesses in the country. Led by Atlanta-based Home Depot, Inc. and Fullerton, California-based HomeClub, Inc., the retail home improvement industry was dominated by massive warehouse stores and discount pricing, two of the determinative characteristics of success that prevailed as the 1990s began.

Despite its promise as a rising contender, Orchard Supply adopted neither of these characteristics. The retail chain emphasized merchandise selection and customer service over pricing. It eschewed the vast floor spaces used by its most intimidating rivals, opting instead to stock twice the number of products in half the square footage typical of industry stalwarts Home Depot and HomeClub. Instead of attempting to attract the classic "do-it-yourself" customers who remodeled their own kitchens and bathrooms, Orchard Supply targeted the "fix-it" shopper, or those customers concerned with completing the smaller tasks associated with repairing and maintaining a home. "Our customers are more likely to repair a leaky faucet than to build a deck," Jenkins explained early on during the 1990s. "Orchard is a hardware store, not a home center."

By operating as such, Orchard Supply distinguished itself from its larger competition and the scores of competitors smaller than the San Jose-based company. Occupying the middle tier of home improvement retailing, Orchard Supply was positioned midway between independent hardware stores and the much larger warehouse home centers, giving the company a viable market niche that would serve as its foundation in the future. As it headed toward this future, the company generated roughly half of its sales from female customers, a rare phenomenon in the home improvement industry. This exception from the norm was also attributed to the differences between Orchard Supply Stores and the larger, more impersonal warehouse stores. Typically, home center stores derived their greatest percentage of sales from lumber and building materials, whereas Orchard Supply relied on plumbing products, housewares, and the 10,000-square-foot nursery that adjoined each unit to generate the bulk of its sales.

It was this successful and unique retailing formula that Jenkins sought to expand throughout California during the 1990s. At the beginning of the decade, all Orchard Supply stores—typically 40,000-square-foot locations with 10,000-square-foot nurseries—were located within 300 miles of the company's 282,000-square-foot distribution center in San Jose, a territory that embraced northern and central California. As Jenkins charted the company's expansion in 1990, he intended to restrict such expansion to California, an area he referred to as "the world's seventh largest market," and to open between two and five stores per year during the ensuing five years. Jenkins was envisioning a 50-unit Orchard Supply chain by 1995.

As the company set forth, the expansion projections announced by Jenkins in 1990 were met nearly precisely. By 1992, Orchard Supply's distribution center in San Jose had become too small to service the company's pressing need to keep its stores' shelves fully stocked. A new, 350,000-square-foot warehouse was established in Tracey, California, giving the company a massive warehouse that was situated equidistant from its expanding chain of stores in central and northern California. By 1993, the company operated more than 40 stores, yet the need to expand further still prodded Jenkins and the rest of Orchard Supply management. To fund this expansion, the company needed cash, so in April 1993 Orchard Supply became a publicly traded company, completing an initial public offering of 3.8 million shares of common stock at $14 per share.

The cash raised from the conversion to public ownership would be desperately needed as Orchard Supply picked up the pace of its expansion and came head to toe with the industry's largest and most successful home improvement chains. Sales for fiscal 1993 climbed to $365 million, continuing the company's impressive string of annual revenue gains, and net income rose to $33,000 after wallowing in the red for two years, but before the year's financial results were announced in January 1994, Jenkins completed a deal that greatly overshadowed the importance of the encouraging financial figures. Although Jenkins regarded the transaction as "a low-risk situation," the contracts signed at the end of 1993 paved the way for Orchard Supply's entry into the most lucrative home improvement market in the United States.

1993 Entrance into Southern California

In December 1993, Orchard Supply acquired seven former Builders Emporium stores, paying a hefty $20 million for the properties. For Jenkins, the price was worth it because six of the stores were located in the Los Angeles area and another near Santa Barbara, giving the company entry into the southern California market for the first time. As Builders Emporium stores, each unit had generated $10 million in sales annually, a volume the stores were expected to realize once they were converted to the Orchard Supply format. The acquisition, according to Jenkins, enabled Orchard Supply to achieve "critical mass," providing the momentum to propel the company into the mid-1990s and toward accelerated growth.

Ranging between 29,000 square feet and 71,000 square feet, the former Builders Emporium locations were converted into Orchard Supply stores during the first few months of 1994. Meanwhile, Jenkins began laying out ambitious expansion plans for the coming years. Looking ahead, he anticipated opening either 14 or 15 stores in 1994 and then ten stores per year from 1995 forward, as he sought to turn what industry observers were hailing as the high-service alternative to warehouse stores into one of the massive chains vying for supremacy in the fiercely competitive market. By the end of 1994, 14 new stores

had been added to the Orchard Supply chain, lifting sales for the year to $441.6 million and net income to more than $1 million.

The pace of expansion ebbed considerably in 1995, when five Orchard Supply stores were added to the chain, but the company's financial growth picked up the slack, rising robustly as stores were added to the lucrative southern California market. Net income in 1995 (the company's 1996 fiscal year) soared from $1.1 million to $10.4 million, and sales increased 21 percent, reaching $532.4 million. To maintain this rate of growth, further expansion was needed, as was the money required to fund the establishment of new stores, so in March 1996 the company sold $11 million shares of stock, providing it with the resources to continue dotting the California map with Orchard Supply stores.

With the money raised through the March 1996 stock offering, Orchard Supply planned to open between five and ten new stores in 1996 and another five to ten stores annually for the next several years, nearly all of which were expected to be located in southern California. To support this growth, plans for the establishment in 1997 of a second distribution facility, also in southern California, were under way as the company headed toward the late 1990s. By April 1996, Orchard Supply was a 60-unit chain, nearly three times the size of the company Jenkins inherited a decade earlier. As Jenkins surveyed the road ahead from this point in the company's history, his confidence was high yet not overly optimistic. "Looking forward," Jenkins remarked in April 1996, "we do not anticipate our sales and earnings increases will maintain as rapid a pace as last year. We do, however, feel that the company is well-positioned for growth."

Principal Subsidiaries

Orchard Supply Hardware Corporation.

Further Reading

Altman, Brad, "Orchard Blooms in California Sun," *Chain Store Age Executive with Shopping Center Age,* May 1990, p. 30.

Cory, Jim, "Critical Mass," *Hardware Age,* September 1994, p. 40.

Davey, Tom, "Orchard Supply Wants Four Hardware Stores in This Area," *The Business Journal Serving Greater Sacramento,* December 10, 1990, p. 2.

"Orchard Records Successful Year, Prepares Stock Offering," *Do-It-Yourself Retailing,* April 1996, p. 21.

"Orchard Supply Acquires 9 Former BE Stores," *Hardware Age,* December 1993, p. A-9.

Schober, William, "Orchard Supply Gears Up for the Fast Track," *Building Supply Home Centers,* May 1994, p. 27.

Shuster, Laurie, "Getting Serious about Casual Furniture," *Home Improvement Market,* June 1996, p. G6.

——, "Orchard Raises Cash To Expand in So. California," *Home Improvement Market,* April 1996, p. 10.

—Jeffrey L. Covell

Oshman's Sporting Goods, Inc.

2302 Maxwell Lane
Houston, Texas 77023
U.S.A.
(713) 928-3171
Fax: (713) 967-8276

Public Company
Incorporated: 1946
Employees: 3,700
Sales: $342.8 million (1995)
Stock Exchanges: American
SICs: 5941 Sporting Goods & Bicycle Shops

Creator of a unique retail format in the sporting goods industry, Oshman's Sporting Goods, Inc. operates a chain of relatively small retail specialty sporting goods stores and a chain of massively sized specialty retail sporting goods stores featuring athletic facilities that allow customers to play with merchandise before they purchase merchandise. For a company founded in 1931, the chain of smaller stores are vestiges of its past, with the exponentially larger stores measuring between 50,000 and 85,000 square feet representing the company's future. Oshman's Sporting Goods did not begin recasting itself as an operator of megastores until 1990, when the first SuperSports USA store opened its doors, but during the first five years of the company's focus on developing large retail units the megastores have increased their importance quickly, generating more than 50 percent of Oshman's Sporting Goods' total sales in 1995. As the 1990s progressed the number of the company's smaller, 8,000-square-foot to 12,000-square-foot stores declined, while the number of its enormous SuperSports USA stores increased. At the end of 1995, there were 109 traditional Oshman's Sporting Goods stores and 24 SuperSports USA stores.

Early History

The Oshman retail business began in 1919, when Jake S. Oshman opened his first store, a dry goods establishment called "Oshman's Dry Goods." Jake Oshman's greatest success,

however, was not achieved in the dry goods business, but in another retail business that would make the Oshman family name known to millions of consumers across the United States. Jake Oshman embarked on the road that would carry him toward national recognition and his signal business success in 1931, when he opened his first sporting goods store in downtown Houston. Founded as a proprietorship, Jake Oshman's sporting goods business was incorporated 15 years later, in 1946, as the country emerged from World War II and embarked on an economic boom period that would at last bring an end to a decade-and-a-half of economic hardship and give the nation's citizens unprecedented amounts of discretionary income and leisure time. Though geographic expansion would come slowly, Oshman's Sporting Goods thrived during the postwar economic rebirth, steadily building a presence in its home state of Texas before entering into neighboring Sun Belt states.

Decades would pass before Oshman's Sporting Goods began to resemble a retail chain, but despite its relatively small size, the business founded and built by Jake Oshman recorded encouraging success during its formative decades. The company's rapid growth and its bid to become one of the country's largest sporting goods chains began nearly four decades after the first Oshman store opened its doors and after its founder, Jake Oshman, left the company. The company's push toward a national presence was orchestrated by another individual, Alvin Lubetkin, who was first introduced to the Oshman family business through the courtship of one of Jake Oshman's daughters, Marilyn Oshman. Lubetkin, a Harvard-educated broker who worked on Wall Street, married Marilyn Oshman in 1960. He then left his job in New York to join Oshman's Sporting Goods a year later at Jake Oshman's request.

Father and son-in-law worked together in Houston, with Lubetkin learning the retail trade from Jake Oshman. Before long, however, the arrangement fell apart and, after one year, Lubetkin quit and returned to working as a broker, later explaining, "Jake Oshman was not easy to work for." But the business separation was not permanent. In 1964, Jake Oshman once again asked his son-in-law to join Oshman's Sporting Goods, this time offering Lubetkin greater responsibility in running the business than he had extended three years earlier. Lubetkin accepted the offer and soon was given more responsibility than he could have expected. Six months after inviting his son-in-law to join the company, Jake Oshman died, paving the way for Lubetkin's ascension to the top of Oshman's Sporting Goods' managerial ladder.

1970 Public Offering

Under Lubetkin's reign of command, Oshman's Sporting Goods blossomed into a national chain with units scattered throughout the Sun Belt states and stretching from coast to coast. Lubetkin's ambitious expansion program began in earnest in 1970, when he took the 11 stores composing the Oshman's Sporting Goods chain public in an initial public offering of stock. The conversion to public ownership marked the beginning of a new era in Oshman's Sporting Goods' history, one that would be dominated by the company's explosive growth and its entry into new territories, as four decades of prosaic growth gave way to two decades of rapid expansion. Looking back from this pivotal juncture in Oshman's Sporting Goods' development, Jake Oshman had taken 39 years to establish a handful of stores, creating a stable, modestly sized business bounded by Texas's borders. Ahead, as the next chapter of Oshman's Sporting Goods' history unfolded, were years of exponential financial growth and physical expansion. In a little more than a decade, Oshman's Sporting Goods' annual sales would leap from the $19 million generated in 1970 to nearly $250 million, and earnings would soar from $883,000 to $7.5 million.

Financial and physical growth was achieved during this period by Lubetkin's emphasis on penetrating new markets through the establishment of new Oshman's Sporting Goods units. Although the proliferation of stores through internal means played a significant role in Oshman's Sporting Goods' growth following the public offering in 1970, growth through external means also contributed to the transformation of the company from a regional chain into a national chain. Lubetkin led Oshman's Sporting Goods through a series of acquisitions following the 1970 public offering that enabled the company to reach the robust pace of expansion that made the Oshman name a national contender in the retail sporting goods industry. In 1972, the company acquired five corporations operating as "Stan's Sports" and purchased Mid-Valley Sports Center. After abandoning the wholesale business in 1974, Oshman's Sporting Goods acquired 24 retail stores from Edison Brothers Stores, Inc. in 1977, and then continued the acquisition spree during the 1980s, acquiring 33 sporting goods stores from Zale Corporation in 1981 and 18 L&G Sporting Goods stores from Lucky Stores, Inc. in 1982.

In the midst of this campaign to add to the company's stature through acquisitions, Oshman's Sporting Goods entered into a new retail niche by acquiring the exclusive rights to the name, trademarks, and service marks belonging to the venerated and esteemed Abercrombie & Fitch Company. Lubetkin made the move in 1978, one year after Abercrombie & Fitch had entered into bankruptcy. He then opened the first revised store bearing the Abercrombie & Fitch name in 1979, establishing the store on Wilshire Boulevard in Beverly Hills. There, Oshman's Sporting Goods' management began superintending the revival of a retailer known for high-priced, prestigious merchandise such as $150 wooden ducks and $25,000 handcrafted Italian rifle sets,

devoting as much effort to the growth of Abercrombie & Fitch as they did to the growth of Oshman's Sporting Goods units.

Despite the efforts of Lubetkin and others, Abercrombie & Fitch proved to be a perennial money loser, dashing hopes that two separate retail vehicles would drive Oshman's Sporting Goods' growth during the 1980s and beyond. Aside from the dismal performance of Abercrombie & Fitch, however, profits were pouring in from the flourishing chain of Oshman's Sporting Goods stores. Since the public offering in 1970 the chain had grown enormously, ranking as the second largest specialty sporting goods retailer in the United States by the mid-1980s, with stores stretching from Sacramento, California to Florida. There were six stores in Hawaii, Oshman's Sporting Goods stores in every Sun Belt state except Mississippi, and stores slated to open in Japan. Annual sales were nearing $300 million, and the number of Oshman's Sporting Goods units was projected to eclipse 200, excluding the nearly 30 Abercrombie & Fitch stores that were part of the company's operations. On nearly all fronts, the business founded by Jake Oshman more than a half century earlier was performing admirably, but in a few short years Oshman's Sporting Goods was in trouble.

Before the luster of Oshman's Sporting Goods' business began to fade, the company sold Abercrombie & Fitch, divesting the floundering enterprise in 1988. Not long after shedding what had been a drag on the company's profits, Oshman's Sporting Goods' nearly 200-store chain began to demonstrate flagging profitability itself, as the dynamics of the retail industry as a whole began to change. In 1989, Oshman's Sporting Goods reported a $1.5 million loss, marking the beginning of what would turn out to be a consecutive string of annual losses that would force Lubetkin and other company executives to reexamine Oshman's Sporting Goods' approach to retailing sporting goods. A new, much larger retail force—"megastores"—had entered the sporting goods fray, stores four to five times larger than the conventionally sized stores that composed Oshman's Sporting Goods' chain, and their pernicious effect on smaller competitors was swift and decisive. Commenting later on the negative impact megastores had on Oshman's Sporting Goods' business, Lubetkin explained to *Footwear News,* "I could blame this on the recession, but the real issue is that some other people out there had developed a better mousetrap. When someone put a 40,000- to 50,000-square-foot superstore next to my 10,000-square-foot store it was painful."

1990 Birth of SuperSports USA

Clearly, something needed to be done to arrest Oshman's Sporting Goods' deteriorating financial health and to reposition the company as a competitor able to thrive in the retail sporting goods industry of the 1990s, but the company's management and board members were undecided on what that something should be. One possibility involved adopting the strategy that threatened to destroy Oshman's Sporting Goods' 193 retail stores. In March 1990, the company opened an 80,000-square-foot SuperSports USA store in Houston that aped the retail trend of the times, but Lubetkin added a twist to the megastore's concept by including athletic facilities within the massive stores that allowed customers to try various sporting good items before they purchased them. Amid the shelves and racks displaying a full line of sporting goods were mini-basketball courts, batting cages, golf simulators, putting greens, boxing rings, racquetball courts, ski decks, climbing walls, archery ranges, and in-line skating areas, offering customers the opportunity to "play before you pay," as the company termed it.

Another SuperSports USA store was opened in 1990, but Lubetkin and the company's board of directors were divided as to whether the megastore strategy was the approach to be adopted for Oshman's Sporting Goods' revival. Lubetkin and others favored the megastore strategy as the company's best opportunity to effect a turnaround, while other board members deemed the creation of a chain of massive retail stores too costly, particularly given the company's anemic financial condition. Following annual losses in 1989 and 1990, Oshman's Sporting Goods registered a $1.9 million loss in 1991 and a $679,000 loss in 1992, which heightened the need to find a solution.

As the number of traditionally sized stores composing the company's chain dwindled during the early 1990s, falling from a peak of 193 to 165 by the end of 1992, Oshman's Sporting Goods tentatively moved forward with the megastore concept, opening three more SuperSports USA stores in 1992. Board members were still arguing over whether the company should pursue the megastore concept, however, lending a rancorous air to board meetings during the early years of the decade that did not disappear until a new chairman took over in April 1993.

Marilyn Oshman, daughter of founder Jake Oshman and the former wife of Lubetkin (the couple divorced in 1977), took the reins of command in April 1993 and sided with her ex-husband on the course the company should follow in the years ahead. After months of debate, the megastore concept was fully embraced, touching off a new era in the company's history that would witness the closing of money-losing, traditionally sized stores and the opening of additional SuperSports USA stores. Although company officials resolved not to abandon their small retail stores entirely (a point underscored by Lubetkin when he told *Discount Store News,* "Oshman's won't ever be just a superstore chain [because] we've got some good little stores that generate pretty good income"), the future of the company was vested in the growth of its SuperSports USA stores.

Three more SuperSports USA stores were opened in 1993, giving the company a total of eight megastores by the end of the year, but staggering losses continued to hound Oshman's Sporting Goods. The company lost $19.4 million in 1993 as the number of its traditional stores fell to 153, causing widespread concern among those in charge of Oshman's Sporting Goods' fortunes. Looking for a saviour, the company's board of directors found one when Marilyn Oshman walked into a meeting in mid-December 1993, although at first those in attendance were startled by Oshman's attire. Oshman entered the meeting wearing camouflage clothing from head to toe, presenting herself more as a curious apparition than the company's chairman, prompting those gathered around the meeting room's table to ask, "Are you going hunting?" Oshman, as she later related the reaction and her response, answered, "Not exactly—not in the traditional sense. But I am hunting—I'm hunting for a profit."

Oshman vowed to wear camouflage clothing every day until Oshman's Sporting Goods turned an annual profit, which she did until the end of 1994, when the company climbed out of the red and posted $290,000 in earnings. During the year, the company had opened four more SuperSports USA stores, giving it a total of 12. Then ten more were opened in 1995, when Oshman's Sporting Goods generated $342.8 million in sales and an encouraging $1.9 million in earnings.

Future Growth Projections

As the company planned for the late 1990s and the beginning of the 21st century, the results of its move into the megastore category were decisive. Between 1990 and 1995, sales from the company's SuperSports USA stores increased from $15.5 million to $164.5 million, a figure that represented 50.3 percent of the company's total sales. For the future, Oshman's Sporting Goods planned to close traditionally sized stores that no longer generated sufficient profit to justify their operation and to accelerate the development of its megastore chain. The company anticipated opening seven new SuperSports USA stores in 1996, 12 in 1997, 14 in 1998, and 16 in 1999, intent on establishing a 72-store SuperSports USA chain by the end of the decade.

Principal Subsidiaries

J. S. Oshman and Co., Inc.; Oshman Ski Skool, Inc.; The Best of Oshitch, District of Columbia; Oshitch Company; Oshitch of Maryland, Inc.; Oshitch of Virginia, Inc.; URAFAN Corp.

Further Reading

Creno, Glen, "Oshman's Unveils Arizona Superstore," *Knight-Ridder/ Tribune Business News,* May 19, 1996, p. 51.

Gibbons, William, "Zelnik Seeks To Acquire Abercrombie," *Daily News Record,* July 24, 1987, p. 1.

Greenbaum, Jessica, "The Prestige of the Thing," *Forbes,* May 9, 1983, p. 183.

Hartnett, Dwayne, "Oshman's Sporting Goods Acquires Sportstown Stores," *Knight-Ridder/Tribune Business News,* August 14, 1995, p. 81.

Heiderstadt, Donna, "Oshman's Megatransformation," *Footwear News,* July 31, 1995, p. 45.

Lee, Sharon, "Oshman's Hits Northeast with Big Princeton Unit," *Footwear News,* February 29, 1988, p. 47.

Lettich, Jill, "Oshman's Refines the Superstore," *Discount Store News,* September 21, 1992, p. 6.

Lustigman, Allysa, "Marilyn Oshman: Chairman of the Board, Oshman's Sporting Goods (The SGB Interview), *Sporting Goods Business,* May 1994, p. 28.

Oberbeck, Steven, "Texas-Based Sporting Goods Chain May Move to Utah," *Knight-Ridder/Tribune Business News,* September 17, 1995, p. 91.

"Oshman's Cuts Back," *Discount Store News,* February, 18, 1991, p. 43.

"Oshman's Planning To Close 33 Stores Over Next 2 Years," *Daily News Record,* December 29, 1993, p. 3.

"Oshman's To Add 6 Superstores," *Discount Store News,* January 3, 1994, p. 6.

Pybus, Kenneth, "In a League of Her Own," *Houston Business Journal,* July 21, 1995, p. 16.

—Jeffrey L. Covell

Park-Ohio Industries Inc.

23000 Euclid Avenue
Cleveland, Ohio 44117
U.S.A.
(216) 692-7200
Fax: (216) 692-7051

Public Company
Incorporated: 1907 as Park Drop Forge Company
Employees: 2,800
Sales: $371.4 million (1995)
Stock Exchanges: NASDAQ
SICs: 2656 Sanitary Food Containers; 3089 Plastics
Products, Not Elsewhere Classified; 3411 Metal Cans;
3462 Iron & Steel Forgings; 3291 Abrasive Products;
5088 Transportation Equipment/Supplies

Entering its 90th year of operation in 1997, Park-Ohio In-
·dustries Inc. is a Cleveland, Ohio-based conglomerate with
operations in ten states. Under the direction of former dissident
shareholder Edward F. Crawford since mid-1992, the company
has been transformed from a consistent money-loser and takeover target into a profitable turnaround specialist. The firm's
diverse interests encompass industrial products like forged and
machined engine parts, induction heating systems, and industrial rubber components as well as consumer goods like outdoor
furniture and lawn care products.

Foundation and Development

Park-Ohio was created through the 1967 merger of Park
Drop Forge Co. and Ohio Crankshaft Co. These two Cleveland
companies experienced a similar pattern of development during
the first half of the 20th century. Established in 1907, Park Drop
Forge was the older of the two firms. It manufactured forgings
for crankshafts, camshafts, and other engine parts used in large
diesel locomotives, trucks, and buses. Dwight Goddard served
as Park Drop Forge's first president and was succeeded by
George C. Gordon in 1913. With its specialization in custom

forging, Park Drop Forge expanded into new modes of transportation as they developed. In 1927, for example, the company's
motor forgings were used in the *Spirit of St. Louis,* helping to
make possible Charles Lindbergh's historic solo transatlantic
flight. By the late 1950s, Park Drop Forge had more than 500
employees, sales of $9 million, and profits of $900,000.

Park Drop's future partner, Ohio Crankshaft, was established by William C. Dunn and Francis S. Denneen in a Cleveland garage in 1920. This company's sales of crankshafts and
camshafts for diesel engines increased so quickly that it was
able to move into a new building in 1922. Growth during the
1930s was fueled by the development of a proprietary metalworking process using high-frequency electrical current. Ohio
Crankshaft created its TOCCO division in 1934 to produce and
sell equipment used in this process. To keep up with demand for
the new machines, the company added two plants during the
1930s and erected a fourth plant during World War II.

By the mid-1950s, Ohio Crankshaft's forged parts could be
found in tugboats, construction and oil drilling equipment,
tractors, trucks, trains, and aircraft brakes. The company generated sales of $20 million in 1956.

Merger in the 1960s

CEO Richard S. Sheetz and President George Bricmont
guided Park Drop Forge's postwar acquisition of its local competitor. Having accumulated a controlling 51 percent stake in
Ohio Crankshaft, Sheetz and Bricmont merged the two companies via a 1967 stock swap. The unified companies' cooperation
bred rapid growth. Taking into account the 1971 acquisition of
Growth International, Inc., Park-Ohio's sales increased from
$46.2 million in 1968 to $89.9 million in 1973. Net income
grew from $1.4 million to $4.6 million during that same period.
The merger added Bennett Industries, Inc., a manufacturer of
steel and plastic containers for the chemical, oil, and food
industries; Castle Rubber Co., a maker of specialty rubber
goods; and Globe Steel Abrasive Co., a producer of metallic
cleaners used in steel fabrication.

Spurred by the decade's energy crisis and spearheaded by
President Bricmont, Park-Ohio acquired oil and natural gas

interests to become energy self-sufficient. By the late 1970s, the company's more than 200 wells throughout Ohio, Pennsylvania, and New York were producing 37 trillion cubic feet of natural gas and 1.5 million barrels of oil. The company's multifaceted strategy worked well through the 1970s. Revenues nearly doubled from $90 million in 1973 to $159 million in 1978, and net income grew even faster, from $4.6 million to $10.3 million.

Early 1980s Recession Heralds Tough Decade

Park-Ohio's many years of prosperity came to an end in the early 1980s, when recession hit the midwestern "Rust Belt" especially hard. Prices of natural gas and oil—by this time a significant segment of the company's business—went into a precipitous decline. At the same time, the conglomerate's Ohio Crankshaft subsidiary lost its single biggest client, accounting for more than two-thirds of annual volume. Not surprisingly, Park-Ohio's sales and profits began to decline. After peaking at more than $200 million in the early 1980s, revenues dipped to less than $150 million in 1983, the year the company suffered a net loss of $5.6 million.

In light of the economic environment, Park-Ohio asked employees at two Ohio Crankshaft plants to accept wage, vacation, and benefit concessions. Workers, who considered the plants' steadily shrinking employee rolls and work rule changes "union-busting" tactics, balked at the proposals. In July 1983, more than 100 United Auto Worker members employed at the Ohio Crankshaft factory in Cleveland went on a protracted strike marred by violence and frequent legal tangles. Production at the Cleveland TOCCO plant was transferred to a new facility in Alabama, and Park-Ohio hired replacement workers at the crankshaft facility.

Although the national economy improved over the course of the decade, Park-Ohio's performance only worsened. The company ended up in the red in five out of the six years from 1986 to 1992, accumulating more than $87 million in losses. In 1989, Value-Line downgraded the company's stock to a speculative investment. Led by local businessman Edward F. Crawford, some unhappy shareholders began to call for management changes. After a series of late 1980s suits and countersuits, Crawford won a seat on Park-Ohio's board of directors in 1989.

In 1988, the company hired Stanley V. Intihar away from a 30-year career with TRW's automotive division. Intihar led a return to Park-Ohio's traditional manufacturing focus, selling the company's money-losing energy interests to Atwood Resources Inc. for $29 million in 1988. The company took a $29.7 million loss on the transaction. Intihar succeeded Richard S. Sheetz, a 24-year veteran of Park-Ohio's chief executive office, in 1991. The new leader quickly spun off unprofitable steel abrasives operations and announced his intention to focus on what he considered the "core business," Bennett Industries. Although they reduced revenues to $120 million by 1992, these divestments freed up sorely needed capital for debt reduction, new production equipment, and other physical plant improvements.

But before these actions could bear fruit, Intihar resigned without comment. Park-Ohio Director Thomas McGinty assumed corporate leadership on an interim basis. Combined with

all of its other weaknesses, the vacancy at the top made Park-Ohio particularly vulnerable to hostile takeover. Over the course of the next few months, the company thwarted several buyout overtures while sorting out its options. In the middle of 1992, the board of directors and shareholders voted to ratify a plan formulated by one of their newest colleagues, Edward Crawford. Crawford proposed that the firm purchase his privately held Kay Home Products and elect him chairman, chief executive officer, and, incidentally, lead shareholder. The subsequent stock swap was the first step in Park-Ohio's transformation from a weak business riddled with red ink into an aggressive, efficient turnaround expert.

Reorganization Brings Return to Profitability in 1990s

Although he was only 53 years old in 1992, Crawford had started out in business in 1962 with a steel container concern. Under the aegis of Crawford Group, Inc., he later diversified into roofing materials and, eventually, into consumer leisure goods. By the early 1990s, his Kay Home Products manufactured barbecue grills, patio tables, and lawn spreaders. It brought Park-Ohio $15.5 million in annual revenues, $405,600 in profits, and a measure of diversification to even out the parent company's cyclical core businesses.

Within six months of taking the helm at Park-Ohio, Crawford had begun a sweeping reorganization. He reduced the board of directors from ten to nine members, brought in a new generation of managers, and instituted $400,000 worth of cost savings each month. Although the company still suffered a loss on 1992, Crawford's first address to his fellow shareowners emphasized that Park-Ohio enjoyed a low level of debt and high capacity for profitable growth.

Crawford was also credited with bringing the nine-year strike at Ohio Crankshaft (by this time the longest walkout in UAW history) to its conclusion. Union officials and management agreed that the key to the settlement was Park-Ohio's dismissal of its hard-line, anti-union law firm. By the end of 1992, the parties had ratified a three-year agreement that featured company-funded health and retirement benefits as well as pay increases. About half of the original picketers had endured the record-breaking conflict.

Acquisitions, New Products Expected in the Mid-1990s and Beyond

In 1993, Crawford set the firm on a path of growth through acquisition, targeting local companies, for the most part, that had untapped potential or that complemented Park-Ohio's core operations. Within that year alone, the firm made seven separate acquisitions, increasing annual sales to $149 million by the end of 1993 and, perhaps more important, returning the parent company to the black with a $6 million profit.

Flush with his success, Crawford set a sales target of $500 million for the end of the decade and then made a large stride toward that goal with the 1995 acquisition of RB&W Corp. (formerly Russell, Birdsall & Wood). This $60 million stock swap, Crawford's largest transaction to date, was the company's only acquisition for the year. Park-Ohio gained another

$8 million toward its $500 million sales goal with that year's acquisition of northeast Ohio's Geneva Rubber Co. In 1996, the conglomerate began to fine-tune its family of companies through the sale of Bennett Industries, Inc. to a subsidiary of Australia's Southcorp Holdings Ltd. Crawford said that he planned to use the proceeds of the divestment for new acquisitions. In the fall of 1996, in fact, Park-Ohio made a $170 million cash bid for Sudbury Inc., a northeast Ohio firm with about $300 million in annual sales.

Although corporate transactions were clearly Crawford's primary expansion strategy, Park-Ohio also sought growth through product diversification. In the spring of 1996 the company created a new subsidiary, Park-Ohio Biomedical Group, to manufacture a patented prescription drug container. Created by a team of physicians, this vial featured a one-piece child safety cap that was purported to be easier for arthritic and elderly adults to remove.

Tangible signs of Crawford's successful turnaround abounded. Park-Ohio's stock appreciated from about $2 in late 1990 to more than $17 in early 1996. And not only did the company stay in the black, but its net income quadrupled from $6 million in 1993 to $24 million in 1995. Sales more than doubled during the same period, from $147 million to $371 million. It appeared mid-decade that the company had finally found a reliable formula for profitable growth.

Principal Subsidiaries

Ajax Manufacturing Company; Blue Falcon Forge, Inc.; Castle Rubber Company; Cicero Flexible Products; General Aluminum Mfg. Company; Gilchrist Kustom Molders, Inc.; National Automatic Pipeline Operators, Inc. (50%); Park-Ohio Bio-Medical Group, Inc.; The National Pipe Line Company (60%); RB&W Corporation; Steel Abrasives, Inc.; TOCCO, Inc.

Further Reading

Gerdel, Thomas W., "Chairman Resigns from Park-Ohio," *Cleveland Plain Dealer*, November 15, 1991, p. 2E.

——, "Suitor Makes Conditional Bid for Park-Ohio," *Plain Dealer*, March 4, 1992, p. 2G.

Karle, Delinda, "Investors Seek Park-Ohio Board," *Plain Dealer*, December 16, 1988, p. 9C.

Livingston, Sandra, "Ohio Crankshaft, UAW Near Pact," *Plain Dealer*, May 30, 1992, p. 1F.

"Park-Ohio Industries Inc.," *The Insiders' Chronicle*, June 29, 1992, p. 2.

Phillips, Stephen, "Park-Ohio Names CEO, Ends Merger Talks," *Plain Dealer*, May 3, 1991, p. 2E.

Rollenhagen, Mark, "UAW Ends 9-Year Strike at Park-Ohio," *Plain Dealer*, June 1, 1992, pp. 1B, 3B.

Rose, William Ganson, *Cleveland: The Making of a City*, Kent, Ohio: Kent State University Press, 1950, pp. 665, 848.

Sabath, Donald, "Acquiring Chief Exec Celebrates," *Plain Dealer*, October 27, 1994, p. 1C.

——, "Companies Have Much in Common," *Plain Dealer*, October 27, 1994, p. 1C.

——, "Largest Shareholder To Take Over Park-Ohio," *Plain Dealer*, July 9, 1992, p. 8G.

——, "Park-Ohio Industries Begins Turnaround, Chief Says," *Plain Dealer*, February 19, 1993, p. 2E.

——, "Park-Ohio Industries Says Plan Is To Grow through Acquisitions," *Plain Dealer*, October 2, 1993, p. 8F.

——, "Park-Ohio on the Prowl, Buys 5.4 Percent Stake in Sifco," *Plain Dealer*, December 6, 1994, p. 1C.

——, "Park-Ohio Planning Changes, Acquisition," *Plain Dealer*, May 19, 1992, p. 1G.

——, "Park-Ohio Rejects Takeover Offer in Spite of Shareholder Urging," *Plain Dealer*, March 27, 1992, p. 6F.

——, "Park-Ohio To Sell Bennett Industries Unit to Australians," *Plain Dealer*, May 30, 1996, p. 1C.

——, "Park-Ohio Unveils Easier-To-Open Prescription Vial," *Plain Dealer*, March 29, 1996, p. 1C.

Sabath, Donald, and Yerak, Becky, "Park-Ohio in Hunt for Sudbury," *Plain Dealer*, September 4, 1996, pp. 1C, 2C.

Sullivan, Elizabeth, "Police Role in UAW Strike Tangles Issues," *Plain Dealer*, August 25, 1985, p. 1A.

Van Tassel, David D., and Grabowski, John J., eds., *The Encyclopedia of Cleveland History*, Bloomington: Indiana University Press, 1987.

Weiss, Barbara, "Manufacturing Main Target for Park-Ohio," *Metalworking News*, May 9, 1988, pp. 4–5.

—April Dougal Gasbarre

Philipp Holzmann AG

Taunusanlage 1
60299 Frankfurt am Main
Germany
(069) 262-1
Fax: (069) 262-433

Public Company
Incorporated: 1917
Employees: 47,355
Sales: DM$14.09 billion (1995)
Stock Exchanges: Frankfurt
SICs: 1541 General Contractors—Industrial Buildings
and Warehouses; 1622 Bridge, Tunnel, Elevated
Highway Construction; 1623 Water, Sewer, and
Utility Lines Construction; 1629 Heavy Construction,
Not Elsewhere Classified

Philipp Holzmann AG is Europe's largest construction company, the second-largest international building contractor in the world (after France's GTM Enterpose), and a global leader in the design and construction of bridges and tunnels, industrial facilities, and public, residential, and commercial buildings as well as prefabricated housing, wooden structures, and building restoration work. As one of the most prominent construction companies in the history of German industry, Philipp Holzmann has played a central role in many of the world's major construction projects, completing structures in more than 70 countries worldwide since its founding. Typical Holzmann projects in the 1990s ran the gamut from high-rise banks, telecommunications towers, marinas, airports, and printing houses to cooling towers, warehouses, gasification plants, waste incineration plants, and the restoration of the U.S. Capitol building. In more recent history, Holtzmann helped construct such noteworthy projects as the 60-story One Peachtree Center in Atlanta and the tallest building in the world (upon completion), Malaysia's Petronas Towers. In 1995, Holzmann maintained branches and offices in 37 German cities and through its 60-odd subsidiaries and associated companies operated in nine foreign countries, with active construction projects from Mongolia to Mali.

Besides general construction work, which comprised 70 percent of Holzmann's total output or sales in 1995, Holzmann's secondary business activities (roughly one-fifth of its business output) are divided between its operations in the construction of transportation systems and the extraction of raw materials; its energy and environmental technology operations; and its services sector. Holzmann's transportation/raw materials group includes its marine, highway, and railway construction operations as well as its raw materials quarrying operations, sand and gravel pits, and raw materials mixing and batching facilities. Its energy and environmental technology group offers such services as waste and water treatment, flue gas cleaning, composting, soil cleaning, and groundwater remediation. Holzmann's services sector is involved in such services as providing integrated construction planning services, adding value to newly acquired real estate by erecting appropriate structures, arranging private financing for infrastructure projects, and managing facilities through technical administrative building services. Each of Holzmann's four sectors is in turn divided into four phases or "fields of activity": (1) design, planning, consulting, and research, (2) project development, (3) construction, and (4) management, service, operation, and maintenance.

19th Century Origins

Philipp Holzmann was founded as a small family enterprise by Johann Philipp Holzmann near Frankfurt, Germany, in 1849. A number of German construction firms that Holzmann would later acquire were also founded during and even before this period: stone facade producer Zeidler & Wimmel (acquired by Holzmann before 1980), for example, was established in the late 18th century and participated in the construction of Berlin's famous Brandenburg Gate; power station builder Steinmüller Group (acquired in 1989) was founded in 1855; and road builder Berneburg GmbH (acquired in 1987) was laying pavement well before the turn of the century. Holzmann's early growth was closely linked to the construction of the German national railroad system, but throughout the century it participated in the erection of several German architectural landmarks, including Frankfurt's Opera House (begun in 1873) and Munich's Palace of Justice (1892).

By the latter part of the 19th century, Holzmann was constructing railways and railroad terminals all over the world, beginning with the Wettstein Bridge in Basel, Switzerland, in 1877 and then in 1882 Amsterdam's Central Station railway terminal. In the 1880s, Holtzmann performed the stonemasonry work for Berlin's historic Reichstag building and later completed the Baghdad Railroad in Iraq and the Dar-es-Salaam railway in eastern Africa. By the mid-1890s, Holtzmann was employing more than five thousand workers and had established one of the earliest examples of a corporate employee health insurance program. For its work on the Anatolian Railroad in Turkey, it was granted economic concessions to the lands surrounding the railroad between 1906 and 1914, which it used to develop irrigation projects for growing cotton for export to Germany. In 1906, Holtzmann began establishing subsidiaries in South America that in subsequent years undertook major power plant, bridge, sewer system, subway, and other civil engineering projects in Argentina, Brazil, Chile, Colombia, Peru, and Uruguay. Although originally founded as a sole proprietorship, Holzmann grew during the 19th century into a limited partnership, then a general partnership, and finally a GmbH (limited liability company) before officially becoming a joint stock corporation (*Aktiengesellschaft*) in 1917.

20th Century Innovations and Expansion

Before World War I interrupted Holzmann's international markets, Holzmann had constructed the first skyscraper in Buenos Aires; the port system for Buffalo, New York; and the New York barge canal. It invented the so-called Berlin method of cladding building foundation ditches around the turn of the century and at about the same time introduced a shield tunneling system using compressed air. It also continued to build many historically significant buildings, bridges, tunnels, and dams in Germany, from the Kathreiner House in Berlin and the Kiel Canal to the City Hall in Hamburg. Like many German companies, Holzmann suffered substantial losses in assets and manpower during World War II but within five years of the war's end had managed to resume its halted overseas operations. Moreover, its many construction projects within Germany during the 1950s and 1960s coupled with its own recovery from the devastating effects of the war contributed to the prolonged boom now referred to as Germany's "Economic Miracle." In the same postwar period, Holtzmann branched out from its traditional fields of commercial, civil, and marine construction into such new areas as road building and industrial prefabricated construction.

In the early 1970s, Holzmann expanded into the Arabian countries, and soon projects in Saudi Arabia were accounting for three-quarters of Holtzmann's international revenues. As the decade progressed, however, war and political turmoil in Iran and Iraq coupled with weak oil prices forced Holzmann's management to reconsider its heavy emphasis on the Middle East. In the mid-1970s, Holzmann consequently began scaling back its presence in the region while evaluating U.S. firms for a strategic acquisition that would open that vast market to its engineers. By 1980 Holzmann had reduced its Middle East operations to 56 percent of total foreign operations and a year later to 35 percent.

In 1982 CEO Hermann Becker recalled for *Business Week* Holzmann's thinking during this period: "We began to worry; what happens if the market collapses, maybe for political reasons?... We started to diversify regionally and to look for markets with generally the same characteristics as our home market, mostly [those] free from political problems, where we could expect economic growth in the long term."

As early as 1973, Holzmann had participated in a small joint venture in Gary, Indiana, that convinced management that no extensive U.S. operations would be possible without a subsidiary on American soil. In its hunt for likely acquisition targets, one American firm stood out. Several years earlier Holzmann had been involved in a joint venture to construct a military training center in Saudi Arabia with J. A. Jones Construction of North Carolina—a state with which CEO Becker became familiar while imprisoned there as a German POW in World War II. Jones's 60-year history had ranged from the early construction of textile mills in North Carolina to the erection of housing projects for the U.S. government in the 1930s to military-related construction during World War II—including the Oak Ridge, Tennessee, diffusion plant used to produce uranium for the first atomic bombs. After World War II, Jones became involved both domestically and internationally in everything from constructing residential housing, industrial buildings, dams and powerhouses, nuclear power facilities, and highways to the ultramodern East Wing of the National Gallery of Art in Washington, D.C. Moreover, Jones had been involved in 80 percent of all construction performed for the U.S. armed services during the Vietnam war. By the time of Holzmann's acquisition, Jones had risen to become the 13th-largest builder in the United States.

The addition of Jones's operations did not come cheaply. Sizable down payments from Holzmann's Middle Eastern oil customers, however, as well as the large accumulation of reserves permitted by German tax law had left Holzmann flush, and for a lump sum of $75 million it bought up Jones and all its subsidiaries. In exchange for Jones's sophisticated international purchasing operations, American-style high-rise construction expertise, and experience constructing breweries, refineries, and chemical plants, Holzmann helped its American partner improve its civil engineering capacities and its ability to take on projects over $100 million in cost. It also convinced Jones to abandon its cost-plus bidding practice (in which the builder receives a relatively fixed two to three percent of a project's costs as profit) for the lump sum method (in which Jones's profit on a project increased the more it held down project costs).

Significantly, the Jones acquisition had been accomplished without the rancor that often accompanies corporate takeovers. Holzmann left Jones's management team in place and worked with them to smooth over early difficulties. Within three years Jones was accounting for more than one-third of Holzmann's total revenues ($1.35 billion of $3.33 billion). By 1981, the purchase had helped raise North America's share of Holtzmann's total operations to 56 percent, up from 38 percent in 1980, and increased the companies' total revenues by 55 percent over 1980. By taking over its parent company's purchasing operations, Jones was also managing approximately $25 million worth of Holzmann's purchases annually by 1982.

Holzmann continued its international expansion in the years that followed. It added Lockwood Greene Engineers in 1980–81; pursued a Mexican joint venture in the early 1980s; acquired the Steinmüller Group in 1989 to form the core of its Energy and Environment Technology sector; and added French builder Nord France S.A. between 1989 and 1991. Between early 1995 and the critical acquisition of J. A. Jones 16 years earlier, Holzmann was involved in no fewer than fifty expansionary moves, from partial share purchases and outright acquisitions to the launching of numerous subsidiaries and joint ventures.

Holzmann's later acquisitions did not all work out as splendidly as J. A. Jones, however. Nord France quickly turned into a financial quagmire, draining DM500 million ($232.2 million) from Holtzmann's coffers between 1989 and 1994, before turning the corner in 1995. Holtzmann's German holdings—from window manufacturer Zenker-Fenster to building technology subsidiary Scheu + Wirth AG and steel builder Stahlbau Lavis Offenbach—all had losing years as well. The setbacks, exacerbated by a slump in the worldwide construction industry in the early 1980s, prompted a German construction industry analyst to remark to the *Wall Street Journal,* "I don't know of any other German company that's had so much bad luck with acquisitions."

The 1990s and Beyond

The reunification of eastern and western Germany in 1990 promised to rescue Holtzmann from that bad luck by opening up lucrative new markets in infrastructure and other construction in the states of the former East Germany. In a small irony, it also enabled Holtzmann to open its branch offices for the new eastern German states in the same locations they had occupied at the end of World War II. In its 1994 annual report, Holtzmann's management described its participation in the eastern German projects as not only a business opportunity but an "obligation" and vowed to continue committing a "disproportionate" percentage of its business activity to these internal projects. Reflecting this, Holtzmann's output within Germany rose from DM4 billion to DM9.1 billion between 1989 and 1990—DM4.1 billion of which was committed to the new eastern German *Länder* (states) alone. And while 53 percent of Holtzmann's business was devoted to German projects in 1990, by 1995 that figure had risen to 69 percent.

The booming growth of the Pacific Rim economies in the 1990s also offered Holtzmann new construction opportunities. By 1990, Asia was the second-largest market for transborder construction contracts in the world, generating $27 billion in contracts to foreign construction companies in 1990 alone. Holtzmann adopted a grassroots strategy of establishing local subsidiaries in Asian countries in order to capitalize on local expertise in construction markets and subcontracting networks. While public infrastructure projects have historically been a special forte of German construction firms, in the mid-1990s an increasing number of these projects involved a "build-operate-transfer" (BOT) arrangement. In these contracts (devised by the Turkish government in the 1980s) the construction firm not only performs the actual construction but also operates the finished facility until it turns a profit, then transfers it to the local government. Holtzmann's involvement in a 1995 joint venture project for the construction of the massive Birecik hydroelectric dam project in

Turkey exemplified the typical BOT contract. Like other major international builders, in the mid-1990s Holtzmann also offered private financing arrangements for such public infrastructure projects in order to win contracts from governments leery of underwriting the full cost of huge construction projects.

Announcing that "South East Asia is *the* growth market of the future," Holtzmann explored the Hong Kong market in 1990 through a joint arrangement with Hong Kong contractor Hsin Chong to create a third company, Hsin Ching Philipp Holzmann Civil Engineering. In 1995, Holtzmann's decision in 1980 to recruit Chinese workers for an Iraqi office building project redounded to its benefit when China, which traditionally uses byzantine negotiation procedures and stiff financial requirements to discourage foreign business, awarded Holtzmann its first Chinese contract, for a resort in Zhaoquing City. By the mid-1990s, Holtzmann was operating in Thailand, India, and Malaysia and was exploring business opportunities in Vietnam, Myanmar (Burma), the Philippines, Laos, and Indonesia. In 1995, Asia accounted for 13 percent of Holtzmann's total foreign output, up from eight percent the previous year. In the mid-1990s, Holtzmann also announced plans to revive the South American construction business it had maintained before World War II.

In the fall of 1994 Hochtief AG, Germany's second-largest construction company, announced its intention to increase to 35 percent the 20 percent stake it had acquired in Holzmann in 1981. Although the *Wall Street Journal* described the competition between Germany's two biggest builders as "fierce," they had in fact worked together on projects before and had reached their current stature by very different paths. Holzmann, for example, was more active in foreign markets than Hochtief (33 percent versus 25 percent, respectively, of total business activity in 1993) and was particularly strong in the world's largest construction market, the United States, while Hochtief was the leader in Australia. Hochtief was the smaller of the two firms but adjusted for size was the more profitable, and according at least to an industry analyst with DB Research GmbH its management seemed to "work more professionally" than Holzmann's. More importantly, while Holzmann's foreign orders had declined between 1989 and 1994, Hochtief's had grown, as had its reputation in such areas as airport construction.

To Holzmann, the long-term import of Hochtief's threatened share increase was unambiguous: a 35 to 40 percent share of Holzmann's stock would give Hochtief a majority of votes at Holzmann's shareholder meetings and effective control of the company. Holzmann reacted by raising more capital to fend off, some said, Hochtief's attempted hostile takeover. Publicly, it stated that although it was ready to work with Hochtief, particularly in foreign projects, it intended to remain an independent company. In January 1995 the Federal Cartel Office—Germany's arbiter in antitrust matters—announced it was denying Hochtief's bid to increase its stake in Holzmann from 20 to 35 percent. Hochtief appealed the decision, but the Cartel Office remained unmoved and rejected Hochtief's bid again in late 1995, claiming that the merger of the two companies would unfairly dominate Germany's construction industry, a vital component of the German economy. Holzmann hailed the decision as "an important event in the 145-year history of the enterprise and the decisive prerequisite for its independence." Hochtief appealed the decision to the Berlin court of appeals, with the first hearings scheduled for late 1996, and vowed to carry its case, if necessary, all the way to Germany's supreme court.

But financial misfortunes continued to plague Holzmann in the mid-1990s. A severe post-reunification construction slump, building projects running up 1995 operating losses approaching DM100 million, and unexpected losses in income from its office and commercial rental properties had forced Holzmann to renege on an earlier promise to pay shareholders a "good dividend" for 1995. Unfortunately, less than three months after this announcement, Holzmann disclosed that 1996 dividends were going by the boards as well. Write-downs and other costs of its property investments had created an unanticipated loss of DM460 million, and payouts to shareholders were simply impossible. Some industry analysts claimed that Holzmann's heavy losses had as much to do with poor management as an unpredictable property market, citing Holzmann's heavy investments in the Swiss-based property development group, Vebau, and its failure to readjust its properties' values down to market levels.

In the wake of these financial setbacks, Holzmann's chief financial officer resigned in May 1996 and was replaced with the finance director of Deutsche Babcock, a German power plant engineering firm hurting from the evaporation of modernization projects in eastern Germany. In answer to speculation that Holzmann was planning to acquire Deutsche Babcock to help in its fight with Hochtief, current chairman of the board Lothar Mayer frankly admitted that Holzmann was seeking "as much as possible" of Deutsche Babcock, a merger that if concluded would create a new German power plant, engineering, and construction megafirm.

With Germany's five-year reunification construction boom played out, Holtzmann confessed publicly in June 1996 that it faced "very difficult years" in 1996 and 1997, causing some to speculate that the company would cancel dividends for a third year in a row. In spite of its difficulties, however, Holzmann entered the late 1990s a still wealthy—if besieged and fallible—global giant. From the depths of a stagnant German construction market, Holzmann had nevertheless managed to post revenues of DM14.1 billion in 1995, an *increase* of eight percent over 1994, and continued growth in its Chinese, Thai, British, South African, Spanish, and U.S. operations offered additional cause for optimism. While the financial setbacks of the mid-1990s seemed to prevent Holzmann from conclusively escaping the threat of takeover, its ample DM1.7 billion in equity capital, its steadily expanding global markets, its technical expertise in executing complex construction projects, and, perhaps most important, its long history of resilient growth sustained its status as a dynamic leader in the international construction market.

Principal Subsidiaries

J. A. Jones Inc. (U.S.); Deutsche Asphalt GmbH; Philipp Holzmann-Held & Francke Bau AG; Stahlbau Lavis Offenbach GmbH; Imbau Industrielles Bauen GmbH; INTECH Verwaltungsgesellschaft mbH; Zeidler & Wimmel GmbH & Co.; Zenker-Fenster GmbH & Co. KG; Josef Möbius Bau-Gesellschaft (Gmbh & Co.; 50%); Holzmann Gleisbau GmbH; Philipp Holzmann Austria G.m.b.H.; Philipp Holzmann Bau Gesellschaft m.b.H. (Austria); Philipp Holzmann BauProjekt AG; Philipp Holzmann Iberica, S.A. (Spain); Nord-France-Gruppe (57.9%); Tilbury Douglas Plc (United Kingdom; 29.5%); Steinmüller-Lavis Structural Steel (Pty) Ltd. (South Africa; 68.5%); Philipp Holzmann U.S.A.; Holzmann Videocon Engineers, Ltd. (India); Philipp Holzmann Nederland B.V.; Holzmann (Malaysia) Sdn. Bhd.; Philipp Holzmann (Thai) Ltd. (49%); Jones Capital Corp. (U.S.); Rea Construction Company (U.S); Lockwood Greene Engineers, Inc. (U.S.; 80%).

Further Reading

Ascarelli, Silvia, "German Construction Rivals Tighten Ties: Hochtief Bets Bigger Will Be Better with Holzmann," *Wall Street Journal,* October 3, 1994, p. A15.
——, "Hochtief Intends to Boost Stake in Rival Holzmann," *Wall Street Journal,* September 20, 1994.
Barham, John, "Dam Developers Wear Down Bureaucrats' Hostility to BOT," *Financial Times,* December 7, 1995.
"Both Partners Work for Successful Marriage," *Engineering News-Record,* June 3, 1982, pp. 30–34.
Deckard, Linda, "Land Purchase Clears the Way for Cologne Arena," *Amusement Business,* April 6, 1992.
"Fields of Activities and Business Segments," corporate brochure, Frankfurt, Germany: Philipp Holzmann AG, 1995.
Fisher, Andrew, "Holzmann Falls into Unexpected Loss," *Financial Times,* April 16, 1996.
——, "Holzmann Loss Shocks Market," *Financial Times,* April 17, 1996.
J. A. Jones, Inc., "Reflections of the Past," corporate document, 1890–1980, Charlotte, N.C.: J. A. Jones.
Lindemann, Michael, "Holzmann Move Fuels Talk of Babcock Merger," *Financial Times,* (London), May 15, 1996.
——, "Holzmann Reveals Further Losses," *Financial Times* (London), May 22, 1996.
——, "Holzmann Warning Gives Succour to Hochtief," *Financial Times,* (London), June 27, 1996.
Maynard, Debra, "New Framework in the Making," *Asian Business,* December 1991.
"Philipp Holzmann: Creating a Haven in U. S. Construction," *Business Week,* August 30, 1982, pp. 84–85.
Sellmeyer, Sheri, "German Business Makes Its Mark," *Business North Carolina,* November 1988.

—Paul S. Bodine

▲ PREUSSAG

Preussag AG

Karl-Weichert-Allee 4
D-30625
Hannover, Niedersachsen
Germany
511 56600
Fax: 511 5661901

Public Company
Incorporated: 1959
Sales: DM29,598 million (1995)
Employees: 65,227 (1995)
Stock Exchanges: Berlin Bremen Düsseldorf Frankfurt
    Hamburg Hannover Munich Stuttgart
SICs: 1000 Metal Mining; 1200 Coal Mining; 1311
    Crude Petroleum and Natural Gas; 1781 Water Well
    Drilling; 1794 Excavation Work; 2800 Chemicals and
    Allied Products; 6719 Holding Companies, Not
    Elsewhere Classified

Preussag AG is the holding company for an international group of firms operating in five major business areas: the steel and nonferrous metals mining and mining services industry; the natural gas/crude oil exploration and production industry and the mining and oil drilling services, engineering, and technology industries; the steel, scrap, tank car, nonferrous metal, and chemical trading and transport industry; the shipbuilding and plant engineering and technology industry; and the building engineering and components industry. Its 210 businesses operating out of offices in Germany and 82 cities worldwide run the gamut from the production of steel and steel products, mining shaft and tunnel construction, port operations services, and uranium mining to tin smelting, tank car leasing, shower screens, air conditioning units, ship construction and repair, and hydroelectric power plants. Five of its largest business divisions are Preussag Stahl AG (steel), Preussag Energie GmbH (crude oil and natural gas), Preussag Handel GmbH (steel trading and handling), VTG Vereinigte Tanklager und Transportmittel GmbH (railroad tank cars), and Preussag Noell Group (engi-

neering and technology). In the early 1990s Preussag ranked among the three largest metals industry firms worldwide, the 12 largest global steel companies, and as the eighth-largest crude steel producer in Western Europe. Within Germany it was the third-largest German corporation and the fourth-largest energy and utilities firm.

Prussian Steel: 1923–45

Preussag AG was founded in Berlin in December 1923 as Preussische Bergwerks-und Hütten-Aktiengesellschaft (Prussian Mine and Foundry Company) out of a collection of iron, lead, zinc, coal, oil, amber, and potash mining, foundry, and processing works formerly owned by the German state of Prussia. Liberated by the Prussian government from the restrictions imposed by the state budget, the new company's management was charged with building Preussag through the efficiencies and profit opportunities of the free market. Despite antiquated equipment dating to the prewar era and a German economy still reeling from the punitive reparations imposed by the Versaille Treaty of 1919 Preussag's diverse operations began to thrive, and by 1925 it was employing 31,000 workers. Only when the hyperinflation of the Weimar years began to stabilize in the late 1920s, however, was Preussag able to fill its backlog orders, increase production, and enlarge its plant capacity. By continuing to rationalize and mechanize its operations, almost all Preussag's businesses were reporting increased sales by 1928, and by 1929 gross profits stood at 26.6 million reichsmarks (RM).

Nevertheless, in 1929 the Prussian parliament decided to form Vereinigte Elektrizitäts und Bergwerk AG (VEBA AG) out of Preussag, Hibernia, and the Preussischen Elektrizitäts-AG in order to stimulate foreign investment in the three firms. Although Preussag alone claimed a share capital of RM140 million no foreign investors rose to the Prussian government's invitation. The U.S. stock market crash at the end of the year signaled the beginning of a worldwide depression, and by 1931 Preussag's gross profits had fallen to RM11 million. When Adolf Hitler was elected chancellor of Germany in 1932 he initiated a military and infrastructural expansion that offered Germany's steel industry some protection from the stagnant world steel market, and by 1933 Preussag's gross profits had

Company Perspectives:

Our core skills are in steel production, crude oil and natural gas production and associated services, in our specialised logistic services and in plant engineering, here particularly in environmental, energy, handling, storage and conveying technology. Sophisticated shipbuilding is another strong area. In building engineering, our products have established a very good market position. By building on this foundation, we want to achieve our growth aims by expanding our range of products and services and also by strengthening our market position both nationally and internationally.

bounced back to RM60.1 million. However, the National Socialists' emphasis on German economic self-sufficiency as well as the general scarcity of foreign currency forced the German iron and steel industry to begin smelting, increasing amounts of low-quality native ore, and by 1934, when Preussag established its petroleum and petroleum products subsidiary Preussag Handel Gesellschaft mbH, German foreign trade in raw materials and semifinished products had fallen under rigid government control.

With the implementation of Hitler's four-year economic plan in 1936—which effectively placed the German economy on a war footing—the German iron and steel industry had largely subordinated its production and investment decisions to the state's industrial policy. Benefiting from the armaments-led expansion of the economy, however, between 1935 and 1938 Preussag's gross profits rose from RM78 million to almost RM100 million, and its work force climbed to 34,000. On the eve of World War II, Preussag opened the Düsseldorf operation of its Preussag Handel Gesellschaft metal trading subsidiary and at the height of the war in 1942 began developing a major pit coal field in Ibbenbüren in northwestern Germany. Hibernia, one of Preussag's two sister firms in the VEBA group, had converted some of its operations to armaments manufacture during the prewar buildup but unlike many German armaments firms escaped the wrath of Allied bombing until 1944. During the war, shipbuilder Howaldtswerke-Deutsche Werft AG (HDW) of Kiel, which would become a major Preussag acquisition in 1989, produced fifty U-boats for the German navy. As the war progressed, Allied air raids, the loss of labor personnel to military conscription, and plant relocations hampered the productivity of many German businesses. Following Germany's surrender in 1945, Preussag was placed under the control of the Allied occupation government, all its possessions in eastern and central Germany were lost to the Soviet-controlled government of eastern Germany, and its operations in western Germany were partly destroyed.

From the Rubble: 1945–59

In the immediate postwar years, the Allied powers pursued a policy of *Entflechtung,* or decartelization, in which many German firms were dismantled and large industry groups were broken up into separate companies with a maximum permitted share capital of RM100,000 each. As Preussag began reconstructing its shattered operations in 1946–47, the historical alliances between German ore, coal, and steel production were being dismembered, and German steel companies were divested of their raw materials mining operations.

In 1948, however, the institution of the U.S.-sponsored Marshall Plan and the reform of Germany's currency system (in which the reichsmark was replaced with the deutsche mark [DM]) signaled the West's intention to allow the devastated German economy to recover, thereby bolstering the West against the increasing threat posed by the Soviet Union. In 1951 the dismantling of German plants was halted and bans, controls, and restrictions on German industry were lifted. Preussag immediately began construction of a coal power plant in Ibbenbüren, and as European reconstruction spurred a boom in the demand for steel Preussag's work force grew to 22,800. In 1952, the lifting of limits on German steel production finally enabled German steel companies to once again become competitive in the world market. Preussag moved its headquarters from Berlin to Hannover, and with the German ''economic miracle'' now underway, Preussag's Ibbenbüren power station came on line in 1954.

Privatization and Expansion: 1959–89

By the late 1950s Preussag was beginning to reestablish itself as an essential part of the German raw minerals industry, but as a subsidiary of the still state-run company VEBA it faced severe limitations: expansion through acquisition was impossible and, unlike public, stock-selling companies, it could not turn to the financial markets to generate the capital needed for investment or financing. With the government of the Federal Republic of Germany its sole shareholder, Preussag could only raise funds by incurring debt through bank loans. While Preussag's fellow VEBA subsidiary, Hibernia, had managed to recover sufficiently from the war to prosper within the framework of a state-run enterprise, Preussag had not, and in December 1958 the German Bundeskabinett, in an attempt to spread the interest in German companies to a wider portion of the public (specifically, Preussag employees and low-income individuals), decided to initiate a partial privatization of Preussag, with VEBA retaining only 22.4 percent of Preussag's shares. In 1959, Preussag's controversial initial public offering raised DM75 million, and within a day of the stock sale Preussag shares were worth more than DM100 million, with roughly two hundred thousand investors registering purchases of the company's stock.

As world demand for steel began to decline around 1960 and the overproduction of steel of the 1950s created a global glut that lasted until the end of the 1960s, a newly privatized Preussag turned to diversification and acquisition. It founded Elektro-Chemi Ibbenbüren GmbH (ECI), a manufacturer of chloro-alkaline products, with the Dutch firm KNZ in 1960; purchased Europe's largest railroad tank car and transportation services agent, VTG Vereinigte Tanklager and Transportmittel GmbH, of Hamburg, a year later; and acquired its first shares in KIAG of Düsseldorf in 1962. Preussag also founded two offices of its Preussag Stahlhandel iron and steel products/metal services subsidiary in 1962 and then a year later a Stahlhandel operation in Hamburg. In 1963, Preussag's VTG subsidiary purchased the inland waterway shipbuilding operations of the Fanto, Luise, and Comos companies as well as an industrial tank plant in Amsterdam. Its aggressive expansion continued in 1964 with acquisition of container ship construction facilities on the North Sea and the purchase of the remaining shares of KIAG two years later.

In the mid-1960s the collapse of Germany's capital markets and a general recession in the national economy brought the first significant slowdown of Germany's postwar boom. Ironically, the introduction of new steelmaking technologies was enabling German steelmakers like Preussag to lift Germany's total steel production to more than 16 million tons just as worldwide demand for steel was bottoming out. Nevertheless, in the remaining years of the decade Preussag acquired France's largest railroad tank car leasing business through its VTG subsidiary (1966); purchased a three-quarters interest in zincing firm Berliner Grossverzinkerie (1966); expanded into the stationary and mobile fire extinguishing and protection markets with the purchase of Minimax GmbH (1966); established Preussag Energie GmbH to explore for and produce crude oil and natural gas (1968); and expanded its marine and shipbuilding holdings by founding container shipbuilder OSA (1968).

In 1969 Preussag turned to the U.S. market to form a joint venture with Kaiser Aluminum and Chemical Corporation to build an aluminum smelter on the Rhine River near Duisberg. Kaiser provided the technical expertise for the erection and operation of the new Kaiser-Preussag Aluminum GmbH facility, which by 1975 claimed a capacity of 143,000 tons. Ten months later Preussag announced another venture with Kaiser, acquiring a 50 percent interest in its aluminum smelting, fabricating, and sales operations in Germany, Switzerland, Italy, and Belgium under the name Kaiser-Preussag Aluminum. Finally, at the end of 1969, VEBA agreed to sell its remaining interest in Preussag to the Westdeutsche Landesbank, making Preussag a wholly public corporation for the first time in its 47-year history.

With share capital now totaling DM315 million and a workforce of 20,600, in the early 1970s Preussag acquired zincing firm Verzinkerei Bollmeyer of Neumünster; formed Kavernen Bau- und Betriebs-GmbH of Hannover with Salzgitter AG for the planning, construction, and operation of underground storage facilities; established two new subsidiaries, Preussag Anlagenbau GmbH, a pipeline and plant engineering and construction firm, and Preussag Stahl AG, its steelmaking subsidiary; established a large container tank operation through a joint venture between subsidiary VTG and a Dutch firm; formed a lead industry joint venture, Preussag-Boliden-Blei GmbH, with the Swiss firm Boliden; and acquired the zincing operations of Zinkelektrolyse Nordenham. Several economic trends conspired to make the 1970s a difficult decade for Germany's steel producers, however. Revaluations of the deutsche mark, burdensome wage levels, and governmentally imposed financial controls squeezed steelmakers' margins, and the onset of the worldwide oil crisis in 1973 drove manufacturing costs higher, further reducing demand. The increased use of thinner gauges of steel and the substitution of other materials for traditional steel-based applications joined with the rise of new, low-priced steel-making countries and slumps in critical steel-using industries to hand the European steel industry its worst drought since World War II. In its 50th anniversary year, Preussag moved to

repair the structural weaknesses exacerbated by the poor economic climate and in 1974 sold off its consumer goods and brand-name product businesses.

By 1975 Preussag had begun testing projects for new technologies in its oil business, dissolved its partnership with Kaiser Aluminum, established a helicopter service business through its VTG subsidiary, and acquired an interest in a French industrial tank firm. It also established a British subsidiary, began constructing an offshore drilling supply base in northwestern Germany, and in a joint venture with the German firms Metalgesellschaft AG and Salzgitter AG founded a study group to explore the offshore extraction of raw materials.

As the second oil crisis of the 1970s began in the latter half of the decade, the West German government began offering Germany's beleaguered steel companies financial inducements to stimulate industry mergers and cooperative arrangements. Preussag turned to new foreign markets to bolster declining revenue in its traditional European base. Between 1976 and 1985, for example, it began a copper exploration operation on the Pacific island of Fiji; participated in the building and operation of two lead mines in Canada; initiated oil drill-boring projects in Egypt and the United Arab Emirates; acquired a crude oil field operation in the Gulf of Mexico, and participated in an offshore drilling platform joint venture in mainland China. Preussag subsidiaries were meanwhile introduced in Brazil, Nigeria, Gabon, Denmark, and Saudi Arabia. Closer to home, the firm acquired zincing firm Großverzinkerei Schörg GmbH and a majority interest in the construction firm Bauer Grundbau, founded the zincing firm Preussag-Weser-Zink GmbH with French metals producer Penarroya, and began developing natural gas fields in northern Germany. (A decade later Preussag and Penarroya merged their lead, zinc, and special metals businesses as a France-based Preussag subsidiary named Metaleurop, forming the world's largest lead-processing company.) Preussag's 1977 purchase of Patino N.V., a Dutch metals, mining, and mineral processing company, also positioned it a year later to gain a majority interest in Amalgamated Metal Corporation of the United Kingdom. By 1979 Preussag's sales stood at US$1.66 billion, and in 1980 its stock began trading on Germany's eight stock exchanges.

A public relations setback in the mid-1980s, however, inaugurated a string of publicity embarrassments that would dog Preussag for the next ten years. In 1984 the European Community fined Preussag and five other European zinc producers for violating antitrust laws by fixing prices and restraining production. Then in 1988 the U.S. government accused Preussag and four other firms of constructing a poison gas plant in Libya and a chemical arms factory in Iraq, if true, a violation of international trade law. Preussag denied the allegations, claiming it had built a desalinization plant for Libya and nothing more. Within three years, German federal prosecutors officially charged Preussag employees—though not the firm itself—with breaking export laws by selling Iraq $16 million worth of equipment for its chemical weapons program. Finally, in April 1995 2,000 U.S. veterans of the Gulf War sued Preussag and several other German firms for their alleged Iraqi chemical weapons work, a claim Preussag officials continued to describe as "substanceless."

As the world steel industry moved gradually toward the recovery that would finally take hold in the late 1980s, Preussag enjoyed its best postwar year ever in 1981 while adding German container shipbuilding businesses to its stable (1980), initiating crude oil and natural gas projects in the United States (1981), achieving technological advances in its oil machinery production capabilities (1982), jettisoning its freight forwarding holdings (1983), and restructuring its construction engineering and technology operation (1984). With sales topping US$4.44 billion in 1985, Preussag continued its ambitious expansion by buying a tin mining business in Indonesia, increasing its holdings in the U.K.-based Amalgamated Metal Corporation and the Swedish firm Boliden, solidifying its presence in the fire protection technology industry, and gaining a majority interest in the German metals trading firm W. & O. Bergmann GmbH. Expansion also necessitated consolidation, however, and in the closing years of the 1980s Preussag sold off coal acid holdings and closed exhausted ore mines; spun off its metal refining businesses to its new Metaleurop subsidiary formed in a joint venture with Penarroya; consolidated its W. &. O. Bergmann holdings; broke its UB Metall operations into four metal industry subsidiaries; and restructured its VTG container shipbuilding operation.

"Realignment": 1989–96

The biggest restructuring of all, however, occurred in 1989, when, under new chairman Erwin Moeller, Preussag converted itself into a holding company comprised of four legally independent business units centered on its four core businesses: coal, crude oil, natural gas, and plant construction. It then merged with the 50-year-old, state-held steel firm Salzgitter AG, creating a DM27 billion conglomerate employing 70,000 workers. The two monumental moves enabled Preussag to post sales of US$15.3 billion in 1990, and with the formation of two new subsidiaries—Preussag Anthrazit GmbH (coal mining) and Preussag Noell Wassertechnik GmbH (offshore engineering and technology)—as well as the new markets opened up by Germany's reunification, Preussag's announcement that it was "optimistic about overall developments" seemed to understate its position.

. The readiness with which Preussag expanded and consolidated its businesses in the years since privatization seemed only to increase in the 1990s. It made acquisitions in the limestone, oil drilling, automobile recycling, mining transport, plaster board, industrial freight forwarding, lead oxide, transport services, engineering, and petroleum industries between 1991 and 1994 and with the purchase of air-conditioning manufacturer Hagenuk Fahrzeugklima GmbH began an association with Hagenuk that would soon lead to a short-lived and ill-starred entrée into the telecommunications business. As another recession struck the European steel industry in the mid-1990s, Preussag was forced to admit that it had "joined the ranks of the other steelmakers, which are all posting large losses." Consequently, in 1993 Chairman Michael Frenzl announced Preussag's intention to further expand its international base—which already accounted for 44 percent of total sales—with a special focus on the North American and Asian markets, as part of a new restructuring plan intended to buffer Preussag from the intense competition of the European steel market. In three short years this policy would result in new ventures in Kazahkstan, Russia, China, Croatia, Brazil, and Albania. Moreover, Preussag's submarine-building subsidiary, HDW, landed naval contracts in southeast Asia, and Preussag Energie pursued new projects in Colombia, Ecuador, Tunisia, Australia, Cuba, Argentina, and Syria. In 1995 Preussag launched Preussag North America as a holding company to promote the establishment of new U.S. ventures, such as its acquisition a few months later of an interest in the Indiana-based steel mill operator Steel Dynamics Inc. By 1994–95, Preussag's foreign sales had edged up to 48 percent of total turnover, and its still-young North American and Asian markets were accounting for roughly 14 percent of international sales, with plans to double Asian sales to DM2.4 billion by the turn of the century.

A second thrust of the restructuring program was to streamline Preussag down to its "core competences"—now steel, energy, logistics, shipbuilding, and plant and building engineering and technology. Rail car construction, auto supply, mobile radio, automated transportation systems, telecommunications, and other loss-leading or niche-threatened businesses were therefore discarded in a series of "strategic disinvestments." Free to concentrate on its historical strengths, in the mid-1990s Preussag found a partner for Metaleurop, its long-troubled French subsidiary, and opened two new blast furnaces, an electric steel plant, and an oxygen steel plant in Germany.

Principal Subsidiaries

Preussag Stahl AG; Preussag Energie GmbH; Preussag Handel GmbH; VTG Vereinigte Tanklager und Transportmittel GmbH; Verkehrsbetriebe Peine-Salzgitter GmbH; Hansaport Hafenbetriebsgesellschaft mbII; Deutsche Tiefbohr AG; Kavernen Bau- und Betriebs-GmbH, Preussag Anthrazit GmbH, Uranerzbergbau-GmbH; Elektro-Chemie Ibbenbüren GmbH; US-Steel Service Companies; DEUMU Deutsche Erz- und Metall-Union GmbH; Howaldtswerke-Deutsche Werft AG; HDW-Nobiskrug GmbH; KERMI GmbH; Wolf Klimatechnik GmbH; Peiner Umformtechnik GmbH; Dr. C. Otto Feuerfest GmbH.

Principal Operating Units

Preussag Noell Group; FELS Group; Metaleurop Group; Deilmann-Haniel Group; W. & O. Bergmann Group; AMC Group; Lehnkering Group; Transwaggon Group; Algeco Group; Preussag Wasser and Rohrtechnik Group; Minimax Group.

Further Reading

Althaus, Sara, "Preussag to Cut 800 Jobs in Shake-up," *Financial Times,* August 20, 1996.
"Bonn Government Sets Salzgitter Sale to Preussag for Reported $1.06 Billion," *Wall Street Journal,* October 2, 1989.
"Bonn Names Four More Firms Linked by U.S. to Libya," *Washington Post,* January 10, 1989, p. A16.
Dennis, Sylvia, "Germany—Preussag Sells Off Hagenuk Operation," *Newsbytes News Network,* October 5, 1995.
"EC Fines Six Companies for Antitrust Violations," *Wall Street Journal,* August 8, 1984.
Genillard, Ariane, "Preussag Blames Loss on European Steel Downturn," *Financial Times,* June 22, 1993.

"German Cars to Be Recycled," *New York Times,* November 28, 1994, p. D3.

"Kaiser Aluminum Plans Venture in Germany with Preussag A.G.," *Wall Street Journal,* February 24, 1969.

"Large German Concern Recently Bought 29% of Patino N.V.'s Stock," *Wall Street Journal,* May 31, 1977.

Marquis, Julie, "German Submarines Ready to Dominate Arms Market," *Los Angeles Times,* February 27, 1996, p. D11.

Peel, Quentin, "Preussag Profit Tumbles to DM193m," *Financial Times,* February 10, 1994, p. 18.

Peel, Quentin, and Lionel Barber, "Germany's Private Steelmakers Revolt," *Financial Times,* February 3, 1994.

"Preussag AG Acquires 26% of Patino N.V.," *Wall Street Journal,* March 29, 1977.

"Preussag to Buy Stake in U.S.," *Wall Street Journal,* November 15, 1995, p. A14.

"Reshaping for Preussag," *Financial Times,* November 11, 1988.

Roth, Terence, "Bonn Government Sets Salzgitter Sale to Preussag for Reported $1.06 Billion," *Wall Street Journal,* October 2, 1989, p. A11.

"West Germany Holds Seven for Aiding Iraq on Poison Gas Facilities," *Los Angeles Times,* August 18, 1990, p. A27.

"World-Wide: German Prosecutors Charged," *Wall Street Journal,* March 29, 1991, p. A1.

—Paul S. Bodine

Pubco Corporation

3830 Kelley Avenue
Cleveland, Ohio 44114-4534
U.S.A.
(216) 881-5300
Fax: (216) 881-8380

Public Company
Incorporated: 1958 as Publishers Company Inc.
Employees: 220
Sales: $47.6 million
Stock Exchanges: NASDAQ
SICs: 3955 Carbon Paper & Inked Ribbons; 2621 Paper
    Mills; 5311 Department Stores; 3531 Construction
    Machinery

Pubco Corporation is a diversified company with an unusual mix of interests. As its name implies, the firm operated as a printing and publishing group from its inception until the early 1980s. But after a 13-month bankruptcy reorganization, the business was reincarnated as a holding company that specialized in acquiring troubled firms and returning them to profitability. Under the direction of Robert Kanner, who acquired a majority stake in Pubco in 1983, the company began to resemble an investment house. It bought controlling stakes in retailers and an apparel manufacturer, then shed its once-core printing businesses in the early 1990s. By 1996, Pubco's diverse interests included business supplies, computer and data processing products, and construction implements. Although Kanner's investment strategies returned the company to profitability in the mid-1980s, Pubco suffered four successive annual shortfalls from 1991 to 1994, culminating in a $10.2 million loss in the latter year. It was hoped that a 1996 corporate reorganization would effect efficiencies and maintain the profitability achieved in 1995.

Postwar Creation and Early Development

Pubco was founded in 1958 as Publishers Company Inc., a Washington, D.C., firm that published and sold encyclopedias,
Bibles, and devotional books door-to-door. After just two years in business, the company made the first of a string of acquisitions, adding Massachusetts' Books, Inc., in 1960. The 1962 additions of Kaufman Printing, Inc., and Merkle Press Inc. gave the budding conglomerate expertise in virtually every facet of the publishing business, from editing to printing to distribution. Publishers' top executives, President Charles W. Lockyer and Chairman E. A. Merkle, brought more than a dozen companies, most of which were involved in printing and publishing, into the fold over the course of the decade. Most significant of these were Buxton & Skinner Printing Company, a label printer in St. Louis whose customers included brewing giant Anheuser-Busch Company, Inc.; Redson Rice Corp., a Chicago-based printer of direct mailers and catalogs; and Tabard Press Corp., a New York City company that specialized in time-sensitive projects like periodicals and annual reports. These acquisitions propelled Publishers' sales from $15.5 million in 1963 to nearly $45 million by 1969, while profits burgeoned from $82,000 to more than $1 million during the period.

The company also dabbled in some extraneous businesses in the late 1960s and early 1970s. In 1968, for example, it formed Publishers Broadcasting Corp. (later renamed Camptown Industries, Inc.). This affiliate owned and operated a Florida campground, four radio stations, a sports facility, and an ice plant. Publishers Company's 1973 name change to Pubco Corp. may have reflected the firm's unusual diversification.

Notwithstanding its foray into broadcasting and entertainment, the holding company retained its primary focus on printing and publishing. Merkle remained Pubco's largest subsidiary, contributing over half the company's revenues in the mid-1970s. In addition to its contracts to print publications for several national labor unions, Merkle printed regional editions of *Time* and *Sports Illustrated* magazines. But when this core business's physical plant began to decline mid-decade, the resulting reduction in printing quality drove away customers. Pubco's bookselling operations went into a tailspin during the same period, incurring three successive losses in the mid-1970s. Profitability vacillated throughout the latter years of the decade; even an injection of capital via a 1979 initial public offering couldn't lift the company out of its doldrums. Back-to-back dips into the red ink in 1981 and 1982 forced Pubco to seek bankruptcy protection under Chapter 11.

Early 1980s Turnaround

In 1983 Cleveland turnaround specialist Robert H. Kanner accumulated two-thirds of Pubco's equity and set out to transform it into a vehicle for the acquisition and revitalization of other troubled companies. Kanner had already established a reputation for wringing optimal performance from distressed firms by the time he rescued Pubco. A Wharton School of Finance dropout, his credo was "Appreciate what nobody else sees, buy what nobody else wants." A twentysomething Kanner embarked on this career in 1976, when he bought an east Cleveland doughnut shop. He acquired five struggling, often bankrupt, companies at "bargain basement" prices over the course of the next five years, culminating with the late 1970s purchase of Buckeye Business Products Inc.

Kanner applied the same strategy to virtually every business he encountered, regardless of the target company's industry segment or compatibility with existing holdings. As he told *Ohio Business* magazine's Michael Moore, three standards guided his business conduct: "Purchase for *cash,* generate *cash,* and accumulate *cash.*" Kanner achieved these goals by reducing employment levels, liquidating assets, and often consolidating headquarters operations at his home base in Cleveland, Ohio. He also amassed a cadre of trusted managers, including George Hahn and Stephen Kalette, along the way. Within 17 months of the Buckeye Business Products transaction, Kanner had squeezed $3.5 million in cash from this manufacturer of printer ribbons and other office supplies. That was enough to buy him a controlling stake in Pubco, which emerged from bankruptcy in February 1983.

Kanner installed himself as president and moved Pubco's headquarters from Washington, D.C., to Cleveland. Charles W. Lockyer stayed on as Pubco's chairman and chief executive officer for a transitional period after the takeover. Kanner shed the money-losing Merkle Press divisions, but retained Buxton & Skinner in St. Louis, Redson Rice in Chicago, and Tabard Press in New York. By the end of Kanner's first year at the helm, Pubco had realized a $3.6 million profit. Within just two years, Pubco had regained its ranking among the leading publicly held printing companies in the United States.

Having achieved profitability, Kanner wasted no time returning to his acquisition strategy using Pubco as a holding company. Over the course of the next decade, he created a web of interrelated businesses under Pubco. Late in 1984 Pubco acquired regional mass merchant Hornsby's Stores Inc. and its supplier, Century Wholesale Co. Kanner liquidated some of the Chicago-area chain's stores and leased the remainder to another retailer, effectively transforming the subsidiary into a profitable real estate management company. Pubco went on to purchase a controlling interest in women's apparel manufacturer Bobbie Brooks Inc. early the following year. Once a well-known name in ladies' fashion, Bobbie Brooks had recently emerged from Chapter 11 only to record a $1.4 million loss on $65 million in 1984 sales. The new management pared nearly 200 employees as well as the label's sportswear and swimwear lines, retaining only the Main Line Fashions outerwear business. The Bobbie Brooks trademark was licensed to clothing manufacturer Garan, Inc. By 1986, the remade Bobbie Brooks was enjoying rising sales and a return to profitability.

In the meantime, Pubco had also acquired the Kline Bros. chain of 18 women's clothing stores in the Midwest. Completed in 1985, the $8.5 million purchase added $75 million in annual revenues to Pubco's coffers. In 1988 Kanner doubled Pubco's stake in Bobbie Brooks to 65 percent by swapping Kline Bros. for equity in Bobbie Brooks. Pubco also transferred its printing operations to Bobbie Brooks at this time. Although shares of both Pubco and Bobbie Brooks were publicly traded on the NASDAQ exchange, Kanner maintained effective control over the parent company and its subsidiaries by virtue of his 75 percent stake in Pubco.

Fueled by these acquisitions, Pubco's sales and profits grew rapidly during its first few years under Kanner. Annual revenues increased from about $36 million to over $100 million, and net profit rebounded from a negative position to $4.5 million.

Evolution Continues in Early 1990s

Although Kanner has been lauded as a brilliant "company doctor" able to revive businesses on the brink of demise, he was unable to find a cure for the pandemic that struck his patient in the early 1990s. That era's economic recession hit the retail segment particularly hard and brought a fresh gush of red ink at Pubco. The company recorded four consecutive losses from 1991 to 1994 for a total shortfall of over $18 million. In response, Pubco beat a rather disorganized retreat from both the printing and retail sectors via liquidations in 1993 and 1994. After dipping to $25 million in 1992, annual revenues stabilized mid-decade at about $47 million, by which time Bobbie Brooks had become Pubco's core affiliate and chief acquisition vehicle.

Kanner made efforts to simplify Pubco's ownership structure and consolidate some of his personal holdings during this same period. He sold Buckeye Business Products to Bobbie Brooks and added computer and data processing supply manufacturer Aspen Imaging International, Inc., to Brooks's roster. Formerly headquartered in Colorado, Aspen's offices were moved to Kanner's Cleveland headquarters. In 1993 Brooks acquired a controlling interest in Allied Construction Products, Inc., a suburban Cleveland manufacturer of construction goods.

In 1996 Kanner proposed a plan to merge Pubco and its heretofore partially owned affiliates. The reorganization would effectively eliminate Bobbie Brooks as a corporate entity, leaving Buckeye Business Products and Aspen Imaging International as wholly owned subsidiaries of Pubco and Allied Construction Products as an 85 percent-owned affiliate. Brooks stockholders would be compensated with an increased stake in the parent company, as Kanner's share would be reduced from 71 percent to 65 percent. Given the fact that Kanner held a majority of the voting shares, it appeared likely that the transaction would be ratified. The CEO and his fellow shareholders hoped to achieve economies by eliminating the superfluous layer of management represented by Bobbie Brooks and thereby carry on the profitability achieved in 1995.

Principal Subsidiaries

Century Wholesale Co.; PC Real Estate Corp.; Pubco Management Co.; Bobbie Brooks, Inc. (90%); Brooks Management Co. (90%); Allied Construction Products, Inc. (85%); Aspen Imaging International, Inc. (62%).

Further Reading

"Bobbie Brooks, Pubco Swap Stock, Shops," *Plain Dealer,* February 2, 1988, p. 7D.

Bullard, Stan, "Kanner 'Family' Filling up Space," *Crain's Cleveland Business,* October 18, 1993, pp. 3–4.

Gerdel, Thomas W., "Pubco Buys Discount Chain in Chicago," *Plain Dealer,* December 18, 1984, p. 9C.

Karle, Delinda, "$25 Million Is Bid for Control of Cook United Inc.," *Plain Dealer,* January 9, 1985, pp. 5B, 7B.

——, "Pubco Puts Emphasis on Returns from Ashes," *Plain Dealer,* March 8, 1985, pp. 17B, 18B.

——, "Winning with the Losers," *Plain Dealer,* March 8, 1985, pp. 17B, 18B.

——, "Bobbie Brooks, Pubco Improve Earnings in '86," *Plain Dealer,* April 1, 1987, p. 2C.

——, "Hahn Named President of Pubco, Bobbie Brooks," *Plain Dealer,* March 10, 1988, p. 2C.

McReynolds, Rebecca, "Pubco-Bobbie Brooks: Apparel's Odd Couple," *Crain's Cleveland Business,* October 14, 1985, p. 27.

Moore, Michael E., " 'Doctor' Kanner Cures Sick Firms," *Ohio Business,* January 1985, pp. 54–55.

—April Dougal Gasbarre

Quality Food Centers, Inc.

10112 Northeast 10th Street
Bellevue, Washington 98009
U.S.A.
(206) 462-2178
Fax: (206) 462-2146

Public Company
Incorporated: 1954
Employees: 4,200
Sales: $729.8 million (1995)
Stock Exchanges: NASDAQ
SICs: 5411 Grocery Stores

The largest independent supermarket chain in the Seattle/ Puget Sound area of Washington State, Quality Food Centers, Inc. (QFC), operates more than 60 supermarkets in western Washington. QFC's stores are open 24 hours and stock a wide breadth of traditional grocery store merchandise, as well as specialty items, such as espresso, flowers, and take-out food. An extensive remodeling program was implemented during the mid-1980s when the QFC chain comprised approximately 20 stores. During the ensuing decade, as the number of stores tripled, the company recorded the greatest financial growth in its history. Annual sales climbed from $136 million in 1985 to $730 million ten years later, when QFC officials were considering expanding beyond western Washington for the first time in the company's history.

Origins

QFC began its rise to prominence as a grocery store chain in 1954 in Seattle, and the retailer confined its expansion to the surrounding Puget Sound region for the first 40 years of its existence. The first three decades of the company's existence were decidedly quiet, at least compared to frenetic activity that would take place later in its history. At first, expansion was pursued methodically and financial growth was realized slowly, but beginning in the mid-1980s both yardsticks of the chain's magnitude—its financial and physical growth—began to rec-

ord prodigious jumps. The agent of change responsible for QFC's dramatic burst of growth was Stuart M. Sloan, who first joined QFC in 1986.

Prior to joining QFC, Sloan spent two decades honing his skills as a retailer in the Seattle area. A graduate of the University of Washington, Sloan served as the president of Schuck's Auto Supply for nearly 20 years, developing a talent at the auto supplies chain for spearheading the pace of expansion that he would later orchestrate at QFC. During his first year as president of Schuck's in 1967, the auto supplies chain comprised eight retail units. By the time he left the company in 1984, Schuck's had grown dramatically under Sloan's watch, blossoming into a chain boasting 58 retail units. Annual sales at the company mirrored its physical expansion, swelling from $1 million in 1967 to $60 million by the time of Sloan's departure in 1984. From Schuck's, Sloan moved on to another Seattle-based retailer in 1984 named Pick N Save Corporation, but his tenure there as executive vice-president was brief, lasting two years.

1986 Leveraged Buyout

In January 1986, Sloan and the president of QFC, Jack Croco, teamed up with a group of investors to buy QFC, spending $34 million in a leveraged buyout that marked the beginning of a definitive new era in the retailer's history. Immediately upon assuming control over QFC, Sloan implemented a series of changes that quickly reshaped the image of the approximately 20 retail units composing the QFC chain. Some of the changes introduced in 1986 were prompted by a market research study of the grocery stores' customers. According to the information gleaned from the study, typical QFC customers during the mid-1980s did not regard QFC stores as their primary grocery shopping destination because the merchandise selection was not broad enough. Sloan responded to the news by adding various specialty items to the stores' shelves, including cold cuts, baked goods, flowers, and espresso, which in addition to drawing more customers to QFC stores also boosted profits since the sale of specialty items yielded higher profit margins than traditional grocery store products.

The revenue generated from the sale of specialty items grew strongly during the remainder of the decade, rising to 12 percent of total sales by the beginning of the 1990s as Sloan transformed QFC into a chain that customers would regard as a one-stop shopping destination. To further bolster this perception in customers' minds, Sloan opened the stores 24 hours a day in 1986 and began remodeling existing units. Although the push to remodel QFC units had begun before the Sloan era—12 of the 22 stores composing the chain in 1987 had been remodeled during the previous six years—the reconstruction of store units represented one of the hallmarks of Sloan's tenure at QFC. During his first decade of control over the grocery chain, Sloan increased the chain's total square footage consistently and substantially by remodeling existing units and by either acquiring or erecting additional stores, but during the first several years of his stewardship the remodeling of stores was of singular importance in his mind. The company's penchant for acquiring stores would manifest itself later, particularly during the mid-1990s.

Sales by the end of 1986 amounted to $158 million, up from the $136 million generated in 1985. As the company prepared for 1987, plans were announced to remodel or enlarge eight stores and open two new stores during the year and establish another two stores in 1988. In March 1987, Sloan took the company public, making an initial public offering of 1.3 million shares. The proceeds gained from the public offering were used to pay off the debt incurred from the $34 million leveraged buyout completed the year before, putting the company in the enviable position of being debt-free as it embarked on what would become a prodigious expansion program. Despite QFC's conversion to public ownership, Sloan retained resolute control over the future direction of the chain by holding on to a 61 percent stake in the company after the stock offering.

Annual sales grew significantly following the 1987 public offering. In 1988, the company earned $7 million on $231.5 million in sales and the following year earned $12.8 million on $318.7 million in sales. After opening three new stores in 1990, two of which were acquired, QFC comprised 27 stores by 1991, when earnings swelled to $20.6 million and sales rose to $395 million. Three new stores were scheduled to open in 1991, each containing more than 30,000 square feet of retail space and one, a 38,000-square-foot store, offering the chain's first Asian food take-out service, a leased department that was called Asian Choice Kitchen. By the end of 1991, the company was planning to open two new stores in 1992, but those plans were exceeded when the company acquired two existing grocery stores and erected one of its own, giving it a total of 33 stores by the end of the year.

After the expansion completed in 1992, which included the remodeling of six stores, the chain's total square footage had increased 18 percent during the year. Although the company was expanding at a robust pace—the chain's total square footage doubled between 1986 and 1992—expansion had not been achieved at the expense of the stores' profitability or by saddling the company with debilitating debt, the two common side effects of rapid growth. Instead, expansion had been funded solely with cash generated by the company's network of stores, leaving it debt-free, and its sales per square foot ranked well above the figures recorded by most other grocery store operators in the country. During the early 1990s, QFC stores collected annual sales of $756 per square foot, a total that compared favorably against the industry average of $552 in sales per square foot.

Animated Expansion During Mid-1990s

Following the 18 percent increase in square footage realized in 1992, Sloan increased the chain's square footage by 19 percent in 1993, when five stores were opened during the year. The stores added in 1993 brought the total number of QFC stores to 40 by the year's end, or roughly twice the number constituting the chain when Sloan arrived in 1986. Regarding plans for future expansion, the company's management was reticent, preferring to keep its specific plans out of the press and offering only that QFC would continue to increase total square footage through acquisition and store remodeling in the Puget Sound region. Comments from the company's executive management at annual shareholder meetings, however, did offer a peek into the minds of QFC's senior management. At the 1993 shareholders meeting, statements by Dan Kourkoumelis, QFC's president and chief operating officer, and Sloan revolved around future expansion. Kourkoumelis, who first joined QFC as a box boy in 1967, summed up the expansion philosophy that had predicated the company's operation in the past, explaining, "We are aggressive, yet opportunistic in selecting our new store locations. We are highly selective. We will not grow for growth's sake." Sloan's words pointed more to the future expansion philosophy of QFC and were decidedly less restrained. "We remain committed to our aggressive expansion plans," he informed the gathering of shareholders. "I don't want anyone to miss that. We're not backing off; we're going full bore," he said.

True to his words, Sloan greatly accelerated QFC's expansion plans as the company entered the mid-1990s. On the heels of reporting $518 million in sales for 1993, Sloan greeted shareholders in 1994 with the announcement, "We can double the number of stores we have," citing the existence of "great growth opportunities" in the Puget Sound region. It was a bold pronouncement, though without a proposed deadline for completion, but Sloan achieved great strides toward reaching his ambitious goal in 1994. In three separate deals completed during the year, Sloan added seven new locations to the QFC chain, including a transaction that represented the largest acquisition in the company's history. In May 1994, QFC agreed to acquire five of the six stores operated by Johnny's Food Centers, all of which were located south of Seattle and in neighborhoods where QFC did not operate stores. By itself, the acquisition increased QFC's total square footage 15 percent, accounting for the bulk of the 22 percent increase in square footage recorded in 1994 and perpetuating the company's record of increasing total square footage at least 17 percent each year for the previous five years.

Once the Johnny's Food Centers stores were added to QFC's fold, the chain comprised 45 stores. Given the company's rapid pace of expansion and the increasing role acquisitions were playing in its expansion strategy, industry analysts were beginning to speculate whether or not QFC could maintain the high profit margins it had become renowned for as it quickly added to its store count. Responding to this concern, Sloan explained, "We are building our business for the long-term, and we recognize and accept the fact that there will be some short-term pains that we must endure on a quarter-to-quarter basis as we strive to produce long-term gains.'' Sloan, in other words, was not going to be deterred from his plan to double the number of QFC stores, and in late December 1994 demonstrated his commitment to expansion by announcing an acquisition more than twice the size of the Johnny's Food Centers acquisition. The acquisition, which was completed in March 1995, added 12 grocery stores operated by Lynnwood, Washington-based Olson's Food Stores, four other stores in various stages of development, and the rights to several future sites. The addition of the Olson's Food Stores lifted QFC's store count to 57, added $150 million in annual sales to the company's growing revenue volume, and strengthened the company's second-place ranking in the Seattle area from a 13.5 percent market share to a 18.5 percent market share.

Trailing only Safeway, which controlled 27 percent of the market in the Seattle area, QFC recorded the greatest physical growth in its history in 1995. Total square footage during the year leaped 46 percent, by far eclipsing any annual gains achieved previously. In the years ahead further expansion seemed assured as Sloan began to hint at embracing a much broader expansion strategy. In mid-1995, halfway toward collecting $730 million in sales for the year, he noted, ''We are not confined geographically. We plan on expanding, developing, and acquiring other stores outside [the Puget Sound] area.'' Sloan hinted further about QFC's future expansion strategy, stating ''We have no immediate plans, but we could also see ourselves outside of Western Washington.''

Sloan's plans to expand beyond Western Washington, which were offered as a possibility in 1995, crystallized in September 1996, when the company announced its intentions to expand outside of the Puget Sound area and concurrently announced it was going to form a holding company for QFC. According to

industry observers, the formation of a holding company signalled QFC's intention to significantly stretch the boundaries of its operating territory. As QFC charted its course for the late 1990s, company representatives were reportedly scouting locations in several Northwestern states and in the metropolitan Portland, Oregon, area in particular, which represented a dramatic shift in strategy for the regional supermarket chain. Whether expansion into neighboring states was to occur remained to be seen, but QFC's stalwart position in the Puget Sound area augured well for the extension of the company's presence into distant markets.

Further Reading

Baljko, Jennifer L., ''QFC Mapping Surprising Expansion Strategy,'' *Supermarket News,* September 30, 1996, p. 4.

Cohn, Cathy, ''QFC Making Its Initial Public Stock Offering,'' *Supermarket News,* March 16, 1987, p. 44.

Enbysk, Monte, ''QFC Maps a Regional Expansion,'' *Supermarket News,* May 1, 1995, p. 7.

Jones, Jeanne, ''QFC Targets Controlled Expansion after Lightening Growth Last Year,'' *Supermarket News,* May 13, 1996, p. 6.

''QFC Planning to Double Store Count,'' *Supermarket News,* April 25, 1994, p. 4.

Spector, Robert, ''QFC Sees Big Growth Opportunities,'' *Supermarket News,* May 10, 1993, p. 177.

Taylor, John H., ''Actions Speak Louder,'' *Forbes,* October 12, 1992, p. 121.

Tosh, Mark, ''QFC's Shopping Spree,'' *Supermarket News*, September 5, 1994, p. 1.

Wolcott, John, ''QFC, Costco, Fred Meyer . . .,'' *Puget Sound Business Journal,* August 21, 1992, p. 18.

Zweibach, Elliot, ''QFC Set to Merge with Olson's,'' *Supermarket News,* January 2, 1995, p. 1.

——, ''Quality Food Names Sloan CEO, Issues Two-for-One Stock Split,'' *Supermarket News,* April 29, 1991, p. 6.

—Jeffrey L. Covell

R.G. Barry Corp.

13405 Yarmouth Road, N.W.
Pickerington, Ohio 43147-9257
U.S.A.
(614) 864-6400
Fax: (614) 866-9787

Public Company
Incorporated: 1947
Employees: 3,000
Sales: $136.6 million
Stock Exchanges: New York
SICs: 3142 House Slippers

Best known for its Dearfoams brand slippers, R.G. Barry Corp. ranks among the world's leading manufacturers of washable house slippers. Offered under the Angel Treads, Madye's, and Snug Treds trademarks, Barry's comfort footwear is distributed through mass merchandisers, department stores, and women's specialty stores. The company also exports its products throughout North America and Europe. In the mid-1990s, approximately 20 percent of R.G. Barry's equity continued to be held by members of the founding Zacks family. The company was guided at that time by Gordon Zacks, who had served as president and chief executive officer of the company since the mid-1960s.

Having endured volatile swings in profitability and undergone several reorganizations throughout the 1980s and early 1990s, R.G. Barry sought stable sales and earnings growth through new product introductions in the mid-1990s. In 1993, the firm launched a line of "heat-to-go" products that incorporated a heat-retaining, microwaveable insert. These items included the Lava Buns stadium seat, ear muffs, a back warmer, scarf, and tabletop bread warmer. Company officials and industry analysts expected R.G. Barry to continue to record sales and income increases in the mid- to late-1990s in part by applying this proprietary technology to products for the medical, industrial, and military markets.

Post–World War II Creation and Early Development

The business was founded in 1945 in a Columbus, Ohio-area basement. That is when three partners—Aaron Zacks, his wife Florence, and a colleague, Harry Streim—created Shoulda-Moulders Co., a maker of slippers, bathrobes and pillows. Two years into the endeavor, the partners changed the company name to R.G. Barry Co., a veiled reference to their three sons. The "R" stood for Harry's son Richard, the "G" for Aaron and Florence's son Gordon, and Barry referred to his sibling.

Despite his prominence in the company moniker, Barry did not follow his parents into the family business, instead he went on to found the Max & Erma's restaurant chain. It was Gordon who joined the company upon his 1955 graduation from Ohio State University's College of Commerce. Knowing his son's penchant for learning by doing, Aaron Zacks assigned Gordon to establish a new corporate manufacturing division in New York. Gordon's operation lost money its first year, while the headstrong entrepreneur became acclimated to the intricacies of manufacturing. This "trial by fire" would prove vital to the younger Zacks's professional development. In 1957, Gordon was summoned back to R.G. Barry's suburban Columbus headquarters when his father's health began to fail. Aaron Zacks suffered a fatal heart attack in 1965, thrusting his relatively inexperienced 32-year-old son into the company presidency.

After taking a course on corporate management from the American Management Association, Gordon Zacks pared R.G. Barry's interests to Dearfoam slippers, then sought to boost its business via acquisitions. Over the course of the 1960s, the firm added operations in Puerto Rico, Tennessee, Texas, North Carolina, and New York, and expanded its family of brands to include Bernardo brand ladies' imported Italian sandals. In 1971, R.G. Barry acquired Maine's Quoddy Products Inc., retailer of hand-sewn Quoddy moccasins.

This strategy of diversification within the footwear industry was very successful; company sales doubled over the course of Gordon's first five years at R.G. Barry's helm. However, Gordon Zacks's early achievement may have endowed him with a bit of vainglory. In a 1985 interview with *Business First-Columbus*'s Bill Atkinson, he admitted that "When I think I'm right I have great faith and confidence in my own judgment.'' While admirable to a certain degree, that egoism would later threaten R.G. Barry's fiscal health.

Introduction of Mushrooms in 1970s

Emboldened by his success, Zacks directed the development of a new line of women's comfort shoes. Dubbed Mushrooms, the footwear was five years in the making and was backed by a marketing program that took another three years to fine-tune. Zacks boasted that it was ''one of the most successful marketing programs in the history of the shoe industry.'' Backed by hundreds of thousands in advertising dollars, R.G. Barry's sales and earnings ''mushroomed'' throughout the 1970s, peaking at over $120 million and $3.8 million, respectively, in 1978.

This relatively small, central Ohio company's successful diversification out of its traditional house slipper niche caught the attention of U.S. Shoe Corp., a billion-dollar southern Ohio shoemaker and retailer. U.S. Shoe responded to Barry's incursion on its market by developing a competing brand, Candie's, which it supported with a multimillion-dollar advertising campaign. Despite the odds—R.G. Barry had a mere fraction of the financial and market clout of its multifaceted competitor—Zacks struggled to maintain his company's hard-won position in women's shoes. As Barry Zacks commented in Atkinson's 1985 piece, ''[Gordon] began to equate success or failure with his own personal success.'' By the early 1980s, his firm had 22 Mushrooms stores in California, Florida, Michigan, and Washington, D.C. During this period, R.G. Barry also expanded the Quoddy chain to 43 stores. The company supported its greatly expanded retail activities with the addition of three manufacturing plants and a network of warehouses, but Zacks failed to take into account the vagaries of popular taste. His bold growth plan soon began to look more like a hasty overexpansion, especially in contrast to U.S. Shoe's ongoing success. Zacks reflected on his skirmish with U.S. Shoe in the 1985 interview with *Business First-Columbus*: ''We were holding our own, but we were bleeding to death.''

After four years of declining earnings and slipping sales, Zacks conceded defeat in 1982. That year, the company took a $12.5 million loss on the sale of its degenerating Mushrooms chain to none other than U.S. Shoe, which converted the retail outlets to its Candie's format. R.G. Barry incurred an $8.5 million loss in 1982. Zacks must have taken some consolation in the fact that his giant rival licensed the Mushroom trademark from his firm for $1 million per year. Barry continued its retreat back to the core Dearfoams slippers with the 1983 spin-off of its Quoddy retail chain to Wolverine World Wide, Inc., manufacturer of Hush Puppies shoes. Two years later, the company sold its Bernardo operations to Jumping-Jacks Shoes, Inc.

Reorganization and Retrenchment in 1980s

Over the course of the next three years, R.G. Barry worked to pare operating expenses and reinvigorate its neglected slipper line. A 1983 restructuring—one of many to come over the ensuing decade—shuttered three plants and reduced employment by 28 percent, from 3,200 to 2,300. Hoping to take advantage of the lower labor and production costs available overseas, the company launched an import division in 1983 and

began moving manufacturing operations from the northeast United States to the Southwest and Mexico. By mid-decade, it had shifted its production ratio from 100 percent domestic to 20 percent domestic and 80 percent foreign.

R.G. Barry also worked to broaden its appeal in the slipper market from a near exclusive emphasis on women to include men and children. A licensing program used the popular Cabbage Patch Kids and Care Bear characters to appeal to children, while Dearfoams developed a line of slippers for men. Other lines with designer names like Oscar de la Renta and Christian Dior commanded higher price points. Barry also redesigned and repackaged its line of women's Dearfoams with particular focus on the product's ''giftability.'' The footwear was such a popular gift that the vast majority, 80 percent, of R.G. Barry's annual sales were concentrated in the fall holiday shopping season. The company emphasized the luxuriousness of its Dearfoams with its first-ever celebrity advertising campaign featuring Zsa Zsa Gabor. In the latter years of the decade, R.G. Barry broadened its retail distribution from its core in department stores to mass merchandisers like K-Mart and Wal-Mart. By the end of the decade, CEO Zacks was able to boast that his company had ''fresh and exciting products in every price point.''

These strategies appeared successful. Although sales declined from $141.1 million in 1981 to $86 million in 1986, the company recovered from its loss position to effect a $4.3 million profit in the latter year. Barry's sales increased steadily to $122.8 million by 1989, but its net income fluctuated erratically throughout the latter years of the decade, from a low of only $23,000 in 1988 to $3.7 million in 1989.

Under pressure from increased foreign and domestic competition, the company slid into the red the following year, incurring total losses of $8.3 million in 1990 and 1991. Zacks mandated two ''major restructurings'' in the span of two months in late 1990 and early 1991. The company reduced its inventory, reorganized its sales force, installed an integrated database system, cut its administrative support staff and laid off 370 U.S. employees. Zacks estimated that this ''right-sizing'' would save the company $6 million to $7 million in operating costs each year. In one of its most surprising moves, R.G. Barry shareholders elected U.S. Shoe Chairman Philip G. Barach to a seat on the board of directors in 1991.

New Products, Global Expansion
Pace Mid-1990s Growth

In the midst of these operational shifts, the company also laid the groundwork for the launch of a whole new class of products. In cooperation with Columbus's Battelle Memorial Institute, R.G. Barry developed a flexible, microwaveable pouch that could retain its heat for up to eight hours. Dubbed ''ThermaStor,'' the product won a spot on *R&D* magazine's listing of 1994's top inventions. These units were used in cold-weather accessories like scarves, gloves, and vests as well as household and leisure articles like breadbaskets and stadium seats. The products were offered under the ''Heat to Go'' brand at mass merchandisers and under the venerable Dearfoams label in department stores. Barry boosted its manufacturing capacity in this segment with the 1994 acquisition of Vesture Corp., whose "microcore" was similar to Barry's own ThermaStor, but utilized a different technology.

Analyst Bart Blout told *Business First-Columbus*'s Carrie Shook that "This technology has far-reaching applications and hundreds of products will be created with it—from shoes to toys." Not only did this open up a completely new and unique segment of the consumer market to R.G. Barry, but it also held great potential for the development of products for the medical, industrial, commercial, and military segments. In 1995, Barry and Battelle formed a joint venture known as ThermaStor Technologies, Ltd. to explore these opportunities. Barry also focused on the development of international markets in the mid-1990s, establishing operations in Europe, Asia, Canada, and Mexico.

R.G. Barry's financial performance improved dramatically in the 1990s. Sales increased from $101.8 million in 1992 to $136.6 million in 1995; profits grew to a record-breaking $6.3 million in the latter year.

Principal Subsidiaries

Vesture Corp.; ThermaStor Technologies, Ltd. (50%).

Further Reading

Atkinson, Bill, "Anatomy of a Mistake," *Business First-Columbus,* November 18, 1985, pp. 12–13, 19.

"Barry Has Quarter, Year Loss Disposing of Mushrooms," *Footwear News,* February 28, 1983, p. 4.

"Barry Quarter in the Chips, As Annual Net Plummets," *Footwear News,* February 25, 1985, p. 48.

"Barry Quarter, Year Profit Up Sharply," *Footwear News,* February 26, 1990, p. 26.

Foster, Pamela E., "R.G. Barry Moving Some Jobs to Texas," *Business First-Columbus,* February 18, 1991, pp. 1–2.

Jackson, William, "Ohio Sends Manufacturing South: Mexico Wooing U.S. Corporations," *Business First-Columbus,* July 16, 1990, p. 1SU.

Lilly, Stephen, "Barry Shareholder Alleges Insider Trading," *Business First-Columbus,* January 16, 1995, pp. 1–2.

"R.G. Barry Lays Off 27; 344 More to Go," *Footwear News,* December 10, 1990, p. 24.

"R.G. Barry Puts Barach on Board," *Footwear News,* August 26, 1991, p. 4.

"R.G. Barry Uses Celebrity, Zsa Zsa Gabor, for First Time in an Ad Campaign," *Columbus Dispatch,* December 20, 1988, p. 3D.

Rieger, Nancy, "Barry Sees Profit Boom," *Footwear News,* April 17, 1989, pp. 2–3.

Seckler, Valerie, "Sickly Retail Scene Seen Affordable Slippers' Boon," *Footwear News,* June 27, 1988, pp. 2–3.

Shook, Carrie, "New Products Heat Up R.G. Barry," *Business First-Columbus,* August 22, 1994, pp. 1–2.

"Warming Trend," *WWD,* May 31, 1994, p. 22.

Wessling, Jack, "Barry Plans to Close or Sell Two Slipper Plants," *Footwear News,* September 3, 1984, pp. 2–3.

——, "Barry Returns to Black in '83," *Footwear News,* July 30, 1984, pp. 2–3.

——, "Barry Sets Designer Slippers," *Footwear News,* May 7, 1990, p. 23.

——, "Critter Pulled in by a Nose," *Footwear News,* February 4, 1991, p. 58.

—April Dougal Gasbarre

The Reader's Digest Association, Inc.

Reader's Digest Road
Pleasantville, New York 10570
U.S.A.
(914) 238-1000
Fax: (914) 238-4559
Internet: http://www.readersdigest.com

Public Company
Incorporated: 1922
Employees: 6,300
Sales: $3.09 billion (1996)
Stock Exchanges: New York
SICs: 2721 Periodicals; 2731 Book Publishing; 3652
   Prerecorded Records and Tapes; 7372 Prepackaged
   Software; 7812 Motion Picture and Video Production

The Reader's Digest Association, Inc. is a worldwide publisher and distributor of magazines, books, recorded music, and home video packages, almost all of which are sold by means of direct-mail marketing. Its major publication is the monthly general-interest magazine *Reader's Digest*, which is the world's most widely read magazine with a global readership of over 100 million, and is available in 47 editions and 18 different languages. The company's remaining products include millions of condensed books, how-to and reference books, home entertainment in music and video form, and other special interest magazines. The company also operates QSP, Inc., a subsidiary which is a major fund-raising organization for schools and organizations throughout the United States and Canada. To market its many products, the Reader's Digest Association employs use of an extensive consumer database that is considered to be one of the best in the world.

The Early Years

Reader's Digest was founded in 1922 through the joint efforts of DeWitt Wallace and Lila Bell Acheson Wallace. DeWitt Wallace was born on November 12, 1889, in St. Paul,

Minnesota, to a father who was a college professor and who later became president of Macalester College. Throughout his years of early adulthood, DeWitt Wallace read widely, and got in the habit of making notes from his reading to retain ideas. In a job handling inquiries about an agricultural textbook, he began wondering if his reading notes might be useful to others were they to be published. Thus, he conceived the idea of condensing magazine articles and reprinting them in a digest magazine.

In the early 1900s, Wallace produced a 128-page book on farming, providing information about agricultural bulletins available to farmers. He sold 100,000 copies of the book by traveling through five states in an old car, selling the book to banks and feed stores that would give the book to customers as a gift. Due to his success with the book, he saw a market for that type of publication among the public as a whole, and sought to publish condensed versions of articles in a magazine form.

World War I temporarily interrupted Wallace's plans. In October 1918, he was severely wounded in battle in France. During his months of recuperation, he focused on reading from a variety of magazines, distilling the articles down to their essentials. On his return home to St. Paul, he continued to work on digesting other magazine articles, putting together 31 summarized articles in a sample of the type of digest magazine he thought would sell. The cost of printing the sample was paid for with money borrowed from his brother and father. He showed his sample to several publishing houses with the hope that they would use his idea and hire him as editor, but all of them turned him down.

In January 1922, Wallace finally published the magazine on his own, aided by his wife, Lila Bell Acheson Wallace. Acheson had been born in Canada in 1889, but spent most of her early life in the United States while her father preached in a number of midwestern towns. In 1921, she married DeWitt Wallace, and together they began selling his magazine idea to readers by direct mail. The couple rented an apartment in Greenwich Village in New York City, with Lila retaining her job as a social worker to pay the rent. DeWitt Wallace sent out letters to potential subscribers, offering his magazine idea for sale and promising a money-back guarantee if readers were not satisfied. These solicitations brought in 1,500 subscriptions at $3 each,

Company Perspectives:

The Reader's Digest Association, Inc., is built on a heritage of service and quality. Today our company is a leading global publisher and one of the world's foremost direct mail marketers. Our magazines, books and home entertainment products provide customers with hours of reading, listening and viewing pleasure. The legacy of service and quality lives on—timeless ideals guiding us in our mission: to develop, produce and market high-quality, profitable products that inform, enrich, entertain and inspire people all over the world.

generating enough money to finance the first edition and possibly the second.

The first edition of the *Reader's Digest* was dated February 1922, and contained 64 pages. Its small measurements, about 5.5 inches by 7.5 inches, allowed readers to carry it in a pocket or purse and was a unique innovation among magazines at the time. The lead article was by Alexander Graham Bell and was on the importance of self-education as a lifelong habit.

DeWitt Wallace spent much of the magazine's first year in the New York Public Library reading articles to summarize in future issues, while Lila Wallace kept her job. The first edition was judged to be a success when there were no cancellations of subscriptions after its release. By September 1922, the couple was able to rent a garage and apartment for their editorial offices, choosing to live in Pleasantville, New York, where they had been married in 1921. Additional promotional letters brought in new subscribers, and within a year of its first edition, circulation had risen to 7,000. After four years, circulation was up to 20,000, and by 1929 it had risen to an astounding 216,000 subscribers.

The Mid-1900s: A Growing Enterprise

Initially, *The Digest* kept a low profile, partly for fear that envious magazines might stop allowing it to reprint their articles. DeWitt Wallace seemed to have a very good notion of what his readers wanted, and circulation continued to grow, reaching over one million in 1936 and three million in 1939. An edition began appearing in England in 1938. Due to the rapid increase in the size of operations, in 1939 the Wallaces moved their facilities to Chappaqua, New York, located close by, but retained their mailing address in Pleasantville, because of the euphonious nature of its name. The address has remained at Pleasantville ever since.

In 1950, condensed books under the *Reader's Digest* name first appeared. These books, which presented abbreviated versions of popular novels, were an immediate success. Therefore, nine years later the company diversified even further when a series of phonograph record albums of music that was culturally sophisticated yet broadly popular appeared under the *Reader's Digest* banner.

Foreign-language editions of *The Digest* carried advertising from their inception, but in the United States advertising was not introduced until 1955. Furthermore, the magazine did not accept advertising for alcoholic beverages until the late 1970s, and it never ran advertisements for cigarettes. Instead, it began warning readers of the dangers of smoking, well before the surgeon general made his report in 1964.

The Digest owed its initial appeal and continued success to DeWitt's ability to choose articles that reflected the values of its many readers. Many of those readers later told of the hope and inspiration they drew from the optimistic spirit that pervaded *The Digest*. That spirit reflected the outlook of DeWitt Wallace, who based the magazine's content on what he wanted to read. Even as the publication grew in size and popularity, he retained strict editorial control.

When the magazine became successful, DeWitt Wallace kept up the task of editing it and managing its finances. His wife designed the corporate headquarters and purchased many artworks that are still part of the company's collection. She also had a hand in selecting the graphics that adorned the back cover of *The Digest*. In 1956, she formed the Lila Wallace Reader's Digest Fund to support the arts and make them accessible to persons of all income levels. A DeWitt Wallace Reader's Digest Fund was also formed for the purpose of providing education programs for young people.

The 1970s and 1980s: The Changing Face of the Association

In 1973, after over half a century of work, the Wallaces retired, although DeWitt Wallace kept in close contact with the editorial and corporate offices. He died on March 30, 1981, at the age of 91. Lila Wallace survived him by three years. The Wallaces never had children, and therefore most of their stock in the company was willed to charities, including Macalester College. This stock was non-voting, however, and almost all of the Wallace's voting power was placed with the two Wallace trust funds, of which the association management owned three percent.

About the time of Lila Wallace's death in 1984, George Grune became head of The Reader's Digest Association. The company was not performing very well, and in a successful effort to improve profitability, he took the company public and began a cost-cutting program that included the termination of foreign editions of the *Reader's Digest* that were losing money, the divestiture of weak divisions, and the reduction of the work force from 10,000 to 7,500. He also decreased the rate at which advertising was being lost.

Members of the staff who had worked during the Wallace years became concerned that Grune's methods departed from Wallace's idea that the company was an association of readers and not just a for-profit venture. There was no doubt that Grune had improved profits; in five years profits increased sevenfold. After years of higher profits, several of the charities that owned non-voting shares of the association's stock sold some of their shares to the public in order to take advantage of the high price the stock would bring. After the sale, in February 1990, 21 percent of the total stock was publicly held, these all being class

A non-voting shares. Nearly all of the class B voting shares (98 percent) were still held by the trust funds, with the remainder held by employees of the association.

As the 1980s drew to a close, The Reader's Digest Association remained a global company, with operations located in 50 cities throughout the world. *Reader's Digest* continued as its premiere publication, accounting for nearly a third of the company's revenues. *The Digest* also served to introduce subscribers to other products sold by the company, such as the condensed books and audio or video tapes.

To maintain its subscribers' loyalties, editors of *The Digest* kept coverage diverse and of high quality. The publication was earning nearly 70 percent of its revenues from circulation, which was a very high figure given that most magazines rely more heavily on advertising for revenue. But because *The Digest* did not rely so much on its advertisers, its content did not have to be targeted to a market desired by the advertisers, leaving editors free to select articles having the broadest appeal.

In the late 1980s, the association had acquired several special-interest magazines, such as *Travel Holiday, The Family Handyman, New Choices for the Best Years,* and *American Health.* In 1990, it expanded this line by purchasing the British magazine *Money,* which was renamed *Moneywise,* and by starting up a French magazine, *Budgets Famille.* The special-interest-magazine line, along with other Reader's Digest books and home entertainment, accounted for the revenues not brought in by the *Reader's Digest* magazine. The company's books were either released individually or in series. Series books included such new product lines in the United States as the AMA Home Medical Library, while general individual books included reference books, how-to books, cookbooks, travel guides, and others.

The 1990s and Beyond

As the global economy was restructured in the 1990s, The Reader's Digest Association made attempts to keep pace. Its products were already well known in 11 of the 12 countries that made up the European single market, although *Budgets Famille* was suspended in May 1990 after six issues because it did not meet circulation or advertising objectives. The company began formulating plans to expand into the new markets of Eastern Europe that were beginning to be important in world trade. For example, when the Berlin Wall was opened in 1989, employees of *The Digest* started distributing complimentary copies of the German-language version of *Reader's Digest* and collecting names for a mailing list of potential subscribers. Then in late 1991, *Reader's Digest* became available in Russian- and Hungarian-language editions to serve readers in those countries. In this way, the association continued to keep pace with an ever-changing world.

In fiscal 1991 the company boasted record sales figures, despite the fact that it was operating in a weak economic climate due to worldwide uncertainty caused by the Persian Gulf War. Aiding the Association in its success were two acquisitions made that year. Both David & Charles, a British book publisher and one of the United Kingdom's leading book clubs, and Joshua Morris Publishing, Inc., an international book publisher

with a focus on children's materials, contributed to the Reader's Digest Association's strong financial standing in the early 1990s.

In 1992, as Reader's Digest celebrated its 70th anniversary, the company updated the strategic plan that had been set in place when Grune first took over in 1984. Even greater emphasis was placed on expanding into new markets around the globe, with use of the *Reader's Digest* magazine as an entry tool. The company committed to the idea of releasing at least one new edition of the magazine in each of the following years. Also emphasized in the newly updated plan were cost control measures which led to a ten percent work force reduction at the company's headquarters in Pleasantville in 1993. The structure of the company itself was also reorganized into three main operating divisions: Reader's Digest Europe, Reader's Digest U.S.A., and Reader's Digest Pacific, each of which became responsible for the business in its own market area.

The corporation's rejuvenation efforts soon began to show evidence of success. In 1993, after 55 years in the United Kingdom, that edition of *Reader's Digest* magazine became the area's best-selling and most widely read magazine. That same year, *Fortune* magazine called the Reader's Digest Association the United States' most admired publishing company. In the United States, the ABC television network aired a special program entitled "Reader's Digest: On Television," which helped the company's books and home entertainment segment begin to flourish once again, after a slump during the previous few years. Furthermore, in a move designed to coincide with the world's progression into the information age, Reader's Digest began to pursue the development of interactive CD-ROM products.

By 1995, James P. Schadt had succeeded Grune as Chairman and CEO of the Reader's Digest Association. Schadt, who moved up from the rank of president upon Grune's retirement to fill the new leadership role, had been with the company throughout its restructuring phase. His position as president was filled by Ken Gordon, a longtime Reader's Digest employee and the head of the U.S.A. operating division. Together, the two continued to focus both on strengthening Reader's Digest's business in the United States, and expanding throughout the world.

1995 also offered unique opportunities for Reader's Digest to participate in cooperative endeavors with other companies. Reader's Digest teamed up with the Meredith Corporation, known widely for its *Better Homes and Gardens* and *Ladies' Home Journal* products, as a means of expanding its consumer database. The company also entered into partnerships with Microsoft, to produce CD-ROMs based on Reader's Digest reference books, and with Dove Audio to produce audio books.

Other operations of the association contributed to the company's total revenue. These operations included a subsidiary, QSP, Inc., which provided fund-raising services for schools and youth groups through the sale of subscriptions to magazines, music products, and candy. Nearing the end of the century, *Reader's Digest* remained the world's best-selling and most widely read magazine. Despite the magazine's popularity, however, it was the books and home-entertainment division that generated the bulk of the association's profits by the late 1990s.

Furthermore, with the increasing popularity of the internet, an entirely new avenue of product development and distribution was opening up for Reader's Digest. As the company began pursuing such avenues, while also continuing its expansion into new markets each year, Reader's Digest seemed to possess great potential for future growth and diversification.

Principal Subsidiaries

QSP, Inc.

Principal Operating Units

Reader's Digest Europe; Reader's Digest U.S.A.; Reader's Digest Pacific; Reader's Digest Special Markets.

Further Reading

Ferguson, Charles W., "Unforgettable DeWitt Wallace," *Reader's Digest,* February 1987.

Lynn, Matthew, "Revolution in Pleasantville," *Management Today,* April 1996, p. 62.

Milliot, Jim, "Publishers Discuss Finances, The Future at Conference," *Publishers Weekly,* December 20, 1993, p. 10.

Moraais, Richard C., "Hate Selling," *Forbes,* June 5, 1995, p. 142.

Pogrebin, Robin, "A Magazine Only a Mother Could Love? Seeking Younger Audience, Reader's Digest Tries to Lose its Stodgy Image," *The New York Times,* July 22, 1996, p. C1.

Rothman, Andrea, "The Man Who Rewrote Reader's Digest," *Business Week,* June 4, 1990.

—Donald R. Stabile
—updated by Laura E. Whiteley

REED ELSEVIER
Reed International PLC

6 Chesterfield Gardens
London W1A 1EJ
United Kingdom
(0171) 499 4020
Fax: (0171) 491 8212
Internet: http://www.r-e.com/

Public Company
Incorporated: 1903 as Albert E. Reed & Company Ltd.
Employees: 25,000
Sales: £1.93 billion (1995)
Stock Exchanges: London Amsterdam New York
SICs: 2711 Newspapers: Publishing, or Publishing &
    Printing; 2721 Periodicals: Publishing, or Publishing
    & Printing; 2731 Books: Publishing, or Publishing &
    Printing; 2741 Miscellaneous Publishing; 7375
    Information Retrieval Services; 7389 Business
    Services, Not Elsewhere Classified

Originally a paper manufacturer and later a conglomerate, Reed International PLC is now a holding company with a half-interest in publishing giant Reed Elsevier PLC, which was formed in 1993 from the combined publishing operations of Reed International and the Dutch publisher Elsevier N.V. Through Reed Elsevier, Reed International co-owns companies in the areas of scientific, professional, business, and consumer publishing. Reed Elsevier is one of the largest publishing groups in the world.

Origins with Paper Mill in Late 19th Century

The beginnings of the company date to 1894, when Albert Reed bought Upper Tovil paper mill at Maidstone, Kent. He was then 48 and already successful in paper manufacturing. After going into the paper business as a boy he had become a manager, and then part owner, of a number of paper mills in different parts of the country, but Upper Tovil was the first that was entirely his. It had been badly damaged in a fire when he bought it, so he was able to install new machinery before reopening it.

Over the years Reed had experimented with different materials and machinery to produce types of paper suitable for the half-tone blocks that were then being introduced. At his new mill he specialized in these papers and soon built up a good trade with the publishers of illustrated magazines. Within two years he had more than 100 employees and had installed a new machine. When Upper Tovil had been expanded to its limit, Reed bought other mills, owning seven by 1903. In that year the business was incorporated as Albert E. Reed & Company Ltd., to enable more capital to be raised.

One of the firm's best customers in its early days was the publishing business of Harmsworth Brothers. This connection chiefly fueled Reed's growth from 1904 onward. Alfred and Harold Harmsworth, shortly to become Lord Northcliffe and Lord Rothermere, respectively, had built up the most dynamic publishing business in London. Only 15 years after launching their first magazine, *Answers,* they controlled a string of magazines and newspapers, including the successful *Daily Mail.* They had one failure, however, a new paper aimed at women, called the *Daily Mirror.* To save it they decided to relaunch it in 1904 for a general readership as an all-picture paper, using a new grade of fine newsprint introduced by Reed. In this form the *Daily Mirror* became a success, and the Reed paper business grew with it. By the outbreak of World War I in 1914, the *Daily Mirror* was the largest selling daily newspaper in the world, and Reed was supplying the newsprint not only for that but also for several national newspapers. The company took over more paper mills in the United Kingdom and invested in pulp mills in Norway and in Newfoundland, Canada.

World War I put a temporary stop to Reed's growth. Supplies of pulp from Scandinavia were cut off, newspapers became smaller, and Reed was forced to close some of its mills. At the same time the Newfoundland venture proved uneconomical. Reed sold it to his friends, the Harmsworths, who were developing their own pulp mill nearby.

Soon after World War I another financial crisis was precipitated by Albert Reed's death in 1920. His twin sons, Ralph and Percy, were determined to carry on the business, but a large sum had to be found to pay the duty on their father's estate and, in any case, some members of the family wanted to turn their shares into cash. Once again, the Reeds turned to their largest customer. Lord Northcliffe had died, but Lord Rothermere agreed to buy a large block of shares in Reed, through the Daily Mirror and Sunday Pictorial companies, which he now controlled. The Reed brothers still had voting control, but Rothermere's holding of around 40 percent of the equity rendered him a major influence in its affairs. He seems to have made little use of this influence, having had many other business commitments, but half a century later this shareholding was to change the nature of Reed's business.

The Reed brothers began to implement the plan for the company that their father had conceived during the war. This was to sell their remaining overseas operations and most of their U.K. mills and concentrate their resources on a single, modern plant, using the largest machines available. In this way they hoped to undercut all competition. A site was selected at Aylesford, a few miles downriver from Tovil, and the new mill began production in 1922.

The new strategy worked well. Despite the Depression the Aylesford plant was steadily expanded and, by 1939, was the largest of its kind of Europe. Newsprint remained the company's chief product, but from 1929 onward Reed also made kraft paper from which it produced corrugated board and paper sacks. With these new products the company captured a large share of the packaging market.

Crisis in the 1950s

During World War II production had to be drastically reduced because of lack of pulp and did not regain prewar levels until 1950. The next few years were a boom period for Reed. The company added to its newsprint and kraft manufacturing capacity, expanded into new forms of packaging, entered the paper tissue market in a joint venture with Kimberly-Clark, and invested some of its profits in pulp mills overseas. Within seven years Reed's work force doubled to 14,000.

In the late 1950s, however, conditions changed for the worse. First the government put an end to the price-fixing arrangements that Reed had with other paper manufacturers, and then to the tariffs that had shielded the U.K. paper industry from Scandinavian competition. This latter change was the result of U.K. membership in the European Free Trade Area and was to be introduced over several years, but its implications were clear from 1959. Without the tariffs, newsprint and kraft made from imported pulp would be unable to compete with Scandinavian products. Reed would have to make major changes.

It was unfortunate that the company had to face this crisis with a relatively untried management. Sir Ralph Reed had retired in 1954, ending the era of family control, and his most able colleague, Clifford Sheldon, had died a few years earlier. The new chairman, Lord Cornwallis, and managing director, P. G. Walker, both came from outside the paper industry. They took prompt steps to reduce the company's dependence on imported pulp, but could not prevent a slide in profits. In 1960, the company's largest shareholder decided to intervene.

This was no longer Lord Rothermere, who had sold his shares in the *Daily Mirror* in the 1930s, but a new group that had been created from the nucleus of the *Mirror*. The latter paper and the *Sunday Pictorial* had declined in the 1920s under Rothermere's ownership but had recovered under his successors. In the late

1930s a new team led by Guy Bartholomew and including Cecil King, a nephew of Lords Northcliffe and Rothermere, had completely restyled the two papers. Now they were aimed at younger, working class readers. Through a mixture of populist style and radical campaigning on social issues, they captured most of this market during the unsettled war years and increased their hold on it in the more prosperous times that followed. The combined circulation of both papers rose from around one million in the 1930s to more than five million in the 1960s.

Conglomerate in the 1950s and 1960s

From the large profits that flowed from this success, Cecil King, who became chairman in 1951, began to build a broad-ranging publishing group. It bought further newspapers, in Scotland and abroad, and a stake in one of the first commercial television companies in the United Kingdom, Associated TV, which proved to be highly lucrative. King next turned his attention to magazines. In 1958 he bought Amalgamated Press, the magazine group founded by his uncles, then Associated Iliffe Press, and finally Odhams Press. This included newspapers as well as the Odhams, Newnes, and Hulton magazine groups. When the Mirror and Pictorial companies became the International Publishing Corporation (IPC) in 1963, it was by far the largest publishing group in the United Kingdom. It had four mass circulation newspapers, all of the leading women's magazines, a host of specialized magazines and directories, and no less than 25 printing plants.

Through this period of upheaval the Mirror and Pictorial companies had held on to their shares in Reed, which they saw as a substantial asset, to be protected and developed. When its future began to look uncertain, King obtained voting control of Reed by transferring to it all of the pulp and paper mills owned by Mirror and Pictorial. In 1963, while retaining the chairmanship of IPC, he made himself chairman of Reed and installed one of his senior managers, Don Ryder, as managing director.

Don Ryder was a former financial journalist who had shown a flair for management. Under his vigorous lead, Reed expanded and diversified. Its success in packaging and its growing overseas interests had already reduced its dependence on the U.K. newsprint and kraft business, and Ryder speeded up this process by a series of takeovers. First he bought companies in other branches of the paper and packaging industry. Then in 1965 he successfully bid for The Wall Paper Manufacturers (WPM), a large but sleepy company that then had a virtual monopoly of the wallpaper market in the United Kingdom. It also included a paint business and Sanderson fabrics. In the same year, Reed bought Polycell Holdings, which made Polyfilla and other decorating products. With these brands Reed acquired instant dominance of the fast-growing do-it-yourself market. Then, through further takeovers, Ryder took Reed into bathroom equipment and other building products. By 1970 the company could be described as a conglomerate. Its work force had grown to 56,000. The enlargement of its share capital had freed it from IPC's control, and its market value had risen well above that of IPC.

Meanwhile, IPC had run into difficulties. The worst of these concerned the *Daily Herald,* a Labour Party newspaper owned jointly by Odhams and the trade unions, which lost money steadily. IPC persuaded the trade unions to relinquish their share and relaunched the paper as the *Sun*. This was no more successful and was finally sold to Rupert Murdoch at a very low price. In addition, there were serious losses on the printing side of IPC. Many of the works it had acquired in its takeovers were found to be obsolete and had to be closed down or modernized at further cost.

Finally, King's activities created a problem. Instead of tackling the company's financial difficulties, he became increasingly preoccupied with politics. The *Daily Mirror* had helped to get the Labour government elected in 1964, and afterward King felt that it should listen to his views. When it did not, he turned on Labour with irrational fury. In 1968, on the front page of the *Daily Mirror,* King demanded the prime minister's resignation. King's colleagues at IPC felt that he was misusing the paper's power and forced him to resign.

Tough Times in the 1970s

King was succeeded by Hugh Cudlipp, a brilliant editor but a poor businessman. Afterward, he admitted that his chairmanship of IPC was "uninspired." The company's decline continued and takeover rumors began. As IPC still owned 27 percent of Reed, and Ryder could not allow it to fall into unfriendly hands, he and Cudlipp agreed in 1970 that Reed should take over IPC.

The combined company was named Reed International, incorporating part of IPC's name, and its turnover made it the thirtieth largest U.K. company. Its work force numbered 85,000, and its business spanned more markets than at any time before or since. Reed's position in most of these markets, however, was far from secure.

The U.K. paper business was still contracting, and Reed had to close down some operations in the 1970s. Its Canadian pulp and paper business was only intermittently profitable. The printing business inherited from IPC continued to lose money, even after the older plant was closed, and Reed failed to deal with its overmanning. WPM faced increasingly tough competition in wall coverings and saw its market share steadily eroded. Newspaper circulations in the United Kingdom were declining and all of IPC's nationals lost ground. It was the *Sun's* recovery under Murdoch that hit the *Mirror* hardest.

In the early 1970s Ryder kept profits moving upward, by rationalizing in the weaker areas and increasing investment in the stronger ones. Indeed, his reputation as a manager was so impressive that at the end of 1974 he was plucked from Reed by the government to head its new National Enterprise Board. His successor, Alex Jarratt, continued to implement Ryder's policy, but it was no longer working. In 1975–1976 the company's profits fell by more than 50 percent, and in the next few years made only a partial recovery.

Only in 1978 did the company recognize that the expansion policy initiated by Ryder had failed in the long run. Turnover had grown tenfold in his 11-year reign, but profits had grown much more slowly, and the outlook was poor. Jarratt decided to dispose of its unprofitable parts. Most of the overseas subsidiaries were sold, and the work force was reduced to 60,000. Nevertheless, 1980–1981 saw another halving of profits, and another round of cutbacks began, this time mainly in the U.K. paper division.

Revitalized as Publishing Group in the 1980s

In 1982 a new chief executive was appointed, Leslie Carpenter, who had come up through the magazine division of the company. The next annual report pointed out that 60 percent of the company's trading profit was coming from the 40 percent of its turnover that lay in publishing. From that time onward, new investment was concentrated in this area. Local newspaper chains were acquired in the United Kingdom, together with publishing and exhibition companies in the United States, where the Cahners subsidiary, a magazine publisher wholly owned since 1977, was thriving.

At this time the company's publishing activities still included U.K. national newspapers. Despite the introduction of photocomposition, these were far less profitable than the magazines. In 1984 Reed decided to float them as a separate company. "National newspapers do not sit easily in a large commercial corporation," said Carpenter. The move was forestalled by a takeover bid for the newspaper group, which was accepted. This was from Robert Maxwell, who had already bought the Odhams gravure printing works from Reed.

Reed was thus left with a flourishing magazine business on both sides of the Atlantic and a miscellany of less profitable manufacturing businesses—the much-reduced paper and packaging division, as well as paints and building products. During Carpenter's time as chief executive there were further disposals in the manufacturing area, and the final moves to abandon manufacturing were made under his successor, Peter Davis, who became chief executive in 1986.

The most significant change came in 1987. In that year the paints and do-it-yourself division was sold, and Octopus Publishing was bought. Octopus, which cost Reed £540 million, was the largest publishing business the company had acquired since IPC. It was a diversified international publishing group with a major presence in mass market nonfiction books, fiction and general trade books, children's books, educational books at both the primary and secondary level, and in business and technical books, and greatly increased Reed's strength in these areas. Its founder, Paul Hamlyn, moved to Reed with the business and became the company's largest noncorporate shareholder.

Paper and packaging, for so long Reed's sole business, was the last of the manufacturing divisions to go. It was bought in 1988 by its own management, taking the name Reedpack, and two years later was sold again to a Swedish company, Svenska Cellulosa. Reed also sold its North American paper group to Daishowa Paper Manufacturing Co., Ltd. in 1988 for C $594.

With Reed now a purely publishing concern, Davis quickly moved to bolster the company's position through acquisitions. In 1989 Reed purchased the U.K. consumer magazine *TV Times* for £123 million. Later that same year, £535.4 million was spent to buy the Travel Information Group, a U.S. travel guide producer, from the News Corporation. The following year Reed enlarged its presence in the area of legal publishing with the purchase of the American firm Martindale-Hubbell for £189 million. Martindale-Hubbell was subsequently merged into Reed's existing legal publisher, R. R. Bowker, and complemented Butterworths, the legal publisher in the United Kingdom, also owned by Reed. In 1991 Marquis Who's Who, publisher of biographical directories, and the National Register Publishing Co., publisher of business directories, were purchased from the Macmillan directory division for US $145 million.

Davis became chairman of Reed in 1990. By the following year, thanks to Davis's acquisitions, Reed had grown to become the third largest publisher in Europe, trailing only Germany's Bertelsmann and France's Hachette. Although 1991 sales were only slightly higher than sales when Davis took over, profits had increased from £100 million to £251 million.

Reed-Elsevier Joint Venture Formed in 1993

In 1992 Davis made his boldest move yet by engineering a "merger" with the Dutch publisher Elsevier N.V., which was the world's leading publisher of scientific journals. At the start of 1993, Reed International and Elsevier were transformed into holding companies, each holding equalized stakes in a joint venture. To reflect Reed's larger capitalization, Reed gained a 5.8 percent stake in Elsevier. Both companies held a 50 percent stake in the newly formed Reed Elsevier PLC, which became the parent company for all of Reed's and Elsevier's publishing businesses. Also newly created was Elsevier Reed Finance BV, which became the parent company for the companies' financing and treasury companies. Reed International held 46 percent of Elsevier Reed Finance, and Elsevier held 54 percent. The Reed Elsevier joint venture immediately vaulted into the list of the top ten publishing companies in the world, with combined annual revenue of US $4.5 billion.

Tensions between the Anglo and Dutch partners surfaced since the agreement, and although the joint venture continued into the mid-1990s, Reed International and Elsevier had not formally merged. The most noteworthy dispute came in 1994 when Davis resigned in a power struggle won by the Dutch. Initially, Davis served as co-chairman of Reed Elsevier, along with Pierre Vinken, who was also chairman of Elsevier. Davis was slated to become sole chairman when Vinken retired in 1995. But the Dutch pushed for a collective style of leadership whereby the four-person executive committee (two from Reed, two from Elsevier) would manage collectively. When the board voted for the Dutch approach, Davis resigned and was succeeded as Reed International chairman by the second-in-command, Ian Irvine.

Meanwhile, Reed Elsevier concluded a couple of significant acquisitions. In 1993 Official Airline Guides was bought from the bankrupt Maxwell for US $425 million. The American market was targeted next. First, both Reed International and Elsevier had their stock placed on the New York Stock Exchange. Later that year, Reed Elsevier took a huge plunge into the online publishing world by acquiring Lexis/Nexis, which offered a number of online information services, from Mead Corp. for US $1.5 billion. The purchase instantly doubled the amount of Reed Elsevier revenue derived from electronic publishing from ten to 20 percent.

By 1995 Reed Elsevier operated four main publishing segments: Scientific, which included both scientific and medical offerings; Professional, which included legal, reference, and educational areas; Business, which included travel publishing, information services, and exhibition operations; and Consumer, which included magazines, newspapers, and books. The Consumer segment was the most troublesome of these and did not fit well with the other three segments. Much of the Consumer segment was put up for sale in 1995. Subsequently, newspaper businesses in the Netherlands and the United Kingdom and consumer magazines in the United States and the Netherlands were sold in five separate transactions for £751 million (US $1.1 billion). Reed Elsevier also attempted to sell Reed Consumer Books but could not secure an acceptable offer. Reed Elsevier planned to improve Reed Consumer's performance, then attempt to sell it again.

Since its establishment, Reed Elsevier's sales have continued to grow, reaching £3.65 billion in 1995, a 20 percent increase over 1994. Operating profits were improving as well, with the operating margin standing at 22.7 percent in 1995. As a result, Reed International faced a bright future heading into the 21st century. It was expected that Reed Elsevier would continue to grow, using the cash from the sales of the consumer properties to make additional significant acquisitions.

Principal Subsidiaries

Reed Elsevier PLC (50%); Elsevier Reed Finance BV (46%).

Further Reading

"Bigger, Better? Reed and Elsevier," *Economist,* September 19, 1992, p. 83.

Blackhurst, Chris, "Dinosaur's New Lease on Life," *Management Today,* January 1992, p. 12.

Chapters from Our History, London: Reed International, 1990.

DuBois, Martin, and Guyon, Janet, "Britain's Reed Agrees To Merge with Elsevier," *Wall Street Journal,* September 18, 1992, pp. A2, A7.

Evans, Richard, "Playing House: After Nearly Three Years, Reed and Elsevier Still Haven't Consummated Their Marriage," *Financial World,* August 1, 1995, p. 37.

Hayes, John R., "The Internet's First Victim?," *Forbes,* December 18, 1995, p. 200.

Hochwald, Lambeth, "Reed Elsevier: The Dancing Elephant," *Folio: The Magazine for Magazine Management,* September 1, 1994, p. 58.

House, Richard, "A Marriage for the '90s," *Institutional Investor,* February 1993, p. 99.

Hudson, Richard L., "Reed Elsevier Enters Big Leagues of On-Line Services," *Wall Street Journal,* October 6, 1994, p. B4.

Marcom, John Jr., "Down to Earth, Mostly," *Forbes,* October 29, 1990, pp. 57, 61.

Pope, Kyle, "Reed Elsevier May Use Its Cash Hoard on Acquisitions, Possibly in the U.S.," *Wall Street Journal,* March 14, 1996, p. A15.

Prokesch, Steven, "Britain's Low-Profile Publishing Giant: Reed International, Big in America, Treads Carefully as It Grows," *New York Times,* February 9, 1992, p. F5.

Reed International: Developments in a Company History, 1960–1974, London: Reed International, 1980.

Skeel, Shirley, "Reed All About It," *Management Today,* October 1992, p. 62.

Steinmetz, Greg, and Narisetti, Raju, "Reed Elsevier Wins Bidding for Lexis/Nexis," *Wall Street Journal,* October 5, 1994, pp. A3, A11.

Sykes, Philip, *Albert Reed and the Creation of a Paper Business, 1860–1960,* London: Reed International, 1980.

—John Swan
—updated by David E. Salamie

REVLON

Revlon Inc.

625 Madison Avenue
New York, New York 10022
U.S.A.
(212) 527-4000
Fax: (212) 527-5000
Internet: http://www.revlon.com

Public Company
Incorporated: 1933 as Revlon Products Corporation
Employees: 7,000
Sales: $1.94 billion (1995)
Stock Exchanges: New York
SICs: 2834 Pharmaceutical Preparations; 2844 Perfumes,
    Cosmetics & Other Toilet Preparations; 3421 Cutlery;
    5122 Drugs, Drug Proprietaries & Sundries; 3999
    Manufacturing Industries, Not Elsewhere Classified;
    8731 Commercial, Physical & Biological Research

Revlon Inc. is the leading mass-market cosmetics company in the United States, marketing products under such familiar brands as Revlon, ColorStay, Age Defying, Almay, and Ultima II. Revlon also sells skin care products (such as Moon Drops, Eterna); fragrances (Charlie, Fire & Ice); personal care products (Flex, Outrageous); and professional products (Roux Fancifull, Realistic). Although recently returning to the public company fold, Revlon is still controlled by Ronald Perelman, who gained control of the company in a nasty hostile takeover in 1985.

Formed as Nail Polish Company in 1932

Revlon's first beauty item was nail enamel. Opaque and long-lasting, it was an improvement over the more transparent, dye-based products of other manufacturers. Revlon's nail polish owed its superiority to the use of pigments, which also allowed a wider color range than the light red, medium red, and dark red then available. Initially, the revolutionary ''cream enamel'' came from the tiny Elka company, in Newark, New Jersey, a polish supplier to beauty salons for whom Charles Revson

began to work as a sales representative in 1931. Charles Revson and his older brother, Joseph Revson, distributed Elka nail polish as Revson Brothers. Within a year, however, Charles Revson decided to open his own nail polish company, going into partnership with his brother and a nail polish supplier named Charles R. Lachman, who contributed the ''l'' to the Revlon name. Revlon was formed on March 1, 1932.

Revson had a keen fashion instinct, honed by his seven years of sales experience at the Pickwick Dress Company in New York. Coupling this with his experience at Elka, he noted that the permanent wave boom was making beauty salons more popular, and that demand for manicures was rising in tandem. He therefore targeted beauty salons as a market niche—a fortunate choice whose importance would grow.

Within its first nine months, the company boasted sales of $4,055. There was a sharp rise in sales to $11,246 in 1933, the year the company incorporated as Revlon Products Corporation. At the end of 1934, the company grossed $68,000. By 1937, sales had multiplied more than 40 times.

In 1937 Revson decided to enlarge his market by retailing his nail polish through department stores and selected drugstores. This gave him access to more affluent customers as well as those with a moderate amount of money to spend on beauty products. Formulating a maxim he followed for the rest of his life, Revson steered clear of cut-rate stores, selling his product only at premium prices.

Advertising helped Revson stick to this rule. Its use was a fateful step for the industry; never again would major cosmetics companies attempt to sell beauty items without it. Revson began by labeling his nail enamels with evocative names like Fatal Apple and Kissing Pink, that were descriptive while offering the promise of novelty. The company's first commercial advertisement appeared in *The New Yorker* in 1935. Aimed carefully at the upper-income clientele Revson was trying to attract, the advertisement came with a price tag of $335, constituting Revlon's entire advertising budget for the year.

By 1940 Revlon had a whole line of manicure products. Lipstick, Revlon's next major item, appeared in 1940. A per-

---

Company Perspectives:

Revlon is one of the world's best known names in cosmetics and is a leading mass market cosmetics brand. The company's vision is to provide glamour, excitement, and innovation through quality products at affordable prices. To pursue this vision, the company's management team combines the creativity of a cosmetics and fashion company with the marketing, sales, and operating discipline of a consumer packaged goods company. The company believes that its global brand name recognition, product quality, and marketing experience have enabled it to create one of the strongest consumer brand franchises in the world, with products sold in approximately 175 countries and territories.

---

fectionist by nature, Revson made sure that its quality was the best he could produce. Its introduction was marked by a full-color advertising campaign stressing the importance of cosmetics as a fashion accessory, and featuring the novel idea of "matching lips and fingertips." The campaign's success showed in the 1940 sales figures; reaching $2.8 million, they more than doubled those of 1939.

World War II brought shortages of glass bottles and metal lipstick cases. Paper had to be substituted. Also in short supply were aromatic oils, fixatives, and packaging materials, which had previously been imported from Italy, Ethiopia, and France. Since the shortages affected the entire industry, secrecy was replaced by mutual cooperation; new synthetics and domestic sources of supply were shared, and a new U.S. aromatics industry was born.

During wartime, patriotic activities replaced expansion. In addition to cosmetics, Revlon turned out first-aid kits, dye markers for the navy, and hand grenades for the army. Characteristically, Revson's military products were the best his company could produce. His attention to detail was rewarded in 1944 with an army-navy production award for excellence.

By the end of the war, Revlon listed itself as one of America's top five cosmetic houses. Expanding its capabilities, the company bought Graef & Schmidt, a cutlery manufacturer seized by the government in 1943 because of German business ties. Costing $301,125, this acquisition made it possible for Revlon to produce its own manicure and pedicure instruments, instead of buying them from outside supply sources.

Postwar Promotions and Television Sponsorships Spurred Further Growth

Postwar sales strategy, too, was influenced by increases in spending and department store credit sales. Returning interest in dress sparked the company's twice-yearly nail enamel and lipstick promotions, which were crafted in anticipation of the season's clothing fashions. Each promotion featured a descriptive color name to tempt the buyer, full-color spreads in fashion magazines, color cards showing the range of colors in the promotion, and display cards reproducing or enlarging consumer ads. Packaging was designed specifically for each line.

The Fire and Ice promotion for fall 1952 was one of the most successful. Its features included the cooperation of *Vogue*, which planned its November issue around the lipstick and nail enamel; "push" money given to demonstrators in stores without Revlon sales staff to insure full retail coverage; and radio endorsements written into scripts for performers such as Bob Hope and Red Skelton. These efforts produced excellent publicity and helped to raise 1952 net sales to almost $25.5 million.

The company received its next boost from its 1955 sole sponsorship of the CBS television show, "The $64,000 Question." Though initially reluctant to go ahead with this project, Revson was persuaded by the success of rival Hazel Bishop, whose sponsorship of "This is Your Life" was providing serious competition for Revlon's lipsticks. Attracting a weekly audience of 55 million people, "The $64,000 Question" topped the ratings within four weeks of its debut. Revlon's advertising budget for the year, $7.5 million, proved Charles Revson's adage that publicity had to be heavy to sell cosmetics; as a result of the television show, sales of some products increased 500 percent, and net sales for 1955 grew to $51.6 million, from $33.6 million one year previously.

In November 1955 an allegation of wiretapping was filed against Revlon by Hazel Bishop. In testimony given in a hearing before the New York State Legislative Committee to Study Illegal Interception of Communications, the charge was denied by Revlon controller William Heller, who nevertheless admitted "monitoring" employees' telephones for training purposes. Underscoring the denial of Hazel Bishop's charges, a Revlon attorney added a denunciation of wiretapping for industrial espionage, and promised cooperation in efforts to stop it.

Also in November 1955, Revlon reorganized as Revlon, Inc. A month later, in December 1955, the company went public. Initially offered at $12 per share, Revlon stock reached $30 within weeks, and the company was listed on the New York Stock Exchange at the end of 1956.

Meanwhile, the success of "The $64,000 Question" soon spurred a spinoff called "The $64,000 Challenge." The two shows helped to raise the company's net sales figures to $95 million in 1958, and to $110 million in 1959. The three-year bonanza came to an end, however, in 1959, amidst charges that both shows had been rigged. At the resulting congressional hearings, the shows' producers and the Revsons blamed each other. Nevertheless, the committee's verdict cleared Revlon of any blame in this matter.

Segmented Product Line in the 1960s

As the 1960s began, Charles Revson became aware that his company was in danger of locking itself into a narrow, upper-middle-class image that could restrict sales. To avoid this, he borrowed a technique from General Motors, and segmented his product line into six principal cosmetics houses, each with its own price range, advertising program, and image. Princess Marcella Borghese aimed for international flair; Revlon was the popular-priced house; Etherea was the hypoallergenic line; Natural Wonder served youthful consumers; Moon Drops catered to dry skins; and Ultima II was the most expensive range. Top-priced lines were sold only in department stores, while others were available in other outlets. This strategy allowed the company to cover a wide market area without in-house conflict.

Early attempts to diversify into other fields were unsuccessful. For instance, Knomark, a shoe-polish company bought in 1957, sold its shoe-polish lines in 1969. Other poorly chosen acquisitions, such as Ty-D-Bol, the maker of toilet cleansers, and a 27 percent interest in the Schick electric shaver company were also soon discarded. Evan Picone, a women's sportswear manufacturer which came with a price tag of $12 million in 1962, was sold back to one of the original partners four years later for $1 million.

The company's first successful acquisition came in January 1966, when Revson bought U.S. Vitamin & Pharmaceutical Corporation in exchange for $67 million in Revlon stock. The buyout brought Revlon a company with annual sales of $20 million, most of them coming from a drug used to treat diabetes. Within a year, U.S. Vitamin proved its worth with its acquisitions of Laboratorios Grossman, a Mexican pharmaceutical company; a comparable concern in Argentina; and another in Chile. In 1971 Revson traded U.S. Vitamin's diabetes drug and $20 million cash for a group of drugs Ciba-Geigy was required to divest for antitrust reasons. Another U.S. Vitamin acquisition was Nysco Laboratories, and its Nyscap process for timed-release medication. This, in turn, led to the introduction of vasodilation drugs. Fully disposable injectables, introduced in 1968, also came from U.S. Vitamin.

The company had begun to market its products overseas at the end of the 1950s. By 1962, when Revlon debuted in Japan, there were subsidiaries in France, Italy, Argentina, Mexico, and Asia. The Revlon debut in the Japanese market was typical of its international sales strategy. Instead of adapting its ads and using Japanese models, Revlon chose to use its basic U.S. advertising and models. Japanese women loved the American look, and the success of this bold approach was reflected in the 1962 sales figures, which were almost $164 million.

By 1967, expanding worldwide markets produced sales of $281 million, showing a 5.7 percent increase over the figure of almost $266 for 1966. Planning further expansion, Revlon spent $12.5 million on improvements to existing facilities plus a new cosmetics and fragrance manufacturing plant in Phoenix, Arizona.

During the 1960s the company consisted of four divisions: international, professional products, Princess Marcella Borghese, and U.S.V. Pharmaceutical. In 1968 Revson decided to add two more divisions: the cosmetics and fragrances division, headed by Joseph Anderer, and the Revlon Development Corporation, which was concerned chiefly with long-range planning concepts and strategies for marketing opportunities and headed by Evan William Mandel.

Acquisitions and Restructuring in the 1970s

The 1970s began with annual sales of about $314 million. The cosmetics division, its six lines separately aimed, advertised, and marketed, was the industry leader in all franchised retail outlets. Revlon fragrances, such as Norell and Intimate for women and Braggi and Pub for men, had also become familiar to U.S. consumers. Revlon also had a new line of wig-maintenance products called Wig Wonder.

An important 1970 acquisition was the Mitchum Company of Tennessee, makers of antiperspirants and other toiletries. Mitchum joined the Thayer Laboratories subsidiary, formerly Knomark. Mitchum-Thayer division's widely publicized products required a 1971 advertising budget of $4 million.

In 1973 Revlon introduced Charlie, a fragrance designed for the working woman's budget. Geared to the under-30 market, Charlie models in Ralph Lauren clothes personified the independent woman of the 1970s. Charlie was an instant success, helping to raise Revlon's net sales figures to $506 million for 1973, and to almost $606 million the following year.

High profits apart, 1974 was a difficult year. Charles Revson began to suffer from pancreatic cancer. Determined to leave a worthy successor, he picked Michel Bergerac, a president of International Telephone and Telegraph's European operations. Terms of Bergerac's contract included a $1.5 million signing bonus, an annual salary of $325,000 for five years, bonuses, and options on 70,000 shares.

Company profitability was Bergerac's chief interest. Impressed with Revson's experienced management team, he induced them to stay by introducing the Performance Incentive Profit Sharing Plan, which allotted each executive points based on profit objectives achieved for the years 1974 to 1976. He also cut company spending with tighter inventory controls, and instituted an annual saving of $71.5 million by the elimination of 500 jobs. Bergerac installed a management-information system, requiring that all managers report monthly on problems, sales, and competition.

Bergerac tried to reduce Revlon's dependence on the increasingly crowded cosmetics market, by acquisition. His first major purchase came in 1975. Coburn Optical Industries was an Oklahoma-based manufacturer of ophthalmic and optical processing equipment and supplies, which cost 833,333 Revlon common shares. Barnes-Hind, the largest U.S. marketer of hard contact lens solutions, was bought in 1976, and strengthened Revlon's share of the eye-care market. Other acquisitions included the Lewis-Howe Company, makers of Tums antacid, acquired in 1978, and Armour Pharmaceutical Company, makers of thyroid medicines, acquired in 1977. These health-care operations helped sales figures to pass the $1 billion mark in 1977, bringing total sales to $1.7 billion in 1979.

By the late 1970s company pharmaceutical research and development had extended into plasma research and new drugs for the treatment of osteoporosis and hypertension. The markets for soft contact lenses and their rinsing solutions were also growing. Bergerac compounded a successful 1979 by buying Technicon Corporation, a leading maker of diagnostic and laboratory instruments for both domestic and international markets, in 1980.

During the mid-1970s Bergerac also organized the six cosmetics lines into three groups for easier administration. Revlon, Moon Drops, Natural Wonder, and Charlie now belonged to group one. Group two was comprised of Flex hair-care products and other toiletries, and group three included Princess Marcella Borghese and Ultima II, the prestige cosmetic brands sold in upscale department stores. The domestic cosmetics operations also included the government sales division, carrying almost all the beauty lines through military exchanges and commissaries in the United States and overseas. By the mid-1980s, Revlon's health-care companies, rather than Revlon's beauty concerns, were innovating and expanding. Reluctant to initiate beauty-product development or department store promotions, Revlon lost ground to Estée Lauder, a privately held company whose marketing strategy of high prices with accompanying gifts had earned it almost universal center-aisle department store space. This caused Revlon's share to drop from 20 percent to ten percent of department store cosmetics sales.

Drugstore and supermarket sales were also suffering; Natural Wonder, a low-priced line, lost 24 percent of its supermarket volume in 1983 alone, and competitor Noxell's inexpensive Cover Girl line was claiming more drugstore sales. Comparisons of profits from total operations told the story: $358 million in 1980 sank to $337 million in 1981, which fell to $234 million by 1982.

Takeover by Ronald Perelman in 1985

By 1984, industry analysts believed that Revlon would be worth more if it were broken up and sold. Within a year, this opinion was borne out by a takeover bid from the much smaller Pantry Pride, a subsidiary of Ronald Perelman's MacAndrews & Forbes Holdings. In defense, Bergerac accepted a $900 million offer for the cosmetics businesses from Adler and Shaykin, a New York investment company. The rest of Revlon was to go to Forstmann Little & Company, a management buyout corporation, for about $1.4 billion. These sales, however, were disallowed by a Delaware judge, who ruled that the deal was not in Revlon's shareholders' best interests. On November 5, 1985, at a price of $58 per share, totaling $2.7 billion, Revlon was sold to Pantry Pride, becoming a private company and giving the name of Revlon Group to the former Pantry Pride. The highly leveraged buyout—engineered with the help of junk bond king Michael P. Milken—saddled Revlon with a huge $2.9 billion debt load, which was an albatross around the company's neck for years to come.

Perelman immediately began to divest the company of the health-care businesses. By 1987, only National Health Laboratories remained. By the end of 1988, Perelman had recovered $1.5 billion of his borrowed funds, partly by selling the eye-care businesses to the British firm of Pilkington for $574 million.

Divested companies were replaced with others geared to the Perelman objective—restoring the luster to the original beauty business. Costing about $300 million, Max Factor joined the Revlon lineup in 1987, along with its Halston perfume and its Almay toiletries. Other newcomers were Yves Saint Laurent fragrances and cosmetics; and Charles of the Ritz, Germaine Monteil, and Alexandre de Markoff followed soon after. In 1989 Perelman spent another $170 million to acquire Betrix, a German makeup and fragrance maker.

Other innovations of the 1980s meshed with national trends. The concern of a burgeoning older population with health and fitness led to wider company research on skin-care products as well as on makeup. International concerns for animal rights found a response in Perelman's Revlon, which abandoned the Draize test in 1989, after closing its animal testing center in 1986. Revlon also sought to improve the company image when it signed up supermodels Cindy Crawford and Claudia Schiffer for its advertising in the late 1980s and early 1990s.

During the late 1980s fears of an approaching recession made bankers generally wary of highly leveraged transactions, and Revlon's junk bonds began to lose value. Internal problems stemmed partly from the department store market, where an attempt by Revlon to economize by grouping its Ritz, Monteil, and Borghese prestige brands at one counter failed. Other problems included the introduction of No Sweat, a deodorant which, despite its $12 million introductory advertising budget, failed to garner market share; the reformulation of Flex, a popular shampoo which lost market share when Revlon introduced a new formula with new packaging and a higher price; and a two percent shrinkage in the fragrance market, affecting the entire industry.

Revlon Finally Turned the Corner in Mid-1990s

By 1990 Revlon held only 11 percent of the U.S. mass-market cosmetics market. Losses were mounting year after year thanks in large part to the money that had to be spent each year to service the debt. In 1991 alone, $131.6 million went toward debt service, contributing to an operating loss of $241.7 million ($226.9 million of which stemmed from extraordinary restructuring charges). Perelman was forced to sell still more assets to keep Revlon from defaulting on its loans.

In addition to selling 80 percent of National Health Laboratories by 1992, Perelman had to also sell off some assets from the core cosmetics area. In 1991 Max Factor and Betrix were sold to Procter & Gamble for $1.14 billion in cash. Sold off the following year were the high-end Halston and Princess Marcella Borghese brands. Unfortunately for Perelman, such moves were not enough to gain the confidence of Wall Street. In 1992 Perelman tried to sell 11 million shares of Revlon stock, in an initial public offering (i.p.o.), at about $18 to $20 per share. The i.p.o. failed, a victim of a sluggish stock market, poor Revlon earnings, and the huge debt that continued to weigh down the cosmetics giant.

To shore up sagging sales, Revlon CEO Jerry Levin boosted Revlon's advertising budget by 25 percent in 1992, to $200 million. Much of this money was spent on television advertising, with less spent on print ads and in-store promotions than in the past. While the Revlon line was promoted in this fashion and through mass-market retailers, the company's only remaining premium brand, Ultima II, was shifted down from upscale stores to J.C. Penney and Dillard's department stores. Early indications were positive for these moves as overall market share for the Revlon Group hit 14.7 percent in 1992. And in 1993 the company was finally able to report operating income (of $51.5 million) although debt service remained high at $114.4 million.

Meanwhile the company started to develop successful new products. The ColorStay line of longer lasting cosmetics was introduced in 1994 with the debut of ColorStay lipsticks, which soon captured the top spot in its category. The Age Defying line of cosmetics for women over 35 soon followed and also proved popular. By 1995 overall market share had reached 19.4 percent and what *Advertising Age* called the "reborn cosmetics juggernaut" unseated Maybelline from the number one position in cosmetics. Net sales were improving steadily from $1.59 billion in 1993 to $1.73 billion in 1994 to $1.94 billion in 1995. And while debt service remained high ($137.7 million in 1995), it was finally exceeded by operating income ($145.1 million).

Backed by what was clearly a remarkable, though long-time-in-coming, turnaround, Perelman felt confident enough to try another initial public offering in early 1996. This time he succeeded and Revlon once again became a public company, although Perelman retained 99.7 percent of the voting stock. About 15 percent of overall shares were sold in the initial public offering, raising about $150 million. The capital raised suggested the beginning of another chapter in Revlon's compelling history.

Principal Divisions

Revlon Consumer Products Worldwide; Revlon Professional Products Worldwide.

Further Reading

Berman, Phyllis, "Revlon without Revson," *Forbes,* June 26, 1978.

Cole, Robert J., "High-Stakes Drama at Revlon," *New York Times,* November 11, 1985.

Light, Larry, and Laura Zinn, "Painting a New Face on Revlon," *Business Week,* April 6, 1992, pp. 26–27.

Light, Larry, and Monica Roman, "Why Perelman Faces Life without Makeup," *Business Week,* April 1, 1991, pp. 71–72.

Morgenson, Gretchen, "The Perils of Perelman," *Forbes,* December 10, 1990, pp. 218–22.

Ono, Yumiko, "Revlon Swings to Profit on Sales of Makeup Line," *Wall Street Journal,* July 31, 1996, p. B8(E), p. B5(W).

Ramirez, Anthony, "The Raider Who Runs Revlon," *Fortune,* September 14, 1987.

"Revlon's Formula: Smart Words, Quality, and Freud," *Business Week,* August 12, 1950.

Sloan, Pat, "Cosmetics Competitors Try to Slap Down Revlon," *Advertising Age,* December 4, 1995, p. 38.

——, "Revlon Redistributes to Win Wider Appeal," *Advertising Age,* August 19, 1991, p. 12.

Spiro, Leah Nathans, and Ronald Grover, "The Operator: An Inside Look at Ron Perelman's $5 Billion Empire," *Business Week,* August 21, 1995, cover story.

Tobias, Andrew, *Fire and Ice: The Story of Charles Revson—The Man Who Built the Revlon Empire,* New York: William Morrow & Company, 1976, 282 p.

Zinn, Laura, Sunita Wadekar Bhargava, and Elizabeth A. Lesly, "The New Ron Perelman Has an Old Problem," *Business Week,* June 14, 1993, pp. 94–95.

—Gillian Wolf
—updated by David E. Salamie

Richardson Electronics, Ltd.

40W267 Keslinger Road
P.O. Box 393
LaFox, Illinois 60147-0393
U.S.A.
(708) 208-2200
Fax: (708) 208-2550

Public Company
Incorporated: 1947
Sales: $235 million (1996)
Employees: 540
Stock Exchanges: NASDAQ
SICs: 3671 Electron Tubes; 3674 Semiconductors &
Related Devices; 5065 Electronic Parts & Equipment

Richardson Electronics, Ltd., is one of the fastest growing, highly specialized international distributors of power semiconductors, electron tubes, electronic security systems, and various other electronic components. Presently, Richardson Electronics has four core businesses, the Electron Device Group, the Solid State and Components Group, the Display Products Group, and the Security Systems Group. Having created for itself a niche to distribute products which control electrical power, and amplify and switch signals within the industrial and telecommunications industries, the company has established an international customer base with over 55 sales offices, including 18 overseas locations in such countries as Brazil, England, France, Italy, Spain, and Germany, and most recently in Taiwan, Holland, Thailand, and Australia. Sales continue to climb rapidly and, despite some anti-trust litigation brought against the company during the early 1990s by the American government, Richardson Electronics continues an aggressive expansion program within the electron tubes and semiconductor industry.

Early History

At the end of World War II, Arthur Richardson, a man with extensive experience in the burgeoning electronics industry, decided to establish his own electronics firm. Recognizing the trends of the future, specifically the growth of the vacuum tube industry, Richardson wanted to take advantage of what he thought would be a gigantic burst in consumer demand. The ambitious entrepreneur's approach was somewhat unique. Many people, not only those within the electronics industry but family and friends, advised him that market growth was being created by semiconductors, which would ultimately render the tubes obsolete. But Richardson clearly saw that the semi-conductor technology in the late 1940s and early 1950s was developing at a much faster rate than most companies within the industry would be able to keep up with. As a result, that meant a large market for the older tube technology, and Richardson intended for his company to fill the gap.

During the late 1950s and early 1960s, the company concentrated on distributing vacuum tubes and component parts for the semi-conductor industry. Sales continued to increase, but gradually, especially compared to the skyrocketing growth seen in other areas of the burgeoning electronics markets. Arthur Richardson was a cautious and careful manager, sticking to the distribution of materials that he knew best. In some ways, Richardson Electronics was left behind during this period of time and didn't take advantage of the wide variety of opportunities in the worldwide electronics boom and insatiable consumer demand. But Arthur Richardson would have it no other way—vacuum tubes and small component parts were the wave of the future, according to the company founder, and one just had to believe in the potential of that niche market.

Arthur Richardson had always encouraged his son to become involved in the management of the company, but the young man resisted his father's desires and pursued his own dreams. Edward J. Richardson attended the Iowa State University School of Veterinary Medicine and began to prepare himself for a life in the country. Having been raised in LaFox, Illinois, there were plenty of chances to observe the livestock in the area, and from the earliest years of his childhood Edward was enamored with the physiology of barnyard animals. While in the middle of his studies at Iowa State, however, Edward suffered a debilitating bout with mononucleosis and was forced to miss two consecutive semesters. Bored with nothing to do at home, the young man finally agreed to work at his father's

Company Perspectives:

Richardson has developed one of the most technically adept sales support teams in the distribution industry. The Company now routinely services customers from the design-in through replacement stages. This well-rounded approach has enabled Richardson Electronics to reach an unparalleled position in the electron tube and power semiconductor distribution industry.

company. When Edward joined the business in 1961, Richardson Electronics employed only three workers, and annual sales amounted to $53,000. Telling his father that he would only help out at the firm on a temporary basis, and fully intending to return to veterinary school, little did Edward know at the time that his destiny had already been decided.

The more time he spent at the company the more Edward was intrigued both by the company's products and his father's vision of what an electronics firm should be. As the older Richardson began to delegate more and more responsibility to his son, it became clear that there was no returning to veterinary school. Edward Richardson assumed the position of Vice President and Director in 1965 and later, when his father retired, became President in 1974. By this time, Edward was completely convinced by his father's vision, and by the predictions of the elder Richardson that were coming true within the electronics industry. The father guided his son through the middle and late 1970s, and when he died Edward was well prepared to lead the company. One of the first decisions that he made after the death of his father involved the addition of power semiconductors and RF components to the company's product line.

Growth and Expansion during the 1980s

Until the beginning of the 1980s, Richardson Electronics had concentrated on the replacement market, namely, selling replacement electronic power tubes to radio and television stations and electronic maintenance firms. Television and radio stations, which used power grid tubes to broadcast both visual and audio signals, were the historic core of the company's business since the tubes usually lasted only one or two years at most and then required replacement. By the early 1980s, however, Edward Richardson recognized the advent and potential of newer technologies, such as the RF and microwave, and began to direct his firm toward supplying original equipment manufacturers, who were rapidly becoming the larger percentage of new customers. When many of the electron tube manufacturers exited the industry at this time due to increased competition, Richardson began to acquire product lines or companies that would ensure his own company's ability to provide a continuous supply of electron tubes to customers. Over a period of just a few years, Richardson Electronics acquired 17 various electron tube manufacturers located throughout the United States.

The implementation of such an aggressive acquisition strategy worked better than expected: sales shot up to $15 million and the number of employees increased to over 35. With revenues gained from a higher sales volume, Richardson Electronics opened its first overseas office in London, England. Almost overnight, business exploded in both England and continental Europe, especially with the introduction of solid-state components and closed-circuit television. Confident of his success in foreign markets, Edward Richardson decided to establish a joint venture in China for the manufacture and distribution of electron tubes. Richardson Electronics invested large amounts of capital, and committed its engineers to spending a significant amount of time training and guiding their Chinese counterparts in the intricacies of electron tube manufacturing. Unfortunately, when the Americans returned to the United States, the quality of the products being manufactured dropped dramatically, and the company had a difficult time from that point forward in getting the quality of the products made in China to conform to Western standards. As a result, the joint venture was only able to sell approximately $1 million worth of products during the early years of its operation.

By 1988, the company had completed its acquisition program and had grown from a relatively small operation into a business with sales of over $150 million, almost exclusively in the electron tube market. That year, the U.S. Justice Department filed suit against Richardson Electronics, accusing the company of numerous anti-trust violations. Alleging that Richardson was creating a monopoly for itself in the field of manufacturing power grid tubes, and in the process eliminating all possible competitors, the Department of Justice vigorously litigated the company. After three years of intense and sometimes bitter court proceedings, the Department of Justice stipulated that the company had to obtain permission before acquiring any company involved in the rebuilding, manufacturing, or distribution of power grid tubes.

The decision of the court had an enormous effect on the way Richardson Electronics conducted its business. Management had always thought of the company as a distributor rather than a manufacturer. Yet during the 1980s, Richardson Electronics had acquired numerous firms primarily engaged in the manufacture of electrical component parts. The results of the anti-trust suit brought against the company led to a selloff of almost all of the manufacturing-related acquisitions made during the 1980s. Richardson Electronics was forced, in large measure, to return to its role as a distributor. Research and development was given a very small portion of the budget, and the company returned to copying products that were originally manufactured by other firms but had been discontinued.

The 1990s and Beyond

By the early 1990s, Richardson Electronics had decided to capture a larger portion of the overseas market, and opened offices in Canada, Mexico, England, France, Italy, Spain, Germany, Japan, and Singapore. Sales generated from overseas operations were becoming a significant percentage of the total figures, with the offices in England, Germany, and Singapore leading the surge. Yet, as usual in the course of business development, there were difficulties along the way. The Mexico City office had initially performed quite well, but because of the political upheaval and the depressed economic conditions during the early 1990s, the company's business in Mexico declined suddenly and rapidly. Management decided to retain a presence in the capital city, but scaled back operations until more promising conditions suggest an expansion of operations. In 1995, management decided to recommit itself to its fledgling operation in China, which since its inception had never generated more that $1 million in sales. The company opened a new office in Shanghai, and sent engineers over to China on extended contracts to ensure that the level of quality control remained high. Industries which manufactured heating equipment and electronic broadcast components needed the kinds of tubes that Richardson Electronics was distributing. Anticipation of better sales volumes for the China office were high in 1995, and the plant appeared to be fulfilling its promise by the middle of 1996.

During the early and mid 1990s, partially as a result of the anti-trust suit, the company implemented a thoroughgoing restructuring program. Richardson Electronics was divided into four distinct groups, the Electron Device Group, the Solid State and Components Group, the Display Products Group, and the Security Systems Division. The Electron Device Group was the business upon which the company was founded, and continued to specialize in providing tubes, especially power grid tubes, for a broad spectrum of industries. Approximately 80 percent of all the company's business in these products involve the replacement of tubes in existing equipment. By the end of fiscal 1995, the company reported over $100 million in sales generated from the Electron Device Group, comprising approximately 50 percent of the firm's total business.

Although not as large nor as important as the Electron Device Group, the remaining three business units were growing rapidly in the mid 1990s. The Solid State and Components Group, which specializes in the distribution of power semiconductors, has grown at a rate of 25 percent annually from 1993 to 1995. Richardson Electronic was fortunate to enter the market when it was expanding at a phenomenal rate, and created a niche for itself as a specialized distributor of semiconductors to the RF and microwave manufacturers. The Display Products Group, specializing in replacement cathode ray tubes for data display applications, primarily in computer terminals, reported an increase in sales of 41 percent from 1994 to 1995. The smallest of the company's four business units, the Security Systems Division specializes in closed-circuit television for corporations, schools, and apartment buildings. The securities

business is growing at a rate of about 20 to 30 percent annually, and Richardson Electronics has made a major commitment to increase its sales during the mid and late 1990s. According to management, one of the most promising markets for the company is the diagnostic imaging sector of the medical market. Richardson Electronics began providing X-ray tubes and X-ray image intensifiers and related component parts directly to hospitals in 1994. In 1995, the company reported a total of $5 million in sales in this sector, and by the end of fiscal 1996 reported an increase in sales to $10 million. With such a promising beginning, the company acquired TubeMaster, a firm specializing in the reloading of X-ray tubes and X-ray image intensifiers, and projected sales of $25 million by the end of fiscal 1997.

By the middle of 1996, Richardson Electronics had 55 offices around the world, and approximately 50 percent of its sales generated from overseas operations. New offices have been opened in Brazil, Taiwan, and Korea, and management has plans for continued expansion to take advantage of new markets in India, Holland, Thailand, and Australia. Edward J. Richardson, faithful to the vision of his father, had built Richardson Electronics into the most successful electron tube distributor in the world.

Principal Subsidiaries

TubeMaster Inc.

Further Reading

"Business Briefs," *Rubber World,* May 1996, p. 11.

Murphy, H. Lee, "China Next Up on Richardson's Agenda for Overseas Growth," *Crain's Chicago Business,* October 23, 1995, p. 29.

——, "Out with the Old, In with New at Richardson," *Crain's Chicago Business,* October 17, 1994, p. 25.

——, "Richardson Pulls Plug on Manufacturing," *Crain's Chicago Business,* August 8, 1994, p. 13.

"Richardson Electronics, Ltd.," *Wall Street Corporate Reporter,* April 29–May 5, 1996.

"Richardson Electronics, Ltd.," *Wall Street Transcript: CEO Interviews,* May 22, 1995.

Trigg, Lee, "Richardson Finds Business Can Exist in a Vacuum," *Business Journal of Kane County,* May 1996, p. 26.

—Thomas Derdak

Ross Stores, Inc.

8333 Central Avenue
Newark, California 94560
U.S.A.
(510) 505-4400
Fax: (510) 505-4322

Public Company
Incorporated: 1982
Employees: 11,935
Sales: $1.42 billion (1995)
Stock Exchanges: NASDAQ
SICs: 5651 Family Clothing Stores

One of the leading off-price retailers in the United States, Ross Stores, Inc., operates a chain of roughly 300 Ross "Dress for Less" stores in 18 states. Although Ross operates one of the largest chains of its kind in the country, it reached this stature late in its corporate life. When the chain was purchased in 1982 by a group of investors that included Mervin Morris, founder of the Mervyn's chain, it comprised only six units in the San Francisco Bay area. During the ensuing decade, the chain grew robustly under the stewardship of Stuart Moldaw and Don Rowlett who converted the junior department stores to off-price retail units, one of the first of their kind in California. During the mid-1990s, Ross "Dress for Less" stores offered brand and designer name apparel for the entire family at prices 20 percent to 60 percent below the prices charged by competing department stores and specialty shops. Of the 292 stores in operation in early 1996, 134 were located in California, by far the most important market for the company.

Origins

The roots of the Ross retail chain stretch back to 1957, when the first Ross junior department store opened. However, the first definitive year in the company's history occurred nearly 30 years after its birth. In 1982, the year that separated the two distinct eras in Ross' history, two retailers with a wealth of experience in the off-price retail industry purchased the Ross enterprise when the chain comprised six junior department stores in the San Francisco Bay area. With these six stores, purchased with the help of venture capital partners, the two entrepreneurs made no mistake about their intentions, quickly developing a retail empire that would boast 107 stores three years later, 156 stores by the end of the 1980s, and nearly 300 stores by the mid-1990s. The orchestrators of this rapid expansion and the two pivotal figures who erased three decades of sleepy growth to engender a dramatically more dynamic Ross retail chain were Stuart Moldaw and Donald Rowlett, the duo who spearheaded the acquisition of the Ross business in August 1982.

Stuart Moldaw, who became chairman of Ross following the acquisition, was not new to the off-price retail scene. Prior to his involvement with Ross, Moldaw founded Pic-A-Dilly, an off-price retail chain, Country Casuals, and The Athletic Shoe Factory. Rowlett, who was selected as the new president of Ross, was no novice either, having created and developed F.W. Woolworth's off-price subsidiary, J. Brannam, into a 36-unit chain. Together, these two retail veterans had visions of creating a powerful off-price retail chain in an area of the country where the off-price concept was virtually nonexistent. Elsewhere, particularly along the East Coast and in the Midwest, off-price retail stores were enjoying burgeoning popularity during the early 1980s, but in California they were conspicuous by their absence, at least as Moldaw and Rowlett saw it. Considering the pace at which Moldaw and Rowlett expanded the Ross chain shortly after acquiring it, the two were intent on pioneering the concept in California and saturating markets before rival off-price chains recognized the opportunities that existed in California.

Early 1980s: Moldaw and Rowlett Era

Such was the attraction of the six-unit Ross chain to Moldaw and Rowlett—its location in California. Little else, beyond the chain's limited name recognition in the San Francisco area, would contribute to its success for the remainder of the 1980s and the 1990s. Success was realized from the changes instituted by Moldaw and Rowlett, the first of which was recasting the six-unit chain as a different type of retailer. The two shifted the chain's focus away from its junior orientation to create an off-price format stocking branded apparel for men, women, and

Company Perspectives:

Ross Stores' mission is to offer competitive values to customers by focusing on the following key objectives: achieve an appropriate level of brands and labels at strong discounts throughout the store; meet customer needs on a more regional basis; deliver an in-store shopping experience that reflects the expectations of the off-price customer; manage real estate growth to maintain dominance or achieve parity with the competition in key markets.

children, as well as domestics merchandise, shoes, and accessories at sharply reduced prices. Once the stores were dedicated toward attracting a broader customer base and outfitted with a broader merchandise selection, Moldaw and Rowlett made their second decisive move by quickly adding to their store count. Two Ross "Dress for Less" stores were opened in the fall of 1982 and 18 stores the following year, more than tripling the size of Ross in little more than a year.

Much of the physical growth recorded during the first full year of Moldaw's and Rowlett's leadership was accomplished by acquiring existing stores in strip malls and free-standing locations abandoned by other retailers. This acquisition strategy would continue to be used by the company as its geographic scope of operations broadened, severing the chains that had fettered it to Northern California for three decades. By the end of 1983, Ross "Dress for Less" stores were situated in Southern California and the first store beyond the state's borders—a store in Reno, Nevada—was opened, touching off a march across the map that in a few short years would extend the company's presence from coast to coast.

Early in 1984, plans called for the establishment of 20 stores in California, Arizona, Washington, and Oregon, but by the end of the year Ross had opened twice as many, opening stores in California, Washington, Utah, Arizona, Texas, and Oklahoma. Much of the growth realized during the year was realized from the acquisition of 15 stores from the Handyman division of Edison Brothers Stores, which added Ross "Dress for Less" stores in Texas and Oklahoma. The acquisition, completed in July, was concluded in the same month that Ross corporate headquarters were moved to a 494,000-square-foot facility in Newark, California, that also served as the company's distribution center.

From this location in Newark, the company's expansion would be plotted into the 1990s, as the number of stores, each stocking a list of brand and designer names that rivaled most department stores and specialty stores, increased exponentially. Though its merchandise compared favorably with the selection offered by department stores and specialty stores, Ross charged substantially less than traditional retailers, selling its merchandise for as much as 60 percent below competitors' prices. The enormous savings to be realized lured customers through Ross' stores, convincing management, in turn, that the only obstacle checking the company's financial growth was the number of stores it operated. More stores meant more revenue and greater

profits, so Moldaw and Rowlett focused their efforts on expansion, making an initial public offering of stock in 1985 to help fund the opening of additional stores. At the time of the public offering, there were 107 Ross "Dress for Less" stores, an impressive total given the company's total store count of six three years earlier, and an extensive operating territory the company could call its own. After entering Washington, Utah, Arizona, Texas, and Oklahoma, in 1984, Ross entered new markets in Colorado, Florida, Georgia, New Mexico, and Oregon in 1985. By the end of the year, sales were up an encouraging 79 percent, swelling to $375.9 million.

Mid-1980s Tumble

The company's record-setting growth in 1985, which included the addition of 41 stores, was followed by an equally impressive 1986, when 39 stores were opened and new markets were penetrated in Maryland, North Carolina, and Virginia. By this point, there were 121 Ross "Dress for Less" stores scattered throughout 16 states, 40 percent of which had been open for less than a year. Fueled by this new growth, annual sales had shot past the $500 million mark by the end of 1986 and future revenue growth seem assured as expansion plans were laid for the company's penetration into new markets. In 1986, however, the company suffered its first major setback when it was forced to shutter 25 unprofitable stores located primarily in Texas and Oklahoma, where anemic economic conditions crimped Ross' profits. For the year, Ross reported a crippling $41.4 million loss, $39.4 million of which stemmed from the stores closures in Texas and Oklahoma.

On the heels of this debilitating loss, the company lost one of its two chief architects when Rowlett resigned from the company in 1987, but it was not long before Ross gained a new architect to rebuild the company and carry it into the 1990s. Following Rowlett's departure, a company veteran, Norman A. Ferber, who was serving as Ross' executive vice-president of merchandising, marketing, and distribution, was appointed as Ross' president and chief operating officer. Less than a year later, in January 1988, Ferber was also named Ross' chief executive officer, taking charge of the company as it was undergoing a series of changes to quickly restore its profitability.

Responding to the $40 million loss in 1986, Moldaw and Ferber drastically cut back on expansion in 1987, opening only 11 stores and situating those stores in markets where Ross "Dress for Less" stores were already located or in close proximity. The days of adding one new state after another to the company's geographic fold were over. Instead of trying to dot the country with store after store, Ross executives focused their expansion in three principal markets, the West Coast, the Washington area, and Florida, and devoted more time to developing a profitable merchandising strategy. Hoping to rescue their company from the red, company officials eliminated the domestics departments in Ross stores and added cosmetics and fragrance departments. Additionally, executives added "high-end" clothing to Ross' merchandising mix, upgrading their inventory with items such as men's sport coats and women's silk dresses.

By the end of 1987, management could point to positive results. For the year, Ross recorded an $11.5 million gain after the more than $40 million loss the year before. Encouraged by their initial success, Moldaw and Ferber continued to refine Ross' merchandising strategy as the 1980s progressed. By 1989, 95 percent of the company's 140 stores contained full cosmetic and fragrance departments staffed with beauty consultants, one of the new and decidedly upscale features adopted by Ross as it repositioned itself for consistent profitability. In the chasm separating discount stores and traditional department stores, off-price retailers occupied the middle ground, but as the 1990s neared Moldaw and Ferber were tipping the balance toward the department store end of the scale by adopting the trappings of more upscale retail outlets. Like many off-price chains, Ross had never divided, or "departmentalized," its retail floor space into merchandise categories to any great extent, but as the company entered the 1990s chrome and wood partitions were used with increasing frequency to delineate various departments. Among the other changes reshaping the chain was a refocused inventory strategy, as Ross "Dress for Less" stores began stocking a lesser variety of merchandise but bolstered their supply of merchandise lines that remained, creating a narrower and deeper inventory for stores to stock.

1990s Expansion

Along with these changes came a renewed commitment to expand the chain. In 1989, when Ross ranked as the third-largest off-price retailer in the country, company officials announced plans to open 100 to 150 stores during the ensuing five years. As the early 1990s progressed, the chain went a long way toward achieving this ambitious goal. In 1990, 29 new stores were opened, giving it a total of 185 stores in 18 states by the end of the year and opening up new markets in Philadelphia and in Boise, Idaho. Another 20 stores were opened the following year, as annual sales jumped from $804 million to $930 million, and another 23 stores were added to the chain in 1992, when sales eclipsed the billion dollar mark, reaching $1.04 billion.

As sales were slipping past $1 billion, Moldaw and Ferber began test marketing a "Home Accents" department, which featured picture frames, china, ceramic ware, and crystal. The concept was introduced in 20 stores early in 1992 and quickly registered sufficient success to warrant its incorporation into other existing Ross "Dress for Less" stores. With 223 stores by the end of 1992, the company planned to put Home Accents departments in nearly all of its existing locations by the end of 1993, giving its a high-profit-margin vehicle to fuel its financial growth in the years ahead. By the end of 1995, when the total number of stores had increased to 292, 282 stores contained Home Accents departments.

Entering the mid-1990s, Ferber, who was named chairman in 1993, was focusing the chain's growth in existing markets. Twenty stores were opened in 1993, another 32 stores in 1994, and 17 stores in 1995, with each successive wave of openings giving Ross a more entrenched market position. With 292 stores

by the end of 1995, Ross was collecting nearly $1.5 million a year in sales, having experienced considerable financial growth during the previous decade. Equally as impressive was the company's profitability, which had been strengthened substantially by the changes adopted in the wake of Ross' mid-1980s debacle. In 1995, the company earned more than $43 million, with the average sales per square foot climbing to $230 from an average of $214 million in 1991. That the company recorded this increase during a national recession that crippled many retailers throughout the country boded well for its future, fueling confidence that the "new" Ross was well-positioned to reap the rewards of the late 1990s. As the company prepared for the late 1990s, it gained new management to lead it toward its future. Effective September 1996, Michael Balmuth, Ross' executive vice president of merchandising, was selected as the company's chief executive officer, replacing Ferber, who stayed on as chairman. As the change of command was underway, Balmuth, who joined Ross in 1989 as senior vice-president and general merchandise manager, could look forward to taking the helm of a company with justifiably strong expectations for consistent if not animated growth in the future.

Principal Subsidiaries

Ross Assurance Group, Ltd.

Further Reading

"Balmuth Named CEO of Ross Stores," *Daily News Record,* June 11, 1995, p. 10.
Gilbert, Les, "Ross Doing Well in Coast with Off-Price Format," *Footwear News,* July 23, 1984, p. 66.
"Going Public Should Help Ross Reach Coast-to-Coast," *Discount Store News,* August 5, 1985, p. 18.
Kahn, Hal, "Ross Stores Inc. CEO to Resign in September," *Knight-Ridder/Tribune Businesss News,* May 31, 1996.
Krein, Pamela, "Ross Stores to Close 25 Money-Losing Units in Southwest," *Discount Store News,* March 16, 1987, p. 39.
MacIntosh, Jean, "Refocused Strategy Puts Off-Pricer Ross Stores Right on the Money," *Daily News Record,* October 27, 1988, p.6.
Meek, Pamela, "Ross Goes Further Upscale in Prototype," *Discount Store News,* September 25, 2989, p. 1.
Paris, Ellen, "A Touch of Class," *Forbes,* February 5, 1990, p. 148.
Radwell, Steven, "Dayton Hudson Sells Its 4 Plum Stores," *Daily News Record,* February 22, 1984, p. 1.
Razzano, Rhonda, "Ross Stores Realigns Mix, Redirects Strategies: Off-Price Recovers from Oil Patch Setback," *Chain Store Age Executive with Shopping Center Age,* May 1989, p. 25.
"Ross Unveils Aggressive Plan: 25 New Stores Set for 1994," *Discount Store News,* March 7, 1994, p. 6.
Ruben, Howard, "Ross Stores Plays the Off-Price Game," *Daily News Record,* February 14, 1984, p. 10.
Rutberg, Sidney, "Ross Stores Loss Fails to Chill Optimism," *WWD,* June 25, 1987, p. 6.

—Jeffrey L. Covell

Saudi Arabian Oil Company

Post Office Box 5000
Dhahran 31311
Saudi Arabia
(3) 673-5002
Fax: (3) 873-8190
Internet: http://www.careermosaic.com/cm/aramco

State Owned Company
Incorporated: 1988
Employees: 50,000
SICs: 2911 Petroleum Refining; 1382 Oil & Gas
    Exploration Services; 1381 Drilling Oil & Gas Wells

With production capacity of about ten million barrels of crude oil per day, the state-owned Saudi Arabian Oil Company (also known as Saudi Aramco) is without question the world's largest producer of crude oil. In the years immediately preceding and following the Persian Gulf crisis, the company worked to broaden its operations from the wellhead to include refining, marketing, distribution, and even retailing. By the mid-1990s, Saudi Aramco considered itself "a fully integrated global oil enterprise." In addition to its largely domestic quest for vertical integration, the oil company pursued joint ventures to extend its geographic reach into North America, Asia, and Europe.

Saudi Aramco is responsible for exploration, development, and production in a tract of land which covers some 16 percent of the 2.2 million square kilometers that constitute the Saudi Arabian peninsula. The company's 260 billion bbl of recoverable crude oil reserves constituted 26 percent of the world's total reserves in the early 1990s. Clearly, Aramco's crude oil operations, which account for 95 percent of total production, are vital not only to the Saudi Arabian economy but also to global energy needs. The state-owned business also had natural gas reserves of 180 trillion cubic feet (tcf). Its assets include the world's largest onshore and offshore oilfields. Revenues generated through the export of Aramco crude oil production constitute over half of total Saudi government revenues, and have helped transform the country from, as one observer has noted,

"a third world country in an inhospitable desert region, to one that is on the threshold of joining the ranks of developed nations."

Early-20th-Century Origins

The incorporation of Saudi Aramco on November 13, 1988, was largely a cosmetic operation, performed in order to remove the final legal attachments of the Arabian American Oil Company (Aramco) to the original U.S. company registered in Delaware on January 31, 1944. However, the history of the Aramco concession, upon which the company's fortune has been forged, dates back to the early 1930s. In 1932 Standard Oil (California) (Socal), now known as Chevron, employed the energies of Harry St. John B. Philby, a close friend of Saudi King Ibn Saud, to obtain permission for Socal to conduct a geological survey in the eastern parts of the Saudi Peninsula. Although granting rights over Saudi Arabia's natural resources to a foreign company was against King Ibn Saud's better judgment, his need for money left him no alternative. King Ibn Saud insisted that no geological appraisal could take place until the full terms of a concession had been agreed. The king's fear was that Socal would discover that Saudi Arabia was barren before it had committed any capital. On May 29, 1933, the concession agreement was signed by the king's minister for finance, Abd Allah al Sulaiman, and the Socal representative, Lloyd N. Hamilton, at the royal palace in Jiddah.

In November 1933 the California Arabian Standard Oil Company (Casoc) was formed to manage operations within the concession on behalf of Socal. The original concession stretched from the Persian Gulf to, and including, the western province of Dahna. In 1939 the concession was further enlarged to around 440,000 square miles to include Saudi Arabia's share of the neutral zone.

However, before any crude oil was discovered in its new Saudi concession Socal was already experiencing problems in marketing its growing Bahraini oil production. Socal opted for the quickest solution to this problem, which was to merge operations with a company which owned marketing facilities near the source of production, but which was short of crude. In

1936 Socal struck a deal with the Texas Company, now known as Texaco. The new joint venture was named Caltex, and was charged with managing all of Texaco's marketing assets from the Middle East to the Pacific. As a part of the deal, Texaco was given half ownership of Casoc.

It took three years before the exploratory drilling of the Dammam Dome, a group of prominent limestone hills near what is presently called Dhahran, was rewarded. In March 1938 the seventh exploration well drilled on the Dammam Dome identified the Arab Zone, as the explorers named it. Crude oil exports started in the same year. The oil was piped from the well to the makeshift port of al-Khobar and, from there, was transported by sea to the Bahrain refinery. In the following year the now prolific Ras Tanura export terminal was used for the first time by Socal's tanker, the *D. G. Schofield.*

World War II

The advent of World War II impeded Casoc's operations. Production at the newly constructed Ras Tanura refinery lasted only six months before it was closed in June 1941 and all dependents of American employees were sent home for the duration of the war.

The war years from 1940 to 1944 were significant, however, for the progressive rationalization of Casoc's management structure under the guidance of its new president, F.A. Davies. Davies had visited Saudi Arabia as a Socal representative in 1930 and had been closely involved in operations ever since. His election, together with that of a new board of directors in August 1940, marked the company's first step toward independence from Socal. Casoc set up its headquarters in San Francisco at 200 Bush Street. Symbolically, the final confirmation of the company's new identity came on January 31, 1944, when Casoc was renamed the Arabian American Oil Company.

The postwar years of the late 1940s witnessed the scramble to expand production from the Aramco concession and to establish a market for it. Between 1944 and 1949 Aramco expanded capacity in all spheres of operation, in no small way aided by the military cooperation in allocating materials and even providing transport. The strategic importance of oil had been proven in the defeat of Adolf Hitler, and the U.S. government had even set aside funds for possible direct investment in the Middle East to secure supplies. Aramco shunned the offer of direct government involvement but with its aid achieved a 25-fold increase in crude oil supply from 20 thousand barrels per day in 1944 to 500 thousand barrels per day in 1949. The Ras Tanura refinery's distillation capacity was expanded from 50 thousand barrels per day to 127 thousand barrels per day between 1945 and 1949, in part to supply the increasing requirements of the U.S. Navy.

Secure access to world markets was fostered in two ways. First, with regard to the European market, Aramco attempted to improve the competitiveness of its crude oil vis-a-vis Soviet and U.S. exports by cutting down on the time and, ultimately, costs of transporting crude from the Persian Gulf. In 1946 Aramco began to build, through its affiliate, the Trans-Arabian Pipe Line Company (Tapline), a 1,068-mile-long pipeline connecting the Abqaiq oilfield to the Mediterranean port of Sidon, Lebanon.

Secondly, Aramco tried to merge operations with the Standard Oil Company of New Jersey, later Exxon, and the Socony-Vacuum Oil Company, now known as Mobil. Harry Collier, the chairman of Socal at that time, supported the choice of these two companies not only because of their unrivaled marketing assets in the Far East but also because the choice satisfied King Ibn Saud's explicitly stated wish that Aramco should remain American to avoid an extension of British influence in the region. Between 1946 and 1948 the two companies wrestled with the legal obstacle posed to the merger by the Red Line Agreement. This obstacle was overcome in December 1948. The companies' shares in Aramco and Tapline were divided as follows: Socal, Texaco, and Standard Oil of New Jersey each owned 30 percent and the Socony-Vacuum Company owned the remaining ten percent.

Also in 1948 Aramco gave up its concessionary rights over the Saudi Arabian part of the neutral zone. This move was made in response to the severe terms accepted by the American Independent Oil Company (Aminoil) in the auction for the concession rights over the Kuwaiti half of the neutral zone. Unwilling to match Aminoil's offer, Aramco decide to preempt similar demands by the Saudi king by giving up the land. In return for this unilateral gesture, Aramco received a reaffirmation of its offshore concession rights in the Persian Gulf. In the auction that resulted from Aramco's cessation, the Pacific Western Oil Company agreed to terms even more onerous than those applied to Aminoil.

However, Aramco did not completely avoid compensating the government for the dramatic increase in the value of its concession. Over the late 1940s and the first half of the 1950s Aramco was progressively forced to relinquish small parts of its concession. Also, on December 30, 1950, following the example of Venezuela in 1948, the Saudi government authorized an increase in the government's share to 50 percent of Aramco's profits net of exploration, development, and production costs.

Growth Slows in 1950s

The expansion of Aramco's operations continued through the 1950s, albeit at a slower pace. Crude oil production only increased from 761 thousand barrels per day in 1960 to 1.2 million barrels per day in 1959, despite an increase of 38 billion barrels to a total of 50 billion barrels in the Saudi Arabian proven recoverable reserves during the same period. This expansion of oil reserves was primarily attributable to two discoveries made by Aramco, the onshore Ghawar and the offshore Safaniya oil fields, in 1951. The onshore and offshore discoveries were the largest on record at the time and have remained unequaled to this day. 1951 marked Tapline's first full year in operation. By 1965 Tapline enabled Aramco to market some 44 percent of its total crude oil exports to Europe, a greater share than that of nearer markets in Asia.

Aramco's activities during the 1950s were distinguished from those of the postwar years by the mature approach that underlay them. The U.S. lesson of the waste caused by over-rapid exploitation of oil reservoirs was not ignored by Aramco. In the early 1950s Aramco began to implement oilfield pressure maintenance programs. At the Abqaiq oilfield, gas reinjection facilities started operation in March 1954, and in February 1956 a similar water program was started. An added advantage with the gas program was that not only was Aramco able to utilize associated gas but that also the associated gas could be stored instead of burned off at the source.

Corporate Control at Issue in 1960s

Both Aramco's and Saudi Arabia's revenues increased dramatically during this period as a result of the expansion of crude oil exports and of rising posted prices. Like Aramco, Saudi Arabia ploughed these revenues into the development of infrastructure. As Saudi Arabia was overwhelmingly dependent on oil for revenues, it was vitally important that revenue stability was achieved to foster long-term development plans. Unlike the Aramco partners, however, the Saudi government had no influence on the two factors, production and price, that determined their revenues. The struggle for control, or the "participation" issue, emerged strongly in the 1960s.

Even though the general office had been moved to Dhahran and two representatives from the Saudi government were included on the board of directors, control of Aramco still rested firmly with the four partners. On August 9, 1960, the chairman of Standard Oil of New Jersey, Munroe Rathbone, decided unilaterally to shave 14¢ off the posted price, a cut of some seven percent, in order to increase its competitiveness in Europe vis-a-vis Soviet crude exports. Not only did the chairman refuse to consult the Aramco board, but he also rejected the advice given him from, among others, the New Jersey company's representative on the Aramco board, Howard Page. Other companies followed suit with the price cut and fueled the outrage of the oil-exporting countries. One dissenting voice that rose above the rest was that of Sayyid Abdullah H. Tariki, the Saudi director general of petroleum and mineral affairs and member of the Aramco board. Tariki immediately set about arranging secret negotiations with other producer countries. The preparatory negotiations proved instrumental in the formation of OPEC in 1960. As it turned out, the formation of OPEC was to be decisive in the battle for control of Aramco.

On November 30, 1962, the General Petroleum and Mineral Organization of Saudi Arabia (Petromin) was founded. Its aim was to foster Saudi participation in all areas of the oil industry, including operations in the Aramco concession. Although Petromin was not producing any crude oil, by 1970 it had joint interests in many concessions and operated a refinery at Jiddah and a fertilizer plant in Dammam. The evolution of Petromin over the 1960s was central to the government's attempts to wrest control from the Aramco partners.

The weakness of the crude oil market continued through the 1960s due to the emergence of Iran as the second major producer in the region. The freezing of posted prices over the 1960s meant that an oil exporter's only means to protect its revenues from being eroded by inflation was to increase production. The companies operating in the gulf, including the Aramco partners, were each put under a great deal of pressure by concessionaire governments to increase production and maintain prices. These incompatible aims could only be satisfied if incremental world demand could be equitably divided between the producers. Howard Page was so concerned to appear to be representing the Saudi case for an increase in its market share that he refused the opportunity to

involve Standard Oil of New Jersey in the very profitable exploration strategy being conducted in Oman, fearing that the company might be identified as aiding a direct competitor to enter the market. Between 1960 and 1970 Iran's production increased by 258 percent or 2.8 million barrels per day compared to the Saudi increase of 189 percent or 2.5 million barrels per day. However, by 1970 both Saudi and Iranian oil production had reached around 3.8 million barrels per day.

Aramco's fortunes were, and always have been, inextricably bound with those of the Saudi government. One way for both to overcome the constraint on revenue expansion imposed by the glutted crude oil market of the 1960s was to diversify into other markets. Expansion and progressive modernization of the Ras Tanura refinery increased crude oil throughput to 380,000 barrels per day in 1970, improved the quality of products, and enabled the blending of new products such as aviation gasoline. Aramco also began to establish the infrastructure necessary for the sale of liquid natural gas (LNG). Between 1962 and 1970 production of LNG increased 18-fold from 2,900 barrels per day to 52,100 barrels per day.

Tightening Markets Presage Gradual Government Takeover

The supply conditions in the crude oil market became markedly tighter in the early 1970s. In 1972 Aramco managed not only to increase production by an unprecedented 1.2 million barrels per day to six million barrels per day but also succeeded in increasing the posted price. The market conditions placed the government in a much stronger position from which to negotiate with the Aramco partners over Saudi participation.

In March 1972, after employing every delaying tactic possible, Aramco accepted the principle of 20 percent state participation in order to preempt unilateral action. The principle was worked out in detail in October 1972, when it was agreed that Saudi participation should be phased in from 25 percent on January 1, 1973, to 51 percent on January 1, 1982, and that compensation should be made for the updated book value of Aramco's assets.

By 1973, however, other oil-exporting countries had obtained or imposed terms far in excess of the Saudi government's demands. Negotiations restarted and continued through to 1980. In 1973 the Saudi interest in Aramco was increased to 60 percent. Between 1976 and 1980 the 100 percent Saudi takeover of Aramco was agreed upon and the financial provisions were made retroactive to January 1, 1976. By the terms of the agreement the Aramco partners received a service fee of 18 to 19 cents per barrel and were obliged to market the crude that Petromin could not sell through its own channels.

The oil price rises of 1973–1974 had a dramatic effect on revenues. The effect on government revenues of increases in the oil price, taxation, and production—from 3.8 million barrels per day in 1970 to an all-time high of 9.9 million barrels per day in 1980—was such that the economy could no longer absorb the funds available to it and was, therefore, generating a surplus.

With their newly acquired interest, the Saudi government began to involve Aramco in the reinvestment of that surplus. In 1975 Aramco was given the task of constructing and operating a gas system that could fuel Saudi Arabia's drive towards industrialization. The master gas system (MGS), as it came to be known, started operation in 1980. In January 1977 Aramco formed a subsidiary, the Saudi Consolidated Electric Company (SCECO), to construct and operate an electric grid system for the Eastern Province. As a result of the agreement between the government and Aramco, SCECO became an independently managed company on January 1, 1983.

Although Aramco had become state-owned, the close ties between the original Aramco partners and the government were not lost. Their relationship was fostered through joint ventures outside Aramco's scope of operations. Mobil continued to hold a 29 percent interest in Petrolube and a 30 percent stake in Luberef. Both the Saudi-American joint ventures were formed to build lubricating oil refineries in Jiddah in the 1970s, and are still responsible for their operation. The other three of the original Aramco partners, Exxon, Texaco, and Gulf, are involved in industrial projects with the Saudi Arabian Basic Industries Corporation (SABIC) in Jubail.

Revenues, Profits and Production Fall in 1980s

However, Aramco's boom years of the 1970s and early 1980s did not last. The oil price rises of 1973 and 1979–1980 led to inter-fuel substitution, such as the substitution of oil for gas, and conservation measures being implemented by the Organization for Economic Cooperation and Development (OECD) countries that brought about a collapse in world oil demand. Coupled with the sharp increase in oil supplies from non-OPEC regions, such as the North Sea, from 32.9 million barrels per day in 1980 to 37.8 million barrels per day in 1985, Saudi Arabia was faced with the no-win choice of either cutting production to maintain the official selling price or cutting prices and flooding the market. Between 1980 and 1985 Saudi Arabia cut production from 9.9 million barrels per day to four million barrels per day.

By 1985 Saudi Arabia was tired of shouldering the full burden of price defense and looking on as its revenues declined. In September 1985 Sheikh Yamani, in conjunction with the Aramco partners, instituted a dramatic change of policy to regain Saudi Arabia's share of the crude oil market. Between August 1985 and August 1986 Saudi Arabian production increased from 2.2 million to 6.2 million barrels per day, and the spot price of many world crudes fell to less than $10 from their previous 1985 levels of around $26 to $29 per barrel. The real price of oil had returned to levels not seen since before the oil price shocks of 1973–1974.

Aramco did not emerge unscathed from the drastic fall in oil revenues. Between 1982 and 1989 Aramco's personnel fell from 57,000 to 43,000. Following the meeting of the Aramco board of directors in San Francisco on April 8 and 9, 1987, the decision was taken to cut its own membership from 20 to 13. Three Americans and four Saudis, among them the ex-oil minister Sheikh Yamani, were removed, leaving two representatives from each of the four original Aramco partners and five Saudi officials.

The trauma of the 1986 oil price crash led to a change in management, Hisham Nazer replacing Sheikh Yamani, and a change in oil policy. The primary aim of Saudi policy after the

unbridled competition of 1986 was to secure market share just as it had been in the oil market glut of the 1960s. To secure long-term supply contracts, Hisham Nazer depended heavily on the close relationship between Aramco and the original shareholders. In his first attempt Nazer signed a 1.25 million barrels per day long-term supply arrangement with the four majors involved in the formation of Aramco, Chevron, Texaco, Mobil, and Exxon, on February 3, 1987. This agreement soon broke down, however, in the face of further price competition, and Nazer turned his attention to the possibility of securing market share through downstream integration—ownership of all phases of the industry from the wellhead to the service station.

In 1988 the first overseas downstream joint venture was concluded by the newly incorporated Saudi Aramco. On November 10, 1988, Saudi Aramco and Texaco signed an agreement committing themselves to the conditions of the joint venture named Star Enterprise. Aramco's share of the joint venture was to be managed by its subsidiary Saudi Refining Incorporated. From January 1, 1989, U.S.-based Star Enterprise was given the responsibility of operating Texaco's refining, distribution, and marketing assets in the east and gulf coasts. Texaco's assets were substantial in these areas and included three refineries—Delaware City, Convent, and Port Arthur—with combined distillation capacity of 625,000 barrels per day and, most importantly, 11,400 service stations. In return Saudi Aramco paid $1.5 billion and committed itself to supplying up to 600,000 barrels per day and to supplying a 30 million barrel inventory. By the mid-1990s, Star Enterprise ranked as America's sixth-largest gasoline marketer. Aramco made subsequent acquisitions of 35 percent of South Korea's Ssangyong Oil and a 40 percent stake in Petron, the Philippines' leading refiner and marketer.

King Fahd Ibn Abdulaziz Al-Saud formally incorporated Saudi Arabian Oil Co. by Royal Decree in 1988. The decree established a monarch-chaired Supreme Council and a board of directors led by the country's minister of petroleum and mineral resources. In addition to domestic government officials and top Aramco managers, the board included Exxon and Chevron chairmen into the early 1990s.

Persian Gulf Crisis, Management Shift Highlight Early 1990s

As a result of the 1990 Persian Gulf crisis, Saudi Aramco emerged as one of the most influential participants in the global oil industry. Within just a few weeks of Iraq's invasion of Kuwait, Saudi Aramco increased its daily production by over 2.5 million barrels per day. The conflict devastated Kuwait's oil-producing infrastructure and international sanctions prevented Iraq from trading oil, thereby eliminating over 4.5 million barrels of oil production per day and triggering what *Oil and Gas Journal* called "one of the most severe crises in the world's oil supplies since World War II." In fact, *Petroleum Economist* magazine asserted that Saudi Aramco "rescued the world from an oil supply crisis" by accelerating its plan to increase crude oil production capacity to ten million barrels per day from a target date of 1995 to 1992.

The company resumed its quest for vertical integration in the aftermath of the war, merging another state-owned firm, Saudi Arabian Marketing & Refining Co. (Samarec) in June 1993, moving into the ranks of the world's ten largest refiners. *Oil and Gas Journal's* L.R. Aalund noted that Samarec has "passed an acid test during the Gulf War when they supplied all allied air, land, and sea forces with their total fuel needs." Less than one month later, the company added state-owned Petromin to its roster, thereby merging majority interests in Petromin Lubricating Oil Refining Co. (a.k.a. Luberef) and Petromin Lubricating Oil Co. (a.k.a. Petrolube), both joint ventures with Mobil Oil Corp.

After nine years as Saudi Arabia's minister of Petroleum and Mineral Resources, Hisham Nazer was succeeded by Saudi Aramco President and CEO Ali Naimi in 1995. The appointment by King Fahd was interpreted as an acknowledgement of the company's growing clout, and as a sign of a new emphasis on the domestic petroleum industry. Aramco Vice-President for International Operations Abdullah Jumaa advanced to acting president and CEO of Aramco upon Naimi's promotion. Despite recent decades' wholesale changes in the ownership, management, and function of Aramco, its place in Saudi Arabia and the world is assured for the foreseeable future.

Principal Subsidiaries

Aramco Services Company (U.S.A.); Petromin Lubricating Oil Refining Co. (50%); Petromin Lubricating Oil Co. (50%).

Further Reading

Aalund, L.R., "Saudi Arabia," *The Oil and Gas Journal,* August 16, 1993, pp. 38–44.

George, Dev, "Safaniya, POEC, And The Saudi Power Play," *Offshore Incorporating The Oilman,* November 1991, p. 11.

"King Of Oil Surges Ahead," *Petroleum Economist,* December 1991, pp. 6–9.

Longrigg, S.H., *Oil in the Middle East,* Oxford, England: Oxford University Press, 1969.

Mangan, David, Jr., and Marshall Thomas, "Saudi Aramco Report Stresses Join Ventures," *The Oil Daily,* June 21, 1991, pp. 1–2.

Mollet, Paul, "Aramco Man Gets The Top Job," *Petroleum Economist,* September 1995, p. 36.

Naimi, A.I., "Saudi Aramco Staying On Course with Strategy for the '90s," *The Oil Daily,* November 21, 1991, p. 5.

"Saudi Aramco Describes Crisis Oil Flow Hike," *The Oil and Gas Journal,* December 2, 1991, pp. 49–51.

Seymour, I., *OPEC: Instrument of Change,* London: Macmillan Press Ltd., 1980.

Yergin, D., *The Prize: The Epic Quest for Oil, Money and Power,* New York: Simon & Schuster, 1990.

—Adam Seymour
—updated by April Dougal Gasbarre

Schlumberger

Schlumberger Limited

277 Park Avenue
New York, New York 10172-0266
U.S.A.
(212) 350-9400
Fax: (212) 350-9564
Internet: http://www.slb.com/

Public Company
Incorporated: 1956
Employees: 51,000
Sales: $7.62 billion (1995)
Stock Exchanges: New York Paris London Amsterdam
   Brussels Frankfurt Basel Geneva Lausanne Zürich
   Tokyo
SICs: 1381 Drilling Oil & Gas Wells; 1389 Oil & Gas
   Field Services, Not Elsewhere Classified; 3533 Oil &
   Gas Field Machinery & Equipment; 3577 Computer
   Peripheral Equipment, Not Elsewhere Classified; 3671
   Electron Tubes; 3674 Semiconductor & Related
   Devices; 3675 Electronic Capacitors; 3679 Electronic
   Components, Not Elsewhere Classified; 3823
   Industrial Instruments for Measurement, Display &
   Control of Process Variables & Related Products;
   3824 Totalizing Fluid Meters & Counting Devices;
   3825 Instruments for Measuring & Testing of
   Electricity & Electrical Signals; 3829 Measuring &
   Controlling Devices, Not Elsewhere Classified; 6719
   Offices of Holding Companies, Not Elsewhere
   Classified; 7372 Prepackaged Software; 8711
   Engineering Services; 8713 Surveying Services

As oil is found all around the world, so is Schlumberger Limited providing a range of oil field services that includes the pinpointing of oil reserves, both on- and offshore; the drilling of boreholes; precise determination of the depth and extent of oil and gas pockets; the pumping and monitoring of oil flow; and the rehabilitation of old or discontinued wells. In addition to its large market share of such services, Schlumberger's Measurement & Systems Group is the world's largest manufacturer of meters for gas, water, and electric utilities; develops and supplies electronics transactions systems, such as smart cards; and builds systems for semiconductor design and manufacture.

Founding an "Electrical Prospecting" Firm in 1919

Schlumberger was the creation of two brothers of that name, Conrad, born in 1878, and Marcel, younger by six years. Rooted in the Alsace region of France, the Schlumberger family had made its mark in both politics and business; the Schlumberger brothers' great-grandfather served as prime minister under Louis Philippe and their father, Paul Schlumberger, later amassed a fortune in the textile industry. Conrad Schlumberger early displayed a genius for science and, by 1907, had become a professor of physics at the École des Mines, while his brother Marcel pursued mechanical engineering and business. Conrad became interested in the electrical resistance generated by different types of rock formation and was soon testing his results on the family's summer estate in Normandy. In 1914 Conrad successfully completed the first commercial application of this technique, locating a body of copper ore for a client in Serbia. World War I brought all experimentation to a halt, but in 1919 Conrad and Marcel Schlumberger set up a modest business in Paris to pursue the further evolution of electrical prospecting, as it was called.

At this point the brothers received crucial financial backing from their father, who made it clear that he considered their work a type of scientific inquiry, and only secondarily a means to monetary rewards. This scientific bias has remained strong at Schlumberger, which has always depended on its technological superiority. Bolstered by this aid, which eventually reached Ffr 500,000, Conrad resigned from his teaching position in 1923 to devote his energy to the new company, Société de Prospection Électrique. In that same year the brothers received their first order from an oil company, resulting in the successful mapping of an oil-rich salt dome in Romania.

A few years later the Pechelbronn Oil Company of France asked the Schlumbergers to make such measurements not from ground level, but from the interior of an already drilled bore-

Company Perspectives:

Our people, their motivation and dedication to customer service worldwide, in a safe and clean environment, are our main asset. Our commitment to technology and quality is the basis for our competitive advantage. Our determination to produce superior products is the cornerstone for our future independence of action and growth.

hole. Conrad asked Henri Doll, his son-in-law and longtime technical supervisor, to design the necessary equipment, and in September 1927 the men compiled the first "wireline log" by lowering an electrical recording device down a Pechelbronn oil well and measuring the resistance every few feet. The results were accurate, meaning that oil deposits could now be located and measured without resorting to expensive and time-consuming mechanical coring.

The world did not immediately beat a path to the Schlumberger door, however. By the time logging teams had been sent to Venezuela, the United States, and the Soviet Union, the Great Depression had taken hold, and drilling activity had come to a virtual halt. The Venezuelan tests went so well that Royal Dutch Shell became interested and ordered additional work to be done in Romania, Sumatra, and Trinidad. Furthermore, the Soviet Union proceeded with its drilling in the Baku oil fields regardless of the Depression, and there the Schlumbergers landed sufficient orders to get them through the first lean years. An ardent socialist, Conrad Schlumberger was pleased to do business in Soviet Russia.

Successfully Expanded into U.S. Market in 1932

The young company's biggest break came with its introduction to the U.S. market in 1932, when Shell asked it to run logs in California and on the Texas gulf coast. These again proved successful and Schlumberger was soon picking up business among the many wildcatters in Texas and Oklahoma. In 1934 the brothers founded Schlumberger Well Surveying Corporation in Houston, Texas, to meet the growing demand for their services, and this U.S. division soon became the largest and most profitable of the parent company's worldwide business.

Once under way, Schlumberger expanded rapidly, despite the Depression. The brothers had a long technological lead on any would-be competitors, an advantage the company has maintained to this day by consistently hiring top engineering talent and spending liberally on research and development. In addition, Schlumberger remained very much a family organization, with the resulting high degree of trust and unity helping to keep employees motivated and loyal. This became of greater importance after the death, in 1936, of Conrad Schlumberger. Marcel Schlumberger assumed control of a burgeoning business, which was already doing more than 1,000 logs a month in North America alone, but he soon had help from other members of the extended family.

As world depression gave way to World War II and France was overcome by Germany, Marcel Schlumberger worked with Jean de Ménil to move the corporation from Paris to Trinidad. De

Ménil, the husband of Conrad Schlumberger's daughter Dominique, was a banker who became head of Schlumberger's financial affairs in 1939. De Ménil is generally credited with managing the move to Trinidad. De Ménil remained overseas and eventually became head of Schlumberger's South American and Middle Eastern businesses, operating out of the Houston office.

Although information is sparse, it is clear that the war was not good for Schlumberger's business. It was necessary to retreat before the Nazi advance, and the war effectively scattered key members of the Schlumberger family. Doll, the company's top technician, fled to Connecticut, where he formed a company called Electro-Mechanical Research that went on to do important work for the Allied war effort. Schlumberger eventually bought out Electro-Mechanical, and Doll emerged as the head of all technical research for Schlumberger worldwide. On the other side of the Atlantic Ocean, Marcel's son-in-law René Seydoux spent two years as a German prisoner of war before assuming control of all European operations. In Houston Pierre Schlumberger, Marcel's son and the only male heir of either of the founders, began to rebuild the U.S. business in 1946 and guided it back to a position of leadership.

Thus fragmented by war, the Schlumberger family was held together largely by Marcel, whose devotion to the business became legendary. In 1940, when it was clear that France would soon fall and many thought that the Schlumbergers would be ruined, Marcel Schlumberger was offered $10 million for his business by the head of rival Halliburton Oil. It is said that Marcel did not even respond to the suggestion, but instead showed his guest to the door.

When Marcel Schlumberger died in 1953, the remaining Schlumbergers were unable to decide on a successor. The firm was left divided, roughly between Doll, who controlled technical research; de Ménil, who controlled the business in South America and the Middle East; Seydoux, who controlled the company's European business; and Pierre Schlumberger, who ran the company's U.S. operations.

Incorporated in the Netherlands Antilles in 1956

Pierre Schlumberger, the natural candidate to follow his father as president, strongly favored incorporating the company and selling stock to raise capital needed to take advantage of the booming postwar economy. Other family members resisted the idea, fearing a loss of both control and quality, but in 1956 Schlumberger Limited was formed in Curaçao, Netherlands Antilles. That location was chosen for tax purposes. Pierre became president and Henri Doll was named chairman.

The new corporation was headquartered in Houston. It remained under family control, as it does to this day, but it began to sell stock, and the fresh capital allowed Schlumberger to expand rapidly at a time when postwar U.S. oil drilling was at its peak. As the undisputed technical leader in the field, Schlumberger charged what it pleased, and when the initial financial statements were made public in 1958 they showed a first year profit of $12.2 million.

The next 25 years may someday be thought of as the company's golden age. By carefully managing the high profits earned by its wireline business, Schlumberger diversified slowly into a number of related fields, giving each acquisition the time and resources needed to make it healthy. Aside from a pair of French electronics firms, the company's first significant purchase was the 1959 acquisition of Forages et Exploitations Pétrolières (Forex), a French oil drilling company. A complementary deal was the 1960 formation of Dowell Schlumberger, a joint venture with Dow Chemical to provide oil well completion services such as cementing and flow stimulation. Schlumberger was now a complete oil services company, able to set up drilling operations anywhere in the world.

As oil drilling gradually fell from its 1957 peak, Pierre Schlumberger and his advisors thought it prudent to expand further into the electronics field. This was a natural extension, as Schlumberger had always used sophisticated electrical monitoring devices and was at home in the electronics field. Accordingly, the firm made a major acquisition in 1961 when it swapped stock with Daystrom, a manufacturer of various electronic instruments primarily for military use. With $90 million in sales, Daystrom was nearly as large as Schlumberger ($130 million), but did not turn a profit for several years after. The parent company pursued many other electronics concerns, eventually absorbing 11 French companies and several in England and the United States. Most of the newcomers required years of work before paying dividends; in 1966, for example, 42 percent of Schlumberger's $343 million in sales was generated by the electronics division, whose operating deficit held down overall corporate profit to $28 million.

After a few wobbly years in the early 1960s, the Schlumberger board of directors decided that Pierre Schlumberger should step down as president. Promoted to his place was Jean Riboud, a longtime friend of the Schlumbergers, particularly Marcel. Riboud guided Schlumberger for the next 20 years, during which time the company's net income and worldwide reputation rose with equal regularity.

Riboud immediately moved corporate headquarters from Houston to New York City and reorganized the now diffuse company on the basis of product lines rather than geography. In 1970 Riboud further diversified the Schlumberger portfolio with the $79 million purchase of Compagnie de Compteurs, an aging French manufacturer of utility meters, which also took a few years to become profitable. By 1980 it had made Schlumberger the largest meter manufacturer in the world and formed the heart of one of the company's four divisions.

The 1973 OPEC oil embargo spurred a massive worldwide increase in oil exploration and drilling, with Schlumberger positioned to benefit from every new well. Its wireline services helped to find new oil, Forex-Neptune drilled the wells, and Dowell Schlumberger kept them pumping. In the space of five years Schlumberger sales jumped from 1972's $812 million to a robust $2.2 billion in 1977, with profit exceeding $400 million in 1977. Schlumberger earned spectacular profits by delivering a superior and much-needed product.

Unwise Acquisitions and an Oil Glut Deflate Profits in the 1980s

The boom years at Schlumberger reached their peak in 1982. At that time the company had sales of $6.3 billion and profits of

$1.35 billion, a staggering 21 percent ratio that made Schlumberger the most profitable of the world's 1,000 largest corporations. The firm's hold on the wireline logging business rivaled that of IBM's in computers, with seven out of every ten logs in the world taken by Schlumberger. Its drilling operation was the world's largest, and it produced more utility meters than anyone else.

As 1982 drew to an end, however, a close observer would have noticed that Schlumberger's quarterly profits were slipping, and they continued to do so as a world recession and greater oil conservation combined to put the brakes on oil exploration. In addition, Chairman Riboud had made a tactical mistake, and he was about to make a second. In 1979 Riboud paid $425 million to buy the leading American semiconductor manufacturer, Fairchild Camera and Instrument Corporation. Schlumberger hoped that Fairchild's technical expertise would help keep it ahead of the pack in its various fields, but the move was a failure from the beginning. Fairchild lost money and drained valuable research and development dollars from the rest of Schlumberger; the parent company was forced to write off much of Fairchild's assets and sell the rest to National Semiconductor in 1987, at a loss of $220 million.

Schlumberger's, and Riboud's, second mistake came in 1985, when it paid $1 billion for SEDCO, another enormous drilling company. Riboud apparently assumed that the oil glut would soon turn around; it did not. Riboud died in 1985 and was succeeded by Michel Vaillaud, who was ousted the following year by the board of directors, during a year that turned out to be the first one in which Schlumberger posted a loss ($1.6 billion) since incorporation. Next in the chairman's seat came 30-year Schlumberger veteran Euan Baird, a Scottish geophysicist and the first non-Frenchman in history to run the company.

Turnaround Engineered by Baird in the Late 1980s and 1990s

As the oil glut continued, Baird quickly moved to turn the company around by refocusing on the core oil field services and measurement and systems business groups. In addition to selling Fairchild, other noncore businesses were divested. Schlumberger also underwent a restructuring to cut costs and become more cost-effective to survive in the difficult economic environment.

At the same time Baird was creating a leaner Schlumberger, he also invested heavily in research and development to keep the company at the technological forefront. From 1987 into the early 1990s, research and development spending was 37 percent higher than before Baird took over. The result was successful innovations, such as EB-Clean and Maxis.

EB-Clean, introduced in 1990, was an additive used in a well bore to enlarge cracks. After it drained away, more oil and gas was able to flow through the now larger cracks. The additive was developed by a joint venture with Dow Chemical called Dowell Schlumberger, which Schlumberger later owned outright when it bought Dow's half in 1993 for $800 million in cash and warrants.

Maxis, also developed in the early 1990s, was a premium imaging system that provided much clearer, more detailed, and faster evaluations of potential well sites than previous systems had done. When rival Western Atlas introduced a competitive system, Schlumberger was ready with a new Maxis Express unit that was smaller and 50 percent cheaper to operate.

In addition to new product development, Baird also actively sought out acquisitions to enhance Schlumberger's oil field services core. Soon after becoming chairman, Baird moved the company into a new area of oil field services, seismic data, which involved using and measuring sound waves bounced off the earth's surface to search for oil-bearing formations. In 1986 the Norwegian firm GECO, one of the world's top seismic companies, was acquired. Five years later Schlumberger acquired 51 percent of Prakla Seismos, a leader in onshore seismic operations, from the German government. In 1992 Seismograph Service Limited was purchased from Raytheon Co. The following year, Schlumberger purchased the remaining 49 percent of Prakla. All of the company's seismic operations were then combined within a Geco-Prakla division. The seismic area proved to be highly competitive and not immediately profitable, but by 1995 Schlumberger's focus on improvements to seismic technology had begun to pay off.

Another important acquisition came in 1992 when GeoQuest Systems Inc. was purchased, also from Raytheon. GeoQuest specialized in computing and information technology services geared to hydrocarbon exploration and production. In late 1994 Schlumberger formed a joint venture, Omnes, with Cable & Wireless plc to provide communications and information technology systems for oil, gas, and other companies with operations in remote areas.

Baird had successfully turned Schlumberger around from that bleak year of 1986, as evidenced by 1994 and 1995 revenue of $6.7 billion and $7.6 billion, respectively, and net income of $536.1 million and $649.2 million, respectively. Schlumberger's wireline testing services remained the industry's unchallenged leader, and its growing stable of electronic subsidiaries should help keep the company at the forefront of technical innovation. So long as oil remains one of the primary sources of energy, it seemed likely that oil companies would turn for advice to Schlumberger.

Principal Operating Units

Oilfield Services; Measurement & Systems; Omnes.

Further Reading

Allaud, Louis, *Schlumberger: The History of a Technique,* New York: Wiley, 1977.

Auletta, Ken, *The Art of Corporate Success: The Story of Schlumberger,* New York: Penguin Books, 1984.

Brown, Stanley H., "It's a 'Slumber-Jay' and It's a Money Gusher," *Fortune,* September 1973.

Hager, Bruce, "How Euan Baird Is Pumping Life Back into Schlumberger," *Business Week,* July 9, 1990, pp. 52–53.

Headden, Susan, "Drilling Deep for Dollars: Oil Services Giant Schlumberger Uses New Technology To Coax Out Crude," *U.S. News & World Report,* July 10, 1995, pp. 40–41.

Reingold, Jennifer, "Reading the Rock: Schlumberger Outmaneuvers Its Competition To Keep the Lead in Oil Field Services," *Financial World,* March 15, 1994, pp. 26–27.

Schlumberger: The First Years, New York: Schlumberger, 1979.

"This Is Schlumberger," New York: Schlumberger, 1988.

Toal, Brian A., "The Path to Profits: Schlumberger Ltd.'s Oilfield Services Group Is Integrating New Technologies and Services To Fit Client Needs," *Oil and Gas Investor,* December 1993, pp. 60–63.

—Jonathan Martin
—updated by David E. Salamie

Sealright Co., Inc.

7101 College Boulevard, Suite 1400
Overland Park, Kansas 66210
U.S.A.
(913) 344-9000
Fax: (913) 344-9005

Public Company
Founded: 1883
Employees: 1,788
Sales: $295.07 million (1995)
Stock Exchanges: NASDAQ
SICs: 2656 Sanitary Food Containers, Except Folding;
   3565 Packaging Machinery; 3556 Food Products
   Machinery; 3081 Unsupported Plastics Film & Sheet;
   3089 Plastics Products, Not Elsewhere Classified

Sealright Co., Inc. is the largest manufacturer of frozen dairy dessert packaging in North America, the third-largest company in the larger U.S. sanitary food container industry, and the fifth-largest company in the overall U.S. container industry by revenues. Sealright designs and manufactures rigid (paperboard) and flexible (plastic) packaging for the food, dairy, beverage, and household products industry. Best known for the round tapered paperboard containers used by premium ice cream manufacturers like Haagen Dazs and Kemp's, in 1992 Sealright's shipments to the $10 billion U.S. frozen dessert industry were its most important business segment. In the mid-1990s the company sought to supply the packaging for an ever-larger proportion of the 1.6 billion gallons of ice cream, ice milk, frozen yogurt, water ices, and sherbet sold annually in the United States while continuing an aggressive expansion into other nondairy packaging markets.

Sealright's rigid packaging operations produced five basic paperboard-based containers in the mid-1990s: Bulkan, a one-to six-gallon cylindrical container used to package bulk frozen dessert for restaurants and dip-store frozen dessert shops like Baskin-Robbins; Convocan, a smaller cylindrical container used to package ice cream and other frozen desserts for super-

market and retail sales; Nestyle, a small, round, tapered container used for retail ice cream, frozen snack food, cookie, and carryout food sales and designed to be "nested" inside other Nestyle containers for compact shipping; Ultrakan, a cylindrical container whose dimensions and composition can be matched to the customer's needs and the product's market; and Vektor, like Ultrakan a customizable container, but with flat sides for more prominent graphics.

Sealright's flexible packaging operations manufacture soft plastic food storage products (such as its Pinch-N-Seal reclosable package for the dried fruit market) for the snack foods, bakery, candy, condiment, household goods, personal care, and medical supplies industries. Sealright is also engaged in package labeling and the manufacture of aseptic packages for puddings, fruit, and sauces (in which the package and its contents are sterilized separately). In 1996 Sealright maintained manufacturing plants in Fulton, New York; Akron, Ohio; Los Angeles and San Leandro, California; and Raleigh and Charlotte, North Carolina; as well corporate, engineering, and packaging technology operations in Kansas City, Missouri.

19th-Century Beginnings

Sealright was founded in 1883 by Forrest Weeks as the Oswego Falls Pulp and Paper Company in Fulton, New York. While apprenticing to become a blacksmith, Weeks discovered the natural power of the Oswego Falls (northwest of Syracuse, New York, on Lake Ontario) and resolved to harness it by establishing a wood pulp mill there. The venture was a success, and in 1898 Weeks added a paper mill, in which paper sheet was made by turning the wood pulp generated by his mill into a cellulose fiber and then stripping it of impurities with a chemical reagent. In the following years Weeks made his son-in-law H. Lester Paddock a partner and in 1901 added a new cylindrical paper machine. Oswego's principal early product was newsprint for the newspaper industry, but Weeks and Paddock soon branched out into butcher wrapping paper, wallpaper, and a high-quality paperboard (like paper, made from wood pulp, but thicker), which quickly became known as "Fulton Board." Because of its natural sanitary qualities it was used in milk bottle caps to prevent spoilage.

Company Perspectives:

The future begins with a belief in the power of customer partnerships. We expressed that belief in 20 words we call Vision Sealright: 'The new Sealright and its people will grow and prosper through multifaceted, enduring relationships with leading consumer-products companies worldwide.' Vision Sealright affirms our commitment to focusing on our customers' needs at all times and on meeting and exceeding their expectations. Vision Sealright recognizes that the new Sealright, its employees, and its stockholders will grow and flourish worldwide with our customers as we help them succeed and profit.

In the early years of the new century Paddock came across a new kind of cylindrical paper container made of a spirally wound paper with superior properties for sanitary uses. Because the container, "Liquid-Tight," was ideally suited for moist dairy products like cottage cheese and ice cream—a market Oswego was already supplying—Paddock acquired the rights and brought the inventor, Dr. Wilbur L. Wright, into the company. The new product was christened "Sealrights." Extolling the product's ability to save housewives from the "every-day household tragedy" of spoiled food, Oswego's early advertising savvily stressed the hygienic benefits of food "untouched by human hands" and also enjoined shoppers to send Oswego the names of any dealer not yet stocking Sealright-packaged goods—"we will see that he is supplied."

Because of the rapid success of the Sealright product line, Oswego incorporated the Sealright Company as a subsidiary in 1917, and the company was soon operating under the moniker Oswego Falls-Sealright Co. Inc. In 1917 its paper containers were being used for everything from draught beer to oysters. Anticipating the day when its paperboard milk bottle cap liners would become obsolete, in 1921 Oswego introduced the first milk container made entirely of paper. Trademarked as the Sealright Kone bottle, it was the true precursor of the modern assembly-line-produced paper milk carton. In the same year Oswego added the first of what would become seven new factory facilities in Fulton, New York.

1920s: Rapid Growth

By the mid-1920s, consumers still purchased ice cream almost exclusively at traditional ice cream parlors. To broaden Oswego's markets, Eugene W. Skinner, hired in the previous decade to manage the company's marketing, ran a single-page ad in the popular *Saturday Evening Post* in 1926 to convince consumers that ice cream, hygienically packaged in Sealright containers, was now a luxury that could be enjoyed in the comfort of one's own home. Anticipating a tough door-to-door sales campaign to follow up on the ad, Skinner instead found himself so inundated with orders that Sealright's Fulton plant had to scramble to keep production flowing. Buoyed by new growth, Oswego expanded into Canada in 1926 with Sealright Canada Ltd., opened Sealright Pacific Ltd. in Los Angeles in 1931, and added a Kansas City division in 1932.

Oswego's deft marketing and exploitation of new consumer preferences enabled it to survive the years of the Great Depression. Indeed, as Oswego's plants continued to churn out Sealright containers throughout the 1930s, Fulton, New York, became known as "the city the Depression missed." Two new product lines helped to keep Oswego ahead of the packaging innovation curve. Its trademarked "Nestyle" carton offered a variation on its paper-based approach to packaging ice cream and cottage cheese for home storage, and its descriptively named Bulkan ("bulk" + "can") container for bulk ice cream packaging subtly suggested the thrust of Oswego's corporate goal: to render obsolete the traditional practice of packaging dairy products in returnable and reusable metal cans. Combining its proprietary Bulkan assembly machine with a cleverly to-the-point marketing slogan—"Sealright Sanitary Service"—Oswego drove the final nails into the coffin of the U.S. metal dairy-product can industry.

In clear anticipation of today's standard all-paper squeeze-to-open milk carton, Sealright introduced heat-sealed paperboard pouring hoods for the glass milk bottle industry in 1939. Trademarked as the Sealon Hood, the product took advantage of emerging plastics technology, which enabled a thin plastic coating to be bonded to paperboard. World War II furthered Oswego's goals by providing it with a wide open overseas military market for paper-packaged food goods while the U.S. government diverted all metal for consumer goods to the war effort. Sealright continued to apply plastic coatings to its products after the war's end, introducing the familiar square-shaped no-wax paper milk carton in 1948 in response to customer complaints that wax coatings tended to dissolve into the milk. Promoted as "another first from Sealright," these Sealking containers enabled dairies to package milk in one-gallon "twin packs," complete with a handy carrying strap. The product's marketing slogans—"pour one, store one"; "with patented aluminum shield protection"; and "exclusive flame sterilized carton"—struck all the appropriate chords: improved sanitation for spoilable dairy products, convenient storability, and the benefits of modern manufacturing technology in the home. Plastic-coated beverage cups were a natural extension and filled the need for a disposable beverage cup that did not spoil the flavor with the taste of paper. Soon Sealright was using plastic coatings in its cylindrical and Nestyle paperboard containers as well. Like the metal can before it, the days of the glass dairy bottle appeared to be numbered by the 1950s, and Sealright began proclaiming from billboards around the nation that "36 million" Americans used Sealright products every day.

Postwar Era

Although Sealright had for years been a closely held public corporation, in the 1940s it began operating as a publicly traded company and enjoyed sales growth of 63 percent in the decade after World War II. The rapid pace of change in the dairy product and packaging industries began to overtake even Sealright in the 1960s, however. Its traditional customers, small- and medium-sized dairies, began to give way to large consolidated dairy producers, and mergers and sellouts left Sealright (now known as Sealright-Oswego Falls Corporation) struggling to maintain itself as a major supplier. The demise of the glass bottle milk packaging industry, which, ironically, Sealright had done so much to bring about, eliminated such traditional Sealright product lines as milk bottle caps, closures, and Sealking paper hoods for glass milk bottles. Adjusting to the new environment, Sealright introduced its Plastyle-brand plastic-coated paper milk carton in 1957, which proved such a success that forty years later it was still in production. Now under the stewardship of Henry C. Estabrook, in the early 1960s Sealright also pursued such nontraditional markets as aluminum foil and fiber oil container production.

1960s: Association with Phillips Petroleum

Although Sealright's sales rose from $58 million in 1961 to $63 million in 1962, they dropped back down to $60 million a year later, and in 1964 Sealright agreed to a $37.8 million exchange of stock with Phillips Petroleum, the eighth-largest oil company in the United States and a major supplier of the polyethylene-based plastic coatings used in Sealright's containers. Besides giving Sealright (renamed Sealright Co., Inc.) the financial security of a large corporate parent, the acquisition strengthened it in the areas of oil can container manufacture and new patent acquisition and enabled it to develop new varieties of plastic and coated paperboard containers using resins from Phillips's plastics division. In 1968 Sealright branched out into the production of clear polyvinyl chloride bottles for the shampoo, mouthwash, lotion, and household chemicals markets and, more importantly, unveiled its round Convocan ice cream container package, which gave consumers the option of seeing the ice cream itself through a transparent window in the lid. The Convocan, moreover, could be assembled, filled, and sealed in the ice cream manufacturer's plant on Sealright's proprietary machinery, cutting the expense of shipping and storing preconstructed containers and, not accidentally, increasing Sealright's sales of production machinery to its customers.

The Convocan led in the 1970s to the introduction of Sealright's Ultrakan package, a tall, round, rigid-walled container that utilized Convocan's in-the-plant assembly concept by exploiting Sealright's huge inventory of aging milk carton machines to create packaging for such new uses as oatmeal and stuffing mixes. Sealright engineers next set about designing a more compact and efficient version of the packaging system for customers who needed to be able to assemble the packaging for their products in their own production facilities. Two holdover products from the 1930s—the Bulkan and Nestyle containers—helped Sealright become the market leader in the manufacture of ice cream shop bulk containers and nested containers, respectively, in the 1980s. Sealright's round container concept was expanded from its original ice cream niche to products as diverse as finger foods and cereal. By the mid-1980s Sealright was designing and manufacturing most of the machines used by its customers to assemble, fill, and seal containers. Typically, it leased the machines to ice cream makers, shipping the semifinished containers' walls, bottoms, and covers to the plants for final assembly.

After eighteen years as a corporate subsidiary in 1982 eleven of Sealright's managers joined with private investment company George K. Baum in a leveraged buyout of all Sealright stock from Phillips Petroleum. After an initial public stock offering four years later, Sealright was again a publicly traded company, and Sealright's now familiar tapered Convocan ice cream container

was becoming synonymous with the increasingly popular high-quality "premium" and "superpremium" ice creams exemplified by producers like Haagen Dazs and Ben & Jerry's. Market research surveys were showing that four out of five consumers preferred ice cream served from round containers to traditional square cartons, and two-thirds preferred see-through container tops. Sealright's sales seemed to corroborate the findings: its round windowed ice cream containers were typically accounting for three-quarters of Sealright sales per year.

1980s: Diversification

Sealright's management was wary of relying too heavily on a single line of packaging for its future growth, however, and in the 1980s it set about diversifying its product mix so its paperboard packaging customers would never comprise more than 50 percent of sales. "We want to be able to offer food companies a fuller line of packaging," Vice-President of Finance John Wempe explained in 1988. "It's to our advantage to make a variety of packages." To that end, in 1986 Sealright acquired Packaging Industries Inc. of California, a manufacturer of flexible (i.e., elastic or pliable) packaging for the food industry. The purchase spawned Sealright's Flexible Packaging Group, enabling it to produce flexible packages for such products as snack foods, sauces, puddings, and candy. By 1989 the percentage of Sealright's sales accounted for by frozen dessert packaging had fallen to 62 percent, followed by nondairy food packaging at 23 percent and nondessert dairy product packaging at nine percent. In 1990 Sealright, now headed by former Phillips veteran Marvin W. Ozley, added Jaite Packaging of Akron, Ohio (founded as a flour sack and grain bag mill in the early 1900s), a producer of labels for soft drink bottles as well as a printer and converter of flexible packaging for condiments, household goods, candy, snack foods, medical supplies, cheese, and meat. Energized by the acquisition, by 1995 Sealright had made its goal of a fifty-fifty split between its dairy and dry grocery packaging sales a reality.

In 1992 Sealright expanded its new Flexible Packaging Group again, acquiring Venture Packaging Inc., a North Carolina manufacturer of wraparound sleeve labels for beverage bottles as well as bags for disposable diapers, label application machines, and laminates for the snack food, bakery, and processed meat industries, and Styrotech, Inc., a North Carolina-based producer of beverage bottle sleeve label application equipment. The following year, it announced plans to construct a 400,000-square-foot frozen dessert packaging plant in DeSoto, Kansas, and in 1994 introduced its fifth major packaging product type, the Vektor container, a square-shaped container with rounded edges and a "billboard"-style front panel for more striking graphics, which could be assembled from parts in the customer's plant.

Competitive Pressures, 1990s

In the early 1990s, competition in the U.S. packaging industry intensified, and Sealright was forced to sharply reduce its prices to preserve market share, exacerbating already strained profit levels caused by excess plant capacity and weakening demand in the frozen dessert industry. New federal product labeling regulations were also forcing Sealright's customers to use up their inventories of outdated containers before restocking, and more significantly, Sealright's principal customers—small, regional ice cream makers—were losing business to huge national firms. Although Sealright could claim roughly five hundred customers nationally, half its sales went to thirty-five firms, and these were increasingly situated on the east and west coasts. Sealright's chief competitors had already abandoned the regional approach to manufacturing—in which plants producing identical product types are distributed regionally to serve specific geographic areas—but Sealright itself still divided its operations between the Midwest and the two coasts. After six years of steady growth in profits and sales through 1991, Sealright's profits consequently dropped to only $1.1 million in 1993 before plummeting to a net loss of $.8 million 1995, one of Sealright's worst years ever.

Within six months of replacing Marvin Ozley as Sealright's CEO in mid-1995, Charles F. Marcy, a food industry veteran, announced a major restructuring of Sealright's organization and market strategy with the goal of returning the company to its historical profit levels by 1998. The company's work force was to be cut by 12 percent; its information systems/customer communications operations would receive a $7 million facelift, and the firm would concentrate on cost-cutting procedures and new partnerships with major customers that would enable it, now reincarnated as a customer-driven "specialty packaging manufacturer," to be more responsive to market forces and expand into the Pacific Rim and South America. Crucially, the company would also abandon its regional, decentralized structure of three rigid packaging and five flexible packaging plants for a centralized approach in which a single plant would manufacture a particular packaging product for the company's entire market. In early 1996, Sealright's Fulton, New York, and Los Angeles facilities thus absorbed the frozen dairy dessert container manufacturing operations of the brand new De Soto, Kansas, plant, which was converted into the firm's new headquarters and R & D center. Explaining Sealright's situation to Kansas City newspapers, Marcy said, "we have become so decentralized that we have the same activity going on in three or four or five different places. By centralizing more, we can create tremendous economies of scale. . . . The truth of the matter is we're in too many businesses. We're looking to consolidate down to a much more manageable product portfolio where we can really add value. . . . We need to concentrate on the key customers with the greatest potential for growth."

Less than a year into the restructuring, the signing of two new international contracts seemed to suggest that Sealright's goal of leaping from a $300 million U.S. packager to a $400 million multinational by the turn of the century was feasible. In April 1996, the company announced it would be supplying McDonald's South African and Chinese restaurant operations with its packaging forming and Quikspread condiment dispensing equipment, and less than a month later it announced a $3.5 million contract with Australia's Coca-Cola Amatil firm to produce 650 million beverage bottle labels for the Australian market. The deal complemented Sealright's existing six-year-old presence in Australia's frozen dessert packaging market and appeared to set the stage for an even larger Sealright presence internationally in the years to come.

Principal Subsidiaries

Jaite Packaging, Inc.; Sealright International, Inc.; Venture Packaging, Inc.; Indopak (d.b.a. Packaging Industries, Inc.); Sealright Packaging Co. of Australia, PTY. Ltd.

Further Reading

Burket, David, "Sealright Names New President and CEO," *Business Wire,* July 27, 1995, p. 1.

——, "Sealright Sales Up, Earnings Down for Second Quarter," *Business Wire,* July 16, 1993.

Fairchild, David, "Sealright Continues Streamlining with an Eye on International Deals," *Kansas City Business Journal,* December 22, 1995, p. 5.

Gose, Joe, "Diet? KC Screams for Rich Ice Cream," *Kansas City Business Journal,* June 25, 1993, p. 1.

Grossman, Steve, "Sealright CEO Stepping Down after Thirty Years," *Kansas City Business Journal,* February 3, 1995, p. 5.

Heaster, Randolph, "Sealright to Trim 180 Jobs at New Plant," *Kansas City Star,* December 15, 1995, p. B1.

Hine, Thomas, *The Total Package: The Evolution and Secret Meanings of Boxes, Bottles, Cans, and Tubes,* Boston: Little, Brown, 1994.

Lilley, Valerie, "Sealright Designs Sauce System for McDonalds in South Africa, China," *Kansas City Business Journal,* April 26, 1996, p. 40.

——, "Sealright to Supply Coca-Cola Labels to Australia," *Kansas City Business Journal,* March 29, 1996, p. 7.

"Merging for New Markets," *Chemical Week,* July 18, 1964, p. 24.

Neher, Megan, "Sealright Eliminates 180 Jobs," *Lawrence Journal World,* December 15, 1995, p. 5.

Pfautsch, Larry, "Sealright Completes Flexible-Packaging Acquisition," *PR Newswire,* December 31, 1992, p. 1.

"Phillips Divests Again," *Chemical Week,* November 10, 1982, p. 19.

"Phillips Petroleum Maps Deal for Milk Container Concern," *New York Times,* July 7, 1964.

"Pinch Can Stimulate Bottom Line," *Food Processing,* August 1995, p. 82.

"Rounding Out the Business," *Dairy Foods,* December 1993, p. 60.

"Sealright," *Fortune,* March 12, 1990, p. 90.

"Sealright Announces Australian Manufacturing Plant," *Business Wire,* May 4, 1994.

"Sealright Announces Companywide Restructuring Designed to Strengthen Customer Relationships, Improve Competitiveness, Cut Costs," *Business Wire,* December 14, 1995.

"Sealright Co., Inc.," *Barron's,* January 27, 1992, p. 56.

"Sealright Co., Inc.: Registers Common for Initial Public Offering," *Standard & Poor's News,* February 21, 1986.

"Sealright Co.: It Scooped Out a Niche Packaging Ice Cream," *Barron's,* April 18, 1988.

"Sealright Co.: Package Maker Diversifies to Leave Little to Chance," *Barron's,* January 21, 1991, p. 50.

"Sealright Sales Up, Earnings Down for First Quarter; Company also Announces Reduction in Force," *Business Wire,* April 18, 1994.

"Sealright Shareholders Approve Sale of Firm to Phillips Petroleum," *Wall Street Journal,* September 30, 1964, p. 19.

"Suppliers for McDonald's Award $500,000 Contract," *Wall Street Journal,* May 6, 1996.

The Sealright Story, Overland Park, Kan.: Sealright Co., Inc., 1995.

Vanac, Mary, "Kansas' Sealright Consolidation Puts Ohio's Jaite Packaging at Risk," *Akron Beacon Journal,* December 15, 1995.

—Paul S. Bodine

Security Capital Corporation

184 West Wisconsin Avenue
P. O. Box 3097
Milwaukee, Wisconsin 53201-3097
U.S.A.
(414) 273-8090
Fax: (414) 277-6406

Public Company
Incorporated: 1993
Total Assets: $3.44 billion (1996)
Employees: 1,094
Stock Exchanges: NASDAQ
SICs: 6712 Bank Holding Companies; 6036 Savings
   Institutions, Not Federally Chartered

Security Capital Corporation is a bank holding company formed in 1993 to enable its subsidiary, Security Bank S.S.B., a state-chartered service bank, to convert itself from a mutual savings bank to a public stock corporation. In 1993 Security Bank was the second-largest thrift institution in the state of Wisconsin and the largest in the city of Milwaukee. Nationally, it ranked 13th among all U.S. state-chartered savings institutions in 1995, and its holding company, Security Capital Corporation, ranked 177th among all U.S. bank holding companies. In addition to making home mortgage and home equity loans to the consumer market, in the mid-1990s Security engaged in a wide range of financial activities, including originating commercial loans, investing in mortgage-backed securities, and offering commercial leasing, insurance, and investment services. In 1996, Security Bank maintained 42 branch offices, ten lending offices, and five subsidiaries in six midwestern states.

Community Thrift: 1913–1965

A year before the outbreak of World War I in 1914, a German-descended entrepreneur named Theodore Mueller founded the Security Loan and Building Association in a one-room storefront in Milwaukee, Wisconsin, and began translating customers' deposits into loans for the growing Milwaukee homebuilding market. To enhance Security's budding image as a safe and reliable thrift, in 1915 Mueller adopted the lion emblem (the "picture of strength") that would remain the bank's corporate symbol of financial invulnerability for the next eight decades. Before Security's first decade was out, however, the U.S. banking industry had become embroiled in the most disastrous period of its history: 5,700 U.S. banks alone closed between 1921 and 1929, and the stock market crash of 1929 inaugurated another prolonged string of failures. Due in part perhaps to the reputation for hard work and pay-your-debt financial responsibility attributed to Milwaukee residents, Mueller's savings and loan (S&L) remained solvent until the onset of the Great Depression forced Congress to radically rewrite the rules of American banking.

While the Depression was beginning to force a new epidemic of bank closures—including several hundred S&Ls—Congress passed the Banking Act of 1933, which sought to eliminate banks' imprudent mixing of their traditional deposit-taking and loan-making functions with more speculative ventures. More importantly for savings and loans like Security, the act also created the Federal Home Loan Bank System (FHLB), which amounted to a kind of Federal Reserve system for S&Ls: federally chartered S&Ls could now receive government-guaranteed insurance for withdrawals, seasonal shifts in business, expansion, and special circumstances. Moreover, for the price of a premium, state-chartered S&Ls like Security could now also conduct business with the full backing of the federal treasury through the new Federal Savings and Loan Insurance Corporation (FSLIC).

Buoyed by the new federal guarantees, Security weathered the 1930s and officially rechristened itself Security Savings and Loan Association in 1940. Reflecting a concern for civic involvement that would characterize the bank through much of its history, in 1944 Security invested $2 million in U.S. government securities. The sizable investment not only helped the federal government finance the war effort but enabled Security to enter the postwar era flush with valuable liquidity. In 1948 the federal government again transformed the topography of the S&L industry by creating the Federal National Mortgage Association (or "Fannie Mae" as it came to be called) to buy Federal

Company Perspectives:

Security Capital Corporation has a tradition of strength and performance, achieved by focusing on a vision of profitable growth without sacrificing basic values or sound financial principles. Our Corporate Objectives: maintain the trust and loyalty of our shareholders and customers by continuing to follow our traditional standards of financial integrity; grow profitably through expansion of product lines and through prudent acquisition of quality institutions that share Security's vision and values; provide a full range of basic, progressive, competitive and superior quality financial services; maintain a dedication to exceptional customer service; recruit, develop, motivate and retain employees of exceptional ability, character, diversity and dedication; fulfill our responsibilities to local communities, the State and the Nation by performing in a manner which contributes to economic and social progress.

Housing Authority (FHA) and Veterans Administration (VA) home mortgage loans from financial institutions. By thus interjecting itself into the lender-borrower market for home loans, Fannie Mae created a so-called secondary market for home mortgages, which—much like stocks and bonds—would now have a tradeable, independent value in the financial marketplace. This, along with other federal incentives to stimulate home loans to returning GIs, led to a housing boom in the late 1940s and 1950s that solidified Security's already thriving niche in the Milwaukee mortgage lending industry.

In addition to continued steady growth both in customers and assets, the 1950s and early 1960s were watershed years for Security for two other reasons: in 1951 it moved to the office on Milwaukee's near south side that would remain its trademark headquarters until the early 1970s, and between 1957 and 1961 it elected the two directors—William G. Schuett Sr. and Joseph F. Schoendorf Jr.—who would play the most central roles in Security's coming boom years. The "go-go" growth that characterized the 1960s in Wall Street's financial markets was about to engulf Security Savings and Loan and transform a distinctly local S&L into a regional banking leader.

Wisconsin S&L: 1965–90

When William Schuett was elected Security's president and CEO in 1965 he inherited a Wisconsin S&L climate that was suddenly brand new. A bill signed by Governor Warren Knowles in the fall permitted state-chartered S&Ls to set up or acquire branch offices if they could demonstrate that the new location was needed and not presently serviced by a competitor. Security—now operating with nearly $120 million in assets—promptly requested approval from the state S&L commission to establish a branch office on Milwaukee's northwest side. Within weeks of the commission's OK, it got the green light to acquire Aetna Savings and Loan, a small, $100,000-in-assets lender based in Milwaukee's critical downtown business district. By the end of fiscal year 1966, Security's assets stood at $131.2

million, and it was perched on an industrywide catapult that would see U.S. S&L assets triple between 1965 and 1975.

In 1967 Security continued its campaign of expansion that by 1996 would number thirteen acquisitions. With the purchase of Sherman Savings and Loan and Atlas Savings and Loan, both of Milwaukee, Security now claimed five branches, and by the end of the fiscal year its assets had grown by a third to $174.4 million, net savings had climbed to almost $39 million, and reserves stood at a comfortable $3.5 million. Virtually overnight Security had become the second-largest S&L in the state. In 1968 Security benefited from two government moves—one federal, the other state—to bolster the home mortgage industry. Fannie Mae became a private organization to enhance its effectiveness in the home mortgage secondary market, and the Government National Mortgage Association (or "Ginnie Mae") was created to absorb some of the subsidy functions for FHA loans previously handled by Fannie Mae. Meanwhile, the Wisconsin supreme court ruled that state S&Ls could now open branches throughout the state, freeing them from the traditional maximum radius of one hundred miles from their main office. In 1968, Security closed 1,436 mortgages valued at $31.3 million and executed more single-family home mortgages than any other S&L in the state. A new branch was opened, assets grew to almost $183 million, and Security was soon claiming that of its 11,000 mortgages only 27 were delinquent.

Security formed its first subsidiary in 1968 when Schuett unveiled the Security Real Estate and Management Corporation, which was charged with managing and liquidating real estate properties acquired by Security through foreclosure. The move reflected Schuett's eagerness to exploit another new loophole in the traditionally straitjacketing regulations governing the S&L industry: Security could now begin to vertically integrate itself into the full range of S&L-related activities, pumping additional assets into its bottom line. In an interview with the Milwaukee *Sentinel* Schuett credited the thrift's growth in part to new marketing and market research techniques but primarily to a "young, highly trained, intelligent and efficient" management team bent on capitalizing on Wisconsin's new liberalized banking environment.

Security broke the $200 million threshold in assets in 1969, closed 1,613 loans (89 percent of which were mortgage loans), and in early 1970 acquired Surety Savings and Loan of Wisconsin, thereby raising Security's net assets to $234 million and giving it seven locations in the Milwaukee area. By the end of 1970, Schuett's team had closed a record 1,823 home loans, added another outlying branch, and completed a $1 million facelift of its downtown Milwaukee office. *American Banker* was now rating Security the fourth fastest-growing S&L in the country and the 89th largest of the nation's top one hundred S&Ls. In 1971 Security definitively broke out of its metropolitan boundaries, exploiting the 1968 state supreme court decision by opening a branch office in Madison, the state capital. Moreover, in Milwaukee's banking community Schuett was establishing a reputation as an aggressive, forward-thinking executive now known respectfully by some as Security's "Baron von Schuett."

Federal efforts to ensure a stable, expanding home-lending market had led to the Emergency Home Finance Act of 1970, which authorized the Home Loan Bank System to use federal subsidies to reduce the interest rates on home mortgages. More importantly, the act created regulations that would extend the secondary market for FHA and VA home mortgages into the conventional home mortgage market. To offset the government's growing influence, Schuett began promoting private mortgage guarantee insurance, and in 1971 Security announced an agreement with Milwaukee's Mortgage Guarantee Insurance Corporation (MGIC) to attract more capital to the home mortgage market by offering guaranteed 100 percent payment for any delinquent Security mortgage loan insured by MGIC. Schuett announced that "what we are beginning here is a true private secondary market for conventional mortgages." Besides attracting more customers for now more secure home loans, private home mortgage insurance offered S&Ls a new way to build assets: defaulted mortgages now had a guaranteed market value and in the form of mortgage-backed securities could be traded like stocks in the financial markets.

S&Ls were finally emerging as major thrift organizations in the Milwaukee area, and by the end of fiscal year 1971, Security alone boasted assets of nearly $300 million with nearly three thousand executed mortgages (almost all for single-family homes) and could further claim it had not lost a dollar on loans since 1965. Throughout the 1970s, Security continued to build up its assets, diversify its loan products, and expand to new markets through acquisition. Meanwhile, some states were beginning to allow S&Ls to offer adjustable rate mortgages to help them weather periods of rising interest that eroded the profitability of fixed rate mortgages, and, in another break with the past, the Housing and Community Development Act of 1974 significantly loosened the regulations on the kinds and amounts of loans S&Ls could make. In 1975 Security created Security Investment Resources Inc., a subsidiary formed to offer annuities, mutual funds, and insurance-related products to an increasingly nontraditional S&L market. By 1976, Security had merged with Community Savings and Loan of Wauwatosa, Wisconsin, and Franklin Savings and Loan of Wausau and surpassed the $500 million mark in assets.

Bad loans, high interest rates, and the weak economy of the late 1970s had left many U.S. S&Ls with long-term, fixed-rate mortgages that yielded little interest and ate away at the industry's profitability. With two watershed federal banking laws—the Depository Institutions Deregulation and Monetary Control Act of 1980 and the Garn-St. Germain Depository Institutions Act of 1982—Congress hoped to resuscitate the S&L industry by allowing it to diversify into new activities. The upper limits of the rates thrifts could pay for deposits were eliminated, and S&Ls could now offer nonresidential real estate, commercial, and personal property loans as well as adjustable rate mortgages. But the liberalized environment also encouraged unscrupulous operators to freely enter the S&L business, acutely aware that any losses they accumulated on risky loans were fully guaranteed by federal funds. By 1989 one in six U.S. S&Ls was bankrupt, and in August 1989 Congress passed a $50 billion S&L bailout that forced hundreds of failing S&Ls to go under or find buyers while restoring the S&L industry's traditional emphasis on mortgage lending. In addition, a new Savings Association Insurance Fund (SAIF) was created to replace the bankrupt FSLIC.

On the strength of its management and enormous assets ($1 billion by 1980), Security weathered the industry shakeout and continued its geographical and vertical expansion. It merged with Wisconsin S&Ls in Cudahy, Antigo, Oconomowoc, West Allis, Green Bay, and Rhinelander and formed five subsidiaries: Security Financial and Leasing Services, Inc. (to lease office equipment, trucks, railroad cars, and other property to midwestern corporations), Security Financial and Mortgage Corporation (to offer mortgage banking services), Security Insurance and Financial Services, Inc. (a full-service insurance agency), Security Commercial Credit Corporation (a commercial loan originator), and Wisconsin Real Estate Asset Management, Inc. (a corporation to develop an office and distribution plant for Security in Milwaukee). In 1986 and 1987, the Federal Home Loan Bank-Chicago formally requested that Security assume the management of two distressed midwestern thrifts, which it did, and while the national S&L industry as a whole was struggling through years of consolidation and instability, Security posted a decade of consecutive profits (1983 to 1993).

Regional Bank: 1990–1996

In 1990, Security Savings and Loan officially changed its name to Security Bank S.S.B. (state-chartered service bank) and within two years had completed its transformation from a state-chartered mutual S&L to a state-chartered savings bank. The move allowed it to escape the jurisdiction of the Federal Office of Thrift Supervision (saving $300,000 annually in fees in the process). More importantly, however, it anticipated a decision in late 1992 by the Wisconsin commissioner of S&Ls to allow S&Ls and savings banks to create bank holding companies, which would in turn allow the depositors of the old mutual S&Ls to become shareholders in a public stock company formed as a subsidiary of the newly created holding company. While a mutual thrift's depositors are in fact its owners, once they become shareholders they traditionally show more active interest in the thrift's management because they now own a share in the company's growth. Moreover, an initial public offering (IPO) generates huge inflows of cash and because mutual thrifts are allowed to set the initial share price well below the market price both the depositors and management gain a significant windfall when the stock becomes publicly traded. The resulting increase in financial strength and the ability of the new corporation to offer stock rather than taxliable cash to companies it wishes to acquire would make much more realistic Security's vision of further expansion through mergers.

In 1993 Security formed the Security Capital Corporation as the holding company to execute its conversion from a mutual thrift to a public company. Depositors approved the conversion in December, and at the IPO depositors and bank employees were offered $270 million worth of shares with special stock reservations and awards to Security's top executives. In January 1994 Security began trading on the NASDAQ stock exchange. The IPO was quickly greeted by protests from critics who argued that Security's generous provisions of stock to Security's management (the top five executives received a total of $7.9 million in free stock) were "indecent" and disproportionate to the remuneration packages of top executives at other Wisconsin banks. Security's management countered that because Security had been a mutual thrift for so long its management had missed out on the financial rewards of stock ownership and awarding large blocks of stock to executives only redressed a long-standing inequity. In 1996, Security also settled, for $12 million, a class action suit brought by depositors who claimed that Security's reservation of large blocks of stock to "insiders" prevented them from buying all the stock they wanted.

Security's predictions of the renewed growth made possible by the stock conversion seemed to be borne out as early as 1995 when it reported that its net income had risen to $20.3 million, $2.1 million higher than the year before. As the bank settled into its new structure, it continued to overhaul and fine-tune its business. A new retail banking division was formed in 1994 to link its 42 branch offices into a network of full-service financial service centers offering everything from traditional home and home equity loans to commercial, real estate, and educational loans as well as investment services and life insurance. With the traditional distinctions between commercial, credit card companies, credit unions, savings banks, and S&Ls fast dissolving, competition grew fiercer, and in 1995 Security added four lending offices; opened an industrial loan and thrift subsidiary in Minnesota; closed its Security Financial and Mortgage Corporation subsidiary; and combined its Security Commercial Credit Corporation and Security Real Estate and Management Corporation subsidiaries into their parent, Security Bank. It also moved swiftly to embrace the new technology transforming the banking industry: a new consumer lending software system allowed statistical modeling and database marketing techniques to build a precise profile of potentially profitable customers, a 24-hour home equity loan banking phone service enabled Security to service customers in regions where it had no offices, and a "data warehouse and management central information system" linked the laptop computers of loan agents in the field with terminals in branch offices.

Halfway through CEO Schuett's first year as newly named chairman of the board, Security was claiming its most successful year ever, with total assets for fiscal year 1996 of $3.44

billion, a newly announced fourth stock repurchase program, and a new corporate slogan, "Your Lifetime Bank," that declared Security's intent to leave its days as a single-market, home loan S&L far behind.

Principal Subsidiaries

Security Bank, S.S.B., Security Investment Resources, Inc., Security Financial and Leasing Services, Inc., Security Insurance and Financial Services, Inc., Security Mortgage and Financial Services, Inc., Security Financial and Mortgage Corporation.

Further Reading

Bronstein, Barbara, "Security Capital Settles Suit over Conversion for $12 Million," *American Banker,* March 19, 1996, p. 14.
Curran, John, "Does Deregulation Make Sense?," *Fortune,* June 5, 1989, p. 181.
Doherty, Chuck, "Security Bank Plans Public Stock Sale," *Milwaukee Sentinel,* July 3, 1993.
Gallagher, Kathleen, "Bill Targets 'Indecent' Thrift Stock Profits," *Milwaukee Sentinel,* January 7, 1994.
Meigs, J. C., "What's Wrong with Our Banking System?" *Consumers' Research Magazine,* March 1, 1991.
Norman, Jack, "S&L Deals Yield Windfall Profits for Executives," *Milwaukee Journal,* December 12, 1993, pp. 1–2.
——, "Security Bank's Depositors Approve Conversion," *Milwaukee Journal,* December 19, 1993.
——, "Security to Reap $270 Million in IPO," *Milwaukee Journal,* September 28, 1993, pp. 6–7.
——, "3 Wisconsin Savings and Loans to Convert to Savings-Bank Status," *Milwaukee Journal,* October 15, 1992.
Spivak, Cary, "Going Public Pays Off for Execs," *Milwaukee Journal-Sentinel,* p. 1.
"2 More S&Ls Apply to Switch to Savings Bank Charters," *Milwaukee Journal,* July 22, 1992.
Williamson, Tammy, "Post-Conversion, Thrifts Are Still Seeking Acquisitions," *Business Journal Serving Greater Milwaukee,* January 1, 1995, p. 8.
——, "Area Bankers Looking to Avoid Becoming 'Dinosaurs'," *Business Journal Serving Greater Milwaukee,* January 1, 1996, p. 14,

—Paul S. Bodine

SEIKO CORPORATION
Seiko Corporation

6-21, Kyobashi 2-chome
Chuo-ku
Tokyo 104
Japan
(03) 3563-2111
Fax: (03) 3563-8496
Internet: http://www.seiko-corp.co.jp/

Public Company
Incorporated: 1881 as K. Hattori & Co., Ltd.
Employees: 1,182
Sales: ¥342.01 billion (US $3.22 billion)
Stock Exchanges: Tokyo
SICs: 3873 Watches, Clocks, & Clockwork Operated
  Devices & Parts; 5094 Jewelry, Watches, Precious
  Stones & Precious Metals, Wholesale

Seiko Corporation is the nucleus of the Seiko group. It is one of the world's largest clock and watch manufacturers. In the 1996 fiscal year, Seiko produced about 209 million watches and 25 million clocks. Seiko Corporation, formerly Hattori Seiko, is the only public company of the group. Its function is to market watches, clocks, jewelry, eyeglasses, and other products made by the manufacturing components of the group: Seiko Instruments Inc. and Seiko Epson Corporation. The watches of the Seiko Corporation are marketed with a multibrand strategy that includes Seiko, Lassale, Jean Lassale, Pulsar, Lorus, and Alba. From the jeweled Jean Lassale styles to the models that incorporate pagers or miniature televisions or computers, they are intended to serve a wide variety of needs.

Late 19th and Early 20th Centuries

In 1881, in Uneme-cho, Kyobashi, part of Tokyo's Ginza district, Kintaro Hattori, a jeweler, established K. Hattori & Co., Ltd. Although 21 years old, Hattori was already an eight-year veteran of the business world. According to the company typescript, "A Brief History of Hattori Seiko Co. Ltd.," it was enough experience to lead him to observe, "On a rainy day, every retail shop will have less customers. However, jewelers can make good use of these slack days by repairing timepieces and thus not waste precious time."

Near the end of the 19th century, increasing railroad traffic produced growing demand for accurate timepieces. In 1884 the adoption of the worldwide 24-hour time zone system, with its reference meridian at Greenwich near London, produced a standardization of time that further increased that demand. In 1892 Hattori established the Seikosha clock manufacturing plant in Ishiwara-cho, Tokyo. Initially employing ten workers, the firm made primarily wall clocks, which, at that time, was the most popular type of timepiece. In October 1893 the plant was moved to its present site in Taihei-cho, Tokyo. Two years later, the main office was moved to new facilities at Ginza that included a clock tower that stood more than 50 feet high. As tall buildings were a rare sight in Tokyo at the time, the tower garnered much attention.

The firm added pocket watches to its product line in 1895. Alarm clocks were added in 1899 and table clocks in 1902. As the market expanded, the company began exporting clocks to China, and by 1912 China received 70 percent of Japan's total export of timepieces. In 1913, Hattori opened its first overseas branch, in Shanghai.

To satisfy in part the growing demand for pocket watches Hattori introduced its first line of wristwatches, which were sold under the Laurel brand name. The wristwatch gained in popularity worldwide and, by the end of the World War I, had replaced the pocket watch as the standard portable timepiece.

In 1917, K. Hattori & Co., Ltd. became a public company. In September 1923, an earthquake hit Tokyo, destroying the Seikosha plant. Hattori tried to compensate hundreds of customers, who had lost a total of 1,500 timepieces left for repair, with replacement clocks and watches. In 1924, annual production was less than ten percent of the 1922 output. In 1924, also, the Seikosha plant introduced the first Seiko brand wristwatch.

In 1927, Kintaro Hattori, at age 69, was honored as the imperial nominee to the House of Peers. Also at this time,

Company Perspectives:

The history of Seiko's timekeeping technology is the history of quartz—our pioneering quartz technology changed the very nature of the timepiece industry. Today, we market a range of quality watches, clocks, and consumer products through an international network of subsidiaries and affiliates, making the Seiko name synonymous with added value and technological innovation throughout the world.

Hattori launched its first ladies' wristwatch, the smallest ever produced in Japan.

Using the microengineering expertise acquired in its clock and watch production, the Seikosha plant began producing camera shutters in 1930. Eventually, Hattori became one of the world's largest suppliers of camera products, although its brand names do not appear on the products.

Marketing Other Companies' Products in the 1930s

In 1934, Kintaro Hattori died, and his eldest son, Genzo Hattori, became president. Genzo Hattori chose to satisfy market needs by adopting a unique corporate structure. It allowed private plants to develop products to be marketed by K. Hattori. In 1936 K. Hattori & Co., Ltd. marketed a total of 2.06 million clocks and watches, the highest figure since the opening of the Seikosha plant; Japan's total watch and clock production came to 3.54 million. In 1939 the company started marketing Braille pocket watches.

As Japan entered World War II, K. Hattori's normal marketing activities were hindered, as reflected in the Seiko group's 1945 production figures. Only 6,260 clocks and 13,318 watches were produced by K. Hattori's affiliates for marketing by K. Hattori. Production was slowed in part because members of the Seiko group, like many other Japanese companies, were ordered to produce military items, such as time fuses and ammunition.

By 1953, however, K. Hattori & Co., Ltd. had recovered to its prewar sales level. In that year, the company purchased a total of 2.46 million watches and clocks from group plants, representing 54.3 percent of Japan's total production, and exported 101,000 watches and clocks. By the late 1950s, the firm's watches were gaining international attention, and Hattori had begun marketing watches in the United States and other countries. The company marketed its first self-winding wristwatch in 1955. Utilizing conveyor-belt production technology, by 1959, production of watches reached three million per year.

Expanding Overseas in the 1960s

In 1964, Chairman Genzo Hattori died. Shoji Hattori, president since 1946, recognized the need for the company to strengthen its global marketing after a visit to Europe in 1962, during which he was asked if there was a watch industry in Japan. Seiko, with the reputation earned by its quartz clock, became the official timer of the Olympic Games in Tokyo, an honor previously held by the Swiss. The company supplied the

games with 1,278 stopwatches, made up of 36 different styles plus the world's first portable quartz chronometers. The sponsorship of various events, including tennis, golf, soccer, track, and other sports, resulted in increased international recognition. Its quartz technology allowed production of a full range of precision timing equipment, designed to meet the needs of sports competitions under varied conditions. This expertise has since helped the firm to become the sponsor or official timer of more than 150 international sports events annually.

Like other Japanese companies, K. Hattori employed a global marketing strategy and looked to overseas expansion. With advertising of new styles and substantially lower prices, it successfully challenged the Swiss in Asian markets, in Hong Kong, Bangkok, and Singapore. Hattori (Hong Kong) Ltd., a new subsidiary, was established in 1968. Marketing was then directed to Britain, West Germany, France, Spain, Italy, and Greece. In the mid-1960s the United States, initially a difficult market for the Japanese to penetrate, presented an additional challenge. Rather than competing with cheap American brands or with high-priced Swiss watches, K. Hattori entered the mid-range of the market, offering jewel-lever watches with an average price tag of $50.

In 1969 K. Hattori began marketing the world's first quartz watch, under the Seiko name. The watch resulted from a "technology contest" between Suwa Seikosha and Daina Seikosha, two K. Hattori affiliates. The new watch, Seiko Astron 35SQ, was encased in 18-karat gold and featured an accuracy within five seconds per month. Developed and manufactured at the Suwa Seikosha plant, it was launched to the Japanese market with a retail price of ¥450.000.

Seiko Brand Soars in Popularity in the 1970s

By the early 1970s, a few years after the introduction of the world's first quartz wristwatch, the Seiko brand soared in popularity, and Seiko adopted the slogan, "Someday all watches will be made this way." About that same time, the company scored a publicity coup when it once again served as official timer of an Olympics, this time the 1972 winter games in Sapporo. Also in 1972, Hattori marketed the world's first ladies' quartz watch, also made at Suwa Seikosha. A year later, it introduced the first Seiko liquid-crystal display (LCD) digital quartz watch. Also manufactured at Suwa Seikosha, the product included built-in illumination and six-digit numerical readout that displayed the time in hours, minutes, and seconds.

In 1970, the firm established Seiko Service Centre (Australia) Pty. Ltd. and Seiko Time Corporation in the United States, the latter adding a Canadian office in the following year. In 1971, the firm expanded into the United Kingdom with Seiko Time (U.K.) Ltd. Seiko Time GmbH was established in West Germany in 1972. Global expansion of the sales effort continued with the opening of Seiko Time Ltda., Brazil, in 1974; Seiko Time (Panama) S.A. in 1977; Seiko Time S.A., Switzerland, in 1978; Seiko Time AB, Sweden, in 1979; and Hattori Overseas (Hong Kong) Ltd. in 1979.

In 1975 the company introduced its plastic ophthalmic lenses. Initially, in 1977, the lenses were exported to a U.S. supplier but since 1986 have been marketed in the United States under the Seiko name. Also in 1975, the firm began marketing digital quartz chronographs.

In 1974, Shoji Hattori died, and Kentaro Hattori, Shoji's nephew and Genzo's oldest son, took over as president. The year 1977 saw record earnings and new products for Hattori Seiko, many of which appeared under brand names other than Seiko. The firm developed Lorus clocks for the export market in 1977. The clock line, which included a pendulum wall clock, a battery transistor wall clock, and alarm clocks, was first sold to countries in Southeast Asia. In the same year, the firm began marketing the digital quartz calculator, a digital quartz world timer, digital quartz alarm chronograph, quartz watches with 100-meter-depth water resistance, and quartz watches with five-year batteries.

In 1978, Seiko introduced twin quartz watches, with two crystals, which offered accuracy within five seconds per year, and quartz divers' watches with 600-meter-depth water resistance, followed in 1979 by the ultra-thin quartz watch with 0.9 millimeter movement, along with the analog alarm quartz watch. In addition, K. Hattori introduced the Alba brand in Japan, which included digital quartz, and began exporting the Alba analog and digital quartz to Southeast Asia. On the other side of the globe, it began marketing the Pulsar brand watches in the United States. The United States also saw the first Lorus quartz watches in 1983.

Difficult Times in the 1980s

Despite the busy production years of the 1970s, success came to a sudden halt in the 1980s. During the decade's first few years, profits were far less than those of the late 1970s. "In a boom that has sent prices of many high-technology companies to record levels, Hattori's shares have fallen to the mid-700-yen range (about US $3.50), barely half their top price in 1978," reported *Business Week,* June 15, 1981.

The firm acquired Jean Lassale, a Swiss subsidiary, and developed a product that combined Seiko's quartz movements with a very thin Swiss-style case. By seeking higher profit margins from luxury products, the company expected to make up for declining profit margins on its less expensive products. The Jean Lassale purchase was part of a pricing strategy to offer a more expensive line to complement lower- and medium-priced watches and appeal to a wider range of customers.

As the yen began to rise in the mid-1980s, competition tightened and the company faced difficult times. New competitors entered watchmaking, from fashion designers to companies who bought watch parts from other watchmakers. With marketing and manufacturing handled by separate companies, trying to compete was difficult.

In 1983, the company changed its name from K. Hattori & Co. Ltd. to Hattori Seiko Co., Ltd., partly to further promote the Seiko name. Watches that featured a black-and-white liquid crystal display TV screen entered the market in 1982. The intention, according to Ichiro Hattori, was not to fill a niche for a frivolous product but to promote the company's name and image. The success of the Seiko TV watches proved that some people liked their watches to do more than tell time. Consequently, in 1984, Hattori Seiko introduced the world's first

computer wristwatches, manufactured at Seiko Instruments & Electronics Company. At the same time, Hattori Seiko launched the world's first LCD battery-operated, pocket color television.

Reijiro Hattori, Kentaro's brother, became president of Hattori Seiko in 1983. Kentaro remained as chairman. Four years later, Reijiro stepped up to chairman when Kentaro died. Ichiro Hattori, president of Seiko affiliates Seiko Instruments Inc. and Seiko Epson Corporation, also died that year. Hattori Seiko then appointed for the first time a non-Hattori family person to the top. Shiro Yoshimura became president. In 1989 Hattori Seiko introduced a new subsidiary, Hattori (Thailand) Ltd. In an effort to prepare for a new global economy, the Seiko name was brought into heavy use throughout the world. In June 1990, the parent firm changed its name from Hattori Seiko Co., Ltd. to Seiko Corporation.

Posting Losses in the 1990s

Seiko continued to introduce innovative products in the 1990s. In 1990 the Seiko Scubamaster hit the market, incorporating a dive table into a computerized diver's watch. In the following year came the Seiko "Perpetual Calendar," the world's first quartz watch with a full automatic 1,100-year calendar. Also introduced in the early 1990s were the Seiko Kinetic series of battery-free quartz watches and the Seiko MessageWatch.

The Kinetic watches used wrist motion to power what Seiko called the world's smallest and most powerful microgenerator. Prices started at $495 retail. The MessageWatch was more than a decade in the making and was originated by a small San Francisco firm, AT&E Corp. When this company ran into financial difficulties in 1991, Seiko and Seiko Epson (both of which were already backers of AT&E) bought the start-up's assets for $19 million. Seiko then developed a new version of the watch, which it test-marketed in Los Angeles in 1994. The MessageWatch was a digital watch designed to receive messages through FM radio waves. The customer had to buy the watch for $80, plus sign on for additional services at monthly rates. The services included paging, weather reports, voice mail alerts, stock market prices, lottery numbers, ski conditions, and sports scores. Under development were enhanced offerings such as traffic information and vehicle navigation systems.

Seiko also kept its name in the international spotlight with frequent participation in major sporting events as official timer. Most significant of these were the 1992 Barcelona and 1994 Lillehammer Olympics. Although the company lost out in the bidding for the 1996 Atlanta games to rival SMH, maker of Swatch watches, Seiko was scheduled to return as official Olympic timer for the 1998 Nagano Olympics. Other major sporting events timed by Seiko during this period included the 1990 FIFA World Cup (of soccer) held in Italy; the 1990 and 1994 Commonwealth Games in New Zealand and Canada, respectively; and the 1994 Asian Games in Japan.

While the company garnered the above achievements, it was simultaneously hit extremely hard by the deep Japanese recession that started in late 1991 and by economic difficulties in its export markets, notably Europe. Sales stagnated early in the decade (¥422 billion in 1990, ¥428 billion in both 1991 and

1992) and then fell to a lower plateau (¥378 billion in 1993, ¥335 billion in 1994, ¥331 billion in 1995, and ¥342 billion in 1996). Profitability disappeared as Seiko posted five consecutive full-year net losses, culminating in a ¥11.15 billion loss in 1996. The losses stemmed in part from restructuring efforts and other adjustments made by Seiko's subsidiaries, which resulted in extraordinary losses, such as the ¥5.6 billion loss in 1996.

The most important restructuring move, and a possible harbinger of future restructurings, came in 1996 when Seiko and the affiliated Seikosha Co. Ltd. created a vertically integrated company, Seiko Clock Inc., that would manufacture and market Seiko clocks. At the same time, another vertically integrated subsidiary, Seiko Precision, Inc., was created to manufacture and market such products as camera shutters, printers, and system equipment, all previously made by Seikosha. As a result of these changes, Seikosha was dissolved. More important, Seiko would now be able to exercise greater control over all aspects of these business lines, a development of critical importance in such a difficult operating environment.

Through the difficult 1990s, Seiko had continued its history of innovation; there was no reason to believe the future would be any different. The company could look forward to more prosperous times ahead as economies recovered from their downturns and people once again clamored for the unique products Seiko offered. And the 1998 Nagano Olympics would certainly provide an ideal platform for Seiko to reestablish its preeminent position in the timekeeping industry.

Principal Subsidiaries

Seiko Clock Inc.; Seiko Precision, Inc.; Seiko Sales (Japan) Inc.; Seiko Australia Pty. Ltd.; Seiko Belgium S.A.; Seiko do Brasil Ltda. (Brazil); Seiko Canada Inc.; Seiko France S.A.; Seiko Deutschland GmbH (Germany); Seiko Optical Europe GmbH (Germany); Seiko Hong Kong Ltd.; Hattori Overseas Hong Kong Ltd.; Seiko Nederland B.V. (Netherlands); Atlantic Time, S.A. (Panama); Seiko Sweden AB; Jean Lassale S.A. (Switzerland); Hattori Overseas Taiwan Co., Ltd.; Ho Chien Trading Co., Ltd. (Taiwan); Muang Thong Seiko Ltd. (Thailand); Seiko Europe Limited (U.K.); Seiko U.K. Limited; Seiko Corporation of America (U.S.A.); Seiko Optical Products, Inc. (U.S.A.).

Further Reading

Armstrong, Larry, "It's 10 PM. Do You Know What Your Bank Balance Is?," *Business Week*, December 26, 1994.

Boyer, Edward, "A Family Rift Roils Seiko," *Fortune*, November 12, 1984.

Minard, Lawrence, and Willoughby, Jack, "Japan's Dark Horse Computer Company," *Forbes*, October 22, 1984.

Shuster, William George, "Seiko Corp. Sets Record with 'Olympic' Campaign," *Jewelers Circular Keystone*, November 1991, p. 112.

——, "Seiko Works To Improve Image, Gain Market Share," *Jewelers Circular Keystone*, February 1991, p. 170.

—Kim M. Magon
—updated by David E. Salamie

Seneca Foods Corporation

1162 Pittsford-Victor Road
Pittsford, New York 14534
U.S.A.
(716) 385-9500
Fax: (716) 385-4249

Public Company
Incorporated: 1949
Employees: 3,091
Sales: $290.1 million (1994)
Stock Exchanges: NASDAQ
SICs: 2033 Canned Fruits & Vegetables; 2037 Frozen
    Fruits & Vegetables; 4522 Air Transportation—
    Nonscheduled

A familiar name to consumers throughout the United States, Seneca Foods Corporation processes fruits and vegetables, marketing its canned, frozen, bottled, and packaged products under the "Seneca" brand name, as well as under several other brand names, including "Libby's," "Nature's Favorite," and "TreeSweet." During the mid-1990s, Seneca operated out of 25 manufacturing plants and warehouses stretching between Washington State and New York, where fruits and vegetables were processed and packaged and then sold to wholesale and retail grocery companies.

By the early 1970s, Seneca represented a sprawling corporate entity, with manufacturing and warehouse facilities spread across the country. In all, there were six independent operating divisions composing Seneca at the time, three of which were involved in the company's mainstay business—food processing—with another engaged in the transportation business, and the remaining two divisions devoted to businesses outside the food industry. The company was well-grounded in the food processing business, its market standing underpinned by modestly-sized, yet strongly positioned operations that processed and packaged sizeable quantities of fruit juices and concentrates, vegetables, and in lesser quantities, table wine. Scores of bushels of apples, grapes, and other fruits were processed, bottled, canned, and frozen by the company's three food divisions

each year, while its non-food divisions, comprising a trucking company, a textile company, and a paint company, provided diversified strength, giving Seneca a well-rounded foundation from which to grow.

The 1970s

As Seneca entered the 1970s, much of what constituted the company had recently been added to its operations. Though Seneca had been established in 1949, it would be two decades before the company began to take on the look of a diversified food processor, with many of the characteristics that described the company from the 1970s forward being adopted after the 20th anniversary year of the Seneca business. This was true not only for the company's non-food businesses, but also for the fruit and vegetable processing and storage facilities that predicated Seneca's existence. Beginning in the 1970s, Seneca added significantly to its business scope and magnitude through a series of acquisitions that bolstered its business and paved the way for the growth to come during the ensuing decades.

At the outset of the 1970s, The company's largest business unit was its Seneca division, which represented the original part of the company founded during the late 1940s. Producing more than three million cases of consumer products and generating more than $10 million in sales each year by the beginning of the decade, the Seneca division comprised two manufacturing plants, one in Dundee, New York and another in Westfield, New York, and two warehousing operations, one in Penn Yan, New York and another in Geneva, New York. At the Dundee manufacturing plant, the company formulated, packaged, and distributed an extensive line of frozen concentrated fruit juices and fruit drinks, bottled and canned juices, and a frozen non-dairy coffee creamer. All of the bulk grape juice and grape concentrates that were formulated into finished products at the Dundee plant were produced at Westfield, where Seneca operated a grape processing plant. Also included within the range of operations at Westfield was another use for the grapes processed by the company, a relatively new business area for Seneca, yet one that was expected to increase in importance as the decade unfolded. At Westfield, Seneca had entered the wind production business, marketing a line of dry, high-quality table wine sold under the Boordy Vineyards label.

The second-largest business unit after the Seneca division was the company's Marion division, one of the new additions to the company as the 1970s began. A contributor of nearly $10 million in annual sales to Seneca's revenue volume, the Marion division was the result of an acquisition completed in May 1970, when the company purchased the Marion Canning Company. With the acquisition of Marion Canning Company, Seneca gained two manufacturing plants, both of which were located in the company's home state of New York. Together, the plants in Marion and Williamson processed two million bushels of apples and 5,000 tons of string beans, as well as lesser quantities of rhubarb, plums, seckel pears, and crab apples. Among this roster of various fruits and vegetables, apples were by far the most important product in the Marion division's business, specifically the use of apples to make apple sauce. Through the Marion division, Seneca ranked as the third-largest producer of apple sauce in the United States, all of which was packed under the "Seneca" label, selling enough of the fruit compote to control eight percent of the national market. Though the division represented a new facet to Seneca's operations at the beginning of the decade, considerable resources were devoted to its development immediately following the acquisition of Marion Canning Company, when an expansion program was initiated that was expected to increase the division's volume 50 percent by 1973.

The third and smallest food processing division operating under the Seneca corporate umbrella was the Prosser division, which produced most of the same consumer products packed by the Seneca and Marion divisions, but, unlike the two larger divisions, was located across the country in Prosser, Washington. The Prosser plant, which produced 13,000 tons of grapes and 500,000 bushels of apples annually, had been constructed in 1964, then expanded in 1968 and 1970. The division drew its strength from its location in the heart of the Yakima Valley, the epicenter of grape and apple production in the United States. On average, Concord grape and apple yields per acre were three times the per acre yields recorded in other major producing areas in the country. Despite its prime location, the Prosser division had recorded several years of serious financial losses following the establishment of its processing plant in 1964, but by 1968 the division had begun to record success, demonstrating consistent profitability by the beginning of the 1970s, when it collected more than $4 million in sales annually.

Combined, Seneca's three food processing divisions—Seneca, Marion, and Prosser—generated $24 million in annual sales at the beginning of the 1970s, $10 million of which was derived from the sale of products marketed under the "Seneca" label. Of the $24 million in total volume, more than half—$13 million—was collected from sales to retail customers, while the balance was derived from sales to institutional and industrial customers. This aspect of Seneca's business only told part of the story, however, because the company relied on another important business segment to fuel its growth: Seneca's non-food companies.

1970 Acquisition of Rochester Group, Inc.

Of Seneca's non-food businesses, the smallest was the company's transportation division, a captive trucking firm that operated 15 tractor-trailer combinations to service Seneca's food divisions on the East Coast. Seneca's transportation division was its lone non-food business—an enterprise that allowed the company "to get another squeal out of the pig," as one Seneca executive noted—until the company completed another acquisition six months after purchasing Marion Canning Company. In November 1970, Seneca acquired Rochester Group, Inc., giving it its first genuine non-food processing businesses, since the company's trucking fleet was directly involved with the production of fruit and vegetable consumer products.

With the acquisition of Rochester Group, Inc., Seneca greatly increased its presence outside the food industry, gaining control of Tapetex Products and Lehman Brothers Corporation. The larger of the two new companies, Tapetex Products operated as a textile converting company, specializing in the production and sale of materials used as linings in men's apparel and used as exterior fabrics for men's and women's outwear garments. Each year the company handled between 30 and 35 million yards of material, enough to generate between $12 and $15 million annually and eclipse the revenue volume of Seneca's largest food processing division.

The other company obtained through the acquisition of Rochester Group, Inc. was Lehman Brothers Corporation, which generated $4 million in sales annually—a total roughly equal with the sales collected by the Prosser division—but earned a higher percentage of profit than any other Seneca division. From its manufacturing plant in Jersey City, New Jersey, Lehman Brothers Corporation produced a full line of interior and exterior paints, enamels, and varnishes, selling its products to more than 500 independent wholesale and retail outlets primarily under the Ox-Line label.

Such was the composition of Seneca's operations as the 1970s began, its scope expanded and diversified significantly through the May 1970 acquisition of Marion Canning Company, which spawned its second-largest business unit, the Marion division, and the November 1970 acquisition of Rochester Group, Inc., which marked the arrival of Tapetex Products, Lehman Brothers Corporation, and nearly $20 million in annual sales into the company fold. Though sweeping and definitive changes had occurred during a six-month period in 1970, a respite from the comprehensive additions executed during the first year of the decade was not taken by Seneca's management. In 1971, Seneca entered into a joint venture project known as Snake River Vineyards, investing enough money to become a one-third participant in the wine production venture. Under the terms of the deal, 1,700 acres of grapes, projected to start producing in 1973, were all under contract to Seneca, complementing the 200,000 gallon winery constructed in 1971 at Penn Yan where the bottling and distribution of "Boordy Vineyards" wine were being conducted.

1973 Acquisition of S. S. Pierce

On the heels of this joint venture agreement, Seneca completed an acquisition that at the very least equaled the importance of its Marion Canning Company and Rochester Group, Inc. acquisitions. In March 1973, Seneca acquired Boston, Massachusetts-based S. S. Pierce Company, a food and beverage producer with $50 million in annual sales. The acquisition immediately doubled Seneca's revenue volume, increasing the company's sales to $110 million, and gave it ownership over several sizeable and profitable companies. Included within the

S. S. Pierce acquisition was the company's Institutional Food Service division, which by itself generated $20 million in annual sales from the production of a broad line of dry grocery and frozen food products for restaurants, schools, hospitals, and caterers in New England. Another $10 million in annual sales were added to Seneca's volume through another S. S. Pierce business unit—its Wine and Spirits division—which bottled and distributed a complete line of hard liquors and low-priced domestic wines under the "S. S. Pierce" label.

Rounding out the collection of companies gained by Seneca through its acquisition of S. S. Pierce were State Line Potato Chip Company, Kennett Canning Company, and Lincoln Food, Inc. The smallest of these three companies was Kennett Canning Company, a $4.5 million-in-sales firm that grew and canned more than five million pounds of mushrooms annually under the "S.S. Pierce" label. Second-largest was S. S. Pierce's State Line Chip Company, which manufactured and sold retail size packages of potato chips, popcorn, corn chips, and other snack products. This company added another $5 million in annual sales to Seneca's revenue volume, contributing half of the $10 million generated by Lincoln Foods, Inc., a processor and distributor of a full line of "hot packed" bottled and canned fruit juices and fruit drinks sold under the "Lincoln" and "Bessey" labels.

The acquisition of S. S. Pierce marked a singular achievement in Seneca's history, enabling the company to broaden and entrench its market presence with the swipe of a pen. The significance of the acquisition had a pervasive effect on the then 24-year-old company, making its arrival known on all levels of Seneca's operations, including the name under which it operated. Four years after the acquisition, Seneca adopted the corporate title of its most integral acquisition, changing its name from Seneca Foods Corporation to S. S. Pierce Company, Inc. in December 1977.

Three days after the name change, the company sold its 33.3 percent interest in Snake River Vineyards, letting go of its involvement in the joint venture on the first day of 1978. Another important divestiture was completed in 1983, when S. S. Pierce sold Lehman Brothers Corporation, the paint business acquired in the 1970 acquisition of Rochester Group, Inc. The company continued to operate as S. S. Pierce Company, Inc. until resurrecting the original name of the company in November 1986, when S. S. Pierce Company, Inc. once again conducted business as Seneca Foods Corporation.

The 1990s

During the 1990s, Seneca continued to add to its juice processing capabilities through acquisitions, but the early years of the decade were also notable for the departure of one of the company's long-held, non-food businesses. In August 1993, ten years after Lehman Brothers Corporation had been sold, Seneca divested the other company obtained through the purchase of Rochester Group, Inc. in 1970, Tapetex Products. A contributor of 13 percent of Seneca's $257 million in total sales during its last year with the company, the Tapetex division was sold for $8.4 million, which facilitated a series of acquisitions that were completed during the ensuing months. In November 1993, the company purchased the Wapato, Washington, juice processing business belonging to Sanofi Bio-Industries for $3.3 million, then in December 1993, Seneca acquired certain assets, including manufacturing facilities located in Eau Claire, Wisconsin, owned by ERLY Juice, Inc. and WorldMark, Inc., producers of products marketed under the "TreeSweet" brand.

Less than year after obtaining the trademarks, inventory, and accounts receivable belonging to ERLY Juice and WorldMark, Seneca completed another acquisition, purchasing M. C. Snack, Inc., a snack food maker of apple chips, based in Yakima, Washington in August 1994. Four months later, in February 1995, Seneca made a pivotal move that represented the highlight of the year for the company and ranked as perhaps the single most important development during the first half of the 1990s. On February 10th, the company formed an alliance with Pillsbury and, for $86.1 million, obtained six vegetable processing plants and a 20-year agreement that named Seneca as the primary supplier of "Green Giant" canned and frozen vegetables. Under the terms of the agreement, Pillsbury would continue to be responsible for the sales, marketing, and customer services functions associated with the "Green Giant" brand, but Seneca would take over the vegetable processing and canning operations previously conducted by Pillsbury.

In a year that saw Seneca widen its lead as the number one marketer of frozen concentrated apple juice, the alliance with Pillsbury represented a definitive move, elevating the importance of vegetable processing in Seneca's business. In the years ahead, vegetables would play a substantial role in the company's future, providing a promising area of growth to complement Seneca's strong position in the fruit processing industry. As the company moved toward late 1990s and its 50th anniversary year, it did so as a leading market competitor, strengthened by the integral acquisitions it had completed during its first four decades of existence.

Principal Subsidiaries

SSP Company, Inc.; Marion Foods, Inc.; Seneca Foods-International, Ltd.

Further Reading

Halversen, Kirsten, "Seneca Joins Chiquita Frupac in Marketing Branded Apples," *Supermarket News,* September 13, 1993, p. 40.
"Seneca Foods Corporation," *Wall Street Transcript,* April 5, 1971, p. 23, 730.
"Seneca Foods Corporation," *Wall Street Transcript,* June 18, 1973, p. 33, 448.

—Jeffrey L. Covell

Shionogi & Co., Ltd.

1-8, Doshomachi 3-chome
Chuo-ku, Osaka 541
Japan
(81) 6 202-2161
Fax: (81) 6 229-9596

Public Company
Incorporated: 1919
Employees: 6,950
Sales: ¥359.5 trillion (US$3.4 billion) (1995)
Stock Exchanges: Tokyo Osaka Nagoya Fukuoka
    Sapporo
SICs: 2833 Medicinals and Botanicals; 2834
    Pharmaceutical Preparations; 2835 Diagnostic
    Substances; 2879 Agricultural Chemicals, Not
    Elsewhere Classified

Shionogi & Co., Ltd., ranks among Japan's leading developers, producers, and exporters of pharmaceuticals. From its inception in the late 1870s until World War II, Shionogi developed a reputation as an all-around manufacturer of over-the-counter drugs, pharmaceuticals, and other health-care-related products. But in the radically-changed postwar Japan, Shionogi began to acquire the state-of-the-art technology necessary to compete with overseas suppliers of the then-new "wonder drugs," primarily by licensing products from prominent American pharmaceutical manufacturers such as Eli Lilly and Merck.

Despite the sudden focus on antibiotics, however, the company did not stop developing and producing its broad lines of pharmaceutical products. While Shionogi has continued to invest in new technology and technical expertise in order to remain on the cutting edge of antibiotic development and production, the company has also continued to expand its facilities for the manufacture of other products and for laboratory research. Development of new products and services and improvement of production methods have been important parts of the company's operations since its early years.

Following a sharp downturn in the antibiotics market, Shionogi strove mightily to diversify into diagnostics, clinical testing services, veterinary products, and agricultural and industrial chemicals in the early 1990s. To that end, the drug manufacturer has established new research and development operations and boosted research staff. A new facility—the Institute for Medical Science—opened in 1988 and extended Shionogi's thrust into basic research. Its current emphasis is on exploring the cause of disease and linking those findings to the development of products to combat those causes. One especially exciting outcome of this program, guided by Shionogi President Yoshihiko Shiono, was an anti-AIDS drug which was expected to be in clinical trials until 2000. The company hoped that internal drug development would be productive enough to allow it to phase out its handling of other manufacturers' wares by 1996.

Late-19th-Century Origins

In 1878 Osaka was already a center of commercial activity, a logical place for a wholesaler of traditional Japanese and Chinese medicines and herbal remedies to open a business. Gisaburo Shiono began supplying local distributors with the herbal and folk remedies that had been in popular use in Japan and China for more than 1,000 years. Eventually he introduced something new: medicines and drugs manufactured in the United States and Europe. This development was a more radical step than simply importing pharmaceutical products for wholesale distribution. The decision required confidence on Shiono's part in his countrymen's willingness to accept a Western-style approach to the treatment of illness.

His confidence turned out to be well placed. In the quarter-century since their government's barriers to trade with those countries had been lifted, Japanese consumers' initial resistance to the infiltration of Western ways into their culture had waned. Some groups still tried to stem the tide of curiosity and interest in Occidental lifestyles and products, but consumers were ready for the Western nations' innovations, which also had the blessing of the newly restored imperial government.

The Shiono family business found a ready clientele in Osaka-area merchants. Within his first two decades of wholesaling both Oriental and Western-style medications, Gisaburo Shiono began to develop new products in-house. By the turn of the century, his reputation for quality and dependability had brought sufficient profits to the company to enable him to build his own research laboratory. Difficulties with transportation and supply lines cropped up as a result of the nation's brief wars with China and Russia, but Shionogi retained a hard-won reputation of quality and service. Early in the 20th century, the company added a new dimension to its wholesale medication business: drug manufacture.

The drug trade proved both profitable and brisk, and the company grew even faster than before. Not even Japan's entry into World War I slowed it down. On the contrary, the demand for pharmaceutical products increased as battlefields became impromptu testing grounds for improvised treatment of injuries under emergency conditions. That situation held true not only during both world wars, but also through far-ranging flu epidemics and disasters such as the Great Kanto Earthquake of 1923.

As Western-style medical practice spread throughout Japan, the company increasingly enhanced its reputation as a reliable supplier to hospitals and pharmacies. However, it was the discovery and development of antibiotics during World War II that was pivotal in Shionogi's business.

Post-World War II Foray into Antibiotics

Like many other Japanese companies whose premises and personnel were devastated during the country's defeat in World War II, Shionogi began working immediately to reorganize and restore its product lines and rekindle the interest of a civilian market for its goods and services. Unlike some companies, Shionogi had the advantage of consistent management. Shiono had looked ahead to groom successors from within the family circle to take over responsibility as needed. President Yoshihiko Shiono and Senior Managing Director Motozo Shionogi, both direct descendants of the founder, continued to guide the company into the mid-1990s.

After an unprecedented military defeat during World War II, Japan still had many businesses that had survived the war and were determined to thrive under peacetime occupation by the invading forces. Those business and industrial leaders encountered no opposition from the occupation authorities or the new government based on the revised constitution that took effect in 1948. Instead, they received help, encouragement, and guidance—the latter in the form of principles of efficient, far-sighted business practices such as those recorded in the writings of W. Edwards Deming. Those principles had been all but ignored when offered to already-prosperous Western businesses.

Shionogi's management decided to specialize in antibiotics at a time when worldwide attention was drawn to the dramatic role they had played in combating diseases formerly considered incurable and in reducing the incidence of fatal infection from battlefield injuries. With the resumption of Japanese self-governance in the early 1950s, Shionogi already had plans underway for expansion into worldwide markets. The company's research laboratories took their first steps toward the successful synthesis of a sulfanilamide at that time. Launched in 1958 under the name of Sinomin, Shionogi's first sulfa drug was popular from the start, encouraging the company to increase its focus on development of original products.

In addition to originating products, Shionogi also formed relationships with overseas manufacturers to handle their products for other Far Eastern markets as well as Japan. A notable example was the line of cephalosporin antibiotics developed by Eli Lilly.

Astute management, especially financial management, has helped keep the company profitable overall despite recurrent problems. Because of the elaborate bureaucracy that new products intended for public use in Japan must face, much time has been lost in introducing new products; this condition has been true since before the turn of the century. Changes in the system to shorten the waiting period were reportedly planned in 1990, but there were no plans to abolish the system altogether.

The Japanese national health system was the source of another set of roadblocks; it periodically lowered drug-reimbursement prices, thus limiting the profits Shionogi could make on sales made within the country. This policy provided strong motivation to further build up the company's international business. However, other factors such as fluctuations in the value of the yen and the effectiveness of competitors marketing campaigns also affected profits on overseas sales from time to time.

Licensure to market other manufacturers' products continued to be profitable overall. Examples include dilevalol, an antihypertensive, a long-acting sulphate preparation, and an ultrasound contrast imaging agent from Molecular Biosystems. Shionogi also handled Molecular Genetics's drugs for veterinary practice. In 1988 Schering-Plough began marketing a new oral antibiotic developed by Shionogi.

Renewed Emphasis on Basic Research Highlights 1980s

Shionogi emphasized expanding its internal operations in basic research as well as in development of new products and product applications rather than building up business by acquiring overseas companies or participating with them in joint ventures to any great extent in the 1980s. The company expanded geographically through the creation of wholly owned subsidiaries in several countries, including the United States, Germany, and Taiwan. This emphasis on company control enabled Shionogi to keep a close rein on the policies and procedures associated with its products and to safeguard the reputation it has long held for top-quality production and service.

Achievement through basic research has long been a major goal for Shionogi, which has also used its findings to develop a number of innovative products. In 1986, for example, Shionogi became the first of Japan's pharmaceutical companies to place biotechnology-based drugs on the market. Two years later, in order to expand its activities in antibiotics research and to examine the nature and causation of certain diseases, the company established a new laboratory and technical resource center, the Institute for Medical Science, in Osaka near its other laboratories. An eminent virologist headed the research teams exploring three basic areas: immunology and the causes of diseases such as cancer and viral ailments; cells, proteins, and genes; and instrumentation. About one-fourth of the company's employees were engaged in some aspect of research and development by the dawn of the new decade.

This new emphasis seemed to be bearing fruit in the late 1980s, as sales increased 22 percent from ¥177 billion in 1984 to ¥216.1 billion in 1989. Growth of net income during this period was just off the pace, at 18.9 percent. But as Shionogi and its president, Yoshihiko Shiono, soon realized, a pharmaceutical company's financial outlook hinges on the development of proprietary drugs and diagnostics.

Difficult Trading Environment In 1990s

Although Shionogi had worked hard to boost its research and development operations, top executives failed to recognize a distinct decline in demand for and prices of antibiotics, which had remained the company's primary product focus. Launched in 1989, the internally developed antibiotic Flumarin quickly soared to a top position among the world's antibiotics. Sales of Flumarin buffered the impact of the downturn in the antibiotics market on Shionogi but weren't enough to prevent revenues from flattening in the early years of the decade. Sales increased by less than 12 percent from 1990 to 1995, and perhaps more tellingly, net income declined from ¥11.8 billion in 1990 to ¥7.3 billion, recovering to ¥11.5 billion in 1995. Shionogi's stagnant finances meant that the company had less money to invest research and development, thereby reducing its potential for new products.

This is not to say that the drug company made no significant moves. In 1992, it acquired full ownership of Japan Elanco Company, Ltd. from former joint venture partner Eli Lilly and Co., including the latter company's multinational hard-gelatin capsule production. And in 1996, the company formed a joint venture with Bristol-Myers Squibb to bring a treatment for hypertension to market. In spite of its difficult financial posi-

tion, Shionogi has also made valiant attempts to expand its research focus from antibiotics to treatments for heart and neurological diseases, cancer, and viral diseases. Its most promising new development was a Human Immunodeficiency Virus (HIV) inhibitor along the lines of AZT. A new gene therapy laboratory focused on treatments for AIDS as well as cancer. It would be 1999 or later before the medical and fiscal efficacy of the drug would become known. Citing Shionogi's dearth of so-called "blockbuster" new drug developments and its scant penetration of global markets, analysts at Lehman Brothers and Merrill Lynch forecast that the company's sales would remain flat and its net income would actually decline through 1998.

Principal Subsidiaries

Taiwan Shionogi & Co., Ltd.; Shionogi U.S.A., Inc.; Shionogi & Co. GmbH (Germany); Shionogi Qualicaps, Inc. (United States); Shionogi Europe B.V. (Netherlands); Shionogi Qualicaps, S.A. (Spain).

Further Reading

100th Anniversary of Shionogi, Osaka: Shionogi Seiyaku Kabushiki Kaisha, 1978.
"Cut and Bruised; Japanese Drug Houses," *The Economist,* September 1985, p. 82.
Fujisawa and Shionogi, Tokyo: DIA Research Institute, 1985.
Shigeru, Endo, "Shionogi Beefs Up Drug R&D To Cure Ailing Performance," *Nikkei Weekly,* August 3, 1995, p. 10.
"Successful Drugs A Major Factor Behind Winners And Losers in R&D Spending Increases," *Nikkei English News,* August 19, 1996.
Takeda and Shionogi, Tokyo: DIA Research Institute, 1990.
Tanaka, Kentaro, "Biotechnology in the R&D Activities of Shionogi Today," *Business Japan,* July 1988, pp. 92–93.

—Betty T. Moore
—updated by April Dougal Gasbarre

Simpson Investment Company

1201 Third Avenue, Suite 4900
Seattle, Washington 98101
U.S.A.
(206) 224-5193
Fax: (206) 224-5060

Private Company
Incorporated: 1895 as Simpson Logging Company
Employees: 7,300
Sales: $1 billion (1995 est.)
SICs: 2621 Paper Mills; 2421 Sawmills & Planing Mills,
General

One of the oldest and largest privately owned companies in the Pacific Northwest, Simpson Investment Company operates as the holding company for Simpson Paper Company and Simpson Timber Company, subsidiaries involved in pulp and paper production and timber harvesting and manufacture, respectively. During the mid-1990s, Simpson Paper operated ten mills in eight states and Simpson Timber owned 770,000 acres of timberland in Washington, Oregon, and California, as well as manufacturing facilities and nurseries in Washington and California.

Origins of the Founder

Although Simpson Investment represented the corporate dynasty of the Reed family, whose legacy of leadership nearly spanned a century, the company was not founded by a member of the Reed family. Instead the diversified forest products giant was formed by Solomon Grout Simpson, a Canadian-born fortune-seeker who scored his greatest success in the logging business and lent his name to what would become one of the oldest and largest privately owned companies in his adopted home state of Washington. Born in 1843, Sol Simpson grew up in Cote St. Charles, Quebec, a burgeoning timber port town situated along the St. Lawrence River. His parents had left Yorkshire, England in the early 19th century and settled in the suburban Montreal community of Cote St. Charles. Like his parents, Sol Simpson demonstrated a peripatetic bent once he

reached early adulthood, but before he embarked on a life away from Cote St. Charles he spent his teenage years working as a timber raftsman in his home town, shepherding fir and spruce logs down the Ottawa and St. Lawrence rivers.

In Sol Simpson's mind, life as a timber raftsman in Cote St. Charles paled against the riches to be found in Carson City, Nevada, where the young Canadian moved in 1865 at the age of 22. Simpson arrived in Carson City intent on unearthing caches of gold and silver from the mines nearby, but luck was not on his side and the once-hopeful fortune-seeker was forced to look elsewhere for money to survive in his adopted country. Simpson began grading roads and logging in Carson City following his failure to find a treasure trove of gold and silver, then he settled down in Carson City, eventually marrying a local woman.

Simpson spent eight years in Carson City honing his logging and road-grading skills before moving to Seattle, Washington, with his wife and young daughter in 1878. In his new town, Simpson graded railroad beds and hauled timber for the Seattle & Eastern Railroad and the Port Blakely Mill Company, earning distinction for his use of horses to pull wagons rather than oxen, the conventional beast of burden used to haul heavy loads. Using horses to transport timber proved to be quicker than using oxen, a discovery that one timber industry historian described as, "not only revolutionary, so far as the West Coast woods was concerned, but downright heretical, practically indecent." Whatever the historical significance, Simpson's innovative approach earned the respect of his customers and gave him the confidence to form his own company.

1890: The Company Is Founded

In 1890 Simpson formed his own company, naming it S.G. Simpson Company, a sole proprietorship construction firm that counted road graders and horses as its primary assets. Initially, the newly formed company was closely allied with the, its chief, if not sole customer. Five years after its formation the company was incorporated and changed its name to Simpson Logging Company. Nearly from the outset, Simpson Logging was a thriving enterprise, its business nearly entirely predicated on the orders issued forth from the Port Blakely Mill Company. Profit-

Company Perspectives:

For as far into the past as anyone can determine, human beings have drawn benefit from natural resources—for shelter and safety; comfort and commerce; recreation and renewal. But people have a unique ability to change their environment—for better or for worse. No natural law ensures htat we do the right things or make the right choices. We have only our knowledge, our responsibility and our commitment. At Simpson, we've always taken our responsibility to the environment very seriously. As our knowledge has grown, we've made some changes. But our commitment to protect the resources on which we all depend has never wavered.

ability was the norm shortly after Simpson Logging's incorporation, as were dividend payments. By 1898, the company was producing a half million board feet of logs per day from eight logging camps and through 80 miles of tracks used by two railroads. Shortly thereafter, company-owned housing was erected and a company-owned store was opened, as Simpson Logging took on the trappings of a full-fledged lumber enterprise quickly after its creation.

It was at this point in the young company's history that the Reed era began, although it would be several years before the first member of the family was handed the reins of control over Simpson Logging. The Reed legacy began in 1897 when Sol Simpson and Mark Edward Reed, at age 31, met for the for the first time, one a successful leader of a promising logging company and the other a failure at the same venture. Fours years before Sol Simpson and Mark Reed met, Reed and a friend had founded a logging company that fell victim to the financial panic of 1893 and was remembered, according to one long-time timber industry observer, as "one of the quickest logging failures in Puget Sound history." For someone who would go on to be eulogized as one of the most important personalities in the history of the Pacific Northwest timber industry, Mark Reed's first failure stood as an anomaly in an otherwise distinguished career, but before accolades from timber industry pundits were thrown his way, the patriarch of the Reed dynasty labored to rise through the ranks of the modestly sized Simpson Logging enterprise.

Reed was hired on as a foreman of one of Simpson Logging's camps shortly after he met Sol Simpson and four years later married one of Simpson's daughters. When Reed joined Simpson Logging, the company still relied on Port Blakley Mill Company for an overwhelming percentage of its business, but by 1902 Simpson had grown tired of the arrangement and severed the ties that connected his company from his former employer. The decision by Simpson made Simpson Logging a commercial logger exclusively, giving the company independence and enabling it to sell its logs to the highest bidder.

Early 20th Century: Reed Family Gains Control

Several years later, in 1906, when the company employed 300 people at five separate camps and cut 300,000 board feet of logs a day, Simpson died and Reed assumed the responsibilities associated with managing the timber operations, though he was not yet named president of the company. That title was bestowed on Reed in 1914 when he assumed full control over the company and began to spearhead the transformation that would turn a log supplier fettered to its 19th-century roots into a diversified, dominant forest-products corporation.

Dominant became an adjective applied to Simpson Logging long before "diversified" became descriptive of the Shelton, Washington-based operations. During the years following the conclusion of the First World War, Reed established Simpson Logging as the dominant independent logger in the Puget Sound. Shortly after orchestrating this ascension, Reed began to direct the company into other, timber-related businesses, touching off an era of diversification that would become one of the hallmarks of Mark Reed's tenure at Simpson Logging.

After a year of construction, the company opened its first sawmill, the Reed Mill, in 1925, marking its entry into the hemlock lumber manufacturing business. Capable of producing 150,000 board feet per day, the Reed Mill was joined two years later by the Reed Shingle Mill. After these additions, Mark Reed moved Simpson Logging into the business that would rank as the company's largest enterprise during the 1990s. For members of the Reed family who depended heavily on the revenue generated from this business, Mark Reed's preliminary thoughts were remarkably prescient. As Reed contemplated the first steps that would lead to the formation of Simpson Paper Company, he remarked, "I feel confident that the pulpwood industry is going to be a very important factor in the development of the Northwest in years to come." Reed went on to presage developments that would affect his company more than a half century later, sounding more and more like a 1990s timber executive by stating, "If this industry could be successfully operated on the waste material from our lumbering operations, we would bring about real conservation."

1920: The First Steps toward Diversification

While Reed was pointing out the need to diversify and vertically integrate the operations of his timber company, he was negotiating a deal that moved Simpson Logging into the pulp and paper business. With the help of other financial backers, Reed formed the, giving Simpson Logging a minority interest in the newly formed company's sole asset: a sulfite pulp mill situated next to the Reed Mill in Shelton. Although by this time Simpson Logging still operated chiefly as a commercial logger, the push towards transforming the company into a diversified forest-products company had begun. In the years ahead, diversification would pick up pace but only after the company endured the economic hardships of the 1930s.

During the Great Depression, Simpson Logging was one of only a handful of operators in the Western Washington forest products industry to keep its facilities operating continuously. Though the company withstood the pernicious affects of a devastatingly weak national economy, it did so only by striking a deal with employees to cut their wages and by adhering to Mark Reed's policy of accumulating zero debt. Reed's dictate was instrumental to Simpson Logging's survival, but the patriarch of the Reed family never saw his company emerge from the economic doldrums of the 1930s. Reed died in 1933 at the nadir of the economic downswing and in his place his son Frank Campbell Reed assumed the reins of command, becoming president and chief executive officer of Simpson Logging.

By the mid 1930s, the prospects for the company began to brighten, instilling sufficient confidence in Frank Reed and his brother William Garrard Reed to complete several acquisitions. The company acquired 50 percent interest in the, converting the railroad from a common carrier to a private carrier, and purchased timberland. But by the late 1930s economic conditions soured again and the company was forced to abandon plans for expansion. Full recovery did not occur until the United States entered World War II in 1941.

Once the country was at war, the Office of Price Administration (OPA) froze the prices of logs, plywood, and lumber, barring forest-product companies like Simpson Logging from charging whatever its customers were willing to pay. As it turned out, the intervention by the OPA occurred when the price of logs was low and the prices of plywood and lumber were high, making commercial logging far less profitable than the manufacturing side of the timber business. Quickly and artificially, the dynamics of the timber industry were changed, forcing commercial loggers to either exit the business altogether or adapt to the changes. Simpson Logging opted to change with the times and spent the war years completing two acquisitions that bolstered its involvement in the manufacturing end of the timber industry. In 1941, the company acquired the Henry McCleary Timber Company, gaining a plywood mill and a door plant, and in 1943 the Olympic Plywood Company was purchased, adding another shingle mill to Simpson Logging's operations.

As these events unfolded, Simpson Logging underwent another leadership change. In late 1942, Frank Reed died in a fire that razed his home, leaving his younger brother William as the next Reed to steward the fortunes of Simpson Logging. William (Bill) Reed's contributions to the development of the family-owned company were as important as his father's and, in essence, quite similar. Mark Reed had led the company toward diversification; his son Bill would continue the transformation of Simpson Logging into a diversified, forest-products company, creating the foundation that would support the company during the 1990s. Shortly after his promotion to the top position of the Simpson Logging, Bill Reed presided over the completion of two acquisitions that set the tone for the company's progress during the second half of the 20th century. In 1945, the company entered the redwood business with the purchase of Del Norte, California-based Requia Timber Company and the following year Simpson Logging signed the 100-year Shelton Cooperative Sustained Yield Unit (CSYU) agreement with the U.S. government. The CSYU agreement paved the way for the future of Simpson Logging by unifying 116,000 acres of company-owned land and 112,000 acres of land owned by the U.S. Forest Service. Under the terms of the agreement the combined acreage was placed under a forest management plan that provided for continuous harvesting and restocking, ensuring that the supply of timber on the land would be perpetual and creating a sustained production of 90 million board feet a year for the next century.

Post-World War II Expansion

During the second half of the 20th century, Simpson Logging expanded at a rapid pace. The company swallowed up timberlands in Washington, Oregon, and California, acquired sawmills, established subsidiary operations in Canada, and made its all-important entry into the pulp and paper business, the largest component of Simpson Investment during the 1990s. Although the company had acquired its first interest in the pulp and paper business during the mid-1920s with a minority stake in Rainer Pulp and Paper Company, the move into pulp and paper did not begin in earnest until the early 1950s. In 1951, the company acquired Lowell, Washington-based, a maker of lithographic paper, book paper, and label paper used for canned goods and fruit boxes in the western United States. The acquisition of Everett Pulp & Paper touched of a three-decade-long acquisition spree that increased Simpson Logging's role as a pulp and paper producer, enlarged its timberland holdings, and moved the company into a number of business areas not directly related to the timber business. It was Bill Reed's objective during his tenure to make Simpson Logging a more integrated forest-products operator and an industry leader in return on assets; his work during the 1950s and 1960s accomplished just that, as Simpson Logging expanded and diversified aggressively.

While the company moved resolutely forward on all fronts, several organizational changes occurred that charted the evolution of Simpson Logging from the 1950s to the 1990s. The first of these changes that facilitated Simpson Logging's transformation into Simpson Investment Company took place in 1956 when Simpson Timber Company was formed as the parent company for Simpson Logging Company, Simpson Redwood Company, which had been founded two years earlier, and the rapidly expanding Simpson Paper Company. In 1959, Simpson Paper Company merged with Vicksburg, Michigan-based Lee Paper Company, forming Simpson Lee Paper Company, and the following year Simpson Logging Company and Simpson Redwood Company were merged into Simpson Timber Company.

Structured as such, Simpson Timber entered the 1960s well on its way toward becoming a leading forest-products company on the West Coast. The company opened a paper mill in California in 1961, established a timber subsidiary in Saskatchewan, Canada, in 1965, and late in the decade bought several companies that brought the forest-products company into business areas outside the timber industry. A furniture company, a leasing company, and a machine tool manufacturer were acquired, but the only acquisition that remained a part of the company's operations into the 1990s was the 1967 purchase of Eugene, Oregon-based Gil-Wel Manufacturing. Later renamed the Simpson Extruded Plastics Company, Gil-Wel Manufacturing was a small manufacturer of extruded thermoplastic pipe used primarily for irrigation purposes.

During the 1970s, Simpson Timber acquired two paper mills in California, one in 1972 that became the company's Shasta Mill and the other in 1979 that became its San Gabriel Mill. Other developments during the decade included the establishment of another timber subsidiary in Canada, where Simpson Timber Co. (Alberta) Ltd. first began operating in 1973, and the acquisition of a plastics plant in Sunnyside, Washington, that was merged into Simpson Extruded Plastics Company. The

1970s also brought an end to another era of Reed leadership. Bill Reed stepped aside as chairman in 1971, handing the reins of command to his son, William G. "Gary" Reed, Jr., who had served as an executive for the company since the 1960s.

As Simpson Timber entered the 1980s, its acquisition program continued unabated, with Gary Reed, Jr. adding mills, timberlands, and plastics manufacturing facilities to the company's fold at a pace commensurate with the rate of expansion established during his father's tenure. Three pulp and paper mills were acquired during the first half of the decade, one in Pennsylvania in 1980, another in California in 1982, and a third in Ohio in 1983. The first half of the 1980s also were highlighted by the acquisition of four plastic plants. In 1982, the company acquired a Visalia, California plastic plant from Gifford-Hill Company, Inc. and in 1985 purchased three plastic plants belonging to Western Plastic Company, giving Simpson Extruded Plastics Company new facilities in Tacoma, Washington, and in Union City and Downey, California.

Midway through the 1980s, another company-wide reorganization altered the structure of Simpson Timber, creating the framework of the company that would carry it into the 1990s. In 1985, Simpson Extruded Plastics Company's name was changed to reflect the recent additions of the three Western Plastics Company plants, becoming PWPipe. Next, more pervasive changes were effected, giving the Reed-owned enterprise a different corporate title. Simpson Investment Company was adopted as the new name for the holding company, replacing the Simpson Timber Company name, which was used thereafter as the name for the company's timber operations. In addition to owning Simpson Timber Company, Simpson Investment Company also served as the holding company for the Simpson Paper and PWPipe companies.

During the latter half of the 1980s, Simpson Investment acquired three pulp and paper mills, two facilities to be used by its PWPipe subsidiary, and a timber company located near Arcata, California, as well as 117,000 acres of northwestern Oregon timberland from the Times Mirror Land and Timber Company. Once these acquisitions were completed, Simpson Investment officials could look back on a century of business, as the company entered the 1990s and celebrated its centennial anniversary year.

One Hundred Years in Business

By the time of its 100th birthday, the Reed-owned enterprise ranked as one of the largest producers of fine papers in the United States, while its timber business—the original part of the business founded in 1890—had thrived for decades by pursuing a strategy of acquiring inexpensive tracts of land, consistently replanting the harvested timberland, and planning for long-term cultivation. As opposed to a century earlier, Simpson Investment entered the 1990s dependent on its pulp and paper business to generate the bulk of its revenue rather than its commercial logging operations. Though this shift in the company's orientation mirrored the changing character of the forest-products industry during the 20th century, the first half of the 1990s proved to be an inopportune time for profits in the pulp and paper business. The early years of the decade were marked by declining pulp prices and a surfeit of products on the market, which crimped profits at Simpson Investment's most important subsidiary, Simpson Paper Company. As a result, the paper subsidiary was forced to consolidate, shuttering two pulp mills in California in 1993 and another in Pennsylvania in 1994, the year Simpson Paper Company's headquarters were moved from San Francisco to Seattle.

Despite the slump in profits derived from the paper industry, Simpson Investment entered the mid 1990s as a powerful, diversified forest-products company. The company ranked as the second-largest privately held company in Washington and as one of the largest forest-products companies on the West Coast. In 1995, the company narrowed its focus by selling its PWPipe subsidiary to Mitsubishi Chemical America Corp. The divestiture enabled Simpson Investment to concentrate its resources on the company's widespread paper and timber interests, operated by Simpson Paper Company and Simpson Timber Company, respectively. As Simpson Investment prepared for the late 1990s and the new century ahead, its pulp and paper business was supported by ten mills scattered across eight states. The company's timber subsidiary owned 770,000 acres of timberland in Washington, Oregon, and California and operated three sawmills, a plywood mill, and a door plant in Washington, and two sawmills, a manufacturing plant, and two nurseries in California. With these properties composing the holdings of Simpson Investment and its two subsidiaries, the family-owned company charted its course for future, intent on continuing the legacy of independence and success spawned from the efforts of Solomon Grout Simpson.

Principal Subsidiaries

Simpson Paper Company; Simpson Timber Company.

Further Reading

Denne, Lorianne, "Simpson Paper Takes Steps While Rival Firms Embroiled," *Puget Sound Business Journal*, June 4, 1990, p. 17.
"Mark E. Reed," *Puget Sound Business Journal*, April 29, 1991, p. 15.
Sather, Jeanne, "Simpson Investment Co. Still Keeping Low Profile," *Puget Sound Business Journal*, June 24, 1994, p. 42.
Spector, Robert, "It Never Came Easy for Simpson Dynasty Founder," *Puget Sound Business Journal*, June 24, 1991, p. 30.
——, *Family Trees: Simpson's Centennial Story*, Bellevue, Wash.: Documentary Book Publishers Corporation, 1990.
Tucker, Rob, "Simpson Investment to Sell Plastic-Pipe Subsidiary to Mitsubishi," *Knight-Ridder/Tribune Business News*, July 5, 1995, p. 7.

—Jeffrey L. Covell

Six Flags Theme Parks, Inc.

400 Interpace Parkway
Building C, 3rd Floor
Parsippany, New Jersey 07054
U.S.A.
(201) 402-8100
Fax: (201) 402-5580

Private Company
Incorporated: 1961 as Six Flags Over Texas
Employees: 1,300
Sales: $650 million (1995 est.)
SICs: 7996 Amusement Parks; 6719 Holding Companies, Not Elsewhere Classified

Six Flags Theme Parks, Inc., is the second-largest theme park operation in the United States. Marketing itself as ''Bigger than Disneyland, closer to home,'' the company has ten parks spread throughout the country and draws an estimated 22 million patrons per year. According to the company's marketing slogan, 85 percent of the U.S. population lives within a day's drive of one of the company's parks. Long known for introducing the public to the latest in thrill ride technology, Six Flags boasts some of the tallest and fastest roller coasters in the world. In addition to its hallmark thrill rides, the company is known for its affiliation with Time Warner, which can be seen in the many Looney Tunes characters and Warner Brothers film properties that have become increasingly prominent in the park during the 1990s.

Early History

The company that introduced steel roller coasters, log flumes, and whitewater rides to the world was founded by Angus Wynn in 1961. Three years before the grand opening of his first amusement park, Six Flags Over Texas, Wynn, a Texas real estate developer, and his partners held a brainstorming session to try to find a way to finance their latest project, a sprawling industrial park located on 7,500 acres of land between Dallas and Fort Worth. Having exhausted all of their cash and credit to purchase the land, the group needed money to develop their dream, the Great Southwest Industrial District. As the conversation at the meeting turned to Disneyland, which had opened three years earlier, one of the partners suggested to Wynn that he open an amusement park himself to generate the needed funds. Wynn took the advice seriously. Later that year, he paid a visit to the southern California park and returned to Texas convinced that the idea for the project was viable. Construction began in 1960 and was completed on August 15, 1961, at a cost of $3.4 million. Wynn's original name for the park, ''Texas Under Six Flags,'' was meant as a reference to the state's early history. A few proud and zealous members of the Daughters of the Texas Revolution soon objected to the name, however, arguing that the state of Texas was never ''under'' anything. Wynn quickly agreed and changed the name to ''Six Flags Over Texas.''

The first Six Flags park, like its Disney forerunner, featured a variety of attractions designed to entertain customers of all ages. For the less thrill-seeking patrons, the park featured a Western venue—including an Indian village, saloon, jail, and a ''Fiesta Train''—as well as a petting zoo and a goat ride. More fast-paced rides included the ''Astrolift'' roller coaster and the ''Missile Chaser.'' A variety of shows and music presented in an amphitheater rounded out the entertainment.

Wynn's marketing strategy in those early days was not unlike the approach of the 1990s. He tried to portray his amusement park as a closer and more affordable alternative to his better known Disney competitor. The people of Texas responded positively to his message. Although Wynn projected that 500,000 people would enter the gates at the $2.75 admission price (for anyone taller than four feet), his expectations proved to be too conservative: the park drew more than one million that first year, managing to pay off all construction costs and make a profit. As had been his original intent, Wynn and his partners used the cash to get the industrial park back on its feet. Even after such a successful debut, the park was intended to have a life span of only about ten years, at which time it would be swallowed up by the industrial development. As attendance and revenue continued to increase during those first few years, however, Wynn quickly came to realize that the amusement park itself was of great value.

During the 1960s, the burgeoning amusement park increased its attendance each year as it introduced a number of rides that would form the backbone of the amusement park industry into the 1990s. For instance, on June 15, 1963, Six Flags unveiled the world's first log flume ride. The first-ever steel roller coaster, Arrow Development's Runaway Mine Train coaster, opened at Six Flags Over Texas three years later.

In 1966 Wynn sold his amusement park business to Penn Central. With the new owners came a more abundant supply of capital for geographical expansion and park additions. In 1967 Six Flags made its first move beyond the Texas state line, opening a Six Flags Over Georgia, in Atlanta. A future president and chief executive officer of the company, Larry Cochran, who began his career with Six Flags as a part-time draftsman helping to design and build the first park, was appointed vice-president and general manager of the new facility.

The 1970s: An Era of Expansion and Innovation

As theme parks became more popular with the American public, evolving into a full-scale, nationwide industry, Six Flags continued to expand its operations. The 1970s saw the company add five parks to its stable. In 1971, the company built a new park in Eureka, Missouri, called Six Flags Over Mid-America. Four years later, Six Flags opened its second park in Texas, AstroWorld/WaterWorld, located in Houston. In 1978, the company made its first entrance into the East Coast market, opening Six Flags Great Adventure in Jackson, New Jersey. Six Flags Magic Mountain, in Valencia, California, purchased in 1979, brought the park to the other coast.

As the decade drew to a close, Six Flags began developing another first in the industry: the whitewater rapids ride. Bill Crandall, manager of the AstroWorld park, discovered the idea for the ride that would later become commonplace in theme parks across the country while watching the kayak competition in the Munich Summer Olympic Games in 1972. Fascinated with the artificial river used for the kayak competition, he believed that a ride simulating the fast-paced action of the event would provide a unique experience for his park patrons. Crandall enlisted the services of Intamin, a top Swiss ride manufacturer, to design and build the first ride of its type in the world. The product of their efforts, Thunder River, opened for business in Houston in 1980 and has since been emulated in amusement parks throughout the world.

The 1980s: A Decade of Transition

With the new decade came an era of revolving-door ownership for the company. At least four corporate entities held a significant stake in the company between 1981 and 1990. The first major change came in 1982 when Penn Central sold the company to Bally Corporation. Under the direction of the new owners, Six Flags added its seventh park, opening Six Flags Great America in Gurnee, Illinois in 1984. Three years later, Cochran and Wesray Capital Corporation, a group of New Jersey investors that included former U.S. Treasury Secretary William Simon, took the company private through a $617 million leverage buyout. The unstable combination of junk bonds and bank loans used to finance the purchase gave what Larry Cochran, who took over as president and CEO, called a "lousy

capital structure," according to an interview with Tim O'Brien of *Amusement Business*. As a result of such short capital reserves, the company accumulated a massive debt load and was forced to pay shareholders the 16 percent interest on their notes in additional bonds in lieu of cash payments, a move that would cut substantially into profits for the remainder of the decade.

Financing problems aside, Six Flags managed a strong performance at the gate in a decade that saw the megaparks, such as Disneyworld and Epcot Center, rise to the forefront of the industry. Six Flags, along with other mid-sized parks such as Great America and Great Adventures, attempted to carve out a profitable niche by offering an entertainment experience that was less expensive and closer to home than the Disney giants— a marketing strategy an increasing number of young families found appealing. To increase its appeal with this segment of the market, the company acquired the rights to Warner Brothers animations, Looney Tunes, which includes such popular characters as Bugs Bunny and the Roadrunner. By the end of the decade, combined annual attendance at the parks had grown to nearly 17 million, generating revenue of around $400 million.

The Early 1990s: New Ownership Spurs Growth

In June 1990, Time Warner increased its interest in the financially strapped amusement park, acquiring a 19.5 percent share of the company, at a cost of $19.5 million. The partnership grew out of an extensive campaign to promote the 50th anniversary of the legendary Looney Tunes character Bugs Bunny at the Six Flags parks. The entrance of the entertainment and communications conglomerate not only gave the company a much needed influx of new capital but a chance for increased usage of the Warner cartoon characters as well. Time Warner's family of magazines and cable television programs also represented avenues for new advertising.

While Six Flags attempted to strengthen its appeal to younger patrons with the help of Bugs Bunny and friends, it also directed much of its energy toward cultivating its long-time relationship with the older, thrill-seeking crowd. As the company ushered in the new decade, it opened new coasters at six of its seven theme parks in an attempt to keep up with the industry-wide push toward taller, faster, and more thrilling rides. Chief among the new additions was the $5.5 million Texas Giant, a 4,920-foot-long wooden-track coaster that featured a top speed of 62 miles per hour and a top lift of 150 feet, making it one of the tallest coasters in the world. With at least 12 of the nation's 40 most popular roller coasters, according to a 1990 edition of the trade newsletter "Inside Track," Six Flags soared to a record-high $431.3 million in revenues, a record ten percent jump from the previous year. Interest charges stemming from the 1987 bond issue, however, resulted in a net loss of $25.4 million for the year.

Two years later, Six Flags again changed owners. This time, however, the transition was aided by an infusion of more than $150 million, courtesy of Time Warner and two New York investment firms who acquired the theme park chain for an estimated $710 million. According to the terms of the agreement, Time Warner paid $31.5 million to up its stake in the company to 40 percent, and the Blackstone Group and Wertheim Schroder & Company contributed $150 million to acquire a

50 percent share. The deal brought what had long been the missing ingredient to the company's bottom line success: financial stability.

With most of its long-term debt retired and a steady flow of cash, the company could now, as Cochran told O'Brien of *Amusement Business,* get back to what it does best, "managing the parks and growing them to their potentials." Toward that end, Six Flags and Time Warner joined forces to develop the $8 million "Batman—the Ride," which combined the latest in coaster technology with the thematic backdrop from the popular movie "Batman Returns," released a month after the ride opened. As guests approached the ride, which first opened at Six Flags Great America in May 1992, they found themselves in the middle of "Gotham City Park," complete with flowers, beautiful landscape, and an audio track playing sounds of children playing and birds chirping. As they continued their journey, though, patrons entered the dilapidated section of the simulated city, the air filled with unpleasant sounds, including distress signals from a police car that has smashed into a fire hydrant. Their only escape can be found in the batcave, where they are whisked away, with their feet dangling, on a car suspended below the tracks on a ride described as a high-speed chair lift that completes a series of loops. According to some industry experts, the looping, suspended coaster represented the biggest technological breakthrough in more than 15 years.

"Batman—the Ride" was typical of new President and Chief Executive Officer Bob Pittman's attempt to live up to the Six Flags tradition of ride innovation and, at the same time, give the regional chain of parks a more recognizable national identity. Between 1991 and 1995, Time Warner invested more than $200 million toward reaching that goal, developing several new thrill rides with themes borrowed from among the communications conglomerate's many businesses. Coasters themed with movies such as "The Right Stuff" and children's rides featuring the Warner Brothers character Yosemite Sam represented a few of the more prominent examples of this crossover campaign.

Pittman, who took over in December 1991, combined this synergistic strategy with a direct assault on the industry leader, the $2.8 billion Disney, through an aggressive $30 million advertising campaign launched in 1992. The media blitz centered around what Pittman, the then 36-year-old founder of MTV, called a "classic second-place strategy." As he told *Forbes* magazine's Lisa Gubernick, "We know we aren't Disney, but we want people to think of us on the Disney scale so they understand we're not some dinky kiddie park." Accordingly, the new broadcast and cable television ads boasted that the company's seven parks were "bigger, faster, closer" than Disneyland. With six of the seven parks larger than the 80-acre home of Mickey Mouse and Donald Duck, 84 percent of the country within 300 miles of a Six Flags park, and an average roller coaster speed of 65 miles per hour, Pittman's claim was not without strong evidence.

The Mid-1990s and Beyond

As Six Flags entered the mid-1990s, it looked to boost its appeal as a regional destination resort by broadening its entertainment package. Although it continued to develop innovative roller coasters and theme rides for the thrill seekers among its potential customers, it also tried to compliment its traditional business with new attractions and services. In 1995, for instance, Six Flags Over Texas purchased the Wet 'n Wild waterpark in Arlington, becoming the third company park to have a separate-gate, company-owned waterpark attraction as a neighbor. Such deals gave the company added marketing power and strengthened the appeal of a multiple-day ticket. Another avenue of diversification for Six Flags launched that year was the concept of the Outlet Center. With the intent of attracting parents and empty nesters who have dropped off their children and grandchildren at the park, Six Flags opened its first outlet center at its Jackson, New Jersey facility. The company planned to add similar stores, which sell a variety of Six Flags and Time Warner merchandise, to its other parks based on the success of the pilot store.

In April of that same year, Time Warner sold 51 percent of its share in the company to Boston Ventures for $1 billion. The deal, as Six Flags spokesperson Eileen Harrell told O'Brien, was heralded as a "best of both worlds" decision, enabling the company to "become a self-financing entity" while maintaining its "access to the large inventory of Time Warner properties." Although Time Warner remained as the largest single stockholder of the company and planned to co-manage the company with Boston Ventures, Pittman, who helped the company to raise annual attendance levels to 22 million, planned to leave the company the following year.

Further Reading

Gubernick, Lisa, " 'We're Bigger, Faster, Closer'," *Forbes,* May 25, 1992, pp. 232–233.
O'Brien, Tim, "Cochran's 30-Year Tenure with Six Flags Is Truly a Success Story," *Amusement Business,* March 25–31, 1991, pp. 45–46.
——, "The Granddaddy of Six Flags Parks Celebrates a Big 30th Anniversary," *Amusement Business,* March 25–31, pp. 49–50.
——, "Indoor Coaster Set for Two Six Flags Parks," *Amusement Business,* March 11, 1996, pp. 32–33.
——, "Pittman: Six Flags To Continue Backing Big Promises with Major Investments," *Amusement Business,* April 17, 1995, pp. 21–22.
——, "Time Warner Characters To Remain at Six Flags," *Amusement Business,* April 24, 1995, pp. 1–2.
"Six Flags Unveils Rides, Water Park," *Travel Weekly,* July 17, 1995, pp. 38–39.
Stanley, T.L., "How Long Can the Ride Continue?" *Brandweek,* September 11, 1995, pp. 34–37.

—Jason Gallman

Smead Manufacturing Co.

600 E. Smead Boulevard
Hastings, Minnesota 55033
U.S.A.
(612) 437-4111
Fax: (612) 437-9134
Internet site: http://www.smead.com

Private Company
Founded: 1906
Employees: 2,500
Sales: $217 million (1995 est.)
SICs: 2678 Stationery, Tablets, and Related Products

Smead Manufacturing is the largest U.S. producer of stationery products in the approximately $1.24 billion (1991) U.S. stationery supplies market, which is comprised of three basic product groups: tablets, pads, and related products (62 percent of industry sales in 1987); stationery items (26 percent of industry sales); and loose sheets of filler paper. In the mid-1990s, Smead was the 18th-largest privately held industrial company in the state of Minnesota, and in 1996, *Working Woman* magazine ranked Smead as the 31st-largest women-owned business in the United States.

Smead's primary product line is office filing products, from manila folders, expanding files, and top tab and end tab filing systems to color-coded indexing systems, records management software, high-density mobile shelving, and electronic tracking, imaging, and bar code technologies. Other typical Smead products include ring binders, medical X-ray jackets, steel rotary filing components, file pockets, hanging files, and report covers. In the mid-1990s it offered over 2,000 individual filing products and accessories as well as records management consulting services and customized product services such as customer-specified file prelabeling.

Like other firms in the stationery industry, Smead converts rolled paper stock bought in bulk from paper and paperboard mills into stationery products using automated technology and sells its finished products to office products retailers and contract stationers. Ranked in general terms as a mid-sized stationery converter, Smead has traditionally competed with the stationery products divisions of large paper manufacturing companies as well as other publicly and privately held independent stationery makers such as Duplex Products, Inc., Avery Dennison Corporation, and Stuart Hall Co. In the mid-1990s, Smead, whose stock is entirely owned by the Hoffman family, maintained seven manufacturing plants in the states of Minnesota, Georgia, Texas, Ohio, Utah, California, and Wisconsin.

"A Better Mousetrap": 1906–40

The Smead Manufacturing Company was founded in 1906 by Charles Smead, a former salesman for the St. Louis-based wholesale office supply firm of G. D. Barnard and Co. Regarded by his employer as "one of the best men on the road," Smead had begun casting about for an alternative to the then standard practice of securing office file envelopes with rubber bands, which almost always deteriorated before the envelope itself wore out. Smead's innovation was the "bandless file," an envelope designed with durable metal clasps. None of the office supply firms Smead offered it to were interested, however, and Smead resolved to strike out on his own. Operating at first out of a small room above the offices of the Hastings *Gazette,* Smead's entire plant-cum-office initially consisted of a printing press, a rack of type, two die-stamping machines, a punch machine, and a few round-cornering machines, which were all hoisted into the 20-by-40-foot room through a window at the rear of the building.

With all of six employees, Smead Manufacturing began commercial production of its bandless files in 1908, but less than a year and half after the product hit the market Smead died, leaving the firm in the hands of his three partners: Otto Ackerman, John Heinen (the registrar of deeds for Dakota County), and Irving Todd (the publisher of the *Gazette*). In 1916 the three sold the firm to P. A. Hoffman, one of the original six Smead employees, and by 1918 Hoffman had moved the fledgling operation to a larger site. For the next decade, Hoffman presided over Smead's growth into a significant player in the stationery

Company Perspectives:

Businesses preparing for the 21st century are finding that new technologies and work processes are redefining the way information is stored and retrieved within their organizations. Computers, fax machines and sophisticated workflow techniques have all improved office efficiency, but they've also created an explosion of information that needs to be kept organized. To be successful in the new millennium, it will be essential to develop and maintain well designed records management systems. Flexibility and ease of use will continue to be the factors that describe the systems that keep organizations running smoothly. Smead has been designing and manufacturing innovative records management systems and techniques for more than 90 years. As we look to the future, our commitment to our customers remains the same; to provide the highest quality systems and supplies for all types of records management, with the same ultimate purpose—keeping you organized.

market and developed his reputation as a respectful, businesslike manager with a keen eye for improving Smead's productivity. (He was known to point at boxes of packaged product and comment, ''that carton has been here two days,'' prompting Smead staff to improve delivery times.) When he suffered a debilitating stroke in 1928, his son and employee Harold Hoffman was promoted to help him run the firm. On the strength of the younger Hoffman's leadership, Smead weathered the Depression until by the eve of U.S. involvement in World War II it had expanded from a single facility to seven separate plants.

Crisis: 1941–55

With the general filing needs of the mainstream business market increasingly covered by its catalog, Smead continued to specialize its product lines to satisfy the unique filing requirements of individual industries. From the early success of the bandless file Smead had added new office filing products—from file folders, dividers, and file pockets to brief covers, binder covers, pressboard folders, and such innovations as the now universal top tab filing system. The outbreak of World War II launched a new boom in paper demand, and the U.S. paper industry as a whole enjoyed a significant sales boost throughout the war. By 1942, for example, Dennison Manufacturing Company—which would become a major Smead competitor in the postwar years—had surpassed its pre-Depression sales levels, and International Paper began supplying nitrate pulp for explosives and waterproof paperboard (or ''V-board'') for food shipments to Allied troops. For Smead, the war's end meant the beginning of an aggressive expansion, which by 1953 included new plants in Logan, Ohio (north of Dayton); Stillwater, Minnesota (on the Wisconsin border); and nearby River Falls, Wisconsin. Unable to service its rapidly expanding customer base from Minnesota alone, Smead also opened sales and warehousing operations in Chicago and Toronto in the postwar years.

The company also introduced new filing systems to meet the increasingly paper-flooded, space-constrained needs of the modern office. High-density shelf filing systems that increased the amount of records that could be stored in a limited space by almost 100 percent were introduced, color-coded index systems that made file organization and identification easier were unveiled, and new filing accessories and standardized indexing techniques to enhance filing efficiency and reduce misfiling errors were developed and marketed. By 1955, Smead could claim 325 employees and sales of $4 million.

Besides marking the onset of a period of rapid expansion at Smead, the end of World War II also had a personal significance for the Hoffman family. In September 1944, Harold Hoffman, then serving his 16th year for his father as Smead's de facto president, had married Ebba Benson, a Minnesota native working as a supervisor for thermostat-maker Honeywell in Minneapolis. When the elder Hoffman died at age 74 in 1954, Harold was officially named Smead's president. Less than 15 months later, however, Hoffman suffered a fatal heart attack while attending a business meeting in Buffalo. Smead's future was suddenly very much in doubt.

Turnaround: 1955–70

After her husband's death, Ebba Hoffman was confronted with the daunting responsibility of choosing between abandoning the Hoffman family's 40-year stake in the Smead name by selling out to a competitor or becoming that rarity in the American business scene of the 1950s—a female owner of a large industrial enterprise. Complicating her decision was the financially precarious condition of the company itself. Despite Smead's confident expansion in the decade after World War II, growth in the paper industry was slow throughout the 1950s, Smead's capital resources were depleted by credit obligations, its profits were thin and getting thinner, and the death of P. A. and Harold Hoffman (neither of whom left wills) had saddled the family with estate taxes that only exacerbated the already heavy debt load brought on by Smead's expansion. As Ebba Hoffman herself described the crisis years later: ''There was no money. I had to go to the bank to borrow money to live on.''

Although she had limited formal education, Hoffman had management experience from her days with Honeywell, a desire to see the company survive as a legacy for her heirs, and more than a passing knowledge of the business and its dealers. More immediately, with the health of the Hoffman family estate now in doubt, she needed a job to support her children, Sharon Lee and John Peter. Thus, when a Smead executive asked Hoffman how soon he could move into her husband's former office, she curtly suggested it might be longer than he hoped and decided to announce her decision to direct the company. In her first months, she decelerated Smead's expansion program, shut down several unproductive plants and warehouses, and discovered a talented Smead engineer whom she charged with improving and diversifying Smead's products and designing the new equipment needed to make them.

Within three years of her husband's death Hoffman had extended Smead's operations to the West Coast through the acquisition of the manufacturing and distribution operations of the Yale Filing Company of Los Angeles. It would operate as a division of Smead until 1969 when Hoffman decided to abandon the Yale name and fully merge its operations with Smead. In 1962 she unveiled a new 140,000-square-foot factory and headquarters building for Smead at its Hastings home. A strike by Smead workers the same year forced Minnesota governor Elmer Andersen to call in police officers to protect Smead's plant. When Hoffman refused to give in to workers' demands, Governor Anderson threatened to recall his troopers. Hoffman's response was to invite him to do just that: she refused to "give the company away" just to please the State of Minnesota. Her reputation for toughness was reinforced again when a Smead executive mistakenly allowed company inventories to climb so high that Hoffman was forced to borrow money to underwrite the error: mistake or not, Hoffman abbreviated the manager's Smead career.

By 1964 Smead's business in the Midwest had grown so large that a new manufacturing plant was constructed in Logan, Ohio, as well as an expanded warehouse and sales facilities, designated the Central Distribution Center, in Chicago. The Logan facility now enabled Smead to manufacture and store its products—from raw materials to finished goods—under one roof. Throughout the 1960s Smead modernized its catalog— which now offered more than three thousand products—to include filing systems and products for the emerging computer industry and new products designed for specific industries. Folders were developed that allowed computer tapes to be handily stored indefinitely; specialized check file guides were designed for the filing needs of the bank and building and loan industries; and wallets and pockets were marketed to hold marriage licenses, reports, and virtually any other document. Smead's growing sophistication in anticipating its customers' needs through research and development also resulted in the creation of color coded filing systems and the Smead "Terminal Digit Indexing System," which quickly claimed market share among insurance firms, medical record librarians, and government agencies.

By avoiding new debt and business ventures outside Smead's traditional niche, Hoffman had guided the company's sales by the late 1960s to a 300 percent increase over 1955, making the period the most productive in company history. Production, sales volume, and inventory were all on the rise, and in 1968 Smead enlarged its new Hastings plant by 30 percent and drew up plans for the expansion of its administrative offices and computer system, which now performed everything from accounting, interplant communication, and analysis to inventory and quality control. Moreover, Smead's West Coast operation was expanded through the purchase of a larger plant in Pico Rivera, California. In 1970, Smead's sales finally passed the $14 million mark. Four years later, Smead gained a small but symbolic place in America's cultural iconography when resigning President Richard Nixon was shown departing from the White House with one of Smead's ubiquitous filing boxes under his arm; Smead's penetration of the U.S. filing supplies market seemed complete.

At the Top: 1970–96

Despite the stagflation and economic uncertainty of the 1970s, between 1970 and 1981 Smead's revenues grew at a compound annual rate of 18 percent, breaking past the $80 million mark in 1981. Between 1975 and 1981 alone, Hoffman increased Smead's plant and warehouse capacity by three-quarters, funding the entire expansion through reinvested profits. A new 75,000-square-foot plant (Smead's fifth) was opened in McGregor, Texas, in 1971 to expand Smead's ability to service its customers in the Southwest. As a result of such determined reinvestment, Smead's year-in, year-out profits were only "adequate," one Smead executive admitted, "but ... *consistently* adequate." By 1981, Hoffman could claim that Smead had not endured a single year of earnings decline since she assumed the company's reins.

Befitting a mature industry that has tapped its potential market, the U.S. stationery products industry experienced flat sales throughout the 1980s and early 1990s and relied on growth in the general economy to enhance sales. Increasing public awareness of the impact of heavy paper use on the environment; the growing use of personal computers in both homes and offices, reflecting a general shift toward the so-called paperless economy; and a spate of corporate downsizings beginning in the 1980s meant potentially smaller markets for office stationery and filing systems. Smead adjusted to the threatening trends, however, adopting a ten to 30 percent recycled-paper content requirement for its paper products (without increasing its prices) and moving to position itself not as a mere supplier of filing supplies and stationery but as a forward-thinking innovator of "total filing solutions" for "records and document management." To that end, in the late 1980s it introduced bar code tracking methods that virtually eradicated misfiling errors. It also introduced "Smeadlink," an integrated software program that enabled users to index, track, and retrieve their entire range of business documents, from faxes, scanned documents, labels, and file tabs to E-mail and electronic and hardcopy paper documents. The product represented an aggressive attempt to single-handedly position Smead as a bridge between the "old" world of paper files and the digital age of paperless communication.

Smead also sought to reduce labor costs and expand its production capacity. In 1993 it announced it was moving some of the one thousand jobs at its Hastings and River Falls facilities to a leased plant in Mexico but hoped to minimize the impact of the move on its U.S. workers by reassigning them to different jobs and transferring to Mexico only those jobs currently held by retiring U.S. workers. In 1996, it announced that a year-long search for a site for a new $14 million manufacturing facility had concluded with the selection of Cedar City, Utah. When operational in 1997, the plant would employ 225 semiskilled workers and would give Smead the capability to provide one-day service to the West Coast and Denver.

At age 84, Ebba Hoffman—still chairwoman and president of Smead and the first woman elected to the Minnesota Business Hall of Fame (1977)—continued to groom her daughter, Sharon Lee Hoffman Avent, to one day succeed her, promoting her to senior executive vice-president in 1995.

Further Reading

Feyder, Susan. "Smead to Move Some Work to Mexico," *Minneapolis Star Tribune,* August 12, 1993, p. 3D.
George, Gina, "Privately Held Industrial Companies," *Minneapolis-St. Paul CityBusiness,* July 28, 1995, p. 25.

Jones, Lara, "Filing Products Maker Closes on 80 Acres for New Plant in Cedar City," vol. 25, *Enterprise/Salt Lake City,* May 6, 1996, p. 11.
——, "Smead Manufacturing to Launch $14 Million Utah Plant," *Enterprise/Salt Lake City,* April 22, 1996, p. 1.
Kurschner, Dale, "Top Rank Minnesota," *Corporate Report—Minnesota,* July 1, 1996, p. 91.
"Mrs. Ebba C. Hoffman Celebrating 40 Years of Leadership and Dedication to the Smead Manufacturing Company" (company brochure), Hastings, Minn.: Smead Manufacturing Company, 1995.

"Smead: A History of Continued Growth . . . Since 1906" (company history), Hastings, Minn.: Smead Manufacturing Company.
"Smead Announces Management Shift," *Hastings (Minnesota) Star Gazette,* December 14, 1995.
Youngblood, Dick, "Smead's Products, Leader All Business," *Hastings (Minnesota) Gazette,* October 25, 1981.

—Paul S. Bodine

Smith✛Nephew

Leadership in Worldwide Healthcare

Smith & Nephew plc

---

2 Temple Place, Victoria Embankment
London WC2R 3BP
England
+44 (0) 171 836 7922
Fax: +44 (0) 171 240 7088

Public Company
Incorporated: 1937 as Smith & Nephew Associated
    Companies Limited
Employees: 12,223
Sales: £1.02 billion (1995)
Stock Exchanges: London
SICs: 3841 Surgical and Medical Instruments; 3842
    Surgical Appliances and Supplies; 3089 Miscellaneous
    Plastics Products; 2844 Toilet Preparations; 3827
    Optical Instruments and Lenses; 2393 Textile Bags;
    5047 Medical and Hospital Equipment; 2830 Drugs

Smith & Nephew plc is the fifth-largest health care products supplier in a worldwide market worth £5 billion. Its main competitors include Johnson & Johnson, 3M, Bristol Myers-Squibb, and Baxter. The company's return on investment is consistently among the best in Britain.

Victorian Origins

Thomas James Smith was born in 1827. He trained as a pharmacist, first as an apprentice in Grantham, Lincolnshire and then, in 1854 and 1855, at London's University College, where Lord Lister, the antiseptic innovator, also studied. In 1856 he was admitted into the newly formed Royal Pharmaceutical Society and in August he bought his first shop at 71 White-friargate, Hull.

Smith soon became involved in the wholesale trade of bandages and related materials. Smith took advantage of his proximity to the docks and fishermen of Hull and began supplying hospitals with cod liver oil, valued for its therapeutic value in cases of rickets, tuberculosis, and rheumatism (vitamins had not yet been identified). At the time, doctors' visits were expensive and pharmacists were often the first ones consulted. Most medicines did not require a prescription, and factory-made pills were only beginning to displace concoctions produced by doctors and pharmacists.

Smith's father lent him £500 in 1860 so he could convert two cottages on North Church Street into a warehouse. It was such a good year that he sought even larger accommodations in 1861, renting some buildings at 10 North Churchside, which he bought in 1880 with the help of another £500 loan from his father. Business was so good because he had traveled to Norway on a Norwegian gunboat to buy 750 gallons of cod liver oil. It was a shrewd business deal, as the Norwegian product was both cheaper and better tasting than the previous supply from Newfoundland; the solid fat (stearine) had been processed out of it. At the same time, Smith's marketing efforts generated many new accounts among the hospitals of London. By 1880, he had even shipped on once to Cairo. At the encouragement of a correspondent, Smith registered his oil under the brand name Paragon Cod Liver Oil, to punctuate its outstanding qualities. Two larger competitors established factories in Norway after medical opinion swung decidedly in favor of the Norwegian product.

T.J. Smith never married; in 1896, a few months before his death, his 22-year-old nephew Horatio Nelson Smith (named after T.J.'s father) became a partner. H.N. was known for his long hours and direct, inquisitive manner. H.N. had apprenticed for six years making draperies. The firm, now known as T.J. Smith & Nephew, shifted its production away from cod liver oil in favor of bandages. And in 1907 it was registered as a limited liability company. When H.N. joined the company in 1896 staff numbered three. But when he signed a contract with the Turkish government in 1911 after the outbreak of the war with Bulgaria, employment reached 54. Soon thereafter a small local competitor, Lambert & Lambert, was acquired.

Smith & Nephew bought sanitary towel manufacturer SASHENA Limited in 1912 (the name an acronym for "Sanitary Absorbent Safe Hygienic Every Nurse Advocates"). The line was later known as, incorporating the 1925 acquisition of a half share of a German mill for producing cellulose sanitary towels, which had been developed to cope with the scarcity of cotton (S&N sold them under the trade name "Lilia," which had originally referred to an industrial cellulose towel product). As James Foreman-Peck records in his book *Smith & Nephew in the Health Care Industry,* the materials and methods for their manufacture were similar to surgical dressings, and women, buoyed by suffrage and a heightened role in the work force, were becoming more affluent. In 1954, the line continued with the introduction of the Lil-lets brand of tampons.

Configuring for Modern Times

World War I provided a huge demand for bandages. S&N staff increased to 1,200 as the company obtained contracts with several of the Allied governments as well as the American Red Cross. S&N's textile capacity was also used for producing certain military paraphernalia, such as weapons belts. In addition, legislation in the early 1920s, which stipulated that miners and factory workers have access to first aid kits in the workplace, offered S&N a natural opportunity. Nevertheless, after the Great War, production was scaled down considerably, to 183 employees. And the Great Depression spurred many administrative changes that helped shape S&N into a modern manufacturing corporation. Marketing efforts became more specialized. The company was incorporated as Smith & Nephew Associated Companies Ltd. (SANACO) in 1937.

Smith & Nephew often looked to Germany for technological innovations; H.N. Smith's knowledge of the German language appears to have served him well. In 1930, the company obtained the British rights to Elastoplast bandages, made from a specially woven cloth coated with adhesive, from Lohmann AG. The bandage, though more expensive than others, provided a quick and very effective fix for varicose ulcers in particular, noted various journals.

Smith & Nephew introduced a similar bandage called the Cellona plaster of Paris bandage in 1930. Though it seemed more expensive than the materials it would replace, the effort saved from making messy casts offset the costs and the bandage's light weight made patients more comfortable and healed them faster. And concerns over industrial accidents made the product's introduction timely. The bandages were later named Gypsona.

Much of Gypsona's complex manufacturing process originated with German companies. Several other types of bandages soaked in various types of medicines were co-opted from Germany and the United States. In 1946, a waterproof version was developed, and a new line known as Ultraplast (which later earned a Royal Warrant) came with the 1958 purchase of the Scottish company Wallace Cameron. In 1961, Elastoplast bandages controlled three-quarters of the market.

Cold War Diversification

In the 1950s, S&N had to decide whether to modernize its textile operations in Britain or buy textiles from the Far East. It and the unions agreed to the former, though a media campaign to enlist the support of other employers was necessary. S&N's mills subsequently earned a great reputation for efficiency. Interestingly, its mills in England and France were poised to produce denim when the enduring blue jeans fashion trend arrived from America. The automation of the company's mills included the purchase of one of the earliest commercially available computers in the 1950s, called the Leo. Its 1963 replacement was so large that S&N leased processing time until the 1970s.

Before its 1951 purchase of, S&N had been previously dependent on technology developed outside the company. Herts, which before World War II was the U.K. subsidiary of Beiersdorf, was best known for PAS and other of the earliest oral treatments for tuberculosis. However, like other research firms S&N were to acquire later, Herts lacked the resources to develop and promote them properly on its own. After the merger, Herts also worked on psychotropic drugs and, closer to S&N's core business, breathable membranes for covering wounds, the first of which was called Airstrip and was introduced in 1952. In addition to guaranteeing itself a supply of these types of films, S&N was also able to license these processes to other firms.

S&N entered the hypodermic syringe market in 1954 with the purchase of S. & R.J. Everett & Co. S&N set up a recycling service to provide a more thorough sterilization than the boiling the hospitals had been doing, but disposable syringes made this obsolete.

Through Lilia Limited, S&N formed a joint selling company with Arthur Berton Ltd., makers of the Dr. White's Brand, in 1955. Three years later both Arthur Berton and Southalls (Birmingham) Ltd. were acquired, making Lilia-White (Sales) Ltd. the leader of the sanitary protection market. To bolster its position, S&N bought Johnson & Johnson's Wrexham sanitary protection factory in 1962. This line contributed the second largest turnover to S&N; health care products remained first. Sanitary protection products made up the second largest portion of S&N's profits after health care products. The company also sold cosmetics and children's clothing.

The group bought No. 2 Temple Place in 1962 to house its headquarters. New products of the 1960s included disposable products and washable cotton blankets to prevent the spread of infection in hospitals. It introduced a standardized nurse's uniform, which was more efficient to produce than the myriad styles then existing among hospitals. A huge leap in efficiency was realized by a joint venture with Johnson & Johnson and a regional Scottish hospital board to develop individually wrapped sterilized dressings, which saved the hospitals the considerable expense of installing and running sterilizing equipment. Total group sales in 1964 were £28.3 million.

In 1968, the giant Unilever conglomerate tried unsuccessfully to purchase S&N in an emotional contest with S&N management, who initiated a campaign for the hearts and minds of its shareholders, touting the company's family tradition as well as its superior financial performance. The tactic worked well when Unilever's plan to slash dividends came to light.

The 1970s were characterized by pressures on margins and volume. The National Health Service, which accounted for much of the firm's U.K. business, became more demanding and cost-conscious; international competitive pressure also increased. This resulted in increased resources for research and development in the next decade. New buildings at the company's venerable Hull site were constructed in 1981 and 1986. Marketing and sales operations for the Health Care division were brought to Hull in 1982, joining the rest of the company's functions.

In the mid-1980s, S&N began licensing OpSite, a skin covering, through Johnson & Johnson. The 1985 purchase of the American company Affiliated Hospital extended S&N's product line into rubber gloves and steel trolleys. 3 Sigma Inc., another U.S. company, was also purchased. In 1987, sports injury specialist Donjoy Inc. and Sigma Inc., which made peristaltic infusion pumps, were added. Phizer Hospital Products Inc.'s United Medical Division, which made special surgical dressings in Florida, was acquired in 1988. In 1986, the company bought Richards of Memphis, Tennessee, which specialized in trauma and orthopedics, for £192.7 million.

S&N's 1989 purchase of Ioptex in for $230 million suffered from bad timing: soon thereafter, prices for the company's cataract replacement lenses fell by nearly two-thirds, thanks to U.S. government intervention. Smith & Nephew sold the company to Allergan for £11 million in 1994, pulverizing the company's profit that year.

But an example of S&N's good fortune was illustrated by Nivea brand moisturizing cream. Overseas rights for the Nivea brand of moisturizing cream passed to Smith & Nephew with the acquisition of Herts Pharmaceuticals Ltd. in 1951. Soon it contributed almost as much as Elastoplast bandages to S&N's consumer sales. In 1992, Beiersdorf paid £46.5 million to buy back U.K. and Commonwealth rights for what was estimated to be the largest toiletry brand in the world. Smith & Nephew continued to earn a 17 percent royalty on U.K. Nivea sales without having to spend any money on advertising. In the 1960s, the brand was extended with "Nivea Lotions" and an upscale skin care line known as "Nivea Visage" competed with L'Oréal in the 1990s.

Searching for Twenty-First-Century Markets

The transformation of S&N into a modern multinational corporation occurred under chief executive Eric Kinder in the 1980s. S&N's international trade dated back to T.J. Smith's early days; companies had been established in Canada in 1921 and in Australia and New Zealand in the early 1950s. Kinder felt the company needed to extend its export markets beyond post-Imperial Commonwealth countries. By the late-1990s, S&N had substantial holdings in Europe and Asia. Sales in the U.K. accounted for 54.1 percent of the group's total in 1980; ten years later, that figure had dropped to 23.6 percent, with the United States as the company's biggest market.

The company broadened its European reach. In 1987, S&N bought the Spanish firm Alberto Fernandez S.A., which made latex products such as gloves and prophylactics. In France the company bought Cogemo S.A., makers of continuous passive motion machines, and Sanortho S.A., which made orthopedic implants. A German distribution venture with B. Braun GmbH was set up in 1985, and expanded to include Switzerland in 1988. But newly developing countries in Asia seemed to offer the best opportunities for growth. S&N's division in Japan,

established in 1990, achieved sales of more than £30 million in five years. In the 1990s, S&N forecast that China and India would be among the ten largest health care markets within thirty years. By 1995, the company had three offices in China, with plans to eventually manufacture bandages there. Sales in Africa, Asia, Australia, and the Pacific were worth £151 million in 1994, still quite less than the £239 million garnered in the United Kingdom. The United States remained the largest market, providing S&N with 40 percent of its sales, or £470 million. Continental Europe accounted for £205 million in sales, up from £37 million in 1984.

At the same time as the geographic range was expanded, the commodity status of certain product lines had to be redressed in order to improve the company's profit margins. In 1991, John Robinson took over as chief executive, succeeding Kinder, who then served as chairman. Under Robinson, the company specialized in products for tissue repair and protection ("wound management"), rather than the grab bag of medical supplies it once offered. Its research goals have been progressing, an executive told *Management Today,* "from replacement to repair to regeneration." In 1993, S&N moved its research center from an Essex mansion to a new site in York Science Park, convenient to York University, an esteemed research institution.

Sacramento-based Cedaron Medical Inc. licensed its Dexter computerized physical therapy system in 1994 to Smith & Nephew, which hoped to succeed by offering a high-tech solution at a lower than average price. The rehabilitation equipment market was growing at least five percent a year at the time of the acquisition, and industrial hand injuries such as carpal tunnel syndrome, which was then beginning to get its share of press attention, seemed a precipitous omen for the Dexter.

Smith and Nephew committed at least $10 million to a 1994 joint venture with California's Advanced Tissue Sciences Inc. to culture cartilage cells for joint replacement applications. This project held the potential to open a vast new market and save patients from expensive and painful surgery. ATS benefited from the S&N's ability to fund the project through years of testing. The product was not expected to be marketed until the end of the century. But after years of consistently respectable earnings and long-term investments in many new areas of technology. The company's future seemed assured.

In 1993, Smith & Nephew finally decided to withdraw from competition with cheaper imported denim and cotton. Nevertheless, after years of consistently respectable earnings and long-term investments in many new areas of technology, its future success in its designated specialty seems assured.

Principal Subsidiaries

Smith & Nephew Pharmaceutical Ltd.; Smith & Nephew United Inc.; Smith & Nephew Richards, Inc. (USA).

Principal Divisions

Health Care; Medical Fabrics; Therapy Equipment; Toiletries.

Principal Operating Units

Smith & Nephew North America; United Kingdom and Europe; Africa; Asia; and Australasia.

Further Reading

"Advertorial Blitz Pushes S&N's Simple Skincare," *Marketing Week,* March 31, 1995, p. 15.

Auguston, Karen, "Giving Customers What They Want, When They Want It," *Modern Materials Handling,* September 1995.

Beresford, Philip, "Winners & Losers: MT250," *Management Today,* June 1991, pp. 32–42.

Borzo, Greg, "Glove Shortage Creates Anxiety," *Health Industry Today,* November 1991, pp. 1, 14–15.

Braly, Damon, "Traditional Burn Dressings Market Slowed by Growing Synthetics Usage," *Health Industry Today,* December 1993.

Ferguson, Anne, "Smith & Nephew's Specialty," *Management Today,* April 1986, p. 64.

Foreman-Peck, James, *Smith & Nephew in the Health Care Industry,* Aldershot, Hants: Edward Elgar, 1995.

Heller, Robert, et. al., "Britain's Best Managed Eight," *Management Today,* April 1986, pp. 58–67.

Hoggan, Karen, "Nivea: Smooth Operator," *Marketing,* August 30, 1990, pp. 18–19.

Larson, Mark, "Cedaron Signs Licensing Deal with British Firm," *The Business Journal Serving Greater Sacramento,* February 21, 1994.

Latham, Valerie, "Nivea Spreads Range," *Marketing,* April 1, 1993, p. 5.

Lorenz, Andrew, "Why Focus Favors Smith & Nephew," *Management Today,* January 1996, pp. 32–36.

Lucas, Spencer, "Driven to Success: Ken Harvey Relied on Enthusiasm—Not Experience—To Get Ahead at Smith & Nephew Richards," *Memphis Business Journal,* December 18, 1995, p. 1A.

"Sanitary Protection Products," *EIU Retail Business,* No. 437. July 1994.

Sewell, Tim, "An Investment Pays Off," *Memphis Business Journal,* May 15, 1995.

Silverman, Suzann D., "A Joint Effort," *International Business,* August 1994, pp. 68–70.

"Smith & Nephew in Good Health," *Management Today,* June 1991, p. 36.

Upton, Richard, "The Bottom Line: Smith & Nephew Sticks to the Well-Tried Remedies," *Personnel Management,* July 1987, pp. 37–39.

—Frederick C. Ingram

Sports & Recreation, Inc.

SPORTS & RECREATION, INC.

4701 West Hillsborough Avenue
Tampa, Florida 33614
U.S.A.
(813) 886-9688
Fax: (813) 886-9001

Public Company
Incorporated: 1988 as SRI Holdings, Inc.
Employees: 5,900
Sales: $525.7 million (1995)
Stock Exchanges: New York
SICs: 5941 Sporting Goods & Bicycle Shops

Operator of the tenth-largest sporting goods chain in the United States, Sports & Recreation, Inc., is a specialty retailer of brand name sporting equipment and athletic footwear. During the mid-1990s, Sports & Recreation operated 84, 50,000-square-foot stores in 29 states, the majority of which were located in smaller, mid-sized markets. The company began as a subsidiary of Brunswick Corporation in 1979, then after a decade of modest physical growth began expanding rapidly during the 1990s. After going public in 1992, when the company operated 20 stores, Sports & Recreation more than quadrupled the number of its stores during the ensuing three years, extending its geographic presence during the period from a 12-state area to include 29 states. The increase in the company's annual sales during this three-year span mirrored the magnitude of its physical growth, soaring from $167 million to $525 million by 1995.

Late 1970s Origins

The genesis of Sports & Recreation occurred in Skokie, Illinois, at the corporate headquarters of Brunswick Corporation during the late 1970s. Brunswick executives discussed the idea of diversifying their bowling and billiards business and starting a sporting goods retailing business. As a result of their discussions, Brunswick created the predecessor organization to Sports & Recreation, a subsidiary retail business formed in 1979 and headed by James Bradke. The business began with one store located on Florida's west coast, where the company's store units would be confined for nearly a decade. Although the company was renowned for the rapid expansion of its stores during the 1990s—indeed, some would charge that the company was overambitious in its effort to open more stores—growth was initially slow for the Bradke-led, Brunswick subsidiary.

During the company's first decade, corporate activity centered largely on simply securing the finances to develop the business. Financial stability first became a concern in 1982 when Brunswick found itself facing a hostile takeover. In the process of shielding itself from the unsolicited advances of a corporate suitor, Brunswick sold the sporting goods business it had established three years earlier, spinning it off to Bradke and other investors for $3 million. Bradke took two other executives with him when he left Brunswick and renamed the new, independent company Sports & Recreation Inc.

Expansion Begins in 1988

With Bradke serving as chairman and chief executive officer, Sports & Recreation set out on its own as an operator of three sporting goods stores. Five years after leaving Brunswick's corporate umbrella, the number of stores operated by Sports & Recreation had increased to five. The desire to develop Sports & Recreation into a genuine chain was touched off, according to one industry analyst, by the encroachment of a rival sporting goods retailer into Bradke's territory. In 1988, when Florida-based sporting goods retailer Sports Authority opened a superstore near Sports & Recreation's corporate headquarters, the gauntlet had been thrown down directly on Bradke's home turf. He answered with an aggressive move, directing an exhaustive expansion program that stood in sharp contrast to the years of slow expansion. During a five-year period following the opening of the Sports Authority store near Sports & Recreation's executive offices, Bradke quintupled the chain's store count, broadened its geographic scope extensively, and as a result created a formidable competitor for Fort Lauderdale-based Sports Authority.

Each based in Florida and each executing ambitious expansion programs, Sports Authority and Sports & Recreation at first glance appeared to be following the same course toward securing the national lead in the retail sporting goods industry.

453

Company Perspectives:

The Company's business strategy is to offer its customers the best value in sporting goods through a wide assortment of quality name brand merchandise, superior customer service and everyday low prices.

However, upon closer examination, each were pursuing different corporate strategies. Sports Authority and other operators of massive retail "superstores" selected sites for their stores in major metropolitan markets, thereby following a general rule of thumb in the sporting goods industry that superstores required a population base of more than two million people to prosper. Accordingly, as sporting goods superstores proliferated during the late 1980s and early 1990s, the push was on to establish a presence in markets such as Detroit, Chicago, and Atlanta.

However, Sports & Recreation broke with tradition and concentrated its expansion on smaller markets. Bradke and his management team moved into second-tier markets such as Oklahoma City, Memphis, and Charlotte, North Carolina, establishing their stores in markets with populations ranging between 300,000 and one million and avoiding the race to secure a foothold in big city markets. "We try to be very selective about the places we go," Bradke said, explaining Sports & Recreation's atypical expansion strategy. "We keep looking at all markets and look for a path of least resistance. We look for communities that seem to have a sporting goods flavor."

As the company dramatically picked up the pace of its expansion, it did so under several different names. Instead of operating its stores under the Sports & Recreation banner, the company's stores were graced with signs that were intended to strengthen the local, "hometown" image of Sports & Recreation's stores. Building on such names as "Sports Unlimited," "Sports & Rec," and "Sports," the stores then also adopted the local community name where a particular store was located. Accordingly, the chain included stores operating under names such as "Tampa Sports," "Oklahoma City Sports & Rec," and "Jacksonville Sports Unlimited."

Before expansion could begin in earnest, however, Bradke still needed a solid financial foundation to support the establishment of massive superstores in secondary markets. The number of stores had increased to eight by the time Bradke had finally secured an arrangement with outside investors. In September 1989, a Luxembourg investment banking company named Investcorp bought a majority interest in the company, thereby facilitating the establishment of additional stores. With the financial strength provided by Investcorp's backing, Bradke was able to obtain the capital needed to expand at the pace he desired. "We really haven't had to use their [Investcorp's] money for expansion," he noted at the time, "but their backing did help us to get other outside financing."

Once Investcorp had financially allied itself with Sports & Recreation, the push was on to extend the company's presence beyond Florida markets and create a national chain. Between 1989 and 1991, the company's financial growth told the tale of its physical growth, as Sports & Recreation quickly grabbed the attention of industry observers who were drawn by the prolific growth registered by the Tampa-based company. Annual sales during the two-year period shot up from $70 million to $138.9 million, nearly doubling while earnings rose from $4.8 million to $9 million. By 1992, when sales continued to rise robustly to $167.4 million, the Sports & Recreation chain comprised 20 stores spread across a 12-state area that bounded the southeastern and southwestern United States. Expansion was increasingly extending the company's presence farther north and west, as the company aimed at becoming a nationwide retailer.

In the early 1990s, Sports & Recreation was recording the greatest growth in its history during the worst of economic times for retailers throughout the country. Indeed, Sports & Recreation stood as the darling of the sporting goods retail industry, growing by leaps and bounds and benefitting, to a certain extent, from the sagging business of other retailers. Just as the company was preparing to mount its ambitious expansion campaign, other retailers were moving in the opposite direction by shuttering some of their outlets. Bradke noted as much in an interview with *Sporting Goods Business,* explaining that "due to the decline of many department stores, there are a lot of large businesses available and a lot of them have base rental rates that can be taken over at a very good price."

1992 Public Offering

Conditions during the early 1990s were ripe for Sports & Recreation's expansion, at least as far as Bradke perceived the situation. "There are opportunities," he remarked in 1991, "that have never been available before"; opportunities he did not intend to pass up. To obtain the financial means to expand his chain of stores further, Bradke took Sports & Recreation public in September 1992, making an initial public offering of stock at $17.50 per share. The public offering raised $68 million, which was used to pay off debt and to finance expansion that was expected to double the chain's size within the ensuing two years.

By the beginning of 1993, the money raised from the public offering had erased nearly all of the company's $31 million in long-term debt and left Bradke with $17 million in cash to open additional stores. Plans for 1993 called for the establishment of at least 12 stores and a 25 to 35 percent growth rate for each year thereafter, but even these lofty expectations were exceeded during the next two years as Bradke engineered a spree of store openings.

Initially, the spate of store openings was well-received both by those at the company's headquarters and by outside investors. The first full-year after the September 1992 public offering was the best financial year in the company's history. Sales were up 43 percent to $239 million, net income was up an enormous 124 percent to $11.3 million, and the company's stock, which began trading on the NASDAQ market at $17.50 per share, was trading at $43.25 per share at the end of 1993. The glowing financial results prodded Bradke forward, leading to the opening of more than 15 stores in 1994 and the announcement that 23 to 25 stores were slated to open in 1995 and another 28 to 32 stores were scheduled for debut in 1996. Quickly, however, forecasts for the future soured, and Bradke's hopes for rampant growth were dashed. A little more than two years after drawing praise for leading Sports & Recreation toward the best financial year in its history, Bradke found himself without a job and the company he had founded moving ahead without him.

Mid-1990s Downturn Brings New Management

Before Bradke's departure, 28 stores were opened in 1995, bringing the total store count by the end of the year to 80. The feverish expansion that had taken place during the early 1990s, however, had begun to take its toll on Sports & Recreation. The company had more than quadrupled its store count during a period when the sports apparel and athletic footwear business was shrinking. As industry sales dipped, Bradke surged ahead with expansion, which by 1995 had saddled Sports & Recreation with mounting debt and bloated inventories, prompting a dramatic drop in the value of the company's stock. Between December 1995 and February 1996 the value of Sports & Recreation's stock was cut in half, plunging to $5 per share and precipitating Bradke's termination.

Bradke was fired by Sports & Recreation's board of directors in February 1996 and replaced by Stephen Bebis, who previously had been in charge of a Canadian chain of home improvement stores named Aikenhead. Upon being named as Sports & Recreation's new chairman and chief executive officer, Bebis announced, "I will be an agent of change, but I see my role as re-engineering what already is a good company into one that continues growing while throwing off strong profits." Specifically, Bebis put the construction of a new corporate headquarters on hold for two to three years and cut back the expansion plans for 1996 laid out by Bradke. Instead of opening as many as 16 stores in 1996, Bebis resolved to open only three stores and focus his efforts on controlling the company's inventory and upgrading the chain's computer systems. As Bebis adjusted to his role as the new leader of Sports & Recreation, many of his plans revolved around curbing the chain's growth and taking the time to bring about order and structure to the free-wheeling growth of the company during the 1990s, but his vision for Sports & Recreation's future was bold. Sports & Recreation headed into the late 1990s in pursuit of becoming the largest sporting goods chain in the country.

Principal Subsidiaries

Sports & Recreation Holdings of PA, Inc.; Guide Series, Inc.

Further Reading

Albright, Mark, "New CEO Prepares Game Plan for Tampa-Based Sports & Recreation Inc.," *Knight-Ridder/Tribune Business News,* February 14, 1996, p. 21.
——, "Sports & Recreation Inc.," *Knight-Ridder/Tribune Business News,* March 15, 1996, p. 31.
Boyd, Christopher, "Agassi vs. Courier," *Florida Trend,* October 1993, p. 60.
Gaffney, Andrew, "Unlimited Boundaries," *Sporting Goods Business,* June 1991, p. 38.
"New Equity Backs Sports Unlimited," *Sporting Goods Business,* April 1991, p. 24.
Smith, Katherine Snow, "Sports Retailer Hits Homers One Customer at a Time," *Tampa Bay Business Journal,* March 25, 1994, p. 1.
"Sports & Recreation Floats IPO," *Footwear News,* September 28, 1992, p. 22.
"Strong Getting Stronger," *Sporting Goods Dealer,"* June 1996, p. 22.

—Jeffrey L. Covell

Standex International Corporation

6 Manor Parkway
Salem, New Hampshire 03079
U.S.A.
(603) 893-9701
Fax: (603) 893-7324
Internet: http://www.standex.com

Public Company
Incorporated: 1955 as Standard International Corporation
Employees: 5,121
Sales: $569 million (1995)
Stock Exchanges: New York
SICs: 3556 Food Products Machinery; 3441 Fabricated
Structural Metal; 3593 Fluid Power Cylinders &
Actuators; 3494 Valves & Pipe Fittings, Not
Elsewhere Classified

Standex International Corporation is the third-largest food products machinery manufacturer in the United States and the seventh most profitable manufacturer of business supplies by return on equity. A highly diversified conglomerate, Standex is the corporate umbrella for three operating groups—Institutional Products, Industrial Products, and Graphics/Mail Order—that produce, market, and distribute 17 product categories, from hydraulic cylinders, relays, and inductors to food service equipment, industrial hardware, commercial printing, and mail order gift packages. The end-users of Standex products range from supermarkets, automobile factories, Sunday schools, and fast food restaurants to water purification plants, government voting sites, chiropractors, computer manufacturers, and prisons. Led by the six product lines of its Institutional Products Group, in 1995 Standex International operated 87 plants and warehouses in 14 countries, including Australia, Italy, Ireland, France, Spain, and Germany.

Postwar Origins

The origins of Standex International may be traced to shortly after World War II, when Bolta Plastics, a vinyl sheeting company, was founded by John Bolten Sr.; his son, John Jr.; Samuel Dennis III, and Daniel Hogan, a former Navy officer and Bolten Sr.'s son-in-law. In less than a decade, Bolten and his partners grew Bolta from a $1 million-a-year startup to a mature $28 million concern. In 1954, General Tire and Rubber bought the company for $4 million, and within a year Bolten and partners had reinvested the money in Standard Publishing, a Cincinnati-based publisher of religious materials founded in 1866, and Roehlen Engraving, a Rochester, New York-based manufacturer of steel-engraved embossing rollers for creating decorative impressions on tiles, upholstery, and other surfaces. They renamed the business Standard International Corporation; Standard Publishing and Roehlen Engraving later became the core of Standex's Graphics/Mail Order and Industrial Products groups, respectively.

Through early acquisitions like Everedy cookware, Lestoil and Bon Ami cleansing product manufacturers, and Coca-Cola bottling franchises in South America, Standard initiated a strategy of growth that by the mid-1990s had totaled more than 125 acquisitions. In a 1979 interview with *Forbes* magazine, Hogan, who had early on succeeded Bolten Sr. as company president, described the ''five laws'' that guided Standex's acquisition policy during his tenure: 1. Beware of the time of the hump—when a company inflates its earnings in anticipation of a sale. 2. The price of an acquisition varies inversely with the square of the distance from New York. 3. Companies that have made money for ten years in a row will probably make it again in the eleventh. 4. Companies with loss carryforwards have a demonstrable capacity for losing money. 5. Concentrate on small private businesses that have some sort of proprietary position in their market and which are for sale because of estate problems or lack of professional management.

Almost without exception, all the companies Standex acquired grew at a faster, more profitable rate within the conglomerate than they had on their own. By focusing only on market leaders in basic U.S. industries that were largely unaffected by rapid technological change, Standex immediately positioned itself at the forefront of a new industry segment every time it acquired a company. ''If you look at our stable of companies,'' Hogan told the *Boston Globe* in 1983, ''you'll find that in every case they have a definite niche and a small industry dominant position, in some cases almost a monopolistic position.''

Company Perspectives:

Standex's policy of balanced diversification—coupled with aggressive management and conservative financial techniques—has enabled the company to achieve above average growth in sales and earnings since its founding in 1955.

Going Public in the 1960s

In 1964, Hogan's management team took Standard International public and began defining the product groups in which it believed the company had the most expertise and around which its acquisition strategy should coalesce. From these early decisions the three basic product groups that would characterize Standex's product identities and market niches for the next three decades were established: industrial products such as pumps, electronic assemblies and switches, and "texturizing" systems for product surfaces; institutional products like restaurant china, casters and wheels, and commercial cooking and refrigeration equipment; and graphics/mail order/consumer products such as religious publications, election forms, mail order food goods, and bookbinding systems.

Early on, Standard adopted a corporate policy of balanced acquisition, ensuring a strong, even cash flow by acquiring cash-generating businesses (like Crest Fruit, purchased in April 1972) at the same time as capital-intensive companies (like Master-Bilt, added in November 1971). Exploiting high inflation rates to largely nullify the four- and five-percent interest charged on the loans it used to fuel its expansion, between January 1967 and June 1968 alone Standard acquired 11 new companies. Standard's growth strategy, however, was coupled with a policy of unceremoniously dumping companies whose profitability or competitiveness in their market niches showed signs of slipping. Through a system of tight financial controls in which all banking matters and cash requests passed through corporate headquarters, Standard focused on unusual requests for cash from it subsidiaries to weed out those potentially ripe for divestiture.

Beyond financial matters, however, Standard encouraged subsidiaries to run their businesses in an independent, entrepreneurial fashion. Indeed, in 1996 Standex's corporate headquarters would consist of only 46 people, managing everything from banking, taxes, and legal affairs to insurance, audits, and investor relations.

Rapid Expansion in the 1970s

Renamed Standex International in 1973, the company continued to fill out its three basic product groups throughout the 1970s and 1980s, adding the firms that would constitute the roughly 25 businesses in its 1996 roster of manufacturers. Between 1969 and 1970, Standex acquired Jarvis and Jarvis (now Jarvis Caster Group, Standex's industrial caster and wheel manufacturer), United Service Equipment Co. (now USECO, a manufacturer of food service feeding systems for hospitals, prisons, and schools), and Mason Candlelight (a producer of candles and candle lamps for table top lighting). In 1971

Standex added Spincraft, a Wisconsin firm specializing in the power spinning of metals, and Master-Bilt Refrigeration, a manufacturer of commercial refrigeration equipment ranging from ice cream dipping cabinets to refrigerated warehouses. Within a year, Standex had also added General Slicing Machine Company, a manufacturer of commercial refrigeration equipment, and Crest Fruit Company, a mail-order grapefruit distributor. The company also continued to weed out unprofitable or uncompetitive units—usually at a profit. Of the 25 businesses Standex divested in its first 40-odd years, only one was sold for a loss.

Between 1971 and 1975, Standex's net sales rose from $119 million to $176 million, a 48 percent leap. Industrial products comprised one-third of all sales, followed by consumer products at 28 percent; graphics (i.e., its publishing and printing operations) at 22 percent; and institutional products at 17 percent. In the same period, Standex acquired industrial engraving plants in West Germany, France, and Australia to capitalize on its library of 100,000 industrial embossing master rolls. In 1977 Standex added further to the core of firms with the acquisition of Barbecue King of Greenville, South Carolina (a manufacturer of commercial cooking equipment) and, a year later, the Wire-O Corporation (a producer of wire book binding products), H. F. Coors (a California-based manufacturer of china and cookware), and Williams Manufacturing (a Chicago producer of chiropractic and traction tables that would become the core of Standex's Williams Healthcare Systems operation).

Standex's strategy of maintaining a mix of varied manufacturers through a rolling series of acquisitions and divestitures amounted to a kind of self-investing diversified mutual fund; the conglomerate could count on the positive performance of any given segment of its product line to offset the shaky performance of any other. Indeed, when appropriate acquisition targets were unavailable or too expensive, Standex literally did invest in itself, choosing to repurchase huge blocks of its own stock rather than invest in other companies. It thus spread the risks of dramatic cyclical downturns throughout the corporation's operations and virtually assured enhanced shareholder value and steadily rising quarterly dividend payments. In fact, through April 1996, Standex had paid dividends in every quarter since it had become a public corporation in 1964, with a clockwork-like 32 dividend increases.

The business press began describing Standex as a "miniconglomerate" and "one of the best of the small conglomerates," but company management preferred the term "diversified manufacturer," claiming there had never been a "grand plan" to create a multinational conglomerate. As Hogan told *Forbes* magazine in 1979, when Standex acquired new companies "we just thought we were making good investments. Then we found out we were a conglomerate."

In 1977, Standex's sales broke the $200 million mark for the first time, and in the following year management launched a program of intensive capital spending that by 1981 had topped $70 million. It added commercial food service equipment manufacturer Barbecue King of South Carolina (later renamed BK Industries) to its stable in 1977, acquired the company's British operation in 1979, and opened a manufacturing facility for its Industrial Products Group in Kent, England, that was soon producing more than 20 million reed switches a year for electronic applications.

As the 1970s wound down, Standex's plans for future expansion were centered on a single giant purchase in a new product area or several small acquisitions to its existing business lines. Preferring to pay cash for its new purchases, Standex arranged a four-year, $12 million loan through three banks in 1979, and the following year added James Burn Bindings Ltd., a British book binding operation, to its Graphics/Mail Order Group.

Challenges in the 1980s

A rash of mergers and acquisitions in the 1980s coupled with rising interest rates, however, put a brake on Standex's expansion plans. As Wall Street corporate raiders drove the asking prices for available companies skyward, acquisitive conglomerates, even those who, like Standex, were looking only for long-term investments in niche-leading companies, were branded guilty by association. In contrast to its 30 acquisitions during the 1970s, Standex acquired only 11 firms in the 1980s.

Partly as a result of this inactivity, by 1984 Standex's total debt-to-capital ratio had fallen from 38 percent in the mid-1970s to 20 percent, and it had accumulated $100 million of potential debt capacity for acquisitions. Sales broke the $375 million mark in 1984, and for perhaps the first time in its 30-year history Standex had no money-losing businesses. And for all its emphasis on development-through-acquisition by 1984 more than 60 percent of Standex's historical expansion growth had come through internal growth. In May, Standex's management joined with a Boston investment firm in an attempt to acquire Standex through a $250 million friendly leveraged buyout. By putting up a percentage of the purchase price and borrowing the rest, with the company itself offered as collateral, Standex's management hoped to buy up its stock and take the corporation private, thereby avoiding the requirement to disclose financial information to the Securities and Exchange Commission and its own shareholders. Within weeks, however, Standex management had withdrawn the offer, citing new uncertainty about the economy. In 1985 Standex nevertheless began aggressively repurchasing its stock on the open market, and by 1996 a total of 17,860,000 shares had been bought back at a cost of over $200 million, reducing the number of outstanding common shares by 57 percent from 1985 levels.

After 37 years at the helm, Daniel Hogan stepped down as president in 1985, leaving the $480 million firm in the hands of Thomas L. King, a Standex veteran of 24 years and, like Hogan, an Ivy Leaguer and former Navy man. King continued to collect the companies' that would comprise Standex's mid-1990s corporate roster. Federal Industries, a Wisconsin-based manufacturer of refrigerated and nonrefrigerated display cases for the food service industry was added to the Institutional Products Group in 1986; and Custom Hoists Inc., a manufacturer of hydraulic cylinders for dump trucks and other vehicles, joined the Industrial Products Group in 1988.

The 1990s and Beyond

In 1991, Sapemo S.A.'s multiple ring binding product line was incorporated into the James Burn International bookbinding operations and, a year later, Standex acquired Toastwell, a St. Louis-based manufacturer of commercial toasters, waffle irons, griddles, and food warmers, for its Institutional Products Group. In mid-1995, Metal Products Manufacturing of Milwaukee, Oregon, was acquired to extend Standex's Snappy Air Distribution product line (Institutional Products Group) into the Pacific Northwest. Reflecting the diversity of the product lines Standex sought for acquisition, in 1989 Standex acquired the assets of a massage/traction table manufacturer and two years later bought the entire product line of a Christmas tree stand manufacturer (making Standex, by 1996, the world leader in that market niche).

In June 1995, Tom King retired as Standex's CEO after ten years at the helm, giving way to Edward J. Trainer, a former president of the Institutional Products Group. Standex's prospects for the remainder of the 1990s appeared quite positive. Revenues, net income, earnings per share, return on equity, return on sales, and book value per share all hit record highs in fiscal 1995. Almost half of all sales came from the three components of its Institutional Products Group—Institutional Products, Air Distribution Products, and Commercial Products—and another quarter was generated by the four operations in its Industrial Products Group—Roehlen/Europe, Roehlen/North America, Standex Precision Engineering, and Standex Electronics. In the mid-1990s, Standex added new product lines to its Master-Bilt subsidiary and increased the capacity of its cooler and pipe, duct, and fitting manufacturing operations. Its European subsidiaries, which duplicated its U.S. product lines, experienced renewed growth, and it initiated a marketing campaign in the South American market, expanded the "quality circle" program it launched in 1982, and continued to explore potential new acquisitions to the corporate stable. The company's essential identity, however, remained fundamentally unchanged; as former CEO Dan Hogan put it laconically in 1983, "we manufacture widgets and we sell them and that's all we do."

Principal Subsidiaries

Crest Fruit Co.; Custom Hoists, Inc.; James Burn/American, Inc.; Standex Financial Corp.; SXI Limited (Canada); Keller-Dorian Graveurs, S.A. (France); S.I. de Mexico S.A. de C.V. (Mexico); Standex International FSC, Inc. (Virgin Islands); Standex International GmbH (Germany); Standex Holdings Limited (U.K.).

Further Reading

Cook, James, "Haphazard Conglomerate," *Forbes,* March 19, 1979, p. 38.
Delamaide, Darrell, "Profits Upturn Underway at Standex International," *Barron's,* March 1, 1976.
Hebert, Ernest, "Thomas L. King: Standex International," *Business New Hampshire,* July 8, 1987.
Hussey, Alan F., "Big Fish, Small Ponds: Standex's Winners Range from Electronics to Chiropractor's Tables," *Barron's,* November 12, 1984.

Pillsbury, Fred, "Buy Homely Philosophy has Paid Off for Standex," *Boston Globe,* November 29, 1983.

Stein, Charles, "Officers Bid for Standex," *Boston Globe,* May 4, 1984.

——, "Standex Officers Withdraw Offer," *Boston Globe,* June 16, 1984.

Troxell, Thomas N., Jr., "Acquisitions Spur Gains for Standex International," *Barron's,* March 6, 1978, 28–29+.

——, "New Hampshire's Larger Manufacturers Size Up the New Year," *New Hampshire Business Review,* December 27, 1991.

——, "Salem-Based Firm Plies Global Market," *New Hampshire Business Review,* March 23, 1990.

Wallace, Glenn, "Diversification Stands at Standex: Founder's Philosophy to Endure," *Manchester Union Leader,* January 20, 1992.

—Paul S. Bodine

Sun Sportswear, Inc.

6520 South 190th Street
Kent, Washington 98032
U.S.A.
(206) 251-3565
Fax: (206) 251-0527

Public Company
Incorporated: 1981 as Sun Shirts, Inc.
Employees: 508
Sales: $93.9 million (1995)
Stock Exchanges: NASDAQ
SICs: 2329 Men's/Boys' Clothing, Not Elsewhere
   Classified; 2339 Women's/Misses' Outerwear, Not
   Elsewhere Classified; 2369 Girls'/Children's
   Outerwear, Not Elsewhere Classified

The largest producer of silkscreened apparel in the United States, Sun Sportswear, Inc., designs, sources, prints, markets, and sells an extensive collection of imprinted, dyed, and decorated casual sportswear for men, women, and children. During the mid-1990s, Sun Sportswear sold its proprietary and licensed designs to roughly 30 national and regional chains, including Wal-Mart, Target Stores, K-Mart, Montgomery Ward, JC Penney, and Sears. The company conducted its business by purchasing blank T-shirts, sweatshirts, sweatpants, tank tops, nightshirts, and similar apparel items and screenprinting designs on those garments. For its licensed designs, the company owned the rights to use or distribute certain characters and trademarks that included "Looney Tunes," "Major League Baseball," "Pocahontas," "The Lion King," "101 Dalmatians," "Garfield," "Batman Forever," and "Winnie the Pooh." For its proprietary designs, Sun Sportswear relied on concepts developed by its merchandising staff and internal graphics design department.

Founded in 1981

In March 1981, David A. Sabey, Richard Lentz, and James A. Contini entered into business together with the establishment of Sun Sportswear's predecessor, Sun Shirts, Inc., a small firm that began business as a T-shirt designer in suburban Seattle, Washington. From the company's founding date forward, Sabey and his successors steered Sun Sportswear in new directions by adding product lines, penetrating new markets, and redefining the company's business strategy. The changes initiated transformed the modestly sized, T-shirt designer into the largest producer of silkscreened casual sportswear in the United States in little more than a decade. Absent from the proceedings that marked the rise of the company they had helped found were Lentz, founder of Union Bay Sportswear, and Contini, a graphic artist. Before Sun Sportswear's inaugural year of business was through, Sabey bought out his partners and assumed full control over the company. Under Sabey's stewardship, the whirlwind of changes that shaped Sun Sportswear into the preeminent leader in its industry ensued.

Initially, Sun Sportswear contracted with other manufacturers to supply screenprinted tops to coordinate with pants sold through Lentz's Union Bay Sportswear. With Lentz's departure and the arrival of three hand presses in 1982, however, the scope of the business changed. Beginning in 1982, the company operated by creating its own designs, screenprinting those designs on blank T-shirts purchased from outside sources, and selling the garments to small, regional retail chains, gift and surf shops, and mass merchandisers, deriving nearly all of its business from sales to male customers. A decade later, Sun Sportswear's business would be dramatically different, as a series of pivotal, evolutionary steps transformed the company into a proprietary and licensed designer of casual sportswear for massive retail chains that drew the bulk of its business from female customers. The first important step toward this end was taken in 1983 when the company expanded beyond T-shirts and started to become more of a full-line sportswear company, changing its name from Sun Shirts, Inc. to Sun Sportswear, Inc. to reflect this change. Concurrent with this significant diversification, the company resolved to develop a customer base comprising mass merchandisers and forego the practice of distributing T-shirts to small retail chains, gift shops, and surf shops. Sabey and his executive staff decided to develop long-term relationships with mass merchandisers such as Target Stores and Wal-Mart who operated retail outlets on a nationwide basis. The decision to eschew smaller retailers and target the country's largest mass merchandise chains was a significant one in Sun Sportswear's

Company Perspectives:

Sun Sportswear is recognized for its ability to attract retail shoppers' interests. We accomplish this by offering a well-designed product line and fresh, attractive artwork that sells our screen printed goods.

history, paving the way for the high-volume, low-cost casual sportswear designer the company would eventually become.

By the mid-1980s, Sun Sportswear was gradually making its way toward becoming a contender in the national market for silkscreened garments, having altered it business strategy meaningfully during its first half decade of existence. The company purchased undecorated apparel items from domestic and foreign producers and then, through its internal art staff, created designs that were applied to the garments at Sun Sportswear's production facility in Redmond, Washington. Operating as such, the company existed exclusively as a proprietary designer, scoring its greatest success with its creation of "Rude Dog" in 1986, by which time Sun Sportswear had expanded its production capabilities to include five hand presses and five automatic presses. Initially, "Rude Dog" was emblazoned as a character on T-shirts, but as the popularity of the Sun Sportswear-created figure grew enormously after its introduction, "Rude Dog" appeared on a plethora of items, including skateboards, beach towels, and socks.

By the end of the 1980s, the "Rude Dog" character had turned into a valuable revenue-generating engine of its own, enjoying such widespread popularity that the apparel items decorated by Sun Sportswear could not satisfy consumer demand. The character was licensed to other manufacturers as a result, appearing on 21 different types of consumer products and giving Sun Sportswear a welcomed yet unanticipated boost to its business. Despite the phenomenal success of "Rude Dog" as a licensed character, Sun Sportswear's most important move in the market for licensed products came not as a licensor but as a licensee. For the first six years of its existence, Sun Sportswear derived all of its business from designs created by its own team of artists, with "Rude Dog" ranking as the biggest success. In 1987, however, the company added licensed designs to its product line and opened the door to a lucrative market that in less than half a decade would account for roughly half of its total sales volume. The decision to produce and sell licensed designs stood as a watershed development in the company's history, equalling the significance of the diversification beyond the T-shirt market and the development of a mass merchandiser customer base in 1983.

1987 Entry into Licensed Designs

Sun Sportswear's entry into the licensed design arena was effected in August 1987, when one of the company's largest customers, Wal-Mart, helped it gain the license for the "California Raisin" characters from Applause Licensing Co., based in Woodland Hills, California. With the highly marketable "California Raisin" characters gracing its casual sportswear garments, Sun Sportswear enjoyed an appreciable increase in

sales, convincing Sabey and the company's management that the rewards to be gained in producing licensed designs merited further investment. Other licensed designs entered Sun Sportswear's fold after the "California Raisins" deal was brokered, including "Garfield" the cat and a "Batman" license in 1989, when Wal-Mart and Target Stores suggested Sun Sportswear as a more capable supplier than the previous licensee.

Although the licensed segment of Sun Sportswear's business represented a new and promising avenue of growth for the company, it by no means abandoned its mainstay proprietary design business. By 1988, the company's internal design staff was creating 1,200 designs a year and more than 2,000 designs by the following year, as Sun Sportswear executives strove to beat back the capricious nature of garment designs by flooding markets with a vast and ever-changing product line. By continually adding to and revamping its proprietary product line and by negotiating for licenses for popular characters and trademarks, Sun Sportswear kept moving forward and surpassing competitors, recording encouraging financial growth along the way. Annual sales, which amounted to $28.9 million in 1987, more than doubled the following year to $59 million, as revenues from the recently added licensed line of garments came pouring in and the consistent effort to refreshen the proprietary line paid off in financial gains.

To accommodate the company's rapid growth and the increasing number of customers located east of the Mississippi River, a second production facility was purchased in 1988, when Sun Sportswear acquired a warehousing and manufacturing property in Johnson City, Tennessee. On the heels of this acquisition, the company stood poised for a banner year, its position as one of the country's largest silkscreeners firmly established. Sun Sportwear by this point purchased roughly 65 percent of its blank garments from manufacturers predominately located in the southeastern United States, and the remaining 35 percent were imported, primarily from Pakistan, Portugal, and Costa Rica. Once decorated, either with designs created by the company or with licensed designs, the garments were sold to 30 major mass merchandisers, with K-Mart, Wal-Mart, and Target Stores ranking as the company's three largest customers by far.

Women's and Girls' Apparel Launched in 1989

Perhaps more remarkable than the company's consistent and rapid growth in a market driven by whimsical and fleeting fashion trends was that nearly all of the growth achieved during the 1980s was realized from selling to only half of the American population. Since its inception, Sun Sportswear had relied nearly exclusively on male customers for its business, but in June 1989 another opportunity for growth came about when the company began test marketing apparel items targeted for women and girls. By the end of its first year, the women's and girls' apparel division generated $3 million in sales, a modest contribution when compared with the $73.2 million generated in revenues for the year, but expectations ran high, leading company officials to project that eventually women's and girls' apparel would account for between 25 percent and 30 percent of the company's total sales. In this projection the company was wrong, for during the 1990s, when the sales of men's and boys' apparel began to flag, the women's and girls' division picked up the slack, eventually accounting for nearly 70 percent of Sun Sportswear's total business.

Before Sun Sportswear officials realized the riches they had tapped by targeting female customers, the company made one more significant move in 1989. In October, Sun Sportswear filed with the Securities and Exchange Commission for an initial public offering of 1.7 million shares. The sale of Sun Sportswear stock to the public, which was completed in October, represented 21 percent ownership of the company, with Sabey retaining the remaining percentage of ownership. With the money yielded from the public offering, an amount that was expected to bring in as much as $20 million, Sabey intended to finance Sun Sportswear's recent expansion, including $2 million to purchase new equipment for the company's new office and printing facility located on a 9.6-acre site in Kent. The remainder of the funds were earmarked for repaying loans associated with the acquisition of the Johnson City facility and for future expansion, giving Sun Sportswear some of the financial resources it would need to maintain its leadership role in the decade ahead.

Sun Sportswear entered the 1990s on a strong note. The company's product line of screenprinted knit cotton T-shirts, sweatshirts, sweatpants, shorts, and woven T-shirts generated $73.2 million in sales in 1989, a 24 percent increase over the previous year's total. The acquisition in early 1990 of the apparel licensing rights to use the National Wildlife Federation logo on T-shirts and sweats kept the company moving in a positive direction, but from there things began to sour. As the onset of a national economic recession began to appear in headlines across the country, laggard consumer spending, retail inventory reductions, and the popularity of licensed characters not owned by Sun Sportswear combined to negatively affect the Kent-based company's business. In August 1990, as a result of waning sales, the company trimmed its work force by 126 at its screenprinting plants in Kent and Johnson City. Then in April 1991 the company announced it would suspend screenprinting operations at its Johnson City facility altogether. The company continued to use the Johnson City plant as a warehousing hub, but the production was shifted to the manufacturing facility in Kent, where Sun Sportswear management anxiously awaited the return of more prosperous economic conditions.

More prosperous economic conditions did not arrive soon enough, particularly for Sabey, who found himself mired in serious financial difficulties during the early years of the 1990s. Since the establishment of Sun Sportswear, Sabey had greatly expanded his business interests by acquiring a fashionable department store chain based in the Pacific Northwest called Frederick & Nelson. As Sun Sportswear struggled during the early years of the decade, recording a $517,000 loss in 1992, Sabey's Frederick & Nelson department store chain suffered from more pernicious financial difficulties and slipped into bankruptcy as the recession worsened. The financial troubles of Sun Sportswear's chairman resulted in a new majority owner for the company and the return of more prosperous economic times for the country's largest producer of silkscreened garments.

1993 Resignation of Sun Sportswear's Founder

In January 1993, Sabey transferred to Seafirst Corp. 67.7 percent of Sun Sportswear's shares to pay part of his debt to the Seattle-based bank and announced his resignation as chairman effective January 22, 1993. To replace Sabey, Seafirst selected Larry C. Mounger, a Sun Sportswear director who had joined the

company's board in 1991. For Seafirst, Mounger, and Sun Sportswear, the timing was perfect. Less than two weeks before Sabey's resignation was scheduled to take effect, Mounger had sold his family-owned business, Pacific Trail Inc., a 48-year-old outerwear firm founded by his father. Despite the propitious turn of events that made Mounger available to guide the fortunes of Sun Sportwear, Mounger had no intention of becoming the company's chairman and chief executive officer. "I was going to retire, manage my own investments and possibly buy, but not run, a business," Mounger later remembered to a reporter from the *Puget Sound Business Journal.* "I had no idea in the world when I was closing Pacific Trail that this would happen."

Despite his surprise, Mounger wasted no time in making his presence known at Sun Sportswear. He quickly developed a 100-day strategy for the company and explained his objectives. "Number one, we've got to turn this company around and increase profits in 1993," Mounger explained in a *Puget Sound Business Journal* interview. "Number two, we've got to grow the top-end and increase our customer base." To achieve these goals, Mounger instituted tougher quality control standards, closed the Johnson City plant, and concentrated the company's focus on its core business of screenprinting. By the end of the year, Mounger could point to tangible proof that the changes undertaken during his watch had worked. After recording a loss of $517,000 for 1992, Sun Sportswear's net income rebounded significantly, jumping to a $2.7 million gain. Sales were up as well, rising from $70.6 million to $104.8 million. For the first time since its initial public offering in 1989, Sun Sportswear entered a new calendar year supported by growth on all fronts.

After Sun Sportswear's president resigned in early 1994, Mounger assumed his post to reign as the company's chairman, chief executive officer, and president. Occupying the company's three top executive positions, Mounger moved resolutely forward in 1994, intent on sustaining the positive momentum built up in 1993. More than $2 million was spent on the latest screenprinting technology, with another $2 million slated for investment in late 1994, giving the company a total of 15 screenprinting presses. With the acquisition of additional presses, Sun Sportswear stood well-positioned for anticipated growth, but 1995 would prove to be a difficult year for the company. Sales were invigorated by the popularity of the company's licensed rights to the "Pocahontas" and "Lion King" characters, but the effects of a strike by major league baseball players caused sales of Sun Sportswear's "Major League Baseball" designs to decline. For the year, sales dipped to $93.9 million and the company plunged once again into the red, recording a $3.7 million loss.

As the company struggled through 1995, a leadership change was effected. Just as quickly as he had arrived, Mounger was gone by October, with the only explanation for his sudden departure coming from a company announcement that Mounger had resigned "to have more time to pursue community service and other personal goals." In Mounger's place, William S. Wiley was selected as president and chief executive officer. Wiley, who had been a consultant to the company's reengineering efforts for the six months prior to his arrival at Sun Sportswear as president and chief executive officer, was charged with guiding the company into the late 1990s and steering it toward consistent profitability. As Wiley and his executive team charted their course for the late 1990s, the one undeniably healthy aspect of Sun Sportswear's business was its women's and girls' apparel division. Since its inception in 1989, the division had developed into a $67-million-a-year business, accounting for nearly 70 percent of the company's total sales in 1995. In February 1996, the women's/girls' and men's/boy's divisions were combined, giving both segments the leadership that had orchestrated the women's and girls' division's robust growth. Structured as such, Sun Sportswear headed toward the late 1990s, intent on maintaining its lead as the largest screenprinting producer in the United States.

Further Reading

"Baseball Strike Pushes Sun Sportswear into Red," *Daily News Record,* May 3, 1995, p. 10.

Farnsworth, Steve, "Sun Sportswear Ends Up with New Majority Owner," *WWD,* January 7, 1993, p. 13.

"Larry Mounger Resigns Posts at Sun Sportswear; Succeeded by William S. Wiley," *Daily News Record,* October 6, 1995, p. 4.

Marlow, Michael, "Sun Shines," *Daily News Record,* June 4, 1996, p. 20.

Prinzing, Debra, "Mounger Shining Up Sun Sportswear's Strategy," *Puget Sound Business Journal,* February 12, 1993, p. 11.

——, "Sabey Slates an IPO for Sun Sportswear," *Puget Sound Business Journal,* October 30, 1989, p. 1.

Spector, Robert, "Larry Mounger Finds His Place in the Sun; Sun Sportswear CEO Enjoys Living in the World of Bugs Bunny, Garfield and Betty Boop," *Daily News Record,* May 2, 1994, p. 20.

——, "Sun: Expecting To Shine Again," *WWD,* July 18, 1990, p. 9.

"Sun Cuts 126 Jobs in Two Facilities," *Daily News Record,* August 1, 1990, p. 4.

——, "Sun Sportswear Pouring Millions into Technology: CAD, New Presses and Bar Codes Keep Sun on Top," *WWD,* September 22, 1994, p. S13.

——, "Sun Sportswear Profits Drop 53% in First Period," *Daily News Record,* April 24, 1991, p. 10.

"Sun Sportswear Profits Soar on 'Pocahontas' Licensed Biz," *Daily News Record,* August 10, 1995, p. 10.

"Sun Sportswear Sees Flat Net in Quarter," *WWD,* October 17, 1990, p. 12.

—Jeffrey L. Covell

Swank Inc.

6 Hazel Street
Attleboro, Massachusetts 02703
U.S.A.
(508) 222-3400
Fax: (508) 226-9598

Public Company
Incorporated: 1897 as the Attleboro Manufacturing Co.
Employees: 1,500
Sales: $140.1 million (1995)
Stock Exchanges: NASDAQ
SICs: 3172 Personal Leather Goods, Not Elsewhere
   Classified; 3911 Jewelry & Precious Metal; 3961
   Costume Jewelry; 3965 Fasteners, Buttons, Needles,
   & Pins; 2844 Toilet Preparations; 5136 Men's and
   Boy's Clothing; 5137 Women's and Children's
   Clothing

Swank, Inc. is one of the United States' leading manufacturers of men's and women's jewelry and leather goods. Swank's customers are mainly major retailers such as department stores, specialty stores, and mass merchandisers, through which the company's products are marketed under the brand names Pierre Cardin, Colours by Alexander Julian, Anne Klein, Anne Klein II, Guess?, and Swank. Most of the company's retail items are offered at various price points and in numerous styles, so as to appeal to a broad range of consumers. Swank's products are also sold internationally throughout over 50 countries, and through numerous factory outlet stores in the United States that distribute its excess and out-of-line merchandise.

The Early Years

The beginnings of Swank, Inc. can be traced to the year 1897, when Samuel M. Stone and Maurice J. Baer founded the Attleboro Manufacturing Company to produce and sell jewelry for women. The two men took over a building in Attleboro, Massachusetts, that had been constructed decades earlier as a forge to turn precious metals into jewelry. Unfortunately, less than a year after Stone and Baer began production, one of the largest fires in the town's history claimed an entire block of buildings, destroying their small enterprise. Many of the company's employees helped fight the fire and were able to salvage a portion of the machinery and finished jewelry. Therefore, the Attleboro Manufacturing Company was able to resume its operations with the remaining equipment and material in another building nearby, which came to be the center of production for the next century.

Within ten years, the Attleboro Manufacturing Company was enjoying a good deal of success in producing women's jewelry and decided to begin expanding into new markets. In 1908, Baer formed a new division, called Baer and Wilde, to oversee the production of men's jewelry, while Stone remained in charge of Attleboro Manufacturing. The new Baer and Wilde division operated with marginal success alongside the Attleboro Manufacturing Company until 1918, when the Kum-A-Part cuff button was designed and became an immediate success. The item became one of the company's first major products, and its sudden popularity facilitated significant growth for the company.

By the time the United States became involved in World War I, the Attleboro Manufacturing Company was large enough to handle the production of thousands of metal identification tags, better known as "dog tags," for the military. While this was the company's most notable contribution to the war effort, it also profited from the production of numerous other emblems for the U.S. government during those years. It was then that the demand for production of men's jewelry surpassed that of women's, and the women's line was terminated. The company was then able to focus its resources completely on the manufacture of men's collar buttons, pins, and holders, as well as tie clips, dress sets, and other men's jewelry items.

Post-World War I: Swank, Inc. Is Born

After production of the women's jewelry line was halted, the company focused solely on the manufacture and marketing of its men's items. Although its men's products were already in high demand, the company pushed even harder to gain more

Company Perspectives:

The Company is dedicated to maintaining style and quality leadership in the broad diversity of products it markets.

market share through the implementation of a new marketing plan and increased advertising. The new marketing plan was originated by Stone in the late 1920s and dictated that the Attleboro Manufacturing Company employ seven wholesale dealers in different major cities throughout the United States to handle the sale and distribution of the men's jewelry line. This action helped the company more easily distribute its products nationwide and also increased its advertising range.

The name Swank actually appeared in 1927 on a print advertisement for a men's collar holder, but it was almost another decade before it became the corporate name. By 1936, Stone's marketing plan was so successful that the company invited the seven dealers to form a new corporation, Swank Products, Inc. The merger not only gave the company a new name, but also gave it a national sales organization of its own, which already had direct contact with thousands of jewelry retailers across the country. These connections were an unusual and important asset for a newly formed corporation and aided in the ease and speed in which Swank shifted to operation on a national level.

In 1941, the company changed its name once again and became Swank, Inc., a designation which stuck for the next 50 years and beyond. Shortly after the name change, the United States' involvement in World War II caused Swank to temporarily stall the production of its regular retail items while it instead manufactured tools for the military. Also produced during the war were precision parts for automatic weapons, and the bronze stars and purple hearts that were awarded to U.S. servicemen for heroism in action. These contributions enabled Swank to maintain steady work during the years of the war, which left the company in solid financial condition at its conclusion.

Expansion into the 1950s and Beyond

During the years following World War II, Swank's product line was diversified by the addition of personal leather goods, gifts, and fragrances. The company first began producing items such as wallets, belts, and other accessories for men, a move which considerably increased Swank's annual sales. It also started producing and marketing fragrances under the Royal Copenhagen name.

In 1966, Swank strengthened its blossoming leather products division with the acquisition of the Prince Gardner Company of St. Louis, Missouri, a manufacturer of men's and women's leather goods marketed under the Prince and Princess Gardner brand names. In 1970, Swank purchased another leather goods manufacturer, Crestline Manufacturing Company of South Norwalk, Connecticut. Crestline continued to produce wallets, belts, and accessories under the Swank, Pierre Cardin, and L'Aiglon labels, and soon achieved a strong reputation for the high quality of its products. The following year, Swank rounded out its leather division with the addition of the Alco Leather Manufacturing Corporation of San Francisco, California.

The sudden increase in production demands due to Swank's new additions prompted the company to invest a large amount of capital into expanding and renovating its facilities in the 1970s. First came a move into a new distribution center in Taunton, Massachusetts, after Swank outgrew its original warehouse nearby. Soon after, the Crestline division operations were moved into a modern manufacturing facility, which was designed specifically to handle the immense production demands that came with being the largest belt manufacturer in the country. Finally, another new plant was constructed in 1978 to accommodate the Prince Gardner division's rapid growth.

After ensuring its ability to handle increased production, Swank entered the 1980s with intentions of broadening its product lines and initiating further growth within the company. It was at that time that Swank reintroduced its women's jewelry line, which had been the company's initial product 80 years earlier. Much of the new women's product was marketed under the Anne Klein brand name, as a means of gaining immediate consumer recognition and approval. Also reintroduced in the early 1980s, after an absence of nearly a decade, was a sales incentive program for Swank's salespeople. The incentive program encouraged employees to sell from all of Swank's major product areas, rather than only from those that were easiest to sell. Available products at that point in time were jewelry, leather accessories, belts, fragrances, and gifts such as pen sets and clothing.

In 1985, Swank further expanded its men's leather accessories line with the addition of new items carrying labels by Reed St. James and Colours by Alexander Julian. A new line of women's jewelry under the brand name 90 Park was also introduced. Sales of these items, coupled with the rising success of earlier products and the sales incentive program, helped Swank reverse two years of annual declines and achieve $157.8 million in sales in 1987. This success was also attributed to a decrease in overhead spending throughout the year, and the fact that the women's jewelry division was steadily gaining popularity and generating more sales. Shortly thereafter, Swank began experiencing declines, which continued for almost five years. Thus, in 1989 the company sold the assets of its Prince Gardner division.

The 1990s and Beyond

By 1991, annual sales had dropped by more than $30 million since the record high in 1987. The company managed to achieve increases in sales for the next two years, although 1992 marked the sale of the company's Royal Copenhagen fragrance line, as Swank struggled to lower its expenses and turn the past few years around. After paying much attention to consumer buying trends in the early 1990s, Swank decided to take advantage of the growing corporate trend toward casual dress. While still maintaining its traditional product lines, in 1994 Swank sought a license to produce and market casual products under the Guess? brand name, such as men's and women's costume jewelry and leather goods. Swank also began offering many of its products at various price points and in numerous styles, so as to appeal to a broad range of consumers.

These measures were successful and aided Swank in overcoming the years of declines in an extremely competitive retail environment. The company posted $143.4 million in 1994 sales, while at the same time managing to pay off over half of the largest debt in company history. The remaining debt was scheduled for repayment in 1995, signaling Swank's belief that another strong year lay ahead.

Meanwhile, Swank's new lines of Guess? products were generating increased sales in the leather accessories and jewelry divisions. Unfortunately, those two areas alone accounted for 96 percent of Swank's 1995 sales, leaving the company reliant upon a narrow base of products. Furthermore, a weakening in consumer interest in high-priced fashion jewelry initiated a shift in production toward more competitively priced career-oriented items, which eroded the year's profit potential. 1995 sales dropped by $3 million from those the previous year, prompting Swank chairperson Marshall Tulin to hand down the positions of president and chief operating officer to his son, John, after stating his belief in the 1995 chairman's message that "it was time to let younger minds handle daily operations."

Entering the end of the century, executives at Swank committed themselves to continued efforts at rejuvenating the company. A goal was set to increase margins on the goods sold, and the company began cutting costs and making efforts to manage its assets in a manner that would maximize stockholder returns as methods to achieve that goal. In his first stockholder address as president and CEO, John Tulin stated his belief that while much work remained, the improvement seen in 1996 signaled that the company's efforts were in the correct direction.

Further Reading

"Swank Back in the Black in 4th Quarter and Year," *WWD,* March 9, 1992, p. 17.
"Swank: Eighty-Eight Years of Progress," Attleboro, Mass.: Swank, Inc., 1985.
"Swank's Sales Grow on Trees," *Sales & Marketing Management,* May 19, 1980, p. 16.
Thompson, Michael, "Jewelry's Public Companies: Slim Profits, Aggressive Plans," *Jeweler's Circular-Keystone,* July 1988, p. 126.

—Laura E. Whiteley

TAB Products Co.

1400 Page Mill Road
Palo Alto, California 94304
U.S.A.
(415) 852-2400

Public Company
Incorporated: 1954
Employees: 1,070
Sales: $152.69 million (1996)
Stock Exchanges: American
SICs: 5021 Furniture; 5112 Stationery & Office Supplies

TAB Products Co. is a leading records management company which manufactures and markets office filing and furniture systems that are sold worldwide. The company provides information storage and retrieval solutions to office environments where efficient access to information is critical to success.

1950s Founding

The company was founded and incorporated in Delaware in 1954 by two former IBM salesmen. Its initial purpose was to market desktop, punch card, and other computer-related file boxes and containers. In these early years, TAB was known for its role as a pioneer in lateral filing systems. An early example of the company's client service process is provided by the total records management system created for Montgomery Ward in the 1970s. TAB's work team studied and recommended systems for Montgomery Ward's departments, including personnel, purchasing, legal, corporate files, credit, accounting, traffic, claims, and corporate systems. The resulting recommendation, implemented throughout Montgomery Ward's 27-story headquarters, was TAB's Spacefinder System, a combination of equipment and color-coded software.

Similarly, in 1977 TAB provided records management systems to two New Jersey State government agencies: the Division of Gaming Enforcement of the New Jersey Department of Law and Public Safety and the Division of Taxation. When gambling began in Atlantic City, the Division of Gaming Enforcement was responsible for instituting a massive system to monitor and fight corruption. Such a system included the processing of prospective employee disclosure statements, with a minimum of seven police checks as well as individual credit checks for each employee. TAB designed a dual filing system, facilitating the dispersal of results of individual investigations to separate investigate units and different filing cabinets.

Also in 1977, the initiation of personal income tax in New Jersey brought TAB together with the Division of Taxation. To manage massive quantities of returns, TAB designed a records management system calling for returns to be batched in groups of 100, and stored in Open Unit Spacefinder storage boxes, which were then placed on TAB mobile file trucks. Other New Jersey government departments—including the Department of Agriculture, the Housing Finance Agency, the Department of Environmental Protection and Transportation, and the State Tax Court—took advantage of TAB's tailored records-handling systems in this epoch.

During the decade from the early 1970s to the early 1980s, TAB's financial status was less than desirable. The company could not seem to sustain earnings momentum; only once in the decade did TAB see two successive years of increased earnings. However, with the advent of computer technology, and TAB's decision to enter that market, the financial picture improved considerably, if slowly. In the early 1980s, TAB changed its direction to adjust to technological changes in the office environment. Having previously specialized in manual filing storage equipment, the company directed significant resources toward its emergence as a supplier of electronic data entry and storage devices. When computer terminal technology began to move forward, for example, TAB made its move into hardware electronics. Fifteen-inch, 132-unit screens became the wave of the future, but compatibility with previous systems led to usage problems. TAB's Electronic Office Products (EOP) Division entered the market with a terminal demonstrating the new measurement specifications, as well as brilliance and clarity features.

As a result of expenses associated with Tab's entry into the computer market, the company initially absorbed heavy losses.

Company Perspectives:

TAB provides information storage and retrieval solutions in office environments where efficient access to information is critical to success TAB not only provides good ideas based on 45 years' experience, but also provides the products, services, installation, and training that improve the way work flows as the result of those good ideas. Comprising systems from forms to electronic technologies, the common value of all TAB solutions—and a business goal since day one—is their ability to help people do business better.

In 1981, the Electronic Office Products Division incurred a deficit of about $1.2 million, and the next year its deficit almost doubled. The deficits reflected major outputs in marketing due to the buildup of a sales force to supplement independent distributors and promote the new computer terminal. Through direct sales, TAB could provide large quantity discounts which would be impossible through the mediation of distributors. In early January of 1982, orders for the computer terminals leapt about 50 percent to 500 or 600 a month, and the company's finances continued to improve during the year.

As a result of the financial upswing, the EOP Division increased its sales force and began to introduce new products. Despite its losses during the development period, by 1982 TAB had reduced its debt-to-equity ratio from over 60 percent to 40 percent, and 1982 cash flow exceeded $5 million after interest expense and dividends. The move into computers was also reflected in the company's revenue and net income figures in the late 1970s and early 1980s; revenue jumped from $50.3 million in 1977 to $89 million in 1981, with a relatively small increase in net income from $2.3 million to $3.2 million, due to marketing outlays. During this same period, stock increases were proportionally high, increasing from a range of two and one-half to four and five-eighths in 1977, to a range of ten and one-eighth to 29 and three-quarters in 1981.

What computers were to the late 1970s, color-coding became in the mid-1980s. According to *The Office,* studies showed that color-coding systems read faster than letters or numbers. In fact, a 1980 study by TAB Products estimated that the average cost of each misfile was $80, and that most firms misfiled between one and five percent of their records regularly. Having introduced color-coding in the early 1970s, TAB became an outspoken advocate of color-coding as a source for saving thousands of company dollars each year. Large and diversified filing systems could more easily be managed with color-coded file folders, increasing worker productivity and minimizing the losses created by file misplacement and search time.

One of TAB's most successful color-coding solutions was presented to the California State Automobile Association in 1984. This San Francisco-based Inter-Insurance Bureau insured over 1.2 million members. With such broad service, the agency's work routine entailed daily charging of 10,000 files to various departments. To manage the quantity, the Auto Association turned to TAB Products' color-coded filing system and Unit

Spacefinders, resulting in a dramatic 25 to 30 percent improvement in productivity. A five percent staff reduction was made possible, resulting in more efficient utilization of personnel.

Another color-coding solution was presented to the Sacramento, California, law firm of Wintraub Genshlea Hardy Erich & Brown. In 1982, this firm became one of the city's largest, through the merger of two practices. TAB designed a system for the speedy combination of two filing systems, seeking to avoid misfiling errors and incompatibility issues. The system provided for the usage of TAB Unit Spacefinders, "unit boxes" suspended from framework, and an alphabetical, color-coded filing system. Through TAB's design, 9500 filing inches were made available where there had previously been only 7000. In April of 1985, the law firm moved to a spacious new building, where it continued to utilize TAB equipment systems.

Supplementing its production of computer products and forms-handling equipment, TAB began to tap the rapidly growing market for computer furniture, work stations, and clustered work centers for open office arrangements. In 1985, TAB began a relationship with Wurlitzer, the maker of keyboard instruments. Having suffered dramatic losses, Wurlitzer began making a line of wood office furniture, which in turn was purchased and marketed by TAB. In the same year, Dennis Searles was promoted to president and chief operating officer, with Harry Le Claire continuing as chairman and chief executive officer. The mid-1980s were also characterized by a number of stock buybacks.

Reorganization in the 1980s

In 1986, TAB was reorganized as a corporation in Delaware. The company began to look outward to expand its offerings, acquiring a 20 percent interest in Acctex Information Systems. Together, the two companies developed a PC-based laser optic filing system. Competition in this market was fierce—with approximately 40 companies developing products—but TAB was seen as a leading contender due to its focus on price, its outsourcing policy, and its partnership with Acctex.

By the close of fiscal year 1987, revenues had more than doubled during a decade of diversification and growth. The company now earned $124 million, as compared to $56 million in 1978. Office-filing systems and supplies were responsible for $71.5 million, or almost 60 percent of 1987 revenues. This category of TAB products now included products from individual file cabinets to enormous mobile filing systems, as well as folders, tabs, and accessories. W. B. Brooksby told *Barron's* that the open furniture market was the fastest growing segment of the furniture market, comprising approximately $7 billion, as compared with about $250 million for office files and supplies. To profit from the new trend, TAB started to focus increasingly on clustered work centers, interchangeable panels, bases, and tops. To generate continued interest in its products, TAB introduced the Designer Series of cabinets, with a wide range of interchangeable components such as drawers, shelves, racks, and hanging frames.

Success was short-lived. By 1989, net earnings fell 43 percent over the previous fiscal year, and revenue decreased by 1 percent. TAB officials told the *Wall Street Journal* that sales declined primarily due to a delay in the renewal of government contracts with the General Service Administration (TAB had been supplying office furniture to the government for over 20 years). However, by 1991, TAB was awarded two federal contracts worth over $20 million.

Shortly before his death, founder Harry Le Claire began a process of reorganization, cost-cutting, and management changes which caused Steven Wilson, of Reich & Tang, to tell *Barron's* that the company was a favored investment pick. In addition, in 1991, the company downsized its stock significantly, repurchasing about one-third of its shares, including 31 percent from Le Claire's estate. Repurchased shares were to be used for employee benefit plans and other corporate purposes. Having spent the majority of its existence moving forward with direct sales but with no particular success, TAB seemed poised for a change.

The 1990s and Beyond

By 1996, TAB was ready to strengthen its board again, electing three new officers to bring the total up to eight members. Fiscal 1996 results showed a dramatic 126 percent increase over the previous year, with net earnings of $2.76 million. Revenues for fiscal 1996 were $152.69 million, a 2 percent increase over fiscal 1995. President and CEO Michael Dering attributed the improvements to increased revenues, improved gross margins, and lower operating expenses.

In July 1996, President and CEO Michael Dering announced his immediate resignation, further heralding a new era in management at TAB Products. Dering had demonstrated leadership during the years immediately following Le Claire's death, and would now take the office of president and chief executive officer at Publications Systems Company, a wholly owned subsidiary of Bell and Howell, Inc. John W. Peth, executive vice-president and chief operating officer, became acting president and chief executive officer, and an external and internal search for Dering's permanent replacement commenced. With no successor named in late summer of 1996, TAB's future direction remains in the balance. It is likely that the company will continue to do what it has done for over 40 years—solve office problems with management systems and materials—with varying levels of success, but continued perseverance.

Principal Subsidiaries

TAB Sales Corp. International (St. Thomas, Virgin Islands); TAB Products of Canada, Limited (Toronto, Ontario); TAB Products Pty Ltd (St. Leonards, Australia); TAB Products (Europa) B.V. (Amsterdam, Netherlands).

Further Reading

"An Automobile Association Adds Color-Coded File System," *Office,* March 1984, p. 46.

"Color-Coded File Indexing," *Office,* September 1979, pp. 144–152.

"Color-Coding Reduces Misfiles at Law Firm," *Office,* September 1983, pp. 124, 177.

"Dividend News," *Wall Street Journal,* February 2, 1984, p. 50.

"Effective Filing Systems Aid Information Flow," *Small Business Report,* January 1988, pp. 28–30.

"Efficient Records Are Mandatory for New Jersey Law and Gaming Agencies," *Office,* November 1981, p. 115.

Gordon, Mitchell, "Storage Specialist: Tab Products' Stress on Electronics Seems to be Paying Off," *Barron's,* June 14, 1982, p. 48.

"Keen Eye for Value: Taking the Long View Pays Off for a Money Manager," *Barron's,* August 3, 1992, pp. 13–17.

"People," *Los Angeles Times,* February 22, 1985, p. 43.

Rader, Ron, "Slow to Develop but Big Screen, 132-Column Units Setting Trend," *Computerworld,* October 26, 1981, pp. 41–42.

"Tab Products Buy-Back," *Wall Street Journal,* October 28, 1991, p. B4.

TAB Products Co. Annual Report, Palo Alto, Calif.: TAB Products Co., 1995.

"Tab Products Co: From Filing to Helping Outfit the Modern Office," *Barron's,* March 14, 1988, pp. 65–66.

"Tab Products Earnings Fell 43 Percent in Fiscal 1989," *Wall Street Journal,* June 29, 1989, p. 12.

"Tab Products Gets Contracts," *Wall Street Journal,* September 10, 1991, p. C17.

"Tab Products May Buy Shares," *Wall Street Journal,* July 16, 1984, p. 2.

"Tab Products Stock Buyback," *Wall Street Journal,* July 15, 1985, p. 27.

"Tab Products Stock Purchase," *Wall Street Journal,* March 26, 1991, p. B2.

"Who's News," *Wall Street Journal,* April 19, 1996, p. B16.

"Who's News," *Wall Street Journal,* October 7, 1991, p. B9.

"Wurlitzer to Produce Office Furniture Line," *Wall Street Journal,* February 5, 1985, p. 51.

—Heidi Feldman

TABACALERA, S. A.

Tabacalera, S.A.

Alcala 47
E-28014 Madrid
Spain
(1) 532 7600
Fax: (1) 522-7586

State-Controlled Company
Incorporated: 1887 as Compañia Arrendataria de
  Tabacos
Employees: 7,300
Sales: Pta 783.1 billion (1994)
Stock Exchanges: Madrid

Tabacalera, S.A., is one of Spain's largest and oldest companies, and is a dominant force in its principal area of activity, the manufacture and distribution of tobacco products. Protected for more than 300 years by a government-enforced monopoly, the company was able to build an almost unassailable position in the tobacco market, even after the controlling monopoly was dismantled in the mid-1980s. From its base in the tobacco industry, Tabacalera then began to expand into new product markets, in response to changes brought on by Spain's membership in the European Economic Community (EEC) and the worldwide decline in tobacco consumption. Tabacalera entered the food industry, among other endeavors, in a diversification process that was initially accompanied by a number of problems. Nevertheless, the company's widespread manufacturing operations and an extremely well-developed distribution network, complete with a large fleet of trucks, provide it with a continued strong base on which to operate.

The Early Years: 16th- through 18th-Century Trade

Tabacalera is one of the oldest companies in the world, with its roots in the period of Spanish colonization of Central and South America. Tobacco was one of many substances unknown in Europe before being discovered by the conquistadores as they pushed the new boundaries of Spanish domination south from their first settlements in Mexico during the 16th century. Regarded initially as a curiosity with supposedly medicinal properties when ground and inhaled, tobacco was used in Europe only in small quantities during the 16th century.

One of the main features of Spanish colonial expansion was the government's determination to retain tight control of the economic traffic between the colonies and Spain. Aimed mainly at ensuring a steady flow of mineral wealth from American mines, this policy limited the number of ports in the colonies that could ship goods to Spain, while also limiting the number of ports in Spain that could receive the goods. At the Spanish end, the government designated Seville as the central port for trade with the colonies, and it was controlled by the Casa de Contratacion—the hiring house for seafarers—which was established in 1504. Because of this designation, Seville became the center of tobacco imports from the Americas, and was one of the first places in Europe where the tobacco plant was cultivated. In the early 17th century, a factory for processing tobacco was built on the banks of the Guadalquivir River near Seville to cater to the growing popularity of snuff—powdered tobacco—among Sevillans.

In 1636, the Spanish government moved to ensure its control of the growing tobacco trade by establishing a monopoly over the production and sale of tobacco in the kingdoms of Castille and Leon. The government decreed that tobacco trade would be controlled by a newly formed body, the Estanco del Tabaco. Despite considerable changes to its structure and powers in the following three and a half centuries, the Estanco del Tabaco formed the foundation of what became present-day Tabacalera, S.A.

Tobacco use grew steadily during the late 17th and early 18th centuries, and in 1725 the Estanco del Tabaco decided to build a new factory in Seville to accommodate the increasing demand. Although construction began in 1728, disputes over the plans and other problems delayed completion of the new factory until 1770. Upon completion, however, the size of the new Royal Tobacco Factory of Seville, along with its proximity to the tobacco port, made it the most important tobacco manufacturing plant in the world at the time.

Restructuring Efforts in the 19th and 20th Centuries

As popular tobacco tastes changed in the early 19th century, the Royal Tobacco Factory in Seville restructured its operations to begin producing cigars in addition to powdered snuff tobacco, which had been produced exclusively for years. The shift to cigar manufacture, brought on by changes in consumer tastes, required a highly labor-intensive process and demanded a large, cheap work force to hand-roll the tobacco leaves. This demand was satisfied by using large numbers of women in the factory, marking one of the first instances of women's large-scale involvement in Spanish industry. This provided the inspiration for the main character in Merimée's novella *Carmen*, which in turn inspired Bizet's opera of the same name.

The demand created by the emergence of cigars as a popular form of tobacco prompted the Estanco del Tabaco to invest heavily in expanding its production capacity during the 19th century. With a second factory already established at Cadiz, the Estanco opened nine more new factories throughout Spain during the 19th century, creating one of the country's biggest and most productive industrial enterprises.

In the mid-19th century, the Spanish government began looking for ways to change the managerial structure of the company. It wished to take advantage of the more sophisticated economic environment, in which direct state control appeared outdated and seemed to hamper delivery of the highest possible profit to the state. Beginning in 1844, various proposals were put forward until finally the operations were placed under the control of a strictly corporate entity in 1887. At that time, the state transferred its monopoly to the central bank, the Bank of Spain, which formed a company called the Compañia Arrendataria de Tabacos. This company leased the management of the monopoly from the bank. The new corporate structure was aimed at achieving the greatest efficiency from the operation by distancing it from the government, while at the same time ensuring the continued supply of revenue to the state from the tobacco operations.

The leasing company controlled the tobacco monopoly for the next 60 years, throughout the tumultuous Spanish Civil War of the 1930s and the final victory of the fascists in 1938. When the contract between the company and the bank came up for its regular review in the early 1940s, the government changed the legal structure of the company once again, opting this time to turn it into a company wholly owned by the state. Thus, In March of 1945 a limited company was formed: Tabacalera, Sociedad Anonima, Compañia Gestora del Monopolio de Tabacos y Servicios Anejos was formed. This change set in place the corporate structure that the company retains today.

The Late 1900s: Responding to Global Economic Change

After three-and-a-half centuries of operating in the comfortable environment of a state-enforced monopoly, Tabacalera was presented with one of its greatest challenges in January 1986, when Spain opted to join the European Economic Community (EEC). As part of the requirements for joining the community, the Spanish government was obliged to relinquish its monopoly of tobacco production and sales. This process involved the partial privatization of Tabacalera, S.A. The state transferred all of its assets and acquired rights in the tobacco monopoly to Tabacalera, in exchange for shares issued by the company that left the state with a 53 percent controlling stake of the company's capital.

Under the new laws of the EEC, Spain's wholesale import and tobacco trading activities were liberalized, giving anybody the right to carry out these activities, but under strict guidelines. Although Tabacalera continued to manage the Spanish monopoly for tobacco products manufactured outside the EEC, and although the state retained control of the retail sales monopoly through its concessionaires, the breaking of the local production monopoly struck at the heart of Tabacalera's operations. This fundamental change, coupled with the upcoming single European market, made it clear that the company had to do more than simply continue making and selling tobacco products if it was to survive. The urgency of change was made even more pressing by signs that tobacco sales could no longer be counted on to rise due to heightened anti-smoking sentiment worldwide.

In 1987, under the presidency of Candido Velazquez Gaztelu, Tabacalera launched a wide-ranging diversification plan aimed at ensuring the company's future in the less secure post-monopoly commercial environment. Velazquez pushed the company into two new areas—food manufacturing and retail distribution—on the basis that these two sectors were best suited to Tabacalera's existing operational structure.

Tabacalera took its first tentative step into the food industry in 1986 by setting up a snack foods operation, Nabisco Brands España y Portugal, as a joint venture with RJR Nabisco. Two years later, Tabacalera actually purchased the company when Kohlberg Kravis Roberts took over RJR Nabisco. In the same time period, Tabacalera bought a group of companies controlled by the Spanish food group Instituto Nacional de Industria. These companies gave Tabacalera access to a wide range of food markets, such as Spain's leading milk concentrate and liquid milk producer, Lactaria Española (LESA); meat and preserves company Carnes y Conservas Españolas S.A. (CARCESA); deep-frozen foods producer Frioalimentos (FRIDARAGO); and Congelados Ibericos S.A. (COISA). Tabacalera also bought a controlling share in a pulses company, Comercial Industrial Fernandez (COIFER S.A.), and a stake in a marine cultivation company, called Acuicultura. Tabacalera also made a strong move into retail distribution, purchasing 75 percent of retailing business Distribuciones Reus S.A. (DIRSA), a company with 325 supermarkets and over 500 franchised shops. DIRSA was also the owner of another company with a chain of more than 100 supermarkets.

The diversification program made Tabacalera one of Spain's leading producers of items such as biscuits, powdered and concentrated desserts, and milk packaging, while it also gave the company a leading position in the tomato sauces, pulps, conserves, juices, and pulses markets and control of one of the largest networks of retail outlets in Spain.

Unfortunately, rather than assure Tabacalera a secure hold on a broader range of operations, the swiftness of the diversification program brought with it a number of serious problems. Namely, in the rush to acquire new businesses, the company had bought a number of operations which were heavy loss-makers. Tabacalera planned to use the economies of scale provided by such a large group to turn the troubled subsidiaries around, but after two years it became clear that the worst of them were largely unsalvageable and would only hamper the group's efforts to become more flexible.

Therefore, Velazquez's successor as chairman, Miguel Angel del Valle Inclan, took office in 1989 and began a process of rationalizing the group's food and distribution activities. He described Velazquez's diversification program as "too ambitious", as reported by Reuter News Service on June 21, 1990. The new aim was to keep only the profitable food subsidiaries, divest the rest, and acquire businesses in other sectors so that the company's revenue from non-tobacco activities would match its tobacco revenue.

Accompanying these moves into different markets, Tabacalera also updated its core tobacco operations during the 1980s to account for changes in the market. Spanish smokers had begun to give up their traditional preference for black tobacco in favor of blond Virginian tobacco. By 1985, Virginian tobacco sales in Spain had already risen to 44 percent of the total tobacco sales, and were on the verge of surpassing those of black tobacco. Tabacalera responded by reorganizing its cultivation and processing operations to produce more Virginian tobacco, which provided a higher profit margin. The company took consideration of this consumption change when it began building a new factory at Cadiz in 1984, much bigger and more efficient than the company's existing plants. Furthermore, in preparation for the challenges likely to emerge due to the upcoming single European market in 1993, the company signed an agreement with Tabaqueira de Portugal in 1989 to allow cross-marketing of the two companies' brands in their respective countries. In December 1990 Tabacalera also announced a modernization plan, which would involve the termination of 1,500 jobs to produce a leaner company in time for the advent of the single market.

The 1990s and Beyond

In 1990, Tabacalera sold the DIRSA retail chain for Pta 12 billion to the French Promodes group, after owning it for only two years. In the same year, the company sold its interest in FRIDARAGO, and gave up its management of the Tabacos de Filipinas company, which had incurred losses of Pta 1.4 billion in 1989 and 1990.

The main problem brought on by the diversification was the milk company, LESA, which continued to lose money despite Tabacalera's investment of large sums to improve it. The company provided more than Pta 8 billion to LESA in the two years following the purchase, but by 1990 the milk producer still showed a huge loss of Pta 5.2 billion. Tabacalera put LESA up for sale, and by April 1991 was holding advanced talks with the French group Union Laitière Normande over the sale of the subsidiary. Also in 1991, Tabacalera changed the name of its Nabisco Brands subsidiaries to Royal Brands.

After cleaning out the bulk of its unprofitable food operations, Tabacalera attempted to consolidate the lucrative remain-

ing businesses by merging the Royal Brands subsidiary with the Carcesa operation to create a leaner, more efficient food division. Under del Valle, the company also began to diversify into other areas: particularly real estate and tourism. In 1990, Tabacalera took a 33 percent stake in a joint venture to build a Pta 10 billion tourist complex in the Canary Islands. It also began to take advantage of its widespread real estate holdings by leasing them out, as well as by using its distribution network to deliver other companies' products. The most lucrative of these contracts was that of the West German company Quelle, Europe's biggest mail-order house, who chose to use Tabacalera's trucks for its Spanish deliveries.

The changes brought about by Spain joining the EEC, combined with the challenges posed by the European single market, caused the question of Tabacalera's relationship with the state to be raised once again. In August 1990, del Valle had stated his belief that the arrival of the single market was a good time to consider whether the state should continue to be the company's major shareholder. The question was sharpened when Spanish legislation was passed in 1990 banning almost all forms of tobacco advertising. Later that year, Spanish newspapers reported that Tabacalera desired a reduction in the state's stake, which would allow the company to be quoted on Spanish stock exchanges by the end of 1992.

The growing debate reached its peak in April 1991, when del Valle was forced out of office in what the *Financial Times* (April 10, 1991) described as "the climax of a political confrontation with the Finance Ministry." He was replaced by German Calvillo Urabayen, president of another government-controlled body: Fomento de Comercio Exterior. Meanwhile, many news sources were giving the impression that the Spanish government was actually considering the idea of selling a portion of its stake in Tabacalera, as well as its stakes in other large state-controlled companies, as a means of earning money to reduce the country's deficit.

By 1993, however, Tabacalera remained a company that was primarily held and controlled by the government. Rather than wait to see if a government business privatization plan would affect the company and help generate growth, Tabacalera instead focused its attention once again on continued restructuring efforts. It entered into a joint venture with RJR Nabisco Holdings Corp. in July 1993, in which each company held a 50 percent stake in the Royal Brands food operations. The deal was structured so that RJR Nabisco would have the option of purchasing the remaining 50 percent of Royal Brands in early 1994, which it did in May of that year. In selling Royal Brands off, Tabacalera signaled its renewed focus on its tobacco products and its desire to continue divesting other peripheral operations acquired in the 1980s.

The following year, Tabacalera was facing a mature market in its homeland of Spain. Although existing Spanish laws gave the company unique distribution rights which translated to a monopoly of sorts, the company knew that it needed to expand globally in order to sustain growth. Therefore, it purchased a 51 percent stake in Culbro Corp.'s General Cigar Company, which gave Tabacalera an entry into the United States' cigar market, which was one of the world's largest and fastest-growing markets. The purchase helped Tabacalera position itself for future growth and distribution expansion, even in the face of the fact that Spain's government was still see-sawing on the idea of relinquishing a portion of its controlling stock in Tabacalera to the public.

By mid-1996, Tabacalera had made moves to sell off the remainder of its food businesses and focus solely on the production and distribution of tobacco, the product it began with over three centuries earlier. The company launched a new cigarette brand in France, called Montecristo, in its continued effort to expand distribution beyond the borders of Spain.

Despite the initial difficulties caused by an over-zealous diversification program a decade earlier, by the closing years of the 20th century Tabacalera appeared to have emerged in a good position to face the more competitive environment of a single European market. Its profits were healthy, its core tobacco business was reorganized to accommodate a changing market, and its expansion into other less lucrative sectors was successfully abandoned. The question of the company's future relationship with the state remained the only unresolved issue, but posed no immediate problems. Therefore, it appeared that Tabacalera would be well-positioned to continue as a powerful industrial group into not only 21st-century Europe, but the entire world.

Principal Subsidiaries

Servicio de Venta Automatica, S.A.; Exportadora de Tabaco de Ceuta y Melilla, S.A. (TABACMESA); La Lactaria Española, S.A. (LESA Group); Hebra Promocion e Inversiones, S.A.; I.T. Brands Corp.; Interprestige, S.A.; Tabacalera France S.A.R.L.; Tabapress, S.A. (93%); Darsa Gaditana, S.A. (89%); Food Premier, S.A. (51%); CITA Tabacos de Canarias, S.A. (CITA Group) (50%); Grupo Tabaquero Canario, S.A. (50%); Tabaco Canary Islands, S.A. (50%); BAT España, S.A. (B.A.T.E. Group) (50%); RJR España, S.L. (50%); Eagle Star Gestora de Fondos de Pensiones, S.A. (49%); Inbatex Holdings Worldwide, S.A. (31%); Compania Española de Tabaco en Rama, S.A. (CETARSA) (20%)

Further Reading

Du Bois, Peter C., "A U.K. Analyst is Bullish on Spain," *Barron's*, July 3, 1989, p. 36.
Phalon, Richard, "Smoke Rings," *Forbes*, August 28, 1995, p. 92.
"RJR Nabisco Buys Full Stake in Spain's Royal Brands," *Reuter Business Report*, May 9, 1994.
Schwimmer, Anne, "Spanish Issues Expected," *Pensions & Investments*, October 28, 1991, p. 38.
"Tabacalera, Selling Stakes in Food Firms, Focuses on Tobacco," *Wall Street Journal*, September 20, 1996, p. B5C.
Torres Mulas, R. & D. Hortas, *Tabacalera: 350 Años Despues*, Madrid: Tabacalera, 1987.
Welling, Kathryn M., "Ahead of the Herd," *Barron's*, February 13, 1995, p. 22.

—Richard Brass
—updated by Laura E. Whiteley

TCBY Enterprises Inc.

1100 TCBY Tower
425 West Capitol Avenue
Little Rock, Arkansas 72201-3439
U.S.A.
(501) 688-8229

Public Company
Incorporated: 1981 as This Can't Be Yogurt, Inc.
Employees: 875
Sales: $121.57 million (1995)
Stock Exchanges: New York
SICs: 5812 Eating Places; 2024 Ice Cream & Frozen
    Desserts; 5451 Dairy Products Stores; 6794 Patent
    Owners & Lessors

TCBY Enterprises Inc. is the first national frozen yogurt store chain. Borrowing a formula from the fast food industry, it has used franchising as a tool for explosive growth. Although some observers felt frozen yogurt to be merely a health food fad, TCBY's endurance, the proliferation of imitators, and the appearance of frozen yogurt in established ice cream chains like Baskin-Robbins have proven the wisdom of the company's concept. TCBY is the largest company of its kind, operating nearly 2,800 locations in 29 countries.

Finding the Right Idea for the 1980s

Frank Hickingbotham was born in McGehee, a small town in southeastern Arkansas, in October 1936. After attending college in nearby Monticello (concurrently serving as a Baptist lay minister in rural communities), he held various jobs, including junior high school teacher and principal of his hometown high school. He began selling insurance, eventually leaving the high school, then entered the restaurant business through Quality Enterprises, a group he had formed with some associates. During the 1970s, he bought a string of AQ Chicken restaurants and dabbled in other food service businesses, including two trucking companies and a frozen pie shell company. He bought Dallas-based cake mix maker Old Tyme Foods Company in 1979.

Already an experienced entrepreneur, Hickingbotham was looking for ways to fill up his time after selling Old Tyme Foods in 1981. It was at a Dallas Neiman-Marcus department store that he discovered frozen yogurt. According to his wife, Georgia, it was the best she had ever tasted. He concurred, uttering, according to company legend, what was to become the company's name: "This can't be yogurt!" What made the product unique was that it had no aftertaste, and it was this very product that Hickingbotham was to sell at TCBY: he used the same supplier as Neiman-Marcus, Arthur's Ice Cream Specialties, Inc., and TCBY bought it for $2.6 million at the end of 1983 (whereupon its name changed to Arthur's Foods, Inc.).

Hickingbotham opened the first frozen yogurt restaurant in Little Rock, Arkansas, in 1981. His son Herren, who was aiming for a career in securities sales, served as manager of the first store. Hickingbotham tapped his brother-in-law, Walt Winters, to run the second one, which opened quickly thereafter. The third store was managed by his youngest son, Todd. The franchise's first full year of business was 1982, in which $1.8 million in sales was achieved. After more than doubling the next year to $5.2 million, annual sales nearly doubled for the next few years, reaching $70 million in 1986.

Hickingbotham cleaned up frozen yogurt's bohemian image, which had previously been marketed typically in the countercultural surroundings typical of the fringe of university campuses. Hickingbotham gave the product a mainstream image that would sell in middle America. The stores, housed mostly in strip malls, were decorated in green and beige and outfitted with real or fake plants, all designed to appeal to the product's core audience of 18-to-49 year-old women.

Hickingbotham originally called his store This Can't Be Yogurt, emphasizing the product's utility as an ice cream substitute. However, competitor I Can't Believe It's Yogurt, Inc. sued him over the similarities with its own name, and Hickingbotham was forced to pay $775,000 and change the name to The Country's Best Yogurt, salvaging, at least, the initials. (In France, the brand is known as "Tous Ces Bons Yogourts.") As part of the settlement, TCBY bought three I Can't Believe It's Yogurt stores in the Houston area.

A Mid-1980s Initial Public Offering

TCBY went public on the National Market System exchange in May 1984. It then bought its supplier, Arthur's Foods (later known as Americana Foods) with the resulting capital. It organized itself into divisions. Administrative employees doubled to 32, and a computerized accounting system was installed.

TCBY began building company-owned stores in Orange County, California, in order to fuel franchise development on the West Coast. The waffle cone made its debut in October 1984. Belgian waffles and crepes were also made in each store to accompany the frozen yogurt. During 1984, the number of stores increased from 41 to 102. Arkansas, Georgia, and Florida were hot spots for franchises. Sales and franchise revenues leaped from $2.3 million to $7.4 million, and net income increased more than fivefold to just over $1 million.

In the spring of 1985, TCBY had 118 stores. By the end of the year it had 242 (17 company-owned), and annual sales had more than doubled to $17.1 million; net income tripled. Its manufacturing subsidiary, now known as Americana Foods, Inc., began construction on a new $5 million plant in Dallas. Martin-Brower, best known for distributing McDonald's products, became TCBY's distributor (ProSource Distribution Services acquired this business from Martin-Brower in 1995). A new headquarters building in Little Rock and a corporate jet were purchased. The company's stock was one of the very hottest in the United States in terms of appreciation. In addition, TCBY reported more than 500 franchising inquiries per week.

In 1986, TCBY enlisted diminutive Hollywood veteran Mickey Rooney to pitch its products on television. "All of the pleasure, none of the guilt" was the company's catch phrase, hammering home the low fat content of its frozen yogurt in comparison to ice cream. (By definition, ice cream contained at least 10 percent fat—20 percent in the case of premium varieties, while TCBY's yogurt only had four percent.) "Say goodbye to ice cream" was another theme of its television advertising. By 1987, 500 TCBY shops populated nearly every state. Finding the field open, Hickingbotham had been able to expand his chain with very little competition.

The End of the 1980s

The year 1989 was an important one, and the last good one for five years. The company had 1,582 stores, and earnings and share value ($28 a share) had continued to rise. In 1990, no new franchises were opened in the first year of a period of consolidation that lasted two more years. Competing frozen yogurt chains, like Freshens and Columbo proliferated, and ice cream giant Baskin-Robbins added frozen yogurt to its own repertoire.

Some angry franchisees and investors, upset by falling profits and perceived corporate apathy, brought lawsuits against the company. Although a judge characterized one such suit as "tenuous," they highlighted franchisee distress. According to *Restaurant Business*, the real cause for falling profits across the industry was the huge increase in the number of players, combined with a global recession. On the whole, frozen yogurt consumption had actually gone up. TCBY continued to lead the frozen yogurt segment in 1992, with a market share of about 45 percent, and ranked behind Dairy Queen, Friendly, and Baskin-Robbins among dairy dessert chains.

In 1992, TCBY hired Charles Cocotas and Thomas Tipps to help reverse its fall. The former, whose prior experience included time as president and chief operating officer at the successful Boston Chicken chain, served as a friendly, straightforward liaison between the company and franchisees as president of TCBY Systems, Inc., Tipps led Americana Foods.

New Venues for the Turn of the Century

The company's international phase had begun in 1986, with the creation of TCBY International. About the same time as Tipps and Cocotas were hired in 1992, this division was made more important, and Hartsell Wingfield was brought in to lead it. With franchisees concerned about oversaturation at home, most of the company's growth came from abroad. In spite of initial worries about the Middle East, a region with a long history with yogurt, the formula stayed the same universally. In China, the product took on the poetic name "angel ice king" in order to avoid the connotations of the Chinese translation of "yogurt": sour milk. The company has formed many international partnerships to accommodate its international operations. Master franchisee for China, Hong Kong, and Macao was Top Green International, a veteran import-export firm whose owners came from both sides of the Pacific.

Although national name recognition of the TCBY brand peaked at 74 percent in 1995, declining grocery store distribution, the sale of the company's refrigerated yogurt business, and store closings depressed sales and franchising revenues from $152.47 million in 1994 to $121.57 million, and the company lost money. (Fortunately, this trend was reversed in 1996.) TCBY decided to sell most of its 42 company-owned stores by May 1996, as well as its Fresno, California–based specialty vehicle manufacturer, Carlin Manufacturing, Inc.

The company continued exploring new marketing avenues, particularly nontraditional locations including airports, convenience stores, and restaurant chains, mostly fast food. Such high-volume locations as hospitals and airports were most highly prized. A&W Restaurants, Wall Street Restaurants, and CITGO convenience stores developed bundled units with TCBY in 1996, following the lead of Burger King and other established chains. 7-11 Stores in Hong Kong also began carrying TCBY products. Hotel operator Marriott was the largest operator of such locations. An earlier cooperative agreement to bring Mrs. Fields cookies into TCBY stores failed as volumes did not justify the increased equipment costs of about $8,000.

More than 40 percent of U.S. stores embraced the widely promoted TCBY Treats concept, which brought additional products including hand-dipped frozen yogurt, ice cream, and Paradise Ice brand shaved ice into the stores. These new offerings were accompanied by a change in color scheme from green to burgundy and new interior fixtures. In the mid-1990s, TCBY had also tested a low calorie lunch menu known as Sensible Temptations, but, like the Mrs. Fields experiment, high start-up costs made many franchisees reluctant to try it. Sara Lee and Ultra Slim-Fast products were also tested.

Americana Foods made yogurt for private labels as well as TCBY's own novelty items (frozen yogurt bars and sandwiches) and hardpack products for grocery store sales. With help from the Mid-America Dairymen cooperative, TCBY also began marketing refrigerated TCBY Traditional Style Yogurt. Sales of grocery items did not appear to benefit from the brand name as well as expected. The marketing rights for this line were sold to Mid-America Dairymen in 1995.

TCBY's spirits in 1995 prompted some takeover rumors by analysts who said the company's days as a fast-growing start-up in a wide-open field were over. However, such strengths as its strong financial position, good distribution system, and high brand recognition, suggest an auspicious future.

Principal Subsidiaries

American Best Care, Inc.; Riverport Equipment and Distribution Company; AIMCO; TCBY Systems, Inc.; TCBY International; TCBY Specialty Products; Americana Foods Limited Partnership.

Principal Divisions

Franchise Services; Franchise Development; Operations; Finance; Administration.

Further Reading

Alva, Marilyn, "Coming Attractions: TCBY Joins Videos on Blockbuster Shelves," *Restaurant Business,* July 1, 1992.

Barrier, Michael, "Cold Product, Hot Company," *Nation's Business,* September 1988, pp. 77–79.

Carson, Teresa, "The Frozen Yogurt Race Is Red Hot," *Business Week,* March 7, 1988, p. 67.

Casper, Carol, "Ice Cream and Yogurt Market Segment Report," *Restaurant Business,* May 1, 1992, pp. 209–230.

Dunnavant, Keith, "Has TCBY Found Its Way?" *Restaurant Business,* April 10, 1994.

——, "Meltdown," *Restaurant Business,* January 20, 1992.

Frank, Stephen E., "Insiders at Specialty Retailers Purchase Shares in Their Own Troubled Businesses," *Wall Street Journal,* August 3, 1994.

Fucini, Joseph J., and Suzy Fucini, *Experience, Inc.,* The Free Press, 1987.

Garrett, Echo M., "The Accidental Franchiser," *Venture,* May 1989.

Hebel, Sara, "Dan Charleton," *Advertising Age,* September 20, 1993, p. 44.

Jaffe, Aaron L., "TCBY Sees Sweet Potential of India's Massive Market," *Asian Wall Street Journal Weekly,* September 25, 1995, p. 4.

Kamis, Tali Levine, "Tickling Chinese Taste Buds," *The China Business Review,* January/February 1996, pp. 44–47.

Kochak, Jacque, "Ice Cream and Yogurt Market Segment Report," *Restaurant Business,* May 1, 1991, pp. 229–252.

Koeppel, Dan, "TCBY Turns Soft as Competition Heats Up," *Adweek's Marketing Week,* July 30, 1990, p. 8.

Moreau, Andy, "TCBY Troubles Mounting: Shareholders Seek to Broaden Lawsuit," *Restaurant Business,* March 1, 1992, p. 48.

Pamplin, Claire, "Ice Cream Here," *Convenience Store News,* February 13, 1995.

Scarpa, James, "Hot Growth for Frozen Yogurt Chain," *Restaurant Business,* March 1, 1989.

Schmuckler, Eric, "A Fatty Stock," *Forbes,* June 26, 1989, p. 133.

"TCBY," *Franchising World,* July/August 1989, pp. 49–50.

"TCBY Builds Pre-Fab Units, Shoots for 200 New Stores," *Restaurant Business,* September 1, 1987, p. 26.

"TCBY Treats Customers to New Menu and Decor," *Restaurants & Institutions,* March 1, 1995.

Walters, Dixie, "TCBY Fattens Up Its Bottom Line," *Arkansas Business,* April 5, 1993, pp. 1, 14–15.

——, "TCBY Pushes International Borders," *Arkansas Business,* September 19, 1994, pp. 1, 16.

Whalen, Jeanne, "At Counter: Ice Cream Giants Stir for Summer," *Advertising Age,* May 9, 1994.

Whittemore, Meg, "Less a Parent, More a Partner," *Nation's Business,* March, 1994, pp. 49–54.

Williams, Jeff, "TCBY Growth Melts Away," *Arkansas Business,* July 17, 1995, pp. 1, 14–15.

Zellner, Wendy, "Flaring Tempers at the Frozen Yogurt King," *Business Week,* September 10, 1990, pp. 88, 90.

—Frederick C. Ingram

TDK Corporation

1-13-1, Nihonbashi
Chuo-ku
Tokyo 103
Japan
(03) 278-5111
Fax: (03) 3278-5358
Internet: http://www.tdk.co.jp

Public Company
Incorporated: 1935 as TDK Electronics Corporation Ltd.
Employees: 26,830
Sales. ¥541.42 billion (US$5.11 billion, 1996)
Stock Exchanges: Tokyo Osaka New York Amsterdam
   London Paris Zurich
SICs: 3675 Electronic Capacitors; 3679 Electronic
   Components, Not Elsewhere Classified; 3695
   Magnetic & Optical Recording Media; 5065
   Electronic Parts & Equipment

TDK Corporation is the world's largest manufacturer of high quality audio and video tape. In addition recording media have been critical to the company's phenomenal growth. Beyond the view of the average consumer's eye, however, is a company that is a world leader in a number of other product markets as well. TDK's research and development department has been responsible for many discoveries in the application of magnetic materials over the years, and the company continues to drive the cutting edge of this technology in the 1990s. In addition to TDK's imposing presence in magnetic recording media markets, the company's sales have been increasingly made up of electronic components such as ferrite cores and magnets; coil and assembled components including electric convertors and hybrid integrated circuits; ceramic components; and high-tech assembly systems capable of the exceptional precision necessary in the manufacture of circuit boards and other delicate components.

Originated as a Marketer of Ferrite Technology

The success of TDK (the initials stand for Tokyo Denki Kogaku Kogyo) parallels the commercial development of a remarkably versatile material known as ferrite, a magnetic material with ceramic properties. Ferrite is composed of ferric oxide and any of a number of other metallic oxides, but usually zinc. Ferrite can be produced in several variations, each with somewhat different properties, and it can be categorized in two groups: hard and soft. Hard ferrite can be easily and permanently magnetized. Soft ferrite, on the other hand, does not stay magnetized for any great length of time, but has other properties that make it suitable for many electronics applications. In the 1990s TDK supplied about half of the world's ferrite.

Ferrite was invented in 1933 by two Japanese scientists, Dr. Yogoro Kato and Dr. Takeshi Takei, at the Tokyo Institute of Technology. Two years later a man named Kenzo Saito founded the TDK Corporation to market the scientists' discovery. Saito had been searching for a manufacturing business that he could establish in his hometown, which was wholly dependent on agriculture. When Kato and Saito met by chance, each was impressed by the other, and soon Kato granted Saito the use of the ferrite technology he and Takei had developed.

TDK's first application was a soft ferrite product, marketed as an "oxide core" and employed in transformers and coils. The demand for ferrite was very limited at this time, however, and TDK's first years were hard. But as the number of electrical appliances in the world increased, demand for TDK's ferrite cores increased dramatically. Early in its history, TDK made research and development a priority by exploring the dimensions of ferrite and finding new ways to employ it. Soon, the use of ferrite cores became widespread in consumer electronic products such as radios and televisions, markets that grew considerably during the 1940s and 1950s. Saito left TDK in 1946 and later became a member of the Diet.

Diversified Manufacturing and Expanded Overseas in the 1950s and 1960s

Eventually TDK branched into the manufacture of materials other than ferrite. In 1951 the company began to produce ceramic

477

capacitors. These components are used to store electrical energy, inhibit the flow of direct current, or facilitate the flow of alternate current, and are widely used in the production of electronic devices. Establishing itself as a key components manufacturer, TDK would benefit as the Japanese electronics industry grew.

In 1952 TDK introduced its first magnetic recording tape. TDK's line of recording tape eventually became the industry standard: at one point it accounted for half of the company's sales. In Japan TDK led the development of recording tape, becoming the first domestic manufacturer of audiocassettes in 1966. Two years later the company defied skeptics when it produced the world's first high-fidelity cassettes, marketed by TDK as Super Dynamic (SD) tape. Meanwhile, a TDK researcher named Yasuo Imaoka was looking for a material that could be used to replace chromium dioxide in video and audiotapes. Chromium dioxide, while offering excellent sound quality, is rare and expensive. Imaoka and his team came up with a process that combined ferric oxide with metal cobalt. The resulting material was named Avilyn, and it had a greater coercivity—a measure of magnetic substances—than chromium dioxide. Avilyn videotapes hit the market in 1973. The formula was soon improved by using cobalt hydroxide instead of metal cobalt, and the resulting Super Avilyn audiotapes revolutionized the industry when TDK unveiled its SA line, the first nonchrome high-bias tape, in 1975. In 1985 the Japanese Council of Industrial Patents named Avilyn as one of the country's top 53 inventions of the century.

As TDK developed technological innovations, its marketing strength also improved. The company entered foreign markets as early as 1959, opening a representative office in New York City. TDK opened a second American office in Los Angeles four years later. TDK's international operations grew extensively during the late 1960s and the 1970s. In 1968, TDK set up a subsidiary in Taiwan to manufacture ferrite cores, ceramic capacitors, and coil components. Over the course of the next ten years, TDK established subsidiaries in West Germany, Hong Kong, Great Britain, Brazil, Korea, Mexico, the United States, Singapore, and Australia. To ease trade imbalances and to insulate the company from currency fluctuations, TDK set up manufacturing facilities in many of these countries. TDK or its subsidiaries began producing magnetic heads in the United States in 1972 and audiotape a year later, ferrite cores in Korea in 1973, ferrite magnets in Mexico in 1974, ferrite cores in Brazil in 1979, and videotape in the United States in 1980. By the mid-1980s nearly half of TDK's business was generated outside of Japan.

VCRs Spur Tremendous Growth

In the mid-1970s TDK's already impressive growth rate took off for a number of reasons. Technological developments in consumer electronics created new demand for the company's expertise in ferrite and other materials. More sensitive audio equipment created strong demand for TDK's SA tapes, and the introduction of videocassette recorders (VCRs) to the consumer market created new demand for both the software (videotapes) and hardware (magnetic tape heads and other components) that TDK was capable of producing. The company's sales went through the roof as the videocassette market expanded 60 percent each year in the late 1970s.

Videocassettes and audiocassettes made up half of TDK's sales in the early 1980s. In 1983, however, an oversupply of videotapes sent prices into a downward spiral. While TDK's audiotapes sales continued to improve, revenue from videotape declined even though total volume increased. Just as the videotape crunch was at its worst, Yutaka Otoshi, the former chief of the tapes division, took over as TDK president and CEO. Otoshi increased TDK's research and development budget from 3.4 percent to 5 percent of sales to ensure the company's technological edge. New products such as the compact 8mm camcorders and players and recordable optical videodiscs were expected to give a boost to the market. Nonetheless, Otoshi focused on expanding TDK's nontape business. As he told *Business Week* in 1983, "we have never thought it was a good idea to concentrate too much on one product."

R&D Successes in the 1980s

In 1984 TDK launched its Components Engineering Laboratory (CEL) in Los Angeles. At this lab TDK's researchers worked with marketing personnel to develop custom prototypes of transformers, microwave products, and other components for use by American customers. In addition to customization, the new lab reduced the time required to go from product development to full-scale production. TDK's research efforts also resulted in the development of a number of new products in the 1980s. The company made breakthroughs in the development of thin-film heads for increased recording sensitivity, in multilayer hybrid circuits that allow equalization in headphone cassette players to be performed in one-third the usual space, and in sensor technology.

Another area in which TDK excelled in the 1980s is the field of anechoic chambers—rooms lined with a material that absorbs radiowaves. Anechoic chambers are used to measure the electromagnetic emission of electronic products and also a product's vulnerability to interference from such emissions. TDK's success with anechoic chambers grew out of its experience with microwave absorption. The company first began research in that field in 1964 and by 1968 had marketed its first ferrite-based microwave absorbers. The popularity of microwave ovens, which use a ferrite and rubber compound to keep the cooking process inside the oven, bolstered TDK's bottom line. In 1975 the company applied its expertise in microwave absorption to anechoic chambers, and in the 1980s, as demand for these facilities grew on the back of a booming electronics industry, TDK became a major force in the field.

In 1987 the company embarked on a joint venture with the Allen-Bradley Company, of the United States, to produce motor magnets for the automobile industry. Allen-Bradley/TDK Magnetics began production at a plant in Oklahoma in April of that year. TDK benefitted from its partner's long-standing relationship with American automakers, and Allen-Bradley benefitted from TDK's magnetics expertise.

The late 1980s also saw the miniaturization of and increased demand for higher-density circuits and components. Manufacturers of these products required extremely precise equipment for their production facilities. TDK's Avimount and Avisert automated assembly equipment was in greater demand as a result. Sales in 1988 were up 25 percent over the previous year and were expected to continue to rise.

TDK's focus on broadening its nontape products was successful; by 1988 the nontape sector accounted for 64 percent of the company's total sales. But TDK did not neglect its recording-media development. TDK's floppy discs garnered a respectable market share partly based on the company's excellent reputation in audio and video recording media. In 1987 the company introduced digital audio tape (DAT)—tapes able to play and record music digitally, like compact disks—in Japan and prepared to enter foreign markets as soon as copyright problems were settled. In 1988, it introduced a top-of-the-line videotape called Super Strong, a new product that allowed TDK to raise prices and still maintain market share.

TDK continued to grow on its own and make acquisitions when appropriate. In 1988 the company acquired Display Components Inc. (Discom), of Westford, Massachusetts. The purchase allowed Discom access to TDK's advanced production techniques while TDK received Discom's state-of-the-art magnetic field technology.

Overseas Production and Increased R&D Mark the 1990s

In 1989 TDK purchased a large American manufacturer of mixed-signal integrated circuits, Silicon Systems Inc. (SSI), for $200 million, further diversifying its range of products. SSI proved to be a problematic acquisition for TDK, however. SSI struggled during its first few years under TDK, even after a $100-million-plus infusion from the parent to help SSI beef up its U.S. production. By the mid-1990s, even this had not provided SSI with the capacity it needed to compete with the giants of the semiconductor industry. Rather than sinking more money into the troubled firm, TDK decided to sell SSI in 1996 and found a willing buyer among these same giants, namely Texas Instruments Inc. Terms were $575 million in cash plus a long-term note that could bring TDK another $50 million in contingent payments. This sale did not mark TDK's complete withdrawal from semiconductor-related areas, however. Not included in the deal were SSI's Communications Products Division and TDK Systems Division, leaving TDK with such products as PC cards and integrated circuits for telecommunications. These were not insignificant, as evidenced particularly by TDK's success in the area of fax/modem PC cards, a product that experienced explosive sales growth in the mid-1990s as the Internet and online services became everyday business and personal tools.

In the early to mid-1990s, TDK had to contend with a glut in the videotape market and the consequences of an extremely strong yen, both of which depressed company sales, and consequently earnings. TDK moved aggressively to cut costs, consolidating Japanese production of blank audio and videotapes in one factory in 1993. To mitigate the effects of the strong yen, TDK shifted much of its production overseas. Ferrite products began to be manufactured in Dalian, China, in 1993. By 1995, more than half of TDK's audio and videotapes were produced outside Japan—in Luxembourg, the United States, and Thailand. In May 1996, TDK announced a plan to shift all its floppy disk manufacturing overseas, some to a California subsidiary, some to several Southeast Asian companies. And in the fall of 1996, a new plant in Hungary began manufacturing transformers, ferrite cores, and other components.

Under the guidance of President Hiroshi Sato, TDK further bolstered R&D by spending six percent of overall sales on new product development. One product area targeted was that of ceramic filters for mobile telecommunications, another high growth sector. Overall, R&D was directed to make TDK even less dependent on the mature areas of magnetic products and tapes. An example of the company's search for nontape revenue was the joint venture with Duracell International Inc. announced in early 1996, whereby the two companies would jointly develop and manufacture ion electrode sets, a key component in the increasingly popular lithium-ion rechargeable battery.

The production shifts and emphasis on new products began to pay off in 1996, with TDK posting healthy increases of 11.6 percent in net sales and 41.1 percent in operating profit over 1995. The company cited electronic components for computers, home electronics, and telecommunications products as the main contributors to these gains.

As it moved into the late 1990s, TDK was well positioned in the five areas in which it operated: magnetic products, ceramic and assembled components, recording devices, recording media, and semiconductor-related products. The company, which was built largely around the merits of one material—ferrite—had long since become a diverse, broad-based high-tech company. As technology continued to race ahead, TDK, with its experience and dedication to creativity, was expected to remain an industry leader.

Principal Subsidiaries

Iida TDK Co., Ltd; Tsuruoka TDK Co., Ltd.; Yuza TDK Co., Ltd.; Kisagata TDK Co., Ltd.; Yashima TDK Co., Ltd.; Ujo TDK Co., Ltd.; TDK Service Co., Ltd.; TDK Design Core Co., Ltd.; TDK-MCC Co., Ltd.; Iwaki Kogyo Co., Ltd.; Yuri TDK Co., Ltd.; Konoura TDK Co., Ltd.; TDK Core Co., Ltd.; Ouchi TDK Co., Ltd.; TDK Distributor Co., Ltd.; Sakata TDK Co., Ltd.; Honjo TDK Co., Ltd.; Kofu TDK Co., Ltd.; Yuzawa TDK Co., Ltd.; Toso TDK Co., Ltd.; TDK (Australia) Pty. Ltd. (55%); TDK do Brasil Ind. e Com. Ltda.; (Brazil); TDK Dalian Corporation (China); TDK Electronics Europe GmbH (Germany); TDK Hong Kong Co., Ltd.; Korea TDK Co., Ltd. (50%); TDK Recording Media Europe S.A. (Luxembourg); TDK (Malaysia) Sdn. Bhd.; TDK de Mexico S.A. de C.V.; TDK Singapore (Pte) Ltd.; TDK Electronics (Taiwan) Corp. (80.24%); TDK UK Ltd.; TDK Electronics Corporation (U.S.A.); TDK U.S.A. Corporation; TDK Corporation of America (U.S.A.); TDK Magnetic Tape Corp. (U.S.A.).

Further Reading

McCartney, Scott, "Texas Instruments to Buy TDK Unit, Broadening Its Role in Chip-Making," *Wall Street Journal,* June 5, 1996, p. B8(W), p. B4(E).

Sprackland, Teri, "How Silicon Systems Turns Yet into Dollars," *Electronic Business,* January 21, 1991, pp. 38–39.

"TDK Agrees to Buy Si Systems," *Electronic News,* April 17, 1989, p. 25.

"TDK Launches New Round of Product Development," *Tokyo Business Today,* July 1995, p. 18.

—updated by David E. Salamie

TI Group plc

Lambourn Court
Abingdon
Oxon OX14 1UH
United Kingdom
171-499-9131
Fax: 171-493-6533
Internet: http://www.tigroup.com

Public Company
Incorporated: 1982
Sales: US$2.5 billion (1995)
Employees: 22,600
Stock Exchanges: London
SICs: 3714 Motor Vehicle Parts and Accessories; 3317 Steel Pipe and Tubes; 3568 Power Transmission Equipment, Not Elsewhere Classified; 6719 Holding Companies, Not Elsewhere Classified

TI Group plc is a holding company for an international specialized engineering group of firms with three core business activities: the manufacture of mechanical seals for leak-prevention applications in the process, aerospace, marine, and automotive industries (John Crane International); the manufacture of small-diameter tubing and fluid-carrying systems for the refrigeration and automotive industries (Bundy Corporation); and the manufacture of aircraft landing gear, hydraulic systems, and propellers for the military and commercial aircraft industry (Dowty Aerospace). In 1995 its operations comprised roughly 125 companies with about 350 manufacturing and customer service facilities in 115 countries with sales outside of the United Kingdom comprising 85 percent of its total revenues. In the 1990s TI was ranked as the second-largest specialized engineering firm in Great Britain, Europe's fifth-largest fabricated metal product manufacturer (excluding machinery and transportation equipment), and one of Europe's top ten largest specialist engineering groups.

From Metalbashing to Bikes and Kettles: 1919–40

TI Group plc was founded as Tube Investments Ltd. in Birmingham, England, in July 1919 out of four Midlands steel tubing manufacturers and distributors who agreed to merge as a public limited committee to more effectively compete in the British tube making industry. That industry, which manufactured such basic industrial products as gas, water, and oil pipes, had been only a few decades old when in 1903 the two largest tube makers in Scotland and England, Stewarts & Menzies and Lloyds, respectively, agreed to merge to form Stewart & Lloyds Ltd. By 1907 the United Kingdom's crowded tube making market consisted of 50 to 60 principal firms turning out about 300,000 tons of iron and steel tubes a year.

When Tube Investments (or "Tubes," as it soon came to be called) came on the scene twelve years later with £1 million in assets and two thousand employees, it began to specialize in the manufacture of precision and other high-quality steel tubes. Throughout the 1920s, TI worked its business niche until by the end of the decade it had become Stewart & Lloyd's only real rival for dominance of the U.K. tube industry. To avoid inefficient competition and redundant research efforts the two firms formed an alliance in 1930. The Depression led to a massive dropoff in demand for British tubes, however, and by 1932 U.K. tube exports were less than half 1929 levels. The export slump continued until 1937, but demand for small-diameter tubes for gas companies and the construction industry kept domestic orders up, and between 1934 and 1939 the production of hot rolled strip for tubes by British firms jumped from 158,000 to 293,000 tons. In 1936, TI and Stewart & Lloyds teamed up to acquire the British Mannesmann Tube Company of Newport on the Welsh coast (which Stewart & Lloyds took over completely in 1938) and then joined forces again in 1938 to provide the capital for the construction of Jarrow Tube Works Ltd. near Newcastle-upon-Tyne.

To broaden its position outside the competitive tube industry, by 1939 TI had diversified into non-tube engineering products, bicycle manufacture, and domestic products and appliances, including kitchen kettles, cookers, and heaters.

Losing Ground: 1940–86

As World War II raged to its conclusion, Sir Ivan Arthur Rice Stedeford was named TI's chairman and managing director in 1944, and he quickly began scouting for postwar opportunities for expansion and diversification. TI's first Asian-Pacific investment was completed in the 1940s with the founding of Tube Investments of India Ltd., an independent, public-stock corporation, in Madras, India. Between 1945 and 1951 the postwar U.K. Labour government nationalized Britain's steel companies, but under the succeeding Conservative governments virtually all these firms were reprivatized between 1953 and 1961. TI took advantage of the volatile climate by adding to its steel holdings throughout the decade. In 1954 it purchased the century-old Round Oak steelworks, the equally historical Park Gate steelmaking business of Sheffield a year later, and—through a joint venture with the U.S. metal industry giant Reynolds Metals Co.—the British Aluminum Co. in 1959. Despite efforts by TI's management in 1955 to begin establishing long-range investment strategies for the corporation, global economic trends began to threaten TI's position as an international steel products leader. Germany and Japan's rapid postwar economic recoveries and the entrée of new developing countries with low labor and manufacturing costs had transformed the international marketplace, and with the decade-long steel glut that began in 1960 TI's ongoing profitability was suddenly a much more tenuous proposition.

In 1960 TI expanded further into the bicycle manufacturing market by purchasing Raleigh Industries, a Nottingham-based bicycle maker, which by 1989 was accounting for half of all bicycle sales in the United Kingdom and at its peak was producing two million cycles annually from its 65-acre plant. In 1963, Sir Stedeford stepped down as TI's chairman after nearly two decades at the helm and was replaced by Lord Plowden who also assumed the position of TI's managing director. TI's second major venture with a U.S. firm followed in 1965 when it agreed to manufacture motor control and switch equipment with General Electric under the brand name Simplex-GE, and in the same year TI acquired Radiation, an unfortunately named manufacturer of gas cookers and water heaters. In 1967, a new Labour government nationalized the U.K. steel industry again, and TI lost the Park Gate steelworks with its Round Oak plant becoming an associate company jointly owned by TI and the government-run British Steel Corporation.

Still struggling with the intensified competition of the steel products industry in the 1970s TI continued reshuffling its corporate deck to find the right mix of profitability and diversification. Its non-tube making holdings still included Raleigh bikes and the gas appliance manufacturers New World and Glow-worm, the electrical cooker and shelf goods producers (respectively) Creda and Russell Hobbs, and the cookware and solid fuel heating manufacturers (respectively) Tower Housewares and Parkray. But following TI's acquisition of Steel Service & Engineering Ltd. of Canada in early 1970, no fewer than eleven British firms were added before year's end, and in the next three years TI purchased an additional six firms. As the United Kingdom joined the European Community to increase international trade opportunities, TI acquired a majority interest in Allen West & Co. Ltd. in 1973, which was later merged in the Simplex-GE joint venture. After Lord Plowden was replaced by Sir Brian Kellett as managing director in 1974, TI moved to increase its holding in British Aluminum and added a gas cylinder division in 1979. Although by the end of the decade TI was still among the thirty largest companies in the United Kingdom it was still far from clear whether its postwar mix of aluminum, machine tools, domestic appliances, and other consumer products was still viable. Its traditional core business—commodity tube making—which traditionally provided only low added value, remained a riskily sizable segment of its operations, and only 15 percent of its manufacturing was being performed outside the United Kingdom.

The first steel industry strike in the United Kingdom since 1926 erupted in 1980, and the recession in the British engineering industry that followed led to a devastating £10 million loss for TI in 1981. The strength of the British pound sterling throughout the recession years only added salt to TI's wounds by rendering its products less attractive to overseas customers, who accounted for roughly half the company's annual sales. Moreover, rising production costs and falling demand for aluminum forced TI's British Aluminum subsidiary to close its smelter at Invergordon, Scotland, in 1981, and with Raleigh's far-flung bicycle division continuing to bleed the corporate balance sheet, TI's domestic appliances operations seemed to be the only business keeping TI out of bankruptcy court.

By 1982 it was plain that radical steps were needed, and beginning with a symbolic name change from Tube Investments to TI Group plc, TI's management began simultaneously divesting and expanding to resuscitate the group's unfocused operations. King Fifth Wheel of Pennsylvania had been acquired in 1981—transforming TI overnight into the world's largest producer of aircraft engine rings—and under new managing director Ronnie Utiger, TI also jettisoned its primary and semifinished commodity-type products, culminating in the 1982 sale of its two-decade-old interest in British Aluminum Co. In July 1982 TI entered the promising computer-controlled lathe making machinery industry with the purchase of the Alfred Herbert company. Despite such considered moves, by the mid-1980s the fortunes of TI's 25 companies were still unclear: its machine tool line, which had been underperforming for a full decade, lost £2 million in 1984, the government's imposition of a value-added tax had damaged sales in TI's Parkray solid fuel heating business, the once-promising U.S. gas cylinder division was faltering, and in 1985 Raleigh cycle—which lost £30 million between 1980 and 1985 alone—suffered a 30 percent drop in demand. A year after Utiger took over the chairmanship in 1985, domestic appliances still accounted for 25 percent of TI's annual sales, specialized engineering (aircraft engine rings, mechanical seals, and vacuum furnaces) close to 25 percent, the newly divisionalized automotive products group about 20 percent, steel tubes 15 percent, and Raleigh cycles 14 percent.

By enlarging TI's position in such growth businesses as automobile mufflers/exhaust systems (making TI one of Europe's top three producers) and car seat mechanisms, Utiger had clearly stabilized TI. By mid-1985, however, Evered, an acquisitive U.K. miniconglomerate, had managed to gain a 20 percent stake of TI stock, further weakening TI's already weak standing in London's financial market and notifying Utiger that even more drastic change was in order.

Clean Sweep: 1986–96

In July 1986 Utiger's hired Christopher Lewinton, a former chairman of Wilkinson Sword, to create a new direction for the company as TI's new CEO. Lewinton went to work studying TI's troubles and soon issued a new corporate mission statement declaring bluntly that "TI's strategy is to become an international group concentrating on specialised engineering businesses, operating in selected niches on a global basis. Key businesses must be able to command positions of sustainable technological and market share leadership." The company's headquarters were relocated from Birmingham to London, and before the year was out the consumer goods subsidiaries Russell Hobbs and Tower Housewares had been shown the door. Four months later the long-suffering Raleigh was sold for £18 million, and appliance makers Glow-worm and Parkray were unloaded for another £63.5 million. In May and June New World appliances was sold to Birmid Qualcast, and Creda was auctioned off to General Electric plc. With domestic appliances now disposed of, Lewinton turned to TI's slow-moving tube and machine tool holdings: TI Machine Tools was sold off in October 1987 and Cold Drawn Tubes and Seamless Tubes were dismissed in March 1988.

Lewinton's unceremonious amputation of at least two arms of TI's historical product mix had its upside too: TI's promising automotive division was bolstered with the acquisition of Armco Inc., an automotive brake and fuel line producer, in January 1987, and eight months later TI purchased Chicago-based Houdaille Industries Inc., then promptly resold it all save for the real target of Lewinton's interest: Chicago-based John Crane International—the world's largest producer of mechanical seals for the industrial process, marine, and automotive industries and the inventor of the forerunner of modern mechanical seal technology. Next, in April 1988, Lewinton acquired Bundy Corporation—a Detroit-based producer of small-diameter tubing and fluid-carrying systems for the automotive and refrigeration industries (founded in 1922). In less than nine months, Lewinton had acquired the two businesses that by 1996 would account for 80 percent of TI's total sales. Moreover, the traditional product mix that at the beginning of Lewinton's reign had forced TI to depend on the U.K. market for more than half its sales had been traded in for a new international model that by 1996 drew less than 25 percent of its sales from the United Kingdom and fully 43 percent from North America.

The key to Lewinton's strategy was his discovery that for almost a half century TI had simply been in the wrong line of work. Its appliance businesses situated TI in the consumer goods industry, but, as Lewinton later explained, "TI's basic culture was engineering. I therefore decided to focus on its basic culture and build the engineering business." The Crane and Bundy additions, however, were meant to be complemented by a third new product group, and it was Lewinton's attempt to determine what that business would be that led to the only missteps in his massive course correction plan. The acquisition of heat-treated furnace maker Thermal Scientific in August 1988, for example, turned into a disappointment and by 1992 had been sold off, and a plan to acquire Spirax Sarco, a manu-

facturer of steam traps, fell apart when its management spurned TI's overtures. By 1990, TI had moved to a larger headquarters in Abingdon near Oxford and could boast 300 manufacturing and customer service facilities in 114 countries. The third cog in the wheel that would complement Bundy and Crane, however, remained elusive until 1992 when Lewinton narrowed his short list down to one firm: Dowty Aerospace, founded as a manufacturer of actuators in Cheltenham, England, in 1931 by George Dowty, who within a few years would invent the first retractable landing gear for aircraft.

Despite Dowty's resistance, TI concluded its takeover of Dowty in June 1992 for £510 million, capping the second phase of Lewinton's rebuilding strategy and earning TI a place in the prestigious FT-SE 100 index of British companies. Even with a prolonged slump in the aerospace industry, Dowty began to emerge as the diversification vehicle Lewinton had wanted. In June 1993, Dowty's landing gear business was fused in a joint venture with Messier-Bugatti, the landing gear subsidiary of the French Snecma Group. Although closing the deal, which created Messier-Dowty International, forced TI to sacrifice some of Dowty's profit potential in a sector—aerospace—that was supposed to be a crucial component of the "new TI," the venture instantly propelled TI to the forefront of the global landing gear industry. By the mid-1990s, Messier-Dowty landing gears were installed in more than 14,000 aircraft and 40 percent of the world's civil jets and warplanes. Dowty's promising polymer engineering business—which comprised industrial and automotive applications such as gaskets and sealing technology—was meanwhile absorbed into TI's John Crane operations, and Dowty's high-tech propeller business began to pay an unexpected dividend when it edged toward global market leadership.

In the 1990s TI moved aggressively into more international markets, extending its network to 115 foreign countries. In the Latin American market (including Mexico), Crane, Bundy, and Dowty were generating US$2.65 billion in sales by 1995 through operations in Venezuela, Colombia, and Argentina and spearheaded by TI's Brazilian mechanical seal, landing gear, automotive fuel and brake line, and refrigeration condenser businesses. TI's North American holdings (including Mexico) added another US$2.1 billion to its balance sheet and by 1995 was generating 43 percent of TI's total sales. In this, TI's largest market, Crane's mechanical seals were being sold to Amoco, General Motors, the U.S. Navy, and DuPont, and major customers for Bundy's brake, fuel line, and other automotive systems included Ford, Chrysler, Mercedes-Benz, and Toyota. Meanwhile, in the early 1990s Messier-Dowty won a contract to supply the nose landing gear for the U.S. Navy's F/A-18E/F fighter, the world's largest combat aircraft program, as well as a US$4 million contract to supply all rigid tube requirements for the Lockheed Martin's Atlas Space Vehicle Program in 1996.

In Europe, the fall of the Iron Curtain in the early 1990s had opened new markets in an Eastern Europe hungry for TI's high-tech product lines. In the Czech Republic, for example, John Crane purchased the mechanical seals firm Lutin in March 1996, and Bundy set up a brake and fuel line plant near Prague to supply the Czech auto industry. Bundy's Hungarian refrigerator condenser plant also began supplying Central Europe's largest refrigeration manufacturer, Samsung-Calex, with condensers in the mid-1990s, and in Russia Dowty moved into that country's cable laying machinery industry through a contract with the Russian Ministry of Post and Telecommunications.

Sales to the Asian-Pacific region, an area specially targeted in Lewinton's grand strategy, grew to £150 million (15 percent of total sales) by 1995 through operations in Australia, China, Hong Kong, India, Indonesia, Japan, New Zealand, Singapore, and South Korea. TI's John Crane Tianjin Ltd. subsidiary became the largest manufacturer of seals in mainland China, and TI's Chinese Dowty operations supplied spare parts and technical support to more than fifty Chinese airlines. In 1995, John Crane won its first mass transit intercarriage gangway assembly contract in the Asian market from the city of Hong Kong, Dowty Aerospace landed a US$8.7 million contract to establish an aircraft landing gear repair facility for the Indian Navy, and Messier-Dowty received an order from India Airlines for the overhaul of the landing gear for its Airbus fleet. In 1994–95, TI formed three major joint ventures—with Sembawang Group of Singapore, Tubemakers of Australia Ltd., and Murugappa Group of India—to solidify its growing presence in the Asian-Pacific market.

TI's turnaround was not entirely seamless, however. In 1995, a whistleblowing employee at one of Dowty's subsidiaries alleged that the U.S. Air Force had been the victim of repeated overcharging by TI subsidiaries in several aircraft part contracts. TI maintained its innocence, and the case was dismissed for lack of jurisdiction. Moreover, while TI had indisputably resurrected itself financially, some industry analysts questioned the permanence of its recovery. Its large presence in the automotive parts industry increased its dependence on a notoriously boom-and-bust automobile industry, and its penchant for acquisitions regularly seemed to threaten its cash reserves. In 1996, the Morningstar stock analysis service praised TI for becoming more profitable but described the company overall as only a "steady . . . but far from spectacular" performer.

By 1995 TI's virtually unprecedented corporate transformation was nearly complete. Only £100 million of its £1.5 billion in sales came from companies in its possession when Lewinton took over in 1986, and only steel tube maker Accles & Pollock (itself founded at the beginning of the century) remained from the original 1919 Tube Investments merger. Sentimentality had never been part of Lewinton's game plan, however, and in September 1996 when he moved to double TI's holdings in John Crane's polymer engineering business with the purchase of the Swedish firm Forsheda, he also sold off Accles & Pollock. TI had come full circle.

Principal Subsidiaries

(I) John Crane (includes Polymer Engineering): John Crane Inc. (U.S.); Dowty O Rings North America Inc. (U.S.); Dowty Palmer-Chenard Inc. (U.S.); John Crane Marine USA; John Crane Canada Inc.; John Crane UK Ltd.; Deep Sea Seals Ltd.; Dowty Woodville Polymer Ltd.; Lapmaster International Ltd; (II) Bundy (includes smaller engineering companies: Bundy Corporation (U.S.); Huron Products (U.S.); Titeflex Corporation (U.S.); Bundy of Canada; Bundy UK Ltd; Lewis & Saunders Inc. (U.S.); VARI-FORM Inc. (Canada); (III) Dowty Aerospace (includes TI Aerospace): Messier-Dowty Inc. (Canada); Dowty Aerospace Aviation Services Sterling - Dowty Aerospace Corp. Inc. (U.S.); Dowty Aerospace Yakima - Dowty Decoto Inc. (U.S.); Dowty Aerospace Los Angeles - Hydraulic Units Inc. (U.S.); King Fifth Wheel (U.S.); Dowty Aerospace Propellers; Dowty Aerospace Hydraulics; Dowty Aerospace Gloucester Ltd.; Messier-Dowty International Ltd. (U.K.; 50%); Messier-Dowty Ltd. (IV) Parent and other: Dowty Group plc; TI International Holdings Ltd.; Dowty (USA) Holdings Inc.; TI Group Inc. (U.S.).

Further Reading

Burn, Duncan, *The Economic History of Steelmaking, 1867–1939,* Cambridge: Cambridge University Press, 1961.
Campbell, Colin, "TI Wins Battle for Dowty," *London Times,* June 11, 1992.
Carr, J.C., and W. Taplin, *A History of the British Steel Industry,* Oxford: Basil Blackwell, 1962.
Cook, Nick, "Anglo-French Team Sets Its Sights on the USA," *Interavia Business & Technology,* May 1994.
Cowe, Roger, "TI Subsidiaries Face $20 Million Fraud Suit," *Guardian,* February 18,1995.
"Kohlberg to Buy Back 6 Houdaille Divisions," *Chicago Tribune,* September 29, 1987.
Lorenz, Andrew, "Why TI Group Went West," *Management Today,* April 1996, p. 35.
O'Connor, Matt, "Houdaille Oks British Buyout Bid," *Chicago Tribune,* August 26, 1987.
Rodger, Ian, "TI Group Tackles World of New Technology with Old Survivors," *Financial Times,* December 14, 1983.
A Short History of TI Group plc, company document, Abingdon, UK: TI Group plc, May 1995.
Tieman, Ross, "TI's Anglo-French Venture Will Create World Leader," *London Times,* June 25, 1993.
Travers, Nicolas, "TI's Long Road from 'Metalbashing' to Hi-Tech," *Chief Executive* (U.K.), July/August 1986, pp. 12–15.
Wilkinson, Terence, "TI Group Engineers High-Tech Turnaround," *Independent* (London), February 13, 1989, p. 21.
——, "TI's Quest for a Global Culture," *Independent* (London), August 21, 1990, p. 19.

—Paul S. Bodine

Times Mirror

The Times Mirror Company

Times Mirror Square
Los Angeles, California 90053
U.S.A.
(213) 237-3700
Fax: (213) 237-3714
Internet: http://www.latimes.com

Public Company
Incorporated: 1884
Employees: 26,902
Sales: $3.4 billion (1995)
Stock Exchanges: New York Pacific
SICs: 2711 Newspapers; 2731 Book Publishing; 2721
  Periodicals; 8741 Management Services; 4833
  Television Broadcasting Stations; 4841 Cable and
  Other Pay Television Services

The Times Mirror Company ranks among the top five newspaper companies in the United States. Regarding itself as a news and information company, Times Mirror is comprised of three business segments: Newspaper Publishing, which houses the publishers of *The Los Angeles Times, The Baltimore Sun, The Hartford Courant* and other newspapers; Professional Information, a group of publishers of science, health, legal, and technical books, as well as a software developer; and Consumer Media, the company's popular magazine segment, publishing such popular periodicals as *Field & Stream, Popular Science, Ski, Yachting,* and others, including art book publisher Harry N. Abrams). From its unassuming beginnings as a four-page daily newspaper saved from an early demise by a printing and binding company, The Times Mirror Company has demonstrated a high degree of resourcefulness. Following a spate of acquisitions in the 1980s, the company was in the midst of a traumatic downsizing by the mid-1990s. Under the direction of former General Mills, Inc. Vice-Chairman Mark Willes, the company shut down *New York Newsday* and the Baltimore *Sun's* evening edition, spun off "nonessential" businesses, and slashed over 1,700 jobs from its work force. The change in management was said to be heavily influenced by descendants of co-founder Harry Chandler, who continued to hold over half of the company's voting stock in the mid-1990s. Notwithstanding its financial difficulties, the Times Mirror Co. and its newspapers enjoyed a reputation for quality journalism, having won eight Pulitzer Prizes from 1990 to 1995. Media watchers hoped that cost-cutting fervor would not bring that tradition to an end in the waning years of the 20th century.

Late 19th Century Origins

The Mirror Printing and Binding House, established in 1873 primarily for commercial printing, agreed in 1881 to print a new daily newspaper called the *Los Angeles Daily Times,* soon renamed the *Los Angeles Times.* The publishers abandoned the project shortly after it was launched, although the printers kept the newspaper going. Seven months later, Civil War veteran General Harrison Gray Otis was named full-time editor. In 1884 Otis and Colonel H.H. Boyce purchased both the newspaper and the printing company, incorporating them into The Times-Mirror Company. The hyphen was dropped before long. Two years later, Otis fully acquired the concern that declared itself "a new and hopeful candidate for a share of the patronage of the community." The newspaper set out, through its headlines and stories, to attract new residents and businesses to the sleepy town of Los Angeles. Over time, the newspaper found itself promoting a free harbor at San Pedro, in 1891, and construction of the city's first freeway, in 1930.

Acquisitions Begin Mid-20th Century

By 1948 Times Mirror had made its first acquisition, purchasing the Publishers Paper Company of Lake Oswego, Oregon. (In the 1980s, Publishers Paper would emerge as the third-largest newsprint producer in the United States, and about 70 percent of the newsprint produced by Publishers Paper in the early 1990s was sold to Times Mirror.) Another major acquisition came in 1961 when Times Mirror absorbed Englewood, Colorado-based Jeppesen Sanderson, the world's leading publisher of air navigation information and flight-training systems. Also that year, Times Mirror acquired the H.M. Goush Company, a producer of modern travel maps and pioneer of the accordion-fold map, in San Jose, California.

Company Perspectives:

To remain successful and grow in a new global marketplace, Times Mirror is committed to sustaining editorial excellence—in other words, doing what we do best—and growing through innovation. We recognize that among our greatest strengths is our reputation for editorial excellence, and we will continue to build on that reputation. In addition, we recognize that our businesses will only flourish and grow if we have superior competitive offerings. To this end, we have made focusing on innovation a cornerstone of our over-all business strategy. Innovation is the engine that will drive our growth—whether it's a new way of doing old things better, the creation of a new product, or the creation of a new business. All of our businesses are committed to growing through innovation.

By 1963 Times Mirror was expanding into other specialized publishing, acquiring New York City-based Matthew Bender & Company, the largest publisher of legal forms and legal treatises in the United States. Two years later the company acquired Chicago-based Year Book Medical Publishers, publishers of medical reference books. Times Mirror bought the 17-year-old art book publisher Harry N. Abrams, Inc., of New York City in 1966. The following year, Times Mirror acquired the C.V. Mosby Company of St. Louis, Missouri, which since became the world's leading publisher of health-science books.

The company's entrance into magazine publishing came in 1967 when it acquired *Popular Science, Outdoor Life, Golf Magazine,* and *Ski Magazine.* Within 20 years of that acquisition, Times Mirror Magazines, Inc. had more than nine million readers and operated two national book clubs with annual sales in excess of two million books. Times Mirror's other strategic move into complementary media came in 1968 when it purchased Co-Axial Systems Engineering Company and its seven cable franchises in southern California, with a base of 5,700 subscribers. Times Mirror embarked on rapid growth in cable that soon included the acquisition of smaller systems in southern California and on Long Island, expanding its subscriber base to 22,000. Its most substantial increase in subscribers would come with the 1979 purchase of Communications Properties, Inc., then the nation's eighth-largest cable operator.

In 1970, Times Mirror acquired the 91-year-old *Dallas Times Herald,* as well as *Newsday*—the tabloid-sized Long Island, New York, daily, that had become the prototype for the nation's suburban press. The company's next major foray into new media was the formation of Times Mirror Broadcasting in 1970 that initially was comprised of KDFW-TV, Dallas, Texas, then known as KRLD-TV; KTBC-TV in Austin, Texas; KTVI-TV in St. Louis, Missouri; WVTM-TV in Birmingham, Alabama; WHTM-TV in Harrisburg, Pennsylvania; WSTM-TV in Syracuse, New York; and WETM-TV in Elmira, New York.

In 1977 the purchase of Southern Connecticut Newspapers Inc. gave Times Mirror control of two of the oldest Connecticut newspapers, *The Advocate* of Stamford and *Greenwich Time.*

The acquisition of The Sporting News Publishing Company of St. Louis, Missouri, that year gave Times Mirror control of *The Sporting News,* a weekly magazine dating back to 1886 that eventually narrowed its focus to become known as "Baseball's Bible."

Times Mirror's 1978 acquisition of Graphic Controls Corporation of Buffalo, New York, was another bid to strengthen the company's presence in the medical-information field with its production of recording charts, instrument marking systems, disposable medical products, and coated imaging papers. Times Mirror kept returning to its roots, however, for acquisitions that strengthened both its editorial muscle and revenue base. In 1979 Times Mirror acquired *The Hartford Courant* of Connecticut, the nation's oldest continuously published newspaper. *The Courant*'s proud heritage included reproducing the full text of the Declaration of Independence in July 1776, when the paper was 12 years old. In 1980 Times Mirror acquired *The Denver Post.* Four years later, in 1984, the company acquired Call-Chronicle Newspapers, Inc., now *The Morning Call,* serving a nine-county region in eastern Pennsylvania and in New Jersey.

Restructuring in the 1980s

To celebrate the advent of its second 100 years in business, Times Mirror adopted a new logo in 1984—a stylized version of the eagle that had appeared on the front of the *Los Angeles Times* and its other publications. In that year, Times Mirror's profit of $420.8 million was an increase of 13 percent from a year earlier. The company's 1984 revenues were a record $2.8 billion, also up 13 percent from the prior year. Newspaper publishing remained the single biggest revenue contributor.

In 1984 Times Mirror began a restructuring process that ended two years later in a flurry of buying and selling. In 1986 Times Mirror paid $600 million for A.S. Abell Company, owner of *The Baltimore Sun.* Times Mirror paid Dow Jones & Company $135 million for Richard D. Irwin Inc., a textbook publisher, in 1988. It also added *Broadcasting* (sold in May 1991) and *The National Journal* to its magazine holdings for $75 million and $10 million, respectively, during the restructuring, while selling the struggling *Dallas Times Herald* for $110 million. The company disposed of five television stations, a cable system in Las Vegas, Nevada, and a number of its non-media holdings. Times Mirror sold off $1 billion in assets and spent $750 million on acquisitions for its core print- and electronic-media businesses during the three-year restructuring.

In 1985 *Newsday* expanded and began to publish *New York Newsday,* an edition targeted to the Brooklyn and Queens boroughs of New York City. In 1986 the company sold H.M. Goush Company and the national book clubs. After 1986 Times Mirror turned its attention to capital expenditures, particularly in its newspaper operations, where equipment had to be updated. In 1987 it launched a five-year $385 million capital-investment plan, bringing new plant and facilities to the *Los Angeles Times.*

In 1987 David Laventhol succeeded Robert Erburu as president of *Times Mirror* although Erburu continued as chairman and chief executive officer of the company. Also that year, Times Mirror bought four magazines from Diamandis Communications for $176.5 million: *Field & Stream, Yachting, Home Mechanix, and Skiing Magazine.* The acquisition came at a time when Times Mirror began experimenting with new start-up publications, such as *Sports Inc.*, which folded after a 15-month trial for lack of advertiser support.

The company sold the money-losing newspapers Denver *Post* and *Dallas Times Herald* in separate deals for a total of $205 million to Dallas publisher William Dean Singleton. Among the other assets sold as part of the restructuring was an 80 percent interest in Publishers Paper.

By 1990 Times Mirror had become the 12th-largest multiple cable system operator in the country and operated four network television affiliates. It had spent $1.5 billion acquiring new businesses throughout the 1980s—$583 million on newspaper properties; $595 million on book, magazine, and other publishing acquisitions; $235 million on cable TV systems; and $82 million on broadcast properties. Capital expenditures during the decade totaled $2.53 billion—more than half of which was concentrated in its newspaper operations. During that same period, revenues grew from $1.87 billion to $3.52 billion.

Financial Challenges in 1990s

Notwithstanding the high capital investments of the 1980s, Times Mirror's core newspaper segment, which continued to account for close to 60 percent of its overall corporate revenues, struggled. A nationwide advertising slump adversely affected all of United States media, beginning in the second half of the 1980s. Newspaper segment operating profits declined 61 percent the first nine months of 1990 compared to the same period a year earlier. In the same period, net income fell 40 percent to $134.9 million. Although it received a boost in circulation when workers at New York City's *Daily News* went on strike, Times Mirror's *New York Newsday* continued to lose money—a cumulative $150 million through 1995 by some analysts' estimates. The losses at *New York Newsday* helped hold the media company's profit margins under nine percent in the early 1990s. Perhaps more telling in a decade when some asserted that Wall Street had as much influence on public media companies as editors, Times Mirror's earnings per share declined over 15 percent, while the publishing industry gained an average of ten percent.

After the newspaper giant's revenues fell to a five-year low of $3.36 billion with a dismal profit margin of 5.2 percent in 1994, the company (prodded, many analysts said, by the Chandler family, which continued to control more than half its voting stock) brought in 54-year-old Mark Willes as CEO. As vice-chairman of General Mills Inc., Willes had earned a reputation as a staunch defender of the bottom line and the nickname "The Cereal Killer." The new leader wasted no time reinforcing that image; within just a few months, he had shuttered *New York Newsday* and the Baltimore *Evening Sun,* divested the company's cable venture, and announced job reductions of 1,000 for the rest of the company, with the axe falling hardest on the flagship *Los Angeles Times.* Some observers accused Willes of downsizing for the good of the stock, not the newspapers. But there was no arguing with the economic reality that newspaper circulation was on the decline while newsprint prices and other costs continued to rise.

Offsetting Willes' penchant for cost-cutting was a drive for growth. Noting that "You can never ultimately save your way to prosperity," Willes did invest in on-line services and electronic publishing. Indeed, Times Mirror's 1995 financial performance seemed to vindicate Willes approach. The company netted over $1.2 billion on $3.4 billion in revenues. Even after accounting for restructuring costs, the company earned its highest profit margin since 1989. Times Mirror stock shot from a ten-year nadir of $17 per share early in 1995 to almost $40 by spring 1996. Furthermore, the CEO has forecast year-over-year earnings per share increases of 50 percent, 40 percent, and 30 percent for 1996 through 1998.

Principal Subsidiaries

Baltimore Sun Co.; Hartford Courant Co.; Jeppesen & Co, GmbH; Jeppesen Sanderson, Inc.; Los Angeles Times; Matthew Bender & Company, Inc.; Morning Call, Inc.; Mosby-Year Book, Inc.; Harry N. Abrams, Inc.; Times Mirror Higher Education Group, Inc.; Times Mirror International Publishers US Inc.; Times Mirror Magazines, Inc.

Principal Operating Units

Newspaper Publishing; Professional Information; Consumer Media.

Further Reading

Case, Tony, "Still Strong: Despite Rising Newsprint Prices and Declining Circulation, Newspaper Companies Boosted Their Profitability in 1995," *Editor & Publisher,* January 6, 1996, pp. 15–24.

——, "Defending the 'Revolution'," *Editor & Publisher,* March 30, 1996, pp. 8–15.

Cohen, Adam, "Decline of the Times," *Time,* July 31, 1995.

Cohen, Roger, "New Aggressiveness at Times Mirror," *The New York Times,* December 3, 1990.

Grover, Ronald, "Times Mirror's Page-One Turnaround Story," *Business Week,* June 20, 1988.

Hart, Jack R., *The Information Empire: The Rise of the Los Angeles Times and Times Mirror Corporation,* 1981.

Hodges, Jane, and Keith Kelly, "Times Mirror's New-Media Coaster Ride," *Advertising Age,* January 29, 1996.

Kelly, Keith J., "Times Mirror Shifts Course," *Advertising Age,* June 5, 1995, p. 38.

Kimmelman, John, "The High Cost of Prestige," *Financial World,* February 28, 1995, pp. 36–37.

Lubove, Seth, "Chandler Versus Chandler," *Forbes,* November 20, 1995, pp. 43–45.

Olney, Warren, "Profits or Pulitzers?" *Los Angeles Magazine,* June 1996, pp. 34–38.

Reilly, Patrick, "Waiting for the Pay-Off," *Advertising Age,* May 24, 1989.

Thompson, Mark, "Times Mirror Tries to Deliver its Future," *MEDIAWEEK,* June 26, 1995, pp. 46–48.

"Top 100 Media Companies," *Advertising Age,* June 29, 1987.

"Willes Tops in Newspaper Pay," *Editor & Publisher,* April 20, 1996, p. 5.

—Diane C. Mermigas
—updated by April Dougal Gasbarre

Tops Appliance City, Inc.

45 Brunswick Avenue
Edison, New Jersey 08818
U.S.A.
(908) 248-2850
Fax: (908) 248-2719

Public Company
Incorporated: 1970
Employees: 1,900
Sales: $421.3 million (1995)
Stock Exchanges: NASDAQ
SICs: 5064 Electrical Appliances, Television & Radio
Sets; 5722 Household Appliance Stores; 5731 Radio,
Television & Consumer Electronics Stores

Starting with a tiny store in New Brunswick, New Jersey, Leslie S. Turchin developed Tops Appliance City, Inc. into one of the leading retailers of home appliances and consumer electronics in New York and New Jersey, with eight megastores. The company ranked seventh nationwide among consumer electronics chains in 1993, and the following year recorded the highest sales volume per square foot of any publicly held retailer in the United States. The company was unable to maintain such momentum, however, in the fiercely competitive greater New York City metropolitan market and faced some challenges in the mid-1990s.

Private Company, 1970–1991

Turchin started out in the electronics and appliance business at the age of nine, working part-time in his father's store in Linden, New Jersey, a gritty, industrial city south of Elizabeth and Newark. After high school he worked in the family business full-time, but had to leave, he told a reporter, "because my father wouldn't pay me a living wage. He only paid me $125 a week gross, while my rent was $145 a month." Turchin joined Sears, Roebuck and Co. at the age of 23 as an appliance salesman in 1965, and he then joined Kelvinator Inc. as a regional sales representative in 1969.

Armed with a $25,000 grubstake, Turchin, at the age of 27 or 28, went into business himself in 1970 by purchasing Tops TV & Appliance in downtown New Brunswick. This "closet-sized" 1,800-square-foot store, across the street from a closed Sears, was in an area later cleared for urban renewal. "When I started," Turchin related to an interviewer, "it was me, one full-time salesman, one part-time bookkeeper and a part-time driver, and we used to get a driver's helper—a stew bum off the street."

Turchin remained there until 1979, when he more or less traded some New Brunswick real estate for a shopping center in nearby Edison that included a closed W.T. Grant's. He recorded sales of $9 million in the first year and eventually was able to take over the entire Grant building, a 45,000-square-foot structure that, arguably, was the first superstore in the consumer electronics industry.

Tops Appliance City reached $158 million in sales in 1985. In 1987 it ranked 13th nationwide among major appliance retailers. A second New Jersey store opened in Secaucus in December 1986 and a third in East Hanover in April 1988. By the following year Tops, having made a name for itself by deep discounting of television sets and video hardware, also was catering to the high-end audio market and looking to cellular telephones and home office equipment like facsimile machines for further growth.

By the time the fourth Tops Appliance City opened in Lakewood in May 1990, the company was selling 100,000 color television sets, 104,000 air conditioners, 90,000 boom-box radios, and 75,000 washing machines per year. Revenues rose from $211.9 million in 1988 to $266.2 million in 1989 and $293.7 million in 1900. Net income of $1.8 million in 1988 rose to $4.1 million in 1989 but dipped to $2.3 million in 1990. In 1991, Tops Appliance City's last full year as a private company, revenues were $300.3 million and net income was a record $5.3 million.

Ingredients of Success

The components for Tops Appliance City's success included high-powered salesmanship, customer service, user-friendly

---

Company Perspectives:

Tops' business strategy is to be the dominant retailer of home appliances and consumer electronics in each of its markets by developing customer loyalty through a marketing program that emphasizes price, service, and selection.

---

store locations and environment, low costs, and bargain prices. Turchin urged his sales force not only to make the sale but to get the customer's repeat business. Tops vowed to undercut any rival's price, offering a $100 reward if it failed to do so, and gave its salespeople carte blanche to bargain with shoppers seeking further price concessions. To raise profit margins in the face of its low prices, management pressed the sales force to pitch lucrative extended warranty contracts. Presiding over his enterprise from a plain desk by the front window overlooking the sales floor of the flagship Edison store, Turchin cast an intimidating and frequently foul-mouthed presence—one he furthered by shaving his head and pumping iron.

Tops Appliance City's huge stores were airy, clean, bright, and logically laid out, with an emphasis on disciplined product presentation, attractive in-store displays, and efficient checkout procedures. It offered the full line of models from each of its vendors in all of its major product categories, but with greater inventory depth at the middle to higher price levels than most retailers. Merchandise was deployed by size, increasing in bulk from the front to the back. Eventually the company began placing all impulse products within reach of consumers on the retail floor. "People want to see the merchandise stacked up, pick up the one they like and walk out with it," Turchin told an interviewer. "That works great in certain product categories."

On the other hand, Turchin added, some products "require knowledgeable sales personnel to walk the customer through the various manufacturers' selections. If you have 300 different televisions on display, you do have to have knowledgeable people available to answer questions." Tops's sales people were trained to specialize in a certain product category, explain the options to prospective customers, and demonstrate them on the floor.

Tops Appliance City assigned 70 people to customer service to assure patrons of fast, hassle-free shopping. It offered free delivery and the removal of old appliances, cartons, and packaging. To keep its costs low, it typically placed its stores in existing buildings, and it used its high-volume trade to whittle suppliers' prices. To cut down pilferage, all workers, including executives, were checked by a security guard before leaving the warehouse.

Perhaps Tops's most distinctive feature was its belligerent advertising. In newspaper ads the company promised to "humiliate" its competitors. Noisy radio commercials in the same in-your-face vein ended with the signature phrase "Fuggedaboudit!" delivered in impeccable Brooklynese. Television commercials, which began with the opening of the Lakewood store, featured "Topsy"—a cartoon character, wearing a pro-

peller beanie, who resembled the company founder—performing antics such as loading a pile of rival retailers into a car and hurling it over a cliff with the epithet, "So long, LOSERS!"

Tops Appliance City struck below the belt at competitor Nobody Beats the Wiz! by placing its logo in the urinals of Tops's men's restrooms. When threatened with a lawsuit, the company halted this practice. In 1996, however, the Wiz charged Tops in federal court with falsely claiming that its prices were lower. Earlier, in 1993, New Jersey had collected $90,000 from Tops to settle its charge that the company had not made good on a number of the claims it had advertised. In 1994 Tops agreed to pay a $36,000 fine and change some advertising practices that the state of New York found to be deceptive, including, said the attorney general's office, "phony discounts and items for sale when there was only one of each item available in each store."

Going Public and Moving into New York

Goldome Strategic Investments Inc., a venture capital arm of Goldome Savings Bank of Buffalo, New York, which later became GSI Acquisition Co. L.P., took a 49 percent stake in Tops Appliance City when Tops became a limited partnership in 1988. To retire debt and raise capital for future expansion, Tops became a public company in August 1992, collecting about $24.4 million from the initial sale of its stock. Turchin retained about 37 percent of the shares and GSI kept more than 35 percent. GSI's holdings were turned over to Westinghouse Electric Corp. in 1993 as part payment for a GSI loan from Westinghouse Financial Services Inc.

Tops Appliance City opened its first New York store in October 1992. Located in Hawthorne, north of New York City in prosperous Westchester County, it featured the company's biggest home office department, including new Apple Macintosh Performa computers to which a specially trained sales force had been assigned. (Tops was one of the first consumer electronics retailers to make a major commitment to computers.) The store also featured a "home entertainment" room adjacent to the selling areas for audio and big-screen television. Also new for Tops, and exclusive to this location, was a 4,400-square-foot home fitness area offering treadmills and stationary bicycles and gyms.

Tops Appliance City entered the Long Island market by opening its sixth store in Westbury in September 1993. A store in New York City's borough of Queens was added a year later. (The company also opened its fifth New Jersey store, in Union, in late 1993.) The expansion of the Tops chain placed the company second to Nobody Beats the Wiz! in its field in the metropolitan area and enabled its revenues to rise from $344 million in 1992 to $411.4 million in 1993 and $461.6 million in 1994. Expansion entailed higher costs, however. Net income rose from $1.8 million in 1992 to $4.7 million in 1993 but dropped to a minuscule $217,000 in 1994. A share of company stock, $14 when the company went public in 1992, rose as high as $30 in 1993 but fell to a low of $5 in 1994.

Redirection in the Mid-1990s

Tops Appliance City appeared to have fallen into deep trouble in the mid-1990s. National firms like Best Buy, Circuit City, and Incredible Universe were poised to enter the volatile, low-margin New York market, which had seen high-profile retailers like Crazy Eddie and Newmark & Lewis fall by the wayside. After discounting store expansion, Tops Appliance City's revenues fell by 15 percent in 1994. With sales volume continuing to drop, Turchin turned over day-to-day operations in June 1995 to a newcomer, Robert Gross, who became chief executive officer. Turchin was said to have become more and more withdrawn since the death of one of his two sons in 1994.

In an open letter to Tops customers, posted on the store doors and also advertised in newspapers, Gross announced a 45-day lowest-price guarantee, the longest in the market. He promised that the products Tops advertised would be in stock, offering either a rain check or a product upgrade if they were not. All products would now bear a computer-printed fact tag and a fixed price. To cut costs, however, the company established a $30 delivery charge for major appliances.

Under Gross's management, Tops Appliance City's sales force abandoned its practice of diverting customers' attention from low-end advertised specials to higher-margin goods and its pressure to take out extended warranty contracts. Sales personnel began cutting shoppers some slack, allowing them to browse the floor unaided. Fixed, final prices, at a reduction of about ten percent, replaced the higher ones that customers had been expected to bargain down. This eliminated the haggling that women especially disliked, according to Gross, who said women seldom shopped at Tops even though they were making 50 to 60 percent of the buying decisions in consumer electronics. Another move to a kinder, gentler Tops was the elimination of the Topsy cartoon character after a study found that it alienated 80 percent of the women surveyed.

At the end of 1995 Tops's primary products were major appliances such as refrigerators, air conditioners, washers and dryers, vacuum cleaners, housewares, and home fitness equipment; and consumer electronics such as television sets, videocassette recorders, camcorders, personal computers, and home and car audio equipment. It offered a broad range of high-quality, nationally recognized brand names within each product category, displaying in excess of 5,000 products and maintaining more than 9,000 products in inventory. During 1995 major appliances accounted for 50 percent of sales, consumer electronics comprised 46 percent, and extended-service plans and miscellaneous income made up the remaining 4 percent. A commercial sales division, established in 1995, accounted for about 11 percent of revenue by selling to small and independent retailers, builders and landlords, corporate buying groups, clubs, and others.

Customers were able to pay for their purchases by cash, check, or credit card, which included Tops's own proprietary credit card. In 1995 25 percent of all sales were paid for with this card. Other credit cards accounted for 50 percent of sales, and other forms of payment were used for 25 percent of sales.

Tops's eight stores were located in heavily populated areas easily accessible from major highways and with adequate parking for high sales volume. They ranged in size between 45,000 and 120,000 square feet. Only the Queens building (and the adjacent land) were owned by the company; the others were leased. The Edison store and the company's 547,000-square-foot warehouse and distribution center at its headquarters, also located in Edison, were being leased from Turchin. Deliveries to customers' homes were being made using trucks owned by independent owner-operators.

Tops Appliance City ended 1995 with a nine percent fall in revenue to $421.3 million. When considering that the Queens store had been open all of the year but only part of 1994, the comparable store-by-store drop in sales was 20 percent. The company incurred a net loss of $1.9 million for the year, jeopardizing, and probably dooming, its plan to open a ninth store in Brooklyn in late 1996. The company's long-term debt at the end of 1995 was $80.6 million.

In June 1996 Tops laid off about 100 managers and corporate staff to reduce expenses. Gross assumed the job of chief financial officer in addition to his other duties. In a prepared statement the company said that the job reductions and "other programs already implemented" were expected to reduce selling, general, and administrative expenses to about $82 million in 1996 from $97 million in 1995.

Tops Appliance City's prospects were bleaker than ever at midyear 1996. Revenue of $150.6 million in the first half of the year was down about 25 percent from $203.5 million during the same period in 1995. The company lost $5.7 million during the first half of 1996.

Further Reading

Bryant, Adam, "Riding High on a Low-Cost Strategy," *New York Times,* January 31, 1993, Sec. 3, p. 8.

Halverson, Richard, "Tops Touts Subdued Attitude," *Discount Store News,* October 16, 1995, pp. 8, 108.

Hisey, Pete, "Crusty Tops Founder Declares War on the Competition," *Discount Store News,* May 17, 1993, pp. 3, 16.

Jaccoma, Richard, "Tops in New York," *DealerScope,* November 1992, pp. 14–16.

Nielsen, John, "The 20 Fastest Growing Private Companies," *Business for Central New Jersey,* September 4, 1989, p. 1+.

Olenick, Doug, and C. Thomas Veilleux, "New Head at Tops," *HFN,* June 5, 1995, p. 1+.

Olson, Thomas, "WEC Swaps for Stock," *Pittsburgh Business Times,* October 11, 1993, p. 1.

Pinkerton, Janet, "Wheelin' and Dealin'," *DealerScope,* July 1994, pp. 10–11.

Veilleux, C. Thomas, "Tops Loses VP, Plans Cutbacks," *HFN,* June 10, 1996, p. 67.

—Robert Halasz

TRACOR

Tracor Inc.

6500 Tracor Lane
Austin, Texas 78725
U.S.A.
(512) 926-2800
Fax: (512) 929-2241

Public Company
Incorporated: 1955 as Associated Consultants and
    Engineers, Inc.
Employees: 9,400
Sales: $886 million (1995)
Stock Exchanges: NASDAQ
SICs: 3812 Search & Navigational Equipment; 8711
    Engineering Services

Tracor Inc. is ranked among the top 15 defense electronics companies in the United States. The company sells its products, systems, and services primarily to the U.S. Department of Defense, although management has recently initiated a strategy to enter commercial markets in the fields of civil aviation, information systems, and commercial imagery systems. Almost untouched by the decline of the defense budget over the last five years, Tracor has created a niche for itself in the Department of Defense's operations and maintenance areas. An industry leader in many defense technology markets, Tracor provides such items as mission planning systems, intelligence information systems, automatic test systems, weapons and combat, and integration and support systems, weapons testing systems and support and electronic countermeasure systems to the different branches of the American Armed Forces. With its acquisition of Vitro Corporation and GDE Systems in 1994 and 1995, respectively, and AEL in 1996, almost overnight the company became the leader in providing engineering and support services for the U.S. Army's strategy plan for battlefield digitalization.

Early History

The roots of the company can be traced back to July 1955, when four ambitious, intelligent, and highly creative associates, who were teaching and conducting extensive research in the area of acoustical research at the University of Texas, decided to transform their late-night moonlighting at the laboratory into a full-time business venture. The four young men included physicists Jess Stanbrough, Chester McKinney, and Richard Lane, and mechanical engineer Frank McBee. The partners approached Harry Polland, an attorney in Austin, to look after the legal aspects of their new firm, named Associated Consultants and Engineers, Inc. The new company's first contract, an industrial noise abatement project for Eastern State Petroleum & Chemical Company, was worth a total of $5,000. During the next two years, the firm garnered numerous small contracts and began to make a reputation for itself as a reliable and creative enterprise.

In 1957, after much discussion among the founding members of the firm, it was decided to change the name to Texas Research Associates, Inc. While the name change was intended to reflect the company's growing concentration on research and development in a wide variety of fields, the partners maintained their focus on acoustical research and sonar technology. That same year, the company received a grant of approximately $200,000 from the Union Carbide Corporation to design, develop, and manufacture a new liquid transistor. With this grant, the founders realized that their new enterprise was going to be a successful business venture. They immediately began to form a skeleton organization to take care of the financial and administrative aspects of the firm's growth. The company purchased its first computer and constructed a facility to house administrative offices and research laboratories. New and bigger contracts with the U.S. Navy began to arrive, mostly involving additional research in sonar technology. One of the new contracts involved a long-term program for the firm to evaluate the U.S. Navy's sonar capabilities and, based on the information gathered, to implement a plan for the design and development of sonar equipment and its use.

During the late 1950s and early 1960s, another firm based in Austin, Texas, was making a name for itself in the burgeoning field of defense electronics. Formed by four men, including physicist O. J. Baltzer, mechanical engineer Marcel Gres, mathematician Gene Smith, and accountant George Strandtmann,

Company Perspectives:

At Tracor, we believe mutual dedication to excellence in performing every task we undertake, large or small, is the key to our future. We accomplish excellence by carrying out our responsibilities to: achieve profitable growth consistent with the best in our industry; provide high-quality, innovative technological products, systems, and services which give the best value to our customers; ensure the highest standards of integrity in all activities; create a safe, pleasant, and motivating work environment providing both job fulfillment and career growth opportunities for employees; and support the communities in which we have operations to develop a better environment for all citizens to enjoy. Growth at Tracor is through excellence.

Textran Corporation was growing in much the same way as Texas Research Associates. Contracts from the U.S. Armed Forces, especially the Navy, had made Textran Corporation one of the most rapidly growing defense firms in the country. Knowing one another's reputations, and acquainted with the technological developments in both firms, the eight men met and decided that it was in everyone's best interest to merge the two companies and share both financial resources and scientific talent. In 1962 Texas Research Associates, Inc., merged with Textran Corporation to form Tracor, Inc.

Immediately after the merger, the new company embarked on an aggressive strategy of acquisition. The firm's first acquisition, Rudmose Associates, Inc., a well-known and financially successful manufacturer of audiometers, was incorporated into Tracor quickly and efficiently. The company's entire product line, and its president, renowned physicist Wayne Rudmose, were brought to Austin. New manufacturing operations were established at 6500 Tracor Lane, just east of downtown Austin. Wayne Rudmose was asked to become more involved in the company's research and development activities, and Tracor, Inc., was soon winning larger and larger contracts from the U.S. Department of Defense.

Growth through Acquisition, 1960s and 1970s

By the early 1960s, Tracor had grown larger and more rapidly than any of its founders had expected. Having reached a level of financial security the directors of the company were comfortable with, Tracor made its first public stock offering in 1964. Primarily implemented to fund the purchase of Sulzer Laboratories, a Rockville, Maryland-based defense industry contractor specializing in crystal frequency standards, the public offering was an enormous success. The day Tracor began trading on the OTC exchange, approximately 110,000 shares were sold at an opening price of $19.50.

With such impressive successes, Tracor continued its growth through acquisition strategy for the remainder of the decade. Tracor purchased companies across the United States in order to build a broader and firmer manufacturing base within the defense electronics industry. Firms specializing in the de-

sign and manufacture of analytical instruments and electronic components were single-mindedly pursued by Tracor management. Many of the companies purchased during this time were leading manufacturers in electronic components for the automobile, electronics, and home appliances markets.

During the 1970s, the company's growth through acquisition program continued without interruption. At the same time, Tracor was introducing innovative products to the defense electronics industry, including graphic display software for electronic defense systems and a noise monitoring system for the U.S. Navy. When some of the acquisitions made during the 1960s began to falter, Tracor management sold them immediately and concentrated the company's resources on strengthening its traditional product lines in defense electronics. By the mid-1970s, Tracor had increased its market share in numerous domestic markets and, with ever-increasing sales, began a strategic plan to enter foreign markets and cultivate overseas customers. By the end of fiscal 1975, the company reported that it had surpassed the $100 million milestone in sales for that year.

Transition and Reorganization during the 1980s

By the beginning of the 1980s, Tracor had developed an international reputation in the defense electronics industry, with customers in Europe and the Middle East. The election of Ronald Reagan as president of the United States, and the subsequent U.S. military build-up under his direction, also helped to strengthen Tracor. Throughout the early and mid-1980s, Tracor's future prospects seemed assured.

In a development that the management of Tracor could not avoid, however, the company was suddenly purchased by Westmark Systems, Inc., in 1987 for just under $900 million in a leveraged buyout that included junk bonds and significant bank debt. Westmark was created by a group of bondholders to acquire and build a consortium of high-quality defense companies. Retired U.S. Navy admiral Bobby R. Inman was hired to manage the entire operation; although he had no experience in the corporate arena, Inman was highly regarded because of his previous tenure as deputy director of the Central Intelligence Agency.

From the beginning, Inman had trouble on his hands. Manufacturing difficulties and cost overruns began to cut into Tracor's profit margins, especially in the area of electronic components. Quality control and new product delays also began to plague the company, with overall sales declining precipitously in 1988 and 1989. Inman was unable to meet the large debt created by the buyout, and he could not foresee the beginning of the end of the Cold War and the decrease in defense spending by the U.S. government that would follow.

In 1990 the bondholders at Westmark, thoroughly dissatisfied with Inman's performance, replaced him with James E. Skaggs. Skaggs had worked for 37 years in the aerospace industry, with extensive experience in computer-based electronic systems at major corporations such as AlliedSignal, AMEX Systems, NASA, and System Development Corporation. Given a free hand by the bondholders, Skaggs brought in his own management team, sold off or closed the company's unprofitable product lines, streamlined and consolidated operations, implemented strict quality control measures, and reduced the company's operating costs. Under his direction, as the company began to stabilize, a petition was filed for a reorganization under Chapter 11 of the Bankruptcy Code.

By December 1991, less than two years after Skaggs had replaced Inman, the reorganization was complete. Westmark had disappeared, and two companies had been formed from the bankruptcy reorganization: Tracor and Littlefuse. Tracor comprised the defense systems manufacturing capability of the former company while Littlefuse concentrated on electronic components. In January 1992, the bondholders became shareholders of Tracor when shares began trading on the NASDAQ exchange. Although the price per share ranged from $2.00 to $4.00 during the first year of its new life, Tracor was obviously a much healthier company. By the beginning of 1993, the company's stock had more than doubled in value to $9.00 per share.

Revitalization and Growth during the 1990s

In 1993 Tracor made two major acquisitions, GDE Systems, Inc., and Vitro Corporation. GDE Systems was a worldwide market leader in the application of advanced digital technology in the design, development, and manufacture of highly sophisticated electronic defense systems such as soft copy mapping, charting, and geodesy systems, automated mission planning systems, test program sets, integrated maintenance, and diagnostic systems. Vitro Corporation had developed a reputation within the defense industry for its systems engineering and integration support to the U.S. Navy. After both GDE Systems and Vitro were fully integrated into Tracor, the company's annual sales increased by 28 percent from 1994 to 1995, from $694 million to $886.9 million.

In 1995 almost 90 percent of the company's sales were to various agencies of the U.S. government, most notably the Department of Defense and the Armed Services. The company played a key role in developing defense systems for the U.S Navy, engineering and manufacturing almost all the technology for the Polaris, Poseidon, and Trident missile systems. Since the beginning of World War II, the company has provided engineering services for every guided missile system used on Navy ships. Recently, Tracor has designed and installed the control system for the launching of ship-based Tomahawk cruise mis-

siles. In addition, the company designs, develops, manufactures, installs, and maintains the advanced radio communications systems for all of the U.S. Navy's AEGIS class of cruisers and destroyers, which is projected to form the backbone of the Navy's fighting fleet during the first part of the 21st century.

In addition, the company provides avionics maintenance for the U.S. Air Force and 16 foreign air forces, including electronic systems aboard the F-16 fighter jet, the C-17 transport, and the B-2 bomber. In May 1996 Tracor won a major contract from the U.S Department of Defense to design and manufacture the Explosive Standoff Minefield Breacher system for the both the Army and Marines. The new system is designed to detonate and neutralize large minefields to clear the way for the safe passage of armored personnel carriers and infantry.

Largely insulated from reductions in the defense budget due to its focus on the operation and maintenance of electronic defense systems, Tracor intends to take advantage of growing government expenditures on maintaining the combat-readiness of the U.S. Armed Forces. Through a strategic policy of acquisition and consolidation, Tracor is positioning itself to continue playing a major role in the electronic systems market of the defense industry.

Principal Subsidiaries

Tracor Aerospace, Inc.; Tracor Applied Sciences, Inc.; Tracor Flight Systems, Inc.; Vitro Corporation; GDE Systems, Inc.

Further Reading

Dornheim, Michael, A., "Litton Teams to Market Integrated EW Systems," *Aviation Week & Space Technology,* July 5, 1993, pp. 64–65.

Kelly, Kevin, "The Education of Bobby Inman," *Business Week,* December 18, 1989, p. 50.

"Purchase of AEL Planned for about $115 Million," *Wall Street Journal,* October 3, 1995, p. B4(E).

"Vitro Wins Naval Contract for Systems Engineering," *Wall Street Journal,* January 22, 1996, p. B4(E).

"Westmark to Sell Assets for $120 Million in Stock," *Wall Street Journal,* March 13, 1996, p. B4(E).

—Thomas Derdak

Travel Ports of America, Inc.

3495 Winton Place
Rochester, New York 14623
U.S.A.
(716) 272-1810
Fax: (716) 272-9952

Public Company
Incorporated: 1979 as Roadway Motor Plazas, Inc.
Employees: 1,204
Sales: $165.2 million (1996)
Stock Exchanges: NASDAQ
SICs: 5411 Grocery Stores; 5541 Gasoline Service
Stations; 5812 Eating Places; 7011 Hotels & Motels;
7538 General Automotive Repair Shops

Travel Ports of America, Inc., operates around-the-clock, full-service travel plazas that provide customers with motor fuel, automotive supplies and repairs, groceries, food service, and motel rooms. These plazas serve both truck drivers and the general public. In 1996 Travel Ports operated 15 full-service travel plazas, a mini-travel plaza, and a fuel terminal in New York, New Jersey, New Hampshire, Pennsylvania, Indiana, and North Carolina. The company was planning to open one or two more each year.

Travel Ports was among a half-dozen or so large chains that were increasingly dominating the "travel plaza" or "travel center" industry. These facilities, some of them with 40,000 square feet of floor space or more, were well lighted on the outside and tastefully landscaped to provide a secure environment and reassuring image. They offered not only the basic one-stop services that truckers had always sought—gas, meals, beds, and automotive supplies—but also shops selling souvenirs and consumer electronics, automatic teller machines, and even chapels. They had, in effect, become small cities.

Roadway Motor Plazas, 1987–91

Incorporated in 1979 as Roadway Motor Plazas, Inc., the company made its first public offering of common stock in 1986 and was subsequently listed on the NASDAQ exchange. E. Philip Saunders was its chairman, CEO, and principal stockholder, and John M. Holahan was its president and chief operating officer. Among the suppliers of petroleum products to the company was W. W. Griffith Oil Co., Inc., owned and operated by Saunders. A fuel-purchase agreement with Griffith Oil extended to January 1996. Griffith Oil later came to be owned by Sugar Creek Corp., also owned and operated by Saunders. In early 1996 Sugar Creek was running a chain of 105 Sugar Creek convenience stores and self-service gas stations in western New York.

By the end of 1987 Roadway was operating 13 24-hour, full-service motor plazas and four mini plazas, one family restaurant, one fuel terminal, and one truck-operating subsidiary in New York, New Jersey, North Carolina, South Carolina, and Pennsylvania. Roadway and other chains were cleaning up the once-seedy truck-stop image, inviting in the general public.

Roadway Motor Plazas had net sales of $45.9 million in fiscal 1986 (ending April 30, 1986) and net income of $642,000. In fiscal 1987 net sales advanced to $64.2 million and net income to $913,000. In fiscal 1988 net sales rose again to $116.7 million, and net income to $1.2 million, which remained a company record until fiscal 1994. The sale of diesel fuel accounted for 45 percent and 62 percent of net sales in fiscal 1987 and 1988, respectively. The company's long-term debt was $20.9 million at the end of fiscal 1988.

At the close of 1986, Roadway Motor Plazas acquired travel plazas from Smoky Mountain Truckstop, Inc., of Asheville, North Carolina, for $3,346,444 and LaBar Enterprises, Inc., of Berwick, Pennsylvania, for $12,990,233. The Smoky Mountain facility, on a 19-acre site at Exit 37 from Interstate Route 40, included a 136-seat restaurant and a general store as well as fuel pumps and a truck-service area.

LaBar Enterprises, owned by James C. LaBar of Bloomsburg, Pennsylvania, had sales of about $86 million in 1986. It consisted of ten truckstop facilities, a fuel terminal, a family restaurant, and four other related businesses, including a truck-leasing subsidiary and a Navistar truck dealership in New Jersey, Pennsylvania, and South Carolina. Most of the assets of the truck-leasing unit were sold in 1987 to Hertz Penske Truck

Leasing Inc. for $15.6 million. Also in 1987, Roadway sold 23 gas stations acquired as part of the LaBar deal to United Petroleum Facilities, Inc., for $2.6 million and Allied Petroleum Marketers, Inc., a related Delaware business, to Stanley W. Mann for $225,000.

In June 1987 Roadway opened its 19th motor plaza, a leased truckstop located in Hamburg, New York. In November 1987, however, Roadway terminated the lease agreement and ceased doing business at the location because the lessor was unable to perform certain obligations, which resulted in revenues that were less than what had been projected.

Roadway acquired Pecan Shoppe of Harbor Creek, Inc., a business located on Interstate 90 outside Erie, Pennsylvania, in 1987 for $263,000. This facility was acquired with the intention of building a major new travel plaza on the property. In October 1989 Roadway acquired about 72 acres of land adjacent to this property. Construction of the travel plaza, which opened in August 1995, was to be financed through a combination of cash generated from operations and bank financing.

In 1988 Roadway subleased the New Cumberland, Pennsylvania, mini-plaza it had acquired from LaBar to Capital Petroleum Inc. and vacated its Big Earl mini-plaza in Bloomsburg, Pennsylvania, which it had sold to a real-estate developer for a $670,000 profit. Also in 1988, Roadway entered into an agreement to purchase 23 acres for $575,000 from Dahlstrom and Grove Associates, Inc., in order to build a major new facility on Interstate 81 in Greencastle, Pennsylvania. This travel center, the first constructed by Roadway, opened in December 1989.

Roadway sold various vehicle assets of P. L. Lawton, Inc., a company acquired in December 1986, to K. J. Transportation Inc. in April 1988 for $3 million. In November 1988 Roadway vacated its leased facilities in Rochester, selling its equipment, furniture, and inventories, transferring them to other locations, or returning them to vendors for reimbursement of original cost.

During fiscal 1989 Roadway phased out its truck sales division, selling its inventory of new and used trucks or returning them to Navistar. This subsidiary continued to operate Roadway's truck service and repair business out of its shop in Bloomsburg. Roadway also sold its Belles Spring Restaurant in Mill Hall, Pennsylvania, which historically had been unprofitable.

In early 1989 Roadway acquired L & G Truckers City, Inc., for $4,252,741 in mortgages, thereby gaining its first facility in Indiana, a 36-acre full-service travel center in Porter. At the same time the company leased a 24-acre motor plaza at Lake Station, Indiana.

In June 1991 Roadway signed a franchise agreement with Choice Hotels International that identified its location in Greencastle, Pennsylvania, as a Friendship Inn and utilized the Choice Hotels national registration system. Under this agreement Roadway was required to remit monthly a royalty fee of two percent and a marketing fee of two percent of gross room revenue. Also in 1991, the company closed its Hickory Run truck stop at White Haven, Pennsylvania.

Roadway's revenues rose from $109.6 million in fiscal 1989 to $125.5 million in 1990 and a record $144.9 million in 1991. In 1989 the company had net income of $903,000. The following year it lost $587,000, but in 1991 it returned to profitability, earning $136,000 in net income.

Travel Ports of America, 1992–95

Roadway was renamed Travel Ports of America in late 1991. The company sold its facility at Loganton, Pennsylvania, in August 1992 for net book value, receiving a mortgage on the property for a portion of the purchase price. In October 1993 it sold its Allentown, Pennsylvania, facility for a sum in excess of net book value and again received a mortgage on the property for a portion of the purchase price.

Travel Ports acquired certain assets of the Exit Three Truck Stop in Greenland, New Hampshire, in April 1994 for an undisclosed amount of cash. It later signed a new 20-year lease on the property, with two five-year extensions, and it also had purchase options throughout the term of the lease. In mid-1994 it took out a $2.5-million loan to cover the acquisition and certain improvements to the facility.

Travel Ports sold its facility at Fairplay, South Carolina, in June 1995 for net book value and received a mortgage on the property for a portion of the purchase price. In 1996 it leased an existing motor plaza in Baltimore.

Revenue figures for fiscal years 1992, 1993, and 1994 were remarkably alike, with net sales and operating revenues ranging between $137.6 million and $137.9 million. Net income was $554,000 in 1992, $783,000 in 1993, and $1,358,000 in 1994.

Net sales rose to $153.3 million in fiscal 1995, and net income to $1.9 million. Net sales rose to $165.2 million in fiscal 1996, but net income dropped to $1.7 million, a circumstance that management blamed on severe winter weather. The long-term debt was $19.8 million at the end of fiscal 1995.

Travel Ports in the Mid-1990s

The principal products sold at Travel Ports in the mid 1990s were diesel fuel, gasoline, and motor oil and other lubricants. Services and repairs were provided for trucks only. Truck washers, truck scales, and paved parking areas large enough to accommodate a number of oversized vehicles were also available at some or all of the company's facilities. Repair facilities were not available at Belmont, New York, or Lake Station, Indiana. Tires and commonly needed parts were in stock at most locations.

Each Travel Ports facility, with the exception of the one at Mahwah, New Jersey, included a 24-hour, family-style restaurant where customers were served a variety of ''home-cooked'' meals. The company operated most of its restaurants under the name ''Buckhorn Family Restaurants.'' Food products were purchased from unaffiliated sources, with meals prepared and cooked in on-site kitchens.

Motel accommodations were available to both truck drivers and the general public. Rooms generally contained double beds, basic furniture, a color television set, and a full bathroom. Rates ranged from $25 to $30 a night. Public laundry facilities were also available. The Maybrook and Dansville, New York, motels operated under a franchise from Days Inn, and the Greencastle, Pennsylvania, motel under a franchise from the Friendship Inn division of Choice Hotels International.

Travel Ports was operating both travel and convenience stores. Travel stores carried a wide array of products often purchased by truck drivers, including health and beauty aids, snacks, tobacco products, western-style clothing and footwear, electronic products, and gift items. Convenience stores, generally located near the gasoline pump islands and used more by the general traveling public, offered bread, milk, beverages, snacks, and other items. An ATM machine was available at all these locations.

Diesel fuel accounted for 64 percent of Travel Ports' revenues in fiscal 1994 but only 30 percent of gross profit. Restaurants accounted for 11 percent of revenues and 30 percent of gross profit. Stores accounted for eight and 11 percent, respectively; shops for six and 13 percent; gasoline for seven and three percent; and motels for one and three percent.

Of Travel Ports' travel plazas in fiscal 1995, the ones in Binghamton and Fultonville, New York; Greencastle, Blooms-burg, Harborcreek, and Milesburg, Pennsylvania; Paulsboro, New Jersey; Candler, North Carolina; and Porter, Indiana, were owned. The ones in Dansville and Maybrook, New York; Mahwah, New Jersey; Lake Station, Indiana; Greenland, New Hampshire; and Baltimore were leased. The company owned its mini-plaza in Belmont, New York, and its fuel storage facility in Berwick, Pennsylvania. It was leasing its headquarters in Rochester, New York.

In 1995 E. Philip Saunders was still chairman and chief executive officer, and John M. Holahan was president and chief operating officer. At the end of January 1996 Saunders held about 31 percent of the company's common stock and Holahan about nine percent. Institutions held about 16 percent.

Further Reading

"Roadway Motor Plazas Buys LaBar Enterprises," *Wall Street Journal,* January 6, 1987, p. 22.
"Roadway Motor Truck Assets," *Wall Street Journal,* July 23, 1987, p. 51.
Travel Ports of America, Inc. Annual Reports, Rochester, N.Y.: Travel Ports of America, Inc., 1995, 1996.

—Robert Halasz

U.S. TRUST

U.S. Trust Corp.

114 West 47th Street
New York, New York 10036
U.S.A.
(212) 852-1000
Fax: (212) 852-1140

Public Company
Incorporated: 1853 as the United States Trust Co. of
New York
Employees: 2,558
Total Assets: $476.8 million (1995)
Stock Exchanges: NASDAQ
SICs: 6022 State Commercial Banks; 6091 Nondeposit
Trust Facilities; 6712 Bank Holding Companies

U.S. Trust Corp., the nation's oldest trust company, is a bank holding company that, through subsidiaries, provides financial services to individuals and institutions in four principal business segments: asset management, private banking, special fiduciary, and corporate trust. U.S. Trust considers itself to be a specialty market financial services company rather than a traditional bank. Its principal line of business is investment management, fiduciary and private banking services to affluent individuals and families. In 1995 it had $47.4 billion in assets under its management and $203.8 billion in assets under its administration.

Servant to the 19th Century's Superrich

In 1853 a group of influential business leaders raised $1 million to create the United States Trust Co. of New York, the nation's first trust company. The creation of a financial company that would act as executor and trustee for the funds of individuals and institutions was an innovative idea, for such trust functions, to the extent that they existed at all, were being performed by individuals, not institutions. Following passage of a bill by the state legislature chartering U.S. Trust, the company's founders selected a board of trustees that included 30 prominent New York industrialists, merchants, bankers, and

civic leaders. Joseph Lawrence was elected president and John Aikman Stewart was named secretary. U.S. Trust began, in its first year, an unbroken tradition of paying an annual dividend.

U.S. Trust's founders included many of the wealthiest men of their day. Among them were the renowned inventor, industrialist, and philanthropist Peter Cooper; Marshall Field, founder of the famed department store; and Erastus Corning, a leading railroad developer and a manufacturer of iron and steel. The company's first office was established at 40 Wall Street; it moved across the street to 48 Wall Street four years later.

In spite of the star-studded cast of tycoons among its founders, U.S. Trust did not thrive as a trust company during its early years. Most Americans of means held their assets in local real estate or business ventures rather than in cash. There was little opportunity to invest in stocks because few businesses were publicly held. U.S. Trust protected itself against failure by also engaging in more typical banking and investing activities, making commercial and personal loans, purchasing mortgages, and engaging in other investments. By 1886 it led all New York City institutions in deposits, with $30 million.

Emerging capital markets made it possible for U.S. Trust to float large bond issues to finance major construction projects and industrial growth. Beginning with the New York Central Rail Road in 1855, the company's corporate clients issued securities financing such monumental ventures as the construction of many of the nation's railroads and the building of the Panama Canal. U.S. Trust served as corporate trustee for these transactions, handling the administration, processing, and recordkeeping for the securities involved.

In 1887, U.S. Trust acquired two small buildings at 45 and 47 Wall Street, which were razed for a new nine-story building headquarters at 45 Wall Street, opened in 1889. This address was to remain U.S. Trust's home for the next 100 years. The same conservatism and stability was reflected in the company's management. After 11 years as secretary, Stewart left U.S. Trust at President Lincoln's urgent request to become assistant treasurer of the United States. He returned to the company after the Civil War, serving 37 years as president and another 24 years as chairman of the board before retiring at the age of 102.

496

Surviving Panics and Depressions

U.S. Trust was a rock of strength as financial panics gripped Wall Street in 1857, 1873, 1884, 1893, and 1907. By the turn of the century the creation of large and widely scattered enterprises meant that wealthy investors and businessmen were no longer able to manage their own assets unaided and had come to rely on financial professionals to provide expert advice on managing their investments. Among U.S. Trust's accounts during the 1880s and 1890s were those of William Waldorf Astor, Jay Gould, and Oliver Harriman. The need for professional financial management became even greater with the ratification of the 16th Amendment to the U.S. Constitution in 1913, establishing the federal income tax.

By the time U.S. Trust celebrated its seventy-fifth anniversary in 1928, its trusteed assets totaled more than $1 billion, far exceeding those of any other trust institution. The company's emphasis on stability served it well during the stock market crash of 1929 and the depression that followed. As controlling stockholder of certain troubled firms, it at times found itself running an insurance company, a machinery maker, a food processor, a molasses company, and a coal mining company. To settle the estate of one customer, it merged three small cement companies it controlled into the General Portland Cement Co. U.S. Trust also provided more personalized service, such as advising clients on schools and careers for their children. It began, for the first time, to advertise in 1958, placing ads in newspaper society pages, *The New Yorker,* and the programs of the Metropolitan Opera and the New York Philharmonic Society.

By 1962 U.S. Trust held more than $6 billion of assets in its vaults. Its personal trust funds and investment portfolios totaled 8,000, plus endowment funds for such universities and colleges as Princeton, Amherst, Middlebury, Williams, Wellesley, and New York University. It also advised on the management of state pension funds worth another $3 billion. The company earned a record $3.7 million in 1962, of which 60 to 75 percent came from management fees and the remainder from interest on loans and its own investments. In 1959 it marked a new era of prosperity by moving into a new 27-story headquarters building erected on its 45 Wall Street site. Six armored trucks carried $60 billion in cash, securities, bonds, and jewelry into the building.

U.S. Trust was managing more than $8 billion in assets by 1965, of which $2.5 billion was in personal trusts, $2.2 billion in investment management accounts, $1.5 billion in institutional- and pension-fund money, and $1.8 billion in custodian accounts (in which it acted mainly as a bookkeeper). It also held several billion dollars in advisory accounts, to which the company gave investment advice but did not hold the assets in its vaults. It had operating income of $20 million in 1964 and net income of $4.25 million, both records. Eighty-five percent of its gross income came directly or indirectly from trust and investment operations and estate handling. Banking operations, however, were more profitable, and one way the company was drumming up business in this field was to sell investment services to institutions such as other banks and insurance companies, because these services traditionally drew in deposits. By 1977 banking was supplying half of the company's earnings. In a reorganization, U.S. Trust Co. became a subsidiary of a new parent holding company, U.S. Trust Corp., in 1978.

Travails of the 1970s

The 1970s was not a good decade for stocks, but U.S. Trust's performance was particularly poor. Whereas the company's gross income doubled between 1969 and 1976, to $86.2 million, its net income hardly budged. In 1976 three big New York City employee pension funds left U.S. Trust because of what was termed "inadequate performance." To expand its business, the bank opened offices in Beverly Hills and Palm Beach and also, to tap the Eurodollar lending market, on Grand Cayman Island. But U.S. Trust suffered another embarrassing setback in 1979, when 41 municipal bond certificates worth $397 million vanished from its vault. A big New York City pension fund, which owned the certificates, did not learn of the loss until months later and, although the bonds were nonnegotiable and no loss was suffered, the fund promptly fired the bank as custodian of more than $8 billion in bonds.

As an economy measure, U.S. Trust pulled out of international lending by closing its London and Geneva branches in 1979. To cut costs even further, U.S. Trust cracked down on its own customers in 1980. The "poor relations" (those with assets below $2 million) lost certain services, such as having a bank officer drive to Connecticut to walk the poodle or relying on the company to write and mail checks to the gas and electric companies. On the other hand, U.S. Trust opened an office in a four-story midtown townhouse for clients who did not want to come down to Wall Street to cash a check. Daniel P. Davison, the bank's new president, made it clear that his goal was to obtain the commercial banking business of its trust customers, especially the 150 families with net worth of $10 million or more.

Restructuring in the 1980s

In 1981 U.S. Trust moved its computer operations center to the East Village to modernize its computer systems and to serve an increasing number of clients. The building also housed the bank's growing securities processing businesses. In 1984 U.S. Trust formed a new subsidiary, Financial Technologies International, to market and license computer software products and services to financial institutions.

Continuing its restructuring, U.S. Trust announced in 1987 that it would no longer make basic business and real estate loans and would seek buyers for virtually all of its commercial, industrial, and real estate portfolios, valued at about $275 million. Since the bank had steadily disengaged itself from large corporate lending as well, this action restricted its corporate banking activities to serving securities industry and financial institution clients, both noncredit businesses. In 1986 U.S. Trust ranked twentieth among trust companies in assets under management, $14.3 billion, and tenth in trust income, $130.5 million. Trust income accounted for 42.4 percent of the company's total operating income that year.

Acquisitions and Divestitures of the 1990s

U.S. Trust moved its headquarters from Wall Street in 1989 to a brand new building in midtown, on West 47th Street. It maintained its downtown presence, however, with a new private banking office at 111 Broadway. The bank was also expanding elsewhere, opening new offices for its Florida subsidiary in

Naples and Boca Raton in 1992 and 1994, respectively, and for its California subsidiary (founded in 1986 with the acquisition of Summit Management Co., Inc.) in Costa Mesa in 1993. A Dallas-based investment firm, Denker & Goodwin, was acquired in 1989 to form the basis of a full-service Texas trust subsidiary with banking powers. Delafield, Harvey, Tabrell, Inc., an investment advisory firm, was acquired in 1992 and became the company's New Jersey subsidiary. U.S. Trust of Connecticut, headquartered in Stamford, opened in 1993 and added offices in Greenwich and Hartford in 1996. The 1993 purchase of Capital Trust Corp. paved the way for the creation of U.S. Trust Co. of the Pacific Northwest, with offices in Portland, Oregon.

U.S. Trust acquired Campbell, Cowperthwait & Co., a Manhattan-based investment advisory firm specializing in high-quality growth stocks, in 1992. Three years later it acquired the individual account business of J. & W. Seligman and Co. and purchased J. & W. Seligman Trust Co. In early 1996 U.S. Trust opened a new office in Garden City, Long Island. In 1995 Chase Manhattan Corp. purchased U.S. Trust's institutional custody, mutual funds servicing, and unit trust businesses for $368.5 million worth of Chase common stock. Chase also agreed to purchase U.S. Trust Corp. of New York, the parent company's security processing and related back-office business. This sale of about one-third of U.S. Trust's business allowed the company to focus on its core businesses: asset management, private banking, and fiduciary.

Because of its venerable history U.S. Trust was long regarded as standoffish if not downright snobbish, but in 1987 it reduced its account minimum from between $1 million and $2 million to $250,000 in liquid assets for individually managed new clients. By 1994 the company had more than 30 salespeople, compared with only one in 1980. It offered 25 mutual funds, with a minimum of only $1,000 to open such an account. Those with truly deep pockets could count on the personal service for which U.S. Trust had always been noted, such as a home mortgage in 24 hours.

In 1995 fiduciary and other fees provided 59 percent of U.S. Trust's total income. Interest on loans accounted for 23 percent; interest on investment securities, ten percent; interest on short-term investments, six percent; and other income, two percent.

Of loans of $1.46 billion that year, private banking accounted for 95 percent, of which two-thirds was for residential real estate. Loans to financial institutions accounted for four percent. Deposits averaged $2.68 billion during the year, of which 56 percent was interest bearing. The company's long-term debt was $26.5 million in March 1996.

Principal Subsidiaries

Campbell, Cowperthwait & Co., Inc.; CTC Consulting Inc.; Mutual Funds Service Co.; UST Fiduciary Services, Ltd.; UST Securities Corp.; U.S. Trust Co. of California, N.A.; U.S. Trust Co. of Connecticut; U.S. Trust Co. of Florida Savings Bank; U.S. Trust Co. International Corp.; U.S. Trust Co. of New Jersey; U.S. Trust Co. of New York (Grand Cayman), Ltd.; U.S. Trust Company of the Pacific Northwest; U.S. Trust Co. of Texas, N.A.; U.S. Trust Financial Services, Inc.

Principal Operating Units

Investments; Personal Investment; Fixed Income Investments.

Further Reading

"Banker to the Rich," *Forbes,* April 1, 1963, p. 40.

Bennett, Robert A., "Brahman's Banker," *New York Times,* January 20, 1980, Sec. 3, p. 9.

"Chasing the Coupon Clippers," *Forbes,* March 1, 1977, pp. 56–57.

"Compound Trouble for U.S. Trust," *Business Week,* January 28, 1980, p. 42.

Crowley, Lyle, "Inside the Private World of Private Bankers," *Bankers Monthly,* November 1990, pp. 27–28.

Hertzberg, Daniel, "Tranquil Aura at U.S. Trust Obscures Vexing Problems for Old-Line Banker," *Wall Street Journal,* October 26, 1979, p. 18.

"Making Risk-Taking Pay at U.S. Trust," *Business Week,* March 20, 1965, pp. 138–140, 144, 146.

Schifrin, Matthew, "Affirmative Action," *Forbes,* January 3, 1994, pp. 58, 62.

Sudo, Philip T., "U.S. Trust Co. To Sell Portfolio of Business, Real Estate Loans," *American Banker,* July 14, 1987, pp. 1, 30.

U.S. Trust: A History of Growth with a Commitment to Personal Service, New York: U.S. Trust Corp., 1996.

"U.S. Trust Centennial," *Newsweek,* April 20, 1953, pp. 80–81.

—Robert Halasz

Uni-Marts, Inc.

466 East Beaver Avenue
State College, Pennsylvania 16801-5690
U.S.A.
(814) 234-6000
Fax: (814) 234-8712

Public Company
Incorporated: 1981
Employees: 2,700
Sales: $327.01 million (1995)
Stock Exchanges: American
SICs: 5411 Grocery Stores; 5541 Gasoline Service
Stations; 5172 Petroleum Products, Not Elsewhere
Classified

Uni-Marts, Inc., is the ninth-largest convenience store chain in the United States in sales and among the top 100 U.S. companies in the larger grocery store industry. In 1996 Uni-Marts operated 407 stores in the mid-Atlantic states of Pennsylvania, New York, New Jersey, Maryland, Delaware, Virginia, West Virginia, and Ohio, with three-quarters of its stores located in its home state of Pennsylvania. In addition to the roughly 3,500 products for sale in the typical Uni-Mart store—ranging from dairy products and dry grocery goods to magazines, candy, beverages, and cigarettes—about three-quarters of Uni-Marts's stores offered self-serve gasoline pumps. In 1995 Uni-Mart sales were divided between general "c-store" merchandise (55 percent) and gasoline sales (44 percent). Through an aggressive growth strategy that blended new store construction and block acquisitions from such chains as Li'l General, Open Pantry, Shop-N-Dine, Handy Market, and Stop-N-Go, by the mid-1990s Uni-Marts had grown into a prominent player in the roughly $86 billion U.S. convenience store industry. Of the 1,500 companies running the 65,000 U.S. convenience stores in the early 1990s, 140 vied directly with Uni-Marts for the small town and rural market.

1970s Origins

Uni-Marts, Inc. was founded in 1972 by Henry D. Sahakian, a Christian Armenian from Iran who moved to the United States in 1956 to study mechanical engineering at Pennsylvania State University in the town of State College. After graduating, he used a modest nest egg left him by his father to found Unico, a builder of student housing projects for the university. The venture was a success, but Sahakian sought new challenges and, noting the rapid growth of Southland Corporation's 7-Eleven convenience stores throughout the region, flew to the chain's Dallas headquarters to personally petition for an exclusive territory of stores. When Southland offered him only a single store, Sahakian turned to Munford, Inc., the Atlanta-based owners of the Ma-jik Market convenience store chain, which granted him a 20-year license for convenience stores in the state of Pennsylvania.

Between 1973 and 1974, Sahakian opened nine Ma-jik Mart stores in such small Pennsylvania communities as Clearfield, Chester Hill, Bellefonte, Curwensville, and Altoona. To gain a stake in the industries supplying his stores, Sahakian acquired Meadow Pride Dairy in 1975, Long's Dairy in 1976, Royale Dairy in 1980, and Valley Farms Dairy in 1988. By 1990, Sahakian's dairy operations alone—which processed and distributed milk and other beverage products to Uni-Mart stores and other customers—reached a sales peak of $22.7 million in 1990, or nine percent of Uni-Mart's total revenues. In 1994, after almost 15 years in the dairy business, Sahakian sold the dairy operations off to Pittsburgh's Schneider's Dairy for $6.1 million, enabling Sahakian to concentrate exclusively on his core business—convenience stores.

By 1977 Sahakian's 30 Ma-jik Marts were generating $10 million in annual sales, and he decided to incorporate them as Unico Ma-jik Markets, Inc., a wholly owned subsidiary of his Unico Corporation. He next expanded into southeastern Pennsylvania, New Jersey, and Delaware and turned to a new sideline, food manufacture. Soon a Unico division was turning out Chunkee Foods sandwiches and Dino's Pizzas, and in 1980 Dino's ads were featuring the familiar face of Penn State football coach Joe Paterno. After less than a decade in business,

Company Perspectives:

It is Uni-Marts' mission to provide friendly, efficient service to our valued customers, offer quality products in a clean atmosphere, and return a reasonable profit to our stockholders.

Sahakian moved Unico's corporate headquarters to a new 28,000-square-foot office building in State College in 1980.

Incorporation in the 1980s

Despite an empire that now numbered 90 stores, Sahakian had become frustrated with his franchisee status with Munford. The amount of income returned after receipts were sent to Atlanta was simply disproportionate to the effort he and his stores expended. He consequently broke with the chain in 1981, terminating his franchise agreement and reestablishing Unico and his Ma-jik Market stores as Uni-Marts, Inc., a name chosen in an office contest. Munford sued, but Sahakian eventually prevailed, winning independence for his chain and its 695 employees. The move proved to be a propitious one for the 1980s became the decade in which the convenience store concept came into its own, exploding from 30,000 U.S. stores in 1976 to 75,000 by 1986. By 1992, two-thirds of all Americans were shopping at convenience stores at least once a week. Faced with this thriving new form of competition, supermarkets reacted by staying open around the clock, and major oil companies like Texaco and Mobil opened convenience stores inside their gas stations. The convenience store market quickly became saturated, and once-dominant firms like Southland, Circle K, National Convenience Stores, and Cumberland Farms fell by the wayside.

In this climate, the success of Sahakian's stores would have seemed all the more remarkable if its underlying strategy had not by now become so apparent: while the big chains claimed the urban markets, small towns were still mostly occupied by independent mom-and-pop stores ill-equipped to compete with Sahakian's vast economies of scale. Uni-Mart's 1993 annual report described the firm's approach plainly: "Uni-Marts' strategy is to locate many of its convenience stores in small towns and rural areas where there are fewer competitors and lower operating costs." By avoiding the competition and crime of the big city for an untapped market with seemingly limitless growth potential, Sahakian had grown from 92 stores in 1982 to 208 four years later, breaking the $100 million level in sales for the first time in 1986.

Sahakian's "small town strategy" not only created a booming business in an industry choked by competition, it also represented a kind of throwback to the pre-supermarket era of the 1920s when the U.S. grocery industry was still dominated by mom-and-pop stores and so-called economy stores. Like these forerunners, Uni-Marts were sometimes the only stores for miles and therefore served not only as a quick-stop filling station/minigrocery but a community gathering place (some larger Uni-Marts featured in-store seating). As Sahakian told *Forbes* magazine in 1995: "We're not afraid to go into small towns. We are their gas station, their restaurant, their drug store, their newspaper stand."

To cement the community's attachment to his stores, Sahakian encouraged Uni-Mart store managers to stock up to 100 products with a local appeal—from refrigerated bait for active fishing communities to work gloves for blue-collar towns. Even among the standard roster of products sold in each Uni-mart, managers of the company's five geographic regions were allowed to modify their stores' product mix to their communities' preferences. In Uni-Marts' headquarters town, State College, Pennsylvania, for example, fast food and snack products sold strongly while beer, deli products, and chicken tended to do well in, respectively, New York state, Pittsburgh, and Lancaster county, Pennsylvania. As Uni-Marts's advertising and sales promotions manager Barb Robuck put it in 1993, "Every geographic area has a little niche. You have to put in the right product and food, but you also must be careful with how you advertise. We can't sit here and put together a corporate product."

Uni-Mart stores themselves ranged in size from 1,200 to 3,000 square feet, with an average of 2,400 square feet. Smaller stores were designed to be run by a single worker at a cash register station located, for better security, facing the store's aisles, and although the convenience store industry is synonymous with around-the-clock hours, Uni-Mart's less crowded markets allowed it to maintain 24-hour operations in only two-thirds of its stores. While the company's prices were in some cases somewhat higher than supermarkets', they were often more competitively priced than other convenience stores. Besides the standard items like deli foods and hot dogs, dairy products, health and beauty aids, tobacco, and candies and snacks, in 1987 Uni-Marts began stocking freshly baked pizza among its fresh, ready-to-eat food goods. Hot Chester Fried Chicken soon followed and, after Uni-Marts consolidated its pizza programs in 1994, freshly baked Valerio's Pizza. To encourage repeat business and further individualize Uni-Marts from other convenience stores many Uni-Marts also offered money order and utility bill payment services, free check cashing, videocassette rentals, and nontraditional food items like cappuccino coffee and yogurt.

If Uni-Marts could rightfully claim, as its slogan put it, that it was "more than a convenience store"—that it was in fact a modern-day "town store" with all the connotations of community involvement that entailed—its community service programs were the proof. Beginning in 1987, it began a series of programs to link its stores closely to their communities while polishing its overall corporate image. It sponsored local Little League teams and fireworks displays, created a nationwide customer service WATTS line ("1-800-UNI-MART"), and contributed money to Pennsylvania State University as well as local charities. Among its more traditional promotional strategies was a player-of-the-game program for Penn State football games, a seniors' club to award free items after a certain number of purchases, and instant-win lottery games. The company also worked hard to foster a team attitude among employees, from forming company softball teams, sponsoring corporate golf outings, and holding annual conventions for store managers to awarding employees for outstanding customer service, providing scholarship programs for employees' families, and faithfully promoting from within.

Responding to Challenges in the 1990s

Uni-Mart's public relations slate was not entirely unblemished, however. Uni-Mart had reportedly alienated some public decency groups by refusing to discontinue sales of such magazines as *Playboy* and *Penthouse* in its stores. Sahakian himself rejected the charge that Uni-Mart unethically sold pornography to the communities it claimed to care about: "I hate censorship," he stated in a 1995 *Forbes* interview, adding "I came to this country because of freedom, and I'm not going to give it up."

As with most convenience stores, cigarette sales historically accounted for a considerable percentage of Uni-Mart's corporate profits (as high as 32 percent of all non-gasoline merchandise sales in 1984). Early on, however, Sahakian had taken note of declining U.S. smoking rates and the likelihood of increasing cigarette taxes and began looking for something to fill the 24 percent hole in merchandise sales that cigarettes occupied by 1994. One solution seemed to be so-called private label cigarette brands, which allowed convenience stores to market and prominently display lower cigarette prices in a way supermarkets could not imitate. Capitalizing on consumers' desire to pay less for tobacco, between 1991 and 1995 convenience stores' market share in cigarette sales rose from 36 to 47 percent.

Sahakian predicted, however, that even short-term pricing victories would not keep cigarette sales from declining to almost negligible levels by the early part of the 21st century. The real answer, he decided, was fast food. In 1994, Sahakian entered into an experimental arrangement with Blimpie's International, a submarine sandwich chain, in which Uni-Marts became in effect a Blimpie franchisee, with Uni-Mart employees making and selling Blimpie subs while performing the traditional duties of a Uni-Marts store. The idea of two companies cooperatively capitalizing on each other's brand name, known as co-branding, stemmed in part from Sahakian's decision in late 1991 to replace the ten to 12 companies that provided the unbranded gasoline sold in its some 300 gas station/convenience stores with a single major gas supplier, Getty Petroleum. In exchange for agreeing to use Getty brand gasoline exclusively in 90 percent of its existing gas station/convenience stores, Uni-Mart leased 141 GettyMart gas station/convenience stores for its chain, increasing its retail network by 42 percent and expanding into Virginia and new areas of Pennsylvania.

If Uni-Marts could gain more repeat customers by offering branded gasoline, Sahakian reasoned, why not new repeat customers for branded fast food? The Blimpie experiment was successful, and in 1994 Uni-Marts entered into co-branding relationships with Blimpie's and Burger King, with Arby's to follow in 1995. Using portions of the $6 million raised from its 1994 sale of its dairy operations to add fast food installations to its stores, by late 1995 Uni-Marts was operating twenty-one Blimpie stores, five Arby's stores, and three Burger King stores, with plans to add 25 to 30 new fast food c-stores every year. Based on early results, Uni-Mart predicted that the new prepared food operations (which offered partial menus of the fast food chains' full restaurants) would have a "positive impact" on the chain's customer traffic as well as adding a needed profit buffer to the razor-thin margins

of its traditional c-store merchandise. Not coincidentally, Uni-Marts could also now side-step its historical reliance on cigarette sales for corporate revenues.

Not all of Uni-Marts' expansionary plans bore fruit, however. In late 1995 the company attempted an unsolicited stock swap with Dairy Mart Convenience Stores that would have produced the third-largest convenience store chain in the United States—1,300 stores with annual revenues in excess of $900 million. The acquisition at first appeared a natural; like Uni-Marts, Dairy Mart, a Connecticut-based chain of 900 stores in 11 states, offered both convenience store and gas station services to rural and small markets. Moreover, Uni-Marts already owned a block of Dairy Mart stock. Dairy Mart, however, fiercely resisted the move, buying the stock of its former chairman to gain a controlling vote over the deal, which it promptly rejected.

Despite the setback, Uni-Marts continued to add value to its operations in the mid-1990s. In 1995 the company signed an agreement with a Pennsylvania credit union to operate automatic teller machines in 155 of its stores, giving customers one more reason to walk through the door and money to spend if they stayed. An extension of Uni-Mart's co-branding concept was also unveiled in 1996: a "convenience center" in State College in which a Uni-Mart served as the anchor store in a one-stop business cluster that included a bank, a Mail Boxes Etc. copying and shipping franchise, a bagel shop, and a drive-through Burger King.

The company also aggressively pursued the integration of technology into its operations, which had begun as early as 1982 when electronic devices for ordering groceries were installed in its stores. A pilot program was launched in 1993 in which a store's cash register would be linked to a PC that would automatically enter rung-up sales into a computer at Uni-Marts's headquarters, promising improved "real-time" control of inventory and sales data. In 1996 the company also adopted an inventory management system that enabled it, in conjunction with its wholesaler, to use computers to more efficiently design optimal "shelf sets" for the goods merchandised in Uni-Mart stores. The system promised to improve Uni-Marts's product merchandising by enabling it to more effectively limit the space devoted to slow-moving items while more efficiently arranging the space allocated to each vendor's products.

Uni-Marts also continued to ensure its stores' compliance with Environmental Protection Agency (EPA) regulations on the replacement of environmentally damaging chlorofluorocarbon (CFC) refrigerants in its store refrigeration systems and other EPA regulations governing the upgrading of filling station gasoline holding tanks. With 90 percent of its tanks upgraded to meet these standards by 1995, Uni-Mart turned its attention to installing high-volume fueling equipment throughout its chain.

Between 1985 and 1995, Uni-Marts's revenues and profits had quadrupled, and Sahakian himself had seen his 6.3 million Uni-Mart shares rise to $26.3 million in value. With an uninterrupted 25-year history of profitability behind it and a realizable goal of 1,000 stores ahead, Uni-Mart's 1996 corporate slogan—

"Proud Past, Bright Future"—seemed to aptly encapsulate the company's status as it entered its anniversary year.

Further Reading

Fox, Bruce, "Uni-Marts Prepares for C-Store Challenge," *Chain Store Age Executive,* August 1994, pp. 26, 32.

"Gasoline Fuels Record 1993 C-Store Profits," *National Petroleum News,* June 1994, p. 42.

"Getty Petroleum Corp.," *The Oil and Gas Journal,* December 16, 1991, p. 33.

"Hey, Buddy, Can You Spare a Billion?" *Progressive Grocer,* September 1995, p. 50.

Kelley, Kristine Portnoy, "Despite the Weather, C-Store Beverages Boast Strong '92," *Beverage Industry,* July 1993, p. 16.

Kovski, Alan, "Retailer Uni-Marts Withdraws Its Offer to Buy Dairy Mart," *The Oil Daily,* December 5, 1995, p. 3.

Lane, Randall, "The Sleepier, the Better," *Forbes,* November 6, 1995, pp. 84, 88.

Marano, Ray, "Uni-Marts Shuns Consumer Apathy, Expands Retail Outlets 42 Percent," *Pittsburgh Business Times,* November 25, 1991, p. 2.

Turcsik, Richard, "Butts Are Dragging," *Supermarket News,* September 12, 1994, p. 59.

"Unsolicited $48 Million Bid Launched for Dairy Mart," *Wall Street Journal,* November 16, 1995, p. 12.

"Uni-Marts Dairy Sale Finalized," *National Petroleum News,* June 1994, p. 42.

"Uni-Marts, Inc.," *Fortune,* August 10, 1989, p. 90.

"Uni-Marts Plans Remodels, Pump Upgrades in 1995," *U.S. Oil Week,* February 6, 1995.

—Paul S. Bodine

United Parcel Service of America Inc.

400 Perimeter Center Terraces North
Atlanta, Georgia 30346
U.S.A.
(404) 913-6000
Fax: (404) 913-6593
Internet: http://www.ups.com

Private Company
Founded: 1907 as American Messenger Co.
Employees: 335,000
Sales: $21 billion (1995)
SICs: 4215 Courier Services Except by Air; 4513 Air
    Courier Services

Known in the industry as "Big Brown," United Parcel Service of America Inc. (UPS) is the world's largest package-delivery company. The Atlanta-based business delivered more than three billion items throughout more than 200 countries and territories in 1995. In addition to its fleet of 147,000 vehicles, the company operates one of the world's top ten airlines by virtue of its more than 500 company-owned and chartered aircraft. Under the direction of CEO Kent C. Nelson in the late 1980s and early 1990s, UPS strove mightily to maintain its dominant position in parcel post and insinuate itself throughout the world.

Roots in the Early 20th Century

UPS was founded in 1907 in Seattle, Washington, by 19-year-old Jim Casey as a six-bicycle messenger service. He set the future tone of the company by mandating that it be employee-owned. Casey delivered telegraph messages and hot lunches and sometimes took odd jobs to keep his struggling business going. By 1913 UPS consisted of seven motorcycles. With Casey's tacit approval, UPS drivers joined the International Brotherhood of Teamsters in 1916. In 1918 three Seattle department stores hired the service to deliver merchandise to purchasers on the day of the purchase. Department store deliveries remained the center of UPS's business until the late 1940s.

In 1929 UPS began air delivery through a new division, United Air Express, which put packages onto passenger planes. The Great Depression ended plans for an overnight air service, and UPS terminated United Air Express in 1931; the company did not resume air service until the 1950s. In the late 1940s the urban department stores that UPS serviced began following their clients to the new suburbs. More people owned cars and picked up their own parcels. UPS's revenue declined.

Casey decided to change direction and expand the common-carrier parcel business, picking up parcels from anyone and taking them to anyone else, charging a fixed rate per parcel. The company's initial customers were primarily industrial and commercial shippers, although the firm also serviced consumers. The company had offered common-carrier service in Los Angeles since 1922, and in 1953 UPS extended it to San Francisco, Chicago, and New York. UPS delivered any package meeting weight and size requirements to any location within 150 miles of these bases. After this initial expansion, UPS frequently appeared before the Interstate Commerce Commission (ICC) to expand its operating rights.

UPS scaled its operations to fit its market niche, refusing packages weighing more than 50 pounds or with a combined length and width of more than 108 inches, limitations that would increase in concert with the company's capabilities. Its average package weighed about ten pounds and was roughly the size of a briefcase, making sorting and carrying easy. UPS competed with scores of regional firms but most had not limited the size and weight of their packages. They ended up with the heavier packages, higher overheads, and lower volumes.

A New Generation of Leadership for the 1960s

Casey resigned as chief executive officer in 1962 and was succeeded by George D. Smith. UPS more than doubled its sales and profits between 1964 and 1969, when the company made $31.9 million on sales of about $548 million. The company remained privately owned, its stock held by several hundred of its executives. UPS in 1969 served 31 states on the east and west coasts. It had just gotten ICC approval to add nine Midwestern states and soon got approval for three more states.

Company Perspectives:

Corporate Mission Statement. Customers: Serve the on-going package distribution needs of our customers world-wide and provide other services that enhance customer relationships and complement our position as the foremost provider of package distribution services, offering high quality and excellent value in every service. People: Be a well-regarded employer that is mindful of the well-being of our people, allowing them to develop their individual capa-bilities in an impartial, challenging, rewarding and cooper-ative environment and offering them the opportunity for career advancement. Shareowners: Maintain a financially strong, employee-owned company earning a reasonable profit, providing long-term competitive returns to our share-owners. Communities: Build on the legacy of our company's reputation as a responsible corporate citizen whose well-being is in the public interest and whose people are re-spected for their performance and integrity.

Only the lightly populated states of Arizona, Alaska, Hawaii, Idaho, Montana, Nevada, and Utah were without UPS service. The firm kept a low profile, avoiding publicity, and refusing interviews of its chief executives. UPS officials believed only one parcel shipping company could exist in the United States, and it hoped that keeping a low profile would prevent anyone from copying its methods.

The firm's secrecy policy was possible because it was closely held. Its 3,700 stockholders (a number raised to 23,000 by 1991) were its own top and middle managers and their families. Stockholders wanting to sell sold their stock back to the company. Because management owned UPS, the company could make long-range plans without the pressure for instant profits faced by many publicly owned firms. Most managers started as UPS drivers or sorters and came up through the ranks, creating great loyalty. The company's management structure was relatively informal, stressing partnership and the involve-ment of management at all levels.

In 1970 Congress considered a reform of the U.S. Postal Service that would allow it to subsidize its parcel post opera-tions with profits from its first-class mail. This would allow it to lower prices and compete more directly with UPS. UPS hired a public relations firm and for the first time officially announced its earnings, trying to build a case that it was an integral part of the U.S. economy and that the postal reform would be disrup-tive. UPS handled 500 million packages in 1969, for 165,000 regular customers. The company claimed that 95 percent of all deliveries within 150 miles were delivered overnight. The com-pany centered operations around a five-day-a-week cycle. Driv-ers made deliveries in the morning, made pickups in the after-noon, and returned to operations centers around 6:00 PM. Their packages were immediately sorted and transferred for delivery.

UPS trucks are painted brown to avoid showing soil and are cleaned every night. Trucks are assigned to specific drivers, who the company treats as future managers and owners. The

company had 22,000 drivers in 1969, and most were kept on the same route to develop a relationship with customers. Some drivers, however, found UPS management inflexible, resulting in occasional local strikes.

In 1976 UPS tried to replace, gradually, all of its full-time employees who sorted and handled packages at warehouses with part-time workers. Teamsters locals in the South, Midwest, and West accepted the idea, but 17,000 UPS employees from Maine to South Carolina went on strike. The strike caused chaos for east coast retailers as their suppliers were forced to send Christmas goods through the overburdened U.S. Postal Service. UPS even-tually reached agreement with the Teamsters, but its labor rela-tions continued to be spotty. Because management owned the business, it tended to drive its employees hard, and many drivers complained of the long hours and hard work. To maximize driver performance, the company kept records of the production of every driver and sorter and compared them to its performance projections. Drivers' routes were timed in great detail.

In 1976 UPS launched service in Germany with 120 delivery vans. It quickly ran into trouble because of cultural and lan-guage differences. UPS eventually adapted by hiring some German managers and accepting the German dislike of working overtime. George C. Lamb Jr. succeeded Harold Oberkotter as UPS chairman in 1980.

Competition Intensifies in 1980s

UPS continued to grow rapidly, aided by trucking deregu-lation in 1980. By 1980 UPS earned $189 million on revenues of $4 billion, shipping 1.5 billion packages. Federal Express Corporation, however, which began operations in 1973, was siphoning off a growing amount of UPS's business. Federal shipped packages overnight by air, and many businesses began shipping high-priority packages with Federal. UPS had the resources to challenge Federal, but it meant taking on signifi-cant debt, something the conservatively run UPS was reluctant to do. In 1981 it had only $7 million in long-term debt and a net worth of $750 million. To compete with Federal, UPS bought nine used 727 airplanes in 1981 from Braniff Airlines for $28 million. It opened an air hub in Louisville, Kentucky, but was hesitant about directly challenging Federal because of the huge cost of building an air fleet. It decided to stick with two-day delivery rather than overnight delivery, hoping that many busi-nesses would be willing to let packages take an extra day if it meant savings of up to 70 percent. It called its two-day delivery Blue Label Air and spent $1 million in 1981 to promote it—a large sum for UPS, which had rarely advertised. In 1982 UPS ran its first-ever television ads, trying to convince executives that two-day service was fast enough for most packages.

The recession of the early 1980s helped UPS because many companies shifted to smaller inventories, shipping smaller lots more frequently and demanding greater reliability. Package volume grew by six percent in 1981. Because of the recession, the Teamsters accepted a contract in 1982 that limited wage increases to a cost-of-living adjustment, which then was di-verted to pay the increased cost of medical benefits. When UPS then released information showing its net income rose 74 per-cent in 1981, labor relations worsened. Bitterness continued between UPS management and drivers as company profits swelled 48 percent to $490 million in 1983. UPS and the Teamsters secretly negotiated for two months in 1984 and reached a three-year agreement providing for bonuses and increased wages. The move averted a probable strike by 90,000 employees. Despite this labor tension, UPS's employee turnover remained remarkably low at four percent. Many workers were recruited as part-time employees while college students and were offered full-time positions after graduation.

In 1982 UPS decided to offer overnight air service, charging about half of Federal's rate. By 1983 its second-day and next-day services were shipping a combined 140,000 packages a day. In 1982 UPS earned $332 million on $5.2 billion in sales. It had a fleet of more than 62,000 trucks. Mail-order firms and catalog houses were the fastest growing part of UPS's business. Jack Rogers became UPS chairman in 1984.

Despite labor troubles, a *Fortune* survey found UPS's reputation the highest in its industry every year from 1984 to 1991. It was by far the most profitable U.S. transportation company, making more than $700 million in 1987 on revenue of $10 billion. Federal Express, however, had 57 percent of the rapidly growing overnight package business; UPS had only 15 percent. Federal was highly automated and used electronics to track packages en route and to perform other services. UPS still did most jobs manually, but was rapidly switching to the use of electronic scanners at its sorting centers and to computers on its trucks. UPS introduced technology methodically, buying a software firm and a computer design shop to create the necessary equipment. It then field-tested its new gear at a 35-car messenger service it owned in Los Angeles. It launched a $1.5 billion five-year computerization project, trying to create a system that tracked packages door-to-door, which Federal was doing already. UPS's healthy river of cash flow enabled it to pay $1.8 billion for 110 aircraft in 1987. The purchase made it the tenth-largest U.S. airline. The company launched its first wide-range television advertising campaign in 1988, spending $35 million to publicize the slogan, "We run the tightest ship in the shipping business." Despite these expenses, the company still had only $114 million in long-term debt and continued to finance large projects out of its cash flow.

By 1988 UPS's ground service was growing by seven percent to eight percent per year, and air service was growing by 30 percent per year. UPS handled 2.3 billion packages per year, compared with 1.4 billion for the U.S. Postal Service. The 300-plane fleet of the UPS overnight service handled 600,000 parcels and documents per day, making $350 million on $2.2 billion in sales in 1988. UPS continued building an overseas air network, but in West Germany, where it had 6,000 employees, it delivered only on the ground. The company shipped eight million packages overseas in 1988, losing $20 million in the process. UPS bought its Italian partner, Alimondo, in 1988, hoping to use it and its German base to expand through Europe. The company also bought nine small European courier companies to expand air service. Its overseas acquisitions cost UPS less than $100 million. UPS and rival Federal Express both were losing money on overseas operations, but UPS had an advantage: Federal could not match its $6.5 billion in assets and $480 million in cash with minimal debt. UPS hoped this would give it greater staying power as the two companies struggled to build a global delivery network. Meanwhile, UPS slowly won some Federal customers by giving volume discounts, which it previously had refused to do. The overseas shipping war escalated as Federal bought Tiger International, Inc., a major international shipper that UPS used for some of its foreign deliveries.

New Leadership Invigorates 1990s

Kent C. Nelson succeeded Jack Rogers as chairman and CEO in 1989. Nicknamed "Oz" for 1940s-era band leader Ozzie Nelson, the 52-year-old had spent his entire working life at UPS, starting with the company only two days after graduating from college. The new leader undertook a gradual, but complete transformation of UPS that extended from its innermost workings to its public image.

Challenged by competitors large and small, UPS launched a plethora of new services in the early 1990s. These ranged from timed and same-day deliveries to less expensive two- and three-day services. The company's Worldwide Logistics subsidiary offered clients everything from inventory management to warehousing and, of course, delivery. Powerful and costly technical systems, often developed internally by a 4,000-member staff, backed up these expanded operations. UPS's DIAD (delivery information acquisition device), for example, combined a barcode scanner, electronic signature capture, and cellular tracking network in a single handheld tool. By 1992, the corporation was investing more money in computers than in ubiquitous brown vehicles. These internal changes reflected the company's traditional focus on super-efficiency as well as its newfound emphasis on customer satisfaction.

In contrast to its secretive early years, the UPS of the 1990s was a bold global marketer. The company embarked on the largest advertising campaign in its history in 1996, spending an estimated $100 million in conjunction with its sponsorship of the Centennial Olympics held in Atlanta, Georgia (which, not coincidentally, had become UPS's headquarters in 1991). UPS hoped that the worldwide recognition enjoyed by the Olympic rings would rub off on its brown trucks, which were not well known outside the United States.

That recognition was vital to the success of UPS's international operations, which continued to lose money into the mid-1990s. By 1995, in fact, losses on the company's European assault totaled nearly $1 billion. But backed by its patient and confident employee/stockholders and a hefty bank account, UPS was able to wait out publicly held Federal Express, which had limited its European service to intercontinental deliveries by mid-decade. In stark contrast, UPS had expanded its international network to include 200 countries and territories worldwide. Undaunted by its massive losses, UPS announced plans to invest more than $1 billion in its European operations from 1995 to 2000, and it infused another $130 million into its Asian operations. The company hoped to profit on its piece of the $25 billion European parcel post market by the end of the century.

This global push fueled a 69 percent increase in sales over the course of Kent Nelson's first six years at the helm of UPS. At the same time, however, it played a significant role in the reduction of the company's overall profit margin from eight percent in 1987 to 4.8 percent in 1995. As the company approached its ninetieth anniversary in 1997, it looked forward to reaping the rewards of its global investment.

Principal Subsidiaries

United Parcel Service Co.; United Parcel Service Deutschland Inc.; United Parcel Service General Services Co.; UPS Customhouse Brokerage, Inc.; UPS International General Services Co.; UPS International, Inc.; UPS Truck Leasing, Inc.; UPS Worldwide Forwarding, Inc.; UPS Worldwide Logistics, Inc.; UPICO Corp.; UPS Aviation Services, Inc.; Diversified Trimodal, Inc.; Merchants Parcel Delivery; Trailer Conditioners, Inc.; II Morrow, Inc.; Red Arrow Bonded Messenger Corp.; UPS Air Leasing, Inc.; Roadnet Technologies, Inc.; UPS Telecommunications, Inc.; UPS Properties, Inc.; UPINSCO, Inc.; Sonic Air, Inc.; Velleb, Inc.; ADI Realty Co.; Alko Corp.; Bardale Co.; Basplas Corp.; Brastock Corp.; Brookind Corp.; Buckroe Corp.; Burdence Corp.; Chasreal, Inc.; Cleve Co.; Cova Corp.; Dakkel Corp.; Dalho Corp.; Darico, Inc.; Daven Corp.; Deerfield Corp.; Denado Corp.; Dullesport Corp.; Edison Corp.; Elsil Corp.; Evind Corp.; Fardak Corp.; Galanta Co.; Kylou, Inc.; Labar Corp.; United Parcel Service Pty. Ltd. (Australia); UPS Pty. Ltd. (Australia); United Parcel Service Speditionsgesellschaft Mbh (Austria); UPS Transport Gmbh (Austria); United Parcel Service (Bahrain) Wll; United Parcel Service (Belgium) NV; United Parcel Service (Bermuda) Ltd.; UPS Do Brasil & Cia; United Parcel Service Canada Ltd.; United Parcel Service Cayman Islands Ltd.; UPS De San Jose, SA (Costa Rica); UPS Denmark AS; United Parcel Service Finland Oy; United Parcel Service France Snc; Prost-Transports SA Speditionsgesellschaft mbH (Germany); United Parcel Service Deutschland Inc. (Germany); UPS Air Cargo Service Gmbh (Germany); UPS Grundstuecksverwaltungs Gmbh (Germany); UPS Transport Gmbh (Germany); UPS Transport Gmbh II (Germany); UPS Worldwide Logistics Gmbh (Germany); UPS Parcel Delivery Service Ltd. (Hong Kong); United Parcel Service Cstc Ireland Ltd.; United Parcel Service of Ireland Ltd.; United Parcel Service Italia, Srl; United Parcel Service Co. (Japan); UPS Japan Ltd.; UPS Yamato Company, Ltd. (Japan); United Parcel Service Jersey Ltd.; United Parcel Service (M) Sdn. Bhd. (Malaysia); United Parcel Service (Transport) Sdn. Bhd. (Malaysia); United Parcel Service De Mexico, SA de CV; Prost-Transports Nederland BV; United Parcel Service Nederland BV; UPS Norge AS (Norway); UPS of Norway, Inc.; UPS of Portugal, Inc.; United Parcel Service Co. (Singapore); United Parcel Service Singapore Pte Ltd.; United Parcel Service Co. (South Korea); Sociedad Inversora Sanrelman, SA (Spain); United Parcel Service Espana Ltd. Y Compania, Src (Spain); UPS Spain, Sl; United Parcel Service Sweden AB; United Parcel Service (Switzerland); UPS International, Inc. (Taiwan); UPS Parcel Delivery Service Ltd. (Thailand); Atexco (1991) Ltd. (United Kingdom); Atlasair Ltd. (United Kingdom); Carryfast Ltd. (United Kingdom); IML Air Services Group Ltd. (United Kingdom); United Parcel Service of America (United Kingdom); UPS (UK) Ltd. (United Kingdom); UPS Ltd. (United Kingdom); UPS of America Ltd. (United Kingdom).

Further Reading

"Behind the UPS Mystique: Puritanism and Productivity," *Business Week,* June 6, 1983.

Bonney, Joseph, "UPS Bets a Billion," *American Shipper,* January 1993, p. 26.

Day, Charles R. Jr., "Shape Up and Ship Out," *Industry Week,* February 6, 1995, pp. 14, 17–20.

Duffy, Caroline A., "UPS Toes the Line with Its Package-Tracking Technologies," *PC Week,* June 28, 1993, p. 211.

Gillam, Carey, "Delivering the Dream," *Sales & Marketing Management,* June 1996, pp. 74–78.

Greenwald, John, "Hauling UPS's Freight," *Time,* January 29, 1996, p. 59.

"James E. Casey," *Puget Sound Business Journal,* April 2, 1993, p. 2A.

Lyne, Jack, "UPS COO Jim Kelly: Bold Days for 'Big Brown,' " *Site Selection,* August 1995, pp. 53–54.

Madden, Stephen J., "Big Changes at Big Brown," *Fortune,* January 18, 1988.

"The Quiet Giant of Shipping," *Forbes,* January 15, 1970.

"Why United Parcel Admits Its Size," *Business Week,* July 18, 1970.

"The Wizard Is Oz," *Chief Executive (U.S.),* March 1994, pp. 40–43.

—Scott M. Lewis
—updated by April Dougal Gasbarre

Vermeer Manufacturing Company

P.O. Box #200
Pella, Iowa 50219-0200
U.S.A.
(515) 628-3141
Fax: (515) 621-7731

Private Company
Incorporated: 1948
Revenue: $430 million (1996 est.)
Employees: 2,300
SICs: 3523 Farm Machinery and Equipment; 3531
    Construction Machinery

An industrial leader in the design and production of specialized machinery for agriculture, construction, and tree care, Vermeer Manufacturing Company (VMC) is one of the world's most successful privately held equipment companies. From revolutionizing the tree care industry with stump cutters and tree spades to the one-of-a-kind large round hay baler in 1971, Vermeer's technological advances have always taken the industry by storm. The 1990s were no exception with the debut of its most recent innovation—"trenchless" boring equipment—which helped Vermeer capture the mid- to large-sized trenching market. VMC's four divisions (agricultural, contract, environmental, and underground) working around the clock six days a week, produced over 100 different kinds of heavy equipment for domestic and international customers and shipped an average of 1,000,000 parts per month.

An Inventor Tries His Hand, the 1940s and 1950s

While the 20th century's industrial revolution spawned technological wonders like the first turbo-prop engine in 1942 and the "Big Inch" oil pipeline from Texas to Pennsylvania in 1943, few advances were made in the field of agriculture. Then a gentleman farmer named Gary Vermeer, with acres of prime land in Pella, Iowa, began tinkering with farm equipment to help things run smoother in harvesting and storing grain. Though he was more than adept at using the tools of his ances-

tors, Vermeer sought to increase harvests and make the process more efficient and less strenuous.

With many area farmers fighting in World War II overseas (including Vermeer's brother Elmer), Vermeer harvested grain for himself and neighbors using early inventions like a corn elevator and manure loader. Yet neither alleviated the back-breaking work of shoveling out wagons, so Vermeer designed a wagon hoist to elevate the grain and let gravity do the rest. When Vermeer built four of his newfangled wagon hoists during the winter, neighbors responded enthusiastically.

By 1948 Vermeer and a cousin had manufactured the popular wagon hoist from a 2,500-square-foot factory on the west side of Pella. Yet this initial taste of entrepreneurial pride was soured a bit with the introduction of hydraulic wagon hoists, which pretty much wiped out the market for mechanical hoists. Undaunted, Vermeer, now 31, continued to seek out ways to make life easier and more profitable for farmers like himself. His next innovation was a right-angled power-take-off (PTO) drive for hammermills (machinery used to mix and grind feed). The PTO drive helped keep the hammermill's wide tractor belts in place which often loosened and flew off the equipment, sometimes with dire consequences. After placing a small ad in a local circular, Vermeer received over 1,000 responses and began producing 100 PTOs drives a week. Before long, Vermeer and his cousin were joined by 18 new employees to keep up with demand.

By the 1950s President Harry Truman had survived an assassination attempt, price and wage controls were lifted, and Gary turned his designing skills to trenching. Like his father and grandfather before him, Vermeer had acres of bottomland requiring dikes and tiling. Within weeks of setting his mind to the task, Vermeer built a trencher/tiler propelled by a PTO drive much like the hammermills. What began as an agricultural tool in 1951—known as the "Model 12"—soon developed into self-propelled and crawler trenchers, and became the basis for a host of other construction equipment.

When Vermeer began selling products worldwide through New York exporters, the company created Vermeer Holland (in 1955) as a manufacturing and distribution facility for European

---

Company Perspectives:

Guiding Vermeer through the competitive world of manufacturing is our "4 Ps" philosophy. Imagine a steering wheel superimposed on a "machine" called Vermeer. People, Product, *and* Profit *are the wheel's essential components, giving the machine direction. At the center of the steering wheel is the fourth P,* Principles, *biblical principles providing connectedness to the other 3 Ps and about which they revolve.*

clients. As a reward for the company's immense growth, Gary instituted a cash incentive program for employees. In 1956 Vermeer again revolutionized an industry—this time in tree care—with the debut of a stump cutter that chewed up stumps in minutes and was operable by just one person instead of several. A prize to landscapers and builders, VMC's stump cutter rendered older, hard-to-handle versions obsolete. As the U.S. economy faced tumultuous times with unemployment of nearly 5.2 million in 1958 and a 116-day steelworkers' strike in 1959, VMC managed to not only keep its work force (now numbering 67) occupied but to continue design of a new breed of industrial equipment.

To Build A Better Mousetrap: The 1960s and 1970s

The dawn of the 1960s brought John F. Kennedy to the presidency and a stunning scientific discovery that later became commonplace in cutting-edge technology—the first laser (light amplification by stimulated emission of radiation) device. This decade also marked more firsts for Vermeer: its 300 or so employees now enjoyed a profit-sharing program; six international locations handled sales and shipping of VMC products; and several new developments in trenching equipment and tree care were on the way. The current trencher line consisted of two PTO-driven machines and three crawler units. Still seeking a better way, the company retooled its track trenchers and developed a rubber-tired machine, both of which could be fitted with attachments such as backfill blades, backhoes, cable plows, concrete cutters, loaders, and even climatized cabs.

Then came the TM-700 tree spade in 1965, a machine for moving trees. The TM-700 was an unusual contraption that dug up, moved, and replanted trees—complete with roots. Again Vermeer's ingenuity produced an industry original—this time one that safely transported and relocated trees bringing instant shade for homeowners and companies alike. Within two years VMC came out with several more tree spades, accommodating both large (up to a 94-inch root ball diameter) and small trees (up to 20-inch diameters). The tree spades were especially popular with landscapers and tree nurseries as a simple and effective way to harvest and replant trees.

In the first part of the 1970s amidst worldwide inflation came Vermeer Manufacturing's biggest contribution to agriculture, the large round hay baler—the first of its kind and the forefather of all round balers since. When one of Gary's neighbors talked about leaving the farming business due to the difficulty of providing feed for his cows, it started the former to thinking about alternate ways to put hay. Characteristically, Vermeer decided to design a hay baler by factoring in several key components: it had to be operable by one person; produce hay bales weighing about a ton; and wind the hay tight enough to shed water. Along with one of his engineers, the two drew a model with chalk and had their first prototype up and running in six weeks. Once again VMC was the toast of the town, revitalizing the farming industry.

Unfortunately, the hay baler's introduction was overshadowed by injuries and deaths when farmers operated the heavy machines improperly, tried to free up clogged intakes, or moved the one-ton-plus hay bales themselves. Vermeer made several adjustments, yet lawsuits temporarily clouded the remarkable machine's recognition. Conversely, others credited the invention with reducing the overall number of deaths related to hay baling—and round hay balers became a common site on farms worldwide. VMC sold more than 85,000 large round hay balers in the next 25 years and every round baler produced in subsequent decades was based on the company's design and technology.

By 1972 Vermeer Manufacturing had exclusive dealerships in Denmark, Egypt, England, France, Germany, Holland, Italy, Saudi Arabia, and Switzerland to sell its ever-increasing line of goods. To help Gary Vermeer continue his evolution from small-town inventor to owner of a global conglomerate came the arrival of a second generation of Vermeers. In 1974 Gary's second son, Robert, was appointed to the board of directors, followed in 1975 by his older brother Stanley. Robert began his VMC career as a vice-president in finance, while Stanley worked in the "experimental" department. A year later in 1976 as VMC's work force grew to 685, Gary's youngest child, Mary, joined VMC's board, while continuing to live and teach in Omaha, Nebraska.

For his efforts on behalf of the community, Gary was awarded the Pella Community Service Award in 1977. Not one to sit on his laurels, Vermeer and his company forged ahead with another discovery—the brush chipper—in 1978. The rugged brush chipper once again endeared VMC to the green industry as the compact machine was able to grind up a variety of materials from large trees (up to a 12-inch diameter) to storm damage brush and the annual disposal of Christmas trees. VMC's chippers turned unsightly waste into environmentally-friendly wood chips used in landscaping beds and around trees for installation and moisture retention. Vermeer's original green industry baby, the stump cutter, now came in several different sizes with patented forged-steel teeth, higher torque, and better maneuverability.

High-Tech Innovations: 1980s and 1990s

Though antipollution measures began to take shape in the mid-1960s, the early 1980s marked more comprehensive and stringent regulations on waste disposal by the Environmental Protection Agency (EPA). Because Vermeer used a metalworking coolant called TRIM Sol and produced between 220 and 2200 lbs. of waste per month (about 71,500 gallons per year), the company was classified as a "small-quantity generator" (SQG) of hazardous waste. To comply with stricter environmental codes, VMC adopted an in-plant coolant management system rather than ship its waste to a facility in Alabama. The system not only recycled coolant and reduced waste, but provided the company with many long-term benefits including increased water purity, improved tool efficiency, less maintenance, and a better bottom-line. Within six months of purchasing the new coolant management system, VMC recouped its cost and went on to save $100,000 in waste disposal costs for the year. By the time the EPA instituted the Resource Conservation and Recovery Act (RCRA) in 1986, VMC was saving $150,000 per year in reduced coolant purchases, labor costs, and machine downtime.

On the family front, Stanley, who began work in the Industrial Engineering department in 1979 was promoted to president of the company in 1982, the same year Mary came to VMC full-time in market research and human relations. Robert was named executive vice-president and secretary-treasurer in 1984, the same year Gary was honored as Iowa Inventor of the Year. Gary was honored again in 1986 with induction to the Iowa Business Hall of Fame, while son Stanley left the company to concentrate on charity work. When Stanley departed, Robert took the reins of the 786-employee strong company as CEO and chairman. Three years later, in 1989, Mary was appointed COO and president.

Before the end of the decade, VMC still dominated the hay baling industry and had added a silage baler to its product line, as well as improvements like automatic twine-tying and weaving systems and bale ejectors and monitors. In 1991 VMC introduced the company's biggest breakthrough since the original round hay baler in 1971. The cutting-edge technology that had produced the first PTO-driven trenchers soon turned them into indispensable tools for utility companies across the nation with the advent of "trenchless" drilling and boring equipment. Having perfected traditional trenching equipment, VMC took its innovation a step further to design and build machines to dig without damaging or destroying topsoil. This was achieved through a line of directional boring equipment called Hammerhead Moles (handheld pneumatic piercing tools) and Navigators (heavy underground construction equipment).

The Hammerhead Moles and Navigators were capable of digging below-surface tunnels and holes through which a wide range of products (pipelines for gas and water; fiber optic cables for television, telephones, and computers) were be connected— without damage in heavily trafficked areas by roadways, commercial buildings and suburban areas—even beneath rivers and lakes. At the same time trenchless technology caught fire, VMC created Vermeer University in 1991, an in-house schooling program. Vermeer University provided a myriad of classes for employees and dealers including technical (mastering computers, equipment operation and service, industrial safety) and professional (sales, career enhancement, personal growth and development). Within three years Vermeer University had over 600 people enrolled in 25 different classes.

As sales for trenchless equipment continued to boom, so did Vermeer's expansion. Just two years after the new technology's introduction, VMC added two more plants and over 900 new employees. Estimated sales for 1993 reached over $270 million, a remarkable achievement for a family-owned and -operated company regarded as a "niche" manufacturer. The next year, 1994, sales were around $320 million according to *Off-Highway Research*, no doubt helped by another environmentally-friendly piece of equipment—the Brawny TG-400—a large tub grinder. Designed to eliminate heavy organic waste, the Brawny TG-400 was a hit with landfills, construction companies, and contractors as the EPA tightened regulations on dumping and burning.

In 1995 the company reorganized into four separate divisions to help maintain what Robert called the "family team atmosphere." The new quads consisted of Agricultural (hay balers, hydraulic rakes, mowing equipment); Contract (specialized machinery like tractor weldments, jay tools, graders, scrapers, and log skidders for Caterpillar, John Deere, Fiat-Hitachi and more); Environmental (green industry tree spades, log splitters, brush chippers, tub and stump grinders); and the largest, Underground (traditional rubber-tired trenchers, trench compactors, and the Navigator and Hammerhead lines). Each division was housed in one of VMC's seven Pella facilities and employed over 2,000 nonunion workers (averaging 12-plus years with the company) drawn from Pella and five neighboring counties—even extending into Missouri. The facilities covered in excess of 1.4 million square feet or 33 acres on Highway 102, just outside the city limits. A major advantage to having its facilities close together was the ability to shift workers from one division to another during in cyclical slowdowns to prevent layoffs and rehirings. In its continuing quest "to find a better way," Vermeer's four divisions combined the best of human and mechanical innovation with state-of-the-art equipment to design, cut, shape, and mold over 200 tons of steel or 70 miles of welding wire per day (over 20,000 miles of welding wire annually).

With industrial products distributed through 75 domestic and 66 international dealers and agricultural dealers numbering more than 442 in the U.S. and Canada, VMC's name and reputation were known worldwide for its superior parts and service. Sales for 1995 topped $350 million and part of VMC's secret for success was a very simple yet effective business strategy: carry no long-term debt. When analysts projected flat sales for industrial and agricultural machinery in 1996, the Vermeers proved them wrong with their best year ever—taking in sales of well over $400 million.

As VMC approached the 21st century, Chairman Emeritus Gary Vermeer was semi-retired and spent an increasing amount of time managing his nearby 2,000-plus acre farm. "He started as a farmer and he was always a farmer at heart," Robert told the *Des Moines Register* in February 1996, "it's just that the factory grew faster than the farm." A month later, Gary was given national tribute when he was inducted into the Construction Equipment Hall of Fame along with steam shovel inventor William Smith Otis, Link-Belt founder William Dana Ewart and others. With Robert and Mary at VMC's helm and a third generation of Vermeers coming of age, the sky was the limit to find bigger and better solutions to agricultural, environmental and industrial needs.

Further Reading

"The Construction Equipment Industry in North America—Vermeer, April 1996," *Off-Highway Research*, April 1996.

Elbert, David, "Manufacturing Biggest Part of Pella Economy," *Des Moines Register*, February 19, 1996, p.8B.

——, "Rooted Deep in Pella Soil," *Des Moines Register*, February 19, 1996, pp. 1B, 8B–10B.

——, "Trenchless Borers are Hottest Product," *Des Moines Register*, February 19, 1996, p.8B.

"Iowa Manufacturer Maximizes Productivity and Minimizes Waste Control with Coolant Management," *Modern Machine Shop*, March 1995, pp. 128–131.

Landberg, Lynn, "Stump Cutter is Self-Propelled," *Construction Equipment*, August 15, 1991, p. 71.

Newendorp, V.W., "Electrohyraulic System Controls and Powers Baler," *Hydraulics & Pneumatics*, August 1989, pp. 53–54.

Osenga, Mike, "Vermeer Continues to Find a Way," *Diesel Progress, Engines & Drives*, March 1996, pp. 12–16.

Schneider, R.T., "HSTs Keep on Shrinking," *Hydraulics & Pneumatics*, July 1995, pp. 38–39.

—Taryn Benbow-Pfalzgraf

VF Corporation

1047 North Park Road
Wyomissing, Pennsylvania 19610
U.S.A.
(610) 378-1151
Fax: (610) 375-9371

Public Company
Incorporated: 1899 as Reading Glove & Mitten
    Manufacturing Co.
Employees: 64,000
Sales: $5.06 billion (1995)
Stock Exchanges: New York
SICs: 2325 Men's and Boy's Trousers and Slacks; 2339
    Women's and Misses' Outerwear, Not Elsewhere
    Classified; 2329 Men's and Boy's Clothing, Not
    Elsewhere Classified; 2326 Men's and Boy's Work
    Clothing; 2331 Women's and Misses' Blouses and
    Shirts; 2322 Men's and Boy's Underwear and
    Nightwear; 2340 Women's and Children's
    Undergarments

VF Corporation is one of the world's largest publicly owned fashion apparel manufacturers, designing and producing a diverse array of clothing products for both the U. S. and international markets. The company consists of numerous divisions, each of which is responsible for a different set of product lines, including jeans, sportswear, intimate apparel, and occupational clothing. Lee Apparel, the firm's largest division, along with Wrangler and Marithé & François Girbaud, manufacture denim and other casual apparel for adults and children. Bassett-Walker specializes in activewear, such as sweatshirts, jogging suits, and jackets, while JanSport, Jantzen, Nutmeg, and H. H. Cutler manufacture the company's different sportswear lines. Vanity Fair produces lingerie and loungewear items for women, and Healthtex is a leading producer of children's wear. The Red Kap division markets a wide variety of occupational apparel for industrial use.

The Early Years

The company's beginnings can be traced to the year 1899, when six men formed the Reading Glove and Mitten Manufacturing Company in Reading, Pennsylvania, and began producing and selling knitted and silk gloves. Of the founders, two men had previous experience in the garment industry as hosiery manufacturing executives, while a third, John Barbey, was a banker and controlled the company's financial operations. After 12 years of slow growth, John Barbey purchased his partners' interests in the company in 1911 and changed its name to Schuylkill Silk Mills. The following year, Barbey's son joined the firm as general manager.

In 1914 the company expanded into the manufacture of silk lingerie, and after three years of successful sales, the Barbeys decided to conduct a contest to find a brand name for their lingerie line. The winner received a $25 prize for the name "Vanity Fair." With hopes of establishing a national reputation for the company's merchandise, the Barbeys launched an extensive advertising campaign that emphasized the superior quality and style of Vanity Fair lingerie. This direct-to-the-consumer approach was considered innovative in that time period, because most other lingerie was of mediocre quality and was sold without brand names primarily through jobbers. The Barbeys' campaign was successful, and as the Vanity Fair brand name became more well known, the company once again changed its name to Vanity Fair Silk Mills, Inc. in 1919.

By the early 1920s, the rising success of the lingerie product line prompted Vanity Fair to discontinue its glove manufacturing operation and devote itself exclusively to the business of making lingerie. In 1937 it moved its manufacturing operation from Reading to Monroeville, Alabama.

Innovation and Expansion in the Mid-1900s

Upon his father's death in 1939, J. E. Barbey assumed the presidency of Vanity Fair, a position which he held for the next quarter century. During that time, he led the company through turbulent times, such as the economic changes that came with World War II. In 1941, the war brought about an embargo on

Company Perspectives:

Our mission is to provide above average shareholder returns by being the most responsive apparel company in the world. With leading brands, unparalleled customer service, global strength and a shared management vision, we are well on our way to achieving this goal.

silk, and the company began using rayon in the production of its lingerie. Throughout the rest of the 1940s, Vanity Fair perfected the use of other new types of lingerie fabrics, and subsequently introduced products made from a nylon tricot material in 1948.

These innovations changed the face of the lingerie industry. Nylon tricot was soon considered to be an ideal lingerie fabric due to its strength, wearing power, elasticity, and ease-of-care features. Its use also enabled the company to produce lingerie with a variety of fashionable features and in many popular colors. As a result, in 1950 Vanity Fair became the first lingerie manufacturer to receive the Coty Award for Design. Throughout the next decade, the company achieved steady growth through its production of lingerie and foundation garments. Then in 1969, as sales growth for these items was beginning to top off, Vanity Fair attempted to offset the effects by expanding into the robe and loungewear market.

Vanity Fair made two major acquisitions in 1969, including the purchase of the H. D. Lee Company, Inc., a manufacturer of men's and boys' jeans and casual pants. Also acquired at that time was Berkshire International, one of the world's largest producers of women's hosiery.

H. D. Lee had been established in the midwestern United States in 1860 as a wholesaler called the H. D. Lee Mercantile Company. In the early 1900s, the firm began selling overalls that it obtained from a supplier in the eastern United States. Because deliveries from this supplier were often unreliable, Lee began manufacturing its own overalls, jackets, and dungarees in a factory in Salina, Kansas. It also introduced the Lee Union-All, a garment designed to protect an entire suit or uniform. The Union-All became the official doughboy fatigue uniform during World War I. Beginning in the 1920s, Lee launched a series of innovative fabrics and apparel, including heavy-duty denim and Lee Rider cowboy pants. In the 1940s, Lee improved its cowboy pants with a tighter fit and the Tighter Rider brand became the best fitting cowboy pants available. The company established its International Division in 1959, and was rewarded a Presidential ''E'' citation in 1964 for making an outstanding contribution to the export expansion program of the United States.

Berkshire International also traced its roots back to the early 1900s, when it was founded as Berkshire Knitting Mills, a manufacturer of cotton stockings. The company's production process applied paraffin wax to cotton thread to give the woven stockings the luster of silk. Berkshire developed into the world's largest manufacturer of women's hosiery, thanks in part to the popularity of motion pictures featuring beautiful actresses

in short skirts and stockings, as well as to the outbreak of World War I, which fueled domestic production.

After acquiring the Lee Company and Berkshire International, Vanity Fair changed its name to VF Corporation as a means of reflecting its expansion into these new areas. VF Corporation was designated the parent company of H. D. Lee and Berkshire International, and a new subsidiary was formed under the Vanity Fair name to house the intimate apparel business. In 1971, VF acquired Kay Windsor, Inc., a manufacturer of budget-priced, ready-to-wear women's dresses and sportswear. This business encountered difficulties during the 1970s due to the growing popularity of women's pantsuits, however, and its division was discontinued in 1982.

In 1979, VF established an International Division to manage its growing operations overseas. The need for this new division had arisen as the export of Vanity Fair intimate apparel to Europe and the Far East soon grew to include many of the products from the Lee Company and Berkshire International.

An Industry Leader in the 1980s

Although the jeans market was beginning to experience diminished demand, VF entered the 1980s in a more profitable position than either of the two other major jeans makers, Levi Strauss or Blue Bell, Inc. VF's success was attributed to less dependence on foreign markets; earnings from other areas, such as lingerie; million-dollar investments in capital improvements; and tighter inventory controls. VF also benefited from Levi Strauss's decision to expand the distribution of its products to mass-merchandise outlets. Independent retailers that had previously carried the Levi's brand angrily responded to this development by stocking the Lee brand instead. Due to the rising demand for Lee's products, several of VF's Berkshire International sites were converted to jeans manufacturing facilities, as Lee became VF's largest operating division.

In 1982, Lawrence Pugh joined VF as president and chief executive officer, and became its chairman the following year. At that time, Robert Gregory was the president of the Lee division, and joined Pugh in an effort to inject new life into the sluggish jeans market. The two men embarked upon a marketing strategy to set Lee apart from other jeans industry leaders by segmenting production into men's and women's lines. VF became one of the first producers to manufacture stretch jeans for women, as well as dressier, more expensive jeans, which began competing with the designer lines that had become popular. VF developed the Ms. Lee brand, which soon became the best-selling line of women's jeans in the United States.

Meanwhile, VF was also segmenting and upgrading its Vanity Fair lingerie lines with more fashionable items to appeal to younger women. In addition to introducing new products, Pugh increased spending for advertising, expanded the company's retail distribution channels, and increased the size of the VF sales force.

Continuing to diversify, in 1984 VF acquired Modern Globe, Inc., a manufacturer of men's and women's cotton undergarments since 1917. VF also purchased Troutman Industries, Inc., a manufacturer of men's casual slacks, and Bassett-Walker, Inc., a producer of fleece activewear. Bassett-Walker had been founded in 1936, and by 1960 had become one of the largest manufacturers of knitted outerwear in the United States. The addition of these companies to VF's corporate portfolio helped the parent company continue to diversify, which allowed it to avoid reliance upon any one product or market segment.

In 1986, VF became the United States' largest apparel manufacturer and domestic jeans supplier when it acquired the Blue Bell Holding Company, a competitor that was the producer of Wrangler jeans. Blue Bell was also a major manufacturer of work clothes, and after acquiring the H. D. Bob Company in 1940 and Casey Jones in 1943, Blue Bell had begun manufacturing garments for the military in World War II. After the war, the company had applied the production methods it used in making military garments to the manufacture of casual clothing and western-style wear. In 1947, the brand name Wrangler was developed for this rapidly growing product line.

VF's friendly purchase of Blue Bell was viewed as an ideal marriage between two companies that had similar manufacturing cultures. The merger offered VF an opportunity to expand more deeply into menswear, while also having available resources to broaden its distribution channels to include mass merchants and discount stores. Furthermore, when VF acquired Blue Bell, it purchased not only the Wrangler product line, but also Blue Bell's other holdings: the Rustler jeans product line, Jantzen and JanSport swimwear and sportswear, Red Kap occupational apparel, and licenses to the Marithé and François Girbaud upscale sportswear collections.

Although VF had grown considerably in size due to its many acquisitions throughout the 1980s, declining jeans sales finally caught up to it in 1989. In the past, whenever one division's sales had slowed, VF had managed to survive the slump by relying on strong sales in its other divisions. This time, however, the company was paying the price for its decision three years earlier to begin marketing its Lee jeans through mass merchandisers and discount outlets. Just as competitor Levi Strauss had found when it attempted the same thing, the marketing error of moving into the discount realm ended up alienating department store buyers, who began refusing to carry the Lee line due to the lower-quality image it now possessed. Without the aid of department and specialty stores, VF found itself amidst a marketplace already dominated by low-cost importers with widely recognized brand names and large consumer advertising budgets. The Lee division traditionally had not given retail stores significant advertising support and found itself at a sizable disadvantage. As a result, both sales and profits in the jeans area fell significantly.

Compounding the company's problems was the growing popularity of a new line of casual men's apparel called Dockers, which had recently been introduced by Levi Strauss. The Dockers brand cut severely into VF's sales of jeans. VF had not changed its basic Lee Rider style, and had been so involved in rejuvenating its jeans business that it had neglected to notice that other manufacturers had expanded into different trouser lines that took advantage of new apparel trends.

The 1990s and Beyond

In the early 1990s, VF not only began taking further measures to rejuvenate its jeans sales, but also started focusing on the market segment of women aged 25 to 44. It continued to offer

increased marketing for its women's jeans lines, while also emphasizing support for other women's apparel such as the JanSport and Jantzen lines. In 1990, the company purchased the manufacturing operations of intimate apparel brands Vassarette and Form-O-Uth from Munsingwear, and added them to the intimate apparel division. The following year marked the acquisition of Healthtex, Inc. a leading manufacturer of children's wear.

With a diverse array of products under its corporate umbrella, as well as numerous distribution options, VF instituted a program to strengthen relationships with its retailers and better understand the needs of its consumers. First, VF began investing more time and money into researching the buying patterns, needs, and lifestyles of its consumers, so as to better serve them. The company then offered its retailers increased advertising and merchandising support based on the results of its consumer research. The information obtained through market research was also helpful in determining which brands to emphasize at any given point in time. Furthermore, VF's proprietary Market Response System was introduced, providing an electronic link between retailers' sales floors and corresponding VF divisions and allowing VF to keep its products in stock at all times.

VF also saw continued growth as a result of its ongoing acquisition program. In 1992, the company purchased three European intimate apparel companies: Valero, Vivesa and Jean Bellanger Enterprises, which together added eight new international brand names to the VF portfolio. These additions, combined with the success of newly developed products throughout the year, helped VF break the $3 billion mark in annual sales for the first time in the company's history.

Following that record year, Lawrence Pugh handed down his role as president to M. J. McDonald, while still remaining at the company's helm as chairman and chief executive. Together, the two led VF through a year of rejuvenated jeans sales, with the exception of the Girbaud division, which began experiencing a decline. Also engineered in 1993 were the acquisitions of Nutmeg Industries, Inc. and the H. H. Cutler Company, both of which helped VF become a leading supplier of licensed sports apparel. VF's Bassett-Walker division actually benefited from these acquisitions as well, as it became the main supplier of knitwear for the two companies, and therefore increased its output for the year.

1994 was a year characterized by cooperative endeavors between different VF divisions and other well-known companies. For example, H. H. Cutler teamed up with Disney to create playwear featuring characters from the movie *The Lion King,* all of which sold out quickly and prompted the creation of similar items the following year featuring *Pocahontas.* Also, H. H. Cutler and Healthtex combined to introduce a Fisher-Price brand of children's discount clothing. Jantzen worked with Nike, Inc. to develop a new line of performance swimwear, while Nutmeg readied itself to launch some of its 1995 sports apparel under the Lee Sport name.

Unique projects and ideas such as those above, coupled with VF's conservative financial strategies and high level of brand name recognition by consumers, enabled the company to break the $5 billion mark in annual sales for 1995. At the end of the year, Pugh once again handed down one of his roles at VF to

M. J. McDonald, who added the responsibilities of being chief executive officer to his list of duties as company president. Pugh remained with the company as its chairman.

Entering the late 1990s, a good majority of VF's products were competing in mature markets, which dictated that the company's future growth was contingent on deriving ways to gain market share. In VF's favor was the evolving trend in many businesses toward dressing more casually at work. But rather than rely solely on such consumer trends and buying patterns, VF began actively formulating new methods to reach consumers and provide them with the best customer service possible, while at the same time increasing name brand recognition. For example, the company began testing a new interactive touch-screen computer program in stores called the Lee Fit-Finder, aimed at helping customers determine the best sizes and styles for their individual body types.

The company continued focusing on a combination of new product development, cost reduction, and inventory management measures to further strengthen relationships with retailers and enable the firm to respond more effectively to market needs. VF's goal had long been to provide the right styles and quantities of products at the right prices on the retail shelf at all times. The ability to meet this goal will be a key determinant in the success of VF's future activities, as it strives to maintain its leadership position, build market share, and increase share-holder value. With products available in almost every type of distribution channel, and with a history of being extremely adept in reacting to industry occurrences in positive and productive manners, VF Corporation entered the end of the century with potential for continued growth and success.

Principal Divisions

Bassett-Walker; H. H. Cutler; Marithé & François Girbaud N. A.; Healthtex; JanSport; Jantzen; Lee Apparel; Nutmeg; Red Kap; Vanity Fair; Wrangler; VF Intimate Apparel—Europe; VF Jeanswear—Europe; VF Asia/Pacific.

Further Reading

Agins, Teri, ''Bottom Line: Once-Hot Lee Jeans Lost Their Allure In a Hipper Market,'' *The Wall Street Journal,* March 7, 1991.

Eklund, Christopher S., and Christine Dugas, ''Lee + Wrangler + Rustler = A New Blue-Jeans King,'' *Business Week,* August 11, 1986.

Ozzard, Janet, ''Mackey McDonald: Positioning VF for the Next Century,'' *Daily News Record,* April 25, 1996, p. 5.

People, Product, Pride . . . The History and Heritage of VF Corporation and Its Divisions, Wyomissing, Penn.: VF Corporation, 1991.

—Sandy Schusteff
—updated by Laura E. Whiteley

Virco Manufacturing Corporation

2027 Harpers Way
Torrance, California 90501
U.S.A.
(310) 533-0474
Fax: (310) 538-0114

Public Company
Incorporated: 1950
Employees: 2,550
Sales: $224 million (1995)
Stock Exchanges: American
SICs: 2531 Public Building & Related Furniture; 2522
   Office Furniture Except Wood

Virco Manufacturing Corporation is the country's largest producer of furniture for the classroom, with a market share of approximately 50 percent. Virco is also engaged in the manufacture of chairs, folding tables, computer-support furniture, wood and steel office furniture, and juvenile furniture. Virco's products can be found in meeting rooms, schools, restaurants, hotels, government facilities, convention centers, or military installations throughout the United States. A fully integrated company, all furniture fabrication, welding, assembling, and shipping is done by Virco.

Early History

Virco was founded by two brothers named Julian and Philip Virtue. The Virtue boys had dropped out of high school in the early 1920s and had at first found work at the S and M Lamp Company in Los Angeles. Industrious and ambitious young men, however, Julian and Philip began conducting experiments with chrome plating in the backyard of their family home in their spare time. Together they successfully chrome plated furniture at first for friends and family and then for local businesses. Soon they quit their jobs at the lamp works in order to focus on starting their own chrome-plating company.

In August 1926, their U.S. Plating Company opened for business. Owned and operated by the Virtue brothers, the company grew rapidly during the late 1920s. By the end of the decade business was so good that the owners moved from a small shack in their own backyard to a plant near downtown Los Angeles. Within a short time, the business also outgrew this facility, and the company once again relocated to a larger factory on West Century Boulevard.

Unlike most U.S. businesses, the U.S. Plating Company continued to grow during the Great Depression of the 1930s. While many firms went bankrupt due to an overextended line of credit, and others failed because of diminishing customers, the operation run by the Virtue brothers found a niche specializing in providing custom nickel plating for other furniture manufacturers. Julian recognized, however, that it would not only be advantageous, but more lucrative, for the company to begin manufacturing furniture on its own. Although Philip was initially reluctant to take such a large risk at the height of the Depression, with the possibility of losing their standing customers, he was finally convinced by his brother's enthusiasm and long-standing business acumen. By the mid-1930s, the company was making furniture for beauty parlors, producing upholstered tubular steel chrome-plated chairs for business offices, and dinette sets for restaurants and family dining rooms. Revenues continued to increase and, as the country began to pull itself out of the economic hardships, the company garnered for itself a reputation as one of the best run businesses in the city of Los Angeles.

The company continued to grow during the Second World War. When America entered the conflict in December 1941, the U.S. military was almost wholly unprepared to engage in a war both in Europe and the Pacific. Although preparations to train, feed, house, transport, and arm millions of soldiers for both theaters began immediately, it was many months before America was ready to fight the enemy. One of the most pressing needs of all was furniture. The Navy needed furniture for its dining halls and sleeping quarters on all its ships, and the Army and Marine Corps needed bunkbeds for its barracks throughout military installations across the United States. From southern

California to Georgia, the U.S. Plating Company supplied the armed services with thousands upon thousands of bunkbeds. A steady demand from the military during the course of the war dramatically increased the company's revenues.

The Postwar Years and a New Company

The years after World War II seemed very promising for the U.S. Plating Company. Revenues continued to increase because of sustaining contracts with the United States government to supply furniture for military installations. In addition, the company added corporate accounts to its growing list of furniture clients in the Los Angeles metropolitan area. Yet suddenly, and without explanation, at the height of U.S. Plating Company's success, Julian Virtue left the firm. Some speculated that the brothers had fought, but neither Philip nor Julian ever mentioned such a disagreement.

Whatever the reason for his departure from U.S. Plating Company, Julian Virtue was determined to establish his own business. In 1950, after having left the firm, he formed the Virco Manufacturing Company. Not wanting to start completely from scratch, Julian Virtue decided to purchase an existing business, the Slauson Aircraft Company. Virtue had become acquainted with Slauson Aircraft during the war when that company had been manufacturing cartridge casings for the Army and Marines. After the war had ended and the entire industrial base of the United States had reverted to a peacetime economy, management at Slauson had made the decision to produce furniture for primary and secondary schools. When Julian acquired the company in 1950, Slauson Aircraft's sole client was the Los Angeles School Board, an important contract in the school furniture industry.

Not content to manufacture school furniture exclusively, largely due to the fact that the sale of school furniture was dictated by the seasonal scheduling of each academic year, Virtue initiated an aggressive and comprehensive diversification program. The company's product line soon expanded to include such items as folding chairs and folding tables, which quickly brought in ever-increasing revenues. At the same time, in concert with his diversification program, Virtue decided to expand the company's markets to include not only the greater Los Angeles metropolitan area but customers throughout the entire country. Within a very brief period of time, Virco had established a nationwide distribution network for its product line. Still, its founder was not quite satisfied with the company's sales volume. In 1954 he acquired Dunn Furniture Company in Conway, Arkansas, which significantly enhanced Virco's ability to manufacture its product line in both the eastern and southern regions of the United States, while at the same time reducing its shipping and freight costs to better serve its growing customer list.

During this time, Julian Virtue's son, Robert, began working for the company during summer vacations and school holidays while in high school and college. Robert was dedicated to assisting his father in managing the company. After graduating from the University of California in 1954 and serving two years in the U.S. Navy, the younger Virtue returned to the firm and starting working on a full-time basis. Like his father in many respects, particularly in his ambition, Robert Virtue soon worked his way up the management ladder by learning all the necessary ingredients of the company's success, including marketing, strategic planning, accounting, operations, and management.

By the beginning of the 1960s, Robert Virtue had become an essential part of his father's management team at Virco. The father and son leadership duo led the company into ever-expanding markets for its educational furniture, including large regions in the Southern part of the United States. By the time Virco was taken public in 1964, and listed its stock in the over-the-counter market, sales hot shot up dramatically. Yet high labor costs and intense competition within the furniture industry, especially in office and educational furniture, reduced the company's profit margins during the late years of the decade. In order to remain competitive, the father and son team had to think of a way for Virco to lower its costs, while simultaneously increase its market share in office and educational furniture.

Expansion and Acquisition in the 1970s and 1980s

Julian and Robert Virtue decided to open a plant in San Luis, Mexico, directly across the border from Yuma, Arizona. Opened amid much fanfare in 1971, the new facility not only significantly decreased Virco's labor costs while providing jobs to Mexican workers. Planned, constructed, and operated according to the "twin plant" or *maquiladora* concept, as it is called in Spanish, the endeavor was jointly sponsored by the United States and Mexican federal governments. The terms of agreement allowed American companies to build and operate manufacturing facilities in Mexico, paying native employees a fair wage, and then importing either finished products or fabricated parts on a duty-free basis. The *maquiladora* employees performed labor-intensive tasks which not only enabled Virco to retain its competitive pricing edge in markets throughout the United States, but also helped to substantially increase the company's profitability and drive up its price per share on the stock market. By the end of the decade, Virco had grown large enough to gain listing on the American Stock Exchange.

During the 1980s, Virco implemented a strategic plan to increase the manufacturing capacity of plants in California, Arkansas, and Mexico. At the company's headquarters in Torrance, California, management concentrated on expanding its production per day of a wide variety of chairs and educational furniture. At the Dunn Furniture plant in Conway, Arkansas, management decided not only to improve its manufacturing capacity, but to transform the facility into a major packing and distribution center. Virco's plant in San Luis, Mexico, was also thriving, and additional improvements to the facility allowed the company to hire a total of nearly 1,200 *maquiladora* workers.

In addition to these operational improvements, in 1984 Virco purchased a large plant owned by the Haywood-Wakefield Corporation in Newport, Tennessee. An old, well-established manufacturer of traditional furniture line products, Haywood-Wakefield had fallen on hard times and gone out of business. Julian Virtue, now retired but still active on a day-to-day basis and serving as chairman emeritus to his son Robert's position as president and chief executive officer, had known of the demise of Haywood-Wakefield through his extensive network of contacts within the furniture industry. In providing his son Robert with advice, Julian Virtue suggested that Virco acquire a part of the manufacturing facilities Haywood-Wakefield had put up for sale. The extensive plant at Newport significantly increased Virco's production capacity, and the facility began to manufacture melamine plastic chair seats and backs almost immediately. Employment at the plant rose quickly, to approximately 200 workers, and soon the Newport operation was sending its products to Los Angeles and Conway, Arkansas, for final assembly.

The 1990s and Beyond

During the early 1990s, Virco continued growing in an increasingly competitive market. Net sales from all its products increased from $191 million in 1992 to $205 million in 1993, with educational sales representing 53 percent of corporate revenues. Management attributed its success to an aggressive pricing strategy combined with the improvement of on-time delivery of customer orders. During the same time, the company moved its western region operations into a larger manufacturing and warehousing facility in Torrance, California, allowing a significant reduction in materials handling and distribution expenses. This consolidation involved a discontinuation of two facilities in the greater Los Angeles area. Also during the same period, Virco's manufacturing facility in Conway, Arkansas, was expanded twice, specifically to increase the company's capacity to produce hard plastic components for various lines of its furniture. In February 1993, Virco's San Luis, Mexico, manufacturing operation was damaged by fire. Although the damage was minor, and repairs were completed not long afterward, management at the company decided in 1995 to put the facility up for sale in order to improve its profit margins while reducing operating expenses.

In 1995, Virco reported net sales of $224 million. The company introduced a new line of computer furniture that became very popular, as well as a new product line of lightweight tables and chairs. Sales of educational furniture continued to increase, and Virco's domination of the market seemed a foregone conclusion for the near future. Although the company moved from selling its shares on the over-the-counter market to the American Stock Exchange in 1977, the Virtue family still retained a major interest and consequently continues to manage the company in the mid-1990s.

Principal Subsidiaries

Virsan SA de CV.

Principal Divisions

Torrance Division; Conway Division.

Further Reading

Allegrezza, Ray, "Home Work: Convergence of Living And Office Space Brings Innovative New Furniture," *Home Furnishing Network,* May 6, 1996, p. 18.

Allegrezza, Ray, "Rx for Little Guys: Adapt or Perish," *Home Furnishing Network,* June 24, 1996, p. 15.

Finegan, Robert, *California Furniture, The Craft and the Artistry,* Los Angeles: Windsor Publications, Inc., 1986.

Hill, Dawn, "Neat Work Habits," *Home Furnishing Network,* May 6, 1996, pp. 20–23.

"More Gainers Than Decliners," *Home Furnishing Network,* March 21, 1996, pp. 12–17.

O'Brian, Bridget, "Insiders Snap Up Furniture Firms' Stock," *The Wall Street Journal,* August 28, 1996, p. C1(E).

"White Elephant to the Rescue," *Business Month,* September 1990, p. 80.

—Thomas Derdak

W. H. Brady Co.

P. O. Box 571
Milwaukee, Wisconsin 53201-0571
U.S.A.
(414) 358-6600
Fax: (414) 438-6951
Internet: http://www.whbrady.com

Public Company
Incorporated: 1939
Employees: 2,400
Sales: $314.36 million (1995)
Stock Exchanges: NASDAQ
SICs: 2891 Adhesives & Sealants; 2672 Coated &
   Laminated Paper, Not Elsewhere Classified; 3999
   Manufacturing Industries, Not Elsewhere Classified

W. H. Brady Co. is an international manufacturer of coated films and identification labels, signs, and related products for the global industrial, commercial, governmental, public utility, medical, semiconductor, and computer markets. In 1995 Brady was the ninth-largest adhesives and sealants manufacturer in the United States, and its Industrial Products Division was the fortieth-largest miscellaneous manufacturing industry.

Brady's expertise lies in three interrelated operations: creating and applying coatings, such as adhesives, to cloth, paper, metals, and plastic films; converting these coated materials into products such as industrial labels and tape products through lamination, printing, die cutting, perforating, and other processes; and designing lettering machines, computer software, portable printers, and other equipment. In the mid-1990s, Brady manufactured and marketed roughly thirty thousand products, ranging from wire identification markers, medical and splicing tape, factory safety signs, adhesive letters, and bar code labels to data collection equipment, portable label printers, data storage tapes, and computer floppy disk supplies and components such as wipes, springs, and reinforcement rings.

Brady comprises three main global groups: the Identification Systems and Specialty Tapes Group, which consists of Brady Precision Tape Co., Coated Products Division, and Industrial Products Division; the Graphics Group, Brady's safety and facility identification division; and the Seton Group, Brady's direct marketing operation for selling products to 1.5 million end users. Brady's prominent customers have included NASA, Boeing, Hollywood's film industry, IBM, PepsiCo, General Electric, and the Alaskan oil pipeline. In addition to U.S. operations in Wisconsin and Connecticut, in 1996 Brady maintained manufacturing or customer service operations in fifteen foreign countries including England, South Korea, Germany, Canada, Australia, Italy, France, and Japan. In 1996 these international operations accounted for about 44 percent of Brady's annual sales.

Origins, 1914

W. H. Brady traces its origins to founder W. H. (Will) Brady's early career as a salesman for an Ohio remembrance advertising firm that manufactured calendars, yardsticks, and other promotional items on which advertising messages were printed. After turning down a promotion to the company's New York office, in 1914 Brady founded the W. H. Brady Company in Eau Claire, Wisconsin, Brady's hometown. His first product was promotional photographic calendars sold to offices and stores, but he soon followed with elaborate color displays for ice cream parlors, printed glass beer signs, point-of-purchase displays, and pre-billboard roadside advertising.

After a decade and a half of growth, the stock market crash of 1929 and the depression that followed drove many of Brady's customers out of business, forcing him to sell his home and, with his parents' support, enroll in college. In the midst of this crisis, an unusual promotional gimmick saved the firm. Candy-maker Webster's Famous Fudge included in its fudge packages a small, paperboard card that contained rows of perforated circles, each of which concealed a prize number. When customers exposed a winning number by pushing out one of the circles on the card, they won four free candy bars. The product fit neatly into Brady's printing, die-cutting, and laminating capabilities, and, aided by the cross-country marketing efforts of Will Brady's oldest son Fred, Brady-manufactured push (or punch) cards, as they were

<h2>Company Perspectives:</h2>

Find a niche and work to own it. Risk trying the untried. View every customer as your ultimate employer. Above all, stick to it.

called, were soon being used to sell everything from cigars and cigarettes to beer and turkeys. Throughout the 1930s and 1940s, Brady manufactured millions of push cards and became their largest producer in the United States. In 1939 Brady was incorporated and declared that its new purpose was to carry on the business of printers, publishers, and painters of advertising matter and, in general, to engage in advertising businesses of all kinds.

Postwar New Product Lines

As World War II erupted, Will Brady yielded leadership to his two sons, Fred and Bill Jr., who from 1942 to 1955 shared direction of the company. The war brought shortages in the paperboard Brady used to make push cards, which was only partially offset by stopgap contracts such as printing morale booklets for the Red Cross. In 1944, however, while working at Milwaukee electrical control manufacturer Cutler-Hammer, Bill Jr. discovered the wire marker card—an adhesive card from which numbered cloth strips could be pulled and wrapped around electrical wires for identification purposes. The self-adhesive (or "pressure-sensitive") tape technology on which the wire marker card was based was still relatively new, but there was an urgent need for a clear and easy way to identify the ever-more dense masses of wiring being installed in ships, planes, and other military equipment. Moreover, the printing, die-cutting, and laminating processes for the paperboard backings on which the wire markers were placed were the same ones Brady used to make push cards. The new Brady markers were quickly embraced by the war industries; among their uses was the identification of wiring for the Manhattan Project construction work.

Sensing an untapped market, Brady began sending its four-page sales brochure to electrical manufacturers around the country and was quickly bombarded by inquiries. It began improving its markers' flexibility and applications by adapting them to customers needs: it made wire markers easier to remove from their backing, for example, and improved the type of material used for the backing itself. After the war's end, wire markers continued to eclipse push cards as Brady's main product, and Brady began performing the typesetting for the marker's label, offered new marker sizes and numbering systems, and introduced new marker types—from circular labels and Underwriters Laboratories seals of approval to small safety signs, pipe and conduit markers, and foil-, epoxy-, and vinyl-based markers that could resist oil, acid, and temperature extremes. Brady's first Caution and Danger safety signs appeared in 1949, and Brady's fallout shelter and radiation hazard signs enjoyed brisk sales during the 1950s and 1960s when the threat of nuclear weapons and radiation was at a peak.

At the same time, Brady was developing proprietary machines that could laminate, die cut, print, and cut to length in a single operation, boosting production volumes and cutting unit production costs. Because it was inexpensive for Brady simply to mail potential customers samples of its markers, it was not until after 1950 that it developed a national sales force. By the late 1940s Brady nevertheless claimed distributors in over 125 cities, most of which were local outlets of national electrical firms. By 1967 the two hundred distributors Brady claimed in the early 1950s had grown to more than one thousand.

National Presence, 1950s

By the early 1950s, Brady had become a national presence and chose "identification specialists" as the way to describe its specialized product niche to the increasingly interested industrial consumer. In desperate need of more production space, it moved permanently from Chippewa Falls, Wisconsin, to a new facility in Milwaukee in late 1952. The move hastened the pace of new product development, which averaged one new product every one to two months. The thirteen products listed on the company's letterhead in 1954, for example, had grown to twenty-one by 1956, and between 1944 and 1969 alone Brady introduced more than eighty new products in a variety of materials, sizes, and colors. By the late 1960s, Brady was offering ten thousand stock items in thirty-five distinct product groups.

Brady's 1953 introduction of Blue Streak Release—an adhesive so effective that labels and markers could be dramatically increased in size without loss of adhesion—was another major step forward in Brady's labeling capability. It also led Brady into a new product group—coatings—that would eventually form a crucial component of its product line and signaled Brady's desire to control as many stages of the label production process as it could. To manufacture its coatings, Brady engineers designed and built proprietary machinery that was used to produce a vinyl tape product suitable for making warning stripes for factory floors. Brady could now free itself of its traditional dependency on 3M, its major tape supplier, and by supplying its own tape could now determine the characteristics, price, and quality of the materials it used in production.

In 1955 profits surpassed the $1 million mark for the first time, and two years later Brady—with Bill Jr. now alone at the helm—expanded into another new product line: nameplates. Thousands of consumer products, from power tools to washing machines, required plates that identified the manufacturer or displayed ratings or instructions. The sale of its aluminum and polyester nameplates (Quik-Plates and Poly-Plates, respectively) gave Brady a new niche in another lucrative market.

The same year, yet another innovation, the Markermatic automatic wire marker application system, solidified Brady's position in the expanding identification products industry. When loaded with a wire marker card, Markermatic automatically peeled back the card's adhesive starter strip, picked off an individual marker, wrapped it around the wire, and returned for the next pass—at a rate of one thousand markers an hour. The machine proved to be a substantial source of lease income for Brady while simultaneously promoting the adoption of its wire marker brands. As Bill Jr. later remarked, "Markermatic made us king of the hill in our industry. Customers perceived us as the leader." Quickly capitalizing on the product's success, Brady followed with Printermatic (an automatic label printer), Wrap-matic (a device for wrapping tape around cylindrical objects), and Aisle Markermatic (a machine, resembling a floor polisher, for the precision-marking of factory lanes).

Overseas Expansion, 1960s

With the establishment of Brady Canada on the outskirts of Toronto in 1958, Brady moved into the international marketplace, which within forty years would generate nearly half its annual sales. In the following years Brady added a nameplate manufacturing operation in Mexico (Uquillas-Brady) and a marketing/distribution operation in England (Simpson-Brady), which by 1962 had evolved into Brady England, Brady's first overseas facility. Although Brady claimed to have no strategic plan for its foreign expansion, a pattern nevertheless emerged. It first established a sales presence in the new foreign market, followed it by building a warehouse to maintain stock for the market, graduated to a leased manufacturing plant managed by local staff, and finally moved on to a new factory owned by a full-fledged subsidiary.

In 1966 Brady opened Brady Europa, a warehouse/factory in Belgium, and in the early 1970s, it bought out its ailing Australian distributorship to form Brady Australia. A formal international division was established in 1972 when Brady Sweden and Brady Germany joined the fold. Discovering that its foreign operations tended to thrive only when it established a subsidiary, rather than merely a distributorship, Brady opened a combined sales/warehouse/factory as Brady France in 1980. By the end of the year, Brady's international subsidiaries were accounting for 20 percent of the company's annual sales—the level at which they stayed for years, despite the addition of Brady Japan in 1987.

The 1960s and 1970s were a time of both continued growth and difficult transitions. Brady's new microscopic, fireproof component markers were being launched into orbit on Gemini space missions, and Brady had presciently seen the potential of the computer market as early as 1962 when it began selling computer-printable wire markers.

Before the end of the decade Brady was manufacturing labels, markers, drafting aids, and keypunch-hole correction seals specifically for the still-infant computer industry. Annual sales broke the $10 million mark in 1968, driven by a robust annual growth rate of 18 percent between 1953 and 1969, and Brady's policy of plowing profits back into new product development continued to reap benefits. By the 1990s, Brady was investing roughly four percent of annual revenue into new product R & D, and its expectations for such innovations were high. In 1989, for example, Bill Brady Jr. announced that he expected new products to account for 25 percent of Brady sales every year.

Corporate Reorganization for the 1970s

Brady's hierarchic management structure was meanwhile showing signs of obsolescence, and its sales force, overwhelmed by the sheer number of products Brady now offered, could only show a limited part of the company's product line to each customer. Partly as a result of these problems, in 1971

Brady experienced a decline in sales for the first time since the wartime years of push cards and morale booklets.

Brady's answer to its troubled business structure was to scrap it in favor of a group of individual divisions, each focusing on a specific product line and market: the Nameplate Division, the Data Processing Division, and the Industrial Products Division, each with its own sales, marketing, and manufacturing units. Rather than conform to a top-down corporate plan, each division manager established his or her own pace for the division, which operated virtually as an independent company.

As the company adjusted to its new structure in the 1970s, product innovation forged ahead. Circuit tracers, hot stampers, nameplates made of specialized materials, and portable wire marker books were added to the Brady catalog in the 1970s. More importantly, typewriter lift-off correction tape and BOT/EOT markers for detecting the beginning and end of recorded data on computer tapes provided Brady with two lucrative new markets to pursue, and it was soon a major player in both. In 1977 Brady unveiled its LiteTouch membrane switches, in which electricity-conducting inks and adhesives enabled consumers to turn on microwave ovens, dishwashers, and sewing machines with a touch of the finger. Ironically, given Bill Brady Jr.'s disdain for government intervention, major federal legislation in the 1970s helped to further boost demand for Brady products. The Occupational Safety and Health Act of 1970 imposed a series of regulations regarding signage, safety warnings, and hazard identification in the workplace, and a related law in 1977 required all trucks carrying hazardous materials to sport high-visibility warning signs. By 1980, Brady had climbed past the $50 million sales plateau.

Not all of Brady's new product gambles bore fruit. In 1969 it introduced Phodar, a method for manufacturing printed circuit boards using dry resist techniques rather than the traditional liquid resist method. It had to abandon the product in 1972, however, when DuPont's competing brand won the battle for market share and Brady's engineers were unable to overcome Phodar's poor shelf life limitations. The same year Brady unveiled Kalograph, an instant, one-step label maker that promised to enable customers to create their own custom industrial labels. The product's high cost, however, combined with its inability to create black lettering and its labels' tendency to fade in sunlight, undermined Kalograph's early promise, and in 1979 Bill Jr. finally pulled it from the marketplace, making it the most expensive failure in Brady's history.

Growth in the 1980s

After the lull in acquisitions of the 1970s, Brady began shopping for potential targets again in the 1980s. Small- to mid-sized, privately owned businesses with stock product lines and technologies similar to Brady's were scrutinized, and between 1981 and 1987 Brady acquired the Weckesser Corporation, a manufacturer of plastic wiring accessories (later sold); the M. C. Davis Co., a maker of miniature and subminiature coils; the MPV Co., a manufacturer of hard protective coatings; Browncor International, a distributor of shipping and packaging supplies; Revere Products, a direct marketer of maintenance products; and, most importantly, the Seton Name Plate Corporation, a manufacturer of nameplates and a business-to-business direct marketer, established in 1956. The Seton acquisition allowed Brady to supplement its traditional niche-focused sales and distribution network with blanket mail order sales through Seton's industrial catalog, which in 1988 alone reached eight million potential customers. Brady soon was establishing Seton subsidiaries in England (1985), Canada (1986), and Germany (1988).

Now operating six domestic divisions and eight international subsidiaries, Brady's annual sales grew 350 percent through the 1980s to $175 million, and profits soared past the $10 million mark. In 1984 Brady became a private/public hybrid when it sold 500,000 shares of nonvoting stock to avoid the estate taxes due when Bill Brady Jr.'s heirs inherited his stake in the company. That moment came in 1988 when Bill Jr., the Brady Co.'s second founder, died, and a longtime Brady insider, Paul Gengler, took over direction of the company. Brady retired its family-run reputation permanently in 1994 by hiring Katherine M. Hudson, a vice-president at Eastman Kodak, to lead it into the 21st century. An aggressive, hands-on executive with a ready sense of humor, Hudson announced her intention to quadruple annual sales to $1 billion, improve earnings, and exploit new opportunities for joint ventures, acquisitions, and geographic expansion, particularly in such new markets as Italy, Brazil, and the Far East.

A year into her tenure, Hudson announced that Brady's far-flung operations would be reorganized into three international divisions: the Identification Systems and Specialty Tapes Group, the Signmark Group (renamed Graphics Group in 1996), and the Seton Group. A year later Brady acquired Varitronic Systems, a U.S. manufacturer of high-tech printing systems, and two British firms: TechPrint Systems Limited, a printer producer, and the Hirol Company, a manufacturer of printing systems and die-cut parts for electronics, telecommunications, and medical testing markets. Brady also sold off its nameplate and medical wound care operations to concentrate on its core businesses and entered into a joint venture with a South Korean marker equipment firm. It was also continuing to push the technological envelope of labeling and coating product design. Between 1980 and 1996 it introduced bar code software; a fully automated labeling machine for circuit boards and electrical components; and the Bradywriter printer, which allowed customers to print their own marker legends in house. It also began offering an express custom sign-making service; computer systems to exactly match customers color samples; installation, training, and contract services for Brady products; and integrated product groups that widened the number of labels and markers customers could choose from.

Principal Subsidiaries

Brady USA; Seton; Brady Precision Tape Co.; Varitronics Systems, Inc.; W. H. Brady, Inc. (Canada); Seton, Inc. (Canada); W. H. Brady Co. Ltd. (England); W. H. Brady (Germany); Seton Limited (England); W. H. Brady S.A.R.L. (France); Seton GmbH (Germany); Nippon Brady K.K. (Japan); Seton S.A. (France); W. H. Brady Pty. Ltd. (Australia); Seton Australia Pty., Ltd. (Australia); W. H. Brady, N. V. (Belgium); W. H. Brady Co. (Hong Kong); W. H. Brady, N.V. (Italy); Seton Italia Srl (Italy); W. H. Brady Pty. Ltd. (New Zealand); TechPrint Systems Limited (TechPress II Limited) (United Kingdom); W. H. Brady Pte Ltd. (Singapore); W. H. Brady Co. (South Korea); Brady AB (Sweden); Brady Financial Co.

Further Reading

"CEO Interview—Katherine M. Hudson, W. H. Brady Co.," *Wall Street Transcript Digest,* May 8, 1995.

Grube, Lorri, "Katherine M. Hudson, Chief Executive," *Chief Executive,* January/February 1995, p. 29.

Gurda, John, *Sticking to It: A History of the W. H. Brady Co., 1914–1989,* Milwaukee: W. H. Brady Co., 1989.

Holley, Paul, "Global Spending Slows Earnings at W. H. Brady," *Business Journal Serving Greater Milwaukee,* May 18, 1996, p. 7.

Joshi, Pradnya, "W. H. Brady Labels Its Fiscal Year Exceptional," *Milwaukee Journal Sentinel,* September 14, 1995, p. 1.

——, "W. H. Brady Wants Growth to Continue," *Milwaukee Journal Sentinel,* August 14, 1995, p. 3.

Kirchen, Rich, "With New Owner, Former Brady Unit Sticks to Growth Track," *Business Journal Serving Greater Milwaukee,* April 8, 1995, p. 7.

Shapiro, Joshua, "An Unusual Climb at Kodak Wins Her a Place at the Top," *New York Times,* January 30, 1991, p. 8.

—Paul S. Bodine

Waldenbooks®

Walden Book Company Inc.

100 Phoenix Drive
Ann Arbor, Michigan 48106
U.S.A.
(313) 913-1100

Wholly Owned Subsidiary of Borders Group, Inc.
Incorporated: 1933
Employees: 450
Sales: $963.4 million (1995)
SICs: 5912 Books, Periodicals & Newspapers; 5942
   Book Stores

Walden Book Company Inc., a subsidiary of the Borders Group, Inc., is a leading U.S. mall-based book retailer, with over 1,035 Waldenbooks stores located in all 50 states and the District of Columbia. To offset a trend of falling attendance in malls in the 1990s, Waldenbooks was introducing its own version of a superstore during this time, establishing such outlets as Waldensoftware, Waldenkids, and Waldenbooks & More across the country in suburban areas. Despite downsizing and restructuring in 1994 and 1995, Waldenbooks has continued to dominate the book world and when combined with its sibling, Borders Books & Music, the two booksellers were second only to Barnes & Noble in sales in 1995 and gaining quickly.

Company Origins

Today's Waldenbooks traveled through many incarnations since its origins in March 1933. As the Great Depression raged and forced banks to close their doors, Lawrence W. Holt and Melvin T. Kafka bravely founded a company in New York City, one they believed would help people cope with the effects of the Depression. Specifically, Holt and Kafka's new company lent popular books for three cents a day, saving people the cost of purchasing. Since most people needed some release and entertainment during that time, Holt and Kafka's book rental libraries seemed to be a proposition that couldn't lose.

A former sales manager for Simon & Schuster, Holt was no stranger to the publishing and bookselling industry. Kafka and

Holt opened several rental libraries within major department stores in the northeast, beginning with Read's in Bridgeport, Maine; Filene's in Boston; and G. Fox Department Stores in Hartford, Connecticut. As interest grew, the partners expanded and dozens of rental libraries sprouted throughout city shopping districts on the East Coast.

By 1948, there were 250 rental libraries doing a brisk business, as well as many leased book departments in stores selling books. This year the company relocated its 15 employees from New York to a new headquarters at 179 Ludlow Street in Stamford, Connecticut, closer to its many outlets.

From Library to Bookseller

In the early 1950s, cheap paperback books became the rage. Publishers, able to produce in mass quantities, could afford to sell paperbacks for as little as 25 cents apiece. In turn, demand mushroomed and Hoyt and Kakfa considered converting their rental libraries to retail outlets. Though the partners' plans to take the company retail hadn't been finalized, Melvin Kafka decided he was ready to step aside and retire. Selling his half of the burgeoning company to his partner, Holt then charged full-speed ahead with changing empire.

By 1960, Walden's leased book departments numbered 150 throughout the United States, in addition to its hundreds of rental libraries. Two years later, the company went forward with its retail plans and opened its first "Waldenbooks" store in the Northway Mall in Pittsburgh, Pennsylvania. The company name, incidentally, was Hoyt's respectful nod to Henry David Thoreau, as Hoyt was born and raised near Walden Pond in Massachusetts. Hoyt had no idea just how widespread the Waldenbooks name would become in the coming decades. The flagship Waldenbooks turned out to be a significant departure for Hoyt and the company in two ways. First, focus was on selling rather than renting or loaning books, and second, the outlet was located in a suburban area mall, signalling a move away from the downtown shopping districts which had always been Walden's bread and butter. By 1969 Waldenbooks had opened 53 retail stores and maintained 71 leased outlets in major departments stores, bringing in sales of $4.4 million. The company's phenomenal success brought the attention of larger companies, and Walden was acquired by Carter Hawley Hale (CHH), a retail conglomerate based in Los Angeles. Following in his father's footsteps, Russell L. Hoyt became CEO, while Hoyt Sr. maintained his role as chairman of the board.

Rapid Expansion in the 1970s

The 1970s were a time of extraordinary growth for Waldenbooks, with new stores opening around the country at the rate of one per week. By 1974, the company had outgrown its corporate offices on Ludlow street and began looking for a more suitable location in Stamford. The next year, Russell L. Hoyt stepped down as CEO and was replaced by Arthur Coons, an executive with parent company Carter Hawley Hale. Still looking for a new corporate headquarters, Walden set its sights on North Stamford, a mostly residential area. Picking up the option to buy an eight-acre plot on High Ridge Road, the company initiated the purchase in November 1976. Yet this proved a Herculean task, complicated by strict zoning laws which allowed for few area businesses and none above a point called Bull's Head, where the desired land tract was located. In the meantime, Waldenbooks had opened its 500th store in 1978. The Bull's Head zoning war between Walden and the city of Stamford was finally settled after more than a year, and in March, the company triumphantly broke ground on High Ridge Road. Forty-five years after its founding, construction began on Walden's new 63,000-square-foot, two-and-a-half story corporate headquarters at 201 High Ridge Road, which became home to the company's 275 employees.

January 1979 marked a changing of the guard at Waldenbooks, as Harry T. Hoffman, formerly president at the Ingram Book Company, was named president. On the 29th of that month, the company moved into its spacious new headquarters in North Stamford. With stores in 44 states, Waldenbooks had become a force to be reckoned with in the bookselling industry. In 1980 alone, a stunning 90 new bookstores were opened and a new face appeared around the home office as Charles Cumello joined the company as a vice-president, controller, and, some believed, heir apparent to Harry Hoffman. The opening of a new store in Burlington, Vermont, the following year brought Waldenbooks its 735th store, and two other significant milestones, first, as the only national bookseller with stores in every U.S. state, and second, the industry's first centralized warehouse linked by a computerized cash register system to each of Waldenbook's retail outlets for ease in inventory control, ordering and sales reporting.

A New Parent in the 1980s

Celebrating its 50th anniversary in 1983, Walden was operating 830 stores nationwide and was continuing to thrive. However, during this heady time of corporate takeovers, Walden became once again drawn into the leveraged buyout fray. When its parent company, Carter Hawley Hale was pursued by another retail giant, The Limited, Inc., General Cinemas expressed an interest in Waldenbooks, making the CHH takeover less attractive to The Limited, Inc. Then General Cinemas pulled out and sold its option for Waldenbooks to Kmart, which made an offer of $295 million for the company's 845 bookstores in July 1983. In turn, Waldenbooks then made a purchase of its own, buying three New York-based Brentano's bookstores, which sold literary classics and related gift items.

Under the parentage of Kmart, Waldenbooks continued to expand. After years of limited, proprietary publishing from the marketing department, the company officially established its own imprint, Longmeadow Press, in 1984. Moreover, the first Waldenbooks & More outlet opened in 1985 along with the launch of a new full-service "mini-bookstore" called Reader's Market within Kmart stores. The 1,000th Waldenbooks store was opened in 1986, the year the company purchased Washington, D.C.'s historic Globe Bookstore. The following year, Waldenbooks acquired the Canadian chain of Cole's bookstores and also introduced "Waldensoftware" and "Waldenkids" retail outlets. By 1989, the company's home office could no longer house its ever-growing occupants. Complete renovation and construction of a 120,000-square-foot addition to the High Ridge Road facility was soon completed, consolidating all 750 employees under one roof.

As Waldenbooks entered its sixth decade, the company was still breaking new ground in the bookselling industry. Not only had Waldenbooks cracked $1 billion in sales, but Hoffman and his managers were clearly looking to the future and intending to dominate it with new retailing innovations. A new motto, "Waldenbooks—Your Guide to Great Reading," was coined, and in March 1990 the company launched its "Preferred Reader" program. The first of its kind, this "frequent buyer club" charged a small annual fee and rewarded patrons with points for every purchase, a ten percent discount on all merchandise, and $5 certificates for every $100 spent. Within months, Waldenbooks had signed up one million members and by the end of the year had approached the five million mark. At nearly the same time, the company had also installed a toll-free book ordering service, direct to its central warehouse in Nashville, Tennessee, making nearly 100,000 titles available to members of the Preferred Reader program for quick delivery. The latter move answered critics who chastised the chain for not carrying a larger variety of titles, particularly more serious literature.

Reorganizing in the 1990s

In 1991, Harry Hoffman retired and, as expected, Charles Cumello was named president and CEO of Waldenbooks. Claiming the company needed to get "back to basics," Cumello immediately set about focusing on books, drastically reducing sidelines such as toys, games, and videos at the company's 1,300 stores. The company also planned to open ten more Brentano's bookstores (not to be confused with the Midwestern Kroch's and Brentano's chain) and unveiled its first true "superstore" in Madison Heights, a suburb of Detroit.

As the superstore concept, in general, became more popular, large department stores anchoring malls lost business, causing mall stores to feel the pinch. Indeed, Waldenbooks found itself in tough times as mall-based stores accounted for only 20 percent of the burgeoning bookselling industry. In response, the company initiated another two firsts in 1992: the debut of its combination Waldenbooks/Waldenkids store, located in North Wales, Pennsylvania; as well as another superstore called Basset Book Shops, which opened in June in Stamford, to be followed by another 18 to 20 stores.

Change of another kind was fast approaching. In October 1992 Waldenbooks' parent company, Kmart, purchased Borders Books & Music, another growing bookstore chain. Though both Waldenbooks and Borders were to be operated as separate divisions of Kmart, overlap was inevitable as Kmart converted the Basset Book Shops into the more recognized and proven Borders Books & Music stores.

To combat stagnant sales in 1993, Waldenbooks began an extensive restructuring plan to close underperforming stores, bolster others, and seek out new opportunities for its combination and superstores. By 1994, Waldenbooks had targeted 187 underperforming stores of its 1,100 for closure. Of these, 74 ended business in 1994, another 45 or so were slated to close in 1995, 27 expected losses and the remainder were examined and believed capable of operating profitably. Despite the company's downsizing, it was still considered a stable "cash cow" in the bookselling industry. In May 1994, Waldenbooks, Borders Books & Music, and Planet Music, Inc. formed their own company called Borders Group, Inc. and became the second largest book retailer in the United States, with more units (though lower sales) than leader Barnes & Noble. In November, Bruce A. Quinnell, chief operating officer and executive vice-president, was promoted to president of Waldenbooks and the company announced it would vacate its long-time home office in Stamford to consolidate headquarters with Borders in Ann Arbor, Michigan, the next year.

In May 1995 Waldenbooks and Borders initiated a very successful public offering of 35.9 million shares for $14.50 each with proceeds going to Kmart Corporation. While its former parent initially retained 13 percent of the new company, the Borders Group announced an agreement in July to purchase the remaining 5.39 million shares held by Kmart; the transaction was completed in August. Through continued belt-tightening and the adoption of Borders' advanced computerized sales and order management system, Waldenbooks was poised for a resurgence in the mid-1990s. Sales for 1995 stood at $963.4 million, and Waldenbooks looked forward to a more bountiful year in 1996.

Principal Operating Units

Brentano's, Coopersmith's, Longmeadow Press, Waldenkids, Waldensoftware.

Further Reading

"After Nearly 50 Years, It's Time to Say, So Long, Stamford," *WW Today,* Summer 1995.
"Borders Group, Inc.—Booking Profits," *United States Equity Research (Retailing),* June 22, 1995.
Mutter, John, "Kmart Names Bruce Quinnell COO at Waldenbooks," *Publishers Weekly,* April 11, 1994, p. 15.
O'Brien, Maureen, "Charting the Course for Waldenbooks," *Publishers Weekly,* March 2, 1990, pp. 52–55.
O'Brien, Maureen, "Walden Claims One Million-Plus in Preferred Reader Program," *Publishers Weekly,* July 6, 1990, p. 11.
O'Brien, Maureen, "Walden's Harry Hoffman Takes Early Retirement," *Publishers Weekly,* March 22, 1991, p. 8.
O'Brien, Maureen, "An Interview with the New Chief at Waldenbooks," *Publishers Weekly,* July 5, 1991, pp. 30–31.
"Walden's Basset Division Joins Superstore Chase," *Publishers Weekly,* April 6, 1992, p. 11.

—Taryn Benbow-Pfalzgraf

![Washington Federal Savings logo]

Washington Federal, Inc.

**425 Pike Street
Seattle, Washington 98101
U.S.A.
(206) 624-7930
Fax: (206) 624-1893**

Public Company
Incorporated: 1917 as Ballard Savings and Loan
    Association
Employees: 411
Total Assets: $4.57 billion (1995)
Stock Exchanges: NASDAQ
SICs: 6712 Bank Holding Companies; 6035 Federal
    Savings Institutions

One of the largest savings and loan institutions in Washington, Washington Federal, Inc., operates as the one-bank holding company for Washington Federal Savings, a thrift that traces its roots to 1917. Washington Federal was formed by Washington Federal Savings in 1994 to effect a reorganization completed in February 1995, when Washington Federal Savings officially became a wholly owned subsidiary of Washington Federal. During the mid-1990s, Washington Federal operated 89 branch offices scattered throughout a five-state area surrounding its headquarters in Seattle, Washington, with 30 offices located in Washington, 20 offices located in Idaho, 21 offices in Oregon, 11 offices located in Utah, and seven offices located in Arizona. During its rise from a fledgling, state-chartered savings and loan association in 1917 to a formidable, federally chartered savings and loan in 1990s, Washington Federal carved a distinct niche for itself by remaining a traditional bank while others in its industry pursued frequently destructive business strategies. Throughout its history, Washington Federal achieved its consistent record of growth by obtaining funds primarily through savings deposits from the general public and by providing low-risk, single-family housing loans. In addition to its mainstay Washington Federal Savings subsidiary, Washington Federal also owned another subsidiary, First Insurance Agency, Inc., which provided general insurance services to the public.

Founded in the Late 1910s

Concurrent with the United States' entry into the First World War, the predecessor to Washington Federal entered into business itself, taking root in a bustling section of Seattle known as Ballard. The community of Ballard, like the city it was a part of, was growing by leaps and bounds. Its mostly Scandinavian residents and its predominate businesses of fishing and milling, added to the Northern European flavor of the community. Aside from providing the perfect setting for a largely immigrant, Scandinavian neighborhood, the fishing and milling industries supported many of Ballard's families and fueled the community's growth, creating the need for financial institutions, which historically had played in integral role in the development of burgeoning communities. One such financial institution, the Ballard Savings and Loan Association, was the predecessor organization to the Washington Federal of the 1990s.

Ballard Savings and Loan was organized on April 24, 1917, beginning business as a savings and loan institution to serve the surrounding and rapidly expanding milling and fishing community. The thrift was created to take deposits and provide single-family home loans, a mission it would pursue throughout its existence. Like the conservative residents that populated Ballard, Ballard Savings and Loan wavered little from its original objectives of the late 1910s, remaining steadfast to its original principles and business strategy into the 20th century as other financial institutions, and particularly savings and loans, adjusted their strategies to conform with prevailing banking trends. Ballard Savings and Loan's self-restrained and conservative business approach held it and its future parent company, Washington Federal, in good stead from the thrift's first days of business into the 1990s, enabling it to weather the numerous financial storms punctuating the 20th century. The steadfastness with which Ballard Savings and Loan Stuck to its principles was never more important than during the thrift's 12th year of business, when the collapse of the stock market touched off the decade-long Great Depression. In response to the economic chaos that ensued, Ballard Savings and Loan assuaged the fears of its customers by vowing to only collect interest on home loans and promising it would not move aggressively toward repossession as long as the property was kept in good repair and the taxes and assessments were paid. Before the financial panic of the 1930s gave way to the economic boom years of the 1940s, more than half of the country's financial institutions collapsed, financially ruined by the devastating affects of an anemic national economy. Ballard Savings and Loan, however, persevered and made it through the Great Depression without a loss to any of its depositors.

Aside from distinguishing itself as one of the minority of financial institutions to survive the Great Depression, Ballard Savings and Loan also joined the ranks of federally chartered financial institutions during the decade. In 1935, the state-charted savings and loan converted to a federal charter and adopted Ballard Federal Savings and Loan Association as its official corporate title. Revitalized economic conditions and population growth in the Seattle area during the 1940s and 1950s eliminated any lingering effects of the economically moribund 1930s, giving Ballard Federal Savings and Loan a two-decade-long opportunity to build on the pace of growth established during its inaugural decade. The thrift opened its first branch office in an outlying area of metropolitan Seattle, Lynnwood, Washington, in May 1958. The following month Ballard Federal Savings and Loan completed its first merger, the first of many to come.

Post-World War II Expansion

In June 1958, Ballard Federal Savings and Loan merged with Washington Federal Savings and Loan Association of Bothell, a deal that marked the departure of ''Ballard'' from the association's corporate title and the adoption of Washington Federal Savings and Loan Association as the new corporate title. The decision to take on Washington Federal as the new name for the thrift was a telling one, one made at the time because of the greater geographic stature the new title lent to the financial institution. In the wake of this signal deal, Washington Federal made good on the geographic presence its new name suggested and embarked on the most prolific era of growth in its history, beginning its rise with more than $35 million in assets. Much of the association's physical expansion was achieved through external means, rather than by establishing its own branches. Although Washington Federal continued to add its own branches from 1958 forward, the thrift's greatest geographic leaps were made overnight, with the quick stroke of a pen on a contract ceding Washington Federal control over an already established network of branches. But Washington Federal also expanded through internal means, opening its first downtown Seattle office in April 1961 and another branch office in nearby Rainier Valley two years later.

By the end of the 1960s, roughly one decade after assets amounted to $36 million, Washington Federal's assets had eclipsed the $100 million mark to reach $101 million. Though the 1960s had engendered vigorous financial growth for Washington Federal, the physical and financial growth recorded during the 1970s far exceeded the thrift's animated rise during the 1960s. As would be the case for the ensuing two decades, Washington Federal achieved its greatest strides by acquiring other financial institutions, such as the 1971 merger with Seattle

Federal Savings and Loan Association, a thrift formed by ten Seattle businessmen one year before Washington Federal first opened its doors. The union with Seattle Federal Savings and Loan added three branches offices to Washington Federal's slowly expanding network of branches, giving the thrift a total of eight branch offices at the beginning of the decade. The boost to Washington Federal's assets was more explosive. A scant few months after assets had nudged past the $100 million plateau, Washington Federal's asset total leaped to $173 million by virtue of the merger with Seattle Federal Savings and Loan.

An equally beneficial merger was completed in late 1978 when Washington Federal merged with First Federal Savings and Loan Association of Mount Vernon, a thrift founded by prominent Pacific Northwest businessmen in August 1934. The merger added 10 new branch offices to Washington Federal's fold, extending its territory of service up to the Canadian border and lifting assets to $733 million. By the end of the 1970s, after recording a phenomenal increase in assets, Washington Federal stood positioned as one of the venerable and most stable financial institutions in the state of Washington, its conservative, low-risk lending policy proved to be a winning formula. In the decade ahead, the thrift's growing presence in Washington would be extended throughout a four-state area, as Washington Federal built upon the momentum achieved during the 1960s and 1970s to develop into a formidable power in the western United States.

Strong Growth During the 1980s

In 1982, Washington Federal become a public company supported chiefly by its customers who purchased 62 percent of the subscription offering. Concurrent with the switch from private to public ownership, Washington Federal converted from a federal mutual to a federal stock association. As a public company, Washington Federal, embarked on a decade that would prove disastrous for the savings and loan industry, but conversely constructive for Washington Federal. During the 1980s, when many of the nation's thrifts fell by the wayside after embracing imprudent investment strategies, Washington Federal bucked the industry-wide trend and grew significantly stronger. According to analysts who monitored the savings and loan industry during the 1980s, Washington Federal's success was attributable to its emphasis on providing single-family housing loans and to its location in the Pacific Northwest where the housing industry flourished during the 1980s. Buoyed by its prime location and its concentration on providing low-risk loans, Washington Federal increased its asset total from $705 million following its public offering to $2.2 billion by 1988. Perhaps more encouraging to the thrift's management was the percentage Washington Federal earned on its swelling assets. By the end of the 1980s, Washington Federal was recording the highest return on assets of any savings and loan institution in the United States, distinguishing itself with a percentage that was between two and two-and-a-half times the figure averaged by regional banks in the country.

As was the case throughout the thrift's history, stability was the primary characteristic describing Washington Federal during the late 1980s. For the previous two decades, the association had been led by the same four executives, a constancy that permeated throughout the organization. With this cadre of management at the helm, Washington Federal once again resumed its acquisition program and completed several deals that extended the thrift's presence beyond Washington's borders. In July 1987, the thrift made a bold move into Idaho by acquiring United First Federal and Provident Federal Savings and Loan Association, both of which were headquartered in Boise, Idaho. The acquisition of the two financial institutions gave Washington Federal 22 new branch offices in Idaho. Another four offices in Idaho were added a little more than a year later when Washington Federal purchased Boise-based Northwest Federal Savings and Loan Association. One month after the acquisition of Northwest Federal Savings and Loan was completed in August 1988, Washington Federal moved resolutely into Oregon by acquiring the 13 branch offices operated by Corvallis, Oregon-based Freedom Federal Savings and Loan Association.

Acquisitions in the 1990s

Entering the 1990s, Washington Federal's acquisitive pace picked up speed, as the thrift bolstered its presence in the four-state area surrounding its headquarters in Seattle. In June 1990, Washington Federal acquired the eight branch offices belonging to Family Federal Savings Association, then merged with Idaho Falls, Idaho-based First Federal Savings and Loan Association and added three more offices to its growing branch network. Next, on the last day of 1991, Washington Federal concluded an agreement with First Western Savings Association, an Oregon-based Metropolitan Savings Association, to acquire its deposits in Eugene, Oregon, and its deposits and leased buildings in downtown Portland, Oregon. By this point, Washington Federal was nearing $3 billion in assets and continuing to draw praise for its industry-leading return on assets, leading one industry analyst to remark to a *Financial World* reporter that "they [Washington Federal] are the pinnacle of the industry in terms of return on equity."

The deal struck with First Western Savings also gave Washington Federal two branch offices in Las Vegas, adding the state of Nevada to the thrift's expanding service territory. Another state was added to the Seattle-based company's geographic scope in March 1993 when Washington Federal acquired First Federal Savings Bank of Salt Lake City, Utah. The purchase of the Salt Lake City bank lifted Washington Federal's assets by $352 million, its deposits by $294 million, and gave the thrift ten new branch offices in Utah. In 1994, when the talks of forming a holding company for Washington Federal turned to action, the thrift opened seven new branch offices—three in Washington, two in Arizona, and one each in Oregon and Utah—and acquired the deposits at two branch locations

operated by Great American Federal Savings Association in Tucson, Arizona.

In November 1994, Washington Federal, which had shortened its name in May 1992 from Washington Federal Savings and Loan Association to Washington Federal Savings, formed Washington Federal, Inc., the holding company for the thrift and another subsidiary, First Insurance Agency, Inc., a provider of general insurance services. During the next several months the Washington Federal system was reorganized to create the structure for the new holding company. On February 3, 1995, the work was completed and Washington Federal became the new parent company for the 78-year-old thrift, with its inaugural year of existence highlighted by another year of strong growth for its consistently stable subsidiary. By the end of 1995, assets had increased an encouraging 20 percent, climbing from $3.8 billion to $4.6 billion, and the number of branch offices operated by Washington Federal had risen to 89. As Washington Federal charted its course for the late 1990s and its 80th year of business, there was every expectation that the enviable achievements of its past would continue to describe its future. Reliable, conservative, and embracing the same business philosophy formulated during the late 1910s, Washington Federal moved toward the late 1990s and beyond, intent on holding sway in the western United States as one of the region's dominant banks.

Principal Subsidiaries

First Insurance Agency, Inc.

Further Reading

Barrett, Amy, "Washington Federal: The Old-Fashioned Way," *Financial World,* March 17, 1992, p. 16.

Chithelen, Ignatius, "Buying Opportunities," *Forbes,* December 23, 1991, p. 189.

Hawkins, Robert, *The Old Neighborhood,* Seattle: Washington Federal, Inc., 1985.

Hornblass, Jonathan, "Washington Federal Shows Throwback Can Win," *American Banker,* June 28, 1994, p. 9.

Neurath, Peter, "Same Old Washington Fed: Dollars Keep Coming," *Puget Sound Business Journal,* January 22, 1990, p. 14.

Pascual, Beatriz, "Washington Federal Savings and Loan Association," *Puget Sound Business Journal,* February 13, 1989, p. 18.

Schultz, Ellen, "Savings and Loans with a Winning Formula," *Fortune,* January 1, 1990, p. 27.

"Washington Federal Savings and Loan Association," *Puget Sound Business Journal,* January 27, 1995, p. 24.

—Jeffrey L. Covell

Washington Mutual, Inc.

1201 Third Avenue
Seattle, Washington 98101
U.S.A.
(206) 461-2000
Fax: (206) 461-2062

Public Company
Incorporated: 1994
Employees: 4,364
Total Assets: $21.63 billion (1995)
Stock Exchanges: NASDAQ
SICs: 6712 Bank Holding Companies; 6036 Savings
    Institutions Except Federal

Owner of the third-largest savings and loan in the United States, Washington Mutual, Inc. operates as the bank holding company for Washington Mutual Bank, its chief operating subsidiary, and various other financial services businesses. Included under Washington Mutual's corporate umbrella during the mid-1990s were Washington Mutual Bank fsb, a federal savings bank, Washington Mutual Life Insurance Company, a life insurance company, Murphey Favre, Inc., a securities brokerage service, and Composite Research & Management Co., an investment advisor firm. Founded in 1889, Washington Mutual registered rampant growth during the 1990s as it expanded throughout the Pacific Northwest. In 1996, the bank nearly doubled its size by acquiring Irvine, California-based American Savings Bank.

19th Century Origins

The birth of the financial institution responsible for forming Washington Mutual, Inc. occurred shortly after the near-death of the city that would feed the growth of one of the United States' largest savings and loans. In 1880, Seattle was a small town in Washington Territory just about to begin its rise toward becoming the Pacific Northwest's most influential commercial hub. With a population of 4,000 at the beginning of the decade, Seattle was little more than a settlement situated in the upper reaches of a

sprawling territory that was yet to be incorporated into the United States. Before the decade was through, however, statehood would arrive and Seattle, after nine years of growth, would transform itself into a burgeoning metropolis. The population of Seattle leaped from 4,000 in 1880 to 40,000 by 1889, the year Washington was admitted to the Union as the 42nd state and the year the city of Seattle was reduced to a pile of ashes.

On June 6, 1889, a glue pot in the basement of a downtown building boiled over and touched off the "Great Seattle Fire," engulfing the downtown district in flames. Before the raging blaze was extinguished, 25 city blocks were razed—120 acres in total—destroying the heart of the city and erasing a decade of robust growth. Overnight, Seattle had been turned into a pile of smoking rubble. Just as the city was shedding the vestiges of its pioneer roots, it was time to rebuild, time to begin anew. It was also the time for the formation of the city's newest financial institution, an enterprise created specifically to help in rebuilding the city of Seattle.

Statehood, the Great Seattle Fire, and the establishment of Washington Mutual, Inc.'s predecessor all occurred in 1889. In September 1889, 15 weeks after flames had turned to ashes, a group of Seattle's business leaders convened to discuss the prospects of forming a building loan company. In attendance were shipbuilders, lawyers, doctors, bankers, and politicians, some of whom had recently arrived in Seattle whereas others had been denizens of the city for years. It was September 21, 1889, and the group of prominent citizens were intent on forming a financial institution that would answer the demand for the resources to build or rebuild houses, something commercial banks were reluctant to finance at the time. Officially established that evening was a general building loan business, a company incorporated as Washington National Building Loan and Investment Association. Washington National began its business while the city of Seattle still remained visibly scarred by the early summer fire.

Initially led by Edward Oziel Graves, who was the former assistant treasurer for the U.S. Treasury's Bureau of Engraving and Printing, Washington National was supported by one employee during its inaugural year, Ira Hill Case, who occupied one desk in a second-floor office shared by a dozen other

Company Perspectives:

Washington Mutual's mission is to be the premier diversified financial services organization in the western states.

businessmen representing an equal number of divergent business interests. The beginnings were modest, to be sure, but not long after its creation, Washington National made banking history. The association's first loans were approved in February 1890, one of which was an amortized home loan, perhaps the first of its kind in the United States. Washington National went on to approve more than 2,000 amortized home loans during the ensuing 20 years, becoming a much-used source for home mortgage loans.

Created as a building loan business, Washington National represented one of 3,500 building and loan associations in the United States at the time of its establishment, but when the company began to flounder after the turn of the century it chose to distance itself from the building society movement. In 1908, the enterprise changed its name to Washington Savings and Loan Association and embarked on a course that gradually steered the newly named financial institution toward the mutual banking field. Along with the name change came additional sweeping changes, as new leadership restructured Washington Savings and Loan to invigorate business. Membership fees were eliminated, the terms of interest and loan repayment schedules were precisely established, an aggressive advertising program was launched, and customers were granted the freedom to withdraw deposits at any time, with any interest accrued up to the day of withdrawal. The changes implemented spurred the institution's growth, igniting a five-year period of unprecedented expansion. Between 1908 and 1913, the number of loans granted by Washington Savings and Loan soared from 300 to 2,700. Assets increased 11-fold, jumping from $346,576 to more than $4 million, and the number of accounts operated by the association leaped from 400 to 2,700. Helped in large part by this growth spurt, Washington Savings and Loan ranked not only as the oldest savings institution in Washington, but also as the state's largest savings institution, providing the association with firm footing as it entered a new phase in its development.

World War I Conversion into a Mutual Bank

In 1917, while the country's newspapers covered the progress of war overseas, Washington Savings and Loan converted into a mutual savings bank and once again changed its name. Rechristened Washington Mutual Savings Bank, the recast institution boasted more than 16,000 depositors at the time of the United States' entrance into World War I and benefitted substantially from the century's first epic military struggle. During World War I, Washington Mutual's assets rose 68 percent, recording a gain of more than $4 million, and real estate loans registered an even greater increase, by 250 percent.

After the conclusion of the war, recessionary economic conditions hobbled Seattle's economic growth, but despite the anemic financial situation Washington Mutual's deposits in-

creased strongly, rising from $15 million in 1921 to more than $26 million two years later. Such encouraging growth came to a stop by the end of the decade, however, as the Wall Street stock market crash of 1929 gave way to a decade-long economic depression that wrought devastation for the U.S. banking industry. Though the years were difficult, Washington Mutual persevered, avoiding the financial ruin that swept away many of the country's financial institutions. It was during the first months of this unrivaled economic plunge that Washington Mutual completed the first acquisition in its history, acquiring Continental Mutual Savings Bank in July 1930.

By the end of the 1930s, Washington Mutual was just shy of 100,000 depositors and about to benefit once again from the economic growth engendered by the century's second great military struggle. During World War II, Washington Mutual, by then more than a half-century old, sold nearly $30 million in war bonds. In 1941, the bank merged with Coolidge Mutual Savings Bank, increasing its resources to more than $77 million and its deposits to more than $72 million, and gaining Washington Mutual its first branch office, the quarters formerly occupied by Coolidge Mutual, which became known as the Times Square Branch. After the war, when banking legislation permitted mutual banks to establish branches in their home county, Washington Mutual opened two banking offices, one in 1947 and another in 1948.

During the 1950s, the promulgation of additional banking legislation paved the way for mutual banks to establish statewide networks of service, but despite the opportunity to do so Washington Mutual did not move outside the greater Seattle area until 1964. Branches were established in the Seattle area during the intervening years, however, with five Washington Mutual offices opening their doors between 1955 and 1961. When Washington Mutual finally did move outside the Seattle area, the stage was set for an era of geographic expansion that extended the bank's presence throughout Washington. From 1964 forward, the physical growth of Washington Mutual was driven by internal expansion and by external means, as the bank took on the role of an aggressive acquisitor. This chapter in the bank's history began with the acquisition of Citizens Mutual Savings Bank in 1964.

Statewide Expansion Begins in 1964

Citizens Mutual Savings Bank's existence as a mutual bank was only hours old when Washington Mutual sealed the deal to purchase the eastern Washington-based financial institution. Founded in 1902 as Citizens Savings and Loan Society, the thrift operated as a savings and loan up until its acquisition by Washington Mutual, acquiring the Pullman Savings and Loan Association the year prior to the 1964 Washington Mutual acquisition. With its base in Spokane and the newly acquired Pullman Savings and Loan adding a presence in Pullman, Citizens Savings and Loan represented an opportunity for Washington Mutual to expand into eastern Washington, but banking legislation at the time did not permit a mutual bank to merge with a savings and loan. To clear this obstacle, Citizens Savings and Loan converted into a mutual bank in 1964, as Washington Mutual had done 47 years earlier, changing its name to Citizens Mutual Savings Bank just prior to its merger with Washington Mutual. Once completed, the transaction extended Washington

Mutual's presence beyond the greater Seattle area for the first time, giving the bank branches in Pullman and Spokane and establishing a pattern the Seattle-based concern would follow in the years ahead.

The year after the Citizens Mutual Savings Bank acquisition, Washington Mutual completed a similar deal when Liberty Savings and Loan Association converted into a mutual bank to facilitate its acquisition by Washington Mutual. Established in 1919, Liberty Savings and Loan Association became Liberty Mutual Savings Bank in 1965, giving Washington Mutual branch offices in Yakima, Kennewick, and Grandview, Washington. The same scenario was played out in 1973 when the Grays Harbor Savings and Loan Association converted into Grays Harbor Mutual Savings Bank just before its acquisition by Washington Mutual, adding a branch office in Grays Harbor to the Seattle-based bank's growing empire.

Against the backdrop of these acquisitions, Washington Mutual expanded geographically through internal means by establishing branch offices on its own. Between 1965 and 1973, the bank opened 15 branch offices in the Seattle area and in regions across the state, building itself into a dominant force in Washington State. Swelled by acquisitions and internal expansion, Washington Mutual entered the 1980s as a venerable yet rising financial institution, its near-century of business in the Seattle area and two decades of statewide expansion generating considerable momentum for the decade ahead. During the 1980s, this momentum would not be checked, as the bank diversified quickly, entering new sectors of the financial industry at a yearly pace. Though industry observers would charge that the bank spread itself in too many directions during the decade, the far-flung expansion effected during the 1980s proved to be the catalyst for Washington Mutual's animated growth during the 1990s.

1982 Arrival of Killinger

During the 1980s, the subsidiary companies that would compose The Washington Mutual Financial Group came into bloom. The proliferation of diversified financial subsidiaries grouped under the Washington Mutual corporate umbrella began in 1982 when the bank acquired Murphey Favre, Inc., Composite Research & Management Co., and formed Washington Mutual Insurance Services. Murphey Favre was the Northwest's oldest securities brokerage firm, Composite Research & Management Co. operated as an investment advisor and portfolio management firm, and Washington Mutual Insurance Services was a full-service retail insurance agency. Beginning with these three subsidiaries, Washington Mutual formed or acquired a host of other operating companies that carried the bank into a variety of new business areas, including travel services, real estate partnerships, junk bonds, and commercial construction loans.

None of the subsidiary companies either acquired or formed during the 1980s was more important to the future of Washington Mutual than the 1982 acquisition of Murphey Favre, a distinction entirely due to the arrival of a young Murphey Favre executive named Kerry K. Killinger. At the time of the 1982 acquisition, Killinger was 32 years old and had served as a securities analyst and investment broker for the company before being named executive vice-president. Once brought into the Washington Mutual fold, Killinger rose quickly through the

bank's executive ranks, becoming president in 1988 and chief executive officer two years later. During Killinger's rise, Washington Mutual was moving in a different direction, as the bank began to decline and suffer from waning profitability. With earnings slipping late in the decade, a new program aimed at restoring profitability and invigorating growth was launched, one that would dramatically amplify the magnitude of Washington Mutual's geographic scope.

1990s: Unprecedented Growth

During Washington Mutual's 100th anniversary year, the new strategy was adopted, a program of growth spearheaded by Killinger, who informed the *Puget Sound Business Journal* that in the coming years it was Washington Mutual's goal "to be the premier consumer bank in the Northwest." Toward this objective, Killinger turned to a "back-to-basics" approach by focusing on consumer loans and checking accounts. Once Killinger was named chairman of Washington Mutual in 1990, the bank's bid to become the dominant financial institution in the region began in earnest, as the newly named chairman, president, and chief executive officer orchestrated an acquisition campaign that swallowed up competitors at a rate of about two per year. For the first time in the bank's history, it extended its presence beyond Washington's borders, compensating for its belated entry into the regional banking arena by expanding aggressively at a time when the savings and loan industry in general was faring poorly.

In 1991, Washington Mutual ranked as Washington's largest independently owned financial institution, with $8 billion in assets and 84 financial centers and 17 home loan centers in its home state, Oregon, and Idaho. These impressive figures would soon be dwarfed by the magnitude of the bank four years later, as Washington Mutual's acquisition spree ignited its growth, carried the bank into Montana and Utah, and necessitated the formation of Washington Mutual, Inc. as a holding company in August 1994. Between 1991 and 1995, Washington Mutual's profits more than doubled, leaping from $80.6 million to $190.6 million, its deposits increased from $5.4 billion to $10.6 billion, and its assets swelled from $8 billion to $21.6 billion. Meanwhile, the number of branch offices operated by the bank had increased dramatically, reaching a total of 248 financial centers and 23 loan centers by the end of 1995. The first half of the 1990s represented a period of growth unrivaled in Washington Mutual's history. As the bank entered the late 1990s it did not slow its pace of growth, rather, its pace increased.

In early 1996, Washington Mutual acquired Coos Bay, Oregon-based Western Bank, giving it 42 branch offices in 35 communities and $787 million in assets. Next, the bank acquired Ogden-based Utah Federal Savings Bank, adding another $123 million in assets to its growing coffers. The bank appeared to be continuing its aggressive campaign to dominate the Pacific Northwest, an objective Killinger touched on when he said, "Our strategy calls for continued growth through selective acquisitions of consumer banks, commercial banks, and other financial service businesses that offer long-term value to our shareholders." Killinger put his words into action in July 1996 when Washington Mutual completed the largest acquisition in its 107-year history. After searching for an entry into the lucrative California market for two years, Killinger found his target in Irvine, where the

158-branch American Savings Bank was headquartered. In a $1.4 billion deal completed at the end of July, Washington Mutual acquired American Savings Bank and nearly doubled its size, making it the third largest savings and loan in the United States. Buoyed enormously by the acquisition of American Savings Bank, Washington Mutual entered the late 1990s intent on continuing its ambitious expansion program. Further acquisitions in the California market were expected, as the venerable financial institution with its $42 billion in assets charted its course for its third century of business.

Principal Subsidiaries

Washington Mutual Bank; Washington Mutual Bank fsb; WM Life Insurance Company; Murphy Favre, Inc.; Composite Research & Management Co.

Further Reading

Chan, Gilbert, "Seattle Thrift Buys American Savings Bank of California," *Knight-Ridder/Tribune Business News,* July 23, 1996, p. 7.

Epes, James, "How WaMu Accounts for Enterprise Bank Buy," *Puget Sound Business Journal,* June 9, 1995, p. 13.

Kapiloff, Howard, "Wash. Mutual Faces Big-League Challenges in California," *American Banker,* July 25, 1996, p. 12.

Killinger, Kerry, "One-Stop Shopping at Washington Mutual," *Bottomline,* November 1987, p. 27.

Morgan, Murray, *The Friend of the Family,* Seattle: The Washington Mutual Financial Group, 1989.

Neurath, Peter, "Good 'Bad News' for Bank," *Puget Sound Business Journal,* January 22, 1990, p. 18.

Pulliam, Liz, "Expansion of Washington Mutual Took Off with New Chairman," *Knight-Ridder/Tribune Business News,* July 23, 1996, p. 72.

"Seattle-Based Washington Mutual Inc. To Acquire Oregon's Western Bank," *Knight-Ridder/Tribune Business News,* October 12, 1995, p. 10.

"Washington Mutual To Acquire American Savings Bank Through Merger, Creating West Coast Banking Powerhouse," *PR Newswire,* July 22, 1996, p. 7.

Wolcott, John, "What Puts the Wham in WAMU?," *Puget Sound Business Journal,* September 2, 1991, p. 20.

—Jeffrey L. Covell

Washington Scientific Industries, Inc.

2605 West Wayzata Boulevard
Long Lake, Minnesota 55356
U.S.A.
(612) 473-1271
Fax: (612) 473-2945

Public Company
Incorporated: 1950 as Washington Machine & Tool
    Works, Inc.
Employees: 150
Sales: $30.4 million (1995)
Stock Exchanges: NASDAQ
SICs: 3469 Metal Stampings, Not Elsewhere Classified;
    3569 General Industrial Machinery, Not Elsewhere
    Classified; 3829 Measuring & Controlling Devices,
    Not Elsewhere Classified

Washington Scientific Industries, Inc. (WSI), manufactures complex, high-precision machine parts and subassemblies for a range of industries, including automotive, medical, agricultural, marine, engine, and computer. The company operates primarily on a contract basis for companies that outsource the manufacture of specialty machined parts. WSI was heavily dependent on the computer disk-drive market until the 1990s, when it restructured and diversified.

1950s Origins

WSI was incorporated in Minnesota in 1950 as Washington Machine & Tool Works, Inc. The fledgling venture was established to serve as a contract manufacturer for aerospace, communications, and industrial markets. The company's name came from the street on which it was originally located, Washington Avenue, in Minneapolis. WSI's founders planned to profit by emphasizing their expertise in the design and production of high-precision machined parts and assemblies that larger companies lacked the resources or expertise to manufacture. For several years during the 1950s, then, WSI profited as a sort of high-tech machine shop, contracting the manufacture of specialized parts.

Although WSI served several different companies in various industries, its big break came when it began contracting with International Business Machines (IBM). IBM began hiring WSI in the mid-1950s to manufacture parts for its computer systems. The partnership with IBM eventually became the core of WSI's business and helped it to grow into a multimillion-dollar company during the 1960s and 1970s. IBM hired WSI primarily to build high-precision disk-drives and motor assemblies for its mainframe computers, but also to build other precision parts. As IBM's growth surged with the computer industry, WSI enjoyed steady sales gains. The expertise it developed working with IBM, moreover, allowed it to get contracts with other computer system makers, making computer components WSI's primary emphasis.

In need of expansion capital to keep up with rising demand, WSI went public in 1958 (the company changed its name to Washington Scientific Industries, Inc. in 1960). When it went public, WSI was generating roughly 50 percent of all of its revenue from IBM. In fact, every year throughout the 1960s, 1970s, and much of the 1980s, IBM supplied more than 50 percent of WSI's sales, and in some years contributed more than 75 percent. Parts of WSI's operations effectively became an extension of the IBM organization, churning out specialized parts in assembly-line fashion that IBM incorporated into its hugely successful mainframe computer systems.

In addition to its thriving (mostly computer-related) parts contracting business, WSI realized gains in developing and producing its own products. Specifically, in 1960 WSI started developing a hydraulic motor. The effort led to the creation of WSI's Fluid Power Division and, later, its Transmission Devices Division. Those units manufactured proprietary hydraulic and mechanical power-transmission products that eventually grew to represent a substantial portion of WSI's sales and, at times, contributed significant profits. In an effort to establish its fluid power products, WSI purchased Von Ruden Manufacturing Co. in 1973. Von Ruden was a Texas-based manufacturer of transmission devices used in agricultural and industrial applications. The operation became the hub of WSI's power-transmission business.

Contracting Business

Throughout the 1960s and 1970s, though, WSI concentrated on its contracting business, particularly for computer components and its lead buyer, IBM. As computer system sales shot up, WSI boosted its sales past $10 million annually. From a relatively small, specialty precision machine operation, WSI expanded to become a high-volume manufacturer. It often produced large runs of parts and assemblies under long-term contracts with IBM, but also with other computer equipment producers; WSI's customer base eventually included industry giants like Johnson & Johnson and Deere & Company as well as venerable Japanese conglomerates like Sony and Toshiba.

As WSI's contracting business ballooned, its power-transmission segments waned, particularly in the wake of the recession of the late 1970s and early 1980s. The units were stung by, among other problems, weak demand from the agricultural sector. WSI consolidated the Fluid Power Division and the Transmission Devices Division in 1983 into one unit, dubbed the Power Components Division, which remained stationed in Texas. That part of WSI's business continued to languish during the 1980s, however, and eventually became a drag on its bottom line. Indeed, while WSI's contract manufacturing businesses regularly pulled in profit margins well in excess of 10 percent, the power-transmission business eked out margins closer to 5 percent.

WSI's contracting business remained strong, and by the mid-1980s the company's annual revenues were swelling toward the $20-million mark. To meet growing demand and to get closer to some of its customers, WSI purchased Rogers & Oling, Inc. in 1985. That firm was a manufacturer of precision machined parts for the computer and aerospace industries. It was operated as part of WSI's California operations (Washington Scientific Industries of California, Inc.). The California operation encompassed two manufacturing plants; one for high-volume, continuous-run products, and another for low-volume, more specialized parts.

The purchase of Rogers & Oling reflected a change of management, and strategy, at WSI. In 1985 the company promoted Clifford Dinsmore to head the company as president and chief executive. Evidencing the influence of IBM over WSI was the fact that Dinsmore was a former employee of IBM, where he had worked as a purchasing troubleshooter. It was through IBM that he became acquainted with WSI, which hired him away in 1974 and made him a vice-president. Although Dinsmore had worked for IBM and wanted to maintain a good relationship with that customer, he was also wary of WSI's dependence on a single company for more than half of its revenue.

In fact, by the mid-1980s WSI was depending on IBM for about 75 percent of its annual shipments. The relationship had reached the point at which WSI more closely resembled a subsidiary of IBM than a hired contractor. WSI's main business had become churning out precision parts and components for IBM's mainframes, particularly its high-end 3380 units. Dinsmore feared that a downturn in IBM's business, the computer industry, or both could seriously hurt WSI. Furthermore, he realized that IBM was in a position of power over WSI and could effectively dictate profit margins and other contract terms. Not surprisingly, in fact, WSI's profits by the mid-1980s were relatively meager and inconsistent: only $376,000 in 1986 from $24.5 million in sales, $1.7 million in profits in 1987, and just $69,000 in profits in 1988. To make matters worse, the undeniable reality by the late 1980s was that the mainframe industry was increasingly under pressure from personal computers and workstations, which were becoming more powerful and were being networked to form powerful, inexpensive, mainframe-like systems.

Engineering a Turnaround in the 1980s

Realizing the gravity of the overall situation, Dinsmore launched a new strategy designed to reduce WSI's dependence on IBM and the mainframe industry. His plan was to diversify into new markets and to pursue relationships with other large manufacturers. Indeed, because it was among the largest companies in the contracting industry, WSI was uniquely positioned to serve big companies that often needed high-volume production runs.

Dinsmore also wanted to move away from WSI's low-volume, specialty business and focus on safer, more profitable long-term contracts to produce high volumes of parts and assemblies. The idea was to pursue contracts that required a production volume large enough to merit WSI's high-tech process engineering, which was one of the company's competitive advantages. WSI engineers would work with a client to develop a process to manufacture a part and then help the customer install sophisticated machining equipment and implement rigorous statistical process control systems. The engineers would work with the customer to tweak and continuously improve the system throughout the life of the contract.

In keeping with his new strategy, Dinsmore, in 1988, shuttered WSI's plant in Pasadena, California, which primarily manufactured complex parts in short production runs. It shifted its focus in California to its larger facility in Covina. WSI shut down its power-transmission unit by selling off the still-flailing Power Components Division. Dinsmore believed that the unit no longer complemented WSI's goal of focusing on process engineering and contracting, rather than on product development, marketing, and distribution.

Among the most significant moves initiated by Dinsmore in the late 1980s was the 1988 buyout of Advanced Custom Molders, Inc. (ACM), a Texas-based manufacturer of precision molded plastic components. ACM brought with it three plants and about 270 employees. The company was profiting at the time by serving the growing list of manufacturers that were setting up low-cost production plants just across the border in Mexico and then bringing the goods back into the United States. WSI invested heavily in ACM, installing a dozen high-tech automated injection-molding machines, among other measures. The addition of ACM helped WSI to increase its sales to $73.6 million in 1990.

By 1990, Dinsmore had succeeded in reducing the total portion of its revenue base contributed by IBM to less than 50 percent, despite continued sales gains to the giant computer company. And Dinsmore was steadily moving toward his original goal of increased diversification and an emphasis on process engineering. But the effects of the company's restructuring seemed to be having a negative impact on its bottom line. Indeed, despite hefty revenue growth, WSI's net income slumped to $56,000 in 1990 before plunging to a net deficit of $4.77 million in 1991.

Part of WSI's problem stemmed from ACM, which was failing to live up to expectations. In an effort to whip the subsidiary into shape, WSI shuttered one of ACM's three plants and restructured the entire operation late in 1991. Augmenting WSI's losses at ACM was a downturn in defense markets, particularly the aerospace industry in California. A few months after WSI closed the ACM plant, therefore, Dinsmore announced that the company was going to terminate operations at its Covina, California plant and move all manufacturing to its Minnesota facilities.

Despite WSI's efforts to restructure, the company continued to lose money, posting net losses of $1.2 million in 1992 and $5.6 million in 1993 (partly as a result of restructuring charges). WSI finally decided to jettison the entire ACM division, selling it off in June of 1993 to Moll Plasticrafters, L.P. One month later Dinsmore resigned as president and chief executive. His shoes were filled temporarily by George J. Martin. Martin had served as president and chief executive of WSI from December 1983 to January 1985 before leaving to head PowCon, Inc., a manufacturer of electronic welding systems. WSI hired Martin back as chairman of the board.

Martin brought in Michael J. Pudil in November of 1993 to act as president and chief executive. Pudil had previously worked as general manager and vice-president of a division of Remmele Engineering, Inc., which was a contract manufacturer involved primarily in machining metal. Pudil went to work consolidating all of WSI's manufacturing operations in Long Lake, Minnesota, a process already under way when he was hired. WSI sold one of its Minnesota plants, leaving the entire company with just one manufacturing plant. Thus in a few short years WSI decreased its assets from seven production facilities in three states to just one factory in Minnesota.

As its assets declined, WSI's sales dropped from more than $60 million during the early 1990s to about $30 million by 1994. Still, the company's strategy remained basically the same: to manufacture high-precision machined parts for a number of companies in different industries. To that end, by 1995 the company had succeeded in reducing its dependence on IBM, which was accounting for less than 25 percent of WSI's sales. WSI posted its first profit—$945,000—in five years in 1995 and proclaimed in its 1995 annual report that "WSI's future appears more promising than at any point within the past five years." In 1996 the company was focusing on strengthening its internal operations and boosting profit margins.

Further Reading

Ewen, Beth, "Languishing WSI Division Is Sold to General Manager," *Minneapolis-St. Paul CityBusiness,* September 18, 1989, p. 4.

Hequet, Marc, "WSI's Identity Crises," *Corporate Report Minnesota,* June 1990, p. 29.

Khermouch, Gerry, "Washington Scientific Machines a Special Niche; Aims for Multiyear Engineering Accords," *Metalworking News,* July 23, 1990, p. 1.

Peterson, Susan E., "Washington Scientific Says It Will Close Owatonna Plant," *Star Tribune,* June 28, 1994, Section D, p. 4.

Savitz, Eric J., "In Big Blue's Shadow: Washington Scientific Thrives There," *Barron's,* February 5, 1990, p. 44.

—Dave Mote

Wawa Inc.

260 Baltimore Pike
Wawa, Pennsylvania 19063
U.S.A.
(610) 358-8000
Fax: (610) 358-8878

Private Company
Incorporated: 1968
Employees: 10,000
Sales: $838 million (1995)
SICs: 2026 Fluid Milk; 2099 Food Preparations, Not
    Elsewhere Classified; 5194 Tobacco & Tobacco
    Products; 5411 Grocery Stores

With 515 outlets in 1996, Wawa Inc. was one of the largest privately held convenience-store chains in the United States. These 24-hour-a-day stores were located for the most part in suburban areas of the five mid-Atlantic and New England states in which the chain operated. All but about 50 were within 90 miles of Philadelphia, however, and the majority were in New Jersey. They emphasized high-quality delicatessen and salad-bar items and low-price cigarettes. The company also was engaged in dairy and wholesale cigarette businesses.

Textile and Dairying Origins

Wawa's origins go back to 1803, when the Millville Manufacturing Co. was founded. This enterprise operated textile mills in several states, including major plants in southern New Jersey. In the late 19th century Millville owner George Wood became interested in dairy farming, and he imported cows from Guernsey in the Channel Islands of the United Kingdom. A Philadelphia resident, Wood had bought a summer home for his family in Wawa, a suburb west of Media, in 1890, and he established a small plant there to process his dairy products. (Wawa is the word for goose in the native American Lenni Lenape language, and a goose appears on the corporate logo.) Pasteurization was unknown then, but using strict sanitary methods, Wood produced a raw milk, Certified Wawa Milk, that was recommended as safe by many Philadelphia doctors.

By the 1960s Millville Manufacturing had ceased operations, and consumers were buying milk from supermarkets rather than relying on Wawa Dairy Farms for home delivery. Deciding to counter the supermarket trend, Grahame Wood, Jr., grandson of George Wood, opened the first Wawa Food Market in Folsom, Pennsylvania.

Featuring brand-name milk, butter, and ice cream from the dairy, it was an immediate success. Two more stores were added by the end of the first year of operation. The 1968 edition of Dun and Bradstreet's *Million Dollar Directory* listed Wawa Dairy Farms as having 250 employees and $9 million in annual sales. In that year Wawa Dairy Farms and Wawa Food Markets merged into the Millville Manufacturing Co., whose principal assets consisted of real estate in southern New Jersey, to form Wawa Inc.

With the added resources of Millville's real estate, Wawa's number of stores reached 40 by the end of 1968 and 80 by the end of 1970. Some of these were operating around-the-clock by the late 1970s. By the end of the decade sales had reached $140 million a year, and the number of employees had grown to 2,200. Grahame Wood was chairman and chief executive officer, and Richard D. Wood, Jr., a cousin, was president.

In 1977 Wawa began testing a paperless cash-access system at 12 Pennsylvania stores. Customers who presented a Provident National Bank card to a Wawa clerk and entered their personal security number on a separate keyboard could withdraw up to $25 a day from their bank accounts. ATM services were developed in later years, and all Wawa stores had ATMs by 1995.

Convenience with a Wholesome Image

Traditionally the best-selling convenience store items have been gasoline, beer, and cigarettes. Only a very few Wawa stores sold gasoline, however, and none sold beer (as much a reflection of local zoning prohibition as corporate philosophy), lottery tickets, or sex-oriented magazines. Even cigarettes were restricted to displays behind smoked glass. Instead Wawa specialized in high-quality perishables, including lunchtime sandwiches, and became the first convenience store operator to offer fresh, prepackaged entrees.

The typical convenience store customer was seen as a young blue-collar male, but Wawa found it could do well among working women as well by keeping its stores neat and clean and by carrying a much greater selection than most of its rivals. These goods included produce—absent from most convenience stores—and a large selection of delicatessen items. In 1985 the company began test-marketing Lite Bite salads, its first product directly targeted to working women. These salads were made in the stores themselves and prepared from Wawa's own produce. Wawa reported sales of about $360 million in 1986 and was opening some 50 locations a year in the late 1980s. Sales per store, which averaged $11,000 a week in 1979, had jumped to $20,000 a decade later.

Wawa's stores, which averaged 3,000 square feet, contained—in contrast to most of its competitors—no aisle or countertop displays. "The conventional merchandising wisdom in a convenience store is to get the customer to buy something she didn't really walk in to buy," Frederic Schroeder, Wawa's vice-president for marketing, told a *Chain Store Age Executive* reporter in 1987. "But our No. 1 aim is to get the customer in and out quickly. Architecturally, we made the checkout area remote from the sandwich/deli area. This is more labor-intensive, but we feel it makes it much more comfortable for the consumers to shop our stores. We also removed the beverage area from the deli, also to make it easier for customers to get in and out of our stores."

In terms of Wawa's merchandise mix, Schroeder went on to say, "We started putting much more emphasis on poultry in our deli area, and on offering lower-sodium foods and foods with a lower fat content. We also continue to promote our produce heavily, and we've added more single-serve fruit juices. . . . Our studies show that in our stores we have over 85 percent of what is available in the average supermarket, and approximately 70 percent of this is selling for comparable prices."

In order to stimulate slow dinnertime business, Wawa tested in 50 stores during 1989–1990 a Fresh Buffet line of chilled entrees, priced from $2.99 to $3.99. Working in partnership with Key Fresh, a division of Keystone Frozen Foods, Wawa offered customers these items in a special refrigerated case, set at very precise temperatures. Shelf life from day of manufacture was approximately ten to 14 days, which translated to about seven days at store level if delivered promptly. A freshness indicator showed how long a package had been in the case. The first six items were chicken Mexican, chicken Oriental, chicken Mornay, beef teriyaki, and two types of lasagna. Wawa found that the buyers tended to be women and customers with higher incomes than typical convenience store patrons. This line was dropped, however, in favor of promoting the more profitable sale of hoagie sandwiches and cigarettes.

By the end of 1990 the Wawa chain had grown to about 485 stores in Connecticut, New Jersey, Pennsylvania, Maryland, and Delaware. This period was, however, a difficult one for Wawa. According to Ralph Wood, company profits declined

from about 1987 to mid-1991, and the number of customers actually fell in 1989 and 1990. Better management was one reason credited for the subsequent turnaround: the turnover of store managers dropped from 30 percent in 1987 to under ten percent in 1991.

Wawa in the 1990s

In 1991 prepared foods (as opposed to packaged items) were accounting for 25 percent of Wawa's sales, with the average gross margin per location, after spoilage, 55 percent. The biggest sales and profit category was deli, mostly sliced meats and cheeses and including local favorites such as hoagie sandwiches. Wawa also was selling a line of low-sodium deli meats and cheeses. Women accounted for about 40 percent of the chain's customers.

Wawa's deli facilities were making more than 50,000 sandwiches a day in 1992, when it had the hoagie declared the official sandwich of Philadelphia through a promotion that secured 30,000 signatures to support the designation. On Hoagie Day—May 6, 1992—the company celebrated by building a 500-foot-long sandwich. Wawa stores were making 174,000 hoagies each week for their customers. Two years later, the company celebrated its 30th anniversary as a convenience store enterprise with a promotional blitz. Because its start-up coincided with Ford Motor Company's introduction of the wildly popular Mustang, Wawa gave away one 1960s Mustang a day for 30 days.

Wawa began a program of eliminating ozone-layer-depleting chlorofluorocarbons (CFCs) in 1988. Wawa-owned refrigerated units like walk-in coolers and deli/dairy cases in its stores were being slowly replaced or converted, with completion of the project scheduled for 1996. The company was installing scanning in all of its stores by the end of 1995 and had installed personal computers and software from Park City Group at each of its locations.

In the early 1990s Wawa's expansion slowed to some 20 store openings a year. Instead the company emphasized remodeling, at $300,000 per store. Although store size stayed about the same, sometimes the company had to buy the lot next door to increase parking for the growing number of customers, who brought the weekly sales level per store to $35,000 in July 1994.

To gauge its customer service, Wawa had what it called its 155-second rule, denoting the average time a customer was in a convenience store. All operations in a Wawa store were geared to get the customer in and out during that time. To meet this standard, the company was working on better ordering systems for the deli sections, speeding up the checkout process, and possibly using telephone and fax ordering to spread out preparation time. It also recognized the need to add more counter space for customers.

An Associated Press survey of Wawa's stores in 1996 found yuppie favorites like kiwis, mineral water, pasta salad, cappuccino, and yogurt available along with the predictable cookies and candy bars in its stores. Some of the larger ones had installed espresso bars where customers could order their coffee with frothy, steamed milk or one of 20 kinds of Italian syrup.

Wawa also offered its own special coffee blend, which had become its leading ready-to-serve around-the-clock product. The company was also developing an English-muffin-based line of breakfast sandwiches. In order to compete better with fast-food outlets as well as supermarket chains, Taco Bell burritos and Pizza Hut personal-pan pizzas had been added to the deli counters, and a downtown Philadelphia food court that opened in 1994 offered fast food only in a choice of Taco Bell, Pizza Hut, or two Wawa house formats—Hoagie Time or Coffee Time.

Wawa's plans, as of 1994, called for 1,000 stores by the year 2000, spending $5 million to $6 million per year over a six-year period. To meet its stores' growing demand for milk and juice, the company also was expanding its dairy and warehouse operations. The land behind the dairy would be used for a new refrigerated warehouse, and additional storage silos were also planned. The remodeled dairy, doubled in capacity, would offer the latest in state-of-the-art computerized processing, new equipment for solution recovery, and recycling of solvents. "We also want to make our dairy more visitor friendly," Richard Wood told a reporter. "When everything is finished, we hope to offer tours to schoolchildren."

At least ten more Wawa stores were expected to be selling gasoline by the year 2000, on larger properties than its current superstores, which averaged about 5,000 square feet. The company felt that getting into the gas business was necessary to compete with oil-company convenience store chains like Sun Co. Inc.'s A-Plus. Wawa had gas pumps in about 30 outlets during the 1970s but dismantled them in all but two outlets by the early 1980s because profits were too low.

Further Reading

Brooke, Bob, "Wawa Wants to Double the Number of Its Stores," *Philadelphia Business Journal,* September 30, 1994, pp. 3–4.

Dowdell, Stephen, "Convenience Chain Sets Rollout of Chilled Entree," *Supermarket News,* December 3, 1990, pp. 1, 42.

Hussey, Anita, "C-Store Competition: Fighting for the Foodservice Dollar," *Progressive Grocer,* February 1991, pp. 130–32.

"Waiting for a Wawa," *Evansville Courier,* June 30, 1996, pp. E1–E2.

Wallace, David, "Fattening Up on Value, Sandwiches," *Philadelphia Business Journal,* October 7, 1991, p. 11.

"Wawa Sets Sites on Female Market Segment," *Chain Store Age Executive,* July 1987, pp. 18, 20, 22.

—Robert Halasz

West Fraser Timber Co. Ltd.

1100 Melville Street, Suite 1000
Vancouver, British Columbia V6E 4A6
Canada
(604) 895-2700
Fax: (604) 681-6061
Internet: http://www.westfrasertimber.ca

Public Company
Incorporated: 1966
Employees: 5,500
Sales: C$1.49 billion (1995)
Stock Exchanges: Toronto Vancouver
SICs: 2400 Lumber & Wood Products

With an emphasis on being a low-cost producer, West Fraser Timber Co. Ltd. has grown into Canada's second-largest forest products company, with operations centered in British Columbia. The company and its subsidiaries own or jointly own ten sawmills, two medium density fiberboard (MDF) mills, a custom cutting facility, a newsprint mill, a linerboard and kraft paper mill, and two pulp mills. Together, these businesses produced 1,600 million board feet (MMfbm) of dimension lumber, 450,000 metric tons (one metric ton equals 1,000 kilograms or 2,204 pounds) of linerboard and kraft paper, 280,000 metric tons of bleached chemi-thermomechanical (BCTMP) pulp, 120,000 metric tons of newsprint, and 110 million square feet of MDF. Other West Fraser products include such specialty wood products as fingerjoint studs and woodchips used in pulp manufacturing.

West Fraser's timber cutting rights in British Columbia and Alberta provided the company with nearly six million solid cubic feet—with a solid cubic foot equal to roughly 35 cubic feet—of allowable annual cut (AAC) in 1996. This accounted for nearly 75 percent of the company's sawlog needs. The company is able to meet 100 percent of its pulp and paper operations' fiber requirements internally. West Fraser's Revelstoke Home Centres Ltd. subsidiary owns and operates a chain of 33 retail home improvement stores located in British Columbia, Saskatchewan, and Alberta and operating under the names "Revelstoke Home

Centre" and "Revy Home & Garden." Revelstoke also owns a lumber trading and distribution facility. Other businesses in which West Fraser holds an interest are a window manufacturer; two lumber re-manufacturers; a maker of wooden I-beams, associated products, and energy-efficient housing units; and a producer of genetically-enhanced seed.

Henry H. (Hank) Ketcham III, son of one of West Fraser's cofounders, is chairman, president, and CEO of the company, which achieved profits of C$95.8 million on C$1.49 billion in 1995. Most West Fraser products are sold as commodities. Canadian sales accounted for 38 percent of West Fraser revenues; the United States represented 36 percent of sales, the Far East generated 14 percent, and Europe accounted for nine percent of the company's 1995 revenues. Faced with dwindling AAC and other resources, West Fraser has begun to diversify its geographical base beyond British Columbia. In 1995, the company purchased the Ranger Forest Products division of Alberta Energy Co. for C$393 million.

Building a Timber Business through the 1950s through 1970s

In 1955, Washington natives and brothers William, Samuel, and Henry Jr. (Pete) Ketcham left their father Henry Sr.'s Seattle wholesale lumber company to strike out on their own. The brothers each pooled $15,000 toward a total price of $58,000 to buy a small, 12-employee planing mill in Quesnel, located in the Cariboo Mountains area of British Columbia. The original intent of the company, called West Fraser, was to supply lumber to Henry Sr.'s wholesale store. With the post–World War II building boom still fueling demand, however, the brothers soon began to acquire more sawmills. Each sawmill was accompanied by its own timber cutting rights, and by the mid-1960s, the company had developed into a full-fledged lumber company. In 1966, the Ketcham brothers incorporated their company as West Fraser Timber Co., with Sam Ketcham serving as president and Pete Ketcham acting as chairman.

West Fraser next launched a chain of retail stores, in part to provide a market for its lumber products, but also to add a stable revenue source as the company competed in a lumber industry vulnerable to peaks and valleys in its commodity prices. As the 1960s ended, West Fraser consolidated its operations around two principal mills in Quesnel and Williams Lake. In the decade that followed, West Fraser pursued a reputation as a low-cost producer, including narrowing its sales focus primarily to the United States and Canada and avoiding high-grade specialty products. Equally important to West Fraser's growth strategy was its determination to avoid excessive debt and to plow its profits back into the company. Much of West Fraser's income went into modernizing its existing mills, even as new plants were acquired. The company also concentrated its logging operations on British Columbia's largely untouched interior region, where logging and road building costs were as much as half of those on the more heavily logged coast.

When Sam Ketcham was killed in a helicopter crash in 1977, the company brought in the first of two presidents from outside the family, while Pete Ketcham continued as chairman. By then, West Fraser had begun to step up its diversification efforts. A major move toward this end came in 1979, when the company entered a 50 percent joint venture with Daishowa Canada Co., subsidiary of Daishowa Paper Manufacturing Co. of Japan, to build the Quesnel River pulp mill. Two years later, West Fraser purchased a 40 percent interest in Eurocan Pulp & Paper Co., a division of Finland's Enso-Gutzeit Oy, with its Kitimat, B.C., pulp and paper mill, two sawmills, and interest in other sawmills. West Fraser was now a fully integrated forest products company, grown to eight sawmills and a chain of ten building supply stores.

Growth throughout the 1980s

By 1981, Canada plunged into the recession, which crippled the logging industry, hitting especially hard in British Columbia. Yet, while other companies in the lumber industry were struggling to survive, West Fraser was achieving its greatest growth. Still a private company, West Fraser continued to pursue its policy of reinvesting its earnings—between 1983 and 1986, the company's retained earnings grew from C$65 million to C$100 million. Much of this income was put to work modernizing and maintaining the company's mills and other plants, giving it a further edge against the competition as a low-cost supplier. Throughout the recession, the company remained in the black, with only Eurocan posting a loss in 1983. The following year, however, West Fraser stepped up its ownership of Eurocan Pulp & Paper to 50 percent, and Eurocan was restructured as a joint venture.

In 1985, when then-president Chester Johnson left the company to head up BC Hydro, a new Ketcham, Henry (Hank) III, took over as West Fraser's president and CEO. A graduate of Brown University, Hank Ketcham had long been groomed for this role, joining the company in 1973 as a mill hand, then working in the company's shipping department before becoming manager of West Fraser's Dawson Creek mill. Ketcham took the company public the following year, in part to pay down debt accrued from increasing its share of Eurocan, and also to sort out succession issues. The company, however, continued to be run as a relatively small family operation. Corporate staff numbered as few as six, and the majority of the company's employees were non-union, making it unique in the industry— yet protecting the company from wildcat strikes plaguing the rest of the logging industry.

The company's C$367 million in 1986 revenues were still fairly small compared to the industry's powerhouses. However, West Fraser's lumber output of nearly 1,000 MMfbm had already made it Canada's third-largest producer. With the lumber industry bouncing back as the recession ended, West Fraser continued its policy of investing heavily in its growth. In 1988, the company added a third pulp line to its Quesnel plant, increasing its share of the output to 150,000 metric tons. Next, the company more than doubled the size of its retail operation by buying up the Revelstoke chain of home and building supply stores. West Fraser's own stores were merged under the Revelstoke brand name. The following year, the company completed a major expansion of Eurocan, building a second berth at that plant's deep-sea terminal and increasing its production by more than 25 percent to 450,000 metric tons, costing the company $125 million. Rounding out the 1980s, West Fraser teamed up with limited partnership Whitecourt Newsprint Company to form the Alberta Newsprint Company joint venture, opening a newsprint mill in Whitecourt, Alberta, in 1990. More acquisitions were to follow. By the mid-1990s, the company would double in size.

Continued Growth in the 1990s

As the new decade began, however, the company saw its earnings drop drastically. Despite revenues of $540.5 million in 1990, net income fell to just under $3.5 million—down from $28.4 million in 1989. This was due to the high cost of stumpage rates, that is, the royalty fees paid to the British Columbian government for each tree felled, which had been raised in a memorandum of understanding between the Canadian and U.S. governments. A slump in building starts as the 1990s recession took hold also caught the industry with an oversupply, forcing prices to drop. In addition, the Eurocan expansion continued to prove expensive for the company, as it struggled to produce at capacity, while absorbing the high costs of de-inking needed to meet the growing demand for recycled newsprint.

The slump in earnings proved temporary. By 1992, the company's earnings rose to $10 million. However, in that year, the company's Revelstoke division faced new pressures when two U.S. companies, Home Depot and Eagle Hardware & Garden, announced plans to bring their home and building supply warehouse stores to Canada for the first time. The chains' plans to expand in the Alberta and Vancouver markets forced Revelstoke, by then the fourth largest Canadian home center chain with 30 stores, to roll out its own warehouse concept, called Revy's, and West Fraser announced plans to spend some $200 million in order to build 15 warehouse stores in the next several years. The company also closed several of the smaller Revelstoke stores, converting some of these buildings to the warehouse concept, while leasing out others.

West Fraser was fueling its growth in other ways, too. In November 1993, the company moved to buy out its Finnish partner, paying C$95.8 in cash and two million shares of common stock to purchase Enso-Gutzeit Oy's 50 percent share of Eurocan (Enso subsequently sold its shares, representing ten percent of West Fraser's outstanding stock, to Canadian investors). The move added 30 percent to West Fraser's lumber capacity, bringing it to an annual output of 1,300 MMfbm. West Fraser was now the second largest lumber producer in Canada, trailing only fellow Vancouver-based company Canfor Corp. Despite a poor performance by the Quesnel River pulp plant, which posted its first-ever operating loss, 1993 saw West Fraser's earnings rebound, to $53.4 million.

The company again pushed to expand its operations in 1994, building a new sawmill in Prince Rupert, B.C. The company also added a value-added plant to its Terrace sawmill, allowing it to produce higher-grade, custom-cut hemlock lumber, while pumping capital into major upgrades of two existing sawmills. At the end of the year, West Fraser added to its retail operation by buying up Eagle Hardware & Garden's Canadian assets, which included two undeveloped Eagle sites, for C$30 million, allowing Revelstoke to consolidate its position in the Vancouver market. The British Columbian logging industry, meanwhile, began to see tightening restrictions on AACs, as B.C.'s resources dwindled and pressure built to enact tighter environmental controls. In British Columbia, allowable logging had already been cut from 85 million solid cubic meters to 70 million solid cubic meters, with forecasts suggesting a further reduction to 59 million solid cubic meters by the turn of the century. West Fraser itself responded to environmental controls by voluntarily giving up its rights to a 317,000-hectare area of the Kitilope Valley wilderness area north of Vancouver. West Fraser's 1994 year end revenues rose to C$1.28 billion, generating a net income of C$82.6 million.

West Fraser next moved to ensure its logging supply. China was viewed as a strong source for lumber. "We believe finding a lot more wood in Canada is not going to be possible," Hank Ketcham told the *Christian Science Monitor,* "If you want to have a growing forest-products company, you better go find some wood someplace, and [that's] why were looking outside of Canada." China held a natural attractiveness to the lumber industry: its forests—actually plantations—grew as much as 15 times faster than those in the colder North American region. The company, however, made a more immediate move to guarantee its lumber supply by purchasing the Ranger Forest unit of Alberta Energy for C$394 million.

The Ranger acquisition brought the company three businesses involved in producing and marketing dimension lumber, MDF, and BCTMP. Assets included a sawmill in Blue Ridge, Alberta, with a capacity of 220 MMfbm per year; an MDF plant in Blue Ridge and a pulp mill in Slave Lake, Alberta; and an added 1.1 million solid cubic meters of timber rights. Speaking of the acquisition to *Pulp & Paper,* Ketcham said: "Not only are we acquiring modern and efficient mills with an exceptional timber base ... we also achieve our long-term goal of geographic diversification." The Alberta expansion was also seen as attractive because of the lower stumpage fees and higher AAC rates available there. The company continued to expand internally as well, constructing a new C$150 million MDF plant in Quesnel, scheduled to open in late 1996.

Revenues rose again for 1995, nearing C$1.5 billion and providing C$95.8 million in revenues. In July 1996, Pete Ketcham died of cancer at the age of 73. Hank Ketcham was named chairman, while remaining as its president and CEO, continuing the Ketcham legacy of low-cost operations and controlled expansion that has allowed West Fraser to rise to the top of its industry.

Principal Subsidiaries

West Fraser Mills Ltd.; Blue Ridge Lumber; Eurocan Pulp & Paper; Quesnel River Pulp Company (50%); Ranger Board Ltd.; Revelstoke Home Centres Ltd.; Slave Lake Pulp; Westpine MDF; West Fraser Building Supplies Ltd.; Canadian Woodworks Ltd. (49%); Forwest Wood Specialties Inc. (49%); Burns Lake Specialty Wood Ltd. (14%); Nascor Incorporated (26%); Vernon Seed Orchard Company (30%).

Further Reading

Annett, Marg, and Annett, William, "West Fraser Timber's Intangible Assets," *BC Business,* September 1987, p. 10.
Cagampan-Stoute, Caroline, "The Strong Silent Type," *Canadian Papermaker,* July 1994, p. 16.
"History of the Company," West Fraser Timber Company, http://www.westfrasertimber.ca/story/comphist.htm.
Langan, Fred, "Canada's Foresters See Green in China," *Christian Science Monitor,* April 18, 1995, p. 8.
"West Fraser Builds for Long Term," *Financial Post,* April 3, 1991.
"West Fraser to Buy Alberta Energy's Ranger Forest Unit," *Pulp & Paper,* August 1995, p. 17.

—M. L. Cohen

West Marine, Inc.

500 Westridge Drive
Watsonville, California 95076
U.S.A.
(408) 728-2700
Fax: (408) 728-2736

Public Company
Incorporated: 1993
Employees: 3,000
Sales: $224.2 million (1994)
Stock Exchanges: NASDAQ
SICs: 5551 Boat Dealers; 5961 Catalog & Mail-Order
   Houses; 6719 Holding Companies, Not Elsewhere
   Classified

West Marine, Inc., is the leading distributor of marine sup-plies to recreational boaters, and the largest and most profitable boat supply chain in the nation. Marine supplies for sailboats and powerboats—including recreational boating supplies, sporting goods, and sophisticated navigational equipment—are sold through three divisions: Store (retail and wholesale, 74 percent), Catalog (retail, 15 percent) and Port Supply (whole-sale, 11 percent). The company was founded as West Marine Products, Inc., in Palo Alto in 1975 by Randolph Repass, a former engineer with a love of boating and a vision for a customer-friendly, product-heavy marine supply store. Through its stores, the company—now based in Watsonville, Califor-nia—sells boating clothes, navigational equipment, life jackets, and other marine supplies.

Company Origins

West Marine's success is largely due to the visionary leader-ship of its founder, Randolph Repass. Repass first tasted the boating supply business through his homespun operation of West Coast Ropes—a garage-based business selling rope used for boating lines—in 1968. Raised by a family that was very involved with recreational and sport boating in Boston's south suburbs, Repass had studied electrical engineering at Duke University, then moved to California's Silicon Valley to work as an engineer for Fairchild Cameraq and Instruments in 1966. At Fairchild, Repass was critical of management's reluctance to give employees the free rein he felt they needed to excel at their jobs. He left Fairchild for a technology company, Nortec, where he didn't stay long either. By 1973, married with two children, Repass started his own consulting firm, Semiconductor Engi-neering Associates. When Repass purchased a 13-foot sailboat for $250—the best he could afford at the time—he went shop-ping for boating supplies and found that most stores were lacking in both product selection and trained personnel. Repass correctly identified a need for a marine accessories retailer carrying a wide selection of products. When he opened the first West Marine store in Palo Alto in 1975, it was indeed the first retailer of its size and selection in the underserved industry.

Repass's business philosophy encompasses a liberal and car-ing attitude toward both the customer and the employee. "Em-ployee empowerment" is a key concept at West Marine, and Repass involves all employees in the company's success by means of a stock option after their first year of employment. Customers appreciate West Marine's innovative return policy, which provides for replacement, refund, or repair of any item with no time limit. West Marine was one of the first companies in the country to implement such a liberal return policy.

In its first year of existence, West Marine carried approxi-mately 600 marine supply items. Business was not instantly successful. In fact, during the first year it was not uncommon for an entire day to pass with no customers, and the company's bills were paid with the earnings of Repass's consulting business. Repass lived on a boat in Santa Cruz and spent numerous evenings in a sleeping bag behind the store counter. However, he worked hard to keep the atmosphere upbeat and staff spirits high, and longtime employees remember both the hard work and the fun of those early days. Repass's hard work and initial investment of $25,000 paid off, and West Marine began to grow quickly in the late 1970s and early 1980s. By 1983, the com-pany had ten stores, and by 1992, a second distribution center was opened in Charlotte, North Carolina, and 27 stores were in

---

Company Perspectives:

West Marine's mission is to supply and service boating-related products that provide outstanding value to retail, catalog, and wholesale customers. The company is committed to treating all of its customers better than they expect to be treated, and it strives to be regarded as the best in the industry. The company strives to provide a supportive environment for its employees; actively works to reduce its impact on the environment and to improve and protect the marine environment; and earns a reasonable profit proportional to its success and its mission.

---

operation. The mail order business was added in 1979. In 1982, needing more space, the company moved its headquarters from Palo Alto to Santa Cruz.

Aggressive Expansion in the 1990s

West Marine reached a turning point in 1989 as a result of recurrent financial difficulties. With 15 stores and a presence in the professional market, it was time to move in a new direction. Repass took three months off to build a house, spend time with his family, and reflect on the company's future. He returned with renewed vigor and plans to develop the company into a "category killer" (meaning that West Marine stores would carry approximately twice as many items as its closest competitors). The company updated its computer system to produce daily store reports and real-time inventory checks for its telemarketing staff, and also hired a new group of managers, including Crawford Cole—a former auto industry executive—as president. In 1988 the company moved its headquarters from Santa Cruz to its current location in Watsonville, California.

In 1990 West Marine had 15 stores, all in the West. In 1991 the company began a process of rapid expansion in an attempt to increase its penetration across the 8,000 miles of shoreline in the continental United States, opening some 31 additional stores by 1994. Between 1992 and 1995 the number of stores increased by an average of 39 percent annually, with new stores established in Florida, Long Island, New England, the Gulf, and the Great Lakes. With pre-opening expenses of about $625,000, most West Marine stores became profitable after two years. The company also diversified its service units, planning half-size stores for smaller communities. Sales from its Port Supply Wholesale Division increased 35 percent (to $20.3 million) in 1993. Net income for 1993 was $3.5 million on sales of $122.8 million, which constituted a 116 percent increase in net income and a 127 percent increase in sales over the previous year.

In 1993 West Marine, Inc., was formed as a parent company for West Marine Products, Inc., and incorporated in California. By 1994, comparable-store sales had leaped by 15.8 percent over the previous year, and the stores' initial stock of 600 items had mushroomed to some 18,000 items. 1994 sales were $124.4 million—a 44 percent increase from $88 million the year before. The majority of the increase was accounted for by the 17 store openings that year.

Going Public in 1994

In November 1994 West Marine went public at a price of $14 per share. With 56 stores and approximately seven percent market share, West Marine was recognized as number one of the four industry leaders—joining Boat America Corp., E&B Marine, Inc., and Boater's World—which together represented 16 percent of the $2.2 billion boating supplies industry. To provide expert management, the company bolstered its executive personnel in marketing, merchandising, and inventory. Harvey Durand, whose background was in drug and grocery stores, was hired as president and chief operating officer, and Dennis Hawkins was hired to oversee merchandising and marketing.

In 1994 the ratio of store to catalog sales remained constant, with catalog sales growing 27 percent to $25.2 million. Mail-order catalogs comprised 900 pages, displaying 19,000 items, and were sent to 3,000,000 people. Net income in 1994 was $6 million, a 71 percent increase over 1993. Earnings increased 52 percent to 91 cents a share, and revenue surged 38 percent to $169.9 million. Between 1991 and 1995 the company's sales increased at an annual rate of 25 percent, and earnings increased by 47 percent.

In April 1995 Crawford Cole took over as CEO, and Randy Repass became chairman. Cole targeted 90 markets for new stores, and identified 200 potential new markets. Eighteen new stores were opened in 1995, including first stores in North Carolina, Maine, and Michigan. Cole also publicly announced plans to continue expanding the product line. In the year prior to Cole's assumption of leadership, West Marine had begun to move beyond the sailing industry, aggressively targeting the powerboat market with several hundred products. The power boating market represented a major growth area for the company, since it is substantially larger than the sailing market (accounting for 85 percent of all boat registrants in 1995).

Later that year West Marine moved its West Coast distribution center from Watsonville to a much larger facility in Hollister, California. At this time, a typical West Marine store carried about 10,000 of the 25,000 items offered by the company, and ranged from 5,000 to 15,000 square feet in size. Since the nearest competitor at this time offered about 14,000 items, West Marine retained its status as category leader. The company ranked 85th on *Forbes*'s "200 Best Small Companies in America" roster for 1995.

Acquisition of E&B Marine in 1996

In July 1996 West Marine finalized its acquisition of competitor E&B Marine, which became a subsidiary. The company issued approximately 600,000 shares ($30 million) in exchange for E&B's stock, and assumed $6 million in long-term debt. The acquisition approximately doubled West Marine's store size and market penetration by adding 62 stores (bringing the total number of stores to more than 130), expanded product selection, increased catalog sales to over $300 million, and helped the company achieve economies of scale. Furthermore, the merger allowed West Marine to instantly achieve two goals: penetrating East Coast markets and accessing powerboaters. E&B Marine originated on the East Coast (with its headquarters in New Jersey), and its primary customer was the small power-boater. In fact, the acquisition lent West Marine a sales presence in 40 markets where it was not previously operating, with very little market overlap. Overall, the merger allowed West Marine to eliminate its closest competitor, accomplish two years of growth in a single year, and become almost four times as large as its nearest remaining competitor (Boat U.S., with approximately $90 million in 1996 sales).

At the same time, West Marine faced a challenge in assimilating the new stores, in that E&B stores were typically much less profitable than West Marine's. To accommodate the merger, West Marine cut back on its continuing expansion plans for 1996 and early 1997. The opening of the company's 150th store in San Francisco, in July 1996, was celebrated with Grand Opening festivities. Grand Opening profits benefitted the San Francisco Baykeeper organization, a local nonprofit group.

Principal Subsidiaries

E&B Marine, Inc.; West Marine Products, Inc.

Further Reading

Beckett, Gary, "West, E&B Forge a $300 Million Giant," *Soundings: Trade Only,* May 1996, pp. 1, 73.

"Community Update, San Francisco," Montgomery Securities, April 29, 1996.

Cropper, Carol Marie, "Some Stocks that Waft on the Summer Breezes," *New York Times,* March 3, 1996, p. 3.

Finnerty, Brian, "West Marine Inc.: Sailing Its Way to a Leading Market Position," *Investor's Business Daily,* July 13, 1994.

Galarza, Pablo, "Boat-Supply Retailer Launching More Stores," *Investor's Business Daily,* April 5, 1995.

"Investment Analysis," Needham & Company, Inc., February, 1995.

Mencke, Claire, "Retailer Builds Lead in Boat Gear Business," *Investor's Business Daily,* February 2, 1994, p. A3.

Morris, Keiko, "Randy Repass: Rough Waters Cleared, West Marine Hopes for Clear Sailing," *Entrepreneurial Award Finalist,* May 20, 1996.

Much, Marilyn, "High Sails: West Marine Powers Ahead by Putting Customer First," *Investor's Business Daily,* August 25, 1995.

"Small Caps: Review & Outlook," PaineWebber, May 1996.

Turner, Nick, "West Marine's Randy Repass: A Profitable Odyssey from Silicon Valley to the Sea," *Investor's Business Daily,* May 13, 1996.

—Heidi Feldman

Westamerica Bancorporation

1108 Fifth Avenue
San Rafael, California 94901
U.S.A.
(415) 456-8000
Fax: (415) 257-8127

Public Company
Incorporated: 1972 as Independent Bancshares
    Corporation
Employees: 841
Total Assets: $2.49 billion (1996)
Stock Exchanges: NASDAQ
SICs: 6712 Bank Holding Companies; 6021 National
    Commercial Banks

Westamerica Bancorporation is a northern California bank holding company comprised of two principal subsidiaries: Westamerica Bank and Bank of Lake County, both community banks serving individuals and business clients. The holding company also oversees the operations of Community Banker Services Corporation and Westcore, which perform certain administrative functions. Westamerica Bancorporation operates more than 50 branches in 12 California counties including Marin, Napa, and Sonoma. From a handful of small community banks in the early 1970s operating under a bank holding company organization, Westamerica had expanded by the mid-1990s to a position as one of the largest networks of community banks serving northern California and as a market share leader in many of the local areas it served.

Formed in 1972 under the name of Independent Bankshares Corporation, the holding company consolidated three previously unaffiliated banks: Bank of Marin, Bank of Sonoma County, and First National Bank of Mendocino County, which was formerly known as First National Bank of Cloverdale. The new structure began operations in 1973.

Foundings of the Constituent Banks

The three individual banks which formed the 1972 holding company and many of the subsequent additions to the Westamerica network are invested with their own community banking history. Many of these individual banks trace their roots to banks which were formed by local business people to provide specialty financing for the local community business base. Many of these California businesses—often involved in agriculture—faced problems securing loans from big city banks which had strong ties to the interests of their railroad customers.

The First National Bank of Mendocino County provided the holding company with its oldest bank charter dating to 1886. The Foster family of Marin County was one of the original families instrumental in founding the Mendocino bank which was formerly known as the First National Bank of Cloverdale. The bank was founded to provide financing for the people involved in agricultural interests in the Mendocino area where sheep ranching was a dominate industry. The Bank of Marin County was formed by businessmen involved in the dairy business and other local merchants.

The Bank of Somona County served the western portion of the county, where cattle ranchers and dairy farmers were the major economic players. The bank was a major financier for the area's apple growers who produced the red-and-yellow skin Gravenstein apples primarily used to make applesauce.

In the 1920s, prominent pear growers, including the Bucknell family, were involved in creating the Bank of Lake County, formerly called the Bank of Upper Lake. That bank expanded and branched as the local economy grew along the shores of Clear Lake.

Vaca Valley Bank's roots are linked to the Gibson family and its local business interests in newspapers and publishing in Solano County and the surrounding area. Westamerica Chairman David L. Payne's grandfather, Luther Gibson, was chairman of Vaca Valley Bank. Payne became involved in the newspaper and publishing side of the Gibson family business in the late 1970s and continued the family tradition in banking in the later part of the 1980s.

Company Perspectives:

As we grow, we remain fully committed to what has made Westamerica a successful community bank—delivering outstanding individual service to customers by understanding their financial needs and meeting those needs effectively. This is more critical today than ever before, as we and all community banks face heightened competition and changing customer needs. Most importantly, community banking at Westamerica has always been about people—our customers, our employees, and our shareholders. We are committed to providing innovative financial services to our individual customers and such niche markets as small businesses and professionals. It is the energy, hard work and commitment of each of our employees who serve our customers that will enable Westamerica to grow and prosper.

Though their origins are more recent, other banks in the Westamerica network also trace their history to the growth in their local communities. Napa Valley Bank was founded upon the expanding wine and tourism industries in the area in the 1960s. CapitolBank in Sacramento County and Gold Country Bank in Nevada County were fueled by the influx of retirees when that area in the western foothills of the Sierra Nevada mountain range became an attractive relocation spot for older citizens in the 1970s.

Acquisitions of the Holding Company

During the 1970s, the parent company, Independent Bancshares Corporation, followed a conservative acquisition policy which entailed purchasing community banks in a county-by-county stepping-stone pattern. In 1974, the company acquired Bank of Lake County, a California state-chartered bank which operated in the county adjacent to where Westamerica's existing operations were located. Gold County Bank in 1979 and Vaca Valley Bank in 1981 were each purchased by exchanging shares of the company for the shares of the acquired banks.

These six banks were consolidated in mid-1983 into a single subsidiary bank, First National Bank of Mendocino County, which subsequently changed its name to Westamerica Bank. The company recorded below industry average earnings and investment return benchmarks during the remainder of the 1980s. The company's performance during this time was impacted by stiff competition from larger banks and other financial institutions such as brokerage firms, mutual funds and insurance firms as well as problem real estate loans. The company became a target for takeover in the late 1980s but successfully fought those moves and remained independent.

The 1990s

Fueled by a series of acquisitions, reorganizations, and mergers, the 1990s ushered in a period of earnings growth and enhanced investment performance. The company's asset base almost doubled in the period from the end of 1990 to mid-1995.

During the 1990s, the company operated in an economic environment marked by slow growth in the affluent markets it served and in a banking environment marked by consolidation among large banks at one end of the spectrum and community banks at the other end, where Westamerica positioned itself.

Within this environment, Westamerica pursued a two-pronged growth strategy by expanding existing bank operations and by acquiring other community banks. The company purchased the $60 million asset-based John Muir National Bank in 1992.

The following year, the company acquired Napa Valley Bancorp, a bank holding company with an asset base of $600 million and with banking operations in geographical markets in which Westamerica competed. The acquired bank holding company consisted of a number of subsidiaries: Napa Valley Bank, Suisun Valley Bank, an 88 percent interest in Bank of Lake County, and a 50 percent interest in Sonoma Valley Bank. Westamerica also gained additional back office operations with the Napa Valley Bancorp Services subsidiary which provided data processing and other services to the network of acquired banks.

Over the next 12 months, Westamerica melded and reorganized Napa Valley's operations and assets. Suisun Valley was merged into Westamerica Bank, the name of Napa Valley Bancorp Services was changed to Community Banker Services Corporation and the 50 percent interest in Somona Valley Bank was sold and the proceeds were used to improve Westamerica's financial base. Through a series of financial transactions, the company consolidated its mortgage banking operations into Community Banker Services and purchased the remaining 12 percent interest in Bank of Lake County from outside investors.

The company next completed three significant acquisitions in 1995. In January, the company purchased the $170 million in assets held by PV Financial, which owned PV National Bank. CapitolBank Sacramento with its $139 million asset base was bought in June and North Bay Bancorp, the parent of $108 million Novato National Bank, was acquired the following month.

The bank also purchased two Bank of America branches and opened a new branch in Contra Costa County's Concord, "a market with strong demographics where no suitable acquisition opportunity was available," the company stated in its 1995 Annual Report. In April 1996, the Napa Valley Bank subsidiary was merged into the Westamerica subsidiary.

Leaders and Strategies in the 1990s

In a research report dated July 18, 1995, issued by the brokerage firm Dain Bosworth Inc, the author Thatcher S. Thompson attributed "the success of Westamerica's acquisition policy" to three factors: "disciplined pricing, cost control and high credit quality standards." Many Wall Street securities analysts credit David L. Payne for Westamerica's turnaround and successful strategy in the 1990s. Payne assumed the position of chairman in 1988 and of chief executive officer and president in 1989. Payne had been a director of the company since 1985 and his grandfather had been chairman of the Vaca Valley Bank.

In the 1990s, Westamerica's growth was marked by a renewed emphasis upon its roots in community banking. With many of the banks in its network tracing their lineage to local businesses, Westamerica has continued to emphasize serving the local small business community. The individual banks have attempted to retain their local identity and their local bank managers have been given the authority to tailor and price their products and services for the needs of the individual and small businesses in the local community. In an official filing with the Securities and Exchange Commission, Westamerica said its individual banks emphasized "big bank resources with small bank resourcefulness."

Westamerica's bankers have maintained strong personal contacts with local small business clients. Thompson's July 18, 1995 report for Dain Bosworth recognized Westamerica's local bankers as a "top-notch sales force."

"Westamerica's hard-driving bankers sell, sell, and then sell some more" was the headline of a November 29, 1994 article in *The America Banker* which described how the bank's staffers toted pagers, cellular phones, and laptop computers when they called upon their existing and potential local small business customers. The article noted that the meet-the-customer approach had helped Westamerica achieve a position as a super-community bank which could effectively compete with California banking giants such as First Interstate, Wells Fargo, and BankAmerica Corp.

The bank also has created niche products and services for its individual customers, particularly affluent professionals and people over the age of 50 years. Payne described his strategy as "working my niches and working them well" in an article in the April 17, 1995 issue of the *Business Journal* for Sacramento, California. "We aren't everything to everybody, and we don't try to be," Payne told the publication.

One niche product which Westamerica created was its "VIP Banking" service for the 20 percent of its customers who represent 80 percent of its profits. Another example of niche marketing was cited by a research report issued in June 1993 by the Minneapolis-based brokerage firm of Piper Jaffray and authored by Steven R. Schroll. That report noted that checking account packages for people 50 years and older provided Westamerica with a deposit base which was "much more stable, less expensive, and thus a much more desirable source of funding" than the average individual account at other banks.

Under Payne's leadership, Westamerica also strengthened its financial foundation. Although labeled as a "Rich Kid" in an October 4, 1991 article in *The American Banker,* the article's author Sam Zuckerman wrote that Payne had gained respect since becoming Chairman in late 1988 for tackling the problem of troubled loans to the construction industry. Within 18 months, Zuckerman described Payne as one of the banking industry's "rising stars" and as "an up-and-coming banking executive" in a January 21, 1993 article in *The American Banker.*

The acquisitions of the 1990s engineered under Payne's stewardship received high marks from banking industry executives and observers. Westamerica avoided loan quality problems by focusing its acquisition targets among high quality banks. Payne "hasn't been bottom-feeding, buying problem banks for a good price. He buys good banks," said banking competitor Harold Giomi, President of Sunrise Bank of California in Roseville, in the *Business Journal* article of April 17, 1995.

The acquired banks were quickly integrated into Westamerica's organization. A February 28, 1994 article in *The American Banker* described how a team approach "enabled Westamerica to consolidate in just 60 days" the operations of the acquired Napa Valley Bancorp. and noted that Westamerica retained 95 percent of Napa Valley's existing business.

Westamerica's "expense reduction campaign" and "strict cost control" were cited in the Dain Bosworth July 18, 1995 research report as major factors which contributed to the bank's improved earnings and return on investment in the 1990s. The ranks of personnel were kept to a minimum as evidenced by the less than one dozen employees working at the bank holding company's headquarters in the mid-1990s. While company assets significantly expanded, the total number of employees declined in the first half of the 1990s decade.

Branch efficiency and productivity were another area of cost control. Westamerica shut branches which did not meet profitability and growth benchmarks. Acquired and existing branches which overlapped were closed. Back-office operations throughout the system also were consolidated.

Westamerica's plans for the last half of the 1990 decade were addressed by Payne in the April 17, 1995 *Business Journal* article. Payne stated, "Our longer-term plan is to expand further in the Sacramento market," where, the article noted, economic growth is forecast to outpace the rate in the San Francisco bay area and the northern California coastal regions according to some demographic economists.

Payne provided a more detailed outline of Westamerica's future strategy in the 1995 Annual Report. Payne reported that Westamerica would pursue its growth-by-acquisition strategy but promised to "apply strict criteria" including a "profitability within six months" standard for each acquisition.

He described the evolving shape of community banking and the products and services the customers want and need: "They want to be able to bank from home 24 hours a day and have access to well-trained representatives, not prerecorded messages." To deliver round-the-clock service with "knowledgeable and responsive" employees, Payne noted that "technology is playing a larger role in this effort" so that employees can "answer customers needs more quickly, whether to process a loan or deposit, or to simply fulfill a service need."

Befitting a network of community banks, many of which were spawned by local business people, Payne noted that Westamerica's bankers embrace the entrepreneurial bent of their customers and thus operate within "a sales and service culture that motivates and rewards performance." Westamerica's bankers receive compensation linked to their achievement of performance goals "from the number of outside calls each branch office must make each week, to how quickly our bankers must respond to customer requests," Payne stated in the 1995 Annual Report.

Payne noted that Westamerica would continue to adhere to stringent cost control by "further streamlining our back office functions and reducing our cost structures."

Such a blueprint for further growth at Westamerica could be a double-edged sword. Thompson at Dain Bosworth noted that while Westamerica was well positioned to continue its growth by acquisition and internal cost control, these strengths made Westamerica an attractive takeover candidate. Thompson forecast, "acquisition of this company is certainly a possibility; however, as long as earnings continue to grow and small bank opportunities remain abundant, we think it is more likely we will see Westamerica in the ranks of the consolidators as opposed to the consolidated."

Principal Subsidiaries

Westamerica Bank; Bank of Lake County; Community Banker Services Corporation; Westcore.

Further Reading

Mark Anderson, "Westamerica Targets Local Area for Future Expansions," *Business Journal (Sacramento),* April 17, 1995, p. 1.

Racine, John, "Acquisition Targets Also Aim at Small Business," *The American Banker,* November 29, 1994, p. 9.

——, "Westamerica's Hard-Driving Bankers Sell, Sell, and Then Sell Some More," *The American Banker,* November 29, 1994, p. 9.

Schroll, Steven R., "Westamerica Bancorporation," Minneapolis: Piper Jaffray Inc., June 1993, pp. 1–2.

Strachman, Daniel, "Teamwork Enabled Westamerica to Consolidate in Just 60 Days," *The American Banker,* February 28, 1994, p. 4A.

Thompson, Thatcher S., "Westamerica Bancorporation," Research Report, Seattle: Dain Bosworth Inc., July 18, 1995, pp. 1–11.

Zuckerman, Sam, "Banking's Rising Stars: David L. Payne," *The American Banker,* January 21, 1993, p. 21.

——, "Westamerica's Rich Kid Makes Believers," *The American Banker,* October 4, 1991, p. 1.

—Lynn W. Adkins

Williams-Sonoma, Inc.

100 North Point Street
San Francisco, California 94133
U.S.A.
(415) 421-7900
Fax: (415) 983-9887

Public Company
Incorporated: 1956
Employees: 6,900
Sales: $644.7 million (1995)
Stock Exchanges: NASDAQ
SICs: 5961 Mail Order Houses; 5719 Miscellaneous
   Homefurnishings Stores

Williams-Sonoma, Inc., has become virtually synonymous with home furnishings through its mail-order catalogs and retail stores. In less than forty years, Williams-Sonoma has grown to a $664 million company, making it the U.S. leader in retail specialty home furnishings. Retail store sales, through more than 200 stores in the company's three chains—Williams-Sonoma, Pottery Barn, and Hold Everything—account for 58 percent of annual sales. Catalog sales—through the Williams-Sonoma, Pottery Barn, Gardener's Eden, Chambers, and Hold Everything catalogs, which ship more than 125 million catalogs each year—account for approximately 41 percent of sales. In collaboration with Time-Life, Williams-Sonoma also publishes the Williams-Sonoma Kitchen Library Series. Each of the 24 (and counting) cookbooks in the series features a single subject, simple recipes, and lavish photographs. More than five million copies of the cookbooks have been sold, primarily through the company's retail stores, since the inception of the series in 1992. Advertising is performed almost exclusively by the company's catalogs.

Each of Williams-Sonoma's divisions is focused on a specialty market. The flagship Williams-Sonoma catalog feature a range of 300 professional, often exotic products for the kitchen. The more than 120 Williams-Sonoma retail stores, the largest of the company's retail store chains, feature an expanded 3,000-item line of kitchenware, including cookware, cookbooks, cutlery, dinnerware, and custom-built French stoves. Pottery Barn, the next-largest division, with 57 stores in its retail chain, sells a near-complete line of carpets, lighting, window treatments, furniture, and other home furnishings through its catalogs and retail stores. Hold Everything, with 35 retail stores in 1995 and its own mail-order catalog, offers a unique line of storage and organization products for the home. Williams-Sonoma's home furnishings offerings are rounded out by mail-order catalogs Chambers, which offers bed and bath products, and Gardener's Eden, which specializes in gardening equipment and accessories. The company has been led by chairman and CEO W. Howard Lester since 1978. Founder Charles E. (Chuck) Williams, chairman until 1986, continues to guide the company's merchandise selection as vice-chairman.

Start with a Passion for Cooking

After serving as an Air Force aircraft mechanic in North Africa and India during World War II, Charles Williams moved to Sonoma, California, where he worked as a self-taught carpenter. A passionate cook, Williams made a trip to Paris in the early 1950s aboard the famed Ile de France cruise ship. While in Paris, he discovered a range of cookware and accessories unknown to the rather bland American kitchen of the period. In 1956, tired of his carpentry career, Williams bought and began to renovate a building in Sonoma that included a failed hardware store. Williams proceeded to dispose of the store's traditional hardware supplies and to stock it instead with the professional quality cooking equipment he had discovered overseas.

The store caught on quickly, becoming popular with many professional and serious cooks. Encouraged by friends such as Julia Child and James Beard—who would be instrumental in sparking an interest in fine cooking in the United States—Williams moved his store to San Francisco, renaming it Williams-Sonoma in honor of its original location. Throughout the next decade, Williams's store prospered, attracting customers from around the country. Williams continued making trips to Europe, discovering new products to bring back to his store.

By the late 1960s, the nature of houseware sales in the United States had changed. Interest in international cuisine was on the rise, generating interest in professional quality cooking equipment. Led by Macy's, department stores were making their kitchenware departments increasingly fashionable. Williams was not impressed by these new departments. "It wasn't that much," he told the *San Francisco Business Times*. Serious cooks continued to flock to the Williams-Sonoma store, and by the early 1970s, Williams, exhausted from shouldering the burden not only of stocking and operating the store, but also from running the business end, began to look for help. One frequent customer and close friend was Edward Marcus of the Nieman-Marcus retail chain. Marcus suggested that Williams either sell his company, or expand it himself. Williams decided to expand, and in 1972, Marcus and Williams formed a corporation, Williams-Sonoma, Inc.

Williams continued to handle the purchasing and merchandising, while Marcus brought in a team of executives to guide the company's business end. A second store was opened in Beverly Hills by 1973. In that year, the company brought out its first mail-order catalog. As Williams told *Gentry,* the catalog was "a learning experience. We found that we could sell items by catalog that wouldn't sell in the stores. We could tell a story that couldn't be explained in the store, especially where the item and its use weren't intuitively obvious." Unlike in the stores, where customers merely saw the products on the shelf, the catalog, called *A Catalog for Cooks,* featured photographs of the products in use. The first mailing of the catalog went to 5,000 people. Sales took off, and the catalog's mailing list quickly went nationwide.

The corporation added stores, too. By 1977 the Williams-Sonoma chain had grown to five stores. The following year Marcus, who held one-third of the company, died, and a change in management led the company into trouble. With $4.9 million in sales, the company carried a debt of $700,000 and posted a net loss of $173,000. "[The new management] proceeded to run it the wrong way," Williams told the *San Francisco Business Times,* "In a year's time, the company was in financial difficulty. I decided to sell. If it was going to have these kinds of financial problems, I didn't want it. I'd never had those kinds of problems before. I'd never borrowed money. For years, I never had credit because I paid cash."

New Ownership for the 1980s

In 1978 Williams sold the company for $100,000 to W. Howard Lester, a former IBM salesman and founder of several computer services firms, and his partner, James McMahan. With the sale came the requirement that Williams remain in charge of selecting merchandise and running the catalog.

Williams-Sonoma turned around quickly under Lester. Within five years, the retail chain grew to 19 stores. Catalog mailings reached 30 million customers by 1983, and catalog sales accounted for more than 75 percent of the company's $35 million in annual revenues. In 1982 the company's catalog sales expanded when it acquired the Gardener's Eden catalog, then posting $100,000 in annual sales. In order to finance further expansion, Lester took the company public in 1983, with an initial public offering of one million shares at $23 per share. Lester retained about 22 percent of the company; Williams, who

continued to lead the company's catalog, held about 1.9 percent of the company's stock.

With the money raised in its IPO, the company established a new distribution and warehouse facility in Memphis, Tennessee. Over the next three years, the retail chain grew to 31 stores in 14 states, and the company opened a second retail chain, Hold Everything, which would grow to five stores. The company also sought to expand its catalog business, introducing a catalog featuring table settings and a second catalog featuring more exotic cookware, both of which did poorly. Coupled with the catalog losses, the move to Memphis cut heavily into the company's profits, which were down to $445,000 in 1983 from a net of $1.5 million in 1982. By 1984, with sales reaching nearly $52 million, earnings had sunk to a mere $38,000.

This setback proved short-lived. By 1985, sales climbed to $68 million, earning the company a net of $2.4 million. The company continued to expand, adding 14 Williams-Sonoma stores by the end of the following year. Expansion went beyond Williams-Sonoma. In 1986 the company acquired the struggling Pottery Barn, a chain of 27 retail home furnishings stores, from The Gap for $6 million. Pottery Barn was also added to the company's growing line of catalogs, which by then included Hold Everything and Gardener's Eden. Meanwhile, the retail end was contributing a growing percentage of the company's sales, up to 36 percent by that year. By the end of the 1986 fiscal year, the company's sales climbed past $100 million.

The company continued to grow aggressively, raising the number of Williams-Sonoma stores to 64 in 1988. A joint venture with Tokyo Department Store brought the first Williams-Sonoma store—and the Catalog for Cooks—to Japan. The company's sales surged to $136.8 million, and net earnings of $3.4 million, by year-end 1987. To guide this burgeoning empire, Lester brought in former Pillsbury Co. president Kent Larson as Williams-Sonoma president. Under Larson, the company formed a joint venture with Ralph Lauren to open a chain of Polo/Ralph Lauren Home Collection stores. A fifth catalog was added to the Williams-Sonoma ranks in early 1989. This catalog, called Chambers, featured bed and both products. By then, retail sales accounted for 53 percent of Williams-Sonoma's sales.

Between 1986 and 1989, the company added an average of 12 stores per year, bringing the total number of Williams-Sonoma, Pottery Barn, and Hold Everything retail units to 102 in the United States, with another unit in Japan. Not all of Williams-Sonoma's ventures were successful, however. After one year, the company and Ralph Lauren agreed to dissolve their joint venture partnership. An attempt to establish a Gardener's Eden retail chain also failed, in part because of the inherently seasonal nature of that market. Nevertheless, the company's revenues, led by its growing Williams-Sonoma retail chain, continued to make steady gains, rising from $174 million in 1988 to $287 million in 1990.

Williams-Sonoma's rapid expansion, and the economy's turn into the recession of the early 1990s, badly hurt earnings. The company's $11.2 million net profit in 1990 fell to $1.6 million and $1.8 million in the next two years, while revenues increased slowly, to $312 million in 1991 and $344 million in 1992.

Recovering after the 1990s Recession

Yet Williams-Sonoma's troubles proved short-lived. Management was restructured, the company introduced new merchandising strategies and catalog designs, and catalog production was brought in-house. The company also slowed expansion of its retail chains, focusing instead on improving store design and on increasing store square footage. In 1992 the company joined with Time-Life Books to create the first in a series of Williams-Sonoma Kitchen Library cookbooks. Sold initially only through Williams-Sonoma retail stores, the first four books offered simple recipes, clear instructions, and tips on cooking techniques for pasta, pies and tarts, grilling, and hors d'oeuvres. The books sold well, adding to Williams-Sonoma's image as a resource for the serious and even not-so-serious cook.

By year-end 1993, the company had posted a strong turnaround. Revenues rose to $410 million, and earnings again climbed past $11 million. A chief architect of the turnaround was executive vice-president Gary Friedman. Friedman introduced major changes throughout the company's retail operations. The Catalog for Cooks was redesigned from digest to full size which, as Lester explained to the *San Francisco Chronicle,* "gives you a lot more punch. You can show bigger recipes and more dramatic photographs on major ideas." The new design spurred an increase of 40 percent on the catalog's sales. Next came a reorganization of the Williams-Sonoma store chain, including grouping in-store promotions around monthly themes—so that, for example, if the theme for the month was pasta, the largest share of in-store displays featured pasta-related merchandise. Within several months, the reorganization helped boost per-store sales by over 20 percent. For the Pottery Barn division, which had lost more than $5 million in 1992, Friedman introduced even more dramatic changes, including replacing more than 80 percent of the retail stores' merchandise, while increasing square-footage in new and future stores. The newly designed Pottery Barn reflected Friedman's own frustration when trying to furnish his home, as he told the *Austin American-Statesman.* "It was a confusing proposition," Friedman said. "I needed a place where I could find everything I needed." To the *Dallas Morning News,* Friedman added: "I wanted a store that would sell me window treatments, lamps, sofas and chairs." The Pottery Barn redesign proved immediately successful, and helped spark the division's growth from combined store and catalog sales of $103 million in 1992 to $165 million in 1993.

With total catalog sales rising to $200 million, Williams-Sonoma rolled out new formats for its Williams-Sonoma flagship chain and its Pottery Barn chain. The expanded Williams-Sonoma stores featured professional demonstration kitchens, larger cookbook libraries, tasting bars, and a food hall featuring high-quality foods and the company's own line of private-label foods. The new format for Pottery Barn stores included an average 10,000 square feet—about triple the size of older Pottery Barn stores—featuring a design studio, lighting gallery, and interior finishings shop. The company also started construction on a 300,000 square-foot addition to its 750,000 square-foot Memphis distribution and warehouse facility. The company also entered an agreement with Time-Warner and Spiegel to introduce a 24-hour television shopping network.

With the implementation of these latest changes, Williams-Sonoma was once again on the fast tract. Sales in 1994 reached $528.5 million, for net earnings of $19.6 million. The following year, with the number of Williams-Sonoma, Hold Everything, and Pottery Barn stores topping 200, revenues jumped again, to $644.7 million. Industry analysts began to look to the still relatively tiny Hold Everything store chain to spur even higher growth for the company. Williams-Sonoma's predictions in 1995 called for the company to reach $1 billion in sales by the turn of the century. If the company continues its success of the mid-1990s, Williams-Sonoma should easily reach that goal, and beyond.

Principal Divisions

Williams-Sonoma; Hold Everything; Gardener's Eden; Pottery Barn; Chambers.

Further Reading

Breyer, R. Michelle, "Pottery Barn Bringing New Format to City," *Austin American-Statesman,* August 19, 1995, p. D1.

Fisher, Lawrence M., "A Store for the Gourmet Cook," *New York Times,* July 30, 1986, p. D1.

Garry, Michael, "Upscale Image Reaps $35 Mil for Williams-Sonoma," *Merchandising,* September 1984, p. 17.

Halkias, Maria, "Mending Cracks at Pottery Barn," *Dallas Morning News,* July 6, 1995, p. 1D.

Joss, John, "The Kitchen God's Life," *Gentry,* January/February 1994, p. 61.

Meeks, Fleming, "Williams-Sonoma," *Forbes,* February 18, 1991, p. 60.

Shaw, Jan, "Williams Learned to Delegate, but He Hasn't Given up Working," *San Francisco Business Times,* December 19, 1988, p. 12.

——, "Williams-Sonoma Cooks Up Growth," *San Francisco Business Times,* November 28, 1988, p. 1.

Springer, Bobbi, "Cooking on Four Burners," *San Francisco Business Magazine,* July 1989, p. 44.

—M. L. Cohen

WMX Technologies Inc.

3003 Butterfield Road
Oak Brook, Illinois 60521
U.S.A.
(708) 572-8800
Fax: (708) 572-3094

Public Company
Incorporated: 1968 as Waste Management, Inc.
Employees: 73,200
Sales: $10.25 billion (1995)
Stock Exchanges: New York Chicago Frankfurt London
   Switzerland
SICs: 4941 Water Supply; 4952 Sewerage Systems; 4953
   Refuse Systems; 6719 Holding Companies, Not
   Elsewhere Classified; 8711 Engineering Services

WMX Technologies Inc., a holding company, is a leading international provider of environmental and related services. In the mid-1990s it operated the world's foremost network of waste recycling, collection, processing, transfer, and disposal facilities. Through Waste Management, Inc., it was the leading recycler and manager of solid wastes in North America. Waste Management and Chemical Waste Management, Inc. were treating, storing, and disposing of chemical and hazardous wastes. Wheelabrator Technologies, Inc. was providing a wide array of environmental services, principally in converting trash to energy and developing clean air and water systems. Waste Management International plc was engaged in a wide range of solid- and hazardous-waste management and related environmental services worldwide. Rust International, Inc., was engaged in a variety of environmental, engineering, and industrial services.

Family Predecessors, 1894–1968

WMX Technologies derived from a family business started by Harm Huizenga, a Dutch immigrant who arrived in Chicago during the World's Fair of 1893 and began hauling garbage the following year at $1.25 a wagonload. His son Tom started

buying into his father's business in the 1920s and, late in the decade, opened his own company, which he called Ace Scavenger Service. In the 1930s he formed, in partnership with other Dutch-Americans—many of them related to the Huizengas—Chicago and Suburban Disposal (C&S) to consolidate routes in the western suburbs of Cicero and Berwyn.

In the 1950s an expanded trust brought together five firms, including Ace, C&S, and Arrow Disposal. Dean Buntrock, a Huizenga son-in-law, joined Ace in 1956, which at the time had about 15 trucks and annual revenue of $750,000 a year. He subsequently took charge of two of the companies and expanded into Milwaukee with a third. In 1965 Arrow Disposal, and Buntrock personally, invested in a small but growing Florida waste-disposal business operated by another relative, H. Wayne Huizenga.

Headlong Expansion

Waste Management was formed in 1968 as a holding company to tie together the 20 or so family-controlled businesses engaged in the collection and disposal of solid waste. The process of consolidation was not completed, however, until 1971. Buntrock, Wayne Huizenga, and an employee, Larry Beck, emerged with the largest stakes in the new entity, which established its headquarters in Oak Brook, a Chicago suburb. Buntrock became chairman and president, Huizenga vice-chairman, and Beck senior vice-president. (Beck and Huizenga retired in 1984; Huizenga subsequently bought a controlling interest in Blockbuster Entertainment Corp., which became the nation's largest video-rental chain.)

Company revenues rose from $5.7 million in 1968 to $10.4 million in 1970, while net income increased from $323,000 to $688,000 in that period. In June 1971 Waste Management made its first public offering of common stock, raising about $4 million. That year it had revenues of just under $17 million and a net income of $1.25 million, serving 14,000 industrial and commercial customers and 40,000 private householders in six states. Waste Management operated 200 trucks and maintained 13,000 waste-storage containers in 1971. It also operated 17 sanitary landfills in five states. In southern Florida, where the water table

---

Company Perspectives:

The mission of WMX Technologies, Inc. is to be the acknowledged worldwide leader in providing comprehensive environmental, waste management and related services of the highest quality to industry, government and consumers using state-of-the-art systems responsive to customer need, sound environmental policy and the highest standards of corporate citizenship. In fulfilling this mission, we shall provide a rewarding work environment for our people, cooperate with the relevant government agencies, and promote a spirit of partnership with the communities and enterprises we serve as we strive to be a responsible neighbor, while increasing shareholder value.

---

was too close to the surface to allow disposal of organic wastes in the ground, the company built the nation's first private solid-waste reduction center, a mill that reduced, after reclaiming metals and paper fibers, all garbage and trash into small particles suitable for spreading upon the surface without the necessity of cover.

Waste Management wasted no time expanding still further. In the first nine months of 1972 it gathered 133 other firms into its fold. These were local operations whose owners were allowed to continue as managers. By the end of the year the company was serving 60,000 industrial and commercial accounts and 600,000 households in 19 states and the Canadian province of Ontario. Revenues reached $82 million for the year, and net income $5.7 million. A second major stock offering during the year raised $25 million more, which, like the first infusion of funds, went to retire debt and to finance the purchase of equipment and disposal sites. With very few exceptions, Waste Management's acquisitions were paid for in stock rather than cash. No dividends were paid out at this time.

By the end of 1974 Waste Management had operations in 32 states and the District of Columbia. It owned 32 sanitary landfills and leased 21 others in 16 states and Ontario. Revenues that year came to $158 million, and net income to $9.3 million. Waste collection and storage services accounted for about 80 percent of revenues, and transfer and disposal services for the remainder.

As Waste Management expanded into international and liquid-waste operations, its revenues and income continued to increase rapidly. Between 1971 and 1980 Waste Management grew at a compounded annual average rate of 48 percent. The company began paying dividends in 1976 and never missed a quarter thereafter. In 1980, the year the company passed its main competitor, Browning-Ferris Industries Inc., in annual sales, it had revenues of $656 million and net income of $59 million. Its revenues reached $965 million in 1982, with net income of $106 million. By 1983 Waste Management's 4,200 trucks constituted the largest garbage fleet in the world.

International Operations

Waste Management entered the international field in 1977, when it won a five-year, $242 million contract to dispose of the

solid waste in Riyadh, the capital of oil-rich Saudi Arabia. In 1981 the company won similar contracts for Jeddah, Saudi Arabia's chief port, and Buenos Aires, Argentina. In the next few years it added Cordoba, Argentina; Caracas, Venezuela; and Brisbane, Australia to its list of overseas municipal clients. By 1989 the company had about 10 big landfills in Europe and through a subsidiary, Ocean Combustion Service, was burning toxic waste on incinerator ships plying the North Sea. By 1990 Waste Management International had operations in 23 countries.

Chemical and Hazardous Wastes

In 1976 the U.S. Congress passed two landmark acts for the definition, classification, and handling of chemical and hazardous wastes. When tough regulations implementing this legislation went into effect in November 1980, Waste Management was ready to serve manufacturers that had accumulated these wastes as a byproduct and were willing to pay as much as 35 times the rate for ordinary trash removal. The company already had eight disposal sites for this material, each with its own chemical laboratory to analyze and monitor incoming waste. Six of them were trenches or pits in soil considered so impermeable that liquids could not seep out and contaminate groundwater. Two were deep-well injection sites where liquid wastes were pumped into porous-rock formations far beneath the surface of the earth. One of these, near Emelle, Alabama, became, at 2,730 acres, the largest such site in the world.

By the early 1980s, Waste Management had become the largest hazardous-waste handler in the United States and the nation's largest handler of chemical wastes for private industry and the Department of Defense. Its chemical- and hazardous-waste operations were contributing close to $100 million to the company's revenues and more than one-fifth of profits.

In 1980 Congress passed "Superfund" legislation giving the Environmental Protection Agency authority and funds to clean up abandoned hazardous-waste sites deemed to be environmental or public-health problems. Waste Management, through its Chemical Waste Management subsidiary, received the EPA's first clean-up contract under Superfund, in Gary, Indiana, and later moved on to major work in Greensboro, North Carolina, and Seattle, and for the cleanup of contaminated materials from the Exxon *Valdez* tanker spill in Alaska.

Chemical Waste added low-level nuclear wastes to the materials it was equipped to dispose of by purchasing Chem-Nuclear Systems Inc. of Kirkland, Washington, in 1983. This gave Waste Management a nuclear-waste disposal facility in Barnwell, South Carolina—one of only two such sites in the nation—as well as two more chemical-waste sites. Additionally, a Denver Superfund project called on the company to transport and dispose of 500,000 tons of radium-contaminated soil and debris from 44 separate locations.

Waste Management acquired, in 1984, 60 percent of Service Corporation of America, the third-largest handler of solid and hazardous waste in the United States, for $220 million in cash. Among the facilities acquired were Waste Management's first hazardous-waste incinerator (in Chicago), a landfill for the disposal of PCBs in Model City, New York, and a double-lined hazardous-waste landfill in Fort Wayne, Indiana. The deal also added 21 landfills to Waste Management's existing 68.

Lawsuits, Fines, and Bad Publicity

A front-page *New York Times* article published on March 21, 1983, touched off, after 15 years of spectacular success, Waste Management's first crisis. It reported that the company had, within the last two years, been cited by state and federal authorities for violations at toxic-waste sites in at least seven states. Former employees charged that the company was responsible for illegal dumping of hazardous wastes at four separate sites. Waste Management also was accused of improperly attempting to influence the EPA and destroying or altering evidence of its violations. In the wake of these allegations, many shareholders dumped the stock, causing a loss of $860 million in the company's overall market value in just two days.

A number of these charges proved well-founded. Waste Management admitted to storing impermissible levels of PCBs at its Vickery, Ohio, site, where investigators found millions of gallons of toxic waste had seeped into the sandstone surrounding five of the deep wells on the property. The company paid $12.5 million in fines and promised to spend another $10 million to bring the site into compliance with regulations. In 1985 it paid out $600,000 for illegally storing PCBs at Emelle. Waste Management later paid fines of $9.25 million for violations at its Chicago hazardous-waste incinerator, which was shut down after a 1991 explosion and written off entirely in 1993.

Waste Management also was accused of a number of illegal business practices aimed at restraint of trade, including intimidating customers and harassing competitors. In 1988 it paid $2 million in fines for collusion to allocate garbage-collection territories in Toledo, Miami, and Fort Lauderdale. Two California company units pleaded guilty in 1990 to price-fixing charges and were fined $1.5 million. Company president Philip Rooney later said Waste Management's legal woes were an inevitable consequence of its size and its decentralized structure of formerly independent local operations.

Full-Line Environmentalists

Waste Management bounced back from these problems and continued to grow throughout the 1980s, earning $562 million in 1989 on revenues of $4.5 billion. Improving its image as well as exploring another possible pathway to profit, the company rapidly expanded its recycling of paper, glass, plastics, and metals. By 1990 its Recycle America subsidiary, formed in 1986, was the nation's largest recycler, with curbside pickup programs serving 1.2 million households.

By mid 1989 Waste Management was operating 123 landfills, of which 60 were undergoing expansion, and it had another 80 new landfills under development. With an estimated one-third of the nation's functioning 6,000 landfills nearing capacity and growing public opposition to new ones, Waste Management's plentiful supply of real estate gave the company what it perceived as great bargaining power. At the same time, because of growing public resistance to landfills, Waste Management saw future growth to come from dealing with waste at its source. In the early 1990s Buntrock traveled to big corpora-

tions, proposing to provide in-house management of all their waste problems. He signed contracts with Alcoa, Boeing, General Electric, General Motors, Du Pont, Hoechst Celanese, and Navistar International.

In 1993 Waste Management reorganized itself into a publicly traded holding company named WMX Technologies. As such, it held a controlling interest in four other publicly traded companies: Chemical Waste Management, Waste Management International, Wheelabrator Technologies, and Rust International, as well as full ownership of Waste Management of North America. This network was testimony to WMX's ambition to dominate every sphere of waste collection and disposal. Wheelabrator's major business in 1993, for example, was its 14 plants burning trash at high temperatures, generating electricity for six million people. (Chemical Waste also had three incineration sites where hazardous organic waste was being burned.) Rust International was one of the nation's leading environmental engineering and consulting firms as well as a leading design and construction company.

Downsizing in the 1990s

Ironically, because of WMX's great scope the consolidated company soon found it was engaged in ruinous competition with itself. For example, its customer base of 11 million homes enthusiastically supported recycling, which was removing 15 to 30 percent of the waste that once went to landfills. This meant less profit for WMX, because of the weak commodities market for recycled material. Trash-to-energy incineration also reduced the demand for landfill space, as did the weak economy of the early 1990s and, partly for this reason, an unexpected drop in the output of industrial wastes by big manufacturers. In 1993 WMX's revenues fell for the first time, and its profits declined by 47 percent. Worst hit was Chemical Waste, which took a $363-million writeoff because of deferrals in the disposal of hazardous waste. The value of WMX's common stock plunged from $17.5 billion to $12.6 billion in 1993. (Chemical Waste and Rust International ceased to be publicly traded companies when WMX bought their available shares during 1993–95.)

In May 1994 Rooney announced plans to sell $1 billion of WMX's $19 billion in company assets over the next 18 to 24 months. It sold Rust International's hazardous-waste and nuclear-waste cleanup operations to OHM Corp. for stock valued at about $77.8 million and Rust's pulp-and-paper industrial-process engineering and construction division to Raytheon Co. for $118 million. Waste Management International took a $148-million writeoff in 1995 to dispose of operations and dismiss 300 workers. In 1996, however, WMX entered the New York City garbage business for the first time by buying Re-Source NE, Inc., the city's largest recycling and waste-processing company. Rooney succeeded Buntrock as WMX's chief executive officer in June 1996.

WMX Technologies in 1995

WMX Technologies ended 1995 with revenue of $10.25 billion, up 7.3 percent from 1994, but net income, at $654.6 million, was down 15.7 percent for the year. Solid-waste management and related services (Waste Management) accounted for 53 percent of revenue during the year; international waste management and related services (Waste Management International) for 17 percent; trash-to-energy, waste treatment, air quality, and related services (Wheelabrator) for 14 percent; engineering, industrial and related services (Rust International) for 10 percent; and hazardous-waste management and related services (Chemical Waste Management) for six percent. The company operated 790 collection facilities with a fleet of 28,500 vehicles, 227 transfer stations, 208 material-recycling facilities, and 195 land disposal sites. It also had 16 trash-to-energy facilities and seven cogeneration and independent power plants in North America. In addition, it was operating 550 water, wastewater, and biosolid projects and had installed more than 12,000 industrial water-treatment systems worldwide. Engineers, scientists, and technical personnel were operating in 35 countries. Long-term debt was $6.42 billion at the end of the year.

Principal Subsidiaries

Chemical Waste Management, Inc.; Rust International Inc.; Waste Management, Inc.; Waste Management International plc; Wheelabrator Technologies Inc. Waste Management and Chemical Waste Management were wholly owned by WMX Technologies. The others were at least half-owned by WMX.

Further Reading

Bonner, Raymond, "Giant Waste Company Accused of Illegal Acts," *New York Times,* March 21, 1983, pp. A1, D10.

Bukro, Casey, "Piled-Up Expectations Squeeze Waste Behemoth," *Chicago Tribune,* May 16, 1994, Sec. 4, p. 3.

Burck, Charles G., "There's Big Business in All That Garbage," *Fortune,* April 7, 1980, pp. 106–108, 110, 112.

Chakravarty, Subrata N., "Dean Buntrock's Green Machine," *Forbes,* August 2, 1993, pp. 96–100.

Ellis, James E., "Cleaning Up after Waste Management," *Business Week,* January 24, 1994, pp. 99, 102.

Foley, Brian F., and Clarke, Philip R., III, "Waste Management, Inc.," *Wall Street Transcript,* December 24, 1973, pp. 35437-35440.

Jacobson, Timothy C. *Waste Management: An American Corporate Success Story.* Washington, D.C.: Gateway Business Books, 1993.

Lancaster, Ron, "Waste Management Says It Has Disposed of Most Problems, but Some Voice Doubts," *Wall Street Journal,* October 4, 1983, p. 60.

Melcher, Richard A., "Back to the Nitty-Gritty," *Business Week,* June 17, 1996, pp. 76, 80.

Morais, Richard J., "A Jagged Line, but the Direction Is Up," *Forbes,* October 24, 1994, pp. 54–55, 58.

Powers, Mary B., "Rust Gets a New Shine," *ENR,* June 14, 1993, pp. 22–24, 26.

Weiner, Steve, "Garbage In, Profits Out," *Forbes,* December 12, 1988, pp. 47, 50.

—Robert Halasz

THE YASUDA TRUST AND BANKING CO., LTD.

The Yasuda Trust and Banking Company, Limited

2-1, Yaesu 1-chome
Chuo-ku
Tokyo 103
Japan
(03) 3278-8111
Fax: (03) 3281-6947

Public Company
Incorporated: 1925
Employees: 5,011
Total Assets: ¥23.78 trillion (US $223.63 billion) (1996)
Stock Exchanges: Tokyo Osaka London
SICs: 6021 National Commercial Banks; 6022 State
    Commercial Banks & Trust Companies; 6211 Security
    Brokers, Dealers & Flotation Companies

Since establishing its first overseas branch some two decades ago, Yasuda Trust and its subsidiaries have been actively engaged in financing, money market operations, trustee operations, and the trading and underwriting of securities. Central to these operations is the Bank's worldwide network of 26 offices. In Japan, Yasuda Trust enjoys valuable relationships with numerous corporate and individual clients, serving their needs through its network of 58 branches nationwide.

The Yasuda Trust and Banking Company, Limited is a leading Japanese financial institution specializing in pension trust management, real estate services, and securities-related services, in addition to offering banking services. It is one of only a limited number of Japanese firms licensed to engage both in banking and in trust management. Although it has suffered through a particularly troubled period in the early and mid-1990s, Yasuda has been one of the most consistently successful trust banks and has made significant contributions to the Japanese economy through both trust management and industrial financing.

Zaibatsu *Period, 1923–1945*

Yasuda was once one of the most powerful industrial groups, called *zaibatsu,* in Japan. The Yasuda group was built mainly on financial services, including banking, insurance, and lending. Yasuda decided to enter the trust business soon after the passage of the trust banking laws in 1923. In 1925, several financiers, led by Yasuda, established the Kyosai ("mutual aid") Trust Company. Yasuda quickly expanded its interest in the trust bank and, the following year, changed its name from Kyosai to Yasuda.

Unlike other *zaibatsu,* which diversified into manufacturing, transportation, and natural resources as well as banking, Yasuda remained solely dedicated to finance. At this point, the Yasuda group consisted of the Yasuda Bank, the Yasuda Fire & Marine Insurance Company, Yasuda Mutual Life Insurance, and the new Yasuda Trust Company.

The 1930s was a tumultuous period for Japanese industry. Government regulation of the economy remained unsophisticated, and because many basic monetary functions were handled by the competing *zaibatsu,* much of the regulation that existed was uncoordinated. But despite frequent and, occasionally, serious recessions, Yasuda and the other *zaibatsu* grew larger and stronger.

This trend was checked, however, when a quasinational socialist military group rose to power. One of the goals of this group was decreasing the power of the *zaibatsu.* But by 1940, the wartime economy required the concentration of industry, and the *zaibatsu* were once again allowed to absorb smaller companies, in the name of economic efficiency. The Yasuda group, however, and Yasuda Trust in particular, avoided amalgamation throughout the war, although it did take over certain accounts from other institutions. As a powerful financial institution, Yasuda was nonetheless intimately involved in war finance.

Postwar Period of Growth

When the war ended in 1945, the American occupation authority dissolved the *zaibatsu* into thousands of smaller enter-

Company Perspectives:

The Yasuda Trust and Banking Company, Limited, ranked among the world's leading trust banks, was founded in 1925 and proudly celebrated its 70th anniversary in May 1995. As a trust bank, it maintains a unique position in the Japanese financial industry, handling asset and pension fund management, real estate brokerage and development, and stock transfer agency and other trustee-related business as well as commercial banking.

prises. Ties between the Yasuda companies were cut, and each was forced to change its name. The Yasuda Bank, the center of the group, became the Fuji Bank. In 1948, under new trust laws, Yasuda Trust was reincorporated as Chuo Trust & Banking, taking its name from the Chuo, or "central," district of Tokyo, where it was headquartered.

Japan's industrial organization laws were relaxed in 1952, and with the enactment of the Loan Trust Law, Chuo changed its name back to Yasuda. This law enabled Yasuda to tap a new, stable market for long-term beneficiary certificates of variable denominations. In this way, customers, mostly private individuals, provided the bank with additional capital for long-term industrial financing.

Using its trust and long- and short-term finance products, Yasuda forged close relationships with Japan's largest industrial companies, including Hitachi, Nippon Steel, the Nissan Motor Company, and Marubeni, a general trading company once associated with Sumitomo. The companies of the former Yasuda group reestablished ties through cross-ownership of stock to form the new postwar Fuyo industrial group.

Yasuda adopted an extremely cautious approach to trust and asset management. Much of this caution was required by law, but Yasuda set out to build a reputation for conservative management. As a primary manager of funds for Japan's largest and fastest growing companies, Yasuda benefited directly from the rapid expansion of Japan's heavy industries during that country's first period of industrial growth (1955–1970). As the bulk of the company's income was spread-based, rather than fee-based, Yasuda grew at an exponential rate.

Such conservative management, however, made Yasuda a largely faceless institution, distinguished only by its smooth and predictable growth and its affiliation with the influential Fuyo group. Still, many of Yasuda's competitors gained similar reputations.

Slower Growth in the 1970s and 1980s

The entire Japanese economy was profoundly affected by two events in the early 1970s. The first was the Nixon Administration's decision in 1971 to abandon the Bretton-Woods system of currency valuation. This resulted in a sharp appreciation of the yen against the dollar and slowed Japanese export-led growth. The second was the OPEC oil embargo of 1973, which drastically raised production costs at all levels of the Japanese economy.

Whereas many less conservative financial institutions were seriously jeopardized by the effects of these crises, Yasuda's growth was merely slowed. Though Yasuda was exposed to contracting sectors such as steel and shipbuilding, its investments were diversified enough that it was able to reorient itself to the new economic environment quickly. This lesson became institutional policy and was instrumental in avoiding a similar crisis during the second oil crisis, in 1979.

Yasuda recognized many years in advance that financial management opportunities in Japan were becoming saturated. Japan's second period of industrial growth (1970–1985) flooded Japanese financial institutions with capital at the same time that it exhausted investment opportunities; Japanese investments were no longer competitive with foreign projects.

To effect a stable entry into foreign financial markets, Yasuda had established "intelligence-gathering" offices in major foreign markets as early as the 1960s. Often, these offices were jointly operated with fellow Fuyo members, or even competitors, such as Mitsui, Mitsubishi, and Sumitomo. When its clients began to investigate the establishment of foreign-registered subsidiaries, Yasuda was able to offer good intelligence and management services specifically tailored for Japanese companies in these markets.

A major obstacle to growth in Yasuda's home market was government regulation. In response to an ongoing effort by the banking, trust, and securities industries, this regulation was gradually being relaxed. Much of this activity, however, was limited to the banking industry. Yasuda prepared for increased competition in Japan by establishing strengths in six distinct areas of long-term growth potential.

In the area of pension management, Yasuda took advantage of the trend in which the ratio of employees to pensioners, five to one in the late 1980s, was projected to fall to two and a half to one by the year 2020. With more than ¥2.2 trillion in pension fund assets in 1988, Yasuda had compiled the best investment record of any Japanese trust bank and was well positioned to maintain its position. In addition, because Japanese business was devoting less money to investment, despite record earnings, Japanese companies enjoyed greater liquidity than ever before. Yasuda responded by creating new corporate cash management services. Yasuda also established its expertise in real estate development, international finance and market services, and leadership in the Tokyo investment market.

Difficulties in the 1990s

Like many Japanese financial institutions, Yasuda entered a prolonged period of declining fortunes in the early 1990s. Unsound lending practices in the late 1980s, the bursting of the Japanese economic bubble in late 1991, and increasing competition engendered by the ongoing deregulation of the Japanese financial industry conspired to halt Yasuda's growth and to raise the possibility of Yasuda being taken over by a stronger rival. Net income steadily declined during the first three years of the decade from ¥52.4 billion in 1989 to ¥48.7 billion in 1990, to ¥34.2 billion in 1991, and to ¥21.5 billion in 1992.

In an effort to reverse this downslide, Yasuda begin in April 1992 a three-year four-goal plan for growth, called the New Century Plan Action II. The plan first sought to clarify and strengthen Yasuda's core specialties, which were identified as asset management, pension and public fund management, and real estate and related development services. A second goal involved restructuring the company's banking business to increase the volume of highly profitable floating-rate long-term loans; to do so, branches would be bolstered and the customer base broadened. The plan's third goal aimed to enhance marketing operations to develop new financial instruments. The final goal sought to improve Yasuda's risk management capabilities to cope with the rapidly changing environment that all Japanese financial institutions faced.

With the Japanese economy continuing in recession and the bank's problem with nonperforming loans (mainly from the late 1980s) growing worse, Yasuda was only able to stay barely profitable during the plan period. Net income stood at ¥8.8 billion in 1993, then came in at ¥9.7 billion in 1994 and ¥9.3 billion in 1995. Under a new three-year plan launched in April 1995, Yasuda sought to address the nonperforming loans issue by reducing their balance, which by September 30, 1995 had reached 15.5 percent of all loans. The value of the nonperforming loans had reached ¥1.49 trillion (US $14.75 billion), the highest such figure among all of Japan's trust and long-term credit banks.

During the 1996 fiscal year, Yasuda wrote off ¥202.53 billion (US $1.9 billion) in nonperforming loans and set aside another ¥238.74 billion (US $2.24 billion) in reserves for loan losses. As a result, the bank posted a net loss of ¥199.5 billion (US $1.88 billion) for the year. Yasuda also announced a restructuring plan in April 1996 that would involve some streamlining of personnel in an attempt to strengthen prospects for improved future performance.

As Japanese banking troubles reached a peak in the mid-1990s, many analysts predicted a period of consolidation in the industry, a development that would also tend to follow from the deregulatory moves of the government. For Yasuda, it was said that its affiliated city bank, Fuji Bank, was the most likely suitor. Also possible, however, was that Yasuda, by aggressively handling its portfolio of nonperforming loans, could recover on its own during the late 1990s.

Principal Subsidiaries

Yasuda Bank and Trust Company (U.S.A.); Yasuda Trust Europe Limited (U.K.); Yasuda Trust and Banking (Switzerland) Ltd.; Yasuda Trust & Banking (Luxembourg) S.A.; YTB Financial Futures (Singapore) Pte. Ltd.; Yasuda Trust Asia Pacific Limited (Hong Kong); Yasuda Trust Australia, Limited; YTB Finance (Aruba) A.E.C.; YTB Finance (Curaçao) N.V. (Netherlands Antilles).

Further Reading

Commins, Kevin, ''Japanese Bank Pushes US-Asia Joint Ventures,'' *Journal of Commerce and Commercial,* May 7, 1990, p. 3A.
Morishita, Kaoru, and Ishibashi, Asako, ''Weak Banks Enter Quest for White Knights,'' *Nikkei Weekly,* December 4, 1995, pp. 1, 19.
Neustadt, David, ''Yasuda Builds Business with Top Developers,'' *American Banker,* February 13, 1990, p. 9.

—updated by David E. Salamie

Yucaipa Cos.

10000 Santa Monica Boulevard, 5th Floor
Los Angeles, California 90067
U.S.A.
(310) 789-7200

Private Company
Employees: 57,000 (est.)
Sales: $11 billion (1995 est.)
SICs: 5411 Grocery Stores; 6799 Investors, Not
     Elsewhere Classified; 6719 Holding Companies, Not
     Elsewhere Classified

Yucaipa Cos. is an investment firm specializing in leveraged buyouts of grocery stores and supermarkets. By the mid-1990s, it held controlling interest in three major regional supermarket chains operating more than 600 stores in 11 states. These chains—Ralphs Grocery Co., Dominick's Finer Foods, and Smith's Food & Drug Centers—had number one or number two market shares in Los Angeles, Chicago, Salt Lake City, Phoenix, Las Vegas, and Albuquerque. Stores controlled by Yucaipa operated under the names of Ralphs, Food 4 Less, Food Co., Cala Foods, Bell Markets, Dominick's Finer Foods, Falley's, and Smith's Food & Drug Centers. In 1995, the three chains employed approximately 57,000 people and had estimated revenues of about $11 billion. Ronald Burkle is the chairman and managing partner of Yucaipa Cos.

Early History

The grocery business has been putting food on Ronald Burkle's table for a long time. His father worked for, and eventually became president of, Stater Brothers, a southern California supermarket company. Ronald Burkle went to work at his father's store in 1966, when he was only 13, boxing groceries after school. In college, Burkle studied dentistry, but found his real interest was the stock market. He dropped out of California State Polytechnic University in 1973 and returned to Stater. While moving up in the company, he played the market as much as he could and watched the beginning of the leveraged buyout activity in the late 1970s. By 1981, when he was 28, Burkle was vice-president in charge of administration for Petrolane Properties, Stater's parent.

When Petrolane decided to sell Stater that year, Burkle convinced his father and other management personnel to back him in making an offer for the company. With Berkshire Hathaway putting up half the equity, Burkle's team made a bid—22 percent less than Petrolane's bankers had promised they could get for the company. Burkle was fired the day his bid was rejected.

The 1980s

Undeterred by the Stater experience, Burkle began buying. He started with a small candy company and then added a Chevrolet car dealership in southern California. But he concentrated on grocery stores, investing in supermarket stocks and making money as chains began consolidating.

In 1986, Burkle bought his first grocery chain, Jurgensen's, a small, gourmet food chain in Los Angeles. This was soon followed by the purchases of Cala and ABC Markets. By 1989, Yucaipa was operating 24 stores, including Food 4 Less warehouses in the San Bernardino and Moreno Valley areas of California and Falley's Inc. in Kansas and Missouri. It also franchised Food 4 Less warehouses in 17 states.

That year Breco Holding Company merged with Yucaipa Holding Company. Breco operated 70 stores in California, and its senior executives had worked with Burkle at Stater Brothers. The merger, which cost $375 million, created a chain of nearly 100 stores, including the 24 in the Los Angeles-based Boys Market chain, the Hispanic-oriented Viva Mart stores introduced by Boys in 1988, and other supermarkets in the Los Angeles and San Francisco Bay areas. The combined company, according to the *Los Angeles Times,* was expected to have revenues of $1 billion per year. Burkle became chairman of the combined company.

At the same time, another Burkle company, Yucaipa Food Corp., announced it was buying Almac's Inc., Rhode Island's largest grocery chain. Yucaipa announced it would operate the stores independently under their current management. Burkle told *The Boston Globe* Yucaipa had no plans to divest of any stores and that the company expected to spend "well into ten figures" remodeling existing stores and adding new stores over the next two years.

Acquisitions in the Early 1990s

Burkle's purchases followed a pattern. He targeted businesses in Watts and East Los Angeles, inner-city black and Hispanic neighborhoods, which other large chains, such as Von's and Lucky's, had abandoned. As a result, although security costs were higher, the stores could charge higher prices to cover those costs, so long as they offered what customers wanted.

By the early 1990s, Burkle had consolidated his various enterprises into Yucaipa Cos. and was operating his supermarket chains under his Food 4 Less Supermarkets, Inc. subsidiary. Financier George Soros invested $75 million in equity in Food 4 Less, becoming Yucaipa's first outside investor.

In 1991, Burkle began negotiating with American Stores for its Alpha Beta grocery chain, one of the largest in southern California and valued at around $400 million. American was forced to sell its Alpha Beta stores as part of an antitrust settlement when it bought the Lucky Stores chain in 1988. With $400 million in financing from Bankers Trust New York Corp., Citicorp, and Manufacturers Hanover Corp., Burkle bought 145 Alpha Beta stores for about $250 million. The buyout doubled the size of the Food 4 Less unit to about 215 stores, 22,000 employees, and $3 billion in annual sales in the southern part of the state, and put Yucaipa in second place, behind Von's, in the number of supermarkets in the greater Los Angeles area. Although most of the Alpha Beta stores were small (less than 30,000 square feet), and at least 40 were marginal, Burkle did not close them down. Instead, he began converting many of those that were borderline to Viva stores and promised to keep the others open. During the next three years Food 4 Less Supermarkets spent more than $120 million upgrading and renovating the Alpha Beta chain. In exchange, the United Food and Commercial Workers Union asked its members to give up triple-time pay for certain holidays and was considering a training wage below the negotiated starting salary of $8 an hour.

Later in the year, Burkle sold the Almac's chain in Rhode Island to Leonard Green, netting Yucaipa $75 million on its $5 million investment in just two years. That sale helped to reduce the company's debt of more than $500 million. But with Yucaipa's operations generating about $115 in cash flow, it was easily able to cover interest payments.

The year 1992 was difficult for businesses in Los Angeles. A total of 36 of the Food 4 Less stores were damaged during the riots in Watts and south-central Los Angeles, and the slow economy in the state affected sales throughout the chains. In December 1992, Food 4 Less instituted its "Caring 4 You" program in its southern California stores to handle employees' workers' compensation problems and questions. The program was created by management and unions; the company hoped to keep costs down and avoid lawsuits, and the unions wanted to be sure members got their benefits without a lot of hassle.

Under the program, representatives from Health Management Center West, an employee assistance company, worked with employees injured on the job to make sure they got appropriate medical attention, investigated late checks, and helped with cumbersome paperwork. A coordinating committee of management and union representatives met monthly to make sure the program was running smoothly.

The coordinating committee also instituted a temporary labor program, providing employees with jobs they could perform while they were healing from their injury. Employees received full pay for the temporary jobs, which were not open positions that could be filled by another employee and could last no longer than six weeks. As Linda McLoughlin Figel, a company vice-president, explained in a 1993 *Stores* article, "There are things we would like to have done in the stores, that have fallen on the back list of priorities. If a person is normally loading trucks it may be he can check orders or sweep trucks out. We are doing it in conjunction with the unions because we don't want to take away from existing union jobs."

Southern California was the country's largest retail market based on dollars spent, and it was probably the most competitive. As price wars heated up in 1993 among supermarkets, drug stores, discount units, and clubs, Food 4 Less Supermarkets took a different tack for its 250 stores, focusing on good service, an efficient distribution system, and a diverse mix of products other than food. "We know we can't be all things to all people," Vice-President Larry Ishii told *Supermarket Business* in its December 1993 issue. "What we *can* be is a complete supermarket chain, and we need to stress our strengths to the customer." Because of the small size of many of its outlets, the company concentrated on providing space to products that had high consumer demand. That meant highlighting toothbrushes, toothpaste, and shampoo, and cutting back on upscale brands of cosmetics.

To improve scheduling and delivery of its merchandise, the company invested in vehicle locators and computers/recorders for its trucks. The software for the onboard trip computer/recorders made it possible to develop a seasonal delivery schedule based on a customer's volume swings and to plan routing each day to each customer's door. The technology improved fuel efficiency by ten percent and raised the rate of on-time deliveries from 80 to 92 percent.

As part of its ongoing expansion strategy, Food 4 Less moved into the San Diego market. Plans called for opening 26 new stores—Boys Market, Viva, Alpha Beta, and Food 4 Less warehouses—as part of a $60 million capital spending program.

As the largest employer in inner-city Los Angeles, the Yucaipa stores also attempted to differentiate themselves from their competitors by their commitment to their communities. For example, over a three-year period, the Boys Viva Supermarket Foundation and Alpha Beta contributed about $10 million to the Los Angeles Unified School District to support after-school interscholastic athletics programs.

The year 1994 saw the introduction of the company's new private-label brand, EQuality. The new line offered 250 health and beauty care items and general merchandise at prices 15–30 percent lower than national brands. The first items introduced in the stores were cough and cold remedies, vitamins, baby wipes, toothbrushes, and nail products. But even before these were on the shelves, an earthquake hit Los Angeles in January. Food 4 Less had to close 34 stores briefly where the loss of electricity damaged or spoiled merchandise.

The big action in 1994, however, was more buyouts and consolidation. In June, Yucaipa bought Smitty's Super Valu, Inc., a 28-store chain operating in Phoenix and Tucson, for $138 million. And in September, Yucaipa announced the management-led buyout of Ralphs Grocery Co. for $1.5 billion. Ralphs was to be merged with Food 4 Less in the largest supermarket merger in California history. The merger made good sense; Ralphs operated conventional-format stores in middle and upper-middle income areas, whereas Food 4 Less operated price impact warehouse stores that were doing well and conventional stores that were doing less well.

Yucaipa paid Ralphs stockholders $525 million, assumed $980 million of Ralphs' debt, and became the majority stockholder in the new company, which kept the Ralphs Grocery Co. name. After all, as Ralphs president Al Marasca explained to *Supermarket News,* "We've been here since 1873, and we're the oldest supermarket chain west of the Mississippi, with a strong customer franchise and a fine reputation for how we operate."

Ralphs was also a pioneer in the supermarket industry. In the late 1950s it was the first major chain to centralize its meat-cutting. Ralphs chairman and CEO, Byron Allumbaugh, initiated the experiment when he started at the company. In a 1996 *Supermarket News* article he recalled, "Stores used to get beef hanging on hooks and disassemble it in the stores—a massive, labor-intensive job. I always thought there had to be a simpler way. So we set up a disassembly factory at a central location. There we did all the major production work centrally and put beef in smaller pieces in shrink-wrap and shipped it to the stores for the final cuts."

The first scanners west of the Mississippi appeared in Ralphs checkout aisles in 1974. "Scanning changed the whole world of food retailing," Allumbaugh told *Supermarket News.* "For the first time, food retailers knew more about what they sold than the manufacturers. All of a sudden we had the information that helped us set up stores, reorder, decide what to promote. Before that, manufacturers told us what to sell, how to set it up on the shelves, and how to promote. It was now a whole different world." Ralphs was also one of the first supermarkets in the country to use a computer (in 1958) and to use that technology to transmit orders between company headquarters and the headquarters of its suppliers.

Ralphs was owned by its founding family for 95 years. But, in 1968, the family sold the company to Federated Department Stores. Twenty years later, Federated was the target of a hostile takeover by the Canadian company, Campeau Corporation. Shortly afterward, Ralphs executives and Campeau Corporation separated Ralphs from Federated in a leveraged buyout. In 1992, to pay off a debt, Campeau gave Ralphs stock to Edward J. DeBartolo, and the supermarket chain became part of his mall development company. Within a year DeBartolo began selling

off assets, and Allumbaugh and Ralphs began looking for a merger partner.

At the time of the merger announcement in 1994, Ralphs had 370 conventional stores and Food 4 Less operated 133 conventional Alpha Betas, 24 conventional Boys, 15 conventional Vivas, and 30 Food 4 Less warehouse outlets in the southern part of the state. The company planned to close about 20 stores, primarily Alpha Betas, and eventually operate 360 stores. Conventional stores would all be called Ralphs and the warehouse, price-impact format would operate as Food 4 Less. In the process, the names Alpha Beta and Boys, which had been around for more than 70 years, as well as the six-year-old Viva name, would disappear.

Before the merger could be completed, however, the California state attorney general required that the company sell 27 stores. As he told *Supermarket News* in December, "We view this merger as potentially problematic from an antitrust perspective in that the combination of Ralphs and Yucaipa Cos. stores could have adversely reduced competition in a number of neighborhoods. A significant reduction in competition within a neighborhood can result in higher prices for consumers."

Delays in the Ralphs merger did not stop Yucaipa from bidding on other chains, and in November Burkle announced Yucaipa had acquired three stores in southern California from the bankrupt Megafood chain. These were reopened by the end of the year as Food 4 Less warehouse stores.

1995 and Beyond

As *Business Week* reported in its May 8, 1995 issue, consolidation was the word in the supermarket industry. The reasons for this were low multiples, low inflation in food prices, and new technologies. "With technology, there are a lot of things we can do now that would have been impossible a few years ago," Burkle told *Business Week.* For example, Yucaipa eliminated Food 4 Less's distribution centers and replaced them with automated racking systems. Big grocery chains were also learning from other large retailers how to use sophisticated information systems to study consumer buying patterns to target their advertising and even to link up with frequent-flier programs.

Yucaipa started the year by announcing it was buying Dominick's Finer Foods, the second largest grocery chain in the Chicago area, with about 100 stores. In addition to Yucaipa, the investment group for the $750 million deal included senior managers from Dominick's and financiers George Soros and Leon Black. The DiMatteo family, who founded Dominick's in the mid-1920s, kept a minority interest in the company. According to a February 6, 1995 *Supermarket News* story, the purchase increased Yucaipa's sales base by close to $9.25 billion. This included $2.5 billion from Dominick's, $5.5 billion from the merger of Food 4 Less and Ralphs, $300,000 from stores in northern California, $650,000 from Smitty's Super Valu in Arizona, and $300,000 from Falley's in the Midwest. Although Dominick's would remain a separate chain with Burkle as chairman and CEO, Yucaipa expected to make the most of the buying power of its three companies in working with suppliers.

The Ralphs/Food 4 Less merger became final in June 1995, with Burkle as chairman, Byron Allumbaugh remaining as

CEO, and Al Marasca continuing as president and COO. George Golleher, who joined Yucaipa in 1989 with the Breco merger and was president and CEO of Food 4 Less, assumed the newly created position of vice-chairman. Yucaipa now operated more than 500 supermarkets, controlling 30 percent of the southern California market, 24 percent of the Chicago market, and 24 percent of the Phoenix market. While continuing to look for more acquisitions, Burkle also addressed the needs of each of his companies and divisions.

For Dominick's this meant making better use of software systems for accounting and delivery and expanding the chain into the suburbs. In Arizona, increased market share was the goal, as Yucaipa spent about $25 million to remodel 17 Smitty's stores. The Midwest region, with 38 stores, continued to absorb the ten Food Barn locations it purchased in 1994. That region operated six conventional stores under the Falley's name and 32 Food 4 Less outlets.

In the San Francisco Bay area, where it operated 25 stores, Yucaipa concentrated on opening more warehouse-size stores under the Food Co. name. The name difference was necessary because another company had the license for the Food 4 Less name in that part of the state. "With only six warehouse stores there now, we don't have enough volume to operate a distribution facility," Burkle explained in a July 3, 1995 *Supermarket News* article. "Opening more warehouse stores [instead of conventional format Cala Foods and Bell Market stores] will add enough volume to enable us to look at opening a perishables warehouse."

For the new Ralphs, the focus was on the conversions and improving same-store sales. A big ad campaign using radio, TV, and newspapers stressed the merger and the savings to be passed on to customers as a result of the new company's buying powers. Ralphs also had to sell the 27 stores required by the state attorney general and it announced that it was closing or selling up to 16 other stores. In addition, the company planned to spend more than $130 million on capital expenditures in 1995, including five new Food 4 Less stores and four new Ralphs units. By October, most of the conversions to the Ralphs name had been completed, and by the end of the year, 20 Ralphs stores had been changed to the Food 4 Less format.

In January 1996, Ralphs named George Golleher as CEO, succeeding Byron Allumbaugh, who resumed his former position as chairman. Al Marasca remained president and COO, with responsibility for all of the company's stores. As part of the management change, Burkle stepped down as chairman. The same month, Burkle handed over the position of CEO at Dominick's to Robert Mariano, the company's president, but remained as chairman.

Although most of the conventional stores had been converted to Ralphs stores, many of the older, smaller Alpha Beta units did not realize the anticipated five percent sales boost. The early part of the year saw Ralphs lay off some 1,000 employees, about 3.8 percent of its work force. Most of these were part-time workers at 28 stores the company closed because of underperformance or because they were competing with another chain store for customers. As Jonathan Ziegler of Soloman Brothers explained in a March 11 article in *Supermarket News*, "After an

LBO, a company needs to sharpen its cost structure, and Ralphs will really have to fine-tune its operations to make them more productive." The company anticipated rehiring a large portion of these workers as it opened new stores during the year.

Ralphs responded to concerns about price competitiveness with its "Extra Savings Every Day" marketing campaign. The program was aimed at communicating the value, prices, and expanded products available since the merger. The campaign included double coupons, customer testimonials, and more Sunday ads, and emphasized the fresh produce now available.

In May 1996, Smitty's Supermarkets, Inc. merged with Smith's Food and Drug Centers, Inc., a public company. Smith's issued stock to Smitty's shareholders and entered into a management services agreement with Yucaipa. Under the agreement Burkle became CEO of Smith's and Yucaipa gained several director seats. The new company operated 149 stores in Arizona, Utah, Nevada, New Mexico, Texas, Idaho, and Wyoming, and had number one or number two market shares in its four principal markets of Salt Lake City, Phoenix, Las Vegas, and Albuquerque.

The company appeared focused on taking advantage of both its loose structure and large size through a "best practices" program, in which store and chain representatives came together to study issues ranging from marketing to real estate to management information systems. "We have 35 or 40 projects at some stage of development right now as we attempt to facilitate bringing all the companies together," Tom Dahlen, senior president of Food 4 Less explained in an April 1996 issue of *Supermarket News*.

In just ten years, Burkle increased Yucaipa's holdings from a single, small gourmet chain to more than 600 stores generating annual sales of more than $11 billion. With that type of sales base, Yucaipa did not appear concerned about its debt payments.

Principal Subsidiaries

Ralphs Grocery Co.; Dominick's Finer Foods; Smith's Food and Drug Centers, Inc.

Further Reading

Bredin, Alice, "Workers' Compensation," *Stores,* April 1993, p. 40.
Goodwin, William, "Supermarket Buyout Deal on Horizon," *American Banker,* March 19, 1991, p. 1.
Hawkins, Phil, "Credit Markets (6/1/95)," *Investors Business Daily On-Line,* May 31, 1996.
Orgel, David, "Sage Reflections," *Supermarket News,* May 6, 1996, p. 42.
"R.I. Grocery Chain Sold to California Firm," *Boston Globe,* May 18, 1989, p. 61.
Ross, Julie Ritzer, "Yucaipa Acquisitions Create Major Supermarket Force," *Stores,* October 1995, p. 32.
Schifrin, Matthew, "The Boxboy's Revenge," *Forbes,* October 14, 1991, p. 129.
Schine, Eric, "At the Food Chains, It's All Gulp and Swallow," *Business Week,* May 8, 1995, p. 85.
——, "Up from the Cereal Aisle," *Business Week,* February 27, 1995, p. 46.

Silverstein, Stuart, "Alpha Beta Stores Sold to Boys, Viva Markets Owner," *Los Angeles Times,* April 6, 1991, p. 1.

"Smith's Food & Drug Centers," Stock Reports, Chicago: Morningstar, Inc., August 1996.

"Smith's Food & Drug Centers, Inc. Completes Merger with Smitty's Supermarkets, Inc. and Recapitalization," *PR Newswire,* May 23, 1996.

"Smith's Foods To Buy Back Shares in Merger," Reuter, May 23, 1996.

"Smitty's Gets a New Owner, Expansion To Accelerate," *Discount Store News,* June 20, 1994, p. 4.

Weinstein, Steve, "The New Ralphs," *Progressive Grocer,* November 1995, p. 32.

White, George, and Johnson, Greg, "Bagging a Deal," *Los Angeles Times,* September 15, 1994, p. D1.

Williams, Linda, "Parent of Boys Market, Claremont Firm To Merge," *Los Angeles Times,* May 10, 1989, p. IV–2.

Zwiebach, Elliot, "A Banner Year for Yucaipa: After 12 Months of Mergers and Acquisitions, The Company Is Taking Steps To Make It All Pay Off," *Supermarket News,* July 3, 1995, p. 1.

——, "Food 4 Less, Ralphs in \$1.5 Billion Pact," *Supermarket News,* September 19, 1994, p. 1.

——, "Food 4 Less, Ralphs Knot To Be Tied This Week," *Supermarket News,* June 12, 1995, p. 1.

——, "Ralphs Sees Big Savings in Food 4 Less Tie," *Supermarket News,* September 26, 1994, p. 4.

——, "Ralphs Taps Golleher as CEO, Details Growth Plans," *Supermarket News,* January 29, 1996, p. 1.

——, "Ralphs, Yucaipa Will Divest 27 Units for Deal To Proceed," *Supermarket News,* December 19, 1994, p. 4.

——, "Smith's Completes Smitty's Merger Plan," *Supermarket News,* May 27, 1996, p. 4.

Zweig, Phillip, "Buy 'Em Out, Then Build 'Em Up," *Business Week,* May 8, 1995, p. 84.

——, "Leon Black: Wall Street's Dr. No," *Business Week,* July 29, 1996.

—Ellen D. Wernick

ZERO *Corporation*

Zero Corporation

444 South Flower Street, Suite 2100
Los Angeles, California 90071-2922
U.S.A.
(213) 629-7000
Fax: (213) 629-2366
Internet: http://www.zerocorp.com

Public Company
Incorporated: 1952 as Zierold Sheet Metal Co.
Employees: 1,800
Sales: $206.25 million (1996)
Stock Exchanges: New York
SICs: 3089 Plastics Products, Not Elsewhere Classified;
    3499 Fabricated Metal Products, Not Elsewhere
    Classified; 3585 Refrigeration & Heating Equipment;
    3161 Luggage

Zero Corporation is a leading designer and manufacturer of enclosure, cooling, and other systems, primarily for the electronics industry. Zero products include electronic cabinets, card cages, backplanes, power supply, and such thermal management systems as closed-loop air conditioning systems and motorized impellers. Sales to the electronics and related industries account for nearly 75 percent of Zero's annual revenues. Zero is also a leading worldwide designer and manufacturer of air cargo containers, systems, and accessories for companies including American, United, Airbus, and others. On the consumer level, Zero manufactures the world-famous line of Zero Halliburton luggage; these distinctive metal suitcases, briefcases, and carrying cases are sold in more than 30 countries. With manufacturing plants in the United States, Europe, and Mexico, Zero serves a customer base of over 20,000, none of which accounts for more than five percent of Zero's annual sales, which reached $206 million in 1995 (fiscal year ended 3/31/96). Throughout its history, Zero has been so successful at capturing the largest share of its market that the "zero case" has become a generic term.

Scrap Metal Origins

German immigrant Herman Zierold founded a small sheet metal business in Los Angeles in the early part of the century. By the end of the Second World War, Zierold's company had ten employees and annual sales of about $300,000; Zierold himself delivered his company's precision aluminum and sheet metal products. In 1951, Zierold sold his business to Jack Gilbert, who renamed the company Zierold Manufacturing Co. Gilbert had dropped out of high school after his father died during the Depression. Working a variety of jobs, including a stint with Douglas Aircraft during the Second World War, Gilbert decided to go into business for himself. Gilbert's interest was in the nascent electronics industry and the need for precision sheet metal products. "I looked at 30 or 35 companies," Gilbert told *Forbes,* "until I found Zierold Metal Co. Zierold was into precision aluminum work, and that was the future in sheet metal."

Gilbert offered Zierold $350,000 for the company, with a $50,000 down payment raised by mortgaging his home. Gilbert and Zierold agreed that Zierold would finance the rest; if Gilbert missed installments, the business would revert back to Zierold. According to Gilbert: "Herman went down the street and made a bet with a scrap dealer that he'd have the business back in a year." By the time Gilbert paid off the last of his installments, however, Herman Zierold was accepting stock in the company instead of cash.

In the postwar years, Los Angeles and other areas were overcrowded with sheet metal companies, but Gilbert's former association with Douglas led him in a direction that would help Zierold stand out from the rest. From friends at Douglas, Gilbert learned that company was purchasing precision aluminum boxes to cover their electronic systems, paying as much as $600 for a custom-made box to house electronic components. As Gilbert told *Forbes,* "I couldn't believe it. I thought those parts ought to sell for about $35."

Gilbert set out to produce a box that was simple and inexpensive to make, developing a process to make deep-drawn boxes. In the deep-drawn process, aluminum was subjected to pressures high enough to press—rather than stretch—the metal

Company Perspectives:

Zero Corporation's primary business is protecting electronics, where it serves the system packaging, thermal management and engineered case requirements of the telecommunications, instrumentation and data processing markets. Zero also serves the air cargo industry and produces the famous line of Zero Halliburton cases for consumers worldwide. With a global distribution network serving over 21,000 customers, Zero is strategically positioned for continued profitable growth.

around a die, creating a seamless box. Because the metal was pressed, causing its molecules to flow around the die, the process eliminated the weaknesses associated with stretching metal. By developing his own dies, Gilbert was able to produce boxes in standardized sizes far more quickly and cheaply than if the boxes needed to be custom-made. Gilbert began taking orders from the aerospace and electronics industries for boxes of various sizes. The company bore the cost for designing and building the dies, which at the time cost between $300 and $1,200, eating into the profits, if any, of an order and placing a heavy financial burden on the company.

By the mid-1950s, the strain of producing the dies forced Zierold to turn business away. Gilbert sought financing, but he worried about losing control of the company. A Small Business Administration loan, however, kept the business afloat, and in 1957, Zierold received new help in the form of a $250,000 investment by Alfred Reddock, a venture capitalist. After Reddock agreed to join the company's board of directors, Zierold gained the credibility it needed to go public, which it did in 1959. A name change soon followed. For years, many of the company's customers had been mistaking "Zierold" for "Zero," going so far as to make out checks to the company under that name. In response, Gilbert changed the company's name to Zero Manufacturing Co.

Over the next decade, the company continued building its collection of dies. An acquisition offer in the mid-1960s by Bendix led Zero to expand its operations beyond California. With no intention to sell, Gilbert nonetheless met with Bendix in order to discover the reasons behind that company's interest in Zero. Learning that Bendix was intent on acquiring sheet metal operations located near the Californian, southern, and New England aerospace markets, Gilbert traveled to manufacturers in those areas, signing on such large concerns as Martin Marietta and Raytheon as Zero customers. Soon after, Zero opened manufacturing facilities in Massachusetts and Florida. Despite gaining such large companies as customers, Gilbert remained determined that no company would account for more than five percent of Zero's sales; as a result orders generally averaged $10,000 or less.

A Brief Stumble in the 1970s

Gilbert next sought to diversify the company's operations. In 1969, Zero purchased the Halliburton luggage-making operations from the Halliburton oil service company. The Zero Halliburton line soon gained worldwide fame. Sales of the line of luggage and cases for photographic equipment rose from $200,000 at the time of the acquisition to nearly $3 million by the end of the 1970s. The company next moved into producing aircraft hydraulic systems and related aircraft devices. Zero's reputation was also enhanced by being chosen to build the cases that would transport moon rocks gathered from the first lunar landing back to Earth.

Yet the company stumbled in the early 1970s. Pursuing a plan to round out the company's operations, Zero made a number of other acquisitions seeking to bring the company into the heating and cooling business. However, a downturn in the economy, and especially in the electronics industry, cut deeply into Zero's profits and caused the company to post operating losses—including a $2 million write-off from selling its new acquisitions—in the first two years of the new decade. By 1973, Zero again turned profitable, earning $600,000 on sales of $22 million. The company changed its name again, to Zero Corporation. The company's success, particularly the success of its deep-drawn manufacturing process, had already caused the zero box to become a generic name in the electronics and aerospace industries.

Zero's collection of dies had grown to over 1,500, which gave the company an edge over competitors making costlier custom-made enclosures, while discouraging others from entering the field in direct competition with Zero. By the late 1970s, nearly all of Zero's die collection had been fully amortized. Sales, with customers including 35 of the 50 largest computer manufacturers in the United States, such as IBM, Burroughs, and Digital Equipment, reached $66 million by 1979, with net earnings of $4.7 million, and a five-year compounded growth rate of 25 percent. The following year, Gilbert retired from full-time management of the company and was replaced by Howard W. Hill. Two years later, Hill was joined by Wilford "Woody" Godbold, a former mergers and acquisitions specialist with Gibson Dunn & Crutcher, a Los Angeles law firm. Godbold, who was raised in Hawaii, went to Stanford as an undergraduate, and received a law degree from UCLA after a stint in the Navy, had served as Zero's corporate counsel before joining the company as executive vice-president. When Hill retired in 1985, Godbold took over as chief executive officer.

The 1980s and Beyond

Under Godbold, the company again began a series of acquisitions to diversify operations, buying eight companies in the first half of the decade for a total outlay of about $20 million. These new acquisitions—for example, the 1985 purchase of Contempo Engineering Co. of Glendale, California, a maker of air conditioning systems for computer installations—centered primarily on the electronics industry. The company's customer base grew to include 187 of the 200 largest electronics manufacturers, giving Zero an 85 percent share of the enclosure market. Zero's production facilities had grown to include 16 plants in the United States and England. By then, rather than contracting Zero to custom-make a die, many manufacturers were designing their electronics equipment to fit one of Zero's 1,700 basic dies, which had expanded to provide capacity for some 40,000 box sizes ranging from a few inches to six-foot boxes used to house

Stinger missiles. "But there always seems to be one more size

Stinger missiles. "But there always seems to be one more size we haven't made," Godbold told the *Los Angeles Business Journal,* and Zero continued to design and produce custom dies for new orders. Most orders involved short production runs, producing high margins for the company—generally nine to ten percent, compared to three percent among most metal manufacturers.

Zero's 1985 sales topped $117 million, bringing net earnings of $11.5 million, which included a $7 million gain from the sale of its Ocean Technology subsidiary. Aiding Zero's growth was the growth of its subsidiaries, particular its Electronics Solutions subsidiary, a computer manufacturing subcontractor acquired in 1985. Between 1987 and 1988, revenues jumped from $139 million to $171 million, with a rise in earnings to $16 million in 1988.

However, a slump in the electronics industry, and cuts in defense spending as the Cold War ended, coupled with a slide into a recession as the 1990s began, slowed Zero down. Sales, which neared $200 million in 1990, fell to $160 million. Per share income also dropped, from $1.02 to $0.62. In an effort to cut operating costs, Godbold moved its Los Angeles factory to Salt Lake City, slashing the company's expenses for workers' compensation, health care, and wages. The company consolidated a number of its remaining California plants to cut operating costs further. Godbold, who served as chairman of the California Chamber of Commerce, was widely criticized for the move. Yet, as Godbold told *World Trade,* "It wasn't an easy thing for us, but the costs of doing business in the state were eating us alive. We had to do it to remain competitive."

The Utah move helped spur the company's sagging profits. Zero also began a new wave of acquisitions, including the 1993 purchase of J.H. Sessions & Sons of Connecticut, which manufactured case hardware such as handles and hinges and other materials for annual sales of $4 million. Orders from the airline industry also picked up—after a long slump due not only to the recession, but also to fears of terrorism surrounding the Gulf War—including a contact to supply baggage/cargo systems to 50 of United Airlines' Airbus planes. Yet the company's foreign sales were hurt by the slide into the European recession, which saw international revenues drop from over $21 million in 1992 to $15.5 million in 1994.

Total sales grew only at four percent between 1992 and 1995, as compared to the company's former 18-year, 25 percent average growth rate. Nonetheless, Zero remained solidly profitable, with net earnings climbing from $9.7 million in 1991 to nearly $15 million by 1994. In 1995, Zero began acquisitions of three new companies, Precision Fabrication Technologies, which manufactured modular enclosures, data communications products, and accessories for the electronics and telecommunications industries; Electro-Mechanical Imagineering, Inc. (EMI), a maker of enclosure, mounting, and protective devices for closed-circuit television security devices; and G.W. Pearce & Sons Ltd., a UK-based deep-drawn aluminum products manufacturer. Combined, these acquisitions added $16 million to Zero's revenues. Total revenues reached $206 million in fiscal year 1996, producing net earnings of nearly $17 million.

Several more acquisitions followed in the first half of 1996. The Zero Halliburton line expanded to include cases for the booming mobile computing market. In January 1996, Zero launched a new subsidiary, Zero Integrated Systems, to design, engineer, and manufacture completely integrated electronic systems, as well as to provide cost analysis and quality testing services. After more than forty years, Zero had at last moved inside the box.

Principal Subsidiaries

Air Cargo Equipment; Electronic Solutions; Integrated Systems; McLean Engineering; McLean Europe; McLean Midwest; Nielson/Sessions; Samuel Groves & Co. Limited (Birmingham, England); Stantron/PFT/EMI; Zero Enclosures.

Further Reading

Akst, Daniel, "Zero No Mere Cipher in Electronics Packaging," *Los Angeles Times,* September 10, 1985, part 4, p. 5A.
Cole, Benjamin Mark, "Zeroing in on Profits," *Los Angeles Business Journal,* November 22, 1993, p. 12.
Merwin, John, "Getting Rich on Little Nothings," *Forbes,* September 1, 1980, p. 104.
Thuermer, Karen, "California Rebuilds Economy, Image with the Help of Exports," *World Trade,* April 1996, p. 62.
"Utah Proves to Be the Right Place for Revitalizing Profits," *Barrons,* October 11, 1993.
"Zero Corp. Carves out Expanding Niche in Field for Computer Cases," *Barrons,* February 6, 1978, p. 42.

—M. L. Cohen

INDEX TO COMPANIES

Index to Companies

Listings in this index are arranged in alphabetical order under the company name. Company names beginning with a letter or proper name such as Eli Lilly & Co. will be found under the first letter of the company name. Definite articles (The, Le, La) are ignored for alphabetical purposes as are forms of incorporation that precede the company name (AB, NV). Company names printed in bold type have full, historical essays on the page numbers appearing in bold. Updates to entries that appeared in earlier volumes are signified by the notation (**upd.**). Company names in light type are references within an essay to that company, not full historical essays. This index is cumulative with volume numbers printed in bold type.

Burger and Aschenbrenner, **16** 486
Burger Boy Food-A-Rama, **8** 564
Burger Chef, **II** 532
Burger King Corporation, **I** 21, 278; **II**
556–57, **613–15**, 647; **7** 316; **8** 564; **9**
178; **10** 122; **12** 43, 553; **13** 408–09; **14**
25, 32, 212, 214, 452; **16** 95–97, 396;
17 69–72 (upd.), 501
Bürhle, **17** 36
Burke Scaffolding Co., **9** 512
BURLE Industries Inc., **11** 444
Burlesdon Brick Co., **III** 734
Burlington Air Express, Inc., **IV** 182
Burlington Coat Factory Warehouse
Corporation, **10 188–89**
Burlington Homes of New England, **14** 138
Burlington Industries, Inc., **V** 118,
354–55; **8** 234; **9** 231; **12** 501; **17**
73–76 (upd.), 304–05
Burlington Mills Corporation, **12** 117–18
Burlington Northern Air Freight, **IV** 182
Burlington Northern, Inc., **V 425–28**; **10**
190–91; **12** 145, 278
Burlington Northern Railroad, **11** 315
Burlington Resources Inc., **10 190–92**; **11**
135; **12** 144
Burmah Castrol PLC, **IV** 378, **381–84**,
440–41, 483–84, 531; **7** 56
Burmah Oil Co., **15** 246
Burmeister & Wain, **III** 417–18
Burn & Co., **IV** 205
Burn Standard Co. Ltd., **IV** 484
Burnards, **II** 677
Burnham and Co., **II** 407–08; **6** 599; **8** 388
Burns & Wilcox Ltd., **6** 290
Burns Cos., **III** 569
Burns Fry Ltd., **II** 349
Burns International Security Services,
III 440; **13 123–25**
Burpee Co. See W. Atlee Burpee Co.
Burr & Co., **II** 424; **13** 340
Burrill & Housman, **II** 424; **13** 340
Burris Industries, **14** 303
Burroughs Corp., **I** 142, 478; **III** 132,
148–49, 152, 165–66; **6** 233, 266,
281–83. See also Unisys Corporation.
Burroughs Mfg. Co., **16** 321
Burroughs Wellcome & Co., **I** 713; **8** 216
Burrows, Marsh & McLennan, **III** 282
Burry, **II** 560; **12** 410
Bursley & Co., **II** 668
Burt Claster Enterprises, **III** 505
Burthy China Clays, **III** 690
Burton Group plc, **V 20–22**
Burton J. Vincent, Chesley & Co., **III** 271
Burton, Parsons and Co. Inc., **II** 547
Burton Retail, **V** 21
Burton Rubber Processing, **8** 347
Burton-Furber Co., **IV** 180
Burtons Gold Medal Biscuits Limited, **II**
466; **13** 53
Burwell Brick, **14** 248
Bury Group, **II** 581
Bush Boake Allen Ltd., **IV** 346
Bush Terminal Company, **15** 138
Business Depot, Limited, **10** 498
Business Expansion Capital Corp., **12** 42
Business Men's Assurance Company of
America, **III** 209; **13** 476; **14 83–85**; **15**
30
Business Science Computing, **14** 36
Business Software Association, **10** 35
Business Software Technology, **10** 394

Businessland Inc., **III** 153; **6** 267; **10** 235;
13 175–76, 277, 482
Busse Broadcasting, **7** 200
Büssing Automobilwerke AG, **IV** 201
Buster Brown, **V** 351–52
Butano, **IV** 528
Butler Cox PLC, **6** 229
Butler Manufacturing Co., **12 51–53**
Butler Shoes, **16** 560
Butterfield & Swire, **I** 469, 521–22; **6** 78.
See also Swire Pacific Ltd.
Butterfield, Wasson & Co., **II** 380, 395; **10**
59; **12** 533
Butterley Company, **III** 501; **7** 207
Butterworth & Co. (Publishers) Ltd., **IV**
641; **7** 311; **17** 398
Butz Thermo-Electric Regulator Co., **II** 40;
12 246
Buxton, **III** 28
Buzzard Electrical & Plumbing Supply, **9**
399; **16** 186
BVA Investment Corp., **11** 447
BVA Mortgage Corporation, **11** 446
Byrnes Long Island Motor Cargo, Inc., **6**
370
Byron Jackson, **III** 428, 439
Bytrex, Inc., **III** 643

C & O. See Chesapeake and Ohio Railway.
C.&E. Cooper Co., **II** 14
C.&G. Cooper Co., **II** 14
C.A. Pillsbury and Co., **II** 555
C.A. Reed Co., **IV** 353
C.A. Swanson & Sons, **II** 479–80; **7**
66–67
C&A Brenninkmeyer KG, **V 23–24**
C&E Software, **10** 507
C&R Clothiers, **17** 313
C&S Bank, **10** 425–26
C&S/Sovran Corporation, **10** 425–27
C. Bechstein, **III** 657
C. Brewer, **I** 417
C.D. Haupt, **IV** 296
C.D. Kenny Co., **II** 571
C.D. Magirus AG, **III** 541
C.E. Chappell & Sons, Inc., **16** 61–62
C.E.T. See Club Européen du Tourisme.
C.F. Hathaway Company, **12** 522
C.F. Mueller Co., **I** 497–98; **12** 332
C. Francis, Son and Co., **III** 669
C.G. Conn, **7** 286
C.H. Dexter & Co., **I** 320
C.H. Knorr Co., **II** 497
C.H. Masland & Sons. See Masland
Corporation.
C.H. Musselman Co., **7** 429
C.H. Robinson, Inc., **8** 379–80; **11 43–44**
C-I-L, Inc., **III** 745; **13** 470
C. Itoh & Co., **I 431–33**, 492, 510; **II**
273, 292, 361, 442, 679; **IV** 269, 326,
516, 543; **7** 529; **10** 500; **17** 124
C.J. Devine, **II** 425
C.J. Lawrence, Morgan Grenfell Inc., **II**
429
C.J. Smith and Sons, **11** 3
C.L. Bencard, **III** 66
C. Lee Cook Co., **III** 467
C.M. Aikman & Co., **13** 168
C.M. Armstrong, Inc., **14** 17
C.M. Barnes Company, **10** 135
C.M. Page, **14** 112
C.O. Lovette Company, **6** 370
C/P Utility Services Company, **14** 138
C.R. Bard Inc., **IV** 287; **9 96–98**

C. Reichenbach'sche Maschinenfabrik, **III**
561
C. Rowbotham & Sons, **III** 740
C.S. Rolls & Co., **I** 194
C.T. Bowring, **III** 280, 283
C.V. Buchan & Co., **I** 567
C.V. Gebroeders Pel, **7** 429
C.V. Mosby Co., **IV** 677–78
C.W. Holt & Co., **III** 450
C.W. Zumbiel Company, **11** 422
Cable & Wireless plc, **15** 69, 521
Cable and Wireless (Hong Kong). See
Hongkong Telecomminications Ltd.
Cable and Wireless plc, **IV** 695; **V**
283–86; **7** 332–33; **11** 547; **17** 419
Cable Communications Operations, Inc., **6**
313
Cable News Network, **II** 166–68; **6**
171–73; **9** 30; **12** 546
Cablec Corp., **III** 433–34
Cableform, **I** 592
Cabletron Systems, Inc., **10 193–94**; **10**
511
Cablevision Systems Corporation, **7**
63–65
Cabot Corporation, **8 77–79**
Cabot-Morgan Real Estate Co., **16** 159
Cadadia, **II** 641–42
Cadbury Schweppes PLC, **I 25–26**; **II**
476–78, 510, 512, 592; **III** 554; **6**
51–52; **9** 178; **15** 221
Caddell Construction Company, **12** 41
Cadence Design Systems, Inc., **6** 247; **10**
118; **11 45–48**, 285, 490–91
Cadence Industries Corporation, **10** 401–02
Cadillac Automobile Co., **I** 171; **10** 325
Cadillac Fairview Corp., **IV** 703
Cadillac Plastic, **8** 347
Cadisys Corporation, **10** 119
Cadmus Communications Corp., **16** 531
Cadoricin, **III** 47
CAE Systems Inc., **8** 519
Caesar-Wollheim-Gruppe, **IV** 197
Caesars World, Inc., **6 199–202**; **17** 318
Caf'Casino, **12** 152
Café Grand Mère, **II** 520
CAFO, **III** 241
Cagiva, **17** 24
Cahners Publishing, **IV** 667; **12** 561; **17**
398
CAI Corp., **12** 79
Cailler, **II** 546
Cain Chemical, **IV** 481
Cains Marcelle Potato Chips Inc., **15** 139
Caisse Commericale de Bruxelles, **II** 270
Caisse de dépôt et placement du Quebec,
II 664
Caisse des Dépôts, **6** 206
Caisse National de Crédit Agricole, **II**
264–66
Caisse Nationale de Crédit Agricole, **15**
38–39
Caja General de Depositos, **II** 194
Cal Circuit Abco Inc., **13** 387
Cal-Van Tools. See Chemi-Trol Chemical
Co.
Cal/Ink, **13** 228
Cala, **17** 558
Calais Railroad Company, **16** 348
Calcined Coke Corp., **IV** 402
Calco, **I** 300–01
CalComp Inc., **13 126–29**

CIPSCO Inc., 6 469–72, 505–06
Circa Pharmaceuticals, **16** 529
Circle A Ginger Ale Company, **9** 177
Circle International, Inc., **17** 216
Circle K Corporation, II 619–20; **V** 210;
7 113–14, 372, 374
Circle Plastics, **9** 323
Circuit City Stores, Inc., 9 65–66,
120–22; **10** 235, 305–06, 334–35,
468–69; **12** 335; **14** 61; **15** 215; **16** 73,
75; **17** 489
Circus Circus Enterprises, Inc., 6 201,
203–05
Circus World, **16** 389–90
Cirrus Logic, Incorporated, 9 334; **11**
56–57
Cisco Systems, Inc., 11 58–60, 520; **13**
482; **16** 468
CIT Alcatel, **9** 9–10
CIT Financial Corp., **II** 90, 313; **8** 117; **12**
207
CIT Group/Business Credit, Inc., **13** 446
CIT Group/Commercial Services, **13** 536
Citadel General, **III** 404
CitFed Bancorp, Inc., 16 105–07
CITGO Petroleum Corporation, II
660–61; **IV 391–93**, 508; **7** 491
Citibanc Group, Inc., **11** 456
Citibank, **II** 227, 230, 248, 250–51,
253–55, 331, 350, 358, 415; **III** 243,
340; **6** 51; **9** 124; **10** 150; **11** 418; **13**
146; **14** 101
CITIC. *See* China International Trade and
Investment Corporation.
Citic Pacific, **16** 481
Citicorp, II 214, **253–55**, 268, 275, 319,
331, 361, 398, 411, 445; **III** 10, 220,
397; **7** 212–13; **8** 196; **9 123–26 (upd.)**,
441; **10** 463, 469; **11** 140; **12** 30, 310,
334; **13** 535; **14** 103, 108, 235; **15** 94,
146, 281; **17** 324, 559
Cities Service Co., **IV** 376, 391–92, 481,
575; **12** 542
Citinet. *See* Hongkong Telecommunications
Ltd.
Citivision PLC, **9** 75
Citizen Watch Co., Ltd., III 454–56,
549; **13** 121–22
Citizen's Electric Light & Power
Company, **V** 641
Citizen's Federal Savings Bank, **10** 93
Citizen's Fidelity Corp., **II** 342
Citizen's Industrial Bank, **14** 529
Citizens and Southern Bank, **II** 337; **10**
426
Citizens Bank, **11** 105
Citizens Bank of Hamilton, **9** 475
Citizens Bank of Savannah, **10** 426
Citizens Building & Loan Association, **14**
191
Citizens Federal Savings and Loan
Association, **9** 476
Citizens Financial Group, **12** 422
Citizens Gas Co., **6** 529
Citizens Gas Fuel Company. *See* MCN
Corporation.
Citizens Gas Light Co., **6** 455
Citizens Gas Supply Corporation, **6** 527
Citizens Mutual Savings Bank, **17** 529–30
Citizens National Bank, **II** 251; **13** 466
Citizens National Gas Company, **6** 527
Citizens Saving and Trust Company, **17**
356

Citizens Savings & Loan Association, **9**
173
Citizens Savings and Loan Society. *See*
Citizens Mutual Savings Bank.
Citizens Telephone Company, **14** 257–58
Citizens Trust Co., **II** 312
Citizens Utilities Company, 7 87–89
Citizens' Savings and Loan, **10** 339
Citroën. *See* Automobiles Citroen.
City and St. James, **III** 501
City and Suburban Telegraph Association
and Telephonic Exchange, **6** 316–17
City and Village Automobile Insurance
Co., **III** 363
City Auto Stamping Co., **I** 201
City Bank Farmers' Trust Co., **II** 254; **9**
124
City Bank of New York, **II** 250, 253
City Brewery, **I** 253
City Centre Properties Ltd., **IV** 705–06
City Finance, **10** 340
City Finance Company, **11** 261
City Ice Delivery, Ltd., **II** 660
City Investing Co., **III** 263; **IV** 721; **9** 391;
13 363
City Light and Traction Company, **6** 593
City Light and Water Company, **6** 579
City Market Inc., **12** 112
City Mutual Life Assurance Society, **III**
672–73
City National Bank of Baton Rouge, **11**
107
City National Leasing, **II** 457
City of London Real Property Co. Ltd., **IV**
706
City of Seattle Water Department, **12** 443
The City Post Publishing Corp., **12** 359
City Products Corp., **II** 419
City Public Service, 6 473–75
City Savings, **10** 340
City Stores Company, **16** 207
Cityhome Corp., **III** 263
Civic Drugs, **12** 21
Civil & Civic Pty. Ltd., **IV** 707–08; **17**
286
Civil Service Employees Insurance Co., **III**
214
Clabir Corp., **12** 199
Claire's Stores, Inc., 17 101–03
Clairol, **III** 17–18; **17** 110
Clairton Steel Co., **IV** 572; **7** 550
CLAM Petroleum, **7** 282
Clancy Paul Inc., **13** 276
Clara Candy, **15** 65
Clarcor Inc., 17 104–07
Clares Equipment Co., **I** 252
Clark & Co., **IV** 301
Clark & McKenney Hardware Co. *See*
Clarcor Inc.
Clark & Rockefeller, **IV** 426
Clark Bros. Co., **III** 471
The Clark Construction Group, Inc., 8
112–13
Clark, Dietz & Associates-Engineers. *See*
CRSS Inc.
Clark Equipment Company, I 153; **7**
513–14; **8 114–16**; **10** 265; **13** 500; **15**
226
Clark Estates Inc., **8** 13
Clark Filter, Inc., **17** 104
Clark Materials Handling Company, **7** 514
Clark Motor Co., **I** 158; **10** 292
Clarkins, Inc., **16** 35–36
Clarkson International Tools, **I** 531

CLASSA. *See* Compañia de Líneas Aéreas
Subvencionadas S.A.
Claussen Pickle Co., **12** 371
Clayton & Dubilier, **III** 25
Clayton Brown Holding Company, **15** 232
Clayton Homes Incorporated, 13 154–55
Clayton-Marcus Co., **12** 300
Clean Window Remodelings Co., **III** 757
Cleanaway Ltd., **III** 495
Cleancoal Terminal, **7** 582, 584
Clear Shield Inc., **17** 157, 159
Clearing Inc., **III** 514
Clearwater Tissue Mills, Inc., **8** 430
Clef, **IV** 125
Clements Energy, Inc., **7** 376
Cleo Inc., **12** 207–09
Cletrac Corp., **IV** 366
Cleveland and Western Coal Company, **7**
369
Cleveland Electric Illuminating Company.
See Centerior Energy Theodor.
Cleveland Fabric Centers, Inc. *See* Fabri-
Centers of America Inc.
Cleveland Iron Mining Company, **13** 156.
See also Cleveland-Cliffs Inc.
Cleveland Oil Co., **I** 341
Cleveland Paper Co., **IV** 311
Cleveland Pneumatic Co., **I** 457; **III** 512
Cleveland Twist Drill Company **I** 531. *See*
also Acme-Cleveland Corp.
Cleveland-Cliffs Inc., 13 156–58; **17** 355
Clevepak Corporation, **8** 229; **13** 442
Clevite Corporation, **14** 207
CLF Research, **16** 202
Clifford & Wills, **12** 280–81
Cliffs Corporation, **13** 157
Climax Molybdenum Co., **IV** 17–19
Clinchfield Coal Corp., **IV** 180–81
Clinical Assays, **I** 628
Clinical Science Research Ltd., **10** 106
Clinton Pharmaceutical Co., **III** 17
Clipper Group, **12** 439
Clipper, Inc., **IV** 597
Clipper Manufacturing Company, **7** 3
Clipper Seafoods, **II** 587
Clorox Company, III 20–22, 52; **8** 433
Clouterie et Tréfilerie des Flandres, **IV**
25–26
Clover Leaf Creamery, **II** 528
Clover Milk Products Co., **II** 575
Clovis Water Co., **6** 580
CLSI Inc., **15** 372
Club Aurrera, **8** 556
Club Européen du Tourisme, **6** 207
Club Méditerranée SA, I 286; **6 206–08**
Clubhôtel, **6** 207
Cluett, Peabody & Co., Inc., **II** 414; **8**
567–68
Clyde Iron Works, **8** 545
Clydebank Engineering & Shipbuilding
Co., **I** 573
Clyne Maxon Agency, **I** 29
CM Industries, **I** 676
CM&M Equilease, **7** 344
CMB Acier, **IV** 228
CMB Packaging, **8** 477
CME. *See* Campbell-Mithun-Esty, Inc.
CML Group, Inc., 10 215–18
CMP Properties Inc., **15** 122
CMS Energy Corporation, IV 23; **V**
577–79; **8** 466; **14 114–16 (upd.)**
CN. *See* Canadian National Railway
System.

Mid-South Towing, **6** 583
Mid-Texas Communications Systems, **6** 313
Mid-Valley Dairy, **14** 397
Mid-West Drive-In Theatres Inc., **I** 245
Mid-West Paper Ltd., **IV** 286
MidAmerican Communications Corporation, **8** 311
Midas International Corporation, I 457–58; **10 414–15**, 554
MIDCO, **III** 340
Midcon, **IV** 481
Middle South Utilities, **V** 618–19
Middle West Corporation, **6** 469–70
Middle West Utilities Company, **V** 583–84; **6** 555–56, 604–05; **14** 227
Middle Wisconsin Power, **6** 604
Middleburg Steel and Alloys Group, **I** 423
Middlesex Bank, **II** 334
Middleton Packaging, **12** 377
Middleton's Starch Works, **II** 566
Middletown Manufacturing Co., Inc., **16** 321
Middletown National Bank, **13** 467
Midhurst Corp., **IV** 658
Midial, **II** 478
Midland Bank plc, II 208, 236, 279, 295, 298, **318–20**, 334, 383; **9** 505; **12** 257; **14** 169; **17 323–26 (upd.)**
Midland Brick, **14** 250
Midland Cooperative, **II** 536
Midland Counties Dairies, **II** 587
Midland Electric Coal Co., **IV** 170
Midland Enterprises Inc., **6** 486–88
Midland Gravel Co., **III** 670
Midland Industrial Finishes Co., **I** 321
Midland Insurance, **I** 473
Midland International, **8** 56–57
Midland Investment Co., **II** 7
Midland Linseed Products Co., **I** 419
Midland National Bank, **11** 130
Midland Railway Co., **II** 306
Midland Southwest Corp., **8** 347
Midland Steel Products Co., **13** 305–06
Midland United, **6** 556
Midland Utilities Company, **6** 532
Midland-Ross Corporation, **14** 369
Midlands Electricity, **13** 485
Midlands Energy Co., **IV** 83; **7** 188
Midlantic Corp., **13** 411
Midrange Performance Group, **12** 149
Midrex Corp., **IV** 130
Midvale Steel and Ordnance Co., **IV** 35, 114; **7** 48
Midway Airlines, **6** 105, 120–21
Midway Manufacturing Company, **III** 430; **15** 539
Midwest Agri-Commodities, **11** 15
Midwest Air Charter, **6** 345
Midwest Biscuit Company, **14** 306
Midwest Com of Indiana, Inc., **11** 112
Midwest Dairy Products, **II** 661
Midwest Express Airlines, **III** 40–41; **11** 299; **16** 302, 304
Midwest Federal Savings & Loan Association, **11** 162–63
Midwest Financial Group, Inc., **8** 188
Midwest Foundry Co., **IV** 137
Midwest Manufacturing Co., **12** 296
Midwest Refining Co., **IV** 368
Midwest Resources Inc., 6 523–25
Midwest Steel Corporation, **13** 157
Midwest Synthetics, **8** 553
Midwinter, **12** 529

Miele & Cie., **III** 418
Miguel Galas S.A., **17** 268
Mike-Sell's Inc., 15 298–300
Mikemitch Realty Corp., **16** 36
Mikko, **II** 70
Mikko Kaloinen Oy, **IV** 349
Mikon, Ltd., **13** 345
Milani, **II** 556
Milbank Insurance Co., **III** 350
Milbank, Tweed, Hope & Webb, **II** 471
Milcor Steel Co., **IV** 114
Miles Druce & Co., **III** 494
Miles Kimball Co., **9** 393
Miles Laboratories, I 310, **653–55**, 674, 678; **6** 50; **13** 76; **14** 558
Miles Redfern, **I** 429
Milgo Electronic Corp., **II** 83; **11** 408
Milgram Food Stores Inc., **II** 682
Milk Producers, Inc., **11** 24
Milk Specialties Co., **12** 199
Millbrook Press Inc., **IV** 616
Miller Brewing Company, I 218–19, 236–37, 254–55, 257–58, **269–70**, 283, 290–91, 548; **10** 100; **11** 421; **12** **337–39 (upd.)**, 372; **13** 10, 258; **15** 429; **17** 256
Miller Chemical & Fertilizer Corp., **I** 412
Miller Companies, **17** 182
Miller Container Corporation, **8** 102
Miller Freeman, **IV** 687
Miller, Mason and Dickenson, **III** 204–05
Miller, Tabak, Hirsch & Co., **13** 394
Millet's Leisure, **V** 177–78
Milliken & Co., V 366–68; **8** 270–71; **17** **327–30 (upd.)**
Milliken, Tomlinson Co., **II** 682
Millipore, **9** 396
Millstone Point Company, **V** 668–69
Millville Electric Light Company, **6** 449
Milner, **III** 98
Milton Bradley Company, **III** 504–06; **16** 267; **17** 105
Milton Light & Power Company, **12** 45
Milton Roy Co., **8** 135
Milwaukee Electric Manufacturing Co., **III** 534
Milwaukee Electric Railway and Light Company, **6** 601–02, 604–05
Milwaukee Insurance Co., **III** 242
Milwaukee Mutual Fire Insurance Co., **III** 321
Minatome, **IV** 560
Minemet Recherche, **IV** 108
Mineral Point Public Service Company, **6** 604
Minerals & Chemicals Philipp, **IV** 79–80
Minerals & Metals Trading Corporation of India Ltd., IV 143–44
Minerals and Resources Corporation Limited, **IV** 23; **13** 502. *See also* Minorco.
Minerals Technologies Inc., 11 310–12
Minerec Corporation, **9** 363
Minerva, **III** 359
Minerve, **6** 208
Mines et Usines du Nord et de l'Est, **IV** 226
Minet Holdings PLC, **III** 357
Mini Stop, **V** 97
Mining and Technical Services, **IV** 67
Mining Corp. of Canada Ltd., **IV** 164
Mining Development Corp., **IV** 239–40
Mining Trust Ltd., **IV** 32

MiniScribe, Inc., **6** 230; **10** 404
Minister of Finance Inc., **IV** 519
Minivator Ltd., **11** 486
Minneapolis General Electric of Minnesota, **V** 670
Minneapolis Heat Regulator Co., **II** 40–41; **12** 246
Minneapolis Millers Association, **10** 322
Minneapolis-Honeywell Regulator Co., **II** 40–41, 86; **8** 21; **12** 247
Minnesota Cooperative Creameries Assoc., Inc., **II** 535
Minnesota Linseed Oil Co., **8** 552
Minnesota Mining & Manufacturing Company, I 28, 387, **499–501**; **II** 39; **III** 476, 487, 549; **IV** 251, 253–54; **6** 231; **7** 162; **8** 35, **369–71 (upd.)**; **11** 494; **13** 326; **17** 29–30
Minnesota Paints, **8** 552–53
Minnesota Power & Light Company, 11 313–16
Minnesota Sugar Company, **11** 13
Minnesota Valley Canning Co., **I** 22
Minnetonka Corp., **II** 590; **III** 25
Minolta Camera Co., Ltd., III 574–76, 583–84
Minorco, **III** 503; **IV** 67–68, 84, 97; **16** 28, 293
Minstar Inc., **11** 397; **15** 49
Minute Maid Corp., **I** 234; **10** 227
Minute Tapioca, **II** 531
MIPS Computer Systems, **II** 45; **11** 491
Miracle Food Mart, **16** 247, 249–50
Mirage Resorts, Inc., 6 209–12; **15** 238
Miramar Hotel & Investment Co., **IV** 717
Mircali Asset Management, **III** 340
Mircor Inc., **12** 413
Mirrlees Blackstone, **III** 509
Mirror Group Newspapers plc, IV 641; **7** 244, 312, **341–43**
Mirror Printing and Binding House, **IV** 677
Misceramic Tile, Inc., **14** 42
Misr Airwork. *See* AirEgypt.
Misrair. *See* AirEgypt.
Miss Clairol, **6** 28
Miss Selfridge, **V** 177–78
Misset Publishers, **IV** 611
Mission Energy Company, **V** 715
Mission First Financial, **V** 715
Mission Group, **V** 715, 717
Mission Insurance Co., **III** 192
Mississippi Chemical Corporation, **8** 183; **IV** 367
Mississippi Drug, **III** 10
Mississippi Gas Company, **6** 577
Mississippi Power & Light, **V** 619
Mississippi River Corporation, **10** 44
Missouri Book Co., **10** 136
Missouri Gas & Electric Service Company, **6** 593
Missouri Pacific Railroad, **10** 43–44
Missouri Public Service Company. *See* UtiliCorp United Inc.
Missouri Utilities Company, **6** 580
Missouri-Kansas-Texas Railroad, **I** 472; **IV** 458
Mistral Plastics Pty Ltd., **IV** 295
Mitchel & King Skates Ltd., **17** 244
Mitchell Construction, **III** 753
Mitchell Energy and Development Corporation, 7 344–46
Mitchell Home Savings and Loan, **13** 347
Mitchell Hutchins, **II** 445
Mitchell International, **8** 526

Mitchells & Butler, **I** 223
Mitchum Co., **III** 55
Mitchum, Jones & Templeton, **II** 445
MiTek Industries Inc., **IV** 259
MiTek Wood Products, **IV** 305
Mitel, **15** 131–32
MitNer Group, **7** 377
Mitre Sport U.K., **17** 204–05
Mitsubishi, **V** 481–82; **7** 377
Mitsubishi Aircraft Co., **III** 578; **7** 348; **9** 349; **11** 164
Mitsubishi Bank, Ltd., **II** 57, 273–74, 276, **321–22**, 323, 392, 459; **III** 289, 577–78; **7** 348; **15** 41; **16** 496, 498
Mitsubishi Chemical Industries Ltd., **I** 319, **363–64**, 398; **II** 57; **III** 666, 760; **11** 207
Mitsubishi Corporation, **I** 261, 431–32, 492, **502–04**, 505–06, 510, 515, 519–20; **II** 57, 59, 101, 118, 224, 292, 321–25, 374; **III** 577–78; **IV** 285, 518, 713; **6** 499; **7** 82, 233, 590; **9** 294; **12** **340–43 (upd.)**; **17** 349, 556
Mitsubishi Electric Corporation, **II** 53, **57–59**, 68, 73, 94, 122; **III** 577, 586; **7** 347, 394
Mitsubishi Estate Company, Limited, **IV** 713–14
Mitsubishi Gas Chemical Company, **I** 330; **8** 153
Mitsubishi Heavy Industries, Ltd., **II** 57, 75, 323, 440; **III** 452–53, 487, 532, 538, **577–79**, 685, 713; **IV** 184, 713; **7** **347–50 (upd.)**; **8** 51; **9** 349–50; **10** 33; **13** 507; **15** 92
Mitsubishi International Corp., **16** 462
Mitsubishi Kasei Corp., **III** 47–48, 477; **8** 343; **14** 535
Mitsubishi Kasei Industry Co. Ltd., **IV** 476
Mitsubishi Marine, **III** 385
Mitsubishi Materials Corporation, **III** 712–13; **IV** 554
Mitsubishi Motors Corporation, **III** 516–17, 578–79; **6** 28; **7** 219, 348–49; **8** 72, 374; **9 349–51**
Mitsubishi Oil Co., Ltd., **IV** 460–62, 479, 492
Mitsubishi Paper Co., **III** 547
Mitsubishi Petrochemical Co., **I** 364; **III** 685
Mitsubishi Petroleum, **III** 760
Mitsubishi Pulp, **IV** 328
Mitsubishi Rayon Co. Ltd., **I** 330; **V** **369–71**; **8** 153
Mitsubishi Sha Holdings, **IV** 554
Mitsubishi Shipbuilding Co. Ltd., **II** 57; **III** 513, 577–78; **7** 348; **9** 349
Mitsubishi Shoji Trading, **IV** 554
Mitsubishi Shokai, **III** 577; **IV** 713; **7** 347
Mitsubishi Trading Co., **IV** 460
Mitsubishi Trust & Banking Corporation, **II** 323–24; **III** 289
Mitsui, **16** 84
Mitsui and Co., **I** 282; **IV** 18, 224, 432, 654–55; **V** 142; **6** 346; **7** 303; **13** 356
Mitsui Bank, Ltd., **II** 273–74, 291, **325–27**, 328, 372; **III** 295–97; **IV** 147, 320; **V** 142; **17** 556
Mitsui Bussan K.K., **I** 363, 431–32, 469, 492, 502–04, **505–08**, 510, 515, 519, 533; **II** 57, 66, 101, 224, 292, 323, 325–28, 392; **III** 295–96, 717–18; **IV** 147, 431; **9** 352–53
Mitsui Gomei Kaisha, **IV** 715

Mitsui Group, **9** 352
Mitsui House Code, **V** 142
Mitsui Light Metal Processing Co., **III** 758
Mitsui Marine and Fire Insurance Company, Limited, **III** 209, **295–96**, 297
Mitsui Mining & Smelting Co., Ltd., **IV** **145–46**, 147–48
Mitsui Mining Company, Limited, **IV** 145, **147–49**
Mitsui Mutual Life Insurance Company, **III** 297–98
Mitsui O.S.K. Lines, Ltd., **I** 520; **IV** 383; **V 473–76**; **6** 398
Mitsui Petrochemical Industries, Ltd., **I** 390, 516; **9 352–54**
Mitsui Real Estate Development Co., Ltd., **IV 715–16**
Mitsui Shipbuilding and Engineering Co., **III** 295, 513
Mitsui Toatsu, **9** 353–54
Mitsui Trading, **III** 636
Mitsui Trust & Banking Company, Ltd., **II** 328; **III** 297
Mitsui-no-Mori Co., Ltd., **IV** 716
Mitsukoshi Ltd., **I** 508; **V** **142–44**; **14** 502
Mitsuya Foods Co., **I** 221
Mitteldeutsche Creditbank, **II** 256
Mitteldeutsche Energieversorgung AG, **V** 747
Mitteldeutsche Privatbank, **II** 256
Mitteldeutsche Stickstoff-Werke Ag, **IV** 229–30
Mitteldeutsches Kraftwerk, **IV** 229
Mixconcrete (Holdings), **III** 729
Miyoshi Electrical Manufacturing Co., **II** 6
Mizushima Ethylene Co. Ltd., **IV** 476
MJB Coffee Co., **I** 28
MK-Ferguson Company, **7** 356
MLC Ltd., **IV** 709
MLH&P. *See* Montreal Light, Heat & Power Company.
MML Investors Services, **III** 286
MNC Financial. *See* MBNA Corporation.
MNC Financial Corp., **11** 447
MND Drilling, **7** 345
MNet, **11** 122
Mo och Domsjö AB, **IV** 315, **317–19**, 340
Moa Bay Mining Co., **IV** 82; **7** 186
Mobay, **I** 310–11; **13** 76
Mobil Communications, **6** 323
Mobil Corporation, **I** 30, 34, 403, 478; **II** 379; **IV** 93, 295, 363, 386, 401, 403, 406, 423, 428, 454, **463–65**, 466, 472–74, 486, 492, 504–05, 515, 517, 522, 531, 538–39, 545, 554–55, 564, 570–71; **V** 147–48; **6** 530; **7** 171, **351–53 (upd.)**; **8** 552–53; **9** 546; **10** 440; **12** 348; **16** 489; **17** 363, 415
Mobile and Ohio Railroad, **I** 456
Mobile Communications Corp. of America, **V** 277–78
Mobile One, **16** 74
Mobira, **II** 69; **17** 353
Mobley Chemical, **I** 342
Mobu Company, **6** 431
Mobujidosha Bus Company, **6** 431
MOÇACOR, **IV** 505
Mocatta and Goldsmid Ltd., **II** 357
Mochida Pharaceutical Co. Ltd., **II** 553
Moctezuma Copper Co., **IV** 176–77
Modar, **17** 279
Modell's Shoppers World, **16** 35–36
Modern Equipment Co., **I** 412

Modern Furniture Rental, **14** 4
Modern Maid Food Products, **II** 500
Modern Patterns and Plastics, **III** 641
Modernistic Industries Inc., **7** 589
Modine Manufacturing Company, **8** **372–75**
MoDo. *See* Mo och Domsjö AB.
Moen Incorporated, **12 344–45**
Moët-Hennessy, **I** 271–72; **10** 397–98
Mogul Corp., **I** 321; **17** 287
Mogul Metal Co., **I** 158
Mohasco Corporation, **15** 102
Mohawk & Hudson Railroad, **9** 369
Mohawk Airlines, **I** 131; **6** 131
Mohawk Rubber Co. Ltd., **V** 256; **7** 116
Mohr-Value Stores, **8** 555
Moilliet and Sons, **II** 306
Moist O'Matic, **7** 535
Mojo MDA Group Ltd., **11** 50–51
Mokta. *See* Compagnie de Mokta.
MOL. *See* Mitsui O.S.K. Lines, Ltd.
Molecular Biosystems, **III** 61
Molex Incorporated, **II** 8; **11 317–19**; **14** 27
Moline National Bank, **III** 463
Molinos de Puerto Rico, **II** 493
Molinos Nacionales C.A., **7** 242–43
Molins Co., **IV** 326
Molkerie-Zentrak Sud GmbH, **II** 575
Moll Plasticrafters, L.P., **17** 534
Molloy Manufacturing Co., **III** 569
Mölnlycke, **IV** 338–39
Molson Companies Ltd., **I** 273–75, 333; **II** 210; **7** 183–84; **12** 338; **13** 150, 199
Molycorp, **IV** 571
Mon-Dak Chemical Inc., **16** 270
Mon-Valley Transportation Company, **11** 194
MONACA. *See* Molinos Nacionales C.A.
Monarch Food Ltd., **II** 571
Monarch Marking Systems, **III** 157
MonArk Boat, **III** 444
Mond Nickel Co., **IV** 110–11
Mondadori. *See* Arnoldo Monadori Editore S.p.A.
Mondi Paper Co., **IV** 22
Monet Jewelry, **II** 502–03; **9** 156–57; **10** 323–24
Money Access Service Corp., **11** 467
Monfort, Inc., **13 350–52**
Monheim Group, **II** 521
Monier Roof Tile, **III** 687, 735
Monis Wineries, **I** 288
Monk-Austin Inc., **12** 110
Monmouth Pharmaceuticals Ltd., **16** 439
Monochem, **II** 472
Monogram Aerospace Fasteners, Inc., **11** 536
Monogramme Confections, **6** 392
Monolithic Memories Inc., **6** 216; **16** 316–17, 549
Monon Corp., **13** 550
Monon Railroad, **I** 472
Monoprix, **V** 57–59
Monroe Auto Equipment, **I** 527
Monroe Calculating Machine Co., **I** 476, 484
Monroe Cheese Co., **II** 471
Monroe Savings Bank, **11** 109
Monrovia Aviation Corp., **I** 544
Monsanto Company, **I** 310, 363, **365–67**, 402, 631, 666, 686, 688; **III** 741; **IV** 290, 367, 379, 401; **8** 398; **9** 318,

Oster. *See* Sunbeam-Oster.
Österreichische Bundesbahnen GmbH, 6 418–20
Österreichische Creditanstalt-Wiener Bankverein, **IV** 230
Österreichische Elektrowerke, **IV** 230
Österreichische Industrieholding AG, **IV** 486–87
Österreichische Industriekredit AG, **IV** 230
Österreichische Länderbank, **II** 239
Österreichische Mineralölverwaltung AG, **IV** 485
Österreichische Post- und Telegraphenverwaltung, V 314–17
Österreichische Stickstoffswerke, **IV** 486
Ostschweizer Zementwerke, **III** 701
Osuuskunta Metsäliito, **IV** 316
Oswald Tillotson Ltd., **III** 501; **7** 207
Otagiri Mercantile Co., **11** 95
Otake Paper Manufacturing Co., **IV** 327
OTC, **10** 492
Otis Company, **6** 579
Otis Elevator Company, Inc., I 85, **III** 467, 663; **13 384–86**
Otis Engineering Corp., **III** 498
Otosan, **I** 167, 479–80
Otsego Falls Paper Company, **8** 358
Ott and Brewer Company, **12** 312
Ottawa Fruit Supply Ltd., **II** 662
Ottaway Newspapers, Inc., 15 335–37
Otter-Westelaken, **16** 420
Otto Sumisho Inc., **V** 161
Otto-Epoka mbH, **15** 340
Otto-Versand (GmbH & Co.), V 159–61; **10** 489–90; **15 338–40 (upd.)**
Ottumwa Daily Courier, **11** 251
Ourso Investment Corporation, **16** 344
Outback Steakhouse, Inc., 12 373–75
Outboard Marine Corporation, III 329, **597–600, 8** 71; **16** 383
The Outdoorsman, Inc., **10** 216
Outlet, **6** 33
Outokumpu Metals Group. *See* OM Group, Inc.
Outokumpu Oy, **IV** 276
Ovako Oy, **III** 624
OVC, Inc., **6** 313
Overhill Farms, **10** 382
Overland Energy Company, **14** 567
Overland Mail Co., **II** 380–81, 395; **10** 60; **12** 533
Overnite Transportation Co., 14 371–73
Overseas Air Travel Ltd., **I** 95
Overseas Containers Ltd., **6** 398, 415–16
Overseas Petroleum and Investment Corp., **IV** 389
Overseas Shipholding Group, Inc., 11 376–77
Overseas Telecommunications Commission, **6** 341–42
Owatonna Tool Co., **I** 200; **10** 493
Owen Steel Co. Inc., **15** 117
Owens & Minor, Inc., 10 143; **16 398–401**
Owens Yacht Co., **III** 443
Owens-Corning Fiberglas Corporation, I 609; **III** 683, **720–23; 8** 177; **13** 169
Owens-Illinois Inc., I 609–11, 615; **II** 386; **III** 640, 720–21; **IV** 282, 343; **9** 261; **16** 123
Owensboro Municipal Utilities, **11** 37
Oxdon Investments, **II** 664
Oxfam America, **13** 13
Oxford Biscuit Fabrik, **II** 543

Oxford Chemical Corp., **II** 572
Oxford Health Plans, Inc., 16 402–04
Oxford Industries, Inc., 8 406–08
Oxford Instruments, **III** 491
Oxford Paper Co., **I** 334–35; **10** 289
Oxford-AnsCo Development Co., **12** 18
Oxirane Chemical Co., **IV** 456
OXO International, **16** 234
Oxy Petrochemicals Inc., **IV** 481
Oxy Process Chemicals, **III** 33
OxyChem, **11** 160
Ozalid Corp., **I** 337–38; **IV** 563
Ozark Airlines, **I** 127; **12** 489
Ozark Pipe Line Corp., **IV** 540
Ozark Utility Company, **6** 593

P & M Manufacturing Company, **8** 386
P & O. *See* Peninsular & Oriental Steam Navigation Company.
P.A. Bergner & Company, **9** 142; **15** 87–88
P.A. Geier Company. *See* Royal Appliance Manufacturing Company.
P.A.J.W. Corporation, **9** 111–12
P.A. Rentrop-Hubbert & Wagner Fahrzeugausstattungen GmbH, **III** 582
P&C Foods Inc., 8 409–11; 13 95, 394
P&O, **6** 79
P.C. Hanford Oil Co., **IV** 368
P. D'Aoust Ltd., **II** 651
P.D. Kadi International, **I** 580
P.D. Magnetics, **I** 330; **8** 153
P.G. Realty, **III** 340
P.H. Glatfelter Company, 8 412–14
P.L. Porter Co., **III** 580
P.R. Mallory, **9** 179
P. Sharples, **III** 418
P.T. Bridgeport Perkasa Machine Tools, **17** 54
P.T. Dai Nippon Printing Indonesia, **IV** 599
P.T. Muaratewe Spring, **III** 581
P.T. Semen Nusantara, **III** 718
P.W. Huntington & Company, **11** 180
Pabst Beer, **I** 217, 255; **10** 99
PAC Insurance Services, **12** 175
Pac-Am Food Concepts, **10** 178
Paccar Inc., I 155, **185–86; 10** 280
Pace Companies, **6** 149
Pace Express Pty. Ltd., **13** 20
PACE Membership Warehouse, Inc., **V** 112; **10** 107; **12** 50
Pace Pharmaceuticals, **16** 439
Pace-Arrow, Inc., **III** 484
Pacemaker Plastics, Inc., **7** 296
Pacer Tool and Mold, **17** 310
Pachena Industries Ltd., **6** 310
Pacific Aero Products Co., **I** 47; **10** 162
Pacific Air Freight, Incorporated, **6** 345
Pacific Air Transport, **I** 47, 128; **6** 128; **9** 416
Pacific Alaska Fuel Services, **6** 383
Pacific Bell, **V** 318–20; **11** 59; **12** 137
Pacific Brick Proprietary, **III** 673
Pacific Car & Foundry Co., **I** 185
Pacific Cascade Land Co., **IV** 255
Pacific Coast Co., **IV** 165
Pacific Coast Condensed Milk Co., **II** 486
Pacific Coast Oil Co., **IV** 385
Pacific Communication Sciences, **11** 57
Pacific Dry Dock and Repair Co., **6** 382
Pacific Dunlop Limited, 10 444–46
Pacific Electric Heating Co., **II** 28; **12** 194
Pacific Electric Light Company, **6** 565

Pacific Enterprises, V 682–84; 12 477
Pacific Express Co., **II** 381
Pacific Finance Corp., **I** 537; **9** 536; **13** 529
Pacific Gamble Robinson, **9** 39
Pacific Gas and Electric Company, I 96; **V 685–87; 11** 270; **12** 100, 106
Pacific Guardian Life Insurance Co., **III** 289
Pacific Health Beverage Co., **I** 292
Pacific Home Furnishings, **14** 436
Pacific Indemnity Corp., **III** 220; **14** 108, 110; **16** 204
Pacific Lighting, **12** 477
Pacific Lighting Company, **V** 682–84
Pacific Lighting Corp., **IV** 492; **16** 496
Pacific Linens, **13** 81–82
Pacific Lumber Company, **III** 254; **8** 348–50
Pacific Magazines and Printing, **7** 392
Pacific Mail Steamship Company, **6** 353
Pacific Manifolding Book/Box Co., **IV** 644
Pacific Metal Bearing Co., **I** 159
Pacific Monolothics Inc., **11** 520
Pacific National Bank, **II** 349
Pacific Natural Gas Corp., **9** 102
Pacific Northern, **6** 66
Pacific Northwest Bell Telephone Co., **V** 341
Pacific Northwest Laboratories, **10** 139
Pacific Northwest Pipeline Corporation, **9** 102–104, 540; **12** 144
Pacific Northwest Power Company, **6** 597
Pacific Pearl, **I** 417
Pacific Petroleum, **IV** 494
Pacific Petroleums Ltd., **9** 102
Pacific Platers Ltd., **IV** 100
Pacific Power & Light Company. *See* PacifiCorp.
Pacific Recycling Co. Inc., **IV** 296
Pacific Refining Co., **IV** 394–95
Pacific Resources Inc., **IV** 47
Pacific Silver Corp., **IV** 76
Pacific Southwest Airlines Inc., **I** 132; **6** 132
Pacific Steel Ltd., **IV** 279
Pacific Telecom, Inc., V 689; **6 325–28**
Pacific Telesis Group, V 318–20; **6** 324; **9** 321; **11** 10–11; **14** 345, 347; **15** 125
Pacific Teletronics, Inc., **7** 15
Pacific Towboat. *See* Puget Sound Tug and Barge Company.
Pacific Trading Co., Ltd., **IV** 442
Pacific Trail Inc., **17** 462
Pacific Western Extruded Plastics Company, **17** 441
Pacific Western Oil Co., **IV** 537
Pacific-Burt Co., Ltd., **IV** 644
Pacific-Sierra Research, **I** 155
PacifiCare Health Systems, Inc., III 85; **11 378–80**
PacifiCorp, V 688–90; 6 325–26, 328; **7 376–78**
Package Products Company, Inc., **12** 150
Packaging Corporation of America, I 526; **12 376–78**, 397; **16** 191
Packard Bell Electronics, Inc., I 524; **II** 86; **10** 521, 564; **11** 413; **13 387–89**, 483
Packard Motor Co., **I** 81; **8** 74; **9** 17
Packer's Consolidated Press, **IV** 651
Packerland Packing Company, **7** 199, 201
Pacolet Manufacturing Company, **17** 327
PacTel. *See* Pacific Telesis Group.

Prichard and Constance, **III** 65

Pride & Clarke, **III** 523

Pride Petroleum Services. *See* DeKalb Genetics Corporation.

Priggen Steel Building Co., **8** 545

Primadonna Resorts Inc., **17** 318

Primark Corp., 10 89–90; **13 416–18**

Prime Computer, Inc. *See* Computervision Corporation.

Prime Motor Inns Inc., **III** 103; **IV** 718; **11** 177; **17** 238

Prime Telecommunications Corporation, **8** 311

The Prime-Mover Co., **13** 267

PrimeAmerica, **III** 340

Primerica Corporation, I 597, 599–602, 604, 607–09, **612–14**, 615; **II** 422; **III** 283 **8** 118; **9** 218–19, 360–61; **11** 29; **15** 464. *See also* American Can Co.

Primes Régal Inc., **II** 651

Primex Fibre Ltd., **IV** 328

Primo Foods Ltd., **I** 457; **7** 430

Prince Co., **II** 473

Prince Gardner Company, **17** 465

Prince Motor Co. Ltd., **I** 184

Prince of Wales Hotels, PLC, **14** 106

Prince Sports Group, Inc., 15 368–70

Prince Street Technologies, Ltd., **8** 271

Prince William Bank, **II** 337; **10** 425

Princess Cruises, **IV** 256

Princess Dorothy Coal Co., **IV** 29

Princeton Gas Service Company, **6** 529

Princeton Laboratories Products Company, **8** 84

Princeton Review, **12** 142

Principal Mutual Life Insurance Company, III 328–30

Principles, **V** 21–22

Princor Financial Services Corp., **III** 329

Pringle Barge Line Co., **17** 357

Printex Corporation, **9** 363

Printronix, **14** 377–78

Prism Systems Inc., **6** 310

Prismo Universal, **III** 735

Prisunic SA, **V** 9–11

Pritzker & Pritzker, **III** 96–97

Privatbanken, **II** 352

Pro-Fac Cooperative Inc., **7** 104–06

Procino-Rossi Corp., **II** 511

Procor Limited, **16** 357

Procordia, **II** 478

Procter & Gamble Company, I 34, 129, 290, 331, 366; **II** 478, 493, 544, 590, 684, 616; **III** 20–25, 36–38, 40–41, 44, **50–53**; **IV** 282, 290, 329–30; **6** 26–27, 50–52, 129, 363; **7** 277, 300, 419; **8** 63, 106–07, 253, 282, 344, 399, **431–35** (upd.), 477, 511–12; **9** 260, 291, 317–19, 552; **10** 54, 288; **11** 41, 421; **12** 80, 126–27, 439; **13** 39, 197, 199, 215; **14** 121–22, 262, 275; **15** 357; **16** 302–04, 440

Proctor & Collier, **I** 19

Proctor & Schwartz, **17** 213

Proctor-Silex. *See* Hamilton Beach/Proctor-Silex Inc.

Prodigy, Inc., **10** 237–38; **12** 562; **13** 92

Productos Ortiz, **II** 594

Produits Chimiques Ugine Kuhlmann, **I** 303; **IV** 547

Profarmaco Nobel S.r.l., **16** 69

Professional Care Service, **6** 42

Professional Computer Resources, Inc., **10** 513

Professional Education Systems, Inc., **17** 272

Professional Health Care Management Inc., **14** 209

Professional Research, **III** 73

Profimatics, Inc., **11** 66

PROFITCo., **II** 231

Progil, **I** 389

Progress Development Organisation, **10** 169

Progress Software Corporation, 15 371–74

Progressive Corporation, 11 405–07

Progressive Distributors, **12** 220

Progressive Grocery Stores, **7** 202

Progresso, **I** 514; **14** 212

Projiis, **II** 356

Prolabo, **I** 388

Proland, **12** 139

Proler International Corp., **13** 98

Promigas, **IV** 418

Promotional Graphics, **15** 474

Promstroybank, **II** 242

Promus Companies, Inc., III 95; **9 425–27**; **15** 46; **16** 263

Pronto Pacific, **II** 488

Prontophot Holding Limited, **6** 490

Prontor-Werk Alfred Gauthier GmbH, **III** 446

Prophet Foods, **I** 449

Propwix, **IV** 605

Prosim, S.A., **IV** 409

ProSource Distribution Services, Inc., **16** 397; **17** 475

Prospect Farms, Inc., **II** 584; **14** 514

The Prospect Group, Inc., **11** 188

Prospect Provisions, Inc. *See* King Kullen Grocery Co., Inc.

Prospectors Airways, **IV** 165

Protective Closures, **7** 296–97

La Protectrice, **III** 346–47

Protek, **III** 633

Proto Industrial Tools, **III** 628

Protogene Laboratories Inc., **17** 288

Proventus A.B., **II** 303

Provi-Soir, **II** 652

Provi-Viande, **II** 652

Provibec, **II** 652

La Providence, **III** 210–11

Providence National Bank, **9** 228

Providence Steam and Gas Pipe Co. *See* Grinnell Corp.

Providencia, **III** 208

Provident Bank, **III** 190

Provident Institution for Savings, **13** 467

Provident Life and Accident Insurance Company of America, III 331–33, 404

Provident National Bank, **II** 342

Provident Services, Inc., **6** 295

Provident Travelers Mortgage Securities Corp., **III** 389

Provigo Inc., II 651–53; **12** 413

Les Provinces Réunies, **III** 235

Provincetown-Boston Airlines, **I** 118

Provincial Bank of Ireland Ltd., **16** 13

Provincial Engineering Ltd, **8** 544

Provincial Gas Company, **6** 526

Provincial Insurance Co., **III** 373

Provincial Newspapers Ltd., **IV** 685–86

Provincial Traders Holding Ltd., **I** 437

Provinzial-Hülfskasse, **II** 385

Provost & Provost, **II** 651

Prudential Bache Securities, **9** 441

Prudential Corporation plc, II 319; **III 334–36**; **IV** 711; **8** 276–77

Prudential Insurance Company of America, I 19, 334, 402; **II** 103, 456; **III** 79, 92, 249, 259, 265–67, 273, 291–93, 313, 329, **337–41**; **IV** 410, 458; **10** 199; **11** 243; **12** 28, 453, 500; **13** 561; **14** 95, 561; **16** 135, 497; **17** 325

Prudential Oil & Gas, Inc., **6** 495–96

Prudential Refining Co., **IV** 400

Prudential Steel, **IV** 74

Prudential-Bache Trade Corp., **II** 51

PSA. *See* Pacific Southwest Airlines.

PSA Peugeot-Citroen Group, **7** 35

PSCCo. *See* Public Service Company of Colorado.

PSE, Inc., **12** 100

PSI Resources, 6 555–57

Psychiatric Institutes of America, **III** 87–88

Psychological Corp., **IV** 623; **12** 223

PT Components, **14** 43

PT PERMINA, **IV** 492, 517

PTI Communications, Inc. *See* Pacific Telecom, Inc.

PTT Telecom BV, **V** 299–301; **6** 303

PTV. *See* Österreichische Post- und Telegraphenverwaltung.

Pubco Corporation, 17 383–85

Publi-Graphics, **16** 168

Public Home Trust Co., **III** 104

Public National Bank, **II** 230

Public Savings Insurance Co., **III** 219

Public Service Co., **14** 124

Public Service Company of Colorado, 6 558–60

Public Service Company of Indiana. *See* PSI Energy.

Public Service Company of New Mexico, 6 561–64

Public Service Electric and Gas Company, **IV** 366; **V** 701–03; **11** 388

Public Service Enterprise Group, **V** 701–03

Publicis FCB, **13** 204

Publicker Industries Inc., **I** 226; **10** 180

Publishers Paper Co., **IV** 295, 677–78

Publishers Press Assoc., **IV** 607

Publix Super Markets Inc., II 155, 627; **7 440–42**; **9** 186

Puente Oil, **IV** 385

Puerto Rican Aqueduct and Sewer Authority, **6** 441

Puerto Rican-American Insurance Co., **III** 242

Puget Mill Company, **12** 406–07

Puget Sound Alaska Van Lines. *See* Alaska Hydro-Train.

Puget Sound National Bank, **8** 469–70

Puget Sound Power And Light Company, 6 565–67

Puget Sound Pulp and Timber Co., **IV** 281; **9** 259

Puget Sound Tug and Barge Company, **6** 382

Pulitzer Publishing Company, 15 375–77

Pullman Co., **II** 403; **III** 94, 744

Pullman Savings and Loan Association, **17** 529

Pullman Standard, **7** 540

Pulte Corporation, 8 436–38

Puma, **14** 6–7; **17** 244

AB Pump-Separator, **III** 418–19

Punchcraft, Inc., **III** 569

Purdue Fredrick Company, **13** 367

INDEX TO INDUSTRIES

Index to Industries

FINANCIAL SERVICES: NON-BANKS

FOOD PRODUCTS

FOOD SERVICES & RETAILERS

RUBBER & TIRE

TELECOMMUNICATIONS

UTILITIES

WASTE SERVICES

NOTES ON CONTRIBUTORS

Notes on Contributors

ADKINS, Lynn W. Business communications consultant and financial journalist in Chicago, Illinois.

BIANCO, David. Free-lance writer.

BODINE, Paul S. Free-lance writer, editor, and researcher in Milwaukee, specializing in business subjects; contributor to the *Encyclopedia of American Industries, Encyclopedia of Global Industries, DISCovering Authors, Contemporary Popular Writers,* the Milwaukee *Journal Sentinel,* and the Baltimore *Sun.*

BOYER, Dean. Newspaper reporter and free-lance writer in the Seattle area.

COHEN, M. L. Novelist and free-lance writer living in Chicago.

COVELL, Jeffrey L. Free-lance writer and corporate history contractor.

DERDAK, Thomas. Free-lance writer and adjunct professor of philosophy at Loyola University of Chicago; former executive director of the Albert Einstein Foundation.

FELDMAN, Heidi. Free-lance writer and arts management consultant.

GALLMAN, Jason. Free-lance writer and English teacher at Ben Davis High School in Indianapolis, Indiana.

GASBARRE, April Dougal. Archivist and free-lance writer specializing in business and social history in Cleveland, Ohio.

GOPNIK, Hilary. Free-lance writer.

HALASZ, Robert. Former editor-in-chief of *World Progress* and *Funk & Wagnalls New Encyclopedia Yearbook*; author, *The U.S. Marines* (Millbrook Press, 1993).

HECHT, Henry. Editorial consultant and retired vice-president, editorial services, Merrill Lynch.

HEDDEN, Heather Behn. Vocabulary and quality management specialist at Information Access Co.; business indexer and abstractor for Trade & Industry, PROMT, and Industry Express databases; contributor to the *Encyclopedia of Business* and the *Encyclopedia of American Industry*; former staff writer for the *Middle East Times* in Cairo, Egypt.

INGRAM, Frederick. Business writer living in Columbia, South Carolina; contributor to the *Encyclopedia of Business,* the *Encyclopedia of Consumer Brands,* and *Global Industry Profiles.*

McNULTY, Mary. Free-lance writer and editor.

MOTE, Dave. President of information retrieval company Performance Database.

PEIPPO, Kathleen. Minneapolis-based free-lance writer.

PENDERGAST, Sara. Free-lance writer and copyeditor.

PENDERGAST, Tom. Free-lance writer and copyeditor.

PFALZGRAF, Taryn Benbow. Free-lance editor, writer, and consultant in the Chicago area.

SALAMIE, David E. Part-owner of InfoWorks Development Group, a reference publication development and editorial services company.

TROESTER, Maura. Free-lance writer based in Milwaukee.

WERNICK, Ellen D. Free-lance writer and editor.

WHITELEY, Laura E. Free-lance writer based in Kalamazoo, Michigan.

BELMONT UNIVERSITY LIBRARY